Industrial Market Structure and Economic Performance

Third Edition

Industrial Market Structure and Economic Performance

Third Edition

F.M. Scherer

Harvard University

David Ross

Williams College

Houghton Mifflin Company   **Boston**

Dallas   Geneva, Illinois   Palo Alto   Princeton, NJ

Printed in the U.S.A.

Library of Congress Catalog Card Number: 89–80961

ISBN: 0–395–35714–4

Contents

List of Figures

List of Tables

Preface

Many colleagues have urged a third edition of this book, whose first two editions, appearing in 1970 and 1980, have been gratifyingly well received. The market, which speaks louder than words, also said it was time to launch a counterattack on the numerous new entrants who had absorbed the first edition's message on declining dominant enterprises but not the second edition's analysis of optimal product variety. Author Scherer was reluctant to take the needed steps, partly from the belief, perhaps mistaken but not uncommon among authors, that the second edition had just about got matters right. Furthermore, the market plainly demanded changes that lay outside his sphere of comparative advantage. The solution was a joint venture, so we introduce here the team of Scherer and Ross, leaving those who continue to cite the book as Mokyr et al. hopelessly out of date. David Ross had primary responsibility for the book's price-theoretic core, Chapters 6–8 and 10–11, and F. M. Scherer for the remaining chapters.

Important changes have in fact been made. They are of three main types. First, the materials on policy have been integrated into the analytic sections, permitting a more rigorous approach to policy questions and making the applications of theory more immediate. Second, during the past decade there has been an explosion of work on the theory of industrial organization and continuing, though less dramatic, progress in our empirical knowledge of how structure, conduct, and performance are related. Although the sheer mass of materials necessitated greater selectivity than in previous editions, we believe we retain our claim to providing the most comprehensive integrated synthesis of current knowledge. Third, where appropriate, we provide more extensive use of mathematics and other accouterments of modern economic analysis.

Despite this third evolutionary change, we have continued to present the material in a form comprehensible to well-motivated readers with no more background in economics than a solid undergraduate microeconomic theory course. Our role model is Benjamin Franklin, who said of his own path-breaking work on the physics of electricity:

If my hypothesis is not the truth itself, it is at least as naked. For I have not with some of our learned moderns disguis'd my nonsense in Greek, cloth'd it in algebra, or adorn'd it with fluxions. You have it *in puris naturalibus*.[1]

Our fluxions (Isaac Newton's word for the differential calculus) have for the most part been confined to footnotes and a proliferation of appendices, where the reader can take them or leave them.

Since the development of this book has been cumulative, our debts grow with compound interest. Richard Caves, Richard Levin, and Richard Schmalensee commented on parts of the third edition manuscript. The second edition benefited from critical comments by Schmalensee, Ronald Braeutigam, William

---

[1]Letter to John Perkins dated February 4, 1753, quoted in Esmond Wright, *Franklin of Philadelphia* (Cambridge: Harvard University Press, 1986), p. 72.

Comanor, James Rahl, Erich Kaufer, Martin Howe, Frederic Jenny, David Qualls, Bradley Gale, John Kwoka, and Stephen Sosnick. Critical comments on the original manuscript during the late 1960s came from Comanor, Kaufer, Shorey Peterson, Jesse Markham, Thomas Kauper, W. G. Shepherd, Darius Gaskins, Ben Branch, John Cross, Saul Hymans, Harold Levinson, Sidney Winter, Ronald Teigen, Michael Klass, and James Denny. Research assistance for this edition was ably provided by Dan Pryor, Matthew Tropp, Amy Whritenour, and Andreas Beckmann; and on earlier editions, by Louis Hawkins, Lowell Seyburn, Thomas Schick, Tom Scherer, Catherine Conrad, and Ed Klotz. The third edition was written while Scherer taught at Swarthmore College and Ross at Williams College.

The authors are, as usual, responsible for errors, but urge readers to call remediable blunders to our attention. We apologize to purchasers of the second edition whose early bindings deteriorated after modest use. We hope that our move to a new publisher will mean greatly improved production quality, including durability whose optimal value can hardly be less than the average reader's lifetime.

F. M. Scherer
David Ross
August 1989

Introduction

This book systematically explores the field of economics traditionally known as *industrial organization,* although, especially in Europe, the term *industrial economics* is often applied in its stead. "Industrial organization" is a curious name, distinctive mainly in its inability to communicate to outsiders what the subject is all about. The field has little to say directly about how one organizes and directs a particular industrial enterprise, although there are business school courses, sometimes with the same name, built directly upon its intellectual foundations.[1] But in its mainstream, industrial organization is concerned with how productive activities are brought into harmony with the demand for goods and services through some organizing mechanism such as a free market, and how variations and imperfections in the organizing mechanism affect the success achieved in satisfying an economy's wants.

Any economy, whatever its cultural and political traditions may be, must decide what products to supply and how much of each to produce, how scarce resources will be apportioned in producing each, and how the end products will be divided up or distributed among the various members of society. There are three alternative methods to solve this bundle of problems. First, decisions can be made to conform with *tradition.* The economic organization of manors in Europe during feudal times and the caste system of occupational selection in India are prominent examples. Second, the problem can be solved through *central planning.* Illustrations include output and input planning for most industries in the Soviet Union and the elaborate controls the U.S. Department of Defense imposes over its contractors. Finally, there is the *market system* approach, under which consumers and producers act in response to price signals generated by the interplay of supply and demand in more or less freely operating markets.

The field of industrial organization is concerned primarily with the third of these approaches—the market system approach. This is not to deny a substantial overlap with other fields, such as comparative economic systems, which specializes in analyzing the operation of centrally planned, hybrid socialist, and traditional economies. Many of the structural features we will examine are of equal concern to the central planner. Likewise, our understanding of free market processes can be sharpened by studying the resource allocation methods of socialist and centrally planned economies. Still, to remain within manageable scope, this book respects the accepted division of labor, confining its coverage to market processes.

On similar grounds of manageability and convenience, our focus must be narrowed even more. We shall have little to say about the operation of labor markets, whose study is the domain of the labor economist, or about the banking, insurance, and other financial intermediary industries, which are the province of money and banking specialists. Primary emphasis will be placed on the manufacturing and mineral extraction sectors of industrialized economies, with secondary emphasis on wholesale and retail distribution, services, transportation, and the so-called public utilities sectors. Manufacturing occupies center stage partly

1. See, for example, Michael E. Porter, *Competitive Advantage: Creating and Sustaining Superior Performance* (New York: Free Press, 1985).

because of further division of labor traditions (that is, public utility and transportation economics are often considered separate specialties) and partly because of its size and strategic importance in the economy. The majority of our empirical analyses will be drawn from work on the U.S. economy, although comparisons to other nations will be offered frequently, and the theories we shall develop are applicable to all market-oriented industrialized nations.

The Scope and Method of Industrial Organization Analysis

In the field of industrial organization, we seek to ascertain how market processes direct the activities of producers in meeting consumer demands, how those processes can break down, and how they adjust, or can be adjusted, to make performance conform more closely to some ideal standard. Many of these questions are also the concern of microeconomic theory, or, at least, of the market theory and welfare economics branches of microeconomic theory. How does industrial organization analysis differ from microeconomic theory? In fact, there is a fair amount of overlap, but there are also important differences in goals and methodology.

Both fields are concerned with explaining why things happen — why, for instance, prices are lower under one set of conditions than under another, or how some variable such as price will change in response to changes in other variables. Both view the type of market organization that links producers with consumers as an important variable. They differ mainly in the richness of the variables they attempt to subsume and in their concern for applying predictions and explanations to concrete real-world cases. Microeconomic theorists thrive on simplicity and rigor; they are happiest when they can strip their models to the barest essential assumptions and variables. Industrial organization economists are more inclined toward explanations rich in quantitative and institutional detail. To be sure, they should prefer a simpler theory over a more complex one when the two have equal explanatory power. But when a tradeoff must be made, the pure theorist will sacrifice some explanatory power for elegance, while the industrial organization specialist tilts in the opposite direction.[2]

Another perspective is provided by Joseph A. Schumpeter's concept of "economic analysis." A science, wrote Schumpeter, is any field of knowledge that has developed specialized techniques of fact finding and interpretation or analysis.[3] What distinguishes the scientific economic analyst from other people who think, talk, and write about economic topics, according to Schumpeter, is a command of three main techniques: history, statistics, and theory — theory being defined as a "box of tools" or a set of models that permits one to deal analytically with broad classes of cases by focusing on certain properties or aspects they have in common.[4] As we shall see repeatedly, industrial organization economists must have a command of all three techniques to make the most of their trade. They must be at home in microeconomic theory to forge rigorous predictive links between fundamental assumptions and their behavioral consequences. They must use modern statistical methods to extract appropriate generalizations from data on industrial structure and performance. And they need some familiarity with the methods and results of historical research, both to perceive the broader flow of events over time and to extract from a tangle of institutional detail the causes of departures from the norm. In short, all three horses in Schumpeter's methodological troika are required to pull the industrial organization cart. Pure theory is only one member of the team.

Why should economists be interested in industrial organization problems? There seem to be two main reasons.

First, studies in the field have a direct and continuing influence on the formulation and implementation of public policies in such areas as the choice between private and public enterprise, the regulation or deregulation of public utility industries, the promotion of competition through antitrust and free trade policies, the stimulation of technological progress through patent grants and subsidies, and much else. The field's attraction to policy-oriented economists was especially strong between 1887 and 1915, when the antitrust laws and the first federal regulatory agencies were in their formative stages, and between 1933 and 1940, when new developments in economic theory interacted with depression psychosis to stimulate a reassessment of the proper role for competitive market processes. After World War II the excitement abated somewhat as economists turned their attention to such new issues as macroeconomic stabilization and the problems of underdeveloped nations. In the 1970s, however, interest revived sharply. This renaissance, which continued into the 1980s, appears to have four main roots: increasing skepticism over the effectiveness of governmental regulation, which led in turn to a deregulation movement; the recognition that market organization significantly affects international trade (for example, through the working of commodity cartels and industrial strategies aimed at gaining comparative advantage); growing doubts over the adaptability and responsiveness of industrial enterprises, especially in Europe and North America; and an intensified debate regarding the nature of structure-performance links and their implications for evolving antitrust policies.

A second reason for toiling in the industrial organization vineyard is that it is intellectually exciting. One thing that will become evident as this volume unfolds is the considerable remaining ignorance concerning many facets of an industrialized market economy's functioning. The theory, data, and methodology needed to fill these voids are gradually becoming available. It is likely therefore that an able person doing research on industrial organization problems will advance the frontiers of knowledge, and lucky ones may trigger or achieve major breakthroughs. To those who relish the quest for knowledge, this is an attractive prospect.

2. For a less typical tradeoff by a leading theorist, see Paul A. Samuelson, "Succumbing to Keynesianism," *Challenge,* vol. 27 (January/February 1985), pp. 10-11: ". . . it is better to have a theory with imperfect foundations that gives some fit to the facts than to have an impeccable theory that doesn't at all fit the facts."

3. Joseph A. Schumpeter, *History of Economic Analysis* (New York: Oxford University Press, 1954), p. 7.

4. Schumpeter, *History,* pp. 12-16. See also Joan Robinson, *The Economics of Imperfect Competition* (London: Macmillan, 1933), p. 1.

An Introductory Paradigm

Before turning to the tasks at hand, it is useful to have a simple model of our broad approach to industrial organization analysis. We begin with the fundamental proposition that what society wants from producers of goods and services is good performance. Good performance is multidimensional. It embodies at least the following goals, not necessarily listed in order of importance:

a. Decisions as to what, how much, and how to produce should be efficient in two respects: Scarce resources should not be wasted, and production decisions should be responsive qualitatively and quantitatively to consumer demands.

b. The operations of producers should be progressive, taking advantage of opportunities opened up by science and technology to increase output per unit of input and to provide consumers with superior new products, in both ways contributing to the long-run growth of real income per person.

c. The operations of producers should facilitate stable full employment of resources, especially human resources. Or at minimum, they should not make maintenance of full employment through the use of macroeconomic policy instruments excessively difficult.

d. The distribution of income should be equitable. Equity is notoriously difficult to define, but it implies at least that producers do not secure rewards in excess of what is needed to call forth the amount of services supplied. A subfacet of this goal is the desire to achieve reasonable price stability, for rampant inflation distorts the distribution of income in widely disapproved ways.

These goals may not be completely consistent with one another. Later chapters will identify conflicts that cannot be resolved without invoking basic value judgments. Still, to the extent possible, good industrial performance implies maximum satisfaction of all four goals. Measuring the degree to which the goals have been satisfied is also not easy, but relevant indicators include the magnitude of price-cost margins, rates of change in output per hour of work and price levels, the size of gaps between actual and minimum feasible unit costs, and the variability of employment over the business cycle.

With this ultimate focus, we seek to identify sets of attributes or variables that influence economic performance and to build theories detailing the links between these attributes and end performance. The broad descriptive model of these relationships used in many industrial organization studies was conceived by Edward S. Mason of Harvard during the 1930s and elaborated by numerous scholars.[5] It is illustrated schematically in Figure 1.1. *Performance* in particular industries or markets is said to depend upon the *conduct* of sellers and buyers in such matters as pricing policies and practices, overt and tacit interfirm cooperation, product line and advertising strategies, research and development commitments, investment in production facilities, legal tactics (for example, in enforcing patent rights), and so on. Conduct in turn depends upon the *structure* of the relevant market, characterized by the number and size distribution of sellers and buyers, the degree of physical or subjective differentiation distinguishing competing sellers' products, the presence or absence of barriers to the entry of new firms, the shapes of cost curves, the degree to which firms are vertically integrated from raw material pro-

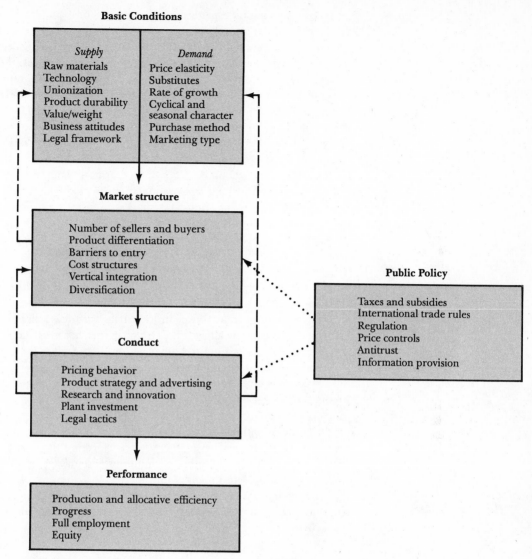

Figure 1.1
The Structure-Conduct-
Performance Paradigm

duction to retail distribution, and the extent of firms' product line diversification (conglomerateness).

Market structure is in turn affected by a variety of *basic conditions.* For example, on the supply side, basic structure-determining conditions include the location and ownership of essential raw materials; the nature of the relevant technology (for example, batch versus continuous process production, or high versus low elasticity of input substitution); the degree of work force unionization; the durability

5. Mason's seminal works are "Price and Production Policies of Large-Scale Enterprise," *American Economic Review,* vol. 29 (March 1939), pp. 61-74; and "The Current State of the Monopoly Problem in the United States," *Harvard Law Review,* vol. 62 (June 1949), pp. 1265–1285.

of the product; the time pattern of production (for example, whether goods are produced to order or delivered from inventory); the value/weight ratio of the product; and so on. A list of significant basic conditions on the demand side must include at least the price elasticity of demand at various prices; the availability of (and cross elasticity of demand for) substitute products; the rate of growth and variability over time of demand; the methods employed by buyers in purchasing (for example, acceptance of list prices as given versus solicitation of sealed bids versus haggling); and the marketing characteristics of the product sold (for example, specialty versus convenience versus shopping goods).[6] Other germane basic conditions are the general framework of law within which industries operate and the dominant socioeconomic values of the business community, such as whether sympathies run toward aggressive individualism or cooperation.

As the solid arrows of Figure 1.1 suggest, we shall be concerned mainly with causal flows running from market structure and/or basic conditions to conduct and performance. That is, we seek theories that permit us to predict ultimate market performance from the observation of structure, basic conditions, and conduct. To cite an example pursued further in Chapter 8, we may find that the current technology calls for a capital-intensive production process, which implies a short-run cost structure with high fixed costs and low variable costs. This encourages aggressive pricing conduct even in industries with few sellers when demand is price inelastic and cyclically volatile, which in turn has important ramifications in terms of price-cost margins and other performance indicators.

To be sure, not all influences flow from basic conditions and market structure toward performance. There are also important feedback effects (dashed arrows in Figure 1.1). For instance, vigorous research and development efforts can alter an industry's technology, and hence its cost conditions and/or the degree of physical product differentiation. Or sellers' pricing policies may either encourage entry or drive firms out of the market, thereby transforming the dimensions of market structure. In this sense, both basic conditions and market structure variables are *endogenous,* that is, determined within the whole system of relationships and not fixed by outside forces. Some interpretations see the influences running from structure to conduct and performance as being so weak, and the feedbacks affecting structure as so strong, that they doubt the predictive power of the structure-conduct-performance paradigm. The evidence on this point will be addressed carefully in due course. Even if a relatively pessimistic verdict emerges, the paradigm is useful as a kind of "hat rack" for organizing relevant theories and facts. Those who doubt the paradigm's power should feel free to accept it in that weakened form.

Thus, the basic conditions—market structure—conduct—performance paradigm will provide both theme and counterpoint for the analysis that follows. The book's organization centers on a structure-conduct-performance trichotomy. After Chapter 2 lays preliminary groundwork, Chapters 3 through 5 describe the structures of industries in the United States and abroad and investigate their determinants. Chapters 6 through 17 then undertake an extended analysis of conduct in the pricing, product policy, and technological innovation spheres. Chapter 18 assesses the quality of the resulting end performance. As counterpoint to this sequence of themes, we will be continuously concerned with the detailed interactions among basic conditions, market structure, conduct, and performance.

The Role of Public Policies

Ideally, good economic performance should flow automatically from proper market structure and the conduct to which it gives rise. But for a variety of reasons, markets may fail, yielding performance that falls below norms considered acceptable. Then government agencies may choose to intervene and attempt to improve performance by applying policy measures that affect either market structure or conduct, as shown by the dotted arrows in Figure 1.1.

The array of possible policy instruments is large. Costs, investments, prices, and outputs can be influenced by taxes or subsidies. An important dimension of market structure is the presence or absence of viable competitors outside national borders; their ability to compete depends inter alia upon tariffs, import quotas, and other government policies affecting international trade. The government might act to increase (or decrease) the amount of information available to buyers and sellers. Intervention through government regulation, for example, to determine who may operate in the market, thereby shaping market structure, or to control price-setting and other dimensions of conduct, is observable throughout recorded history. Much newer is antitrust policy, which seeks to maintain market structures conducive to good conduct, or to set rules of conduct, such as the avoidance of collusive price fixing, appropriate to desired end performance objectives. Or in extreme cases, the government may choose to do the job of supplying goods and services itself, operating nationalized enterprises according to criteria designed to serve the public interest, or having state-owned companies compete in such a way as to set cost, price, and quality standards that stimulate private rivals to improve their performance.[7]

Many aspects of industrial organization analysis are controversial, but none excite economists' disputative juices more than questions of appropriate public policy. At bottom, the debate turns on ideological value judgments as to the proper role of government. Here, analysis is futile; *de gustibus non est disputandum.*

6. Convenience goods, such as toothpaste, razor blades, and cigarettes, are items purchased with little shopping around because the costs of obtaining price comparisons outweigh the benefits. Shopping goods, such as furniture, major items of clothing, and mortgages, are items whose purchase is infrequent and whose value is high, so that price and quality comparison shopping trips are warranted. Specialty goods are high-value items on which the buyer has been presold, so that he or she will go to considerable trouble to obtain the particular brand desired. See Richard B. Heflebower, "Toward a Theory of Industrial Markets and Prices," *American Economic Review,* vol. 44 (May 1954), pp. 128–129; and Richard H. Holton, "The Distinctions Between Convenience Goods, Shopping Goods, and Specialty Goods," *Journal of Marketing,* vol. 23 (July 1958), pp. 53–56.

7. On the economics of nationalized enterprise, see William G. Shepherd, *Economic Performance under Public Ownership* (New Haven: Yale University Press, 1965); Richard Pryke, *Public Enterprise in Practice* (London: Macmillan, 1971); and Raymond Vernon and Yair Aharoni, eds., *State-owned Enterprise in the Western Economies* (New York: St. Martin's Press, 1981). On using national entities to stimulate the private sector, see W. C. Merrill and Norman Schneider, "Government Firms in Oligopoly Industries," *Quarterly Journal of Economics,* vol. 80 (August 1966), pp. 400–412; and Andrei Shleifer, "A Theory of Yardstick Competition," *Rand Journal of Economics,* vol. 16 (Autumn 1985), pp. 319–327.

But only one layer higher are questions to which economics can make useful contributions, even though scholars still differ strongly in their reading of the relevant evidence. Free and unfettered markets fail; on that there is little disagreement. How seriously they fail is a matter of dispute; our work in this book will attempt to provide a balanced assessment. On the other side, governments as policy implementers also fail, setting wrong objectives and clumsily pursuing the objectives they set, rightly or wrongly. Much of the debate over policy with respect to industrial structure and conduct turns on differing perceptions of the costs and benefits: how serious the market failures are, and how long it takes for market processes to remedy them automatically versus how effective the government is in implementing corrective policy measures, how long correction requires, and how large the costs are of interventions that miss their mark.[8] The effectiveness of government policy is also a fertile subject for research. But even with the best possible appraisals of policy costs and benefits, finding the right balance is difficult, in part because ideology affects the magnitude of intervention costs. The citizens of a democracy tend to get the quality of government they want. If ideological beliefs run strongly against government intervention, few able persons will be drawn into the branches of government that implement policy toward industry, and interventions will tend to be ill-conceived and costly, supporting the case for laissez faire policies. If there is solid support for intelligent intervention, better people will be drawn into the task, and the interventions will be more effective. In this respect there are important differences between the United States, with a traditional (but fluctuating) aversion to government intrusion in economic affairs, and Japan and the nations of Western Europe, whose traditions run more toward strong, interventionist government, which, as a result, channel more of their best talent into making government function effectively.[9]

Among the various instruments of public policy affecting industrial structure and conduct, the two most broadly related to the focus of this book are regulation and antitrust. Each merits a somewhat more extended introduction.

Public Regulation

Regulation may be pervasive, as when price controls were applied to most of American industry to combat inflation during World War I, World War II, and the early 1970s.[10] Or it may be targeted toward specific industries in which the need is perceived to be especially compelling. From an economic perspective, the classic justification of regulation has been advanced for the so-called public utility industries such as electric power and natural gas distribution, local telephone service, bulk commodity railroading, and the transportation of petroleum and natural gas in pipelines. The common element in all of these cases is that the size of an efficient enterprise is so large relative to the size of the market served that competition fails adequately to discipline costs, prices, and product qualities.[11] Regulation governs entry in such markets, attempting to ensure that a minimum-cost structure is achieved, and for the suppliers permitted to operate, prices and service qualities are controlled.

Few industries satisfy the criteria for classic public utility regulation unambiguously, and regulatory intervention has embraced a much wider array of industries. There are three main explanations.

One emphasizes other kinds of market failures such as severe information asymmetries or the presence of externalities — costs or benefits that fall upon parties other than the enterprises making resource allocation decisions. Pharmaceutical testing exemplifies the information asymmetries case. The costs of testing the safety and efficacy of a new drug are large. They are best borne by a single entity, usually the firm responsible for developing and marketing the drug. And the customers — the physician who prescribes the drug and the patient who ingests it — are much less able to assemble the information needed for sound decisions than either the producing firm or some government agency. Yet in its desire to maximize profits, the producing firm has incentives to be less than candid about the drug's therapeutic limitations. Regulation is imposed to elicit more complete information. Environmental pollution is the standard example of external costs that spill over from resource-allocating decision makers to third parties. Emissions-control mandates, fines, and/or taxes are imposed to set matters right. Ideally in such cases, no more regulatory intervention occurs than is needed to solve the specific market failure problem, and in this respect the regulation is much less far ranging than in public utility situations.

Regulation may also take place because, even though markets are working well, those who have political power are displeased with the results, or they may consider some good or service to be too important to be priced and allocated by unfettered market processes.[12] For example, in the 1970s the U.S. government regulated crude oil and natural gas prices and allocations to prevent domestic producers from realizing windfall profits as a consequence of the OPEC cartel's price-raising actions.[13] Most large cities regulate the provision and pricing of taxi services to ensure inter alia that unwary travelers are not "taken for a ride," damaging the city's reputation as a good place to visit and do business. The list of justifications, plausible and not so, could be proliferated almost without end.

8. See Frank H. Easterbrook, "Comparative Advantage and Antitrust Law," *California Law Review,* vol. 75 (May 1987), pp. 983–989.

9. Compare Corwin D. Edwards, *Cartelization in Western Europe* (Washington: U.S. Department of State, 1964), pp. 46–47; A. D. Neale, *The Antitrust Laws of the United States of America* (Cambridge: Cambridge University Press, 1966), pp. 475–476; Milton Friedman, *Capitalism and Freedom* (Chicago: University of Chicago Press, 1962), Chapters I and II; Arthur M. Schlesinger, Jr., *The Cycles of American History* (Boston: Houghton Mifflin, 1986), Chapters 2 and 9; and James Buchanan, *Liberty, Market, and State: Political Economy in the 1980s* (New York University Press, 1985).

10. On World War I, see Simon Litman, *Prices and Price Control in Great Britain and the United States during the World War* (New York: Oxford University Press, 1920). On World War II, see Seymour E. Harris, *Price and Related Controls in the United States* (New York: McGraw-Hill, 1945); Harvey C. Mansfield, *A Short History of OPA* (Washington: Office of Price Administration, 1947); and J. K. Galbraith, "Reflections on Price Control," *Quarterly Journal of Economics,* vol. 60 (August 1946), pp. 475–489. On the early 1970s controls, see Marvin H. Kosters, *Controls and In-*

flation: The Economic Stabilization Program in Retrospect (Washington: American Enterprise Institute, 1975).

11. Important works on the economics of regulation include Alfred Kahn, *The Economics of Regulation,* 2 vols. (New York: Wiley, 1970); Harold Demsetz, "Why Regulate Utilities?" *Journal of Law & Economics,* vol. 11 (April 1968), pp. 55-66; Paul L. Joskow and Roger G. Noll, "Regulation in Theory and Practice: An Overview," in Gary Fromm, ed., *Studies in Public Regulation* (Cambridge: MIT Press, 1981), pp. 1-77; and Richard Schmalensee, *The Control of Natural Monopolies* (Lexington, MA: Heath, 1979).

12. For a historical view, see Jonathan R. T. Hughes, *The Governmental Habit: Economic Controls from Colonial Times to the Present* (New York: Basic Books, 1977).

13. On petroleum, see Joseph P. Kalt, *The Economics and Politics of Oil Price Regulation* (Cambridge: MIT Press, 1981). On natural gas, whose regulation predated the first OPEC price shock, see Ronald R. Braeutigam and R. Glenn Hubbard, "Natural Gas: The Regulatory Transition," in Leonard W. Weiss and Michael Klass, eds., *Regulatory Reform: What Actually Happened* (Boston: Little, Brown, 1986), pp. 137-168.

A third and more skeptical hypothesis states that regulation occurs because there are well-organized vested interests expecting to benefit. It goes on to observe that the producers subjected to regulation are usually better organized and better able to manipulate political levers than consumers. Therefore, the principal beneficiaries of much regulation are not consumers, but producers.[14] This happens in part because producers work through their legislators to have laws passed that correct what they perceive to be a problem. Sometimes the problem is alleged cutthroat competition. In 1887, for example, the desire to lessen competition among railroads drew industry support and legislative drafting help for the Interstate Commerce Act, which established the first U.S. federal regulatory agency.[15] Similar laws were later extended to interstate trucking and inland water shipping on grounds that they should not be able to compete unfettered against the regulated railroads. On other occasions, regulation may be a response to producers' desire to avoid "spoiling the market" through excessive new entry — a motive behind many state occupational licensure laws ostensibly passed to perpetuate high standards of professional competence.

Even when legislators have only the public interest at heart in passing regulatory laws, those who are regulated may end up as beneficiaries by "capturing" the agency regulating them. This happens inter alia because the regulated firms use their political influence to have friendly regulators appointed, because the regulated enterprise has superior technical knowledge upon which regulatory agency staffs come to depend, and because regulators, like most people, seek identification and approval, which they are more likely to find by cultivating a community of interest with the well-organized firms they regulate than with a remote and unresponsive public.

Whatever their motivation, those who oversee the fortunes of the traditional regulated industries are likely to be responsible for determining what prices may be charged. The established principle in U.S. law is that they should permit "a fair return upon . . . the fair value of the property being used."[16] Concretely, this entails establishing a *rate base* reflecting the value of the regulated firm's (or industry's) assets and then authorizing prices sufficient, after noncapital costs are covered, to let the firm expect to realize some specified *allowed rate of return* on its assets. An effort is normally made to set the allowed rate of return high enough so that the regulated firm can raise additional funds, if they are needed, in capital markets.

This essentially cost-plus-profit orientation causes some important problems. For one, utilities that fail to keep their costs at minimum feasible levels are nevertheless likely to have prices approved that are sufficient to cover their costs and provide a return on capital. Also, when the allowed rate of return exceeds the market cost of new capital, profit-maximizing regulated enterprises may have a systematic incentive to choose excessively capital intensive production processes or build peak-load capacity whose unit cost exceeds the value of the service provided.[17] These incentive breakdowns may be corrected to some extent by *regulatory lag* — that is, by the tendency for regulatory price setting to lag behind changing cost conditions, so that unexpectedly rapid cost reduction by a regulated firm enhances profits temporarily while overly rapid cost escalation squeezes them. Regulators might also engage in *incentive regulation,* awarding higher allowed rates of return to firms operating efficiently than to those that do not. But this is seldom done, largely because of the difficulty of establishing absolute or comparative efficiency standards, and perhaps also because there is a natural human instinct to avoid the unpleasant task of punishing laggards. The desire to run a tight ship and serve consumers economically may also affect regulated enterprises' behavior favorably, but there is reason to believe that on balance, regulated monopolists' incentives are not all they should be. The incentive situation is somewhat different when regulators set prices for whole groups of firms in one action, as has been the traditional practice in transportation industry regulation. Then, individual firms that surpass industry efficiency norms may be able to retain the profit benefits from superior performance, but if the firm's costs are large relative to total industry costs, behavioral distortions may again intrude.[18]

Further complexities intrude when regulatory agencies must set not only a general level of prices, but a whole array of prices covering differing kinds and grades of service or product quality, and when the product quality itself must be regulated. We cannot dwell on them here, but advance to our conclusion. It is not easy to regulate an industry well. The cost-plus orientation toward which pricing methods gravitate weakens incentives for efficiency. Unexpected consequences often ensue. Regulatory agencies commonly suffer from severe information handicaps relative to the industries they regulate, leading to mistakes and capture. Opportunities for abuse abound. There are situations in which the alternatives to regulation are sufficiently unattractive so that, despite its flaws, some form of regulation is a sensible policy choice. It has become increasingly clear, however, that in many instances the public would be better off relying upon unfettered market processes as a regulator, even though the market functions a good deal less than perfectly. Considerations such as these led to the deregulation movement of the 1970s and 1980s. As always in periods of rapid policy change, there is danger of overreaction, so that truly beneficial institutions are dismantled along with those that are defective. Finding the right balance is difficult.

Antitrust

Antitrust is often viewed as a form of government regulation, and law school courses on the subject are sometimes found under the rubric "trade regulation." Yet in principle, there are (or ought to be) major philosophical differences. Traditional regulation usually requires a continuing relationship between regulator and

14. See George J. Stigler, "The Theory of Economic Regulation," *Bell Journal of Economics and Management Science,* vol. 2 (Spring 1971), pp. 3-21; Richard A. Posner, "Theories of Economic Regulation," *Bell Journal of Economics and Management Science,* vol. 5 (Autumn 1974), pp. 335-358; and Sam Peltzman, "Toward a More General Theory of Regulation," *Journal of Law & Economics,* vol. 19 (August 1976), pp. 211-240.
15. For contrasting interpretations, see George W. Hilton, "The Consistency of the Interstate Commerce Act," *Journal of Law & Economics,* vol. 9 (October 1966), pp. 87-113; and Thomas S. Ulen, "The Market for Regulation: The ICC from 1887 to 1920," *American Economic Review,* vol. 70 (May 1980), pp. 306-310.
16. *Smyth* v. *Ames et al.,* 169 U.S. 546-547 (1898).

17. Seminal articles on this point were Harvey A. Averch and Leland L. Johnson, "Behavior of the Firm under Regulatory Constraint," *American Economic Review,* vol. 52 (December 1962), pp. 1052-1069; and Stanislaw H. Wellisz, "Regulation of Natural Gas Pipeline Companies: An Economic Analysis," *Journal of Political Economy,* vol. 71 (February 1963), pp. 30-43. The subsequent literature is enormous. For an overview, see Roger Sherman, "The Averch and Johnson Analysis of Public Utility Regulation Twenty Years Later," *Review of Industrial Organization,* vol. 2, no. 2 (1985), pp. 178-193.
18. See Andrew F. Daughety, "Regulation and Industrial Organization," *Journal of Political Economy,* vol. 92 (October 1984), pp. 932-953.

regulatees as market conditions change and compel price and capacity adjustments. Antitrust, on the other hand, is ideally episodic — more like surgical intervention than the steady administration of medicine to treat a chronic disease. Conduct rules are articulated, and violations are penalized at a frequency and intensity just sufficient to achieve adequate deterrence. Or the antitrust authorities intervene to maintain or alter market structures so that good conduct and performance are expected to follow automatically, without further government involvement.

Antitrust in this modern form is a North American invention. Canada passed a Dominion antitrust statute in 1889; the United States adopted its Sherman Act in 1890. These new laws were a distinctive reaction to the turbulent economic changes of the times. The railroads and steamships vastly expanded the scope of many markets; technological and managerial innovations led to much larger business enterprises associated at first with the "trust" form of organization; and price levels were falling, largely as a consequence of monetary stringency associated with the gold standard. Burdened with rising real debt repayment costs and perceiving themselves to be squeezed between the high prices charged for inputs by powerful trusts and the falling prices of their own outputs, farmers and small business owners clamored for legislation that would constrain the trusts' behavior and redress the balance of economic power.[19]

The U.S. Congress and national leaders had mixed emotions about these economic developments. They recognized that the new forms of business organization might be more efficient, yet they wanted to avoid abuses of business power and ensure some semblance of fairness in interactions between big business, small business, and the consumer. Their ambiguity is reflected in the contemporary words of columnist Finley Peter Dunne's fictional Irish immigrant-philosopher, Mr. Dooley, who in turn attempted to summarize President Theodore Roosevelt's views:

"Th' trusts," says [T.R.], "are heejoous monsthers built up be th' enlightened intherprise iv th' men that have done so much to advance progress in our beloved country," he says. "On wan hand I wud stamp thim undher fut; on th' other hand not so fast."[20]

The Sherman Act, which after extensive rewriting in committee passed a crucial Senate vote by a 52-1 margin, contained two main substantive sections. Section 1 prohibits contracts, combinations, and conspiracies in restraint of trade, prescribing penalties for violators of imprisonment and/or a fine up to $5,000 (raised over time to a maximum of $1 million). Section 2 prohibits monopolization, attempts to monopolize, and combinations or conspiracies to monopolize "any part of the trade or commerce among the several States, or with foreign nations," specifying criminal penalties for violation similar to those of Section 1. Of the procedural sections, the most important were Section 4, permitting the Attorney General to institute suits in equity to enjoin illegal practices, and Section 7 (since superseded), permitting private parties injured by actions illegal under Sections 1 or 2 to sue for the recovery of three times the amount of actual damages sustained.

Enforcement of the Sherman Act was lackadaisical during the 1890s. However, when President Theodore Roosevelt took office in 1901, he began a vigorous antitrust campaign continued by presidents Taft and Wilson and supported by a series of key judicial interpretations. At President Wilson's urging, the two remaining pillars of the U.S. antitrust edifice were put in place during 1914.

The Clayton Act was designed to curb specific practices not covered by the Sherman Act and to restrain the growth of monopoly "in its incipiency." Section 2, heavily amended in 1936, prohibited price discrimination that substantially lessened competition, and Section 3 dealt with various related practices. Section 4 superseded Sherman Act Section 7 in authorizing treble damages suits, and Section 5 eased the burden of proving violation for parties suing to recover treble damages. Section 7, amended in 1950, prohibited certain mergers tending to lessen competition, and Section 8 forbade interlocking directorates among competing firms.

For some time prior to 1914, both critics and advocates of antitrust saw the need for an agency that would perform both investigatory and adjudicative functions and possess special competence in business affairs. The Federal Trade Commission Act established such an agency, centered on a panel of five full-time commissioners invested with substantial quasi-judicial powers. Section 5 of the FTC Act also outlawed "unfair methods of competition," leaving it to the Commission and ultimately the Supreme Court to determine what practices were to be covered. Since the creation of the Federal Trade Commission in 1914, U.S. federal antitrust enforcement responsibilities have been divided between two agencies, the FTC and the Antitrust Division of the Department of Justice. Their powers overlap in many but not all relevant areas. The Department of Justice alone has grand jury powers and the ability to demand (or withhold) criminal penalties, making it uniquely effective in ferreting out secret conspiracies. The FTC's membership and procedures were originally intended to expedite the adjudication of complex business questions, but in practice, FTC actions have on average taken longer than Department of Justice cases.[21] A positive attribute of the dual enforcement approach has been a tendency for one agency's oversights or excesses to be corrected by the actions of the other agency.

Antitrust spread more slowly to other parts of the world, but by 1985, most Western industrialized nations had laws broadly similar to those of the United States. Usually they are called *competition policy* laws, accentuating the positive and avoiding the negative connotations of *anti*trust. The United Kingdom enacted price-fixing prohibitions in 1956 and extended the jurisdiction of its Monopolies Commission to mergers in 1965. West Germany adopted a basic antitrust statute in 1957 and tightened merger control provisions in 1973. France had a law curbing price fixing and other restrictive practices as early as 1791, but it was largely ignored until major amendments were passed in 1977. Japan's antitrust laws were derived from provisions imposed by the occupation authorities following World War II. Their enforcement involves a sometimes conflict-ridden give-and-take

19. For insight into the historical background, see Hans B. Thorelli, *The Federal Antitrust Policy* (Stockholm: Stockholms Högskola, 1954); and William Letwin, *Law and Economic Policy in America* (New York: Random House, 1965).

20. Henry F. Pringle, *Theodore Roosevelt* (New York: Harcourt Brace, 1931), p. 245.

21. See Richard A. Posner, "A Statistical Study of Antitrust Enforcement," *Journal of Law & Economics,* vol. 13 (October 1970), pp. 374–381.

between the responsible agency, the Fair Trade Commission, and the Ministry of International Trade and Industry, which is more inclined to favor exemptions from procompetitive rules. At the multinational level, the 1957 Treaty of Rome, which created the European Economic Communities, contained explicit competition policy provisions. They have for the most part been vigorously enforced.

The Interweaving of Analysis and Policy

One can scarcely understand the rationale for such policy interventions as antitrust and regulation without comprehending how market performance is related to structure and conduct. The links between structure, conduct, and performance are in turn illuminated by careful study of important real-world policy cases. In this edition, therefore, we integrate our approach to what might otherwise be considered separate topics. Chapter 5 combines an analysis of merger motives and consequences with an evaluation of leading merger antitrust cases. After Chapters 6 through 8 lay an analytic foundation, Chapter 9 reviews antitrust policies toward price fixing and related restraints. Further foundation-building sets the stage for the analysis in Chapter 12 of alternative approaches to structural monopoly conditions, including both antitrust and some forms of regulation. Price discrimination behavior and its legal status are discussed together in Chapter 13. In Chapters 14 and 15, the complex policies governing pricing relationships between vertically linked (for example, seller and buyer) firms are investigated. No attempt is made to provide a systematic survey of traditional public regulation institutions, which merit the book-length treatment they receive elsewhere. However, several propositions central to understanding the logic of public regulation will be taken up as we develop a theory of how various types of markets function.

The Welfare Economics of Competition and Monopoly

Competition has long been viewed as a force that leads to an ideal solution of the economic performance problem, and monopoly has been condemned through much of recorded history for frustrating attainment of the competitive ideal. To Adam Smith, the vital principle underlying a market economy's successful functioning was the pursuit of individual self-interest, channelled and controlled by competition. As each individual strives to maximize the value of his own capital, said Smith, he

. . . necessarily labours to render the annual revenue of the society as great as he can. He generally, indeed, neither intends to promote the public interest, nor knows how much he is promoting it. . . . [H]e intends only his own gain, and he is in this, as in many other cases, led by an invisible hand to promote an end which was no part of his intention.[1]

Smith's "invisible hand" is the set of market prices emerging in response to competitive forces. When these forces are thwarted by "the great engine of . . . monopoly," the tendency for resources to be allocated "as nearly as possible in the proportion which is most agreeable to the interests of the whole society" is frustrated.[2]

Much of Smith's detailed analysis is obsolete. Yet his arguments on the efficacy of free competition remain intact, a philosophical lodestar to nations relying upon a market system of economic organization. Economists have, to be sure, amended their view of competition since Smith's time, and they have developed more elegant models of how competitive markets do their job of allocating resources and distributing income. One objective of this chapter is to survey these modern views. In addition, we shall examine some of the qualifications and doubts that have led to the partial or complete rejection of Smith's gospel in many parts of the world.

Competition Defined

We must begin by making clear what is meant by *competition* in economic analysis. Two broad conceptions, one emphasizing the conduct of sellers and buyers and the other emphasizing market structure, can be distinguished. Adam Smith's widely scattered comments, dealing with both conduct and structural features, typify the dominant strain of economic thought during the eighteenth and nineteenth centuries.[3] On the conduct side, Smith considered the essence of competition to be an *independent striving* for patronage by the various sellers in a market. The short-run structural prerequisites for competitive conduct were left ambiguous. Smith observed that independent action might emerge with only two sellers, but it was more likely (that is, collusion among the sellers was less likely) with

1. Adam Smith, *An Inquiry into the Nature and Causes of the Wealth of Nations* (New York: Modern Library edition, 1937), p. 423.

2. Smith, *Wealth of Nations,* pp. 594–595. See also pp. 61, 147, and 712.

3. For admirable surveys of the development of economic thought on the nature of competition, see George J. Stigler, "Perfect Competition, Historically Contemplated," *Journal of Political Economy,* vol. 65 (February 1957), pp. 1–17; J. M. Clark, *Compe-*

tition as a Dynamic Process (Washington: Brookings, 1961), Chapters 2 and 3; Paul J. McNulty, "A Note on the History of Perfect Competition," *Journal of Political Economy,* vol. 75, Part 1 (August 1967), pp. 395–399; and *idem,* "Economic Theory and the Meaning of Competition," *Quarterly Journal of Economics,* vol. 82 (November 1968), pp. 639–656.

twenty or more sellers.[4] Competition in Smith's schema also had a long-run dimension that could be satisfied, despite short-run aberrations, as long as it was possible for resources to move from industries in which their returns were low to those in which they could earn comparatively high returns. This in turn depended upon a structural condition: the absence of barriers to resource transfers. Recognizing that resources were often fairly immobile in the short run, Smith and his followers conceded that the full benefit of competitive market processes might be realized only in the long run.

As mathematical reasoning began to penetrate economics during the nineteenth century, a different, essentially structural concept of competition came to the forefront. In modern economic theory, a market is said to be competitive (or more precisely, purely competitive) when the number of firms selling a homogeneous commodity is so large, and each individual firm's share of the market is so small, that no individual firm finds itself able to influence appreciably the commodity's price by varying the quantity of output it sells. In mathematical jargon, price is a *parameter* to the competitive seller — it is determined by market forces and not subject to the individual seller's conscious control. The parametric character of price to the competitive firm is fundamentally a subjective phenomenon. If market demand curves are smooth and continuous, it is not strictly true that a small seller's output changes have *no* effect on the market price. They simply have such a minute effect that the influence is *imperceptible* to the seller, who can therefore act as if the effect were in fact zero.[5]

This technical definition of competition differs markedly from the usage adopted by businesspeople who, following Adam Smith's lead, are apt to view competition as a conscious striving against other business firms for patronage, perhaps on a price basis but possibly also (or alternatively) on nonprice grounds. Failure to recognize these implied semantic distinctions has often led to confusion in policy discussions. To keep such confusion at a minimum, we adopt the term "rivalry" to characterize much of the activity businesspeople commonly call "competition." The essence of rivalry is a striving for potentially incompatible positions (for example, if Firm A sells 100 units of output to Jones, Firm B cannot satisfy that part of Jones' demand) combined with a clear awareness by the parties involved that the positions they seek to attain may be incompatible. Under this dichotomy, it is possible for there to be vigorous rivalry that cannot be called pure competition. The jockeying for position in the automobile market among General Motors, Ford, and Honda is an obvious example. At the same time, there can be pure competition without rivalry. For instance, two Iowans growing corn on adjacent farms are pure competitors but not rivals in the sense implied here. Since the market for corn is so large relative to the two farmers' potential supply, it can readily absorb their offerings with scarcely a ripple in the Chicago Board of Trade price. Neither farmer can consider the neighbor's output decisions as having any adverse impact on his or her own economic position.

Violations of the principal structural preconditions for pure competition give rise to a rich variety of sellers' market types. For present purposes it suffices to identify the six most important types, using the two-way classification based upon the number of sellers and the nature of the product presented in Table 2.1. The distinction between homogeneity and differentiation in this classification hinges

Table 2.1   Principal Seller's Market Structure Types

	Number of Sellers		
	One	A Few	Many
Homogeneous products	Pure monopoly	Homogeneous oligopoly	Pure competition
Differentiated products	Pure multiproduct monopoly	Differentiated oligopoly	Monopolistic competition

on the degree of substitutability among competing sellers' products. Homogeneity prevails when, in the minds of buyers, products are perfect substitutes. Products are differentiated when, owing to differences in physical attributes, ancillary service, geographic location, information, and/or subjective image, one firm's products are clearly preferred by at least some buyers over rival products at a given price. The distinguishing trait of a differentiated product is the ability of its seller to raise the product's price without sacrificing its entire sales volume. Obviously, infinite gradations in the degree of product differentiation may exist, and it is difficult in practice to draw a precise line where homogeneity ends and differentiation begins. Similarly, although pure monopoly ends and oligopoly begins when the number of sellers rises from one to two, it is difficult to specify exactly where oligopoly shades into a competitive market structure. The key to the distinction is subjective — whether or not the sellers consider themselves conscious rivals in the sense defined earlier. If the sellers are sufficiently few in number to have each believe (a) that its economic fortunes are perceptibly influenced by the market actions of other individual firms, and (b) that those firms are in turn affected significantly by its own actions, then the market can be said to be oligopolistic.

Pure monopolists, oligopolists, and monopolistic competitors share a common characteristic: each recognizes that its output decisions have a perceptible influence on price, or in other words, each can increase the quantity of output it sells under given demand conditions only by reducing its price. All three types possess some degree of power over price, and so we say that they possess *monopoly power* or *market power.*

Homogeneity of the product and insignificant size of individual sellers and buyers relative to their market (that is, *atomistic* market structure) are sufficient conditions for the existence of pure competition, under which sellers possess no monopoly power. Several additional structural conditions are added to make competition in economic theory not only "pure" but "perfect."[6] The most important is the absence of barriers to the entry of new firms, combined with mobility of resources employed, or potentially employable, in a market. Conversely, significant

---

4. Smith, *Wealth of Nations,* p. 342.

5. This definition is given for the sellers' side of an industry. The definition of buyers' competition is symmetric. Pure competition exists among buyers when the number of entities buying a homogeneous product is so large, and each buyer's share of the market so small, that each buyer believes variations in the quan-

tity it buys have an imperceptible effect on the market price. When some buyer can perceptibly influence price, *monopsony* is said to exist.

6. This distinction is essentially the one adopted by Edward H. Chamberlin in *The Theory of Monopolistic Competition* (Cambridge: Harvard University Press, 1933), Chapter 1.

entry barriers are the *sine qua non* of monopoly and oligopoly, for as we shall see in later chapters, sellers have little or no enduring power over price when entry barriers are nonexistent. A newer extension of this concept is pertinent when firms can enter a market and then *exit* easily, in the precise sense that their investments can be liquidated without loss more rapidly than producers within the market can react to the entering-and-exiting firms' decisions. When this exit condition is satisfied, markets are said to be *contestable* even if the conditions for pure competition are not met.[7]

Other conditions sometimes associated with perfect competition include perfect knowledge of present and future market conditions and continuous divisibility of inputs and outputs. These are less important, as well as less realistic, for their violation does not necessarily alter the main conclusions generated by the theoretical model of a purely and perfectly competitive market system's operation.

One final terminological point deserves mention, because it is a common source of confusion. The power over price possessed by a monopolist or oligopolist depends upon the firm's size *relative to* the market in which it is operating. It is entirely possible for a firm to be very small in absolute terms, but to have considerable monopoly power. The physician in an isolated one-doctor town is an excellent example. So was the Besser Manufacturing Company, which was found guilty in 1951 of illegally monopolizing the concrete block machinery industry, even though it employed only 465 persons at the time and had sales of less than $15 million.[8] On the other hand, a firm may be enormous in absolute terms, but possess little monopoly power in its principal markets. An example is the Sun (Oil) Company, which had sales of $8.7 billion in 1987 but accounted for only about 4 percent of U.S. petroleum refining and marketing. To postulate a 1-to-1 relationship between monopoly power and absolute size is like confusing pregnancy with obesity. Some superficial manifestations may be similar, but the underlying phenomena could hardly differ more.

The Case for Competition

We proceed now to the principal questions on our agenda. Why is a competitive market system held in such high esteem by statesmen and economists alike? Why is competition the ideal in a market economy, and what is wrong with monopoly?

Political Arguments   We begin with the political arguments, not merely because they are sufficiently transparent to be treated briefly, but also because when all is said and done, they, and not the economists' abstruse models, have tipped the balance of social consensus toward competition. One of the most important arguments is that the atomistic structure of buyers and sellers required for competition decentralizes and disperses power. The resource allocation and income distribution problem is solved through the almost mechanical interaction of supply and demand forces on the market, and not through the conscious exercise of power held in private hands (for example, under monopoly) or government hands (that is, under state enterprise or government regulation). Limiting the power of both government bodies and private individuals to make decisions that shape people's lives and fortunes was a fundamental goal of the men who wrote the U.S. Constitution, which in turn has served as a model for many other nations. As James Madison wrote (under the pseudonym Publius) in Federalist Paper No. 10, nothing was more important to a well-constructed union than avoiding the imposition on all citizens of measures favored by narrow factions.[9] Factions, continued Madison, arise most frequently from the unequal distribution of property, pitting the wishes of "a landed interest, a manufacturing interest, a mercantile interest, a moneyed interest, with many lesser interests" against the common good. The best way to avoid faction-dominated outcomes, said Madison, was to keep the individual factions so small and diverse that they would be "unable to concert and carry into effect schemes of oppression."

A closely related benefit is the fact that competitive market processes solve the economic problem *impersonally*, and not through the personal control of entrepreneurs and bureaucrats. There is nothing more galling than to have the achievement of some desired objective frustrated by the decisions of an identifiable individual or group. Who, on the other hand, can work up much outrage about a setback administered by the impersonal interplay of competitive market forces?

A third political merit of a competitive market is its freedom of opportunity. When the no-barriers-to-entry condition of perfect competition is satisfied, individuals are free to choose whatever trade or profession they prefer, limited only by their own talent and skill and by their ability to raise the (presumably modest) amount of capital required.

The Efficiency of Competitive Markets

Admitting the salience of these political benefits, our main concern nonetheless will be with the economic case for competitive market processes. Figure 2.1(b) reviews the conventional textbook analysis of equilibrium in a competitive industry, and Figure 2.1(a) portrays it for a representative firm belonging to that industry. Suppose we begin observing the industry when the short-run industry supply curve is S_1, which embodies the horizontal summation of all member firms' marginal cost curves. The short-run market equilibrium price is OP_1, which is viewed as a parameter or "given" by our representative firm, so the firm's subjectively-perceived demand curve is a horizontal line at the level OP_1. The firm maximizes its profits by expanding output until marginal cost (MC) rises into equality with the price OP_1. It produces OX_1 units of output and earns economic profits — that is, profits above the minimum return required to call forth its capital investment — equal to the per-unit profit GC_1 times the number of units of output OX_1. Because economic profits are positive for the representative firm, this cannot be a long-run equilibrium position. New firms attracted by the profit lure will enter the industry, adding their new marginal cost functions to the industry's supply curve, and existing firms will expand their capacity, so the industry supply curve shifts to the right. Entry and expansion will continue, augmenting output and driving the price down, until price has fallen into equality with average total cost (ATC) for

7. See William J. Baumol, John C. Panzar, and Robert D. Willig, *Contestable Markets and the Theory of Industry Structure* (New York: Harcourt Brace Jovanovich, 1982).

8. *U.S.* v. *Besser Mfg. Co.*, 96 F. Supp. 304 (1951), affirmed 343 U.S. 444 (1952).

9. *The Federalist Papers*, Mentor Book edition (New York: New American Library, 1961), pp. 77–84.

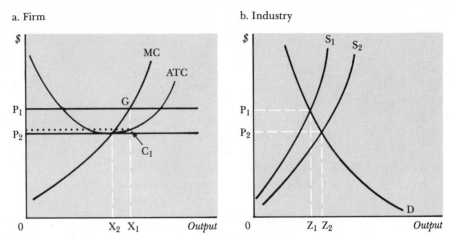

a. Firm   b. Industry

Figure 2.1
Equilibrium under Pure
Competition

the representative firm.[10] In the figures shown, this zero-profit condition emerges with the short-run supply curve S_2, yielding the market price OP_2. The representative firm maximizes its profits by equating marginal cost with new price OP_2, barely covering its unit costs (including the minimum necessary return on its capital) at the output OX_2.

The long-run equilibrium state of a competitive industry has three general properties with important normative implications:

a. The cost of producing the last unit of output — the marginal cost — is equal to the price paid by consumers for that unit. This is a necessary condition for profit maximization, given the competitive firm's perception that price is unaffected by its output decisions. It implies efficiency of resource allocation in a sense to be explained momentarily.

b. With price equal to average total cost for the representative firm, economic (that is, supra-normal) profits are absent. Investors receive a return just sufficient to induce them to maintain their investment at the level required to produce the industry's output efficiently. Avoiding a surplus return to capital is considered desirable in terms of the equity of income distribution.

c. In long-run equilibrium, each firm is producing its output at the minimum point on its average total cost curve. Firms that fail to operate at the lowest unit cost will incur losses and be driven from the industry. Thus, resources are employed at maximum production efficiency under competition.

One further benefit is sometimes attributed to the working of competition, although with less logical compulsion. Because of the pressure of prices on costs, entrepreneurs may have especially strong incentives to seek and adopt cost-saving technological innovations. Indeed, if industry capacity is correctly geared to demand at all times, the *only* way competitive firms can earn positive economic profits is through innovative superiority. We might expect therefore that technological progress will be more rapid in competitive industries. However, doubts concerning the correctness of this hypothesis will be raised in a moment.

The Inefficiency of Monopoly Pricing

Monopolists and monopolistic competitors differ from purely competitive firms in only one essential respect: They face a downward-sloping demand curve for their output. Given this, the firm with monopoly power knows that to sell an additional unit (or block) of output, it must reduce its price to the customer(s) for that unit; and if it is unable to practice price discrimination (as we shall generally assume, unless otherwise indicated),[11] the firm must also reduce the price to all customers who would have made their purchases even without the price reduction. The net addition to the nondiscriminating monopolist's revenue from selling one more unit of output, or its *marginal revenue*, is equal to the price paid by the marginal customer, minus the change in price required to secure the marginal customer's patronage multiplied by the number of units that would have been sold without the price reduction in question.[12] Except at prices so high as to choke off all demand, the monopolist always sacrifices something to gain the benefits of increased patronage: the higher price it could have extracted had it limited its sales to more eager customers. When demand functions are continuous and smooth, marginal revenue under monopoly is necessarily less than price for finite quantities sold. When the monopolist's demand function can be represented by a straight line, marginal revenue for any desired output is given by the ordinate of a straight line intersecting the demand curve where the latter intersects the vertical axis, and with twice the slope of the demand curve, as illustrated in Figures 2.2(*a*) and 2.2(*b*).[13] We will normally use straight-line demand curves in subsequent illustrations because they make it easier to get the geometry of their associated marginal revenue curves exactly right.

Now the profit-maximizing firm with monopoly power will expand its output only as long as the net addition to revenue from selling an additional unit (the marginal revenue) exceeds the addition to cost from producing that unit (the marginal cost). At the monopolist's profit-maximizing output, marginal revenue equals marginal cost. But with positive output, marginal revenue is less than price, and so the monopolist's price exceeds marginal cost. This equilibrium condition for firms with monopoly power differs from that of the competitive firm. For the competitor, price equals marginal cost; for the monopolist, price exceeds marginal cost. This difference has important implications to which we shall return in a moment.

---

10. We assume perfect imputation of all factor scarcity rents here. If the imputation process is imperfect, only the marginal firm — the firm just on the borderline between entering and not entering — will realize zero economic profits.

11. The logic of price discrimination will be explored in Chapter 13.

12. Generally, for the monopolist price is a function $P = f(Q)$ of the quantity Q sold. Total sales revenue $R = PQ$. Marginal revenue is the change in total revenue associated with a unit change in quantity sold, thus, $MR = dR/dQ = P + Q(dP/dQ)$. P in the MR expression is the price paid by marginal consumers; dP/dQ is the change in price necessary to attract them (usually with a negative sign); and Q corresponds approximately to the quantity that would be sold without the price reduction.

13. Proof: Let the demand curve have the equation $P = a - bQ$, where Q is the quantity demanded. Total revenue $R = PQ = aQ - bQ^2$. Marginal revenue $dR/dQ = a - 2bQ$. At $Q = 0$, $P = MR$. The slope $(-2b)$ of the marginal revenue function is twice the slope $(-b)$ of the demand curve.

a. Pure monopolist

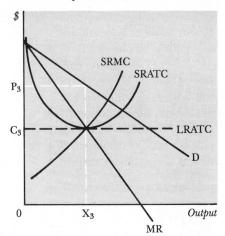

b. Monopolistic competitor

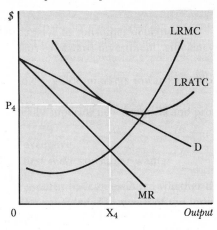

Figure 2.2
Equilibrium under Monopoly

The competitive enterprise earns zero economic profit in long-run equilibrium. Is the firm with monopoly power different? Perhaps, but not necessarily. Figure 2.2(*a*) illustrates one of the many possible cases in which positive monopoly profits are realized: specifically, the per-unit profit margin P_3C_3 times the number of units OX_3 sold. As long as entry into the monopolist's market is barred, there is no reason why this profitable equilibrium cannot continue indefinitely. Figure 2.2(*b*), on the other hand, illustrates the standard long-run equilibrium position of a monopolistic competitor.[14] The crucial distinguishing assumptions are that monopolistic competitors are small relative to the market for their general class of differentiated products and that entry into the market is free. Then, if positive economic profits are earned, new firms will squeeze into the industry, shifting the typical firm's demand curve to the left until, in long-run equilibrium, it is tangent to the firm's long-run unit cost function LRATC. The best option left for the firm then is to produce output OX_4, where marginal revenue equals marginal cost (as in any monopolistic situation) and the average revenue or price OP_4 is barely sufficient to cover unit cost. Thus, while firms with monopoly power *may* secure monopoly profits, they need not, especially under the plausible conditions of monopolistic competition.

We found earlier that in long-run equilibrium, the purely and perfectly competitive firm produces at minimum average total cost. Is this true also of the monopoly? Many textbooks imply that it is not, or that it will be true only by accident. Again consider Figure 2.2(*a*). It assumes that the monopolist operates under constant long-run cost conditions; that is, that plants (or plant complexes) designed to produce at high outputs give rise to roughly the same cost per unit as those designed to produce at low outputs. We shall see in Chapter 4 that many real-world cost functions exhibit this property over substantial output ranges. If so, the firm will invest in a plant complex characterized by the short-run cost function SRATC, with minimum short-run unit costs identical to the minimum long-run cost OC_3 at the profit-maximizing output OX_3. We conclude that it is quite possible theoretically and empirically for monopolists, like their competitive brethren, to operate in such a way as to minimize average total cost. However, this is also not necessary. Figure 2.2(*b*) presents the most widely discussed exception. Since the monopolistic competitor in Chamberlinian equilibrium operates with its demand curve tangent to its LRATC curve, and since the demand curve is downward sloping, the LRATC curve must also have a negative slope at the equilibrium output. It follows that average cost is *not* minimized, for lower unit costs could be realized by expanding the firm's output. The monopolistic competitor does not do so because price (read off the demand curve) falls more rapidly than unit cost beyond the Chamberlinian equilibrium output, so that a higher output would spell negative profits.

In sum, firms with monopoly power may deviate from the zero-profit and minimum-cost conditions associated with purely and perfectly competitive equilibrium, but they need not do so.[15] The only distinction necessarily implied by the theories of pure competition and pure monopoly is that the monopolist's price exceeds marginal cost, while the competitor's price equals marginal cost. This seeming technicality, so trivial at first glance, is the basis of the economist's most general condemnation of monopoly: it leads to an allocation of resources that is inefficient in the sense of failing to satisfy consumer wants as completely as possible.

To see this, we must think more deeply about the meaning of price as it affects the decisions of a consumer just on the margin between buying one more unit of a product and not buying it. A numerical illustration is especially helpful, so let us consider Figure 2.3(*a*). It assumes that the production of a composite commodity "manufactured goods" with the demand curve D_M is monopolized. The industry is assumed (for simplicity) to produce under constant cost conditions, with long-run average total cost and marginal cost equal to $5.00 per unit at any output level chosen. The manufactured goods monopolist maximizes its profits by setting marginal cost equal to marginal revenue, which for the assumed cost and demand conditions requires producing 2 million units and setting a market-clearing price of about $9.70 per unit.

Now in setting this price, the monopolist chokes off the demand of consumers who would have been willing to purchase units (or additional units) at prices below $9.70. Consider some consumer who would purchase an extra unit at $9.60, but not at $9.70. We say that $9.60 is her *reservation price* — the price just low enough to overcome her reservations about purchasing an extra unit. She buys the extra unit at $9.60 because it is worth that much to her; she refrains from purchasing at $9.70 because she considers the unit not worth the higher price. The consumer's reservation price for any incremental unit of consumption indicates in monetary terms how much that unit is worth to her. It is an index of the value of an extra unit

14. Chamberlin, *Monopolistic Competition*, supra note 6, Chapter 5.
15. But firms with monopoly power cannot normally be free of both deviations simultaneously. If they earn zero or negative profits, they will necessarily find it optimal to operate at higher than minimum average total cost. And (ignoring some dynamic complications to be introduced in Chapter 10) if they find it optimal to operate at minimum average cost, they will earn positive monopoly profits.

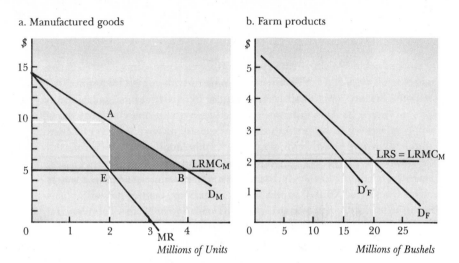

a. Manufactured goods

b. Farm products

Figure 2.3
Resource Allocation with
Competition and Monopoly

of consumption from the consumer's viewpoint and hence, in a social system honoring consumer sovereignty, from the viewpoint of society.[16]

The extra unit of manufactured goods required to satisfy the demand of this marginal consumer can be produced with resources costing $5.00. The marginal social value of the extra unit is $9.60. Marginal value exceeds marginal cost, so it would appear eminently worthwhile to produce that unit. The same can be said for all other units of manufactured goods that would be demanded at prices from $9.60 down to $5.00; their value to marginal consumers (read off the demand curve) exceeds their marginal cost, so they ought to be produced. They are not produced — that is, output is unduly restricted — because the monopolist is unwilling to sacrifice the profits it can secure by charging the higher price ($9.70) and selling fewer units.

For virtually all units of manufactured goods the monopolist does supply, the value to consumers of those units (measured as the demand curve ordinate for any given unit consumed) exceeds the monopolist's $9.70 price. On all but the two-millionth (that is, marginal) unit supplied and demanded, therefore, there is a surplus of value to consumers over the price paid. This is called *consumers' surplus*.[17] With a monopoly price of $9.70, the total consumers' surplus realized is defined by the triangular area in Figure 2.3(*a*) bounded by the vertical axis, a horizontal line at the $9.70 level, and the demand function from its vertical intercept to point *A*. By analogy, the monopolist's profit is called a producer's surplus. It is measured as quantity sold times unit profit, or in Figure 2.3(*a*) as the rectangular area between zero and two million units and between the $9.70 price and the $5.00 cost. If, contrary to its profit-maximizing instincts, the monopolist reduced its price to $5.00, its profit or producer's surplus would be converted into consumers' surplus on the two million units that would have been consumed even at the $9.70 price. This is essentially a redistribution of income. But in addition, two million more units will be demanded, virtually all (given the demand function's slope) at reservation prices exceeding $5.00. Satisfying that demand would add consumers' surplus equal to the triangular area ABE between the demand curve and the $5.00 price line. At the $9.70 monopoly price, this surplus is realized neither by the monopolist nor by consumers. It is in effect lost, and therefore it is called a *dead-weight welfare loss*. It provides a first indication of the inefficiencies associated with monopolistic output restriction. Only through an expansion of manufactured good output to 4 million units, where price equals marginal cost, does some segment of society realize the surplus ABE.

Of course, the resources needed to expand production of manufactured goods must come from somewhere, which (assuming full employment) means that consumption of some other end product must be reduced. The problem of efficient resource allocation is a general equilibrium problem, involving the balance of all sectors in the economy. The analysis of general equilibrium takes us between Scylla and Charybdis: the rigorous models lack intuitive appeal and the intuitive models lack rigor. Because it is so important to understand the common sense of monopoly resource allocation, we opt for an intuitive approach here.[18]

Suppose the economy consists of only two industries, a monopolized manufactured goods industry and a competitive farm products industry. Figure 2.3 shows these two industries in general equilibrium, given the assumed demand functions D_M and D_F, constant-cost production conditions in each industry, and the assumed market structures. (Note that the diagrams are not drawn to the same scale.) The output of manufactured goods is (as before) two million units per year; the output of farm products is twenty million bushels per year. Now suppose we could arrange to transfer resources valued at $100 from the farm products industry to the manufactured goods industry. Since the marginal cost of manufactured goods is $5.00, it will be possible to produce twenty extra units with these resources. To sell the extra production, the price will have to be reduced infinitesimally — for example, to $9.699. The value of the extra manufactured output from the viewpoint of marginal consumers barely willing to pay this new, lower price is 20 units $\times$ $9.699 = $194. However, the loss of farm products owing to the resource transfer must be weighed against this gain. Since the marginal cost of a bushel of farm produce is $2.00, the transfer of $100 in resources forces society to sacrifice fifty bushels of output. To choke off the demand for this output (at least, as a first approximation), the price of farm products must be raised slightly — for example, to $2.001 per bushel. This reduction in quantity demanded comes at the

16. Indirectly, the reservation price measures the utility of a marginal unit to consumers, for when utility-maximizing consumers are in equilibrium, the price of each commodity included in their market baskets equals the marginal utility of that commodity divided by the marginal utility of money.

17. The terminology here follows Alfred Marshall, *Principles of Economics,* 8th ed. (London: Macmillan, 1920), pp. 124 ff. and 467 ff.

18. A more rigorous exposition was included as an appendix to the first and second editions of this book. For a geometric ap-

proach using transformation functions but otherwise paralleling the argument here, see Robert Dorfman, *Prices and Markets* (Englewood Cliffs: Prentice-Hall, 1967) pp. 120–135. For other approaches, see William J. Baumol, *Welfare Economics and the Theory of the State* (rev. ed.; Bell, 1965), Chapters 1–6; Francis Bator, "The Simple Analytics of Welfare Maximization," *American Economic Review,* vol. 47 (March 1957), pp. 22–59; and Tjalling Koopmans, *Three Essays on the State of Economic Science* (New York: McGraw-Hill, 1957), pp. 4–104.

expense of consumers who were willing to buy an extra bushel at $2.00 but not at $2.001. Since they would rather abstain from consuming that bushel than pay $2.001, the value of the farm products foregone at the margin must be about $2.00 per bushel. The total value of farm products sacrificed as a result of the resource transfer is approximately $2.00 × 50 bushels = $100.00. Recapitulating, consumers have benefited from the resource reallocation by a net increase in output value of approximately $194 − $100 = $94.

If it is possible through such a reallocation to increase the value of the overall output bundle, it must follow that the value of output was not maximized in the original (monopoly) equilibrium. Too few resources were allocated to the monopolistic sector, and too many to the competitive sector, relative to the allocation that maximizes the value of output to society. Because it leads to an allocation of resources that fails to maximize the value of the overall output bundle, we say that monopoly misallocates resources, or that it leads to an inefficient allocation of resources.

The same point can be shown in terms of consumers' and producers' surplus. The value of the farm output transferred here is less than $2.001 per bushel. Since before the transfer farm output was sold at a price of $2.00 per bushel, consumers' surplus for the marginal output bundle must have been virtually nil. Because price equals marginal cost in a competitive industry, producers' surplus must also have been nil. But after reallocation, the $100 of resources yield additional manufactured goods valued at $194, so either producers' or consumers' surplus of approximately $94 must be generated by the transfer. If it is possible through reallocation to increase surplus in this way, it must follow that the sum of consumers' plus producers' surpluses was not maximized in the original (monopoly) equilibrium. Failure to maximize the value of the output bundle and failure to maximize the sum of consumers' plus producers' surpluses are conceptually identical manifestations of monopolistic resource misallocation.[19] Although we shall use the surplus concept again later, the output bundle maximization approach is somewhat more convenient for illustrating the relatively drastic changes implied by our two-sector example, so we emphasize the latter here.

If significant value gains can be had by reallocating $100 worth of resources, additional gains must come from carrying the process farther. Let us go all the way, breaking up the manufactured goods monopoly into numerous independent production units and eliminating any barriers to the entry of new resources. With the manufactured goods price initially well above the cost of production, resources will flow (or be drawn) into manufacturing, where the lure of positive profits beckons, and out of farming, where a zero-profit competitive equilibrium prevailed. It might seem that the price of farm products must rise above marginal cost as resources are pulled away and output contracts. This is true as a first approximation, but not as a second, for two reasons. First, a competitive industry simply cannot be in long-run equilibrium if price exceeds marginal cost. Something must give to restore the equality between price and cost. Second, as the price of manufactured goods is reduced to sell an expanding output, a substitution effect in favor of manufactured goods and adverse to farm products is induced. Assuming for the moment that the price of farm products hovers near the marginal cost of $2.00, the *ceteris paribus* (other prices equal) assumption on which the manufactured goods sector's demand function was constructed remains valid, so there will be no shift in D_M. But because of the fall in the manufactured goods price there must be a leftward shift in the farm products demand curve — for example, to D'_F. Ignoring some complications temporarily, let us assume that D'_F represents the final farm products demand curve after all adjustments have occurred, and D_M the manufactured products demand curve. To be in final equilibrium, each competitive industry must have price equal to long-run marginal cost. This implies an output of four million units of manufactured goods with a price of $5.00 per unit and an output of 15 million bushels of farm products at a price of $2.00 per bushel. Resources originally valued at $10 million have been transferred from farm products to manufactured goods production, increasing the value of the aggregate output to society by a substantial amount — specifically, by the triangular area ABE in Figure 2.3(*a*).

Now let us attempt a further reallocation of resources. If we transfer resources valued at $100 from farm products to manufactured products, we sacrifice fifty bushels of farm output. These would have been bought by consumers with reservation prices of $2.00 or slightly higher, so that the value of farm output sacrificed is at least $100 and perhaps a bit more. We gain twenty extra units of manufactured goods saleable only at prices slightly less than $5.00, so the value of the additional manufactured output is less than $100. The value of the output gained is less than the value of the output sacrificed, so the transfer reduces the overall value of output to society. If we transfer $100 of resources in the opposite direction, we obtain fifty more bushels of farm output saleable only at prices slightly less than $2.00 for a gain of less than $100. We give up twenty manufactured units that would have been bought by consumers with reservation prices of $5.00 or higher, implying a value sacrifice exceeding $100. The value of the output added in the farm sector is less than the value of the manufactured goods sacrificed, and so this transfer also reduces the total value of output. Thus, a transfer of resources in either direction away from the competitive equilibrium allocation reduces output value. It follows that the value of output must have been at a (local) maximum in competitive equilibrium. Quite generally, when all sectors of an economy are in competitive equilibrium, with price equal to marginal cost for each firm, the total value of the output, measured in terms of each commodity's equilibrium price, is at a maximum. It is impossible to make any small resource reallocations that yield a higher output value. Because it maximizes output value in this sense, a fully competitive market system is said to allocate resources efficiently.[20] Conversely, a system shot through with monopoly elements is inefficient because it fails to do so. This, in a nutshell, is the heart of the economist's case for competition and against monopoly.

19. Cf. Arnold C. Harberger, "Three Basic Postulates for Applied Welfare Economics: An Interpretive Essay," *Journal of Economic Literature,* vol. 9 (September 1971), pp. 785–797; Robert D. Willig, "Consumer's Surplus without Apology," *American Economic Review,* vol. 66 (September 1976), pp. 589–597; and Jerry A. Hausman, "Exact Consumer's Surplus and Deadweight Loss,"

American Economic Review, vol. 71 (September 1981), pp. 662–676.
20. It is remarkable how acute Adam Smith's insight was on this point, when he observed that the individual producer in a competitive economy necessarily labors to render "the exchangeable value of the whole annual produce . . . as great as possible." *Wealth of Nations,* p. 423.

The analysis thus far has ignored a few complications. To describe the final equilibrium, we need a third approximation. One loose end is that the fall in manufactured goods prices increases the real income of consumers. This income effect will shift both sector demand curves to the right (unless one of the commodities happens to be an inferior good). Monopoly profits are also wiped out, freeing part of money transactions holdings to support those increases in demand.[21] The increased demand for products will be transmitted into increased demand for productive inputs, whose wages will be bid up.[22] This leads to upward shifts in the industry cost functions. With the present model, it is not possible to specify exactly where the final equilibrium will occur after all these effects have worked their way through the system, and therefore the shifted curves are not shown in Figure 2.3. One thing is certain, however. In each sector price will be equal to marginal cost for every producer, and so no further resource transfers can increase the ultimate aggregate value of output. Efficient resource allocation will have been achieved.

While this end result of eliminating monopoly is clearly desirable, another effect is more difficult to assess. Income will have been redistributed, with former monopoly profit recipients losing and other claimants (such as workers) gaining. Whether this is good or bad cannot be determined without a value judgment over which reasonable persons may disagree. There are at least two reasons for thinking that the competitive equilibrium may be preferred over the monopolistic one on equitable grounds, but the case is not airtight. First, society may object to monopoly profits as unearned gains and place ethical value on seeing them eliminated. One trouble with this argument is that the monopoly's original creators may already have reaped their gains by selling out their ownership interests at high capitalized values, leaving secondary and tertiary stock buyers, who before the monopoly's dissolution were receiving no more than a normal return on their money investment, with severe capital losses. Second, of the roughly half of all industrial enterprise common stocks held in 1983 by individual U.S. citizens, 72 percent of the stocks by value were held by families in the top 10 percent of the income distribution.[23] If all families of given size have similar income utility functions, the marginal utility of income must be higher for the multitudes who supply only their labor services than for the wealthy few with substantial monopoly shareholdings. A redistribution of income away from monopolists and toward labor suppliers will therefore add to the sum of utility for all citizens. Yet however appealing this may appear on intuitive grounds, there is no scientific way of making the interpersonal utility comparisons required to support it. Therefore, we tread warily when we say that competition is beneficial not only because it allocates resources efficiently, but also in terms of income distribution equity.

This completes the case based upon orthodox economic theory. Some other criticisms of monopoly can be mentioned more briefly. Monopolists' price-raising propensities may stimulate imports and worsen individual nations' terms of trade.[24] Lacking competitive pressure, firms may not exercise diligence in controlling their costs and therefore waste resources. As Adam Smith observed, "Monopoly . . . is a great enemy to good management."[25] For similar reasons, monopolists may display a lethargic attitude toward technological innovation, although contrary suggestions will be considered shortly. And, finally, enterprises with monopoly power, or those that seek it, may devote excessive resources to advertising, legal stratagems, and the maintenance of excessive capacity; or they may use pricing systems that encourage inefficient geographic locations and unnecessarily high transportation costs. These alleged flaws, we shall find, may be even more serious than the resource misallocation problem. It is only for reasons of orderly presentation that we defer a more detailed examination until later.

Qualifications and Doubts

General equilibrium analysis reveals the superiority of a competitive market system in solving society's resource allocation and income distribution problems under certain assumptions. But can we expect real-world economies to conform to the assumptions of the general equilibrium model? Might there be violations of assumptions stated explicitly or implicitly, or additional considerations not taken into account, that would cause us to modify our judgment? Several qualifications and doubts come to mind.

For one, the whole concept of efficient resource allocation is built upon the fundamental belief that the consumer is sovereign — that individual preferences are what count in the ledger of social values.[26] If, for example, consumers freely choosing in the market demonstrate that they would prefer at the margin to give up fifty bushels of grain to get an additional twenty hair shirts, we conclude that society is really better off because of the shift. Yet in practice our respect for consumer sovereignty is by no means universal — not, in any event, for infants, convicted criminals, dope addicts, the mentally ill, and others whose preferences cannot be trusted to generate rational choices. And in this age of widespread neuroses and psychoses, the line between rationality and irrationality is not all that easy to draw. One might even entertain doubts about the soundness of consumption decisions made by presumably normal, rational adults whose tastes (assumed in the standard theory of consumer behavior to be stable) have been remolded under a barrage of advertising messages. Further qualms intrude when we recognize that there are external diseconomies in consumption, for example, that the purchase of a new hair shirt by Mr. Willoughby may not only increase his utility, but simultaneously reduce the utility of envious neighbors. All this warns us that the theorems of welfare economics are erected upon sandy foundations. This does not

21. Under the previous (second) approximation, payments to all income claimants were $50 million, compared to $59.4 million when the manufacturing sector was monopolized. For monetary equilibrium to be restored, there must either be input and output price increases or a contraction in the money stock.

22. Unless supply functions are perfectly inelastic, the rise in real wages will also call forth increased input supplies, which in turn will permit a general expansion of output, ceteris paribus.

23. See F. M. Scherer, "Corporate Ownership and Control," in John R. Meyer and James M. Gustafson, eds., *The U.S. Business Corporation: An Institution in Transition* (Cambridge: Ballinger, 1988), pp. 46–48.

24. See Lawrence J. White, "Industrial Organization and International Trade: Some Theoretical Considerations," *American Economic Review,* vol. 64 (December 1974), pp. 1013–1020.

25. Smith, *Wealth of Nations,* p. 147.

26. On the consumer sovereignty question, see Tibor Scitovsky, "On the Principle of Consumers' Sovereignty," and Jerome Rothenberg, "Consumers' Sovereignty Revisited and the Hospitality of Freedom of Choice," both in the *American Economic Review,* vol. 52 (May 1962), pp. 262–290; Scitovsky, *The Joyless Economy* (New York: Oxford University Press, 1976); and the debate among G. L. Bach, Steven Hymer, Frank Roosevelt, Paul Sweezy, and Assar Lindbeck in the *Quarterly Journal of Economics,* vol. 86 (November 1972), pp. 635–636, 648–650, 661–664, and 672–674.

mean that their conclusions are wrong. The demonstration of a competitive system's allocative efficiency makes considerable sense even when complications related to advertising, ignorance, and the like are introduced. But blind faith is also uncalled for.

A second assault on the economist's conventional wisdom holds that under conditions known as "natural monopoly," firms can be large enough to realize all economies of scale only if they are monopolists. Under monopolistic (or in weaker cases, oligopolistic) organization, then, costs are lower than they would be if an industry includes many small-scale producers. The consequences are illustrated in Figure 2.4. The long-run average total cost curve available to large or small firms is LRATC, with associated marginal cost curve LRMC. If the industry were atomistically structured, each member firm would operate a small plant designed to produce OF units of output at a unit cost of OP_C. Then the long-run supply curve of the competitive industry would be $P_C S$, and total output would be OX_C. Alternatively, the monopolist would consider its marginal cost possibilities LRMC, choose to produce OX_M units (where marginal cost equals marginal revenue) at an average total cost per unit of OC_M, and let the market clear at price OP_M. Output under monopoly, with its low costs, is higher than output under atomistic competition, with its high costs. Clearly, it cannot be said that consumers are poorly served by the monopoly, even though one might ideally prefer that the monopoly expand its output to OX_A or even (as we shall see in a later chapter) OX_O. Furthermore, on the output OX_C supplied by the small competitors, unit costs are higher than those of the monopoly by $P_C C_M$ per unit, or by area

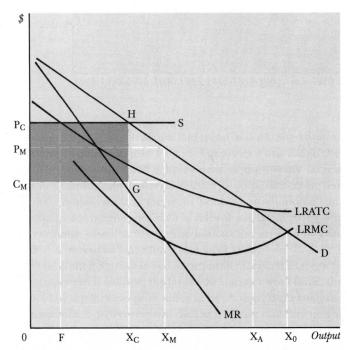

Figure 2.4
Natural Monopoly

P_CHGC_M in total. Excess cost, in this case caused by the too-small scale of production, is a dead-weight loss to society just as the failure to satisfy demand (by restricting output below the level at which price and marginal cost are equated) is. As Figure 2.4 is drawn, monopoly is unambiguously superior to competition, having lower costs and higher output, and hence smaller dead weight losses with respect to each. In a more complex case to be addressed in Chapter 5, monopoly may have lower costs but also supply less output, requiring a tradeoff between the lower dead weight losses associated with its cost structure and the higher dead weight losses stemming from its output restriction. Whether monopolists or oligopolists actually enjoy cost advantages as great as those shown in Figure 2.4, or indeed any at all, is an empirical question. We shall deal with it thoroughly in Chapter 4.

Previously it was suggested that monopolists, sheltered from the stiff gale of competition, might be sluggish about developing and introducing technological innovations that reduce costs or enhance product quality. Yet some economists, following the late Joseph A. Schumpeter, have argued exactly the opposite: firms need protection from competition before they will bear the risks and costs of invention and innovation, and a monopoly affords an ideal platform for shooting at the rapidly and jerkily moving targets of new technology.[27] If this is true, then progress will be more rapid under monopoly than under competition. And, Schumpeter argued, it is the rate of technical progress, not the efficiency of resource allocation at any moment in time, that in the long run determines whether real incomes will be high or low. Suppose, as a hypothetical illustration, that real gross national product this year could be $5 trillion under pure and perfect competition, but that the misallocation caused by monopoly elements reduces it at every moment in time by 10 percent — that is, to $4.5 trillion this year. Suppose furthermore that a purely and perfectly competitive economy can sustain real growth of 3 percent per year, so that in five years the GNP under competition will be $5.81 trillion. How much more rapid must growth be under monopoly to catch up to the competitive potential in five years, starting from the lower monopoly base of $4.5 trillion? The answer is, a monopolistic economy growing at 5 percent will catch up in five years, and it will surpass the competitive system by an increasing margin from then on. Or if a monopolistic economy starting from a 10 percent static allocation handicap could grow at the rate of 3.5 percent per year, it would overtake the competitive system (grown to $9.1 trillion) in twenty years. If in fact growth is more rapid under monopoly than under competition, sooner or later the powerful leverage of compound interest will put the monopolistic system in the lead, despite any plausible starting disadvantage owing to static misallocation. The question is, of course, was Schumpeter right? Is technological progress really more rapid under monopoly? Orderly presentation demands that we leave the issue unsettled, returning to it in Chapter 17.

Since growth could conceivably bring overpopulation, depletion of natural resources, pollution, and generally reduced standards of living, some have

27. Joseph A. Schumpeter, *Capitalism, Socialism and Democracy* (New York: Harper, 1942), especially pp. 88 and 103.

questioned whether a high rate of economic growth is desirable.[28] We cannot resolve that value conflict here, but two observations are warranted. First, for given levels of population, available resources will be stretched farther and real income per capita will almost surely be higher with more rather than less (nonmilitary) technical progress. Second, the logic of monopoly resource misallocation has special twists when applied to natural resources available only in fixed amounts. In certain cases (for example, with zero extraction cost and unchanging demand elasticities over time), the profit-maximizing prices, and hence rates of resource depletion, are the same under monopoly as under competition.[29] In other more plausible cases, monopolies tend to charge higher prices than a competitive industry in the early years, but this means that there will be more of the resource, and hence lower prices, in later years.[30] Thus, if one believes that society is excessively myopic in its rate of natural resource use (which is tantamount to rejecting market-determined interest rates as a guide to dynamic resource allocation), the conservationist bias of monopolists may be applauded. To be sure, the same conservationist result might be achieved with less objectionable income distribution implications through appropriate public policy interventions, for example, through taxes or government-owned land leasing decisions.

It is also possible that monopolistic industry organization might be more conducive to the macroeconomic stability of employment, listed in Chapter 1 as an important performance goal. The hair-trigger price adjustments of purely and perfectly competitive markets could intensify tendencies toward instability, making it more difficult to combat cyclical unemployment through fiscal and monetary measures. The issue is too important to be left to the macroeconomists, who in any event have made little progress addressing it. Yet boundaries must be drawn, and we choose to leave the question for another forum.[31]

The discussion of allocative efficiency thus far has emphasized the monopoly and monopolistic competition cases, deliberately ignoring oligopolistic market structures. We now ask, how much competition is necessary to bring prices into rough equality with marginal cost? Will rivalry among the few, or oligopoly, suffice? This turns out to be an extraordinarily difficult question, for the theory of oligopoly pricing does not yield the neat, confident generalizations derivable under the theories of pure monopoly or monopolistic competition. We shall spend several chapters exploring the theory and evidence before answers can be ventured. In a similar vein is Professor Galbraith's contention that countervailing power — the power of a few large buyers dealing with monopolistic sellers — offers an effective surrogate for competition.[32] Power on the buyer's side will be a focus of Chapter 14.

Particularly important qualifications are required by the conditions associated with monopolistic competition. Because its product is differentiated physically or through other distinctive attributes, the monopolistic competitor faces a downward-sloping demand curve. It therefore seeks an equilibrium in which price exceeds marginal cost, and in addition, production occurs at less than minimum average total cost. But the consumer gets something in exchange: greater variety in the available bundle of goods and services. Again, a tradeoff is required. And as Professor Chamberlin concluded in his pioneering work, "Differences in tastes, desires, incomes, and locations of buyers, and differences in the uses which they make of commodities all indicate the need for variety and the necessity of substituting for the concept of a 'competitive ideal,' an ideal involving both monopoly and competition."[33] This tradeoff problem will be addressed in Chapter 16. We shall see that under monopolistic competition, too much variety may emerge under certain identifiable conditions and too little under others.

The Problem of Second Best

There are many reasons why, in the real world, it is impossible or undesirable to satisfy all the assumptions of the purely competitive general equilibrium model. Given that competition cannot be pure and perfect in all sectors, what policy should be pursued toward the remaining sectors? Is the second-best solution one that encourages maximum conformity to the rules of competition, whenever and wherever possible? The answer suggested by the theory of second best is quite possibly no, but it is difficult to say, because the answer depends upon complex circumstances peculiar to each case.

To provide a preliminary perspective, we return to Figure 2.3. We assume an economy consisting of two sectors, manufactured goods and farm products. The manufactured goods sector is monopolized; there is misallocation of resources, and we want to improve matters. Suppose, however, that there is no feasible way to break up the monopoly, for example, because of scale economies or a reticent Supreme Court. If something is to be done, it must be done in the farm products sector. What to do? Let us, out of desperation, organize the farmers into a monopoly. The farm price will be raised. This will set off a chain of repercussions. Owing to the change in relative prices, a substitution effect will shift the manufactured goods demand curve to the right, drawing resources out of the farming sector. Income effects may induce further shifts and price changes; monopoly profits will rise; wages of some productive inputs will probably fall, shifting marginal cost curves downward; and so on. Suppose, after all the necessary adjustments have been made, the economy settles down into the equilibrium illustrated in Figure 2.5. The price of manufactured goods is $7.00, with 4.25 million units supplied at a cost of $4.00 per unit; and the price of farm products is $2.80, with 11 million bushels supplied at a cost of $1.60 per unit.[34]

28. For various views see E. J. Mishan, *Technology and Growth: The Price We Pay* (New York: Praeger, 1969); D. H. Meadows et al., *The Limits to Growth* (New York: Universe, 1972); and Julian Simon and Herman Kahn, eds., *The Resourceful Earth: A Response to Global 2000* (Oxford: Blackwell, 1984).

29. See Joseph E. Stiglitz, "Monopoly and the Rate of Extraction of Exhaustible Resources," *American Economic Review*, vol. 66 (September 1976), pp. 655–661; the critiques by Tracy R. Lewis et al. and Gordon Tullock, *American Economic Review*, vol. 69 (March 1979), pp. 227–233; and Joseph Stiglitz and Partha Dasgupta, "Market Structure and Resource Depletion," *Journal of Economic Theory*, vol. 28 (October 1982), pp. 128–164.

30. For simulation analyses on petroleum, bauxite, and copper,

see Robert S. Pindyck, "Gains to Producers from the Cartelization of Exhaustible Resources," *Review of Economics and Statistics*, vol. 60 (May 1978), pp. 238–251.

31. The first two editions of this text devoted a full chapter to the questions, but the material appears to have been little read. The (rare?) interested reader is referred to the 1980 edition.

32. John Kenneth Galbraith, *American Capitalism: The Concept of Countervailing Power* (Boston: Houghton Mifflin, 1952), Chapter 9.

33. Chamberlin, *Monopolistic Competition*, supra note 6, pp. 214–215.

34. Marginal costs have fallen by 20 percent, reflecting a commensurate decline in input wages. The diagrams assume a 13 percent average decline in the quantity of inputs supplied.

Figure 2.5
Resource Allocation in a
World of Monopolies

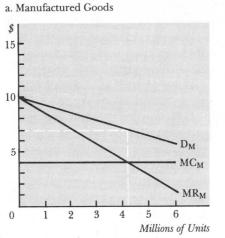

a. Manufactured Goods

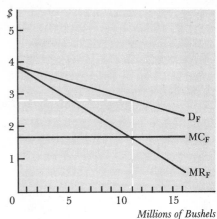

b. Farm Products

Now let us try, as before, to increase the aggregate value of the economy's output by further resource transfers. Suppose we transfer resources valued at $160 out of the farm monopoly into manufacturing. This entails a sacrifice of one hundred bushels of farm produce (since the marginal cost is $1.60) and a gain of forty manufactured good units. The additional manufactured goods can be sold only to consumers with reservation prices below $7.00, and so the value gain must be slightly less than $280. So far, so good. But the farm produce given up has a value to consumers of $2.80 or slightly more per unit, implying a total value sacrifice exceeding $280. The value sacrifice exceeds the gain, and hence the transfer is not worthwhile. It can be seen by similar reasoning that a transfer of resources from manufacturing into farming will reduce the value of output slightly. It follows that the aggregate value of output must be at a (local) maximum in the equilibrium attained by monopolizing both sectors! By abandoning our effort to maintain a world of competition and moving instead to a world of monopolies, we have secured an equilibrium with output value implications closely resembling those of competitive equilibrium.[35]

This happens to be a special case. The data underlying Figure 2.5 were rigged so that the ratio of the monopoly equilibrium price to marginal cost in the manufactured goods sector (7 to 4) is the same as the price/marginal cost ratio in farming (2.80 to 1.60). Or to put the point in a form that will be more convenient in later chapters, prices are marked up above marginal cost so that the monopoly equilibrium *price − cost margins*, defined as (P − MC)/P, in the two industries are identical:

$$(2.1) \qquad \frac{P - MC}{P} = \frac{7 - 4}{7} = \frac{2.80 - 1.60}{2.80} = 0.4286$$

A simple but precise rule of thumb for profit maximization under monopoly is for the monopolist to set its price — cost margin equal to the inverse of its price elasticity of demand:[36]

$$(2.2) \qquad\qquad PCM = \frac{P - MC}{P} = \frac{1}{e}$$

This in turn implies that equal price — cost margins will be set voluntarily by monopolists if, and only if, each firm encounters the same price elasticity of demand in the neighborhood of its equilibrium output. Quite generally, when the supply of production inputs is fixed, and when all producers sell their output directly and only to consumers, a completely efficient (first-best) allocation of resources can be achieved by equating price/marginal cost ratios across all industries. This *rule of proportionality* was proposed by some economists during the 1930s as a possible solution to the monopoly problem, to be enforced by direct government intervention in pricing decisions.[37]

Intervention would in fact be required, since the odds against every producer facing the same demand elasticity values, and hence voluntarily choosing the same price — cost margins, are astronomical. Moreover, enforcing the equal (P − MC)/P rule through public authority will not lead to an efficient allocation of resources under certain highly probable conditions. For one, some goods or services are almost necessarily sold under competitive conditions, frustrating the attainment of a "world of monopolies" solution. The most important example is leisure. The price of leisure to the typical worker-consumer is the opportunity cost he or she incurs by not supplying additional labor services — that is, the wage for additional hours of work. For firms as employers, the marginal cost of labor is the wage paid, unless the labor market is monopsonistic, in which case it exceeds the wage paid. For the world of monopolies solution to be achieved, the price of leisure must be raised above the marginal cost of labor services to firms in the same proportion as all other commodity prices exceed their marginal costs. It is extremely difficult to find a practical way of doing this; direct per-hour subsidy payments by the government to each and every worker obviously fail to meet the practicality test. But unless the price of leisure is raised relative to the wage paid by firms, or unless all workers' labor supply curves are completely inelastic, workers will consume too much leisure and supply too little labor relative to the quantities required for an efficient allocation of resources. Thus, labor inputs, and hence the output bundle available for consumption, will be smaller under a world of monopolies approach to product pricing than it would be if all products were supplied under competitive conditions.

---

35. Cf. Joan Robinson, *The Economics of Imperfect Competition* (London: Macmillan, 1934), Chapter 27.

36. Proof: From note 12 above, marginal revenue MR = P + Q(dP/dQ). This can be manipulated to P[1 + (dP/dQ)(Q/P)]. Price elasticity of demand e is defined as −[(dQ/dP)(P/Q)] = −[1/(dP/dQ)(Q/P)]. Substituting this last expression into the expression for MR, we obtain MR = P(1 − 1/e) = P − P/e.

With MC = MR, we have MC = P − P/e, which rearranges to (P − MC)/P = 1/e.

37. See R. F. Kahn, "Some Notes on Ideal Output," *Economic Journal,* vol. 45 (March 1935), pp. 1–35; and Abba P. Lerner, "The Concept of Monopoly and the Measurement of Monopoly Power," *Review of Economic Studies,* vol. 1 (June 1934), pp. 157–175.

Another complication stems from the elaborate vertical and horizontal inter-relationships characterizing any modern economy. Many products are not sold exclusively to final consumers; they are also used in whole or in part as intermediates by other firms. Consider the case of common salt, and assume (merely to simplify matters) that the only scarce basic resource is labor, which receives an equilibrium wage of $5.00 per hour. Suppose that a hundredweight of salt can be produced using one hour of labor, and that monopolistic salt producers sell their product at $10 per hundredweight, so that the ratio of price to marginal cost is 2. Suppose in addition that the production of a barrel of pickles requires one hundredweight of salt (for which $10 is paid) and one hour of labor (for which the pickle-maker pays $5.00). The combined marginal cost, from the pickle producer's perspective, is $15 per barrel. If the rule of proportionality were enforced, the pickles will be sold at a price twice their marginal cost, that is, at $30 per barrel. But since both salt and pickles enter directly into the market baskets of consumers, a distortion emerges. Two hours of labor will produce salt valued at $20 by the marginal consumer or pickles valued at $30. A reallocation of resources (labor) from the production of salt for final consumption to the production of pickles (requiring, of course, more intermediate salt) will raise the aggregate value of output. Thus, applying the rule of proportionality fails to maximize the value of output when products serve both as intermediates and final consumption goods. Analogous difficulties arise when a particular intermediate good enters into the various end products' manufacturing processes at different stages, or when the intermediate good accounts for varying proportions of the total cost of different end products.[38]

These and similar problems are assaulted in the general theory of second best.[39] The starting point is recognition that one or more of the conditions necessary for a first-best optimum simply cannot be satisfied, for example, because some sectors of the economy are unavoidably monopolistic and others competitive. Violations of the first-best optimum conditions are introduced as constraints upon the problem of maximizing the desired criterion function — that is, of maximizing the aggregate value of output or the sum of consumers' plus producers' surpluses. The second-best problem is to find new decision rules for the sectors a policy-maker *can* control, given the imposed constraints.

The typical result is a set of formidably complex decision rules in place of the simple "price equals marginal cost" conditions customary in first-best problems. The only positive generalization reached by Lipsey and Lancaster in their pioneering article was that, when some first-best optimum condition could not be attained, it was no longer desirable to fulfill the other first-best optimum conditions. An important contribution by Abram Bergson provided insight into the directions a second-best policy might take under certain circumstances.[40] He assumes a competitive labor supply sector, one or more uncontrollable industries that elevate price above marginal cost, and one or more industries controlled by the government in which prices are to be set to achieve an economywide second-best optimum. When the government-controlled output is a substitute in consumption for the output of uncontrolled and distorted industries, the second-best solution typically entails raising the controlled output's price above marginal cost.

The magnitude of the elevation — that is, the ratio of the controlled output's price to marginal cost — turns out to be the weighted harmonic mean of price/cost ratios in the uncontrolled sectors (including labor supply), with the weights being the equilibrium quantity of each uncontrolled industry's output times its elasticity with respect to the controlled output's price/cost ratio. The greater the price/cost distortion for any given uncontrolled industry, the more important that industry is in the economy, and the more that industry's output expands as the substitute-controlled output's price is raised,[41] the higher will be the second-best controlled price/cost markup, ceteris paribus. When the controlled output is a complement in consumption to the uncontrolled output, the controlled output's price may be depressed below its marginal cost in the second-best solution. In a world of mixed substitutes and complements, the direction of the second-best price adjustment depends upon the magnitudes of the uncontrolled industries' price distortions, outputs, and demand cross elasticities.

This is, needless to say, a formidably tough assignment. No central authority could conceivably obtain the masses of information on demand elasticities, cross elasticities, cost functions, and prices needed to devise fully articulated second-best pricing strategies for even a single major industry richly interconnected with other sectors. Even if the data were available, it is doubtful whether second-best actions in that industry alone would do much to offset distortions pervading the rest of the economy. Because it indicates that maintaining competitive pricing whenever possible is not necessarily optimal, but offers little clear guidance toward improved policies in the absence of information seldom if ever attainable, the theory of second best is a counsel of despair.

A "third-best" approach might be to choose among alternative *general* policies, trying to adopt the policy that *on average* has the most favorable resource allocation implications. In the framework of our present concern, the main alternatives boil down to letting monopoly increase in sectors not already monopolized, versus attempting to enforce as much competition as one can consistent with economies of scale, product differentiation, and so forth. When the issue is put this way, the case for competition gains renewed appeal. On the positive side, if one has little or no prior information concerning the direction in which second-best optima lie, eliminating avoidable monopoly power is about as likely to improve welfare as is encouraging new monopoly distortions where none existed previously. And on the negative side, it is easy for a policy that is permissive toward monopoly to get out

38. See Lionel McKenzie, "Ideal Output and the Interdependence of Firms," *Economic Journal,* vol. 61 (December 1951), pp. 785–803; and Richard E. Just and Darrell L. Hueth, "Welfare Measures in a Multimarket Framework," *American Economic Review,* vol. 69 (December 1979), pp. 947–954.

39. The standard reference is R. G. Lipsey and Kelvin Lancaster, "The General Theory of Second Best," *Review of Economic Studies,* vol. 24, no. 1 (1956), pp. 11–32. An almost simultaneous and similar formulation is Marcel Boiteux, "Sur le gestion des monopoles publics astreints a l'equilibre budgetaire," *Econometrica,* vol. 24 (January 1956), pp. 22–40. For a generalization, see Edward Foster and Hugo Sonnenschein, "Price Distortion and Eco-

nomic Welfare," *Econometrica,* vol. 38 (March 1970), pp. 281–297. A two-commodity, one-input proof of the main propositions here is contained in the Appendix to Chapter 2 of the 1980 edition of this text, pp. 599–600.

40. Abram Bergson, "Optimal Pricing for a Public Enterprise," *Quarterly Journal of Economics,* vol. 86 (November 1972), pp. 519–544.

41. This last relationship is probably a special case stemming from Bergson's assumption that price/cost markups in the uncontrolled sector are not influenced by changes in the controlled sectors' price/cost markups.

of hand. Too much monopoly distortion may emerge in formerly competitive sectors, especially in view of the fact that some important sectors (such as the labor-leisure market) will remain competitive. Given the difficulties, a generally procompetitive policy seems more apt to be superior in a third-best sense.[42]

Nevertheless, one might conclude that the whole question of allocative efficiency is so confused and uncertain, once second-best considerations are introduced, that policymakers would be well advised to give up trying to achieve the best possible allocation of resources. Rather, heavier weight might be accorded other criteria such as equity of income distribution, compatibility with political beliefs, conduciveness to production efficiency, and speed of technological progress. It is worth repeating that if this view is adopted, a procompetitive policy is likely to be favored under the first two criteria. Judgment is reserved on the production efficiency and progress issues until the relevant evidence can be examined more carefully.

Doubts Concerning the Profit Maximization Hypothesis

The conclusions of economic theory concerning the allocation of resources and distribution of income under competition and monopoly are based, among other things, upon the assumption that consumers maximize their subjective satisfaction and firms maximize profits. However, the profit maximization assumption has been challenged vigorously on several fronts.[43] The argument, in brief, is that profit maximization is at best unappealing and at worst meaningless to business decision makers operating in an environment of uncertainty, organizational complexity, and conflicting goals. Since these changes could require modifications in performance predictions based upon orthodox price theory and in judgments about the desirability of competition, we must pay them careful heed.

The Effects of Uncertainty   Nearly all the interesting decisions made by business firms require predictions about uncertain future events. Decision makers simply cannot know precisely how strong and how elastic demand will be in the next period, let alone ten years hence, or how far labor unions will carry their struggle for higher wages in forthcoming negotiations, or how rival sellers will react to a price change, or how the long-term bond rate will move in coming years. How should they behave in the face of such uncertainties? Economic theory usually assumes that managers formulate definite expectations about the future values of relevant variables and then plug the expected values into their profit-maximizing decision rules. The expectations presumably include at least an estimate of the most likely, or best-guess, value and perhaps also some notion about the probability of more pessimistic and optimistic outcomes. This is already assuming a lot. Critics have noted that many businesspeople are poorly informed about business conditions in general, know almost nothing about the axioms of probability,[44] and understand only crudely the logic of profit maximization, that is, what variables (such as marginal cost and marginal revenue) must be taken into account and how they must be related. It is scarcely realistic to expect that profit maximization will sprout magically from such barren soil, the skeptics continue. In a famous defense of orthodoxy, Fritz Machlup countered that business managers have an intuitive understanding of what is required to maximize profits, even though they cannot articulate rules matching the economist's price-equals-marginal-cost condition, just as automobile drivers who have never taken a course in differential equations can intuitively solve the problem of passing another car on a two-lane highway. He went on to stress a subjective interpretation of the variables that are manipulated by entrepreneurs:

> It should hardly be necessary to mention that all the relevant magnitudes involved — costs, revenue, profit — are subjective — that is, perceived or fancied by the men whose decisions or actions are to be explained . . . rather than "objective.". . . Marginal analysis of the firm should not be understood to imply anything but subjective estimates, guesses and hunches.[45]

This defense comes close to saying that whatever managers choose to do can be called profit maximization, however remotely it resembles the policies an omniscient maximizer would set. Carried so far, the theory of profit maximization becomes little more than tautology.

Yet even if we assume a close correspondence between business expectations and objective reality, further dilemmas appear. Imagine a decision maker weighing two alternative policies, one offering a best-guess profit expectation of $1 million with a 5 percent chance of bankrupting the firm (whose net worth is currently $4 million), the other an expected profit of $2 million with a 15 percent chance of disaster. Which is the rational choice? It is impossible to say without further information on the attitudes of the firm's owners toward increases in wealth versus total loss of their equity.

Further complications are posed by the interactions among uncertainty, risk aversion, and the decision maker's time horizon. Long-run profit maximization implies maximizing the discounted present value of an enterprise's current and future profit stream. But at what rate shall future profits be discounted? Finance texts advise that the discount rate be derived from the firm's weighted average cost of capital, with the cost of each financing mode evaluated at the rate currently prevailing in securities markets. Yet market rates fluctuate widely from time to

42. For similar arguments, see L. Athanasiou, "Some Notes on the Theory of Second Best," *Oxford Economic Papers,* vol. 18 (March 1966), pp. 83–87; and Y. K. Ng, "Towards a Theory of Third Best," *Public Finance,* vol. 32, no. 1 (1977), pp. 1–15.

43. The literature is enormous. Seminal contributions include Fritz Machlup, "Marginal Analysis and Empirical Research," *American Economic Review,* vol. 36 (September 1946), pp. 519–554; Armen A. Alchian, "Uncertainty, Evolution, and Economic Theory," *Journal of Political Economy,* vol. 58 (June 1950), pp. 211–221; Andreas G. Papandreou, "Some Basic Problems in the Theory of the Firm," in B. F. Haley, ed., *A Survey of Contemporary Economics,* vol. 2 (Homewood: Irwin, 1952), pp. 183–222; Herbert Simon, "Theories of Decision-Making in Economics and Behavioral Science," *American Economic Review,* vol. 49 (June 1959), pp. 253–283; Robin Marris, "A Model of the 'Managerial' Enterprise," *Quarterly Journal of Economics,* vol. 77 (May 1963), pp. 185–209; R. M. Cyert and J. G. March, *A Behavioral Theory of the Firm* (Englewood Cliffs: Prentice-Hall, 1963); Oliver E. William-son, *The Economics of Discretionary Behavior* (Englewood Cliffs: Prentice-Hall, 1964); R. J. Monsen and Anthony Downs, "A Theory of Large Managerial Firms," *Journal of Political Economy,* vol. 73 (June 1965), pp. 221–236; Michael C. Jensen and William H. Meckling, "Theory of the Firm: Managerial Behavior, Agency Costs, and Ownership Structure," *Journal of Financial Economics,* vol. 3 (1976), pp. 305–360; Herbert Simon's Nobel Prize address, "Rational Decision Making in Business Organizations," *American Economic Review,* vol. 69 (September 1979), pp. 493–513; Richard R. Nelson and Sidney G. Winter, *An Evolutionary Theory of Economic Change* (Cambridge: Harvard University Press, 1982); and Harvey Leibenstein, *Inside the Firm: The Inefficiencies of Hierarchy* (Cambridge: Harvard University Press, 1987).

44. For evidence, see Mark J. Machina, "Choice under Uncertainty: Problems Solved and Unsolved," *Journal of Economic Perspectives,* vol. 1 (Summer 1987), pp. 121–154.

45. "Marginal Analysis and Empirical Research," supra note 43, pp. 521–522.

time.[46] What if management is convinced that the current market rate is too low or too high and will soon be overtaken by events? Should expectations of future rates be substituted? How far into the future? How these questions are answered — and unanimous agreement is lacking even in treatises on managerial economics — can have a substantial impact on business firms' conduct.

Consider, for example, the problem of a firm with monopoly power deciding upon its pricing strategy. One possibility is to price so as to realize the highest possible profits today, regardless of future consequences. Alternatively, the firm may choose not to exploit its monopoly power fully today, hoping that a low current price will cement customer loyalties and deter the emergence of new competitors, increasing the probability that the firm will weather whatever storms the uncertain future will bring. The "right" choice in this and more complex dynamic pricing problems, to be explored in Chapter 10, is far from obvious.

That managerial goals can differ strikingly in different market environments is shown by a comparative survey of top managers in 1,031 Japanese and 1,000 U.S. industrial corporations during the early 1980s.[47] The managers were asked how important eight diverse goals were to their organizations. The average rankings for the two panels were as follows:

Goal	American Managers	Japanese Managers
Return on investment	1	3
Higher stock prices	2	8
Increased market share	3	2
Improving products and introducing new products	4	1
Streamlining production and distribution systems	5	4
High net worth ratio	6	5
Improvement of social image	7	6
Improving working conditions	8	7

Achieving high returns on investment and higher stock prices — arguably, indicia of an emphasis on profit maximization — were ranked much higher by the American managers than by the Japanese. Yet it is far from clear that the Japanese were neglecting profits in an equally meaningful sense, for the introduction of superior new products, though possibly reducing current profits, is likely to enhance the firm's future profit-earning potential. And although they may be gained only through patient struggle, larger market shares, we shall see in Chapter 11, are strongly and systematically associated with greater profitability. Whether these differences in stated managerial goals stem from differences in the cost of capital (because of their stronger propensity to save, the Japanese have lower interest rates), differences in business organization (for example, the longer employment tenure of Japanese managers or their closer relationships with banks), or differences in the deeper-seated aspects of culture is a question that warrants careful research.

Organizational Complexity

Another feature of the modern business enterprise that may prevent it from behaving in strict conformity to the profit maximization hypothesis is its organizational complexity. Most large corporations have multiple operating units supervised by one or more corporate-level executives. Within the corporate staff, and often mirrored at the operating level, there are functional components specializing in production, sales, materials procurement, finance, accounting, research and development, and so forth. An elaborate chain of command extends from workers at the operating level to top management and the board of directors — the latter presumably representing stockholder interests. This structure must be tied together by a communications network so that decisions taken at various levels and in the diverse functional specialties mesh. It is here that breakdowns occur. Conflicts among functional groups are bound to arise. David Halberstam documents, for example, the hard-fought goal disparities between MBAs on Ford Motor Company's finance staff, who stressed strategies with clear, quantifiable, profit-maximizing prospects, and the engineering-oriented "product" people, who urged an accelerated pace of design improvement and were more inclined to accept added cost to improve product quality.[48] Such conflicts must often be passed up to higher, and perhaps top, management for resolution. But the information transmission process is subject to attenuation. Top managers cannot possibly digest all the knowledge possessed by every operating-level employee, and so some grasp of special circumstances affecting particular cases must be sacrificed. Furthermore, the content of messages is often distorted to suit the prejudices and fears of both senders and receivers. The more hierarchical filters through which information passes and the sharper the conflict is among specialists, the more distorted the message is likely to become, and the greater is the chance that incorrect choices will be made. Or in the reverse flow from top management to operating levels, the more likely instructions will be misinterpreted or deliberately ignored.

Given this organizational complexity, it may prove very difficult for top management to arrive at and enforce decisions that maximize profits. Complicating matters is the fact that operating-level personnel often care little about profit maximization. Even the best-designed employee bonus and profit-sharing systems seldom instill much zeal for profit maximization below the middle management level. Operating-level employees see little correlation between their individual actions and the size of the profit pie in which they will share, just as individual firms in a competitive industry consider their output decision to have an imperceptible effect on the market price and hence their profits. At the same time, they have many goals that conflict with profit maximization by any criterion. Division chiefs fearing dismissal or playing for time gloss over operating problems until the

46. See, for example, Robert J. Shiller, "Do Stock Prices Move Too Much To Be Justified by Subsequent Changes in Dividends?" *American Economic Review,* vol. 71 (June 1981), pp. 421–436. Compare Terry A. Marsh and Robert C. Merton, "Dividend Variability and Variance Bounds Tests for the Rationality of Stock Market Prices," *American Economic Review,* vol. 76 (June 1986), pp. 483–498.

47. Tadao Kagawa et al., "Strategy and Organization of Japanese and American Corporations," summarized in M. J. Peck, "The Large Japanese Corporation," in Meyer and Gustafson, *The U.S. Business Corporation,* supra note 23, pp. 35–36.
48. David Halberstam, *The Reckoning* (New York: William Morrow, 1986), Chapters 11, 13, 28, 33, 34, and 41.

situation has deteriorated beyond repair. Research and development engineers seek technical sophistication and product refinement for their own sake, even when they add more to cost than to revenues. Production and staff supervisors find make-work jobs for redundant personnel because firing people is unpleasant, and so on.

It is the classic responsibility of top management to ferret out these deviations and to establish a system of controls and incentives that ensures internal conformity with the firm's profit maximization goal. Organizational complexity can frustrate such efforts. But an equally significant obstacle arises out of the very character of the modern business corporation. Like the divisional and functional specialists they command, top managers may pursue the profit goal with less than complete diligence.

One reason for this is said to be the increasing separation between ownership and control of industrial enterprises — a phenomenon alluded to by Lenin[49] and first studied intensively during the early 1930s by Berle and Means.[50] There was a time more than a century ago when individuals managing even the largest U.S. companies held, if not a majority, at least a substantial minority equity interest in their enterprises. Gradually this has changed. Big business has become bigger; the lion's share of industrial output is produced by corporations large under any plausible definition of the word. The ownership of large corporations has been dispersed among thousands of stockholders, no one of whom may own a sufficiently large fraction of the outstanding shares to exercise a significant controlling role. AT&T had 2.8 million common stockholders of record in 1986, Exxon 740,000, and IBM 793,000. The median (250th) firm in terms of stockholder numbers on *Fortune*'s list of the 500 largest industrial corporations for 1956 (the last year such data were reported) had more than nine thousand shareholders.

In their pioneering study, Berle and Means found eighty-eight of the 200 largest American nonfinancial corporations to be "management controlled" in 1929 because no individual, family, corporation, or group of business associates owned more than 20 percent of all outstanding voting stock, and because evidence of control by a smaller ownership group was lacking.[51] Only twenty-two of the corporations were judged to be privately owned or controlled by a group of stockholders with a majority interest. Replicating the Berle and Means methodology, but with a lower 10 percent ownership share threshold, Robert Larner found that by 1963, 161 of the 200 largest nonfinancial corporations had come to be management controlled. He concluded that the "managerial revolution" identified by Berle and Means was "close to complete."[52]

This view of the world has been challenged by Phillip Burch, Edward Herman, Thomas Dye, and others for ignoring the power positions of financial intermediaries and the possibility that family or other interest groups might exercise effective control from a position well below a 10 or 20 percent share ownership threshold.[53] Proceeding under an assumption that control could be exercised with a family stock position of 4 to 5 percent accompanied by extended representation on the board of directors, Burch concluded that in 1965, only 41 percent of the leading 300 industrial corporations and 28 percent of the top fifty merchandising corporations were "probably management controlled."[54] He found that 43 percent of the industrials and 58 percent of the merchandising corporations were "probably family controlled."

Thus, one's conclusion as to whether the separation of ownership and control has advanced nearly to its limit, or less than half of the way, depends upon subtle quantitative distinctions over which reasonable scholars can disagree.

When managers themselves are not major stockholders, the task of representing stockholder interests falls upon the board of directors. A path-breaking study by Myles Mace showed that the role of stock-holding family representatives in U.S. corporations varied widely.[55] Sometimes, Mace found, family members ceased exercising active control in the boardroom when their stock ownership dropped below 50 percent. In other cases they continued to exercise de facto control despite holding only a small fraction of the company's stock. Much evidently depends upon such idiosyncracies as the business ability and interest of family members. When family members did take an active part, it was manifested among other things in bringing family influence to bear on the choice of other board members.

When the board of directors is more clearly controlled by management, the inside chief executive officer (usually the chairman or president) typically selects outside board members. A reputation for not rocking the boat receives heavy weight in selection decisions; few CEOs wish to repeat the experience of General Motors with board member H. Ross Perot, who criticized company policies both within the boardroom and publicly.[56] Nominations are normally validated by an overwhelming margin as stockholders docilely assign their proxies. Except in crisis situations, board members in turn rubber-stamp management recommendations on new managerial appointments and other policies. Thus, through reciprocal self-selection, the management group maintains its control. Mace's 1971 study revealed that outside directors tended to be ill-informed about their corporations' operations and that conventional boardroom ethics discouraged independent action, or even the posing of embarrassing questions.[57] There is reason to believe that outside directors' participation became more active during the 1980s

49. V. I. Lenin, *Imperialism: The Highest Stage of Capitalism* (New York: International Publishers, 1939), p. 59 (originally published in 1917).

50. Adolf A. Berle and Gardiner Means, *The Modern Corporation and Private Property* (New York: Macmillan, 1932). See also the June 1983 issue of *The Journal of Law & Economics* (vol. 26), containing papers from a conference on the fiftieth anniversary of the Berle and Means book's publication; and the special issue of *Journal of Financial Economics*, vol. 20, January/March 1988.

51. Berle and Means, *The Modern Corporation*, pp. 90–118. Other early studies reaching similar conclusions include Raymond W. Goldsmith, *The Distribution of Ownership in the Largest 200 Nonfinancial Corporations*, Temporary National Economic Committee Monograph no. 29 (USGPO, 1940); and Robert Aaron Gordon, *Business Leadership in the Large Corporation* (Washington: Brookings, 1945).

52. Robert J. Larner, *Management Control and the Large Corporation* (Cambridge: Dunellen, 1970), pp. 9–24.

53. Philip H. Burch, Jr., *The Managerial Revolution Reassessed* (Lexington: Heath, 1972); Thomas R. Dye, "Who Owns America: Strategic Ownership Positions in Industrial Corporations," *Social Science Quarterly*, vol. 64 (December 1983), pp. 865–867; and Edward S. Herman, *Corporate Control, Corporate Power* (Cambridge: Cambridge University Press, 1981), pp. 54–65.

54. Burch, *The Managerial Revolution*, pp. 68 and 96.

55. Myles L. Mace, *Directors: Myth and Reality* (Boston: Harvard Business School Division of Research, 1971), pp. 154–174.

56. "GM Plans Offer To Pay $700 Million To Buy Out Its Critic H. Ross Perot," *Wall Street Journal*, December 1, 1986, pp. 1, 13.

57. Mace, *Directors*, pp. 43–71 and 94–101.

through fear of multimillion-dollar liability judgments against directors who approved, after only superficial consideration, actions that adversely affected stockholder welfare.[58] Thus, in a 1987 Harris poll of 400 U.S. corporations' chief executive officers, 36 percent reported that their directors had become "more assertive" during the past five years, while only 2 percent said that the board had become less assertive.[59] Still it almost surely remains true that under noncrisis conditions, boards of directors do not impose much restraint on management's operating discretion.

Although the legal mandates affecting board of directors' makeup and functioning vary widely from nation to nation, there is surprising uniformity in the extent to which, when strong outside ownership interests are absent, inside management calls the tune. In Japan, most corporations' boards consist almost entirely of inside management members.[60] A few members are appointed by banks or affiliated companies, but once they join, they tend to become full-time employees of the company on whose board they sit. In West Germany, large corporations are required by law to have two different boards — an operating board comprising inside management members and a supervisory board with strong representation from both outside interests and delegates selected by the company's workers.[61] In principle, the supervisory board has the power to steer management in directions it might otherwise not choose. In practice, however, its ability to do so is limited by management's control of information and by the tendency of worker representatives to become co-opted as they spend more and more time on corporate policy matters and less with the workers who elected them.

The Multitude of Managerial Goals

Within certain imprecisely defined bounds, then, management may be free to pursue goals not necessarily consistent with maximizing returns to stockholders. What are those goals? How seriously do they conflict with profit maximization?

One possibility is for managers to seek a placid, comfortable, risk-free existence. As J. R. Hicks put it in a much-quoted quip, "The best of all monopoly profits is a quiet life."[62] Such a characterization does considerable justice to the archetypal British business leader of past generations. Whether it reflects the psychology of American, Japanese, and Continental European counterparts, or even the newest generation of British managers, is more doubtful.

A goal emphasized by the leaders of twelve large, successful U.S. corporations is "long-term corporate survival."[63] Donaldson and Lorsch, the interviewers, found that corporate heads often perceived significant conflicts between maximizing short-run profits and their longer-term survival goal. They complained about "the tyranny of quarter-to-quarter profit growth standing in the way of investment for the long term."[64] Since the proper time frame for profit maximization is ambiguous and since the alternative to survival, even for stockholders, can be unpleasant, it is arguable that behavior emphasizing survival serves owner interests too. Nevertheless, as we shall see in Chapter 5, conflicts can arise — for example, if managers of companies in declining industries seek to perpetuate their enterprises by channeling stockholders' funds into the acquisition of firms whose operations are quite different from their own, requiring know-how and managerial skills they may not have.

Managers seek survival not only of the companies they direct but also of their own jobs. Desiring security of job tenure does not necessarily conflict with profit maximization; the manager who keeps the profits rolling in is, after all, a good person to have around. Yet conflicts can arise, especially in decision making under uncertainty. As William Fellner has pointed out, there tends to be an asymmetry in the rewards to hired managers.[65] If risky decisions turn out badly, stockholders lose their assets and managers lose their jobs.[66] If they turn out well, the manager may be promoted or receive a bonus, but the rewards are seldom commensurate with the stockholders' profit gains. Faced with this asymmetry, the hired manager may sacrifice higher expected profits for lower risk than an owner-manager would under otherwise identical circumstances. Also, because the stock market reacts sensitively to changes, managers concerned about their tenure exhibit an apparent preference for lower but more stably growing earnings over higher but fluctuating earnings. One manifestation is the use of accounting discretion to smooth reported earnings — for example, by shifting the reporting of deferable costs from bad to good years.[67] This is most likely innocuous, but other stability-enhancing behavior can have more negative implications. To protect themselves against attention-drawing setbacks, managers tend to accumulate *organizational slack* — inessential resources that are shed only when operating unit profits are under severe pressure. From a study of three divisions of large corporations during the 1970s, Schiff and Lewin estimated that the amount of slack built into divisional budgets averaged 20 to 25 percent of the units' operating expenses.[68] Top managers were said to be aware that such slack existed; however, they were unable to purge it because they lacked the detailed knowledge needed to set cost and profit budgets tight enough to maximize profits, but not so tight as to jeopardize operations.

58. See, for example, Jeremy Bacon and James K. Brown, *The Board of Directors: Perspective and Practices in Nine Countries* (New York: Conference Board, 1977), Chapters 1 and 8; Charles A. Anderson and Robert N. Anthony, *The New Corporate Directors: Insights for Board Members and Executives* (New York: Wiley, 1986); and Winthrop Knowlton and Ira Millstein, "Can the Board of Directors Help the American Corporation Earn the Immortality It Holds So Dear?" in Meyer and Gustafson, eds., *The U.S. Business Corporation,* supra note 23, pp. 169–191.

59. "Changing Roles," *Business Week,* October 23, 1987, p. 28.

60. Peck, "The Large Japanese Corporation," in Meyer and Gustafson, *The U.S. Business Corporation,* supra note 23, pp. 21–22.

61. Bacon and Brown, *The Board of Directors,* supra note 58.

62. Hicks, "Annual Survey of Economic Theory: The Theory of Monopoly," *Econometrica,* vol. 3 (January 1935), p. 8.

63. Gordon Donaldson and Jay W. Lorsch, *Decision Making at the Top* (New York: Basic Books, 1983), pp. 7–8.

64. Ibid., p. 170.

65. William Fellner, *Competition Among the Few* (New York: Knopf, 1949), pp. 172–173.

66. For evidence that adverse deviations from trend profitability lead to a shortening of corporate presidents' tenure, see W. M. Crain, Thomas Deaton, and Robert Tollison, "On the Survival of Corporate Executives," *Southern Economic Journal,* vol. 43 (January 1977), pp. 1372–1375; Michael S. Weisbach, "Outside Directors and CEO Turnover," *Journal of Financial Economics,* vol. 20 (January/March 1988), pp. 431–460; and Jerold B. Warner, Ross L. Watts, and Karen Wruck, "Stock Prices and Top Management Changes," *Journal of Financial Economics,* vol. 20 (January/March 1988), pp. 461–492.

67. See Jacob Y. Kamin and Joshua Ronen, "The Effects of Corporate Control on Apparent Profit Performance," *Southern Economic Journal,* vol. 45 (July 1978), pp. 181–191.

68. Michael Schiff and Arie W. Lewin, "Where Traditional Budgeting Fails," *Financial Executive,* vol. 36 (May 1968), pp. 50–62; and *idem,* "The Impact of People on Budgets," *Accounting Review,* vol. 45 (1970), pp. 259–268. See also Williamson, *Discretionary Behavior,* supra note 43, pp. 85–126. Two of the slack-laden companies studied by Williamson, it is worth noting, were controlled by dominant family ownership groups.

There is reason to believe that U.S. corporations' behavior changed during the early 1980s. Many firms experienced severe pressure on profits from a combination of the deepest recession since the 1930s and sharply rising import competition, stimulated in turn by unusual (and unsustainable) strength of the U.S. dollar vis-à-vis other currencies. They reacted by implementing extensive, deep staff cutbacks.

Another important change in the 1980s was the large number of "going private" transactions, under which whole publicly-owned corporations or parts thereof restructured themselves financially and reverted to essentially private ownership status. Between 1980 and 1987, the total recorded volume of such transactions exceeded $120 billion. Usually, most of the financing for these new organizations came from borrowing, and inside managers tended to hold a substantial share of the relatively small residual common stock interest. Case studies and statistical analyses reveal that operating efficiency improved significantly following the restructurings[69] — presumably because of strengthened incentives attributable to management's ownership stake and the pressure of heavy interest payment obligations. It remains unclear whether less desirable tradeoffs may also have been precipitated by such "leveraged buyouts." In particular, there is evidence that capital investments and research and development spending were cut back, possibly weakening the new organizations' long-run strength.

Being human, most hired managers derive considerable satisfaction from achieving personal prestige and power. Both appear to be correlated more closely with the volume of company sales, employment, and assets than with the volume or rate of profits it earns. There have also been indications that the compensation of top executives is more closely associated with corporate size than with profitability. In view of this, it has been argued that hired managers are more concerned with enhancing sales or the growth of sales than with increasing profits.[70] In the static theory of the monopolistic or oligopolistic firm, maximizing sales revenue is incompatible with maximizing profits except under improbable circumstances (for example, when marginal cost is zero). In more dynamic models, the conflict between sales growth and profitability is less pronounced. Nevertheless, increases in growth beyond some point must impose profit sacrifices as management's ability to control is overstrained, as low payoff investment projects are approved, and as high-cost sources of capital are tapped.

Constraints on Departures from Profit Maximization

In sum, there is no shortage of ways business managers *may* deviate from profit maximization. However, there are also constraints on management's freedom to deviate.

One is the threat of takeover. According to hypotheses first advanced by Robin Marris and Henry Manne, failure to maximize profits will depress company stock prices below their potential value.[71] This may induce some outside entrepreneur to bid for a controlling interest, remove the incumbent management, and redirect the company's energies toward increasing profits and hence raising stock values. During the 1960s, such hostile takeovers evolved from rare to commonplace events in the United States and United Kingdom. After a hiatus, takeover activity exploded during the 1980s and expanded beyond Anglo-American frontiers.

There has been extensive quantitative research on this theory of takeovers and managerial constraint. Early British studies and more recent U.S. analyses show that the stock prices of firms singled out as takeover targets were much lower in relation to the accounting or replacement cost value of assets than firms not subjected to takeover attempts.[72] Analyzing 371 companies on *Fortune*'s list of the 500 largest U.S. industrial corporations for 1980, Mørck et al. found that the ratio of stock prices to assets per share averaged 0.524 for forty takeover targets, compared to 0.848 for nontarget sample members.[73] This can be interpreted as evidence of a selection mechanism disciplining lax managers. However, parallel studies reveal that the takeover targets were at worst only slightly less profitable than their industrial peers in the years preceding initiation of the takeover attempt.[74] The profitability evidence has at least two quite different rationalizations. For one, depressed stock prices may reflect investors' expectations of declining future profitability rather than unsatisfactory past profits. Needless to say, such a hypothesis is difficult to test when a takeover alters the target company's control structure. An alternative explanation is that valuation errors on the stock market, not managerial errors leading to deficient profits, are what nominates companies for a takeover attempt. Those with the most undervalued shares become prime targets. This view is also difficult to substantiate or refute empirically; without a good way of ascertaining future earnings absent the takeover attempt, it is hard to tell whether the company's stock was in fact undervalued. It would not be surprising to learn that reality embodies a mixture of these cases: some takeovers occur because of management shortcomings and some because of misvaluation by the stock market.

69. See Steven Kaplan, "Management Buyouts: Efficiency Gains or Value Transfers?" paper presented at a New York University Salomon Brothers Center conference on *Financial-Economic Perspectives on the High-Yield Debt Market* (December 1988); the testimony of F. M. Scherer before the House of Representatives Committee on Ways and Means, March 1989; and Mike Wright and John Coyne, *Management Buyouts* (London: Croom Helm, 1985).

70. For various approaches, see Edith T. Penrose, *The Theory of Growth of the Firm* (Oxford: Blackwell, 1959); William J. Baumol, *Business Behavior, Value, and Growth* (rev. ed.; New York: Harcourt, Brace and World, 1967), Chapters 5–10; Marris, "A Model of the 'Managerial' Enterprise," supra note 43; J. Williamson, "Profit, Growth and Sales Maximization," *Economica*, vol. 34 (February 1966), pp. 1–16; John Lintner, "Optimum or Maximum Corporate Growth under Uncertainty," and Robert M. Solow, "Some Implications of Alternative Criteria for the Firm," in Robin Marris and Adrian Wood, eds., *The Corporate Economy* (Cambridge: Harvard University Press, 1971), pp. 172–241 and 318–342; Richard Schramm, "Profit Risk Management and the Theory of the Firm," *Southern Economic Journal*, vol. 40 (January 1974), pp. 353–363; George K. Yarrow, "Growth Maximization and the Firm's Investment Function," *Southern Economic Journal*, vol. 41 (April 1975), pp. 580–592; and Robert E. Wong, "Profit Maximization and Alternative Theories: A Dynamic Reconciliation," *American Economic Review*, vol. 65 (September 1975), pp. 689–694.

71. Marris, "A Model of the 'Managerial' Enterprise," supra note 43; Marris, *The Economic Theory of "Managerial" Capitalism* (London: Macmillan, 1964); and Henry G. Manne, "Mergers and the Market for Corporate Control," *Journal of Political Economy*, vol. 73 (April 1965), pp. 110–120. For a more recent exchange of views, see the symposium in the *Journal of Economic Perspectives*, vol. 2 (Winter 1988), pp. 3–82.

72. See especially Ajit Singh, *Take-overs: Their Relevance to the Stock Market and the Theory of the Firm* (Cambridge University Press, 1971); Douglas Kuehn, *Takeovers and the Theory of the Firm* (London: Macmillan, 1975); and (for an early U.S. test) Brian Hindley, "Separation of Ownership and Control in the Modern Corporation," *Journal of Law & Economics*, vol. 13 (April 1970), pp. 185–221. On the extent to which managers can depart from profit maximization before triggering a takeover, see Robert Smiley, "Tender Offers, Transaction Costs and the Theory of the Firm," *Review of Economics and Statistics*, vol. 58 (February 1976), pp. 22–32.

73. Randall Mørck, Andrei Shleifer, and Robert W. Vishny, "Characteristics of Targets of Hostile and Friendly Takeovers," in Alan J. Auerbach, ed., *Corporate Takeovers: Causes and Consequences* (University of Chicago Press, 1988), p. 118.

74. David J. Ravenscraft and F. M. Scherer, "Life After Takeover," *Journal of Industrial Economics*, vol. 36 (December 1987), pp. 149–150. See also Edward S. Herman and Louis Lowenstein, "The Efficiency Effects of Hostile Takeovers," in John Coffee et al., eds., *Knights, Raiders, and Targets* (New York: Oxford University Press, 1988), pp. 211–240; Arthur T. Andersen and T. Crawford Honeycutt, "Management Motives for Takeovers in the Petroleum Industry," *Review of Industrial Organization*, vol. 3 (1987), pp. 1–12; and Timothy Hannan and Stephen A. Rhoades, "Acquisition Targets and Motives: The Case of the Banking Industry," *Review of Economics and Statistics*, vol. 69 (February 1987), pp. 67–74.

An analysis of unusually rich data by Ravenscraft and Scherer raises doubts concerning the efficacy of takeovers in remedying managerial failures.[75] Nine years on average after sixty-two U.S. companies experienced 1960s- and 1970s-vintage takeovers, the operating profitability of the acquired units, appropriately adjusted for accounting valuation changes, had neither improved nor regressed relative to pretakeover profit rates. This evidence runs contrary to the hypothesis that takeover occurs to *raise* profitability. Leaders of the acquiring firms may have overestimated their ability to improve matters, but if so, that too speaks poorly for the role of takeovers as a disciplinary mechanism.

Against the still unconfirmed hope that takeovers discipline management and force profit maximization, there is also the possibility of negative consequences. For one, until the 1980s, large corporations were much less likely to be taken over than smaller firms.[76] Recognition of this induced some firms to enter hastily brokered mergers to increase their size and reduce the probability of takeover. However, financial innovations during the 1980s brought even multibillion dollar corporations under siege, reducing the attractiveness of such defensive strategies. In the 1980s a new criticism surfaced. On the assumption that stock market investors are often short-sighted, it was claimed that the threat of takeover induced managers to emphasize short-run profit maximization over longer-term profit-seeking, with adverse consequences for research and development spending and other far-sighted activities. The evidence on this point has thus far been weak and inconclusive.[77]

When forced into the trenches on the question of whether firms maximize profits, economists resort to the ultimate weapon in their arsenal: a variant of Darwin's natural selection theory.[78] Over the long pull, there is one simple criterion for the survival of a business enterprise: profits must be nonnegative. No matter how strongly managers prefer to pursue other objectives, and no matter how difficult it is to identify profit-maximizing strategies in a world of uncertainty and high information costs, failure to satisfy this criterion means ultimately that a firm will disappear from the economic scene. Profit maximization is therefore promoted in two ways. First, firms departing too far from the optimum, either deliberately or by mistake, will disappear. If the process of economic selection continues long enough, the only survivors will be firms that did a tolerably good job of profit maximization. Second, knowledge that only the fit will survive provides a potent incentive for all firms to channel their behavior in profit-maximizing directions, learning whatever skills they need and emulating organizations that excel at the survival game.

To be sure, the selection process operates imperfectly. The environment is constantly changing, altering the behavior required for survival, so that adaptations learned today may not serve tomorrow. And adaptation by industry members may be sufficiently slow to permit firms performing less than optimally to keep their heads above water for a long time.

Despite these qualifications, it seems reasonable to believe that the natural selection process is a stern master in a competitive environment. That it works equally well under monopoly does not follow. When firms with monopoly power are shielded by entry barriers, product differentiation, government favoritism, or the like, threats to their survival may be sufficiently blunted that the organizations can survive for decades without maximizing profits or minimizing costs. The crucial question remains, How much protection from the forces of natural selection do real-world enterprises enjoy? How far from profit-maximizing norms can they stray and still remain viable?

Quantitative Research   There has been much quantitative research on managerial incentives to conform to, or depart from, profit maximization and on the conditions under which departures occur. The work has three main emphases: managerial compensation patterns, returns on new corporate investment, and the relationship between profitability and corporate ownership structure.

Many studies have investigated whether executive salaries and bonuses are correlated with their companies' profitability. The stronger the correlation, the more one might expect managers' incentives to parallel those of owners. An immediate problem is that greater corporate size undoubtedly requires superior managerial skills, and so a positive association between size and compensation is expected. A related problem is that *levels* of sales or assets and levels of profits are highly correlated, making it difficult to tell whether managers strive for size per se or the higher profits that accompany greater size. Close statistical fit[79] and also some a priori theory[80] suggest a nonlinear size–compensation relationship of logarithmic form. When the size effect is so controlled, the weight of evidence suggests that higher or rising profits imply higher executive compensation, although the regulated electric power and telephone companies may be an exception.[81] Using stock price changes rather than reported profits as his indicator of how well managers served stockholders, Kevin Murphy found for a sample of 461 U.S.

75. Ravenscraft and Scherer, "Life After Takeover," pp. 150–154.

76. See Singh, *Take-overs,* supra note 72, pp. 139–144; and Singh's review of Kuehn's book in the *Journal of Economic Literature,* vol. 14 (June 1976), pp. 505–506.

77. See, for example, Herbert I. Fusfeld, "Corporate Restructuring — What Impact on U.S. Industrial Research?" *Research Management,* vol. 30 (July-August 1987), pp. 10–17; and James F. Mathis and Arthur B. Hill, "How 'Speculator's Capitalism' Affects R&D in the Chemical Processing Industries," *Research-Technology Management,* vol. 31 (May-June 1988), pp. 44–49.

78. See especially Alchian, "Uncertainty," Winter, "Natural Selection;" and Nelson and Winter, *An Evolutionary Theory,* supra note 43.

79. See, for example, George K. Yarrow, "Executive Compensation and the Objectives of the Firm," in Keith Cowling, ed., *Market Structure and Corporate Behaviour* (London: Gray–Mills, 1972), pp. 149–173; and W. J. Boyes and Don E. Schlagenhauf, "Managerial Incentives and the Specification of Functional Forms," *Southern Economic Journal,* vol. 45 (April 1979), pp. 1225–1232.

80. Herbert A. Simon, "The Compensation of Executives," *Sociometry,* vol. 20 (March 1957), pp. 32–35.

81. See, for example, Yarrow, "Executive Compensation," supra

note 79; Geoffrey Meeks and Geoffrey Whittington, "Directors' Pay, Growth and Profitability," *Journal of Industrial Economics,* vol. 24 (September 1975), pp. 1–14; William A. McEachern, *Managerial Control and Performance* (Lexington: Heath, 1975); David H. Ciscel and Thomas Carroll, "The Determinants of Executive Salaries," *Review of Economics and Statistics,* vol. 62 (February 1980), pp. 7–13; the comment by James A. Dunlevy, *Review of Economics and Statistics,* vol. 67 (February 1985), pp. 171–174; John R. Deckop, "Determinants of Chief Executive Officer Compensation," *Industrial and Labor Relations Review,* vol. 41 (January 1988), pp. 215–226; A. D. Cosh and A. Hughes, "The Anatomy of Corporate Control: Directors, Shareholders and Executive Remuneration in Giant U.S. and U.K. Corporations," *Cambridge Journal of Economics,* vol. 11 (December 1987), pp. 285–313; and Edward A. Dyl, "Corporate Control and Management Compensation," *Managerial and Decision Economics,* vol. 9 (March 1988), pp. 21–26. On regulated firms, compare Mark Hirschey and James Pappas, "Regulatory and Life Cycle Influences on Managerial Incentives," *Southern Economic Journal,* vol. 48 (October 1981), pp. 327–334; and Thomas M. Carroll and David H. Ciscel, "The Effects of Regulation on Executive Compensation," *Review of Economics and Statistics,* vol. 64 (August 1982), pp. 505–509.

executives over the years 1964–1981 that annual percentage changes in compensation were positively correlated with stock price changes.[82] Managers who led companies experiencing stock price declines of 30 percent or more saw their pay decrease by 1.2 percent per year on average; those whose stock increased in value by 30 percent or more averaged 8.7 percent annual compensation gains. The shifts are modest, but perhaps at least point managers in a profit-maximizing direction.

It is also important to ask whether the level of executive compensation and the extent of its correlation with profitability are greater under some ownership structures than under others. The research on this point has yielded equivocal results. Using data from the 1920s and 1930s, Stigler and Friedland found no significant correlation between executive compensation levels and a variable (taken from Berle and Means) distinguishing management-controlled from other corporations, taking into account also company size in terms of asset values.[83] A study of U.S. data for 1980 showed that compensation levels were significantly higher in corporations with widely dispersed stock ownership (implying control by inside managers), holding company size and profit rates equal,[84] while a British study obtained the opposite result.[85] With data on forty-eight companies in three U.S. industries, McEachern discovered that compensation was more closely correlated with profitability in corporations controlled by an outside ownership group than in companies controlled by either an inside owner-manager group or by inside managers alone.[86]

Even in very large and diffusely held corporations, stock ownership can be an important component of top managers' wealth. To be sure, managers may own only a tiny fraction of their employer's outstanding shares, but a small share of a large sum can be a lot of money. Studying fifty leading U.S. manufacturing corporations, William Lewellen found that on average, dividends, capital gains on company stock holdings, and changes in the value of stock options averaged 1.36 times fixed dollar (salary plus bonus) compensation for the companies' top three executives over the period 1940–1963.[87] More recent confirming evidence on the compensation and stock holdings of 461 high-level U.S. corporation executives comes from Kevin Murphy.[88] On average, the executives' stock holdings averaged $4.7 million — thirteen times their annual salary plus bonus. Moving from the lowest decile in terms of observed returns to common stockholders to the top quintile, the value of the managers' *own* stock holdings increased on average by some $5 million. Even though heroic efforts by the managers might not achieve such dramatic stock return increases, it seems clear that the typical top executive must have been keenly aware that his or her own wealth was linked to the fortunes of the company's shareholders. However, the link may have been less close in management-controlled corporations, for which McEachern found inside managerial stock holdings to be lower than in companies with strong inside or outside ownership groups.[89]

Although executive salaries and bonuses are correlated with both firm size and the level of profits, the size correlations tend to be the stronger of the two. Consequently, executives might be willing to sacrifice profitability at the margin to enhance sales and hence compensation. One way of doing this is to plow back earnings into growth-oriented investments yielding at the margin a lower return than stockholders could achieve reinvesting more generous dividends in other firms' stocks. Baumol and associates found evidence of such behavior in a statistical study of several hundred U.S. corporations.[90] The average rate of return on plowback investments was estimated to be in the range of 3.0 to 4.6 percent, compared to 14 to 21 percent on new equity capital. Subsequent clarifications revealed that the subset of companies issuing new equity capital realized sizable returns on their plowback too, and that the main locus of depressed plowback returns was firms issuing no new common stock.[91] Further light was shed on the matter by Grabowski and Mueller. They argued that most corporations pass through a life cycle. In the early years, when owner control is often strongest, lucrative investment opportunities call for external financing. But as the firm and its products mature, cash flows increase while investment opportunities dwindle. Investment of internally generated funds may be maintained at high levels despite falling profitability because managers seek to expand in accustomed ways and because earnings reinvested internally are taxed more lightly than earnings paid out as dividends and then reinvested. Testing their hypotheses, Grabowski and Mueller classified 759 U.S. corporations into mature (that is, with the majority of their sales in pre-1940 products) and nonmature categories. They found that the nonmature companies realized significantly higher returns on invested capital in each of three periods from 1957 to 1970. From this they concluded that "managers of mature corporations in technologically unprogressive industries re-invest too large a percentage of their internal funds. Their shareholders would apparently be better off with higher payouts. . . ."[92]

If management-controlled companies reinvest their funds in low-yield projects or otherwise fail to maximize profits, there should be a discernible difference in

82. Kevin J. Murphy, "Corporate Performance and Managerial Remuneration," *Journal of Accounting and Economics,* vol. 7 (April 1985), pp. 11–42. For similar earlier findings, see Robert T. Masson, "Executive Motivations, Earnings, and Consequent Equity Performance," *Journal of Political Economy,* vol. 79 (November/December 1971), pp. 1278–1292.

83. George J. Stigler and Claire Friedland, "The Literature of Economics: The Case of Berle and Means," *Journal of Law & Economics,* vol. 26 (June 1983), pp. 237–268.

84. Rexford E. Santerre and Stephen P. Neun, "Stock Dispersion and Executive Compensation," *Review of Economics and Statistics,* vol. 68 (November 1986), pp. 685–693. Compare Dennis C. Mueller, *Profits in the Long Run* (Cambridge University Press: 1986), pp. 159–161, who found statistically insignificant stockholder control coefficients for a large U.S. sample.

85. John Cubbin and Graham Hall, "Directors' Remuneration in the Theory of the Firm," *European Economic Review,* vol. 20 (January 1983), pp. 345–346.

86. McEachern, *Managerial Control,* supra note 81, pp. 77–84.

87. Wilbur G. Lewellen, *The Ownership Income of Management* (New York: Columbia University Press, 1971), pp. 79–103.

88. Murphy, "Corporate Performance," supra note 82, pp. 26–27.

89. McEachern, *Managerial Control,* supra note 81, pp. 82–83.

90. William J. Baumol, Peggy Heim, Burton Malkiel, and Richard Quandt, "Earnings Retention, New Capital and the Growth of the Firm," *Review of Economics and Statistics,* vol. 52 (November 1970), pp. 345–355. Results for the United Kingdom are similar; see, for example, Geoffrey Whittington, "The Profitability of Alternative Sources of Finance," *Review of Economics and Statistics,* vol. 60 (November 1978), pp. 632–634. For contrasting Canadian results, see Daniel M. Shapiro, William A. Sims, and Gwenn Hughes, "The Efficiency Implications of Earnings Retentions: An Extension," *Review of Economics and Statistics,* vol. 65 (May 1983), pp. 327–331.

91. See Irwin Friend and Frank Husic, "Efficiency of Corporate Investment," *Review of Economics and Statistics,* vol. 55 (February 1973), pp. 122–127, with a reply by Baumol et al., pp. 128–131; and Steven Fazzari, R. G. Hubbard, and Bruce Petersen, "Financing Constraints and Corporate Investment," *Brookings Papers on Economic Activity* (1988, no. 1), pp. 141–195; and James M. Griffin, "A Test of the Free Cash Flow Hypothesis: Results from the Petroleum Industry," *Review of Economics and Statistics,* vol. 70 (February 1988), pp. 76–82.

92. Henry G. Grabowski and Dennis C. Mueller, "Life-Cycle Effects on Corporate Returns on Retentions," *Review of Economics and Statistics,* vol. 57 (November 1975), pp. 400–416.

profitability or stock market returns between such firms and enterprises with more powerful owner control groups. Whether the owner group remains outside or participates actively in management, in which case it might sacrifice profits to enhance its own managerial perquisites, could affect the comparison. So also could the degree of monopoly power, since the managers of firms operating in an intensely competitive environment may have little or no discretion to divert profits to their personal ends. Numerous studies have tested some subset of these hypotheses, but only one has attempted to control for the entire set of plausible behavioral variables. The results have varied widely, depending upon the data analyzed, the range of variables taken into account, and the statistical methodology employed.[93] The most comprehensive study (Mueller's) included as explanatory variables the proportion of common shares held by the top five managers, the control position of outside owners, company market share, company size, diversification, industry structure, industry advertising, and industry innovative propensities.[94] Given these variables, Mueller found that corporations with a strong inside owner group had significantly *lower* 1950–1972 profit trajectories, while the existence of a strong outside owner group made no discernible difference. Whether these results will generalize for other nations, company samples, and analytic techniques remains to be seen.

Implications The last word has by no means been uttered on how assiduously modern industrial corporations strive to maximize their profits. From the voluminous and often inconsistent evidence, it appears that the profit maximization assumption at least provides a good first approximation in describing business behavior. Deviations, both intended and inadvertent, undoubtedly exist in abundance, but they are kept within more or less narrow bounds by competitive pressures, the self-interest of stock-owning managers, and the threat of managerial displacement by important outside shareholders or takeovers. To the extent that deviations do occur, they are apt to be larger when competition is weak and when management is strongly entrenched, either by virtue of its own stockholdings or because no coherent outside ownership coalition exists. If firms with monopoly power do tolerate extensive organizational slack, pay princely managerial salaries, and the like, economic inefficiency must be higher than one would predict under the assumption of strict profit maximization.

Workable Competition

We return now to our original question: how valid is the competitive ideal as a prescription for economic policy? Given all the qualifications and doubts unearthed in the foregoing pages, extreme confidence is hardly appropriate. We may even experience an impulse to return to the womb — to Adam Smith's crude vision of how the market economy does its job. Smith was wrong in numerous details, but details of the system may be less important than the broad scheme of operation. If one stands back and gazes astigmatically at competitive market systems without worrying about the fine points, one sees that they do display generally greater responsiveness to consumer demands and generate more potent incentives for the frugal use of resources than do monopoly market structures. This, rather than the satisfaction of all optimal conditions in a general equilibrium system containing 43 quadrillion equations, may be the core of the case for competition.

Doubts concerning the competitive model's utility as a policy guide prompted a search for more operational norms of "workable competition." The phrase was coined by J. M. Clark, who observed in his seminal article that perfect competition "does not and cannot exist and has presumably never existed" and that the competitive model of theory affords no reliable standard for judging real-world market conditions.[95] Clark went on to argue that some departures from the purely and perfectly competitive norm are not as harmful from a longer-run perspective as was commonly supposed, and he formulated certain minimal criteria for judging the workability of competition. The criteria he chose were influenced by the depression psychosis of the times and are less important than the impact Clark's work had in stimulating other economists.

The result was an explosion of articles on workable competition, many in substantial disagreement with one another. We will not attempt to review the literature here, since the job has been done admirably by Stephen Sosnick.[96] Using Sosnick's general schema, the criteria of workability suggested especially frequently by diverse writers can be divided into structural, conduct, and performance categories.

Structural criteria:

- The number of traders should be at least as large as scale economies permit.
- There should be no artificial inhibitions on mobility and entry.
- There should be moderate and price-sensitive quality differentials in the products offered.

Conduct criteria:

- Some uncertainty should exist in the minds of rivals as to whether price initiatives will be followed.
- Firms should strive to attain their goals independently, without collusion.
- There should be no unfair, exclusionary, predatory, or coercive tactics.
- Inefficient suppliers and customers should not be shielded permanently.
- Sales promotion should be informative, or at least not be misleading.
- There should be no persistent, harmful price discrimination.

93. Contributions since the second edition of this text appeared include James L. Bothwell, "Profitability, Risk, and the Separation of Ownership from Control," *Journal of Industrial Economics,* vol. 28 (March 1980), pp. 303–311; Stigler and Friedland, "The Literature of Economics," supra note 83, pp. 254–258; Harold Demsetz and Kenneth Lehn, "The Structure of Corporate Ownership: Causes and Consequences," *Journal of Political Economy,* vol. 93 (December 1985), pp. 1155–1177; Randall Mørck, Andrei Shleifer, and Robert Vishny, "Management Ownership and Market Valuation," *Journal of Financial Economics,* vol. 20 (January/March 1988), pp. 293–315; and Wi-Saeng Kim and Es-

meralda O. Lyn, "Excess Market Value, Market Power, and Inside Ownership Structure," *Review of Industrial Organization,* vol. 3 (Fall 1988), pp. 1–26.

94. *Profits in the Long Run,* supra note 84, pp. 149–157.

95. J. M. Clark, "Toward a Concept of Workable Competition," *American Economic Review,* vol. 30 (June 1940), pp. 241–256. For an extension, see Clark's *Competition as a Dynamic Process,* supra note 3, especially Chapters 2–4.

96. Stephen Sosnick, "A Critique of Concepts of Workable Competition," *Quarterly Journal of Economics,* vol. 72 (August 1958), pp. 380–423.

Performance criteria:

- Firms' production and distribution operations should be efficient and not wasteful of resources.
- Output levels and product quality (that is, variety, durability, safety, reliability, and so forth) should be responsive to consumer demands.
- Profits should be at levels just sufficient to reward investment, efficiency, and innovation.
- Prices should encourage rational choice, guide markets toward equilibrium, and not intensify cyclical instability.
- Opportunities for introducing technically superior new products and processes should be exploited.
- Promotional expenses should not be excessive.
- Success should accrue to sellers who best serve consumer wants.

Critics of the workable competition concept have questioned whether the approach is as operational as its proponents intended. On many of the individual variables, difficult quantitative judgments are required. How price sensitive must quality differentials be? When are promotional expenses excessive, and when are they not? How long must price discrimination persist before it is persistent? And so on. Furthermore, fulfillment of many criteria is difficult to measure. For instance, to determine whether firms' production operations have been efficient, one needs a yardstick calibrated against what is possible. Finally and most important, how should the workability of competition be evaluated when some, but not all, of the criteria are satisfied? If, for example, performance but not structure conforms to the norms, should we conclude that competition is workable, since it is performance that really counts in the end? Perhaps not, because with an unworkable structure there is always a risk that future performance will deteriorate. If stress *is* placed on performance, what conclusion can be drawn when performance is good on some dimensions but not on others? Here a decision cannot be reached without introducing subjective value judgments about the importance of the various dimensions. And as George Stigler warned with characteristic irony, embarrassing disagreements may result:

To determine whether any industry is workably competitive, therefore, simply have a good graduate student write his dissertation on the industry and render a verdict. It is crucial to this test, of course, that no second graduate student be allowed to study the industry.[97]

To investigate these weighting and consensus problems, Steven Cox obtained from forty-two economists, marketing professors, and business writers responses to questionnaires eliciting evaluations of the quality of fourteen major U.S. industries' 1960–1969 performance, both overall and on four subdimensions — product pricing (defined to approximate the criteria of allocative efficiency), technological progressiveness, cost minimization, and wage-price inflation.[98] There was a moderately high level of agreement among the panelists in their overall performance judgments, with the strongest consensus emerging among the panelists claiming greatest knowledge of the fourteen industries. In evaluations of overall performance, it was clear from a factor analysis that panelists placed by far the greatest weight on whether an industry was technically progressive: the more progressive it was, the higher its performance was ranked. Among the academic economist panelists, high scores on the product pricing subdimension and low advertising expenditures as a percentage of sales (the latter calculated from nonquestionnaire data) also led to significantly higher overall performance ranks. But among the business specialists (that is, business journal writers and marketing professors) the opposite propensity held: industries that spent a *large* fraction of their sales dollar on advertising were ranked more favorably, as were industries yielding what appeared to be supra-normal profits. This shows that the most severe stumbling block in evaluating industrial performance is likely to be securing agreement on what is considered good or bad attributes of performance. Conflicting value judgments concerning performance attributes and their weights undoubtedly underlie many disputes as to the proper public policy toward monopolistic business enterprises.

Conclusion

Readers seeking a precise, certain guide to public policy are bound to be disappointed by this survey, for we have found none. The competitive norm does seem to serve as a good first approximation, but it is difficult to state in advance how much competition is needed to achieve desirable economic performance, nor can we formulate hard and fast rules for identifying cases in which a departure from competition is desirable. We therefore begin our journey with only a primitive road map to guide us. Let us hope that we can avoid going too far astray and end with experience useful in drawing a better map.

97. George J. Stigler, "Report on Antitrust Policy — Discussion," *American Economic Review,* vol. 46 (May 1956), p. 505.

98. Steven R. Cox, "An Industrial Performance Evaluation Experiment," *Journal of Industrial Economics,* vol. 22 (March 1974), pp. 199–214.

Industry Structure

3

We begin our exploration of structure-conduct-performance links by surveying some structural features of modern industrial economies, with emphasis on the United States. In this chapter we cover four main facets of industry structure: (1) the extent to which economic activity as a whole occurs in large enterprises, (2) the extent to which particular markets are dominated by one or a few sellers, (3) the extent to which firms are diversified across multiple product lines, and (4) the degree to which firms are vertically integrated. Our main concern in this volume is with monopoly power, to which the second (market domination) dimension of structure is most closely related. Here we nevertheless take a more sweeping view that encompasses structural dimensions possibly interacting with the orthodox bases of monopoly power. At the same time we shall neglect certain important aspects of market structure — notably, the height of entry barriers, the extent of product differentiation, and the degree of buyer concentration. These are handled more conveniently in later chapters.

The Position of the Largest Corporations

Sheer enterprise size and monopoly are not necessarily synonymous. Nevertheless, there are hypotheses that link variations in economic performance to interactions between overall corporate size and power within particular markets. One may also be apprehensive on social and political grounds about the share of economic activity controlled by large corporations. It is worth the labor therefore to examine the position of the largest industrial enterprises.

In 1984, there were approximately 3.2 million incorporated business enterprises operating in the United States, along with roughly 12.5 million nonfarm partnerships and sole proprietorships. Yet a relatively few firms towered over all the rest. The largest enterprise in terms of sales, assets, and employment in 1987 was General Motors. (AT&T had been larger on all three dimensions until its local operating companies were separated from the parent in 1984 following an antitrust settlement.) General Motors' 1987 assets of $87.4 billion represented 1.5 percent of the assets of all nonfinancial corporations; its work force of 876,000 exceeded the population of seven U.S. states and was of about the same size as the industrial labor forces (that is, in manufacturing and mining) of Austria, Belgium, Holland, or Switzerland.

In 1982, 1,313 U.S. nonfinancial corporations had assets valued at $250 million or more. They controlled 68 percent of the assets of all U.S. nonfinancial corporations. A further breakdown of the distribution of asset holdings by industrial sector is given in Table 3.1. In the communications-electric-gas, transportation, manufacturing, and banking[1] sectors, more than half of all corporate assets were controlled by enterprises with assets of $250 million or more. On the other hand, the agriculture, construction, and services sectors remain the domain of enterprises relatively small as bigness in business goes.[2]

1. Asset sizes in banking and finance are not comparable with those in other sectors, since it is easier to put together and manage a large portfolio of financial assets than a large aggregation of physical assets. Also, financial enterprises must be segregated from nonfinancial corporations to lessen double counting, since a high proportion of financial firms' assets consists of claims against the assets of nonfinancial corporations.

2. The fractions of total corporate assets accounted for by corporations with assets of $100 million or more were 7.8 percent in agriculture, 22.2 percent in construction, and 34.7 percent in services. For all nonfinancial corporations, the figure was 72.9 percent.

Table 3.1   Fractions of Corporate Assets Accounted for by Large
Corporations in 1982

Sector	Number of Active Corporations (all sizes)	Sector Share of 1982 GNP*	Corporations with Assets of $250 Million or More	
			Number	Share of All Sector Assets
All nonfinancial corporations	2,464,303	—	1,314	68.0%
Agriculture, forestry, and fisheries	91,320	2.8%	6	5.6
Mining	36,676	4.1	79	67.3
Construction	282,345	4.0	26	16.5
Manufacturing	259,106	20.5	657	79.5
Transportation	91,856	3.5		
Communications, electric, sanitary, and gas utilities	23,614	5.7	284	91.0
Wholesale and retail trade	839,547	16.0	198	36.4
Services	819,706	14.0	64	27.2
Real estate	295,119	11.8		
Banking, finance, and insurance	461,630	4.2	1,875	78.4

*Includes contributions of unincorporated businesses and government.
Sources: U.S. Internal Revenue Service, *Statistics of Income: 1982,* "Corporation Income Tax Returns"
(Washington: USGPO, 1985), Table 6; and *Survey of Current Business,* vol. 65 (April 1985), p. 20.

Any *aggregate concentration* analysis of this sort is affected by the choice of a size measure, since some measures show considerably more concentration than others.[3] Table 3.2 reports for diverse indices the share of domestic manufacturing activity associated with the largest 100 and 200 U.S. manufacturing corporations, ranked on the basis of value added in manufacture for the census year 1982.[4] Employment is much less concentrated than the other measures, in part because the largest manufacturers are more capital-intensive than their smaller counterparts and partly because the largest companies include a disproportionate number of petroleum refiners, which have particularly high output values in relation to their employment. Payrolls are more concentrated than employment because the largest firms tend to pay relatively high wages and salaries. New capital expenditures vary widely from year to year and, at least in 1982, show less than their characteristically disproportionate concentration because of a sharp recession and an unusual stimulus to capital outlays from 1981 corporate income tax revisions.

In the analyses that follow, we use the most complete data series available. The reader must bear in mind that some measures imply higher degrees of concentration than others.

Table 3.2 Aggregate Concentration Shares in 1982 for Five Different Measures

Size Measure	Share of 100 Largest Manufacturing Corporations	Share of 200 Largest Manufacturing Corporations
Domestic value added	32.8%	43.2%
Domestic plant sales	31.8	44.0
Employment in the U.S.	23.8	32.7
Payroll in the U.S.	31.5	41.5
New capital expenditures	36.2	48.7

Source: U.S. Bureau of the Census, "Concentration Ratios in Manufacturing," *1982 Census of Manufactures,* MC82–S–7 (Washington: USGPO, April 1986), Table 4.

Changes in Aggregate Concentration over Time

Changes over time in the aggregate concentration of manufacturing activity are of special interest. Manufacturing was the original locus of the Industrial Revolution, and as performer of most industrial research and development, it continues to make uniquely important contributions to the overall economy's dynamic progress.[5] Just after the American Civil War, manufacturing was still predominantly the province of relatively small firms serving local markets, and the sector as a whole was much less concentrated in the aggregate than it is today. (Transportation, on the other hand, already showed signs of growing dominance by the large railroad and canal corporations.) At the time, Karl Marx stood alone among well-known economists in predicting that big business would come to dominate the industrial scene. This development Marx attributed to the corporate form of organization, then acquiring its modern trappings, and to the interaction of scale economies with bitter competition. "One capitalist always kills many," said Marx, leading to a "constantly diminishing number of the magnates of capital, who usurp and monopolize all advantages of this process of transformation."[6] The limit was a state in which "the entire social capital would be united, either in the hands of one single capitalist, or in those of one single corporation," although Marx did not explicitly assert that the ultimate limit would ever be attained.[7]

3. On the analytic differences that the choice of a firm size measure can make, see David J. Smyth, William J. Boyes, and Dennis E. Peseau, "The Measurement of Firm Size: Theory and Evidence for the United States and the United Kingdom," *Review of Economics and Statistics,* vol. 59 (August 1977), pp. 290–298; and John D. Jackson and James A. Dunlevy, "Interchanging Measures of Firm Size: An Asymptotic Test and Further Results," *Southern Economic Journal,* vol. 48 (January 1982), pp. 764–768.

4. Value added is defined, ignoring some details on the handling of inventory adjustments, as sales less outside purchases of materials (including energy and certain specialized services).

5. See F. M. Scherer, "Interindustry Technology Flows in the United States," *Research Policy,* vol. 11 (August 1982), pp. 227–245.

6. Karl Marx, *Capital,* trans. Ernest Untermann, vol. 1 (Chicago: Kerr, 1912), p. 836.

7. Marx, *Capital,* p. 688. In a footnote to the fourth German edition (1890), Friedrich Engels called explicit attention to the English and American "trusts" as an attempt to attain single-firm domination of particular industries. See also the more general discussion in Paul M. Sweezy, *The Theory of Capitalist Development* (New York: Monthly Review Press, 1942), pp. 254–269.

During the next sixty years, the industrialized economies of the world evidently moved a considerable distance toward fulfilling Marx's prediction. The first systematic attempt to study trends in aggregate concentration was by Adolf Berle and Gardiner Means.[8] Using the rather meager data then available, they estimated the 200 largest U.S. nonfinancial corporations' share of all nonfinancial corporation assets to be 49 percent at the end of 1929. They also found that the 200 leading firms' assets grew more rapidly than the assets of all corporations between 1909 and 1929. Without committing themselves to a prediction of what actually would happen, they observed that if the observed disparity in growth rates continued, the 200 largest would account for 70 percent of all nonfinancial corporations' assets by 1950 and nearly 100 percent by 1972.[9]

Obviously, this did not happen. There is reason to believe Berle and Means overestimated the relative growth of the largest enterprises between 1909 and 1920 and hence extrapolated too steep a trend.[10] Moreover, aggregate concentration appears to have increased only by fits and starts since 1929. The most solidly grounded long-term series, from quarterly surveys of corporate financial accounts since 1947 and a painstaking reconstruction of diverse data sets for earlier years, has been compiled by the Federal Trade Commission (FTC) and updated more recently by the Census Bureau. The resulting estimates of the one hundred largest manufacturing corporations' share of their corporate universe assets are charted in Figure 3.1. Evidently, there was a sharp upsurge in aggregate manufacturing sector concentration during the late 1920s and into the early years of the Great Depression, a decline associated with the World War II mobilization and postwar boom, another sustained increase as the wartime boom faded into normalcy, a brief period of stability, and then continuing but erratic increases. Analysts and unwary politicians who cite the FTC statistics as reported, without realizing that a major change in reporting procedures was effected in 1973,[11] are apt to conclude that aggregate asset concentration declined appreciably in the 1970s before resuming its upward trend. But in fact, when the noncomparable series are properly spliced (broken line after 1973), one observes continuing but modest increases during the late 1970s and 1980s.

A somewhat different picture is presented with data on manufacturing sector value added, available only since 1947. The value-added statistics are plotted as the lower time series in Figure 3.1. The *levels* of aggregate concentration are lower because, as noted earlier, the largest corporations tend to be more capital intensive than smaller manufacturers. But more importantly, the upward trend in asset concentration after the mid-1960s is not evident in the value-added data. The difference in patterns apparently stems from the greater inclusiveness of the asset data.

The asset data, but not the value-added data, include operations of U.S. corporations' overseas subsidiaries, before 1973 often on a fully consolidated basis, but thereafter on a net equity basis. Throughout most of the period following World War II, overseas investments grew more rapidly for the one hundred largest manufacturers than for their smaller peers, and so rising concentration of domestic plus foreign assets is implied. By 1977, multinational corporations with a home base in the United States generated $161 billion of value added in their majority-owned foreign affiliates, supplementing their domestic value added of $490.5 billion.[12] Eighty-nine percent of the foreign activity was in two broad industrial sectors: manufacturing and petroleum. In 1984, U.S. manufacturing corporations derived 20 percent of their total sales revenues from foreign operations. Sectors with the largest proportions of overseas sales were computers and office equipment (47 percent), drugs (37 percent), and industrial chemicals (30 percent).[13]

Also, the asset data, but not the value-added data, include the value of companies' activities in nonmanufacturing fields — that is, mining, retailing, transportation, finance, and services. Again, the one hundred largest manufacturers appear to have diversified into nonmanufacturing ventures at a brisker pace than their smaller counterparts, so their share of combined manufacturing and nonmanufacturing assets rose while their share of value added in manufacturing alone remained roughly constant.

One's conclusion concerning aggregate concentration trends depends, then, upon whether one focuses on domestic manufacturing activities alone, or includes the overseas and nonmanufacturing endeavors of enterprises whose home base is manufacturing. By the former criterion, aggregate concentration appears to have risen insignificantly since the mid-1960s. With the latter, broader perspective, a continuation of the increasing trend is found.

Expanding the analysis from corporations at home in manufacturing to other nonfinancial enterprises alters the picture in further ways. Because productivity (that is, output per unit of labor and capital input) has tended to grow more rapidly in manufacturing than in other sectors, and because the demand for manufactured goods is relatively price and/or income inelastic, manufacturers' share of national income has declined over time — from 30 percent in 1947 to 18.9 percent in 1987. The weight of the largest manufacturing corporations (which are large relative to the leading enterprises in most other industrial sectors) has therefore declined in aggregate concentration computations spanning manufacturing and nonmanufacturing corporations alike. Lawrence J. White found declining aggregate asset concentration between 1960 and 1977 in banking and life insurance, rising concentration in the retail trades and transportation, and a mixed pattern in electric and gas utilities.[14] Combining data for all sectors, his analysis reveals no clear 1958–1975 trend for the largest nonfinancial corporations and, for financial and nonfinancial enterprises together, a slight aggregate concentration decline during the 1970s.

8. Adolf Berle and Gardiner Means, *The Modern Corporation and Private Property* (New York: Macmillan, 1932), especially pp. 28–40.

9. Berle and Means, *The Modern Corporation*, p. 40.

10. See S. J. Prais, *The Evolution of Giant Firms in Britain* (Cambridge: Cambridge University Press, 1976), pp. 211–212.

11. See David W. Penn, "Aggregate Concentration: A Statistical Note," *Antitrust Bulletin,* vol. 21 (Spring 1976), pp. 91–98.

12. Ned G. Howenstine, "Gross Product of U.S. Multinational Companies, 1977," *Survey of Current Business,* vol. 63 (February

1983), pp. 24–26.

13. U.S. National Science Foundation, *Science and Technology Data Book: 1988* (Washington: USGPO, 1988), p. 45.

14. Lawrence J. White, "What Has Been Happening to Aggregate Concentration in the United States?" *Journal of Industrial Economics,* vol. 29 (March 1981), pp. 223–230. See also William K. Jones, "Confounding the Corporate State: Large Firms in the Postwar Economy, 1947–1977," manuscript, Columbia University School of Law, February 1982.

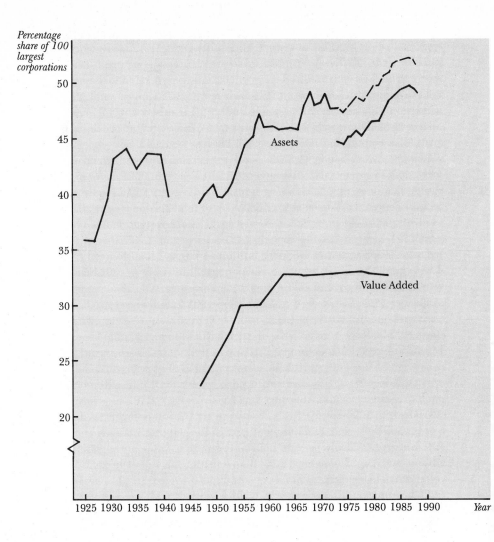

Figure 3.1
The One Hundred Largest
Manufacturing Corporations'
Share of Their Corporate
Universe Assets

*Percentage
share of 100
largest
corporations*

Assets

Value Added

Year

Aggregate Concentration in Other Nations

Is the enterprise size structure and trend in the United States typical or atypical of patterns in other nations? Table 3.3 provides a first rough overview. From diverse public sources, the 1985 employment of the twenty largest industrial (that is, manufacturing and minerals industry) corporations in ten nations was ascertained. Employment is the focus because international comparisons of money-denominated magnitudes such as sales or assets can swing wildly from year to year as exchange rates fluctuate. The nations are arrayed in Table 3.3 in descending order of industrial labor force size as of 1985.

The United States has by a substantial margin the largest leading companies. A rough pattern is evident; the larger the nation's work force, the smaller the average top-10 or top-20 enterprise tends to be. A regression analysis shows that the average size of a top-20 enterprise rises as a square root function of national work force size.[15] Aggregate concentration indices tend to be inversely correlated with nation size, suggesting that scale economies or other imperatives push leading enterprises

Table 3.3 Aggregate Industrial Concentration Patterns in Ten Nations, 1985

Nation	Average Size of Leading Firms (Number of Employees)		Leading Company Employment as a Percent of Total Industrial Employment	
	Top 10	Top 20	Top 10	Top 20
United States	310,554	219,748	13.1%	18.6%
Japan	107,106	72,240	7.3	9.9
West Germany	177,173	114,542	20.1	26.0
United Kingdom	141,156	108,010	23.1	35.3
France	116,049	81,381	23.2	32.5
South Korea	54,416	n.a.	14.9	n.a.
Canada	36,990	26,414	15.3	21.9
Switzerland	60,039	36,602	49.4	60.2
Holland	84,884	47,783	84.5	95.1
Sweden	48,538	32,893	49.4	66.9

Sources: For company data, ELC International, *Europe's Largest Companies: 1987* (Stockholm: A.S. Økonomist Literatur, 1987); *Fortune,* April 28, 1986 (for the largest U.S. industrials); and *Fortune,* August 4, 1987 (for the largest industrials outside the United States). Data on total industrial employment in individual nations are from International Labour Office, *Yearbook of Labour Statistics: 1986* (Geneva: 1986), pp. 46–107; and the *Statistisches Jahrbuch der Schweitz: 1986,* p. 341.

toward being larger relative to their national work forces in small nations than in large nations. However, important deviations from the pattern compel further explanation.

The aggregate concentration ratios for Switzerland, Sweden, and Holland are particularly high because all three harbor very large multinational enterprises — for example, Nestle, Ciba-Geigy, and Hoffmann-LaRoche in Switzerland; SKF and Electrolux in Sweden; and Royal Dutch Shell and Philips in the Netherlands — with more of their employment located abroad than at home. Since the company employment counts include all employees, at home and abroad, while the national work force denominators to which they are related include only domestic employment, aggregate concentration is overstated. For similar reasons, the data force a fair amount of double counting when the subsidiaries of multinational companies are counted once in the nation where they reside and again in the consolidated employment tallies for their parents. Canada is particularly affected in

15. For top 20 companies, the regression equation is:

$$\text{Log}_{10} \text{COSIZE} = 1.57 + 0.492 \log_{10} \text{NATEMP}; R^2 = 0.71;$$

where COSIZE is the average company size and NATEMP is total 1985 national employment in manufacturing and mining industries.

The reader unfamiliar with regression and correlation techniques is referred to the Appendix to Chapter 3 of the second edition of *Industrial Market Structure and Economic Performance* for an elementary introduction.

this respect; six of its twenty largest enterprises were subsidiaries of U.S. petroleum and automobile companies.

In 1985, the year analyzed, the United States was both an important target and source of multinational firms' investments. The subsidiaries of foreign-based companies had 2.85 million employees in the United States, 1.47 million of them, or 6 percent of the relevant U.S. work force cohort, in manufacturing and mining industries.[16] In that year, the net ownership claims of foreign-based enterprises in U.S. subsidiaries amounted to $185 billion, while U.S.-based enterprises had similar claims totalling $230 billion in their own foreign subsidiaries.[17] Data for the late 1980s will undoubtedly reveal a balance in favor of foreign multinationals as foreign firms took advantage of the weak dollar and large U.S. balance of trade deficit by acquiring numerous American companies.

Japan's surprisingly low aggregate concentration ratios in Table 3.3 stem in part from two other important biases. For one, the typical large Japanese manufacturing enterprise contracts out much more work to small supplier companies than do enterprises in other nations. The suppliers are so closely related to, and dependent upon, their customer that they might plausibly be considered an integrated part of the customer even though they are legally independent. More importantly, many Japanese companies are linked by common banking ties, cross-ownership, and tradition into *Keiretsu* family groupings, even though they report as separate and independent corporations. The ten largest Japanese companies counted in Table 3.3 include, for example, the related but separately reporting Mitsubishi Heavy Industries and Mitsubishi Electric companies. These rich intercorporate interrelationships are a legacy of the *Zaibatsu* (literally, money clique) system, under which four family holding companies with ownership interests in hundreds of operating enterprises controlled one-fourth of all paid-in capital in Japanese industry and finance.[18] The Zaibatsu groups were broken up following World War II, but many of the ties remain in less formal guise. By 1960, the three leading Zaibatsu successor groups controlled 7.4 percent of the paid-in capital of all Japanese corporations if only firms with very close interrelations were counted, or 17.3 percent if firms with weak and uncertain Zaibatsu links were included.[19] A government study revealed that in 1972, the pivotal trading companies of six groups held stock in a total of 4,104 companies, including 506 majority ownership positions and 1,057 leading ownership positions.[20] Consolidating only units with majority ownership ties raised the share of all corporate assets held by the one hundred largest Japanese enterprises in 1984 from 20.7 to 24.8 percent.[21]

Intricate intercorporate ties are also found in West Germany, where the banks and certain holding companies play a key role,[22] and in Sweden through the Wallenberg family and their position in the Svenska Enskilda Bank. Unconsolidated tabulations for 1963 show the one hundred largest private companies to have originated 46 percent of manufacturing value added. Yet the Wallenbergs wielded effective control over thirty-two ostensibly separate companies, including eight of the ten largest private sector manufacturers.[23] Value added by firms in which the family had at least a strong minority interest amounted to 14.8 percent of total manufacturing value added in 1963.

The relatively modest aggregate concentration figure for South Korea partly reflects the position of many small, labor-intensive manufacturing firms persisting from the period preceding rapid industrialization. In addition, Korea, like Japan, has several large, widely diversified enterprises (called Chaebol) with extensive majority and minority holdings in separately reporting companies.[24]

These complications make it difficult to compare levels of aggregate concentration across nations with quite different patterns of industrial corporation ownership. Still, despite both conceptual and data availability difficulties, a fairly robust generalization remains: the smaller the nation, the higher aggregate industrial concentration tends to be.

Scattered and less than fully consistent evidence exists on aggregate concentration trends in a diversity of nations. The United Kingdom experienced sharply rising aggregate concentration during the 1960s, but since 1975, the upward trend stopped and may have reversed.[25] The share of sales originated by the one hundred largest West German industrial, construction, and electric power and gas enterprises rose from 33.6 percent in 1954 to 42 percent in 1965 and 50 percent in 1973, but since then, no clear trend has been evident.[26] Aggregate concentration rose in Japan during the 1950s and early 1960s, but a decline is clearly evident in later years.[27] Canada appears to be an exception, with most data series indicating continuing but generally mild increases during the 1970s and early 1980s, although recent aggregate concentration levels are considerably lower than they were during the 1920s and 1930s.[28]

Interlocking Financial and Personnel Ties

In the United States, as in many other nations, aggregate concentration figures have tended to understate the extent to which the control of industrial wealth resides in a relatively few hands. This comes from three main types of intercorporate

16. Ned G. Howenstine, "U.S. Affiliates of Foreign Companies: Operations in 1985," *Survey of Current Business,* vol. 67 (May 1987), pp. 36–51. For rich data on transnational investment, see John Dunning and John Cantwell, *IRM Directory of International Investment and Production* (New York: New York University Press, 1987).

17. Russell B. Scholl, "The International Investment Position of the United States in 1986," *Survey of Current Business,* vol. 67 (June 1987), pp. 38–39.

18. See Richard E. Caves and Masu Uekusa, *Industrial Organization in Japan* (Washington: Brookings, 1976), pp. 59–68, for a survey of the literature.

19. Eugene Rotwein, "Economic Concentration and Monopoly in Japan," *Journal of Political Economy,* vol. 72 (June 1964), p. 268.

20. See the translation of the Fair Trade Commission's "Report on the Investment of General Trading Companies," *Antitrust Bulletin,* vol. 20 (Spring 1975), p. 182.

21. Christian Marfels, "Aggregate Concentration in International Perspective," in R. S. Khemani et al., eds., *Mergers, Corporate Concentration and Power in Canada* (Halifax: Institute for Research on Public Policy, 1987), p. 69. On the declining and then stable trend of Japanese aggregate concentration following World War II, see Tomo Iguchi, "Aggregate Concentration, Turnover, and Mobility among the Largest Manufacturing Firms in Japan," *Antitrust Bulletin,* vol. 32 (Winter 1987), pp. 939–965.

22. Monopolkommission, *Gesamtwirtschaftliche Chancen und Ris-*

iken wachsender Unternehmensgrössen (Baden-Baden: Nomos, 1986), pp. 130–163 and (for an English summary) 446–447. On the role of the banks, see "Three Rich, Powerful Banks Dominate the Economy," *Business Week,* April 19, 1976, pp. 89–98; and "Deutsche Makes Its Mark," *The Economist,* July 25, 1987, pp. 64–65.

23. Alf Carling, *Industrins Struktur och Konkurrensförhallanden* (Stockholm: Statens Offentliga Utredningar, 1968), pp. 128–137; and "The 'Wallenberg Boys' — and How They Grew," *Business Week,* February 25, 1967, pp. 116–122. The Wallenberg family's control was probably dispersed somewhat during the 1980s.

24. "Seoul Orders Conglomerates To Divest Some Holdings," *Wall Street Journal,* July 29, 1987, p. 12; and "Seoul Puts Big Business on a Shorter Leash," *Business Week,* August 17, 1987, p. 51.

25. For the most recent evidence, see Alan Hughes and Manmohan Kumar, "Recent Trends in Aggregate Concentration in the United Kingdom Economy," *Cambridge Journal of Economics,* vol. 8 (September 1984), pp. 235–250.

26. Marfels, "Aggregate Concentration," supra note 21, p. 67; Juergen Mueller and Rolf Hochreiter, *Stand und Entwicklungstendenzen der Konzentration in der Bundesrepublik Deutschland* (Göttingen: Schwartz, 1976), Tabelle 9; and Monopolkommission, *Gesamtwirtschaftliche Chancen,* supra note 22, pp. 95–127.

27. Marfels, "Aggregate Concentration," supra note 21.

28. See Marfels, "Aggregate Concentration," and *Report of the Royal Commission on Corporate Concentration* (Ottawa: Ministry of Supply and Services, March 1978), pp. 18–32.

linkage: control by family groups, the participation of financial intermediaries and interlocking directorates.

A 1930s survey turned up several examples of multicorporation control by family groups with either majority or substantial minority stock holdings.[29] The du Pont family, through its various holding companies, owned roughly 25 percent of the stock of E. I. du Pont de Nemours and about 20 percent of the United States Rubber Company's stock. The du Pont company and affiliates in turn held a 23 percent stock interest in General Motors. To the Rockefeller family and its philanthropic institutions could be traced stock interests ranging between 7 and 24 percent in six of the largest petroleum companies, along with the largest single share interest in the Chase National (now Chase Manhattan) Bank. The Mellon family had dominant ownership positions in Gulf Oil, Alcoa, the Mellon National Bank, the Koppers Company, and the Pittsburgh Coal Co., as well as weaker affiliations with several other major corporations (including Westinghouse Electric). Since the 1930s, the control of these groups has been gradually attenuated as stock was distributed among multiplying heirs, as the heirs sold some of their shares to pay inheritance taxes, and as the corporations issued additional common stock, merged, or (for du Pont, in 1962) were forced by antitrust judgments to disgorge minority holdings (in General Motors).

Control of industrial companies through financial intermediaries has had a cyclical history in the United States. As the twentieth century dawned, J. P. Morgan, George F. Baker of New York's First National Bank, and a few other financial leaders caused their banks to take significant ownership positions and to use them in aggressively shaping individual company policies and indeed whole industry structures.[30] Gradually this exercise of power waned in response to public resentment, the rise of other investment banking houses, and passage in 1933 of the Glass-Steagall Act, requiring separation of investment and commercial banking activities.

In the period following World War II, and especially after new laws required explicit funding of corporate pension obligations and made it clear that common stocks were proper pension fund investments, the fraction of stocks held by financial intermediaries rose steadily. In 1960, institutional investors — that is, pension funds, the managers of individual trust funds, mutual funds, banks, insurance companies, foundations, and educational endowments — controlled 27 percent of U.S. corporations' common and preferred stock. By 1986, the institutions' position had risen to approximately 44 percent.[31] In 1985, institutional investors held 51 percent of the common stocks of the typical top-100 company, 50 percent of the stocks of companies ranked 101 to 500 by outstanding share value, and 37 percent for companies ranked 501 to 1,000.[32]

In one sense, this development reflects the spread of people's capitalism, for pension funds have become the largest single locus of institutional holdings, and entitlement to the ultimate benefits of such investments is spread widely, in rough proportion to the distribution of income. Yet voting rights in such institutionally held securities are seldom passed back to the ultimate beneficiaries. Whatever power stock ownership normally conveys resides mainly in the fund managers, not in the beneficiaries. For the *Fortune* 500 industrial companies of 1981, Thomas Dye attempted to identify strategic ownership positions, defined as entities numbered among the top five listed shareholders and whose holdings were greater than or equal to 1 percent of a company's total shares.[33] Of the 2,156 positions so identified, 486 were held by banks, 860 by financial holding entities (such as trust companies, mutual funds, and employee stock trust managers), 101 by insurance companies, and 122 by pension funds. All told, 73 percent of the strategic ownership positions were traced to financial intermediaries.

For the most part, intermediaries wield the power their control over shares conveys with reticence. The most common practice is to follow the "Wall Street rule" — when fund managers are dissatisfied with the decisions of a company whose shares they hold, they don't complain, they sell. In most instances institutional investors validate management recommendations in proxy voting, although exceptions occur, and the incidence of negative votes has probably been rising.[34] What is less well known is what influence institutional investors exert through face-to-face interaction with operating company management, for example, through informal contacts and formal representation on boards of directors. In 1975, according to a survey by Edward Herman, the 200 largest nonfinancial corporations' boards of directors included 345 bank and insurance company representatives.[35]

Interlocking directorates are a third way in which the control of corporations can be consolidated. The simplest type of interlocking directorate occurs when one person sits on the boards of two or more corporations. Although there has apparently been a decline in the number and richness of interlocks since the early 1900s,[36] such multiple directorships continue to be widespread. A House of Representatives study found that the 463 directors of 29 large industrial corporations held directorates in more than 1,200 different corporations during 1962.[37] Interlocking directorates among competing firms were outlawed by the Clayton Act of 1914, and although the law was not vigorously enforced until 1968, most of the interlocks disclosed by the congressional study probably had little direct effect on competition.

An indirect interlock exists when different directors of some firm (often a financial institution) hold seats on competing firms' boards. For example, the chairman of the board of Morgan Trust Co. served in 1962 on the board of General Motors, while directors of both Ford Motor Company and Chrysler sat on the Morgan

29. U. S. National Resources Committee, *The Structure of the American Economy,* Part 1 (Washington: USGPO, 1939), pp. 160–163 and 306–317. See also "The Mellons of Pittsburgh," *Fortune,* October 1967, pp. 121–122.

30. See David Bunting and Mark S. Mizruchi, "The Transfer of Control in Large Corporations: 1905–1919," *Journal of Economic Issues,* vol. 16 (December 1982), pp. 985–1003; David M. Kotz, *Bank Control of Large Corporations in the United States* (Berkeley: University of California Press, 1978), pp. 28–41 and 51–60; and Edward S. Herman, *Corporate Control, Corporate Power* (Cambridge: Cambridge University Press, 1981), pp. 118–120 and 157–160.

31. F. M. Scherer, "Corporate Ownership and Control," in John R. Meyer and James Gustafson, eds., *The U.S. Business Corporation: An Institution in Transition* (Cambridge: Ballinger, 1988), pp. 46–47.

32. Ibid.

33. Thomas R. Dye, "Who Owns America: Strategic Ownership Positions in Industrial Corporations," *Social Science Quarterly,* vol. 64 (December 1983), pp. 856–867.

34. Scherer, "Corporate Ownership," pp. 50–51.

35. Herman, *Corporate Control,* supra note 30, pp. 130–131.

36. See David Bunting and Jeffrey Barbour, "Interlocking Directorates in Large American Corporations, 1896–1964," *Business History Review,* vol. 45 (Autumn 1971), pp. 317–335.

37. U.S. House of Representatives, Committee on the Judiciary, Antitrust Subcommittee, staff report, *Interlocks in Corporate Management* (Washington: USGPO, 1965), pp. 115–116, 159–164, and 234–255. See also Peter C. Dooley, "The Interlocking Directorate," *American Economic Review,* vol. 59 (June 1969), pp. 314–323.

Trust board. Banks supposedly take pains to ensure that their directors who also sit on competing clients' boards preserve confidences and engage in no unethical practices. Still the potential for abuse exists.

In sum, there are many formal and informal ties that, if exploited fully, could render control of American industry by a few groups more monolithic than it appears in the bare statistics describing aggregate concentration. It is unlikely that a serious breakdown of corporate independence can be traced to these ties, partly because groups with weak minority voting positions may be unable to pull reluctant operating managers along, and partly because the officers of financial intermediaries have a tradition of reticence in exercising whatever power they possess. Yet our ignorance on this subject is great, and so we have only weak insight into the magnitude of the consequences.

Turnover among the Largest Corporations

We have seen that a few very large enterprises account for a considerable share of all industrial activity. Is membership in this elite group a stable phenomenon, or something that slips readily from the grasp of those whose attention and zeal falter? In other words, is turnover among the ranks of the large corporations relatively high or low?

Several studies of turnover among the largest U.S. corporations have been published.[38] In one of the most comprehensive, Collins and Preston compiled lists of the one hundred largest manufacturing, mining, and distribution companies, ranked by assets, for the years 1909, 1919, 1929, 1935, 1948, and 1958.[39] They found that a total of 209 identifiable corporations appeared on these six lists at one time or another. Thirty-six of the top one hundred in 1909 remained among the one hundred leaders of 1958. On average, 2.5 firms disappeared from the list per year.

Why did some drop off the list, while others ascended? A first impression can be gained by considering what happened to the leading ten corporations of 1909. They are ranked in order of 1909 assets, and the figure in parentheses indicates the company's rank or status among the top one hundred in 1987, as determined from an updating by the authors:

1. United States Steel (now USX) (17)
2. Standard Oil of New Jersey (Exxon) (3)
3. American Tobacco (American Brands) (52)
4. International Mercantile Marine (dropped)
5. International Harvester (dropped)
6. Anaconda Copper (dropped)
7. United States Leather (dropped)
8. Armour (dropped)
9. American Sugar Refining (dropped)
10. Pullman Inc. (dropped)

Only one of the 1909 top ten remained among the top ten of 1987, and seven dropped from the list of the leading one hundred. Of these, only one disappeared altogether. After nearly succumbing in the 1921 recession and then struggling along for three more decades, United States Leather was liquidated in 1953.

International Mercantile Marine, renamed United States Lines, was acquired in 1969 by Kidde Inc. and then sold off in 1978 to ocean shipper McLean Industries, which filed for reorganization under the bankruptcy laws in 1986. International Harvester, renamed Navistar, ranked 182nd in terms of assets on *Fortune*'s list of the 500 largest industrials after shedding the farm equipment business with which it started corporate life. Anaconda, though still large enough at the time to remain on the one hundred-largest list, was acquired in 1977 by the Atlantic Richfield Company (now Arco). Having grown too slowly to remain among the top one hundred by an assets measure, Armour merged in 1968 with the General Host Company, which in turn was acquired in 1969 by Greyhound of bus fame. In 1983, most of its original business, fresh meat packing, was sold to ConAgra, Inc., but Greyhound retained the specialty meats lines. American Sugar Refining, renamed Amstar, ranked three hundred twentieth on *Fortune*'s 1987 list before being subjected to a leveraged buyout and sold off in pieces. Having fallen out of the top 200, Pullman was acquired by Wheelabrator Frye in 1980, which spun it off as Pullman-Peabody in 1981, but its traditional railroad car-making business was sold to Trinity Industries in 1984.

These disappearances and declines reflect technological changes; the transition of the American economy into the age of automobiles, aircraft, and electronics from an era that stressed meeting more basic food and clothing needs; and the extensive corporate restructuring that followed an unsuccessful conglomerate merger wave during the 1960s and early 1970s. Other 1909 pacesetters who disappeared from the list of one hundred leaders (and in some cases, from the business scene altogether) include American Agricultural Chemical, American Cotton Oil, American Hide and Leather, American Ice, American Linseed Oil, Baldwin Locomotive Works, Cudahy Packing, General Cigar, Harbison-Walker Refractories, International Salt, U.S. Cast Iron Pipe and Foundry, United Shoe Machinery, Wilson Meat Packing, and Wells Fargo.

A similar picture emerges when we trace the ten largest corporations of 1987 back to 1909:

1. General Motors (not listed in 1909)
2. Sears Roebuck (45)
3. Exxon (formerly Standard Oil of N.J.) (2)
4. IBM (not listed)
5. Ford Motor Co. (not listed)
6. Mobil Oil (not listed)
7. General Electric (16)
8. Chevron (not listed)
9. Texaco (91)
10. du Pont (29)

38. For references to the extensive literature, see the second edition of this volume, p. 55, note 35. For a survey comparing 1917, 1945, 1967, and 1986 rankings, see "Corporate Scoreboard," *Forbes,* July 13, 1987, pp. 121–172.

39. N. R. Collins and L. E. Preston, "The Size Structure of the Largest Industrial Firms," *American Economic Review,* vol. 51 (December 1961), pp. 986–1011. See also Robert J. Stonebreaker, "Turnover and Mobility among the 100 Largest Firms: An Update," *American Economic Review,* vol. 69 (December 1979), pp. 968–973.

The ascendance of General Motors and Ford (already listed among the top ten of 1919) is explained, of course, by the automotive revolution. It in turn propelled three additional petroleum refiners to the top by 1987 — two of them fragments of the original New Jersey Standard Oil Company, broken up after a 1911 antitrust judgment. The most dramatic addition to the top ranks was IBM, which occupied only sixty-eighth place on the 1948 list.

Movement up and down the largest corporation lists depends in part upon shifts in the pattern of demand. In a statistical analysis, Seymour Friedland found a positive correlation between the rate of growth of forty-four leading corporations' assets and the rate at which their home industry group's share of all manufacturing activity changed.[40] The simple correlation coefficient was 0.87 for the 1906–1928 time period and 0.80 for the 1928–1950 interval.

The rate at which companies move onto and off the lists, that is, the turnover rate, has declined over time, at least until recently. This is shown in Table 3.4, which extends the Collins and Preston analysis over two additional intervals, 1958–1977 and 1977–1987. Two measures are given: one showing the rate of exit for all reasons, and the second counting only natural exits, excluding the primary and secondary effects of mergers and government antitrust actions.[41] By either criterion, a decline in the rate of turnover up to the 1940s is apparent. However, a sharp reversal occurred in the turbulent 1977–1987 period. Four reasons for the early decline in turnover can be postulated. First, the largest firms might have become more entrenched by virtue of the power their increased size confers, although it is difficult to articulate a specific mechanism by which this entrenchment process works. Second, the rate of technological change, or the rate of change in demand patterns, might have slowed. This too seems implausible in view of the enormous technological advances made following World War II. Third, the management of large corporations may have become more professionalized, taking a longer-term view of its role and identifying its function not as the sale of certain products, but preservation of the firm qua organization. This implies among other things a willingness to adopt new product lines when the demand for traditional items ebbs. Such a change has almost surely occurred. Finally, as a by-product of their more professional managerial outlook and increased size, large corporations may have become more diversified, hedging against shifts in demand. This too has happened, as we shall see, although with more mixed consequences than one might have supposed.

Concentration in Particular Markets

We turn now to the dimension of structure most closely related to the main concern of this volume: the possession of monopoly power. We begin by considering some principal methods of measuring the phenomenon.

Alternative Monopoly Measures

Some are performance-oriented, such as the *Lerner Index,* defined as:[42]

$$M = (Price - Marginal\ Cost)\ /\ Price.$$

Its merit is that it directly reflects the allocatively ineffecient departure of price from marginal cost associated with monopoly. Under pure competition, $M = 0$. The more a firm's pricing departs from the competitive norm, the higher is the

Table 3.4 Exits from the Top 100 Industrial and Distribution
Corporations, 1909–1987

Time interval	Average number of exits per year for all causes	Average number of natural exits per year
1909–1919	4.0	2.6
1919–1929	3.1	2.1
1929–1935	2.7	2.0
1935–1948	1.5	1.5
1948–1958	1.6	1.7
1958–1977	1.7	1.6
1977–1987	3.0	2.9

Sources: N. R. Collins and L. E. Preston, "The Size Structure of the Largest
Industrial Firms," *American Economic Review,* vol. 51 (December 1961), pp. 986–1011;
supplemented by our research using *Fortune,* April 25, 1988. *Fortune,* © 1988 Time
Inc. All rights reserved.

associated Lerner Index value. A related performance-oriented approach focuses
on some measure of the net profits realized by firms or industries. We shall
make abundant use of such measures in subsequent chapters, particularly in
Chapter 11.

The other main approach is to analyze observable dimensions of industry
structure. Economic theory suggests that the vigor of competition is related positively to the number of firms in the relevant industry, other things (such as the
height of entry barriers) being equal. However, the degree of inequality can also
matter. In an industry with one hundred sellers, does each firm control 1 percent
of the industry output, or do four firms control 80 percent while the remaining
ninety-six produce only 20 percent? A simple measure that copes with inequality
by stressing the position of the largest firms is the market concentration ratio *CR*,
defined as the percentage of total industry sales (or capacity, or employment, or
value added, or physical output) contributed by the largest few firms, ranked in
order of market shares. The most common variant in American studies (referred
to as the four-firm sales concentration ratio *CR*4 and often as *the* concentration
ratio) is the percentage of total industry sales originated by the leading *four* firms.
Concentration ratios are also published for U.S. manufacturing industries with
respect to the leading eight, twenty, and fifty firms.[43] Obviously, concentration

40. Seymour Friedland, "Turnover and Growth of the Largest
Industrial Firms, 1906–1950," *Review of Economics and Statistics,*
vol. 39 (February 1957), pp. 79–83.

41. On the methodology, see Collins and Preston, "The Size
Structure," supra note 39, pp. 996–999. For corrections we made
in reworking their data, see the second edition of this volume, p.
57, note 39.

42. A. P. Lerner, "The Concept of Monopoly and the Measurement of Monopoly Power," *Review of Economic Studies,* vol. 1 (June
1934), pp. 157–175.

43. Concentration ratios for manufacturing industries have
been published since 1972 in a special section of the first summary volume of the quinquennial U.S. *Census of Manufactures.*
More complete tabulations appear in a special report annexed to
that volume. For a summary of earlier U.S. concentration ratio
sources, see Ralph L. Nelson, *Concentration in the Manufacturing Industries of the United States* (New Haven: Yale University Press,
1963), pp. 17–19. Concentration data for nonmanufacturing industries are available only from sporadic industry-specific studies.

data for several different numbers of firms provide more information on industry structure than the ratio for only one set (that is, the top four), and it is often useful to present a concentration table, as in Table 3.5, which provides a breakdown on the U.S. phonograph record and recorded tape industry for 1982. A drawback to the concentration table approach is the awkwardness, both in verbal discourse and statistical analyses, of working with several sets of numbers.

The most popular summary measure that combines elements of both firm numbers and inequality is the so-called *Herfindahl-Hirschman Index*, or *HHI*, given by the formula:[44]

$$\text{HHI} = \sum_{i=1}^{N} S_i^2,$$

where S_i is the market share of the ith firm. When an industry is occupied by only one firm (a pure monopolist), the index attains its maximum value of 1.0 (or 10,000, when the market shares are measured in percentage terms). The value declines with increases in the number of firms N and increases with rising inequality among any given number of firms.[45] By squaring market shares, the HHI index weights more heavily the values for large firms than for small.[46] This means that if precise data on the market shares of very small firms are unavailable, the resulting errors will not be large. However, it is crucial that the largest sellers' market shares be measured accurately. Regular publication of HHI indices for U.S. manufacturing industries was commenced by the Census Bureau with its 1982 report.[47]

Ideally, in choosing which index to use in measuring concentration, one should proceed from a theory showing why seller concentration matters behaviorally. Several mathematical models favor the Herfindahl-Hirschman index.[48] However, other theories equally plausible on a priori grounds yield no clear prediction. One might argue that the choice does not matter much because the principal contenders are all highly correlated with each other. For example, the correlation between four-firm sales concentration ratios and HHI values published for 437 manufacturing industries in 1982 was 0.954.[49] An even higher correlation of 0.992 was obtained when logarithms of the HHI and CR4 values were taken, allowing for

Table 3.5 Concentration Table for the Phonograph Record and Tape Industry

Group of Firms	Percentage of Total Industry Sales
Largest four	61%
Largest eight	71
Largest twenty	81
Largest fifty	87

Source: U.S. Bureau of the Census, *1982 Census of Manufactures,* "Concentration Ratios In Manufacturing," MC82-S-7 (April 1986), p. 7–43.

the nonlinear relationship clearly evident when the data are plotted in the scatter diagram of Figure 3.2. However, Figure 3.2 also reveals that the relationship is horn-shaped, with more variation in the HHI at high levels of four-seller concentration than at low levels.[50] Since the most interesting industries from a theoretical standpoint are often those that are most highly concentrated, this means that the indices may tell somewhat different stories quantitatively just where precision of measurement is most important. Consequently, the best approach may be to proceed empirically, determining which index does the best job explaining important behavioral relationships in statistical analyses. When alternate summary indices are used to predict such performance measures as profitability, no single candidate exhibits clear dominance.[51] Thus, the question of which index is best remains open.

Defining the Relevant Market

Even more important than choosing the proper index of concentration is ensuring that the market for which concentration is being measured is properly defined. If the market is defined too broadly so that firms that are not truly competing are included, concentration ratios will err on the low side; if the market is defined too narrowly, excluding meaningful competitors, concentration ratios will err on the high side.

---

44. On its history, see A. O. Hirschman, "The Paternity of an Index," *American Economic Review,* vol. 54 (September 1964), p. 761.

45. When s_i is defined as the deviation of the ith firm's market share from the industry mean, the variance of market shares is given by $\Sigma s_i^2 / (N - 1)$. A standard formula from statistics has $\Sigma s_i^2 = \Sigma S_i^2 - (\Sigma S_i)^2/N$. But when the S_i are market shares, $\Sigma S_i = 1$, and so $(\Sigma S_i)^2 = 1$. Substituting, we have $\Sigma s_i^2 = \Sigma S_i^2 - 1/N$. Rearranging according to the HHI formula in the text, we obtain:

$$HHI = \Sigma S_i^2 = \Sigma s_i^2 + 1/N.$$

The first term on the right-hand side is the *variance equivalent,* the second the inverse of a *numbers equivalent.* Note that if all firms had equal market shares, $\Sigma s_i^2 = 0$ and the HHI index falls monotonically but nonlinearly with an increasing number of firms.

On this, see M. A. Adelman, "Comment on the 'H' Concentration Measure as a Numbers Equivalent," *Review of Economics and Statistics,* vol. 51 (February 1969), pp. 99–101; and William A. Kelly, "A Generalized Interpretation of the Herfindahl Index," *Southern Economic Journal,* vol. 48 (July 1981), pp. 50–57.

46. There is no a priori reason why the weighting scheme need be quadratic, as with the HHI index. For an approach emphasizing variable exponent weights, see Leslie Hannah and J. A. Kay, *Concentration in Modern Industry* (London: Macmillan, 1977), pp. 41–63. Note that in the limiting case of a zero exponent (in place of the HHI index's 2), one obtains a concentration index that merely counts the number of firms. See also Stephen Davies, "Measuring Industrial Concentration: An Alternative Approach," *Review of Economics and Statistics,* vol. 62 (May 1980), pp. 306–309.

47. HHI indices for 1947, 1954, and 1957 are reported in Nelson, *Concentration in the Manufacturing Industries,* supra note 43,

Appendix A. For Canada, see Department of Consumer and Corporate Affairs, *Concentration in the Manufacturing Industries of Canada* (Ottawa: Information Canada, 1971), Table A-1.

48. See George J. Stigler, "A Theory of Oligopoly," *Journal of Political Economy*, vol. 72 (February 1964), pp. 55–59; Thomas R. Saving, "Concentration Ratios and the Degree of Monopoly," *International Economic Review,* vol. 11 (February 1970), pp. 139–146; John C. Hause, "The Measurement of Concentrated Industrial Structure and the Size Distribution of Firms," *Annals of Economic and Social Measurement,* vol. 6 (Winter 1977), pp. 79–90; Robert E. Dansby and Robert D. Willig, "Industry Performance Gradient Indexes," *American Economic Review,* vol. 69 (June 1979), pp. 249–260; and Roger Clarke and Stephen Davies, "Market Structure and Price-Cost Margins," *Economica,* vol. 49 (August 1982), pp. 277–287.

49. For references to numerous earlier studies finding high correlations, see the second edition of this volume, p. 61, note 52. See also note 51 infra.

50. Cf. John E. Kwoka, "Does the Choice of Concentration Measure Really Matter?" *Journal of Industrial Economics,* vol. 29 (June 1981), pp. 445–453; and Leo Sleuwaegen and Wim Dehandschutter, "The Critical Choice Between the Concentration Ratio and the *H*-Index in Assessing Industry Performance," *Journal of Industrial Economics,* vol. 35 (December 1986), pp. 193–208.

51. See John Kwoka, "The Herfindahl Index in Theory and Practice," *Antitrust Bulletin,* vol. 30 (Winter 1985), pp. 915–947 and the studies examined in Chapter 11 infra. For a simulation analysis approach to the choice problem, see C. Wiriyawit and E. C. H. Veendorp, "Concentration Measures as Indicators of Market Performance," *Quarterly Review of Economics and Business,* vol. 23 (Autumn 1983), pp. 44–53.

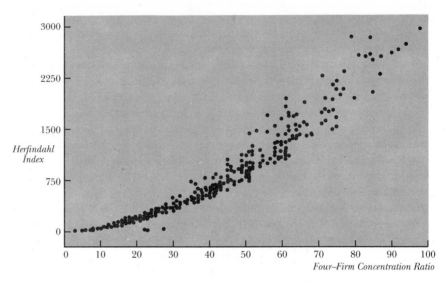

Most studies of market concentration use data collected by national census bureaus. Each census agency has developed or adapted an elaborate system for categorizing the output of business units.[52] In the United States, the basic system is called the Standard Industrial Classification, or S.I.C. Onto it, the Census Bureau has grafted an even more intricately subdivided system organized around a series of seven-digit numbers, each successive digit reflecting a finer degree of classification. Consider, for example, the seven-digit product line 2844515 (suntan and sunscreen lotions and oils). The first digit (2) indicates that this set of commodities is produced in the manufacturing sector of the economy (as opposed to, say, 5 for trade or 0 for agriculture and forestry). The first two digits together (28) reveal that the commodity is produced in the "chemicals and allied products" group of the manufacturing sector. There are twenty such two-digit groups in manufacturing, numbering 20 through 39. The first three digits (284) place our commodity in the "cleaning and toilet products" field. Adding the fourth digit locates it more finely in S.I.C. industry 2844, covering "toilet preparations." In 1982, the manufacturing sector was divided into 450 such four-digit industries, for nearly all of which concentration indices have been published.[53] At a still finer level of detail is the five-digit *product class* 28445 — in this case, a catch-all category covering "other cosmetics and toilet preparations" (shaving preparations, perfumes, dentifrices, and the like having received separate five-digit codes). The 1982 Census of Manufactures enumerated approximately 1,500 five-digit product classes, for most of which concentration ratios are available. Finally, one jumps to the seven-digit *product* or *commodity* level. Examples in the five-digit class 28445 include suntan oils, cleansing creams, lipsticks, aerosol deodorants, nail lacquer, and cosmetic and baby oil. At this level of detail, the U.S. Census of Manufactures identifies some 11,000 items. No concentration ratios are published for them.[54]

Census Bureau industry and product class definitions do not always conform to the market definition criteria economists would prefer. To get its difficult job done at all, the Bureau must use definitions facilitating accurate reporting by business firms, which usually means that it must follow the way firms have grouped together or segregated their production operations. Emphasis is often placed on similarity of production processes, which may or may not reflect product competition interrelationships.

The ideal definition of a market must take into account substitution possibilities in both consumption and production. On the demand side, firms are competitors or rivals if the products they offer are good substitutes for one another in the eyes of buyers. But how, exactly, does one draw the line between "good" and "not good enough" substitutes? The essence of the matter is what happens when price relationships change. If the price of Product A is raised by a small but meaningful percentage and as a result consumers substitute Product B for Product A in significant quantities, then A and B are good substitutes and ought to be included under a common market definition.[55]

A difficulty encountered in implementing this concept is that extensive substitution may occur only within certain relative price ranges and not in others. When the delivered price of coal is $40 per ton, an increase in the price of crude oil from $12 to $18 per barrel may not prompt much substitution because petroleum distillates are more economical as a boiler fuel over the entire $12 to $18 price range.[56] However, as the price of oil is pushed even higher, a point must be reached at which it becomes attractive to substitute coal for oil. In judging whether or not products are substitutes, then, one must make assumptions about the plausible range of prices. In this there are risks of circular reasoning if markets are being defined for purposes of measuring structural monopoly power, for a rational oil monopolist would raise its price until it comes near, without overstepping, the point at which coal begins making substantial inroads. Thus, one must ask whether a given percentage change in price *above the competitive level* would induce

---

52. In U.S. Census practice, four-digit *industry* data are collected by assigning all the activity of particular establishments or plants to the single industry in which the largest sales occur. This sometimes leads to significant amounts of "product contamination," or "wrongly classified activity." The five-digit *product class* data are collected on a product sales basis and are free of such contamination. Some European concentration data series are collected by assigning all the activity of a whole company to the industry in which the firm has its greatest sales volume. Very severe contamination may occur under this procedure.

53. To avoid revealing the data of individual companies, the U.S. Census Bureau sometimes withholds disclosure of certain concentration values, especially in the more highly concentrated industries.

54. But see Dean A. Worcester, Jr., *Monopoly, Big Business and Welfare in the Postwar United States* (Seattle: University of Washington Press, 1967), pp. 70–81, who summarizes an analysis of concentration in selected seven-digit lines.

55. Sometimes this substitutability relationship may be reflected in high values of the *cross elasticity of demand*, defined as the percentage change in the quantity sold, say, of Product B associated with a 1 percent change in the price of Product A, holding Product B's price constant. But cross elasticities are not without inter-

pretational difficulties. Suppose, for example, initial sales of Product A are 1,000 units and sales of Product B are 100 units. Now let the price of A be raised by 10 percent and assume that 30 units of demand shift from A to B. The cross elasticity $(\partial Q_B/Q_B) / (\partial P_A/P_A)$ is 3.0, suggesting high substitutability. But if we assume instead that B reduces its price by a comparable 10 percent and that the same 30 units of demand shift from A to B, the computed cross elasticity $(\partial Q_A/Q_A) / (\partial P_B/P_B)$ is 0.3. In this case, the producer of A is not likely to consider B a very good substitute for its product.

On these and other difficulties encountered in using cross elasticities to delineate market boundaries, see Klaus Stegemann, "Cross Elasticity and the Relevant Market," *Zeitschrift für Wirtschafts-und-Sozialwissenschaften*, no. 2 (1974); and Kenneth D. Boyer, "Degrees of Differentiation and Industry Boundaries," in Terry Calvani and John Siegfried, eds., *Economic Analysis of Antitrust Law* (Boston: Little, Brown, 1979), pp. 88–106. A further analysis of market delineation methods will follow in Chapter 5.

56. In terms of BTUs, 1 ton of coal and 4.3 barrels of oil are roughly equivalent. But even when they are priced at well above 4.3 times the price of coal, petroleum distillates are often preferred because they are easier to transport and use.

significant substitution of coal for oil. This, of course, is difficult. As a result, economists sometimes fall back upon commonsense devices such as searching for a marked qualitative gap in the chain of substitutes, as Mrs. Robinson recommended.[57]

Substitution on the production side must also be considered. Groups of firms making completely nonsubstitutable products may nevertheless be meaningful competitors if they employ essentially similar skills and equipment and if they could move quickly into each others' product lines should the profit lure beckon. The four-digit Census industry "screw machine products" is a good example of a definition satisfying these criteria, for screw machine shops turn out everything from ball bearing races to lamp couplings with equipment readily shifted from one product to another quite different one. Again, however, the application poses practical judgmental problems. How quickly must firms be able to shift among products to be classified in the same market? Given a long enough interval and sufficient investment, shifts in production activity more accurately described as new entry than substitution can occur. A distinction between substitutability and ease of entry (that is, where barriers to new entry are minimal) must be drawn. At the risk of being somewhat arbitrary, we should probably draw the line to include as substitutes only existing capacity that can be shifted in the short run, that is, without significant new investment in equipment and worker training.

In view of these broad principles, how good are the Census Bureau's industry definitions for purposes of identifying structural monopoly conditions? What problems arise? Are there consistent biases in the definitions, and if so, in what direction? And how can they be combatted? As a backdrop for exploring these questions, Table 3.6 presents 1982 sales concentration data for a sample of forty-four U.S. manufacturing industries, mostly defined at the four-digit level. The sample is fairly representative, but excludes vaguely defined catch-all categories and favors the larger, more highly concentrated industries that will reappear frequently in later chapters.

The most important single source of problems is a definition excessively broad or narrow relative to the possibilities for substitution in consumption. Several of the industries in Table 3.6 are plainly too broad. Pharmaceutical preparations, for example, lumps together dozens of drugs, or classes of drugs, for which there are no adequate substitutes (except perhaps debility or greatly extended medical care). Economically meaningful market definitions are more apt to be found in this case at the seven-digit level of product detail. Other industries defined too broadly include aircraft (involving a wide diversity of types ranging from pleasure craft to supersonic bombers), motors and generators (ranging from fractional horsepower types to 500 hp behemoths, each demanding quite different production tooling), and soap and detergents (with several functionally distinct product lines). Industries defined too narrowly include the separate glass container and metal can groups (since cans and bottles are substitutable in many applications); cotton weaving mills (since synthetic fabrics and wool compete in many uses, and looms are often interchangeable between cotton and synthetic blend yarn processing); and synthetic rubber (for which natural and reclaimed rubber, accounting for 32 percent of total rubber consumed in 1982, can sometimes be substituted). Concentration ratios in the primary copper and aluminum (and to a lesser degree

Table 3.6 1982 Concentration Ratios for Representative Industries

S.I.C. Code	Industry Description	4-firm Ratio	8-firm Ratio	Number of Firms	HHI Index*
3711	Passenger cars (five-digit)	97	99	n.a.	n.a.
2067	Chewing gum	95	n.a.	9	n.a.
3632	Household refrigerators and freezers	94	98	39	2745
33310	Primary copper (five-digit)	92	100	7	2483
3641	Electric lamps	91	96	113	n.a.
21110	Cigarettes (five-digit)	90	n.a.	8	n.a.
2043	Cereal breakfast foods	86	n.a.	32	n.a.
3211	Flat glass	85	n.a.	49	2032
3511	Turbines and turbine generators	84	92	71	2602
2082	Beer and malt beverages	77	94	67	2089
39641	Zippers (five-digit)	70	81	n.a.	1452
36512	Household television receivers (five-digit)	67	90	n.a.	1351
3011	Tires and inner tubes	66	86	108	1591
3721	Aircraft	64	81	139	1358
3334	Primary aluminum	64	88	15	1704
2841	Soap and detergents	60	63	642	1306
3691	Storage batteries	56	79	129	989
3523	Farm machinery and equipment	53	62	1787	1468
3221	Glass containers	50	73	41	966
3411	Metal cans	50	68	168	790
2822	Synthetic rubber	49	74	63	935
3562	Ball and roller bearings	47	65	109	724
3312	Blast furnaces and steel mills	42	64	211	650
2211	Cotton weaving mills	41	65	209	645
2041	Flour and other grain mills	40	60	251	551
3674	Semiconductors	40	57	685	597
3144	Women's footwear, except athletic	38	47	209	492
3621	Motors and generators	36	50	349	476
2051	Bread, cake, and related products	34	47	1869	410
2873	Nitrogenous fertilizers	32	57	109	515
3241	Portland cement	31	52	119	469
3541	Metal-cutting machine tools	30	44	865	351
2911	Petroleum refining	28	48	282	380
2834	Pharmaceutical preparations	26	42	584	318
2851	Paints and allied products	24	36	1170	222
2651	Folding paperboard boxes	22	35	457	212
2711	Newspapers	22	34	7520	193
3552	Textile machinery	22	32	511	200
2421	Sawmills and planing mills	17	23	5810	113
2026	Fluid milk	16	27	853	151
2086	Bottled and canned soft drinks	14	23	1236	109
3451	Screw machine products	8	11	1744	30
2335	Women's and misses' dresses	6	10	5489	24
3273	Ready-mixed concrete	6	9	4161	18

*With the underlying market shares measured in percentage terms, the maximum possible value is 10,000. Values not available are in all cases relatively high.

Source: U.S. Bureau of the Census, *1982 Census of Manufactures,* "Concentration Ratios in Manufacturing," MC82-S-7 (April 1986).

57. Joan Robinson, *The Economics of Imperfect Competition* (London: Macmillan, 1934), p. 5.

steel) industries also tend to overstate monopoly power because these metals compete with one another in numerous applications and because the output of domestic scrap reprocessing is omitted from consideration. In 1982, resmelted copper scrap constituted about 23 percent of all domestic copper production by dollar value and reprocessed aluminum 27 percent of aluminum production.

Concentration ratios can also overstate monopoly power by failing to take into account competition from foreign suppliers. Import competition has been regularly rising since the 1950s. For U.S. producers, it increased rapidly during the early 1980s when the dollar was unusually strong, but ebbed in the later 1980s as the dollar's fall forced increases in imported goods prices. For manufacturing as a whole, imports in 1982 averaged 9.1 percent of domestic producer sales. Industries in Table 3.6 for which 1982 imports amounted to 25 percent or more of domestic output included textile machinery (67 percent), women's shoes (72 percent), automobiles (38 percent), semiconductors (35 percent), machine tools (31 percent), and television sets (27 percent).[58]

While failure to consider import competition causes concentration ratios to overstate the degree of structural monopoly power, the implicit census assumption that all markets are nationwide errs in the opposite direction. Certain bulky, low-value commodities cannot be transported economically far from the site of production, so the market definition must be regional or local to be meaningful. Cement is a classic example. Table 3.6 shows that the leading four firms accounted for 31 percent of all nationwide sales in 1982. Yet unless a cement plant was connected to customers by water routes, it cost roughly 45 cents to ship a dollar's worth of cement 350 miles, and for that reason 83 percent of all cement was shipped 200 miles or less in 1977.[59] When the United States is divided into fifty-one regions (essentially on a statewide basis), one finds that in only three of the regions did the leading four cement producers account for less than 50 percent of 1964 sales.[60] Newspapers and ready-mixed concrete are even more extreme, since relevant markets are seldom much larger than a single metropolitan area, so one finds near-monopoly conditions in many local newspaper markets and tight oligopoly in all but the most densely populated ready-mix markets. Because of the centripetal pull of transportation costs, national concentration ratios also understate true concentration in glass containers, nitrogenous fertilizers, petroleum refining, paperboard boxes, and fluid milk. The same would be true for beer and metal cans were it not for the fact that the leading suppliers have a strong presence in nearly all important geographic markets.

Finally, published concentration ratios may misrepresent the extent of structural monopoly power for various idiosyncratic reasons. The bottled and canned soft drinks industry, with a four-firm concentration ratio in 1982 of only 14, provides a particularly strong illustration. Its ostensibly low concentration reflects the organization of the industry into numerous local bottling companies. But most bottlers operate under franchises from nationwide firms like Coca-Cola and Pepsi-Cola that do not let them interpenetrate each other's home territories. A more meaningful index of concentration would be the proportion of the nationwide market commanded by products tied to the leading national firms. Some indication is provided by the fact that product class 20873 — liquid beverage bases for use by soft drink bottlers — had a four-firm concentration ratio of 90 in 1982.

To sum up, concentration ratios understate the true quantum of structural monopoly when markets are defined to include nonsubstitutes, when meaningful markets are local or regional rather than nationwide, when sellers enjoy strong product differentiation advantages within relevant product lines, and when special features like the soft drink franchising system are present. The degree of structural monopoly is overstated when substitutes are excluded from the industry definition and when import competition is significant.

Given these problems, what practical steps can be taken to avoid mistakes in the use and interpretation of concentration ratios? The most important is to recognize that pitfalls exist: concentration indices are at best only a rough one-dimensional indicator of monopoly power, and their use must be tempered with common sense. For statistical work, careful scholars either eliminate poorly defined industries (which may cause other biases) or (preferably) adjust the concentration ratios they use, for example, by employing five-digit or regional concentration ratios when the four-digit national industry is defined too broadly, and by multiplying the ratios for import-impacted industries by the ratio of domestic sales to import sales plus domestic sales.[61] We shall have more to say on such methods in Chapter 11.

The Overall Extent of Seller Concentration in the U.S. Economy

Forewarned of the hazards, we attempt now to assess how concentrated markets are in the American economy as a whole. For many sectors we can do little more than make impressionistic guesses, since adequate quantitative data are totally lacking. Perspective on the relative sizes of the various sectors is provided by the 1982 gross national product share figures in the second numerical column of Table 3.1.

In the agriculture, forestry, and fisheries sectors, industry structures are overwhelmingly atomistic. However, competition is moderated by a heavy overlay of government price supports, marketing orders, acreage restrictions, and other interventions. Also, in logging, the cost of transporting trees to sawmills or pulp mills is sometimes so high that few mills purchase timber in any given forest area. Thus, the structure is characterized by oligopsony (few buyers).[62]

58. See U.S. Bureau of the Census, *U.S. Commodity Exports and Imports As Related to Output: 1982 and 1981* (Washington: USGPO, December 1986), Table 2C. Again, in 1982, imports were unusually high because the U.S. dollar was quite strong. The auto import share is also high because a recession curbed domestic demand, but import quotas negotiated with Japan the previous year served as a floor as well as a ceiling on imports from that nation.

59. U.S. Bureau of the Census, *1977 Census of Transportation,* "Commodity Transportation Survey: Summary," TC77-CS (Washington: USGPO, June 1981), pp. 438–439.

60. Federal Trade Commission, *Economic Report on Mergers and Vertical Integration in the Cement Industry* (Washington: 1966), pp. 29–31. State market boundaries are in most instances too narrow, but they approximate a correct definition more closely than nationwide figures.

61. For methodological guidance, see George J. Stigler, *Capital and Rates of Return in Manufacturing Industries* (Princeton: Princeton University Press, 1963), pp. 206–211; and Leonard W. Weiss, "Corrected Concentration Ratios in Manufacturing — 1972," undated manuscript, University of Wisconsin Department of Economics. Weiss' compendium contains variously adjusted concentration ratios for 1972. Weighted average regional and local concentration ratios for 1963 are presented in David Schwartzman and Joan Bodoff, "Concentration in Regional and Local Industries," *Southern Economic Journal,* vol. 37 (January 1971), pp. 343–348. For import-adjusted 1977 concentration ratios, see C. C. Coughlin and T. G. Watkins, "The Impact of International Intra-Firm Trade on Domestic Concentration Ratios," *Review of Industrial Organization,* vol. 2, no. 3 (1985), pp. 232–250.

62. See Walter J. Mead, *Competition and Oligopsony in the Douglas Fir Lumber Industry* (Berkeley: University of California Press, 1966).

Mining presents a mixed picture. Some mining industries, such as limestone and common sand and gravel, are atomistic nationally, but product values are so low in relation to transportation cost that oligopoly prevails in appropriately defined regional and local markets. Others, such as copper, iron ore, uranium, lead, zinc, gold, and phosphate are moderately to highly concentrated even at the national level. For the higher-value minerals, imports could be a significant check on monopoly power, but for many of the rarer minerals (such as chromium, molybdenum, nickel, and diamonds) concentration is also high in world markets, and international cartels are not uncommon. Crude oil production in the United States borders on atomism, with the four leading producers controlling 35 percent of domestic reserves and 25 percent of output in 1980. However, the price of crude oil in most industrialized nations is determined by the OPEC cartel, which for substantial periods of time since 1973 was able to hold prices well above competitive levels. The four leading soft-coal mining firms originated 25 percent of U.S. production in 1976, and the eight leaders accounted for 34 percent. Higher concentration ratios prevail in spatially narrower coal-mining regions, but with coal prices pulled up by cartel-dominated oil prices and with pollution laws encouraging long-distance shipping of low-sulphur Western U.S. coal, markets have become increasingly nationwide in scope. Thus, loose oligopoly is probably the best characterization of the industry's structure.

Contract construction includes large numbers of small firms and can be termed generally competitive in structure, despite pockets of localized oligopoly.

Competition in the transportation, communications, and electrical and gas utilities sectors is controlled and restrained by formal public regulation. Oligopoly is the predominant market structure in railroading, air transport, intercity bus lines, parts of water transportation, and highway freight carriage between less densely travelled points, while large numbers of firms operate on the high-volume trucking routes and in inland water transportation. Intermodal competition is generally strong, especially since substantial deregulation occurred in the late 1970s and early 1980s. In electricity and gas distribution and local telephone service, natural monopoly has been the rule, although cellular radio communications services have been organized as a tight oligopoly under regulations implemented during the 1980s. Easing of regulatory entry restrictions has transformed inter-city telecommunications into a tight oligopoly. Radio broadcasting is monopolistically competitive except in isolated low-population areas. Over-the-air television broadcasting is oligopolistic, but broadcasters compete with cable services, whose organization tends toward natural monopoly or very tight oligopoly.

Wholesale and retail trade are more difficult to categorize. In metropolitan areas of substantial size (for example, with population exceeding 100,000), market structures are characteristically atomistic or loosely oligopolistic. Despite the rise of the chain store, single-unit ventures continue to thrive. More than a million single-unit retailing firms accounted for 47 percent of all U.S. retail sales in 1982. Chains with 101 or more units made 29 percent of total 1982 sales — an increase from 13 percent in 1954 and 19 percent in 1967.[63] In food retailing, where chain-store operation has had a particularly long history, oligopoly is prevalent in metropolitan area markets. Among 263 U.S. metropolitan areas, four-firm concentration ratios for 1972 ranged from 26 (for Charlestown, South Carolina) to 81 (for Cedar Rapids, Iowa), with a median value of 52.[64] Elements of spatial and subjective product differentiation may fragment metropolitan area retail markets into smaller segments. The urban consumer without an automobile may find it necessary to pay appreciable taxi fares or shop for groceries in a smaller, relatively high-priced neighborhood convenience store. And there are relatively few stores where one can find freshly made German Weisswurst, a concert-quality grand piano, or a serious book on some arcane subject such as the economics of industrial market structure. If a simple verdict had to be rendered, however, it would be that high concentration is more the exception than the rule in retailing.

The pattern in banking is one of loose oligopoly in nationwide credit markets and large cities, with very tight oligopoly or even monopoly confronting individuals in smaller cities and towns. Competition in banking is loosely regulated, and insurance rate-setting is tightly regulated in many states. Concentration is moderate to high in the health and life insurance fields and low in most other fields. The real estate brokerage trades are atomistically structured except in very small towns.

The service industries, including hotels and motels, laundry services, funeral parlors, barber and beauty shops, repair services, legal and medical services, and the like tend toward large numbers of sellers except in small towns.[65] Yet the amount of monopoly power present is much greater than a superficial analysis of market structure might imply. This is so in part because of very strong product differentiation and in some fields (such as medicine and surveying) cartel-like restrictions on new entry. The extensive repair service trades pose special problems. Once the customer has left his or her watch or car or computer with a particular shop, a bilateral monopoly condition exists, and the customer typically lacks bargaining power because the repair person has greatly superior knowledge of what must be done. Also included in the services sector are the various amusement and recreational industries, whose concentration is high except in the largest cities.

The government sector, accounting for 11 percent of gross national product in 1982 (including only activities directly carried out by government bodies and not work contracted to private industry) is much too complex for any blanket statement. Many government services (such as law enforcement and defense) are provided outside the market framework, and it makes little sense to discuss them in terms of a competition-monopoly structural spectrum. In other areas, such as the Postal Service, the Government Printing Office, the Navy's shipyards, and the vast array of schools, government activities coexist with more or less parallel private functions.

It is futile to attempt a precise quantitative summary of how much structural monopoly power exists in the whole of the American economy. Suffice it to say that there is a modest amount of activity (not more than 5 percent of GNP) approaching pure monopoly (most of which is subject to government regulation),

63. *Statistical Abstract of the United States: 1986,* p. 774.

64. Bruce W. Marion, Willard F. Mueller, et al., *The Profit and Price Performance of Leading Food Chains, 1970–74,* study published by the Joint Economic Committee of the U.S. Congress (Washington: USGPO, 1977), pp. 126–132.

65. See U.S. Bureau of the Census, *1982 Census of Service Industries,* "Establishment and Firm Size," SC82-I-1 (Washington: USGPO, May 1985).

somewhat more activity approaching pure competition, and large quantities of oligopoly and monopolistic competition.[66]

Manufacturing Concentration Levels and Trends

Manufacturing, which by standard measures is the largest single sector in the U.S. economy, has been reserved for more thorough analysis. It is the only sector for which comprehensive data on industry concentration exist, permitting detailed structural analyses.

Although it is relatively easy to find examples for very narrowly defined chemical, drug, medical device, and other product categories, monopoly in the sense of a single seller is virtually nonexistent in nationwide U.S. manufacturing industries of appreciable size.[67] The rate at which near-monopolies have faded appears to have exceeded the rate of new appearance by a substantial margin. In 1962 Gillette made 70 percent of domestic razor blade sales, but its position was eroded, first by the appearance of Wilkinson's stainless steel blades and then by Bic's aggressive marketing of disposable razors. Eastman Kodak's 90 percent share of amateur film sales and 65 percent share of all film sales, including instant photo packs, was sharply challenged in the 1980s by import competition from Fuji. General Motors' share of diesel locomotive sales probably remains near 75 percent. For decades Western Electric supplied roughly 85 percent of U.S. telephone equipment, but its position faded rapidly owing to technological changes of the 1970s and the antitrust-induced divestiture in 1984 of affiliated Bell Telephone local operating companies, ending a captive market situation. IBM's 72 to 82 percent share of the digital computer market during the 1960s fell as new rivals captured mini- and microcomputer applications. Xerox's 75 to 80 percent share of electrostatic copier revenues declined with the erosion of its patent position during the 1970s. Rio Tinto Zinc's near monopoly of world borax supplies was eroded when one of its three mines was nationalized by the government of Turkey.[68] During much of the 1960s and 1970s, Boeing controlled roughly two-thirds of noncommunist world jet airliner placements. With the rise of Europe's Airbus Consortium, Boeing's share declined to 50 percent in the late 1980s. Through the second half of the 20th century, the De Beers Organization has controlled 80 to 90 percent of the world's uncut diamond supply.

Oligopoly, on the other hand, is abundant. Table 3.7 shows the distribution of 448 four-digit manufacturing industries in 1982 by four-firm sales concentration ranges. When the leading four firms control 40 percent or more of the total market, oligopolistic behavior becomes likely. Inspection shows that 199 industries, comprising 44 percent of all the industries by number and 39.5 percent by value added, had four-firm concentration ratios of at least that threshold magnitude. Since, abstracting from import competition, four-digit census definitions tend toward excessively broad definitions on average, these figures suggest that something on the order of half of all U.S. manufacturing industry can be characterized as oligopolistic.

Has this distribution of market structures always been present? And is there an observable trend toward increasing or decreasing concentration? Very long run analyses plunge us into the realm of incommensurables. During the first half of the nineteenth century, nationwide concentration of manufactured goods output was undoubtedly much lower than it is now. But markets were predominantly local

Table 3.7   Distribution of U.S. Manufacturing Industries by Four-Firm
Sales Concentration Ratios: 1982

Four-Firm Concentration Ratio Range	Number of Industries	Percentage of All Industries	Percentage of Total Value Added
0–19	86	19.2%	21.7%
20–39	163	36.4	38.8
40–59	120	26.8	19.7
60–79	56	12.5	14.9
80–100	23	5.1	4.9

Source: Adapted from U.S. Bureau of the Census, *1982 Census of Manufactures,* "Concentration Ratios in Manufacturing," MC82–S–7 (Washington: Government Printing Office, April 1986).

then. The railroads had not been built on any significant scale; wagon roads were primitive; and the waterways were circuitous, slow, and often blocked in winter. As a result, competitive contact among geographically scattered manufacturers was modest, and the amount of monopoly power they possessed must have been high. As the railroads expanded their coverage from 9,000 miles of road operated in 1850 to 167,000 miles in 1890, and as the spread of telegraph and then telephone service greatly facilitated communications, something resembling a true national market emerged for the first time.[69] Firms interpenetrated each others' former home territories and competition intensified. Indeed, if we could measure monopoly power in manufacturing directly, we might well find it to have been at a historic low between 1870 and 1890, for there was a sharp increase in concentration following 1880. This was attributable to the rapid internal growth of enterprises that proved themselves fit for the competitive struggle, and even more to an enormous number of mergers among previously independent firms. We will discuss the merger movement in Chapter 5. The main point for present purposes is that it ran its course shortly after the turn of the century, so that the economy of 1904 was structurally quite different from the economy of 1830 or 1870. Whether there was more or less monopoly power in 1904 than in 1830 no one can say with confidence, because the whole economic environment had been transformed so radically.

66. For other estimates of the incidence of competition and monopoly in the U.S. economy, see George J. Stigler, *Five Lectures on Economic Problems* (London: Longman, Green, 1949), pp. 46–62; Clair Wilcox, "On the Alleged Ubiquity of Oligopoly," *American Economic Review,* vol. 40 (May 1950), pp. 67–73; Carl Kaysen and Donald F. Turner, *Antitrust Policy* (Cambridge: Harvard University Press, 1959), pp. 26–43; and W. G. Shepherd, "Causes of Increased Competition in the U.S. Economy, 1939–1980," *Review of Economics and Statistics,* vol. 64 (November 1982), pp. 613–626.

67. A study of 314 four-digit manufacturing industries revealed the average estimated leading firm market share to be 17.5 percent, with a range from 68.7 to 1.1 percent. The average market shares for the second, third, and fourth sellers were 10.0, 7.0, and 5.3 percent, respectively. John E. Kwoka, Jr., "Regularity and Diversity of Firm Size Distributions in U.S. Industries," *Journal of Economics and Business,* vol. 34 (1982), pp. 391–395.

68. "Boring but Nice," *The Economist,* July 28, 1988, p. 60.

69. For a more skeptical view of the railroads' impact, see Robert W. Fogel, *Railroads and American Economic Growth* (Baltimore: Johns Hopkins University Press, 1964).

The gap between 1904 and the present can be bridged in less vague terms thanks to the painstaking labors of G. Warren Nutter.[70] Utilizing numerous published sources and a good deal of guesswork, Nutter estimated that 32.9 percent of all national income originating in the manufacturing sector came from industries in which the four largest enterprises accounted for 50 percent or more of output at one time or another between 1895 and 1904.[71]

Similar figures can be derived from more recent censuses of manufactures. The proportions of manufacturing value added originating in industries with four-firm sales concentration ratios of 50 or higher were as follows:[72]

1947	24.4 percent
1954	29.9 percent
1958	30.2 percent
1963	33.1 percent
1972	29.0 percent
1982	25.2 percent

Were it not for Nutter's original benchmark, one might be inclined to infer that a strong upward trend was operating, at least up to 1963. But since the 1963 high-water mark barely exceeded Nutter's concentration estimate for 1895–1904, it seems more reasonable to assume that some sort of cyclical movement has occurred, with industry concentration falling to unusually low levels during the sellers' market immediately following World War II — a pattern analogous to the one observed for aggregate concentration. Since 1963, however, the cycles have diverged, with market concentration declining while aggregate concentration (measured by value added) remained stable.

Further analysis reveals that much of the postwar increase was the result of events in a few of the largest industries, for example, as the steel, aircraft, farm machinery, computer, and organic chemicals industries moved below or above the 50 percent concentration ratio boundary. Thus, the Nutter approach proves quite sensitive to relatively small concentration changes in particular industries. An alternative view is obtained by computing weighted average concentration ratios for all manufacturing industry, letting each individual industry's four-firm ratio be weighted by the value added originating in that industry.[73] The resulting concentration indices are as follows:

1947	35.3
1954	36.9
1958	37.0
1963	38.9
1972	39.2
1977	38.5
1982	37.1

This approach suggests a much more modest concentration increase between 1947 and 1963, with a reversal materializing in the 1970s.

The clear implication from various censuses following World War II is that concentration in U.S. manufacturing industries increased modestly at most over a period of thirty-five years. Less solid evidence suggests that the increase was slight even when compared to levels prevailing at the turn of the century. As Professor Adelman prophetically concluded in an earlier study of concentration trends, "Any tendency either way, if it does exist, must be at the pace of a glacial drift."[74]

Comparisons with Other Nations

Let us broaden our perspective. Three questions concerning the structure of industry in nations other than the United States are of special interest. Are there consistent patterns in the degree of concentration observed in similar industries across diverse nations? Is concentration higher or lower on average in manufacturing industries outside the United States? And are there discernible trends in manufacturing market concentration abroad?

Because there are substantial differences across nations in industrial classification systems and in the extent to which data are reported for the more finely subdivided classes, it is difficult to answer the first two questions. Inevitably, many industries must be excluded as noncomparable. Even when one attempts to analyze only comparably defined industries, there are pitfalls. For example, it was hardly obvious from inspection that the British industry, "aluminium and aluminium alloys and manufactures thereof" covered almost solely fabricating activity up to 1970, since until then Britain had only one small primary aluminum smelter and imported 90 percent of its requirements. Without such knowledge, one could only be puzzled at the five-firm concentration ratio of 51 for the British industry in 1968 when the aluminum industries of most other nations were highly concentrated.

Such comparability problems were minimized in a study of twelve industries across six nations. The usual national census and trade publications were supplemented by 125 company interviews in the six nations. The standardized three-firm national concentration ratios compiled in this way are arrayed in Table 3.8.

70. G. Warren Nutter, *The Extent of Enterprise Monopoly in the United States: 1899–1939* (Chicago: University of Chicago Press, 1951), especially pp. 35–48 and 112–150. See also Henry A. Einhorn, "Competition in American Industry, 1939–58," *Journal of Political Economy,* vol. 74 (October 1966), pp. 506–511, and Shepherd, "Causes of Increased Competition," supra note 66.

71. Note that one is likely to find more industries with a four-firm concentration ratio exceeding 50 at some time during a ten-year period than in any single year. But there are so many other possibilities for error in a reconstruction job as difficult as Nutter's that it makes little sense to dwell heavily on this particular bias. See the comment by Stanley Lebergott and the rejoinder by Nutter in the *Review of Economics and Statistics,* vol. 35 (November 1953), pp. 349–353.

72. Industries in the ordnance group (formerly set aside under S.I.C. 19) were excluded from both numerator and denominator of the 1947–63 calculations, since no concentration data were published for them. Data did become available for 1972 and later,

but six such industries (all six above the 50 percent threshold) were excluded to maintain consistency. The 1982 figure with the six included is 26.2 percent.

73. The 1947, 1954, and 1958 figures are drawn from testimony of M. A. Adelman in U.S. Senate, Committee on the Judiciary, Subcommittee on Antitrust and Monopoly, Hearings, *Economic Concentration,* Part 1 (Washington: USGPO, 1964), p. 355. Since the calculations were based upon all available information, we include here for 1972 and later years the six ordnance industries with unavailable data earlier. If the six are excluded, the 1982 concentration ratio average falls to 36.7. Because the census industry classification was somewhat more finely subdivided in 1972 and later years, that is, with 448 industries in 1982, as compared to 417 in 1963, average indicated concentration probably would have fallen more in the absence of classification changes.

74. M. A. Adelman, "The Measurement of Industrial Concentration," *Review of Economics and Statistics,* vol. 33 (November 1951), pp. 295–296.

A considerable amount of variation among nations is evident, but one can also see that certain industries — for example, cigarettes, bottles, refrigerators, and batteries — tend to be relatively highly concentrated in every nation, while others, such as weaving, paints, and shoes, tend to be relatively unconcentrated. This qualitative impression is verified quantitatively by correlating the concentration ratios for each nation pair. Using international automobile identification letters to designate the nations, the relevant matrix of intercorrelations is as follows:

	USA	CAN	GB	S	F	D
USA	1.00	.73	.48	.44	.75	.77
CAN		1.00	.59	.50	.76	.62
GB			1.00	.90	.77	.79
S				1.00	.62	.73
F					1.00	.81

All the off-diagonal correlations are positive, and twelve of the fifteen are statistically significant at the 95 percent confidence level or better. Thus, if concentration in some industry is relatively high in one nation, it tends to be relatively high in other nations too.

Table 3.8   Three-firm Concentration Ratios for Twelve Identically Defined Industries in Six Nations, 1970

Industry	United States	Canada	United Kingdom	Sweden	France	West Germany
Brewing	39	89	47	70	63	17
Cigarettes	68	90	94	100	100	94
Fabric weaving	30	67	28	50	23	16
Paints	26	40	40	92	14	32
Petroleum refining	25	64	79	100	60	47
Shoes (except rubber)	17	18	17	37	13	20
Glass bottles	65	100	73	100	84	93
Portland cement	20	65	86	100	81	54
Ordinary steel	42	80	39*	63	84	56
Antifriction bearings	43	89	82	100	80	90
Refrigerators	64	75	65	89	100	72
Storage batteries	54	73	75	100	94	82
Simple average	41	71	60	83	66	56

*Prenationalization value.

Source: F. M. Scherer, Alan Beckenstein, Erich Kaufer, and R. D. Murphy, *The Economics of Multi-Plant Operation: An International Comparisons Study* (Cambridge: Harvard University Press, 1975), pp. 218–219 and 426–428.

A danger in any such analysis is that the small industry sample may not be representative. The Table 3.8 sample clearly is not in at least one respect: the leading U.S. companies in the industries selected tended to operate more plants each than the comparable average for all American manufacturing industries. However, evidence that the results are robust comes from a similar correlation analysis by Frederic Pryor covering larger samples of industries for the six nations of Table 3.8 plus six others. A comparison of his United States versus other national correlation coefficients is presented in Table 3.9, with the size of Pryor's sample given in subscripted parentheses. Except for Sweden, the values are extremely close. Other analyses of this genre all point in the same direction.[75] Sufficient similarity in concentration patterns exists among nations to suspect that some common cluster of concentration-determining forces is at work. We shall take up the search for those common elements in Chapter 4.

Table 3.8 shows a considerably lower average level of industry concentration in the United States than in the five other nations. Whether these results generalize is not completely clear. It appears established beyond question that in small industrialized nations like Sweden, Belgium, Canada, and Switzerland, industry concentration levels are distinctly higher on average than in large nations like the United States, Japan, and Germany.[76] Frequently, the markets of small nations are simply too small to accommodate many viable competitors. Whether this inverse size-concentration relationship persists all the way out to a nation the size of the United States, the largest capitalist industrial country, is less certain. The weight of the evidence from several comparisons between the United Kingdom and the United States supports a conclusion that the U.K. industries are more concentrated.[77] Pryor's study shows a slightly lower average level of concentration in West Germany than in the United States during the early 1960s. However, there is also conflicting evidence.[78] A West German analysis of *three*-firm concentration ratios for 1984 yielded a value-added weighted average of 37.3 percent.[79] This is almost identical to the U.S. *four*-firm value for 1982 of 37.1 percent. The difference in the number of sellers implies that West German concentration would be higher on a comparable basis, probably by about 5 percentage points.[80] The broader German industry definitions, with only 319 categories in comparison to

75. See the second edition of this volume, p. 71, and the references given on p. 73, note 81.

76. Frederic Pryor, "An International Comparison of Concentration Ratios," *Review of Economics and Statistics,* vol. 54 (May 1972), pp. 133–134; *Concentration in the Manufacturing Industries of Canada,* supra note 47, pp. 49–50; Gideon Rosenbluth, *Concentration in Canadian Manufacturing Industries* (Princeton: Princeton University Press, 1957), pp. 75–87; and Alexis P. Jacquemin and Henry W. de Jong, *European Industrial Organisation* (London: Macmillan, 1977), p. 59.

77. See P. Sargant Florence, *The Logic of British and American Industry* (London: Routledge and Kegan Paul, 1953), pp. 130–135; B. Peter Pashigian, "Market Concentration in the United States and Great Britain," *Journal of Law & Economics,* vol. 11 (October 1968), pp. 299–319; and Malcolm Sawyer, "Concentration in British Manufacturing Industry," *Oxford Economic Papers,* vol. 23

(November 1971), pp. 371–374. Compare W. G. Shepherd, "Structure and Behavior in British Industries, with U.S. Comparisons," *Journal of Industrial Economics,* vol. 21 (November 1972), pp. 40–44, who adjusted both U.S. and U.K. concentration ratios to allow for regional markets, excessively broad industry definitions, and the like and found the adjusted U.S. ratios to be higher on average.

78. Pryor, "An International Comparison," supra note 76, pp. 133–134; and Frederic Jenny and André-Paul Weber, "The Determinants of Concentration Trends in the French Manufacturing Sector," *Journal of Industrial Economics,* vol. 26 (March 1978), pp. 193–196, who find "strikingly close" average concentration levels in France and the United States.

79. Monopolkommission, *Gesamtwirtschliche Chancen,* supra note 22, p. 44.

80. Cf. note 67 supra.

Table 3.9   Comparison of Pryor's International Concentration
Correlations with Those from the Smaller Table 3.8 Sample

	Pryor	Table 3.8 Sample
U.S. — Canada	.77(37)	.73
U.S. — Great Britain	.51(72)	.48
U.S. — Sweden	.68(74)	.44
U.S. — France	.74(47)	.75
U.S. — West Germany	.73(67)	.77

Source: Frederic L. Pryor, "An International Comparison of Concentration Ratios,"
Review of Economics and Statistics, vol. 54 (May 1972), p. 136.

448 U.S. four-digit codes, points in the same direction. For Japan, the most comprehensive data suggest marginally lower average concentration than in the United States, but it is unclear whether taking into account intercorporate Keiretsu ties would alter the picture.[81]

More confident conclusions can be reached on concentration trends *within* nations. In Canada, average four-firm ratios increased by nearly 10 percentage points between 1948 and 1965, but from 1965 through 1982 they varied narrowly without trend in the range of 47.8 to 50.8.[82] The best evidence for Japan suggests declining average concentration from 1937 into the 1960s, with a reversal of the trend since then.[83] For the United Kingdom, the trend has been generally upward, but much more rapidly (approximately 10 percentage points on average) between 1958 and 1968 than either before or after.[84] Rising national market concentration has also been the pattern for the founding members of the European Economic Community, as shown in a comparison of unweighted average four-firm ratios for forty-seven broadly defined (three-digit) industries for the years 1963 and 1978:[85]

| | **Average Ratio** | |
	1963	1978
West Germany	18.9	23.1
France	22.3	30.5
Italy	22.0	28.3
Netherlands	35.3	39.7
Belgium	36.6	41.8

However, the formation and extension of the Common Market poses problems in interpreting such national industry trends similar to those engendered by the spread of American railroads and communication systems in the nineteenth century. To show the effect of this development, Yamawaki et al. combined and reworked the data underlying the five individual founding nation averages above to estimate four-firm concentration ratios, assuming those five nations to be a true common market. For 1963, the average ratio was 16.3; for 1978, 18.5.[86] Although transportation costs and remaining trade barriers left the European Community well short of being a single common market in 1978, the overall impact of integration was almost surely to create market structures more competitive than they otherwise would have been.

The Stability of Leading Positions

The concentration ratio is a static index, characterizing market structure for a single, typically short interval in time. We should not be surprised that the identity of the leading sellers in an industry changes occasionally. When turnover among the top firms is rapid, high concentration ratios may conceal or belie the intensity of competition for two reasons. First, the market shares of industry leaders, and hence the concentration ratio, will be lower when computed on, say, a five-year basis than the shares of leaders identified for any shorter interval, since momentary leaders will tend to be firms enjoying unusually and perhaps unsustainably high shares owing to chance factors.[87] Second, the very rapidity of turnover suggests a competitive struggle for position. High turnover is said by some economists to be an indicator of dynamic competition, which may be present even when concentration ratios imply the absence of much competition in a static structural sense.[88]

A first look at the available statistics on leading firm turnover lends some support to the claim that dynamic competition is strong. An analysis of 204 four-digit manufacturing industries showed that the four industry leaders of 1947 continued to be the 1958 leaders in only 19 percent of the cases.[89] In only 6 percent of the

81. Caves and Uekusa, *Industrial Organization in Japan,* supra note 18, pp. 26–28.

82. See the *Report of the Royal Commission on Corporate Concentration,* supra note 28, pp. 34–37; Statistics Canada, "Industrial Concentration," preliminary document 31–402 (1982); and R. S. Khemani, "The Extent and Evolution of Competition in the Canadian Economy," in D. G. McFetridge, ed., *Canadian Industry in Transition* (Toronto: Toronto University Press, 1986), pp. 135–176.

83. Caves and Uekusa, *Industrial Organization in Japan,* supra note 18, pp. 26–28.

84. See Kenneth D. George, "A Note on Changes in Industrial Concentration in the United Kingdom," *Economic Journal,* vol. 85 (March 1975), pp. 124–128; and P. E. Hart and R. Clarke, *Concentration in British Industry,* Occasional Paper No. 32 (London: National Institute of Economic and Social Research, 1980), Chapter 2.

85. Hideki Yamawaki, Leonard W. Weiss, and Leo Sleuwaegen, "Industry Competition and the Formation of the European Common Market," working paper, International Institute of Management (Berlin: August 1986). Because of data gaps, the authors were able to cover only 47 out of the 103 comparably defined three-digit manufacturing industries.

See also Jacquemin and de Jong, *European Industrial Organisation,* supra note 76, pp. 55–58; Mueller and Hochreiter, *Stand und Entwicklungstendenzen,* supra note 26, Chapter 4; and Jenny and Weber, "The Determinants," supra note 78, pp. 194–196. In *Ges-*

amtwirtschaftliche Chancen, supra note 22, p. 58, the West German Monopolies Commission reports that in 277 comparably defined industries, the average value-added weighted four-firm concentration ratio rose from 35.9 in 1978 to 37.3 in 1984.

86. Yamawaki et al., "Industry Competition." See also Sleuwaegen and Yamawaki, "The Formation of the European Common Market and Changes in Market Structure and Performance," *European Economic Review,* vol. 32 (September 1988), pp. 1451–1476.

87. This is the "regression effect" identified by the eminent biologist Francis Galton (1822–1911).

88. For reviews of the various hypotheses, see Jonathan D. Ogur, *Competition and Market Share Instability* (Washington: Federal Trade Commission, 1976); and Richard E. Caves and Michael E. Porter, "Market Structure, Oligopoly, and Stability of Market Shares," *Journal of Industrial Economics,* vol. 26 (June 1978), pp. 289–313. For a simulation analysis showing that high rank stability does not necessarily imply a lack of price competition, see Sherrill Shaffer, "Does Competition Imply Frequent Rank Turnover?" *Scandinavian Journal of Economics,* vol. 88, no. 3 (1986), pp. 511–527.

89. See the testimony of Jules Backman in U.S. Senate, Committee on the Judiciary, Subcommittee on Antitrust and Monopoly, Hearings, *Economic Concentration,* Part 2 (Washington: USGPO, 1964), pp. 562–563. See also Gideon Rosenbluth, "Measures of Concentration," in *Business Concentration and Price Policy* (Princeton: Princeton University Press, 1955), p. 93.

industries did the rank order of the four leaders remain identical between 1947 and 1958.

However, such statistics could be misleading. Most of the market share changes that caused some firms to drop out of the top four and others to enter are small. If, for instance, the firms ranked third and fourth in an industry during some year have market shares of 7.0 and 5.3 percent, while the firms ranked fifth and sixth have shares of 4.2 and 3.4 percent,[90] it does not take a shakeup of dramatic proportions to displace the third- and fourth-ranked firms. And most market shares, Michael Gort found in an analysis spanning the years 1947 through 1954, do not change drastically over such a seven-year interval.[91] Using confidential census data on 205 industries, he correlated, industry-by-industry, the market shares of the fifteen sales leaders during 1947 with the corresponding 1954 market shares. In 74 percent of the 205 cases, the intertemporal correlation was 0.80 or higher. In only 10 percent of the industries was the correlation less than 0.50. Thus, if a firm's market share was low relative to the pack in 1947, it was likely to be low also in 1954, and vice versa.

Moreover, there is evidence that stability of market positions and concentration in the static sense are positively associated. The correlation between the intertemporal correlation coefficients (serving as an index of relative stability) and 1947 four-firm concentration ratios for Gort's sample was 0.52.[92] This result could have a trivial statistical explanation — for example, because there is greater inequality of market shares in more concentrated industries, so that larger absolute and relative deviations are needed to force a change in rank. However, in an analysis that controlled for concentration class biases and a large number of other variables, Caves and Porter found that annual percentage changes in sellers' market shares tended to be smaller with higher concentration levels.[93] Meisel replicated this result and found in addition that firms' market share instability was higher when brand market shares were relatively unstable.[94] Whether brand share instability implies more or less intense competition is a question to which further attention will be devoted in Chapter 16.

It is also possible that market share instability — to some economists a manifestation of competitive vigor — has the paradoxical long-run effect of raising static concentration levels. We shall examine this hypothesis in the next chapter.

The Diversification of American Corporations

Product line diversification is interesting for several reasons: as a prominent structural attribute, as a source of large-firm cost advantages (or disadvantages) (explored in Chapter 4), as a possible influence on firms' pricing (Chapter 10) and research and development decisions (Chapter 17), and as a possible cause of the largest corporations' increasing share of all manufacturing activity.

Between 1950 and 1975, American corporations staged a massive campaign to increase their diversification. Some manifestations are shown in Table 3.10, which compares diversification levels achieved in 1950 and 1975 by the largest 200 manufacturing enterprises, with each year's cohort ranked according to that year's domestic manufactured product sales. The extent of diversification is measured in two ways.

Table 3.10 Diversification of the Top 200 Manufacturing Enterprises of 1950 and 1975, Ranked by Sales

Company Groups, by Current-Year Sales Ranking	Average Number of Lines of Business per Company		Average Numbers-Equivalent Index	
	1950	1975	1950	1975
Companies 1–40	8.10	12.95	2.52	3.69
Companies 41–80	5.03	11.83	2.07	3.95
Companies 81–120	3.53	11.43	1.88	4.83
Companies 121–160	3.15	9.18	1.75	4.28
Companies 161–200	4.00	9.08	2.02	4.32
All 200 Companies	4.76	10.89	2.05	4.22

Source: David J. Ravenscraft and F. M. Scherer, *Mergers, Sell-offs, and Economic Efficiency* (Washington: Brookings, 1985), p. 30.

One is a simple count of the number of manufacturing lines of business in which the companies operated. The lines of business are defined according to standardized industry codes formulated by the Federal Trade Commission. The total number of lines in the FTC code system was 261. No company came anywhere near realizing that maximum; the five most diversified firms in 1975 averaged fifty-three lines of business each. For all 200 companies, the count of lines averaged 4.76 in 1950 and 10.89 in 1975 — a 2.29-fold increase over the quarter-century interval. The larger companies are seen to have operated more lines in each year, although the greatest relative increase in diversification occurred for the middle group of companies ranked 81 to 120. The line of business count averages conceal a fair amount of diversity. In 1950 twenty-five of the largest companies operated in only one manufacturing line, while in 1975 only five of the leaders did so. At the other extreme, twenty-two of the top 200 operated in twenty-one or more lines in 1975, while only two achieved that level of diversification in 1950.

The last two columns of Table 3.10 provide an alternative means of measuring diversification — a "numbers equivalent index" derived as a variant of the Herfindahl-Hirschman index used to measure seller concentration. Where F_{ij} is

90. Cf. note 67 supra.

91. Michael Gort, "Analysis of Stability and Change in Market Shares," *Journal of Political Economy,* vol. 71 (February 1963), pp. 51–61.

92. Gort, "Analysis of Stability," p. 56. See also I. M. Grossack, "Toward an Integration of Static and Dynamic Measures of Industry Concentration," *Review of Economics and Statistics,* vol. 47 (August 1965), p. 56; and the testimony of L. E. Preston in the Senate Subcommittee on Antitrust and Monopoly hearings, *Economic Concentration,* Part 1 (Washington: USGPO, 1964), pp. 68–69. On turnover in banking markets, see Arnold A. Heg-gestad and Stephen A. Rhoades, "Competition and Firm Stability in Banking," *Review of Economics and Statistics,* vol. 58 (November 1976), pp. 443–452; and Michael L. Marlow et al., "Market Structure and Rivalry: New Evidence with a Non-Linear Model," *Review of Economics and Statistics,* vol. 66 (November 1984), pp. 678–682.

93. Caves and Porter, "Market Structure," supra note 88, pp. 306–307.

94. John B. Meisel, "Entry, Multiple-Brand Firms and Market Share Instability," *Journal of Industrial Economics,* vol. 29 (June 1981), pp. 375–384.

the fraction of company i's sales located in the jth line of business, the numbers-equivalent diversification index is calculated as $1/\sum\limits_{j} F_{ij}^2$. It has its minimum value of 1.0 when a company operates in only one line of business. If each of the company's lines were of equal size, the numbers equivalent index would have the same value as the number of lines. The more unequal the lines are in size, the more the index falls back toward unity. We see in Table 3.10 that the average numbers equivalent indices are a good deal lower than the average line counts, implying considerable inequality. For all 200 companies in 1975, the data imply an average company whose eleven lines contributed 41, 20, 12, 9, 5, 4, 3, 2, 2, 1, and 1 percent to its domestic manufactured product sales.

Data of equal quality do not exist for nonmanufacturing corporations. However, there is reason to believe that companies whose home base is manufacturing are more diversified than firms at home in other fields. Under its *Enterprise Statistics* program, the U.S. Census Bureau assigns each reporting company to that single "primary" category among 207 different manufacturing, mining, construction, trade, and service industry categories in which the firm has its largest sales volume. It then splits the company's operating establishments (for example, plants, mines, and stores) into two classes: those specializing in the primary industry category and all others.[95] In 1982, all companies whose primary field was in one or another manufacturing sector category had 65.1 percent of their employment in their primary category and 34.9 percent in other (that is, diversified) categories. Retail trade companies were much less diversified; 92.7 percent of their operating establishment employment was in their primary line. For minerals industry companies, 83.1 percent of employment was in the primary line. Manufacturing companies' diversification was not limited to activities in that sector of the economy. The 471 companies submitting line of business data to the Federal Trade Commission for 1975 operated in 1.37 broadly defined (mostly two-digit S.I.C.) domestic nonmanufacturing lines on average in addition to their eight manufacturing lines.[96]

The increase in diversification that occurred between 1950 and 1975 was accomplished to a considerable degree through merger, as distinguished from internal growth, that is, the internal development of new business specialties. For the 148 of 1950's top 200 U.S. manufacturing companies that survived into 1975, 41 percent of the manufacturing lines operated in 1975 came from diversification mergers, while only 14 percent originated from diversification through internal growth.[97] The remaining 45 percent were lines carried over from 1950 company structures.

The year 1975 has proved to be a high-water mark in U.S. corporations' diversification, for many of the diversification-increasing mergers were unsuccessful. A back-to-basics movement followed in the 1970s and early 1980s, entailing the divestiture of thousands of subsidiaries, most of which had joined the parent through previous diversifying mergers.[98]

The very notion of diversification — movement into new fields — implies a breaking with past product specialization patterns. Still much of this movement was not totally unstructured. Du Pont, which initially specialized in explosives, spread out into other chemical products such as dyestuffs, synthetic fibers, plastics, paints, and then the refining of petroleum products used as inputs to its chemical processes. General Electric expanded its coverage of the electrical product spectrum and drew upon its expertise in steam turbine technology to become a leading manufacturer of turbojet engines. Procter and Gamble diversified into food and paper product lines calling for similar marketing skills and retail distribution channels. Among the 183 to 207 companies Richard Rumelt studied, the fraction whose product line strategies could best be said to entail related business diversification increased from 27 percent in 1949 to 40 percent in 1959 and 45 percent in 1969.[99] Ravenscraft and Scherer show that merger-active companies with a strong orientation toward research and development acquired new research-intensive lines, while firms with high advertising/sales ratios sought out advertising-prone merger partners.[100] Quite generally, the acquisition targets occupied rapidly growing industries.[101] However, the trend in the 1960s and early 1970s was toward increasingly pure conglomerate acquisitions, that is, toward the acquisition of companies operating in lines of business completely different from those of the acquirer. Defining "horizontal" acquisitions as those in which the acquirer operated in the same four-digit industry category as the acquiree, "related business" acquisitions as those in which the new parent had experience in the same two-digit field but not in the same four-digit industry, and "pure conglomerate" acquisitions as those in which the parent had no experience in the same two-digit group, Ravenscraft and Scherer recorded the following levels of U.S. manufacturing sector merger activity (by billions of dollars of assets acquired) between 1950 and 1977:[102]

	Time Period			
Type of Merger	1950–55	1956–63	1964–72	1973–77
Horizontal	1.79	5.43	14.21	8.09
Related Business	0.49	2.97	8.81	5.44
Pure Conglomerate	0.14	2.03	13.46	6.64

Was the diversification-through-merger movement responsible for the increases in aggregate manufacturing sector concentration observed at the outset of

95. U.S. Bureau of the Census, "General Report on Industrial Organization," *1982 Enterprise Statistics,* vol. 1 (Washington: USGPO, 1986), Table 1. Employment in central offices, R&D laboratories, warehouses, and other auxiliary establishments is excluded from the analysis here.

96. Federal Trade Commission, *Statistical Report: Annual Line of Business Report, 1975* (Washington: September 1981), pp. 48 and 212.

97. David J. Ravenscraft and F. M. Scherer, *Mergers, Sell-offs, and Economic Efficiency* (Washington: Brookings, 1986), p. 36. On the United Kingdom, see M. A. Utton, "Large Firm Diversification in British Manufacturing Industry," *Economic Journal,* vol. 87 (March 1977), pp. 96–113; and A. W. Goudie and G. Meeks, "Diversification by Merger," *Economica,* vol. 49 (November 1982), pp. 447–459.

98. See Ravenscraft and Scherer, *Mergers,* Chapter 6.

99. Richard P. Rumelt, *Strategy, Structure, and Economic Performance* (Boston: Harvard Business School Division of Research, 1974), p. 51.

100. Ravenscraft and Scherer, *Mergers,* p. 51. See also Michael Gort, *Diversification and Integration in American Industry* (Princeton: Princeton University Press, 1962), pp. 135–143; Charles H. Berry, *Corporate Growth and Diversification* (Princeton: Princeton University Press, 1975), pp. 91–108; James M. MacDonald, "R&D and the Directions of Diversification," *Review of Economics and Statistics,* vol. 67 (November 1985), pp. 583–590; and (on Canada) Donald J. Lecraw, "Diversification Strategy and Performance," *Journal of Industrial Economics,* vol. 33 (December 1984), pp. 179–198.

101. Ravenscraft and Scherer, *Mergers,* pp. 49–54.

102. Ravenscraft and Scherer, *Mergers,* p. 24.

this chapter? A crude answer can be obtained using the data in Table 3.10 on the 200 largest manufacturers (by domestic sales volume) of 1950 and 1975. The average number of lines they operated increased from 4.76 to 10.89; their average numbers equivalent index went from 2.05 to 4.22. Suppose they had moved from five to eleven lines by acquiring lines whose 1975 sales were uniformly smaller than the sales of lines carried over from 1950. Then, from our previous interpretation of the numbers equivalent index's meaning, the new lines would have contributed 4, 3, 2, 2, 1, and 1 percent to total 1975 manufactured product sales, or a total of 13 percent. But if the lines carried over from 1950 had grown at roughly equal rates between 1950 and 1975, the 1950 company sales shares of those lines would have been 47.1, 23.0, 13.8, 10.3, and 5.7 percent, implying an average 1950 numbers equivalent index of 3.25. Clearly, this is too high, which implies that some of the new acquired lines must have been larger in 1975 than the lines carried over from 1950. If one assumes that the carry-over lines had 1975 sales shares of 41, 12, 5, 3, and 2 percent and that those lines grew at equal rates between 1950 and 1975, a 1950 numbers equivalent value of 2.13 is obtained, which is close to the actually observed average value.[103] This in turn implies that new diversification lines contributed $100 - 41 - 12 - 5 - 3 - 2 = 37$ percent of 1975 domestic manufacturing sales. From the data source underlying the value-added series of Figure 3.1, and interpolating linearly between available 1947 and 1954 values, we estimate that the 200 largest U.S. manufacturers accounted for 34 percent of domestic value added in manufacturing during 1950 and 44 percent in 1975. From our diversification change analysis, we estimate that 37 percent of the 44 percent share in 1975, or 16.3 aggregate concentration percentage points, came from diversification lines. This implies that in 1975, had 200 of the largest manufacturers not increased their diversification, and had their 1950 lines grown no more rapidly in the absence of diversification efforts (which is arguable), the 200 leaders' share of 1975 value added would have been only 28 percent, not the actually observed 44 percent. A strong chain of assumptions is needed to reach this conclusion, but it seems clear that diversification was a very important contributor to the observed growth of aggregate concentration.[104]

Vertical Integration in American Industry

Vertical integration, like diversification, can be viewed both as a static dimension of market structure and as a process of market structure adaptation. Dynamically, firms integrating upstream, or backward, undertake to produce raw materials and semifabricated inputs that might otherwise be purchased from independent producers. Firms integrating downstream, or forward, move toward further finishing of semifabricated products and the wholesaling and retailing operations that put manufactured goods in the hands of consumers. Vertical integration in the static sense describes the extent to which firms cover the entire spectrum of production and distribution stages.

One motive for vertical integration is to reduce costs. A classic example is found in the steel industry. Integration of blast furnaces, converters, and primary reduction mills reduces handling and the need for reheating the molten metal. Vertical integration may also give producers enhanced control over their economic environment. Upstream integration, for example, can help ensure that supplies of raw materials will be available in time of shortage and protect the user from a price squeeze by monopolistic suppliers. Downstream integration gives the firm greater control over its markets, lessening the probability of being ignored or shut out by middlemen. We consider the pricing implications of vertical integration at length in Chapter 14.

Although there is only meager quantitative information on the extent of vertical integration in the U.S. economy, we can gain rough qualitative impressions. We know, for example, that the major petroleum refiners are highly integrated, commanding extensive crude oil reserves, refining facilities, the pipelines through which crude oil and refined products are transported, and in many instances networks of company-owned retail gasoline stations. Glass bottle manufacturers, on the other hand, exhibit very little integration. Most of them buy their sand, natural gas or oil, machinery, and (less consistently) shipping cartons from other companies and sell their output to packers and bottlers, who in turn utilize independent retailers to convey the end products to consumers. Problems arise, however, when we attempt to develop quantitative measures of vertical integration that are comparable across industry lines and between firms.

At first glance, the ratio of value added to sales, which averages about 0.42 for manufacturing industries when measured at the plant level, might seem an appropriate measure. However, it gives misleading comparisons when firms or industries are located at varying stages in the stream of economic activity. Suppose, to use an example coined by Adelman, an economy consists of three disintegrated firms — a raw materials producer, a fabricator, and a distributor — and suppose each contributes one-third of total value added.[105] Assuming further that the raw materials producer buys nothing from outside suppliers, its value added/sales ratio is 1.0, giving the misleading impression that it is totally integrated vertically. The fabricator (buying raw material valued at one-third and adding its own labor, and so forth, valued at one-third) has a value added/sales ratio of 0.5, while the distributor's ratio will be 0.33. The nearer the raw materials end of the production stream a specialist firm's (or industry's) operations are, the higher its value added/sales ratio tends to be, ceteris paribus.

Michael Gort attempted to circumvent such measurement problems in a study of 111 large corporations using confidential 1954 census data.[106] Through qualitative analysis, he identified for each company those four-digit product activities that were auxiliary to the firm's primary (largest) product class, namely, activities that either supplied inputs into the primary production stage or contributed to further downstream fabrication or distribution of the primary product. He then defined an index of integration, namely, employment in the auxiliary industries as a percentage of total company employment. Not surprisingly, he found petroleum industry members to have by far the highest integration index — 67 percent.

---

103. The 1975 shares must be rescaled so that they sum to unity for 1950; this is done by dividing each by 0.63. The resulting 1950 numbers equivalent index is found as:

$$\frac{1}{0.651^2 + 0.190^2 + 0.072^2 + 0.048^2 + 0.032^2} = 2.13.$$

104. Compare the second edition of this volume, p. 78, analyz-

ing data from Gort, *Diversification and Integration,* supra note 100, and finding a lower impact of diversification from 1947 to 1954.

105. M. A. Adelman, "Concept and Statistical Measurement of Vertical Integration," in *Business Concentration and Price Policy* (Princeton: Princeton University Press, 1955), pp. 281–283.

106. Gort, *Diversification and Integration,* supra note 100, pp. 80–82.

Distant runners-up were machinery, with 30.5 percent of employment in auxiliary industries, and food products, with 30.3 percent. The least integrated manufacturers were found in the transportation equipment group (9.7 percent), electrical equipment (12.8 percent), and fabricated metal products (15.0 percent).

An attempt to characterize quantitatively the long-run dynamics of vertical integration has been made by Livesay and Porter.[107] They consulted numerous historical sources to ascertain whether the largest U.S. manufacturing companies in six reference years had moved upstream into raw materials production and downstream into transportation, wholesaling, and retailing. Thirty-eight percent of the companies in their sample had integrated into raw materials production by 1899. The fraction increased to 51 percent in 1909, then grew very slowly to 55 percent by 1948. The proportion of sample companies integrated into retailing rose from 11 percent in 1899 to 26 percent in 1919 and 36 percent in 1929, showing no clear trend thereafter. Thus, it would appear that manufacturers' most important moves toward vertical integration occurred rather early in the century. A limitation of the Livesay-Porter approach is its inability, at least without access to data seldom publicly available, to determine how widespread companies' involvement in nonmanufacturing stages was. Thus, General Electric was evidently considered integrated into retail distribution even though only its major appliances, and indeed only a fraction of them, moved through GE-owned outlets. The auto manufacturers were also counted as active in retailing despite the fact that most of their outlets are independently owned franchised dealerships.

Economists seeking to measure changes over time in the intensity of integration have for the most part had to accept the limitations of value added/sales ratios.[108] Adelman examined such ratios for the manufacturing sector as a whole from 1849 to 1930 and for selected steel makers from 1902 to 1952. He found no clear trend toward either increased or reduced vertical integration.[109] Arthur Laffer computed similar ratios for all corporations in ten broad sectors of the economy from 1929 to 1965 and concluded that there was no discernible time trend in the degree of integration.[110] Consistent with these findings is evidence that only 11 percent of the volume of manufacturing industry mergers between 1950 and 1977 involved discernible vertical integration links.[111] In this respect, as with respect to market concentration, the structure of American industry has changed surprisingly little since early in the century.

107. Harold C. Livesay and Patrick G. Porter, "Vertical Integration in American Manufacturing, 1899–1948," *Journal of Economic History,* vol. 29 (September 1969), pp. 494–500.

108. Using an approach based upon input-output table relationships, Ruth J. Madigan, "The Measurement of Vertical Integration," *Review of Economics and Statistics*, vol. 63 (August 1981), pp. 328–335, finds an upward trend in integration between 1947 and 1972 for 96 companies. However, her detailed example, for Certain-Teed Corporation, shows rising integration from what appear to be diversification mergers, and index values for the larger sample jump around in ways that suggest difficulty identifying the industries served.

109. "Concept and Statistical Measurement," supra note 105, pp.

308–311. See also Irvin B. Tucker and Ronald P. Wilder, "Trends in Vertical Integration in the U.S. Manufacturing Sector," *Journal of Industrial Economics,* vol. 26 (September 1977), pp. 81–94. Some upward drift in the ratio for all manufacturing was evident after 1939, but not to levels appreciably higher than the values attained in 1899 and 1931. In the 1970s and 1980s, a declining trend probably began. See e.g. Bo Carlsson, "The Evolution of Manufacturing Technology and Its Impact on Industrial Structure," *Small Business Economics,* vol. 1 (1989).

110. Arthur B. Laffer, "Vertical Integration by Corporations, 1929–1965," *Review of Economics and Statistics,* vol. 51 (February 1969), pp. 91–93.

111. Ravenscraft and Scherer, *Mergers,* supra note 97, p. 24.

The Determinants of Market Structure

Economies of Scale

What explains the widespread differences in market structure found in diverse industries? Is it necessary for seller concentration to be as high as it is in many manufacturing industries? These questions are our concern in the present chapter. We explore several determinants of market structure, including economies of scale, government policy, growth, and chance.

Concentrated market structures could stem from persistent scale economies, permitting relatively large producers to manufacture and market their products at lower average cost per unit than relatively small producers. Economies of scale are best analyzed in terms of three categories: product-specific economies, associated with the volume of any single product made and sold; plant-specific economies, associated with the total output (possibly encompassing many products) of an entire plant or plant complex; and multiplant economies, associated with a firm's operation of multiple plants. Each deserves extended consideration.

Ball bearing manufacturing provides a good illustration of several *product-specific* economies. If only a few bearings are to be custom-made, the ring machining will be done on general-purpose lathes by a skilled operator who hand-positions the stock and tools and makes measurements for each cut. With this method, machining a single ring requires from five minutes to more than an hour, depending upon the part's size and complexity and the operator's skill. If a sizable batch is to be produced, a more specialized automatic screw machine will be used instead. Once it is loaded with a steel tube, it automatically feeds the tube, sets the tools and adjusts its speed to make the necessary cuts, and spits out machined parts into a hopper at a rate of from eighty to one hundred forty parts per hour. A substantial saving of machine running and operator attendance time per unit is achieved, but setting up the screw machine to perform these operations takes about eight hours. If only one hundred bearing rings are to be made, setup time greatly exceeds total running time, and it may be cheaper to do the job on an ordinary lathe. As the number of parts to be made increases, setup time per unit of running time falls — for example, to 88 percent of running time with 1,000 rings and 9 percent with 10,000 rings. The larger the batch, the lower the average cost (that is, setup plus running time) per unit will be. Analogous savings come with higher volume at other stages of the bearing-making process — for example, in grinding, groove honing, cage stamping, and assembly. If very large quantities (say, a million per year) of a single bearing design can be sold, a still different production approach is likely to be chosen. Even more specialized higher-speed machines are used, and parts are transferred automatically to the next processing stage in a straight-line flow. Computer-guided devices then match completed inner and outer rings with balls to attain the desired tolerances; and the parts are assembled, greased, and packaged without any human intervention. With such an automated straight-line production approach, unit costs may be 30 to 50 percent lower than with medium-volume batch methods. But in order to realize these savings, the production line must be kept running without changeover two shifts per day, and this requires a large and continuous volume.

Product-specific economies of scale also have an important dynamic dimension.[1] When intricate labor operations must be performed, as in shoe stitching and aircraft or computer assembly, or when complex process adjustments must be worked out through trial and error, as in semiconductor fabrication, unit costs fall as workers and operators learn by doing. Figure 4.1 shows actual unit cost data, represented by dots for individual production lots, measured in terms of labor hours used per pound of airframe assembled, for the B-29 bomber of World War II fame. (Unit number 82 was modified to drop the first atomic bomb at Hiroshima.) With unit costs and cumulative volume measured on logarithmic scales, a straight line (dashed) provides a good approximation to the relevant *learning curve*. The cost observations tend to drift above the fitted straight line when model changes were effected and also as production was terminated, with output per month dropping from a peak of eighty aircraft to only ten in late 1945 and early 1946. The fitted B-29 learning curve has a slope of 70.5 percent; that is, unit costs declined on average by 29.5 percent with each doubling of cumulative output. Similar learning curve slopes are observed in large-scale integrated circuit (LSI) production. It is extremely difficult to deposit precisely the right microscopic amounts of material into the various circuit strata, and so at first one is fortunate if one or two chips out of one hundred function properly. But as production experience accumulates, the staff gradually learn how to control the process, and yields rise to as much as 50 or 80 percent while setup time between batches declines. Cost reductions of 25 to 30 percent with each doubling of cumulative output are common. Thus, if the tenth good chip costs $1,000, the thousandth chip will cost approximately $100, the ten-thousandth chip $42, and the millionth chip $6.

An essentially product-specific economy of scale stressed by Adam Smith comes from specialization and the division of labor.[2] With a larger output of some product, workers can specialize more narrowly and build up greater proficiency in their tasks. The automobile assembly line pioneered by Henry Ford is the classic illustration. Its disadvantage is that too narrow and unchanging a task definition turns off workers' minds. Where creative adaptation is important, the trend has been away from such specialization.

For chemical and metallurgical process-type industries such as petroleum refining, iron ore reduction and steel conversion, cement making, the synthesis of chemicals, and steam generation, the most important economies of scale at the *plant-specific* level come from expanding the size of individual processing units. The output of a processing unit tends within certain physical limits to be roughly proportional to the volume of the unit, while the amount of materials and fabrication effort (and hence investment cost) required to construct the unit is more closely proportional to the surface area of the unit's reaction chambers, storage tanks, connecting pipes, and the like. Since the area of a sphere or cylinder varies as the two-thirds power of volume, the cost of constructing process industry plants can be expected to rise as the two-thirds power of their output capacity, at least up to the point where the units become so large that extra structural reinforcement and special fabrication techniques are required. There is considerable empirical support for the existence of this *two-thirds rule,* which is applied by engineers in estimating the cost of new process equipment.[3] Energy usage also tends to rise less

Figure 4.1
Learning Curve for B-29
Bombers Produced at Boeing's
Wichita Plant

*Manhours
Per
Pound
of
Airframe
(Logarithmic
Scale)*

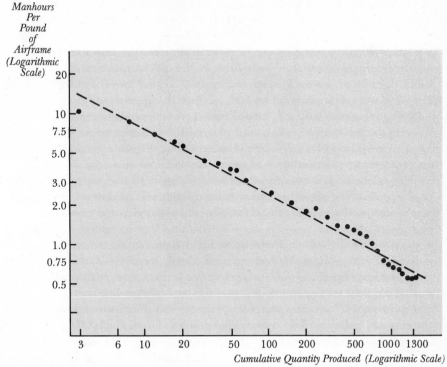

Cumulative Quantity Produced (Logarithmic Scale)

Source: U.S. Army Air Forces, Air Materiel Command, *Source Book of World War II Basic Data: Air Frame Industry,*
vol. I (Washington: 1952).

than proportionately with increases in processing vessel size. The scale-up of machines such as compressors, turbines, conveyors, rolling mills, furnaces and air conditioners, packaging devices, and the like appears to follow similar though less mathematically exact laws: within limits, increases in capacity come at a less than

1. On the theory, see Armen Alchian, "Costs and Output," in Moses Abramovitz et al., *The Allocation of Economic Resources: Essays in Honor of B. F. Haley* (Stanford: Stanford University Press, 1959), pp. 23–40; Jack Hirshleifer, "The Firm's Cost Function: A Successful Reconstruction?" *Journal of Business,* vol. 35 (July 1962), pp. 235–255; Kenneth J. Arrow, "The Economic Implications of Learning by Doing," *Review of Economic Studies,* vol. 29 (April 1962), pp. 155–173; L. E. Preston and E. C. Keachie, "Cost Functions and Progress Functions: An Integration," *American Economic Review,* vol. 54 (March 1964), pp. 100–106; and Sherwin Rosen, "Learning by Experience as Joint Production," *Quarterly Journal of Economics,* vol. 86 (August 1972), pp. 366–382. For empirical studies, see Harold Asher, *Cost-Quantity Relationships in the Airframe Industry* (Santa Monica: RAND Corporation study R–291, July 1956); Leonard Dudley, "Learning and Productivity Changes in Metal Products," *American Economic Review,* vol. 62 (September 1972), pp. 662–669; Boston Consulting Group, *Perspectives on Experience* (Boston: 1972); Douglas Webbink, *The Semi-*

conductor Industry, Federal Trade Commission staff report (Washington: January 1977), pp. 45–62; and Paul L. Joskow and George A. Rozanski, "The Effects of Learning by Doing on Nuclear Plant Operating Reliability," *Review of Economics and Statistics,* vol. 61 (May 1979), pp. 161–168.

2. Adam Smith, *An Inquiry into the Nature and Causes of the Wealth of Nations,* Book I, Chapter I.

3. See F. T. Moore, "Economies of Scale: Some Statistical Evidence," *Quarterly Journal of Economics,* vol. 73 (May 1959), pp. 232–245; John Haldi and David Whitcomb, "Economies of Scale in Industrial Plants," *Journal of Political Economy,* vol. 75 (August 1967), pp. 373–385; Lawrence J. Lau and Shuji Tamura, "Economies of Scale, Technical Progress, and the Nonhomothetic Leontief Production Function," *Journal of Political Economy,* vol. 80 (November/December 1972), pp. 1167–1187; and Richard C. Levin, "Technical Change and Optimal Scale: Some Evidence and Implications," *Southern Economic Journal,* vol. 44 (October 1977), pp. 208–221.

proportional rise in equipment cost. Moreover, the crew needed to operate a large processing unit or machine is often little or no larger than what is required for a unit of smaller capacity, so labor costs per unit fall sharply with scale-up.[4]

Another advantage of increased plant size comes from what E. A. G. Robinson called "the economies of massed reserves."[5] A plant large enough to use only one specialized machine may have to hold another machine in reserve if it insists upon hedging against occasional, essentially random breakdowns in order to sustain production. For a larger plant with numerous machines, a single extra machine may provide almost the same degree of protection at much lower cost relative to total capacity carrying costs. Similarly, the number of repair staff a company must employ to maintain any stipulated level of service in the event of random breakdowns rises less than proportionately with the number of machines in operation, all else being equal.[6] Massed reserves economies can also be realized when unit shutdowns occur regularly and predictably. For example, the violent reactions occurring in a basic oxygen steel-making furnace (BOF) necessitate relining the furnace with new refractory brick every twenty-five to forty days. It is important to maintain a fairly steady flow of steel to keep later-stage rolling mills and other equipment busy. Therefore, in a two-furnace shop, one furnace is usually shut down for relining while the other is working. Adding a third BOF and augmenting the relining crew so that two furnaces are operated while a third is relined doubles sustainable output with an investment increase of only about 50 percent.

Every plant must carry some overhead. Within limits, cost savings can be realized by specializing overhead functions and spreading overhead over a larger volume. A large plant can have one or more specialized cost accountants, production schedulers, stock keepers, nurses, plant guards, and so on. A small plant must often double up such functions, with possible skill losses (but gains in perspective); or if individual capabilities or union rules prevent such doubling up, it may utilize certain specialized workers to less than full capacity; or it may have to make do with more costly part-time help or contracting-out expedients. Every plant must also have a manager, and in a large plant, the manager's salary can be spread over a larger output volume, permitting lower unit costs; or a higher salary can be paid, which presumably will attract managers of superior ability.

There are important interactions between product-specific and plant-specific economies. Most real-world plants produce multiple products, each with its own product-specific cost function. The cost of producing a particular product is influenced not only by that product's volume, but also by the size of the plant in which the product is made. Baumol et al. have devised the term, "economies of scope," to describe the impact on total costs, plant-specific and product-specific, attributable to production of more than one product.[7]

Figure 4.2 illustrates the economies of scope concept three-dimensionally, letting the horizontal plane measure the output of two products, 1 and 2, and the vertical plane the average combined cost of production.[8] The shaded curved surface $ZC_{X2}C_{X1}$ shows the average cost of producing various combinations of 1 and 2. A vertical plane extended along the axis OX_1 at $X_2 = 0$ traces the cost curve ZC_{X1}, showing the product-specific average cost of various quantities of product 1 without any output of product 2. A vertical plane extended along the axis OX_2 traces the comparable curve ZC_{X2} for product 2. Points on the shaded cost surface

Figure 4.2
Average Costs with Two
Products X_1 and X_2 and
Economies of Scope

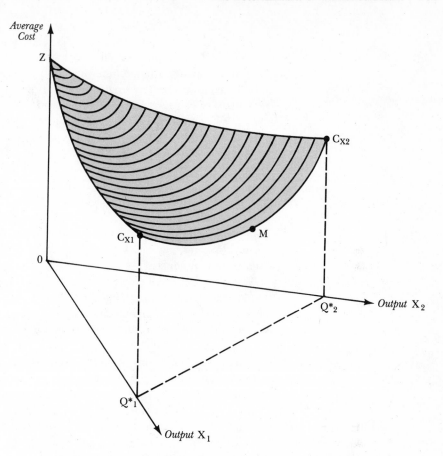

in between these extremes show the combined cost of producing diverse combinations of 1 and 2. If a third vertical plane is constructed to intersect axes OX_1 and OX_2 at 45 degree angles, it cuts the shaded cost surface along line $C_{X1}C_{X2}$, tracing out the implications of producing various linear output combinations of 1 and 2. At its midpoint M, it pinpoints the average cost of producing half as much of product 1 as quantity OQ^*_1 in combination with half as much of product 2 as quantity OQ^*_2. When $C_{X1}C_{X2}$ is convex downward, as shown in Figure 4.2, it is less expensive to produce 1 and 2 together than separately. Economies of scope prevail. Conversely, if $C_{X1}C_{X2}$ were concave downward, contrary to the situation

4. See Lau and Tamura, "Economies of Scale," pp. 1180–1185, who find no increase in labor usage in larger Japanese petrochemical plants.

5. E. A. G. Robinson, *The Structure of Competitive Industry,* rev. ed. (Chicago: University of Chicago Press, 1958), pp. 26–27. See also James G. Mulligan, "The Economies of Massed Reserves," *American Economic Review,* vol. 73 (September 1983), pp. 725–734.

6. See Michael Rothschild and Gregory J. Werden, "Returns to Scale from Random Factor Services: Existence and Scope," *Bell Journal of Economics,* vol. 10 (Spring 1979), pp. 329–335.

7. See William J. Baumol, John C. Panzar, and Robert D. Willig, *Contestable Markets and the Theory of Industry Structure* (New York: Harcourt Brace Jovanovich, 1982), Chapter 4.

8. Figure 4.2 is a heuristic approximation only. In principle, it is dangerous to depict multi-output cost functions in terms of *average* costs because of an "apples and oranges" problem in dividing total cost by, say, $X_1 + X_2$, and because such functions have strange transients at low values of one or another output. It is preferable, as urged by Baumol et al., pp. 50 and 453–457, to work with total costs.

depicted in Figure 4.2, diseconomies of scope would exist; it would be more expensive to produce 1 and 2 together than separately.

Overhead-spreading and other economies at the plant-specific level may continue out to plant output volumes exceeding the threshold at which all product-specific economies for any single product are exhausted. In that case, the quest for economies of scope will lead plants to produce multiple products. Or demand for any single product may be too weak to justify producing at a scale conferring all product-specific economies. Then assigning multiple products to a single plant with economies of scope can offset at least some of the product-specific economy sacrifices attributable to low-volume production. This phenomenon shows up most strikingly in relatively small markets such as Canada, where demand is frequently too limited to let firms achieve all the product-specific economies potentially attainable in manufacturing a given product. As a result, the typical Canadian plant tends to produce a wider assortment of products than its counterpart in the much larger U.S. market, where it is easier to fill a plant with one or a few high-volume products.[9]

Economies of scope may also extend to the operation of multiple plants by a single firm. The multiplant enterprise can employ a more richly specialized array of talent than a single-plant firm, all else equal. It can achieve more specialization within individual plants for given product line breadth. It can mass its cash balance reserves[10] and spread production, market, and financial risks over a larger volume of activity. It may be able to get more mileage out of its expenditures on a field sales force and other marketing instruments. Determining the importance of such multiplant economies must be deferred to a later stage of our analysis.

What Checks the Realization of Scale Economies? It is clear that economies of scale exist and that unit costs fall with increases in product volume, plant size, and firm size, at least within limits. Does this decline in average costs continue indefinitely? There are many reasons for believing that it does not.

In nearly all production and distribution operations, the realization of scale economies appears to be subject to diminishing returns. With a large enough volume, setup costs dwindle to insignificance. Learning curves flatten out as very large cumulative output volumes are attained.[11] Cement kilns experience unstable internal aerodynamics at about 7 million barrels per year capacity. Other scaled-up process vessels and machines become unwieldy or require special structural reinforcement beyond some point, increasing unit costs rather than reducing them. The advantages of mass reserves peter out. Workers and machines become so specialized that they cannot adapt or be adapted to change. And so on.

Sooner or later a point is reached at which all opportunities for making further cost reductions through increased size or volume are exhausted. This point is associated, though not necessarily in a simple way, with the scale at which the largest or most specialized machine or other input can be utilized fully. What complicates matters is that other large-scale processes may not dovetail perfectly with the largest-scale process at its own optimal size. For example, in the mid-1970s a steel-making shop with three 250-ton basic oxygen furnaces could turn out 6 million tons of raw steel per year. Its scale set a floor for the size of a least-cost integrated steel works. Individual blast furnaces large enough to supply such a BOF shop had been built, but they were relatively energy inefficient, and lower costs could be achieved with blast furnaces turning out 2.8 million tons of pig iron, enough (with scrap added) for 4 million tons of raw steel. One such least-cost blast furnace was insufficient to keep a least-cost BOF shop supplied; two were too much; and building a half-size blast furnace to supplement the least-cost facility entailed clear unit cost increases. The *least common multiple* at which the principal iron- and steel-making processes dovetailed was an output of 12 million tons of steel per year, achieved with two BOF shops and three blast furnaces. Barring other complications, this scale constituted the *minimum efficient scale* (MES) for an integrated steel-works — that is, the smallest scale at which minimum unit costs were attained. Equally low unit costs might be enjoyed at capacities representing an integral multiple of the minimum efficient scale — for example, in the present case, at annual capacities of 24 million tons, 36 million tons, etc. These higher capacities could be obtained if a firm built additional 12-million-ton plants in other locations or, less plausibly, by multiplying a single plant's scale. Between these least common multiple values, unit costs were slightly above their minimum owing to the imperfect dovetailing of processes, and the steel-making firm's long-run cost curve had a generally horizontal but scalloped shape beyond 12 million tons annual capacity.

Other considerations may render the doubling and redoubling of least common multiples at a single plant site uneconomic. Psychological surveys show that for reasons still imperfectly understood, workers express less satisfaction with their jobs, and especially with the challenge their jobs offer, in large plants than in small plants.[12] To attract a work force in the face of such alienating job conditions, large plants must in effect buy off their workers with a wage premium — one that has apparently been growing over time. Superior productivity from scale economies provides the wherewithal to pay this premium, but as the least common multiple plant size is exceeded, *further* productivity gains are nil and therefore unavailable to sustain still larger wage premiums. Second, especially in smaller cities and towns, increasing the size of a plant's work force may require expanding the geographic radius from which workers are drawn, which in turn implies higher worker commuting costs and higher offsetting wages. Third, materials flows lengthen and become more complex as plant scales increase, and handling costs rise commensurately, discouraging continued expansion at a given plant site. Fourth, the risks of fire, explosion, and wildcat strikes are at a maximum when all production is concentrated at a single plant site, so firms enjoying sufficient sales

9. See John R. Baldwin and Paul K. Gorecki, "The Relationship between Plant Scale and Product Diversity in Canadian Manufacturing Industries," *Journal of Industrial Economics,* vol. 34 (June 1986), pp. 373–388.

10. See William J. Baumol, "The Transactions Demand for Cash: An Inventory Theoretic Approach," *Quarterly Journal of Economics,* vol. 66 (November 1952), pp. 545–556; and Karl Brunner and Allan H. Meltzer, "Economies of Scale in Cash Balances Reconsidered," *Quarterly Journal of Economics,* vol. 81 (August 1967), pp. 422–436.

11. See Harold Asher, *Cost-Quantity Relationships,* supra note 1, especially Chapters 4 and 7; and Gerald W. Brock, *The U.S. Computer Industry* (Cambridge: Ballinger, 1975), p. 29.

12. F. M. Scherer, "Industrial Structure, Scale Economies, and Worker Alienation," in Robert T. Masson and P. D. Qualls, eds., *Essays on Industrial Organization in Honor of Joe S. Bain* (Cambridge: Ballinger, 1976), pp. 105–121; John E. Kwoka, "Establishment Size, Wages, and Job Satisfaction," in John Siegfried, ed., *The Economics of Firm Size, Market Structure, and Social Performance* (Washington: Federal Trade Commission, 1980), pp. 359–379; and (at the firm level) Lucia F. Dunn, "Work Disutility and Compensating Differentials: Estimation of Factors in the Link between Wages and Firm Size," *Review of Economics and Statistics,* vol. 68 (February 1986), pp. 67–73.

volume usually prefer to expand at other locations once they have achieved the minimum efficient scale (and sometimes even before) at one site. Finally, it is much harder to manage a big plant than a small one, all else being equal. To keep their operations taut and under control, companies characteristically avoid expanding individual plants beyond the size required by equipment scale-up and work force specialization imperatives.

This last point is more general, being applicable at the firm level as well as at the plant level.[13] Any enterprise must have an individual who assumes ultimate executive authority and responsibility. Classical economists referred to this person as "the entrepreneur"; or in President Truman's homelier simile, he or she is the person on whose desk rests the sign "The buck stops here." The entrepreneur or chief executive officer (CEO) is a fixed, indivisible input. And as every sophomore economics student has learned by heart, whenever increasing doses of variable inputs (workers, middle managers, technicians, rolling mills, and so forth) are used in combination with some fixed input, sooner or later diminishing marginal returns take hold. Concretely, as enterprises increase in size, their chief executives are confronted with more and more decisions, and they are removed farther and farther from the reality of front-line production and marketing operations. Their ability to make sound decisions is attenuated, with a consequent rise in costs and/or fall in revenues. The problem is aggravated when the firm operates in a complex or rapidly changing environment, for it is the nonroutine decisions associated with change that press most heavily upon top managers' capacities.[14]

A related hypothesis asserts that as the enterprise increases in size, it becomes more and more difficult to keep each branch's operations in harmony with those of other parts. Hordes of middle managers, coordinators, and expediters[15] proliferate. Not only is the money cost of this bureaucracy far from inconsequential, but organizational sluggishness also rises with complexity. As Robinson puts it, "A mistake made by a platoon commander demands only an instantaneous 'As you were!' A mistake by an Army Commander may require days of labor to set right."[16] The consequence of these management and coordination problems is upward pressure on costs that becomes increasingly intense as plant and firm scales rise. At some critical point, the diseconomies of large-scale management overpower the economies of scale, and unit costs begin rising with output, giving the long-run average total cost curve its U-shape familiar to readers of microeconomic theory texts. The downward segment of the U is governed by orthodox scale economies, the upward thrust by managerial diseconomies.

Overcoming large-scale managerial diseconomies, and hence the long-run average cost function's upward-sloping segment, has challenged some of the most able minds in business enterprise. Staff functions have been organized to supply decision-making information to the chief executive officer in its most useful form and to round out a system of checks and balances reducing the likelihood that important facets of decisions will be overlooked. Communication has been simplified and accelerated by such technological innovations as the telegraph, the telephone, and most recently, computerized information networks. Techniques of cost accounting and budgetary control have been brought to a high state of perfection, giving the CEO a clearer view of the organization's past performance and future plans. Perhaps most important of all, ways have been devised to make the management of large organizations manageable through the decentralization of operating authority and financial responsibility to product line or territorial divisions. The decentralized multidivisional form of corporate organization, that is, the "M-Form," Oliver Williamson suggests, may well have been "American capitalism's most important single innovation of the 20th century."[17]

General Motors Corporation was a pioneer in attempting to stave off managerial diseconomies of scale through decentralization.[18] In a series of reorganizations during the 1920s following patterns developed in the du Pont Company, which had acquired a 23 percent ownership interest in GM, substantial authority and responsibility were delegated to operating divisions, while a strong central staff was established to provide analysis and advice (but in principle, not direction) on matters of policy. Whenever feasible, operating entities were set up as semiautonomous profit centers, with the stern calculus of profit and loss simultaneously guiding the decisions of operating-level executives and providing top management with an indicator of good or bad performance. To charge the system with incentive, key managers were paid bonuses that varied to reflect supervisors' evaluations of how well performance objectives were satisfied. For more than half a century, the system passed the acid test of restraining scale diseconomies. General Motors was not only the world's largest manufacturing enterprise, but also one of the most profitable. Yet it is far from clear that GM's organizational strategy was sufficient to weather the storms of changing market conditions. As early as 1946, Peter Drucker warned presciently that General Motors might be susceptible to a parochialism of view that could leave it unprepared to deal with changes

13. See Robinson, *The Structure of Competitive Industry,* supra note 5, Chapter 3; Nicholas Kaldor, "The Equilibrium of the Firm," *Economic Journal,* vol. 44 (March 1934), pp. 60–76; R. H. Coase, "The Nature of the Firm," *Economica,* vol. 4 (November 1937), pp. 386–405; E. H. Chamberlin, "Proportionality, Divisibility, and Economies of Scale," *Quarterly Journal of Economics,* vol. 62 (February 1948), pp. 229–262; Oliver E. Williamson, "Hierarchical Control and Optimum Firm Size," *Journal of Political Economy,* vol. 75 (April 1967), pp. 123–138; and Michael Keren and David Levhari, "The Internal Organization of the Firm and the Shape of Average Costs," *Bell Journal of Economics,* vol. 14 (Autumn 1983), pp. 474–486.

14. See David Schwartzman, "Uncertainty and the Size of the Firm," *Economica,* vol. 30 (August 1963), pp. 287–296, who finds empirically that the more uncertain the market environment is, as exemplified by the frequency and magnitude of retail price markdowns, the smaller the largest manufacturing firms in an industry tend to be.

On possible technological tradeoffs between achieving minimum unit costs at planned output volumes and flexibility to operate at only modest cost premiums when output deviates widely from the plan, see George J. Stigler, "Production and Distribution in the Short Run," *Journal of Political Economy,* vol. 47 (June 1939), pp. 305–327; and Gerald Aranoff, "Output-Flexibility and Diverse Technology," *Scottish Journal of Political Economy,* vol. 36 (May 1989).

15. For readers untutored in the ways of bureaucracy, an expediter is a person whose desk is between the desks of two coordinators.

16. Robinson, *The Structure of Competitive Industry,* supra note 5, p. 41.

17. See Oliver E. Williamson, *Corporate Control and Business Behavior* (Englewood Cliffs, NJ: Prentice-Hall, 1970), p. 175; building upon Alfred D. Chandler, Jr., *Strategy and Structure: Chapters in the History of the Industrial Enterprise* (Cambridge: MIT Press, 1962).

For quantitative tests of whether "M-Form" organizations are more profitable or in other ways more successful, see Barry C. Harris, *Organization: The Effect on Large Corporations* (Ann Arbor, MI: UMI Research Press, 1983); and Charles W. L. Hill, "Internal Organization and Enterprise Performance: Some UK Evidence," *Managerial and Decision Economics,* vol. 6 (December 1985), pp. 210–216. The results have been equivocal. See also Hill, "Oliver Williamson and the M-Form Firm: A Critical Review," *Journal of Economic Issues,* vol. 19 (September 1985), pp. 731–751.

18. Chandler, *Strategy and Structure,* Chapter 3. In a later and fuller historical synthesis, *The Visible Hand: The Managerial Revolution in American Business* (Cambridge: Harvard University Press, 1977), Chandler deemphasizes the role of General Motors and gives pride of place to General Electric.

in its external environment.[19] By the 1950s, the principle of decentralization was frequently breached, and the central staff showed signs of ossification.[20] Major organizational philosophy changes followed — toward centralization, weakening the product divisions' authority, in the 1970s, and partial decentralization again in the 1980s.[21] In the mid-1980s, General Motors proved less able than its smaller domestic and foreign rivals at adjusting to more intense competition and changing consumer demands; and its market share and profitability deteriorated. It had entered the stage of upward-sloping unit costs — perhaps permanently.

The original General Motors decentralization strategy has been emulated, subject to countless detailed variations, by other large corporations in the United States and abroad. Few if any have succeeded completely in overcoming the problems of large-scale bureaucracy. Interviews with 125 North American and European companies revealed a virtually unanimous consensus that decision-making in the large multiplant firm is slower and that top executives' remoteness from operational details often (but not always) impaired the quality of decision-making.[22] Further difficulties arise when the negotiated prices set to transfer goods or services internally between divisions deviate from marginal cost, and hence distort choices.[23] How well companies cope with the managerial problems of size appears to depend upon the complexity of production and marketing challenges and the abilities of a firm's guiding individuals. A few firms are fortunate to secure leaders with sufficient organizational genius to sustain superior profitability despite what might otherwise be debilitating scale. Others achieve average profits only because production or marketing scale economies are persistent enough to offset managerial diseconomies. Still others, such as the United States Steel Corporation (now renamed USX), have experimented with myriad organizational forms but remain less efficient and profitable than smaller rivals. And in such volatile industries as fashion handbag manufacturing or on-site home-building, where rapid adaptation to changing conditions is vital and orthodox scale economies are exhausted at modest scales, managerial diseconomies severely restrict the sizes firms can attain without experiencing rising unit costs.

We conclude then that the long-run average cost function of industrial firms has a shape something like that shown, in conventional two-dimensional single-output format, in Figure 4.3. Up to some minimum efficient scale OA, economies of scale lead to reductions in unit cost as capacity and output rise. Through decentralization and other organizational techniques, it is possible to increase the firm's size considerably beyond OA at more or less constant costs per unit. But if the enterprise expands too far — that is, beyond scale OB — managerial diseconomies of scale intrude, leading to operation at higher-than-minimum cost per unit.[24]

Transportation Costs   The cost of delivering output to customers (or bringing customers to the place where service is provided) can also limit the size-increasing effect of scale economies. Transportation costs affect cost-scale relationships primarily at the level of a single plant or geographically clustered plant complex. If more output is produced, more must be sold. To sell more, it may be necessary to reach out to more distant customers. This in turn can lead to increased transportation costs per unit sold. The magnitude of the increase depends upon several variables. One is the

Figure 4.3
A Typical Long-run
Unit Cost Function

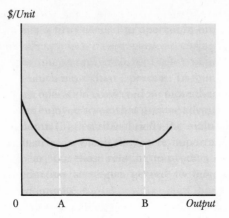

$/Unit

0   A   B   Output

size of the plant in relation to the size of the market served. If the plant supplies only a small fraction of market demand, it may be able to increase sales appreciably without expanding its geographic reach. In this case transport costs will not significantly constrain plant size. A second factor is the nature of the pricing system. Transportation costs absorbed by the producer rise with output when prices are uniform in all markets or when the price in more distant markets is set by more advantageously located rival producers. Such conditions, we will see in Chapter 13, are commonplace. The third variable is the geographic structure of transportation costs. Usually freight charges rise less than proportionately with the distance shipped. The smaller the percentage increase in cost associated with shipping one's output an extra one hundred kilometers, the more weakly transport

19. Peter F. Drucker, *The Concept of the Corporation* (New York: Day, 1946), Chapter 3.

20. See J. Patrick Wright (for John DeLorean), *On A Clear Day You Can See General Motors* (Grosse Pointe, MI: Wright Enterprises, 1979).

21. See "GM Moves To Centralize All Operations," *Automotive News,* September 20, 1971, pp. 1, 36; "Project Center: GM Management System's New Aid," *Chicago Tribune,* February 27, 1977; "General Motors: What Went Wrong," *Business Week,* March 16, 1987, pp. 102–110; "G.M.'s Goodbye to the Bonus," *New York Times,* April 17, 1987, p. D-1; "Humbler G.M. Is Now Listening," *New York Times,* Jan. 30, 1988, p. D1; Ross Perot, "How I Would Turn Around GM," *Fortune,* February 15, 1988, pp. 44–49; and "GM Faces Reality," *Business Week,* May 9, 1988, pp. 114–118.

Similarly, Sears Roebuck, characterized by Chandler as having attained its "final" decentralized structure in 1948, moved in the 1970s toward greater centralization of merchandising decision-making. See "What Sears' New Look Means to Sears," *Business Week,* January 26, 1976, p. 27.

22. F. M. Scherer, Alan Beckenstein, Erich Kaufer, and R. D. Murphy, *The Economics of Multi-Plant Operation: An International Comparisons Study* (Cambridge: Harvard University Press, 1975), p. 324.

23. On this "transfer pricing" problem, see Jack Hirshleifer, "On the Economics of Transfer Pricing," *Journal of Business,* vol. 29 (July 1956), pp. 172–184; John A. Menge, "The Backward Art of Interdivisional Pricing," *Journal of Industrial Economics,* vol. 23 (July 1961), pp. 215–232; Robert G. Eccles, *The Transfer Pricing Problem: A Theory for Practice* (Boston: Harvard Business School, 1985); and (on cross-border transfers in multinational firms) Robin Murray, ed., *Multinationals Beyond the Market: Intra-Firm Trade and the Control of Transfer Pricing* (New York: Halstead, 1981).

24. In a more dynamic treatment of the managerial cost-scale question, Edith T. Penrose argues that one must take into account the process by which firms move from one scale to a larger one. *The Theory of Growth of the Firm* (Oxford: Basil Blackwell, 1959). In her view, expansion at any moment in time is constrained by the inability of the firm's management to cope with the planning and leadership problems created by increased size. Thus, the firm's static cost curve bends upward at a scale only slightly larger than its current scale. But as time passes, management digests the problems caused by past growth and gains the ability to deal with new problems. Thus, the managerial limit to efficient expansion recedes over time and, Penrose argues, there is no single optimal firm size in the long run.

costs constrain plant size. Fourth, the geographic distribution of customers matters. If buyers are distributed evenly over the map, transportation costs will rise less than proportionately with the number of customers served, ceteris paribus, since shipping cost is related to the radius of shipment while the volume of patronage is related to the square of the radius. If, on the other hand, customer density declines sharply away from the home market, transport costs may rise more than proportionately with the volume shipped. Finally, the relationship of the commodity's production cost to its bulk is important. For bulky, low-value commodities like sand or beer bottles, unit transportation costs rise relatively rapidly with distance shipped. For compact, high-value items like integrated circuits and machine tools, they rise slowly.

The combined effect of these influences is illustrated in Figures 4.4(a) and 4.4(b). We assume that increased output must be sold at greater distance by absorbing freight charges. For each diagram, an identical production cost/scale curve UPC is assumed. The minimum efficient scale in terms of production costs alone occurs at output OX. In Figure 4.4(a), unit shipping costs USC rise slowly with increased output. Total cost per unit LRATC is the vertical sum of unit production costs and unit shipping costs. The least-cost scale, taking into account both production and transportation costs, occurs in Figure 4.4(a) at output OY. In Figure 4.4(b), unit shipping costs rise much more rapidly, and this causes a reduction in the least-cost scale to OZ.

Improvements in technology have had important effects on shipping costs and hence on market structure. The expansion of railroad networks during the second half of the nineteenth century caused a fall in unit transportation costs, moving many producers from a position like that of Figure 4.4(b) to one like 4.4(a). The least-cost scale of production thereupon rose, and firms took advantage by building new plants of unprecedented size. The deregulation of rail and trucking rates in the United States during the late 1970s and early 1980s had similar effects in industries that had previously endured relatively high rates.

Figure 4.4
The Effect of Transportation
Costs on The Scale Optimum

a. Scale Optimum with Modest
   Transportation Costs

b. Scale Optimum with Substantial
   Transportation Costs

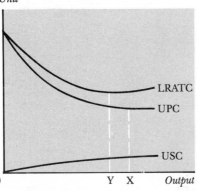

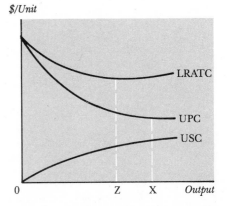

Scale Economies and Vertical Integration

A further complication must be explored. The typical large manufacturing corporation carries out a bewilderingly complex array of activities. Yet, as we have seen in the preceding chapter, it spends more than half its sales dollar purchasing raw materials, components, machines, special services, and the like from other firms. What determines which operations a firm will perform internally and which it will farm out to others? And how does this choice affect the scale of operation?

Of particular interest here are activities entailing minimum efficient scales (MES) large in relation to other facets of the firm's operations. For example, the most costly component of a refrigerator or windowsill air conditioner is its compressor. In the early 1970s, economies of scale in compressor manufacturing persisted out to outputs of 2 to 3 million units per year, not necessarily all of the same design. Scale economies in refrigerator box fabrication and assembly, on the other hand, were exhausted at a plant output of roughly 800,000 units per year.[25] Must the refrigerator assembler be large enough to produce its own compressors at minimum unit cost, or could it buy its compressors from outside specialists and operate efficiently at the smaller assembly-only MES? Similarly, a minimum-cost automobile assembly plant produced only about 200,000 vehicles per year on double-shift operation. But stamping body parts and machining automatic transmissions required larger annual volumes — for example, from 250,000 to 400,000 units per year for each line.[26] Is an auto firm of efficient size one that merely assembles other firms' high-scale-economy parts efficiently, or must it be large enough to span the full range of component manufacturing activities at minimum unit cost? In short, how vertically integrated must the firm be, or obversely, to what extent can it satisfy its needs through outside procurement of high-scale-economy components, perhaps avoiding thereby some diseconomies of managing a large organization?

There are several related answers to these questions. In a seminal article, R. H. Coase observed that the distinguishing mark of a "firm" is the "suppression of the price mechanism."[27] Resource allocation in the market is normally guided through prices, but within the firm the job is done through the conscious decisions and commands of management. Activities are collected in what we call a firm, Coase argues, when transaction costs incurred in using the price mechanism exceed the cost of organizing those activities through direct managerial controls. One reason why market transaction costs may be appreciable is that price shopping, the communication of work specifications, and contract negotiation take

25. Scherer et al., *Multi-Plant Operation,* supra note 22, pp. 80 and 269.

26. See Lawrence J. White, *The Automobile Industry Since 1945* (Cambridge: Harvard University Press, 1971), Chapters 3 and 4; and C. F. Pratten, *Economies of Scale in Manufacturing Industry* (Cambridge, England: Cambridge University Press, 1971), pp. 132–149.

In the 1980s there was a radical change in the U.S. automobile industry's vertical integration patterns. Sharp wage increases under labor contracts negotiated earlier by General Motors, Ford, and Chrysler drove the costs of integrated production above the costs attainable by independent suppliers, often operating in nonunion areas or outside the United States. As a result, the advantages of integration were overwhelmed, and many components produced internally before were contracted out.

27. Coase, "The Nature of the Firm," supra note 13, p. 389. See also Oliver E. Williamson, "The Vertical Integration of Production: Market Failure Considerations," *American Economic Review,* vol. 61 (May 1971), pp. 112–123. For other explanations of vertical integration emphasizing more efficient internal communication and coping with uncertainty, see Kenneth J. Arrow, "Vertical Integration and Communications," *Bell Journal of Economics,* vol. 6 (Spring 1975), pp. 173–183; and Dennis W. Carlton, "Vertical Integration in Competitive Markets under Uncertainty," *Journal of Industrial Economics,* vol. 27 (March 1979), pp. 189–209.

time and effort. Especially when goods or services would have to be contracted for repeatedly in small quantities or when designs are changing in complex ways, it may be cheaper to bring them under the firm's direct span of internal managerial control.

For components, materials, and services whose provision entails compelling scale economies, the choice between integration and disintegration has an important additional dimension. By the logic of specialization and division of labor, one might expect the rewards from vertical disintegration to be especially great, since then, as Professor Robinson argues, "The specialist firm, working for a number of smaller firms, is on a larger scale than any of the individual firms could have achieved for that particular process or product."[28] But precisely because scale economies are so compelling, the number of nonintegrated suppliers is likely to be small. For example, the total U.S. market for household and analogous refrigerators, freezers, and air conditioners in 1972 was large enough to support only five or six least-cost compressor manufacturers. Similar conditions hold with respect to the supply of automobile and truck transmissions, diesel truck and bus engines, specialized paint pigments, and many other intermediate goods. From limited supply sources may follow monopolistic pricing of components bought outside. Even if the monopolistic supplier chooses not to exercise fully its power to elevate prices, buyers recognize their dependence upon the supplier's restraint and fear, naturally enough, that they may not always be so fortunate. To avoid actual or feared monopolistic exploitation, users of high-scale-economy materials or components often decide to undertake internal production, even though they may incur a cost penalty in doing so. In effect, they view the higher cost of vertically integrated production, sacrificing some scale economies, as a less onerous burden than the risk of being gouged by a more efficient but monopolistic outside supplier.

Nor does the story end there. If several firms reason in this way and integrate vertically, the independent supply market will become thinner or even disappear. To be sure, nonintegrated firms may obtain their needed supplies from firms that have chosen to integrate. But although being dependent upon a single independent supply source for some critical raw material or component is unnerving, it is even worse when the supplier is also one's main-line competitor. The situation is unstable. When vertical integration induced by the fewness of supply sources thins the market further, other buyers may be stampeded into integrating too even though they must accept appreciable scale economy sacrifices.

Quite generally, the more prone markets are to a breakdown of competitive supply conditions, either because scale economies limit the number of suppliers or because buyer and seller are locked together in complex coordinating relationships, the stronger is the buyer's incentive to protect itself by integrating upstream.[29] An extreme illustration of this generalization can be seen by comparing the shoe industries of the United States and the Soviet Union.[30] In the United States, more or less workably competitive sources of supply exist for glues, shoe finishing chemicals, sole rubber compounds, paperboard containers, lasts, and special shoe-making machines. U.S. shoe manufacturers are therefore willing to rely upon independent specialists to meet their needs. In the Soviet Union, markets were virtually nonexistent, at least before reforms were initiated in the mid-1980s, and independent suppliers often failed to meet plan requirements, thereby disrupting downstream operations. To avoid such supply problems, Soviet shoe-making firms undertook extensive vertical integration to satisfy their requirements internally. And because glue-making, rubber compounding, and machine-building operations of minimum efficient scale could satisfy numerous efficiently sized shoe plants' needs, the compulsion toward such integration increased the least common multiple. Soviet shoe manufacturing enterprises therefore grew to sizes unnecessary in the United States and Western Europe.

The Measurement of Cost-Scale Relationships

We have proposed viewing economies of scale in terms of the minimum efficient scale (such as OA in Figure 4.3 or OX in Figure 4.4) at which all attainable unit cost savings are realized. The crucial question remains: Is the MES large or small in relation to the demand for an industry's output? Whether there is room for many firms in the market, each large enough to enjoy all scale economies, for only one firm (a *natural monopoly* situation), or for just a few (*natural oligopoly*) depends upon the relevant technology and the size of the market, that is, the output that would be demanded at a price just sufficient to cover minimum unit cost.

There are several techniques for measuring cost-scale relationships. Some are suitable mainly for ascertaining the minimum efficient plant size, some the minimum efficient firm size, and some for both.

One approach is to analyze profitability as a function of size. At the firm level there are abundant data. However, several pitfalls exist. For one, profitability is not necessarily related in any simple way to scale economies, as conventionally defined. Large firms may realize higher profit returns not only because of superior efficiency, but because they possess more monopoly or monopsony (that is, buying) power. Or they may be less profitable because they bear a disproportionate share of the monopoly output restriction burden. Also, profit figures may be sensitive to variations in accounting conventions governing depreciation, the valuation of assets acquired in mergers, and the like. A special accounting problem affecting comparative firm size analyses is a possible tendency for smaller corporations' owner-managers to pay themselves salaries including a generous dose of what would otherwise be called profit. This is done to avoid double taxation. As a result, small firms' reported profits may be biased downward.[31] Finally, the relative

28. Robinson, *The Structure of Competitive Industry,* supra note 5, p. 20. See also George J. Stigler, "The Division of Labor Is Limited by the Extent of the Market," *Journal of Political Economy,* vol. 59 (June 1951), pp. 185–193.

29. For statistical analyses of the determinants of vertical integration, all supporting this generalization, see Kirk Monteverde and David J. Teece, "Supplier Switching Costs and Vertical Integration in the Automobile Industry," *Bell Journal of Economics,* vol. 13 (Spring 1982), pp. 206–213; David Levy, "Testing Stigler's Interpretation of 'The Division of Labor Is Limited by the Extent of the Market,'" *Journal of Industrial Economics,* vol. 32 (March 1984), pp. 377–389; James M. MacDonald, "Market Exchange or Vertical Integration: An Empirical Analysis," *Review of Economics and Statistics,* vol. 67 (May 1985), pp. 327–331; David T. Levy, "The Transactions Cost Approach to Vertical Integration: An Empirical Examination," *Review of Economics and Statistics,* vol. 67 (Au-

gust 1985), pp. 438–445; and Richard E. Caves and Ralph M. Bradburd, "The Empirical Determinants of Vertical Integration," *Journal of Economic Behavior and Organization,* vol. 9 (April 1988), pp. 265–279. For sixteen industry case studies, see Kathryn R. Harrigan, *Strategies for Vertical Integration* (Lexington, MA: Lexington Books, 1983), Chapters 4–11.

30. See Alice C. Gorlin, "Soviet Firms and the Nationalization of the Shoe Industry of the USSR," Ph.D. dissertation, University of Michigan, 1972, especially pp. 214–216; and Scherer et al., *Multi-Plant Operation,* supra note 22, p. 270.

31. See Herman O. Stekler, *Profitability and Size of Firm* (Berkeley: University of California Institute of Business and Economic Research, 1963), pp. 20 and 36–46; and George J. Stigler, *Capital and Rates of Return in Manufacturing Industries* (Princeton: Princeton University Press, 1963), pp. 59–61.

profitability of small versus large corporations appears to vary with the business cycle, with smaller enterprises doing relatively well in boom periods and poorly in recessions.[32]

In Chapter 11 we undertake an extensive review of how profits vary with monopoly power, firm size, the business cycle, and much else. Here a preliminary glimpse of the broad relationships observed for U.S. manufacturing corporations must suffice. Table 4.1 arrays the average after-tax returns on stockholders' equity for all manufacturing corporations in six size classes during six time intervals characterized by widely varying macroeconomic conditions. Data for corporations with assets of less than $10 million are omitted because of possible owner-manager compensation biases. In all six periods the billion-dollar-plus corporations exhibit the highest returns. The differential is most prominent during the relatively normal 1963–65 period and the recessions of 1969–1971 and 1979–1982.[33] Small corporations did best during the late 1960s boom, the 1975–1977 period of recession mixed with open inflation, and the stable-price 1984–1987 economic recovery.

Another measurement approach, appropriate more for plant than firm-level studies, is statistical cost analysis. Multiple regression techniques are used to relate costs to output volume, accounting also for such variables as the capacity utilization ratio, differences in the age of the capital stock (and hence in the embodied technology), differences in input prices, the number of distinct products offered (reflecting economies or diseconomies of scope), cumulative output volume, and so forth. All this is easier said than done. Complete, reliable data are hard to come by. Recent studies using particularly high-powered but data-intensive statistical methods have emphasized regulated industries such as electric power, railroads, trucking, airlines, and telecommunications, on which regulators have imposed unusually stringent cost and output reporting mandates. Since some of those industries are arguably natural monopolies, one might expect the results to show

Table 4.1   Average After-Tax Profit Returns on Stockholders' Equity for U.S. Manufacturing Corporations in Diverse Size Classes, 1963–1987

Asset Size Range	1963–65	1966–69	1969–71	1975–77	1979–82	1984–87
Over $1 billion	13.5%	12.7%	10.3%	13.2%	13.1%	11.7%
$250–1000 million	11.0	12.1	10.4	13.0	10.8	9.0
$100–250 million	11.2	12.0	9.7	12.1	10.5	9.7
$50–100 million	10.4	11.2	8.6	12.0	10.0	10.4
$25–50 million	10.0	11.4	8.2	11.9	9.2	10.4
$10–25 million	9.9	11.0	7.9	12.4	9.9	11.1

Source: Federal Trade Commission and (after 1981) U.S. Bureau of the Census, *Quarterly Financial Report for Manufacturing, Mining, and Retail Corporations* (Washington: Government Printing Office, various years). The entries are unweighted averages of quarterly rates of return. Because of the midyear change in business conditions, the 1966–69 period includes only the first two quarters of 1969, while the 1969–71 period includes the last two quarters of 1969.

relatively large minimum efficient scales, as many in fact do.[34] On manufacturing industries, for which less sophisticated analyses have been necessitated by more meager data supply, the most common finding has been a long-run average total cost curve similar to Figure 4.3, showing distinct economies of scale at relatively small plant sizes, a range of intermediate sizes over which unit costs did not differ appreciably, and (in a minority of cases) diseconomies of scale for very large plants. With few exceptions, the minimum efficient scale revealed in studies of U.S. manufacturing industries has been small relative to industry size. It would be hazardous to generalize from this result, however, since, assuming cost-minimizing behavior, industries with sufficiently numerous plants to permit a reliable statistical cost analysis should be those with small minimum efficient scales relative to national product demand.

A third empirical approach is the so-called survivor test, developed in its modern form by George Stigler.[35] The logic is simple: firm or plant sizes that survive and contribute increasing fractions of an industry's output over time are assumed to be efficient; those that supply a declining share of output are deemed too large or too small. This test of efficiency clearly covers a broader range of variables than mere production and distribution scale economies. As Stigler observes, under the survivor test an efficient firm size "is one that meets any and all problems the entrepreneur actually faces: strained labor relations, rapid innovation, government regulation, unstable foreign markets, and what not"; and survival may reflect monopoly power or discriminatory legislation as well as conventional scale economies.[36] Several investigators have applied the survivor test to more than a hundred industries.[37] The most prominent result has been the wide range of firm and

32. On the depressed 1930s, see J. L. McConnell, "Corporate Earnings by Size of Firm," *Survey of Current Business,* vol. 25 (May 1945), pp. 6–12. For a more recent British study, see Geoffrey Whittington, "The Profitability and Size of United Kingdom Companies, 1960–74," *Journal of Industrial Economics,* vol. 28 (June 1980), pp. 335–352.

33. The largest corporations' strikingly superior profitability in 1979–1982 is attributable in part to the high returns of characteristically large petroleum companies, whose crude oil operations benefited from the OPEC-led escalation of prices in that period. In 1982, a year of severe recession, petroleum companies accounted for nearly 28 percent of all manufacturing corporations' after-tax profits but only 19 percent of their stockholders' equity. The petroleum companies' return on equity was 13.2 percent, compared to 8.3 percent for nonpetroleum manufacturers of all sizes.

34. Early studies are surveyed in John Johnston, *Statistical Cost Analysis* (New York: McGraw-Hill, 1960); and A. A. Walters, "Production and Cost Functions: An Econometric Survey," *Econometrica,* vol. 31 (January–April 1963), pp. 1–66. On the newer techniques, see Melvyn Fuss and Daniel McFadden, eds., *Production Economics: A Dual Approach to Theory and Applications* (2 vol.; Amsterdam: North-Holland, 1978). Examples of the many newer studies include Ronald R. Braeutigam, Andrew F. Daughety,

and Mark A. Turnquist, "The Estimation of a Hybrid Cost Function for a Railroad Firm," *Review of Economics and Statistics,* vol. 64 (August 1982), pp. 394–404; Jeffrey A. Clark, "Estimation of Economies of Scale in Banking Using a Generalized Functional Form," *Journal of Money, Credit and Banking,* vol. 16 (February 1984), pp. 53–68; Douglas W. Caves, L. R. Christensen, and M. W. Tretheway, "Economies of Density versus Economies of Scale: Why Trunk and Local Service Airline Costs Differ," *Rand Journal of Economics,* vol. 15 (Winter 1984), pp. 471–489; and Merrile Sing, "Are Combination Gas and Electric Utilities Multiproduct Monopolies?" *Review of Economics and Statistics,* vol. 69 (August 1987), pp. 392–398.

35. George J. Stigler, "The Economies of Scale," *Journal of Law & Economics,* vol. 1 (October 1958), pp. 54–71.

36. Stigler, "The Economies of Scale," p. 56.

37. See especially T. R. Saving, "Estimation of Optimum Size of Plant by the Survivor Technique," *Quarterly Journal of Economics,* vol. 75 (November 1961), pp. 569–607; Leonard W. Weiss, "The Survival Technique and the Extent of Suboptimal Capacity," *Journal of Political Economy,* vol. 72 (June 1964), pp. 246–261; and R. D. Rees, "Optimum Plant Size in United Kingdom Industries: Some Survivors Estimates," *Economica,* vol. 40 (November 1973), pp. 394–401.

plant sizes that seem to pass the test. This has been interpreted (somewhat mis-leadingly) by Stigler as evidence that "the long run marginal and average cost curves of the firm are customarily horizontal over a large range of sizes."

Applications of the test also suggest that the minimum efficient plant or firm size is small relative to market size in most industries. Thus, T. R. Saving found that sixty-four of the ninety-one manufacturing industries for which he was able to make 1947–1954 survivorship estimates had minimum efficient plant scales at 1 percent or less of industry value added.[38] However, such tests are not free of ambiguity. Survival patterns are not always stable over time; curious patterns appear (such as survival of only the largest and smallest plants); and the criteria for distinguishing surviving from nonsurviving size groups entail a certain amount of arbitrariness. Tests on the same industries by different scholars have sometimes yielded quite different estimates.[39] Consequently, the survivor method is better reserved as a supplement to, and a check on, other techniques than as one's sole approach to analyzing cost-scale relationships.

Finally, there is the *engineering approach* to scale economies measurement. Many companies employ, either internally or by contracting the task out to specialized firms, engineers who plan and design new production units and plants. The persons who perform these functions accumulate much information on alternative equipment and plant designs and the associated investment and operating costs. This expert knowledge can be tapped through interviews and questionnaires to estimate cost-scale relationships and minimum efficient scales. Scale economies studies using the engineering approach span a wide range of detail, from those that estimate cost relationships for each individual machine or process and integrate them through a statistical or mathematical model[40] to questionnaires asking little more than the best overall scale of operations. With the simple questionnaire approach, important details may be overlooked, and so considerable on-site interviewing is usually necessary to support confident conclusions — a costly process for both the investigator and informants. As with statistical cost function studies, cost and scale relationships may be complicated by product mix variations. Despite these difficulties, carefully executed engineering estimates undoubtedly provide the best insights into cost-scale links.

There have been several studies using the engineering approach to derive plant scale economies estimates for a substantial sample of industries.[41] Table 4.2 summarizes the findings from an unusually ambitious interviewing program covering twelve fairly representative major industries in seven industrialized nations.[42] Three measures are given: the capacity, output, or employment of a minimum efficient scale plant, assuming mid-1960s best-practice technology; how large a share of total 1967 U.S. output, capacity, or employment such an MES plant would contribute; and the percentage elevation of long-run unit costs as a consequence of building and operating plants at one-third the MES rather than the full MES. Two implications stand out. First, with the exception of the refrigerator-freezer industry, the least-cost plant sizes tend to be quite small relative to the national market — too small to warrant high levels of concentration, assuming that each leading firm operates only one MES plant. By this assumption, the four-firm concentration ratio in brewing would have been 14, in cigarettes 26, and in fabric weaving less than 1. Second, the long-run cost curves in most industries are

Table 4.2 Minimum Efficient Plant Scales as a Percentage of 1967 U.S. Demand, and the Cost Disadvantage of Suboptimal Scale Plants

Industry	Minimum Efficient Scale	Percentage of 1967 U.S. Demand	Percentage by Which Unit Cost Rises at One-third MES
Beer brewing	4.5 million (31 U.S. gallon) barrels per year capacity	3.4	5.0
Cigarettes	36 billion cigarettes per year	6.6	2.2
Cotton and synthetic broadwoven fabrics	37.5 million square yards per year	0.2	7.6
Paints	10 million U.S. gallons per year	1.4	4.4
Petroleum refining	200,000 (42 U.S. gallon) barrels per day crude oil capacity	1.9	4.8
Leather shoes	1 million pairs per year	0.2	1.5
Glass bottles	133,000 tons per year	1.5	11.0
Portland cement	7 million 376-pound barrels per year capacity	1.7	26.0
Integrated steel	4 million tons per year capacity	2.6	11.0
Anti-friction bearings	800 employees	1.4	8.0
Refrigerators	800,000 units per year	14.1	6.5
Automobile storage batteries	1 million units per year	1.9	4.6

Source: F. M. Scherer, Alan Beckenstein, Erich Kaufer, and R. D. Murphy, *The Economics of Multi-Plant Operation: An International Comparisons Study* (Cambridge: Harvard University Press, 1975), pp. 80 and 94.

much less steep at suboptimal plant scales than one is led to believe by the typical textbook illustration. Only in cement are unit costs elevated at one-third MES by anything like the magnitudes suggested earlier in Figures 2.4 or 4.3. In half the industries, the elevation is 5 percent or less. In refrigerators, where realizing all plant-level scale economies requires the highest market concentration, one could

38. Saving, "Estimation of Optimum Size of Plant," p. 580.

39. See William G. Shepherd, "What Does the Survivor Technique Show About Economies of Scale?" *Southern Economic Journal,* vol. 34 (July 1967), pp. 113–122.

40. See for example Hollis B. Chenery, "Engineering Production Functions," *Quarterly Journal of Economics,* vol. 63 (November 1949), pp. 507–531 (on natural gas pipelines); Neil B. MacDonald, W. F. Barnicke, F. W. Judge, and K. E. Hansen, *Farm Tractor Production Costs: A Study in Economies of Scale,* Report for the Royal Commission on Farm Machinery (Ottawa: Queen's Printer, 1969); and Myles G. Boylan, Jr., *Economic Effects of Scale Increases in the Steel Industry* (New York: Praeger, 1975).

41. The pioneering study of this genre, covering twenty industries, was Joe S. Bain, *Barriers to New Competition* (Cambridge: Harvard University Press, 1956), especially pp. 71–83 and 227–249. See also C. F. Pratten, *Economies of Scale in Manufacturing Industry* (Cambridge, England: Cambridge University Press, 1971); and Leonard W. Weiss, "Optimal Plant Size and the Extent of Suboptimal Capacity," in Robert T. Masson and P. D. Qualls, eds., *Essays on Industrial Organization in Honor of Joe S. Bain* (Cambridge: Ballinger, 1975), pp. 128–131.

42. Scherer et al., *Multi-Plant Operation,* supra note 22, Chapter 3.

have an industry with twenty-one plants if one were willing to accept excess production costs of 6.5 percent.

Because engineering approach studies are so time-consuming, less expensive surrogate measures of the minimum efficient plant scale have been sought. One such substitute is the average size of plants comprising the upper half of an industry's sales or employment size distribution, as revealed in census reports. The ratios for such "top 50 percent" plant size averages to total industry size tend to be closely associated with engineering approach share estimates like those in the third column of Table 4.2. The simple correlation coefficients for comparable industries range from 0.59 to 0.89.[43] Average top 50 percent plant size shares were computed for 155 four-digit U.S. manufacturing industries with value added of $75 million or more in 1963. In only fourteen industries did the average sales of the largest plants amount to 10 percent or more of total industry sales.[44]

Thus, economies of scale at the plant level do not necessitate high national concentration levels for most U.S. manufacturing industries. There are, to be sure, exceptions. Middling levels of oligopoly are required in such industries as refrigerators, passenger autos, and tractor manufacturing; and tight oligopoly is probably mandated in a few industries such as turbogenerators, diesel engines, typewriters, and civilian airliner production.

A less sanguine conclusion emerges when we recognize that transportation costs often lead to geographic markets considerably smaller than the nationwide expanse assumed in Table 4.2. Shipping a dollar's worth of beer 350 miles from the brewery, for example, cost approximately 7.8 cents on a representative 1963 haul.[45] This level of transportation cost was sufficient to fragment the United States into five to seven meaningful geographic markets, within which an MES brewery contributed a sufficient share of output to make oligopoly probable. Seven of the twelve industries in Table 4.2 had shipping costs high enough to induce regionalization. Table 4.3 takes the influence of transportation costs into account, estimating the number of regional markets into which the lower forty-eight U.S. states might properly have been subdivided during the 1960s. These estimates are then used to indicate (in the last column) the share of 1967 output an MES plant would have originated in the average regional market. A considerably stronger tendency toward oligopoly — that is, with mean four-seller regional market concentration ratios of 40 or more in five of the seven industries — is revealed. These, it must be stressed, are crude averages. In the densely populated Northeast and North Central states, MES plant market shares would have been lower, while in the sparsely populated Plains states, they would have been higher. Since the Table 4.2 sample was deliberately biased toward industries with relatively high transportation costs, the Table 4.3 analysis probably overstates the average impact of regionalization on concentration. In a survey of U.S. manufacturing industries, Weiss found only 96 (out of 283 candidates) in which the evidence supported dividing the United States into three or more probable regional markets.[46] Still one must not ignore the interaction between shipping costs and scale economies in setting a floor for concentration levels consistent with production and distributional efficiency.

We turn more briefly now to product-specific scale economies. Not much can be said because there have been no systematic quantitative studies like those re-

Table 4.3   The Impact of Regionalization on MES
Plant Market Shares, circa 1967

Industry	Approximate Number of Regional Markets in Continental U.S.	MES Plant Share per Average Regional Market
Beer brewing	6	20.4
Paints	5	7.0
Petroleum refining	5	9.5
Glass bottles	9	13.5
Cement	24	40.8
Integrated steel works	4	10.4
Storage batteries	6	11.4

Source: F. M. Scherer, "Economies of Scale and Industrial Concentration," in Harvey J. Goldschmid et al., ed., *Industrial Concentration: The New Learning* (Boston: Little, Brown, 1974), pp. 28–31; adapted in part from Leonard W. Weiss, "The Geographic Size of Markets in Manufacturing," *Review of Economics and Statistics,* vol. 54 (August 1972), pp. 245–266.

viewed thus far for plant-specific economies. A preliminary grasp on the matter can be had by invoking the "80-20 rule" — a rough empirical generalization indicating that the best-selling 20 percent of a firm's products by number account for 80 percent of total sales, while the more numerous "cats and dogs" items contribute the remaining 20 percent. Observation suggests that the typical sizable U.S. manufacturer manages to exploit most if not all product-specific economies on the best-selling 20 percent of its products, but falls short, and often far short, of realizing minimum costs on the remaining low-volume items. For the latter, demand is insufficient to sustain long, low-cost production runs. In a limited sense, the production of special Bock beers, navy blue acrylic-blend cloth printed with camellia designs, thirty-six-inch steel I-beams, or roller bearings designed for a particular tractor tends toward natural monopoly.[47] This 80-20 generalization is extremely rough. In smaller nations like Canada and Sweden, a considerably larger fraction of all output is manufactured in suboptimal volumes.[48] And in the United States, the ratio varies from industry to industry, depending upon demand and production process characteristics. Thus, in continuous process industries such as cement making and petroleum refining, product-specific scale economy sacrifices are minuscule. But for most if not all microprocessor chips and military or civilian

43. Scherer et al., *Multi-Plant Operation,* pp. 182–183; and Weiss, "Optimal Plant Size," supra note 41, pp. 132–133.

44. Scherer et al., *Multi-Plant Operation,* pp. 434–439.

45. Scherer et al., *Multi-Plant Operation,* p. 90. Since then, transport costs have fallen with deregulation of the trucking and rail industries, but minimum efficient plant scales (ignoring transport costs) have probably risen into the 8 to 10 million barrels per year range.

46. Leonard W. Weiss, "The Geographic Size of Markets in Manufacturing," *Review of Economics and Statistics,* vol. 54 (August 1972), pp. 245–266.

47. The power that goes with monopoly is limited in most such cases (but not for thirty-six-inch I-beams) because competitors can quickly and easily, even if not costlessly, supply similar or identical products by resetting the equipment used to make other products.

48. See Scherer et al., *Multi-Plant Operation,* supra note 22, p. 51, and the references cited there.

aircraft, learning curve economies probably continue out to the total quantity demanded at a price covering minimum cost. Research delineating more precisely the distribution of production volumes by the extent to which product-specific economies are realized, and the cost implications thereof, remains sorely needed.

The Impact of Technological Change and Market Growth

How high seller concentration must be to secure production efficiency depends upon the balance between technology and market size. Both of these variables change over time. In the early 1950s, Joe S. Bain found that a least-cost flat-rolled steel products plant had a capacity of from 1.0 to 2.5 million tons per year.[49] By 1965, the MES capacity had risen to 4.0 million tons. Further advances in blast furnace, basic oxygen furnace, and continuous casting technology raised the optimum further by the late 1970s — most likely to a capacity of about 12 million tons per year. For simpler steel products such as reinforcing bars and narrow strip, on the other hand, the trend was in the opposite direction as least-cost production shifted from large integrated works to "mini-mills" using electric arc furnaces to process scrap steel at capacities of 750,000 tons per year or less.[50]

As in steel, the evidence on technology trajectories and their plant size implications is mixed. Analyzing data on plant construction in twenty-two chemical products lines, Lieberman found that new plant sizes grew by 8 percent per year on average from the late 1950s into the early 1980s.[51] John Blair, on the other hand, explained an observed tendency for the largest plants' share of output to decline between 1947 and 1958 as the result of "decentralizing" technological innovations.[52] These include the substitution of individual electric motors for central motive power; the rise of easily fabricated plastics and light metals; the replacement of specialized machines by more flexible and adaptable units, such as computer-controlled metal-working machines; and the displacement of water and rail transportation by trucks, with greater flexibility and more economical accommodation of less-than-carload shipments. Also, the growing breadth of product lines in some industries and increased demand volatility owing to heightened fashion consciousness have complicated the job of managing plants, precipitating plant size declines. So also have wage and other cost increases in urban centers, inducing a flight to smaller towns where plant sizes are constrained by local labor availability.

The net balance between these conflicting tendencies appears to have favored rising plant sizes. Saul Sands analyzed forty-six industries for which comparable data on physical output and the number of plants were available for the years 1904 and 1947. He found that physical output per plant increased by about 3 percent per year on average.[53] Meanwhile, output in manufacturing was rising at a rate of 3.9 percent per year.[54] These data, not strictly comparable, imply a decline in average plant size relative to market size. However, Sands found in a related study that the largest twenty plants in forty-seven industries originated an average of 42 percent of industry shipments by value in 1904 and 47 percent in 1947.[55] This suggests that, for Sands' more limited but better-matched samples, plant size growth may have outstripped market growth.

Comparable studies for the period following World War II have not been found. A crude picture can be gleaned from aggregate Census of Manufactures data. The overall growth of manufactured goods output can be decomposed into three additive elements: the growth in the number of plants, the growth of average employment per plant, and the growth of output per employee hour (or productivity).[56] Total manufactured goods output grew between 1947 and 1982 at 2.99 percent per year on average. The growth of the three components was as follows:

Number of plants	+1.13 percent per year
Labor hours per plant	−0.48 percent per year
Output per hour of work	+2.55 percent per year

The components do not sum precisely to 2.99 percent because they are drawn from imperfectly comparable sources, but the broad statistical picture is unmistakable. Plants have been declining in average size measured by employment, but with output per hour rising more rapidly than the fall in hours per plant, average output per plant has grown by roughly 2 percent per year. But the growth of manufactured goods output has outstripped average plant growth, leading to a decline in the size of plants relative to total output.

To the extent that industry concentration is influenced by the efficiency imperatives associated with plant scale economies, we should expect concentration to be higher, the smaller markets are, and especially the smaller they are in relation to minimum efficient plant scales. Also, the more rapidly demand grows, the more likely it is that rising plant scale requirements will be outstripped, all else equal, and hence the stronger any trend toward declining concentration, or the weaker a trend toward rising concentration, will be.

The first half of the first hypothesis is supported inter alia by an analysis of 1982 four-firm concentration ratios for the 448 manufacturing industries covered by Table 3.7 (Chapter 3). Four-firm concentration ratios were lower, the larger an industry's value added was, with a correlation coefficient of −0.16 (statistically

49. Bain, *Barriers to New Competition,* supra note 41, p. 236.

50. See, for example, Donald F. Barnett and Robert W. Crandall, *Up from the Ashes: The Rise of the Steel Minimill in the United States* (Washington: Brookings, 1986), pp. 7–10 and 65–67.

51. Marvin B. Lieberman, "Market Growth, Economies of Scale, and Plant Size in the Chemical Processing Industries," *Journal of Industrial Economics,* vol. 36 (December 1987), p. 183.

52. John M. Blair, *Industrial Concentration* (New York: Harcourt Brace Jovanovich, 1972), pp. 95–98 and 114–151.

53. Saul S. Sands, "Changes in Scale of Production in United States Manufacturing Industry, 1904–1947," *Review of Economics and Statistics,* vol. 43 (November 1961), pp. 365–368.

On changing plant sizes and their impact on nineteenth century market structures, see Jeremy Attack, "Firm Size and Industrial Structure in the United States during the Nineteenth Century," *Journal of Economic History,* vol. 46 (June 1986), pp. 463–475.

54. U.S. Bureau of the Census, *Historical Statistics of the United States: Colonial Times to 1957* (Washington: 1960), p. 414, drawing upon a National Bureau of Economic Research study by Solomon Fabricant.

55. Saul S. Sands, "Concentration in United States Manufacturing Industry, 1904–1947," *International Economic Review,* vol. 3 (January 1962), pp. 79–92.

56. Letting Q be total output, N the number of plants, and L the number of work hours expended, it is true by identity that:

$$Q = N \times (L/N) \times (Q/L).$$

Taking logarithms of the variables and differentiating with respect to time, one finds that the annual percentage change in Q equals the annual percentage change in N plus the annual percentage change in L/N plus the annual percentage change in Q/L.

The productivity (Q/L) and output growth data are from U.S. Bureau of Labor Statistics, *Trends in Multifactor Productivity, 1948–81,* Bulletin 2178, September 1983, pp. 12–14. The plant count and employment data are from U.S. Bureau of the Census, *1982 Census of Manufactures,* "General Summary," MC82(1)–1 (March 1986), Table 1. It is assumed that nonproduction employees worked 1,900 hours per year in both 1947 and 1982.

significant at the 95 percent confidence level).[57] To test the *relative* market size hypothesis, R. D. Murphy calculated the ratio of top 50 percent average plant sales to total industry sales as a surrogate measure of the national market share required by an MES plant. For 101 U.S. manufacturing industries in 1963, all with value added of $75 million or more, the top 50 percent ratio and four-seller concentration ratios were strongly related, with correlation coefficients of 0.68 to 0.76, depending upon the functional form tested.[58] The larger the size of industry-leading plants was relative to industry sales, the higher concentration was. This result persists when relative market size statistics derived using the engineering method are employed to analyze seller concentration in the twelve Table 4.2 industries across six national markets: Canada, the United States, the United Kingdom, France, West Germany, and Sweden.[59] The larger the number of MES plants a specific national market could hold, the lower the three-seller concentration ratio was, with a correlation coefficient of -0.67 between the variables in logarithmic form. It seems clear that large market size, absolute or (especially) in relation to MES plant scales, is a significant inhibitor of high concentration.

Numerous statistical studies have disclosed an analogous dynamic relationship between changes in market size and changes in concentration. In one of the first such analyses, Ralph Nelson found that each 100 percentage point increase in an industry's value added between 1935 and 1954 (for example, from a base of 10 to 20, further from 20 to 30, and so forth) was accompanied on average by a 1.45 percentage point incremental decline in the four-seller concentration ratio.[60] Later work has related concentration changes to market growth, holding constant other relevant variables such as the initial concentration level, market size, and the degree of product differentiation. For 165 comparable U.S. manufacturing industries over the years 1947–1977, Mueller and Rogers estimated that the four-firm concentration ratio declined 0.7 percentage points for each 100 percentage point increase in current-dollar value added.[61] The changes were modest, and one may agree with W.G. Shepherd that "it would take a thumping amount of growth to reduce concentration by even a sliver."[62] Yet without the thumping amounts of growth actually experienced, there would have been a stronger upward trend in concentration.

Economies of Multiplant Operation

Although seller concentration increases with the need to operate plants that are large relative to the served market, this is not the only, or perhaps even the main, cause of high concentration. That other influences are at work is shown by the fact that the leading firms in most industries operate multiple plants supplying a similar array of products. The most complete data on multiplant operation patterns in U.S. manufacturing come from the 1963 census. No material changes appear to have occurred since then.[63] Table 4.4 presents the distribution of 417 four-digit industries according to the average number of relevant plants per Big Four seller. (The count excludes warehouses, separate R&D laboratories, headquarters and sales offices, and plants specializing in the products of industries other than the one for which plants are tallied.) In the median industry, the leading sellers averaged 3.25 plants each. The leaders operated a single plant each in only twenty-two industries, or 5 percent of all industries.

Table 4.4   Extent of Multiplant Operation in 417 U.S. Manufacturing
Industries, 1963

Plants per Big Four Member	Number of Industries	Percent of Industries
1.00 to 1.5	78	18.7
1.75 to 2.5	89	21.3
2.75 to 4.0	87	20.9
4.25 to 7.0	87	20.9
7.25 to 10	28	6.7
10.25 to 20	35	8.4
More than 20	13	3.1
All industries	417	100.0

Source: Senate Committee on the Judiciary, Subcommittee on Antitrust and Monopoly, report, *Concentration Ratios in Manufacturing Industry: 1963,* Part 2 (Washington: 1967), Table 27.

Evidently, the preeminent position of most leading firms must be attributed not merely to maintaining large plants, but to operating many of them.[64] From this it does not necessarily follow that high concentration and extensive multiplant operation are strongly associated. In fact, there is little systematic difference in the extent of multiplant operation between leading firms in highly concentrated industries, as compared to those in more atomistic industries. This is shown by the tabulation of 1963 U.S. data in Table 4.5. Leading firms in industries with concentration ratios in the 20 to 39 range operated slightly more plants on average than leaders in the most highly concentrated industries. The most that can be said is that if the industry leaders in both concentrated and atomistically structured industries operated fewer plants, all else equal, there would be less concentration across the board.[65]

57. For an earlier study yielding similar results, see Ralph L. Nelson, *Concentration in the Manufacturing Industries of the United States* (New Haven: Yale University Press, 1963), pp. 46–48.

58. Scherer et al., *Multi-Plant Operation,* supra note 22, pp. 193–194.

59. Scherer et al., *Multi-Plant Operation,* pp. 222–223.

60. Nelson, *Concentration in the Manufacturing Industries,* supra note 57, pp. 52–56.

61. W. F. Mueller and R. T. Rogers, "Changes in Market Concentration of Manufacturing Industries, 1947–1977," *Review of Industrial Organization,* vol. 1 (Spring 1984), p. 6. See also the many similar studies referenced in note 112 infra.

62. Testimony of W. G. Shepherd, Senate Committee on the Judiciary, Subcommittee on Antitrust and Monopoly, hearings, *Economic Concentration,* Part 2 (Washington: 1965), p. 639.

63. See Edward Miller, "Size of Firm and Size of Plant," *Southern Economic Journal,* vol. 44 (April 1978), pp. 863–864.

64. However, the four industry leaders also operate larger plants than their followers — in 1972, fourteen times as large on average as all non-Big Four firms and 2.4 times those of the fifth through eighth largest sellers. See Miller, "Size of Firm and Size of Plant," pp. 867–869.

65. Needless to say, multiunit operation is also extensive among the leading firms in the retail trades. In 1982, the leading four U.S. companies operated an average of 1,188 stores each in food retailing, 937 each in the department store field, 1,024 in drugs, 965 in gasoline retailing, and 190 in the retailing of musical records and tapes. U.S. Bureau of the Census, *1982 Census of Retail Trade,* "Establishment and Firm Size," RC82–I–1 (Washington: February 1985), Table 6.

Table 4.5   The Relationship between Seller Concentration and the Extent
of Multiplant Operation

Four-Firm National Concentration Ratio Range	Number of Industries	Average Number of Plants per Company		
		Four Leaders	Next Four	Rest of Industry
1–19	90	4.4	2.7	1.03
20–39	162	6.1	3.5	1.07
40–64	103	4.7	2.4	1.08
65–100	62	5.9	2.2	1.09

Source: Senate Committee on the Judiciary, Subcommittee on Antitrust and Monopoly, report, *Concentration Ratios in Manufacturing Industry: 1963*, Part 2 (Washington: 1966), Table 27.

The crucial remaining question is, does multiplant operation by leading firms confer economies above and beyond those associated with operating a single plant of optimal scale? And, if so, how significant are they? Or to reverse the focus, how seriously disadvantaged are firms operating only a single MES plant compared to the larger multiplant enterprises?

We shall organize our analysis into three main categories — economies of multiplant production, investment, and physical distribution; economies of risk-spreading and finance; and advantages of sales promotion on a multiplant scale. As we shall see, these have varying performance implications, some entailing clear-cut efficiency gains, some redistributions of income, and some a blend of efficiency, redistributive, and monopoly effects. Two other sets of possible consequences must be dealt with summarily.

For one, economies of scale in conducting research and development may persist into a size range embracing multiple least-cost plants. This possibility is so important that much of Chapter 17 will be devoted to it. We defer further discussion until then.

Second, a multiplant enterprise may be able to economize on management services by having a common central pool of financial planners, accountants, market researchers, labor relations specialists, purchasing agents, lawyers, and the like. There is statistical evidence that size, both absolute and relative, does yield overhead cost savings. For 132 U.S. manufacturing industries, it was possible to secure data on 1977 "general and administrative" costs as a fraction of the reporting companies' sales.[66] These included costs directly traceable to the operating units, averaging 4.82 percent of sales, and those allocated from a common corporate cost pool, averaging 1.48 percent of sales. That cost variable was related through multiple regression to three explanatory variables:

SALES   Logarithm$_{10}$ of industry sales (in thousands)

OPINC   Industry operating income (a measure of profit) as a percentage of sales

CR4   Industry four-firm seller concentration ratio

The resulting regression equation was:

$$(4.1) \quad \text{G\&A} = 13.66 - 1.336 \ \text{SALES} + 0.192 \ \text{OPINC} - 0.022 \ \text{CR4}; \ R^2 = .19;$$
$$\quad (4.85) \quad (2.90) \quad\quad (3.86) \quad\quad\quad (2.13)$$

with t-ratios given in subscripted parentheses. The general and administrative cost burden is lighter in larger industries and heavier in more profitable industries. But most relevant for present purposes, it is smaller in more concentrated industries. On average, moving from an industry with a four-firm concentration ratio of 40 to one with CR4 of 80 reduces the G&A/Sales percentage by 0.90 points, or by 14 percent of the average industry value. Thus, savings appear to come both from operating in large industries and having relatively large shares of a given industry's sales.

However, there is also evidence that decision-making is slower in large enterprises and that transmitting incentives through a complex multiplant organizational structure is more difficult. Interviews with 125 manufacturing firms in six nations suggested that on balance, the managerial and central staff economies associated with multiplant operation were slight, and that in many instances, organizational size beyond some modest multiplant threshold was disadvantageous.[67] Still on this point our knowledge is modest, and much more remains to be learned.

To begin analyzing how multiplant operation affects the costs of production, investment, and physical distribution, it is useful to identify three distinct cases (recognizing of course that hybrids also exist). First is the situation in which a market of considerable geographic expanse is served, and outbound transportation costs are appreciable.[68] Then the firm's least-cost strategy is likely to entail operating multiple geographically dispersed plants, each supplying for the most part only the customers nearest its location. The operating patterns of sizable companies in the cement, petroleum refining, beer, and glass bottle industries provide relatively pure examples. Second is the case of firms with low shipping costs (for example, less than 1.5 percent of plant sales on 350-mile deliveries) but complex product lines. Then each plant of a multiplant enterprise may specialize in some narrow segment of the product array — for example, one plant in women's cemented-sole fashion shoes, another in women's casuals, a third in men's Goodyear welts, a fourth in work shoes, and so on. The third case is a catchall to cover enterprises with multiple plants joined together more or less randomly, usually by merger, without any attempt to enforce either geographic or product specialization. Such combinations are not likely to provide production or distribution economies and can therefore be ignored.

If delivery costs are substantial, as they are for beer or cement or steel reinforcing bars, it is obviously more economical, if one is to serve a large market like the continental United States or the European Community, to have multiple dispersed plants than to ship everything from one giant, centrally located establishment. But this begs the fundamental question: Why does a firm have to serve the

66. F. M. Scherer, "Antitrust, Efficiency, and Progress," *New York University Law Review,* vol. 62 (November 1987), pp. 1004–1006.

67. See Scherer et al., *Multi-Plant Operation,* supra note 22, pp. 321–325, 335, and 339–340.

68. A variant involves plants tied by high input shipping costs or processing weight losses to geographically dispersed raw material sources of modest size. Uranium milling, pulp mills, and tomato canning are examples.

entire geographic expanse? Are there production, investment, and/or distribution cost differences between the situation in which a single company operates five least-cost, geographically dispersed plants and the one in which five independent geographically dispersed firms operate a single MES plant each?

There may be. When demand grows over time and when scale economies can be realized by expanding capacity in large indivisible chunks, excess capacity carrying costs can be reduced, and the scale economy opportunities can be exploited more fully, by playing a kind of investment whipsaw game.[69] First a large investment is made at location A, with other plants reducing their shipping radii to satisfy growing nearby demand more fully and letting plant A serve what would normally be their peripherally located customers. Later, plant B expands and territories are readjusted to utilize its new capacity, and so on. Transportation costs are higher under this coordinated investment staging scheme than with autarkic expansion by each individual plant, jointly or independently owned, but investment carrying costs may be lower by a more than offsetting amount. However, such a scheme will not yield net savings if the individual plants can cover temporary capacity deficits by buying from recently expanded *nearby* competitors at prices approximating marginal cost and if they can sell excess postexpansion supplies to such competitors, or if *local* supply and demand can be equilibrated by charging high prices before major expansions and lower prices immediately thereafter. The more smoothly local markets work in facilitating adjustment to capacity jumps, the smaller are the benefits from coordinated multiplant, multiregion investment staging. In other words, such investment coordination economies are of a second-best character, realizable because local markets fail to balance demand and supply.

Economies may also result from the operation of multiple geographically dispersed plants as an integrated system. For instance, the demand for automobile batteries peaks during the winter months in the northern United States and during the summer in the South. A firm with plants in both areas might be able to maintain less peak-load capacity by shipping north in the winter and south in the summer. In practice, however, this was not normally done in the early 1970s, largely because the costs of carrying additional capacity were less than cross-shipping costs.[70] Similarly, when the short-run average variable cost curve slopes downward at low outputs, production cutbacks in response to a general demand slump can be accomplished more economically by shutting down one or more whole plants in an integrated network than by reducing output at each of many independent plants.[71] Again, this is infrequently observed, in part because cost curves fail to have the requisite shapes and in part because the desire to retain skilled workers argues for spreading the impact of cutbacks rather than concentrating it geographically.[72] As a third illustration, an integrated truck or barge fleet may be used to fuller capacity by coordinating backhauls among several plants or, when shipping costs are not so high as to require plant dispersion, by consolidating the output of several plants to secure lower full truckload or carload rates from common carriers. Numerous cases of this sort were uncovered in interviews with 125 companies. For the most part, however, the savings were small.[73]

The other main interesting mode of multiplant operation occurs when plants specialize in some narrow slice of a product array — for example, small mass-produced ball bearings at one plant, other small ball bearings at a second, large ball bearings at a third, tapered bearings at a fourth, and so on. Plants with a narrow line of products are easier to manage. For a plant of given size, production run lengths will be greater, and hence product-specific economies will be realized more fully, the narrower the line manufactured is. The key interpretive questions are, can the same degree of plant specialization be achieved by single-plant firms choosing to offer only a narrow range of products? And are the plants of multiplant sellers in fact more narrowly specialized than those of single-plant firms?

In answer to the first question, it appears that at least in some industries, there are marketing advantages to being a broad-line supplier. This in turn argues for multiplant operation unless one's product line can be rounded out through purchases from other manufacturers — that is, either from local competitors or perhaps from noncompeting foreign firms. Among twelve industries studied in depth, the compulsions toward broad-line manufacturing were strongest in refrigerators, bearings, and fabrics.[74]

The second question in effect asks whether single-plant producers in multiproduct industries incur not only a marketing disadvantage by failing to offer a broad line, but also cram relatively more low-volume products into the production plans of their only plant and therefore sacrifice product-specific economies as well. Some single-plant firms do experience shorter production runs than their multiplant rivals. However, many exceptions exist, and the shorter runs of some relatively small firms may signify nothing more than deliberate specialization on the low-volume items in which the larger companies have no interest — for example, because their management structures are too hierarchical to cope with the challenges of small-lot production. From the limited evidence available, multiplant size and the attainment of product-specific economies do not appear to be closely correlated. In Canada, where the smallness of the national market often forces companies to operate relatively small plants packed with many individual products, a statistical analysis showed no tendency for industries with high levels of multiplant operation to have more complex within-plant product assortments.[75] In the United States, many large multiplant firms appear to be large because they produce commensurately more products than single-plant rivals, not because they produce a given array of products in higher volume.[76] Nevertheless, the overall picture is quite complex, and we must conclude that there is insufficient hard evidence on this important dimension of multiplant scale economies.

69. See Scherer et al., *Multi-Plant Operation,* pp. 40–48, 143–147, and 290–295, drawing upon the theory developed in Alan S. Manne, ed., *Investments for Capacity Expansion* (Cambridge: MIT Press, 1967).

Analogous to such investment coordination economies are network economies in operating a telephone system, airline, or pickup and delivery system. See Dennis W. Carlton and J. Mark Klamer, "The Need for Coordination Among Firms, with Special Reference to Network Industries," *University of Chicago Law Review,* vol. 50 (Spring 1983), pp. 446–465.

70. Scherer et al., *Multi-Plant Operation,* p. 277.

71. See Don Patinkin, "Multi-Plant Firms, Cartels, and Imperfect Competition," *Quarterly Journal of Economics,* vol. 61 (February 1947), pp. 173–205; and Edward L. Sattler and Robert C. Scott,

"Price and Output Adjustments in the Two-Plant Firm," *Southern Economic Journal,* vol. 48 (April 1982), pp. 1042–1048.

72. Scherer et al., *Multi-Plant Operation,* supra note 22, pp. 280–282.

73. Ibid., pp. 271–274.

74. Ibid., pp. 256–257.

75. Baldwin and Gorecki, "The Relationship between Plant Scale and Product Diversity," supra note 9, p. 376. See also Richard E. Caves, *Diversification, Foreign Investment, and Scale in North American Manufacturing Industries* (Ottawa: Economic Council of Canada, 1975), especially Chapters 5 and 6.

76. Scherer et al., *Multi-Plant Operation,* supra note 22, pp. 316–321.

Capital-Raising Economies

Economies of scale are also encountered when firms raise capital through borrowing and common stock issues. Indeed, this appears to be one of the most persistent advantages of corporate size, with small incremental capital cost savings being enjoyed out to very large scales. A study of debt costs in the 1960s revealed that corporations with assets of $200 million borrowed funds at an average interest rate 0.74 percentage points lower than firms with assets of $5 million. Billion-dollar corporations enjoyed a 0.34-point incremental advantage over their $200 million asset counterparts.[77] At the time, interest rates on long-term Baa corporate bonds averaged 5.5 percent; thus, the savings were substantial in relative terms. Smaller firms pay higher capital costs because they tend to issue new securities in smaller quantities, so that nearly fixed transactions costs are higher per dollar raised, and because, once issued, their securities elicit a less favorable reaction from investors. Archer and Faerber analyzed the transaction costs of 238 common stock issues floated between 1960 and 1962 by corporations of widely varying sizes. Flotation costs ranged from 5 to 44 percent of the total value of the shares sold, varying inversely with both the size of the issue and the size of the issuing company.[78]

Investors demand higher returns from the securities of small corporations as compared to large corporations for several reasons, the most important of which centers on differences in perceived riskiness. Statistical investigations reveal that profitability varies less over time for large individual corporations than for smaller concerns. The standard deviation of annual earnings before tax plus interest as a percentage of assets over the 1960–1968 time period varied on average as follows with respect to the size of 768 U.S. corporations for which complete data were available:[79]

Asset Size	Standard Deviation
$10 million	6.8%
$100 million	4.1%
$1 billion	1.4%

The greater intertemporal stability of large corporations' earnings has at least three possible explanations. First, large multiplant firms may possess more monopoly power than smaller enterprises, all else equal. One consequence may be the ability to pursue an earnings-stabilizing pricing policy. Second, large firms appear more prone to smooth reported earnings through various accounting manipulations. Third, the ability to spread risks increases with size. The effect of a major fire, explosion, or localized wildcat strike is apt to be less devastating for a company with numerous plants than for the single-plant operator. Large multiplant enterprises are likely to offer more distinct products and/or serve more geographic markets, perhaps extending to overseas ventures, and this makes them better able to weather a price war, exchange rate shock, or the loss of an important customer in any single product segment.[80]

The risk-spreading and monopolistic advantages of size work to some extent at cross-purposes, for if the overall sales volume is held constant, one's share in any given narrowly defined market must be inversely correlated with the number of markets or product lines one supplies. Moreover, the less closely related those markets are, the less monopoly power the firm is likely to have, but the greater the earnings stabilization effect will be. To see this, note that the standard deviation of total profits for a firm operating in two markets is given by:

$$(4.2) \qquad \sigma_F = \sqrt{\sigma_1^2 + \sigma_2^2 + 2r\,\sigma_1\,\sigma_2}$$

where σ_1 is the standard deviation of profits in market 1, σ_2 the standard deviation of profits in market 2, and r is the coefficient of correlation between profit movements over time in the two markets. Suppose each market is served by a distinct plant, and for each market the expected (that is, best-guess) value of profits is $1 million per year, with a standard deviation of $400,000. If the plants are organized as independent firms, each finds the standard deviation of its profits to be 40 percent of the mean. If the two markets are influenced so similarly by demand and cost conditions that profit fluctuations between them are perfectly correlated over time, with r $= +1.0$, then combining the two plants into a single multiplant firm will leave the standard deviation at 40 percent of expected profits.[81] But the more different or conglomerate the markets are, the lower their intertemporal earnings correlation r will be. When there is a completely random relationship between profit changes across the two markets, r $= 0$ and $\sigma_F \cong \$566,000$, or roughly 28 percent of expected combined profits. The more markets with randomly related demand and cost movements the firm serves, ceteris paribus, the more its risks will be spread, and the smaller will be the standard deviation of profits as a percentage of expected or average profits.[82]

77. Ibid., p. 287. See also Rudolph C. Blitz, Ben Bolch, Paul Laux, and John Siegfried, "The Effect of Market Structure on the Cost of Borrowing," in Robert L. Wills et al., eds., *Issues After a Century of Federal Competition Policy* (Lexington, MA: Lexington Books, 1987), pp. 333–343; and U.S. Small Business Administration, *The State of Small Business: A Report of the President, 1987* (Washington: USGPO, 1987), pp. 72–91.

78. S. H. Archer and L. G. Faerber, "Firm Size and the Cost of Externally Secured Capital," *Journal of Finance,* vol. 21 (March 1966), pp. 69–83. See also Victor L. Andrews and Peter C. Eisemann, "Who Finances Small Business in the 1980s?", in Paul M. Horvitz and R.R. Pettit, eds., *Small Business Finance* (Greenwich, CT: JAI Press, 1984), pp. 75–96; and Jay R. Ritter, "The Costs of Going Public," *Journal of Financial Economics,* vol. 19 (December 1987), pp. 269–281.

79. These figures were computed using data kindly supplied by Daryl N. Winn and originally analyzed in his article, "On the Relations Between Rates of Return, Risk, and Market Structure," *Quarterly Journal of Economics,* vol. 91 (February 1977), pp. 157–163. They are derived from a regression equation relating the standard deviation of pretax earnings *plus* interest *divided by* assets to the base ten logarithm of assets. The relationship was not precisely log linear, so the estimate for $1 billion corporations is probably biased on the low side.

In "The Effects of Multinational and Export Diversification on the Profit Stability of U.S. Corporations," *Southern Economic*

Journal, vol. 46 (January 1980), pp. 792–805, Joseph C. Miller and Bernard Pras find the stability of profits over time to increase with asset size and diversification into activities abroad, but not with domestic product line diversification. See also Geoffrey Whittington, "The Profitability and Size of United Kingdom Companies, 1960–74," *Journal of Industrial Economics,* vol. 29 (June 1980), pp. 345–349; and for references to earlier studies, the second edition of this volume, p. 105, note 82.

80. For relevant theory, see Björn Wahlroos, "On the Economics of Multiplant Operation: Some Concepts and Extensions," *Journal of Industrial Economics,* vol. 29 (March 1981), pp. 231–245; and David de Meza and Frederick van der Ploeg, "Production Flexibility as a Motive for Multinationality," *Journal of Industrial Economics,* vol. 35 (March 1987), pp. 343–351.

81. The firm's combined profit standard deviation is:

$$\sigma_F = \sqrt{400{,}000^2 + 400{,}000^2 + (2 \times 1 \times 400{,}000^2)}$$
$$= \sqrt{4 \times 400{,}000^2} = 2 \times \$400{,}000$$

Combining the two markets leads not only to doubled profit expectations but also a doubled standard deviation.

82. When r $= 0$ and the individual markets are of identical size, the ratio of the σ_F to the expected value of total firm profits declines by the ratio $1/\sqrt{N}$ with increases in N, the number of markets served.

The variability of profits affects firms' capital cost because investors tend to be risk-averse. They will invest their capital at lower interest rates or dividend expectations — and hence a lower cost of capital to the firm — if they expect the profits or cash flow stream from which they will draw to be stable than if they expect it to be highly variable over time. This is so for at least two reasons.

First, with an extremely variable profit or cash flow profile, there is a greater chance that one or two particularly bad years will plunge the firm into bankruptcy, leaving it unable to cover the interest service on its debt and perhaps wiping out common stock investors' equity.

Second, investors' utility appears to decline with increased variation of returns over time even when bankruptcy is avoided. The exact nature of the capital market risk-reward tradeoff is unclear. One theoretical explanation, widely accepted by corporate finance specialists despite significant empirical anomalies, is the *capital asset pricing model,* or CAPM (pronounced Cap-M). It derives mathematically the logic of risk-averse investors' attempts to maximize their utility by acquiring a financial holdings portfolio with the optimal mix of risky and risk-free assets. Risk is measured operationally as the variability over time in returns to financial investments. As a first approximation, the more a given security's return (that is, the year-to-year change in its market price plus dividends payments) fluctuates, the more risky it is said to be. But investors can insure against certain individual security risks by holding a portfolio with numerous securities, and so at a deeper level of subtlety, the riskiness of a particular security depends upon how its returns over time affect the riskiness and expected return from their complete portfolio. The size of the risk premium $E(P_i)$ for the ith company's security is expressed by the formula:

$$(4.3) \qquad E(P_i) \;=\; \beta_i \, [E(R_m) \;-\; R_F]$$

where $E(R_m)$ is the expected return from a portfolio of all risky assets traded in securities markets, R_F is the rate of interest on riskless securities (for example, short-term government notes), the difference between them is the overall *market* risk premium, and β_i (known to many investors as *beta*) is a coefficient reflecting the so-called *systematic* or *undiversifiable* risk associated with security i. From the underlying mathematical theory, it is readily ascertained that:

$$(4.4) \qquad \beta_i \;=\; r_{im} \;[\, \sigma_i \,/\, \sigma_m \,]$$

where r_{im} is the correlation over time between the returns on security i and the entire market portfolio, σ_i is the standard deviation of security i's returns over time, and σ_m is the standard deviation of the market portfolio's returns. The larger r_{im} is, the more closely ups and downs in security i's returns are synchronized with those of the broader market portfolio, and so the more difficult it is to combine security i with other stocks in one's portfolio and achieve a reduction in *combined* variability through risk pooling. In other words, one cannot readily diversify against risk correlated with the market's aggregate risks. Therefore, the higher r_{im} is, the larger will be the risk premium on security i, and hence the higher the cost of capital to company i will be, all else equal.

Also, for a given r_{im}, the higher the ratio of company i's standard deviation σ_i is relative to the market portfolio standard deviation σ_m, the larger the risk coefficient β_i will be, and so the higher the company's cost of capital will be. The magnitude of β_i is in part related to fundamentals: that is, the more variable a company's earnings are over time, the more variable its stock market returns are likely to be.[83] As we have seen, the variability of earnings declines with greater company size; and as we shall document further in Chapter 11, it also declines with higher concentration of the markets within which a company operates. We therefore expect company β_i values to decline with greater size and concentration — a prediction that is borne out by the evidence.[84] This helps explain why smaller firms pay more for their capital.

The story remains incomplete, however. Quantitative research has shown that small firms pay even more for their common stock capital than one would predict, applying the capital asset pricing model's β_i to account for stock price variability and the correlation of returns with overall market movements.[85] Various explanations have been proposed for this small-firm premium: a tendency for the markets of smaller companies' stocks to be thinner, leading to higher bid/ask differentials; the greater risk of total failure through bankruptcy in small companies; the tendency of stock analysts and investors to devote more research to, and know more about, the securities of larger companies; prudent investor rules (relaxed in the 1970s) that discouraged pension funds from investing in other than blue-chip securities; and (in the 1980s) the growth of index funds including only the Standard & Poors 500 stocks or some other collection of large-firm stocks, implicitly discriminating against the securities of smaller enterprises. For whatever the reason, small firms pay more — for example, averaging the 1964–1978 estimates assembled by Reinganum and Smith, 2 percentage points more annually on common stock outstanding for each move to the next smaller size decile through the first- to sixth-highest deciles, and much more moving from the ninth to the tenth (smallest) size decile.[86]

83. See Donald J. Thompson, "Sources of Systematic Risk in Common Stocks," *Journal of Business,* vol. 49 (April 1976), pp. 173–188; and Robert Jacobson, "The Validity of ROI as a Measure of Business Performance," *American Economic Review,* vol. 77 (June 1987), pp. 470–477.

84. See Timothy G. Sullivan, "The Cost of Capital and the Market Power of Firms," *Review of Economics and Statistics,* vol. 60 (May 1973), pp. 209–217; Anthony J. Curley, J. Lawrence Hexter, and Dosoung Choi, "The Cost of Capital and the Market Power of Firms: A Comment," with reply by Sullivan, *Review of Economics and Statistics,* vol. 64 (August 1982), pp. 519–525; John T. Scott, "The Pure Capital-Cost Barrier to Entry," *Review of Economics and Statistics,* vol. 63 (August 1981), pp. 444–446; and The-Hiep Nguyen and Gilles Bernier, "Beta and q in a Simultaneous Framework with Pooled Data," *Review of Economics and Statistics,* vol. 70 (August 1988), pp. 520–523.

85. For a survey of the literature, see G. William Schwert, "Size and Stock Returns, and Other Empirical Regularities," *Journal of Financial Economics,* vol. 12 (June 1983), pp. 3–12, and the seven papers that follow the survey. See also K. C. Chan, Nai-fu Chen, and David A. Hsieh, "An Exploratory Investigation of the Firm Size Effect," *Journal of Financial Economics,* vol. 14 (September 1985), pp. 451–471.

86. Marc R. Reinganum and Janet K. Smith, "Investor Preference for Large Firms: New Evidence on Economies of Size," *Journal of Industrial Economics,* vol. 32 (December 1983), pp. 213–227. The larger jump in returns for the smallest size decile may come spuriously from classifying companies by the market value of their stock. If the depression was viewed as random and temporary, those with the most severely depressed stock prices may tend also to have particularly high earnings/price ratios. Median market value per company ranged from $4.7 million for the smallest size decile to $1.09 billion for the largest.

In a similar but earlier study using 1961–1969 data, W. W. Alberts and S. H. Archer found annual stock returns to vary from 8.7 percent for companies with mean assets of $6.3 billion to 32.1 percent for companies with mean assets of $5 million. "Some Evidence on the Effect of Company Size on the Cost of Equity Capital," *Journal of Financial and Quantitative Analysis,* vol. 8 (March 1973), pp. 229–242.

Evaluating the welfare implications of these capital-raising scale economies is peculiarly difficult. They are at least in part redistributions of wealth — small company XYZ pays more for its capital, and investor Jones earns more from an investment in XYZ. If so, no real resource saving results, unlike the case in which ABC Company builds its giant petrochemical plant with less steel and instrumentation per ton of capacity than XYZ's small plant. We call such strictly redistributive savings benefitting the larger company *pecuniary economies* to distinguish them from the *real economies* resulting when resources are actually saved.[87] To be sure, for investor Jones, some subjective anguish may be incurred if investing in small companies is riskier than investing in the giants. But if Jones is able to assemble a portfolio of securities that cancels out all but the nondiversifiable risks of general macroeconomic fluctuations, investing in many small XYZs may entail no appreciable added risk burden. Then XYZ pays more while Jones receives more without accepting added risk. Moreover, the resulting wealth redistribution favors those who are already wealthy. In 1983, the top 2 percent of U.S. families ranked in terms of annual income owned 50 percent of all personally held corporate stocks; the top 10 percent held 70 percent.[88] Mitigating the inequities from such redistributions is the increasing tendency for corporate stocks to be held by pension funds, whose benefits flow to a much broader cross section of the population. In 1986, nearly 21 percent of all U.S. corporate common stocks were held by pension funds, and another 5 percent were held by insurance companies.[89] Thus, small firms pay more for their capital and the average wage earner retires more comfortably.

The capital asset pricing model assumes that firms raise their capital in perfect markets, that is, that the interest or earnings pledged per million dollars is the same, whether a million dollars or a half billion dollars are raised. This too is not entirely true. A corporation with assets of $500 million might be able to borrow $50 million at very close to the prime rate, but if it tries to double its assets in a short time frame by borrowing, it will have to pay a steep interest premium, and it might even be unable to find any willing lenders.[90] In a historical variation on this theme, Lance Davis has argued that the rapid growth of industrial concentration in the United States was partly the result of capital market imperfections, giving rise to an environment in which only a few entrepreneurs with especially good banking connections (such as Carnegie, Swift, and Rockefeller) could mobilize the capital sums required to exploit opportunities opened up by market growth and technological change.[91] British industry experienced less concentration during the same period, Davis continues, because capital was more widely accessible. The trend toward rising U.S. concentration ebbed in the early twentieth century as capital markets were perfected.

One final point must be mentioned. Because of its access to capital on superior terms, the large firm may have greater staying power in periods of unusually sharp competition. This advantage includes the ability to weather a severe business recession and to finance predatory ventures such as price wars and lengthy court battles over patent rights. We shall have more to say about such activities in later chapters.

Economies of Large-Scale Promotion

Economies of large-scale promotion and marketing also pose analytic difficulties. One complication is the element of chance associated with sales promotion. A massive advertising campaign may be a spectacular success or a resounding flop, depending upon the ingenuity and luck of the Madison Avenue people in charge. Second, promotional economies of scale may show up not only in the form of lower costs but also in the ability of firms to charge prices higher than those of smaller rivals for comparable products, or in some combination of price premiums and cost savings. Thus, both cost curves and demand curves are affected. Third, and because of the demand curve effect, the benefits realized through large-scale promotion may not redound to the public. It is not clear that consumers gain when one firm's monopoly power is bolstered by a successful promotional campaign, or whether bleary-eyed television viewers are better off from the barrage of messages to which they are subjected. These are matters of considerable controversy, and we shall progress best by dodging them for the present and scheduling a fuller debate in Chapter 16. Here we confine ourselves to the narrower question, To what extent is market structure affected by the private advantages of sales promotion?

Even there, no simple answer can be provided. In his pioneering study of twenty American industries, Joe S. Bain concluded that product differentiation was "of at least the same general order of importance . . . as economies of large-scale production and distribution" in giving established market leaders a price or cost advantage over rivals, and especially over new entrants.[92] However, a later twelve-industry study found that although product differentiation was very important, firms with only a single plant of efficient scale were by no means barred from success.[93] In several industries, single-plant enterprises were able to promote their products on virtually equal terms, realizing all or most scale economies; and in others they could find sizable market segments in which to operate profitably despite a promotional handicap.

To explore further the reasons for these disparate conclusions, let us begin by focusing on advertising, which Bain found to be the most important single basis of large-firm advantages.

One possible source of scale economies is the need to attain a certain threshold level of advertising messages before reaching maximum effectiveness. There are two main reasons why this might be so. First, the average consumer's behavior may not be influenced by a single message, whereas five or six delivered messages (out of a possibly larger number sent) are likely to induce action, if advertising is

87. Pecuniary economies may also be realized when large firms extract from purchased input suppliers volume discounts not associated with any real savings gained by supplying in larger quantities. See Scherer et al., *Multi-Plant Operation*, supra note 22, pp. 260–262.

88. Robert B. Avery et al., "Survey of Consumer Finances, 1983," *Federal Reserve Bulletin*, vol. 70 (September 1984), pp. 687–689.

89. These estimates are from the Flow of Funds section, Federal Reserve System Board of Governors.

90. This in part reflects the "principle of increasing risk" articulated by Michal Kalecki in an article with the same title, *Economica*, vol. 4 (November 1937), pp. 440–447.

91. Lance Davis, "The Capital Markets and Industrial Concen-

tration: The U.S. and U.K., A Comparative Study," *Economic History Review*, vol. 19 (August 1966), pp. 255–272.

92. *Barriers to New Competition*, supra note 41, pp. 142–143 and 216.

93. See Scherer et al., *Multi-Plant Operation*, supra note 22, p. 258. See also Kenneth D. Boyer and Kent M. Lancaster, "Are There Scale Economies in Advertising?" *Journal of Business*, vol. 59 (July 1986), pp. 509–526, who find no evidence of lower advertising costs per sales dollar for brands or firms with larger sales. On cigarettes, which may be exceptional either substantively or in the precision of effects measurement, see Randall S. Brown, "Estimating Advantages to Large-Scale Advertising," *Review of Economics and Statistics*, vol. 60 (August 1978), pp. 428–437.

able to do so at all.[94] Second, when advertising messages are communicated further by word of mouth and peer influence, conditions analogous to those governing chain reactions or the spread of epidemics may apply.[95] A small impulse soon peters out, but one that affects a sufficiently large initial critical mass spreads rapidly and covers a large segment of the population. To the extent that either of these two models of advertising effectiveness is valid, there must exist an advertising response function of the logistic shape illustrated in Figure 4.5. Over the range AB the threshold (no doubt varying for different consumers) is being approached and surmounted, and the sales generated by an additional message rise. But beyond point B average returns fall, at first slowly and then (if oversaturation can occur) precipitously.

Whether there is in fact an increasing returns stage AB in advertising response functions is debated,[96] but even if there is, it alone is not enough to imply an advertising cost advantage for larger firms. If all firms face essentially the same response function, all will find it profitable to carry their advertising to approximately the threshold level B if they advertise at all, and all will thereby enjoy similar sales responses.[97] For economies of scale to exist, there must be some further interacting set of circumstances conferring an advantage upon larger firms — for example, by letting them have different and more favorably configured response functions. This may stem from consumer inertia or from physical barriers to the rapid expansion of sales. For example, one supermarket chain may for a variety of historical reasons operate fifty stores in some metropolitan area, another chain only fifteen. Most of both chains' customers are apt to be tied by force of habit or familiarity with store layout to their regular shopping locales; only a small fraction are movable in any given short period by advertising. And if either chain did attract new customers very rapidly through advertising, congestion would build up in its aisles, curbing patronage gains. The large chain may therefore face a response function like LR_1 in Figure 4.6 while the small chain faces SR_2. If both must send approximately OX advertising messages to achieve a threshold level of awareness, the large chain will cover the population of switchable consumers *and* reinforce the purchasing habits of its (larger) group of regular patrons at a substantially lower advertising cost per sales dollar than the small chain.

Figure 4.5
Advertising Response Function

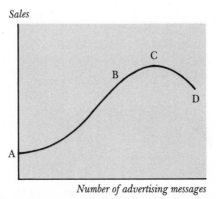

Sales

Number of advertising messages

Figure 4.6
Advertising Response
Functions for Large
and Small Firms

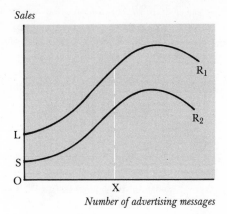

Number of advertising messages

The response functions facing firms of varying size may also differ because advertising has cumulative as well as current effects. It takes a long time to build an image and get consumers in the habit of requesting Kleenex® when what they want is absorbent facial tissue. In the short or medium run, the small firm trying to expand its sales of an essentially equivalent product through vigorous advertising runs into sharply diminishing returns long before it has achieved the size of the well-established sellers it is trying to displace. Even in the long run, equality of effect may be ruled out if more or less permanent marketing advantages accrue to *first movers* — firms that pioneered some product segment or managed through superior skill or luck to come up with a captivating product image, as Miller Lite did in the brewing industry during the 1970s. On this first mover phenomenon we shall have more to say in Chapters 16 and 17.

94. See "Advertising: Frequency and Effectiveness," *New York Times,* June 22, 1976, p. 57.

95. Stephen Glaister, "Advertising Policy and Returns to Scale Where Information Is Passed Between Individuals," *Economica,* vol. 41 (May 1974), pp. 139–156.

96. Julian L. Simon marshals compelling evidence for direct-mail and clip-out coupon methods that diminishing returns set in immediately. *Issues in the Economics of Advertising* (Urbana: University of Illinois Press, 1974), Chapter 1. For beer, there is persuasive experimental evidence of initially increasing returns. See Russell L. Ackoff and James R. Emshoff, "Advertising Research at Anheuser-Busch, Inc. (1963–68)," *Sloan Management Review,* vol. 17 (Winter 1975), pp. 1–15. For other evidence on response function shapes, see Jean-Jacques Lambin, *Advertising, Competition and Market Conduct in Oligopoly over Time* (Amsterdam: North-Holland, 1976), pp. 94–98 and 127–129; William S. Comanor and Thomas A. Wilson, *Advertising and Market Power* (Cambridge: Harvard University Press, 1974), pp. 49–53; and Robert L. Steiner, "Point of View: The Paradox of Increasing Returns in Advertising," *Journal of Advertising Research,* vol. 27 (February/March 1987), pp. 45–53.

97. This is only a heuristic approximation. More exactly, assume that the product price and unit production cost are fixed so that each additional unit of output sold yields a gross margin m, expressed as a ratio of sales. Let A be the number of advertising messages, S the dollar volume of sales $[= s(A)]$, and c the cost of an advertising message. Then the firm maximizes:

$$\pi = m\, s(A) - cA$$

Differentiating, $d\pi/dA = m\, ds/dA - c = 0$ at the maximum. Since ds/dA is the marginal revenue from advertising, this means that the marginal revenue from advertising net of production costs must be set equal to the cost of the marginal advertising message.

To illustrate further, let the advertising response function be characterized by the cubic equation:

$$S = 100 + 20\,A + 4\,A^2 - .333\,A^3,$$

which has the same shape as Figure 4.5 and a maximum (equivalent to point C) at A = 10. If m = 0.25 and c = 4, the profit-maximizing level of advertising is 8.47.

Economies of scale in marketing can also interact dynamically with production scale economies to magnify the handicap of smaller firms. Beer in the United States provides an example.[98] From the time of their reincarnation after the repeal of Prohibition in 1933, a few brewers — notably, Anheuser-Busch, Schlitz, Pabst, and Miller — chose to cultivate a nationwide "premium" image. They set their prices high relative to those of local and regional beers both to sustain that image and to cover the high costs of shipping throughout the nation from Midwestern breweries. But beginning in the 1950s, several things happened. The Big Four built or bought breweries on the East and West coasts, reducing transport costs and (with prices held roughly constant) providing more money to plow into advertising.[99] After a considerable lag, this, coupled with rising affluence and the desire of consumers to trade up to more prestigious beers, led to rapidly growing sales for the national premium sellers. That in turn permitted them to build additional new breweries which, by exploiting a combination of technological advances and scale-up economies, had much lower production costs per unit than those of regional brewers lacking premium image brands. With lower costs, the Big Four (joined later by Coors) could squeeze the premium-popular price differential, enhancing their market shares even more, which in turn permitted them to advertise more heavily in absolute terms than smaller regional rivals but at appreciably lower average outlays per sales dollar.[100] The upshot of these and related interacting developments was an increase in the four-firm concentration ratio in brewing from 21 in 1947 to 85 in 1987.

This overview has skipped over some potentially important tactical details. For one, with respect to what organizational unit are advertising scale economies realized? For supermarket chains, advertising strives to lure consumers into *stores,* but most advertising by consumer goods manufacturers is focused on individual *brands,* not plants or firms. When threshold effects apply in the latter case, they may have to be attained brand by brand, not at the aggregate firm level. Unless there are multibrand interactions, firm size may be irrelevant. Partly related questions are, how does the array of feasible media vary with firm size, and how in turn are costs affected? Giant, a Washington, DC, area retail grocery chain with the largest local market share, cannot sensibly advertise on nationwide network television or in national magazines. A&P, with a much smaller District of Columbia position but broader geographic compass, might.

Multibrand interactions can occur if a favorable reputation from one set of products (for example, Honda's motorcycles) spills over to other products (such as automobiles), or if the media offer discounts for combining a large volume of advertising, perhaps spanning multiple brands, in one place or time period. Discounts do exist. The *New York Times,* for example, offered general contract advertisers volume discounts of 5.5 percent in 1988 for buying the equivalent of one hundred weekday pages in a year as compared to one page.[101] A thirty-second television commercial cost only about twice as much as a ten-second insertion.[102] The discount gained by purchasing longer commercials might be dissipated through diminishing marginal effectiveness as the message drones on, but large advertisers avoid this problem by piggybacking messages for two or more distinct products (for example, for Procter & Gamble, detergent and disposable diapers) in a single bargain-priced time slot. Whether larger advertisers enjoyed further discounts from the television networks for buying an accumulation of insertions over the course of a year has been the subject of heated controversy.[103] The weight of evidence favors a conclusion that such discounts were at best erratic and small.

Potentially more important might be the savings nationwide advertisers enjoy by purchasing network time, which, depending upon the time of day and audience appeal, usually costs less than what one would pay securing the same coverage through individual station spot messages.[104] For regional firms, more costly spot messages may be the only practical option. There is, however, an offsetting consideration. Network advertising is less flexible than local spots; it cannot be adapted to individual market conditions — for example, to emphasize local markets where special sales campaigns are planned or to avoid cities where one has no distribution. Spot advertising offers sufficiently compelling flexibility benefits that some nationwide consumer goods makers employ it almost exclusively, while others use the networks for their base-line advertising and adjust to local market conditions through extensive spot purchases.[105] These considerations imply that the advertising cost disadvantage of regional firms is not nearly as serious as one might infer from comparing rates paid per thousand viewers. But there are undoubtedly cases in which the advertising rate structures do confer an appreciable advantage on larger national firms.

For industries like brewing with high product transportation costs, the chief advantage of multiplant operation may lie not so much in having a more attractive array of advertising options as in capitalizing fully on the image one enjoys. That is, somehow or other, certain products catch on, and once they do, the word spreads — more rapidly, the more mobile the host society is. As with Coors or Heineken beer, this can happen even without any advertising outside one's home territory. Once a product does gain an image transcending local market boundaries, that image is an asset whose full value is captured only through nationwide (or multinational[106]) distribution. If transportation costs are high, this in turn may require the operation of multiple decentralized plants.

A quite different advantage of large scale is sometimes enjoyed by the sellers of complex durable goods. Most consumers are unwilling to buy a particular new

98. Scherer et al., *Multi-Plant Operation,* supra note 22, pp. 248–249.

99. As price-production cost margins rise, there is an increase not only in wherewithal, but also incentive — a phenomenon conforming to the Dorfman-Steiner theorem, discussed further in Chapter 16. For data on the escalation of beer advertising in the early 1950s, see Charles F. Keithahn, *The Brewing Industry,* Federal Trade Commission staff report (Washington: December 1978), pp. 77–78.

100. See Douglas F. Greer, "Product Differentiation and Concentration in the Brewing Industry," *Journal of Industrial Economics,* vol. 19 (July 1971), p. 214.

101. *New York Times,* Advertising Rate Card effective January 1, 1988, p. 12.

102. Simon, *Issues in the Economics of Advertising,* supra note 96, p. 15; and Michael E. Porter, "Interbrand Choice, Media Mix and Market Performance," *American Economic Review,* vol. 66 (May 1976), p. 402.

103. The literature is large. For citations, see the second edition of this volume, p. 111, note 103.

104. See John L. Peterman, "Differences Between the Levels of Spot and Network Television Advertising Rates," *Journal of Business,* vol. 52 (October 1979), pp. 549–561; John C. Hilke and Philip B. Nelson, "An Empirical Note from Case Documents on the Economies of Network Television Advertising," *Review of Industrial Organization,* vol. 4 (Spring 1989), pp. 131–145.

105. Scherer et al., *Multi-Plant Operation,* supra note 22, pp. 247–253; and Hilke and Nelson, p. 133.

106. Richard E. Caves finds spreading the benefits from such intangible assets as a strong brand image or superior marketing skills to be a particularly important explanation of multinational operation. *Multinational Enterprise and Economic Analysis* (Cambridge: Cambridge University Press, 1982), pp. 3–7.

automobile or computer unless they are confident they can obtain prompt, reliable service not only at home, but wherever they may travel or relocate. This can give the manufacturer with a far-flung, high-quality dealer network a sales advantage, although whether it actually does so depends upon how distribution channels are organized. There are economies of scale at the sales and service establishment level. A certain minimum investment in training, specialized testing equipment, and spare parts is necessary. If sales and service outlets are limited to the products of a single manufacturer, for example, through franchise contracts, low-volume manufacturers may be able to maintain efficient outlets only in the larger cities. This can precipitate a vicious cycle as failure to build a strong nationwide service network limits smaller producers' sales, which in turn makes it all the more difficult for them to achieve scale economies at the service level. In the automobile industry, where annual sales of at least 600,000 units per year were needed to have a strong captive dealer network throughout the United States,[107] failure to achieve that volume contributed to the demise of Studebaker, Packard, American Motors, and many other manufacturers. However, the advantage of larger auto firms depended critically upon dealer exclusivity — that is, on a given dealer handling only the products of one manufacturer. As the tendency toward exclusivity broke down during the 1970s and 1980s, in part because foreign automakers supplied superior-quality small cars desired by dealers to round out their lines, the disadvantages of small national volume waned. Similarly, when each mainframe computer manufacturer had to deploy its own field service network, smaller manufacturers were at a disadvantage relative to IBM, whose high volume permitted it to pack geographic space more densely with service branches of efficient size.[108] But when an independent sales and service industry arose with the advent of personal computers, smaller computer makers were able efficiently to distribute their products through multimake outlets. As a partial result, IBM was exposed to much more competition in personal computers than in mainframes, and its market share was correspondingly smaller.

The auto industry also provides the premier example of a further scale economy arising out of the interaction between product differentiation and production. Since the late 1920s, when General Motors vaulted to U.S. industry leadership by changing its model designs frequently while Ford emphasized its unchanging Model T and Model A, periodic restyling has been an important element of interfirm rivalry. The cost of tooling required to stamp the sheet metal for a new exterior body design is considerable — from $16 to $35 million in 1972 for a small, simple car and much more since then because of inflation and growing complexity.[109] For a car line with a new chassis and drive train along with exterior body parts, start-up costs on the order of $700 million were required during the late 1970s.[110] The manufacturer able to spread the costs of this tooling over, say, ten million units in a six-year period enjoys a substantial unit cost advantage over the firm with a much smaller volume. This is in the first instance a product-specific economy of scale, although it may be enjoyed even more fully by manufacturers with multiple models designed to appear different, but using common metal stampings and drive train components "under the skin." With more different car lines selling in larger total volume than those of its domestic competitors, General Motors historically achieved greater common multimodel use of tooling than its rivals, and the cost savings achieved thereby contributed to its superior profitability.[111] However, GM's strategy was not without risks, for in the 1980s it pushed its quest for commonality to the point where its diverse offerings looked so much alike that sales were lost to domestic and foreign rivals appealing to increasingly diverse consumer tastes.

To sum up, in at least some industries, and especially in certain consumer goods industries, there are appreciable economies of scale in several aspects of sales promotion and product differentiation. These advantages of size can create imperatives for market concentration above the level required to realize all narrowly construed production and physical distribution economies.

Nevertheless, the product differentiation sword can also cut in the opposite direction. Through successful product differentiation, smaller firms may be able to carve out for themselves a small but profitable niche in some special segment of the market. Even in the automobile industry, where the disadvantages of small-scale production are so formidable, the makers of Rolls-Royce, Porsche, and copies of such 1930s classics as the Duesenberg and Cord have found viable niche-serving strategies.[112]

How the advantages and disadvantages of size in product differentiation balance out is as always a quantitative question. That modern promotional methods favor the larger seller is suggested by a series of studies relating changes in seller concentration over time to diverse measures of product differentiation potential along with more conventional explanatory variables such as market size, market growth, and initial concentration levels.[113] One striking and robust result is that since World War II, concentration in American manufacturing industries has tended to rise more rapidly in differentiated consumer goods industries than in industries whose products are purchased by knowledgeable business firm users. In the analysis covering the longest period of time, Mueller and Rogers found the following 1947–1977 four-firm concentration index changes and ending levels for 165 four-digit manufacturing industries, divided into four subcategories:[114]

107. See B. P. Pashigian, *The Distribution of Automobiles: An Economic Analysis of the Franchise System* (Englewood Cliffs, NJ: Prentice-Hall, 1961), especially pp. 238–239.

108. See Brock, *The U.S. Computer Industry,* supra note 11, pp. 33–37.

109. See John S. McGee, "Economies of Size in Auto Body Manufacture," *Journal of Law & Economics,* vol. 16 (October 1973), pp. 248–253; and "Choreography on a Stamping Line," *New York Times,* December 24, 1988, p. 35. The inflation-adjusted costs of making exterior body part dies may have fallen more recently as computer-aided design and manufacture techniques make it possible to program die-cutting machines directly from stylists' drawings or plaster models.

110. See, for example, David Halberstam, *The Reckoning* (New York: William Morrow, 1986), p. 550 (on the cost of Chrysler's K-car series).

111. See White, *The Automobile Industry Since 1945,* supra note 26, pp. 20–22 and 48–53.

112. See "Special Cars for Special People," *Fortune,* February 1968, pp. 136–143.

113. The literature is vast and controversy-laden. Pioneering contributions were James A. Dalton and Stephen A. Rhoades, "Growth and Product Differentiability as Factors Influencing Changes in Concentration," *Journal of Industrial Economics,* vol. 22 (March 1974), pp. 235–240; and Willard F. Mueller and Larry G. Hamm, "Trends in Industrial Market Concentration, 1947 to 1970," *Review of Economics and Statistics,* vol. 56 (November 1974), pp. 511–520. Critical but ultimately corroborative contributions include Richard E. Caves and Michael E. Porter, "The Dynamics of Changing Seller Concentration," *Journal of Industrial Economics,* vol. 29 (September 1980), pp. 1–16; and David Levy, "Specifying the Dynamics of Industry Concentration," *Journal of Industrial Economics,* vol. 34 (September 1985), pp. 55–68. For similar but weaker results for France, see Frederic Jenny and André-Paul Weber, "The Determinants of Concentration Trends in the French Manufacturing Sector," *Journal of Industrial Economics,* vol. 26 (March 1978), pp. 193–207.

114. Mueller and Rogers, "Changes in Market Concentration of Manufacturing Industries, 1947–1977," supra note 61, p. 3, updating a similar article by the same authors in the *Review of Economics and Statistics,* vol. 62 (February 1980), pp. 89–96.

Type of Product	Average Change in Concentration	1977 Average Concentration Level
Producer Goods	− 1.7	42.1
Consumer Goods:	+ 6.8	42.5
Low Differentiation	+ 1.6	27.6
Moderate Differentiation	+ 6.1	42.3
High Differentiation	+14.7	62.4
All 165 Industries	+ 1.9	42.3

The tendency for concentration to increase was clearly stronger on average in consumer goods industries, and within that cohort, it rose systematically with the extent of product differentiation, categorized from differences in average advertising/sales ratios. In a multiple regression analysis, Mueller and Rogers discovered, as previous contributions had shown, that changes in concentration were positively and significantly associated with advertising/sales ratios, taking into account also variously lagged initial concentration, industry size, and market growth variables. But more importantly, a variable including only television and radio advertising expenditures had more explanatory power than a variable including all advertising expenditures. Indeed, concentration changes were *negatively* but insignificantly correlated with a variable relating newspaper, magazine, and outdoor advertising outlays to industry sales. What chain of causation lies behind these results remains unclear. They could imply strong economies of scale in the use of television advertising, unusually rapid market share increases for firms that used the new mass media with particular virtuosity, the ability of powerful media to accelerate sales gains for companies with superior products,[115] or some combination of these and other influences. Whatever the mechanism, it seems clear that the modern instruments of promotion and persuasion have led to quite different concentration dynamics for highly differentiated consumer goods.

Conclusions It is difficult to draw simple conclusions concerning the relationship between multiplant economies of scale and the necessity of market concentration. The possibilities are complicated. A fair amount depends upon luck and the specific market segments individual firms choose to serve. Some aspects (such as pecuniary capital-raising economies and product differentiation advantages) call for value judgments as to whether the gains realized by large sellers are also gains to society. Nevertheless, generalizations are useful, and so Table 4.6 attempts to provide an overview of how important multiplant economies were in the late 1960s for twelve U.S. industries studied intensively by one of the authors. It focuses on firms operating in the mainstream of their industries, not in offbeat market niches; and it weighs the various advantages of size according to their strategic importance in the marketplace without adjustments for desirability in terms of some higher social criterion.

Column (1) estimates the overall disadvantage experienced by firms operating only one plant of minimum efficient scale compared to enterprises enjoying all the benefits of multiplant size. Ranges are given to reflect relevant variations in market conditions and historical legacies. Column (2) then estimates how many MES plants a firm needed to operate in order to have not more than a slight overall handicap vis-a-vis companies securing all multiplant economies. *Slight* here implies unit cost sacrifices, or the loss of price premiums (net of promotional costs) of not much more than 1 percent. In four or (less confidently) five industries, multiplant operation conferred no more than slight advantages; in the rest, multiplant firms enjoyed somewhat greater advantages over single-plant general-line rivals. Column (3) describes briefly the main sources of multiplant economies both for industries in which they were important and where they were not. Many facets appear, but those relating to product differentiation and the need for sales and production strategies geared to buyers' preferences for broad-line suppliers predominate.

Column (4) translates the column (2) judgments into an estimate of how large a share of the U.S. market an enterprise needed to realize all but slight untapped advantages of multiplant size. It in effect summarizes the imperatives for high concentration at the nationwide level. In only three of the twelve industries — refrigerators, brewing, and perhaps cigarettes — were oligopolistic national industry structures (that is, with four-firm concentration ratios exceeding 40) compelled. However, in several of the industries, transportation costs were sufficiently high to confine the sales of any single plant to a regional (that is, less than nationwide) market. As a result, achieving the main advantages of size required oligopolistic structures in most glass bottle and many petroleum, steel, and cement markets. Also, in bearings, the estimates assume a firm specializing in ball, roller, or tapered models, not all three. With multiplant firms thus specialized, there would be middling oligopoly levels in ball and roller bearings and high concentration in such specialty lines as tapered or needle bearings. The overall picture then is one of production or marketing compulsions toward oligopoly, usually loose, in more industries than not. On the other hand, oligopoly was rather clearly not necessary for most production in shoes, batteries, paints, and fabrics.

Column (5) indicates the average market share held by individual firms among the industries' three leading producers during 1970. By comparing column (5) with column (4), one gains an impression of the mesh between scale economy-mandated levels of concentration and actual concentration. For brewing, refrigerators, and petroleum refining, the mesh was fairly close.[116] In weaving and batteries, at the other extreme, Big Three members were roughly ten times as large as they needed to be to enjoy all but slight residual advantages of size. For all twelve industries, the average ratio of actual to required market share was 4.4. Thus, to the extent that the twelve-industry sample is representative — and on this little

115. The third explanation is implied by E. Woodrow Eckard, who finds relative prices to have advanced more slowly in high-advertising industries. "Advertising, Concentration Changes, and Consumer Welfare," *Review of Economics and Statistics,* vol. 70 (May 1988), pp. 340–343. It is also possible that high-advertising industries had particularly rapid changes in product designs, which made the standard price indices less reliable. See F. M. Scherer, "The Causes and Consequences of Rising Industrial

Concentration," *Journal of Law & Economics,* vol. 22 (April 1979), pp. 200–205.

116. The column (2) and (4) estimates for petroleum refining are significantly affected by the assumption that it was important to be vertically integrated into offshore oil exploration and production. Such integration became less important by the early 1980s after percentage depletion allowances were abolished and government price controls were removed.

Table 4.6
Evaluation of Firm Size Required to Experience Not More Than
Slight Price/Cost Handicaps

Industry	(1) Overall disadvantage of representative general-line single MES plant firm	(2) Number of MES plants needed to have not more than "slight" overall handicap	(3) Main bases of multi-plant firm's advantage	(4) Share of U.S. market required in 1967	(5) Average market share per U.S. Big Three member, 1970
Beer brewing	Slight to severe, depending upon inherited brand image	3–4	National brand image and advertising; coordination of new plant investments	10–14%	13%
Cigarettes	Slight to moderate (borderline)	1–2	Advertising and image differentiation	6–12	23
Fabric weaving	Very slight to moderate, depending upon product line	3–6	Integration into finishing; broad-line sales force and advertising	1	10
Paints	Slight	1	Integration into raw materials production	1.4	9
Petroleum refining	Very slight to moderate, depending upon regional market position and crude oil access	2–3	Risk spreading on crude oil ventures; coordination of plant investments; advertising and national image	4–6	8
Shoes	Slight to moderate, depending upon product line	3–6	Broad-line sales force and advertising	1	6
Glass bottles	Slight to moderate, depending upon location and products	3–4	Need for central engineering and design staff	4–6	22
Cement	Slight	1	Risk spreading and capital raising	2	7
Ordinary Steel	Very slight	1	Capital raising; plant expansion coordination	3	14
Bearings	Slight to moderate, depending upon product line	3–5	Broad-line customer preferences affecting lot sizes; central engineering	4–7	14
Refrigerators	Moderate	4–8 (incl. other appliances)	Image and market access, affecting production run lengths; warehousing and transportation	14–20	21
Storage batteries	Slight	1	Market access	2	18

Source: F. M. Scherer et al., *The Economics of Multi-Plant Operation: An International Comparisons Study* (Cambridge: Harvard University Press, 1975), pp. 334–36.

corroborating or conflicting evidence exists[117] — actual concentration in U.S. manufacturing industry appears to be considerably higher than the imperatives of scale economies require.

Stochastic Determinants of Market Structure

Up to this point we have assumed that market structures are the more or less determinate result of such variables as technology, the size of the market, the effectiveness of managerial organization, and the receptiveness of consumers to advertising. A quite different view of the processes by which market structures evolve can, however, be postulated. Let us begin by stating the proposition in its baldest, most radical form: the market structures observed at any moment in time are the result of pure historical chance.

This idea is best introduced by a concrete illustration. Suppose an industry comes into being with fifty member firms, each with first-year sales of $100,000 and hence each with a 2 percent starting share of the market. Now suppose the firms begin growing. Each is assumed to have the same average growth prospects as every other firm. But this average is subject to statistical variance. In any given year some firms will be lucky, growing more rapidly than the average, while others are unlucky, growing by less than the average. Let the probability distribution of growth rates confronting each firm be normal, with a mean of 6 percent per annum and a standard deviation of 16 percent. These parameters were chosen to reflect the average year-to-year growth actually experienced between 1954 and 1960 by 369 companies on *Fortune*'s list of the 500 largest industrial corporations for 1955. To repeat, each firm faces the same distribution of growth possibilities, and each firm's actual growth is determined by random sampling from that distribution. What will the size distribution of firms look like a number of years hence?

By applying a bit of probability theory it is possible to estimate the parameters of the resulting firm size distribution. However, insight is enriched by using a computer to simulate the dynamic properties of the growth process model. Each firm's growth in each year was determined through random sampling from a distribution of growth rates with a mean of 6 percent and a standard deviation of 16 percent. The firms' growth histories and the overall industry size distribution were then tabulated at twenty-year intervals. The results of sixteen consecutive simulation runs are summarized in the form of four-firm concentration ratios in Table 4.7.

Contrary to what untutored intuition might advise, the firms do not long remain equal in size and market share, even though their growth prospects are identical *ex ante*. Patterns resembling the concentrated structures of typical manufacturing industries emerge within a few decades. After the growth process has run its course for a century, it is not uncommon to find a single industry leader controlling 25 or 35 percent of the market while its former rivals muddle along with 0.1 percent. For the sixteen simulation runs at the one hundred-year mark, the range of leading firm market shares was 10 to 42 percent, with an average of 21 percent.

117. But see Nicholas Owen, "Scale Economies in the EEC," *European Economic Review*, vol. 7 (February 1976), pp. 143–163, who found national advantage in bilateral European trade flows for some fifty-nine to sixty-three industries to be more closely associated with *plant* size than with *firm* size.

Table 4.7 Four-firm Concentration Ratios Resulting from 16 Simulation Runs of a Stochastic Growth Model

Simulation	Four-firm concentration ratio at year:							
	1	20	40	60	80	100	120	140
Run 1	8.0	19.5	29.3	36.3	40.7	44.9	38.8	41.3
Run 2	8.0	20.3	21.4	28.1	37.5	41.6	50.8	55.6
Run 3	8.0	18.8	28.9	44.6	43.1	47.1	56.5	45.0
Run 4	8.0	20.9	26.7	31.8	41.9	41.0	64.5	59.8
Run 5	8.0	23.5	33.2	43.8	60.5	60.5	71.9	63.6
Run 6	8.0	21.3	26.6	29.7	35.8	51.2	59.1	72.9
Run 7	8.0	21.1	31.4	29.0	42.8	52.8	50.3	53.1
Run 8	8.0	21.6	23.5	42.2	47.3	64.4	73.1	76.6
Run 9	8.0	18.4	29.3	38.0	45.3	42.5	43.9	52.4
Run 10	8.0	20.0	29.7	43.7	40.1	43.1	42.9	42.9
Run 11	8.0	23.9	29.1	29.5	43.2	50.1	57.1	71.7
Run 12	8.0	15.7	23.3	24.1	34.5	41.1	42.9	53.1
Run 13	8.0	23.8	31.3	44.8	43.5	42.8	57.3	65.2
Run 14	8.0	17.8	23.3	29.3	54.2	51.4	56.0	64.7
Run 15	8.0	21.8	18.3	23.9	31.9	33.5	43.9	65.7
Run 16	8.0	17.5	27.1	28.3	30.7	39.9	37.7	35.3
Average	8.0	20.4	27.0	33.8	42.1	46.7	52.9	57.4

The four-firm concentration ratios after a century of growth ranged from 33.5 percent to 64.4 percent, with a mean of 46.7 percent.

Why do concentrated firm size distributions arise from initial conditions that seemingly give each firm an equal chance? The answer, in a word, is luck. Some firms will inevitably enjoy a run of luck, experiencing several years of rapid growth in close succession. Once the most fortunate enterprises climb well ahead of the pack, it is difficult for laggards to rally and rectify the imbalance, for by definition, each firm — large or small — has an equal chance of growing by a given percentage amount. Furthermore, once a firm has, by virtue of early good luck, placed itself among the industry leaders, it can achieve additional market share gains if it should happen again to be luckier than average (as it will be in roughly half of all cases). In ten of the sixteen simulation runs underlying Table 4.7, the leading firm in Year 140 occupied a position among the top four firms in Year 60, and in four cases the Year 140 leader was also the first in Year 60. In Run 13, the leading firm held its leadership position at every single twenty-year benchmark, and in Run 5, the leader led at every twenty-year point but one.

The simulation experiment reported here was designed to conform to the assumptions of Gibrat's Law of Proportionate Growth.[118] Specifically, the population of firms was fixed, and the distribution of growth rates from each firm sampled was independent of both firm size and the firm's past growth history.[119] Stochastic growth processes adhering to Gibrat's Law generate a log normal size distribution of firms — that is, a distribution highly skewed when sales are plotted by the frequency of their actual values, with one or a few firms commanding high sales while most make low sales, but which is normal and symmetric when the logarithms of firms' sales are plotted.[120] Statistical studies reveal that a log normal distribution often fits actually observed firm size data tolerably well.[121] However, the assumptions of Gibrat's Law need not be satisfied rigidly to obtain results similar to those of Table 4.7. There is a whole family of stochastic growth processes that lead to the skewed size distributions typical of real-world industries.[122] All have the common feature of making a firm's size in, say, year t + 1 proportional, subject to random variation, to its size in year t. Other dynamic processes that lack the proportionate growth property exist, but they typically fail to generate realistically skewed firm size distributions.[123] Reasoning backward from observation to hypothesis, Simon and Bonini argue that industry structures must in fact be generated by some such stochastic growth process, since actual size distributions "show such a regular and docile conformity . . . that we would expect some mechanism to be at work to account for the observed regularity."[124]

118. Robert Gibrat, *Les Inegalites Economiques* (Paris: Recueil Sirey, 1931). See also Michal Kalecki, "On the Gibrat Distribution," *Econometrica,* vol. 13 (April 1945), pp. 161–170; and on the general theory of random walks, of which the Gibrat model is a special case, William Feller, *An Introduction to Probability Theory and Its Applications,* 2nd ed., vol. I (New York: Wiley, 1957), pp. 65–87.

119. In one sense, Gibrat's assumptions were violated. A bankruptcy rule was enforced, requiring a firm to drop out of the industry permanently if its sales fell to $30,000 or less. There were only three bankruptcies in the 800 company histories simulated.

For a demonstration that equal starting market shares are not necessary for substantial company rank changes and the emergence of skewed size distributions, see Uriel G. Rothblum and Sidney G. Winter, "Asymptotic Behavior of Market Shares for a Stochastic Growth Model," *Journal of Economic Theory,* vol. 36 (August 1985), pp. 352–366.

120. Proof: Let S_{oj} be the initial sales of the jth firm and e_i the random growth multiplier in the ith year. Then sales in year t are:

$$S_{tj} = S_{oj} e_1 \ldots e_i \ldots e_t;$$

that is, the cumulative product of initial sales times a string of random growth multipliers. Taking logarithms, we obtain:

$$\text{Log } S_{tj} = \log S_{oj} + \log e_1 + \ldots + \log e_i + \ldots + \log e_t.$$

By the central limit theorem, the distribution of the sum of T random variables is asymptotically normal when $T \to \infty$.

121. See P. E. Hart and S. J. Prais, "The Analysis of Business Concentration," *Journal of the Royal Statistical Society,* vol. 119, Part 2 (1956), pp. 150–181; Herbert A. Simon and C. P. Bonini, "The Size Distribution of Business Firms," *American Economic Review,* vol. 48 (September 1958), pp. 607–617; and (for results suggesting that the log normal distribution holds in roughly half the industries studied) Irwin H. Silberman, "On Lognormality as a Summary Measure of Concentration," *American Economic Review,* vol. 57 (September 1967), pp. 807–831.

122. See especially Herbert A. Simon, "On a Class of Skew Distribution Functions," *Biometrika,* vol. 42 (December 1955), pp. 425–440; and Yuji Ijiri and Herbert A. Simon, *Skew Distributions and the Sizes of Business Firms* (Amsterdam: North-Holland, 1977). The distributions are sufficiently similar that it is difficult to find statistical tests distinguishing which of several alternate stochastic processes generated them. See Richard E. Quandt, "On the Size Distribution of Firms," *American Economic Review,* vol. 56 (June 1966), pp. 416–432.

123. Firm size distributions with realistic skewness properties also result from a complex natural selection model embodying random innovative search and imitation, with growth linked to the success of those activities. See Richard R. Nelson and Sidney G. Winter, *An Evolutionary Theory of Economic Change* (Cambridge: Harvard University Press, 1982), Chapters 12–14. For a nonstochastic hypothesis attributing log normal firm size distributions to a particular type of monopoly pricing (to be considered tangentially in Chapter 10), see Dean A. Worcester, Jr., *Monopoly, Big Business, and Welfare in the Postwar United States* (Seattle: University of Washington Press, 1967), Chapters 5 and 6.

124. Simon and Bonini, "The Size Distribution of Business Firms," supra note 121, p. 608.

We are all so thoroughly imbued with the belief that chance favors the well-prepared that it is difficult to accept a model making corporate success the result of mere chance. Still it is not essential to interpret the stochastic growth models quite so literally. There are without doubt aspects of business enterprise in which luck plays a significant role — for example, in the hiring of key executives, in research and new product development decisions, in legal disputes involving key patents, in the choice of advertising campaign themes, or in a thousand and one other decisions among attractive but uncertain alternative courses of action. Given the operation of chance in these elemental decisions, high or low sales growth follows in a more conventionally deterministic manner.

One implication of this milder restatement is the possibility that growth rates for a given firm from year to year will not be independent, as assumed in the Gibrat model. For example, a lucky chief executive officer choice may affect growth favorably for a decade or more. Yet this is not a fatal objection. Ijiri and Simon have demonstrated in a simulation study that size distributions similar to those generated by Gibrat models can also be obtained when there is serial correlation in firms' year-to-year growth rates.[125]

The assumptions of the Gibrat model may also be violated if growth rates, or the standard deviations of growth rates, are correlated with firm size. Independence of size and growth rates implies that small firms operate at neither an advantage nor a disadvantage compared to their larger cousins. If economies of scale persist out to substantial market shares, large firms would possess an advantage that might be exploited *inter alia* in the form of more rapid growth. This, combined with stochastic elements, would lead to even more rapid concentration. Conversely, if small firms could grow more rapidly on average, or if there were a continuous inflow of new firms, the tendency toward increasing firm size inequality would be moderated and under certain conditions checked altogether.

Several empirical investigations have sought to determine whether firm growth rates are correlated with firm size. The results vary widely, depending upon the nation, time period, and statistical methodology. Among other things, one must be wary of sampling biases, since a consistent data series is more likely to include rapidly growing small firms than small companies growing only slowly or declining. The most careful recent studies for the United States reveal that growth rates tend to decline with greater size.[126] The observed correlations are weak, but they constrain tendencies toward rising concentration over time.

There is stronger and more consistent evidence rejecting the Gibrat assumption that growth rate standard deviations are independent of firm size.[127] To the contrary, large firms' growth rates are more stable, that is, with lower standard deviations. This works in the direction of enhancing tendencies toward concentration.[128] Chance will occasionally propel initially small firms to large size. But once a firm enters the large size bracket, the variance of its growth rate diminishes, and so does the chance that it will decline abruptly. Thus, once a high level of concentration is achieved, there are forces tending to sustain it.

A finer-grained analysis suggests that the variability of growth rates may differ not only with firm size, but also from industry to industry, depending upon the nature of the product and the character of competition.[129] One might expect variability to be especially high in industries characterized by a rapid pace of product design change owing to technological or style innovation and also in markets populated by consumers who respond enthusiastically to clever advertising campaigns. The firm with a good design or promotional idea may leap ahead rapidly; the firm that misgauges market sentiments can suffer spectacular market share declines.

Empirical tests of the interindustry difference hypotheses yield equivocal support. Extending an earlier analysis by Weiss,[130] 154 U.S. manufacturing industries whose definitions changed insignificantly between 1947 and 1972 were divided into two broad groupings, those whose product designs changed rapidly and those with little design change. These were in turn subdivided into finer product-type groupings. The average four-firm concentration ratio changes between 1947 and 1972 were as follows (with the number of industries covered indicated in parentheses):

High hypothesized design change group:

Consumer durables (20)	+6.40
Consumer semidurables (33)	+7.00
Durable equipment (19)	−3.95

Low hypothesized design change group:

Nondurable materials (20)	+0.25
Semidurable materials (31)	−1.65
Durable materials (17)	−1.41
Consumer nondurables (24)	+4.96

The overall average concentration change for the high design change group was +3.45 percentage points, compared to +0.53 for the low design change group. This appears to support the design change hypothesis. However, the pattern is not uniform within groups. Rapidly rising concentration is found mainly in the consumer goods industries, as observed in our earlier discussion of advertising. In an

125. Yuji Ijiri and Herbert A. Simon, "Business Growth and Firm Size," *American Economic Review,* vol. 54 (March 1964), pp. 77–89; idem, "Interpretations of Departures from the Pareto Curve Firm-Size Distributions," *Journal of Political Economy,* vol. 82 (March/April 1974), pp. 315–331; Daniel R. Vining, Jr., "Autocorrelated Growth Rates and the Pareto Law: A Further Analysis," *Journal of Political Economy,* vol. 84 (April 1976), pp. 369–380; and Andrew Chesher, "Testing the Law of Proportionate Effect," *Journal of Industrial Economics,* vol. 27 (June 1979), pp. 403–411.

126. See David S. Evans, "Tests of Alternative Theories of Firm Growth," *Journal of Political Economy,* vol. 95 (August 1987), pp. 657–674; idem, "The Relationship Between Firm Growth, Size, and Age," *Journal of Industrial Economics,* vol. 35 (June 1987), pp. 567–581; Bronwyn H. Hall, "The Relationship Between Firm Size and Firm Growth in the US Manufacturing Sector," *Journal*

of Industrial Economics, vol. 35 (June 1987), pp. 583–606; and the earlier references in the second edition of this text, p. 149, note 231.

127. See the references in note 126 above.

128. See Simon, "On A Class of Skew Distribution Functions," supra note 122; and his comment in the *Journal of Political Economy,* vol. 72 (February 1964), p. 81.

129. See Ajit Singh and Geoffrey Whittington, "The Size and Growth of Firms," *Review of Economic Studies,* vol. 42 (January 1975), p. 20; and D. J. Aislabie, "Further Evidence on the Size and Growth of Firms," *Economic Record,* vol. 47 (June 1971), pp. 230–244.

130. Leonard W. Weiss, "Factors in Changing Concentration," *Review of Economics and Statistics,* vol. 45 (February 1963), pp. 70–77. The updating here was done by Tom Scherer.

analysis of finely disaggregated data, Caves and Porter show that complex interactions may be at work: high levels of product research and development destabilized market shares in low-advertising industries, but not in high-advertising lines, while high levels of advertising destabilized market shares in high-advertising, low-R&D lines.[131] This too suggests that turbulence is most likely to induce rising concentration in consumer goods industries, which are much more advertising-prone. A study of aggregated census data revealed that after controlling for consumer goods status, manufacturing industry concentration fell on average between 1963 and 1977 in industries with relatively high research and development intensities.[132] The author's interpretation, stretching beyond the limits of the available data, was that the concentration-increasing effects of high market share turbulence stemming from product change were more than offset by high rates of entry from new firms offering innovative products.[133]

Much more remains to be learned about these important relationships. The random growth hypotheses have considerable appeal, both because chance plainly does play a role in company growth and because actual firm size distributions often correspond to those predicted by stochastic growth models. A full understanding of why market structures become what they do must blend the insights of stochastic growth theory with those derived from more static models stressing economies of scale, managerial diseconomies, the determinants of entry, and other phenomena that will occupy us in later chapters.[134]

The Impact of Government Policies

As framer of the legal environment within which business operates and as the largest single domestic customer for goods and services, government cannot help but influence market structures. Here we examine some areas in which its impact is particularly direct and noticeable. We confine our analysis to the U.S. situation and, in particular, to the role of the federal (as distinguished from state and local) government.

With the advent of World War II, the government's purchase of goods and services expanded enormously. Since then government purchases have remained at generally high levels as an active (but fluctuating) defense procurement program continued and as the government moved into such fields as the exploration of space, interstate highway building, railroad operation, and the development of key technologies. In 1984, for example, the federal government purchased goods and services from the private sector valued at roughly $175 billion, or 5 percent of gross national product.

These expenditures have both direct and indirect effects on the structure of industry. The distribution of prime contracts awarded by the Department of Defense has tended historically to be quite concentrated — more so than aggregate concentration in the economy generally. During various relevant periods, the one hundred largest prime contract recipients obtained the following percentage shares of all defense prime contract awards by dollar volume:

World War II	67 percent
Korean War (1951–1953)	64 percent

Vietnam War (1966–1968)	66 percent
Post-Vietnam (1974–1976)	68 percent
1985–1987	68 percent

From this it does not necessarily follow that aggregate concentration has been raised by government procurement practices, since the largest government contractors are not necessarily the largest companies in the private sector, despite considerable overlap. Further insight is obtained by evaluating the contract status of the fifty corporations leading *Fortune*'s list of the 500 largest industrials for 1982. Those fifty corporations accounted for 34 percent of manufacturing and mineral company sales in 1982 while gaining 44 percent of defense prime contract awards by dollar volume in fiscal years 1985–1987.[135] This suggests that defense procurement has exerted modest upward pressure on aggregate concentration.

At least as important are the indirect effects of government procurement. The pace of technological change has been extremely rapid in the defense, space, and atomic energy fields. Companies winning major government contracts to develop new concepts and equipment could achieve substantial know-how advantages over others in civilian applications of the technology. Generally, the government has attempted to distribute its orders so that at least several firms gain proficiency in new areas. Boeing's rise to leadership in the jet airliner field was based in part upon experience accumulated through the B-47 bomber program, but the Air Force required Boeing to share its B-47 production workload with Douglas (now McDonnell-Douglas) and Lockheed — a decision that helped those companies regain a position in the commercial airliner market after their propeller-driven mainstays fell from favor. The widespread diffusion of government research and development contracts in the semiconductor, radar, and similar electronics fields contributed to the formation of numerous viable competitors. However, this pro-competitive policy has not always worked. Even though IBM received less government money for computer research than rivals Sperry Rand and General Electric during the computer industry's formative period, IBM's rise to industry dominance was not prevented, and IBM's technological position was clearly bolstered by sizable SAGE air defense system development contracts.[136] A skew in computer R&D and procurement contracts toward smaller and new companies did

131. Richard E. Caves and Michael E. Porter, "Market Structure, Oligopoly, and Stability of Market Shares," *Journal of Industrial Economics,* vol. 26 (June 1978), pp. 289–308.

132. Arun K. Mukhopadhyay, "Technological Progress and Change in Market Concentration in the U.S., 1963–77," *Southern Economic Journal,* vol. 52 (July 1985), pp. 141–149.

133. When there is a flow of new entry into the smallest size class, a Yule size distribution is generated. The Yule distribution can be less asymmetric, although under limiting conditions it converges on the log normal distribution. See Simon and Bonini, "The Size Distribution of Business Firms," supra note 121.

134. For a promising start, see Stephen W. Davies and Bruce R. Lyons, "Seller Concentration: The Technological Explanation

and Demand Uncertainty," *Economic Journal,* vol. 92 (December 1982), pp. 903–919.

135. The data are taken from the annual "Largest Industrials" issues of *Fortune,* typically in April of the following year, and U.S. Department of Defense, *100 Companies Receiving the Largest Dollar Volume of Prime Contract Awards,* Fiscal Years 1985, 1986, and 1987 (Washington: Department of Defense Directorate for Information Operations and Reports). See also William Burnett and F. M. Scherer, "The Weapons Industry," in Walter Adams, ed., *The Structure of American Industry,* 8th ed. (New York: Macmillan, 1989).

136. See Kenneth Flamm, *Targeting the Computer* (Washington: Brookings, 1987), pp. 48–49, 93–100, 174, and 177.

help limit IBM's dominance, for example, by encouraging the growth of Burroughs, Control Data, Honeywell, and Cray. And in the jet engine and atomic reactor fields, the government initially supported work by several contractors. However, both industries evolved into near duopolies after some firms dropped out owing to lack of interest and others were denied further support because of unsatisfactory performance.

Certain industries' structures have been shaped by federal government plant construction and sale programs. During World War II, rapid expansion of defense production was achieved in part by the construction of government-owned, contractor-operated plants in key industries. After the war many of these plants, particularly those devoted to raw materials production, were sold to private industry. Because of inconsistent policies, the structural consequences varied widely. In aluminum, what was once a virtual Alcoa monopoly was transformed into a triopoly through the sale of plants (built at a cost of $300 million and operated during the war mainly by Alcoa) to Kaiser and Reynolds at a total purchase price of $100 million. Alcoa, with an antitrust conviction hanging over its head, was excluded from the bidding.[137] The sale of synthetic nitrogen plants was also arranged in such a way as to increase the number of competing sellers.[138] On the other hand, the wartime synthetic rubber program was run under procedures giving a few large companies a patent and know-how advantage in the postwar development of the new industry, and because no attempt was made to prevent multiplant purchases, the sale of twenty-five plants ended with three firms controlling 47 percent of industry capacity. For many plants there was only one bidder. In every other case but one, the successful bidder was the company that had previously operated the plant for the government.[139]

Government also affects industry structure through its role as grantor or guarantor of loans. Small businesses are the sole clientele of the Small Business Administration's loan program, averaging more than $3 billion per year during the early 1980s. Large industrial enterprises have secured government financing support in more spectacular but much less frequent cases — for example, through the $250 million loan guarantee for Lockheed Aircraft in 1971, the $730 million guarantee to support General Dynamics' Quincy, Massachusetts, shipyard operations in 1977, and the $1.9 billion guarantee in 1980 and 1981 to prevent the collapse of automaker Chrysler. Much larger sums were involved in the government's rescue of failing banks during the 1980s. The $4.5 billion Continental Illinois operation in 1984 and the infusion of at least as much into the First Republicbank of Texas in 1988 drew newspaper headlines, but hundreds of smaller banks also received government aid to remain in business or to facilitate merger with healthier institutions. At least initially, few of these bailout interventions were concentration-increasing, and to the extent that companies like Chrysler remained viable when the alternative would have been bankruptcy and closure or merger, the net effect was to maintain market structures more fragmented than those that would have evolved otherwise.

Federal government policies have had complex but important influences on the structure of such mineral-based industries as petroleum, whose members included fourteen of the top twenty-five industrial corporations on *Fortune*'s 1982 list. Three aspects warrant mention. First, Washington's support of the largest petroleum companies' participation in an international cartel dividing up Middle Eastern oil franchises among themselves and the leading European companies retarded (but did not stop) the expansion of smaller producers into world markets. It also sowed the seeds for the formation of OPEC, the most influential cartel in world history, although it is hard to say whether OPEC would have coalesced in the absence of a "Seven Sisters" against whom its efforts were initially directed.[140] Second, as the nation's premier landlord, the government has shaped industry structure through the policies it pursues in leasing mineral exploration and development rights. By requiring large front-end payments before any drilling is done, the bonus bidding system of awarding Outer Continental Shelf oil and gas rights has increased risks and enhanced the relative advantage of giant companies. Thus, in 1972, the eight largest petroleum producers accounted for 63 percent of all OCS production. Onshore, where different leasing methods give rise to much lower front-end costs, the eight leaders' share of production from federal lands was only 38 percent.[141] Compensating to some extent for these biases was the government's policy of granting to smaller refiners preferential crude oil import quotas up to 1973 and preferential entitlements to price-controlled domestic crude oil between 1974 and 1981. Indeed, the entitlements were so lucrative that more than fifty inefficiently small "teakettle" refineries were constructed mainly to take advantage. When the controls and entitlements system was dismantled, most of the artificially stimulated refineries were shut down.[142]

Tax policies influence market structure in myriad ways. Small businesses have been encouraged by gradations built into the federal income tax structure. Thus, in 1988, the tax rate on the first $25,000 of corporate profits was 15 percent, rising to 25 percent for the next $50,000 and reaching the full 34 percent standard rate for profits exceeding $75,000. Taxing stockholders' capital gains at lower rates than ordinary income — a practice abandoned in 1988 — is believed to have enhanced incentives for new venture formation, which has been an important source of new market entry and technological dynamism in the U.S. economy.[143] On the other hand, the heirs of small company owners have often been forced to merge with larger enterprises in order to meet inheritance tax obligations.[144] Concentration-increasing mergers were also facilitated, even if not directly encouraged, by complex tax law provisions making it possible for corporations to

137. See M. J. Peck, *Competition in the Aluminum Industry: 1945–1958* (Cambridge: Harvard University Press, 1961), pp. 11–19.

138. See Jesse W. Markham, *The Fertilizer Industry: Study of an Imperfect Market* (Nashville: Vanderbilt University Press, 1958), pp. 106–107.

139. Compare S. E. Boyle, "Government Promotion of Monopoly Power," with C. F. Phillips, Jr., "Market Performance in the Synthetic Rubber Industry," both in the *Journal of Industrial Economics,* vol. 9 (April 1961), pp. 132–169.

140. See John M. Blair, *The Control of Oil* (New York: Pantheon, 1976), especially Chapters 4 and 9.

141. See, for example, the Federal Trade Commission staff report, *Federal Energy Land Policy: Efficiency, Revenue, and Competition,* Senate Committee on Interior and Insular Affairs print (Washington: Government Printing Office, 1976), pp. 383 and 451A;

Douglas K. Reece, "An Analysis of Alternative Bidding Systems for Leasing Offshore Oil," *Bell Journal of Economics,* vol. 10 (Autumn 1979), pp. 659–669; and James B. Ramsey, *Bidding and Oil Leases* (Greenwich, CT: JAI Press, 1980).

142. Joseph P. Kalt, *The Economics and Politics of Oil Price Regulation* (Cambridge: MIT Press, 1981), pp. 59–61; and Neil Lloyd, "The Impact of the Small Refiner Bias on the Structure of the United States Petroleum Refining Industry, 1973–1986," econometrics seminar paper, Swarthmore College, 1986.

143. See "Venture Capitalists Wary of Tax Plan," *New York Times,* January 9, 1985, Sec. IV, p. 1.

144. J. Keith Butters, John Lintner, and W. L. Cary, *Effects of Taxation on Corporate Mergers* (Boston: Harvard Business School Division of Research, 1951), Chapter 8; and C. C. Bosland, "Has Estate Taxation Induced Recent Mergers?" *National Tax Journal,* vol. 16 (June 1963), pp. 159–168.

escape taxation altogether on mergers effected through security swaps, to write up asset values and thereby increase tax-shielding depreciation charges, and to avoid capital gains taxes otherwise due on cash mergers leading to increased asset values.[145] The capital gains tax avoidance loophole was eliminated in the U.S. income tax reform law of 1986, but other merger-facilitating provisions remain.

Federal antitrust laws seek to restrain increases in market concentration as well as to encourage competitive conduct. Paradoxically, passage of the first U.S. antitrust law, the Sherman Act of 1890, is believed to have stimulated a wave of concentration-increasing mergers around the turn of the century.[146] After a period of uncertainty, the Supreme Court enunciated a hard line against price-fixing agreements in 1897, but not until 1904 were mergers brought squarely under the law's control. If a group of sellers sought to stifle competition during the seven-year interim, they stood a better chance of avoiding legal difficulties by merging than by engaging in more loosely structured conspiracies. A similar but more recent imbalance in the British and German antitrust laws may also have helped precipitate merger waves.[147] Since the 1950s, on the other hand, antitrust enforcement in the United States has almost surely kept the growth of seller concentration to the modest magnitudes documented in Chapter 3. We shall have much more to say about mergers and their antitrust treatment in Chapter 5.

By granting patent rights to inventions, the government may facilitate dominance of a market by one or a few firms and make entry by newcomers difficult or impossible. Chapter 17 will explore the logic of the patent system in detail. Suffice it to say here that patents contributed significantly at one time or another to concentration in such industries as telephone equipment, electric lamps, synthetic fibers, photographic materials, shoe machinery, and certain classes of pharmaceuticals. On the other hand, they have also helped small innovative firms enter and maintain a foothold in numerous industries.

Tariffs have sometimes been called the "mother of trusts."[148] They and other forms of protection such as quotas and orderly marketing agreements can insulate monopolistic or oligopolistic industries from import competition, preserving them in a form that lacks economic justification and blunts incentives to adopt efficiency-increasing measures. On the other hand, they can also foster the development of infant industries to a stage of maturity at which the members can withstand foreign competition unaided. Since few U.S. industries are in their infancy relative to overseas rivals, the first set of effects might be expected to predominate. However, a statistical analysis provides no indication that the extent of tariff protection accorded U.S. manufacturing industries during the 1970s was systematically correlated with seller concentration levels.[149]

Finally, there is a host of special government policies affecting particular industries or segments of the business population. The equipment needed to control air and water pollution from industrial plants and to protect in-plant workers' health is often subject to appreciable scale economies. The enforcement of antipollution and environmental health and safety laws has led to the closure of many small plants in the foundry, cement, paint, pigment, storage battery, coal and uranium mining, and other industries.[150] More stringent enforcement of the laws toward new as contrasted to existing plants has also retarded new competitive entry. The time required to fill out government tax, regulatory, and statistical survey forms is virtually fixed in many cases and rises less than proportionately with organizational size in others. Even though large companies have to complete more forms than small firms, the burden of government paperwork probably falls relatively more heavily on smaller enterprises. The effect of this regressive tax on small firms' ability to survive is undoubtedly modest, but not zero. And by limiting entry into such regulated or licensed industries as mail services, banking, trucking, airlines (until the late 1970s), surveying, taxi cab operation, on-premises airport car rental, and the like, federal and local governmental agencies have often constricted the competitive alternatives available to consumers.

In sum, market structure is shaped in many ways by government policy. We advance now to a more detailed analysis of a further structural determinant and the government policies that influence it.

145. See U.S. Congress, Joint Committee on Taxation, Staff Report, *Federal Income Tax Aspects of Mergers and Acquisitions* (Washington: Government Printing Office, March 1985); and Dennis A. Breen, *The Potential for Tax Gains as a Merger Motive,* Federal Trade Commission staff report (Washington: July 1987).

146. George Bittlingmayer, "Did Antitrust Policy Cause the Great Merger Wave?" *Journal of Law & Economics,* vol. 28 (April 1985), pp. 77–118.

147. For a suggestion that earlier price fixing prohibitions in Germany had the same effect, see Fritz Voigt, "German Experience with Cartels and Their Control during Pre-War and Post-War Periods," in John Perry Miller, ed., *Competition, Cartels, and Their Regulation* (Amsterdam: North-Holland, 1962), p. 204.

148. The original statement was in 1899 by Henry Havemeyer, organizer of the "Sugar Trust," quoted in Richard Zerbe, "The

American Sugar Refinery Company, 1887–1914," *Journal of Law & Economics,* vol. 12 (October 1969), p. 341.

149. Edward J. Ray and Howard P. Marvel, "The Pattern of Protection in the Industrialized World," *Review of Economics and Statistics,* vol. 66 (August 1984), pp. 452–458.

150. See B. Peter Pashigian, "The Effect of Environmental Regulation on Optimal Plant Size and Factor Shares," *Journal of Law & Economics,* vol. 27 (April 1984), pp. 1–28; Ann P. Bartel and Lacy Glenn Thomas, "Predation through Regulation: The Wage and Profit Effects of the OSHA and EPA," *Journal of Law & Economics,* vol. 30 (October 1987), pp. 239–264; and (for a more sanguine view) William A. Brock and David S. Evans, *The Economics of Small Business: Their Role and Regulation in the U.S. Economy* (New York: Holmes and Meier, 1986), Chapters 4 and 5.

Mergers: History, Effects, and Policy

We have saved for separate treatment a set of particularly important market structure-shaping forces — mergers, takeovers, and other legal transformations through which two or more formerly independent firms come under common control. We begin with a historical overview of merger activity in the United States and abroad. We then analyze the motives for merger and the systematic evidence on merger characteristics and consequences. An exploration of government policies toward mergers and takeovers follows.

Broad Trends in Merger Activity

Figure 5.1 splices data from numerous sources to provide a quantitative picture of merger activity in the United States between 1895 and 1988. The focus is on the constant-dollar asset value (or for 1919–1950 (dotted segment), the number) of acquired companies with a home base in manufacturing or mineral extraction industries. For other industrial sectors, data of comparable quality are not available.

U.S. merger activity has been episodic, marked by four prominent waves — one clustered around the turn of the century, one peaking in 1929, a third peaking in 1968, and a fourth, with record-breaking asset acquisition levels, during the early and mid-1980s. Each has its own distinguishing features and merits separate attention.

The Great Merger Wave of 1887–1904

The merger wave that began with recovery from the worldwide depression of 1883 and ended with the depression of 1904 was a reaction of epic proportions to changes in transportation, communications, manufacturing technology, competition, and legal institutions that coincided during the closing decades of the nineteenth century.[1] It was most prominent in the United States, but had weaker parallels in Great Britain and Germany.[2] In the United States, it encompassed at least 15 percent of all plants and employees occupied in manufacturing at the turn of the century.[3] Its outstanding characteristic was the simultaneous consolidation of numerous producers into enterprises dominating the markets they supplied. Ralph Nelson found that of the roughly 3,000 merger-related independent firm disappearances he counted over the 1895–1904 period, 75 percent occurred in mergers involving at least five firms and 26 percent in consolidations of ten or more firms. By way of contrast, 14 percent of all 1915–1920 disappearances involved mergers of five or more firms, and only 1.4 percent ten or more firms.[4] Multifirm consolidations have been extremely rare in the United States since World War II.

1. There is an extensive literature covering this period. See especially Jesse W. Markham, "Survey of the Evidence and Findings on Mergers," in the National Bureau of Economic Research conference report, *Business Concentration and Price Policy* (Princeton: Princeton University Press, 1955), pp. 141–212; Ralph L. Nelson, *Merger Movements in American Industry, 1895–1956* (Princeton: Princeton University Press, 1959); and Naomi R. Lamoreaux, *The Great Merger Movement in American Business, 1895–1904* (Cambridge: Cambridge University Press, 1985).

2. On the United Kingdom, see Leslie Hannah, "Mergers in British Manufacturing Industry, 1880–1918," *Oxford Economic Papers,* vol. 26 (March 1974), pp. 1–17. On Germany, see Richard Tilly, "Mergers, External Growth, and Finance in the Development of Large-Scale Enterprise in Germany, 1880–1913," *Journal of Economic History,* vol. 42 (September 1982), pp. 629–658; with comment by J. M. MacDonald and reply by Tilly in the *Journal of Economic History,* vol. 43 (June 1983), pp. 483–486.

3. This is the estimate by Markham in "Survey," supra note 1, p. 157.

4. Nelson, *Merger Movements,* supra note 1, pp. 28–29 and 53.

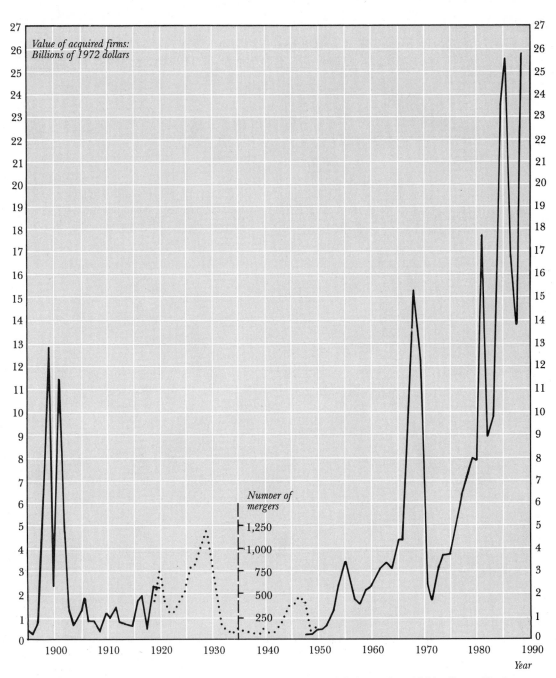

Figure 5.1
Constant-dollar Volume of
Manufacturing and Minerals
Firm Acquisitions, 1895–1985

Source: F.M. Scherer, *Industrial Market Structure and Economic Performance,* Second Edition (Boston: Houghton Mifflin Company, 1980), p. 120; extended using Federal Trade Commission and W.T. Grimm Co. data.

A trailblazer in the "market dominance through merger" game was the Standard Oil Company. Incorporated in 1870, it brought together twenty of the twenty-five existing Cleveland-area petroleum refiners in early 1872. It then embarked upon a sustained program of acquiring competitors in other parts of the nation, adding roughly one hundred more affiliations by merger during the next two decades and capturing a 90 percent share of U.S. petroleum refining capacity.

The pinnacle of the 1887–1904 merger wave was reached with the formation in 1901 of the United States Steel Corporation, combining an estimated 785 plants into the first American industrial corporation with capitalization exceeding $1 billion. Actually, U.S. Steel is better described as a "combination of combinations." During the late 1880s, a series of mergers consolidated more than 200 formerly independent iron and steel makers into twenty much larger rival entities. Most of these new firms were confined to only a few facets of steel making, and after their formation, many mapped out programs of integrating vertically to cover the whole spectrum from ore mining through fabrication. Charles Schwab, then president of Carnegie Steel, foresaw that this would lead to excess capacity and sharp price competition. He communicated his views to J. Pierpont Morgan, who organized a merger among twelve of the prior consolidations and for his labors realized promotional profits estimated at $62.5 million. The result was United States Steel (now USX), which at the time of its creation controlled some 65 percent of all domestic steel ingot-pouring capacity.

Similar developments reshaped many industries, large and small. In an early study of ninety-two large consolidations, John Moody found that seventy-eight gained control of at least 50 percent of total output in their home industry, and twenty-six secured a market share of 80 percent or more. Despite inevitable inaccuracies, his figures have been shown to be substantially correct.[5] The industries affected included copper, lead, railroad cars, explosives, tin cans, tobacco products, electrical equipment, rubber products, paper, farm machinery, brick making, chemicals, leather, sugar, business machines, photographic supplies, and shoe machinery. As Jesse Markham concluded in his 1955 survey, "The conversion of 71 important oligopolistic or near-competitive industries into near monopolies by merger between 1890 and 1904 left an imprint on the structure of the American economy that 50 years have not yet erased."[6]

A sharp decline in merger activity during 1903 and 1904 coincided with two important events — a severe recession, and the emergence of legal precedents in the *Northern Securities* case showing that market-dominating mergers could be prohibited under the antitrust laws.[7] A period of relative quiet continued for a dozen years, interrupted occasionally by such ripples as the formation of General Motors (combining Buick, Cadillac, Oldsmobile, and several other producers to gain 22 percent of the market in 1909, and adding Chevrolet a few years later). In hindsight, the most spectacular episode is "the one that got away." Twice Henry Ford was willing to sell out to General Motors — for $3 million in 1908 and for $8

5. Cf. Markham, "Survey," pp. 158–162, commenting on John Moody, *The Truth About Trusts* (New York: Moody, 1904), and later studies. See also Nelson, *Merger Movements,* p. 102; and Lamoreaux, *The Great Merger Movement,* supra note 1, p. 108.

6. Markham, "Survey," p. 180.
7. *U.S.* v. *Northern Securities Co.,* 120 Fed. 721 (April 1903), 193 U.S.197 (March 1904).

million a year later. But GM was unable to raise the required cash, and so the two leading auto producers remained independent.

The 1916–1929 Merger Movement

Merger activity showed signs of reviving in 1916 and 1917, but was interrupted by the conversion to war production in 1918 and the readjustment recession of 1921–1922. It then rode the stock market boom of the 1920s to heights paralleling, at least in terms of the numbers of companies acquired, those of 1899. Markham estimated that approximately 12,000 firms disappeared through mergers between 1919 and 1930.[8] However, the 1920s wave differed from its turn-of-the-century precursor in several respects.

For one, much of the activity, including many of the largest combinations, occurred in the electrical and gas utility sector. According to Markham, roughly 2,750 utilities, comprising 43 percent of all public utility firms operating in 1929, were swallowed up to create the pyramided holding companies that collapsed during the depression of the early 1930s.

In the manufacturing and minerals sectors, some 8,000 mergers had a less dramatic effect on market structures than a smaller number did during the 1887–1904 merger wave. Mergers creating a single dominant firm were apparently discouraged by the antitrust laws, despite lax enforcement. It is also possible that earlier mergers had exhausted most of the promising opportunities for market dominance. Whatever the reason, simultaneous multifirm consolidations were rarer, and the market share accretions were smaller. Some of the most prominent manufacturing mergers created a relatively large number two firm in an industry previously dominated by one giant. The difference between the 1887–1904 and 1916–1929 merger waves has been characterized by George Stigler as the difference between "mergers for monopoly" and "mergers for oligopoly."[9]

The wave of the 1920s also appears to have entailed more vertical integration and diversification mergers than its predecessor. Carl Eis has estimated that approximately 53 percent of 1926–1930 manufacturing and mining mergers were horizontal (that is, between competitors), with the balance falling largely into the product line extension and vertical integration categories.[10]

The 1960s Conglomerate Merger Wave

In 1950, in response to what appeared to be a resurgence of merger activity, the U.S. antitrust laws were amended to include much tougher restraints against horizontal and vertical mergers. As commensurate court precedents followed, horizontal mergers declined from 39 percent of all manufacturing company acquisitions by asset value in 1948–1955 to 18.7 percent in 1956–1963 and 12.0 percent in 1964–1971.[11] But merger-making itself was not deterred. Instead, it was deflected into new directions — notably, into mergers aimed toward diversification.[12] During the 1960s, acquisition activity rode a renewed stock market boom upward, encouraged by financial innovations such as the use of "funny money" (e.g., convertible preferred stocks and debentures) to buy out target company common shareholders. In constant-dollar terms, as shown in Figure 5.1, the volume of manufacturing assets acquired in 1968 surpassed the prior peak attained in 1899. To be sure, the U.S. economy of 1968 was nearly ten times larger than its 1900 counterpart, and so, in relative terms, the turn-of-the-century merger wave remained unsurpassed in impact.[13]

Table 5.1   Distribution of Large Manufacturing and Minerals Company
Assets Acquired, by Type of Merger, 1948–1979

Type of Merger	Percentage of Total Assets Acquired			
	1948–55	1956–63	1964–71	1972–79
Horizontal	39.0%	18.7%	12.0%	14.9%
Vertical	12.7	20.0	6.6	8.3
Product Extension	36.1	36.9	38.9	28.2
Market Extension	2.1	6.7	7.7	3.0
Pure Conglomerate	10.1	17.7	34.8	45.5

Source: Bruce T. Allen, "Merger Statistics and Merger Policy," *Review of Industrial Organization*, vol. 1 (Summer 1984), p. 80, drawing upon various issues of the Federal Trade Commission's *Statistical Report on Mergers and Acquisitions.* The FTC series covers only *large* mergers, defined as those in which the acquired firm's premerger assets were valued at $10 million or more. Smaller acquisitions amounted to roughly 11.4 percent of small plus large acquisitions by asset value in 1968, 1971, and 1974. See David J. Ravenscraft and F. M. Scherer, *Mergers, Sell-offs, and Economic Efficiency* (Washington: Brookings Institution, 1987), pp. 198–199.

Most of the renewed 1960s merger activity, to repeat, was of a diversifying or conglomerate character. In its manufacturing and minerals industry merger surveys, which provide the basis for Table 5.1, the Federal Trade Commission distinguished among three conglomerate merger variants. *Product line extension* mergers entail the joining of noncompeting products whose marketing channels or production processes are similar — for example, when leading detergent manufacturer Procter & Gamble acquired laundry bleach maker Clorox. Under *market extension* mergers, a firm such as Safeway acquired additional supermarkets in geographic markets it had not served previously. *Other* conglomerate mergers, also called *pure conglomerates,* were those lacking such complementarities — for example, when Beatrice Foods diversified into such fields as luggage manufacturing and auto parts.

Along with the relative decline in horizontal mergers, the most striking change revealed by Table 5.1 is the sharp increase in the proportion of pure conglomerate mergers. As a result of this active conglomerate merger-making, we saw in Chapter 3, the average number of manufacturing lines of business in which the leading U.S. manufacturing enterprises operated more than doubled.[14]

8. Markham, "Survey," pp. 168–169.

9. George J. Stigler, "Monopoly and Oligopoly by Merger," *American Economic Review,* vol. 40 (May 1950), pp. 23–34.

10. Carl Eis, "The 1919–1930 Merger Movement in American Industry," *Journal of Law & Economics,* vol. 12 (October 1969), pp. 280–284.

11. These are drawn from Table 5.1 infra and based upon Federal Trade Commission classifications. Compare the classifications on p. 93 supra, which show larger horizontal merger proportions because smaller mergers are included and the industry categories are often broader.

12. See also pp. 92–94 supra.

13. Cf. Debra L. Golbe and Lawrence J. White, "Mergers and Acquisitions in the U.S. Economy: An Aggregate and Historical Overview," in Alan J. Auerbach, ed., *Mergers and Acquisitions* (Chicago: University of Chicago Press, 1988), pp. 25–39.

14. See Table 3.10 supra and the accompanying text.

The strict enforcement of U.S. antitrust laws deflected merger activity into nonhorizontal categories and restrained increases in seller (that is, horizontal) concentration below what they would have been under unfettered conditions. This in turn is almost surely responsible in part for the glacial change in manufacturing industries' seller concentration ratios reported in Chapter 3 — from an average four-firm value of 36.9 percent in 1954 to 37.1 percent in 1982.[15]

Europe had a quite different experience. Until the 1970s, European antitrust laws regarding mergers were at best much weaker than their U.S. counterparts. Although there was also a rise in diversification mergers,[16] horizontal activity continued at a high rate, and substantial increases in average manufacturing industry seller concentration ratios occurred.[17] The most careful impact analysis available reveals that mergers were responsible for four-firm concentration ratio increases averaging 12.7 percentage points between 1958 and 1971 in 12 important West German manufacturing industries.[18] However, following the enactment of new and tougher anti-merger laws in 1974, three-seller concentration ratio increases in a nearly comparable set of West German industries averaged only 0.8 percentage points over the period 1975–1980.[19]

The Wave of the 1980s

The U.S. conglomerate merger wave of the 1960s, like its predecessors in 1903–1904 and 1929, came to a halt with a decline in stock prices — mild for most companies, but sharp for the securities of companies that had aggressively pursued conglomerate acquisitions. The next major upsurge occurred during the 1980s. It broke new ground not only in absolute activity levels but also in several qualitative respects.

For one, its inception coincided with a stock market slump, not with a boom, as in earlier waves.[20] Despite a 152 percent increase in capital equipment price levels, the Standard & Poor's index for 500 common stocks in 1980–1982 averaged only 24 percent higher than its 1968 value. Stock prices were so low relative to the cost of replacing plant and equipment that it was often less expensive to "expand" by buying other companies than by building de novo. Bargain-seeking merger activity soared. When the Federal Reserve Board switched to an expansive monetary policy in 1983 and a stock market boom ensued, merger activity was again influenced by more traditional stimuli: "If we don't make that XYZ acquisition soon, it will cost us more next year because of rising stock prices." But with the unprecedented collapse of stock prices on October 19, 1987, merger activity did not decline correspondingly, as it had following past stock market crises. Rather, bargain-hunting resumed, led by foreign acquirers who found the combination of relatively low U.S. stock prices and an unusually weak dollar exchange value irresistibly tempting.

A less subtle new characteristic was the explosion of hostile tender offer takeover activity. Hostile takeovers first came to prominence during the 1960s merger wave, but the targets were for the most part small, and "raiding" was viewed as not the sort of thing in which a self-respecting Wall Street financier would participate. The etiquette changed in 1974 when the Morgan-Stanley banking house (lineal descendant of United States Steel merger broker J. P. Morgan) helped International Nickel take over ESB Inc. Other investment banking houses joined the fray, and junk bonds and other innovative financial devices were conceived, permitting relatively small groups to launch credible multibillion dollar takeover bids. As a result, giants such as Gulf Oil, Getty Oil, RCA, Burlington Industries, Trans-World Airlines, and Federated Stores, along with hundreds of smaller publicly traded corporations, were acquired as a direct or indirect ("white knight") consequence of hostile tender offer attempts.[21] The new financing techniques also allowed acquirers to offer cash for the common stock shares of target companies in roughly three-fourths of all recorded cases.[22] Most acquisitions of the 1887–1904, 1920s, and 1960s merger waves, on the other hand, were accomplished through the exchange of new stocks (and/or bonds) for old.

Antitrust policy also swerved in a more permissive direction as the Reagan Administration took office in 1981. Sensing the reduced probability of government challenge, many companies attempted horizontal mergers that would have been inconceivable under prior administrations. The proportion of mergers with significant horizontal overlaps almost surely rose. However, no clear statistical picture can be provided, since President Reagan's appointees to key Federal Trade Commission positions killed the bearer of bad news, cancelling the merger data publication program upon which Table 5.1 and similar analyses were based.[23]

The Motives for Merger

Mergers occur for a myriad of reasons, and in any given case, several different motives may simultaneously influence the merging parties' behavior. Still it is useful to attempt a preliminary sorting-out of the diverse motivating forces.

15. See p. 84 supra. Even before, Leonard Weiss found, increases in concentration attributable to mergers between 1929 and 1958 were small. "An Evaluation of Mergers in Six Industries," *Review of Economics and Statistics,* vol. 47 (May 1965), pp. 172–181.

16. For the United Kingdom, see A. W. Goudie and G. Meeks, "Diversification by Merger," *Economica,* vol. 49 (November 1982), pp. 447–459.

17. See pp. 87–88 supra.

18. Juergen Mueller, "The Impact of Mergers on Concentration: A Study of Eleven West German Industries," *Journal of Industrial Economics,* vol. 25 (December 1976), pp. 113–132; augmented in Mueller and Rolf Hochreiter, *Stand und Entwicklungs-tendenzen der Unternehmenskonzentration in der Bundesrepublik* (Göttingen: Schwartz, 1976).

19. Juergen Mueller, "Sinkender Einfluss der Fusionen auf die Unternehmenskonzentration," *DIW Wochenbericht* (Berlin: Deutsches Institut für Wirtschaftsforschung, December 2, 1982), pp. 598–603.

20. On the macroeconomic correlates of merger activity, see Markham, "Survey," supra note 1, pp. 146–154; Nelson, *Merger Movements,* supra note 1, p. 118; Hannah, "Mergers in British Manufacturing," supra note 2, pp. 8–9; Alan Beckenstein, "Merger Activity and Merger Theories: An Empirical Investiga-

tion," *Antitrust Bulletin,* vol. 24 (Spring 1979), pp. 105–128; R. W. Melicher, Johannes Ledolter, and L. J. D'Antonio, "A Time Series Analysis of Aggregate Merger Activity," *Review of Economics and Statistics,* vol. 65 (August 1983), pp. 423–430; Paul Geroski, "On the Relationship between Aggregate Merger Activity and the Stock Market," *European Economic Review,* vol. 25 (July 1984), pp. 223–233; Golbe and White, "Mergers and Acquisitions," supra note 13, pp. 40–45; and George Bittlingmayer, "Merger as a Form of Investment," Science Centre Berlin working paper, 1987.

21. The most comprehensive source of data on recent U.S. mergers is the annual *Mergerstat Review* (Chicago: W. T. Grimm & Co.). For the years 1980–1987, Grimm & Co. recorded an average of eighteen tender offers per year. This was only 0.7 percent of all merger actions by number, but a much larger (though not estimated) fraction of mergers by dollar volume.

22. See David J. Ravenscraft, "The 1980s Merger Wave: An Industrial Organization Perspective," in Lynn E. Browne and Eric S. Rosengren, eds., *The Merger Boom* (Boston: Federal Reserve Bank of Boston, 1987), pp. 28–29.

23. The data are still collected under the Hart-Scott-Rodino premerger notification program; only the analyses and publication are lacking.

The Monopoly Motive   In horizontal mergers, and especially in the massive consolidations that took place around the turn of the century, the desire to achieve or strengthen monopoly power played a prominent role. Some 1887–1904 consolidations gained monopoly power by creating firms that dominated their industries. Others fell short of dominance, but transformed market structures sufficiently to curb the tendencies toward price competition toward which sellers gravitated in the rapidly changing market conditions of the time.[24] As Thomas Edison remarked to a reporter concerning reasons for the formation of the General Electric Company in 1892:

> Recently there has been sharp rivalry between [Thomson-Houston and Edison General Electric], and prices have been cut so that there has been little profit in the manufacture of electrical machinery for anybody. The consolidation of the companies . . . will do away with a competition which has become so sharp that the product of the factories has been worth little more than ordinary hardware.[25]

Those were days when businesspeople were not yet intimidated by the wrath of trustbusters or public opinion. Now they are more circumspect, and evidence of monopoly-creating intent is harder to find. Also, vigorous antitrust enforcement in the United States and, more recently, abroad has done much to curb competition-inhibiting mergers. Yet exceptions exist. The belief that Youngstown Sheet & Tube Co. had been secretly cutting prices and that its merger with Jones & Laughlin Steel would place Youngstown's price setting in firmer hands was documented in the investigation that led eventually to the merger's approval in 1978 by the U.S. attorney general.[26] A Continental Baking Company vice president's memorandum to his chairman argued for the acquisition of McKee Baking Company as likely to contribute to "the ability to control pricing in a basically noncompetitive atmosphere."[27] Such cases appear to be exceptional, however. Mergers with explicit price-raising intent are likely to escape censure only if they affect markets too small to attract the attention of the antitrust enforcement agencies.[28]

Speculative Motives   Monopoly and speculative motives interacted to propel the great merger wave of 1887–1904. The value of a company's common stock depends upon investor expectations regarding future profits. If competition can be eliminated or reduced through merger, profits will presumably rise, making the new consolidated firm's shares worth more than the sum of the previously competing companies' share values. Entrepreneurs sought to achieve such capital value transformations by arranging competition-reducing mergers. However, many went farther. Because investors were captivated by the prospect of pursuing this road to fortune, and because there were no effective controls on the quality of information disseminated in connection with new stock flotations, promoters arranged mergers with little chance of securing appreciable monopoly power, but simultaneously issued prospectuses, planted rumors, and primed the market to convince investors otherwise. By exciting false expectations, the promoters were able to sell the stocks of newly consolidated firms at prices far exceeding their true economic value — a practice known at the time as *stock watering*. As in honestly monopolistic consolidations, the promoters were paid in newly issued stock for their contribution. Only in this case, the merger makers hastened to sell their shares to unwary outsiders before the bubble burst. And burst it did. Shaw Livermore studied 328 mergers consummated between 1888 and 1905 and discovered that at least 141 were financial failures, 53 collapsing shortly after their formation.[29] Analyzing a smaller sample, Markham found that consolidations promoted by outside banks, syndicates, and the like failed much more frequently than those put together by individuals with a continuing commitment to the affected industry. From this and other evidence, he concluded that the quest for promotional profits was the most important single motive for merger during the frenzied 1897–1899 and 1926–1929 periods.[30]

Alarm over such abuses led to passage of the Securities Act of 1933 and the Securities Exchange Act of 1934, establishing federal regulation of securities issue information and other promotional practices. They and the antitrust laws made it difficult for promoters to repeat the experiences of the 1890s and 1920s. However, speculative motives continue to attract investors, and investors' interest in turn fuels the efforts of merger makers. Most U.S. merger waves coincided with stock market booms, and (more often in error than not) investors have viewed the purchase of merging companies' shares as a vehicle for profiting from continuing price appreciation. Also, for reasons that will be explored in due course, the combined value of merging companies' shares typically rises at the time a merger is announced. This too creates an opportunity for speculative gain, inducing financial intermediaries to arrange mergers with the hope of securing multimillion-dollar fees and participating in the stock price increases.[31]

More can be said. On average, we shall see, the typically conglomerate U.S. mergers of the 1960s and early 1970s did not turn out well financially. However, merger-making is a highly uncertain business. A few merger-prone companies yielded spectacular returns to their investors, especially to those who bought in early, before the boom in conglomerate firm stocks gained momentum. The distribution of long-term gains to early investors in the stocks of the thirteen most merger-prone U.S. manufacturing conglomerates of the 1960s was highly

24. This motive is emphasized and documented through case studies in Lamoreaux, supra note 1. See also George Bittlingmayer, "Did Antitrust Policy Cause the Great Merger Wave?" *Journal of Law & Economics,* vol. 28 (April 1985), pp. 77–118, who argues that tough enforcement of laws against collusive price fixing but weak antimerger enforcement contributed to the magnitude of the 1887–1904 merger wave. On the weakness of scale economy motives, see Anthony P. O'Brien, "Factory Size, Economies of Scale, and the Great Merger Wave of 1898–1902," *Journal of Economic History,* vol. 48 (September 1988), pp. 639–649.

25. *New York Times,* February 21, 1892, p. 2, cited in H. C. Passer, *The Electrical Manufacturers: 1875–1900* (Cambridge: Harvard University Press, 1953), p. 326. See also p. 54 of Passer on the motives for several earlier Thomson-Houston mergers.

26. Author Scherer reviewed the record and prepared an advisory memorandum for Attorney General Bell's consideration.

27. See Stephen Calkins, "Developments in Merger Litigation:

The Government Doesn't Always Win," *Antitrust Law Journal,* vol. 56 (1988), p. 868 note 67.

28. See, for example, David M. Barton and Roger Sherman, "The Price and Profit Effects of Horizontal Merger: A Case Study," *Journal of Industrial Economics,* vol. 33 (December 1984), pp. 165–178, who found substantial price increases following the acquisition of two small competitors by the leading producer of the film used in duplicating microfilm originals.

29. Shaw Livermore, "The Success of Industrial Mergers," *Quarterly Journal of Economics,* vol. 49 (November 1935), pp. 68–96.

30. Markham, "Survey," supra note 1, pp. 163 note and 181.

31. See Richard B. DuBoff and Edward S. Herman, "The Promotional Financial Dynamic of Merger Movements: A Historical Perspective," *Journal of Economic Issues,* vol. 23 (March 1989), pp. 107–133; and (for a more popular examination) John Brooks, *The Takeover Game* (New York: Dutton, 1987).

skewed.[32] Early bird investors holding the median performer among those thirteen firms' stocks over the period 1965–1983 fared only slightly better than persons investing conservatively in a portfolio of all 425 Standard & Poor's industrial company stocks; those who invested late did substantially worse than the S&P portfolio. However, the individual wise enough, or lucky enough, to invest $1,000 in conglomerate Teledyne in 1965 and hold on had shares valued at $65,463 in 1983. In this respect, investing in conglomerate merger-makers' stocks was similar to visiting the roulette tables at Las Vegas. The house odds ensure that most patrons will exit with less money than they had upon entering, but a few will realize big gains, and the prospect of those big gains draws the traffic. So also with conglomerate mergers of the 1960s. There is, however, a difference. At Las Vegas, the house collects at the end of the day. But for those who organized and led conglomerate firms' merger-making activities, the bills for disappointing performance were not presented for years or even decades, if at all. And meanwhile, the living was good.

Normal Business Motives

Any explanation of mergers that ignores such speculative inducements is likely to miss the mark. Yet it must be recognized that there are many normal, wholesome business motives for merger. These compel careful examination.

It is widely believed that mergers serve as an efficient, humane escape route for companies that are otherwise about to fail. This is true, but not very important quantitatively. As a rule, merger makers seek healthy acquisition targets, not basket cases. Among 698 sizable manufacturing companies acquired between 1948 and 1968, only 4.8 percent had negative profits in the year before acquisition occurred.[33] In a 634-company sample including a cross section of both small and large acquisition targets, 5.8 percent had negative operating income (before deduction of interest charges) in the year before acquisition.[34]

Small companies are often acquired because their owner-managers are aging or weary of business pressures and lack heirs or other successors to take their place. Interacting with this motive is the desire of family company owners to diversify their investment portfolios, thereby reducing their risk exposure, and to raise funds for paying the sometimes substantial estate taxes levied when an owner-manager dies.[35]

Tax considerations also affect the urge to merge in a variety of more complex ways. When an acquisition premium is paid above the values at which a company's depreciable assets are recorded in tax accounts, the acquired assets can under U.S. law be stepped up and subjected to higher depreciation charges, shielding the acquirer from tax liabilities. Until reforms were enacted in 1986, acquiring companies making such step-ups could normally escape immediate capital gains taxation. Such tax advantages appear to have been an important consideration in many merger decisions, but not critical enough to determine whether merger would or would not occur.[36] Under the structure of U.S. and many other nations' tax laws, corporate profits are taxed directly when realized by the corporation and again at the personal level when they are distributed as dividends to individual (but not institutional) stockholders. To avoid this double taxation, corporations are tempted to reinvest their profits in merger-making rather than paying them out as dividends. When capital gains are taxed more lightly than dividend income, as was true in the United States until 1989, successful reinvestment increased the value of the company's stock, permitting shareholders to sell some of their shares and realize their gains under the more lightly-taxed capital gains provisions. Expanding upon this theme, Oliver Williamson argued that conglomerate firms achieved efficiencies by reinvesting earnings in internal capital markets better able than external markets to assimilate information on investment opportunities.[37] However, intracompany capital markets are often highly bureaucratic and politicized, and it is unclear whether they actually do a better job allocating capital than is achieved in the give-and-take between a firm and its outside investors.[38]

We saw in Chapter 4 that capital-raising enjoys especially pervasive economies of large scale. When a small firm joins a large firm, the smaller firm is likely to benefit from the larger enterprise's lower cost of capital. Indeed, for small firms without ready access to outside capital markets, stringent capital rationing barriers may be broken. Case studies reveal that this may be one of the most compelling advantages of mergers.[39] However, it has limitations. An argument made for conglomerate companies in the 1960s is that, by pooling risks across a diversity of industries, they could attract capital at lower risk premiums. However, as we shall see, the conglomerates proved to be less than consistent in managing their acquisitions well, and as a result, financial markets came to view them as unusually high-risk, not low-risk, investments.[40] Thus, the desired companywide capital cost savings did not materialize.

Other merger-based economies of scale are even more difficult to evaluate. Distinctions must be made inter alia between horizontal mergers, in which the merging firms produce and sell similar products, and conglomerates, in which the product lines differ, perhaps greatly.

Economies of scale in production are much more likely to be achieved following horizontal (or perhaps vertical) mergers than when unrelated operations are combined. Even then, problems arise.

32. David J. Ravenscraft and F. M. Scherer, *Mergers, Sell-offs, and Economic Efficiency* (Washington: Brookings, 1987), pp. 38–44 and 207–210. For a seminal view on how uncertainty creates incentives for speculative merger-making, see Michael Gort, "An Economic Disturbance Theory of Mergers," *Quarterly Journal of Economics,* vol. 83 (November 1969), pp. 624–642.

33. Stanley E. Boyle, "Pre-Merger Growth and Profit Characteristics of Large Conglomerate Mergers in the United States, 1948–1968," *St. John's Law Review,* vol. 44 (Spring 1970, special edition), pp. 152–170.

34. Ravenscraft and Scherer, *Mergers,* supra note 32, p. 60.

35. Studies showing the importance of estate tax considerations to the sale of small firms include J. K. Butters, John M. Lintner, and W. L. Cary, *Effects of Taxation on Corporate Mergers* (Boston: Harvard Business School Division of Research, 1951), Chapter 8; and C. C. Bosland, "Has Estate Taxation Induced Recent Mergers?" *National Tax Journal,* vol. 16 (June 1963), pp. 159–168. In 1976 the tax law was changed to give small business heirs up to ten years to settle federal estate tax liabilities, lessening the incentive to merge for estate tax reasons.

36. See Alan J. Auerbach and David Reishus, "The Impact of Taxation on Mergers and Acquisitions," in Auerbach, ed., *Mergers and Acquisitions,* supra note 13, pp. 69–88; and Ronald J. Gilson, Myron S. Scholes, and Mark A. Wolfson, "Taxation and the Dynamics of Corporate Control," in John C. Coffee, Louis Lowenstein, and Susan Rose-Ackerman, eds., *Knights, Raiders, and Targets: The Impact of the Hostile Takeover* (New York: Oxford University Press, 1988), pp. 271–299.

37. Oliver E. Williamson, *Corporate Control and Business Behavior* (Englewood Cliffs, NJ: Prentice-Hall, 1970), pp. 121–130, 163–164, and 176–177.

38. Ravenscraft and Scherer, *Mergers,* supra note 32, pp. 213–214; and Joseph L. Bower, *Managing the Resource Allocation Process* (Boston: Harvard Business School Division of Research, 1970), especially Chapter 9.

39. Ravenscraft and Scherer, *Mergers,* pp. 212–213.

40. Ravenscraft and Scherer, *Mergers,* p. 44; and J. Fred Weston, K. V. Smith, and R. E. Shrieves, "Conglomerate Performance Using the Capital Asset Pricing Model," *Review of Economics and Statistics,* vol. 54 (November 1972), pp. 357–363.

When firms that make the same products merge, their plants are already built; not much can be done in the short run to unbuild them and achieve the principal plant-specific economies of scale. Exceptions are most likely to be found in declining or severely depressed industries. When multiple plants are combined, the least efficient units can be shut down and the most efficient units retained or even expanded. However, one must ask, why spend good money to acquire a rival's plants and then shut them down? Several answers exist. For one, production may require a complex mixture of equipment, and following merger, only the best units from each partner will be retained and integrated. For instance, in steel, one company may have good blast furnaces and converters but inefficient rolling mills; another may be stronger in its rolling and finishing operations. Achieving such integration is more easily said than done, as the difficulties following the merger of the Jones & Laughlin and Republic Steel companies testify.[41] We must also ask why the needed rationalization of capacity cannot be achieved through measures short of merger, for example, with the efficient upstream producer selling ingots to an independent firm for rolling and finishing. Plants that will be closed may also be acquired because what is wanted is not production capacity, but brand-name products or captive distribution channels, the demand for which will be served from the most efficient available capacity. Or in the case of the Westphalian cement industry of Germany, competitors may be acquired and then shut down because it is more profitable to buy them out and suppress their price competition than to drive prices below average variable costs, forcing all producers to endure substantial losses until the weakest finally cease operation.[42]

Horizontal mergers leading to no immediate plant closure or expansion may nevertheless yield scale economies over a longer period. There are two principal scenarios. First, a company with many older plants is likely to have more capacity due for replacement at any interval in time than a smaller firm, all else being equal. This may make it easier to carry out large-scale replacement investments, especially when optimal-sized production units come in large indivisible lumps, as in steel, petroleum refining, and cement making. Second, if all firms in an industry experience roughly proportionate demand growth, the company with a large market share, gained inter alia through mergers, can expect to enjoy larger absolute increments of growth, and therefore may be better situated to invest in sizable new plant units. In both cases, the long-run advantage from merger-related size hinges upon the assumption that firms view their sales potential passively and do not strive actively — for example, through price competition — to win whatever sales volume they need to utilize new capacity increments of efficient scale. That business firms may behave in this way, especially in Europe, is suggested by evidence that plant sizes are positively and significantly correlated with leading firms' market shares.[43] But one must not overlook the underlying causation. If mergers do contribute as suggested to the realization of scale economies, it is because entrepreneurs lack the nerve to compete independently in bringing new efficient-size plants on line.

Product-specific economies of scale offer somewhat different opportunities. When merging firms manufacture similar product lines, production assignments might be rearranged quickly to combine and lengthen production runs. An extreme illustration is provided by the 1969 merger of three English antifriction bearing manufacturers — Ransome and Marles, Hoffmann, and Pollard.[44] The first two sold extensively overlapping lines of general-purpose bearings whose dimensions conformed to international standards. Immediately following the merger, production assignments were revamped to eliminate duplication and lengthen runs. Within three years, output per employee had been improved by some 40 percent, partly as a direct result of the increased specialization and partly through simple belt tightening. Further substantial gains were expected from the introduction of automated production lines for high-volume bearings — the first such installations in the United Kingdom.

Several similar but less dramatic cases of postmerger, product-specific scale economy gains were uncovered in a study of twelve industries across six nations.[45] Such gains occurred more frequently, and involved greater savings, in Europe and Canada than in the United States. This was so for at least four reasons, in descending order of importance. First, the much greater size of the U.S. market made it easier to attain most product-specific economies without merger. As the European Common Market achieves greater unification and Canadian-U.S. trade barriers are eliminated, this difference will fade. Second, price competition was typically more vigorous in U.S. industries, generating greater pressure for U.S. producers to specialize in products on which they could capture maximum scale economies. For many European producers, merger was a route to product-specific scale economies compensating for the failure of competition to enforce specialization. Third, because of the U.S. market's vast geographic expanse, the transportation cost that would be incurred if merged but distant plants specialized more narrowly frequently outweighed the cost savings greater specialization might permit. And finally, legal barriers to sizable horizontal mergers probably deterred a few mergers that might have yielded product-specific economies.

From this discussion, an important analytic thread emerges. Plant-specific and product-specific scale economies can and do result from mergers. But for a significant fraction of the cases in which they do, it is because competition has failed to stimulate efficient plant investment, specialization, or closure choices. Mergers are a second-best solution, given the failure of competition. It follows obversely that the more effectively competition is working, the less essential mergers are as a source of production scale economies.

Mergers may also confer advantages in marketing — for example, through the pooling and streamlining of field sales forces, the ability to offer distributors a broader product line, the use of common advertising themes, and (to the extent they exist) the sharing of advertising media quantity discounts. In a survey of sixty-nine U.S. acquisitions, mostly conglomerate, John Kitching found marketing complementarities to be much more important than production economies,

41. See, for example, "LTV's Steel-Industry Gamble," *New York Times,* November 22, 1985; and "LTV, Dragged Down by Steel Subsidiary, Struggles To Survive," *Wall Street Journal,* January 6, 1986.

42. For an elaboration of this and analogous cases, see F. M. Scherer, Alan Beckenstein, Erich Kaufer, and R. D. Murphy, *The Economics of Multi-Plant Operation: An International Comparisons Study* (Cambridge: Harvard University Press, 1975), pp. 164–166. See also Mark W. Frankena and Paul A. Pautler, "Antitrust Policy for Declining Industries," Federal Trade Commission Bureau of Economics Staff Report, October 1985.

43. Scherer et al., *Multi-Plant Operation,* p. 175.

44. Scherer et al., *Multi-Plant Operation,* p. 169.

45. Scherer et al., *Multi-Plant Operation,* pp. 308–321.

and second only in importance to capital-cost economies.[46] However, conflicting evidence emerged from analyses by the Federal Trade Commission, the Economic Council of Canada, and (for the United Kingdom) Gerald Newbould, all of whom found post-merger marketing economies to be relatively unimportant.[47] The Canadian study showed marketing economies to emerge even less frequently than production economies, which were reported in 6.5 percent of the 1,826 surveyed acquisitions and 15.2 percent of the horizontal manufacturing industry mergers.

Complementarities also exist in research and development. One firm may have two or three unusually creative engineers but lack the distribution network needed to derive full commercial benefit from the new products they turn out. Another may have superb marketing channels but find its laboratories populated by unimaginative clods. Together they can make beautiful music. Ideas and money can also be brought together through merger. There is reason to believe that such motives have influenced an appreciable number of mergers, especially those in which small research-based enterprises were acquired.[48] Once such creative individuals are ensconced in the larger, more bureaucratic R&D organizations of large acquirers, however, they often become frustrated. A study by super-computer specialist Control Data Corporation revealed that fewer than 15 percent of the innovative engineers and scientists recruited through acquisitions over a period of twenty-two years remained with the company.[49] More generally, a statistical analysis covering 2,955 lines of business showed that having all of a line's assets stemming from conglomerate mergers was associated with R&D/sales ratios 18 percent lower on average than those prevailing generally in the industry in which the unit operated.[50]

Finally, there is the possibility that mergers infuse superior new management into companies suffering from talent or motivational deficiencies. Or they may permit managerial overhead streamlining.

For the 2,955 lines of business discussed above, there was a weak negative correlation between corporate overhead allocations and merger intensity, implying an average cost reduction of about 0.5 percent of sales for lines originating totally through merger.[51] For the horizontal mergers surveyed by the Economic Council of Canada, economies in administration and management were given top rating in a third of the cases — more than twice as frequently as for plant and materials integration economies.[52]

Yet merger is clearly no panacea for management weaknesses. Merger makers may suffer from hubris, overestimating their ability to manage more complex organizations and to deal with unfamiliar technologies and markets.[53] This failing can be compounded when corporate leaders are motivated by the desire to build an empire through the consummation of numerous mergers. In his sample of thirty-eight British mergers, Newbould found that managerial teething problems were common — so much so that eighteen of the companies said undertaking similar acquisitions was impossible because their managerial resources were insufficient.[54] In the United States, somewhere between 47 and 57 percent of the conglomerate mergers made during the 1960s and early 1970s were subsequently undone through divestiture of the acquired units.[55] That performance of the sold-off units had been unsatisfactory is shown by the fact that their operating income was *negative* on average (compared to +13.9 percent of assets for nondivested units) in the year before sell-off commenced.[56] Case studies of divested conglomerate acquisitions reveal frequent breakdowns in the control mechanisms linking top corporate and operating-level management, especially when operating units were hit by unexpected problems. Incentive failures at the operating level were also common.[57] Thus, it is far from clear a priori that moving relatively small firms into much larger organizations through merger has a net positive impact on the quality of management.

Statistical Evidence on Merger Outcomes

Mergers *may* improve the coalescing firms' efficiency, but they can also increase the burdens of bureaucracy and degrade operating performance. From a priori principles and case study evidence, it is impossible to discern whether the balance of effects is positive or negative, or how large the average merger-induced changes may be. For that, broad-gauged statistical analysis is necessary. Literally scores of statistical studies have sought to measure the net efficiency consequences of merger.

Here we encounter a methodological fork. There have been two main approaches to the quantitative assessment of merger outcomes. One examines stock price movements using the logic of Capital Asset Pricing Theory,[58] while the other analyzes levels and changes in internally generated company performance indices such as profitability, sales, and market shares. The conclusions drawn are in some cases radically different, so we must take care to understand the underlying methodologies and if possible to reconcile the conflicting results.

Stock Price Studies   Many so-called *event studies* have attempted to isolate the economic consequences of merger.[59] The announcement of a forthcoming merger is viewed as an event

46. John Kitching, "Why Do Mergers Miscarry?" *Harvard Business Review,* vol. 45 (November-December 1967), pp. 87–90.

47. Gerald D. Newbould, *Management and Merger Activity* (Liverpool: Guthstead, 1970), p. 178; Economic Council of Canada, *Interim Report on Competition Policy* (Ottawa: Queen's Printer, July 1969), pp. 213–218; and Federal Trade Commission staff report, *Conglomerate Merger Performance: An Empirical Analysis of Nine Corporations* (Washington: Government Printing Office, 1972), pp. 37, 41, and 47–49.

48. See Murray N. Friedman, *The Research and Development Factor in Mergers and Acquisitions,* Study No. 16, U.S. Senate Committee on the Judiciary; Subcommittee on Patents, Trademarks, and Copyrights (Washington: USGPO, 1958). In a survey of venture capital institutions, Robert Premus found that approximately 42 percent of the new high-technology companies in which the funds invested were expected to "go public" with their own stock exchange listings, 26 percent would merge with larger firms, 19 percent would "just survive," and 13 percent would fail outright. *Venture Capital and Innovation,* study prepared for the Joint Economic Committee, U.S. Congress (Washington: USGPO, 1985), p. 35. Premus' percentages for three size categories were weighted to yield the overall averages reported here.

49. William C. Norris, "The Social Costs of Takeovers," *Corporate Report,* September 1983, p. 47.

50. Ravenscraft and Scherer, *Mergers,* supra note 32, pp. 120–121.

51. Ravenscraft and Scherer, *Mergers,* p. 106.

52. *Interim Report,* supra note 47, p. 217.

53. See Richard Roll, "The Hubris Hypothesis of Corporate Takeovers," *Journal of Business,* vol. 59 (April 1986), pp. 197–216.

54. *Management and Merger Activity,* supra note 47, pp. 182–183.

55. Ravenscraft and Scherer, *Mergers,* pp. 164–165; and Michael E. Porter, "From Competitive Advantage to Corporate Strategy," *Harvard Business Review,* vol. 65 (May-June 1987), pp. 43–59.

56. Ravenscraft and Scherer, *Mergers,* pp. 166–168.

57. Ravenscraft and Scherer, *Mergers,* pp. 134–141, 192–193, and 239–279.

58. Cf. pp. 128–129 supra.

59. For surveys of a vast literature, see Michael C. Jensen and Richard S. Ruback, "The Market for Corporate Control: The Scientific Evidence," *Journal of Financial Economics,* vol. 11, no. 1 (1983), pp. 5–50; and Gregg A. Jarrell, James A. Brickley, and Jeffry M. Netter, "The Market for Corporate Control: The Empirical Evidence Since 1980," *Journal of Economic Perspectives,* vol. 2 (Winter 1988), pp. 49–68.

that influences stock market investors' valuations of the acquiring and acquired firms. To isolate that influence, the stock price movements of the subject firms are normalized by estimating regression equations like equation (4.3) on p. 128 above. In effect, overall stock market movements are stripped out, leaving only deviations of the subject firm's stock price from the general market pattern to be analyzed. The result has been a trajectory of normalized merging firm stock prices over time like those shown in Figure 5.2, where the "A" values refer to the acquiring firm and the "a" values to the acquired or target firm. If the merger event had no influence on investors' valuations, the merging firms' normalized stock price trajectories would track, with some random deviation, the solid horizontal "General Market Portfolio" line. But quite typically, systematic deviations are observed.

For the target (usually smaller) firm, normalized stock prices tend to drift downward relative to the general market trend starting between two years and six months before the merger announcement. This is often interpreted as evidence that the target firm's management has strayed from the path of profit maximization or has otherwise run into difficulties. A few weeks before the merger event, target firm stock prices begin drifting upward because of information leaks and/or insider trading. At the time of the merger announcement, the target's stock price jumps upward, reflecting the premium above preannouncement values usually offered to induce the target firm shareholders to tender their shares (in a tender offer takeover) or vote for the merger (in a negotiated merger). When the merger is consummated, of course, the target firm's shares are delisted and no further price observations occur.

For the acquiring (*A*) firm, systematic patterns are less evident. When mergers are effected by offering shares of *A*'s stock in exchange for target *a* shares, *A* share values tend to drift upward relative to the overall market during the year or so before merger announcement. That *A*'s stock is used as the medium of exchange probably reflects the belief of *A*'s managers that the market is valuing their stock

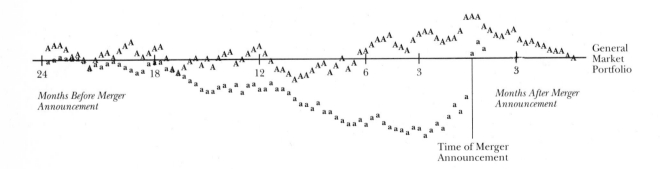

Figure 5.2
Normalized Merging Firm
Stock Prices Over Time

unusually favorably. For cash acquisitions, no systematic preannouncement pattern is apparent. For both stock and cash transactions, the most typical result is that during the ten days or so surrounding the merger announcement, acquirer *A*'s share values neither rise nor fall significantly relative to general market trends.

Thus, in a short window of time around the merger event, target firm shareholders experience significant stock price gains while acquiring firm shareholders are neither better nor worse off. The interpretation given this evidence is that, since a plus added to a zero yields a plus, the combined companies' market value has risen. Market value could rise because the merger is expected to confer monopoly power. But for conglomerate mergers, this is unlikely, and two studies of horizontal merger events in the United States yielded only equivocal evidence of enhanced monopoly profit expectations.[60] That stock market value has increased is viewed as evidence that the merging firms' intrinsic profitability is expected to rise, and if monopoly effects are ruled out, this must mean that the merger is efficiency increasing.

This inference rests upon some key assumptions, in particular, that stock markets are "efficient." Stock market efficiency implies that stock prices at any moment reflect all available information about future economic events and that current prices are unbiased predictors of future prices. Both implications are debatable.

No one denies that the stock market makes mistakes about future values. Indeed, stock prices are believed to move in a *random walk,* sometimes deviating below true (but unknown) values and sometimes rising above them.[61] An alternative interpretation of the "a" trajectory in Figure 5.2 is that the target firm's stock prices have departed randomly from their true values. Thus, it is not *a*'s managers who have erred, but the securities markets. If so, the market's undervaluation of "a" makes it a bargain worth scooping up, for example, through acquisition. Event analysts rule this interpretation out by invoking an axiom of market efficiency, that is, that even if a stock is undervalued, no one can know it is. But if there are actors, for example, the merger opportunity analysts of acquiring firms, who possess information superior to what is impounded in the market, or believe (perhaps wrongly) that they do, an undervaluation or bargain theory of acquisitions cannot be excluded as an alternative to the "*A* can run *a* more profitably than *a*'s managers" theory.

Moreover, there is evidence contrary to the efficient markets assumption that stock prices at the time of merger events are unbiased predictors of the future. The standard merger event study analyzes stock price changes only a few days on each side of the key announcement or other event. But when the coverage was extended to a year following the merger announcement, seven studies surveyed by Jensen and Ruback showed average acquiring firm stock price *declines* averaging 5.5 percent.[62] *Three* years following merger and takeover announcements of the 1970s

60. B. Espen Eckbo, "Horizontal Mergers, Collusion, and Stockholder Wealth," and Robert Stillman, "Examining Antitrust Policy Toward Horizontal Mergers," *Journal of Financial Economics,* vol. 11, no. 1 (1983), pp. 241–273 and 225–240.

61. On random walks generally, see William Feller, *An Introduction to Probability Theory and Its Applications,* vol. 1 (2nd ed.; New York: Wiley, 1957), Chapter III. On stock market valuation errors, see Fischer Black, "Noise," *Journal of Finance,* vol. 41 (July 1986), pp. 530–534.

62. Jensen and Ruback, "The Market," supra note 59, pp. 20–21.

and early 1980s, Magenheim and Mueller found, the average acquiring firm stock price decline was 16 percent.[63] Thus, target firm shareholders gain, but over the longer run, the shareholders of the (typically much larger) acquiring firms seem to lose. A plus added to a (possibly large, and quite uncertain) minus is no longer clearly a plus, so one cannot confidently infer that mergers are value enhancing.

There is no easy escape from these methodological problems. Prudence compels that other kinds of data be employed to see whether the results support or contradict the inferences from stock market event studies. To this task we proceed.

Premerger Profitability   Does the characteristic decline in the normalized stock prices of target firms prior to acquisition imply inefficient management or other problems? Additional light can be shed by examining the premerger profitability of targets. In doing so, it is important to distinguish between voluntary mergers, often initiated by and always consented to by target company management, and mergers induced directly or indirectly by a tender offer to the target's shareholders, bypassing target management. The latter, it should be noted, were much rarer than the former even during the 1980s, when U.S. tender offer takeovers numbered in the dozens compared to more than a thousand voluntary mergers per year.

Most studies of target firm profitability prior to voluntary mergers include only acquired firms listed on major stock exchanges, excluding the typically much larger number of small, privately held targets. The only more comprehensive study is that of Ravenscraft and Scherer,[64] who found that operating income (before deduction of interest expense and taxes) averaged 20.2 percent of assets in the year before acquisition for 634 manufacturing companies, large and small. For all manufacturing companies in the same three years, the comparable average was 10.9 percent. Thus, the targets were nearly twice as profitable on average as their nonacquired peers — a clear contradiction to the hypothesis that acquired firms are poor performers. There is a systematic size bias in the targets' profitability pattern: the smaller the target, the greater was its premerger profitability, apparently because large acquirers are willing to bother with small acquisitions only if they are extraordinarily attractive. But even for the largest acquired companies, average profitability was above all manufacturing norms, although the early 1960s may have been exceptional, with large targets underperforming the manufacturing universe by an appreciable margin.[65]

Tender offer targets appear to be different. Ravenscraft and Scherer found ninety-five targets of 1962–1976 tender offer takeovers to have operating income/assets ratios 3.5 percent lower on average than all manufacturing corporations in the same period (that is, 11.08 percent as compared to 11.49 percent) and 8.1 percent lower than companies in the same two-digit industry groups as the targets.[66] For fifty-six targets of 1975–1983 tender offers, Herman and Lowenstein found the targets to be of above-average profitability when a weighted average was taken, apparently because of the high profits made by a few very large petroleum companies.[67] When a simple average is taken, giving equal weight to the smaller targets, the group may have been slightly less profitable than the overall corporate population from which they were drawn. Thus, there is some evidence of deficient performance by the targets of involuntary merger attempts, but the systematic deficiency was at worst small on average.

These results can be reconciled with the declining trajectory of premerger stock prices for both tender offer and voluntary merger targets. Stock prices depend not only upon current earnings but also upon expectations of future earnings and the growth of such earnings. For voluntary mergers, there is evidence that profitability was rising as the year of merger approached and that a peak may have been reached in the year before merger.[68] This is consistent with the fact that target firm managers (often owner-managers) pick the time when they are to be acquired, and the highest price is apt to be fetched when profitability peaks. If profit ratios were rising to a peak before merger, the increase in profitability had to be decelerating, and since the stock market values profitability *growth,* a decline in the growth rate should be accompanied by a fall in stock prices relative to their trend, which is what event studies show. In other words, the targets were not performing badly, they were simply not continuing to improve their previously superior performance. For tender offer targets, the data suggest no significant change in profit rates during the two years preceding the first tender offer, and the lack of acceleration may again have triggered negative stock market reactions.

Further light is shed by the work of Mørck, Shleifer, and Vishny.[69] For 371 *Fortune* 500 industrial corporations, they analyzed 1980 ratios of companies' stock market value divided by the replacement value of their assets (a ratio called "Tobin's Q"). For the seventeen sample members entering voluntary acquisitions between 1981 and 1985, there was no significant difference between company Tobin's Q ratios and the comparable ratios for the principal industry in which a firm operated. Thus, no inference that the stock market viewed the targets unfavorably is warranted. For eighty companies with no merger but a complete top management turnover, Q ratios were significantly lower than those of the companies' home-base industries, implying unfavorable stock market evaluations and the expected corrective measures, that is, heads rolling. The experience of thirty-one hostile takeover targets was especially interesting. They had relatively low Q ratios, implying a dim stock market view of their prospects. But so did their industries, and indeed, the unfavorable industry effects were larger and more significant than the deviations of company Q ratios from industry average Q ratios. Thus, the companies that became tender offer targets occupied industries that got into trouble, and that, more than individual company shortcomings, seems to have singled them out for takeover attempts.[70]

63. Ellen B. Magenheim and Dennis C. Mueller, "Are Acquiring-Firm Shareholders Better Off after an Acquisition?" in John Coffee et al., eds., *Knights,* supra note 36, pp. 177–181, with comment by Michael Bradley and Gregg Jarrell, pp. 255–256. The 16 percent estimate assumes the most conservative measurement technique.

64. Ravenscraft and Scherer, *Mergers,* supra note 32, pp. 58–64.

65. See Ravenscraft and Scherer, *Mergers,* pp. 56–58 and 67–73; Boyle, "Pre-Merger Growth and Profit," supra note 33; and Robert S. Harris, John F. Stewart, and W. T. Carleton, "Financial Characteristics of Acquired Firms," in Michael Keenan and Lawrence J. White, eds., *Mergers and Acquisitions: Current Problems in Perspective* (Lexington, MA: Lexington Books, 1982), pp. 223–240.

66. Ravenscraft and Scherer, *Mergers,* pp. 68–70.

67. Edward S. Herman and Louis Lowenstein, "The Efficiency Effects of Hostile Takeovers," in Coffee et al., eds., *Knights,* supra note 36, pp. 225–227.

68. Ravenscraft and Scherer, *Mergers,* pp. 72–73 and 113–117.

69. Randall Mørck, Andrei Shleifer, and Robert W. Vishny, "Characteristics of Targets of Hostile and Friendly Takeovers," in Alan J. Auerbach, ed., *Corporate Takeovers: Causes and Consequences* (Chicago: University of Chicago Press, 1988), pp. 114–120.

70. The statistically insignificant firm effect found by Mørck et al. may be an artifact of diversification, since a firm that specializes in some hard-hit industry will have lower Q ratio values than other industry members diversified into industries enjoying greater prosperity and/or stock market favor.

**Postmerger
Performance**

The question remains, how well did acquirers do with the companies they acquired after the mergers were consummated? Here too important methodological problems arise. For one, the typical acquired company is small relative to its acquirer — on average for U.S. mergers of the 1960s, less than one-twentieth the size of its new parent. Thus, its profit contribution is apt to be overwhelmed within the much larger compass of the parent's operations. Also, when mergers occur, acquired entity asset values are often written up to reflect the premiums paid over premerger accounting sums. One must be careful to distinguish changes attributable to the accountants' sleight-of-hand from those reflecting more or less efficient operation of the acquired company's business.

The only study to deal with both of these problems was by Ravenscraft and Scherer.[71] To pinpoint the differences in profitability between lines without merger, pre-1950 lines expanded through merger, and lines joining the parent as a result of diversifying mergers, they used 1974–1976 line of business financial breakdowns filed with the Federal Trade Commission by 471 large U.S. manufacturing corporations. For each of the nearly 6,000 mergers made between 1950 and 1976 and linked to 4,409 reporting lines of business, Ravenscraft and Scherer ascertained the method of asset accounting used. The results from their analysis of these data are complex, but can be summarized as follows:

1. An estimated 47 percent of the acquired units were subsequently sold off. Those units had profits well above their industry norms before merger, but on average, profitability was *negative* in the year preceding sell-off. Thus, disastrous performance declines occurred. The sell-off rate was significantly higher for conglomerate acquisitions than for horizontal and vertical acquisitions.

2. Units whose asset values were restated at the time of acquisition and which were not subsequently sold off experienced modest profitability declines, most of which resulted from accounting revaluations, but a small part of which reflected deteriorating performance.

3. Units whose asset values were not restated and which were not subsequently sold off experienced severe postmerger profitability declines. Before merger, their profitability was more than double industry norms; nine years on average after merger, the ratio of their operating income to assets had fallen to rough equality with industry norms. Horizontal mergers fared insignificantly better than conglomerate acquisitions. Much of the profitability decline was an inevitable regression from unsustainably high premerger values, but some appears to have been the consequence of less efficient postmerger operations.

4. Mergers between companies of roughly equal size had more favorable postmerger sell-off experiences. Their profitability rose slightly relative to premerger values by one measure and was essentially unchanged by another measure.

5. Companies taken over as a direct or indirect result of tender offers suffered significant postmerger profitability declines. However, those declines were attributable almost entirely to accounting manipulations. Abstracting from such accounting revaluations, average operating performance neither improved nor worsened following takeover.

The picture that emerges is a pessimistic one: widespread failure, considerable mediocrity, and occasional successes. Although unusually ambitious in methodology and scope, the Ravenscraft-Scherer study was limited in time and space. It covered only U.S. manufacturing corporations, emphasized conglomerate mergers made during the 1960s and early 1970s, and analyzed post-merger profitability only for the years 1974–1977. Still their findings for larger acquisitions (i.e., tender offer targets and "mergers of equals"), though more detailed, do not differ greatly from those emerging from other studies. Analyzing profits in the fourth through sixth years following 413 mergers made between 1968 and 1978 by U.S. commercial banks, Stephen Rhoades discerned no tendency for profitability either to improve or decline relative to premerger levels.[72] From an ambitious matched analysis of industrial mergers in Belgium, France, West Germany, Holland, Sweden, the United Kingdom, and the United States, Mueller et al. concluded:

No consistent pattern of either improved or deteriorated profitability can therefore be claimed across the seven countries. Mergers would appear to result in a slight improvement here, a slight worsening there. If a generalization is to be drawn, it would have to be that mergers have but modest effects, up or down, on the profitability of the merging firms in the three to five years following merger. Any economic efficiency gains from the mergers would appear to be small . . . as would any market power increases.[73]

The European samples, it is worth emphasizing, contained a much larger proportion of sizable horizontal mergers than can be observed in post-1950 U.S. analyses. Another British study controlling explicitly for merger accounting revaluations, as in the Ravenscraft-Scherer analysis, concluded:

[T]he efficiency gains, which in public policy statements have been assumed to be the saving grace of growth by takeover, cannot . . . be relied upon: strong evidence was reported that the efficiency of the typical amalgamation did not improve after merger . . . it actually appears to have declined.[74]

Further insights consistent with the Ravenscraft-Scherer sell-off evidence are contributed by a study of post-merger market share changes exploiting detailed line of business data for the one thousand largest U.S. manufacturing enterprises.[75] Dennis Mueller found that between 1950 and 1972, merged lines' market shares declined significantly relative to those of lines without sizable mergers. The share erosion was substantially greater for conglomerate acquisitions than for horizontal acquisitions.

71. Ravenscraft and Scherer, *Mergers,* Chapter 4.

72. Stephen A. Rhoades, "The Operating Performance of Acquired Firms in Banking before and after Acquisition," Staff Study No. 149, Board of Governors of the Federal Reserve System, April 1986.

73. Dennis C. Mueller, ed., *The Determinants and Effects of Mergers* (Cambridge: Oelgeschlager, Gunn & Hain, 1980), p. 306.

74. Geoffrey Meeks, *Disappointing Marriage: A Study of the Gains from Merger* (Cambridge: Cambridge University Press, 1977), p. 66. On U.K. mergers, see also Keith Cowling et al., *Mergers and Economic Performance* (Cambridge: Cambridge University Press, 1980); and Manmohan S. Kumar, *Growth, Acquisition and Investment* (Cambridge: Cambridge University Press, 1984), pp. 70–89.

75. Dennis C. Mueller, "Mergers and Market Share," *Review of Economics and Statistics,* vol. 67 (May 1985), pp. 259–267.

To sum up, statistical evidence supporting the hypothesis that profitability and efficiency increase following mergers is at best weak. Indeed, the weight of the evidence points in the opposite direction: efficiency is reduced on average following merger, especially when relatively small firms are absorbed into much larger and more bureaucratic enterprises lacking experience in the targets' specialized lines of business. To be sure, the statistical averages are just that; there is considerable variation from the central tendencies. Individual cases can be found to substantiate virtually all of the efficiency gain hypotheses identifiable in principle. Yet the overall historical record is far from reassuring.

U. S. Policies toward Mergers

Mergers affect market structure, sometimes in dramatic ways. They can create or enhance monopoly power, although most U.S. mergers of recent vintage have had little or no impact on this dimension. They can facilitate the realization of scale economies, and they can either improve or worsen the management of acquired units. Hostile takeovers threaten existing management with displacement, and thus may preemptively influence incumbent managers' behavior. In setting the rules of the game under which mergers take place, governments apply a variety of policy instruments, the most important of which are antitrust (called *competition policy* in Europe), tax policy, and the regulations governing corporate obligations and stockholder rights in response to tender offers. Leaving tax policy questions for public finance treatises, we focus here primarily upon antitrust policies toward mergers and secondarily upon tender offer rules.

Early U.S. Merger Antitrust

The United States was by a considerable span the first nation to adopt systematic antitrust policies toward merger. The Sherman Antitrust Act of 1890 declared "every . . . combination in the form of trust or otherwise . . . in restraint of trade" illegal. The early trusts were largely assembled through merger, so the law was plainly aimed at least in part at mergers. Section 2 of the Sherman Act outlawed monopolization of trade and attempts to monopolize. What these broad prohibitions meant with respect to particular mergers had to be determined through case-by-case adjudication.

After a faltering start, the first decisive antitrust blow against a merger occurred in the *Northern Securities* case.[76] The Northern Securities Company was formed in 1901 to consolidate the joint control of J. P. Morgan, James Hill, and other contemporary tycoons over the Northern Pacific and Great Northern railroads. President Theodore Roosevelt chose to make the combination a test case, and the arrangement was found to have illegally restrained rail transport competition in northern states west of the Mississippi River. The Supreme Court's decision was hardly a paragon of legal consensus, with four justices dissenting in two separate minority opinions from the majority judgment.

Subsequent cases (some to be discussed more fully in Chapter 12) made it clear that the Sherman Act could be used to prohibit mergers only when the merging firms were on the verge of attaining substantial monopoly power. To fill a perceived gap, Congress in 1914 passed the Clayton Antitrust Act, whose stated purpose was "to arrest the creation of trusts, conspiracies and monopolies in their incipiency and before consummation."[77] The principal provision affecting mergers was Section 7, which stated in part:

That no corporation engaged in commerce shall acquire, directly or indirectly, the whole or any part of the stock or other share capital of another corporation also in commerce where the effect of such acquisition may be to substantially lessen competition between [the two firms] or to restrain such commerce in any section or community or tend to create a monopoly of any line of commerce.

This choice of language left a gaping loophole through which able corporation lawyers could navigate their clients. It banned only *stock* acquisitions — the principal large-scale consolidation method of the times. By shifting to the outright purchase of a competitor's assets, companies could escape the law's reach. Direct asset acquisition is not always easy, but the loophole was opened even wider. In three 1926 cases, the Supreme Court ruled that a merger could not be dissolved if the acquiring firm first bought its rival's stock, but liquidated the stock and transformed its position to one of asset ownership before the antitrust enforcement agencies brought suit.[78] Then, in 1934, the Court found that a stock acquisition was safe if converted to asset ownership before a Federal Trade Commission order barring the merger was issued.[79] Moreover, the Supreme Court decided in 1930 that to prove a Section 7 violation, the government had to show nearly as substantial a lessening of competition as in Sherman Act cases.[80] These decisions left Section 7 emasculated. Altogether, only fifteen mergers were ordered dissolved through antitrust actions between 1914 and 1950, and ten of the orders were accomplished under Sherman Act rather than Clayton Act proceedings.

In 1950 Congress, concerned about a perceived new merger wave (which, as inspection of Figure 5.1 shows, was in fact only a modest blip) and about further government merger case defeats, passed the Celler-Kefauver Act. The Act amended original Clayton Act Section 7, removing the asset acquisition loophole and making several wording changes to bring nonhorizontal mergers within the law's reach, to eliminate a previously split infinitive, and to make clear Congress' desire to see a more vigorous antimerger program implemented. Its principal substantive paragraph provides:

76. *U.S.* v. *Northern Securities Co. et al.,* 120 Fed. 721 (1903); 193 U.S. 197 (1904). For background color, see William Letwin, *Law and Economic Policy in America* (New York: Random House, 1965), pp. 182–237. In 1970 a merger between the two was approved. *U.S.* v. *Interstate Commerce Commission et al.,* 396 U.S. 491 (1970).

Since citations to court decisions will be used frequently, a note on standard citation format is in order. U.S. in the citation 193 U.S. 197 above stands for reports of the United States Supreme Court; Fed. is for early reports of the lower Federal courts; F. Supp. is for later citations to federal district courts; and F. 2nd is for later citations to federal appellate courts. The number before the reporting source (that is, *193* in 193 U.S. 197) gives the volume number; the following number the page number on which the case report begins. Additional numbers following commas give the specific page numbers cited.

77. Senate Report no. 698, to accompany H.R. 15,657, 63rd Cong., 2nd sess. (1914), p. 1.

78. *Thatcher Mfg. Co.* v. *Federal Trade Commission, Swift & Co.* v. *Federal Trade Commission,* and *Federal Trade Commission* v. *Western Meat Co.,* 272 U.S. 554 (1926).

79. *Arrow-Hart & Hegeman Electric Co.* v. *Federal Trade Commission,* 291 U.S. 587 (1934).

80. *International Shoe Co.* v. *Federal Trade Commission,* 280 U.S. 291 (1930). On the development of Clayton Act Section 7 interpretations during this period, see David Dale Martin, *Mergers and the Clayton Act* (Berkeley: University of California Press, 1959), especially pp. 104–107.

[t]hat no corporation engaged in commerce shall acquire, directly or indirectly, the whole or any part of the stock or other share capital and no corporation subject to the jurisdiction of the Federal Trade Commission shall acquire the whole or any part of the assets of another corporation engaged also in commerce, where in any line of commerce in any section of the country, the effect of such acquisition may be substantially to lessen competition, or to tend to create a monopoly.

The new mandate was taken seriously by the enforcement agencies and the courts. From late 1950, when the Celler-Kefauver amendment was signed, through 1965, the Justice Department and Federal Trade Commission (with joint responsibility for enforcement) initiated some 173 antimerger complaints under the new law — more than twice as many as they had attempted during the thirty-six-year life of old Section 7. Moreover, the agencies' efforts were rewarded this time with an impressive string of victories in appeals to the Supreme Court. These judgments communicated in the strongest possible way that a tough line was to be taken.

Further legislation strengthened the enforcement agencies' hand. By 1973, both agencies had secured authority to seek preliminary injunctions against mergers — an order which, if granted, is usually lethal because of the merging parties' unwillingness to leave merget agreement terms pending during a long period of litigation. In 1969 the Federal Trade Commission instituted a premerger notification program under which companies agreeing to mergers of appreciable size had to file information on their sales, broken down to the U.S. Census seven-digit product level. This program was sanctioned and extended in the Hart-Scott-Rodino Act of 1976, which required inter alia a 15- to 30-day waiting period following initial notification before the merger could be consummated, giving the enforcement agencies time to study the evidence and decide whether to complain.

The Celler-Kefauver Act's text reveals that the law's main concern is with mergers tending to create monopolies or lessen competition. There are inklings in the underlying debate that Congress wished inter alia to stem the perceived tide toward rising economic concentration by "protect[ing] viable, small, locally owned businesses" — that is, to maintain fragmented market structures for their own sake, and not merely for the sake of minimizing monopoly power.[81] These are not inherently inappropriate goals, but there is not much that economists, or economics texts, can say to illuminate them. We are led therefore, as the courts have increasingly been drawn, to focus on the explicit links between mergers and prospective monopoly power.

Market Definition Precedents

The methods of Celler-Kefauver Act analysis are consciously structuralist. To determine whether a merger violates the law, one must identify the relevant product market (that is, in the law's terms, the "line of commerce") and the relevant geographic market (the "section of the country"). With the market so defined, one must ascertain whether the merger-induced change in market structure, measured in terms of market share or concentration index increases, is sufficient to threaten a substantial lessening of competition.

In its first substantive pronouncement on the 1950 merger law, the Supreme Court provided a list of criteria for identifying the relevant product market:

The outer boundaries of a product market are determined by the reasonable interchangeability of use or the cross-elasticity of demand between the product itself and substitutes for it. . . . However, within this broad market, well-defined submarkets may exist which, in themselves, constitute product markets for antitrust purposes. . . . The boundaries of such a submarket may be determined by examining such practical indicia as industry or public recognition of the submarket as a separate economic entity, the product's peculiar characteristics and uses, unique production facilities, distinct customers, distinct prices, sensitivity to price changes, and specialized vendors.[82]

The Court's criteria are sufficiently broad as to be useless without further clarification. In early substantive reviews, the Supreme Court found relevant markets to include the retailing of men's, women's, and children's shoes separately in individual cities with population exceeding ten thousand;[83] commercial banking in a four-county area around Philadelphia;[84] aluminum electrical conductor wire and cable (excluding copper);[85] glass bottles and metal cans combined,[86] grocery retailing in the Los Angeles area;[87] and beer sales in the state of Wisconsin.[88] In those cases, mergers were found to be illegal when the merging firms' market shares exceeded 20 percent (in thirty-two women's shoe markets), 36 percent of Philadelphia area bank deposits, 29.1 percent (27.8 plus 1.3) in aluminum wire and cable, 25 percent (22 plus 3) in glass and metal containers, 7.5 percent (4.7 plus 2.8) in Los Angeles food retailing, and 24 percent (13.0 plus 10.7) in Wisconsin beer. Some of the market definitions overstepped the bounds of logic and plausibility, and in early cases, the Supreme Court found the shares of defined markets to exceed what was permissable with such consistency that Justice Potter Stewart was provoked in a dissent to exclaim, "The sole consistency that I can find is that in litigation under Section 7, the Government always wins."[89] Nevertheless, the court's decisions exhibit a different sort of consistency: the consistent willingness to accept market definitions that resolve intrinsic uncertainties on the side of preventing mergers with possible anticompetitive effects. This in turn may have been no more than faithful stewardship to the will of Congress.

There is, however, an alternative explanation. No matter what the civics texts say, decisions on matters as complex as mergers represent a rule of men, not laws. The Supreme Court that rendered the decisions cited above was inclined toward overriding laissez-faire presumptions to stem economic concentration, which a majority perceived as undesirable. In 1974, following new and more conservative appointments to the bench, the Court handed antitrust enforcers their first defeat on a merger market definition question.[90] The Department of Justice argued that a merger between two coal companies was objectionable because the partners' combined share of 1967 Illinois production totaled 21.8 percent. The Supreme Court found the merger legal, stating that the relevant measure was not current

---

81. See *Brown Shoe Co.* v. *U.S.,* 370 U.S. 294, 344 (1962); and *U.S.* v. *Von's Grocery Co. et al.,* 384 U.S. 270, 275–278 (1966).

82. *Brown Shoe Co.* v. *U.S.,* 370 U.S. 294, 325 (1962).

83. Ibid. at 337–339.

84. *U.S.* v. *Philadelphia National Bank et al.,* 374 U.S. 321, 359–360 (1963).

85. *U.S.* v. *Aluminum Co. of America et al.,* 377 U.S. 271, 273–277 (1964).

86. *U.S.* v. *Continental Can Co. et al.,* 378 U.S. 441, 456–457 (1964).

87. *U.S.* v. *Von's Grocery Co. et al.,* 384 U.S. 270, 272 (1966).

88. *U.S.* v. *Pabst Brewing Co. et al.,* 384 U.S. 546,548–552 (1966). See also 233 F. Supp. 475, 482 (1964).

89. *U.S.* v. *Von's Grocery Co. et al.,* 384 U.S. 270, 301 (1966).

90. *U.S.* v. *General Dynamics Corp. et al.,* 414 U.S. 486 (1974).

coal *production* shares, but the share of uncommitted coal reserves needed to win new long-term contracts from electrical utilities. And since one of the merging firms had sparse uncommitted reserves, the merger was allowed to stand. The decision signaled to lower courts that market definitions adverse to a pending merger would not be accepted uncritically and that a premium would henceforth be placed on careful economic analysis. The enforcement agencies began losing merger cases on market definition grounds with some regularity, and economists, both in and outside the enforcement agencies, worked to develop market definition principles with a more solid analytic basis.[91]

Economic Principles   The essence of monopoly power is the ability to raise prices above competitive levels. A key market definition question, therefore, is: what boundaries circumscribe the set of firms positioned to thwart attempts by the merging firms persistently to raise prices?

The underlying principles are most easily grasped when the problem is one of geographic market definition, as illustrated in Figure 5.3. Suppose a merger is proposed between Portland cement suppliers A and B, who are located in the vicinity of Philadelphia. Other cement makers C, D, and so forth, are located along a one-dimensional highway extending from Philadelphia westward. Each supplier has production plus local delivery costs of $40 per ton. Shipping a ton of cement costs $2 for every 50 miles of distance traversed. Assuming no persistent physical limits on local supply, the price to Philadelphia consumers if firms A and B compete vigorously should be approximately $40. The ability of merging firms A and B to raise prices locally is constrained by the lure higher prices would create for competitive inroads from more distant suppliers — from C if the Philadelphia price is raised above $42, from D with a price elevation above $44, and so forth. Which firms *are* then in the market, meaningfully constraining the actions of A and B? The question has no answer until a value judgment is made as to *how much* the price can be elevated in Philadelphia (or whatever group of consumers is affected) before one infers that *too much* monopoly power is being exerted. If the line is drawn at 10 percent, that is, $44, then the set of suppliers able to hold the actions of Philadelphia area cement makers within the accepted competitive limits includes only firms A, B, C, and D. Thus, the relevant market is defined to include Philadelphia area firms plus all firms located within 100 miles of Philadelphia. More distant firms E, F, and so forth, are out of the market as defined.

There is a problem in this approach. Suppose that when the merger occurs, firms A, B, C, and D are already participating in a monopolistic scheme to keep prices in Philadelphia at $44 per ton. The monopoly power that merger policy seeks to prevent is already being exercised. Then an unwary analyst might add 10 percent to the observed $44 price and conclude that the relevant market should include all firms able to supply cement to Philadelphians at prices of $48.40 or less. The boundary will be extended beyond 200 miles, adding firms E and F to the calculations of merger impact. It is conceivable that E and F have much larger capacities than A, B, C, and D, so that when one extends the market boundaries to include E and F and sums the included producers' capacities, the shares of A and B in that erroneously defined market are sufficiently small that the merger is considered inconsequential and allowed to proceed, even though it in fact strengthens

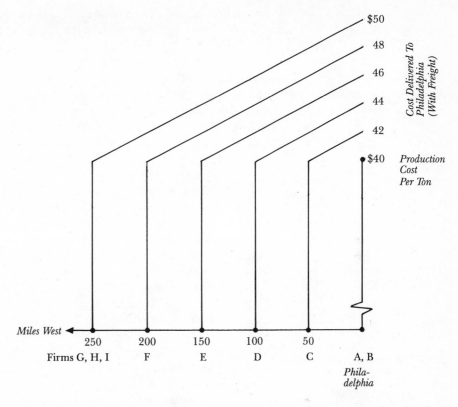

Figure 5.3

Effect of Distance on Delivered
Cost and Geographic Market
Definition

the ability to collude of A, B, C, and D. Conduct can influence market definition if one is not careful, causing errors to be made.

Despite the difficulties, this approach to market definition was adopted in *Merger Guidelines* published by the U.S. Department of Justice in 1982. Specifically, the Department announced:

Taking the location of the merging firm . . . as a beginning point, the Department will . . . expand the provisional market boundaries to include the locations of firms (or plants) that could make significant sales to customers of firms

91. The literature is enormous. Significant contributions include Kenneth G. Elzinga and Thomas F. Hogarty, "The Problem of Geographic Market Delineation in Antimerger Suits," *Antitrust Bulletin,* vol. 45 (Spring 1973), pp. 45–81; Kenneth D. Boyer, "Industry Boundaries," in Terry Calvani and John Siegfried, eds., *Economic Analysis and Antitrust Law* (Boston: Little, Brown, 1979), pp. 88–106; Ira Horowitz, "Market Delineation in Antitrust Analysis: A Regression–Based Test," *Southern Economic Journal,* vol. 48 (January 1981), pp. 1–16; William M. Landes and Richard A. Posner, "Market Power in Antitrust Cases," *Harvard Law Review,* vol. 94 (March 1981), pp. 937–996; the comments on Landes and Posner by Richard Schmalensee, Louis Kaplow, Timothy J. Brennan, and Janusz Ordover, Alan Sykes, and Robert Willig, in *Harvard Law Review,* vol. 95 (June 1982),

pp. 1787–1874; Gregory J. Werden, "Market Delineation and the Justice Department's Merger Guidelines," *Duke Law Journal,* vol. 1983 (June 1983), pp. 514–579; Jonathan B. Baker and Timothy Bresnahan, "The Gains from Merger or Collusion in Product-Differentiated Industries," *Journal of Industrial Economics,* vol. 33 (June 1985), pp. 427–444; George J. Stigler and Robert A. Sherwin, "The Extent of the Market," *Journal of Law & Economics,* vol. 28 (October 1985), pp. 555–586; Noel D. Uri and Edward J. Rifkin, "Geographic Markets, Causality and Railroad Deregulation," *Review of Economics and Statistics,* vol. 67 (August 1985), pp. 422–428; and Jonathan B. Baker, "Why Price Correlations Do Not Define Antitrust Markets," Federal Trade Commission Bureau of Economics working paper no. 149 (January 1987).

previously included . . . in response to a small but significant and non-transitory increase in price. As a first approximation, the Department will hypothesize a price increase of five percent and ask how many sellers could sell the product to such customers within one year.[92]

The "five percent" guideline is arbitrary; in fact, the Justice Department's economists argued initially for a 10 percent standard applied over two years, not one, and in subsequent cases, a 10 percent criterion was often used.[93] Ideally, the price elevation percentage ought to be smaller, the larger the relevant amount of demand affected, and hence the greater the burden of monopoly power on consumers. It ought to be larger, the more uncertain the measurement of a price elevation's impact is. Measuring that impact is relatively easy in delineating geographic markets, since transportation costs are readily calculable,[94] and for mature commodities not subject to turbulent technological or demand changes. In what is believed to have been the first explicit judicial recognition that the extent of price elevation mattered, a U.S. district court set the threshold at 1 percent in defining the relevant geographic market for gasoline — a mature commodity in particularly heavy demand.[95]

Similar procedures were announced by the Department of Justice for identifying product markets. However, it is much more difficult to determine in an antitrust proceeding whether "a significant percentage of the buyers of products already included [in the market] would be likely to shift to . . . other products in response to a small but significant and non-transitory increase in price."[96] Therefore, other approaches continue to be used by the various contending parties, and in early applications of the price elevation approach to merger market definition, the Justice Department was rebuffed by the courts in every case but one.[97]

The main approaches and their problems can be illustrated through an illustration drawn, with considerable artistic license and oversimplification, from a litigated 1987 merger between Owens-Illinois and Brockway, the second- and third-largest U.S. glass bottle manufacturers.[98] Their shares of the glass container market, if it was a market, were 22.7 and 15.0 percent — almost surely enough to render the merger illegal. The key question was: Was "glass containers" indeed the relevant market for antitrust purposes, or should the market include in addition metal cans and especially plastic containers? Plastic containers, the adjudicating court observed, "offer many of the same advantages traditionally unique to glass — such as impermeability to moisture and oxygen, clarity, and heat resistance — in addition to providing . . . the primary attractions of plastic — nonbreakability and lighter weight."[99]

From the court's discussion of numerous applications, it is evident that glass containers had strong advantages over plastics in packaging such products as oxygen-sensitive wine, carbonated beverages, and pickles. Thus, glass would sell even if its price were higher than the comparable plastic container price. Because of carbonation loss, for example, Coca-Cola found it necessary to rotate plastic-bottled but not glass-bottled packages every thirteen weeks. In other applications, plastic would be favored over glass at identical per-unit prices because of its lower product shipping cost (owing to differential weight and breakage) and "squeezability." Thus, as seems typical when differentiated products vie for orders, there was a spectrum of applications, from those in which glass had an intrinsic advantage over plastic to those in which it operated at a disadvantage.

This set of facts is characterized in Figure 5.4. We assume that the price of an average plastic container is fourteen cents. Given the price of plastic containers, demand for an average glass bottle is given by the solid demand curve D_{14}.[100] It lies above the fourteen-cent level at which plastic containers are priced for the first eleven billion bottles of demand per year, reflecting the intrinsic superiority of glass in that range of applications. At prices roughly one cent below those of plastic containers, glass bottles win the contest across a wide quantity range. At still lower prices, however, demand turns more inelastic, reflecting increasing difficulty wresting further applications away from plastics and eventually the fact that demand for *all* containers — glass, plastic, and other — is limited by the demand for the products packaged in them.

The dotted line D_{10} shows what happens to the demand for bottles when the price of the average plastic container is reduced to ten cents. The curve's downward shift shows that to remain competitive, bottles must sell at lower prices.[101] Intrinsic superiority in certain applications is not enough; if the price of plastic falls and bottle prices do not adjust, users for whom the superiority of glass is modest will shift to plastic.

We are now in a position to apply the principal economic methods used to determine whether glass bottles and plastic containers should be placed in the same market for merger evaluation purposes. Three main tests have been proposed: the Justice Department's price elevation test, cross elasticity of demand, and price correlation over time.

The supply curve for glass bottles (reflecting marginal cost) is given by the curve S_G. Given a fourteen-cent price for the average plastic container, and hence the glass bottle demand curve D_{14}, the competitive equilibrium price for bottles is ten cents per unit, and some 28.6 billion bottles are sold. Suppose now a merger among bottle makers gives them the power to raise prices. Will they be restrained from doing so by competition from plastic? Assuming provisionally that the price of plastic containers does not change, the effect of substitute competition is already

92. U.S. Department of Justice, *Merger Guidelines* (Washington: June 14, 1982), p. 8.

93. Calkins, "Developments," supra note 27, p. 857, note 9.

94. For outdated information on shipping costs and a methodology for updating it, see Scherer et al., *Multi-Plant Operation,* supra note 42, pp. 89–90 and 408–413.

95. *Marathon Oil Company* v. *Mobil Corporation et al.,* 530 F. Supp. 315, 322 (1981). Author Scherer was witness for Marathon Oil.

96. *Merger Guidelines,* supra note 92, p. 4.

97. Calkins, "Developments in Merger Litigation," supra note 27, pp. 862–865.

98. *Federal Trade Commission* v. *Owens-Illinois, Inc., et al.,* 681 F. Supp. 27 (1988).

99. Ibid. at p. 31.

100. The demand curve equation is assumed to be:

$$P_{glass} = P_{plastic} + 6.09 - 1.236\,Q + .0507\,Q^2 - .00002719\,Q^4$$

where Q is the quantity of bottles sold (in billions per year). The plotted curve's serpentine shape is chosen as the static analogue of

the well-established dynamic tendency for superior new products to follow a market penetration trajectory over time that closely approximates a logistic curve. See Colin G. Thirtle and Vernon W. Ruttan, *The Role of Demand and Supply in the Generation and Diffusion of Technical Change* (New York: Harwood, 1987), pp. 77–101. A logistic diffusion curve will emerge *inter alia* when consumers' reservation prices are normally distributed and a product's price is reduced relative to substitutes at a constant rate over time.

The supply function's equation is:

$$P = 5 + .0000075\,Q^4.$$

101. The parallel demand shift implies for simplicity that the market for containers of all types has zero price elasticity. This violates reality, but probably not seriously, since the demand for containers is derived from the demand for the products they enclose, there are few substitutes for all containers in this role, and the cost of containers is relatively small in comparison to total product price.

Figure 5.4
Glass Bottles Versus Plastic
Containers

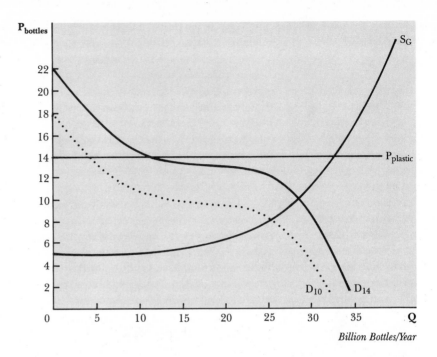

Billion Bottles/Year

reflected in demand curve D_{14}. Suppose the bottle price is raised 10 percent, that is, from $10 to $11. The quantity of bottles demanded will fall to 27.6 billion, or by 3.6 percent. A 10 percent price increase leads to only a 3.6 percent reduction in quantity demanded; glass bottle demand is price inelastic. A full-fledged monopoly would raise the price of bottles into the range of elastic demand.[102] Indeed, the monopoly profit-maximizing price, it can be shown, is $12.50. Thus, according to the Justice Department test, if a merger conferred the ability to set prices collusively, the bottle makers would not be restrained by substitute competition from raising their prices substantially. There is a sufficiently large set of packaging applications for which plastic containers at fourteen cents are weak substitutes that postmerger price-raising would be profitable.

This conclusion is critically dependent upon the assumption that plastic container prices remain at fourteen cents. The record of the Owens-Illinois-Brockway merger case shows that, because of technological changes, the quality of plastic containers was rising and prices were falling over time relative to those of glass bottles. Suppose that at the time of merger, or at some foreseeable time thereafter, plastic container prices were to be ten cents on average, all else equal. Then the demand curve for bottles would be the dotted line D_{10}, and the competitive equilibrium price of bottles would fall to 8.10 cents. The demand for bottles at this equilibrium is visibly more elastic than at the equilibrium with fourteen-cent plastic container prices. With plastic prices at ten cents, a glass bottle monopoly created by merger would raise the profit-maximizing bottle price to 9.18 cents — only 13.3 percent more than the competitive price. If there were doubts whether the merger could create sufficient monopoly power to raise prices all the way to the profit-maximizing level, application of the Justice Department test might not clearly exclude plastic and glass together as a meaningful market, which might in turn mean (if concentration among plastic manufacturers were sufficiently low) that the merger should not be stopped.

Consider now the cross elasticity test. The cross elasticity of demand for glass bottles is given by:

$$\frac{\text{Percentage change in the quantity of bottles sold}}{\substack{\text{Percentage change in plastic container price,}\\ \text{holding bottle prices constant}}}.$$

If the price of plastic containers were to fall from fourteen to twelve cents per unit, that is, by 14.3 percent, holding the price of glass bottles constant at its original competitive equilibrium value of ten cents, the quantity of bottles consumed would fall by 10.3 percent to 25.55 billion units per year.[103] The cross elasticity of demand is found to be 0.75 — a relatively low value, suggesting that glass and plastic are not good substitutes.[104] But if there were a larger decrease in the price of plastic containers, that is, from fourteen to ten cents, the quantity of glass bottles sold would fall by 58 percent, ceteris paribus, implying a cross elasticity of demand equal to 2.03. This is a relatively high value, suggesting, as in the DoJ bottle price elevation analysis, that at relatively low plastic prices, glass and plastic are good substitutes and should be included in the same market!

Finally, some economists have proposed correlating the prices (or changes in the prices) of two commodities over time. If a relatively high correlation is obtained, there is presumably a tendency for prices to tend toward uniformity, allowance being made for transport costs and quality differences. High correlations are said in turn to warrant an inference that the two commodities belong to the same market.[105] Given the assumptions underlying Figure 5.4, this analysis can be performed if one assumes, consistent with the Owens-Illinois case evidence, that plastic container prices have been drifting downward relative to glass bottle prices over time. Holding constant the supply curve for bottles (and hence general price levels), the equilibrium prices of bottles over a range of plastic container prices are as follows:

Plastic (cents)	Glass (cents)
20	12.53
18	11.75
16	10.91
14	10.00
12	9.09
10	8.10

---

102. This is a direct implication of monopoly pricing equation (2.2), p. 35 supra.

103. Because the price of glass bottles changes in response to changes in the price of plastic containers, it is difficult in practice to hold glass prices constant. We are able to do so because we have a well-specified model of the interdependence between glass and plastic prices. Failing to hold the glass bottle price constant will lead to downward-biased cross elasticities.

104. For simplicity, we abstain here from averaging values to obtain *arc* elasticities.

105. Stigler and Sherwin, "The Extent of the Market," supra note 91, p. 555.

If values such as these were observed with roughly equal frequency as technological changes reduced the level of plastic container prices, the simple correlation between the two price series would be 0.999, and the correlation of the series' logarithms would be 0.995. Again, from this longer time perspective, one would conclude that glass bottles and plastic containers belong to the same market.

We see then that the market definition one chooses is sensitive to the methodology used, and that differences in results may hinge upon the size of the price movements assumed, which in turn depend upon the time frame analyzed. Over a short period of time, with plastic prices hovering near fourteen cents per unit, all three market definition methods are apt to yield the same conclusion: that glass bottles and plastic containers occupy separate and distinct markets. But if technological progress is more rapid for one commodity (plastics) than for another, and if a relatively long time frame is adopted, all three methods might indicate that the two commodities belong in the same market. A similar conclusion emerges when there are significant fluctuations over time in the supply conditions for at least one commodity (that is, when plastic container prices move randomly between ten and fourteen cents) uncorrelated with those of the other commodity. Here, as in setting the price elevation threshold for the *Merger Guidelines* test, a value judgment cannot be avoided: How far back into history should the investigation look, and even more importantly, how far into the future should changing market conditions be projected?

Market Structure Changes

Once the thorny question of market definition is settled, the analysis of a merger's effects must determine whether the increase in market concentration is sufficient that a substantial lessening of competition is threatened. This is a point on which the analysis in subsequent chapters will provide some guidance. But in the end, difficult value judgments cannot be escaped. In its first *Merger Guidelines,* published in 1968, the Department of Justice stated that in relatively concentrated markets, for example, with four-seller concentration ratios of 75 percent or more, it would ordinarily challenge mergers involving the following market shares:[106]

Acquiring Firm	Acquired Firm
4%	4% or more
10%	2% or more
15% or more	1% or more

In markets with four-firm concentration ratios of less than 75 percent, its challenges would be directed toward mergers with the following market shares:

Acquiring Firm	Acquired Firm
5%	5% or more
10%	4% or more
15%	3% or more
20%	2% or more
25% or more	1% or more

More stringent standards were enunciated for markets displaying a trend toward rising concentration.

Announcing new merger guidelines in 1982, the Department of Justice shifted its focus to the Herfindahl-Hirschman Index (HHI), which is favored by some (but not all) theories of monopolistic pricing and which conveys a more scientific aura than the humble four-firm concentration ratio.[107] For markets with HHI values above 1800 (corresponding to a situation with six roughly equal-sized sellers), the Department indicated that it was "likely" to challenge mergers increasing the HHI by 100 percentage points or more. A broader array of considerations would be brought to bear in determining whether to challenge mergers adding from 50 to 100 points. For markets with HHI values between 1000 and 1800, a merger challenge was deemed "unlikely" unless the HHI was increased through merger by at least 100 points, but "more likely than not" for mergers with a larger structural impact. For markets with HHI values below 1000, a merger challenge was said to be "unlikely."

The 1987 Owens-Illinois merger with Brockway Glass provides an illustration of the technique. *Assuming* glass bottles to be the relevant market, the leading firms' market shares and their squared values were as follows:

	Market Share (%)	Squared
Anchor/Diamond	23.7	562
Owens-Illinois	22.7	515
Brockway	15.0	225
Ball-Incon	11.4	130
Triangle	8.2	67
Kerr	3.1	10
Gallo	3.1	10
Eleven others (sum)	12.8	19
Total	100.0	1538

The sum of the squared market shares gives the premerger HHI. It lies in the range where, under the Justice Department's guidelines, only mergers increasing HHI by more than 100 points were likely to be challenged. To calculate the merger's impact, one adds the merging firms' shares (22.7 + 15.0 = 37.7), squares the sum (= 1421), and subtracts from that new component of the HHI the firms' squared shares (515 and 225) as independent entities, concluding that the increase in HHI attributable to merger is 681. This exceeds the guidelines by a country mile, and so if glass bottles were the relevant market, the merger would probably have been enjoined.[108] However, since the District Court ruled that the

106. U.S. Department of Justice, *Merger Guidelines* (Washington: May 30, 1968).

107. *Merger Guidelines,* supra note 92, p. 13.

108. Neither the Federal Trade Commission, which challenged the Owens-Illinois-Brockway merger, nor the federal courts, which were called upon to issue a preliminary injunction, are bound by the Justice Department guidelines. However, both have elected to apply them in some instances.

true market was much broader, encompassing plastic, metal, and paper containers as well as glass, the merger was found not to exceed guideline boundaries and was allowed to go forward.

Other Considerations   In its 1982 *Merger Guidelines,* the Department of Justice named numerous other factors that might be considered to modify its basic structural analysis. The most important of these was ease of entry: if new entry were found to be easy, mergers might not be challenged even if the structural thresholds were overstepped. The *Guidelines* also continued the "failing firm" defense that had been part of U.S. merger law since the 1930s.[109] Specifically, mergers that otherwise violated the *Guidelines* could pass muster if one of the merging firms were likely to fail without a possibility of financial reorganization, and if there were no viable alternative mergers offering a less severe impairment of competition.

An important additional consideration was added to the list in a 1984 *Guidelines* revision.[110] The Justice Department announced that if clear and convincing evidence shows that merger is reasonably necessary to achieve significant efficiencies, those efficiencies would be considered in decisions whether to challenge the merger. This was a sharp departure from both the 1982 *Guidelines* and earlier judicial precedents. Thus, in its 1962 *Brown Shoe* decision, the Supreme Court stated:

. . . some of the results of large integrated or chain operations are beneficial to consumers. Their expansion is not rendered unlawful by the mere fact that small independent stores may be adversely affected. It is competition, not competitors, which the Act protects. But we cannot fail to recognize Congress' desire to promote competition through the protection of viable, small, locally owned businesses. Congress appreciated that occasional higher costs and prices might result from the maintenance of fragmented industries and markets. It resolved those competing considerations in favor of decentralization. We must give effect to that decision.[111]

Or as it stated flatly five years later, "Possible efficiencies cannot be used as a defense to illegality."[112] Later Celler-Kefauver Act case opinions by a more conservative Supreme Court were silent on the efficiencies question. Thus, the 1984 *Guidelines* broke new ground.

The logic of an efficiencies defense is illustrated in Figure 5.5. The story begins with a competitively organized industry whose supply curve S_o leads to an equilibrium price of OP_o. Suppose now mergers occur, with two effects: they facilitate cost-saving measures, shifting the supply (summed marginal cost) curve downward to S_m, and they confer sufficient monopoly power that the price is raised to OP_m. The cost saving per time period (shaded area B) is beneficial to society; it releases resources that can be used to produce other goods and services.[113] The elevation of price is detrimental; it imposes a dead-weight loss measured by shaded area A. Ideally, a tradeoff should be made; mergers with benefits B exceeding their dead-weight losses A ought to be allowed; those with the opposite balance of effects should be prevented. And since dead-weight loss triangles tend to be small except under extreme conditions, Oliver Williamson showed in a seminal article,[114] mergers that promise even relatively small percentage cost reductions were likely to pass the test. In Figure 5.5, the cost-saving benefits clearly outweigh the dead-weight losses.

Figure 5.5
Merger Tradeoff Analysis

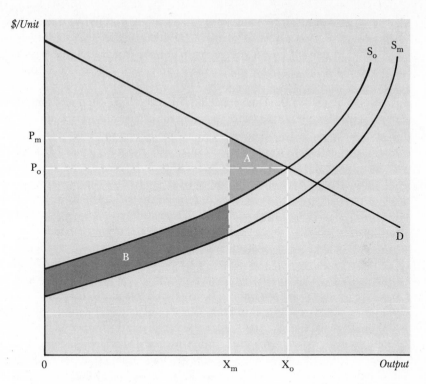

There is, as always, a hitch. It is difficult to predict cost savings (and also price-raising effects) with any degree of confidence. Business executives called into court (or premerger meetings with antitrust enforcers) may have incentives to be less than candid. And because of the uncertainties and hubris afflicting merger decisions, executives may not foresee clearly the effects of their actions. Thus, the New York Central-Pennsylvania Railroad merger was expected to generate cost savings of roughly 4 percent after a five-year shakedown period.[115] The actual result was organizational confusion, costs rising without control, bankruptcy, and eventual quasi nationalization. Similarly, a high Bethlehem Steel Corporation official,

109. See *International Shoe Co.* v. *F.T.C.,* 280 U.S. 291 (1930); *Citizen Publishing Co.* v. *U.S.,* 394 U.S. 131, 136–139 (1969); and *U.S.* v. *Pabst Brewing Co. et al.,* 296 F. Supp. 994, 1002 (1969).

110. U.S. Department of Justice, *Merger Guidelines* (Washington: June 14, 1984), p. 22.

111. *Brown Shoe Co.* v. *U.S.,* 370 U.S. 294, 344 (1962). For a review of the legal precedents, see Andrew G. Berg, "Cost Efficiencies in the Section 7 Calculus," *Case Western Reserve Law Review,* vol. 37 (Winter 1987), pp. 218–272.

112. *Federal Trade Commission* v. *Procter & Gamble Co. et al.,* 386 U.S. 568, 580 (1967). In the *Procter & Gamble* case and even more so in certain later cases, the Federal Trade Commission argued that merger-based efficiencies were *undesirable* because they gave a large acquirer "a decisive advantage in efficiency over its smaller

rivals." *In the matter of Foremost Dairies, Inc.,* 60 F.T.C. 944, 1084 (1962). This position was abandoned following less populist appointments to the Commission.

113. See also pp. 25–27 supra.

114. Oliver E. Williamson, "Economies as an Antitrust Defense: The Welfare Tradeoffs," *American Economic Review,* vol. 58 (March 1968), pp. 18–36; augmented and corrected in the *American Economic Review,* vol. 58 (December 1968), pp. 1372–1376, and *American Economic Review,* vol. 59 (December 1969), pp. 954–959.

115. Compare "The Big Merger Begins To Click," *Business Week,* May 4, 1968, p. 104; "Penn Central Sees a Light in the Tunnel," *Business Week,* November 22, 1969, p. 44; and "The Penn Central Bankruptcy Express," *Fortune,* August 1970, p. 104 ff.

explaining his company's motives for acquiring the Youngstown Sheet & Tube Co. in 1956, testified that Bethlehem (whose capacity was concentrated in the East) could not develop integrated steel-making operations in the Midwest unless it was permitted to take advantage of Youngstown's existing position in the Chicago area.[116] Four years after the merger was prohibited, Bethlehem began constructing its Burns Harbor, Indiana, complex — for three decades the United States' most modern flat-rolled steel-making facility. Meanwhile, Youngstown undertook a $450 million program to modernize and expand its old Indiana Harbor operations.

Deluged with such misinformation, the enforcement agencies and/or courts attempting to weigh merger benefits against costs would make many faulty decisions. And indeed, the Department of Justice is believed to have accepted few if any merger efficiency defenses during the first three years after stating its willingness in principle to entertain such evidence.[117] There are at least two ways out of the dilemma. One would be to require merger proponents to provide compelling evidence of probable efficiencies before a pending merger is approved. Such a policy would have the fringe benefit of forcing merger makers to think through the integration of their acquisitions carefully in advance — an exercise of prudence that is often absent in actual practice. Fewer efficiency-*reducing* mergers might be the result. Alternatively, a two-stage strategy could be adopted. Prospective mergers for which a persuasive efficiencies defense was sustained would be allowed to proceed for a trial period, for example, of three years. At the end of those three years, an after-the-fact evaluation would be conducted to determine whether the promises were substantially realized. If so, the merger would receive permanent clearance. If not, the parent corporation would be required to divest sufficient capacity to establish a viable independent supplier with a market share equivalent to that of the originally acquired entity.

There was a time when this approach would not have worked. In the early decades of Celler-Kefauver Act enforcement, mergers were often consummated, only to be declared illegal after many years of litigation. The enforcement authorities then found themselves in a difficult position: the eggs were scrambled, company lawyers argued, and great damage would be done trying to unscramble them. As a result, the government was forced to back off and accept only a token settlement that failed to restore the competitive status quo ante.[118] However, since then companies and their investment banking advisers have become adept at selloffs, spin-offs, leveraged buyouts, and other reorganizations through which parts of a company are divested and set up as viable, self-standing operations. Exceptions might arise, but there is no reason to believe that a two-stage efficiencies defense approach would be generally infeasible.

Conglomerate Mergers   In the United States, we have seen, most merger activity following the revision of merger law in 1950 was of a conglomerate character. Legal precedents have been shaped to challenge conglomerate mergers in a limited range of situations.

The most important precedent is the *potential competition* doctrine. It is best illustrated by returning to Figure 5.3. Suppose the relevant market with respect to Philadelphia consumers is defined to include all suppliers out to a distance of 100 miles, for example, A, B, C, and D. What then is the status of firm E, located 150 miles away? E is not within the relevant market as defined. But if firms A, B, C, and D were to collude and raise the price of cement in Philadelphia to $47, firm E could profitably ship cement to Philadelphia and make inroads into the cartel's sales, perhaps undermining its price-raising ability. It is therefore viewed under the law as a potential competitor, one waiting in the wings and "so positioned on the edge of the market that it exert[s] beneficial influence on competitive conditions in that market."[119] If one of firms A, B, C, or D were to acquire firm E and bring its pricing under inside control, it could eliminate E's potential competitive threat, and hence might be viewed as lessening competition in the Celler-Kefauver Act sense. Or if an outside firm like E were to acquire an insider, its incentives to act as a cartel-disrupting interloper would change, and again, potential competition would be lessened.

Early potential competition decisions focused on whether outside firms had in fact tried to enter before merger, whether they were likely to enter if prices inside the market were elevated, and whether they were viewed by insiders as genuine entry threats.[120] A Supreme Court whose membership had shifted toward more conservative antitrust doctrines returned to the question in 1964 and defined more precisely the circumstances under which the acquisition of potential competitors could be barred:

Unequivocal proof that an acquiring firm would have entered *de novo* but for a merger is rarely available. . . . Thus, . . . the principal focus of the doctrine is on the likely effects of the premerger position of the acquiring firm on the fringe of the target market. . . . [A] market extension merger may be unlawful if the acquiring firm has the characteristics, capabilities, and economic incentive to render it a perceived potential *de novo* potential entrant, and if the acquiring firm's premerger presence on the fringe of the target market in fact tempered oligopolistic behavior on the part of existing participants in that market.[121]

The last phrase is crucial. Unlike the rules developed for horizontal mergers, it implies an inquiry into whether the *behavior* of sellers within the market entered by merger is such that, but for the outsider's threat, high prices would have been charged. In terms of our Figure 5.3 example, firm E would be a meaningful potential entrant only if the structure within the market is such that price-raising by firms A, B, C, and D is likely, absent the threat from E. This combination of

---

116. See Willard F. Mueller, *The Celler-Kefauver Act: Sixteen Years of Enforcement,* Federal Trade Commission staff report to the Antitrust Subcommittee, House Committee on the Judiciary (Washington: USGPO, 1967), p. 17; and *U.S.* v. *Bethlehem Steel Corporation et al.,* 168 F. Supp. 576, 615–616 (1958). For further examples, see Joseph F. Brodley, "Potential Competition Mergers: A Structural Synthesis," *Yale Law Journal,* vol. 87 (November 1977), p. 64n.

117. It rejected, for instance, a July 1986 demonstration that by taking over an ailing producer of high-fructose corn syrup, Archer-Daniels-Midland Co. achieved *actual* labor productivity gains averaging 34 percent per year over the first three and one-half years following acquisition. Co-author Scherer was consultant to Archer-Daniels-Midland.

For an early indication of the Justice Department's views, see

John E. Kwoka and Frederick R. Warren-Boulton, "Efficiencies, Failing Firms, and Alternatives to Merger: A Policy Synthesis," *Antitrust Bulletin,* vol. 31 (Summer 1986), pp. 431–450.

118. See Kenneth G. Elzinga, "The Antimerger Laws: Pyrrhic Victories," *Journal of Law & Economics,* vol. 12 (April 1969), pp. 43–78.

119. *U.S.* v. *Falstaff Brewing Corp. et al.,* 410 U.S. 526, 532–536 (1973).

120. See *U.S.* v. *El Paso Natural Gas Co. et al.,* 376 U.S. 651 (1964); *Federal Trade Commission* v. *Procter & Gamble Co. et al.,* 386 U.S. 568 (1967) (involving potential competition in a product line extension merger); *U.S.* v. *Penn-Olin Chemical Co.,* 378 U.S. 158 (1964); and *U.S.* v. *Falstaff,* supra note 119.

121. *U.S.* v. *Marine Bancorporation et al.,* 418 U.S. 602, 624–625 (1974).

behavioral plus structural tests imposes a heavier burden of proof on antitrust enforcers than the strictly structural rules applied in horizontal merger cases.[122]

Other early cases blocked conglomerate mergers that strengthened reciprocal dealing power on the part of the merged firms ("Since you sell to our X Division, it behooves you to buy the products of our Y Division"),[123] or that left the merging firms with superior staying power to wage predatory warfare against smaller, less well-financed rivals.[124] As we shall see in Chapters 12 and 13, the predation doctrine was attenuated in later decisions under other sections of U.S. antitrust law, and the so-called deep pocket challenge to conglomerate mergers has fallen into disuse.

During the 1960s, the government was unsuccessful in challenges to conglomerate mergers because they increased aggregate concentration, which was alleged to be undesirable per se, or because they fostered a mutuality of interlocking interests among multimarket suppliers that led the conglomerates to compete less vigorously.[125] To extend the law's reach so widely, the courts concluded, was the job of Congress, not the judiciary. In 1979, Congress rose to the bait, docketing a bill that would bar mergers between two corporations with sales or assets of at least $2 billion each, or between one company with assets or sales of at least $350 million and another with a market share of 20 percent or more in some significant market.[126] The merging firms could avoid the law's bite if they proved that their merger would substantially enhance competition or yield substantial efficiencies. The bill was vigorously opposed *inter alia* by the Business Roundtable, a consortium representing the nation's largest corporations, and failed to muster sufficient support to emerge from committee.

Vertical Mergers

The Celler-Kefauver Act was expressly intended to bring competition-reducing vertical mergers (for example, mergers between a supplier and its customer) under its wing. The first substantive Supreme Court interpretation ruled Brown Shoe Company's acquisition of the Kinney Company illegal not only on horizontal grounds but also because the merger allegedly made it more difficult for shoe manufacturers competing with Brown to sell their shoes to Kinney's extensive network of retail stores.[127] Subsequent cases took an equally tough line against so-called market foreclosing vertical mergers. However, as we shall see in Chapters 14 and 15, heated debate has arisen among economists and legal scholars as to whether vertical mergers and other vertical arrangements are under normal conditions likely to have adverse effects. One consequence has been a less energetic effort to enforce the law against vertical integration mergers. In its 1982 *Merger Guidelines*, the Justice Department announced that it would challenge such mergers only when they facilitated collusion or significantly raised barriers to new entry.[128]

The Vigor of Enforcement

During the first three decades following passage of the Celler-Kefauver Act, enforcement remained consistently vigorous despite inevitable disagreements over where the law's outer boundaries lay. This aggressive stance was adopted by Republican and Democratic administrations alike. With the Reagan government's ascendance to power in 1981, however, a sea change occurred. Key antitrust agency positions were staffed with more conservative individuals, and a stream of new appointments accelerated the federal judiciary's drift toward greater skepticism of government intervention into markets, whether its purpose was ostensibly to stimulate or (through regulation) restrict competition.

The change in policies is shown *inter alia* in statistics on enforcement efforts. Despite record-breaking merger volumes during the 1980s, the number of challenges brought by the Department of Justice and Federal Trade Commission fell from an average of 20.7 per year between 1960 and 1980 to 10.4 in calendar years 1981–1984.[129] During the last two years of the Carter administration, requests for additional information, suggesting careful scrutiny of a merger, were made on 10.8 percent of the transactions for which premerger notification reports were filed, and 2.5 percent of the notified mergers were formally challenged. Between 1982 and 1987, the additional information request rate dropped to 4.0 percent and the challenge rate to 0.7 percent.[130] Among the relatively few enforcement actions brought to court between 1981 and 1987, the Department of Justice won only one. The FTC staff had a somewhat stronger record, securing merger prohibitions in 30 percent of the cases brought before the full Federal Trade Commission for review, and prevailing in five of their six efforts to secure federal district court injunctions.[131]

The Reagan administration also sought new legislation to codify its more lenient policies. Among other things, it proposed that the Celler-Kefauver Act prohibition of acquisitions whose effect "*may* be substantially to lessen competition" (emphasis added) be changed to bite only when "there is a significant probability that such acquisition will increase the ability to exercise market power."[132] In addition to focusing more precisely on monopolistic price-raising effects, the revision would shift a greater burden of proof to the enforcement agencies. With Congress solidly in Democratic party hands, the proposed bills failed to emerge from committee.

As merger antitrust enforcement by federal government agencies waned, other groups came forward to fill the breach. For one, there were increasing efforts by private parties — most typically, competitors to horizontally merging firms — to mount legal challenges. This phenomenon posed an intriguing question. Suppose the consequence of a merger is elevated prices. Why should competitors object? Should they not bask happily under the high-price umbrella? They must have other motives for going to court. One possibility is fear that the merger will increase their rivals' efficiency and hence make the merging firms more potent

122. See Brodley, "Potential Competition Mergers," supra note 116, pp. 17–25.

123. *Federal Trade Commission* v. *Consolidated Foods Corp. et al.,* 380 U.S. 592 (1965).

124. See, for example, *Federal Trade Commission* v. *Procter & Gamble,* supra note 120, at p. 578.

125. See *U.S.* v. *International Telephone and Telegraph Corp. et al.,* 306 F. Supp. 766, 796–797 (1969); and *U.S.* v. *Northwest Industries, Inc. et al.,* 301 F. Supp. 1066, 1092–1096 (1969).

126. S. 600, 96th Congress, 1st sess.; and Senate Committee on the Judiciary, Subcommittee on Antitrust, Monopoly, and Business Rights, Hearings, *Mergers and Economic Concentration,* Parts 1 and 2 (Washington: USGPO, 1979).

127. *Brown Shoe Co.* v. *U.S.,* 370 U.S. 294 (1962).

128. *Merger Guidelines,* supra note 92, pp. 22–26.

129. F. M. Scherer, "Mergers and Antitrust," in Gary Libecap, ed., *Advances in the Study of Entrepreneurship, Innovation, and Economic Growth,* vol. 1 supplement (JAI Press, 1988), pp. 106–107; and "Merger Policy in the 1970s and 1980s," in Robert J. Larner, ed., *Economics and Antitrust Policy* (Westport: Quorum Books, 1988), p. 84.

130. House of Representatives, Committee on the Judiciary, news release, "Rodino Announces Hearing on Antitrust Enforcement," March 2, 1988.

131. Calkins, "Developments in Merger Litigation," supra note 27, pp. 869–874.

132. S. 2160, 99th Congress, 2nd sess.; and Senate Committee on the Judiciary, Hearings, *Merger Law Reform* (Washington: USGPO, 1986).

competitive threats. This, it can be argued, is hardly the sort of thing the antitrust laws were intended to prevent. On the other hand, merger might make it more difficult for nonmerging rivals to secure access to channels of distribution, strengthen the merger partners' ability to wage predatory warfare (a controversial proposition, we have seen), or (in a case that was filed but then withdrawn) give the rivals unfair access to government-subsidized overseas production sources. Considering whether companies ought to be granted "standing" to challenge their rivals' mergers, the Supreme Court concluded in 1987 that increased price competition alleged to follow from merger was not an actionable "antitrust injury" unless predatory, below-cost pricing was shown to be likely, and the Court believed that such predation cases were at best "infrequent."[133] Thus, suits by competitors were rendered more difficult.

Concerned over the Reagan administration's merger policy, a group of state attorneys general began investigating ways by which they, using their state antitrust laws and the right of third parties to sue under the federal law, might challenge mergers with a likely impact in their home jurisdictions. In 1987, they issued their own set of merger guidelines differing in important respects from those of the Justice Department.[134] For market definition, no specific price elevation criterion was articulated. Instead, product substitutes were to be included if they were comparably priced and suitable for substitution to 75 percent of relevant consumers. Geographic markets were to encompass all sources from which relevant consumers purchased 75 percent of their supplies. As under the Department of Justice guidelines, Herfindahl-Hirschman indices were to be used in measuring structural changes, but the thresholds were set lower for industries in which concentration was rising during the previous three years. An efficiencies defense was also to be entertained, but only in markets with HHI values below 1800. At the time this was written, the role of the states as supplemental merger antitrust enforcers was in its infancy. Where it will lead remains to be seen.[135]

Tender Offer Takeovers

Tender offer takeovers pose public policy issues only peripherally related to antitrust. In the United States, the most germane statutes are the corporation laws of the individual states. These vary appreciably from state to state, and during the 1980s, there were significant changes. More often than not, the top management of large corporations was distressed about conditions that made their companies increasingly vulnerable to outside raiders. They sought changes in state corporation laws that made it more difficult to carry out takeovers without management consent — for example, by substantially delaying consummation of a takeover unless a two-thirds majority of stockholders votes in favor, by excluding certain classes of stockholders from voting for takeover, by staggering director terms, by authorizing "poison pills" that make the target less attractive if a takeover succeeds, and so forth.[136] In considering such changes, state legislatures often engage in a "race to the bottom." Seeking the tax revenue advantages of having companies incorporate in their states, they must compete with other states to offer the most attractive charter terms. This tendency figures prominently in arguments for unified federal corporate chartering laws, but such a move has been vigorously and successfully resisted by both the states and corporations reluctant to accept a relative expansion of federal power.

The principal U.S. federal government intrusion into the takeover process occurred when the Williams Act was passed in 1968. Its impetus was the rising tide of tender offer takeovers, including "Saturday night special" offers giving stockholders only a weekend to decide whether or not to tender their shares. Using federal regulation of interstate securities trading as its fulcrum, the Williams Act addressed this problem by requiring that cash tender offers be held open for at least twenty business days so that a more leisurely debate over the takeover's merits could occur. In addition, to increase the transparency of the takeover process, the Williams Act required that any entity purchasing more than 5 percent of a company's shares file with the Securities and Exchange Commission within ten days a report disclosing the purchaser's identity, the number of shares owned, and the purpose of the acquisition. The reports are made public immediately, so the news of a pending takeover attempt diffuses quickly.

With the renewed surge of takeover activity during the 1980s, these 5 percent, ten-day window provisions became highly controversial. A series of insider trading convictions led to the claim that individuals with inside information on what was happening were profiting by buying target company stocks from shareholders unaware that, when the intended takeover was publicly disclosed, they could sell at appreciably higher prices. Legislation was proposed to shorten the time window to one day and trigger public disclosure at 3 percent, rather than 5 percent, of outstanding common stock shares.[137] On fairness grounds, the proposal appeared eminently reasonable. But opponents argued that low ownership thresholds and short windows seriously discourage takeover attempts, which were considered to be an important method of displacing inefficient management teams.[138] When a

133. *Cargill Inc. et al.* v. *Montfort of Colorado,* 479 U.S. 104 (1986).

134. *Horizontal Merger Guidelines of the National Association of Attorneys General* (Washington: March 10, 1987).

135. On early cases, see Robert Abrams, "Developments in State Antitrust Enforcement," *New York University Law Review,* vol. 62 (November 1987), pp. 989–997; and the contributions by Robert Abrams, Lloyd Constantine, and John H. Shenefield in the *Washburn Law Journal,* vol. 29 (1989). On an important action by the State of California, see "Food Store Tie Blocked in California," *New York Times,* September 30, 1988, p. D1; and "Food Mergers Worry Some Officials," *New York Times,* October 3, 1988, p. D1.

Although the state antitrust laws saw little application against mergers during much of the twentieth century, the Texas law apparently blocked the acquisition of Gulf Oil by Standard Oil in 1902 and a merger between Gulf and Texaco in 1905. See Joseph A. Pratt, "The Petroleum Industry in Transition: Antitrust and the Decline of Monopoly Control in Oil," *Journal of Economic History,* vol. 40 (December 1980), pp. 828–831.

136. A key decision upholding the right of states to pass laws discouraging takeovers was *CTS Corp.* v. *Dynamics Corp. of America,* 481 U.S. 69 (1987). For more general analyses, see Margaret E. Guerin-Calvert, R. H. McGuckin, and Frederick Warren-Boulton, "State and Federal Regulation in the Market for Corporate Control," *Antitrust Bulletin,* vol. 32 (Fall 1987), pp. 661–692;

"States vs. Raiders: Will Washington Step In?" *Business Week,* August 31, 1987, pp. 56–57; and "Debate over Impact of Delaware Measure," *New York Times,* February 1, 1988, p. D4.

137. S. 1323, introduced by Senator William Proxmire in the *Congressional Record,* vol. 133, no. 90 (June 4, 1987), pp. S7594–7603.

138. Important conceptual contributions include Sanford J. Grossman and Oliver D. Hart, "Takeover Bids, the Free-Rider Problem, and the Theory of the Corporation," *Bell Journal of Economics,* vol. 11 (Spring 1980), pp. 42–64; Frank H. Easterbrook and Daniel R. Fischel, "The Proper Role of a Target's Management in Responding to a Tender Offer," *Harvard Law Review,* vol. 94 (April 1981), pp. 1161–1204; Lucian A. Bebchuck, "The Case for Facilitating Competing Tender Offers," *Harvard Law Review,* vol. 95 (March 1982), pp. 1028–1056; and Louis Lowenstein, "Pruning Deadwood in Hostile Takeovers: A Proposal for Legislation," *Columbia Law Review,* vol. 83 (March 1983), pp. 249–334.

From 1978 to 1980, buyers "considering" a takeover succeeded in acquiring 21 percent of target firms' shares on average during the ten-day window period; those who previously or simultaneously announced a takeover averaged 37 percent. See Wayne H. Mikkelson and Richard S. Ruback, "An Empirical Analysis of the Interfirm Equity Investment Process," *Journal of Financial Economics,* vol. 14 (December 1985), p. 530.

takeover attempt is publicly disclosed, stock prices jump to the level of the takeover bid, modified upward or downward by the market's judgment of how likely further competitive bidding, or complete failure, are. Before disclosure, the bidder can buy shares at prices 20 to 40 percent less than it will have to pay once its intentions become known. Since the postannouncement price at which shares can be purchased is likely to approach the bidder's estimate of the target's true value, it is mainly on the early predisclosure purchases that the bidder makes a sizable profit. By reducing the number of shares that can be accumulated before disclosure forces stock prices up, window regulations reduce the potential profit from takeover attempts and therefore inhibit investment in what is viewed as a socially desirable, efficiency-enhancing function. The counter-arguments to this analysis stress that, as we have seen, it is less than clear that takeovers actually do improve targets' efficiency on average. If they do not, discouraging takeovers might not be undesirable. And even if one accepts takeovers as efficiency-increasing, one might wish to sacrifice some efficiency benefits to ensure greater fairness in securities markets.

New legislation was also proposed to deal with two-tier tender offers, that is, those in which a relatively high price is offered to secure a majority of the target company's shares, after which the remaining minority is acquired on less favorable terms. Such offers create compelling incentives for shareholders to tender their shares in the first round for fear of receiving lower prices in the mop-up round.[139] The solution proposed in Senate bill 1323 of 1987 was to require that if 15 percent of a company's stock were acquired, additional acquisitions had to be made through a tender offer open to all shareholders. This proposal emulated what was standard practice under the United Kingdom's takeover rules, administered until 1988 by the Takeover Panel, a group without formal suasion powers.[140]

Other controversial practices considered for federal regulation during the late 1980s included *greenmail,* or target company repurchases of stock from declared raiders at prices higher than those at which the company is willing to pay all its shareholders; *poison pills,* and the last-minute creation of *golden parachutes,* permitting displaced top managers to receive princely severance bonuses.

Because there were strongly held views both for and against changes in federal takeover regulations, and because the Reagan administration was committed to a view that mergers and takeovers "improve efficiency, transfer scarce resources to higher valued uses, and stimulate effective corporate management,"[141] a bill embodying substantial changes in the rules died on the floor of the U.S. Senate in June of 1988. The issues are unlikely to disappear, however, so they will continue to occupy the congressional agenda.

Merger Policy in Other Nations

The United States was by a considerable stretch the first nation to have an active structural antitrust policy. In other nations, the concept is newer, and in some cases, there is little to report.[142]

Among European nations, the United Kingdom was the first to adopt merger control laws as a part of its competition policy. The 1965 Mergers and Monopolies

Act assigned to the Monopolies and Mergers Commission (MMC) responsibility for reviewing certain mergers — notably, those involving market shares of 33 percent (later reduced to 25 percent) or greater. In its early years, British merger policy was schizoid, for in 1966 the Labour government created an Industrial Reorganisation Corporation (IRC) to encourage and finance mergers that might build enterprises better able to hold their own in international trade. Its record includes acting as broker in the merger of Britain's two largest domestic auto manufacturers (British Motor Holdings and Leyland); aiding the formation of Europe's third-largest electrical equipment manufacturer through the merger of English Electric and Elliott Automation; and arranging a merger of three firms (including the most prominent price cutter) with a combined 35 percent share of the U.K. ball and roller bearing market.[143] The IRC was allowed to lapse during the 1970s, in part because the Conservative government briefly in power was less attracted toward mergers as a means of forming enterprises large enough to be susceptible to central government control, and partly out of disappointment over how few palpable efficiencies had materialized from major consolidations.[144]

In reviewing mergers referred to it, the Monopolies and Mergers Commission is guided by criteria much broader than those applied in the United States.[145] Its basic mandate is to determine whether a merger "may be expected to operate against the public interest." Its inquiry may include not only the effect on competition and prices, but also prospective efficiencies and how management, employment levels, labor relations, debt service obligations, and overseas control will be affected. It is said that this tabula rasa has been used among other things to prevent mergers that would bring British companies under unwanted foreign control and to favor management teams with close Establishment ties. However, in 1988 the Conservative government announced reforms intended to ensure that only mergers believed to interfere with competition were referred to the Commission.[146] Between 1977 and 1981, the MMC received for review twenty-seven mergers out of 1,019 that had been screened by another government agency. Five binding orders against the reviewed mergers were issued, and nine more were abandoned when it became clear that an MMC inquiry would delay consummation.

139. See Lucian Bebchuck, "The Pressure To Tender: An Analysis and a Proposed Remedy," in John Coffee et al., eds., *Knights, Raiders, and Targets,* supra note 36, pp. 371–397.

140. See Peter Frazer, "The Regulation of Takeovers in Great Britain," in Coffee et al., eds., *Knights,* supra note 36, pp. 436–441. In 1988, responsibility shifted to a Securities and Investment Board with formal powers. On the adoption of parallel European Community rules, see "Europe Acts on Mergers," *New York Times,* December 23, 1988, p. D4.

141. Report of the Council of Economic Advisers, *Economic Report of the President* (Washington: USGPO, February 1985), p. 196.

142. For a broad review, see Organisation for Economic Co-operation and Development (OECD), *Merger Policies and Recent Trends in Mergers* (Paris: 1984), especially Section A.

143. On economies resulting from the bearing industry merger, see pp. 164–165 supra.

144. For a review of the experience following IRC-induced mergers, see Cowling et al., *Mergers and Economic Performance,* supra note 74, Chapter 5.

145. On the recent experience, see John Agnew, *Competition Law* (London: Allen & Unwin, 1985), Chapter 6. On the earlier history, see Alister Sutherland, *The Monopolies Commission in Action* (Cambridge: Cambridge University Press, 1969), pp. 69–70; and C. L. Pass, "Horizontal Mergers and the Control of Market Power in the U.K.," *Antitrust Bulletin,* vol. 17 (Fall 1972), pp. 811–834.

146. See "Anti Antitrust," *The Economist,* December 26, 1987, pp. 9–10; and "Still Playing God," *The Economist,* January 16, 1988, pp. 49–50.

In 1973, West Germany passed merger control amendments to its basic anti-trust law. They were aimed at preventing mergers likely to create or strengthen a shared market-dominating position.[147] This criterion, clarified in 1980 amendments, is both narrower and broader than the thrust of U.S. merger law. It is narrower in the sense that the complex statutory criteria for identifying whether there is shared dominance allow, for instance, a firm with a market share of 17 percent to acquire a competitor with a 15 percent market share in a moderately concentrated industry (for example, with a Herfindahl-Hirschman Index exceeding 1400). Since the HHI change implied by such a merger is 510 points, such a merger would plainly violate the U.S. Department of Justice guidelines. And more generally, mergers that elevate smaller firms to the size of the market-leading enterprise, even in relatively highly concentrated industries, have been deemed consistent with the structural criteria. The German approach is broader because of decisions by the German Supreme Court that a purely conglomerate merger linking a rich parent with a smaller firm dominant in its special market violates the law because it could reinforce the power of the market-dominating partner.[148] This approach was entertained in certain U.S. Federal Trade Commission decisions during the 1960s, but rejected thereafter. The West German law also contains a much broader efficiencies defense than under either U.S. court precedents or the Justice Department guidelines. Mergers that violate the structural criteria must be approved if they will lead to improvements in competitive conditions outweighing the disadvantages of market domination. Between 1974 and the end of 1985, the German Federal Cartel Office rendered judgments prohibiting a total of sixty-nine mergers. Of these, twenty-six were fully enforced, fifteen were reversed by higher courts, five were overturned by the Economics Ministry (which has independent review power), eight were withdrawn or substantially modified by the Cartel Office, and fifteen remained pending under appeal.[149] During the same period, 113 mergers were voluntarily withdrawn by the merging parties following informal discussions with the Cartel Office.

Like Great Britain, France actively encouraged large-scale mergers during the 1960s in the belief that greater scale was required for international competitiveness. In 1977, however, partly because of disillusion over the fruits of that policy but mainly to preempt the Common Market authorities, it created a new Commission on Competition to review domestic mergers entailing market shares exceeding 40 percent. Because of divided political support, the Commission adopted a relatively unaggressive stance, reviewing only four mergers between 1977 and 1981, and approving all four. Its first serious challenge to a merger (between two U.S.-owned companies) was overturned on procedural grounds in 1985.[150]

At the supra-national level, the European Coal and Steel Community treaty of 1951 required that mergers be expressly authorized by the Community's High Authority if they might bring about concentration. During the ECSC's first decade, some 136 cases were considered. None resulted in outright disapproval, although three mergers may have been abandoned voluntarily owing to the High Authority's display of reticence.[151] The Coal and Steel Community's merger control function was subsumed by the European Commission in later years, and after 1962, a number of very large mergers were approved. One joined Thyssen Huette (with 1966 sales of $1.7 billion) and Huettenwerk Oberhausen (with sales of $252 million), creating the world's fourth-largest steel-making concern at the time, with more than 10 percent of total Common Market capacity. In 1973 the Commission approved a major joint venture between the two largest French producers, whose combined 67 percent national market share was the result of numerous earlier mergers. The Commission's published statements placed no emphasis on the likelihood that the joint venture would fuse further the business policies of the two firms, whose price-fixing arrangements were one of Europe's worst-kept secrets.[152]

In 1971 the European Commission moved outside the coal and steel arena to challenge acquisitions by the Continental Can Company's Belgian subsidiary of the largest German and Dutch metal container producers.[153] The decision was overturned by the European Court of Justice in 1973 because of market definition inadequacies. But the Court confirmed the Commission's authority under European Common Market treaty Article 86 to prohibit as an abuse of power horizontal acquisitions by already dominant enterprises. The Commission began screening mergers, and its informal intervention induced significant modifications in flat glass and airline mergers.[154] After protracted debate, the Commission initiated in 1989 a more formal program to review mergers between sizable companies with combined sales exceeding five billion European Currency Units, less than two-thirds of which were made in any single Common Market member nation.[155]

Since 1923 Canadian law prohibited mergers that operate to the detriment of the public. But the burden of proof was that of criminal law standards, and between 1923 and 1986, only one merger was found to overstep the line.[156] In 1986 a new merger law greatly eased the burden of proof, among other things establishing a criterion similar to that of U.S. law: whether the merger substantially lessens competition. Efficiencies, if shown, are to be weighed against the detriments from lessened competition. The efficiencies defense may prove to be more important in Canada than in the United States, since, as we have seen in Chapter 4, Canadian firms have experienced more difficulty than their U.S. counterparts capturing

147. See Ernst-Joachim Mestmäcker, "Competition Policy and Antitrust: Some Comparative Observations," and Juergen F. Baur, "The Control of Mergers Between Large, Financially Strong Firms in West Germany," both in *Zeitschrift für die gesamte Staatswissenschaften,* vol. 136 (September 1980), pp. 398–404 and 444–464.

148. Rheinmetall/WMF merger, German Supreme Court decision, June 25, 1985, discussed in the sixth report of the Monopolkommission, *Gesamtwirtschaftliche Chancen und Risiken wachsender Unternehmensgrössen* (Baden-Baden: Nomos, 1986), pp. 181–183, with English language summary, p. 449.

149. Monopolkommission, *Gesamtwirtschaftliche Chancen,* p. 172, with a table of cases at pp. 424–429.

150. See OECD, *Merger Policies,* supra note 142, p. 25; OECD, *Competition Policy in OECD Countries, 1984–85* (Paris: 1987), pp. 102–103; OECD, *Competition Policy in OECD Countries, 1985–86* (Paris: 1987), p. 115; and Henri Aujac, "An Introduction to French Industrial Policy," in William J. Adams and Christian Stoffaes, eds., *French Industrial Policy* (Washington: Brookings, 1986), p. 28.

151. See Hans Mueller, "The Policy of the European Coal and Steel Community Towards Mergers and Agreements by Steel Companies," *Antitrust Bulletin,* vol. 14 (Summer 1969), pp. 413–448; and Klaus Stegemann, *Price Competition and Output Adjustment in the*

European Steel Market (Tuebingen: Mohr, 1977), pp. 272–276.

152. See the European Economic Community Commission's *Third Report on Competition Policy* (Brussels: 1974), pp. 64–65.

153. See the EEC Commission's *First Report on Competition Policy* (Brussels: 1971), pp. 78–83; and the *Third Report on Competition Policy,* pp. 15 and 28–38.

154. See Dennis Swann, *Competition and Industrial Policy in the European Community* (London: Methuen, 1983), pp. 119–120 and 124–127; and "Europe Inc," *The Economist,* March 19, 1988, pp. 11–12.

155. See the papers by Jean-Francois Verstrynge, Ernst Mestmäcker, Dieter Schwartz, Christopher Bellamy, and Daniel G. Goyder in Barry E. Hawk, ed., *European/American Antitrust and Trade Law* (New York: Fordham Corporate Law Institute, 1989); and Alexis Jacquemin, Pierre Buigues, and Fabienne Ilzkovitz, "Horizontal Mergers and Competition Policy in the European Community," *European Economy,* no. 40 (May 1989).

156. See Chris Green, "Mergers in Canada and Canada's New Merger Law," *Antitrust Bulletin,* vol. 32 (Spring 1989), pp. 253–273; and Bruce Dunlop, David McQueen, and Michael Trebilcock, *Canadian Competition Policy: A Legal and Economic Analysis* (Toronto: Canada Law Book, 1987), pp. 185–206.

economies of scale in the relatively small Canadian market. A unique feature of the new Canadian law is the possibility of ordering as a remedy for concentration-increasing mergers a reduction in the level of tariff protection enjoyed on the merging firms' products.[157]

Under the remnants of the Anti-Monopolies Law imposed upon Japan by the occupying forces following World War II, sizable mergers must be registered with the Fair Trade Commission for review to ensure that a controlling position does not result. The first test case came in 1969, when Yawata Steel and Fuji Iron and Steel, broken apart after the war, proposed to merge and form Nippon Steel Corporation. Yawata had 18.5 percent of Japanese steel ingot capacity at the time, Fuji 17.0 percent. The Fair Trade Commission opposed the merger, angering other government agencies, who threatened to have the FTC stripped of its powers. A compromise was eventually worked out under which the merged Nippon Steel would provide supply assurances until competitors had established their own facilities and spin off a tin-plated steel operation.[158] Between then and 1978, the Fair Trade Commission did not challenge another merger. In at least one later case, cross-ownership reductions were implemented before the FTC gave its approval. A 1977 amendment to the Japanese Anti-Monopoly Act is also believed to have induced appreciable reductions in the extent to which numerous companies held minority stock positions in other firms.[159]

As of 1984, merger control policies had been adopted in four other nations and were being considered by several others.[160] Too little experience exists to permit a careful assessment. Outside the United States, therefore, attempts to avoid monopoly enhancement through merger, or other consequences perceived as undesirable, remain for the most part in a relatively early evolutionary stage. Much more remains to be learned as the substantively diverse policies are implemented in markets embodying equally wide differences in concentration, openness to international trade, business culture, and other relevant attributes.

Conclusion

Few topics in industrial organization economics arouse more passionate debate than mergers and takeovers. Some see mergers as an important source of efficiency; others emphasize their prominence as an outlet for managerial empire-building instincts whose pursuit degrades, not enhances, efficiency; still others focus on mergers' role in altering market structures and enhancing monopoly power. National and international policy responses to the potential monopoly problem are equally diverse. In the chapters that follow, we begin building a theoretical structure by means of which we can better understand the consequences of high seller concentration stemming from mergers and other causes.

---

157. Between June 1986 and January 1989, 331 mergers were reviewed under the new procedures. Seven were abandoned, nine were allowed to proceed after some restructuring, and four were referred to the Canadian Competition Tribunal for formal hearings. See Gordon E. Kaiser, "Competition Law: 1988 Merger Review," *Legal Alert* (Mississauga, Ontario: Insight Press), vol. 8 (April 1, 1989), pp. 157–160.

158. See "Japanese Fair Trade Commission Decision on the Yawata-Fuji Steel Merger," *Antitrust Bulletin,* vol. 15 (Winter 1970), pp. 803–827.
159. OECD, *Merger Policies,* supra note 142, pp. 31–34; and OECD, *Competition Policy, 1984–85,* supra note 150, p. 135.
160. OECD, *Merger Policies,* pp. 12–13 and 45–49.

Economic
Theories of
Oligopoly Pricing

We turn now from market structure to conduct in the market, keeping in mind that the two cannot be divorced completely. A paramount task of industrial organization theory is identifying the links running from market structure to economic performance through such aspects of conduct as pricing behavior, investment, the pace of innovation, and decisions concerning product variety and quality. In this chapter we begin the task.

We have seen that in the manufacturing sector and in parts of mining, finance, and retailing, a few relatively large sellers commonly supply the lion's share of output in the markets they serve. If then we wish to learn how the real-world price system functions, we must understand oligopoly pricing. Chapter 6 reviews what has been learned about oligopolistic behavior in the absence of collusion. Chapters 7 and 8 consider the feasibility of collusive behavior among oligopolists and examine factors that facilitate and limit the power of oligopolists to hold prices persistently above cost.

Oligopolistic Interdependence

Oligopoly pricing is interesting and important not only because it is so prevalent but also because it poses such difficult problems for the economic theorist. When either pure competition or pure monopoly prevails, there are clear-cut solutions to the firm's price and output decision problem, assuming only that managers seek to maximize expected profits and that they hold definite (though probabilistic) expectations concerning future demand and cost conditions. With rivalry among the few, however, this is not so. Each firm recognizes that its best choice depends upon the choices its rivals make. The firms are interdependent and acutely aware of it. Their decisions depend then upon the assumptions they make about rival decisions and reactions—and many alternative assumptions might be entertained. These decisions go a long way toward determining firm profitability and industry performance. Casual observation suggests that in oligopoly virtually anything can happen. Some industries—cigarettes and breakfast cereals come readily to mind—succeed in maintaining prices well above production costs for years. Others, despite conditions that would appear at first glance to encourage cooperative behavior, gravitate toward price warfare.[1]

Economists have developed literally dozens of oligopoly pricing theories—some simple, some marvels of mathematical complexity. Recognizing the wide range of behavior and theoretical predictions, some economists have asserted that the oligopoly problem is indeterminate.[2] This is correct in the narrow sense that one cannot forge unique and compelling mechanistic links from cost and demand conditions to price equilibria. But a more constructive interpretation is this: to make workable predictions, we need a theory much richer than the received

1. The cigarette and breakfast cereal industries are discussed in Chapter 7. Until the 1970s, local gasoline markets offered the classic example of price warfare. A more recent example is the market for cola in Phoenix, Arizona. Although Coca-Cola and Pepsi controlled over 65 percent of the market during the summer of 1988, prices for a six-pack of cola in supermarkets fell to 59¢—barely covering the cost of the aluminum cans. "Coke vs. Pepsi:

A Truce in the Cola Wars," *The Margin*, March/April 1989, pp. 14–15.

2. Cf. K. W. Rothschild, "Price Theory and Oligopoly," *Economic Journal*, vol. 57 (September 1947), pp. 299–302; and R. B. Heflebower, "Toward a Theory of Industrial Markets and Prices," *American Economic Review*, vol. 44 (May 1954), pp. 121–139.

theories of pure competition and monopoly — a theory that includes variables irrelevant to those polar cases. In our quest for a realistic oligopoly theory, we must
develop an understanding of the diversity of cases, acquiring Edward Mason's
"ticket of admission to institutional economics."[3] At the same time, we must retain
the sharply honed tools with which economic theorists traditionally have worked.
We must not expect too much, however. The most that can be hoped for is a kind
of soft determinism: an understanding of broad tendencies and predictions correct
on the average, but subject to occasionally substantial errors.

**The Theory of
Oligopoly Pricing:
Basic Insights**

The basic difficulty facing an oligopolist is uncertainty about rival actions and
reactions. To maximize profits, the firm must infer the particular strategies rivals
will follow in their quest for profits. For the theorist, the challenge is to identify
assumptions that firms might plausibly make and that yield profit maximizing
outcomes mimicking oligopoly behavior and performance. The first noteworthy
attempt to do so was published by Augustin Cournot in 1838, but was not discovered by mainstream economists until forty-five years later.[4] Cournot postulated
that firms choose their profit-maximizing quantity of output, assuming that the
quantities marketed by rivals are fixed. He found that, for any particular number
of firms, there exists a determinate and stable price-quantity equilibrium (that is,
an outcome in which no firm has an incentive to change its level of output, given
the output of rivals). The basic Cournot model is presented in the Appendix. For
the case of n firms having identical marginal costs, each firm has a limited degree
of monopoly power — that is, price is elevated above marginal cost; and the price-
cost margin[5] falls with the number of firms and the elasticity of overall market
demand e:

$$(6.1) \qquad \frac{(P - MC)}{P} = \frac{1}{ne}.$$

Compare this with the profit-maximizing price-cost margin for a monopolist presented in Equation (2.2) (see Chapter 2). The Cournot equilibrium oligopoly
price-cost margin is the monopolist's margin, divided by the number of firms. For
fixed n, the size of the profit margin falls as demand becomes more elastic. As the
number of firms increases, the equilibrium price declines until it approaches marginal cost; that is, the competitive equilibrium is more closely approximated as the
number of rivals increases — a conclusion consistent with ordinary observation.[6] If
marginal costs vary among firms, each firm's market share s_i depends upon its
efficiency; low-cost firms have larger shares:

$$(6.2) \qquad s_i = e(P - MC_i)/P.$$

Finally, the Cournot model provides a direct link between industry performance,
measured by the difference between price and the weighted average industry marginal cost, and a measure of market concentration, the Herfindahl-Hirschman
concentration index:[7]

$$(6.3) \qquad \frac{(P - \overline{MC})}{P} = \frac{H}{e},$$

where $\overline{MC}$ is the weighted average of the sellers' marginal costs.

Thus, Cournot's oligopoly pricing model exhibits a number of the characteristics we intuitively associate with oligopoly. However, before examining the model's logic in more detail, we must note that Cournot's initial premises were unrealistic in important respects. For one, he assumed that the quantity of output supplied is the firm's key decision variable. Firms choose their outputs and then offer them on the market, which (through some unarticulated bidding process) establishes a price just sufficient to equate quantity demanded with quantity supplied. Yet observation suggests that price typically is the decision variable of primary interest to firms with monopoly power.[8] That is, sellers set a price and then let buyers decide whether, and how much, to purchase at that price. As Cournot's earliest critic J. Bertrand observed, if identical firms with equal and constant marginal costs choose their price, assuming the *prices* of rivals to be fixed, the only stable price-quantity equilibrium will be one in which price equals marginal cost.[9]

This objection can be met while preserving the heart of the Cournot model if we assume some degree of product differentiation, so that different producers are able to sell simultaneously in the same market at different prices. To illustrate the modified theory, a numerical example is useful.

We postulate an industry with two firms selling differentiated products. Each company chooses the price for its product, and buyers respond by deciding from whom and how much to purchase. Profits depend upon the price charged and the amount sold, as well as on costs. Figure 6.1 summarizes the possible results of this duopolistic rivalry from the viewpoint of Firm 1. The numerical entries give the net profits (in thousands of dollars per month) realized by Firm 1 for any combination of its own price P_1 and rival Firm 2's price P_2. Three simple but plausible assumptions underlie the equations generating these profit values. First, the two firms share the market equally when their prices are identical. When their prices are not equal, the high-price firm's market share falls with the rise in the percentage difference between its price and its rival's price. Second, the total quantity demanded from the two firms is an inverse linear function of the two prices, weighted by the firms' market shares. No units will be demanded when both firms

3. Edward S. Mason, *Economic Concentration and the Monopoly Problem* (Cambridge: Harvard University Press, 1957), p. 60.

4. A. A. Cournot, *Researches into the Mathematical Principles of the Theory of Wealth*, reprint of the 1927 ed. translated by Nathaniel T. Bacon (New York: Augustus M. Kelley 1838, 1971).

5. See the discussion on p. 35 supra and accompanying notes.

6. From Equation (6.1), as $n \to \infty$, holding e fixed, PCM $\to 0$; as $e \to \infty$, holding n fixed, PCM $\to 0$. In the more general case, where unit costs may rise at production levels below some minimum efficient scale of operation, there is a limit to the number of firms that can earn nonnegative profits in equilibrium. As the minimum efficient scale becomes small relative to demand, equilibrium n rises until, at the limit, price approximates marginal cost. See William Novshek, "Cournot Equilibrium with Free Entry," *Review of Economic Studies*, vol. 47 (April 1980), pp. 473–486.

7. See p. 72 supra. The notation has been simplified here from HHI to H.

8. The use of quantity as the strategic variable has been defended by assuming that firms first choose plant capacities and then engage in price rivalry. David M. Kreps and Jose A. Scheinkman, "Quantity Precommitment and Bertrand Competition Yield Cournot Outcomes," *Bell Journal of Economics*, vol. 14 (Autumn 1983), pp. 326–337. See also C. Davidson and R. Deneckere, "Long-Run Competition in Capacity, Short-Run Competition in Price, and the Cournot Model," *Rand Journal of Economics*, vol. 17 (Autumn 1986), pp. 404–415; and H. Dixon, "The Cournot and Bertrand Outcomes as Equilibria in a Strategic Metagame," *Economic Journal*, vol. 96 (Supplement 1986), pp. 59–70.

9. J. Bertrand, book review of "Theorie Mathematique de la Richesse Sociale" and of "Recherches sur les Principes Mathematiques de la Theorie des Richesses," *Journal des Savants*, vol. 67 (1883), pp. 499–508.

Figure 6.1
Net Profit Matrix for Firm 1

Price Quoted by Firm 2

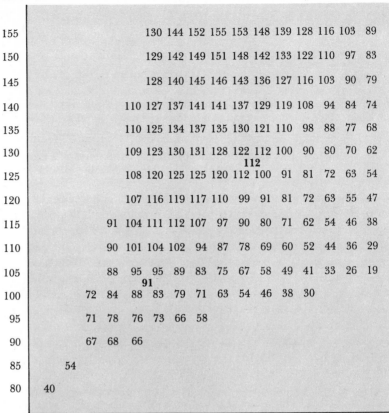

Price Quoted by Firm 1

charge $200 per unit or more. Third, the firms are assumed to have identical U-shaped short-run average total cost curves, with the minimum attainable cost ($65 per unit) occurring at an output of 2,250 units per month.[10] If both firms charge less than $80 per unit, the marginal cost of meeting the resulting heavy demand for each firm would exceed the price received — a problematic range we avoid here.[11] A similar problem arises at prices above $80 per unit when the price differential between the two firms is allowed to become unrealistically wide. Those cells have been suppressed in the table.

Firm 1's Cournot-type decision problem is to pick the value of its own price that maximizes its profits, assuming that the price of rival Firm 2 remains constant. For example, suppose that Firm 2's price is $145 per unit. We read across the row of possible payoffs associated with that price until we find the highest profit (about $146,000) attainable by Firm 1, achieved by setting P_1 at $120 per unit. This is Firm 1's Cournot-optimal decision when Firm 2's price is $145. However, if Firm

2's price should instead be $120 per unit, the best choice under the Cournot assumption is for Firm 1 to quote $110 per unit, earning profits of $119,000 per month. In a similar fashion, we can find Firm 1's Cournot-optimal response to any observed value of P_2. This decision rule, graphed in Figure 6.2 as R_1, is called Firm 1's Cournot *reaction function*, since if rival Firm 2 changes its price from, say, $145 to $120, Firm 1 will react by moving along R_1 from $P_1 = $120 to $P_1 = $110.

A similar profit matrix could be drawn up for Firm 2, although to keep Figure 6.1 legible, it is not shown. Assuming symmetry of cost and demand functions, it would be the transposition of Figure 6.1; that is, the profit to Firm 2 when $P_2 = 120$ and $P_1 = 130$ is the same as the profit to Firm 1 when $P_1 = 120$ and $P_2 = 130$. From Firm 2's profit matrix, we can derive its Cournot reaction function, shown by the line R_2 in Figure 6.2.

Now the stage is set to play through the logic of Cournot rivalry. Suppose Firm 2 has been operating as a monopolist, maximizing its profits (at $220,000 per month) by charging a price of $140 per unit. Firm 1 enters the industry, assumes this price to be fixed, and makes the best of it, moving to its reaction function R_1, which here lies between $115 and $120 — $118 to be precise. But now, the $140 price is no longer optimal for Firm 2. Given Firm 1's presence and its price of $118, the best price for Firm 2 is just over $110 (found by drawing a horizontal line to the P_2 axis from Firm 2's reaction function at the point where a vertical line representing Firm 1's price of $118 intersects). This alters the initial conditions assumed by Firm 1, which therefore moves along its reaction function to a new Cournot-optimal price of $107 per unit. The logic of price-cutting and counter-cutting continues until the two firms reach the point where their reaction functions intersect. There and only there, where each firm is quoting a price of $103 per unit, selling 2,450 units and earning profits of $91,000 per month, will the two firms find no alternative price yielding higher profits, assuming the rival's price to be constant. At this point (boldfaced in Figure 6.1, point C in Figure 6.2), the stable Cournot equilibrium is attained.

It is intuitively appealing to present the Cournot equilibrium as if it resulted from a series of moves played out over time.[12] If the moves were in fact sequential the sellers would quickly discover the inconsistency between their assumption that rivals' decision variables (in this case price) are fixed and the reality of rival reaction functions. As an early critic of the Cournot model, Irving Fisher, observed:

---

10. In mathematical form, Firm 1's market share S_1 is given by the exponential equations:

$$S_1 = .5e^{-3[(P_1 - P_2)/P_2]},$$

when $200 > P_1 > P_2$, and

$$S_1 = .5e^{-3[(P_2 - P_1)/P_1]},$$

when $P_1 < P_2 < 200$. The total quantity Q demanded from both firms is given by $Q = 10,000 - 50S_1P_1 - 50S_2P_2$. Firm 1 sells S_1Q units, and its total revenue is P_1S_1Q. Each firm's total cost function is $C_i = 50,000 + 20q_i + .01q_i^2$, $i = 1,2$. Firm 1's profit, given in Figure 6.1, is $P_1S_1Q - C_1$.

11. Of course, this situation can arise if a firm finds itself in a price war. Whether such a firm rations output or absorbs short-run losses to maintain its market share for the long run depends on the dynamics of the rivalry — a topic to be addressed in Chapter 10.

12. For a discussion of the complications that arise when the Cournot model is interpreted as a multistage process, see James W. Friedman, *Oligopoly and the Theory of Games* (Amsterdam: North-Holland, 1977), Ch. 5.

Figure 6.2
Cournot Equilibrium
for Firms 1 and 2

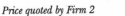

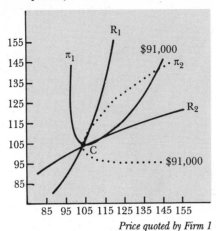

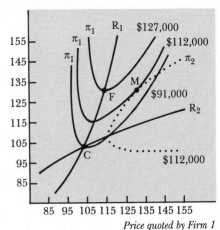

no business man assumes either that his rival's output or price will remain constant any more than a chess player assumes that his opponent will not interfere with his effort to capture a knight. On the contrary, his whole thought is to forecast what move the rival will make in response to his own.[13]

By failing to recognize that rivals will react to its price initiatives, a firm conforming to the Cournot assumption is guilty of myopia. We shall see in later chapters that decision makers do exhibit myopic tendencies in certain rivalry situations. Nevertheless, economists have come to believe that the multi-move Cournot assumption is unrealistic when applied to pricing decisions involving only a few firms.

Constantly beckoning the sellers in an oligopoly is the prospect of monopoly profits. The profit matrix in Figure 6.1 can be interpreted as a topographic map, with each cell indicating the height of a profit mountain. By connecting cells with identical profit levels, we can form contour lines or *iso-profit* curves indicating the set of price pairs P_1 and P_2 that yield Firm 1 a constant level of profit. Figure 6.2(a) shows each firm's $91,000 iso-profit curve (smooth for Firm 1, dotted for Firm 2) cutting the intersection of the two reaction functions. The iso-profit curves for a given firm bottom out at their intersection with the firm's reaction function — that is, they are tangent to horizontal lines intersecting the reaction function for Firm 1 and vertical lines intersecting R_2. Iso-profit curves farther from the origin O indicate higher (constant) profit levels.

From point **C**, by moving diagonally northeast (that is, raising both sellers' prices), it is possible to increase each seller's profits. Such increases are possible up to the point where an iso-profit curve of Firm 1 is tangent to a similar curve for Firm 2 (at point **M** in Figure 6.2(b)). There each firm is charging $128 per unit, and each realizes profits of $112,000 (boldfaced in the profit matrix of Figure 6.1). At point **M**, the sum of Firm 1's profits plus Firm 2's profits is at a maximum, and so we conclude (subject to possible later modifications for asymmetric cases) that $P_1 = P_2 = \$128$ is the *joint profit-maximizing* solution for the duopolists. To reach it, Firms 1 and 2 must cooperate as if they were a unified monopoly. The solution at **M** is not sustainable if one or both of the sellers behave according to the Cournot assumption that its rival's price will remain constant. Thus, if Firm 1 believed, à la Cournot, that Firm 2 would hold its price constant at the joint profit-maximizing value of $128, Firm 1 could achieve higher profits of $127,000 by cutting its own price to $113 (point **F** in Figure 6.2(b), or just above the two "125" entries in Figure 6.1). But then Firm 2's profits would be sharply reduced, and if Firm 2 responded similarly, the reciprocal price cutting would lead back to the Cournot equilibrium point **C**, with prices of $103 and lower profits of $91,000 for each seller. If the firms recognize that their fortunes are interdependent in this way, they would be well-advised to find ways of avoiding Cournot-type behavior and holding their prices at the $128 joint profit-maximizing level.

This was the central point made in 1929 by Edward Chamberlin.[14] Chamberlin asserted that when the number of sellers is small and products are standardized, the oligopolists can scarcely avoid full recognition of their interdependence. Each therefore would be reluctant to take measures that, when countered, would leave all members of the industry worse off. Instead, the firms would set price at the monopoly level:

If each seeks his maximum profit rationally and intelligently, he will realize that when there are only two or a few sellers his own move has a considerable effect upon his competitors, and that this makes it idle to suppose that they will accept without retaliation the losses he forces upon them. Since the result of a cut by any one is inevitably to decrease his own profits, no one will cut, and although the sellers are entirely independent, the equilibrium result is the same as though there were a monopolistic agreement between them.[15]

For the monopoly (that is, joint profit-maximizing) price to emerge, Chamberlin argued, it is essential only that firms *recognize* their mutual interdependence and their interest in a high price. Indeed, it would be unreasonable to expect members of a highly concentrated industry to behave otherwise:

The assumption of independence cannot be construed as requiring the sellers to compete as though their fortunes were independent, for this is to belie the very problem of duopoly itself. It can refer only to independence of action—the absence of agreement or of "tacit" agreement.[16]

This passage, we shall see in Chapter 9, had a profound impact on the intellectual foundations of antitrust policy, for it led economists to recognize that monopoly pricing could occur without explicit collusion if the industry structure is conducive, and that the gatherings in smoke-filled rooms traditionally attacked under the antitrust laws were not an essential ingredient of monopoly behavior.

Chamberlin acknowledged that monopoly prices might not be attained or maintained owing to certain complications. Perhaps most obvious, when the number of sellers becomes sufficiently large that individual firms begin to ignore their direct or indirect influence on price, an abrupt break toward the competitive

13. Irving Fisher, "Cournot and Mathematical Economics," *Quarterly Journal of Economics*, vol. 12 (January 1898), p. 126.
14. E. H. Chamberlin, "Duopoly: Value Where Sellers Are Few," *Quarterly Journal of Economics*, vol. 43 (November 1929), pp. 63–100; incorporated with revisions as Chapter III in *The Theory*

of Monopolistic Competition (Cambridge: Harvard University Press, 1933). Subsequent references are to the sixth edition of the latter.
15. Chamberlin, *Monopolistic Competition*, supra note 14, p. 48.
16. Chamberlin, *Monopolistic Competition*, pp. 46–47.

price is apt to occur. Second, when substantial time lags intervene between the initiation and matching of price cuts, some firms might undercut the monopoly price, risking future profits for the sake of short-term gains. Third, sellers might fail to hold prices at the monopoly level if they are uncertain about the reactions, intelligence, or farsightedness of their rivals. Finally, as we will see in Chapter 7, when costs and/or market shares differ across firms, it is not always easy, even with direct communication, for rivals to agree on a common price. Coordinating pricing under such conditions in the absence of communication is much more difficult. Despite these qualifications, the main impact of Chamberlin's analysis was to show that when sellers are few and products standardized, a monopoly price can be established without formal collusion.

Conjectural Variations Chamberlin's insight can be incorporated into the Cournot model by allowing firms to hold conjectures about how rivals would respond to their own adjustments in output (or price). In the original Cournot model emphasizing *output* adjustments, the effect of a change in production dq_i by firm i on industry output Q was one for one, since other firms' output was assumed to be unchanged.

$$dQ/dq_i = dq_i/dq_i = 1$$

Suppose alternatively that firm i believes that firm j will alter its production in response to i's action, that is, $dq_j / dq_i \neq 0$. Define $Q_i = Q - q_i$, that is, industry output excluding Firm i's production. Then Firm i's estimate of the sum of *all* rival reactions to its own output change is dQ_i/dq_i—called Firm i's *conjectural variation*.[17] Thus, the full effect on total industry output of a one-unit adjustment in production by Firm i will be 1 (the direct effect) plus the conjectural variation (the total rival reaction).

The solution to the Cournot model modified to incorporate conjectural variations is developed in the Appendix.[18] For the case of *n* firms producing an undifferentiated product with identical marginal costs and holding identical conjectural variations, the modified Cournot model yields the following equilibrium condition:

(6.4) $$\frac{(P - MC_i)}{P} = \frac{s_i}{e} [1 + dQ_i/dq_i].$$

If the conjectural variation is negative, Firm i expects its rivals at least partially to offset changes in its output. In the extreme case of $dQ_i/dq_i = -1$, so that the right-hand side of Equation (6.4) becomes zero, the offsetting is complete, and price falls into equality with marginal cost—the equilibrium of pure competition. For values of the conjectural variation greater than 0, Firm i expects rivals approximately to match its output adjustments. Perfect matching by all sellers, if anticipated, would lead each to behave in ways that mimic perfect coordination or collusion, leading in equilibrium to the monopoly price-cost margin for Firm i. As shown in the Appendix, this would occur if $dQ_i/dq_i = (1 - s_i) / s_i$, reducing (6.4) after substitution into the pricing rule followed by a monopolist.[19]

Moving from individual firm Equation (6.4) to the *industry* average price-cost margin requires modeling the interaction of the conjectural variations of each firm.[20] One empirically useful special case emerges when we require firms to hold conjectural variations proportional to their relative market shares:[21]

$$(6.5) \qquad \frac{(P - \overline{MC})}{P} = \frac{1}{e} [A + (1 - A)H].$$

where A is the proportionality factor. If A = 0, conjectural variations for all firms are zero—the original Cournot case. If A = 1, each firm assumes complete matching, yielding equation (2.2)—the monopoly result. As A falls below zero, firms assume an increasing degree of *mutual offsetting,* and price approaches marginal cost. Thus, depending on the behavioral assumptions made by the firms, industry prices can range between the competitive or the monopoly level, regardless of the number or size distribution of firms. Of course, as Chamberlin argued, the behavioral assumptions that firms make are sensitive to market structure. Firms in an atomistic industry are unlikely to believe in output matching by rivals. At

17. Arthur L. Bowley introduced into the Cournot model the partial derivative of rivals' output with respect to the firm's own production in his book, *The Mathematical Groundwork of Economics* (Oxford: Oxford University Press, 1924). Ragnar Frisch named this term the conjectural variation. "Monopoly—Polypole—la Notion de Force dans l'Economie," *Nationalökonomisk Tidsskrft*, vol. 71 (1933), pp. 241–259.

18. The approach to conjectural variations used here, which allows one to isolate structural and behavioral influences on oligopoly pricing, was developed by Keith Cowling and Michael Waterson, "Price-Cost Margins and Market Structure," *Economica*, vol. 43 (August 1976), pp. 267–274; and Roger Clarke and Stephen W. Davies, "Market Structure and Price-Cost Margins," *Economica*, vol. 49 (August 1982), pp. 277–287. Variations on this approach can be found in Roger Clarke, Stephen Davies, and Michael Waterson, "The Profitability-Concentration Relation: Market Power or Efficiency?" *Journal of Industrial Economics*, vol. 32 (June 1984), pp. 435–450; William F. Long, "Market Share, Concentration and Profits: Intra-industry and Inter-industry Evidence," paper presented at the December 1982 Meetings of the Econometric Society; and Dennis Mueller, *Profits in the Long Run* (Cambridge: Cambridge University Press, 1986), Chapter 4.

19. See Equation (2.2) and surrounding text.

20. The inclusion of conjectural variations in the Cournot model does not fully address Fisher's charge of myopia, since there is no guarantee that the modified reaction functions will be consistent with the postulated conjectural variations. One response is to argue that the modified Cournot model is a shorthand description of a more complicated—perhaps multiperiod—interaction among firms. See, for example, B. Douglas Bernheim, "Rationalizable Strategic Behavior," *Econometrica*, vol. 52 (July 1984), pp. 1007–1028. Efforts to model that more complicated interaction will be described in the next section. A second response has been to identify modified Cournot model solutions in which the observed reaction functions are consistent with the conjectural variations. For examples of the latter, see Timothy F. Bresnahan,

"Duopoly Models with Consistent Conjectures," *American Economic Review*, vol. 71 (December 1981), pp. 934–945; Martin Perry, "Oligopoly and Consistent Conjectural Variations," *Bell Journal of Economics*, vol. 13 (Spring 1982), pp. 197–205; and Morton I. Kamien and Nancy L. Schwartz, "Conjectural Variations," *Canadian Journal of Economics,* vol. 16 (May 1983), pp. 191–211. Andrew F. Daughety, "Reconsidering Cournot: The Cournot Equilibrium is Consistent," *Rand Journal of Economics,* vol. 16 (Autumn 1985), pp. 368–379, argues that the original Cournot equilibrium is consistent when viewed in a dynamic context. Charles Holt, "An Experimental Test of the Consistent-Conjectures Hypothesis," *American Economic Review,* vol. 75 (June 1985), pp. 314–325, reports on duopoly experiments that came out closer to the zero conjectural variation Cournot result than the consistent conjectures equilibrium. Gyoichi Iwata, "Measurement of Conjectural Variations in Oligopoly," *Econometrica,* vol. 42 (September 1974), pp. 947–966, estimates conjectural variations for the Japanese flat glass industry.

21. See the Appendix for the derivation of this result. Chapter 11 discusses its use in empirical research. Richard Schmalensee, "Collusion Versus Differential Efficiency: Testing Alternative Hypotheses," *Journal of Industrial Economics*, vol. 35 (June 1987), pp. 399–425, has criticized the definition of A as imposing a negative relationship between dQ_i/dq_i and s_i, thereby requiring small firms to be the main restrictors of output in output-matching equilibria—a counter-intuitive result. Alternative approaches, which involve more complicated interactions between measures of market structure and firm beliefs, have been proposed by J. Cubbin, "Apparent Collusion and Conjectural Variations in Differentiated Oligopoly," *International Journal of Industrial Organization*, vol. 1 (June 1983), pp. 155–163; Frederick Harris, "Testable Competing Hypotheses from Structure-Performance Theory: Efficient Structure Versus Market Power," *Journal of Industrial Economics*, vol. 36 (March 1988), pp. 267–280; and Michael Waterson, *Economic Theory of the Industry* (Cambridge: Cambridge University Press, 1984), pp. 26–28.

the other extreme, firms in an industry with a small number of large rivals may well recognize the benefits from cooperative behavior, and hence are more likely to believe that rivals will be motivated similarly.

Allowing for product differentiation complicates the oligopoly pricing problem even further, although the general conclusions are similar. They suggest that, for particular patterns of product differentiation and firm costs, the number and size distribution of firms, as well as their profitability, are simultaneously determined as functions of the industry members' conjectural variations. Add to these conclusions the observation that a firm's beliefs about rival behavior are influenced by the number and size of rivals, and we are left with the pattern of interactions among market structure, conduct, and performance sketched in Figure 1.1.

To sum up, the basic Cournot analysis predicts a tendency for price to fall toward marginal cost as the number of sellers rises (that is, less concentrated industries are more likely to have prices near the competitive level). The addition of conjectural variations implies oligopoly pricing ranging from competitive to that adopted by a profit-maximizing monopolist. The major challenge facing us is to understand more fully the determinants of the behavioral assumptions made by managers of enterprises in specific industries. In recent years, those struggling with this challenge have turned to the tools of game theory.

The Contributions of Game Theory

From the perspective of the participants, the oligopoly pricing problem shares all the characteristics of a contest or game. The firms are the players.[22] Each seeks to win by choosing a strategy (a move, series of moves, or rules for choosing moves based on the environment and moves of rivals) designed to maximize its payoff, here profit. Each firm recognizes that its profit depends directly on the strategies of its rivals. The logic of such contests falls within the domain of game theory, and most modern oligopoly models are constructed using the tools of game theory.[23]

Among the simplest representations of a game is the payoff matrix, each entry of which indicates the payoff expected by each player for every possible combination of strategies. For example, the following matrix presents Player A's payoff in a two-person zero-sum game.

		B's strategies		
		b_1	b_2	b_3
	a_1	8	-5	-10
A's strategies	a_2	0	-2	6
	a_3	4	-1	5

Player B's payoff is the negative of Player A's. (All payoff pairs sum to zero, hence the name *zero-sum*.) Thus, if A chooses strategy a_2 and B chooses strategy b_3, then A's payoff is $+6$, while B's is -6. Each player's problem is to find a strategy that will maximize his or her payoff, taking the other player's strategies into account. The game theorist's problem is to find a pair of strategies that solves each player's problem. Such a pair constitutes a stable solution for the game in the sense that neither player has an incentive to change strategy, given the opponent's strategy. Such a stable solution is called a Nash equilibrium, after John Nash, who formalized the concept.[24] The Nash equilibrium to a two-person zero-sum game can be found by deriving the best response function for each player and locating the strategies that are common to both. To find his best response function, A examines each column of his payoff matrix (that is, the set of all payoffs available to A once B has chosen the strategy associated with that column), locating the best payoff available to him. The strategy yielding that payoff is A's best response to B's strategy. If B chooses strategy b_1, A finds that the best payoff available in column 1 is 8—the payoff associated with a_1. A's best response to b_2 is a_3, yielding a payoff of -1. Similarly, a_2 is the best response to b_3. Thus, A's best response function consists of the strategy pairs (a_1, b_1), (a_3, b_2), and (a_2, b_3). B solves the analogous problem by examining each row of the payoff matrix looking for her best payoff (that is, the lowest payoff to A in the row) associated with each of A's strategies. These payoffs are -10, when A plays a_1, -2 for a_2, and -1 for a_3. Thus, B's best response function consists of the strategy pairs (a_1, b_3), (a_2, b_2), and (a_3, b_2). The strategy pair (a_3, b_2), the only intersection between the two best response functions, is the Nash equilibrium for this game. If A chooses a_3, B has no incentive to deviate from b_2 (giving her a payoff of $+1$) and move to b_1 (-4) or b_3 (-5); if B chooses b_2, A has no incentive to deviate from a_3 (-1) to a_1 (-5) or a_2 (-2).

Oligopoly games vary greatly in complexity.[25] Most involve *variable sum payoffs*, that is, the total profits available to the industry are not constant, but rise or fall depending upon the decisions of each firm.[26] Strategies can range from simple price or quantity choices to selecting the breadth of a product line and the characteristics of each product. Strategies can involve a single move or an infinite sequence of moves and responses. In some games, the firm has a limited number of strategies at its disposal (for example, price high or price low). More often, there is an infinity of options within carefully defined limits (for example, choose price on the assumption that rival prices remain fixed, as long as revenue at least covers

22. In most oligopolies, a few sellers face many buyers—so many that no one buyer believes she can influence the decisions of the sellers or other buyers. Therefore, buyers are represented passively by a demand curve. The case where oligopolistic sellers face few buyers, bilateral oligopoly, will be treated in Chapter 14.
23. The field grew out of the work of John von Neumann and Oskar Morgenstern, *Theory of Games and Economic Behavior* (Princeton: Princeton University Press, 1944). Applications of game theory to industrial organization are discussed in Martin Shubik, *Game Theory in the Social Sciences* (Cambridge: MIT Press, 1984); James W. Friedman, *Oligopoly and the Theory of Games*, supra note 12; and Drew Fudenberg and Jean Tirole, "Game Theory for Industrial Organization: Introduction and Overview," in Richard Schmalensee and Robert D. Willig, eds., *Handbook of Industrial Organization* (Amsterdam: North Holland, 1989).
24. John F. Nash, Jr., "Noncooperative Games," *Annals of Mathematics*, vol. 54 (September 1951), pp. 286–295. Nash formalized the concept in his Ph.D. dissertation. It is sometimes called the Cournot-Nash equilibrium, since the solution Cournot devised

for his oligopoly model is an example of the equilibrium defined by Nash.
25. Detailed surveys of formal oligopoly models can be found in James W. Friedman, *Oligopoly Theory* (Cambridge: Cambridge University Press, 1983); Carl Shapiro, "Theories of Oligopoly Behavior," in Richard Schmalensee and Robert D. Willig, eds., *Handbook of Industrial Organization* (Amsterdam: North-Holland, 1989); and Jean Tirole, *The Theory of Industrial Organization* (Cambridge: MIT Press, 1988).
26. The types of rivalry encountered in oligopoly seldom conform to the zero-sum assumption. One exception would be cases such as those observed in Japan (see p. 40 supra) in which firms arguably set market share as a primary objective. Then one firm's market share gain must come at the expense of its rivals'. Another exception would be viewing oligopolistic conflict as "games of survival" or "games of ruin," with the winner enjoying the whole of a profitable market. See Shubik, *Game Theory and the Social Sciences*, supra note 23, pp. 295–297.

variable costs). Yet no matter how complex the game becomes, the challenges facing players and theorists are the same as those in the simple zero-sum game presented above. From the individual firm's standpoint, the oligopoly problem is to choose the strategy that maximizes its profit, taking the strategies of rivals into account. From the standpoint of the theorist, the problem is to find a set of firm strategies that are mutually feasible and that solve each firm's problem — that is, to find a Nash equilibrium for the game.

For a more realistic example of the payoff structure encountered in business rivalry, we refer again to Figure 6.1. It should be evident now that Figure 6.1 is simply a large payoff matrix, and that the reaction functions graphed in Figure 6.2 are the best response functions for the two firms. For example, if Firm 2's price is $145 per unit, Firm 1's best response is to charge the price (in this case $120 per unit) that yields it the highest payoff (a profit of about $146,000) of any in that row of the payoff matrix. The Nash equilibrium to the oligopoly game depicted in Figure 6.1 is the intersection of the two best response functions. When both firms set price at $103, earning a profit of $91,000 each, neither firm can increase its profit by unilaterally altering its price. Thus, the equilibrium solutions to the Cournot model are a Nash equilibrium.

As noted, many oligopolists manage to do better, from their perspective, than this equilibrium — achieving results all the way up to the joint profit maximum, point **M** in Figure 6.2. The incentives and conditions that determine whether an oligopoly will reach this joint profit maximum can be seen more sharply if we limit our focus to the two salient price strategy alternatives, $103 and $128. The resulting abbreviated game matrix records the profit outcome for Firm 1 (before the comma) and Firm 2 for each strategy pair:

		Firm 2's price strategies	
		$128	$103
Firm 1's price strategies	$128	112,112	58,123
	$103	123, 58	91, 91

When the firms view one another primarily as rivals for industry profits, emphasizing the degree to which one gains at the other's expense, then the Nash equilibrium, with each charging $103 per unit, has an irresistible magnetism. If Firm 2 quotes a price of $128, Firm 1 will be better off quoting $103 (for a profit of $123,000 versus $112,000 at a price of $128). If Firm 2 quotes a price of $103, Firm 1 will be better off quoting $103 (for a profit of $91,000 versus $58,000 if it raises its price to $128). In the language of game theory, the $103 price *dominates* the $128 price, in the sense that it is the more profitable response, no matter which strategy the other firm plays. Firm 2 follows a similar logic.

Now consider the problem from a different perspective. Each firm can do much better if *both* charge the $128 price. *Cooperation* makes each $21,000 wealthier. Will each firm behave as if both were partners in the business of extracting profits from consumers, as Chamberlin suggested? We will see in Chapters 7 and 8 that the task of agreeing on profit-maximizing cooperative strategies is often far more difficult than arises from a simple payoff matrix like the one presented here. Yet even in this simple game, it seems unlikely that the firms would choose the cooperative solution. Each firm is tempted to cheat on the cooperative solution. If Firm 2 holds true to the $128 price, Firm 1 can raise its profits by cutting price to $103. At the same time, each firm worries that the other will cheat, playing the other for a sucker. Thus, even when both firms view one another more as partners than as rivals, the game's logic appears to compel an outcome that makes both firms worse off than they need to be!

This paradoxical situation is a typical member of the genus called Prisoners' Dilemma games.[27] A digression on the original prisoners' dilemma will provide valuable analogies for subsequent use. Suppose Smith and McAlpin, partners in crime, rob a mail train. Both are caught, but the district attorney is unable to prove her case unless she can obtain a signed confession. She can, however, make lighter charges (for example, possession of stolen goods) stick. The two suspects are interrogated in separate rooms (after being informed of their constitutional rights) and are confronted with specific alternatives. Suppose McAlpin does not confess. If Smith clams up too, both will get one year in prison on the minor charge. On the other hand, if Smith turns state's evidence, then McAlpin receives a ten-year sentence and Smith goes free. Still Smith must recognize that if McAlpin confesses and Smith does not, he ends up with the ten-year term while McAlpin walks out a free man. If both confess, both will get six years in jail. The payoff matrix, with Smith's time in prison (surely a negative payoff from his perspective) listed first, is as follows:

		McAlpin's strategies	
		Don't confess	Confess
Smith's strategies	Don't confess	−1, −1	−10, 0
	Confess	0, −10	−6, −6

Viewed purely in terms of his self-interest, Smith is better off confessing, no matter what McAlpin's choice may be.[28] The same holds true from McAlpin's viewpoint. Thus, the Nash equilibrium to this game has each confessing; both end up with six years in jail, instead of the single year they would serve if somehow they could solve the prisoners' dilemma and deny their guilt despite the strained circumstances.

In terms of their static, single-play structure, the oligopoly price game ($128 versus $103) and the classic Prisoner's Dilemma game are identical. Both have a payoff matrix of the form:

		Player 2's strategies	
		I	II
Player 1's strategies	I	B, B	D, A
	II	A, D	C, C

27. An intuitive introduction is provided by Douglas R. Hofstadter, "Metamagical Themas: Computer Tournaments of the Prisoner's Dilemma Suggest How Cooperation Evolves," *Scientific American*, May 1985, pp. 16–26.

28. We assume that Smith indeed dislikes prison and that he need not fear retribution from McAlpin. Altering either assumption would change the structure of the payoff matrix.

such that A > B > C > D.[29] The Nash equilibrium to games of this form, in which the participants consider themselves to be rivals, leaves both players worse off than they need to be. Even when the players view themselves as partners, the logic of the payoff matrix would seem to drive the players toward strategies that leave both players worse off.

And yet experience suggests that oligopolists often manage to achieve payoffs closer to those associated with strategy I. Nor does oligopoly offer the only example of real-world victories over the logic of the Prisoners' Dilemma. We observe, for example, that nuclear deterrence has been remarkably stable and successful for four decades. There has been no exchange of nuclear weapons leaving all nations worse off, even though successful unilateral attack could allow the initiator to impose its will on the victims, and being attacked unilaterally would (at least in the average citizen's judgment) be disastrous.

One way out of the Prisoners' Dilemma occurs when the players take steps that change the payoff matrix. Paradoxically, *worsening* some of one's own payoff possibilities may improve the likely outcome to the game.[30] For example, after being convicted and fined for price fixing, General Electric announced in 1963 a "price protection" plan—also known as a "most favored customer" plan—under which it guaranteed that if it gave a discount on any new turbogenerator order, it would retroactively grant the same discount on all orders taken within the preceding six months.[31] In effect, General Electric unilaterally lowered the payoff associated with a low-price strategy, that is, it eliminated the attractiveness of defecting from the cooperative solution. In the context of our earlier example, if cutting the price from $128 to $103 required rebates totaling $150,000 to customers of the past six months, the payoff matrix is altered as follows:

		Westinghouse's price strategies	
		$128	$103
GE's price strategies	$128	112,112	58,123
	$103	−28, 58	−51, 91

Keeping the price at $128 is now GE's dominant strategy (some "protection" for customers!). To be sure, this leaves GE vulnerable to a price cut by Westinghouse. But if Westinghouse's main incentive previously for price cutting had been fear that GE would cut its price, that fear is assuaged. Since GE and Westinghouse were engaged in rivalry over many periods (more on that in a moment), Westinghouse also recognized that a price cut undoubtedly would cause GE to abandon the price protection plan.[32] In fact, Westinghouse emulated GE's price protection plan in 1964, further transforming the payoff matrix to encourage cooperation,[33] and both companies maintained the plans until forced in 1976 by the government to abandon them.

Marketing practices of this sort can be quite potent in affecting industry conduct. In a series of experiments designed to simulate conditions in the market for tetraethyl lead and related antiknock gasoline compounds, Grether and Plott found that outcomes deviated more from the competitive equilibrium (although remaining far from the outcome associated with complete cooperation) when such practices as price protection, advance notice of price changes, and delivered pricing were used.[34] Advance notice eliminates rivals' fears that a firm will unexpectedly lower price. Delivered pricing, in which the firm agrees to absorb all freight charges, eliminates rival uncertainty over whether a deviant price quote represents a discount or shipping cost differentials. Other commitments that reduce the attractiveness of undercutting cooperative prices include adopting capacity-dependent technologies and adjusting the firm's financial structure to raise the ratio of debt to equity.[35] Both make it harder for management to expand production, for example, by unilaterally adopting a low-price strategy, without facing unacceptably high operating costs relative to earnings.

That firms can facilitate the collective maximization of industry profits by altering their marketing practices has obvious policy relevance. Coordination of marketing practices may be just as effective in raising profits as agreements to allocate market shares or set prices, while being more difficult to detect and prosecute. However, this brings us no closer to understanding how oligopolists can elevate prices toward the joint profit-maximizing level when the logic of the payoff matrix points to the Cournot, or even the competitive, equilibrium. At first glance, the key would seem to lie in the fact that oligopolistic rivalry is conducted repetitively over time. However, moving to a multiperiod setting does not change the logic implying the dominance of low price strategies. After demonstrating this, we turn to the remaining missing ingredient: the limited information and uncertainty facing firms.

To simplify the discussion, we drop the assumption that our firms produce differentiated products and require them to have constant, identical marginal costs of production.[36] This returns us to Bertrand's variant of the original Cournot

29. A second condition usually is also imposed: $(A+D)/2 < B$. This ensures that it would not be feasible to negotiate a deal in which player 1 plays strategy I, Player 2 plays II, and then Player 1 compensates Player 2 in a way that makes both better off than they would have been had both played I. In multiperiod variants of the Prisoners' Dilemma game, this condition rules out solutions in which the two players benefit from cycling between strategy pairs (I,II) and (II,I) on successive moves.

30. See Thomas C. Schelling, *The Strategy of Conflict* (Cambridge: Harvard University Press, 1960), Chapter 5. The Anti-Ballistic Missile Treaty of 1972 offers an example for nuclear deterrence: by limiting defensive systems, the United States and Soviet Union sought to ensure that each country could inflict unacceptable damage on the other following a unilateral attack by the other—decreasing the temptation for either to cheat on the cooperative outcome.

31. *U.S.* v. *General Electric Co. et al.*, "Plaintiff's Memorandum in Support of a Proposed Modification to the Final Judgment Entered on October 1, 1962, Against Each Defendant," December 1976.

32. In a single-period game, GE might have conditioned its price protection plan on adoption by the other firms in the industry.

33. With a symmetric transformation of Westinghouse's payoffs, the price pair ($128, $128) becomes the Nash equilibrium of the game.

34. David M. Grether and Charles R. Plott, "The Effect of Market Practices in Oligopolistic Markets: An Experimental Examination of the *Ethyl* Case," *Economic Inquiry*, vol. 22 (October 1984), pp. 479–507.

35. James A. Brander and Tracy R. Lewis, "Oligopoly and Financial Structure: The Limited Liability Effect," *American Economic Review*, vol. 76 (December 1986), pp. 956–970; Steven C. Salop, "Practices That (Credibly) Facilitate Oligopoly Coordination," in Joseph E. Stiglitz and G. Frank Mathewson, eds., *New Developments in the Analysis of Market Structure* (Cambridge: MIT Press, 1986); Thomas E. Cooper, "Most-Favored-Customer Pricing and Tacit Collusion," *Rand Journal of Economics*, vol. 17 (Autumn 1986), pp. 377–388; and Eric Maskin and Jean Tirole, "A Theory of Dynamic Oligopoly, I: Overview and Quantity Competition with Large Fixed Costs," and "A Theory of Dynamic Oligopoly, II: Price Competition, Kinked Demand Curves, and Edgeworth Cycles," both in *Econometrica*, vol. 56 (May 1988), pp. 549–569 and 571–599, respectively.

36. The same conclusions would hold using a multiperiod version of the Cournot duopoly model presented above.

model. Instead of two, let there be n firms. If all n firms charge the price that would be quoted by a monopolist, the industry earns π^M profits; hence, each firm earns π^M/n. When prices differ, the low-price firm captures the entire market. If the low price is charged by several firms, the low-price firms split the market evenly. If a firm knows that its rivals plan to charge the monopoly price, it can capture the entire market by setting the price one cent below its rivals. For all intents and purposes, the firm would earn π^M on that move of the game.

The Nash equilibrium to the single-period Bertrand oligopoly game has each firm charging a price equal to marginal cost, the competitive outcome. At any price above that level, a firm could raise its profits by lowering its price an infinitessimal amount, capturing the entire market. Multiperiod versions of static (single-period) games fall into two categories. In a *repeated game*, players must devise strategies for the single-period game in each of T successive periods. A *supergame* is an infinitely repeated single-period game. Having each firm charge the monopoly price is a Nash equilibrium of the Bertrand supergame. To see this, we must confirm that no firm has an incentive to reduce price from the monopoly level. A firm could capture the entire market today by lowering price infinitesimally. However, it would expect its rivals to respond on the next move, driving profits to zero in the next and all subsequent periods. Thus, defecting from the monopoly price earns a total of π^M in profits (the gain from capturing the market on the first move) for the defector. If no firm defects, each earns its share of industry profits, π^M/n, in perpetuity. The present value of receiving one dollar each year forever is the reciprocal of the interest rate r.[37] Therefore, the present value of the firm's share of industry profits is

$$\frac{\pi^M}{nr}.$$

As long as nr $<$ 1, that is, because the number of rivals, or the interest rate, or both, are sufficiently small,[38] the firm has no incentive to price below the monopoly level.

This supergame offers an introduction to the impact of dynamics on game theoretic results, and supergames of this sort have attracted a fair amount of attention among theorists.[39] However, their usefulness has been limited on two counts. First, a puzzling characteristic of supergames is the existence of a multitude of Nash equilibria, with little rationale for expecting one to emerge rather than any other.[40] In the Bertrand supergame, there is no logic that drives firms to the monopoly price, as opposed to other prices. *Any* price at or below the monopoly level will be an equilibrium as long as the resulting industry profit π^* satisfies the condition $\pi^*/nr > \pi^M$.

More worrisome is the fact that supergame results rarely carry over to corresponding repeated games. Consider the repeated Bertrand game with T periods or moves. Suppose (subject to contradiction) that all firms have charged the monopoly price on the first T-1 moves. With only one move left, the game takes on all the characteristics of a single-period model. Under the assumed game structure, what has happened in the past is irrelevant. Defecting is the dominant strategy. If what happens in period T-1 has no effect on period T, then the optimal strategy for period T-1 also depends only on the single-period payoff matrix; defecting dominates. This logic holds for each preceding period back to the start of the game. Hence, the Nash equilibrium to the repeated game is the same as that to the single-period game: competitive pricing prevails.[41]

Why is the past irrelevant in the repeated Bertrand game? Firms learn nothing from it. The shift to a multiperiod structure gains theorists little additional understanding of oligopolistic pricing if firms are assumed to be perfectly informed about the conditions of the game. Time is important to understanding oligopolistic rivalry not in its own right, but because it allows firms to learn from the past and try to influence the future. For time to matter, we must introduce imperfect information into our models—a task we undertake next.

Imperfect Information and Uncertainty

The problem in the classic Prisoners' Dilemma is one of information and communication. If Smith and McAlpin could get together on their stories and remain constantly in touch so that each knows the other is not confessing, both could get off with lighter sentences. It is a wise district attorney who places the prisoners in separate interrogation rooms to foment uncertainty and distrust. Similarly, cooperation is much more likely to emerge in oligopoly pricing when rival managers keep one another informed of their plans and activities (if not in smoke-filled rooms, then through the business press) and when market transactions are sufficiently simple and frequent to be monitored easily.

Absent complete communication, firms are imperfectly informed about market conditions (such as demand and rival costs) and rival intentions. They seek to infer both from past behavior and market outcomes, and each firm recognizes that its own current and past actions will be treated by rivals as signals of its costs and intentions. Added to this stew is the spice of human fallibility. As we will see in

37. A dollar invested today at interest rate r would grow through compounding to $(1+r)^t$ by year t. Therefore, the value today of a dollar received in year t would be $1/(1+r)^t$. The present value (value today) of a dollar received each year in perpetuity would be

$$\frac{1}{(1+r)} + \frac{1}{(1+r)^2} + \frac{1}{(1+r)^3} + \ldots ,$$

which is an infinite series. The sum of the infinite series, $1 + x + x^2 + x^3 + \ldots$, where $0 < x < 1$, is $1/(1+x)$. Substituting $1/(1+r)$ for x and subtracting 1 (the first term), we obtain the present value of a perpetual stream of dollars as $1/r$.

38. Managers who care little about future gains will discount profits in the future more heavily than financial markets. They would replace r with their own subjective interest or discount rate. Thus, myopic managers are more likely to defect from the monopoly price.

39. Basic supergame analysis is introduced in James Friedman, *Oligopoly and the Theory of Games*, supra note 12. It is treated at length by D. Abreu, "Infinitely Repeated Games with Discounting: General Theory," Harvard Institute of Economic Research Discussion Paper No. 1083 (1984); and Drew Fudenberg and E. Maskin, "The Folk Theorem in Repeated Games with Discounting or with Incomplete Information," *Econometrica*, vol. 54 (May 1986), pp. 533–554.

40. Supergames do permit one to see how a particular equilibrium is affected over time by complications such as business cycle shocks and cost asymmetries. For example, see E. J. Green and R. H. Porter, "Noncooperative Collusion under Imperfect Price Information," *Econometrica*, vol. 52 (January 1984), pp. 87–100; Julio Rotemberg and Garth Saloner, "A Supergame-Theoretic Model of Price Wars During Booms," *American Economic Review*, vol. 76 (June 1986), pp. 390–407; and D. Abreu, D. Pearce, and E. Stacchetti, "Optimal Cartel Equilibria with Imperfect Monitoring," *Journal of Economic Theory*, vol. 39 (June 1986), pp. 251–269. Depending on underlying cost conditions, such models can imply price wars during periods of weak or strong demand.

41. This basic argument appears in Reinhard Selten, "The Chain Store Paradox," *Theory and Decision*, vol. 9 (April 1978), pp. 127–159.

Chapters 7 and 8, managers do err in applying their pricing policies to specific situations, or by misevaluating shifts in demand. To rivals, such errors may be indistinguishable from a switch to a more aggressive low-price strategy.

A firm seeks strategies that are robust in this uncertain environment, permitting it to learn from the past without raising its vulnerability to rivals in the future. Theorists seek to understand how these strategies evolve and how they interact to influence market performance. Game theory allows one to derive optimal strategies associated with particular specifications of the imperfect information and uncertainty firms face. Since the mid-1970s, there has been an explosion of formal game theoretic models imposing imperfect information on multiperiod settings.[42] Important insights have also emerged from the controlled experiments and simulations made possible by reducing oligopoly pricing problems to game payoff matrices.

Among the most fruitful of these have been the Prisoners' Dilemma simulation tournaments conducted by Robert Axelrod.[43] Axelrod invited theorists to submit strategies to be used in a series of repeated prisoners' dilemma games, in which each entrant's strategy would engage every other strategy as well as itself. The goal was to devise a strategy that would accumulate the largest total payoff over the entire tournament. Participants knew that the same prisoners' dilemma payoff matrix (for illustration here, our old friend from the oligopoly pricing game):

		Firm 2's price strategies	
		$128	$103
Firm 1's price strategies	$128	112,112	58,123
	$103	123, 58	91, 91

would be repeated each period,[44] and strategies were permitted to take into account the outcomes of previous encounters with individual rival participants. Strategies, submitted in the form of computer programs, ranged in complexity from flipping a coin through the "always defect" strategy found dominant in the finitely repeated game with certainty, to one that involved seventy-seven lines of computer code. Axelrod engaged each program with every other program (including itself) two hundred times, repeating the exercise five times to eliminate any random anomalies.

The program that won, the shortest submitted, was Anatol Rapoport's Tit-for-Tat strategy: Cooperate on the first move; thereafter, do whatever the other player did on the previous move. The essence of the strategy is that it encourages cooperation while minimizing its vulnerability to defection. To see why Tit-for-Tat came out ahead, consider a limited version of Axelrod's tournament in which only two strategies are played: Tit-for-Tat and "always defect." Each strategy participates in two two-hundred-move games: against itself and against the other strategy. When "always defect" is pitted against itself, Players 1 and 2 each price low on each move, so that each player receives a total payoff of 200 x $91 = $18,200:

"Always Defect" vs. "Always Defect"

Move	Strategies		Payoffs	
	1	2	1	2
1–200	$103	$103	$91	$91
Total			$18,200	$18,200

Now consider what happens when Player 1 plays Tit-for-Tat, while Player 2 plays "always defect":

Tit-for-Tat vs. "Always Defect"

Move	Strategies		Payoffs	
	1	2	1	2
1	$128	$103	$58	$123
2–200	$103	$103	$91	$91
Total			$18,167	$18,232

On the first move, Tit-for-Tat prices high, "always defect" prices low, and the payoff is 58 for Tit-for-Tat and 123 for "always defect." On each subsequent move, both players defect. Thus, Tit-for-Tat's total payoff is $18,167, while "always defect" receives $18,232. By winning on the first move and tying ($103, $103) on all subsequent moves, "always defect" wins its head-to-head competition. However, suppose Tit-for-Tat encounters another rival playing the Tit-for-Tat strategy. Because both price high on the first move, both price high on all subsequent moves:

Tit-for-Tat vs. Tit-for-Tat

Move	Strategies		Payoffs	
	1	2	1	2
1–200	$128	$128	$112	$112
Total			$22,400	$22,400

Each player receives payoffs of $22,400. Neither player wins the head-to-head competition, but each does better than either would have playing "always defect." Over the two games, "always defect" receives $18,200 + $18,232 = $36,432, while Tit-for-Tat receives $18,167 + $22,400 = $40,567, winning this minitournament. It is true that playing the "always defect" strategy will guarantee the player at least as high a payoff as its opponent in head-to-head competition. In this sense, "always defect" wins every head-to-head competition with another strategy. However, the victory may be Pyrrhic. For if there is any prospect that an opposing

42. The latest work is surveyed in Fudenberg and Tirole, "Game Theory for Industrial Organization," supra note 23; and Shapiro, "Theories of Oligopoly Behavior," supra note 25.

43. Robert Axelrod, *The Evolution of Cooperation* (New York: Basic Books, 1984). A summary and discussion of Axelrod's findings appear in Hofstadter, "Metamagical Themas," supra note 27.

44. They did not know how many moves there would be in the game.

strategy permits some degree of cooperation, playing Tit-for-Tat will give its player a higher payoff than "always defect." When the goal is to maximize the cumulative payoff rather than the margin of victory over a rival, "always defect" appears to be a stupid strategy indeed.

A number of the participants in Axelrod's tournament understood the basic logic of trying to encourage cooperation, but sought ways to improve on their payoffs by periodically pricing unexpectedly low (to capture the higher profits available when the opposing player maintains the high price). The problem with such defections is that it is not easy to ensure a return by both players to the high price strategy. Suppose Player 1, playing Tit-for-Tat, goes up against Player 2, whose strategy is identical to Tit-for-Tat except that on move 101 she prices low regardless of her rival's previous action:

Tit-for-Tat vs. "Defect on 101"

	Strategies		Payoffs	
Move	1	2	1	2
1–100	$128	$128	$112	$112
101	$128	$103	$58	$123
102	$103	$128	$123	$58
103	$128	$103	$58	$123
		. . .		
200	$128	$103	$123	$58
Total			$20,250	$20,250

For the first 100 moves, both players price high. On move 101, Player 1 prices high, while its rival prices low. On move 102, Player 2 resumes the Tit-for-Tat pattern and prices high; however, Player 1 prices low as dictated by the Tit-for-Tat strategy. This pattern of oscillation will continue until the end of the game. The payoff to each is $100 \times 112 + 50 \times 58 + 50 \times 123 = \$20,250$. The "echo effects" of Player 2's one-shot grab for higher profits reduce the payoffs each player can obtain over the subsequent moves. Axelrod's summary of the result is instructive:[45]

A major lesson of this tournament is the importance of minimizing echo effects in an environment of mutual power. When a single defection can set off a long string of recriminations and counterrecriminations, both sides suffer. A sophisticated analysis must go at least three levels deep. The first level of analysis is the direct effect of a choice. This is easy, since a defection always earns more than a cooperation. The second level considers the indirect effects, taking into account that the other side may or may not punish a defection. This much was certainly appreciated by many of the entrants. But the third level goes deeper and takes into account the fact that in responding to the defections of the other side, one may be repeating or even amplifying one's own previous exploitative choice. Thus a single defection may be successful when analyzed for its direct effects, and perhaps even when its secondary effects are taken into account. But the real costs may be in the tertiary effects when one's own isolated defections turn into unending mutual recriminations. Without their realizing it, many of these rules actually wound up punishing themselves.

The essential characteristics of Tit-for-Tat are that it is "nice," in the sense of being first to offer the cooperative strategy; "provocable," in that it responds to rival defections as soon as possible; and "forgiving," by quickly matching a rival's return to the cooperative strategy.

It is tempting to conclude that these characteristics will prove successful when applied to more general oligopoly pricing environments. This has yet to be demonstrated—either by experiment or formal model. The movement from two players facing two alternative payoffs to N players facing an infinity of payoffs (as is true of most oligopoly pricing games) magnifies the complexity of the interactions manyfold.[46] Even so, we can draw at least two lessons for our analysis of oligopoly pricing from Axelrod's tournaments:[47] First, what happens during the early evolutionary stages of an industry is likely to affect the outcomes of rivalry among enterprises in the mature industry as much through what firms learn about one another's behavior as through the market structure that evolves. Thus, dynamics (the subject of chapter 10) is as important to understanding a mature industry as it is for tracing through the interactions of entry, exit, and investment. The past conditions the present. Second, if repeated game models of oligopoly pricing are to yield useful results, they must incorporate the process by which firms learn about rivals and market conditions. Some efforts in this direction have begun to appear.

To suggest their promise, we return to the repeated Bertrand game, with its n firms and T periods, and add only one element of uncertainty—uncertainty over rival intentions. To simplify the algebra, we assume away the complication of discounting future profits into present value terms. Consider the decisions facing Firm i at the start of the game. While it recognizes the logic of defection, particularly toward the end of the game, it also recognizes that all firms would be better off—even a firm that thought it could defect one move before any rival—holding price at the monopoly level.[48] Suppose it guesses that the probability that all rivals will maintain the monopoly price at least until there are no more than ten periods left in the game is 0.1 (that is, one in ten). Firm i's payoff from defecting (that is, just undercutting the monopoly price) is at most π^M.[49] Firm i's expected payoff from holding price at the monopoly level is

$$.9(0) \ + \ .1(\pi^M/n)(T-10)[50]$$

45. Axelrod, *The Evolution of Cooperation*, supra note 43, p. 38.

46. In theoretical physics, this is known as the many body problem. Starting from the basic laws of motion, it is possible to compute the effects of two interacting bodies on one another. When large numbers of bodies interact, exact solutions for the behavior of the system become impossible. Instead, statistical techniques are used to approximate the paths taken by individual bodies and hence the behavior of the whole.

47. The discussion that follows is influenced strongly by D. Kreps and A. Michael Spence, "Modelling the Role of History in Industrial Organization and Competition," in George R. Feiwel,

ed., *Issues in Contemporary Microeconomics and Welfare* (Albany: State University of New York Press, 1985), pp. 340–378.

48. If one firm defects in the first period, it earns π^M in that period and zero thereafter. If no firm defects throughout the game, then each firm earns $T\pi^M/N$. As long as the number of periods in the game exceeds the number of firms, each firm benefits from cooperation.

49. It would be zero if one of the other firms also decides to defect, resulting in the standard single-period Bertrand price war.

50. The payoff is at least this great, since there remains the possibility that no rival will cheat for some of the last ten periods.

As long as $T > 10n + 10$,[51] Firm i's minimum expected payoff from pricing high in the first period exceeds its maximum payoff from undercutting. Under the conditions specified, Firm i eventually will find it optimal to defect. In the second period, maintaining the monopoly price is attractive if $(T - 1) > 10n + 10$. In some period t, it must be true that $(T - t) < 10n + 10$. However, if we left the game at this point, we would have learned little from Axelrod's tournament. The fact that none of its rivals defected on the first move gives Firm i information about their intentions. He (and they) may raise their estimate of the probability that rivals do not intend to defect (or are playing some version of the Tit-for-Tat strategy). With each passing period in which no defection takes place, each firm's conviction that rivals are not about to defect will be strengthened. Further, the firms are unlikely to know the precise value of T. Failure of rivals to defect may propagate a general perception that T is greater than beliefs about T held at the start of the game. Even if T were known with certainty, for example, because of the announced future introduction of a new superior product, the firms know they may be rivals in oligopoly pricing games involving future generations.

This is an example of a game of incomplete information.[52] Each firm has some information (such as the number of firms) in common with all rivals and some information (such as its intentions) which only it knows. Over the moves of the game, firms seek to infer the private information held by their rivals. The basic approach to devising an optimal strategy has each firm (a) imagining all possible bits of private information the others could have, (b) deriving the strategies rivals would choose based upon that information, (c) attaching subjective probabilities to those possibilities, and (d) choosing best responses to rival moves, based in part on what can be learned about rivals' private information from past moves. Of course, uncertainty can involve any number of dimensions: cost structure, research and development strategies, or new product introductions, to name a few. The mathematics of these games have proved to be daunting. In the games analyzed to date, equilibria are extremely sensitive to the firms' initial probability assessments, and, as in the supergame literature, multiple equilibria emerge in games of any complexity. Yet this research offers the promise of incorporating the insights from experimental and simulation game theoretic results into formal models of oligopoly pricing.

In sum, game theory has yet to yield compelling mechanistic solutions to oligopoly pricing problems. It has helped identify certain general structural characteristics of rivalries involving conflict mixed with incentives for cooperation. It confirms the notion emerging from traditional theory that "anything can happen" in oligopoly, depending upon firm conjectures about rival behavior, and it suggests that those conjectures depend crucially on past interactions in an uncertain environment. Finally, there is the suggestion (emerging most notably from game experiments and simulations) that simple strategies combining cooperative, forgiving behavior with a willingness to retaliate when provoked provide firms with effective means of transcending the complexities and uncertainties of oligopolistic markets. Armed with these generalizations, we are better able to understand the conditions facilitating and impeding solution of the pricing problems faced by real-world oligopolists.

Dominant Firm Behavior

The models presented thus far are intended to characterize rivalry among approximate equals. Yet as we saw in Chapter 3, the largest firms in an industry can be many times larger than their smallest rivals.[53] In some industries, a single firm or jointly acting group of firms holds a dominant position (for the single firm, a market share of 40 percent or more). Smaller rivals are as sensitive to the interests of dominant firms as mice around an elephant. Two models that capture important elements of this asymmetric rivalry problem are von Stackelberg's leader-follower model and Forchheimer's dominant-firm model.[54]

The von Stackelberg model emerges from the Cournot model when one asks, what happens if one firm correctly anticipates the reactions of its rivals? Therefore, we begin by returning to the Cournot model—considering two firms that face linear demand, produce undifferentiated products at identical constant marginal costs, and for whom quantity is the strategic variable.[55] Each firm holds the Cournot conjectural variation, that is, each assumes the other's level of production to be unchanged by its own output decisions. Figure 6.3 presents each firm's Cournot reaction functions. Finding a particular level of Firm 2's production on the vertical axis, we move horizontally to R_1 and then vertically down to the horizontal axis to identify Firm 1's Cournot profit-maximizing response.

Figure 6.3 differs from Figure 6.2 in several important respects. First, because demand is linear and marginal costs constant for each firm in this example, the reaction functions are straight lines. Second, because the rivalry focuses on outputs rather than prices, the iso-profit curves (drawn for Firm 1 in Figure 6.3) curve *toward* the axes, not away; and the closer the curve is to the axis, the *higher* is the level of profit. Holding one's own production fixed, profits rise as one's rival decreases its production (for example, iso-profit curve III represents a higher level of profit than curves I and II); whereas profits rise with an increase in rival price for the case treated in Figure 6.2. Finally, the output reaction curves slope down in Figure 6.3—Firm 1 responds optimally to a decrease in Firm 2's output by raising production—in contrast to the upward-sloping price reaction curves of Figure 6.2.

---

51. Cooperating in the first period pays if

$$.1(\pi^M/n)(T-10) > \pi^M; \; T-10 > n/.1 \rightarrow T > 10n + 10.$$

Suppose an industry has four identical firms that can adjust prices monthly. If each firm has a five-year planning horizon, the relation holds: $5(12) = 60 > 10(4) + 10 = 50$.

52. The basic theory is presented by J. Harsanyi, "Games with Incomplete Information Played by Bayesian Players," *Management Science*, vol. 14 (1967–1968), pp. 159–182, 324–334, and 486–502 respectively. The approach has most commonly been used to model entry. For an application to oligopoly theory, see David M. Kreps et al., "Rational Cooperation in the Finitely Repeated Prisoners' Dilemma," *Journal of Economic Theory*, vol. 27 (August 1982), pp. 245–252.

53. See especially note 67, p. 83 supra.

54. Heinrich von Stackelberg, *Marktform und Gleichgewicht* (Vienna: Springer, 1934); and Karl Forchheimer, "Theoretisches zum unvollständigen Monopole," *Schmollers Jahrbuch* (1908), pp. 1–12. See the discussions in A. J. Nichol, *Partial Monopoly and Leadership* (Philadelphia: Smith–Edwards, 1930); William Fellner, *Competition Among the Few* (New York: Alfred A. Knopf, 1949); and Kalman J. Cohen and Richard M. Cyert, *Theory of the Firm: Resource Allocation in a Market Economy* (Englewood Cliffs, N.J.: Prentice-Hall, 1965).

55. The details of the model are presented in the Appendix. Demand is $P(Q) = 200 - Q$, $Q = q_1 + q_2$. Marginal cost for each firm is 50.

Figure 6.3

Two Firm von Stackelberg
Equilibrium

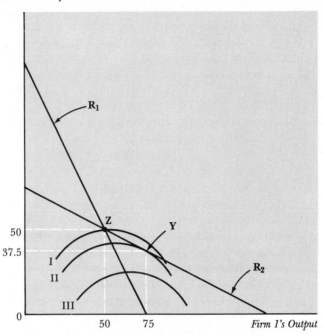

Firm 2's Output

When both firms maintain the Cournot conjectural variation, the equilibrium solution occurs at the intersection Z of the two reaction curves. In this example, both firms produce fifty units (see Appendix). Suppose, however, Firm 1 recognizes that Firm 2 responds according to its reaction curve R_2. There is a range in which Firm 1 can increase its output moving from Z along R_2 (to anticipate Firm 2's response) and thereby reach higher iso-profit curves (closer to the horizontal axis). The limit to this range occurs where an iso-profit curve (in this case, II) is tangent to R_2, that is, where $q_1 = 75$. If Firm 1 were to raise output beyond this level, Firm 2's Cournot response would move Firm 1 to a lower iso-profit curve (one farther away from the horizontal axis). The point of tangency Y (where Firm 1 produces 75 and Firm 2 produces 37.5 units) is the von Stackelberg equilibrium. Firm 1 is called the von Stackelberg leader, since it takes the lead in setting output, while Firm 2 is called the follower—passively taking the leader's output as given.

With identical firms, it is difficult to rationalize why one firm should take the leadership role while the other accepts a follower role, with its reduced market share and profits. The von Stackelberg equilibrium is more suggestive of market outcomes when one firm has a significant competitive advantage over a group of rival firms. To illustrate this case (see Appendix), we assume that one firm, Firm L, has a cost advantage over n rivals. Let marginal cost c_F be constant and the same for each rival; and let marginal cost for Firm L be c_L, with $c_L < c_F$. All firms produce an undifferentiated product; and market demand is linear, that is, of form $P = a - bQ$, where Q is industry output. All firms recognize Firm L's advantage: it could raise output to the point where price falls just below c_F, imposing losses on its rivals but preserving positive profits for itself. We assume that this recognized advantage leads to von Stackelberg behavior — rivals behave as follower firms, holding the Cournot conjectural variation for all other firms in the industry, while the leader incorporates the follower reaction functions into its conjectural variation.[56] In equilibrium, Firm L's output is

$$(6.6) \qquad q_L = \frac{(a - c_L) + n(c_F - c_L)}{2b} ,$$

while output for a typical follower, Firm F, is

$$(6.7) \qquad q_F = \frac{(a - c_F) - (n + 1)(c_F - c_L)}{2b(n + 1)} .$$

In the absence of any cost advantage, these equations become $q_L = (a - c)/2b$ and $q_F = (a - c)/2b(n + 1)$. The leader's market share is $(n + 1)/(n + 2)$, and hence falls with an increase in the number of rivals, although the relative difference in size between the leader and a typical follower becomes more pronounced.[57] For a given number of followers, an increase in the leader's cost advantage over followers, $c_F - c_L$, will increase Firm L's output and decrease each follower's production, thus raising the leader's market share. The interaction of the two effects is a bit more complicated. Table 6.1 presents the leader's market share as a function of the number of followers and the leader's cost advantage (follower unit costs minus the leader's unit costs) for an extension of the von Stackelberg model presented above.[58] For any given cost advantage, an increase in the number of followers initially lowers the leader's market share. Eventually, however, the larger number of rivals so enhances the strategic significance of the leader's cost advantage that its market share begins to rise. As both the cost advantage and the number of disadvantaged rivals rise, the leader's dominance becomes more pronounced.

Table 6.1   Von Stackelberg Leader's Market Share

	Number of Followers					
$c_F - c_L$	1	3	5	7	9	11
0	0.67	0.57	0.55	0.53	0.53	0.52
2	0.68	0.60	0.58	0.59	0.59	0.60
4	0.69	0.62	0.62	0.64	0.66	0.68
6	0.70	0.65	0.66	0.69	0.72	0.76
8	0.71	0.67	0.70	0.74	0.78	0.83
10	0.72	0.70	0.74	0.79	0.85	0.91

56. In this sense, the von Stackelberg model is no less guilty of assuming myopia on the part of follower firms than is the Cournot model. As with the Cournot model, it is possible to obtain results similar to those of the von Stackelberg model using multiperiod cases incorporating far more complicated behavioral interactions among firms.

57. The leader's output is fixed in this case, while output for each follower falls.

58. See note 55 supra. The followers' marginal cost is fixed at 50, while the leader's marginal cost is set at progressively lower levels.

The Von Stackelberg model assumes that followers hold Cournot conjectural variations on output; that is, the followers take the leader's output to be given. In Forchheimer's alternative, the followers are price takers, that is, each rival firm is assumed to be so small relative to market demand that it views changes in its output as having no effect on price. In effect, the rival firms form a purely competitive "fringe." From the perspective of the dominant firm, the strategic significance of the competitive fringe comes from recognition that the fringe firms, setting price equal to their own (upward-sloping) marginal costs, raise output when the price is increased and cut production when price falls. The solution to Forchheimer's model is depicted in Figure 6.4. The supply curve S_f of the competitive fringe is the horizontal sum of the fringe marginal cost curves.[59] The overall market demand function is D. Where S_f intersects D, that is, at price A, the competitive fringe supplies all the market will absorb at that price. Between A and the price at which fringe supply falls to zero, the fringe and dominant firm split the market. Thus, the dominant firm's own effective or residual demand function is the kinked curve formed by AB and (below B) D, found by subtracting from the total quantity demanded at any given price the amount supplied by the fringe.

From its residual demand curve ABD, the dominant firm derives its marginal revenue function MR.[60] It maximizes its profits at the output where MR intersects its marginal cost curve MC, and it sets the price OP that brings the quantity it produces into equilibrium with its residual demand schedule. At OP, the dominant firm produces $OQ^* = PY$ units, leaving the competitive fringe the remaining YZ units (which by construction equals PX). The overall market is in equilibrium, since at P, total industry output (PY + YZ) just equals demand (PZ). The dominant firm's profits depend on the position of its average total cost curve, which has been excluded from Figure 6.4 to preserve the diagram's legibility.

Figure 6.4
Dominant Firm with
Competitive Fringe

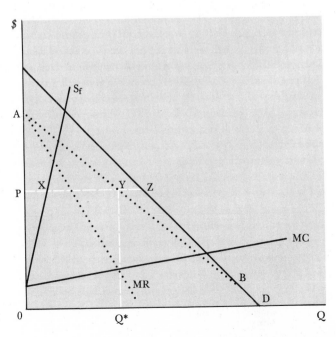

Forchheimer's model is perfectly determinate, given its assumptions about market conditions and firm behavior. However, the equilibrium in Figure 6.4 may not be the end of the story if S_f and MC are short-run cost curves, that is, if they represent supply conditions, given existing plant capacities. In the long run, capacity can be increased and marginal cost curves shifted to the right. Whether the equilibrium depicted in Figure 6.4 will hold in the long run depends upon whether fringe producers are covering their total costs of production. If the marginal fringe producer (that is, the last producer to expand production) is profitable at price OP, it will have an incentive to invest in additional capacity, shifting out the fringe supply curve. This in turn will shift the dominant firm's residual demand curve down and to the left, leading to a smaller market share, lower price, and lower profits. We return to the dominant firm's long-run pricing problem in Chapter 10.

By combining models, behavior over a wide range of asymmetric market structures can be modeled. The dominant firm model has been extended to the case of a dominant k-firm cartel, in which the largest k firms maximize joint profits with respect to residual demand.[61] One also can imagine an oligopoly divided into strategic tiers. Two or three dominant firms might operate with Cournot conjectures with respect to each other, but act collectively as a von Stackelberg leader with respect to a tier of medium-sized firms, which in turn faces the residual demand left by a competitive fringe of small firms.

A curious feature of these dominant firm models is that, in both of the cases presented, market performance is better with the dominant firm than without it. In Forchheimer's model, consumers pay price OP. Without the dominant firm, price rises to OA in Figure 6.4, at the intersection of market demand and S_f, output falls, and thus, consumers are worse off. How can a shift to pure competition be harmful? Consumers are worse off because they no longer have access to the low-cost production of the dominant firm. Of course, consumers would be better off if price could be forced down below OP—best off, abstracting from the second best complications noted in Chapter 2, if price were to fall to the level at which D and MC intersect. Rivalry will not move the industry there unless the competitive fringe firms have access to the same technology used by the dominant firm[62] or unless there is the threat of large-scale entry, a topic to be addressed in Chapter 10.

If an industry consists of a von Stackelberg leader and n follower firms, the resulting market price will be lower than for an industry with $n + 1$ identical

59. We assume rising marginal costs for the fringe firms to guarantee that the fringe remains small relative to the dominant firm. If fringe firms' marginal costs were constant, a price above marginal cost would lead the fringe to expand output so much as to leave nothing for the dominant firm. No such restriction on the dominant firm's costs is necessary.

60. See the Appendix for an example.

61. See T. R. Saving, "Concentration Ratios and the Degree of Monopoly," *International Economic Review*, vol. 11 (February 1970), pp. 139–146; and Gavin C. Reid, "Comparative Statics of the Partial Monopoly Model," *Scottish Journal of Political Economy*, vol. 24 (June 1977), pp. 153–162; D. Encaoua and A. Jacquemin,

"Degree of Monopoly, Indices of Concentration, and Threat of Entry," *International Economic Review*, vol. 21 (February 1980), pp. 87–105; and Leo Sleuwaegen, "On the Nature and Significance of Collusive Price Leadership," *International Journal of Industrial Organization*, vol. 4 (June 1986), pp. 177–188.

62. An outward shift of the competitive fringe's supply curve will reduce price, improving the lot of consumers. However, the total benefit to the economy from such a shift will not be as great as the gain to consumers, since the increase in production in part represents a substitution of higher marginal cost fringe production for dominant firm production.

firms, all holding Cournot conjectural variations. To increase its total profit, as described above, the von Stackelberg leader raises output above the level it would have produced had it held the Cournot conjectural variation. For every unit increase in output by the leader, each follower decreases production by $1/(n+1)$ units (see Appendix). Since there are n followers, the net effect of a one-unit increase in output by the von Stackelberg leader is an increase in industry output of $1 - n/(n+1) = 1/(n+1)$ units. The increase in industry output lowers the market price, benefiting consumers. To the extent that the leader has a cost advantage over followers, the economy also benefits from the increase in the leader's market share: the leader's increased low-cost production partially replaces high-cost follower production.

Will a dominant firm always improve market performance? Far from it. Performance effects depend in good measure upon the source of the dominance. The performance benefits noted here depended on the assumption that the dominant firms had cost advantages over their rivals. Market performance may worsen if the dominant firm's advantage comes from monopsonistic control of key inputs, or other barriers preventing expansion by rivals or entry by other firms. And as we will see in Chapter 7, through price leadership, a dominant firm may make it possible for an industry to support prices approximating the monopoly level even in the absence of a formal collusive agreement.

Conclusion

Let us now try to tie together the principal lessons emerging from this survey. Any realistic theory of oligopoly must take as a point of departure the fact that when market concentration is high, the pricing decisions of sellers are interdependent, and the firms involved can scarcely avoid recognizing their mutual interdependence. Perceptive managers will recognize that their profits will be higher when cooperative policies are pursued than when each firm looks only after its own narrow self-interest. As a consequence, even in the absence of any formal collusion among firms, we should expect tightly oligopolistic industries to exhibit a tendency toward the maximization of collective profits, perhaps even approaching the pricing outcome associated with pure monopoly. However, oligopolistic rivalry is played out in an uncertain, ever-changing environment. While the evolution of this environment permits managers to learn about market conditions and rival intentions, it also poses the constant danger that a rival will undercut the existing pricing structure in search of competitive advantage. Coordination of pricing policies is not easy.

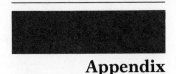

Appendix

The Quantity-Cournot Model

We consider the basic Cournot model in three stages. In the first, there are two firms (a duopoly) each having identical constant marginal production costs and facing a linear industry demand curve. The second stage allows any number of firms. The final stage considers general demand and cost conditions. In all three cases, entry is blocked and the products of each firm are identical in the eyes of consumers.

(a) Duopoly   Each firm chooses its level of production (q_1 and q_2, respectively). The market price is a linear function of industry output

$$(6A.1) \qquad P(Q) = a - bQ,$$

where ($Q = q_1 + q_2$). Firm 1's profit[63] is the difference between its total revenue $- P(Q)q_1 -$ and total cost, which equals the product of constant unit cost c and the number of units produced:

$$(6A.2) \qquad \pi_1 = (a - bQ)q_1 - cq_1.$$

Because price depends upon Firm 2's output as well as its own, Firm 1 cannot determine its profit-maximizing level of production without making an assumption about how Firm 2 will respond. The Cournot model assumes that each firm believes the other will hold its production fixed. Under this assumption, Firm 1 maximizes its profit by differentiating π_1 with respect to q_1, and setting the resulting expression equal to zero (the first-order condition for the existence of a maximum to the profit function):

$$(6A.3) \qquad \begin{aligned} d\pi_1/dq_1 &= P(Q) + (dP/dQ)q_1 - c \\ &= a - 2bq_1 - bq_2 - c = 0. \end{aligned}$$

We can manipulate this equation to obtain a function relating Firm 1's profit-maximizing level of production to Firm 2's output:

$$(6A.4) \qquad q_1 = \frac{(a - c)}{2b} - \frac{1}{2}q_2 .$$

Equation (6A.4) is Firm 1's *reaction function* or *reaction curve*, since it records Firm 1's profit-maximizing responses or reactions to Firm 2's decisions (see Figure 6.2 and

---

63. Firm 2's profit can be found by substituting q_2 for q_1.

accompanying text). Firm 2 solves an identical problem to obtain its reaction function

$$(6A.5) \qquad q_2 = \frac{(a - c)}{2b} - \frac{1}{2} q_1 .$$

The equilibrium solution, that is, the solution to each firm's profit maximization problem that leaves neither firm an incentive to alter its production, lies at the intersection of the two reaction curves. It is found by substituting (6A.5) into (6A.4) and solving for q_1:

$$(6A.6) \qquad q_1 = \frac{(a - c)}{3b} .$$

(b) N-Firm Oligopoly   Suppose that, instead of two firms, there are n firms. Firm 1's profit function again is described by (6A.2); but differentiating leads to a first-order condition containing the outputs of all n-1 rivals:

$$(6A.7) \qquad d\pi_1/dq_1 = a - 2bq_1 - b \sum_{i=2}^{n} q_i - c = 0.$$

We could find the equilibrium solution as before by deriving the reaction functions for each firm and simultaneously solving this system of n equations. However, it is easier to use the fact that each firm faces identical conditions and hence will have the same level of production as each rival in equilibrium. Therefore, we can rewrite (6A.7) as

$$(6A.8) \qquad a - 2bq - b(n-1)q - c = 0, \text{ or } q = \frac{(a-c)}{(n+1)b} .$$

The market price can be found by substituting (6A.8) into (6A.2)[64] and collecting terms:

$$(6A.9) \qquad P = \frac{a + nc}{(n+1)} .$$

As the number of firms becomes large, P comes closer and closer to marginal cost.

(c) General Case   In the general case, we make no assumptions about industry demand and allow for differences in firm costs. Consider the problem facing any one of the firms in this industry, call it Firm i. Firm i's profit is

$$(6A.10) \qquad \pi_i = P(Q)q_i - c_i(q_i).$$

Again, using the Cournot assumption that rival production is fixed, Firm i differentiates (6A.10) with respect to q_i to obtain the first order condition[65]

$$(6A.11) \qquad d\pi_i/dq_i = P + (dP/dQ)q_i - MC_i = 0,$$

where MC_i, marginal cost, is dC_i/dq_i. $P + (dP/dQ)q_i$ is Firm i's marginal revenue.[66] In a manner analogous to the procedure for monopoly,[67] this can be manipulated into

$$P[1 + (dP/dQ)(Q/P)(q_i/Q)] = P - (P/e)s_i,$$

where e is the market price elasticity of demand and s_i is Firm i's market share.

Substituting this last expression into (6A.11) and rearranging terms, we obtain Equation (6.2) from the body of the chapter, relating the firm's market share in equilibrium to its marginal cost:

(6.2) $$s_i = e(P - MC_i)/P.$$

Alternatively, (6.2) can be written as an equation relating the firm's price-cost margin to its market share:

(6A.12) $$\frac{(P - MC_i)}{P} = \frac{s_i}{e}.$$

For the case where each firm has the same marginal cost, $s_i = 1/n$, and (6A.12) simplifies to equation (6.1):

(6.1) $$\frac{(P - MC_i)}{P} = \frac{1}{ne}.$$

Multiplying each side of (6A.12) by the market share s_i and summing over the n firms, we obtain an expression relating the weighted average industry price-cost margin to a measure of market concentration, the Herfindahl-Hirschman concentration index:[68]

(6.3) $$\frac{(P\Sigma s_i - \Sigma MC_i s_i)}{P} = \frac{\Sigma s_i}{e} \longrightarrow \frac{(P - \overline{MC})}{P} = \frac{H}{e}.$$

The Cournot Model with Conjectural Variations

In this section, we relax the requirement that firms assume no rival output changes in response to their own adjustments.

(a) Duopoly Firm 1's profit function remains that given in Equation (6A.2) above. However, now the first-order condition for the existence of a maximum to that profit function must incorporate Firm 1's conjecture about how Firm 2 will react:

(6A.3′) $$d\pi_1/dq_1 = p(Q) + (dP/dQ)[1 + (dq_2/dq_1)]q_1 - c$$
$$= a - [2b + (dq_2/dq_1)]q_1 - bq_2 - c = 0.$$

As before, we solve for q_1 to obtain Firm 1's reaction function

(6a.4′) $$q_1 = \frac{(a - c - bq_1)}{[2b + (dq_2/dq_1)]}.$$

64. $Q = nq$.

65. An equilibrium to the Cournot model exists under quite general conditions, even for differentiated products. The basic requirement is that demand and cost conditions be sufficiently "well behaved" to ensure that a local maximum exists for each firm's profit function at equilibrium rival outputs, or formally, that each firm's profit function be quasi concave in output. This is guaranteed if marginal costs are not decreasing at the equilibrium and industry demand is linear or concave (curving down). See Friedman, *Oligopoly and the Theory of Games*, supra note 12, Chapters 2

and 7, for details. A much weaker condition (but one harder to verify) has been found by William Novshek: Firm i's marginal revenue must not rise with its rivals' output. "On the Existence of Cournot Equilibrium," *Review of Economic Studies*, vol. 47 (January 1985), pp. 85–98.

66. See note 12, p. 21 supra.

67. See note 36, p. 35 supra.

68. For notational convenience, we have suppressed the indices on the summation operator Σ. Note that $\Sigma s_i = 1$.

Equilibrium production is found, as before, by simultaneously solving the system of equations formed by the reaction functions for Firms 1 and 2 (the latter being identical to (6A.4′) with subscripts exchanged). Assuming the two firms to have identical conjectural variations, equilibrium production for Firm 1 (and hence Firm 2) is:

(6A.6′) $$q_1 = \frac{(a - c)}{b[3 + (dq_2/dq_1)]} .$$

Industry output is $2q_1$. Substituting into (6A.1) and simplifying, we obtain

(6A.13) $$P = \frac{a[1 + (dq_2/dq_1)] + 2c}{[3 + (dq_2/dq_1)]} .$$

If the conjectural variation dq_2/dq_1 is zero, the solution is the same as in the original Cournot model. If $dq_2/dq_1 = -1$, each firm expects its rival to offset completely any change in its own production; and the equilibrium price falls to marginal cost c. If the conjectural variation is 1, then each firm expects parallel output matching—as if the two firms were colluding explicitly. Price rises to the joint profit-maximizing level, the level which would prevail if the firms merged into a monopoly: $p = (a+c)/2b$.[69] As the conjectural variation rises between -1 and 1, that is, as rivals move from offsetting to matching behavior, equilibrium output falls and price rises.

(b) General Case (Homogeneous Products)   We return to the general n-firm case discussed above and incorporate into the first-order condition for profit maximization Firm i's conjectural variation, represented as in the text, dQ_i/dq_i:

(6A.11′) $d\pi_i/dq_i = P + (dP/dQ)[1 + (dQ_i/dq_i)]q_i - MC_i = 0.$

As before, we transform Firm i's marginal revenue to obtain an expression in terms of the price elasticity of demand and market share:

$$P + P(dP/dQ)(Q/P)(q_i/Q)[1 + (dQ_i/dq_i)] = P - (P/e)s_i(1 + dQ_i/dq_i).$$

Substituting this back into (6A.11′), we obtain the expression for the price-cost margin reported in the main body of the chapter:

(6.4) $$\frac{(P - MC_i)}{P} = \frac{s_i}{e}(1 + dQ_i/dq_i).$$

In the extreme case of $dQ_i/dq_i = -1$, rivals fully offset production changes by Firm i, the right-hand side of (6.4) is zero, and Firm i operates where price equals marginal cost—the condition characterizing equilibrium under pure competition. For values of the conjectural variation greater than 0, Firm i expects rivals to tend to match its output adjustments. Perfect matching would mimic perfect coordination or collusion, enabling Firm i to achieve a price-cost margin equaling that which would be achieved in the equilibrium under monopoly, that is, $1/e$. To find the conjectural variation that leads to this monopoly result, we set the right-hand side of (6.4) equal to $1/e$ and solve, obtaining

(6A.14) $$\frac{dQ_i}{dq_i} = \frac{(1 - s_i)}{s_i} .$$

Deriving an expression for industry profitability requires one to make assumptions concerning the interaction of all industry members' conjectural variations. Clarke and Davies have developed a formulation that has proved useful in empirical work.[70] They assume that firms' beliefs about individual rival reactions are proportional to their relative production levels:

(6A.15)
$$\frac{dq_j}{dq_i} = A\frac{q_j}{q_i}.$$

Noting that $dQ_i/dq_i = \Sigma_{j\neq i}dq_j/dq_i$, we substitute (6A.15) into (6A.11') to obtain

(6A.11") $\quad d\pi_i/dq_i = P + (dP/dQ)[1 + A\Sigma_{j\neq i}q_j/q_i]q_i - MC_i = 0.$

Since $\Sigma_{j\neq i}q_j = Q - q_i$, we can transform Firm i's marginal revenue to obtain

$$P + P(dP/dQ)(Q/P)(q_i/Q)[1 + A(Q - q_i)/q_i] = P - (P/e)[s_i + A(1 - s_i)].$$

Substituting this expression back into (6A.11") and manipulating terms, we obtain an alternative version of the expression for Firm 1's price-cost margin:

(6A.4')
$$\frac{(P - MC_i)}{P} = \frac{1}{e}[A + (1-A)s_i].$$

Multiplying each side of (6A.4') by the market share s_i and summing over the n firms, we obtain the expression reported in the main body of the chapter, relating the weighted average industry price-cost margin to the interaction of the summary measure of firm conjectural variations and the Herfindahl-Hirschman concentration index:

(6.5)
$$\frac{(P\Sigma s_i - \Sigma MC_i s_i)}{P} = \frac{1}{e}[A\Sigma s_i + (1-A)\Sigma s_i^2]$$
$$\longrightarrow \frac{(P - \overline{MC})}{P} = \frac{H}{e}[A + (1-A)H].$$

A similar derivation can be used for the case where products are differentiated.[71] However, even more restrictive assumptions on the interaction of firm conjectural variations and the nature of product differentiation are required to obtain an expression analogous to Equation (6.5).

The von Stackelberg Leader-Follower Model

(a) Duopoly The discussion of the von Stackelberg model presented in the main body of the text (pp. 221–224) begins with a numerical example of the Cournot duopoly model derived above. The linear demand curve has $a = 200$ and $b = 1$:

$$P(Q) = 200 - Q.$$

Each firm has constant marginal cost of $c = 50$. Therefore, Firm 1's profit is

$$\pi_1 = (200 - Q)q_1 - 50q_1.$$

69. To find the monopoly production level, we return to Equation (6A.4) and assume that $q_2 = 0$. Substituting this level into (6A.1), we obtain the monopoly price.
70. "Market Structure and Price-Cost Margins," supra note 18.

Chapter 11 discusses the empirical applications of their approach.
71. Clarke et al., Stephen Davies, and Michael Waterson, "Profitability-Concentration," supra note 18, pp. 435–450.

With Cournot behavior, each firm assumes that the other will hold its production fixed. Under this assumption, Firm 1's reaction function (graphed in Figure 6.3) can be found by substituting the assumed values for a, b, and c into Equation (6A.4):

$$q_1 = \frac{(200 - 50)}{2} - \frac{1}{2} q_2 .$$

Firm 2 solves an identical problem to obtain its reaction function R_2 (also drawn in Figure 6.3): $q_2 = 75 - (1/2)q_1$. The equilibrium solution lies at the intersection of the two reaction curves. We find this point by substituting the appropriate values into Equation (6A.6): $q_1 = (200-50)/3 = 50$. Since Firms 1 and 2 are identical, we can substitute this result into (6A.7) to find the industry price: $200 - 2(50) = 100$.

   In the von Stackelberg model, one firm (here Firm 2) "follows" the other, maximizing its profits on the assumption that the other's output is fixed, that is, it continues to hold the Cournot conjectural variation. However, the "leader" (here Firm 1) recognizes this follower behavior and incorporates the follower's reaction function into its profit-maximizing problem. In this case, the reaction function is a straight line. Therefore, the slope of R_2 equals Firm 1's conjectural variation: $dq_2/dq_1 = -.5$. To derive Firm 1's profit-maximizing output, we transform its first-order condition (6A.3′) into a function of q_1 only by substituting $-.5$ for dq_2/dq_1 and Firm 2's reaction function for q_2. Doing this, we obtain

$$d\pi_1/dq_1 = 200 - (2 - .5)q_1 - (75 - .5q_1) - 50 = 0,$$

which implies $q_1 = 75$. We substitute this value back into Firm 2's reaction function to obtain $q_2 = 75 - .5(75) = 37.5$. Graphically, this solution occurs when Firm 1 moves to the highest iso-profit curve consistent with Firm 2's reactions, that is, at the tangency between iso-profit curve II and R_2 in Figure 6.3.

(b) Von Stackelberg Oligopoly with n Followers

With identical firms, it is difficult to justify why one should behave as a leader while the others accept the follower role and the reduced market share and profits that result. We turn to the case in which the leader, Firm L, has a cost advantage over n follower firms that are identical to one another, that is, $c_L < c_F$. We use the linear industry demand curve (6A.1). Following Equation (6A.7) above, the first-order condition required to maximize the profits of a typical follower firm, Firm F, is

$$d\pi_F/dq_F = [a - b(q_L - n\, q_F)] - bq_F - c_F = 0.$$

From this, we obtain Firm F's reaction function to Firm L's production:

(6A.4′)
$$q_F = \frac{(a - c_F - bq_L)}{b(n+1)} .$$

Firm L recognizes that all n followers will behave according to this reaction function, so its conjectural variation $dQ_L/dq_L = ndq_F/dq_L = -n/(n+1)$. Firm L's profit-maximizing first-order condition is

$$d\pi_L/q_L = [a - b(q_L - nq_F)] - b(1 + dQ_L/dq_L)q_L - c_L = 0.$$

Substituting in Firm L's conjectural variation and the reaction function for Firm F, we obtain

$$a - bq_L - [n/(n+1)](a - c_F - bq_L) - [b/(n+1)]q_L - c_L = 0,$$

which we can manipulate to obtain

(6.6) $$q_L = \frac{(a - c_L) + n(c_F - c_L)}{2b}.$$

Substituting (6.6) into Firm F's reaction function, we arrive at:

(6.7) $$q_F = \frac{(a - c_F) - (n+1)(c_F - c_L)}{2b(n+1)}.$$

If the leader has no cost advantage over the follower, then these equations simplify into $q_L = (a-c)/2b$ and $q_F = (a-c)/2b(n+1)$. The leader's market share is

$$s_L = q_L/(q_L + nq_F) = (n+1)/(n+2).$$

Forchheimer's Dominant Firm Model

In this section, we work out the algebra of the dominant firm profit-maximizing problem for a numerical example of the case depicted in Figure 6.4. We again assume linear demand, $P = 200 - Q$, where Q is the sum of q_D (dominant firm production) and Q_f (the sum of production by the competitive fringe). Marginal costs for the dominant firm are $MC = 20 + .2q_D$. The horizontal sum of the marginal cost curves for the fringe firms yields the fringe supply curve, S_f, with $MC = 20 + 4Q_f$. The fringe supplies where $MC = P$, implying that

(6A.16) $$Q_f = (P-20)/4.$$

The leader faces the residual demand,

$$Q - q_f = (200-P) - (P-20)/4 = 205 - 1.25P; P \geq 20,$$

(the dashed line AB in Figure 6.4). We rewrite the residual demand to obtain price as a function of dominant firm output

(6A.17) $$P = (205-q_D)/1.25 = 164 - .8q_D.$$

To maximize profits, the dominant firm equates marginal revenue with marginal cost. Marginal revenue is

$$P + (dP/dq_D)q_D = 164 - .8q_D - .8q_D = 164 - 1.6q_D,$$

and the maximizing condition is

$$164 - 1.6q_D = 20 + .2q_D,$$

which we manipulate to obtain $q_D = 80$. We substitute this into (6A.17) to obtain $P = 100$, and into (6A.16) to obtain $Q_f = 20$.

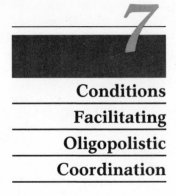

Conditions Facilitating Oligopolistic Coordination

Chapter 6 developed a theory of oligopolistic pricing on the assumption that each firm maximizes its profits based on conjectures about the probable reactions of rivals. An oligopolist's problem would be greatly simplified if managers could meet with their opposite numbers at rival firms and negotiate mutually beneficial prices and market shares. Legal prohibitions on collusion inhibit, but by no means eliminate, such efforts. Even in the absence of direct communication, oligopolists can move their industry in the direction of greater cooperation. Yet antitrust laws are not the only stumbling block to successful collusion. Adopting joint-profit maximizing policies is neither automatic nor easy, especially when industry members have diverse and conflicting opinions about the most favorable price structure. How do oligopolists go about determining mutually satisfactory prices? What coordination and communication processes are available to resolve conflicts? In this chapter we treat oligopoly pricing as a problem in interfirm cooperation and examine five important institutions facilitating oligopolistic coordination: (1) overt and covert agreements, (2) price leadership, (3) rules of thumb, (4) the use of focal points, and (5) the buffering of demand shocks through inventory and order backlog adjustments.

Overt and Covert Agreements

Collusion to secure monopolistic prices and profits is a venerable, if not venerated, institution. It was practiced in ancient Babylon, Greece, and Rome. Adam Smith remarked sagely that "people of the same trade seldom meet together, even for merriment and diversion, but the conversation ends in a conspiracy against the public, or in some contrivance to raise prices."[1] Industry profits can never be higher than when firms set prices at the monopoly level—that is, at the price that would be set if one profit-maximizing enterprise controlled industry output. However, collusive strategies are not without risk. Unsuccessful attempts at collusion can backfire—leading to price wars and heavy losses—not to mention the jail terms and other legal sanctions that can arise in countries where collusive agreements are prohibited. In the United States, nearly every form of agreement, open or secret, to fix prices or restrict output is illegal; but dozens of violations are prosecuted each year, and countless others go undetected.

The variety of collusive pricing arrangements in industry is limited only by the bounds of human ingenuity. Some are casual and short lived, for example, the spontaneous meetings called to terminate price wars. Others endure for decades held together by an elaborate organizational web and binding written contracts. Here only the most important species can be identified.

Social gatherings are an occasion for one of the least structured, but not ineffective, forms of collusion. A well-known example was the Gary dinners held by Judge Elbert H. Gary, chairman of U.S. Steel's board of directors, from 1907 to 1911. Judge Gary once explained that the "close communication and contact" developed at these dinners generated such mutual "respect and affectionate regard" among steel industry leaders that all considered the obligation to cooperate and

1. Adam Smith, *An Inquiry into the Nature and Causes of the Wealth of Nations* (1776; Modern Library Edition, 1937), p. 128.

avoid destructive competition "more binding . . . than any written or verbal contract."[2] A modern variant is the trade association convention held in a resort hotel, where members who have been cutting prices are alternately browbeaten, plied with martinis, and cajoled until they promise to adopt a more cooperative stance in the future.

Informal gentlemen's agreements are also reached on a wide range of specific issues and practices. The best-known examples are, of course, agreements to set and abide by particular prices. If this is impractical, emphasis may be placed on securing mutual adherence to pricing formulas or lists of "representative" prices published by trade associations. When product lines are very complex, firms often find it advantageous to collude on specific product details and on the handling of extras. Until the late 1960s, for instance, American steel producers were fairly successful in abjuring price competition on standard products without resorting to formal collusion. But they found it far more difficult tacitly to coordinate prices for the virtually infinite gradations in finish, temper, gauge, packaging, and the like requested on special order by individual customers. As a result, company representatives held covert meetings to agree on uniform standards, specifications, interpretations, and charges for extras.[3] In the gypsum board industry, price-fixing agreements were supplemented by agreements to use only rail delivery and to charge uniform interest rates to customers granted extended credit.[4] Finally, business executives may meet in smoke-filled rooms to agree on output limitations, market shares, or specific geographic areas or product lines to be regarded as each firm's exclusive sphere of interest. Spheres-of-interest agreements have been especially popular among giant international chemical producers as a means of restricting competition.[5]

Nearly all these dimensions of collusion were present in the electrical equipment conspiracy of the 1950s.[6] It involved at least twenty-nine different companies selling turbine generators, transformers, switchgear, insulators, industrial controls, condensers, and other electrical equipment with total sales of roughly $1.5 billion annually. Although agreements to limit competition had been a recurrent feature of the electrical industry since the 1880s, the schemes of the 1950s were given specific impetus when repeated episodes of price warfare proved incompatible with top management demands for higher profits. Several collusive systems evolved, each tailored to the peculiar features of the particular product line and selling method.

On standardized products such as insulators, standard transformers, and industrial controls, company representatives met and agreed upon prices that each promised to quote in all subsequent transactions until an agreement to change was reached. This was by far the simplest arrangement, but it suffered from the disadvantage of arousing suspicions when all firms submitted identical bids in repeated transactions. A more complex approach was required for products such as turbine generators, since each buyer demands modifications to suit its own special needs, and, as a result, two orders are seldom exactly alike. Collusion in this instance was facilitated by the publication of a pricing formula book half the size of a Manhattan telephone book. By piecing together the prices of each component required to meet a buyer's generator specifications, firms were able to arrive at the book price on which discussions centered.

Some of the most elaborate procedures were devised to handle switchgear pricing. As in the case of generators, book prices served as the initial departure point. Each seller agreed to quote book prices in sales to private buyers, and meetings were held regularly to compare calculations for forthcoming job quotations. Sealed-bid competitions sponsored by government agencies posed a different set of problems, and new methods were devised to handle them. Through protracted negotiation, each seller was assigned a specified share of all sealed-bid business, for example, General Electric's share of the high-voltage switchgear field was set at 40.3 percent in late 1958, and Allis-Chalmers' at 8.8 percent. Participants then coordinated their bidding so that each firm was low bidder in just enough transactions to gain its predetermined share of the market. In the power switching equipment line, this was achieved for a while by dividing the United States into four quadrants, assigning four sellers to each quadrant, and letting the sellers in a quadrant rotate their bids. A "phases-of-the-moon" system was used to allocate low-bidding privileges in the high voltage switchgear field, with a new seller assuming low-bidding priority every two weeks. The designated bidder subtracted a specified percentage margin from the book price to capture orders during its phase, while others added various margins to the book price. The result was an ostensibly random pattern of quotations, conveying the impression of independent pricing behavior.

It seems indisputable that prices and profits were elevated substantially through the electrical equipment conspiracy when it operated successfully.[7] Yet durable success is by no means assured under informal restrictive arrangements. Indeed, the electrical equipment case illustrates the fragility of nonbinding collusive agreements. Parties to the agreements of the 1950s chiseled repeatedly, touching off bitter price wars. As one General Electric executive explained his group's decision to go its own independent way in 1953, "No one was living up to the agreements and we . . . were being made suckers. On every job someone would cut our throat; we lost confidence in the group."[8]

2. From a government antitrust brief cited in Fritz Machlup, *The Political Economy of Monopoly* (Baltimore: Johns Hopkins, 1952), p. 87. See also Donald O. Parsons and E. J. Ray, "The United States Steel Consolidation: The Creation of Market Control," *Journal of Law & Economics*, vol. 18 (April 1975), pp. 208–212.

3. In "Steel Gets Hit with the Big One," *Business Week*, April 11, 1964, pp. 27–28. Although the accused firms denied their guilt at the time, in July 1965 they pleaded "no contest," which in a criminal antitrust case involving large firms is tantamount to an admission of guilt.

4. "Gypsum Trial Shows How Price-Fix Plan Supposedly Operated," *Wall Street Journal*, October 3, 1975, pp. 1, 16.

5. See G. W. Stocking and M. W. Watkins, *Cartels in Action* (New York: Twentieth Century Fund, 1946), Chapters 9–11.

6. See R. A. Smith, "The Incredible Electrical Conspiracy," *Fortune*, April and May 1961; J. G. Fuller, *The Gentlemen Conspirators* (New York: Grove, 1962); and John Herling, *The Great Price Conspiracy* (Washington, D.C.: Luce, 1962).

7. For an argument that the conspiracy was ineffectual see Ralph G. M. Sultan, *Pricing in the Electrical Oligopoly*, vol. I (Boston: Harvard Business School Division of Research, 1974), especially Chapters 6 and 8. David F. Lean, Jonathan D. Ogur, and Robert P. Rogers concluded that turbogenerator manufacturers were more successful in raising profit margins through price leadership after the end of the conspiracy than they were during the conspiracy period. See "Does Collusion Pay . . . Does Antitrust Work?," *Southern Economic Journal*, vol. 51 (January 1985), pp. 828–841.

8. Smith, "The Incredible Electrical Conspiracy," *Fortune*, April 1961, p. 172, quoting Clarence Burke. See also Allan T. Demaree, "How Judgment Came for the Plumbing Conspirators," *Fortune*, December 1969, pp. 97–98, observing that the conspirators had to meet repeatedly to reassure themselves and that, as one company official said, "we wouldn't trust each other outside the damn room."

Two central problems assault the stability of cartels. First, the parties to the conspiracy may have divergent ideas about appropriate price levels and market shares, making it difficult to reach an understanding all will respect. Second, when the group agrees to fix and abide by a price approaching the monopoly level, strong incentives are created for individual members to cheat on the agreement — that is, to increase their profits by undercutting the fixed price slightly, gaining additional orders at a price that still exceeds marginal cost. These two problems often interact, for parties dissatisfied with the original agreement are especially likely to cheat in its subsequent execution.

The Problem of Agreeing on Price

Consider the problem of agreeing on a common price for firms selling identical products. With price matching, each firm should normally expect to obtain the same market share as its competitor, or at least a constant market share based on historical buyer-seller relations, sales force efficiency, or minor product quality advantages. Each producer can estimate its own individual demand curve from knowledge of industry demand.[9] For simplicity, assume that an industry consists of two firms having identical market shares at identical prices. If the industry demand is

$$P = 200 - .02(q_1 + q_2),$$

then the demand for either firm, illustrated by D_1 in Figure 7.1, is

$$P = 200 - .04q_i, \quad i = 1, 2,$$

with marginal revenue schedule MR_i. Assume initially that each firm has the same total cost function. Firm 1 (hence, Firm 2) has total cost

$$TC_1 = 50,000 + 20q_1 + .01q_i^2.$$

The resulting marginal cost, MC_1, is $20 + .02q_1$. If Firm 1 independently sets marginal cost equal to marginal revenue, it will quote a price of $128 per unit (see Appendix) and produce 1,800 units (OP_1 and Oq_1, respectively, in Figure 7.1). Firm 2 will do the same. Thus, each firm, following the logic of profit maximization, will arrive independently at the price that maximizes joint profits. The requirement is that neither firm attempt to change its share of the market.

Figure 7.1
Constant Shares

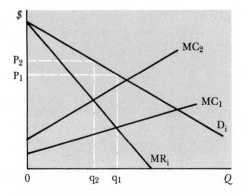

Suppose, however, that Firm 2 has the higher marginal cost function MC_2, derived from $TC_2 = 20,000 + 40q_2 + .02q_2^2$. This might happen because Firm 2 is endowed with poorer natural resources or because it has chosen to build a plant with low initial (and subsequently fixed) capital costs, but with high and more rapidly rising marginal costs. High-cost Firm 2 will find the price of \$147 per unit associated with an output of 1,333 units optimal from its viewpoint, while low-cost Firm 1 (with marginal cost function MC_1) continues to prefer a price of \$128 per unit. There is conflict between the companies in their price and output preferences.

This result is quite general.[10] Whenever producers obtaining equal shares of a market at identical prices have disparate marginal cost functions, their individual price preferences differ.[11] When homogeneity of products precludes any lasting price differential, or when the price differential required for producers of differentiated products to retain their customary market shares is not equal to the difference between favored prices, some means of resolving the conflict must be found. One approach is for the firm preferring the lowest price to impose its will upon the other producers. Because customers will flock to the low-price seller, the firm with the lowest price preference will have a distinct advantage over its rivals. If others attempt to hold price up at the higher levels they favor, they will suffer a severe erosion of sales and market share. Still this mode of price leadership is not always quite so simple. If firms with higher costs do attempt to maintain their prices despite market share losses, the low-price producer may be forced to satisfy more customers, and hence supply more than the quantity of output that maximizes its profits. Or if the high-cost firms are dissatisfied with their profits at the low-cost firm's favored price, they may set price even lower, either out of desperation or in the hope of threatening and coercing the low-cost firm into adopting a more cooperative stance. The result can be an uncontrolled war in which the price is driven well below the low-cost producer's preferred level.[12]

Analogous problems arise when, owing to moderate degrees of product differentiation or differences in capacity, the various members of the industry obtain different shares of the market at identical prices. Figure 7.2 presents the analysis for two firms, each (for analytic convenience) with the same marginal cost function $MC_{1,2}$. Firm 1, with demand curve D_1 and marginal revenue function MR_1, normally sells 60 percent of the duopoly's output. Firm 2 sells the remaining 40 percent, so its demand curve D_2 and marginal revenue curve MR_2 lie to the left of

9. At any given price, each firm's individual demand curve has the same price elasticity as the industry demand curve. Proof: Let $Q(P)$ be industry demand and s be the firm's constant market share. Then $q = sQ(P)$ is the firm's output. Substituting this into the firm's price elasticity of demand, $(dq/dP)(P/q)$, we obtain $(sdQ/dP)(P/sQ) = (dQ/dP)(P/Q)$.

10. For an extensive treatment of the problem of achieving a collusive agreement when costs differ, see Richard Schmalensee, "Competitive Advantage and Collusive Optima," *International Journal of Industrial Organization*, vol. 5 (December 1987), pp. 351–367.

11. An exception would be the special case in which the marginal cost curves happen to intersect each other where they mutually intersect the common marginal revenue curve.

12. See R. L. Bishop, "Duopoly: Collusion or Warfare?", *American Economic Review*, vol. 50 (December 1960), pp. 933–961; and Robert H. Porter, "On the Incidence and Duration of Price Wars," *Journal of Industrial Economics*, vol. 33 (June 1985), pp. 415–426. For examples from U.S. rail freight pricing during the late nineteenth century, see Paul W. MacAvoy, *The Economic Effects of Regulation* (Cambridge: MIT Press, 1965), pp. 129–135; and Robert H. Porter, "A Study of Cartel Stability: The Joint Executive Committee: 1880–1886," *Bell Journal of Economics*, vol. 14 (Autumn 1983), pp. 301–314.

Figure 7.2
Oligopoly Pricing with
Disparate Market Shares

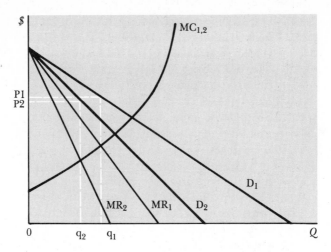

Firm 1's corresponding curves. Equating marginal cost with its own marginal revenue, Firm 1 maximizes profits by producing Oq_1. Reading up to demand curve D_1, we find its preferred price to be OP_1. Firm 2 maximizes its profits individualistically with output Oq_2, which calls for a price of OP_2. Again, the sellers' preferences conflict. The firm with the smaller market share prefers a lower price than its rival with a larger market share.

This conclusion holds when marginal costs rise as output is increased. The high-share firm prefers a higher price in this instance because, in the higher output range where it operates, rising marginal costs discourage expansion more than at lower outputs. More generally, three cases exist for firms with identical marginal cost functions:

1. When marginal costs are rising, the lowest price is preferred by the firm with the smallest market share, ceteris paribus.
2. When marginal costs are constant over the relevant range, differences in market shares do not lead to different price preferences, ceteris paribus.
3. When marginal costs fall with higher output, the lowest price is preferred by the firm with the largest market share, which has an incentive to expand and take full advantage of the low costs associated with high outputs.

One implication of these relationships is that the amount of conflict over preferred price levels may depend upon whether firms price to achieve long-run or short-run objectives. As we have seen in Chapter 4, long-run average and marginal costs tend to be roughly constant over the range of plant sizes and degrees of multiplant operation observed most frequently in manufacturing industry. This suggests the prevalence of no-conflict case (2) when pricing is oriented toward long-run goals. On the other hand, short-run cost curves are more likely to fit the case (1) mold, except in output ranges substantially below designed plant capacity, and so considerable conflict might be expected among firms of diverse size that are pricing to maximize short-run profits.

The ultimate solution to such price preference conflicts, short of merging all producers into a consolidated monopoly, is a *rationalization cartel*.[13] The cartel's members must agree on a common price, the total market-clearing output at that

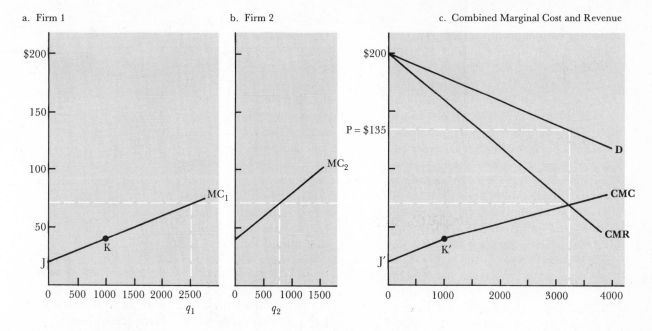

Figure 7.3
The Geometry of A
Rationalization Cartel

price, and the allocation of output and profits across member firms. Making the same numerical assumptions as those underlying Figure 7.1, Figure 7.3 shows how the rationalization cartel's problem is solved geometrically. An algebraic proof follows in the Appendix, Part (b). In panel (a) of Figure 7.3, the marginal cost function of low-cost Firm 1 is shown; panel (b) contains the corresponding marginal cost function for high-cost Firm 2. To arrive at the rationalization cartel solution, the two MC curves are summed horizontally in panel (c). Up to the $40 value at which Firm 2's marginal cost curve begins, the combined cartel marginal cost curve CMC consists only of the segment J′K′ drawn from segment JK of Firm 1's marginal cost function. Beyond point K′, the combined MC curve slope flattens because Firm 2's supply has been added to the incremental supply of Firm 1. From *total* market demand function D in panel (c), the combined marginal revenue function CMR is derived. Joint profit is maximized when CMR = CMC, that is, with a total cartel output of 3,250 units, sold at a price of $135 per unit. To determine how much each firm produces, the CMR = CMC intersection ordinate value of $70 is projected (white dashed line) back to panels (a) and (b), where its intersection with the individual firm MC functions shows that Firm 1 will produce 2,500 units and high-cost Firm 2 only 750 units. With this allocation of output, marginal costs are equalized between the firms and are simultaneously equal to overall market marginal revenue. If marginal costs were not equalized, it would

Table 7.1 Profit Implications of Alternative Market Division and
Pricing Schemes

	Firm 1's Profits	Firm 2's Profits	Joint Profits
Price = $128, each firm produces 1,800 units	$112,000	$73,600	$185,600
Price = $147, each firm produces 1,333 units	$101,522	$87,093	$188,615
Price = $135, with Firm 1 producing 2,500 units and Firm 2 750 units	$175,000	$40,000	$215,000

be possible to reallocate production assignments toward the lower MC firm so as
to produce the same output more economically.

Table 7.1 summarizes the distribution and sums of industry profits under the
equal market shares equilibria at prices preferred by Firms 1 and 2, respectively,
and under the rationalization cartel solution, the latter assuming that each cartel
member sells only its own output at the jointly-determined price. Plainly, joint
profits are higher under the rationalization cartel. Selling only 750 units of output,
however, high-cost Firm 2 fares poorly. But this problem is readily remedied by
having both firms contribute their profits to a common pool and then redistribut-
ing them, e.g., with $125,000 going to Firm 1 and $90,000 to Firm 2. Then each

If, contrary to the assumptions accepted thus far, high-cost Firm 2 could be
shut down altogether and its assets sold so as to avoid the $20,000 fixed cost,
profits could be increased even more. Then, as the Appendix shows, all production would be undertaken by low-cost Firm 1, the price will be set at $140 per unit,
and net profit will rise to $220,000, that is, $5,000 more than with rationalized but
joint production as assumed previously.

firm is better off under the rationalization cartel than it would be under equal
market-sharing at its own preferred price.[14]

Yet even when joint profits are increased through rationalization and profit
pooling, it is by no means certain that all firms will participate willingly. Demonstrating that there are output and profit allocations that make at least one firm
better off without making any other worse off does not guarantee that a group of
strong-willed rivals will agree to any of them. For the high-cost firms, agreeing to
reduce output substantially or to shut down altogether has been likened to disarm-
ing.[15] One never knows whether firms producing most of the output under rationalization will take advantage of their position in the future, demanding a higher
share of total profits. Maintaining production capabilities intact is a good bargaining counter against such demands. As a result, few cartels have gone very far toward the rationalization of production, even when profit pooling is accepted.[16]
The elaborately organized ocean shipping cartels—called "conferences"—afford
the most extreme example on which substantial information exists.[17] For example, the United Kingdom/Australia conference, reorganized in 1966, raised *aver-*

age cargo sizes substantially (reducing unit costs) by prevailing upon participating lines to cut their fleets by twenty-five to thirty ships. The Europe/New Zealand conference averaged a 95 percent capacity utilization rate, despite the fact that markets for the principal cargo—meat and dairy products—are subject to wide seasonal variations.[18] Even they, however, found their ability to maintain high prices undermined by the emergence of competition from nonmember Soviet Union ships.[19]

To sum up, when cost functions and/or market shares vary from firm to firm within an oligopolistic industry, conflicts arise that interfere with the maximization of collective monopoly profits. Hard bargaining lubricated by hard liquor cannot eliminate differences in firms' price and output preferences; it can only provide a favorable environment for compromise, if compromise is possible at all. Because price-fixing negotiations are usually conducted in secrecy, we have little evidence on the amount of internal stress encountered in establishing agreements. But there are indications that it is considerable. In the electrical equipment conspiracy, for example, there were conflicts over pricing policy between the high- and low-cost producers, and over market shares between the bigger firms and two smaller firms—one a new entrant. Both disputes were resolved only when General Electric and Westinghouse made concessions to save the agreement. In OPEC—without doubt the most lucrative cartel of modern history[20]—sharp divisions of

14. As the example is constructed, consumers are *not* better off. Prices are higher and quantities lower under the rationalization cartel than they would have been had the firms accepted Firm 1's equal-shares price. In other cases, consumers could conceivably do better under rationalization than under alternative monopoly solutions. Rationalization benefits consumers when marginal costs are falling continuously over the attainable range of outputs, or when the low-cost firm's marginal cost function is at all relevant outputs below the lowest point on the high-cost firm's marginal cost function.

15. Fellner, *Competition Among the Few*, pp. 218–220 and 232.

16. See John A. Howard, "Collusive Behavior," *Journal of Business*, vol. 27 (July 1954), pp. 196–204, for an analysis of the degree to which rationalization was carried out in certain British industries. An alternative explanation for the paucity of rationalization is that the benefits are modest, for example, because cost conditions vary little from firm to firm, because long-run cost curves are flat, and because most firms in normal years run their plants at or near the level that minimizes average cost.

17. See H. David Bess and Martin T. Farris, *U.S. Maritime Policy—History and Prospects* (New York: Praeger, 1981); Gunnar Sletmo and Ernest Williams, *Liner Conferences in the Container Age: U.S. Policy at Sea* (New York: Macmillan, 1981); J. E. Davies, "An Analysis of Cost and Supply Conditions in the Liner Shipping Industry," *Journal of Industrial Economics*, vol. 31 (June 1983), pp. 417–435; Alan W. Cafrany, *Ruling the Waves: The Political Economy of International Shipping* (Berkeley: University of California Press, 1987); and Lawrence J. White, *International Trade in Ocean Shipping Services* (Cambridge: Ballinger, 1988).

Participation by U.S. lines in shipping conferences had been limited by regulations of the Federal Maritime Commission, and

the ability of North Atlantic conferences to rationalize shipping had been limited by FMC regulations and a 1979 price-fixing conviction against the major shipping lines. However, 1984 legislation expanding the antitrust immunity of U.S. shipping lines appears to have reduced these obstacles. "Ships of State Collide," *The Economist*, June 9, 1979, p. 91 ff.; "From Price Fixing to Price Cutting," *The Economist*, March 29, 1980, p. 106; and "If You Can't Beat Them . . . ," *Forbes*, April 23, 1984, pp. 36–37.

18. Davies, "Analysis of Cost and Supply," p. 431.

19. See "A Harder Crackdown on Rate-Cutting at Sea," *Business Week*, January 29, 1979, p. 42; and "Soviet-Bloc Inroads on World Shipping," *New York Times*, January 30, 1984, p. D8.

20. OPEC certainly has been lucrative. Whether it has operated as a full-fledged profit-maximizing cartel has been a matter of some dispute. On the one hand, James M. Griffin, "OPEC Behavior: A Test of Alternative Hypotheses," *American Economic Review*, vol. 75 (December 1985), pp. 954–963, finds evidence that OPEC members were following a loose market-sharing strategy instead of equating marginal cost to individual marginal revenue. See also P. A. Geroski, A. M. Ulph, and D. T. Ulph, "A Model of the Crude Oil Market in which Market Conduct Varies," *Economic Journal*, vol. 97 (Supplement 1987), pp. 77–86. Others argue that OPEC is in essence endorsing market-determined solutions, or at worst, behaving as a dominant-firm oligopoly with Saudi Arabia acting as the price leader. Edward Jay Epstein, "The Cartel that Never Was," *Atlantic Monthly*, March 1983, pp. 68–77; Paul MacAvoy, *Crude Oil Prices as Determined by OPEC and Market Fundamentals* (Cambridge: Ballinger, 1982); and David J. Teece, "OPEC Behavior: An Alternative View," in J. M. Griffin and David J. Teece, eds., *OPEC Behavior and World Oil Prices* (London: Allen & Unwin, 1982) pp. 64–93.

opinion have regularly complicated the process of setting oil price levels. Heavily populated, underdeveloped nations (for example, Iran and Nigeria in the 1970s) and nations having significant military commitments (Iran, Iraq, and Libya in the 1980s) have sought prices that would generate maximum short-term revenues, while Saudi Arabia and (until the mid 1980s) Kuwait, with much smaller populations and abundant crude oil reserves, have been more concerned with long-run considerations. Differing estimates of the elasticity of demand for OPEC's oil also seem to have contributed to conflicting price preferences. Saudi Arabia in particular appears more sensitive to the stimulus high prices give to discovery and use of non-OPEC energy resources and to the possibility that very high prices reduce the demand for oil.

Given the difficulty of agreeing, there is a tendency to avoid price changes once agreements are reached. Fear of upsetting group discipline led OPEC to forgo or delay several price changes advocated by some member states at ministerial meetings. In his study of six cartels operating legally under Danish laws, Bjarke Fog uncovered an extreme case in which a key product's price was left unchanged for a decade despite rising costs and disappearing profits.[21] Parties to the agreement were reluctant to suggest a price increase for fear of appearing weak to their confederates.

The Chiseling Problem

Once agreement has been reached, a different set of problems arise. The very act of fixing the price at a monopolistic level creates incentives for sellers to expand output beyond the quantity that will sustain the agreed-upon price. The essence of the matter is illustrated in Figure 7.4. Assume, given industry demand curve D_1, that the price is successfully raised from OP_C, as shown in panel (a), to OP_M. To sustain the increase, industry output must be cut from OQ_C to OQ_M. This leaves the typical firm in a situation characterized by panel (b). If it sells only a modest fraction of total industry output, the individual seller may consider the collectively fixed price to be virtually parametric—that is, insensitive to its own output choices. With its output held at Oq_M, its marginal cost is well below the fixed

Figure 7.4
Incentives to Cheat on Cartel Prices

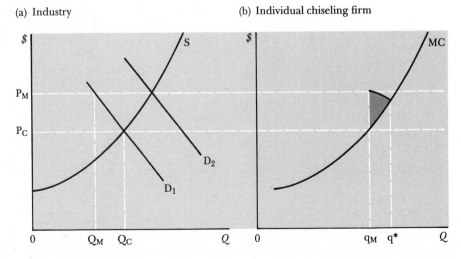

(a) Industry

(b) Individual chiseling firm

price, and so the firm is tempted to break with the agreement, quote a slightly lower price, and enjoy additional business q^*q_M at chiseled prices. Its short-run profits are increased by the shaded area, creating what has been argued is an almost irresistible incentive to cheat. Of course, if every seller were to behave in this manner, the industry price will fall from the agreed-upon monopoly value to the level of all producers' marginal cost, where no further incentive for output expansion remains. Detecting and deterring cheating has been termed *the* central cartel problem,[22] and, because solving it is often difficult, many economists argue that price-fixing cartels are inherently unstable.[23]

A number of solutions to the cartel's price chiseling problem have been suggested.[24] They fall generally into two categories. The first seeks to raise the certainty and size of retribution. For example, cartel members might carry sufficiently high excess production capacity to guarantee that cheating would lead to deep price cuts. The second seeks to eliminate these short-run incentives to cheat by focusing on strategic variables that can be adjusted only in a very public way and with a lag—that is, by controlling the evolution of the long-run supply curve. One example works when the cartel faces growing demand: the firms simply agree to slow the rate at which new capacity comes on line. In the extreme example illustrated in Figure 7.4, capacity remains unchanged so that when demand shifts out to D_2, no firm has an incentive to expand production beyond the level needed to meet demand at market price OP_M; each firm just covers its marginal cost.[25] No firm has an incentive to cheat in this new short run. Long-term cheating would require building very visible capacity above the level agreed to by the cartel. It is not generally remembered, for example, that when OPEC achieved its great price-raising success in 1973 and early 1974, Saudi Arabia had agreed with the ARAMCO group extracting its oil to increase daily capacity from twelve to twenty million barrels per day by 1983. Had the plan not been canceled, OPEC's inability to maintain high prices would almost surely have materialized earlier. Iraq's bombing of Iranian oil shipping terminals during the 1980s also helped restrain output (while complicating the problem of agreeing on how output was to be divided up).

Thus, price-fixing cartels can be stable if they depend less on output restriction than on discouraging entry or expansion by existing firms. New entry is an obvious hazard, emerging when a cartel manages to hold price near monopoly levels. It will be analyzed further in Chapter 10. The added output of new entrants

21. Bjarke Fog, "How are Cartel Prices Determined?" *Journal of Industrial Economics*, vol. 5 (November 1956), pp. 16–23.

22. George J. Stigler, "A Theory of Oligopoly," *Journal of Political Economy*, vol. 72 (February 1964), pp. 44–61.

23. Thus, Milton Friedman argued in 1974 that OPEC would be a flash in the pan. *Newsweek*, March 4, 1974.

24. See Marie-Paule Donsimoni, "Stable Heterogeneous Cartels," *International Journal of Industrial Organization*, vol. 3 (December 1985), pp. 451–467; D. K. Osborne, "Cartel Problems," *American Economic Review*, vol. 66 (December 1976), pp. 835–844; Martin J. Osborne and Carolyn Pitchik, "Profit-Sharing in a Collusive Industry," *European Economic Review*, vol. 22 (June 1983),

pp. 59–74; idem, "Cartels, Profits and Excess Capacity," *International Economic Review*, vol. 28 (June 1987), pp. 413–428; and Ray Rees, "Cheating in a Duopoly Supergame," *Journal of Industrial Economics*, vol. 33 (June 1985), pp. 387–400.

25. Along the new demand curve, P_M does not maximize the cartel's long-run profits. However, absent other means of coordination, this strategy yields profits higher than they would be if all firms freely expanded capacity to meet the growing demand. If capacity expansion occurred at constant unit cost, the price without effective coordination would gravitate continuously toward OP_C.

may drive down price immediately or it may force parties to the original agreement to negotiate a new price, raising renewed coordination problems. In his study of German cartels, Fritz Voigt found that the interaction of entry, chiseling, and bickering among insiders caused numerous price-fixing agreements to be short lived, breaking down after periods of operation as short as a few months.[26]

Of course, even short-lived cartels may yield monopoly profits sufficient to make the effort worthwhile. Furthermore, many business managers (and heads of oil-rich nations) are farsighted enough to recognize that their long-run interests are served best by maintaining industry discipline, and this may be enough to inhibit widespread chiseling. Finally, it is often possible (especially in nations with weak antitrust laws or in international trade) to formalize restrictive agreements in such a way as to greatly reduce the incentives for cheating.

An approach particularly popular because of its effectiveness and compatibility with antitrust policies is the insertion of restrictive provisions into patent licenses. Several types of restriction are possible when one firm or (outside the United States) several firms jointly hold a strong patent position. First, the entry of new sellers can be blocked by refusal to grant licenses. Second, each licensee can be restricted to a specific geographic territory or segment of the market. Third, the price of the patented product can be specified as one of the license terms.[27] And fourth, direct or indirect output restrictions can be included in the licensing agreement. A potent way of damping licensees' incentive to expand output by shading prices is to combine quota restrictions with punitive royalty provisions. For example, in the 1930s, Westinghouse's license to use General Electric's incandescent lamp improvement patents stipulated a royalty of 2 percent for sales by Westinghouse up to 25.4421 percent of the two firms' combined sales, but the royalty rate increased to 30 percent for sales exceeding this quota.[28] Similarly, du Pont's moisture-proof cellophane patent license to Sylvania during the 1930s prescribed a punitive royalty rate of 30 percent or more for sales exceeding some predetermined share of the total cellophane market.[29]

When patent protection is lacking, output restrictions may be enforced through various other formal cartel agreements. One approach is the so-called compulsory cartel, under which a government agency imposes binding production and marketing restrictions upon individual firms. The first true modern cartels (dating back to the late eighteenth century) were of this type, and governments (including that of the United States) have over the years continued to encourage or sanction output restrictions in some industries, particularly for raw materials such as sugar, grain products, milk, citrus fruits, cocoa, and coffee, and for services such as property-liability insurance, maritime shipping, and other modes of transportation. Governments may sanction the formation of export cartels[30] or participation in international cartels which in turn influence relations among member firms in the domestic market. If national laws permit, industry members may enter voluntarily into formal cartel agreements prescribing penalty payments when output quotas are exceeded. Excess production penalties were a prominent feature of the European steel and aluminum cartels following World War I.[31] As a third possibility, work-week limitations written into labor contracts through collective bargaining may be used as a means of restricting output. This approach was successful in the U.S. flat glass industry during the 1920s.[32] The United Mine

Workers were accused of similar attempts in the bituminous coal industry, although the evidence remains disputed.[33]

A cartel tightens its control over member prices and outputs if it can require all members to distribute their output through a central industry sales bureau. During the depression of the 1930s, soft coal producers in the Appalachian mountain region organized an exclusive selling agency with power to apportion sales and outputs among the 137 member firms.[34] In the late 1960s, West German steel makers sold through four privately owned syndicates.[35]

A variant of the central sales bureau method adapted for products purchased under "competitive" bidding is the so-called *bidding* or *tender cartel*. The U.S. electrical manufacturers' conspiracy possessed many attributes of a bidding cartel, although it lacked formal binding agreements and organization. The Water-Tube Boilermakers' Association agreement approved in 1959 by the British antitrust authorities is typical of formally organized bidding cartels.[36] When bids for steam-generating boilers were requested by some buyer (such as the nationalized Central Electricity Generating Board), each member firm submitted to the association director a confidential quotation of the price at which it was willing to fill the order. Using a formula that compared recent with historical shares of the market, the director nominated one firm to undertake the job. The firm nominated could then adjust its quotation downward to meet the lowest quotation, and when the revised bids were officially tendered to the buyer, the nominated firm was usually the winner. Since nomination to be the low bidder depended upon the past allocation of orders rather than price, there was no incentive for member firms to undercut each other's price quotations.

The surest way for firms to achieve the monopoly price is to merge all actual and potential producers into a single firm. In theory, the same result can be accomplished by a rationalization cartel. However, as noted above, convincing every producer to participate in a rationalization cartel is no easy matter.

26. Fritz Voigt, "German Experience with Cartels and Their Control During Pre-War and Post-War Periods," in J. P. Miller, ed., *Competition, Cartels, and Their Regulation* (Amsterdam: North-Holland, 1962), pp. 169–208.

27. Patent license agreements — particularly price restrictions — lie in a gray area of U.S antitrust law. See Louis Kaplow, "The Patent-Antitrust Intersection," *Harvard Law Review*, vol. 97 (June 1984), pp. 1813–1892; Ira M. Millstein, "The Role of Antitrust in an Age of Technology," *Cardozo Law Review*, vol. 9 (March 1988), p. 1208; and U.S. Senate, Committee on the Judiciary, Subcommittee on Technology and the Law, Hearings, *Intellectual Property Antitrust Protection Act of 1987* (Washington: 1988).

28. See Stocking and Watkins, *Cartels in Action*, supra note 5, pp. 308–310; and H. C. Passer, *The Electrical Manufacturers* (Cambridge: Harvard University Press, 1953), pp. 161–164.

29. G. W. Stocking and W. F. Mueller, "The Cellophane Case and the New Competition," *American Economic Review*, vol. 45 (March 1955), p. 43.

30. For a discussion of the International Electrical Association, which was formed to cartelize international trade in electrical equipment, see Barbara Epstein and Richard Newfarmer, "Imperfect International Markets and Monopolistic Prices to Developing Countries: A Case Study," *Cambridge Journal of Economics*, vol. 6 (March 1982), pp. 33–52.

31. G. W. Stocking and M. W. Watkins, *Cartels or Competition?* (New York: Twentieth Century Fund, 1948), pp. 185–186; and R. F. Lanzillotti, "The Aluminum Industry," in Walter Adams, ed., *The Structure of American Industry*, 3rd ed. (New York: Macmillan, 1961), p. 192. For an analysis of the statics and dynamics of quota systems, see Fritz Machlup, *The Economics of Sellers' Competition*, (Baltimore: Johns Hopkins, 1952), pp. 482–488.

32. G. W. Stocking and M. W. Watkins, *Monopoly and Free Enterprise* (New York: Twentieth Century Fund, 1951), pp. 123–124.

33. For conflicting views, see Almarin Phillips, *Market Structure, Organization and Performance* (Cambridge: Harvard University Press, 1962), p. 134; and Reed Moyer, *Competition in the Midwestern Coal Industry* (Cambridge: Harvard University Press, 1964), pp. 162–164.

34. Phillips, *Market Structure*, pp. 125–132.

35. See Klaus Stegemann, *Price Competition and Output Adjustment in the European Steel Market* (Tübingen: Mohr, 1977), pp. 244–253.

36. *In re Water-Tube Boilermakers' Agreement*, L.R., 1 R.P. 285, 1959.

Despite their normally illegal status, there have been many price-fixing and other restrictive agreements in the United States. A fair amount of research has been devoted to analyzing the characteristics of agreements sufficiently transparent or careless to be detected and prosecuted successfully by the antitrust authorities. One prominent feature is the typically small number of sellers and the high degree of seller concentration in the relevant product or geographic market.[37] Evidently, agreement is easier to achieve when the number of sellers is modest — for example, ten or fewer, as Hay and Kelly found in 79 percent of the cases they studied. When a larger number of sellers were involved, a trade association or central sales agent commonly undertook the more complex task of coordinating the participants' behavior.[38] Homogeneity of products appeared more conducive to agreement than heterogeneity — for example, associated either with product complexity or heavy advertising.[39] There is evidence that agreements occurred more frequently in slowly growing or stagnating markets with below-average profits, suggesting that dissatisfaction with profit levels may be an important spur to collusion.[40] However, a statistical study of price fixing before it was outlawed in the United Kingdom provides some reason to believe that *effective* agreements (and not all were) had a tendency to *raise* price-cost margins.[41]

To sum up, restrictive agreements are widespread, and they can assume numerous forms. Some approaches are more successful in yielding monopoly profits than others. None is completely free from the risk of breakdown. Yet their central tendency is quite clearly to elevate prices above the level that would be sustained under independent competitive conduct.

Price Leadership

The paramount problem for firms trying to make the best of an oligopolistic market structure is to devise and maintain communications systems that permit behavior to be coordinated in the common interest. The conflicts that inevitably arise must be resolved without resorting to price warfare. Adjustments to changes in demand and cost conditions must be made so as to elicit unanimous consent and minimize the risk that actions taken in the group's interest will be misinterpreted as Prisoners' Dilemma-style defecting or self-serving aggression. Collusion is communication par excellence, but it is generally illegal in the United States, and the tide of antitrust legislation is running against it in other industrialized nations. Firms have an understandable desire to find alternative means of coordinating their behavior without running afoul of the law. One such means (which lies in the gray area of the American antitrust law) is price leadership.[42]

Price leadership implies a set of industry practices or customs under which list price changes are normally announced by a specific firm accepted as the leader by others, who follow the leader's initiatives. Wide variations are possible in the stability of the leader's position, the reasons for its acceptance as leader, its influence over the other firms, and its effectiveness in leading the industry to prices that maximize joint profits. Economists commonly distinguish three main types of price leadership: dominant firm, collusive, and barometric.[43]

Dominant firm price leadership occurs when a single firm dominates the industry in the conventional sense of the word and sets a price that best serves its own objectives, taking into account the anticipated supply reactions of fringe or follower firms. The mechanics were discussed in Chapter 6. Dominant firm leadership occurs when the leader has a large market share, with other sellers being too small to have a perceptible influence on price, or when one firm is recognized as having a sufficient cost advantage over rivals, and sufficient available capacity, to impose its pricing preferences on the industry.

The concept of price leadership "in lieu of overt collusion" was formulated by Jesse Markham to characterize the kind of leadership especially apt to support a monopolistic solution to oligopolists' pricing coordination problem. According to Markham, collusive price leadership is most likely to emerge when (a) the industry is tightly oligopolistic, (b) sellers' products are close substitutes, (c) cost curves are similar, (d) there are barriers to entry of new rivals, and (e) demand for the industry's output is relatively inelastic (so that price raising pays).[44]

Against collusive price leadership is juxtaposed the notion of barometric leadership, under which, as its name suggests, the price leader does no more than act as a barometer of market conditions, setting prices approximating those that would emerge in any event under competition. Distinguishing characteristics include occasional changes in the identity of the price leader (who is likely in any case to be one of the largest sellers); the absence of leader power to coerce others into accepting its price; a tendency for the leader formally to validate price reductions that other sellers have already initiated through off-list concessions; upward

37. See George A. Hay and Daniel Kelley, "An Empirical Survey of Price Fixing Conspiracies," *Journal of Law & Economics*, vol. 17 (April 1974), pp. 13–38; and Arthur G. Fraas and Douglas F. Greer, "Market Structure and Price Collusion: An Empirical Analysis," *Journal of Industrial Economics*, vol. 26 (September 1977), pp. 29–33. Compare Peter Asch and Joseph J. Seneca, "Characteristics of Collusive Firms," *Journal of Industrial Economics*, vol. 23 (March 1975), pp. 233–235; and James M. Clabault and John F. Burton, Jr., *Sherman Act Indictments: 1955–65* (New York: Federal Legal Publications, 1966), pp. 138–141.

38. Hay and Kelley, "An Empirical Survey," p. 21; and Fraas and Greer, "Market Structure and Price Collusion," pp. 32–39.

39. Hay and Kelley, "An Empirical Survey," pp. 24–25; and Asch and Seneca, "Characteristics," pp. 230–236.

40. Asch and Seneca, "Characteristics," pp. 227–236; *idem*, "Is Collusion Profitable?" *Review of Economics and Statistics*, vol. 58 (February 1976), pp. 1–12; and John P. Palmer, "Some Economic Conditions Conducive to Collusion," *Journal of Economic Issues*, vol. 6 (September 1972), pp. 29–38.

41. Almarin Phillips, "An Econometric Study of Price-Fixing, Market Structure and Performance in British Industry in the Early 1950s," in Keith Cowling, ed., *Market Structure and Corporate Behavior* (London: Gray-Mills, 1972), pp. 177–192.

42. As the legal counsel for the Plumbing Fixture Manufacturers Association is said to have exclaimed after learning of illegal collusion by its members, "I think the industry is stupid. . . . If they only had price leadership . . . which they don't have . . . that isn't violative of anything." Allan T. Demaree,

"How Judgment Came for the Plumbing Conspirators," *Fortune*, December 1969, pp. 97–98.

43. This scheme was proposed by Jesse W. Markham, expanding on an earlier proposal by George J. Stigler. See Stigler, "The Kinky Oligopoly Demand Curve and Rigid Prices," *Journal of Political Economy*, vol. 55 (October 1947), pp. 444–446; and Markham, "The Nature and Significance of Price Leadership," *American Economic Review*, vol. 41 (December 1951), pp. 891–905. For critical comments, which have been largely ignored since, see Alfred Oxenfeldt, "Professor Markham on Price Leadership," *American Economic Review*, vol. 42 (June 1952), pp. 380–384; R. F. Lanzillotti, "Competitive Price Leadership: A Critique of Price Leadership Models," *Review of Economics and Statistics*, vol. 39 (February 1957), pp. 56–64; and Joe S. Bain, "Price Leaders, Barometers, and Kinks," *Journal of Business*, vol. 33 (July 1960), pp. 193–203. A related taxonomy based on noncooperative game theoretic concepts has been proposed by Yoshiyasu Ono, "Price Leadership: A Theoretical Analysis," *Economica*, vol. 49 (February 1982), pp. 11–20.

44. Markham, "The Nature and Significance of Price Leadership," pp. 901–903. Formal models of the use of price leadership to approximate collusive outcomes can be found in W. Bentley Macleod, "A Theory of Conscious Parallelism," *European Economic Review*, vol. 27 (February 1985), pp. 25–44; and Julio J. Rotemberg and Garth Saloner, "Price Leadership," Massachusetts Institute of Technology Department of Economics Working Paper No. 388, September 1985.

leadership only when rising costs or demand warrant price hikes; and occasional lags in following, or outright rejection of, the leader's price initiatives.

In practice, it is difficult to categorize actual cases quite so neatly. This point is best seen by carefully considering how price leadership has operated in several important industries.

Cigarettes

The cigarette industry during the 1920s and 1930s affords a classic example of price leadership used to establish a price structure that (barring miscalculations) tended to yield maximum collusive profits.[45] The Big Three, selling from 68 to 90 percent of industry output, mostly through their Camel, Lucky Strike, and Chesterfield brands, clearly recognized their mutual interdependence. The leading brands were quite similar physically; blindfold tests revealed that experienced smokers could not distinguish among them. There is no close substitute for cigarettes in the minds of most consumers, and so the cigarette manufacturers enjoyed considerable discretion in choosing an overall price level.

Between 1911 and 1921, conditions in the cigarette industry were unsettled owing to several radical changes: the dissolution of the old Tobacco Trust in an antitrust action, the introduction of new tobacco blends, and the initiation of nationwide advertising campaigns. In 1918 American Tobacco tried to lead a price rise, but Reynolds (the largest seller) refused to follow. In 1921, American cut its price and Reynolds retaliated with a further cut, which American and the other sellers matched. This experience apparently had a profound educational impact on American and the other major brand sellers, none of whom challenged Reynolds' leadership again for a decade. Between 1923 and 1941, virtual price identity prevailed continuously among the Big Three's standard brands, although certain other cigarettes of similar size and quality sold in smaller quantities at premium prices, and premium-priced Philip Morris grew through heavy advertising to a 6 percent market share. During this period there were eight standard brand list price changes. Reynolds led six of them, five upward and one downward, and was followed each time, in most cases within twenty-four hours of its announcement. The other two changes were downward revisions during 1933 led by American and followed by the other standard brand vendors. American also attempted to lead a price increase in 1941, but Reynolds again refused to follow and the change was rescinded. Throughout this period, the return on invested capital realized by Reynolds, American, and Liggett & Myers averaged 18 percent after taxes—roughly double the rate earned by American manufacturing industry as a whole.

The 1933 departures from Reynolds' leadership illustrate further the high degree of coordination displayed by the Big Three. Even the most astute price leaders make mistakes, and Reynolds made one in 1931. In June, as cigarette consumption was declining because of widespread unemployment and as leaf tobacco prices reached their lowest level since 1905, Reynolds announced an increase in the net wholesale price of Camels from $5.64 to $6.04 per thousand, or 12.08 cents per pack of 20—ostensibly to generate revenue for the promotion of its new moisture-proof cellophane package. The other leading producers followed immediately—American, allegedly, because it saw "the opportunity to make some money" and Liggett & Myers because its officers concluded that "safety lay in imitation."[46] But this increase, combined with the dire financial straits in which many cigarette smokers found themselves, opened up significant market penetration possibilities for firms selling cigarettes of inferior quality. With the standard brands selling at retail prices of up to fifteen cents per pack, these so-called ten-cent brands increased their share of the market from 1 percent in early 1931 to 23 percent in late 1932. In response, American cut its Lucky Strikes price from $6.04 to $5.29 per thousand in January 1933, and then to $4.85 per thousand (after wholesale discounts) in February 1933. Reynolds and Liggett followed immediately, this time without undercutting.[47] At the same time the Big Three pressured retailers to keep the price differential between standard brands and the ten-cent brands below three cents, and in some chain outlets the price of standard brands fell to ten cents per pack. The counterattack against the intruding ten-cent brands was largely successful; their share of the market dropped from 23 percent in November 1932 to 6 percent in May 1933. Having recovered much of the lost ground, American and Liggett followed Reynolds' increase to $5.38 per thousand in January 1934.

Following World War II the pattern changed. Efforts by the smaller firms to lead price increases were rebuffed. But American Tobacco successfully led several increases, in part because it briefly moved into first place in total cigarette sales and in part because the cigarette brand structure became much more complex. For an appreciable period American had the highest sales volume in nonfilter cigarettes and also exercised price leadership there. Reynolds meanwhile led the price adjustments on filter tips, where most of its volume was concentrated. Then American's market share fell and Philip Morris moved ahead aggressively, asserting price leadership successfully from second place in overall sales soon after its Marlboro brand became the world's best-selling cigarette.[48]

Despite these changes in leadership roles and the proliferation of differentially priced king-size, extra-long, mentholated, and low-tar brands, there was little indication of intensified price rivalry among the cigarette makers.[49] Indeed, despite a doubling of federal excise taxes to sixteen cents per pack in 1983, the reappearance of low-price brands, and falling consumption, the leading U.S. cigarette manufacturers raised prices sufficiently to increase their profits from $3.80 to $11.55 per thousand cigarettes sold between 1980 and 1988.[50]

45. Markham, "The Nature and Significance of Price Leadership," pp. 903–905; William Nicholls, *Price Policies in the Cigarette Industry* (Nashville: Vanderbilt University Press, 1951); and R. B. Tennant, "The Cigarette Industry," in Adams, *The Structure of American Industry*, supra note 31, pp. 357–392.

46. Nicholls, *Price Policies*, pp. 84–85.

47. There is some evidence that outright collusion occurred at this point. The night before American's second price announcement, the A&P Company's national headquarters telegraphed its 15,000 stores to reduce prices of all standard brands to ten cents per pack. In subsequent court testimony, A&P officials denied receiving advance notice from the several rival firms, but said their action was based upon "trade rumors." Nicholls, *Price Policies*, pp. 119–120.

48. "Marketing Observer", *Business Week*, February 24, 1973, p. 48.

49. For the closest thing to a possible exception, see "Cigarette Producers Dabble in Dual Pricing," *Business Week*, March 29, 1976, p. 33.

50. See "Smokers are Starting to Choke on Soaring Prices," *Business Week*, December 19, 1983, pp. 62–63; "Cheap Smokes: The Market That's On Fire," *Business Week*, April 14, 1986, p. 41; and "Contrasts in Tobacco Strategy," *New York Times*, October 27, 1988, p. D1. Nevertheless, there is evidence that price leadership in the cigarette industry has failed to achieve a high degree of market-sharing coordination. In a perfect market-sharing cartel, firm price elasticities would approximate those for the industry (supra note 9). For the industry, generally recognized estimates of price elasticity range between $-.3$ and $-.8$. In contrast, Daniel A. Sumner, "Measurement of Monopoly Behavior: An Application to the Cigarette Industry," *Journal of Political Economy*, vol. 89 (October 1981), pp. 1010–1019, reports estimates of firm price elasticities between -13.5 and -34.5. For a critique of Sumner's methodology, see Jeremy I. Bulow and Paul Pfleiderer, "A Note on the Effect of Cost Changes on Prices," *Journal of Political Economy*, vol. 91 (February 1983), pp. 182–185.

Steel　Largely because of the United States Steel Corporation's initially commanding market share and the cooperative attitudes cultivated at the Gary dinners, a tradition of lock-step followership behind U.S. Steel's price leadership developed during the 1900s.[51] Despite occasional limited sub rosa shading from list prices, the industry's pricing discipline for the next half century was little short of remarkable.[52] The first signs of change began to appear in 1958. Even though a recession had reduced the industry to a 61 percent capacity utilization rate, industrywide wage increases precipitated a clamor for higher prices. U.S. Steel, under attack from a congressional committee for inflationary wage and price behavior, failed to exercise the expected leadership. Eventually Armco, with roughly 4.4 percent of industry capacity, announced an increase, which was followed by U.S. Steel and the rest of the industry. For nearly four years no further general list price changes were attempted. Then, in 1962, U.S. Steel's announcement of a list price increase averaging $6 per ton drew withering criticism from President Kennedy and was rescinded. This experience apparently dampened U.S. Steel's zeal for bearing the onus of price leadership. The following year, price increases were announced on a product-by-product (as opposed to across-the-board) basis in numerous product lines by several smaller producers. The typical reaction of U.S. Steel was to follow with a slightly smaller increase in its own list prices, causing the original leaders to revise their quotations downward and fall into line. Price revisions through 1968 continued to be made on a piecemeal basis, with the initiative coming from several different companies. When U.S. Steel did exercise leadership, it announced cuts mixed with increases, displaying a "new diplomacy" that contrasted vividly with the "bludgeon" approach employed up to 1962.[53]

With price leadership being passed from hand to hand and with price changes announced almost monthly in some product lines, the danger of coordination breakdowns grew. By 1968 the strains could no longer be suppressed. Lacking strong leadership and under mounting pressure from imports, which had captured nearly 20 percent of the American market, steel producers began to engage in increasingly widespread sub rosa price cutting. This was not unprecedented, but another development was. As its domestic market share fell to an all-time low of 21 percent, U.S. Steel abandoned its traditional policy of holding list prices inviolate and joined the "chiselers," offering substantial secret concessions to a number of buyers. The once-rigid steel price structure began to crumble.

These developments led headlong into one of the most fascinating episodes in steel industry history.[54] On November 4, 1968, Bethlehem Steel announced a 22 percent cut in the list price of hot-rolled steel sheets, from $113.50 per ton (excluding extra charges) to $88.50 per ton. Its action, covering a product line accounting for 11 percent of total industry output, was evidently provoked by an under-the-counter offer U.S. Steel made to a major Bethlehem customer. In its announcement, Bethlehem asserted that the reduction was effected "in spite of rising costs to meet current domestic competition." "Prices should go up, not down," the statement continued, but "Bethlehem must be competitive." Within three days all significant producers had joined in the decrease. Three weeks later U.S. Steel in effect sued for peace, quoting a new price of $125 per ton for fully processed hot-rolled steel sheet and simultaneously creating a new semifinished product category, hot-rolled bands, to be priced at $110 per ton.[55] Bethlehem, however, waited nine days before responding. On December 6 it matched U.S. Steel's hot-rolled band price but raised its fully processed product price to only $117 per ton. A week later U.S. Steel revised its price schedules to match the lower response. In February of 1969 Bethlehem then led an increase in prices to $124 per ton for hot-rolled bands and $129 per ton (or after adjustment for extra charge changes, $125) for fully processed sheets. The price war was over. Bethlehem had communicated its message in the most vivid possible terms, and, at least temporarily, it apparently achieved its intended goal of restoring industry discipline.

In the years that followed, the leadership role continued to rotate among industry members, some of them small. A United States Steel price initiative was openly rebuffed on one occasion in 1976[56] and repeatedly thereafter. In 1983, United States Steel publicly renounced its desire to remain the industry price leader, claiming that its effort to prop up prices in periods of weak demand "was destroying the company."[57] Although United States Steel (later renamed USX) continued to lead on occasion, Bethlehem, the second-ranking (and later third-ranking) producer assumed an increasingly active role both in announcing price hikes and in attempting to enforce discipline when others deviated quietly from the industry price line.[58] Despite nearly continuous price and quota restrictions on import competition beginning in 1977, sub rosa chiseling was widespread, and, when the U.S. economy began to emerge from the deep recession of 1982-1983, off-list discounts on flat-rolled products had reached $120 per ton (relative to list prices of $563).[59] Over the years 1982 through 1986, American steel makers recorded net losses totaling $11.6 billion—42 percent of the value of their steel-making assets in 1982.[60]

The old order had changed. What was once a clear example of collusive price leadership had evolved into something more closely matching the barometric

51. For evidence on the level of collusion present in the steel industry around the turn of the century, see Robert Allen, "Accounting for Price Changes: American Steel Rails, 1879–1910," *Journal of Political Economy*, vol. 89 (June 1981), pp. 512–528.

52. See Leonard W. Weiss, *Economics and American Industry* (New York: Wiley, 1961), pp. 293–299; and George J. Stigler and James K. Kindahl, *The Behavior of Industrial Prices* (New York: Columbia University Press, 1970), pp. 71–74.

53. See "U.S. Steel Lifts Prices on Most Types of Plate But Also Trims Quotes on Some Other Items," *Business Week*, March 5, 1966, p. 44; "Did Prices Rise? Steel Users Ask," *New York Times*, September 2, 1965; "Steel Price Step a 3-Prong Attack," *New York Times*, October 17, 1965, Section 3; "U.S. Steel Proves It's the Leader," *Business Week*, December 16, 1967, p. 34; and "Calling the Shots on Steel Prices," *Business Week*, August 10, 1968, pp. 26–27.

54. Accounts of key developments include "Bethlehem Cuts Major Price 22%," *New York Times*, November 5, 1968, p. 67; "Steel Industry Hit By Major Price Cut," *Business Week*, November 9, 1968, p. 35; "U.S. Steel Moves To End Price War," *New York Times*, November 28, 1968, p. 75; "New Split Opens in Steel Pricing," *New York Times*, December 7, 1968, p. 73; "Revolution in Steel Pricing?," *Business Week*, December 14, 1968, p. 41; "Bethlehem Cuts Steel Sheet List," *New York Times*, February 5,

1969, p. 47; and "Steel Heads Up Again," *Business Week*, February 8, 1969, p. 27.

55. The $125.00 price was not directly comparable with the earlier $113.50 price because it included some elements that had previously been priced as "extras." According to the U.S. Steel announcement, the new $125.00 price approximately restored the status quo ante bellum.

56. "Steel Price-Rise Cancellation: Fight for Orders Called Cause," *New York Times*, September 4, 1976, p. 25.

57. "Graham is Trying to Forge a Tougher U.S. Steel," *Business Week*, October 10, 1983, pp. 104–106.

58. See "Dr. Bethlehem's New Steel Formula," *Business Week*, November 15, 1969, p. 39; "Bethlehem Steel's New Price Gambit," May 9, 1970, p. 21; "Steel Rift Caused Price-Rise Delay," *New York Times*, August 14, 1971, p. 1; "A Hold on Steel Prices," *Business Week*, November 4, 1972, p. 33; "Bethlehem, National Lift Prices," *New York Times*, August 9, 1986, p. A29; and "Prices to Rise on Steel Cans, Beverage Industry Exempt," *New York Times*, August 25, 1988, p. D1.

59. "New Rises Seen in '84 Steel Prices," *New York Times*, April 2, 1984, p. D1.

60. American Iron and Steel Institute, *1987 Annual Statistical Report* (Washington: 1988), p. 7.

model. This does not mean that the industry's price leaders had no impact. It seems undeniable that, in the absence of what leadership there was, steel prices in the United States, instead of rising, would have fallen sharply between 1974 and 1978, as they did elsewhere in depressed world markets.[61] During the early 1980s, demand was so slack and import competition so fierce that remaining leadership efforts were powerless to prevent significant price decreases. However, after U.S. producers closed down 27 percent of their 1980 capacity, import threats were blunted by the dollar's decline, and domestic demand recovered from its slump, leadership, most notably by Bethlehem, helped eliminate discounting and raise list prices so that major customers were paying 20 to 30 percent more per ton in 1988 than they paid in 1987.[62]

Automobiles   In his seminal article on price leadership, Professor Markham argued that when oligopolists' products are not homogeneous, multiple pricing policies will be pursued and price leadership may even be meaningless.[63] He cites the automobile industry as an example of individualistic pricing owing to product differentiation. This characterization has certainly not been valid since the 1950s, for price leadership-followership has been an unmistakable feature of the leading U.S. auto makers' conduct. General Motors has long been the acknowledged price leader. Although auto models differ greatly, each company aims specific models toward particular market segments, and each GM rival knows how its models relate to those of GM and therefore how they must be priced. Statistical analysis reveals that the prices quoted by different producers for models of comparable performance and interior space have been quite similar and that, with few exceptions, pricing discipline has been maintained.[64] What product differentiation does is permit modest price differentials to exist without inducing drastic market share shifts. Thus, during the late 1960s, Ford charged $10 to $20 more than Chevrolet for comparable full-sized models (retailing then at now-astounding prices of approximately $2700) and Plymouth $40 to $50 more.[65] Smaller firms such as American Motors (the last of the domestic independent companies to vanish) experienced considerably greater latitude, for example, to reduce prices by as much as $200 relative to General Motors models without evoking retaliation.[66] Reductions of similar magnitude on poorly selling Chrysler models were also tolerated. However, when Chrysler offered substantial rebates to combat an industrywide 1975 model-year sales slump, Ford and General Motors quickly retaliated to protect their market shares.[67]

Traditionally, the principal occasion for list price changes was the day on which new models were introduced, usually in September. Although General Motors was the price leader, production scheduling considerations often required the other producers to announce their new models, and hence their prices, before General Motors did. They then tried hard to anticipate GM's decisions and set their prices accordingly, but if GM's subsequent announcement brought surprises, they beat a hasty retreat, raising or lowering their prices into the desired relationship with those of General Motors.[68] During the mid-1970s, rapid inflation led the auto makers to ease the shock of large annual price increases by shifting to quarterly announcements, in which General Motors continued to play the leading role.

The 1970s also ushered in more important behavioral changes. The 1973 to 1974 and 1979 to 1981 OPEC oil price shocks led consumers to turn by fits and starts toward smaller cars, on which Japanese importers were in a particularly strong position. In 1975, the U.S. Congress passed a law requiring progressive increases in new cars' gasoline mileage from the average of fourteen miles per gallon prevailing in 1974 to eighteen in 1978 and 27.5 in 1985. The handwriting was on the wall: either from demand-side or regulatory pressures, U.S. producers were forced to shift their production mix strongly toward small cars. But small cars had historically been at best marginally profitable,[69] and rapidly rising production costs, among other things because of labor contracts fully indexed against inflation, made it even harder for the U.S. firms to compete profitably against imports. Unless they were willing to accept a more or less permanent deterioration of their profitability, the U.S. automobile makers faced the difficult task of raising small car prices without shifting so much demand to larger substitutes that attainment of the miles-per-gallon regulations was jeopardized.

Macroeconomic developments helped out, but required a change in the price leadership pattern. Between September 1977 and September 1978, the Japanese yen rose in value by 40 percent relative to the U.S. dollar. Japanese compact car makers, led by Toyota, were forced to raise their prices. They did so in four steps during the 1978 model year.[70] General Motors followed in virtual lock step an average of thirty-two days later. Ford in turn followed General Motors, although with the sales of its Pinto lagging because of safety problems, it did not join the fourth price increase. The important point is that the leadership role had been ceded under special circumstances by General Motors to a new group of rivals.

After 1978 the yen moved lower again relative to the dollar, and General Motors resumed the initiative in attempting to keep prices rising in pace with rapid

61. See U.S. Council on Wage and Price Stability report, *Prices and Costs in the United States Steel Industry* (Washington: USGPO, October 1977), Chapters II and III; and Federal Trade Commission staff report, *The United States Steel Industry and Its International Rivals* (Washington: USGPO, November 1977), Chapter 4.

62. "That Disturbing Deal on Steel," *New York Times*, December 14, 1988, p. D-2.

63. Markham, "The Nature and Significance of Price Leadership," supra note 43, p. 902.

64. Stanley E. Boyle and Thomas F. Hogarty, "Pricing Behavior in the American Automobile Industry, 1957–1971," *Journal of Industrial Economics*, vol. 24 (December 1975), pp. 81–95; and Stanley E. Boyle and Michael J. Piette, "Neglected Elements in Vertical Integration Analysis: The Case of Retail Price Preticketing," *Review of Industrial Organization*, vol. 1 (Spring 1984), pp. 69–77. Compare Richard L. Smith II, "The 1958 Automobile Information Disclosure Act: A Study of the Impact of Regulation," *Journal of Industrial Economics*, vol. 28 (June 1980), pp. 388–390.

In "Competition and Collusion in the American Automobile Industry: The 1955 Price War," *Journal of Industrial Economics*, vol. 35 (June 1987), pp. 457–482, Timothy F. Bresnahan contrasts evidence of a price war with evidence of cooperative behavior in the preceding and following years. See also Bresnahan, "Depar-

tures from Marginal-Cost Pricing in the American Automobile Industry: Estimates for 1977–1978," *Journal of Econometrics*, vol. 17 (November 1981), pp. 201–227.

65. Lawrence J. White, *The Automobile Industry Since 1945* (Cambridge: Harvard University Press, 1971), p. 115.

66. "Rambler Takes a Gamble," *Business Week*, February 25, 1967, p. 39.

67. See "GM Also to Offer Rebates up to $500 on Smaller Models," *Washington Post*, January 21, 1975, p. D-1; and "Auto Rebates: A Financial Disaster for Detroit," *Business Week*, March 10, 1975, pp. 72–73.

68. White, *The Automobile Industry*, supra note 65, pp. 109–116 and 126–133; "Detroit's Dilemma on Prices," *Business Week*, January 20, 1975, p. 82; and (on similar machinations for the 1984 model year) Walter Adams and James W. Brock, "The Automobile Industry," in Walter Adams, ed., *The Structure of American Industry*, 7th ed. (New York: Macmillan, 1986), p. 139.

69. See, for example, National Academy of Engineering, *The Competitive Status of the U.S. Auto Industry* (Washington: National Academy Press, 1982), pp. 68–70.

70. See John E. Kwoka Jr., "Market Power and Market Change in the U.S. Automobile Industry," *Journal of Industrial Economics*, vol. 32 (June 1984), pp. 512–515.

cost increases. Between December of 1978 and 1979, it announced seven broad price increases, all followed closely by Ford and somewhat less assiduously by Chrysler.[71] By 1981, the price of the average new U.S. auto had been raised from $3,600 to $8,750 in a decade.[72] However, competition from low-priced imports intensified, the Big Three collectively sustained net losses in 1980 and 1981, and Chrysler was driven to the brink of bankruptcy. Industry discipline eroded, several General Motors initiatives were rebuffed, and competition among the domestic Big Three broke out in the form of rebate offers and bargain loan interest rates.[73]

The pressure was reduced when Japan agreed with the U.S. government in April 1981 to restrict its imports to 1.68 million units for three years (with an increase to 1.85 million in 1984 and 2.3 million from 1985 to 1989). Having gained a reputation for superior quality but limited in the number of cars they could sell, the Japanese producers chose to exploit the advantage conferred by falling yen/dollar exchange rates in the form of higher profit margins rather than reduced prices. This permitted U.S. firms to recoup and implement selected further price increases.[74] Then, from 1985 to 1988, the yen nearly doubled in value relative to the dollar. As in 1977 through 1978, this forced Japanese producers to raise their prices, although by accepting a reduction in previously high profit margins and pushing for ever higher productivity, their cumulative three-year price increase was limited to approximately 30 percent. Again, as in 1977 through 1978, U.S. auto makers followed the Japanese up, but this time by only about a third of the Japanese increases.[75] Whether the new U.S. pricing strategy was intended to increase U.S. producers' combined market share, to defend it against rapidly growing Japanese production within the United States,[76] or some combination of the two remained unclear at the time this was written. Certainly, the nature of price leadership had become more complex.

Ready-to-Eat-Cereals Further evidence on the nature of price leadership in industries with differentiated products can be found in the ready-to-eat breakfast cereal industry.[77] Some products, such as the corn flakes and raisin brans of Kellogg and Post, were recognized by many if not most consumers to be close substitutes; and a retail price differential of one or two cents per package could lead quickly to appreciable market share shifts. Consequently, both price changes and package size changes were matched rapidly, and virtual price identity per ounce was the rule. But cereals come in many grain bases, shapes, and flavors, and such children's cereals as Lucky Charms and Fruit Loops or cereals seen as meeting specific dietary needs like All-Bran and Fibre One could be priced several cents apart on comparable packages before a significant movement toward the lower-priced brand became evident. This, plus the fact that certain other cereals such as Shredded Wheat, Nutri-Grain, and Quaker Oats are fairly unique, gave the cereal makers a band of discretion within which they could vary prices without experiencing much volume change. Also, cereal consumers react more slowly to price signals than, say, steel or automobile buyers, for whom the stakes are sufficiently high on any single transaction that careful price shopping is stimulated. This meant that failure to match a rival's price increase immediately was seldom a serious threat to the rival.

Nevertheless, the Big Three (controlling 76 percent of total ready-to-eat cereal sales in 1982) were also acutely aware that if one firm raised prices above those of similar rival products by more than some discernible amount — usually by more than three or four cents per package — it moved into a "trouble area" or even "greatly weakened its efforts" to maintain volume.[78] Between 1962 and 1970, the Big Three increased their average wholesale prices per pound by fourteen cents — much more than the differential any single company could sustain through individual pricing action. Price leadership facilitated the joint movement to higher prices.

Kellogg was recognized by all as the leader. It normally led increases in rounds covering many but not all the products in its line.[79] Out of fifteen unambiguous price increase rounds between 1965 and 1970, Kellogg led twelve. It was followed nine times by General Mills and ten times by Post; on only one occasion did neither of the two follow. The median lag between the effective date of Kellogg's price increases and those of General Mills and Post was 22 days. General Mills led once and was followed by the other Big Three members; General Foods led twice and was followed once. Quaker, the fourth largest seller, with a 5 to 7 percent market share, tended to pursue a more independent policy, seldom following Kellogg's lead directly but paying close attention to the relationship of its own prices to those of the Big Three. Unlike cigarettes, steel, and automobiles, the price leader in cereals rarely rescinded its price increase when others failed to follow. Rather, it relied upon its product differentiation to prevent a sudden loss of business, hoped for (and waited until) parity was restored in a subsequent round, and in certain cases intensified its promotional activity to compensate for its high price disadvantage. When General Mills or Post failed to follow Kellogg on some round, they tended to make up for the failure by raising prices on a disproportionate share of their product line in a subsequent round. During the 1960s, General Mills also utilized the discretion product differentiation afforded by moving from a price

71. Adams and Brock, supra note 68, p. 140.

72. "Detroit Bows to Sticker Shock," *New York Times*, August 5, 1981, p. D1.

73. See "Chrysler Holds Prices Steady; Ford's Rise is Less than GM's," *New York Times*, January 7, 1981, p. D6; "Ford Won't Match G.M. Price Rise," *New York Times*, April 10, 1981, p. D5; "Major Price Restraints Announced by Chrysler," *New York Times*, September 30, 1981, p. D1; "Incentives Create Disarray in Car Pricing," *New York Times*, October 26, 1981, p. 26; and "G.M. To Cut Prices of Some 1982 Cars by $500 to $2,000," *New York Times*, January 30, 1982, p. 1.

74. See "Is Japan Driving Up U.S. Auto Prices?" *Business Week*, December 5, 1983, p. 117; Clifford Winston and Fred Mannering, *Blind Intersection?: Policy and the Automobile Industry* (Washington: Brookings, 1987), Chapter 4; and Arthur T. Denzau, "The Japanese Automobile Cartel: Made in the USA," *Regulation*, 1988, no. 1, pp. 11–16.

75. See "GM's Price Hikes: Foresight or Folly?" *Business Week*, April 14, 1986, p. 36; "U.S. Auto Makers Get a Lift," *New York Times*, Nov. 9, 1987, p. D1; "G.M. Chief Promises To Hold '88

Car Prices," *New York Times*, February 8, 1988, p. D2; "Carmakers Should Cut Prices Now," Editorial, *Business Week*, March 7, 1988; and "Rising U.S. Auto Prices Could Resharpen the Asian Edge," *International Herald Tribune*, November 9, 1988.

76. In 1989, U.S. plants owned by Japanese firms (solely or in joint ventures with U.S. firms) accounted for 14 percent of domestic production. Planned construction would double the capacity of these plants by 1992. "After a Brief Pause, Japanese Auto Makers Gain on Detroit Again," *Wall Street Journal*, May 23, 1989, p. A1.

77. This analysis is based upon testimony in the Federal Trade Commission's antitrust case, *In re Kellogg Co. et al.*, Docket 8883, especially transcript pp. 27,799–27,925. See also F. M. Scherer, "The Breakfast Cereal Industry," in Walter Adams, ed., *The Structure of American Industry*, supra note 68, Chapter 5.

78. From a 1967 General Mills pricing analysis included in the cereal antitrust case record as CX-GM-278.

79. There were very few clear-cut list price decreases. Of 1,122 list price changes between 1950 and 1972 uncomplicated by package or case size changes, only seventeen were price decreases.

position somewhat lower than Kellogg's early in the decade to a premium price position by the late 1960s. Its internal decision-making memoranda reveal an acute sensitivity as to how far it could push without endangering its market position. All in all, the price leadership pattern in cereals exhibited more flexibility than in well-disciplined industries with more homogeneous products. Yet leadership was sufficiently robust to permit price increases in times of both booming and stagnant demand; and the sub rosa price-shading characteristic of barometric leadership was totally absent.

The strongest challenge to the established structure has come from private-label cereals (on which the supermarket affixes its own company imprint). Because they are sold at lower prices, without the benefit of extensive advertising and other differentiation, their presence limits the extent to which nationally branded marketers can elevate price. In the 1960s, responding to slippage in its branded products, Ralston intensified its efforts to win private-label business. It succeeded in making inroads into Kellogg's Corn Flakes sales, leading Kellogg to deviate from its normal policy to the point of matching Ralston's wholesale price in July 1971. Shortly thereafter, Ralston responded with its own price reduction, accepting a lower price differential than before Kellogg's cut (10 percent versus 16 percent), whether as a result of cost pressures or the chastening effect of Kellogg's cut is uncertain. Such private-label inroads were partly responsible for a seven-point decline in Kellogg's market share during the 1970s and the elevation of Ralston to fifth ranking producer.[80] In 1983, Kellogg tried a different tactic, introducing a "new" cereal, Crispix, virtually identical to Ralston's best-selling branded cereal Chex. The implicit message was that if Ralston's aggressive pricing jeopardized Kellogg's corn flake profits, Kellogg would respond with an attack on Ralston's special domain. Whether as a result of Kellogg's more aggressive stance or because of the long economic recovery of the mid-1980s, private-label gains were largely halted.[81] It is significant that Kellogg, the only relatively undiversified cereal maker, continued during the 1980s to be one of the most profitable large American corporations.

Turbogenerators

The U.S. turbogenerator industry illustrates a quite different approach to reconciling product heterogeneity and the use of price leadership.[82] In May 1963, two and one-half years after it was convicted for illegal price fixing, General Electric announced a new pricing policy for turbine generators.[83] One facet of the policy was the publication of a new and more simplified pricing book that permitted rival Westinghouse rather easily to compute the "book" price of any generator on which the two firms might be asked to bid. GE also announced a standard multiplier it would apply to the book price on each bid, and it communicated its intent not to deviate from the standard "book-price-times-announced-multiplier" procedure in bidding. The multiplier itself varied over time, but changes were publicly announced by General Electric. Consequently, what might otherwise have been a very complex coordination problem was reduced to a matter of Westinghouse's knowing how to calculate the so-called book price and following GE's price leadership with respect to the multiplier.

During the first year after this policy was implemented, Westinghouse evidently misinterpreted how book prices were to be computed, causing General Electric to suspect deliberate price cutting and in retaliation to reduce its price multiplier. But within two months after the GE reduction, Westinghouse re-aligned its prices to the earlier GE multiplier. After GE followed suit, the two companies are said to have applied identical multipliers to identical book prices on their turbogenerator bids for the next twelve years—until the practices were challenged by federal antitrust authorities. In sharp contrast to the history of the 1950s and early 1960s, GE and Westinghouse effected *no* generator price decrease during this period. General Electric led a number of increases, with Westinghouse typically following by announcing an identical multiplier increase within four days (although on one occasion the lag was three months). Thus, by linking price leadership to a simplification of the methods for computing bid prices, General Electric managed to avoid the pricing coordination breakdowns that had materialized even with outright collusion in earlier periods.[84]

Gasoline   Unusually complete information is available on the pricing of gasoline in Ohio during the 1950s. There, the Standard Oil Company of Ohio was said to be a classic barometric price leader. Especially for price decreases, a barometric leader often merely formalizes through list price announcements changes that have already permeated the market through informal departures from the list price. As an executive of Sohio described the price adjustment process in his territory:

> The major sales executives of all companies watch carefully the number and size of subnormal markets. . . . If the number of local price cuts increases, if the number and amount of secret concessions to commercial customers increase, it becomes more and more difficult to maintain the higher prices. . . . Finally, some company, usually the largest marketer in the territory, recognizes that the subnormal price has become the normal price and announces a general price reduction throughout the territory.[85]

For list price increases, the barometric leader must exercise a higher degree of initiative. This is brought out clearly in another Standard Oil of Ohio statement:

> On the other hand, in our own interest we must usually take the lead in attempting higher price levels when we believe that conditions will permit. Having a substantial distribution in our market we are confronted with the fact that few marketers, especially those with a lesser consumer acceptance, can take the lead in increasing prices.[86]

80. The continued penetration of private-label brands may be explained in part by the recessions of the 1970s and early 1980s, which made consumers more price conscious, and by the preoccupation of the major cereal manufacturers with the FTC's antitrust suit (see Chapter 12 infra). About the latter, Kellogg Chairman William LaMothe noted, "We started to pull our punches." "The Snap, Crackle, Pop Defense," *Forbes*, March 25, 1985, p. 82.

81. See "Who's Afraid of Generic Cereals?" *Industry Week*, March 16, 1983, p. 33 ff.; "Licensed Cereals Turn Soggy," *Advertising Age*, June 6, 1985, p. 24; and "Kellogg Pours Out More New Cereals," *Advertising Age*, July 25, 1988, p. 2ff.

82. This account is drawn from the complaint in *Appalachian Power Co. et al.* v. *General Electric Co. et al.*, S.D. New York, December 29, 1971; and from the "Plaintiff's Memorandum in Support of Proposed Modification to the Final Judgment" in *U.S.* v. *General Electric Co. et al.*, Civil No. 28,228, E.D. Pennsylvania,

December 1976. See also Bruce T. Allen, "Tacit Collusion and Market Sharing: The Case of Steam Turbine Generators," *Industrial Organization Review*, vol. 4 (1976), pp. 48–57; and Lean et al., "Does Collusion Pay?," supra note 7.

83. See Chapter 6, p. 212, supra for another important component of the new policy.

84. Lean et al., "Does Collusion Pay?," supra note 7, found statistically significant evidence of higher profit margins on turbogenerator sales during the post-conspiracy price leadership period.

85. Statement of S. A. Swensrud, quoted by George J. Stigler in "The Kinky Oligopoly Demand Curve," supra note 43, p. 445.

86. Edmund P. Learned and Catherine C. Ellsworth, *Gasoline Pricing in Ohio* (Boston: Harvard Business School Division of Research, 1959), p. 25, quoting a company policy statement. See also pp. 42 and 83.

The same statement emphasizes that such initiatives may be rejected by the rest of the industry:

Upward moves in our market are made by us only when, in our opinion, general prices and the economic pressure from industry costs are such that our competitors in their own interest will follow. It is notorious that when we guess wrong, or when we advance our market too far, immediate market disintegration sets in.

The interpretation given these leadership patterns — lowering the list price when market conditions are depressed, while raising it successfully only when demand and cost conditions support the higher level — is that the leader merely acts as a barometer of market conditions and not as an instrument of collusion. As Professor Stigler put it, the barometric firm "commands adherence of rivals to his price only because, and to the extent that, his price reflects market conditions with tolerable promptness."[87]

Evaluation It should be clear from these examples that simple distinctions between barometric and collusive price leadership are not easily drawn. Of the cases examined, gasoline pricing in Ohio and steel pricing after 1965 conform most closely to the barometric model. But although more than one economist has earned a high consulting fee by doing so, it would be misleading to conclude that any leadership pattern displaying barometric characteristics is "competitive." Consider first the matter of price increases. The price an industry can sustain obviously depends upon market conditions, as suggested in the theory of barometric leadership. However, under given supply and demand conditions, alternative institutional arrangements may lead to different price levels. And here the institution of price leadership can be important. As the Standard Oil of Ohio statement quoted previously indicates, even when market conditions are firm, producers with weak market positions might be unable to increase price successfully. An accepted price leader like Sohio can lead the way to prices higher than those attainable if no such firm existed. This price may not be much higher, but there is no guarantee that will not exceed the competitive level by at least a small amount on the average.[88]

Consider too the classic symptoms of barometric price leadership: when the price leader reduces its list price only because sub rosa departures from the list price are widespread. This is also not necessarily harmless. By making a dramatic list price cut, the price leader can often restore industry discipline and discourage further price cutting. It achieves this result in two ways: by providing a rallying point at which prices can be held, and by raising the implicit threat that further off-list pricing will incite additional list price reductions constraining even more the opportunities for profitable operation. The latter was no doubt what Bethlehem Steel had in mind with its hot-rolled steel price cut of 1968. If it failed, the failure must be attributed not to the type of leadership exercised, but to underlying structural conditions — that is, in that particular instance, to the difficulty of holding prices much above those at which numerous foreign steel producers stood willing to sell. This appears to be true more generally for companies described as barometric price leaders. Professor Edmund Learned, for example, observed that if Standard Oil of Ohio "had thought it could reasonably get more it would have tried to do so."[89] We are led to conclude that the intent of ostensibly barometric price leadership may be identical to the intent of collusive price leadership: maximization of joint industry profits. What varies is the success the leader has in achieving that goal, which depends in turn upon seller concentration, the height of entry barriers, and a variety of other conditions to be examined further in Chapters 8 and 10.

In sum, the effect of both collusive and barometric price leadership in oligopoly tends to be the establishment of prices higher than they would otherwise be, other things being held equal. This effect is achieved by sending to other members of the industry clear signals that indicate the way toward the profit-maximizing price in good times and serve as a rallying point in depressed times. Only two important exceptions need to be noted. First, when a price leader in a concentrated industry has lower unit costs than its principal rivals, as was probably true with respect to General Motors in the automobile industry at least until the late 1970s, it may hold the price below levels desired by other sellers. And second, strong price leaders may occasionally resist raising prices to the short-run profit-maximizing level during a boom, partly because long-run profits might be reduced by exploiting temporary conditions to the utmost and partly as an act of economic statesmanship, for example, to cooperate with the government in combating inflation.[90] Taking this latter qualification into account, we find that price leadership tends both to increase prices on the average and to reduce the magnitude of price fluctuations.

Rule-of-Thumb Pricing as a Coordinating Device

Another means of maintaining industry discipline when prices are set or changed is the use of pricing rules of thumb. These typically involve a variant of the full-cost or cost-plus pricing principle, in which a "normal" or desired profit margin or percentage return on invested capital is added to estimated unit costs to calculate the product price. If all industry members have similar costs and adhere to similar rules — or if a price leader adopts a formula and other sellers accept it — then price cutting below full-cost levels is minimized, the behavior of rivals becomes more predictable than it otherwise would be, and efficient producers are virtually assured of realizing at least normal profits.

Business enterprises apparently have been using pricing rules of thumb for a long time, but the concept did not penetrate mainstream economic analysis until it was identified by R. L. Hall and Charles J. Hitch through an interview survey of pricing practices in thirty-eight British firms.[91] Since then an enormous literature

87. Stigler, "The Kinky Oligopoly Demand Curve," supra note 43, pp. 445–446.

88. See also Howard P. Marvel, "Competition and Price Levels in the Retail Gasoline Market," *Review of Economics and Statistics*, vol. 60 (May 1978), pp. 252–258, who found that five years elapsed before a 1965 price increase led by Texaco was fully eroded to competitive levels.

89. Learned and Ellsworth, *Gasoline Pricing in Ohio*, supra note 86, p. 158.

90. See A. D. H. Kaplan, Joel B. Dirlam, and R. F. Lanzillotti, *Pricing in Big Business: A Case Approach* (Washington, D.C.: Brookings Institution, 1958), p. 27.

91. R. L. Hall and Charles J. Hitch, "Price Theory and Business Behaviour," *Oxford Economic Papers*, vol. 2 (May 1939), pp. 12–45.

on the subject has appeared, although little new work has been done in the 1970s and 1980s.[92]

Hall and Hitch and later analysts found several reasons why business managers use cost-based rules of thumb in their pricing decisions. It is a way of coping with (essentially by ignoring) uncertainties in the estimation of demand function shapes and elasticities. Second, many businesspeople justify the practice on grounds of "fairness," in the sense that too high a price is unfair to the customer and too low a price fails to provide a fair margin of profit over cost. Third, calculation and posting of prices are costly, especially for companies selling hundreds or thousands of different products or which introduce new products frequently. Adopting rules of thumb greatly simplifies the pricing problem in such businesses as department stores, automobile repair shops, and metal working shops.

All sorts of full-cost pricing rules are encountered. Here two examples must suffice. In the retail trades, a conventional pricing approach is to seek some standard percentage margin — for example, 40 percent — of price less cost over price. Knowing the wholesale cost W of an item, one finds the retail price by calculating $W/(1 - .4)$. The 40 percent margin in this case must cover all selling and overhead expenses. From the standpoint of promoting industry coordination, this rule has the advantage of basing price on a cost common to all retailers, independent of their selling efficiency.

A quite different, well-known full-cost price rule is the technique used by General Motors with great success until aggressive import competition erupted.[93] GM started with the goal of earning, on the average over the years, a return of approximately 15 percent after taxes on total invested capital. Not knowing how many autos would be sold and hence unit costs (including prorated fixed costs), it calculated costs on the assumption of operation at 80 percent of conservatively rated capacity. A standard price was calculated by adding to unit cost a sufficient profit margin to yield the desired 15 percent after-tax return. The rule would be adjusted across the product line to take account of actual and potential competition, business conditions, long-run strategic goals, and other factors. Actual profit then depended on the number of vehicles sold. Between 1960 and 1979, GM's actual return on stockholders' equity fell below 15 percent in only four years, all marked by recession and/or OPEC-induced gasoline price shocks. The average return was 17.6 percent. After 1979, however, recession and intensifying import competition caused GM frequently to fall short of its target.

Case studies reveal that the use of full-cost pricing procedures is widespread. Only eight of the thirty-eight firms in the Hall-Hitch sample indicated that they used no such rules. Half of the twenty large U.S. corporations studied by Kaplan, Dirlam, and Lanzillotti used some target return on investment approach to pricing major products.[94] In a study of 139 Danish firms, Bjarke Fog found that most used some kind of full-cost pricing scheme.[95] Three-quarters of 166 British firms studied by Skinner used some form of average-cost pricing rule.[96] Applying a simple wholesale cost markup rule, Cyert and March were able to predict *to the penny* the prices actually charged for 188 of 197 randomly selected items sold by a large department store.[97]

At a more aggregate level, empirical studies of corporate income tax shifting provide modest support for the full-cost hypothesis. A standard point in introductory price theory is the demonstration that changes in the corporate income tax have no effect on price in a perfectly competitive industry (or, for that matter, in monopoly). Under a full-cost pricing formula, however, the tax is included as a cost, so higher taxes do raise prices. Using U.S. manufacturing data for 1931 through 1970, Sebold found that as much as 69 percent of corporate income taxes were shifted to consumers.[98]

When pricing decisions are based upon some variant of the full-cost rule, we expect prices to be more responsive to changes in cost than to changes in demand. Industrywide cost changes generate a readily understood signal that price changes are in order. As Richard Heflebower observed, "When factor prices fall, the initiator of a selling price reduction is not suspected of trying to enlarge his share. Or, in reverse, the boldness of the firm which moves to reflect higher factor prices in his selling prices is appreciated, particularly when margins have been squeezed sharply."[99] The adjustment problem is different for demand changes. When demand declines, full-cost pricing may call for price increases to cover higher overhead allocations, but this could be barred by the very weakness of demand. In boom times, full-cost rules dictate little or no increase in prices unless marginal costs have risen sharply owing to pressure on capacity.[100]

Much of the economic literature on full-cost pricing has focused on whether it is inconsistent with profit maximization. Suppose a firm plans its capacity so that average total cost ATC (excluding profit) is minimized at the normal or average output. When profits are maximized, marginal cost MC = marginal revenue

92. For excellent surveys of the literature, see Richard B. Heflebower, "Full Costs, Cost Changes, and Prices," in the National Bureau of Economic Research conference report, *Business Concentration and Price Policy* (Princeton: Princeton University Press, 1955), pp. 361–396; and Aubrey Silberston, "Surveys of Applied Economics: Price Behaviour of Firms," *Economic Journal*, vol. 80 (September 1970), pp. 511–582.

93. See Donaldson Brown, "Pricing Policy in Relation to Financial Control," *Management and Administration*, vol. 7 (February–April 1924), pp. 195–198, 283–286, and 417–422; Albert Bradley, "Financial Control Policies of General Motors Corporation and Their Relationship to Cost Accounting," *National Association of Cost Accountants Bulletin*, vol. 1 (January 1927), pp. 412–433; U.S. Congress, Senate, Committee on the Judiciary, Report, *Administered Prices: Automobiles* (Washington: USGPO, 1958), pp. 104–130; and Kaplan et al., *Pricing in Big Business*, supra note 90, pp. 48–55 and 131–135.

94. Kaplan et al., *Pricing in Big Business*, p. 130; and Lanzillotti, "Pricing Objectives in Large Companies," *American Economic Review*, vol. 48 (December 1958), pp. 923–929. See also R. C. Skinner, "The Determination of Selling Prices," *Journal of Industrial Economics*, vol. 18 (July 1970), pp. 201–217.

95. Bjarke Fog, *Industrial Pricing Policies: An Analysis of Pricing Policies of Danish Manufacturers*, trans. I. E. Bailey (Amsterdam: North-Holland, 1960), p. 217.

96. Skinner, "The Determination of Selling Prices," supra note 94.

97. Richard M. Cyert and James G. March, *A Behavioral Theory*

of the Firm (Englewood Cliffs, N.J.: Prentice-Hall, 1963), pp. 146–147. Somewhat less success in applying similar rules at a different store during 1968 was reported by William J. Baumol and Maco Stewart, "On the Behavioral Theory of the Firm," in Robin Marris and Adrian Wood, eds., *The Corporate Economy* (Cambridge: Harvard University Press, 1971), pp. 118–134.

98. Frederick D. Sebold, "The Short-Run Shifting of the Corporation Income Tax: A Simultaneous Equation Approach," *Review of Economics and Statistics*, vol. 61 (August 1979), pp. 401–409. See also Robert J. Gordon, "The Incidence of the Corporation Income Tax in U.S. Manufacturing, 1925–1962," *American Economic Review*, vol. 57 (September 1967), pp. 731–758; John G. Cragg et al., "Empirical Evidence on the Incidence of the Corporation Income Tax," *Journal of Political Economy*, vol. 75 (December 1967), pp. 811–821; and the exchange of views in the *Journal of Political Economy*, vol. 78 (July/August 1970), pp. 768–777. Tax incidence studies suffer from a number of methodological and data limitations noted by Anthony B. Atkinson and Joseph E. Stiglitz, *Lectures on Public Economics* (New York: McGraw Hill, 1980), especially p. 226; and Harvey S. Rosen, *Public Finance* (Homewood: Irwin, 1988), Chapter 9.

99. Richard B. Heflebower, "Toward a Theory of Industrial Markets and Prices," *American Economic Review*, vol. 44 (May 1954), p. 135.

100. For evidence that concentrated industries do display such pricing rigidity, see Dennis W. Carlton, "The Rigidity of Prices," *American Economic Review*, vol. 76 (September 1986), pp. 637–658; and Chapter 13 of the second edition of this book.

MR and $(P - MC)/P = 1/e$.[101] Since MC = ATC when ATC is at a minimum, we obtain the equilibrium condition $(P - ATC)/P = 1/e$; the profit margin, expressed as a percentage of price, is the reciprocal of the elasticity of demand. Thus, long-run profit maximization is consistent with a full-cost pricing rule. The maximizing rule requires firms to add lower margins in pricing products with close substitutes (that is, with highly elastic demands) than in pricing products whose demand is relatively inelastic, ceteris paribus. Virtually all the available evidence suggests that this is indeed the case.[102]

The problem of short-run price and margin adjustments to changing demand and cost conditions is more complicated. Where the price elasticity of demand is insensitive to price changes, a firm maximizing short-run profits will cut price in a recession (for rising marginal costs) or hold prices fixed (if marginal costs are constant). However, except under a standard volume rule of the type practiced by General Motors, we should expect full-cost prices to rise in a recession, since fixed overhead must be prorated over a smaller volume. Twelve of the thirty-eight British business officials surveyed by Hall and Hitch indicated that they would break away from full-cost rules and cut prices during a severe recession, while an equal number insisted they would adhere to the rules.[103] Fog found only fourteen of sixty-seven Danish firms unwilling to cut prices below full-cost levels when running at less than capacity.[104] McFetridge found that price markups in the Canadian textile industry tended to fall during recessions and rise during periods of increased demand.[105] Similarly mixed historical evidence on the pricing behavior of nine U.S. manufacturing industries was compiled by Markham.[106] Evidently, some, but far from all, industrial pricing is consistent with strict interpretations of the full-cost hypothesis.

One might suppose that observed departures from full-cost pricing rules in times of especially weak or strong demand represent a profit-maximizing response. However, they could just as easily reflect price rivalry that reduces the profits of all firms (although it is initiated by firms myopically trying to increase their individual profits). By adhering rigidly to the rule, a seller no doubt fails to squeeze the most out of its profit-making opportunities at every moment in time.[107] Nor will slavish adherence to full-cost rules be as effective in maximizing joint profits as a carefully administered cartel. But in most real-world oligopolies, and particularly when legal prohibitions inhibit outright collusion, the old Russian adage that "the perfect is the enemy of the good" holds with special force. Poorly coordinated efforts to increase short-run profits under changing and uncertain conditions can, through short-sightedness or misinterpretation, deteriorate into moves and countermoves that reduce rather than increase group profits. If by employing rules of thumb an industry does the best it can on the average under less than ideal conditions, we must conclude that the rules constitute an instrument of long-run profit maximization.[108] Full-cost pricing facilitates oligopolistic coordination by making rivals' decisions more predictable and by providing common pricing guidelines.

When costs vary widely from firm to firm within an industry, coordination through the use of full-cost rules becomes more difficult. One effective and apparently widespread escape is the dissemination by a trade association of industrywide average cost data by product line, function, or component. This information then becomes, by overt or tacit consent, the basis of price calculations.[109] Coordination of pricing decisions is aided also when a trade association develops standard cost accounting systems for the benefit of its members.

One further implication of full-cost pricing rules must be mentioned briefly. Setting a price that affords only a moderate profit margin may not maximize profits during the immediate time period. However, unless an industry enjoys substantial barriers to new entry, a higher price and profit margin policy could attract new entrants, whose additional output will have a depressing impact on future prices and profits. Profits over the long pull may therefore be higher if firms use pricing rules that yield less than the maximum return attainable in any current period, but at the same time discourage new entry. This important aspect of business pricing strategy will be analyzed further in Chapter 10.

Focal Points and Tacit Coordination[110]

As we stressed in the last chapter, a variety of plausible outcomes to the oligopoly pricing game involve pricing above the competitive level. A prime difficulty facing both firms and students of oligopoly pricing lies in choosing among a number of pricing alternatives that lie between the competitive and the monopolistic levels. This multiplicity of outcomes would complicate the coordination problem facing oligopolists — difficult enough when communication is open and free. But the antitrust laws make overt communication hazardous. Insight into how this coordination

---

101. See Chapter 2, note 36. The margin over cost can be derived from this relation:

$$(P - MC) = P/e \rightarrow MC = P(e-1)/e.$$

Thus,

$$(P - MC)/MC = (P/e)/[P(e-1)/e] = 1/(e-1).$$

102. Fog, *Industrial Pricing Policies*, supra note 95, pp. 101–115 and 204–223; Kaplan et al., *Pricing in Big Business*, supra note 90, p. 173; Leonard W. Weiss, *Concentration and Price* (Cambridge: MIT Press, 1989); and Donald G. McFetridge, "The Determinants of Pricing Behaviour: A Study of the Canadian Cotton Textile Industry," *Journal of Industrial Economics*, vol. 22 (December 1973), pp. 141–152.

103. Hall and Hitch, "Price Theory and Business Behaviour," supra note 91, pp. 25–27.

104. Fog, *Industrial Pricing Policies*, supra note 95, p. 120.

105. McFetridge, "The Determinants of Pricing Behaviour," supra note 102, pp. 141–152.

106. Jesse W. Markham, "Administered Prices and the Recent Inflation," in the Commission on Money and Credit compendium, *Inflation, Growth, and Employment* (Englewood Cliffs, N.J.: Prentice-Hall, 1964), pp. 144–173.

107. Simulation studies suggest that under at least some plausible conditions, the use of full-cost rules can lead to near-maximum profits. See William J. Baumol and Richard E.

Quandt, "Rules of Thumb and Optimally Imperfect Decisions," *American Economic Review*, vol. 54 (March 1964); and J. Hadar and D. Hillinger, "Imperfect Competition with Unknown Demand," *Review of Economic Studies*, vol. 36 (October 1969), pp. 519–525.

108. This conclusion is now widely accepted. Through the application of full-cost pricing rules, cartels may "succeed in the maintenance of a monopolistic level of price, in spite of strong temptations for competitive price cutting." Fritz Machlup, *The Economics of Sellers' Competition* (Baltimore: Johns Hopkins University Press, 1952), p. 65. "Our studies . . . lead us to the proposition that firms will devise and negotiate an environment so as to eliminate the uncertainty. . . . In the case of competitors, one of the conspicuous means of control is through the establishment of industry-wide conventional practices." Cyert and March, *A Behavioral Theory*, supra note 97, p. 120. In "Pricing Practices in Small Firms," *Southern Economic Journal*, vol. 30 (April 1964), p. 317, W. W. Haynes reports that trade associations attempt to restrict cutthroat competition by urging wider use of full-cost pricing.

109. See Haynes, "Pricing Practices," pp. 317–319; and Cyert and March, *A Behavioral Theory*, supra note 97, p. 120.

110. A slightly different version of this section appeared as F. M. Scherer, "Focal Point Pricing and Conscious Parallelism," *Antitrust Bulletin*, vol. 12 (Summer 1967), pp. 495–503.

problem can be solved is provided by Professor Schelling's theory of focal points.[111]

The theory is introduced most conveniently through a noneconomic example. Consider the following problem posed by Schelling:

> You are to meet someone in New York City. You have not been instructed where to meet; you have no prior understanding with the person on where to meet; and you cannot communicate with each other. You are simply told that you will have to guess where to meet and he is being told the same thing and that you will have to try to make your guesses coincide.

> You are told the date but not the hour of this meeting; the two of you must guess the exact minute of the day for meeting. At what time will you appear at the chosen meeting place?[112]

Although there are tens of thousands of conceivable meeting places in New York City, a majority of the thirty-six persons on whom Schelling tried this problem chose the information booth at Grand Central Station, and nearly all chose to meet at twelve noon. The reason is that Grand Central Station (at least for New Yorkers as of 1960) and noon have a certain compelling prominence; they are focal points. In a variety of problems, when behavior must be coordinated tacitly — that is, without direct communication — there is a tendency for choices to converge on some such focal point. The focal points chosen may owe their prominence to analogy, symmetry, precedent, aesthetic considerations, or even the accident of arrangement; but they must in any event have the property of uniqueness. In economic problems, round numbers tend to be focal points, as do simple rules such as "split the difference."

The great merit of Schelling's general focal point theory is that it permits us to integrate into the mainstream of oligopoly theory a number of phenomena that might otherwise be deemed mere curiosities. Several specific ways in which focal points enter into oligopolistic price determination can be identified.

First is the practice of *price lining*, widespread at the retail level. Even dollar amounts serve as one focal point for pricing decisions. The automobile salesperson who works out the arithmetic for a rock-bottom price of $12,507.63 is almost pleading to be relieved of $7.63. More common in retailing is the use of odd pricing points such as $19.95, which owe their acceptance to tradition. By setting its price at some such focal point, a firm tacitly encourages its rivals to follow suit without undercutting. Conversely, if one company announces a price that has no such compulsion, a rival is tempted to set its own price just a cent or two below. In a replay of the classic Bertrand model described in Chapter 6, this leads to a further small retaliatory cut, precipitating a downward spiral which, in the absence of focal points, has no clear-cut stopping point. In setting price at a focal point, one in effect asks rhetorically, "If not here, where?" — implicitly warning rivals of the danger of downward spiraling.[113]

Government agencies may inadvertently facilitate price parallelism by setting ceiling prices, for example, as part of anti-inflation campaigns. For instance, a student of French price controls concluded that official ceiling prices provided a focus for individual quotations that might otherwise have differed.[114] In England it was customary, at least until the last few months before the steel industry was nationalized in 1967, for all producers to quote only the maximum prices announced by the Iron and Steel Board.[115]

Turning to still another class of pricing practices, how does one explain the following experience of the U.S. Veterans Administration? On June 5, 1955, five different companies submitted sealed bids to fill an order for 5,640 one-hundred-capsule bottles of the antibiotic tetracycline, each quoting an effective net price of $19.1884 per bottle.[116] The typical purchasing agent's reaction would be that no explanation is needed: call in the Justice Department to investigate a clear-cut case of conspiracy. But although one can never be certain, it is probable there was no direct collusion connected with this transaction. Rather, the bids were influenced by two kinds of focal points. First, there was a past history of price quotations that provided a focal point for the June 5 bids. This facet will be explored more fully in a moment. But second, the curious price of $19.1884 per bottle was arrived at through the application of a series of round number discounts to round number base prices: $19.1884 is the standard trade discount of 2 percent off $19.58, which (after rounding) is 20 percent off the wholesale price of $24.48, which in turn is 20 percent off the $30.60 price charged to retail druggists, which is 40 percent off the prevailing list price of $51.00, which in turn reflected an earlier 15 percent cut from the original list price of $60.00 per one hundred capsules.

When price reductions were effected by the oligopolistic suppliers of antibiotics, they nearly always took one of three forms: a cut to a new even-dollar price, an even percentage reduction in the old price, or rounding off the odd fraction of a cent produced when round number discounts led to a figure like $19.1884.[117]

Round number discounting is apparently not confined to the drug industry, although we have little information on how widespread it is. It was a prominent feature of plate glass mirror pricing, on which some evidence has been assembled. The Mirror Manufacturers Association published a list price booklet for various mirror sizes, and nearly all wholesale transactions were made at round number discounts — for example, 80 percent and then 10 percent off the list price.[118]

What is the significance of round number discounting and quoting as a coordinating device? When products are sold repeatedly in fairly large quantities to well-informed buyers, sellers are anxious to have some means of changing prices once in a while without precipitating a spiral of retaliatory undercutting. By reducing its price a round percentage amount, the initiator tacitly says to its rivals,

111. Thomas C. Schelling, *The Strategy of Conflict* (Cambridge: Harvard University Press, 1960), especially Chapters 2 and 3. On p. 74, Schelling anticipates the application of his ideas to price theory: "In economics the phenomena of price leadership, various kinds of nonprice competition, and perhaps even price stability itself appear amenable to an analysis that stresses the importance of tacit communication and its dependence on qualitatively identifiable and fairly unambiguous signals that can be read in the situation itself."

112. Schelling, *The Strategy of Conflict*, p. 56.

113. Schelling, *The Strategy of Conflict*, pp. 111–112.

114. John Sheahan, "Problems and Possibilities of Industrial Price Control: Postwar French Experience," *American Economic Review*, vol. 51 (June 1961), p. 352.

115. "Steel Price War Rages in Britain," *New York Times*, April 7, 1966. See also Martin Howe, "The Iron and Steel Board Pricing 1953–1967," *Scottish Journal of Political Economy*, vol. 15 (February 1968), pp. 43–67.

116. From exhibit PX-645 in the Federal Trade Commission antitrust case *In re American Cyanamid Co. et al.*, FTC Docket no. 7211 (1959).

117. Federal Trade Commission, *Economic Report on Antibiotics Manufacture* (Washington, D.C.: USGPO, June 1958), p. 190.

118. Almarin Phillips, *Market Structure, Organization and Performance* (Cambridge: Harvard University Press, 1962), pp. 177–196.

"See here, I'm not trying to touch off a war. I think the price should be lower, and I've quoted a good, clean reduction to which we all should now conform." A cut that lacks the prominence of a round number percentage discount or a new round number value is a cut without staying power. There is no magnetic attraction preventing a further change on the next transaction. And since large, well-informed buyers are adept at making prices slide downhill, it is to the interest of sellers to avoid incessant price changes. The way to do so is to ensure that any changes move to a new focal point likely to be respected by rivals.

The theory of focal points can be extended along dynamic heuristic lines. Even a price that has no particular uniqueness or compulsion in its own right may become a focal point simply by virtue of having been quoted repeatedly. The Veterans Administration tetracycline price history is again illustrative. The first VA order for tetracycline was filled by the Pfizer Company as sole bidder at a price of $19.58 less 2 percent trade discount. In the next transaction (March 1955), five firms bid $19.58, but three omitted the 2 percent discount. When all matched the winning bid of $19.1884 net in the third transaction (on June 5), that price obtained the additional prominence of unanimous acceptance. All five firms then adhered to it in responding to four further VA sealed bid requests during the following year. Extensive antitrust litigation produced no evidence that this pattern of identical bidding was the result of outright collusion, nor were meetings and explicit agreements essential under the circumstances. Given a focal point established through past experience, and given the five tetracycline sellers' reluctance to initiate a movement to lower price levels, everything needed for coordinating *tacitly* on identical bids of $19.1884 per bottle was in place.

Order Backlogs, Inventories, and Oligopolistic Coordination

A modern industrial economy exposes firms to frequent unexpected fluctuations in demand and input costs. Yet changes in production are costly. Setup, hiring, and retraining costs increase with frequent production rate alterations; productivity falls with the interruption of routines; and work force morale may suffer. As a result, firms find it undesirable to make hair-trigger changes in production schedules on the basis of noisy demand and cost change signals. They wait for stronger confirmation of shifts, and since the flow of orders is inherently erratic, time is required to distinguish a random short-term aberration from a more persistent trend. Therefore, decisions to change the level of production tend to lag changes in demand. In his pioneering studies of inventory and production cycles, Metzler found the planning period between changes in demand and changes in production to be five months on the average.[119] In the interim, at least as a first approximation, the imbalance is corrected through changes in inventories and/or order backlogs.

Of course, when production is imperfectly synchronized with demand, prices might also be manipulated to clear the market. A monopolist will want to balance the costs of price and production changes against inventory and order backlog carrying costs.[120] Too large an inventory causes excessive capital, storage, and deterioration costs; too small an inventory leads to uneconomic production lot sizes and the loss of sales when items are out of stock. Similarly, too small a backlog reduces production scheduling flexibility; too large a backlog alienates customers. Thus, when inventory levels climb sharply or order backlogs fall, an incentive to reduce price materializes; while when inventories decline or order backlogs grow, firms are tempted to choke off some of the excess demand through a price increase.

When unexpected shocks cause demand to deviate from its expected growth path, formal models of firm behavior suggest that price will vary less when firms hold inventories and order backlogs than when they are constrained to meet demand out of current production.[121] If the costs of having too small an inventory are sufficiently great, then the interpretation of inventories as facilitating production smoothing can be turned on its head: Production may actually vary more than sales, and inventories and sales may be positively correlated (as producers strive to keep inventories from falling too low).

These incentives to limit inventory and backlog fluctuations apply more or less across all industry structures — atomistic, oligopolistic, and monopolized. However, when oligopolists seek uniformly to maximize joint profits, the price (or price structure) is the subject of explicit or tacit bargaining. As we have seen, if the oligopoly has been successful in elevating prices above the competitive level, its members cannot be guided by the rule of expanding output until marginal cost rises into equality with individual firm marginal revenue, for to do so would undermine the jointly accepted price. Uncertainty concerning the position of industry demand functions and how demand is to be shared among the oligopolists under varying circumstances obscures the derivation of individual firm marginal revenue functions.[122] Oligopolists recognizing their common interest in orderly pricing are therefore likely to adopt a passive sales rule, balancing changes in inventories and production to adjust sales to demand at the accepted price and abjuring attempts to force upon the market (or withhold) output in a way that could

119. Lloyd Metzler, "Factors Governing the Length of Inventory Cycles," *Review of Economics and Statistics*, vol. 29 (February 1947), p. 7. The actual period of production, excluding planning time, appears to be much shorter for most manufactured goods. See John A. Carlson, "The Production Lag," *American Economic Review*, vol. 63 (March 1973), pp. 73–86. The lag has probably become shorter with the growing use of computerized inventory and order control systems and "just in time" schemes.

120. The formal theory of profit maximization by a firm which can hold inventories and/or order backlogs and which faces a downward sloping demand curve has been developed by Kenneth J. Arrow, Samuel Karlin, and Herbert Scarf, *Studies in the Mathematical Theory of Inventory and Production* (Stanford: Stanford University Press, 1958). Edwin S. Mills, *Price, Output, and Inventory Policy* (New York: Wiley, 1962), cites three main reasons for carrying inventories: the speculative motive (producing quantities that will not be sold in the current period in anticipation of subsequent price increases); the desire to reduce production costs by smoothing production; and the desire to avoid rejecting orders when imperfectly predictable demand turns out to be especially strong.

121. Formal models focusing on monopoly behavior are developed by Alan S. Blinder, "Inventories and Sticky Prices: More on the Microfoundations of Macroeconomics," *American Economic Review*, vol. 72 (June 1982), pp. 334–348; Richard A. Ashley and Daniel Orr, "Further Results on Inventories and Price Stickiness," *American Economic Review*, vol. 75 (December 1985), pp. 964–975; and James A. Kahn, "Inventories and the Volatility of Production," *American Economic Review*, vol. 77 (September 1987), pp. 667–679. Edward C. Prescott obtains similar results for a competitive industry. See his "Efficiency of the Natural Rate," *Journal of Political Economy*, vol. 83 (December 1985), pp. 1229–1236. Daniel F. Spulber, "Risk Sharing and Inventories," *Journal of Economic Behavior and Organization*, vol. 6 (March 1985), pp. 55–68, shows that the financial costs of fluctuations in demand are reduced when adjustments are extended beyond the manufacturer to include wholesalers and retailers.

122. A geometric elaboration on the sharing problem appears in the first edition of *Industrial Market Structure and Economic Performance*, pp. 149–152.

upset the price equilibrium.[123] Inventories also may serve as a strategic reserve, enabling firms to punish any chiseling on the agreed-upon price by flooding the market with output. When inventories play this role, we would expect a positive correlation between inventories and sales, since at lower levels of demand, excess production capacity obviates the need for inventories to demonstrate a commitment to retaliation.[124]

These motives for avoiding price adjustments are absent in atomistically structured and (rare) purely monopolized markets. Therefore, we should expect oligopolistic industries to rely more heavily than atomistic industries upon inventory and order backlog variations in adjusting to demand fluctuations, ceteris paribus, and less heavily upon price variations. Concretely, prices should be less variable and inventories and backlogs more variable over time in oligopolistic than in atomistic industries. Inventory and backlog variations should be especially pronounced in concentrated industries lacking formal arrangements (such as cartel agreements) for coordinating prices and outputs, but striving nonetheless to take into account mutual interdependence.[125]

This set of conjectures is quantitatively testable for firms that hold inventories and order backlogs. Studies of individual German and French manufacturers indicate that increases in demand lead to increases in production, but the response is weaker when demand shifts are viewed as temporary.[126] Sellers tend not to alter price in response to temporary changes in demand, but do raise prices when increases in demand are viewed as longer-lasting.[127] For U.S. manufacturers, E. S. Mills found that production changes could be predicted quite well from inventory behavior, but that the predicted correlations between price and inventory movements failed to occur.[128] Using two-digit sectoral data for the United States, Alan Blinder found that, in contrast to the predictions of a pure production-smoothing model, production varied more than sales, and that inventories and sales were either uncorrelated or positively correlated over the business cycle.[129]

Little has been done in existing empirical work to explore the role of oligopolistic interdependence. Mills rationalized the lack of correlation between price and inventories by suggesting that prices were insensitive to short-run changes in demand and inventory levels in the quasi-collusive industries he analyzed (cement, rubber tires, shoes, and southern pine lumber).[130] Victor Zarnowitz observed that the more average delivery periods (that is, the ratio of order backlogs to sales) varied, the less variable prices were; and that changes in price were more closely correlated with changes in order backlogs than with changes in wages in the relatively unconcentrated paper and textile industry groups, while changes in wages were by far the more powerful explanatory variable in the relatively concentrated primary metals, machinery, and fabricated metal products groups.[131] Julio Rotemberg and Garth Saloner observed that the degree to which inventories vary with sales increases with industry concentration, suggesting that strategic considerations begin to dominate the benefits of production smoothing more, the greater the degree of oligopolistic interdependence.[132]

Industry case studies also reveal that the ability and willingness to absorb short-run demand shocks through inventory variation have been important in maintaining stable price structures. In the copper industry, for example, companies operating in the atomistically structured scrap-smelting segment typically refuse to hold large inventories; when scrap supplies are high, the output of smelters exercises a depressing influence on prices. However, during the period in which U.S. firms dominated primary copper production,[133] Anaconda, Kennecott, and Phelps Dodge, controlling about 75 percent of total U.S. production, repeatedly shored up the price structure by taking strong inventory positions.[134] For example, during the early 1960s, the Anglo-American producers held 100,000 tons of copper off the world market to stabilize prices at thirty-one cents per pound over a two-year period.[135]

Similar inventory behavior was observable in aluminum before dramatic changes in demand and supply conditions during the 1970s and 1980s transformed the industry's structure and reduced producer control over prices.[136]

123. Of course, this passive policy with respect to price may be accompanied by measures to increase one's share of the market through such nonprice measures as personal selling, advertising, and innovation. See Chapters 15 and 16 infra.

124. Julio J. Rotemberg and Garth Saloner, "The Cyclical Behavior of Strategic Reserves," *Quarterly Journal of Economics*, vol. 104 (February 1989), pp. 73–98.

125. See George A. Hay, "Production, Price, and Inventory Theory," *American Economic Review*, vol. 60 (September 1970), pp. 531–545; "The Dynamics of Firm Behavior under Alternative Cost Structures," *American Economic Review*, vol. 62 (June 1972), pp. 403–413; and Rotemberg and Saloner, "The Cyclical Behavior," pp. 73–99.

126. In surveys of company behavior during the 1970s and 1980s, between 20 and 40 percent of French and German firms typically reported inventories above or below "optimal" levels. Heinz Koenig and Marc Nerlove, "Price Flexibility, Inventory Behavior, and Production Responses," in Walter P. Heller, R. M. Starr, and D. A. Starrett, eds., *Equilibrium Analysis — Essays in Honor of Kenneth J. Arrow*, vol. 2 (New York: Cambridge University Press, 1986), pp. 179–218. During the first quarter of 1987, nearly 50 percent of U.S. firms holding inventories appraised them as too large or too small. Joseph W. Duncan, Marc Nerlove, and David R. Ross, "Expectations, Plans and Realizations of U.S. Manufacturing Firms: Results from the New Dun & Bradstreet Survey," paper presented at the 18th Biennial Conference of the Center for International Research on Economic Surveys, Zurich, Switzerland, September 8–10, 1987.

127. These results are reported for German firms by Seiichi Kawasaki, John McMillan, and Klaus F. Zimmermann, "Inventories and Price Inflexibility," *Econometrica*, vol. 51 (May 1983), pp. 599–610; and for French and German firms by Koenig and Nerlove, "Price Flexibility," pp. 179–218.

128. Mills, *Price, Output, and Inventory Policy*, supra note 120, pp. 124–125 and 258–259. See also M. D. Steuer and A. P. Budd, "Price and Output Decisions of Firms — A Critique of E. S. Mills' Theory," *Manchester School of Economics and Social Studies*, vol. 36 (May 1968), pp. 1–25.

129. Alan S. Blinder, "Can the Production Smoothing Model of Inventory Behavior Be Saved?" *Quarterly Journal of Economics*, vol. 101 (August 1986), pp. 431–453. Blinder's study focused on

twenty sectors, evenly split between durable and nondurable goods manufacturing, for 1959 to 1981. Similar results were obtained by Kenneth D. West, "A Variance Bounds Test of the Linear Quadratic Inventory Model," *Journal of Political Economy*, vol. 94 (April 1986), pp. 374–401. Support for the production smoothing model is reported using data for the automobile industry (1965–1979) by Olivier J. Blanchard, "The Production and Inventory Behavior of the American Automobile Industry," *Journal of Political Economy*, vol. 91 (June 1983), pp. 365–400.

130. Mills, *Price, Output, and Inventory Policy*, supra note 120, pp. 124–125 and 258–259.

131. Victor Zarnowitz, "Unfilled Orders, Price Changes, and Business Fluctuations," *Review of Economics and Statistics*, vol. 44 (November 1962), pp. 380–381 and 390–391.

132. Rotemberg and Saloner, "The Cyclical Behavior," supra note 124, pp. 73–98.

133. Concentration among U.S. copper producers remains high. However, the ability of U.S. firms to control the world market has disappeared. While the largest four firms controlled 60 percent of noncommunist world primary copper production in 1947, that share had fallen to 17 percent in 1974. Margaret Slade, *An Econometric Model of the U.S. Copper and Aluminum Industries* (New York: Garland, 1984), Chapter III.

134. Kaplan et al., *Pricing in Big Business*, supra note 90, pp. 176–181; and Raymond F. Mikesell, *The World Copper Industry: Structure and Economic Analysis* (Baltimore: Johns Hopkins University Press, 1979), especially Chapters 1, 4, and 6.

135. Thomas O'Hanlon, "The Perilous Prosperity of Anaconda," *Fortune*, May 1966, pp. 121 and 235.

136. Merton J. Peck, ed., *The World Aluminum Industry in a Changing Energy Era* (Washington: Resources for the Future, 1988). As of 1953, six firms controlled 87 percent of world primary aluminum production. Slade, *An Econometric Model*, p. 118. By 1981, their share had fallen to 53 percent (Peck, *World Aluminum*, p. 8). The jump in energy prices during the 1970s put most production facilities in the United States, Japan, and Europe at a significant cost disadvantage. The years since then have seen a shift in capacity to low-cost countries, with a concomitant change in the roster of rival firms. See also Steven K. Holloway, *The Aluminum Multinationals and the Bauxite Cartel* (New York: St. Martin's Press, 1988).

When sales fell off sharply because of the Great Depression, Alcoa in 1931 accumulated inventories equal to six months' output before closing down any of its plants. Although other world producers also found themselves holding large stocks, prices remained firm. As Aluminium Ltd. of Canada noted in its 1932 annual report, "World stocks of aluminium are not excessively large. They are in firm hands and do not weigh unduly upon the world market."[137] Following World War II, short-term declines in the demand for aluminum ingot were again absorbed primarily through inventory accumulation rather than price cuts or production shutdown.[138] As new entry into ingot production occurred, pricing discipline broke down in 1971, but inventory buildups again contributed to the avoidance of price declines during the unusually sharp recession of 1975.[139] The mere desire to avoid disruptive price cutting was not, however, a sufficient explanation for the willingness of aluminum producers to accept enormous inventory fluctuations. High fixed costs and the wide gap between marginal costs (six cents per pound in 1948) and price (fifteen cents) made it worthwhile to incur substantial inventory carrying charges in anticipation of future profitable sales when demand recovered.[140] And of course, aluminum ingots are not subject to physical or style deterioration. Inventories of fabricated aluminum products were allowed to vary much less than ingot inventories during the period of dominance by the Big Six producers, partly because of obsolescence risks and partly because the margin between price and variable cost is smaller. It is probable that the palpably weaker pricing discipline seen in many fabricated aluminum product lines can be traced in part to this inventory policy difference as well as to the large number of fabricating firms.

Markham's study of the rayon industry prior to 1950 exhibits both similarities and differences.[141] Short-term fluctuations in demand were regularly absorbed through inventory variations and not production adjustments or price changes. Only when sales declines persisted for several months were cutbacks in production initiated, while price changes were resisted even longer. When demand continued to decline, however, industry discipline was not strong enough to ward off downward price revisions, partly because profit margins fell sharply at below-capacity production rates and partly because smaller firms were unwilling to bear the continued burden of high inventory carrying costs. Still, these recession-inspired price cuts were not nearly as detrimental to industry profits as they might have been in other industries, for they permitted rayon producers to win back a more than proportionate volume of business from substitute fibers whose prices were highly flexible downward during recessions.

Other industries have been less successful in avoiding price competition through their inventory policies. The accumulation of especially large gasoline stocks in local markets has often triggered price wars, despite efforts by the major integrated producers to keep excess supplies out of the hands of firms prone to price cutting.[142] Producers in the relatively unconcentrated textiles industry characteristically accumulate finished goods stocks to smooth out production during slack periods, but when demand continues to be weak and carrying charges mount, they tend to dispose of their inventories at distress prices.[143] And in a large retail department store studied by Cyert and March, price changes were the usual means of keeping inventories in check.[144]

Thus, by letting inventories and order backlogs fluctuate, oligopolistic producers can adjust to short-term demand shifts in a way that minimizes the threat to industry pricing discipline. However, such a strategy carries the concomitant risk that under stress, the fainthearted will dump excessive stocks at disruptive prices. At the same time, large stocks can act as a threat to enforce pricing discipline: when cheating is detected, the dumping of inventories leads to a sobering price war. This inventory response has an advantage over maintaining excess capacity as a commitment to retaliation, since the period of retaliation is limited by inventory depletion, and stock depletion signals that cooperation can once again be viable. Thus, an inventory-based threat against cheating combines the characteristics of the tit-for-tat strategy that has proved so effective in experimental games:[145] The threat is unleashed only when someone cheats, when it is readily and rationally provoked, and when it permits the industry to quickly "forgive" the cheater and return to the former equilibrium.[146] Such a strategy may explain why a number of empirical studies have found that, far from smoothing production, inventory holding has led to more variability in production than in sales.[147] Much more research is needed on this facet of oligopoly behavior.

Conclusion

In sum, there are several means by which oligopolists can coordinate their pricing decisions to approximate the maximization of joint profits. Collusion, although under increasing world-wide antitrust fire and by no means simple to implement, has not vanished. Price leadership facilitates monopolistic pricing when follower firms are willing to cooperate with the leader's decisions. Mutual adherence to full-cost pricing rules is not apt to yield profits as high as under ideal collusive

137. M. J. Peck, *Competition in the Aluminum Industry* (Cambridge: Harvard University Press, 1962), p. 88, n. 6.

138. Peck, *Competition in the Aluminum Industry*, pp. 83–96.

139. See the U.S. Council on Wage and Price Stability staff report, *Aluminum Prices: 1974–75* (Washington: USGPO, September 1976), pp. 132–137 and 151–154.

140. Peck, *Competition in the Aluminum Industry*, p. 88. Because of rapid energy price increases during the 1970s, the ratio of marginal to total unit costs rose sharply, making producers more willing to cut back production in the face of a slump. See pp. 27–30 and 128–130.

141. Jesse W. Markham, *Competition in the Rayon Industry* (Cambridge: Harvard University Press, 1952), Chapters 7 and 8.

142. See Ralph Cassady, Jr., *Price Warfare in Business Competition* (East Lansing: Michigan State University Bureau of Business and Economic Research, 1963), p. 52; Learned and Ellsworth, *Gasoline Pricing in Ohio*, supra note 86, pp. 33–48; and Robert T. Masson and Fred C. Allvine, "Strategy and Structure: Majors, Independents, and Prices of Gasoline in Local Markets," in R. T. Masson and P. D. Qualls, eds., *Essays on Industrial Organization in Honor of Joe S. Bain* (Cambridge: Ballinger, 1976), pp. 155–180.

143. See Weiss, *Economics and American Industry*, supra note 52, p. 143.

144. Cyert and March, *A Behavioral Theory of the Firm*, supra note 97, p. 140.

145. See Chapter 6, pp. 216–219.

146. Julio J. Rotemberg and Garth Saloner, "Strategic Inventories and the Excess Volatility of Production," Massachusetts Institute of Technology, Alfred P. Sloan School of Management, Working Paper 1650–85, April 1985. The use of inventories as a strategic weapon is also discussed in Lanny Arvan, "Some Examples of Dynamic Cournot Duopoly with Inventory," *Rand Journal of Economics*, vol. 16 (Winter 1985), pp. 569–579; Roger Ware, "Inventory Holding as a Strategic Weapon to Deter Entry," *Economica*, vol. 52 (February 1985), pp. 93–101; and in Chapter 10 infra.

147. See Michael Lovell, "Determinants of Inventory Investment," in *Models of Income Determination, Studies in Income and Wealth*, vol. 28 (Princeton: National Bureau of Economic Research, 1964), pp. 177–244; A. S. Blinder, "Retail Inventory Behavior and Business Fluctuations," *Brookings Papers on Economic Activity*, (1981, no. 2), pp. 443–505; and references in Rotemberg and Saloner, "Strategic Inventories." Moheb Ghali, "Inventories, Production Smoothing and the Accelerator: Some Empirical Evidence," *Quarterly Journal of Economics*, vol. 88 (February 1974), pp. 149–157, finds empirical support for production smoothing.

conditions, but it helps keep them higher than they would be under a regime of independent competitive conduct. Firms also can reduce the likelihood of competitive price cutting and achieve cooperative outcomes in a noncooperative environment by setting and keeping prices at focal point values. A complement to all of these coordination methods is the use of inventories and order backlogs to absorb demand fluctuations rather than continually attempting to equate marginal cost with price or marginal revenue.

Appendix

Cartel Pricing When Costs Differ

(a) Market Sharing

The two firms agree to split the market evenly. Hence, if industry demand is

$$(7A.1) \qquad P = 200 - .02(q_1 + q_2),$$

then the demand facing either firm is

$$(7A.2) \qquad P_i = 200 - .04q_i,$$

with marginal revenue $MR = 200 - .08q_i$. We suppose initially that Firm 2 has the same cost function as Firm 1, $TC_1 = 50,000 + 20q_1 + .01q_1^2$, yielding marginal cost of $MC_1 = 20 + .02q_1$. If each firm independently seeks to maximize profit by equating marginal cost to marginal revenue, each will charge the same price and produce the same number of units:

$$(7A.3) \qquad \begin{aligned} 200 - .08q_i &= 20 + .02q_i \\ q_i = (200-20)/(.02+.08) &= 1800. \end{aligned}$$

Substituting into (7A.2), we obtain

$$(7A.4) \qquad P_i = 200 - .04(1800) = 128.$$

Suppose, however, that Firm 2 has $TC_2 = 20,000 + 40q_2 + .02q_2^2$, implying that $MC_2 = 40 + .04q_2$. Now Firm 2 finds a higher price more attractive:

$$(7A.5) \qquad \begin{aligned} 200 - .08q_2 &= 40 + .04q_2 \\ q_2 = (200-40)/(.04+.08) &= 1333 \\ P_2 = 200 - .04(1333) &= 147. \end{aligned}$$

At Firm 1's preferred price of \$128,

$$(7A.5a) \quad \pi_1 = 128(1800) - 50,000 - 20(1800) - .01(1800)^2 = 112,000;$$

and

$$(7A.5b) \quad \pi_2 = 128(1800) - 20,000 - 40(1800) - .02(1800)^2 = 73,600.$$

At Firm 2's preferred price of \$147,

$$(7A.5c) \quad \pi_1 = 147(1333) - 50,000 - 20(1333) - .01(1333)^2 = 101,522;$$

and

$$(7A.5d) \quad \pi_2 = 147(1333) - 20,000 - 40(1333) - .02(1333)^2 = 87,093.$$

(b) Rationalizing Production

Rationalizing production across firms with different costs requires (a) setting total output; (b) selecting the corresponding market-clearing price; (c) allocating output among the participating firms; and (d) allocating profits among the participants.

To explore the algebra underlying Figure 7.3, we assume as before that the *total* market demand equation is $P = 200 - .02(q_1 + q_2)$. To maximize joint profit, we form the combined profit function:

(7A.6)
$$\pi_c = P(q_1 + q_2) - TC_1 - TC_2$$
$$= [200 - .02(q_1 + q_2)] (q_1 + q_2)$$
$$- (50,000 + 20 q_1 + .02 q_1^2) - (20,000 + 40 q_1 + .02 q_2^2).$$

Collecting terms, we obtain:

(7A.7)
$$\pi_c = 180 q_1 + 160 q_2 - .03 q_1^2 - .04 q_2^2$$
$$- .04 q_1 q_2 - 70,000.$$

To find the first order conditions for maximum profits, we differentiate with respect to q_1 and q_2, obtaining:

(7A.8a)
$$\frac{\partial \pi_c}{\partial q_1} = 180 - .06 q_1 - .04 q_2 = 0; \text{ and}$$

(7A.8b)
$$\frac{\partial \pi_c}{\partial q_2} = 160 - .04 q_1 - .08 q_2 = 0.$$

These are solved simultaneously, yielding the profit-maximizing values:

$$q_1{}^* = 2,500, \text{ and}$$
$$q_2{}^* = 750.$$

Returning to the market demand function, we find the equilibrium price to be:

(7A.9)
$$P = 200 - .02 (2500 + 750) = \$135.$$

If each firm sells its own output at this price,

(7A.10a)
$$\pi_1 = 135(2500) - 50,000 - 20(2500) - .02(2500)^2$$
$$= \$175,000; \text{ and}$$

(7A.10b)
$$\pi_2 = 135(750) - 20,000 - 40(750) - .02(750)^2$$
$$= \$40,000.$$

If Firm 2 could be shut down without continuing fixed costs of $20,000 per period, an alternative formulation using only Firm 1's production can be considered:

(7A.11)
$$\pi = q_1 (200 - .02 q_1) - 50,000 - 20 q_1 - .02 q_1^2.$$

The first order condition is:

(7A.12)
$$\frac{d\pi}{dq_1} = 180 - .06 q_1 = 0;$$

which solves for output $q_1 = 3,000$ units and $P = \$140$. Plugging these values into equation (7A.11), we find the profit with only Firm 1 producing to be $220,000.

Conditions Limiting Oligopolistic Coordination

While oligopolists have incentives to cooperate in maintaining prices above the competitive level, there are also divisive forces. As we saw in Chapter 7, the chief challenges to coordination are finding mutually agreeable prices, mitigating the incentives for and impact of cheating, and doing both in an environment in which most, if not all, overt collusive agreements are illegal. In this chapter we examine several conditions that complicate industry members' information processing and create a wedge between sellers' common interests and the interests of individual firms. They include the presence of significant numbers of sellers, heterogeneity of products and distribution channels, the interaction of high overhead costs with adverse business conditions, lumpiness and infrequency of product purchases, opportunities for secret price cutting, and the unraveling of an industry's informal social structure.[1]

Number and Size Distribution of Sellers

One structural dimension with an obvious influence on coordination is the number and size distribution of sellers. Generally, the more sellers a market includes, the more difficult it is to maintain prices above cost, other things being equal. This is so for three main reasons.[2]

First, as the number of sellers increases and the share of industry output supplied by a representative firm decreases, individual producers are increasingly apt to ignore the effect of their price and output decisions on rival reactions and the overall level of prices. As a very crude general rule, if evenly matched firms supply homogeneous products in a well-defined market, they are likely to begin ignoring their influence on price when their number exceeds ten or twelve. It is more difficult to generalize when the size distribution of sellers is highly skewed. Then pricing discipline depends critically upon several variables (to be analyzed subsequently) affecting the rate at which smaller firms can expand their sales through price cutting.

Second, as the number of sellers increases, so also does the probability that at least one will be a maverick, pursuing an independent, aggressive pricing policy. And if market shares are sensitive to price differentials, even one such maverick of appreciable size can make it hard for other firms to hold prices near monopoly levels. As M. J. Peck observed, "[O]ne Henry Ford could introduce a new price policy, whereas fifteen sellers with conservative styles of business might produce results akin to the most 'static' of monopolies."[3]

1. Note that a number of these factors are identified in the guidelines the Federal Trade Commission and Antitrust Division of the Department of Justice follow in evaluating the competitive effects of proposed mergers. U.S. Department of Justice, *Merger Guidelines* (Washington: June 14, 1984), Section 3.4.

2. A fourth reason applies in auction markets, such as construction, where firms must bid on unique projects for which costs cannot be projected with certainty. In such situations, firms generally tack on a premium to their bids to avoid the "winner's curse," the risk that a winning low bid reflects too low an estimate of costs that will have to be absorbed. As the number of bidders rises, the size of the premium the winner can extract decreases.

For a survey of the theoretical developments, see R. Preston McAfee and John McMillan, "Auctions and Bidding," *Journal of Economic Literature*, vol. 25 (June 1987), pp. 699–738. The impact of the winner's curse on bidding for offshore oil leases and construction contracts has been measured by Kenneth Hendricks, Robert H. Porter, and Bryan Boudreau, "Information, Returns, and Bidding Behavior in OCS Auctions: 1954–1969," *Journal of Industrial Economics*, vol. 35 (June 1987), pp. 517–542; and Stuart E. Thiel, "Some Evidence on the Winner's Curse," *American Economic Review*, vol. 78 (December 1988), pp. 884–895.

3. M. J. Peck, *Competition in the Aluminum Industry: 1945–58* (Cambridge: Harvard University Press, 1961), p. 207.

Finally, different sellers are likely to have at least slightly divergent notions about the most advantageous price. Especially with homogeneous products, these conflicting views must be reconciled if joint profits are to be held near the potential maximum. The coordination problem increases with the number of firms. Some economists have suggested that the difficulty of coordination rises nearly exponentially with the number of firms.[4] Their reasoning is as follows. Unless there is a central coordinating agency (such as a cartel sales bureau or a well-accepted price leader), each firm must tacitly or overtly communicate with every other firm over a *modus vivendi* in pricing. The number of two-way communication flows required is given by the combinatorial expression $N(N-1)/2$. With two sellers, the number of channels is one; with six, it rises to fifteen, and so on. Breakdown of any single channel can touch off independent actions threatening industry discipline. Although oligopolists may escape the implications of the formula by building in redundancies and creating central coordination institutions, the difficulty of coordination undoubtedly does increase more than proportionately with the number of sellers.

One point merits further consideration here. Does the presence of numerous small firms operating on the fringe of an otherwise oligopolistic industry affect pricing behavior and profits? Oligopolists who take their interdependence seriously are not apt to counter aggressive moves by fringe firms contributing only a tiny fraction of industry output, since even a doubling of the fringe's sales has a modest proportionate effect on their own sales. They are especially unlikely to respond if the retaliatory cut must apply across the board because of anti-discrimination laws, or because all buyers will demand any price reduction offered to selected customers. Recognizing this, fringe producers will not be deterred from initiating independent pricing actions by fear of retaliation. But over the short run of a year or two, the impact of their actions depends upon the relationship between their production capacity and total industry output.

When demand is strong, fringe members will be able to produce at capacity and sell their output at the price preferred by the industry leaders, or at some mutually accepted price differential. But if a recession occurs, they may find themselves operating well below desired levels at the high market prices the oligopolistic leaders are attempting to maintain. To remedy this, they will bid for additional orders at reduced prices. This pattern has been observed repeatedly in cement, rayon, tin cans, gasoline, steel, and fabricated aluminum products, among others.[5] The reaction of the leading firms depends then upon the magnitude of the fringe's incursions. If the fringe's capacity is small relative to total industry output, so that the shift in market shares is less than approximately 10 percent of total industry output, the leading producers are apt to ignore the incursions and persevere in their efforts to hold the price line. But when larger market share transfers appear imminent, defensive price reductions by the leading firms will normally begin. Whether price cutting will proceed further depends mainly upon three things: the expected duration of the demand slump, the degree to which cost constraints inhibit deeper price shading by the smaller firms, and the responsiveness of fringe producers to the educational message implicit in the leading firms' retaliatory price moves. In general, oligopoly price structure breakdowns are more likely, the higher the proportion of industry capacity in the hands of competitive fringe producers and the more industry leaders find themselves departing from desired operating levels at posted prices.

Product Heterogeneity

Product homogeneity implies that the offerings of rival sellers are alike in all significant physical and subjective respects, so that they are virtually perfect substitutes in the minds of consumers. With perfect homogeneity, there remains only one dimension along which rivalrous actions and counteractions can take place: price. In such cases, oligopolists have a particularly easy task of coordinating their behavior, for they must coordinate along only the one dimension. When products are heterogeneously differentiated, the terms of rivalry become multidimensional, and the coordination problem grows in complexity by leaps and bounds.

Four broad product heterogeneity classes, arrayed in order of increasing dimensionality, can be identified.[6] First, there may be stable interfirm differences in real or subjectively imputed product quality sufficient to require price differentials in market equilibrium. The coordination problem here is two-dimensional, involving both the price level and the amount of the differential. Judging from the amount of conflict over gasoline price differentials between major brand and independent retailers, it is probably more than twice as difficult to coordinate on these two magnitudes together than it is to reach tacit agreements concerning only a uniform price.[7] Second, when sellers are located at varying distances from buyers (that is, there is spatial differentiation) and transportation costs are relatively high, a very complex price structure may be required. Further analysis of this problem is deferred to Chapter 13. Third, product qualities may be dynamically unstable, as in fashion goods industries and fields subject to rapid technological change. Each product change alters the relative competitive position of every producer and requires either a new set of pricing decisions or the acceptance of a rigid, historically based price structure not likely to maximize profits. Fourth, complex products such as airplanes, electrical power generators, buildings, and nonstandardized personal services are sold on a custom-made basis. When no two orders are ever exactly alike or when there is leeway for deviations from the

4. See Almarin Phillips, *Market Structure, Organization and Performance* (Cambridge: Harvard University Press, 1962), pp. 29–30; and Oliver E. Williamson, "A Dynamic Theory of Interfirm Behavior," *Quarterly Journal of Economics*, vol. 79 (November 1965), p. 600.

5. See Samuel M. Loescher, *Imperfect Collusion in the Cement Industry* (Cambridge: Harvard University Press, 1959), pp. 120 and 293; Jesse W. Markham, *Competition in the Rayon Industry* (Cambridge: Harvard University Press, 1952), pp. 78 and 127–136; James W. McKie, *Tin Cans and Tin Plate* (Cambridge: Harvard University Press, 1959), pp. 217–218; Edmund P. Learned and Catherine C. Ellsworth, *Gasoline Pricing in Ohio* (Boston: Harvard Business School Division of Research, 1959), pp. 108 and 149;

and Peck, *Competition in the Aluminum Industry*, supra note 3, pp. 66–72. More recent pricing studies of comparable thoroughness are scarce, in part because the "case study" approach has fallen from favor among economists and partly because government agencies have been less diligent in subpoenaing the necessary data.

6. Compare Richard E. Caves and Peter J. Williamson, "What Is Product Differentiation, *Really?*" *Journal of Industrial Economics*, vol. 34 (December 1985), pp. 113–132, who identify five dimensions of product heterogeneity.

7. See Learned and Ellsworth, *Gasoline Pricing in Ohio*, pp. 133 and 149; and Leonard W. Weiss, *Economics and American Industry* (New York: Wiley, 1961), pp. 411–412.

buyer's product specifications in hundreds of particulars, tacit coordination on joint profit-maximizing strategies becomes extremely difficult to maintain.

Several examples serve to illustrate the range of coordination difficulties associated with static and dynamic product heterogeneity. Perhaps most extreme is the problem of aerospace firms bidding to secure government contracts for the development of new, technologically advanced weapon systems and space vehicles. The choices of government decision makers are necessarily multidimensional. What is sought is the best combination of qualitative design features, time of availability, and expected development, production, and operating costs. A virtual infinity of potential design feature combinations is open to bidders, and each firm's judgment concerning the quality-cost-time tradeoffs most likely to win approval from the customer (itself a bureaucratic maze with internally conflicting preferences) invariably differs from that of its rivals. Effective tacit coordination of bid details under these circumstances is literally impossible, and interfirm rivalry to win attractive new development program contracts has been vigorously independent even when only two firms were bidding.[8] Because of this, and given certain other characteristics unique to the environment of advanced weapons and space systems development, competition for new research and development program contracts often has more desirable behavioral effects when the number of rivals is small than when there are numerous bidders.[9]

For nearly a century, the heavy electrical equipment industry has exhibited the pricing patterns associated with complex, multidimensionally differentiated products. During the closing decades of the nineteenth century, spirited competition prevailed with respect to both product quality and price in the electric traction motor, induction motor, and polyphase generator lines, even though there were only two sellers vying for many of the orders. Harold Passer isolated two main reasons for the strenuous duopolistic rivalry in traction motors: complexity of the product and rapid technological change. Regarding the complexity of railway motors, he observed:

When a product possesses many features and when the possible variations in these features are numerous, it is hard to see how agreement on the product could be tacit. And the process of reaching explicit agreement on the product would have been lengthy and elaborate, if possible at all.[10]

On the other hand, his analysis shows that after an initial period of settling, price competition was mild and stable in the electric arc lamp and incandescent lamp fields, where the products were simpler and more readily standardized.[11]

Contrasting behavioral patterns in static product lines with those in technologically dynamic ones, he observed further:

It is probable that continuous and unpredictable change in the technology of a product and its manufacture introduces the element of uncertainty which accounts for the competitive rather than the monopolistic behavior of the oligopolist. . . . If technological change proceeded at a slower pace . . . the traditional duopoly case, with a fairly homogeneous product and a recognition of mutual dependence, may have resulted. Product competition based on a static technology, in which product choices are made from a perfectly well-known and unchanging set of alternatives, may have an effect on duopolistic behavior different from that based on a rapidly advancing technology.[12]

Of the two disruptive influences stressed by Passer, complexity of the product seems to have been more important, for in the absence of explicit collusive agreements, there were periods of intense price competition in the electrical generator field despite a maturing of the product technology. We recall from Chapter 7 that to facilitate standardized pricing, General Electric developed and published an elaborate pricing formula book with which industry price analysts could build up the prices for thousands of generator component parts into an overall book price. Yet because the typical generator order is so complex, there was considerable opportunity for alternative interpretations of customer specifications, and parties to the conspiracies of the 1950s found mere agreement to follow book pricing techniques an insufficient foundation for effective collusion. They felt compelled to meet and compare calculations before submitting bids. When the meetings were suspended because some company refused to participate, the poor coordination of price calculations was one element leading to sharp price reductions, although as we shall see shortly, there were other contributing factors.

Automobile tires present a different set of pricing coordination problems. Tires are fairly simple products and the industry is quite concentrated.[13] One might expect a high degree of tacit cooperation. Yet the price structure in tires has been described as "chaotic"; tire manufacturers have been subjected to "an almost uninterrupted series of price buffetings"; and profits have been lower on the average than those of other industries with comparable market structures.[14] One apparent reason is the great variety of manufacturers' and private-label grades, complicated by the welter of conflicting sales claims, labels, guarantees, and prices. As of the early 1980s, 2,500 auto tire sizes and styles were available for sale in the United States.[15] A uniform quality grading program administered by the National Highway Traffic Safety Administration has had little effect in standardizing the array of possibilities confronting consumers.[16]

8. For a fascinating account of the two-firm TFX aircraft competition, see Richard A. Smith, *Corporations in Crisis* (Garden City: Doubleday, 1963), Chapters 9 and 10; and Robert F. Coulam, *Illusions of Choice: The F-111 and the Problem of Weapons Acquisition Reform* (Princeton: Princeton University Press, 1977), Chapter II. On another vigorous two-firm competition, see Robert W. Drewes, *The Air Force and the Great Engine War* (Washington: National Defense University Press, 1987).

9. See F. M. Scherer, *The Weapons Acquisition Process: Economic Incentives* (Boston: Harvard Business School Division of Research, 1964), pp. 44–49.

10. Harold C. Passer, *The Electrical Manufacturers: 1875–1900* (Cambridge: Harvard University Press, 1953), p. 263.

11. Passer, *The Electrical Manufacturers*, pp. 62 and 161–162.

12. Passer, *The Electrical Manufacturers*, pp. 352–353. See also Ralph G. M. Sultan, *Pricing in the Electrical Oligopoly*, vol. 1 (Boston: Harvard Business School Division of Research, 1974), pp. 28–36; and vol. 2 (1975), Chapter 12.

13. It is difficult to derive an accurate measure of industry concentration. In 1982, four firms accounted for 67 percent of domestic automobile tire shipments. Since then, there have been a number of mergers among leading tire manufacturers, reflecting massive overcapacity in the late 1970s and early 1980s. The tire market has also become global in scope. See "The Traumatic Tire Business," *New York Times*, July 5, 1985, p. D1; and "Global Fight in the Tire Business," *New York Times*, March 10, 1988, p. D1.

14. A. D. H. Kaplan, Joel B. Dirlam, and R. F. Lanzillotti, *Pricing in Big Business: A Case Approach* (Washington: Brookings Institution, 1958), p. 280. Between 1974 and 1977, the industry's operating income averaged 8.4 percent of assets—consistently less than the median for all manufacturing corporations. Federal Trade Commission, *Statistical Report: Annual Line of Business Report* (Washington, various years).

15. "Tire-Rating System Reliability Disputed, Is Suspended by U.S.," *New York Times*, February 3, 1983, p. A1.

16. The need for quality grading standards was suggested by a Federal Trade Commission staff report. *Economic Report on the Manufacture and Distribution of Automotive Tires* (Washington: USGPO, 1966). The grading program, which includes traction and temperature resistance as well as mileage ratings, went into effect in 1979–1980. The mileage ratings program was dropped in 1983, but reinstated under court order in 1985. See "The 324 Ways to Grade a Tire," *Business Week*, February 19, 1972, pp. 22–23; and "Grading of Tires Resumes," *New York Times*, May 4, 1985, p. A52.

Four brief examples round out the picture. The value of crude petroleum varies with gravity (that is, the proportion of heavier components), sulfur content, and access to low-cost transportation. The price premium or discount that a particular crude oil can command changes over time — for example, with heavier crudes selling at less of a discount when unusually cold winter weather stimulates heating oil demand and with advantageously located crudes (such as those from Libya and Nigeria) selling at a higher premium when the ocean tanker market is tight. Inability to reach and continuously revise their agreement on how large such price differentials should be was a significant source of discontent among OPEC cartel members during the 1980s. The traditionally tight pricing discipline of American steel producers was upset during the late 1960s and mid-1970s by disparate handling of extra charges and especially by the propensity of some firms to sell first-quality steel strip at the much lower prices normally charged for secondary or defective output.[17] In railroading, the Grand Trunk Line provided circuitous and hence slower service than its three major rivals between Chicago and New York City during the 1880s and 1890s. It could attract a substantial volume of perishable commodities like dressed meat only by charging lower rates. Disputes over the size of the rate differential led to two rate wars, in which rate levels fell by roughly 50 percent.[18] And despite a long record of price uniformity among standard-brand cigarettes, the introduction of new king-size and filter-tip cigarettes by the leading producers during the 1950s was followed by several years of widely varying differentials before all firms came together on a uniform price structure.[19]

In sum, when the offerings of rival producers differ over numerous dimensions, the problem of coordinating on a common price structure is much more complex than it is with homogeneous products. Other things being equal, cooperation to maintain high collective profits is less likely to be successful, the more heterogeneous products are. However, some aspects of product differentiation work in the opposite direction. When sellers can build strong brand loyalties, or when economies of scale in product differentiation raise barriers to the entry of new competition, profits may be higher than they would be with homogeneous products. The net effect of these opposing forces depends in a complex way upon the specific character of product differentiation and the degree to which other influences conducive to coordinated pricing operate. The type of heterogeneity most likely to disrupt pricing discipline appears to be the multidimensionality of a product's technical features.

The Extent of Product Heterogeneity in Concentrated Markets

How widespread is product heterogeneity as a structural condition limiting interfirm coordination? To gain insight into this question, an analysis was made of the seventy-six nonmiscellaneous U.S. manufacturing industry groups with four-firm concentration ratios of 60 or more in 1982. Those seventy-six industries presumably have structures most conducive to oligopolistic pricing. Each industry was given a score of from 1 to 4 on four attributes: multidimensionality of its products, the rate of change in product technology, the degree to which there are physical differences in the quality of rival products, and the degree to which consumers subjectively impute quality differences to products as a result of such influences as advertising. (No attempt was made to take geographic or spatial differentiation into account.) With respect to product dimensionality, the following system of scores was used:

1. Standardized technical configuration
2. Some configuration options
3. Complex configuration options
4. Very complex configuration options

On the rate of technological change, physical product difference, and subjective quality difference attributes, the scores varied from 1 for "virtually none" to 4 for "great", with "modest" and "considerable" categories intervening.

The results were as follows. The mean score was 1.87, suggesting a net tendency more toward homogeneity than heterogeneity. Fourteen of the seventy-six industries received a score of 1 on all four attributes, connoting virtually complete product homogeneity both statically and dynamically. Twenty-four industries, or 51 percent of the total, had no score higher than 2, while 32 percent had at least two scores of 1 and none higher than 2. Forty-nine percent of the industries had at least one score higher than 2, indicating a considerable degree of heterogeneity on at least one attribute. There were seventy-one scores of either 3 or 4 altogether. Twenty-five industries had scores of 3 or 4 on the product dimensionality criterion, which probably affects pricing coordination with special force.

Although the analysis is subject to judgmental errors, it seems reasonable to draw three broad conclusions. First, few manufacturing industries conform tightly to the polar case of perfectly homogeneous oligopoly. Second, somewhere between 33 and 50 percent of the concentrated industries supply products heterogeneous enough to pose fairly difficult obstacles to tacit coordination. Third, the predominant pattern in oligopolistically structured manufacturing industries is a modest degree of product heterogeneity engendering slight to moderate coordination problems.

Methods of Coordinating Heterogeneous Product Pricing

Even modest product heterogeneity might undermine pricing discipline were it not for certain devices that facilitate coordination. One considered in Chapter 7 is focal point pricing. Price lining is especially important in consumer goods fields such as clothing, where style changes occur frequently. Adherence to focal points permits sellers to avoid price competition that changes in product design and image would otherwise precipitate. But even when direct price competition is minimized, active quality competition may continue as firms attempt to offer the most attractive qualitative features consistent with a fixed, inflexible price.

Independent pricing behavior may also be headed off through the negotiation of standardization agreements on product features that would seriously complicate tacit collusion if left uncoordinated. In the steel industry, for example, explicit agreements were at one time concluded to secure uniform treatment of extras — that is, complex differences in finish, temper, packaging, and so on.[20]

17. Robert Lamb, "The Mystery of Steel Prices," *Fortune*, March 1977, pp. 158–160.

18. Paul W. MacAvoy, *The Economic Effects of Regulation: The Trunkline Railroad Cartels and the ICC Before 1900* (Cambridge: MIT Press, 1965), pp. 129–135.

19. R. B. Tennant, "The Cigarette Industry," in Walter Adams, ed., *The Structure of American Industry*, 3rd ed. (New York: Macmillan, 1961), pp. 376–377.

20. Cf. p. 236 supra.

Although the layperson might think that cement is cement, cement trade associations found it necessary to negotiate standardization agreements in order to discourage rivalry based upon claims of superior quality. They also published for the guidance of members standardized terms of sale, cash discounts, package charges, refunds for returned bags, and bin-testing cost rules. Differences in any of these categories could undermine a carefully cultivated system of direct and tacit price agreements.[21] Still another common practice (until it was condemned in a series of antitrust decisions) was the maintenance of basing point pricing systems to overcome the intricate problem of quoting transportation charges in industries where such costs constitute a major fraction of the total delivered product price. The basing point system will be examined more fully in Chapter 13.

Strategic Groups

When, as is common, firms in an industry differ from one another along a number of dimensions—such as diversity of product line, degree of vertical integration, quantity and content of advertising, number and types of distribution channels, reputation for product quality, and investments in research and development—they may be viewed as forming strategic groups or clusters based on the degree to which they follow similar strategies.[22] Sellers' prices and profits depend inter alia on the extent of cooperation within their group and the interactions among groups.

In Chapter 7, we saw how differences in the structure of costs inhibits agreement among firms. One case in which cost differences arise is when some firms integrate vertically, and hence are concerned with the impact of pricing and production on downstream and/or upstream stages—a concern not shared by single-stage rivals. Also, a single product firm may view the market differently than will a conglomerate, balancing rates of return and other interests across a host of products.[23] It is often difficult to find common ground when a manufacturer that has patiently built a reputation for quality through advertising and an extensive service organization meets a rival selling heavily discounted merchandise through store brands.

To the extent that an industry includes groups of firms choosing different strategies, it becomes harder for members to reconcile their different preferences for prices, rates of product innovation, expenditures on advertising, and the like. At the same time, the existence of strategic groups can also lead to intraindustry mobility barriers[24] increasing the ability of firms *within* groups to coordinate pricing decisions (by reducing the number of immediate rivals) and offering firms protected niches against aggressive rivals. It is relatively easy to start up a gourmet soup business, or even to supply supermarkets with private-label canned soup. However, it has proved virtually impossible to make a dent in Campbell's lock on the branded canned soup market. Once established, large firm market shares may be relatively easy to defend against smaller rivals, and thus leading firms may be able to pursue cooperative pricing strategies even when there are numerous industry members. Where reputational advantages, trademarks, or established customer relationships make it difficult for other firms to duplicate an innovating firm's marketing strategy, smaller firms may be able to differentiate themselves sufficiently from larger competitors to eliminate profit disadvantages normally associated with sacrificing economies of scale and scope.[25]

Thus, product heterogeneity greatly complicates the way industry members interact with one another. While this inhibits the ability of the industry as a whole to coordinate prices and production, it may permit individual firms or clusters of firms to exploit monopoly power relative to certain classes of buyers.

Dynamic Implications of Cost Structures

The ability of oligopolists to cooperate with one another is also affected in a variety of ways by cost conditions. We saw at the start of Chapter 7 that differences in marginal and average costs across firms increase the difficulty of agreeing on price and market shares. In this section, we examine some dynamic implications of industrial cost structures.

First, consider the role (to be explored further in Chapter 17) of technological innovations. The more rapidly producers' cost functions are altered through technical change and the more unevenly those changes are diffused throughout the industry, the more likely there will be conflict regarding the pricing choices. For example, National Steel, after installing new and more efficient continuous strip mills during the 1930s, became an active price cutter, pulling other steel makers with higher costs along.[26] In the 1970s and 1980s, low-cost minimills played a similar price structure-disrupting role. Between 1971 and 1984, steel product lines in which minimills competed actively had an average constant-dollar price *decline* of 24 percent, while the products requiring technologies not yet mastered by the minimills experienced real price decreases of only 2.6 percent.[27]

The introduction of the mechanized window glass production technique around the turn of the century touched off a struggle for survival in which prices were driven below cost even for the new and more efficient machine methods. After stability was restored through cartel agreements, a second episode of price warfare between glass makers using new continuous process techniques and those employing obsolete methods arose during the early 1930s.[28] The spread of float glass techniques beginning in the late 1960s does not appear to have had a similar impact, in part because the industry structure had already become tightly oligopolistic and partly because the technology was covered during its early phases by

21. Loescher, *Imperfect Collusion*, supra note 5, pp. 134–135. On similar credit term and delivery method agreements in the gypsum board industry, see "Busting a Trust: Gypsum Case Unravels Alleged Price-Fix Plan," *Wall Street Journal*, October 3, 1975, p. 16.

22. Howard H. Newman, "Strategic Groups and the Structure-Performance Relationship," *Review of Economics and Statistics*, vol. 60 (August 1978), pp. 417–427; and Michael E. Porter, "The Structure within Industries and Companies' Performance," *Review of Economics and Statistics*, vol. 61 (May 1979), pp. 214–227. The term "strategic group" was coined by Michael S. Hunt, "Competition in the Major Home Appliance Industry, 1960–1970," Ph.D. diss., Harvard University, 1972, Chapter 2. However, similar ideas can be found in earlier work by individuals concerned with strategic behavior, for example, Alfred D. Chandler, *Strategy and Structure: Chapters in the History of the Industrial Enterprise* (Cambridge: MIT Press, 1962); and Alfred P. Sloan, *My Years with General Motors* (Garden City, NY: Doubleday, 1964), p. 63. For a discussion of the industry structural characteristics that facilitate strategic heterogeneity, see Richard E. Caves and Thomas A. Pugel, *Intraindustry Differences in Conduct and Performance: Viable Strategies in U.S. Manufacturing Industries* (New York: New York University Monograph Series in Financial Economics, 1980).

23. See p. 312 and Chapter 10 infra for discussions of rivalry when the level of diversification varies across firms.

24. Richard E. Caves and Michael E. Porter, "From Entry Barriers to Mobility Barriers: Conjectural Decisions and Contrived Deterrence to New Competition," *Quarterly Journal of Economics*, vol. 91 (May 1977), pp. 241–261.

25. Michael E. Porter, "The Structure Within Industries," supra note 22, pp. 214–227; and Ralph M. Bradburd and David R. Ross, "Can Small Firms Find and Defend Strategic Niches? A Test of the Porter Hypothesis," *Review of Economics and Statistics*, vol. 71 (May 1989), pp. 258–262.

26. See Weiss, *Economics and American Industry*, supra note 7, pp. 296–297.

27. Donald F. Barnett and Robert W. Crandall, *Up from the Ashes: The Rise of the Steel Minimill in the United States* (Washington: Brookings Institution, 1986), pp. 32–35.

28. G. W. Stocking and M. W. Watkins, *Monopoly and Free Enterprise* (New York: Twentieth Century Fund, 1951), pp. 121–126.

Figure 8.1
Low Fixed Cost Firm A

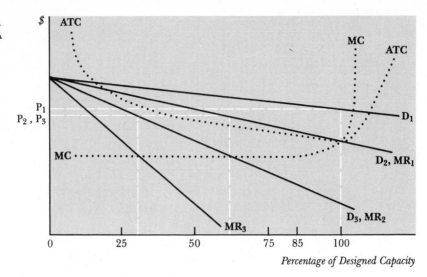

strong Pilkington patents. In the sanitary pottery fixtures industry, conflicts associated with the introduction of tunnel kilns (replacing more costly beehive oven processes) were in part responsible for the failure of producers to eliminate widespread price cutting despite repeated attempts to reach collusive agreements.[29] And in the ocean shipping industry, the introduction of highly efficient containerships during the 1960s undermined long-standing agreements and triggered a wave of price competition.[30]

However, our main focus in this section will be on the interaction of fluctuations in demand with cost structures. There is reason to believe that industries characterized by high overhead costs are particularly susceptible to pricing discipline breakdowns when a cyclical or secular decline in demand forces member firms to operate well below designed plant capacity. This tendency has been especially marked in industries with heavy investments in developed natural resource deposits (such as petroleum extraction and underground coal mining) and those using highly capital intensive production processes (such as railroads, petroleum refining, chemicals, steel, aluminum, cement, glass, and papermaking).[31] It may well spread to other industries as costs traditionally seen as variable take on the characteristics of overhead.[32]

To understand this phenomenon, two questions must be answered. First, why do oligopolists with high fixed costs have stronger incentives to cut prices when demand declines than firms with low fixed costs? And second, if price cutting does break out, how does the cost structure affect the extent to which it will be carried?

We proceed using diagrams comparing two different (not necessarily competing) firms: Firm A, with average fixed costs amounting to 15 percent of average total cost ATC at 85 percent of designed capacity output (Figure 8.1), and Firm B, with average fixed costs equaling 50 percent of ATC at 85 percent of designed capacity output (Figure 8.2). For both firms, marginal cost is assumed to be constant up to 85 percent of designed capacity output, after which it rises sharply.

Figure 8.2
High Fixed Cost Firm B

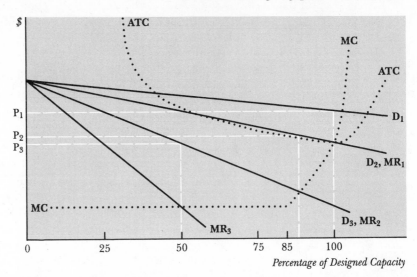

This is consistent with most of the statistical evidence on short-run cost functions.[33] To ensure comparability, average total cost is equal in the two cases at designed capacity output (i.e. at minimum ATC). Identical linear constant-shares demand curves reflecting three stages of the business cycle—prosperity (D_1), a modest recession (D_2), and a severe recession (D_3)—are assumed for the two firms. To keep the drawings as simple as possible, each lower demand curve has twice the slope of its higher neighbor, permitting the marginal revenue curve of one to serve also as a demand curve under more depressed conditions. It follows that the demand curves all have the same elasticity at any given price.[34]

Suppose each firm is operating at 100 percent of designed capacity with demand D_1, maximizing profits under the assumption of rival price matching (and hence constant market shares) by equating MR_1 with MC, and selling at the highly profitable price OP_1. Now a mild recession shifts demand to D_2. For low fixed-cost Firm A, the optimal reaction is a substantial reduction in output to

29. Cf. Phillips, *Market Structure*, supra note 4, pp. 175–176.

30. "Cooling the Rate War on the North Atlantic," *Business Week*, April 29, 1972, pp. 48–52. For background, see Robert Larner, "Public Policy in the Ocean Freight Industry," in Almarin Phillips, ed., *Promoting Competition in Regulated Markets* (Washington: Brookings Institution, 1975), pp. 113–130.

31. In an econometric analysis of business units drawn from the PIMS dataset (see Chapter 11) during the mid-1970s, a time of significant demand fluctuations, Peter R. Cowley found that the level of capacity utilization had a statistically significant positive effect on seller price-cost margins only for the more capital intensive businesses. "Business Margins and Buyer/Seller Power," *Review of Economics and Statistics*, vol. 68 (May 1986), pp. 335–336.

32. Increasingly, firms are coming to regard skilled, experi-

enced workers as assets; and, as noted below, the ratio of production workers to all workers in manufacturing continues to decline. The more payroll comes to be seen as a fixed cost, the greater the incentive to maintain sales in the face of falling demand. See Robert S. Kaplan, "Yesterday's Accounting Undermines Production," *Harvard Business Review*, vol. 62 (July-August 1984), pp. 95–101; and William J. Bruns and Kaplan, *Accounting and Management: Field Study Perspectives* (Cambridge: Harvard Business School, 1987).

33. For surveys of the literature, see J. Johnston, *Statistical Cost Analysis* (New York: McGraw-Hill, 1960), Chapters 4 and 5; and A. A. Walters, "Production and Cost Functions: An Econometric Survey," *Econometrica*, vol. 31 (January-April 1963), pp. 39–51.

34. See Chapter 7, note 9.

about 65 percent of capacity, where MR_2 and MC are equated, and a modest reduction in price to OP_2. Firm A still earns an appreciable, albeit smaller, profit margin. High fixed-cost Firm B's marginal cost situation dictates a reduction in output only to 90 percent of capacity, but a sharp reduction in the profit-maximizing price to OP_2. The previously substantial profit margin is nearly eliminated. Thus, when demand falls below levels that will sustain capacity output, the profit-maximizing enterprise with high fixed costs cuts prices more sharply and suffers more severe erosion of profits than a similarly inclined firm with low fixed costs. This result is quite general, since marginal costs must fall more steeply with reduced output from the point at which ATC is minimized for a firm with higher fixed and lower marginal costs at below-capacity production levels.

We turn the screw tighter now, hitting the firms with a recession that drives demand from D_2 to D_3. For Firm A, since both MR_2 and MR_3 (derived from demand curves with the same elasticity at given prices) cut MC at the same level, no change in price is induced. For Firm B, with a slight curvature in MC in the neighborhood of its intersection with MR_2, a small price reduction follows. Thus, when marginal costs are roughly constant at below-capacity operation, as statistical studies suggest, and when demand curves shift isoelastically, the intensification of an already depressed situation motivates little or no price reduction by oligopolists pursuing joint profit maximization.[35] The full brunt of the recession is borne in reduced output and hence employment of labor and other inputs.

Yet it is precisely when business conditions really turn sour that price cutting runs rampant among oligopolists with high fixed costs. Something more than the marginal conditions for profit maximization must affect producer behavior. The key factor is the relative attractiveness of chiseling on joint profit-maximizing prices at different stages of the business cycle. We saw at the start of Chapter 7 that firms have an incentive to expand output from the cooperative or constant-shares level as long as (1) the prevailing price exceeds marginal cost and (2) the output expansion is limited so as to avoid retaliation, thus permitting an individual firm to move off the constant-shares demand curve along a "rival price constant" curve. Figures 8.1 and 8.2 reveal that for output below 100 percent of designed capacity, the gap between price and marginal cost is greater for high fixed-cost Firm B. And for both firms, the marginal gain from chiseling (the change in output times the difference between the chiseled price, assuming rival prices constant, and the new marginal cost) is greater at recession demands (D_2 and D_3) than during prosperity (D_1).[36]

More compelling in the calculus of managers and owners is their asymmetrical valuation of profit and loss. With the shift in demand from D_2 to D_3, both firms show losses: OP_3 is below ATC at the profit-maximizing output. Firm A's loss is relatively small, by the inflated standards of textbook diagramming—about 5 percent of costs. But Firm B, with its high fixed costs spread over a restricted volume of output, shows an enormous deficit—over 25 percent of costs. With a milder, perhaps more realistic leftward demand shift, Firm B would incur substantial losses, while Firm A would remain in the black. These losses are likely to confront Firm B, or some similarly situated high fixed-cost operator in B's industry, with a financial crisis. Unable to meet interest and dividend payments out of profits, the firm's decision-making horizon shortens.[37] Its managers, with their employment on the line, and owners, with the prospect of bankruptcy looming, turn all their attention to immediate remedies, ignoring the risks of diminished profits from weakened industry discipline in the uncertain future. By chiseling on the joint profit-maximizing price OP_3, operation at higher capacity levels would be possible, overhead could be spread over more units of output, and losses would be reduced or even (if capacity utilization could be increased to 90 percent) eliminated. Some producers in Firm B's straits will choose to take the chance. As Hall and Hitch summarized their interviews with British businessmen during the 1930s, "Usually one entrepreneur is overcome by panic: 'there is always one fool who cuts'; and the rest must follow."[38] Unless they are imbued with a strong sense of group loyalty, the rest will indeed follow sooner or later as price cutters make inroads on their sales, exacerbating the problem of covering overhead costs, and the end result will be a general decline in price away from the joint profit-maximizing level OP_3.

Assuming the persistence of depressed demand state D_3, the limit to which proliferating noncooperative price cutting can be carried is where price falls uniformly to the level of marginal cost. Here again, we find an important difference between industries with high and those with low fixed costs. Price cutting will be checked at higher price levels when marginal costs are high and fixed costs are low than when marginal costs are low and fixed costs are high. The industry characterized by high fixed costs suffers more when demand is depressed both because of stronger inducements to price cutting and a lower floor to price declines.

From this analytic conclusion we are tempted to generalize: The higher fixed costs are, relative to total costs, the more prone an industry is to serious pricing discipline breakdowns during recessions. Unfortunately, the problem is more complicated. Recognizing the temptations confronting them, firms in high fixed-cost industries seem to exercise extraordinary restraint in their pricing actions. In 1982, for example, British breweries responded to the sharpest fall in output since the Great Depression by raising prices.[39] When tacit restraint fails, firms in high fixed-cost industries have an unusually high propensity to scurry into formal collusive agreements. According to Alfred Neal, when the number of sellers is small:

> . . . each seller realizes that if every other seller follows his price, all will make smaller profits or greater losses and no permanent cure to depressed demand

35. If the shifts in demand cause elasticities to change symmetrically, equiproportional price changes will result. This case is ignored here because the changes follow from demand conditions, not from differences in the cost structure, which is our present concern.

36. It is possible to conceive cases in which the marginal incentives for chiseling are at least as great in booms as in recessions, for example, industries with chronic excess capacity, or industries where marginal costs do not rise steeply at designed capacity and where demand becomes more inelastic during booms. See Julio J. Rotemberg and Garth Saloner, "A Supergame-Theoretic Model of Price Wars during Booms," *American Economic Review*, vol. 76 (June 1986), 390–407.

37. For a discussion of the influence of company financial structure on strategic behavior, see James A. Brander and Tracy R.

Lewis, "Oligopoly and Financial Structure: The Limited Liability Effect," *American Economic Review*, vol. 76 (December 1986), pp. 956–970.

38. R. L. Hall and Charles J. Hitch, "Price Theory and Business Behaviour," *Oxford Economic Papers*, vol. 2 (May 1939), p. 25. See also Bjarke Fog, *Industrial Pricing Policies: An Analysis of Pricing Policies of Danish Manufactures*, trans. by I. E. Bailey (Amsterdam: North-Holland, 1960), p. 34; and Alfred C. Neal, *Industrial Concentration and Price Inflexibility* (Washington: American Council on Public Affairs, 1942), p. 87.

39. Keith Cowling presents this and several other examples drawn from Great Britain's recession of the early 1980s. "Excess Capacity and the Degree of Collusion: Oligopoly Behaviour in the Slump," *Manchester School of Economic and Social Studies*, vol. 51 (December 1983), pp. 341–359.

will be achieved, since only the most ruthless price war will eliminate enough capacity to improve the price situation. Under such circumstances, only the most sanguine or the most foolhardy seller would start an open price war (though no one would be averse to making secret concessions up to the point where an open price war threatened to start).[40]

Yet when several firms engage in this sort of brinkmanship, some are likely to lose their footing, pulling the rest along, unless an explicit collusive agreement can be reached quickly to halt the slide. We conclude then that the probability of pricing discipline breakdowns increases with the burden of fixed costs borne by sellers, ceteris paribus, but that recognition of this danger may stimulate institutional adaptations nullifying the tendency.

It is hard to predict a priori the outcome of this tug-of-war between the incentive to look out for one's own short-run interests only and the incentive to cooperate. Some examples show the range of observed behavior.

Railroading is the case par excellence of an industry with high fixed costs and an historical propensity toward pricing discipline breakdowns when competition is left unfettered. The capital of railroads in 1914 has been estimated at 574 percent of gross operating revenues, compared to 94 percent for manufacturing companies.[41] The heavy component of fixed charges for capital sunk in roadbeds, rails, terminals, and rolling stock was accompanied by low short-run marginal cost for adding an extra freight car or two onto an already scheduled train. Because of these cost conditions, rivalry among railroads in the closing decades of the nineteenth century was often marked by oscillation between price warfare and collusive agreements. This pattern was most striking on the key Chicago-New York routes.[42] During the early 1870s, only the New York Central and the Pennsylvania offered through service between Chicago and New York City. By concluding explicit price-fixing agreements, they managed to maintain eastbound traffic rates at roughly fifty-six cents per hundredweight. However, when the Baltimore & Ohio completed its route in 1874, it refused to join the agreement; price shading developed, and the grain rate fell to forty cents that year, twenty cents in 1876, and fifteen cents in 1877. Some shipments moved east for as little as 7.5¢ per hundredweight during the summer of 1879 — a rate that may not even have covered immediate marginal costs, although the evidence is inconclusive. Between 1880 and 1886, the Joint Executive Committee cartel — initially the New York Central, Pennsylvania, B & O, and Grand Trunk lines — succeeded in raising rates to thirty cents per hundredweight under favorable conditions. But the agreements broke down repeatedly until the whole rate structure was subjected to effective regulation by the Interstate Commerce Commission. Robert Porter found that the duration of railroad price wars and the level of prices during favorable periods was quite sensitive to the number of firms in the cartel, which varied from three to five during this period.[43] The New York-Chicago lines were perhaps extreme in the duration and intensity of their competitive price cutting, since entry was important and there were several rail-water interlines vying for business. However, similar price wars of shorter duration occurred on many other segments of the U.S. railroad network.[44]

Turning now to the manufacturing sector, *rayon* manufacturing is a capital-intensive industry whose pricing behavior before 1950 has been analyzed thoroughly.[45] Producers had short-run cost relationships similar to Figure 8.2, with fixed costs amounting to one-third of total unit cost at capacity output, and with average total cost rising to 125 percent of its minimum value for operation at one-half capacity. (In Figure 8.2, the comparable figure is 138 percent.) The first reaction of producers to a decline in demand was typically to sustain capacity production and build up inventories. If the recession persisted, the larger firms restricted output to maintain the price level, but smaller firms tended to shade prices to keep their plants busy. This approach was successful in preserving a semblance of pricing discipline in mild recessions. But if operations fell much below 75 percent of capacity, profit margins were wiped out completely; and after this point, attempts to maintain stable prices proved futile.[46] In the depths of the early 1930s depression, when industry leaders American Viscose and du Pont were operating at only 55 percent of capacity, a formal price-fixing agreement was instituted. Elaborate steps were taken to implement it, but financial pressures on individual firms were so strong that the agreement broke down. Even the largest producers were violating it through off-list selling.[47]

The *cement* industry has a cost structure similar to rayon's.[48] Though the product is essentially homogeneous and the number of sellers in most markets is relatively small, the industry has experienced repeated pricing discipline breakdowns when demand declined generally or locally. Recognizing their inability to collude tacitly with any great success, U.S. cement makers entered into a series of price-fixing arrangements, but these tended to collapse under financial stress. From 1930 to 1932, unfettered price cutting drove down the average realized price per barrel by 30 percent while unit overhead costs were rising.[49] An antitrust judgment in 1948 deprived the industry of its principal collusive device—the basing point system. Strong demand kept prices on the upswing during the early 1950s; but excess capacity began to appear after 1956, precipitating price shading.[50] U.S. industry profits were hard hit by the sharp recessions of 1975 and 1982 through 1983.

40. Neal, *Industrial Concentration*, supra note 38, p. 77.

41. Eliot Jones, "Is Competition in Industry Ruinous?" *Quarterly Journal of Economics*, vol. 34 (May 1920), pp. 484–485. Even in 1987, by which time right-of-way abandonments, depreciation, and inflation had eroded the railroads' asset values, the assets of twelve railroad companies on *Fortune*'s list of the fifty largest transportation companies were 188 percent of revenues, compared to 91 percent for the 500 largest industrial corporations.

42. See MacAvoy, *The Economic Effects*, supra note 18; L. F. Lee and Robert H. Porter, "Switching Regression Models with Imperfect Sample Separation Information—With an Application on Cartel Stability," *Econometrica*, vol. 52 (March 1984), pp. 391–418; and Robert H. Porter, "A Study of Cartel Stability: The Joint Executive Committee, 1880–1886," *Bell Journal of Economics*, vol. 14 (Autumn 1983), pp. 301–314.

43. Robert H. Porter, "On the Incidence and Duration of Price Wars," *Journal of Industrial Economics*, vol. 33 (June 1985), pp. 415–426.

44. For a skeptical view of the extent of rate warfare, see C. Emery Troxel, *Economics of Transportation* (New York: Rinehart, 1955), pp. 428 and 657; and Thomas S. Ulen, "The Interstate Commerce Commission as a Cartel Manager," Ph.D. diss. chapter, Stanford University, 1977.

45. See Markham, *Competition in the Rayon Industry*, supra note 5, pp. 103, 130, and 150–153.

46. Markham, *Competition in the Rayon Industry*, p. 161.

47. Markham, *Competition in the Rayon Industry*, pp. 76–77 and 135–156. The pricing of other synthetic fibers appears to have been more disciplined in the 1950s and 1960s, but during the 1970s industry discipline deteriorated under a heavy burden of excess capacity. "The Losses Pile Up in Synthetic Fibers," *Business Week*, December 6, 1976, pp. 46–47. On a cartel formed to reduce the excess capacity, see R. W. Shaw and S. A. Shaw, "Excess Capacity and Rationalisation in the West European Synthetic Fibres Industry," *Journal of Industrial Economics*, vol. 32 (December 1983), pp. 149–166; and Organisation for Economic Cooperation and Development, *Competition Policy in OECD Countries: 1984–1985* (Paris: 1987), pp. 251–252.

48. Loescher, *Imperfect Collusion*, supra note 5, pp. 59–72.

49. Loescher, *Imperfect Collusion*, Chapters 4 and 5, especially pp. 181–185.

50. Federal Trade Commission, *Economic Report on Mergers and Vertical Integration in the Cement Industry* (Washington: USGPO, April 1966), pp. 16–17.

The *steel* industry is not unlike rayon and cement. Its products are fairly homogeneous, once the "extras" problem is solved; and the fixed costs associated with its capital-intensive, vertically integrated production processes are relatively high. When account is taken of geographic market bounds, the American steel industry is less concentrated than either cement or rayon. Yet up to 1968 and except for some episodes during the 1929-1938 depression, it was more successful than either cement or rayon in avoiding widespread price deterioration, even when operating at less than 65 percent of capacity between 1958 and 1962. The main explanation for this record apparently lies in the extraordinary respect U.S. industry members exhibited for their mutual interdependence. A price structure that permitted producers to avoid outright losses unless output fell below 40 percent of capacity was a contributing factor[51] — at least until import competition forced a general reduction of price-cost margins beginning in the late 1960s. Even then, the downward rigidity of its price structure during the recession of 1975 stood in remarkable contrast to that of European steel makers.[52]

High fixed and low marginal costs also played a part in the *heavy electrical equipment* industry's apparent inability to avoid price warfare without formal collaboration in times of depressed demand. Demand for electrical equipment is cyclical — either feast or famine. In addition to carrying fixed plant and equipment costs, producers maintained staffs of skilled design and production engineers they were reluctant to disperse, and so a significant fraction of labor costs was also viewed as fixed.[53] These conditions contributed to the rivalry that on occasion drove prices as low as 40 percent of book values.

Finally, we consider the *petroleum* extraction and refining industries, which have their own special fixed-cost problems. Much extraction capital is invested in holes in the ground — sunk cost in every sense of the word. Once a well is drilled, the marginal cost of drawing oil from it is for many years practically nil. Refineries are capital-intensive, and to complicate matters, many products emerge from the distillation towers as joint products or by-products with a marginal cost that is either low or indeterminate. Tacit collusion in the sale of refined products is complicated by disagreements over retail price differentials between major and independent brands and by the perishability (through physical deterioration) of local gasoline inventories. Frequent gasoline price wars at the retail and wholesale level have been the result. At the crude oil extraction stage, prices in the United States fell from an average of $1.19 per barrel in 1930 to sixty-five cents per barrel in 1931, descending to twenty-five cents per barrel in some territories during the summer of 1931 as the onset of the Great Depression and the opening up of new fields coincided. However, U.S. crude oil prices exhibited remarkable downward rigidity between 1945 and 1973, mainly because of import restrictions (after 1959) and the cartelized prorationing system, under which Texas producers in particular were required under state and federal laws to restrict their supply when demand fell. Between 1973 and the early 1980s, Saudi Arabia, Kuwait, and Libya, with cash inflows from oil sales exceeding their capacity to spend, played a similar role in supporting OPEC cartel prices at ten to twenty times marginal production costs despite episodes of excess capacity.[54] However, by the mid-1980s, OPEC members found themselves with demand of only fifteen to eighteen million barrels per day against capacity of thirty million barrels. Chiseling became rampant and prices plunged from $34 per barrel in 1982 to as low as $7.50 in June 1986.

To summarize, some industries (like American steel until 1968 and world oil until 1984) have been quite successful in minimizing rivalrous pricing despite high fixed and low variable costs and depressed demand; some have been successful only when the financial pressures on their members were not strong; and some have been unsuccessful even after engaging in collusion. The explanation for these differences appears to lie largely in the presence or absence of other conditions conducive to cooperative pricing. When other factors such as the size distribution of firms, the degree of product homogeneity, the extent of acceptance accorded the price leader, the ability and willingness of producers to carry sizable inventories, and deftness in avoiding antitrust action are favorable, pricing discipline may be maintained despite substantial fixed costs. When they are unfavorable, a heavy fixed cost burden makes independent pricing during business downturns all the more probable. The net balance among these tendencies can only be ascertained through statistical analysis—a task we defer to Chapter 11. To anticipate a fragment of the results, there is evidence that high capital intensity leads on average to lower profit returns, presumably reflecting more fragile pricing discipline. However, the profit-depressing effect of capital intensity is mitigated to some extent when market concentration is particularly high.[55]

To the extent that governments learn to use the tools of macroeconomic stabilization successfully, the interaction of fixed costs with depressed business conditions could become a less important cause of pricing discipline breakdowns. But when recessions do materialize, or when shifts in demand adverse to particular industries occur, fixed costs present a pressing problem to business firms. Whether this problem will become more important depends upon which of two conflicting trends dominates. On the one hand, there is a tendency for payroll costs to take on the characteristics of fixed costs. This is so partly because the work force composition is shifting away from direct laborers and operatives, whose numbers can be varied with demand, to overhead-type employees like managers, salespeople, clerks, and engineers, who are hired to meet longer-term needs and are not laid off as readily in response to short-run production declines. The ratio of production workers to all workers in manufacturing industries declined from 82 percent in 1939 to 76 percent in 1954 and 65 percent in 1982.[56] In addition, unions are increasingly demanding and winning greater job security for direct laborers. This raises the fixed component of cost structures and makes it difficult for producers to absorb demand shocks by maintaining prices and restricting

51. See U.S. Senate, Subcommittee on Antitrust and Monopoly, report no. 1387, *Administered Prices: Steel* (Washington: USGPO, 1958), pp. 45–51.

52. See the U.S. Council on Wage and Price Stability staff report, *A Study of Steel Prices* (Washington: USGPO, 1975), pp. 39–75.

53. See Sultan, *Pricing in the Electrical Oligopoly*, supra note 12, vol. 1, p. 205, note 8.

54. On the history of foreign and domestic crude oil cartels, see Morris A. Adelman, *The World Petroleum Market* (Baltimore: Johns Hopkins, 1972); U.S. Senate, Committee on Foreign Relations, report, *Multinational Oil Corporations and U.S. Foreign Policy* (Wash-

ington: USGPO, 1975); and John M. Blair, *The Control of Oil* (New York: Pantheon, 1976).

55. Robert D. Buzzell and Bradley T. Gale, *The PIMS Principles: Linking Strategy to Performance* (New York: Free Press, 1987), Chapter 7; and David J. Ravenscraft, "Structure-Profit Relationships at the Line of Business and Industry Level," *Review of Economics and Statistics*, vol. 65 (February 1983), pp. 22–31.

56. Computed from the relevant Censuses of Manufactures, vol. I. Employees in central offices and other auxiliary establishments are included in the denominator, with the figure for 1939 estimated from the 1954 value. See also supra note 32.

output.[57] At the same time, there is a trend toward vertical disintegration, in which firms substitute market purchases for in-house production.[58] This has the effect of turning fixed payroll costs into variable materials costs. Also, the maturing and homogenization of entrepreneurial attitudes may exert an influence in the direction of firmer pricing discipline.

A Digression on Cutthroat Competition

Thus far, we have implicitly assumed that when a fall in demand induces price competition among oligopolists, society is the gainer, since monopolistic profit margins are reduced and prices are brought into closer proximity to marginal cost. Nevertheless, this judgment is not universally accepted. It is sometimes argued that competition among oligopolists burdened with high fixed costs has a tendency to become "cutthroat" or "ruinous," and that it should be restrained through price-fixing agreements or mergers. This view was widespread around the turn of the century, but even in recent years it has been propounded by a few American economists and by many prominent scholars abroad.[59]

The cutthroat competition issue has two principal branches. One pertains to industries with chronic excess capacity because superior substitutes have appeared on the scene, or as the aftermath of some unique episode such as a surge of wartime orders or the abandonment of tariff protection. The other branch concerns industries subjected to sharp cyclical or random fluctuations, with vigorous price competition breaking out during troughs of the cycle. Each is worth considering carefully, although in so doing we must depart from the main thread of our analysis.

The Sick Industry Problem

First we have the case of the secularly declining or "sick" industry. Railroading, coal (up to the 1950s in America and 1970s in Europe), civilian ship building, Belgian and Swedish steel, better-quality leather shoes, some branches of agriculture, aluminum in Japan after the 1973 energy shock, and (during the 1920s and 1930s in America and through the 1970s in many western European nations) textile manufacturing are well-known examples.[60] As this range of illustrations suggests, it is not necessary that the market structure be oligopolistic; sick industry problems can occur in atomistically structured fields. There are two chief prerequisites: capacity substantially in excess of current and probable future demands and rigidities that retard the reallocation of capital and/or labor toward growing industries. Then unless there is some artificial restraint such as government price regulation (as in railroading) or tightly knit cartel agreements, competition is likely to drive prices down to levels that yield investors much less than a normal return on their capital. When firms' cost structures include a high proportion of fixed costs, this profitless existence can continue for years or even (as in railroading and coal mining) for decades, since producers find it preferable to continue operation and cover at least their (relatively modest) variable costs than to shut down and have their investments wiped out completely. The burden of stagnating demand may also fall upon the industry's labor force, for if workers are unable or unwilling to acquire new skills and/or migrate to new regions offering more abundant job opportunities, unemployment will be acute and wage rates may fall to low levels. Capitalists almost surely suffer, then, in a sick industry, and laborers may suffer if they lack alternative employment opportunities.

It is standard practice for the afflicted, and frequently also for well-meaning outsiders, to urge that such industries be granted immunity from the rigors of competition to ease the pain of adjustment. Through private- or government-sponsored price-fixing programs, prices can be held at levels that let investors realize a "fair" return on their capital and permit the payment of "just" wages to laborers during the adjustment period. These proposals have a certain amount of appeal on equity grounds. But abandoning the discipline of competition carries a distinct cost. However painful, losses serve the economic function of driving out surplus and inefficient production capacity and compelling the reallocation of resources into more remunerative lines. Monopolistic price-fixing schemes protect the inefficient producers who, under competitive pressure, would exit first from an industry. They almost always retard the adjustment of physical capacity to reduced demand, although it is less clear that labor mobility is necessarily enhanced by downward pressure on wages. In some cases, price-fixing agreements, by permitting positive monopoly profits to be gained, have actually caused capacity to be increased in industries confronted with stagnating demand, aggravating the resource misallocation problem.[61] This perverse effect is particularly likely in cartels allocating numerous members' sales and profit shares in proportion to physical capacity, for by building additional redundant capacity, a firm can increase its profits.[62] For example, efforts by the West European synthetic fibers industry during the late 1970s to rationalize production in the face of weakening demand led to market share gains for the least efficient and financially shakiest firms.[63]

57. The striking cyclical price flexibility observed in Japanese industries may be due to the fact that workers in the larger Japanese enterprises have virtual lifetime tenure in their jobs. Therefore, most labor costs (with the exception of bonus payments) tend to be fixed. See James C. Abegglen, *The Japanese Factory* (Glencoe: Free Press, 1958), pp. 11–25; and Walter Galenson and Konosuke Odaka, "The Japanese Labor Market," in Hugh Patrick and Henry Rosovsky, eds., *Asia's New Giant* (Washington: Brookings Institution, 1976), pp. 613–627.

58. See p. 96 supra.

59. For various views, see Spurgeon Bell, "Fixed Costs and Market Price," *Quarterly Journal of Economics*, vol. 32 (May 1918), pp. 507–524; Jones, "Is Competition in Industry Ruinous?" supra note 41; J. M. Clark, *Studies in the Economics of Overhead Costs* (Chicago: University of Chicago Press, 1923), especially pp. 434–450; L. G. Reynolds, "Cutthroat Competition," *American Economic Review*, vol. 30 (December 1940), pp. 736–747; Loescher, *Imperfect Collusion*, supra note 5 , pp. 191–199; Phillips, *Market Structure*, supra note 4 , pp. 16–19 and 221–242; Romney Robinson, "The Economics of Disequilibrium Price," *Quarterly Journal of Economics*, vol. 75 (May 1961), pp. 199–233; Kojiro Niino, "The Logic of Excessive Competition," *Kobe University Economic Review*, vol. 8 (1962), pp. 51–62; Edgar Salin, "Kartellverbot und Konzentration," *Kyklos*, vol. 16 (1963), pp. 177–202; G. B.

Richardson, "The Pricing of Heavy Electrical Equipment: Competition or Agreement?" *Bulletin of the Oxford University Institute of Economics and Statistics*, vol. 28 (May 1966) pp. 73–92; Sultan, *Pricing in the Electrical Oligopoly*, supra note 12 , vol. 1, Chapter II, and vol. 2, pp. 286–298; Alfred E. Kahn, *The Economics of Regulation*, vol. II (New York: Wiley, 1971), pp. 172–220; Alfred S. Eichner, "Monopoly, the Emergence of Oligopoly and the Case of Sugar Refining: A Reply," *Journal of Law & Economics,* vol. 14 (October 1971), pp. 521–527; M. J. Peck, Richard C. Levin, and Akira Goto, "Picking Losers: Public Policy Toward Declining Industries in Japan," in John B. Shoven, ed., *Government Policy Towards Industry in the United States and Japan* (New York: Cambridge University Press, 1988), pp. 195–239; and Joseph L. Bower, *When Markets Quake: The Management Challenge of Restructuring Industry* (Boston: Harvard Business School Press, 1986), Chapter 4.

60. On Japan, see Akira Goto, "Japan: A Sunset Industry," in Merton J. Peck, ed., *The World Aluminum Industry in a Changing Energy Era* (Washington: Resources for the Future, 1988), pp. 90–120. On Europe, see Bower, *When Markets Quake*, pp. 49–76.

61. Cf. Loescher, *Imperfect Collusion*, supra note 5, pp. 192–194.

62. See Kurt Bloch, "On German Cartels," *Journal of Business*, vol. 5 (July 1932), pp. 213–222.

63. Shaw and Shaw, "Excess Capacity," supra note 47.

The policy maker dealing with such situations faces a value judgment: He or she must weigh the pain associated with competitive pricing against its superior allocative efficiency. It is well known that politicians opt frequently for a narcotic approach. However, there are compelling arguments for the competitive solution. When demand is price elastic, as is often the case for products whose secular decline stems from the incursion of substitutes, or when machinery can be substituted readily for labor (as in coal mining and textiles), keeping prices and wages up through monopolistic restrictions will substantially increase the number of immobile laborers thrown into the ranks of the unemployed. The higher income enjoyed by those who manage to retain their jobs is not likely to outweigh the losses experienced by those who do not. Moreover, it may be possible to satisfy both goals — equity and efficiency — through programs to retrain and subsidize the relocation of workers employed in, or displaced from, declining industries. Extending outright subsidies to investors caught by declining demand, on the other hand, seldom commands much political support (although indirect subsidies, for example, through import barriers, are common). Because, therefore, monopolistic price-fixing schemes do not necessarily ease the lot of workers, because economic efficiency is definitely impaired, and because no premium is placed on avoiding occasional capital losses by investors, most economists are inclined to reject the argument that cutthroat competition in declining industries justifies a deviation from the competitive rule.[64]

Cyclical Competition

The case of temporary cyclical or random demand downturns is more complicated. Here, by definition, capacity is not permanently in excess of demand, and the problem is to avoid the loss or deterioration of capacity needed when demand recovers. Oligopolists operating evenly matched capital-intensive plants in cyclically sensitive, price-inelastic durable goods markets may, in the absence of institutions facilitating collusion, engage in especially bitter competition during recessions. Each company may strive to increase capacity utilization and cover overhead costs by price shading, and none will cease operations, relaxing the pressure of its supply on price, until all are near the brink of collapse.[65] Competition of this character is said to have several potentially undesirable effects.

For one, if the slump persists, some firms can be driven into bankruptcy by their losses. These will not necessarily be the least efficient producers, but those that are weakest financially — for example, the newer and smaller organizations without well-developed banking connections.[66] This is clearly objectionable on equity grounds, and it might at first glance appear that capacity needed to meet future demands is lost. However, the latter supposition is debatable. The financial reorganization following a bankruptcy plea seldom entails the outright dismantling of technically efficient production facilities. Rather, the plants are normally acquired at bargain prices by another solvent firm, which sooner or later restores them to operation, burdened by much lower capital charges. It must be noted too that major bankruptcies are relatively rare. In 1983, at the trough of an unusually severe general business recession, there were 4,433 recorded U.S. manufacturing and mining business failures, out of a total population of 441,000 incorporated and unincorporated manufacturing and mining business enterprises. Two-thirds of the recorded failures had liabilities of more than $100,000, and the total liabilities of failing companies approximated $6.4 billion — 0.3 percent of total manufacturing and mining assets.[67]

Second, it is claimed that the stop-and-go operation of plants and firms associated with financial reorganization or less drastic intrafirm adjustment to sharp competition causes diverse inefficiencies. The maintenance and replacement of machines may be postponed, workers may be laid off, skills deteriorate during layoffs, organizational continuity is lost, and research and development projects may be slowed down or terminated. While all this is possible, it is an empirical question whether the long-run efficiency sacrifices accepted under pressure from temporarily intense price competition are very great. What evidence we have suggests that serious sacrifices are uncommon in ordinary slumps, showing up only during a depression as deep and protracted as that of the 1930s. Indeed, Dennis Mueller found that industrial enterprises adjusted their capital expenditure plans to favor long-term research and development projects at the expense of capital replacement and expansion projects during the U.S. recession of 1958.[68] And during the unusually severe recession of 1982–1983, company-financed R&D outlays increased by 8.5 percent in nominal terms and 4.4 percent in constant dollar terms.[69] Moreover, it is doubtful whether firms would invest more heavily in new equipment and retain more workers on their payrolls under a monopolistic high-price policy (which reduces the quantity of output demanded and capacity utilization rates, ceteris paribus) than they would in a competitive milieu.

An argument heard frequently overseas, but seldom in the United States, is that temporary price-fixing arrangements to control cutthroat competition during recessions prevent permanent increases in market concentration, because otherwise small firms would either fail or head off the inevitable by merging with stronger industry leaders. There is no evidence that small but efficient U.S. firms have been forced in wholesale lots into the arms of their larger rivals during business recessions since the 1930s. However, some reports indicate that a movement toward crisis-induced concentration operated during the relatively mild Japanese recession of 1965 and 1966.[70] The Japanese experience may have differed from that of the United States because of disparate job tenure commitments to workers, fewer antitrust and regulatory restrictions on cooperation among firms and financial institutions in Japan, greater social homogeneity in Japan, or because in

---

64. It is also true that the seriousness of the "sick industry" problem is exaggerated by those who favor monopolistic restrictions on other (typically self-seeking) grounds. As George Stigler suggests, relatively few industries are really "sick," but many are hypochondriacal. *The Theory of Price* (New York: Macmillan, 1952), p. 249.

65. Conversely, an industry whose members operate numerous plants of widely varying efficiency and with a high variable cost component can adapt more smoothly to demand downturns, since less efficient plants will be closed down long before the most efficient plants (and their controlling firms) are threatened with failure.

66. See Phillips, *Market Structure*, supra note 4, pp. 104 and 116, for some spectacular if ancient examples.

67. U.S. Department of Commerce, *Statistical Abstract of the United States* (Washington: USGPO, 1986), p. 522.

68. Dennis C. Mueller, "The Firm Decision Process: An Econometric Investigation," *Quarterly Journal of Economics*, vol. 81 (February 1967), pp. 71–73.

69. National Science Foundation, *Science & Engineering Indicators* (Washington: 1987), p. 294.

70. See "Big Businesses in Japan Are Growing Bigger," *New York Times*, January 24, 1966, p. 37; "MITI May Enforce New Anti-depression Cartel," *Japan Times*, February 9, 1966; and Richard E. Caves and Masu Uekusa, *Industrial Organization in Japan* (Washington: Brookings, 1976), pp. 26–30 and 145–148.

Japan there was a much larger fringe of inefficiently small enterprises.[71] Yet even if the need of small firms to merge were accepted as inevitable, mergers could be channeled in such a way as to minimize adverse structural effects through antitrust policy.

One thing is indisputable. When all-out competition does break out during business slumps, driving price below the unit costs of efficient producers, prices must rise above full cost during booms if average profits over the complete business cycle are to attract a continuing supply of investment. The more volatile downward prices are in recessions, the more volatile upward they must be in booms. This poses several problems. First, wide fluctuations in prices and profits may have destabilizing macroeconomic effects, making it more difficult to maintain aggregate employment at high levels through fiscal and monetary policy.[72] Second, public opinion is often myopic, and attempts by important oligopolistic industries to raise their prices during booms to levels compensating for recession losses could provoke demands for government price controls and other direct intervention. Recognizing the difficulty of controlling such controls once they are imposed, politicians and entrepreneurs alike may prefer some formal price stabilization scheme to a less structured situation in which tacit collusion yields high boom profits but collapses in recessions. Third, some firms may fail under the burden of losses accumulated during hard times, even though long-run profit expectations are favorable. Fear of this contingency can lead risk-averting investors to demand, before committing their capital, a return exceeding the return earned in less volatile industries. If so, an industry subjected to alternating periods of highly profitable operation and price warfare might have to pay more to attract a given amount of capital than more stable industries, other things being equal. With capital costs lower under a price stabilization scheme, producers might conceivably sell their output at lower average prices than they would over a more volatile cycle of price shifts.[73]

A Theoretical Analysis of Price Stabilization Cartels

This last result is by no means assured. To see why, we must plunge more deeply into the analysis of who gains and who loses from price stabilization cartels.[74]

To keep a complex exposition as simple as possible without sacrificing essential insight, we assume that industry demand fluctuates randomly between two states—boom condition D_{BOOM} and slump condition D_{SLUMP}. Each state occurs half the time, that is, with probability 0.5.[75] The demand functions are assumed to be linear and shift in a parallel fashion between boom and slump. The short-run competitive industry supply function S is assumed to be stable and linear over the range of its intersection with D_{BOOM} and D_{SLUMP}. These assumptions are represented graphically in Figure 8.3, with D_0 included to show the mean level of demand, averaging boom and slump.

Figure 8.3 compares two pricing regimes: Case 1, in which prices and output are competitively determined, and Case 2, in which the price is stabilized at the level that would prevail under pure competition with mean demand function D_0. With competitive Case 1, the price rises to OP_B in the boom, and the quantity supplied and demanded is OQ_B. In the slump, the price falls to OP_S, and the quantity demanded and supplied is OQ_S. Under the stabilization cartel, Case 2, the price is OP_0 at all times. During the boom, producers expand output to OQ_B^*, where marginal cost equals price OP_0. Note that at this price the quantity demanded exceeds OQ_B^*, so nonprice rationing must take place. In the slump, the quantity OQ_S^* is demanded at the stabilized price OP_0, and the producers' supply must be restricted through quotas or other devices.

The profitability of the two arrangements can be compared by evaluating expected producers' surpluses—that is, the sum of the surpluses of price over marginal cost (read from the supply curve) for all units produced. Surplus components are designated by capital letters for each relevant area in Figure 8.3. Listing boom values first and slump values second, the expected value of producers' surplus under freely competitive Case 1 is:

$$(8.1) \quad E[PS_1] = .5[E + F + G + H + I + J + K + L + M] + .5[L + M].$$

With the price stabilized at OP_0, the expected value of producers' surplus for Case 2 is:[76]

$$(8.2) \quad E[PS_2] = .5[I + J + K + L + M] + .5[I + L].$$

71. Caves and Uekusa, *Industrial Organization in Japan,* pp. 101–115; and Ken-ichi Imai and Hiroyuki Itami, "Interpenetration of Organization and Market: Japan's Firm and Market in Comparison with the U.S.," *International Journal of Industrial Organization*, vol. 2 (December 1984), pp. 285–310.

72. See G. B. Richardson, *Information and Investment* (Oxford: Oxford University Press, 1960); David McCord Wright, "Some Notes on Ideal Output," *Quarterly Journal of Economics*, vol. 76 (May 1962), especially pp. 176–178; F. M. Scherer, "Market Structure and the Stability of Investment," *American Economic Review*, vol. 59 (May 1969), pp. 72–79; and idem, "Investment Variability, Seller Concentration, and Plant Scale Economies," *Journal of Industrial Economics*, vol. 22 (December 1973), pp. 157–160.

73. Donald Dewey, "Information, Entry and Welfare: The Case for Collusion," *American Economic Review*, vol. 69 (September 1979), pp. 587–594. Whether this is sufficient grounds for tolerating collusion is the subject of several comments in the *American Economic Review*, vol. 72 (March 1982), pp. 256–281.

74. The most general analyses of the problem are Benton F. Massell, "Price Stabilization and Welfare," *Quarterly Journal of Economics*, vol. 83 (May 1969), pp. 284–298; and Stephen J. Turnovsky, "Price Expectations and the Welfare Gains from Price Stabilization," *American Journal of Agricultural Economics*, vol. 56 (November 1974), pp. 706–716. Other contributions, some seminal, include F. V. Waugh, "Does the Consumer Benefit from Price Stability?" *Quarterly Journal of Economics*, vol. 58 (August 1944), pp. 602–614; Walter Y. Oi, "The Desirability of Price Instability under Perfect Competition," *Econometrica*, vol. 29 (January 1961), pp. 58–64; Albert Zucker, "On the Desirability of Price Instability," *Econometrica*, vol. 33 (April 1965), pp. 437–441; Clem A. Tisdell, *The Theory of Price Uncertainty, Production and Profit* (Princeton: Princeton University Press, 1968); the colloquy among Paul A. Samuelson, Oi, and Waugh in *Quarterly Journal of*

Economics, vol. 86 (August 1972), pp. 476–503; Peter Helmberger and Rob Weaver, "Welfare Implications of Commodity Storage Under Uncertainty," *American Journal of Agricultural Economics*, vol. 59 (November 1977), pp. 639–651; David Bigman and Shlomo Reutlinger, "National and International Policies Toward Food Security and Price Stabilization," *American Economic Review*, vol. 69 (May 1979), pp. 159–163; F. Gerard Adams, Jere R. Behrman, and Romualdo A. Roldan, "Measuring the Impact of Primary Commodity Fluctuations on Economic Development: Coffee and Brazil," *American Economic Review,* vol. 69 (May 1979), pp. 164–168; Brian D. Wright, "The Effects of Ideal Production Stabilization: A Welfare Analysis under Rational Behavior," *Journal of Political Economy,* vol. 87 (October 1979), pp. 1011–1033; Stephen J. Turnovsky, Haim Shalit, and Andrew Schmitz, "Consumer's Surplus, Price Instability, and Consumer Welfare," *Econometrica,* vol. 48 (January 1980), pp. 135–152; B. G. Dahlby, "Measuring the Effect on a Consumer of Stabilizing the Price of a Commodity," *Canadian Journal of Economics,* vol. 14 (August 1981), pp. 440–449; David M. G. Newbery and Joseph E. Stiglitz, *The Theory of Commodity Price Stabilization* (New York: Oxford University Press, 1981); David M. G. Newbery, "Commodity Price Stabilization in Imperfect or Cartelized Markets," *Econometrica,* vol. 52 (May 1984), pp. 563–578; and Jay Helms, "Errors in the Numerical Assessment of the Benefits of Price Stabilization," *American Journal of Agricultural Economics,* (February 1985), pp. 93–100.

75. Letting the demand curve shift with a continuous probability distribution having mean D_0 does not alter the results essentially. See Turnovsky, "Price Expectations," pp. 707–709.

76. We assume an allocation system during the slump that lets output be produced by firms with the lowest marginal cost—that is, as in the rationalization cartels described in Chapter 7. Otherwise, producers' surplus will be smaller.

Figure 8.3
Simple Price Stabilization
Cartel

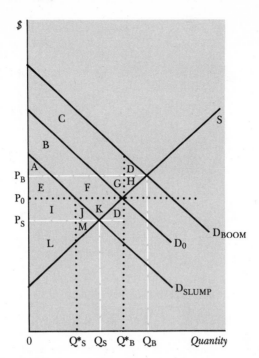

Subtracting, we obtain:

(8.3) $E[PS_1] - E[PS_2] = .5[E + F + G + H + M] - .5I.$

Because, by construction, D_{BOOM} and D_{SLUMP} are equidistant from D_0, $P_BP_0 = P_0P_S$, and so area $E + F$ necessarily exceeds area I.[77] Therefore, the profits earned by letting prices fluctuate competitively (Case 1) are larger than those gained under the stabilization cartel. Such profit sacrifices will not be accepted gladly by cartel members unless they place great weight on being relieved of the risk of price fluctuations. It seems almost inevitable that they will try to improve their lot by using their collective monopoly power to stabilize price at a level exceeding the mean competitive level OP_0.

Whether society as a whole benefits from a stabilization cartel charging OP_0 can be ascertained by assuming (heroically) that producers' and consumers' surpluses are commensurable. The expected value of consumers' surplus for competitive Case 1 is:

(8.4) $E[CS_1] = .5[A + B + C + D] + .5[A + E + I + J].$

For Case 2, it is:[78]

(8.5) $E[CS_2] = .5[A + B + C + E + F + G] + .5[A + E].$

Subtracting (8.5) from (8.4), we find that consumers' surplus is slightly *higher* under the stabilization cartel:

(8.6) $E[CS_1] - E[CS_2] = .5[I + J + D] - .5[E + F + G],$

since area E + F + G exceeds I + J + D by the area of triangle K.[79] However, summing (8.3) plus (8.6), we see that the combined producers' surplus and consumers' surplus under competitive pricing exceeds the surplus under a stabilization cartel by $.5[D + H + J + M]$.[80] Economic welfare clearly is higher with competitively fluctuating prices, and without making consumers worse off there is no way risk-neutral producers can be compensated for the profit sacrifices they would incur if they stabilize the price at OP_0.

Our conclusion concerning producers' profitability is not completely general. It depends in part upon the assumption of parallel demand function shifts, which in turn implies that demand becomes more elastic in the slump. If demand shifts so that its elasticity is the same at any given price during the slump as in the boom, and a fortiori if demand becomes less elastic in the slump, then $P_B P_0 < P_0 P_S$, and the slump producers' surplus gain I − M from stabilization might exceed the boom profit sacrifice E + F + G + H. This is more likely, the less elastic the supply function is in the neighborhood of the equilibria.[81] For industries susceptible to purported cutthroat competition, marginal cost (and hence supply) functions like the one illustrated in Figure 8.2 are plausible, suggesting fairly inelastic supply. On the crucial question of how demand elasticity varies over the business cycle, one finds only conflicting a priori conjectures and virtually no empirical evidence.[82] It seems at least conceivable that a Figure 8.3-type stabilization cartel could under the appropriate conditions be sufficiently profitable that producers, and especially risk-averse producers,[83] would be content not to raise the price above the competitive mean demand level. But the required conditions are sufficiently stringent that one might expect such cases to be rare.

A cartel in which output is rationed during the boom and curbed by producer quotas in the slump is not, however, the only feasible means of stabilizing prices. An alternative is a buffer stock cartel, under which some central authority stabilizes prices by accumulating goods during the slump and disposing of them in boom years. Its operation is characterized in Figure 8.4. The same conditions apply as in Figure 8.3, with one exception: Producers supply output OQ_0 at price OP_0 in both boom and slump. During the slump, the quantity demanded is only OQ_S^* (compared to OQ_S if the price were allowed to fall competitively), and the

77. Nonlinearity of the supply function alters this result, but usually in a direction that strengthens the conclusions reached here. Any nonlinearity is likely to entail a supply function that curves upward. If the supply curve is steeper between its intersection with D_0 and D_{BOOM} than between D_0 and D_{SLUMP}, then $P_B P_0 > P_0 P_S$.

78. We assume here a rationing scheme during the boom that puts output only in the hands of consumers realizing the highest consumers' surplus. That is, no output is sold to consumers with demand ordinates to the right of OQ_B^*. If, as is likely, this condition is not satisfied, consumers' surplus under the stabilization cartel will be less than indicated in Equation (8.5).

79. By construction, the rectangles E + F + G and I + J + K + D' are equal, and D = H = D'.

80. Another way to see this result, following the discussion on p. 25 supra, is to note that the stabilization cartel creates a dead-weight welfare loss triangle of J + M during slumps (the difference between the value and cost of foregone production) and of D + H during booms.

81. For a further analysis, see the first edition of *Industrial Market Structure and Economic Performance*, pp. 203–205.

82. Cf. R. F. Harrod, "Imperfect Competition and the Trade Cycle," *Review of Economics and Statistics*, vol. 18 (February 1936), pp. 84–88; R. F. Bretherton, "A Note on the Diminishing Elasticity of Demand," *Economic Journal*, vol. 47 (September 1937), pp. 574–577; and Richard B. Heflebower, "The Effect of Dynamic Forces on the Elasticity of Revenue Curves," *Quarterly Journal of Economics*, vol. 55 (August 1941), pp. 652–666.

83. See Dahlby, "Measuring the Effect," supra note 74, pp. 440–449; and Helms, "Errors in the Numerical Assessment," supra note 74, pp. 93–100.

Figure 8.4
Buffer Stock Cartel

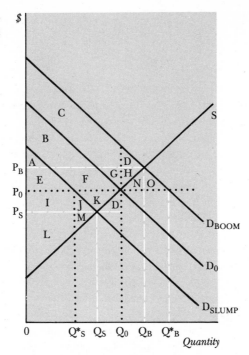

cartel authority must buy and stockpile $Q_0 Q_S^*$ units per time period. During the boom, the quantity demanded at repressed price OP_0 is OQ_B^*, and the cartel covers the gap between production and demand $(Q_B^* Q_0)$ out of its stockpile. If OP_0 is indeed the price associated with mean demand, then stock accumulations during slumps will, over the long run, just balance stock drawdowns during booms.

We proceed now to analyze the gains and losses. With a buffer stock cartel stabilizing the price at OP_0 (Case 3), the producers' surplus is the same in both demand states:

$$(8.7) \qquad E[PS_3] = I + J + K + L + M.$$

Letting competitive Case 1 (Equation 8.1) be the benchmark for comparison, we find

$$(8.8) \quad E[PS_1] - E[PS_3] = .5[E + F + G + H] - .5[I + J + K].$$

Unless supply is perfectly inelastic, area $E + F + G + H$ exceeds $I + J + K$, and the buffer stock cartel is less profitable than uninhibited competitive pricing.

Turning to the consumer's side, a buffer stock cartel yields surplus:

$$(8.9) \quad E[CS_3] = .5[A + B + C + D + E + F + G + H + N + O] + .5[A + E].$$

Subtracting (8.9) from (8.4), we obtain:

$$(8.10) \quad E[CS_1] - E[CS_3] = .5[I + J] - .5[E + F + G + H + N + O].$$

Since the negative term is larger than the positive, consumers are clearly better off under the buffer stock cartel then under freely competitive pricing. Indeed, summing (8.8) and (8.10), we discover that the combined producers' plus consumers' surplus with competitive pricing Case 1 as compared to buffer stock cartel Case 3 is $-.5[N + O + K]$. That is, aggregate welfare is *higher* with the assumed buffer stock cartel than with freely varying competitive prices. This stands in distinct contrast to the results for the more restrictive cartel Case 2. One implication is that it might be possible to compensate producers for their lower profits under the assumed buffer stock cartel — for example, through lump-sum transfers or (more plausibly) by raising the stabilized price above the level associated with mean demand — without entirely dissipating the surplus consumers derive from price stabilization. This is all the more likely if producers are risk averse and hence willing to supply a given output at a lower price when the risk of price fluctuations is lower.[84] On the other hand, costs of administering the stabilization scheme and storing buffer stocks have not been tallied in the analysis, and they might be of sufficient magnitude to deplete an appreciable fraction of the net surplus (that is, $.5[K + N + O]$) realized through stabilization.[85]

Some Broader Considerations

Several practical complications have been ignored to keep the analysis tractable. For one, producers have been assumed to adjust their supply to the price as it is at any moment in time, rather than making predictions about what it will be. This is probably appropriate for industries whose production cycle is short in relation to the business cycle over which demand changes occur, but not for most farm products and manufactured items with long gestation periods (such as turbogenerators and airplanes). Turnovsky has shown that producers will gain, not lose, from a Case 3 buffer stock cartel if they base their competitive output decisions on a naive extrapolation of prior period prices and if high demand in one period tends to be followed by low demand in the next, and vice versa.[86] On the other hand, a buffer stock cartel leaves producers worse off if, in adapting their output decisions, they have "rational" (that is, correct) expectations concerning the supply and demand conditions governing competitive price fluctuations. With either expectational approach, the sum of producers' plus consumers' surpluses continues to be higher under a buffer stock stabilization cartel of the Case 3 type than under freely fluctuating competitive prices.

Recognition that output decisions must be based upon predictions of an uncertain future suggests a second important set of qualifications. For the buffer stock cartel to work as contemplated in Figure 8.4, the cartel authority must be able to predict demand fluctuations (and also supply shifts[87]) sufficiently well that accumulations in slump periods balance disposals in boom periods. This, of course, is easier said than done. And there is the additional complication of distinguishing cyclical fluctuations from long-term trends. Wishful thinking or pressure from

---

84. For conditions under which consumer and producer interests in stabilization are more likely to coincide, see Wright, "Effects of Ideal Price Stabilization," supra note 74, pp. 1011–1033; and Newbery, "Commodity Price Stabilization," supra note 74, pp. 563–578.

85. For a strongly negative view of the welfare gains from price stabilization schemes, see Newbery and Stiglitz, *Theory of Commodity Price Stabilization*, supra note 74, Chapter 2.

86. Turnovsky, "Price Expectations," supra note 74, pp. 710–711.

87. When it is supply rather than demand that is shifting randomly, buffer stock cartels tend to yield higher producers' surplus than freely competitive markets whose mean price equals the stabilized price. See Turnovsky, "Price Expectations," pp. 708–709.

cartel members may delay recognition that the market will not support the existing price in the long run. If the price is too high, the resulting rapid accumulation of stocks will threaten to exhaust the cartel authority's financial resources, unless the price stabilization scheme is backed by substantial government subsidies, as has been true of numerous agricultural support programs in the United States and Europe. As the financial limits of the cartel authority are approached, the very size of the buffer stock contributes to the cartel's undoing, since speculators begin to gamble on the cartel's collapse. For should the cartel authority become bankrupt, the entire weight of the buffer stock will be thrown into the market, causing prices to plummet. This was the experience of the international tin cartel, which collapsed in 1985.[88] Over the preceding eleven years, there had been a steady fall in the consumption of tin. Although the International Tin Council managed to achieve a balance between current supply and demand by the end of 1982, it had already accumulated stocks of 73,000 metric tons and all but used up its cash reserves.[89] A resumption of stock accumulations in 1985, combined with the depreciation of the dollar[90] exhausted the ITC's borrowing ability. Tin prices thereupon fell by nearly 40 percent.[91]

Even in the absence of persistent imbalances between demand and supply, and unless there are significant economies of scale in forecasting or stock holding, it is not at all clear that a cartel authority can do a better job than individual producers in predicting the future and hedging against it. If the cartel authority's forecasting ability is only equal to that of individual producers, and since stabilization at price OP_0 is in many (but not necessarily all) cases less profitable for producers than resort to unfettered competitive markets, producers may choose not to support the cartel unless it offers them an attractive quid pro quo. If demand fluctuations are predictable and if buffering pays, many producers might prefer to hold their own inventories or, if not, to take their chances in the competitive spot market — augmented by futures and options markets, if they exist.[92] To win and maintain support in the face of these handicaps, the cartel authority will almost surely slant its decisions toward stabilizing prices at a level higher than the average under free competition.[93] Producers would then enjoy the best of both worlds — risk avoidance and average returns at least commensurate with what they would be in the competitive market. And for consumers, the attendant elevation of average prices must make the stabilization cartel a less attractive proposition than the pure theory implies.

Skepticism about the risk avoidance benefits of stabilization cartels is also prompted by evidence that the risks of financial failure are not all that great in cyclical industries prone to alleged excesses of cutthroat competition. Eliot Jones studied the financial records of the steel, harvester, sugar refining, tobacco, whiskey, cordage, wallpaper, malt, bicycle, and other manufacturing industries, which entered into large-scale consolidations around the turn of the century in a purported effort to escape ruinous competition.[94] He found that although many of the firms had experienced some lean years, nearly all managed to remain financially healthy. Loescher concluded that the "quite brutal" competition occasionally breaking out in the American cement industry did not impair the industry's long-run health, and that incentives for price warfare were aggravated by the excessive capacity lured into the industry by earlier attempts to stabilize prices at too high a level.[95] Conduct resembling ruinous competition has been extremely rare in the recessions experienced by the United States since World War II. With the possible exception of the electrical turbogenerator industry, from which Allis-Chalmers exited in 1962, leaving inadequate domestic capacity to serve subsequently booming demands,[96] it is hard to find examples of manufacturing industries not declining secularly whose structural or financial health been significantly impaired by episodes of sharp domestic competition.[97] And although members predicted dire consequences from the elimination of cartel-like minimum brokerage commission rules on the New York Stock Exchange, the actual consequence appears to have been more a trimming of manifest inefficiencies (accompanied, to be sure, by the failure of some less efficient firms) than any impairing of the industry's ability to satisfy the demand for its services.[98]

Thus, claims that competition has cutthroat and destructive propensities, and hence that cartelization is warranted, deserve to be taken with several grains of salt. Economic theory nevertheless reveals that certain kinds of price stabilization

88. See Ronald W. Anderson and Christopher L. Gilbert, "Commodity Agreements and Commodity Markets: Lessons from Tin," *Economic Journal*, vol. 98 (March 1988), pp. 1–15; "Tin Council Decides to Maintain Price for Metal Despite Enormous Supplies," *Wall Street Journal*, December 24, 1984, p. 14; "The Great Tin Crash," *The Economist*, November 2, 1985, pp. 15–16; and "Rattle, Rattle," *The Economist*, August 30, 1986, p. 61, for a discussion of the International Tin Council's collapse. Good background discussions appear in William L. Baldwin, *The World Tin Market: Political Pricing and Economic Competition* (Durham, N.C.: Duke University Press, 1983); and Fiona Gordon-Ashworth, *International Commodity Control: A Contemporary History and Appraisal* (New York: St. Martin's Press, 1984), especially Chapter 14. Tin is by no means the only buffer stock cartel to run into problems. For the less than sterling record of the coffee and cocoa stock cartels, see "The Lure of 'Orderly Marketing,' " *Business Week*, May 9, 1977, pp. 67–83.

89. Anderson and Gilbert, "Commodity Agreements," p. 6.

90. The world price of tin was denominated in Malaysian ringgits, which moved with the dollar. The ITC's debt was collateralized with tin holdings on the London Metals Exchange. The dollar's depreciation caused the value of those holdings in British pounds to fall below the level needed to support the ITC's level of borrowing.

91. Anderson and Gilbert, "Commodity Agreements," supra note 88, p. 10.

92. See Ronald I. McKinnon, "Futures Markets, Buffer Stocks, and Income Stability for Primary Producers," *Journal of Political Economy*, vol. 75 (December 1967), pp. 844–861; Benton F. Massell, "Some Welfare Implications of International Price Stabilization," *Journal of Political Economy*, vol. 78 (March/April 1970), pp. 404–417; and Allen B. Paul, ed., "Price Instabilities and Public Policy: Summary of an ERS-University Seminar," U.S. Department of Agriculture Economic Research Service working paper (Washington: January 1976). For a discussion of the role of speculators in price stabilization efforts, see Mario J. Miranda and Peter G. Helmberger, "The Effects of Commodity Price Stabiliza-

tion Programs," *American Economic Review*, vol. 78 (March 1988), pp. 46–58; and Stephen W. Salant, "The Vulnerabilty of Price Stabilization Schemes to Speculative Attack," *Journal of Political Economy*, vol. 91 (February 1983), pp. 1–38.

93. See, for example, "House Documents Link Coffee Groups, U.S. Aides," *New York Times*, November 11, 1977, p. B10.

94. Jones, "Is Competition in Industry Ruinous?" supra note 41, pp. 473–519.

95. Loescher, *Imperfect Collusion*, supra note 5, pp. 192–194.

96. See "Allis-Chalmers To Stop Making Some Generators," *Wall Street Journal*, December 21, 1962. In 1970 it reentered the business, apparently without great start-up difficulties, through a joint venture with West German generator maker Kraftwerk Union. However, after the energy shocks of 1973–1974 and 1979–1981 curbed electricity demand growth, excess capacity emerged again, and there were major plant closures.

97. One possible exception is the U.S. semiconductor industry, whose low profits in the late 1970s led to investment shortfalls that eventually set the stage for severe market share losses to Japanese producers.

98. Contrast the generally sanguine appraisals of Aharon R. Ofer and Arie Melnik, "Price Deregulation in the Brokerage Industry: An Empirical Analysis," *Bell Journal of Economics*, vol. 9 (Autumn 1978), pp. 633–641; Seha M. Tinic and Richard R. West, "The Securities Industry Under Negotiated Brokerage Commissions: Changes in the Structure and Performance of New York Stock Exchange Member Firms," *Bell Journal of Economics*, vol. 11 (Spring 1980), pp. 29–41; and Hans R. Stoll, "Revolution in the Regulation of Securities Markets: An Examination of the Effects of Increased Competition," in Leonard W. Weiss and Michael W. Klass, eds., *Case Studies in Regulation* (Boston: Little, Brown, 1981), pp. 12–52; with the mixed views that preceded deregulation: Kahn, *The Economics of Regulation*, supra note 59, vol. II, pp. 193–209; and H. Michael Mann, "The New York Stock Exchange: A Cartel at the End of its Reign," in Phillips, ed., *Promoting Competition*, supra note 30, pp. 301–327.

schemes — notably, of the buffer stock variety — could, at least in principle and under favorable conditions, yield attractive net benefits. How often the requisite conditions hold is uncertain, and there is clearly a danger that a stabilization cartel will exploit its power to degrade overall economic welfare instead of enhancing it. A skeptical stance seems appropriate. Yet it must also be admitted that there might conceivably be cases — no doubt exceptional — in which the benefits of stabilization arrangements could outweigh their costs.

Lumpiness and Infrequency of Orders

We return now to our main theme. The effectiveness of oligopolistic coordination also depends upon the size distribution over time of buyers' orders. Profitable coordination is most likely when orders are small, frequent, and regular. It is least likely when requests for price quotations on large orders are received infrequently and at irregular intervals.[99]

As we have seen, any decision to undercut a price on which industry members have tacitly concurred requires a balancing of probable gains against costs. The gain is an increased probability of securing a profitable order. The cost involves the likelihood of rival reactions driving down the level of prices on all current and future orders, and hence reducing profits. The gains from price cutting obviously are greater when the order at stake is large relative to total sales than when it is small. Expected costs, on the other hand, probably rise less than proportionately with order size. The amount of information a firm conveys concerning its pricing strategy depends more upon the number of transactions in which it quotes independent prices than upon the size of the transactions. A price cut on a small order transmits as much information as one on a large order. To be sure, rivals may weight more heavily the information on cuts involving substantial revenues. But this need not be true when opportunities to bid for large orders appear only infrequently and irregularly. More typically, competitors will reason, "Well, this was evidently a special case that can hardly be disregarded, but which is also not necessarily a good indicator of what we have to do to win the next round." Three or four departures in close succession on $10,000 orders are more apt to trigger rival retaliation than undercutting the established price on a single, unusual million-dollar order.[100] Consequently, the gains-cost balance will often be conducive to price cutting when a large order is at stake, while it will seldom be so for a small order, other things being equal.

Occasional large orders are particularly attractive to enterprises with short time horizons or high future discount rates — for example, those having difficulty covering high overhead costs during a moderate recession. There is nothing like red ink on the income statement to concentrate the mind. Even if the firm's future is not at stake, the future of senior management undoubtedly is. Such a firm will be favorably disposed toward accepting the risk of uncertain future retaliation if the immediate gain is an order sufficiently large to keep operations humming at capacity for several months. Small companies, it should be noted, will have stronger incentives from this standpoint with respect to orders of a given size than large firms.

The history of the cast-iron pipe industry during the 1880s and 1890s illustrates these relationships well. The product, purchased mainly by municipalities and gas utilities through competitive bidding, was homogeneous; and the number of sellers in the Midwestern market, isolated by high freight costs, was at most fifteen. Phillips describes the problems faced by firms in bidding as follows:

Jobs for a large city on which a bid was submitted might be of sufficient magnitude to keep a shop operating for weeks or months. The fine adjustments within each firm which would allow variations in output according to revenue and costs so as to maximize profits were impossible. In the absence of agreement among firms, the outcome of the bidding made the difference between operating and not operating for a substantial period of time. The firm with excess capacity, bidding on a large job, would be prone to submit any price so long as it was in excess of incremental costs of filling the order. And in view of the sporadic and large-sized jobs, some one of the several firms was apt to have the excess capacity created by a few unsuccessful bids.[101]

The result, at least in the absence of formal collusion, was intense price competition, and several bankruptcies occurred. Another consequence was the formation of a bidding cartel to restrain industry members' competitive zeal. This arrangement was the target of a precedent-setting antitrust decision in 1899.[102] The six leading firms eventually merged, removing them (at least at the time) from the scrutiny of the antitrust authorities.[103]

For a second example we return to the twentieth century. By far the largest single buyer of the antibiotic tetracycline is the federal government. As we observed in the preceding chapter, during 1955 and 1956 the five tetracycline producers settled down into a pattern of submitting identical $19.1884 bids per one-hundred-capsule bottle in Veterans Administration transactions, the largest of which involved 30,000 bottles. Then, in October of 1956, the Armed Services Medical Procurement Agency (ASMPA) made its first tetracycline purchase, calling for 94,000 bottles. Partly because of the unusually large order volume and partly because pricing precedents for the agency were unclear, industry discipline broke. Two firms held to the established $19.1884 price, but Bristol-Myers undercut to $18.97 and Lederle cut all the way to $11.00.[104] Even at this reduced price, Lederle secured before-tax profits of at least $750,000, since the marginal cost of producing an additional one hundred capsules was less than $3.00. This action touched off a series of rival countermoves, although the exact form of the retaliation would have been difficult to predict in advance. In the next VA transaction

99. When there is a regular flow of orders from large buyers in addition to the flow of small orders, systematic price discrimination may arise. This case will be considered in Chapter 13.
100. As we saw in Chapter 6, repeated experience under stable conditions affords an opportunity for rivals to learn to cooperate with and trust one another through some version of the Tit-for-Tat strategy. Rivals can be taught to cooperate by the deft use of threats, rewards, and punishments. See Thomas C. Schelling, *The Strategy of Conflict* (Cambridge: Harvard University Press, 1960), Chapter 5.
101. Phillips, *Market Structure*, supra note 4, p. 103.
102. *U.S.* v. *Addyston Pipe and Steel Co.* et al., 171 U.S. 614 (1899).

103. Bittlingmayer suggests that it is hard to distinguish whether the merger was driven by a desire to maintain coordination, given the lumpiness of orders, or to rationalize production given persistent economies of scale. George Bittlingmayer, "Decreasing Average Cost and Competition: A New Look at the Addyston Pipe Case," *Journal of Law & Economics*, vol. 25 (October 1982), pp. 201–229.
104. See Federal Trade Commission, *Economic Report on Antibiotics Manufacture* (Washington: USGPO, 1958), pp. 195–197. The tetracycline producers were subsequently acquitted of antitrust price-fixing charges. Nor is it likely that Lederle would have cut the price as deeply as it did had a prior collusive understanding existed.

(two weeks later, for 50,400 bottles), four suppliers (including Lederle and Bristol-Myers) quoted $19.1884, apparently because they considered the VA and AS-MPA purchases, which differed in delivery details, to be in different classes. But Pfizer cut to $17.63 (10 percent off the old $19.58 base) less 2 percent trade discount. Nearly a year later, in the next Armed Services purchase (this time for only 14,112 bottles), Pfizer matched Lederle's previous $11.00 price, but Lederle returned to $19.1884. Seven months later, in the third Armed Services transaction, all bidders returned to the $19.1884 level. The overall picture during the two years following Lederle's $11.00 bid was one of considerable disarray in both ASMPA and VA bidding, punctuated by Lederle's persistent adherence to the prebreak price in an apparent effort to signal that it wished to see stability restored at high price levels after it had captured the largest plum.[105]

Lumpiness of orders contributed to the poor pre-1960s pricing discipline of the electrical equipment industry. In the slump year 1958, only thirty-three turbo-generators were ordered from U.S. producers; in relatively prosperous 1960, there were eighty, some on multiunit contracts. A single order was sufficient to keep General Electric or Westinghouse, the industry leaders, busy for as much as a month. For Allis-Chalmers, whose market share averaged 10 percent in the decade before its 1962 exit, a single order might mean a half year's successful operation. Similarly, in Great Britain, where electrical equipment purchasing was concentrated in the governmental Electricity Generating Board, a single turbogenerator order could keep one of the three producers busy for more than a year, and a transformer order might amount to three months' backlog. There too, pricing discipline was fragile because of the struggle for orders to fill capacity voids.[106]

Secrecy and Retaliation Lags

The tendency for sellers to cut prices to secure orders ensuring capacity operation for a substantial period is a special case of a more general phenomenon. The longer the adverse consequences of rival retaliation can be forestalled, the more attractive undercutting the accepted price structure becomes. A common method of attempting to delay retaliation is to grant price concessions secretly. Whenever price exceeds marginal cost under oligopoly and when it appears feasible to keep special concessions secret, producers experience the temptation to engage in secret price shading. If the practice is confined to a small fraction of industry sales, the price cutters may be able to enjoy, more or less permanently, a larger volume of profitable business than they could by adhering faithfully to list prices.[107] But when secret price cutting spreads to more than 20 or 30 percent of total sales volume, list prices will undoubtedly be reduced openly. If further sub rosa shading continues, industry discipline may collapse completely.[108]

Our old friend, the electrical equipment industry, illustrates the latter, more dramatic result. The propensity of manufacturers to enter into secret deals with major buyers aggravated other disruptive conditions described previously. Thus, the proximate cause of the 1957–1958 "white sale" in switchgear, during which prices plunged to 40 percent of book values, was an under-the-counter bargain that turned out not to be secret. In 1956 and early 1957, the conspiracy among switchgear sellers was proceeding swimmingly, and prices had been stabilized at high levels. Then Westinghouse offered a secret 4 percent discount to the president of Florida Power and Light Company on a million-dollar order. General Electric sales representatives learned of the deal and offered to match it. When Westinghouse sales officials heard of the leak, they reacted angrily by cutting prices on another buyer's order. Other firms joined in, and the conspiracy broke down in a torrent of price warfare.[109] A key element in turbogenerator manufacturers' subsequent price protection plan, by which they avoided uninhibited price rivalry from 1964 through 1976, was the publication of all orders and price quotations by General Electric and Westinghouse. They also permitted buyers to have their records inspected and verify that transactions in fact took place at the prices the sellers had publicly announced.[110]

A different pattern has been observed in the steel, rayon, and aluminum industries. Price shading is usually initiated under adverse business conditions by the smaller firms. They are encouraged to act independently in part by knowledge that the details of their concessions will be kept secret, even though industry leaders quickly find out that chiseling is taking place.[111] Thus, it is not so much secrecy per se as the limited scope of the deviations that inhibits retaliation; secrecy is merely a priming element in the process. If covert concessions become fairly widespread, however, industry leaders react by announcing formal list price reductions. In aluminum extrusions, for example, where the independent fabricators entering into secret deals controlled about half the market, off-list pricing normally led to a reduction in list prices because the chiselers made serious inroads into primary producer sales. But in aluminum sheet fabrication, the independents accounted for only about 6 percent of total sales, and primary producers were

105. Tit-for-Tat strategies are conceptually harder to structure when there are more than two rivals. Nevertheless, as the tetracycline example illustrates, cooperation seems to emerge quite readily in real-world and experimental situations. See Robyn M. Dawes and Richard H. Thaler, "Anomalies: Cooperation," *Journal of Economic Perspectives*, vol. 2 (Summer 1988), pp. 187–197.
106. See Richardson, "The Pricing," supra note 59, pp. 73–92.
107. One way to limit the extent of price cutting is by getting the government to regulate the industry. For an example of an industry in which cartel pricing was preserved despite structural characteristics normally associated with competitive markets, see Paul L. Joskow, "Cartels, Competition and Regulation in the Property-Liability Insurance Industry," *Bell Journal of Economics*, vol. 4 (Autumn 1973), pp. 375–427.
108. A number of works attempt to analyze mathematically the dynamic logic of secret price cutting, detection, and deterrence. Among these, the earliest and most influential was George J. Stigler, "A Theory of Oligopoly," *Journal of Political Economy*, vol. 72 (February 1964), pp. 44–61. See also Ronald I. McKinnon, "Stigler's Theory of Oligopoly: A Comment," *Journal of Political Economy*, vol. 74 (June 1966), pp. 281–285; Daniel Orr and Paul W. MacAvoy, "Price Strategies To Promote Cartel Stability," *Economica*, vol. 32 (May 1965), pp. 186–197; G. Warren Nutter and John H. Moore, "A Theory of Competition," *Journal of Law & Economics*, vol. 19 (April 1976), pp. 39–65; Dale K. Osborne,

"Cartel Problems," *American Economic Review*, vol. 66 (December 1976), pp. 835–844; the exchange of views in *American Economic Review*, vol. 68 (December 1978), pp. 938–949; and R. Rothschild, "Cartel Problems: Note," *American Economic Review*, vol. 71 (March 1981), pp. 179–181. Most suffer from naive notions of how business firms learn about sub rosa price shading by rivals, asymmetry in their assumptions as to which firms are potential price shaders, and/or neglect of the tensions and institutional complexity inescapable in Prisoners' Dilemma-type situations with mixed incentives for conflict, cooperation, and dynamic learning. For a critique of the earlier models, see Basil S. Yamey, "Notes on Secret Price-cutting in Oligopoly," in Marcelle Kooy, ed., *Essays in Economics and Economic History in Honour of Prof. H. M. Robertson* (London: Macmillan, 1972), pp. 280–300.
109. See Smith, *Corporations in Crisis*, supra note 8, pp. 132–133.
110. *U.S.* v. *General Electric Co. et al.*, "Plaintiff's Memorandum in Support of a Proposed Modification to the Final Judgment Entered on October 1, 1962, Against Each Defendant," December 1976, pp. 7–10 and 17–18. See also p. 212 supra.
111. See Weiss, *Economics and American Industry*, supra note 7, pp. 295–298; Markham, *Competition in the Rayon Industry*, supra note 5, p. 128; Peck, *Competition in the Aluminum Industry*, supra note 3, p. 69; and U.S. Council on Wage and Price Stability, *A Study of Steel Prices*, supra note 52, pp. 9–15.

inclined to ignore off-list quotations as a minor irritant.[112] Likewise, the three smallest primary aluminum producers, with a combined 8 percent share of U.S. ingot capacity, managed through small discounts to utilize their capacity fully during the 1974–1975 recession. Industry leaders Alcoa, Reynolds, and Kaiser ignored the cuts, adhered to list prices, and cut output back to less than 75 percent of capacity.[113]

Where secrecy prevails, prices can be influenced by rumors. Customers receiving secret price cuts would not want the information to leak if that meant a return to concerted industry pricing discipline. However, they do have an incentive to try to extend the cuts they obtain. Rumors can be a useful bargaining tool. In the U.K. synthetic fiber texturizing industry, customers strengthened their bargaining positions by providing documents indicating that products were being sold at discounted prices while withholding information that the discounted goods were defective.[114]

Secret price cutting, whether pursued to the point of complete breakdown in industry discipline or merely to across-the-board list price reductions, interferes with the maximization of collective profits. Recognizing this, oligopolists have tried to nip the problem in the bud by making it difficult to conceal concessions. They do this through some variant of the so-called open price policy, advocated in 1912 by corporate lawyer Arthur Jerome Eddy.[115] In the typical case, an industry trade association is authorized to collect detailed information on the transactions executed by each member. To ensure full compliance, the association or an independent auditing firm is sometimes empowered to audit company records, and fines may be levied for failure to report sales quickly or accurately.[116] The association then publishes at frequent intervals (for example, weekly) a report describing each transaction, including the name of the seller, the buyer, the quantity sold, and the price. Thus, each member knows shortly after the fact who has been shading prices for whom and can take appropriate retaliatory action. The potential price-cutting firm recognizes in turn that it will be found out quickly, so the incentive for offering concessions in the hope of deferring retaliation through secrecy fades. Maximum knowledge of rival actions provides an exceptionally favorable environment for tacit collusion, as one open price agency, the American Hardwood Manufacturers' Association, boasted to members:

The theoretical proposition at the basis of the Open Competition plan is that . . . *knowledge regarding prices actually made is all that is necessary to keep prices at reasonably stable and normal levels.* . . . by keeping all members fully and quickly informed of what the others have done, the work of the Plan results in a certain uniformity of trade practice. There is no agreement to follow the practice of others, *although members do naturally follow their most intelligent competitors,* if they know what these competitors have been actually doing. . . . The keynote to modern business success is mutual confidence and co-operation. *Co-operative competition, not Cut-throat competition.*[117]

Aware that oligopolistic suppliers are more willing to make price concessions in secret than openly, and because they are better able to control internal corruption (or are less apt to be the subject of front-page headlines when it is discovered), large industrial buyers typically rely upon secret negotiations rather than sealed bidding in their procurement operations. This message has been slow to permeate governmental thinking. Except in procuring complex, technologically advanced equipment such as weapon systems and space vehicles, the federal government and most state and local governments require that purchases of supplies, equipment, and the like be made through sealed competitive bidding. That is, the procurement agency issues a request for bids with detailed specifications of the items desired, and would-be suppliers tender sealed price quotations. These are opened publicly on a predetermined date, and the firm submitting the lowest responsible quotation wins the order. (In case of ties, various procedures may be employed, depending upon time pressures. The winner may be chosen by lot, or the order may be split, or negotiations to secure a lower price may be initiated, or all bids may be rejected and new bids requested.) This approach to procurement has the great advantage of minimizing opportunities for bribery and favoritism. But as Paul Cook observes, "It would . . . be hard to find a device less calculated to foster open and aggressive competition among [oligopolistic] sellers."[118] Any firm tempted to cut its price below the prevailing industry level knows its action cannot escape the attention of rivals, and therefore it must fear retaliation on the next round. It will cut only if the gain appears to outweigh this clear-cut risk. In addition, sellers may be reluctant to cut prices below current levels in a sealed-bid competition because other large buyers will find out and demand similar price reductions.[119]

The Social Scene

We turn last to the relationship between an industry's formal and informal social structure and its ability to coordinate pricing behavior.[120] This set of influences lies beyond the reach of conventional economic analysis, and its effects would be difficult to predict even with a rich multidisciplinary theory. Consequently, the economist is forced, without denying their importance, to view variations in industry conduct and performance owing to differences in social structure as an

112. See Peck, *Competition in the Aluminum Industry*, pp. 66–68.

113. U.S. Council on Wage and Price Stability Staff Report, *Aluminum Prices: 1974–75* (Washington: USGPO, 1976), especially pp. 73 and 121–123.

114. Andrew Likierman, "Pricing Policy in the Texturising Industry, 1958–71," *Journal of Industrial Economics*, vol. 30 (September 1981), pp. 25–38.

115. See Arthur Jerome Eddy, *The New Competition* (Chicago: McClury, 1912). On the steel industry as a forerunner to Eddy's approach, see Donald O. Parsons and E. J. Ray, "The United States Steel Consolidation," *Journal of Law and Economics*, vol. 18 (April 1975), pp. 208–209. For a more modern argument in the same spirit as Eddy's, see G. B. Richardson, "Price Notification Schemes," *Oxford Economic Papers*, vol. 19 n.s. (November 1967), pp. 355–365.

116. For a summary of several cases, see G. W. Stocking, "The Rule of Reason, Workable Competition, and the Legality of Trade Association Activities," *University of Chicago Law Review*, vol. 21 (Summer 1954), pp. 527–619.

117. Phillips, *Market Structure*, supra note 3, pp. 147–148, quoting

from *U.S.* v. *American Column and Lumber Co. et al.*, 257 U.S. 377, 393–394 (1921) (italics in original).

118. Paul W. Cook, Jr., "Fact and Fancy on Identical Bids," *Harvard Business Review*, vol. 41 (January–February 1963), pp. 67–72. See also Vernon A. Mund, "Identical Bid Prices," *Journal of Political Economy*, vol. 68 (April 1960), pp. 150–169.

119. For example, the "most favored nation" clauses in Salk vaccine procurement contracts, requiring that the seller charge no higher price to that buyer than it does to any other buyer, were a significant deterrent to price cutting. See *U.S.* v. *Eli Lilly & Co. et al.*, CCH *1959 Trade Cases*, para 69,536. On similar provisions in tetraethyl lead sales, see Steven C. Salop, "Practices That (Credibly) Facilitate Oligopolistic Coordination," in Joseph E. Stiglitz and G. F. Mathewson, eds., *New Developments in the Analysis of Market Structure* (Cambridge: MIT Press, 1986), pp. 273–279.

120. For a seminal treatment of this problem, see Phillips, *Market Structure*, supra note 3, Chapter 2. See also Richard B. Heflebower, "Stability in Oligopoly," *Manchester School of Economics and Social Studies*, vol. 29 (January 1961), pp. 79–93.

unexplained residual or "noise." We can nevertheless at least identify some conditions that appear either to facilitate or impair collusion.

When conglomerate corporations face other conglomerates in a web of markets, it has been hypothesized,[121] they compete less sharply by allowing each other more or less exclusive spheres of influence. Before World War II, a substantial share of Japanese business activity was concentrated in the hands of a few giant conglomerate *Zaibatsu* groups.[122] Each group was strong in some lines and relatively weak in others. They came into contact with one another in dozens of markets, especially in the heavy industrial sector. In addition, there were frequent social and matrimonial ties among members of the several families dominating the principal Zaibatsu. Students of Japanese economic history disagree on the effect these links had on competitive behavior. Some concur with Corwin Edwards that a live-and-let-live attitude was encouraged by the fear that aggressive action in a market where one had an edge would be countered by aggression in markets where rivals had the advantage.[123] Others found that the principal Zaibatsu were "keen rivals," and that they often refused to cooperate with one another in cartel agreements because of confidence in their own superiority, clique rivalries, and dissatisfaction with agreed-upon prices and output quotas.[124] Perhaps the most balanced view is given by Lockwood, who described prewar Japanese enterprise as:

> . . . a rather indeterminate blend of sharp jealousy and mutual solidarity, of rugged individualism and collusive action. If rivalries were keen, they yet operated in a setting characterized by a propensity among the rivals to cooperate in abating the rigors of the free market.[125]

Among the most conglomerate of Western firms prior to World War II were I.G. Farben in Germany, Imperial Chemical Industries in England, and du Pont in the United States. Their interests touched in hundreds of product areas, and they unquestionably adopted a live-and-let-live policy toward one another, negotiating explicit geographic spheres of influence agreements for products on which they had exclusive patent protection and avoiding aggressive price competition where they did compete directly. Competition among the three chemical giants intensified in the postwar period after the Farben combine was broken up, du Pont's spheres of influence agreements were attacked by American antitrust authorities, and other chemical firms began to diversify and expand into product lines formerly dominated by the Big Three.[126]

We have noted repeatedly the remarkable discipline of American steel producers, who resisted the urge to break from list prices during the late 1950s even when operating at only 60 percent of capacity. The industry's finely honed esprit de corps can be traced back to the Gary dinners of 1907 through 1911.[127] Differences in social structure have much to do with the contrasting performance observed in the European steel industry. During the 1960s excess steel capacity began to appear in Europe. Although they served overlapping market areas and were separated by only moderate transportation costs and tariffs, the Continental and (prenationalization) British sectors reacted differently. On the Continent, prices fell by as much as 25 percent, while British domestic prices held firm despite an influx of imports from hard-pressed Continental producers. British companies adhered to list prices in part because they shared homogeneous goals, had a close-knit industry organization, and because their directors (many of whom attended the same elite schools and belonged to the same social clubs) held cooperative attitudes.[128] On the other hand, entrepreneurs in the European Coal and Steel Community embodied many diverse backgrounds, styles of doing business, and national goals; and a permissive bias toward orderly pricing on the part of ECSC's High Authority was not enough to overcome these obstacles to cooperation. Again, during the steel industry recessions of the mid-1970s and early 1980s, even quotas administered with more or less compulsion through the European Community Commission were insufficient to quench centrifugal national industry instincts, and vigorous price rivalry persisted despite the stabilization effort.[129]

As suggested in the preceding chapter, informal social contacts made at trade association meetings often lead to bonds of friendship and mutual understanding that facilitate tacit and explicit collusion. This was one basis for the rayon industry's cooperative pricing policies; another was the fact that the two leading firms occupied adjacent home office buildings in Wilmington, Delaware.[130] American rayon producers also participated, directly or through affiliates, in cartel arrangements in nations where they were legal, and this collaboration abroad engendered cooperative attitudes in the domestic market. Nor is the pattern unique to rayon. Stocking and Watkins found that the three firms dominating the U.S. sulfur industry competed vigorously between 1913 and 1922. However, they then formed an export cartel (legal under the American antitrust laws) that apparently fostered

121. See e.g., Corwin D. Edwards, "Conglomerate Bigness as a Source of Power," in the National Bureau of Economic Research conference report, *Business Concentration and Price Policy* (Princeton: Princeton University Press, 1955), pp. 331–359; Arnold A. Heggestad and Stephen A. Rhoades, "Multi-Market Interdependence and Local Market Competition in Banking," *Review of Economics and Statistics*, vol. 60 (November 1978), pp. 523–532; John T. Scott, "Multimarket Contact and Economic Performance," *Review of Economics and Statistics*, vol. 64 (August 1982), pp. 368–375; and Allyn D. Strickland, *Firm Diversification, Mutual Forebearance Behavior and Price-Cost Margins* (New York: Garland, 1984).

122. See p. 64 supra.

123. "Conglomerate Bigness," p. 335; and Eleanor M. Hadley, "Concentrated Business Power in Japan" (Ph.D. diss., Radcliffe College, 1949), pp. 7 and 13–14.

124. See G. C. Allen, *A Short History of Modern Japan: 1867–1937* (New York: Praeger, 1963), p. 135; and William W. Lockwood, *The Economic Development of Japan* (Princeton: Princeton University Press, 1954), pp. 228–230.

125. *The Economic Development of Japan*, p. 231.

126. Alfred E. Kahn, "The Chemical Industry," in Walter Adams, ed., *The Structure of American Industry*, 3rd ed. (New York: Macmillan, 1961), pp. 246–252; G. W. Stocking and M. W. Watkins, *Cartels in Action: Case Studies in International Business Diplomacy* (New York: Twentieth Century Fund, 1946), Chapters 9–11; testimony of Joel Dirlam in U.S. Congress, Senate, Subcommittee on Antitrust and Monopoly hearings, *Economic Concentration,* Part 2 (Washington: USGPO, 1965), pp. 755–758; and M. J. Gart, "The British Company That Found a Way Out," *Fortune,* August 1966, p. 104 ff.

127. Cf. pp. 235–236 supra. For a fascinating account of how steel makers brought social and other pressures to bear on nonconformists, see Dan Cordtz, "Antiestablishmentarianism at Wheeling Steel," *Fortune,* July 1967, pp. 105 ff. In "Price Fixing Conspiracies: Their Long-term Impact," *Journal of Industrial Economics*, vol. 24 (March 1976), pp. 201–202, W. Bruce Erickson argues on the basis of three case studies that prolonged explicit collusion creates preconditions favorable to the subsequent development of price leadership or similar oligopolistic coordination methods.

128. See Dennis Swann and D. L. McLachlan, "Steel Pricing in a Recession," *Scottish Journal of Political Economy*, vol. 12 (February 1965), pp. 81–104.

129. See "European Steel Industry Faces Worst Crisis in Memory," *New York Times*, May 23, 1977, pp. 41–42; "The Imperiled EC Steel Cartel," *Business Week*, August 18, 1980, p. 88; "Europe's Bruised Steelmakers," *New York Times*, November 10, 1982, p. D1; and "Unshackled," *The Economist*, July 2, 1988, p. 60.

130. See Markham, *Competition in the Rayon Industry*, supra note 4, pp. 3 and 97–98.

the spirit of cooperation necessary to sustain high domestic prices even during the severe depression of the 1930s.[131] Similarly extensive intertwining of nearly all the U.S. primary aluminum ingot producers in joint bauxite mining and alumina refining ventures overseas was believed by the Council on Wage and Price Stability staff to be a plausible partial explanation for the absence of vigorous price discounting during periods of substantial excess capacity.[132]

Still the existence of an industry association institutionalizing frequent business and social contacts does not guarantee cooperation. Personal antagonisms and distrust arising from all sorts of real and imagined causes can shatter organization harmony. Ralph Cassady found that emotional behavior resulting from fear, anger, hatred, or desperation plays a major part "in many if not all" price wars.[133] Testimony from an antitrust case involving southern U.S. mirror manufacturers vividly illustrates the problems that can arise. At a trade association meeting in 1954, several producers got together to negotiate an increase in prices.[134] One participant described his experience as follows:

I had never expressed myself to him, my actual feelings at all times. So when we got in this meeting . . . I just decided to tell him, "John, you are the one that started this price war to begin with." I can't recall just the exact things that took place, but he as much as said I was a damn liar, that I started it. I said, "What do you mean, I started it, Mr. Messer?" He said, "You shipped mirrors into Galax, Virginia, and I want you to retract and quit accusing me of starting this price war, when you are the one that did it.". . . Mr. Messer turned so red I thought he was going to have a stroke.

Another participant recalled:

I thought they were going to come to blows. The luncheon meeting had been very congenial, but after the first two or three minutes in this meeting . . . it looked like there might be a free-for-all break out at any time.

An agreement was in fact reached by all save Mr. Messer, but during the following month the agreed-upon price was undercut on nearly 70 percent of all transactions. In his analysis of this case, Phillips concludes that "in a psychological sense, it is doubtful that these men were capable of agreeing on anything."[135] The uniqueness of the case is shown by the fact that the western and northern branches of the mirror industry, with similar market structures, managed to avoid price warfare without engaging in known collusion.[136] However, the problem of mutual distrust does not seem to be an unusual one. Fog observes that in Denmark, where formal price-fixing agreements were legal,

. . . cartel agreements are not always the expression of cordial co-operation among firms. In many cases it is rather a deeply rooted distrust that necessitates the signing of binding agreements, as the firms dare not place confidence in a gentleman's agreement.[137]

Similar coordination problems arise when an industry includes a maverick of significant size—that is, a strong-headed, individualistic entrepreneur whose values or business methods differ from those of other industry members. Ernest P. Weir, president of National Steel, was such a figure, and during the 1930s his aggressive pricing policies contributed significantly to some of the industry's rare pricing discipline breakdowns. Henry Ford played the role during the early decades of the auto industry, as did his friend Harvey Firestone in the rubber tire industry. The purchase of the New York Yankees by George Steinbrenner and the Atlanta Braves by Ted Turner was a major factor behind the bidding war for free-agent players in major-league baseball. The emergence of a maverick willing and able to disrupt industry tranquility seems to depend more on chance than on identifiable structural or behavioral preconditions, and this imparts an additional element of randomness into predictions of industrial performance. Nonetheless, really striking cases appear to be rare, perhaps because large, less aggressive firms will often pay a handsome acquisition price to eliminate small rivals actively promoting price competition. As the president of a cement manufacturing company wrote to the head of a rival concern, "The most effective way to cure a bad situation is to buy up the offenders."[138]

Conclusion

To summarize, cooperation to hold prices above the competitive level is less likely to be successful, the less concentrated an industry is; the larger the competitive fringe is; the more heterogeneous, complex, and changing the products supplied are; the higher the ratio of fixed or overhead to total costs is; the more depressed business conditions are; the more dependent the industry is on large, infrequent orders; the more opportunities there are for under-the-counter price shading; and the more relations among company executives are marred by distrust and animosity. None of these links is strictly deterministic; all reflect central tendencies subject to random deviation. It is in part because of this complexity and randomness that oligopoly poses such difficult problems for the economic analyst.

131. Stocking and Watkins, *Monopoly and Free Enterprise*, supra note 28, pp. 126–128.

132. Council on Wage and Price Stability, *Aluminum Prices: 1974–75*, supra note 113, pp. 23–26, 226–227, and 232.

133. Ralph Cassady, Jr., *Price Warfare in Business Competition* (East Lansing: Michigan State University Bureau of Business and Economic Research, 1963), pp. 53–55.

134. Phillips, *Market Structure*, supra note 3, pp. 183–193, draw-

ing upon the record of *U.S.* v. *Pittsburgh Plate Glass Co. et al.*, 260 F. 2d 397 (1958); 360 U.S. 395 (1959).

135. Phillips, *Market Structure*, p. 193.

136. Phillips, *Market Structure*, p. 192.

137. Fog, *Industrial Pricing Policies*, supra note 38, p. 155.

138. Loescher, *Imperfect Collusion*, supra note 5, p. 120, note 76. See also Reed Moyer, *Competition in the Midwestern Coal Industry* (Cambridge: Harvard University Press, 1964), pp. 82 and 157.

9

Antitrust Policy
Toward
Price-Fixing
Arrangements

We have seen how price-fixing arrangements can lead to monopoly prices, and we have explored the conditions under which they thrive or fail to secure their desired goals. Now we probe more deeply into their legal status in the United States and abroad.

The Evolution of U.S. Law

Section 1 of the U.S. Sherman Act, passed in 1890, prohibits "every contract, combination . . . or conspiracy in restraint of trade or commerce among the several states." An extended series of court decisions has interpreted this language as making illegal *per se* all agreements among competing firms to fix prices, to restrict or pool output, or otherwise directly to restrict the force of competition. Such agreements have been singled out for judicial treatment different from the *rule of reason* approach taken with respect to a variety of other practices. Under a *per se rule,* it is only necessary for the complainant to prove that certain conduct occurred and that it fell within the class of practices "so plainly anticompetitive" that they are illegal on their face.[1] No detailed inquiry into the conduct's economic rationale and consequences is required. Under the rule of reason, on the other hand, the courts undertake a broader inquiry into facts peculiar to the contested practices, the reasons why they were implemented, their competitive significance, and their impact on consumers.

Emergence of the Per Se Rule

The per se rule against overt agreements in restraint of trade was initially articulated in the *Trans-Missouri Freight Association* decision—the first price-fixing case to be appealed to the U.S. Supreme Court. In an effort to eliminate the freight rate wars toward which they were inclined, eighteen railroads operating west of the Missouri River entered into formal agreements establishing the rates each line would charge. In reply to a suit brought in 1892 by the U.S. district attorney in Topeka, the railroads advanced two main defenses: that they were exempt from Sherman Act prohibitions by virtue of their status as carriers regulated under the Interstate Commerce Act of 1887, and that the rates they fixed by agreement were in any event legal because they were "reasonable." Both defenses were sustained by the lower courts. As the district court judge observed:

When contracts go to the extent only of preventing unhealthy competition, and yet at the same time furnish the public with adequate facilities at fixed and reasonable prices, and are made only for the purpose of averting personal ruin, the contract is lawful.[2]

---

1. *National Society of Professional Engineers* v. *U.S.*, 435 U.S. 679, 692 (1978).

2. *U.S.* v. *Trans-Missouri Freight Association et al.*, 53 Fed. 440, 451 (1892). For an economic analysis of the very first case, see

John J. Siegfried and Michelle Mahony, "The First Sherman Act Case: Jellico Mountain Coal, 1891," working paper, Vanderbilt University, December 1988.

However, this interpretation, as well as the ruling exempting regulated railroads from the Sherman Act's reach, was rejected by the Supreme Court in a 5 to 4 decision. Speaking for the majority, Justice Peckham found that the language Congress used in the Sherman Act could not be construed to admit a test of reasonableness:

When . . . the body of an act pronounces as illegal every contract or combination in restraint of trade or commerce . . . the plain and ordinary meaning . . . is not limited to that kind of contract alone which is in unreasonable restraint of trade, but all contracts are included in such language, and no exception or limitation can be added without placing in the act that which has been omitted by Congress.[3]

He went on to note that while preventing ruinous competition among the railroads might be socially desirable, it would be impossible for the courts to determine whether the rates set through interfirm agreements were reasonable, and that recognition of this difficulty might have prompted Congress to prohibit *all* agreements in restraint of trade and not just unreasonable ones. His view of the judiciary's role in carrying out the stated intent of Congress is revealed most clearly in this passage:

It may be that the policy evidenced by the passage of the act itself will, if carried out, result in disaster to the roads. . . . These considerations are, however, not for us.[4]

In a case following shortly thereafter, the per se rule was reiterated on a new and different logical plane. Six producers of cast-iron water and gas pipe, accounting for about two-thirds of total sales in the Middle West and West, formed a bidding cartel that rigged the prices quoted to buyers in certain cities, reserved other cities as the exclusive domain of a single seller, and pooled contributions made to a central fund in implementing the scheme. The cast iron pipe industry gravitated toward price warfare because of sharp fluctuations in order volumes, the large size of individual orders, and a cost structure characterized by persistent scale economies, high overhead, and low marginal costs at less than full capacity operation.[5] Hearing the case for the Circuit Court of Appeals, Judge (later President and Supreme Court chief justice) William Howard Taft went beyond a literal reading of the words used by Congress in Sherman Act Section 1, attempting to build a per se prohibition upon the common law prevailing in America and England at the time. He argued that the common law permitted restraints of trade which were merely ancillary to some legitimate cause, but that it voided those contracts whose *main* object was to restrict competition. Taft insisted that past decisions inconsistent with this view had been erroneous, "set[ting] sail on a sea of doubt" in their attempt to determine how much restraint of competition was in the public interest.[6] Observing that the pipe producers' agreements were clearly not ancillary, Taft concluded that the reasonableness of the agreements was irrelevant:

It has been earnestly pressed upon us that the prices at which the cast-iron pipe was sold . . . were reasonable. We do not think the issue an important one, because . . . we do not think that at common law there is any question of reasonableness open to the courts with reference to such a contract. Its tendency was certainly to give the defendants the power to charge unreasonable prices, had they chosen to do so.[7]

He added in the next line that "if it were important, we should unhesitatingly find that the prices charged in the instances which were in evidence were unreasonable." This afterthought muted the force of Taft's opinion as precedent, for while citing the material quoted here approvingly, the Supreme Court on appeal placed more emphasis on the unreasonableness of the prices charged than on Taft's harmonization of the common and statutory law.[8]

The per se prohibition's scope was attenuated and muddied somewhat during the next three decades as the Supreme Court applied a rule of reason to Sherman Act monopolization cases (considered in Chapter 12) and as decisions were rendered in borderline areas. A forceful restatement had to await the *Trenton Potteries* decision in 1927. The defendants, some twenty-three manufacturers controlling roughly 82 percent of the bathroom bowl market, published standardized price lists through a trade association committee, discussed prices at frequent association meetings, and exhorted one another not to sell at off-list prices. Evidence compiled in the criminal trial suggested that the exhortations were not very successful. Pricing discipline of the association members was weak, and, for many members, adherence to list prices was apparently more the exception than the rule. Hearing the case on appeal, the Supreme Court directly addressed the question of whether reasonableness of the prices actually charged was a relevant consideration in determining the defendants' guilt or innocence. It first distinguished price-fixing cases from other cases in which a rule of reason had been applied, observing that the meaning of reasonableness "necessarily varies in the different fields of the law." It then went on to conclude:

The aim and result of every price-fixing agreement, if effective, is the elimination of one form of competition. The power to fix prices, whether reasonably exercised or not, involves power to control the market and to fix arbitrary and unreasonable prices. The reasonable price fixed today may through economic and business changes become the unreasonable price of tomorrow. . . . Agreements which create such potential power may well be held to be in themselves unreasonable or unlawful restraints, without the necessity of minute inquiry whether a particular price is reasonable or unreasonable as fixed and without placing on the Government in enforcing the Sherman Law the burden of ascertaining from day to day whether it has become unreasonable through the mere variation of economic conditions.[9]

In rejecting "day to day" scrutiny of prices, the Court in effect concluded that Sherman Act enforcement was to follow clear-cut and simple rules, avoiding the more intrusive regulatory approach assigned the Interstate Commerce Commission in monitoring railroad pricing. The Court's emphasis on the process of attempting to

3. *U.S.* v. *Trans-Missouri Freight Association*, 166 U.S. 290, 328 (1897).

4. 166 U.S. 290, 340 (1897). On the absence of a significant stock market reaction to the decision, see John J. Binder, "The Sherman Antitrust Act and the Railroad Cartels," *Journal of Law & Economics*, vol. 31 (October 1988), pp. 443–468.

5. See George Bittlingmayer, "Decreasing Average Cost and Competition: A New Look at the Addyston Pipe Case," *Journal of Law & Economics*, vol. 25 (October 1982), p. 202, who argues that because of natural monopoly conditions, the "firms could not be-

have competitively even if they wanted to." See also Almarin Phillips, *Market Structure, Organization and Performance* (Cambridge: Harvard University Press, 1962), pp. 99–118.

6. *U.S.* v. *Addyston Pipe & Steel Co. et al.*, 85 Fed. 271, 284 (1898).

7. 85 Fed. 271, 293 (1898).

8. *Addyston Pipe & Steel Co. et al.* v. *U.S.*, 175 U.S. 211, 235–238 (1899).

9. *U.S.* v. *Trenton Potteries Co. et al.*, 273 U.S. 392, 396–398 (1927).

fix prices and its neglect of whether the pottery makers actually had the power to carry out their agreements has been criticized by Professor (now appellate judge) Richard Posner as a "cops and robbers" approach to antitrust.[10] The decision is nevertheless viewed as the basic precedent in U.S. price-fixing cases, prohibiting explicit pricing conspiracies per se, whether or not they are effective.

Still the courts, like other human organizations, do not always hew faithfully to the rules they have enunciated. A significant break from the *Trenton Potteries* precepts occurred only six years later when the U.S. economy was in the trough of the Great Depression. An industry hit especially hard by the slump was coal mining. Prices of bituminous coal fell by 25 percent from 1929 to 1933, while output was reduced 38 percent. More coal mining firms reported losses than profits. To cope with these conditions, 137 producers in the Appalachian Mountain region formed in 1931 a new company, Appalachian Coals, Inc., to serve as exclusive selling agent for member firms. Its members accounted for 12 percent of all soft coal production east of the Mississippi River and 54 percent of production in the Appalachian territory and immediately surrounding states. The agency was instructed to get the "best prices obtainable" for member output, and if all output could not be sold, to allocate orders among the member mines. In effect, it served as a kind of sales cartel, but with far from complete control over the relevant market. When the government brought suit, a district court found Appalachian Coals in violation of Sherman Act Section 1, citing the *Trenton Potteries* decision as precedent.[11] But on appeal the Supreme Court reversed. Chief Justice Hughes, speaking for an eight-member majority, pointed to the "deplorable" economic condition of the industry; stated that the purpose of the Sherman Act was to prevent *undue* restraints of interstate commerce; and called for the judiciary to engage in "close and objective scrutiny of particular conditions and purposes . . . in each case" to determine whether or not defendants were merely adopting reasonable measures to protect commerce from injurious and destructive practices.[12] He concluded that Appalachian Coals would not be able to fix the price of coal in consuming markets because of competition from nonmembers. Hughes suggested further that the Appalachian Coals type of selling agency was clearly no worse than a full-blown consolidation of coal producers through merger, which was not likely to be declared illegal under prevailing antitrust interpretations, and toward which the mines might be driven if not allowed to pursue the less drastic selling agency alternative. Thus, the injunction against Appalachian Coals was quashed. But since no experience under the proposed scheme had been accumulated, the Supreme Court ordered the District Court to retain jurisdiction and to take remedial action if Appalachian's operations should in fact prove to impose an undue restraint upon commerce. No review was actually made, since Congress subsequently authorized explicit price restoration measures under the National Industrial Recovery Act of 1933, the Bituminous Coal Conservation Act of 1935, and the Bituminous Coal Act of 1937.

The *Appalachian Coals* decision is now considered an anomaly with no status as a precedent. After disillusion with cartelization as an antidepression weapon set in during the mid-1930s,[13] the Court returned to a clear per se rule against explicit price-fixing arrangements. The return came in another case involving depression-inspired pricing practices, this time in the gasoline industry. Independent refiners had been dumping gasoline in the midwestern market at panic prices, demoralizing the whole price structure. During 1935 and 1936, some twelve to eighteen major refining companies organized themselves into a committee and agreed to take surplus gasoline from the independents, disposing of it in a more orderly manner so as not to depress prices. Each major firm chose one or more independent "dancing partners," whose surplus it was to acquire. In a subsequent antitrust trial, the defendant firms admitted that their scheme contributed to a rise in prices, but argued that the surplus disposal program's influence on prices was minor compared to the effect of general economic recovery, and that the increase in prices was reasonable in view of the excessively low levels to which prices had fallen during the depression. They were found guilty by a jury; and the Supreme Court on appeal sustained the jury's verdict with respect to twelve corporate defendants. Following an unconvincing attempt to rationalize its *Appalachian Coals* opinion, the Court stated that:

> . . . for over forty years this Court has consistently and without deviation adhered to the principle that price-fixing agreements are unlawful per se under the Sherman Act and that no showing of so-called competitive abuses or evils which those agreements were designed to eliminate may be interpreted as a defense. . . . If the so-called competitive abuses were to be appraised here, the reasonableness of prices would necessarily become an issue in every price-fixing case. In that event the Sherman Act would soon be emasculated; its philosophy would be supplanted by one which is wholly alien to a system of free competition; it would not be the charter of freedom which its framers intended. . . . Any combination which tampers with price structures is engaged in an unlawful activity. . . . Congress . . . has not permitted the age-old cry of ruinous competition and competitive evils to be a defense to price-fixing conspiracies.[14]

Since then, the Supreme Court's gasoline case approach has been followed consistently. Included under the per se prohibition have been not only express price-fixing agreements but also conspiracies seeking indirectly to limit price competition, such as agreements to restrict output, to divide markets up into exclusive spheres of influence, to allocate customers by seller, to follow standardized pricing formulas or methods, and to boycott or exclude from the market firms declining to abide by industry pricing norms.[15]

Borderline Cases   There remain certain gray areas in which a rule of reason has been applied or at least considered. An important early decision came in 1918, when the Supreme Court found that the Chicago Board of Trade did not violate the Sherman Act

10. Richard A. Posner, *Antitrust Law: An Economic Perspective* (Chicago: University of Chicago Press, 1976), pp. 40–41 and 76. See also Phillips, *Market Structure, supra* note 5, pp. 171–176.

11. *U.S.* v. *Appalachian Coals, Inc. et al.*, 1 F. Supp. 339 (1932).

12. *Appalachian Coals, Inc.* v. *U.S.*, 288 U.S. 344, 359–360 (1933).

13. See, for example, L. S. Lyon, P. T. Homan, et al., *The National Recovery Administration* (Washington: Brookings, 1935); J. M. Clark, "Economics and the National Recovery Administration," *American Economic Review*, vol. 24 (March 1934), pp. 11–25; Karl Pribam, "Controlled Competition and the Organization of American Industry," *Quarterly Journal of Economics*, vol. 49 (May 1935), pp. 371–393; Leonard Kuvin, "Effects of N.R.A. on the Physical Volume of Production," *Journal of the American Statistical Association*, vol. 31 (March 1936), pp. 58–60; and Ellis W. Hawley, *The New Deal and the Problem of Monopoly: A Study in Economic Ambivalence* (Princeton: Princeton University Press, 1966), Chapters 1–7.

14. *U.S.* v. *Socony-Vacuum Oil Co. et al.*, 310 U.S. 150, 218–221 (1940).

15. For an admirable survey of the cases, see A. D. Neale, *The Antitrust Laws of the U.S.A.* (2nd ed.; Cambridge: Cambridge University Press, 1970), Chapter II.

enforcing a rule requiring that members buy or sell grain when the exchange was not in session (for example, at night) only at the most recent closing price. The Court stated:

The legality of an agreement or regulation cannot be determined by so simple a test as whether it restrains competition. Every agreement concerning trade, every regulation of trade, restrains. To bind, to restrain, is of their very essence. The true test of legality is whether the restraint imposed is such as merely regulates and perhaps thereby promotes competition, or whether it is such as may suppress or even destroy competition. To determine that question the Court must ordinarily consider the facts peculiar to the business to which the restraint is applied; . . . the nature of the restraint and its effect, actual or probable.[16]

Superficially, this opinion implies a willingness to apply a rule of reason in borderline cases, where it is not obvious whether an agreement merely establishes conditions conducive to competitive trading or actually suppresses competition. However, the case was badly litigated, and as a result the courts failed to distinguish between the rule's effect on grain prices, which at worst was minute, and its much more significant effect in protecting board members from the competition of off-exchange transactions on which they received no commissions.[17] In so doing the Court may unwittingly have set the stage for a presumption that dealers on an organized exchange were somehow different from others engaged in the hurly-burly of trade, meriting special antitrust immunity that persisted for half a century.[18]

Similar immunities were for a long time enjoyed by such professions as medicine, dentistry, law, architecture, and civil engineering. The lines between rule of reason and per se cases and the criteria for deciding rule of reason cases were clarified as those immunities came under challenge.[19]

Thus, the National Society of Professional Engineers defended its rules prohibiting competitive price bidding among members by arguing *inter alia* that the avoidance of competition encouraged high-quality engineering and hence ensured public safety. This argument was rejected as beyond the bounds of rule of reason analysis, which "precludes inquiry into the question of whether competition is good or bad. . . . [W]e may assume that competition is not entirely conducive to ethical behavior, but that is not a reason, cognizable under the Sherman Act, for doing away with competition."[20]

The law's substance and procedural mandates were clarified in a case involving a more temporary profession—college football. The National Collegiate Athletic Association performed an essential function in setting rules for the conduct of college football games, and as such, its rule-making was not to be rejected per se. However, the television broadcasting rules in question were found to have curtailed programming and blunted the ability of member schools to respond to consumer preferences, and thus the NCAA "restricted rather than enhanced the place of intercollegiate athletics in the Nation's life."[21] Specifically, the NCAA rules reduced the number of games available for television broadcasting and raised the price paid by the networks per game. They prevented top-ranked schools from having as many of their games televised as market demand would support, and smaller colleges were unable to offer their games for broadcasting by local stations. These effects were seen by the Supreme Court as sufficiently restrictive on their face that the NCAA had to assume a "heavy burden" in defending them. And the Court found the NCAA's defenses — its desire to protect "live attendance" at games and to maintain "competitive balance" among teams — to have little or no demonstrated connection with the broadcasting restrictions.

A practice that received the Supreme Court's blessing delineates the boundaries further. Broadcast Music, Inc., (BMI) and the American Society of Composers, Authors and Publishers (ASCAP) took copyright assignments from musical composers and licensed to television and radio broadcasters a package of rights to all their composers' works at fixed royalty rates, distributing the proceeds back to composers on the basis of measured usage of individual works. Since each represented thousands of composers, the activities of ASCAP and BMI were clearly a form of price fixing. Yet in the Supreme Court's view, they had at least two persuasive merits. For one, neither group prevented composers from licensing their copyrights individually with the using broadcasters; the blanket license was an option to the individual licenses still available. But for a broadcaster using many compositions by many composers, work-by-work licensing entailed substantial negotiation costs; these could be economized by taking advantage of the package license. Thus, the blanket licensing was not coercive, and it did not "facially" restrict competition or decrease output, but it did offer potential benefits.[22] It could not therefore automatically be found anticompetitive, and so the Supreme Court referred the question back to the lower court for "a more discriminating examination." On reconsideration, the appellate court declined to engage in a full-scale balancing of benefits against costs. Since the blanket licensing arrangements were not per se illegal, those who challenged them had to bear the burden of proving that they restrained competition among copyright owners. But since individual licensing was feasible, the court concluded, that burden had not been borne, and so the arrangements were allowed to stand.[23]

From these cases emerges a three-tier approach for dealing with restrictive agreements. Certain classes of agreements, for example, hard-core price fixing, are deemed so restrictive that they are illegal per se if shown to exist. Other agreements may have redeeming features that render them appropriate for rule of reason analysis, but if preliminary scrutiny shows that they are restrictive and anticompetitive on their face, the inquiry can cease, and illegality will be presumed.

16. *Board of Trade of the City of Chicago* v. *U.S.*, 246 U.S. 231, 238 (1918).

17. See Richard O. Zerbe, "The Chicago Board of Trade Case, 1918," *Research in Law and Economics*, vol. 5 (1983), pp. 17–55.

18. In 1974 the scope of Chicago Board of Trade members' collective commission fixing was narrowed in an antitrust consent decree. Antitrust and Congressional attack on the practices of New York Stock Exchange brokers led to the phased elimination of fixed commissions beginning in 1972. See H. Michael Mann, "The New York Stock Exchange: A Cartel at the End of Its Reign," in Almarin Phillips, ed., *Promoting Competition in Regulated Markets* (Washington: Brookings, 1975), pp. 301–327.

19. A key early case was *Goldfarb* v. *Virginia State Bar Association*, 421 U.S. 773 (1975).

20. *National Society of Professional Engineers* v. *U.S.*, 435 U.S. 679, 695, 696 (1978). For a more complete review of the cases, see Lawrence A. Sullivan, "The Viability of the Current Law on Horizontal Restraints," *California Law Review*, vol. 75 (May 1987), pp. 836–855.

21. *National Collegiate Athletic Association* v. *Board of Regents of the University of Oklahoma et al.*, 468 U.S. 85, 120 (1984).

22. *Broadcast Music, Inc. et al.* v. *Columbia Broadcasting System et al.*, 441 U.S. 1, 19–20 (1979).

23. *Columbia Broadcasting System, Inc.* v. *ASCAP et al.*, 620 F. 2d 930 (1980), cert. den. 450 U.S. 970 (1981).

Only those that pass through the first two screens qualify for more careful balancing of benefits and costs.

Explicit Exemptions

In addition to the borderline cases treated under rule of reason analysis, several species of price fixing have been accorded explicit statutory exemption from the antitrust laws. Several of the earliest attempts to enforce the Sherman Act were directed against labor unions, including railroad union supporters of the famous 1894 Pullman strike.[24] However, Section 6 of the Clayton Act exempted from antitrust the activities of labor and agricultural or horticultural organizations whose objective was the mutual help of members.[25] The efforts of workers to secure higher wages through unionization received further support under the Norris-LaGuardia Act of 1932 and the National Labor Relations Act (Wagner Act) of 1935. Currently binding judicial interpretations have not permitted the exemption to be extended beyond the bounds of particular employer-employee wage and working conditions bargains. Attempts by unions to collude with unionized employers in fixing end product prices or driving nonunion firms out of business were ruled violations of the Sherman Act.[26]

In addition to the exempting language of Clayton Act Section 6, joint activities of agricultural cooperatives were further shielded from antitrust through the Capper-Volstead Act of 1922 as long as they do not "unduly" enhance farm product prices. Responsibility for enforcing the Act was assigned to the Department of Agriculture, which during the 1930s also acquired the power to issue *marketing orders* binding farm goods handlers and processors to abide by farm cooperative price and output restrictions. With a mandate to serve farm interests, the department has shown little concern about the impact of cooperatives' price-fixing activities on consumers.[27]

The 1918 Webb-Pomerene Act exemption from antitrust of price fixing and other agreements pertaining solely to export sales is a mercantilist remnant common to the antitrust policies of most industrialized nations. Although its intent was partly to permit small domestic firms to penetrate foreign markets more effectively and to secure economies of scale through coordinated marketing, an equally important objective has been to alter the terms of trade and enhance payments balances by allowing domestic producers to exploit whatever power over export prices they might collectively possess. Originally, the Webb-Pomerene provisions required that export cartel agreements be monitored by the Federal Trade Commission to ensure that they do not intentionally or artificially affect prices in the domestic market. However, the Export Trading Company Act of 1982 shifted primary jurisdiction to the Department of Commerce, at the same time giving veto power to the Department of Justice in cases of abuse or injury to domestic competitors. The Webb-Pomerene exemptions were invoked with surprising infrequency, covering only about 4 percent of U.S. exports by value in 1965 and 1.5 percent in the late 1970s.[28]

In the early years of American antitrust, Sherman Act bans on price-fixing agreements applied with equal force to regulated and unregulated industries. Indeed, as we have seen, the first substantive Supreme Court decision found price fixing illegal in railroading, the first federally regulated industry. Gradually, however, grants of immunity were written into the principal statutes governing regulated industries, e.g., for the railroads, the Reed-Bulwinkle Act, passed over President Truman's veto in 1948. More recently, the wheel has turned as the antitrust agencies won court injunctions against price fixing and other restrictive practices in a number of industries previously assumed to be exempt by virtue of being regulated, and as efforts to deregulate such industries as transportation proceeded.

In 1984, concerned that the United States was lagging behind international competitors in the performance of industrial research and development, Congress passed the National Cooperative Research and Development Act. It creates an important exception to the antitrust laws, requiring that appropriately registered joint ventures among competitors to carry out research and/or development be judged under a rule of reason standard balancing the benefits of joint work against any potential anticompetitive effects. Experience with the new law was too limited at the time this was written to evaluate how successful the courts would be in undertaking such rule of reason analyses.[29]

Remedies and Penalties in Price-Fixing Cases

Under the Sherman Act, the Department of Justice possesses two weapons for attacking price-fixing conduct. It can institute a civil suit (that is, a suit in equity), the end result of which may be a court injunction against illegal practices; or it can seek a criminal indictment leading to punitive fines and/or prison sentences. Because the legal proscriptions against express price-fixing agreements are so clear, the Justice Department has tended to emphasize criminal sanctions against pricing conspiracies. The criminal route has the advantage of secret grand jury proceedings and the possibility of offering immunity to individuals involved in the conspiracy, inducing the provision of evidence that would otherwise be difficult to elicit. This advantage is compelling; efforts by the Federal Trade Commission to detect and prosecute hard-core price-fixing violations without it have been generally unsuccessful.

Until 1955, the maximum fine assessable for Sherman Act violations was $5,000 per count. This was so low that it was often more profitable to violate the

24. *U.S.* v. *Debs et al.*, 64 Fed. 724 (1894).

25. For a review of the debate over the labor exemption's appropriateness, see Robert H. Lande and Richard O. Zerbe, "Reducing Unions' Monopoly Power: Costs and Benefits," *Journal of Law & Economics*, vol. 28 (May 1985), pp. 297–310.

26. An important Supreme Court decision was *Pennington* v. *United Mine Workers et al.*, 381 U.S. 657 (1965), 257 F. Supp. 815 (1966). It is analyzed in Oliver E. Williamson, "Wage Rates as a Barrier to Entry: The Pennington Case in Perspective," *Quarterly Journal of Economics*, vol. 82 (February 1968), pp. 85–116.

27. For diverse views, see Willard F. Mueller, Peter G. Helmberger, and Thomas W. Paterson, *The Sunkist Case: A Study in Legal-Economic Analysis* (Lexington: Lexington Books, 1987), especially Chapter 2; and Thomas M. Lenard and Michael P. Mazur, "Harvest of Waste: The Marketing Order Program," *Regulation*, May/June 1985, pp. 19–26.

28. See the testimony of Willard F. Mueller in U.S. Senate, Committee on the Judiciary, Subcommittee on Antitrust and

Monopoly, hearings, *International Aspects of Antitrust* (Washington: USGPO, 1967), pp. 31–60; David A. Larson, "An Economic Analysis of the Webb-Pomerene Act," *Journal of Law & Economics*, vol. 13 (October 1970), pp. 461–500; and Joel Davidow, "Cartels, Competition Laws and the Regulation of International Trade," *Journal of International Law and Politics*, vol. 15 (Winter 1983), pp. 351–376.

29. For analyses of early registrations, see Barry Bozeman, Albert Link, and Asghar Zardkoohi, "An Economic Analysis of R&D Joint Ventures," *Managerial and Decision Economics*, vol. 7 (December 1986), pp. 263–266; and John T. Scott, "Diversification versus Cooperation in R&D Investment," *Managerial and Decision Economics*, vol. 9 (June 1988), pp. 173–186. For an argument that the exemption did not go far enough, see Thomas Jorde and David Teece, "Innovation, Cooperation and Antitrust," paper presented at a University of California, Berkeley, Conference on Antitrust, Innovation and Competitiveness, October 1988.

law and risk being caught than to refrain from violations. In 1955 Congress raised the maximum fine to $50,000 per count. In 1974 the ceiling was raised again to $100,000 for individuals and $1 million for corporations, and price-fixing violations were made a felony (rather than a misdemeanor, as they had been until then). The average fine per case rose from $116,465 for cases initiated during the early 1960s to $629,398 for cases instituted during the early 1980s.[30]

A more potent deterrent may be the imposition of prison sentences. This penalty was used infrequently at first. Between 1890 and 1940, jail sentences were imposed in only twenty-four cases, thirteen involving trade union leaders and eleven business executives. All the businessmen imprisoned during this period had perpetrated acts of racketeering accompanied by overt threats, intimidation, or violence.[31] Only since the late 1950s have business officials been incarcerated for simple price fixing. Even then, judges were traditionally reluctant to treat white-collar antitrust violators as harshly as, say, burglars, embezzlers, and other nonviolent garden-variety criminals. Thus, the longest price-fixing sentence up to 1974 was ninety days, and more often than not, suspended sentences were issued. However, in extending the maximum Sherman Act violation sentence from one to three years in 1974, Congress made clear its intent to escalate the stakes; and the Department of Justice began urging significant jail terms as a regular matter in hard-core collusion cases. In twenty cases initiated between 1975 and 1979, fifty-one persons were sentenced to prison terms ranging from ten days to three years, with an average term of 130 days per person convicted.[32]

Clearly, the deterrent effect has been strengthened. There is reason to believe that, at least for larger corporations employing attorneys aware of the antitrust law's sting, conduct that could lead to per se convictions has been discouraged or at least driven more deeply underground. Statistical studies suggest that prices and/or price-cost margins fall following price-fixing indictments.[33]

Even more potent may be the impact of a relatively recent development. Clayton Act Section 4 (which amended Section 7 of the original Sherman Act) permits persons injured by antitrust law violations to sue for the recovery of three times the amount of damages sustained. Clayton Act Section 5 permits treble damage plaintiffs to draw upon prior antitrust judgments resulting from government-initiated cases in proving that a violation has occurred. These provisions were used infrequently, and without much success, until after World War II. Then a series of favorable Supreme Court decisions simplified the problems of obtaining evidence, forming classes of aggrieved plaintiffs, and proving damages. The number of private treble damages suits increased from eighty-three per year on average in the 1940s to 221 in the 1950s, 696 in the 1960s, and 1,314 in the 1970s.[34] During the 1970s, the number of private filings exceeded by seventeen times the number of cases initiated by the federal government antitrust agencies. Most treble damages cases are settled "out of court" by negotiation for relatively modest sums, with a median value of $50,000 for a sample of seventy-one settlements surveyed by Salop and White.[35] However, some of the suits have yielded spectacular payments — for example, roughly $500 million in the numerous cases following a massive electrical equipment price-fixing conspiracy during the 1950s and at least equal amounts in the wake of proven price fixing by cardboard carton manufacturers.[36]

The risk of having to pay treble damages for antitrust law violations almost surely creates a strong deterrent effect against price fixing. However, the treble damages law also carries problems. Treble damages suits have proliferated in connection with other substantive areas of antitrust law, including matters on which the perceived balance of costs against benefits is less lopsided and per se rules have been found inappropriate. Analyzing a sample of 2,357 cases, Salop and White discovered that although horizontal price fixing was complained of more often than any other alleged violation, price-fixing allegations were levied in only 21 percent of the suits.[37] Even though relatively few cases — 3.4 percent in the Salop-White sample — continue all the way to court judgments favoring the plaintiffs, the risk of treble damages awards as a consequence of nonhard-core conduct could encourage more conservative, less aggressive business behavior. There is also a temptation for nuisance suits to be filed in the expectation that target companies will offer an out-of-court settlement (including an appreciable fee for the plaintiff attorneys, who often act as entrepreneurs in initiating the action). Salop and White found that 70.8 percent of the cases in their sample were settled "out of court," with attorney fees amounting to 20.3 percent of the average sum paid out as a damages settlement.[38] The trebling of damages could in principle create incentives for injured parties to forego taking measures that would eliminate or minimize losses incurred as a consequence of others' behavior. It is said, for example, that electrical power utilities failed to combat known price fixing by electrical equipment manufacturers because elevated equipment prices increased the asset base upon which, under the prevailing scheme of price regulation, their allowable

30. See Joseph C. Gallo, Joseph L. Craycroft, and Steven C. Bush, "Guess Who Came to Dinner: An Empirical Study of Federal Antitrust Enforcement for the Period 1963–1984," *Review of Industrial Organization*, vol. 2 (1985), p. 120.

In 1989, legislation to raise the maximum fine to $10 million was under consideration.

31. See James M. Clabault and John F. Burton, *Sherman Act Indictments, 1955–1965* (New York: Federal Legal Publications, 1966), p. 104; and Richard A. Posner, "A Statistical Study of Antitrust Enforcement," *Journal of Law & Economics*, vol. 13 (October 1970), pp. 365–420.

32. Gallo et al., "Guess Who," pp. 123–124.

33. See Robert M. Feinberg, "Antitrust Enforcement and Subsequent Price Behavior," *Review of Economics and Statistics*, vol. 62 (November 1980), pp. 609–612; Dosoung Choi and George C. Philippatos, "Financial Consequences of Antitrust Enforcement," *Review of Economics and Statistics*, vol. 65 (August 1983), pp. 501–506; and Michael K. Block, Frederick C. Nold, and Joseph G. Sidak, "The Deterrent Effect of Antitrust Enforcement," *Journal of Political Economy*, vol. 89 (June 1981), pp. 429–445.

34. Steven C. Salop and Lawrence J. White, "Private Antitrust Litigation: An Introduction and Framework," in White, ed., *Private Antitrust Litigation: New Evidence, New Learning* (Cambridge: MIT Press, 1988), p. 4.

35. Ibid., p. 13.

36. See Charles A. Bane, *The Electrical Equipment Conspiracies: The Treble Damages Actions* (New York: Federal Legal Publications, 1973), pp. 250–265; "Cardboard Makers To Pay $300 Million To End Pricing Suit," *New York Times*, May 2, 1979, p. 1; "Fact-Finding Backed in Mead Price-Fixing," *New York Times*, June 2, 1982, p. D2; "Mead Corp. Settlement," *New York Times*, September 8, 1982, p. D14; and Robert C. Goldberg, Craig Hakkio, and Leon Moses, "Competition and Collusion, Side-by-Side: The Corrugated Container Antitrust Litigation," undated manuscript. Exact damages figures are not available, since many of the companies settled the claims against them without a public announcement of the amounts changing hands.

37. Salop and White, "Private Antitrust," supra note 34, p. 6.

38. Ibid., pp. 7 and 14. Attorneys representing the government are also not immune from opportunistic conduct. In the 1976 debate over antitrust law amendments permitting state attorneys general to sue for treble damages on behalf of all state residents injured by an alleged collusive scheme, it was argued that poorly grounded suits might be brought by ambitious, publicity-seeking politicians. The *parens patriae* law ultimately enacted gave the courts discretion to award attorney fees to respondents who defended themselves successfully against suits brought in bad faith or for oppressive reasons.

profits were calculated.[39] Similarly, the Pillsbury Company was able to collect an unusually large award from folding carton manufacturers because the bidding system it used — requiring a carton maker to bid on *all* of the forty to sixty carton types it planned to purchase — excluded smaller, nonconspiring companies from the bidding and hence left it peculiarly vulnerable to the price-raising efforts of the conspirators.[40] Because there is no provision in antitrust treble damages law equivalent to the "contributory negligence" doctrine of tort law, Pillsbury's misguided procurement system turned out to be a source of gain.

These dangers are real. Proposals for reform include requiring unsuccessful plaintiffs to pay all litigation costs, the award of only single damages for nonhardcore violations,[41] the introduction of a contributory negligence defense, and the complete elimination of private damages suits and substitution of fines (paid to the federal treasury) commensurate with the monopoly profits realized by lawbreaking corporations. Yet the private damages approach also has compelling advantages — notably, decentralizing initiative to buyer groups and private law firms with superior access to information and more legal talent than a government enforcement agency can normally command. Whether the right balance has been struck is likely to remain controversial.[42]

Controversy will also continue over an anomaly in the U.S. treble damages law. In 1977, the Supreme Court ruled that under normal circumstances, final consumers could not sue to recover damages for the elevation of prices resulting from monopolistic behavior more than one stage removed in the distribution chain.[43] In the case at hand, there was an alleged price-fixing arrangement by concrete block manufacturers, who sold to masonry contractors, who contracted with general contractors carrying out projects for the State of Illinois and various county and city governments. To allow the State of Illinois as final consumer to sue, the Supreme Court argued, would be to subject the price fixers to multiple liability, since there was no question that the first-stage masonry contractor buyers could recover trebled damages for the overcharges they sustained. And attempting to apportion the damages among the several stages in the chain, it continued, would be excessively difficult. Since at least some, if not all, of the elevated prices attributable to price fixing are likely to be passed on by middlemen to end consumers under either competitive or monopolistic pricing,[44] the *Illinois Brick* decision lets middlemen recover damages for losses they have not sustained, while the presumed beneficiary of antitrust law — the consumer — is unable to be made whole. Attempts by Congress to change the law in the late 1970s were successfully resisted by business interests, but the problem will continue to demand attention.

Antitrust Abroad: A Comparison

While the per se rule was emerging in America during the early part of the twentieth century, most European nations had no statutory antitrust laws at all, and cartels flourished. The few laws that did exist related only to abuses of individual or collective monopoly power, and they were seldom enforced. Following World War II, there was an international antitrust legislation boom. Now nearly every

Western nation has some kind of antitrust law, or to use a term accentuating the positive, *competition policy*. Examining the approaches adopted abroad puts the U.S. laws in perspective and brings out more clearly the underlying philosophy, advantages, and drawbacks of the American system. No nation's laws are completely typical, and a superficial survey of all would add little value. We therefore focus mainly on the British system, adding only a brief overview of several other national systems to highlight some differences.[45]

Prior to World War II, the British had no significant statutory law concerning price-fixing arrangements and cartels. The applicable rules were those of common law which, in the *laissez faire* spirit of the nineteenth century, had gradually given increasing weight to the principle of free contract, permitting businesses to enter freely into contracts with one another, including contracts and agreements restricting competition. In emphasizing this right, the courts implicitly sacrificed the right of individual citizens to enjoy the benefits of free and unrestricted competition. Recognizing the antisocial potential of restrictive agreements, the British courts refused to provide positive support by enforcing such contracts against parties (for example, price chiselers) who breached them. But they also would not intervene to overturn restrictive agreements or award damages to an injured third party unless some explicitly unlawful act of violence, intimidation, molestation, or fraud was perpetrated in connection with the restriction.[46]

The first major change came in 1956, when Parliament approved the Restrictive Trade Practices Act.[47] The act required agreements in restraint of trade

39. See William Breit and Kenneth G. Elzinga, "Antitrust Enforcement and Economic Efficiency: The Uneasy Case for Treble Damages," *Journal of Law & Economics*, vol. 17 (October 1974), pp. 337–338.

40. Multi-District Litigation 250 (the Folding Carton case) (Northern District of Illinois). Co-author Scherer was advisor to the court in assessing the validity of damages claims.

41. In the first such changes, the Export Trading Company Act of 1982 and the National Cooperative Research Act of 1984 limited plaintiffs to single damages against agreements registered under the acts, but shown in subsequent litigation to step beyond the bounds of the law.

42. For a thoroughgoing debate on the issues, see the papers in the conference volume edited by White, *Private Antitrust Litigation*, supra note 34.

43. *Illinois Brick Co. et al.* v. *Illinois et al.*, 431 U.S. 720 (1977). On a successful challenge to one facet of *Illinois Brick*, see "Court Allows States Wide Antitrust Law to Shield Consumers," *New York Times*, April 19, 1989, p. 1.

44. Under competitive pricing at the first buying stage, the added costs will be passed on fully if the supply function is horizontal. There will be less passing on, the more closely the supply function approaches the vertical. Under purely monopolistic pricing with straight-line demand functions, half of the added costs will be passed on if the marginal cost curve is horizontal; less than half will be passed on if the marginal cost curve is upward-sloping.

45. There is now a vast comparative literature. A useful source is the Organisation for Economic Cooperation and Development loose-leaf compendium, *Guide to Legislation on Restrictive Business Practices*. Its periodical updating appears to have lagged in recent years, but new developments are summarized in annual OECD publications, *Competition Policy in OECD Countries* (before 1983, titled *Annual Reports on Competition Policy in OECD Member Countries*).

46. A key decision was *Mogul Steamship Co.* v. *McGregor, Gow, and Co.*, 21 Q.B.D. 544 (1888), 23 Q.B.D. 598 (1889).

47. Valuable surveys on the act and its interpretation include R. S. Stevens and B. S. Yamey, *The Restrictive Practices Court* (London: Weidenfeld, 1965); the Symposium on Restrictive Practices in *Oxford Economic Papers*, vol. 17 n.s. (November 1965); Dennis Swann, Denis P. O'Brien, W. P. Maunder, and W. S. Howe, *Competition in British Industry* (London: Allen & Unwin, 1974); John Agnew, *Competition Law* (London: Allen & Unwin, 1985); and J. Douglass Klein, "Cooperation and the *Per Se* Debate: Evidence from the United Kingdom," paper presented at the American Economic Association meetings, December 1987.

among suppliers of goods to be registered with a Registrar of Restrictive Practices;[48] it authorized the registrar to challenge any agreements that appear contrary to the public interest; and it established a special Restrictive Practices Court, with streamlined procedures and a membership including both judges and laypeople, to determine whether challenged agreements should be prohibited. Parties to a challenged agreement bear the burden of proving to the court that their agreement provides positive benefits covered under one or more of eight *gateways* and of showing in addition that the benefits from the agreement outweigh the harm. The gateways include such defenses as the following: The agreement is necessary to protect the public against injury; it is necessary to counteract measures taken by competitors not party to the agreement; it is necessary to negotiate fair prices with powerful suppliers; it is necessary to sustain the level of export earnings; its removal would have serious and persistent adverse effects on local employment and unemployment; it does not materially restrict competition and is unlikely to do so; and its removal would deny the public substantial benefits or advantages. This is a rule of reason approach, but one much broader than what has evolved in the United States. The Restrictive Practices Court has broad discretion to determine whether or not an agreement is, on balance, socially desirable or undesirable.

Despite the breadth of certain gateways and legal traditions far from hostile to cooperation among business enterprises, the Restrictive Practices Court demonstrated its willingness to adopt a hard line. By the end of 1964, more than 2,400 agreements had been registered, and thirty-two cases had been contested before the Court. Of these thirty-two, only nine led to decisions in favor of the companies; the other twenty-three agreements had to be discontinued or substantially revamped. In more than seventy-five other cases the court rendered uncontested decisions, typically against the restrictions in question. By 1986, the number of "goods" (that is, not service) registrations had climbed to 4,557, with twelve agreements surviving in thirty-five contested cases. In its very first contested price-fixing case, the court accepted as a valid defense the contention of the British Cotton Yarn Spinners Association that theirs was a declining industry, and that painful pockets of localized unemployment would develop if their pricing schemes were rejected. But the court held that the benefits of the agreement were outweighed by the harm — notably, the retention of inefficient and unnecessary capacity in the industry.[49] This ringing (and to most observers unexpected) declaration of faith in competitive market processes, supplemented by hard-line decisions in several subsequent cases, led to the voluntary abandonment of more than a thousand other restrictive agreements and the modification of hundreds more.

Nevertheless, in at least a few cases, the Restrictive Practices Court has been willing to accept price-fixing agreements as reasonable. These decisions are of special interest because they show how far the court can go in weighing benefits against costs. They therefore provide a valuable contrast to the American scene.

The first[50] involved a bidding cartel among six steam boiler manufacturers, with facts similar to the *Addyston Pipe & Steel* case of U.S. fame. Overhead costs were high; demand was cyclical; orders often came in substantial chunks; and a single customer (the government's Electricity Generating Board) placed 83 percent of all domestic orders. One attempted defense, pleading that price fixing was necessary to maintain industry capacity and support research and development during recessions, was rejected after an analysis of the evidence. Another defense, urging the need to create countervailing power to deal with the monopsonistic Electricity Generating Board, was struck down on a technicality, though it may have influenced the court's ultimate decision. The court's approval was formally premised on its acceptance of an argument that cooperation was required to compete more effectively in export markets. The decision, applying to both domestic and overseas transactions, is consistent with the approach of the U.S. Webb-Pomerene and Export Trading Company Acts, except that American law prohibits extension of an export cartel's influence to the domestic market.

Price fixing by nut and bolt manufacturers was approved in order to save small-lot purchasers the trouble of shopping around, after a finding that the prices fixed were reasonable.[51] A cement industry agreement was authorized when the court concluded that the industry was charging reasonable prices and that it would be able to attract capital at lower costs (and hence charge lower prices) if the uncertainties created by substantial cyclical fluctuations in an environment of high overhead costs were ameliorated through collusion.[52] The American cement industry, advancing similar arguments in defense of less extensive collusive arrangements, was found to be violating the U.S. laws.[53] An agreement among magnet manufacturers was endorsed when the court concluded that desirable cooperation in research and development would be inhibited unless the firms could also cooperate in pricing.[54] Under the U.S. Cooperative Research Act of 1984 and earlier precedents, R&D joint ventures that extend their reach into product price fixing are illegal. A purchasing cartel among sulphuric acid producers was approved in order to countervail the power of the American sulphur export cartel.[55] And as a last example, price fixing by ceramic tile makers was sanctioned to enforce standardization of tile sizes, allowing alleged economies in production.[56]

Several of the price-fixing agreements approved by the British Restrictive Practices Court could not have survived an American antitrust challenge. Some of the court's permissive decisions have been sharply criticized for defective economic reasoning; and commentators have argued that the benefits claimed were dubious at best, so that a per se prohibition would have caused no serious social

48. Under 1973 amendments, the Registrar's Office was taken over by an Office of Fair Trading with expanded jurisdiction. The registration of agreements concerning services (but not professional services) as well as goods was also required beginning in 1973.

49. *In re Yarn Spinners' Agreement*, L.R., 1 R.P. 118 (1959). Shortly after the decision, the Conservative government passed a law providing compensation for yarn spinning firms required to close plants because of price competition. There was also a wave of horizontal and vertical mergers among textile makers.

50. *In re Water-Tube Boilermakers' Agreement*, L.R., 1 R.P. 285 (1959).

51. *In re Black Bolt and Nut Association's Agreement*, L.R., 2 R.P. 50 (1960).

52. *In re Cement Makers' Federation Agreement*, L.R., 2 R.P. 241

(1961). An executive of one U.K. firm told co-author Scherer in 1970 that the cartel rules introduced so many inflexibilities, it was questionable whether even the cement producers really benefited. Nevertheless, an attempt by the registrar to overturn the agreement's approval because of changed circumstances was unsuccessful. See Arthur Beacham, "Cement Revisited," *Bulletin of Economic Research*, vol. 27 (November 1975), pp. 104–108.

53. *Federal Trade Commission* v. *Cement Institute et al.*, 333 U.S. 683 (1948).

54. *In re Permanent Magnet Association's Agreement*, L.R., 3 R.P. 119 and 392 (1962).

55. *In re National Sulphuric Acid Association's Agreement*, L.R., 4 R.P. 169 (1963).

56. *In re Glazed and Floor Tile Home Trade Association's Agreement*, L.R., 4 R.P. 239 (1963).

losses while saving substantial legal costs.[57] The court's procedures have been criticized as slow and inefficient,[58] although they are clearly much more expeditious than their U.S. counterparts, dispatching contested cases in from six to thirty-five hearing days. More importantly, the court can levy fines only against firms that have violated its explicit orders, and there is reason to believe that many agreements have been driven "underground," where the worst that can happen is that they will be discovered and subjected to *future* prohibition.[59] Also, as experience was accumulated with the restrictive practices law, firms found ways to revise their agreements so as to achieve the desired effect without violating the law's formal prohibitions. Cadbury Schweppes and J. Lyons, for example, converted a clearly illegal quota system in the distribution of citrus concentrate into an arrangement with the same effect, but winning court approval, by agreeing that Cadbury purchase 43 percent of its concentrate requirements from Lyons, with substantial penalties for falling below the 43 percent figure.[60] A 1979 government review criticized the law for emphasizing "form" over "effect," but urged no substantial reorientation because business firms had attuned their practices to the existing precedents.[61] In 1988, however, the Department of Trade and Industry recommended major changes to emphasize "effect" over "form," to eliminate the registration system but give the Office of Fair Trading substantial subpoena powers, and to increase fines for anticompetitive behavior.[62]

The original West German antitrust statute, passed in 1957, outlaws price-fixing agreements, but permits exceptions to ease the adjustment problems of secularly stagnating industries; to reduce costs through joint research and development, marketing, or production specialization arrangements; to promote exports or facilitate imports; and to cope with "exceptional circumstances" in the economic situation. Exceptions on efficiency grounds are supposedly granted on the condition that prices not be increased, although a statistical study reveals that abnormal price increases have in fact tended to occur in exempted industries.[63] In 1973 the law was amended to exempt agreements promoting the efficiency of small and medium-sized firms (that is, with a combined market share of less than 15 percent). Other amendments made clear that in nonexempt areas, "concerted actions" as well as restrictions of a contractual nature were prohibited. After a slow start, enforcement of the law has been vigorous — probably second only to that of the United States. Unlike its British counterpart, the German Federal Cartel Office (Bundeskartellamt) is armed with abundant subpoena powers so that, for example, its staff was able in September 1971 to burst in upon cement industry executives *in flagrante delicto* — using a slide projector to display agreed-upon sales quotas for upcoming months. Amendments in 1968 authorized fines commensurate with the excess profits gained through violation. Early applications included fines totalling DM 48 million against nine synthetic fiber producers and DM 7 million against seven breweries fixing prices in the Dortmund area.

Article 85, Section 1, of the 1957 Treaty of Rome (which established the European Community) prohibited all interfirm agreements that have the effect of preventing, restraining, or distorting competition within the Common Market. Among the offenses explicitly mentioned are agreements fixing prices and restricting output. Section 3 of the same article then provides an escape hatch permitting the exemption of agreements that contribute toward improving the production or distribution of goods or promoting technical progress, as long as consumers receive a fair share of the resulting benefits and competition is not substantially eliminated. Interpretation of this rule of reason approach was delegated to the EC Commission and the Court of Justice. In 1962 the commission set up a system for the registration of restrictive agreements, but it also operates a parallel surveillance system, and if unregistered but presumptively illegal agreements are discovered, the companies involved can be fined heavily. At the time this was written, its subpoena powers were still being tested following a successful effort in 1987 by chemicals maker Hoechst, a West German firm, to obtain a local court order temporarily barring commission employees from entering its premises to search for documents.

A generally tough line was taken toward straightforward price fixing and market-sharing agreements covering a significant share of community output, and beginning with action against an unregistered cartel among quinine sellers in 1969, fines of growing severity were imposed upon violators. The commission has been more tolerant of specialization agreements—for example, when one firm supplies the combined market demand for certain product variants and yields the market for other variants to rivals—as long as the number of suppliers is not reduced unduly. Specialization agreements among small and medium-sized firms with a national market share of 10 percent or less (revised in 1985 to 20 percent of Common Market sales) were given block exemption in a 1972 ruling. An important test of the commission's policies occurred in the late 1970s when the synthetic fibers industry was suffering from severe excess capacity, and the Commissioner for Industrial Affairs recommended that a "crisis cartel" be formed. The commission as a whole was reluctant to give its formal approval, especially to the cartel's market-sharing provisions. The arrangement broke down in 1980—because of legal uncertainties, according to one commentator, but also because of Italian firms' reluctance to cooperate, according to another.[64] However, in 1984 a capacity closure agreement was approved by the commission, subject to conditions that the

57. See Alister Sutherland, "Economics in the Restrictive Practices Court," *Oxford Economic Papers*, vol. 17 n.s. (November 1965), pp. 422–423; and J. P. Cairns, "Benefits from Restrictive Agreements: The British Experience," *Canadian Journal of Economics and Political Science*, vol. 30 (May 1964), pp. 228–240.

58. I. A. MacDonald, "The Restrictive Practices Court: A Lawyer's View," *Oxford Economic Papers*, vol. 17 n.s. (November 1965), pp. 372–375.

59. Agnew, *Competition Law*, supra note 47, pp. 133–135.

60. See Thomas Sharpe, "British Competition Policy in Perspective," *Oxford Review of Economic Policy*, vol. 1 (Autumn 1985), p. 87.

61. *Review of Restrictive Trade Practices Policy* (the so-called Leisner Report) (London: HMSO, 1979).

62. "Competition Law: Tougher," *The Economist*, March 12, 1988, p. 56.

63. See David B. Audretsch, "Legalized Cartels in West Germany," working paper, Science Centre Berlin, January 1988.

64. Compare Dennis Swann, *Competition and Industrial Policy in the European Community* (London: Methuen, 1983), pp. 95–96;

Joseph Bower, *When Markets Quake: The Management Challenge of Restructuring Industry* (Boston: Harvard Business School Press, 1986), p. 78; and R. W. Shaw and S. A. Shaw, "Excess Capacity and Rationalisation in the West European Synthetic Fibers Industry," *Journal of Industrial Economics*, vol. 32 (December 1983), pp. 151–153.

Similar uncertainties beset European petrochemical producers, who were informally encouraged by the Commissioner for Industrial Affairs to form a cartel, but had difficulty agreeing among themselves on a formula for capacity reduction and were fined by the Commission for unauthorized agreements. See, for example, Bower, pp. 181–186; Organisation for Economic Co-Operation and Development, *Competition Policy in OECD Countries, 1985–86* (Paris: 1987), pp. 256–257; and "Europe Fines 23 Concerns," *New York Times*, December 22, 1988, p. D15. Some petrochemical plant closures were authorized as bilateral specialization agreements. Conflicts between the directorate responsible for competition policy and those concerned with industrial policy are not uncommon.

"parties' marketing behaviour" would not be affected and that consumers "derive a fair share of the benefit resulting."[65]

The Canadian antitrust code dating back to 1889 included from its beginning provisions authorizing criminal penalties (that is, fines and/or imprisonment) for anyone who "conspires, combines, agrees or arranges with another person . . . to prevent, limit or lessen, unduly, the manufacture or production of a product, or to enhance unreasonably the price thereof." The words *unduly* and *unreasonably* suggest a rule of reason approach. But in leading cases the courts held that the public has a vested interest in the maintenance of competition and that every agreement which "materially interferes with competition in a substantial sector of trade" is detrimental to the public interest.[66] This comes close to the U.S. philosophy. Amendments effective in 1976 stipulated that proof of violation does not require a showing that complete or virtual elimination of competition is likely, and bid-rigging agreements were singled out as per se illegal.[67] At the same time antitrust coverage was extended to services as well as goods; and civil remedies such as injunctions, the reduction of tariffs on offending products, and suits for damages were made available as substitutes for, or complements to, criminal sanctions.

Japan's postwar antitrust laws provide exemptions from price-fixing prohibitions on a number of grounds—for example, to deal with temporary business recessions or structural crises such as the shock imparted by OPEC oil price increases, to rationalize production, for exports and imports, and to aid small businesses.[68] No single case is typical, but events in the aluminum industry illustrate one of the exceptions.[69] With the rise in petroleum prices, Japan's aluminum industry, lacking its international rivals' access to low-cost hydroelectric power, became hopelessly noncompetitive. The Ministry of International Trade and Industry (MITI) recommended a capacity reduction cartel, which was approved by the Fair Trade Commission (responsible for cartel law enforcement). Together MITI and the five aluminum producers drew up a mutual capacity reduction plan aimed at cutting back aluminum ingot capacity by 530,000 tons, that is, 32 percent of 1978 capacity. The plan was lubricated by permission from MITI to import from Japanese-owned offshore sources 400,000 tons of low-cost aluminum duty-free, permitting the companies to maintain their product-rolling operations at home. The capacity reduction goal was surpassed by 1982, and as of 1987, ingot capacity reductions totaling 80 percent had been achieved. How crucial the cartel was to this achievement is unclear; the Japanese producers' costs were so high that cutbacks would have been necessitated under any circumstances. But the cartel undoubtedly transformed what might otherwise have been a rout into a relatively orderly withdrawal.

Although exceptions such as this one exist, the trend in Japan has been toward greater efforts to discourage restrictive agreements. In 1963, according to Fair Trade Commission estimates, 28 percent of Japanese manufacturing output was covered by cartel agreements; by 1973, the comparable figure had fallen to 18 percent.[70] In 1977, the Fair Trade Commission was authorized to levy fines ("surcharges") for violations, and in 1981 fines were imposed for the first time.[71] Another important precedent was solidified in 1984. There has often been tension between the Fair Trade Commission, with its procompetition mandate, and MITI, which has perceived cartelization as a useful tool in its export-building portfolio. The conflict escalated when the Fair Trade Commission initiated criminal price-fixing charges in 1974 against twelve petroleum companies, who defended themselves *inter alia* by insisting that they were acting under "administrative guidance" from MITI. The dispute wended its way to the Japanese Supreme Court, which ruled in 1984 that agreements contrary to the Antimonopoly Act were exempt when they conformed to bona fide administrative guidance, but that the specific petroleum company price-fixing activities did not follow such administrative guidance and were therefore illegal.[72]

The Per Se vs. Rule of Reason Question Revisited

From this brief survey, we find that the United States is extreme in the extent to which it applies a per se prohibition against price fixing and similar restraints of trade. Has it made the best policy choice?

Given the complexity of the links between market structure, conduct, and performance, it seems almost certain that there are at least some conditions under which agreements to fix "reasonable" prices will permit better economic performance than unfettered competition. Leading candidates include high overhead cost industries subjected to severe cyclical or secular shocks and industries that would be unable to cooperate in desirable cost-saving programs without some mitigation of price competition. The key question is not whether such cases exist, but how frequently they occur and whether the social benefits realizable through a policy that seeks to allow restrictive agreements only in those cases exceed the social costs of the policy. Obviously, we have no solid estimates of either benefits or costs. The authors' best reading of the case study evidence, including the standard works on such "cutthroat competition" industries as railroading before 1887 and soft coal mining, is that the gains from permitting restrictive agreements on a selective basis would be modest. Or to put the point negatively, price competition does seem to have done its job in forcing "sick" industries to shed high-cost capacity, and the chief rationale for assertions to the contrary is the natural propensity for those whose oxen are gored to raise the loudest, most persuasive cries of distress. It is also doubtful whether the gains from full-blown "rationalization" cartels

65. Organisation for Economic Co-Operation and Development, *Competition Policy in OECD Countries, 1984–1985* (Paris: 1987), pp. 251–252.

66. See OECD, *Guide to Legislation*, supra note 45, "Explanatory Notes on Legislation: Canada," pp. 2–3, and the selection of court decision excerpts in section 3.0; and Bruce Dunlop, David McQueen, and Michael Trebilcock, *Canadian Competition Policy* (Toronto: Canada Law Book Inc., 1987), pp. 121–131.

67. Ministry of Consumer and Corporate Affairs, *Proposals for a New Competition Policy for Canada: Second Stage* (Ottawa: Consumer and Corporate Affairs Canada, March 1977), pp. 202 and 207.

68. In 1972, there were nine authorized depression cartels, ten rationalization cartels, 175 export and two import cartels, and 604 small business cartels. See Richard E. Caves and Masu Uekusa, *Industrial Organization in Japan* (Washington: Brookings, 1976), pp. 141–148. By 1987, the number of small business cartels had fallen to 226. However, twenty-two industries had quali-

fied for "special measures" cartels attributable to the energy shock. See Leonard W. Weiss, "The Legal Cartels of Japan," paper presented at the meetings of the American Economic Association, December 1987.

69. See M. J. Peck, Richard Levin, and Akira Goto, "Picking Losers: Public Policy Toward Declining Industries in Japan," *Journal of Japanese Studies*, vol. 13 (Winter 1987), pp. 79–123.

70. Weiss, "The Legal Cartels," p. 2.

71. OECD, *Competition Policy . . ., 1984–1985*, supra note 65, p. 130.

72. Ibid., pp. 131–132. The defense is not a new one. It was attempted by the Athenian grain dealers in approximately 386 B.C. in justifying their conspiracy to buy grain from importers at low prices, stockpile it, and sell it in times of scarcity at prices above the permissible maximum. The defense failed, and the sentence was death. See *Lysias*, Loeb Classical Library (Cambridge: Harvard University Press, 1930), pp. 490–503.

would be large, for vigorous competition is often as effective an inducement to product specialization as cartelization.[73] The need for cartelized cooperation is least pressing in a market as vast as the United States, where the conflict between scale economies and competition is seldom acute.[74]

Let us nevertheless grant for the sake of argument that the benefits of a selective restriction policy would be finite and positive. If the full-blown rule of reason approach required to implement the policy were itself costless, it should be adopted. But it is not costless. There are definite costs in the form of added uncertainty, more complex adjudication, and an enhanced probability of erroneous and irrational choices.

A relatively unimportant cost would be the increased uncertainty business firms would face as to which agreements are illegal. At least in borderline areas, it would be impossible to proceed with confidence until an official opinion is rendered. This is not a serious problem, however, for companies could always avoid legal uncertainty by refraining from brinkmanship.

Much more impressive would be the costs of adjudicating and enforcing the policy, for each case would become, in the jargon of the antitrust law firms and economic consultants who would be significant financial beneficiaries, "the big case." Even with relatively simple per se rules, elaborate proceedings are often needed merely to establish whether or not a prohibited act was perpetrated. A full-fledged rule of reason case would surely have to go farther, analyzing past industry structure and performance and projecting future trends. A thorough investigation of this sort conducted under traditional antitrust procedures would be so costly in terms of money and, more important, high-level talent that the enforcement agencies would find the number of cases they could undertake sharply limited. As Professor Mason argued, "The demand for a full investigation of a market situation or a course of business conduct is a demand for nonenforcement of the antitrust laws."[75]

If approval of price-fixing arrangements were made contingent upon the reasonableness of the prices fixed, one would run squarely into the dilemma perceived by the Supreme Court in its *Trenton Potteries* opinion: "The reasonable price fixed today may through economic and business changes become the unreasonable price of tomorrow."[76] To place upon the enforcement agencies and courts "the burden of ascertaining from day to day whether [the price] has become unreasonable through the mere variation of economic conditions"[77] could break the back of an already bowed and groaning camel, and it would entail a substantial increase in the degree to which government intervenes in the affairs of business.

These problems are in part symptoms of a fundamental deficiency: the unsuitability of U.S. judicial processes for making balanced judgments on issues as technical and complex as the reasonableness of a price-fixing scheme. This in turn is the consequence of several problems. For one, the rules of evidence applied in antitrust cases are cumbersome in the extreme. If delay is deemed advantageous, as it often is, counsel can stretch out proceedings to prodigious lengths by challenging the authenticity and materiality of each document and nit-picking the testimony of witnesses. Second, jurists are seldom trained in economics, and many lack the knowledge to separate sense from nonsense in the contending parties' briefs or to get a firm analytic handle on the conduct and performance variables at issue. The brightest judges do amazingly well, but the middle ranks turn in performances that could merit no more than a C+ on an undergraduate theory examination. Third, the whole adversary process on which the courts operate is best suited for reaching either-or decisions: Is the defendant guilty, or not? Is the contract valid, or not? It is much less adept at ascertaining, say, how much competition is optimal out of a continuous spectrum of possibilities.[78] Nor is it well suited for weighing many conflicting considerations to reach a decision that on balance, out of alternatives A through N, J best serves the public interest. Indeed, the facts and arguments are often so complex that they swamp the judge's ability to comprehend and integrate them logically. He or she may then arrive at a decision on the basis of raw instinct, working backward from that point to develop a line of reasoning which, however strained, supports the conclusion. It is for this reason, Derek Bok suggests, that one frequently encounters antitrust decisions that hold *all* the arguments in a case to support the conclusion taken, even though questions of industrial conduct are almost never that simple.[79] Decisions reached in this manner by overtaxed jurists will almost surely be erroneous a significant fraction of the time. And decisions approving restrictive agreements when they are undesirable, if an accurate balance were to be struck, constitute an additional cost of an open-ended rule of reason approach.

Yet the art of policy design calls for more than merely comparing well-known possibilities in the context of existing institutions. It is at least as useful to seek new, dominant alternatives. Substantively, the courts might be required to ascertain not whether prices are fixed at reasonable levels, but whether the structure and organization of an industry are such that price fixing would on average be expected to improve performance.[80] Procedurally, a heavy burden of proof might be imposed upon those who seek to justify price-fixing arrangements, as was done in the U.S. college football television case. At the same time, the adjudicative system might be reformed, for example, along lines similar to the British Restrictive Practices Court. A special antitrust court could be established with streamlined procedures, rules of evidence suitable to economic investigations, and a membership chosen for its knowledge of business and economics rather than the usual bar association credentials. Procedures could be streamlined even more by having the contending parties jointly prepare a common document that defines the issues, advances and criticizes the arguments and counter arguments, and analyzes relevant statistical evidence, going as far as possible toward the point where an intelligent decision on the disputed matters can be rendered.

---

73. On the economic effects of the European synthetic fibers cartel in its early stages, see Shaw and Shaw, "Excess Capacity," supra note 64, pp. 153–166.

74. See pp. 164–165 supra. On specialization agreements in a much smaller economy such as Canada, see Klaus Stegemann, "The Exemption of Specialization Agreements," *Canadian Public Policy*, vol. 3 (Autumn 1977), pp. 533–545.

75. Edward S. Mason, *Economic Concentration and the Monopoly Problem* (Cambridge: Harvard University Press, 1957), p. 398 (1927). He concedes that many rule of reason cases might not have to be quite so thorough.

76. *U.S.* v. *Trenton Potteries Co. et al.*, 273 U.S. 392, 297 (1927).

77. 273 U.S. 392, 398 (1927).

78. For a superb discussion of this problem, see Derek C. Bok, "Section 7 of the Clayton Act and the Merging of Law and Economics," *Harvard Law Review*, vol. 74 (December 1960), pp. 291–299.

79. Bok, "Section 7," p. 270.

80. See Almarin Phillips, *Market Structure*, supra note 5, pp. 235–240; and Posner, *Antitrust Law*, supra note 10, pp. 55–77.

To be sure, some sacrifices must be accepted to reduce the cost of implementing a full-fledged rule of reason. As noted earlier, cold economic logic did not always carry the day at the British Restrictive Practices Court. Yet the incidence of mistakes is probably not any higher than it would be under more thorough but cumbersome (and hence confusing) procedures. More important, the Restrictive Practices Court procedures sacrifice certain safeguards by abandoning traditional rules of evidence and by placing strict limits on what can be appealed to higher courts. To make the system work efficiently, a considerable amount of discretion is allowed the court of primary jurisdiction. A rule of men is to some extent substituted for the more plodding rule of law. It is here that U.S. traditions depart most strongly from those dominating European competition policy.

The difference between nations is summarized perceptively by A. D. Neale, a British observer:

One of the profoundest institutional differences between the two countries is the absence in the United States of anything corresponding to the amorphous but recognizable assemblage of public bodies and personages that we know in Britain as "the Establishment," and this has much to do, as both cause and effect, with American distrust of authority *per se*. In general the possession of power by established authorities arouses a much lesser degree of anxiety or resentment in Britain, where the emphasis is much more on the use of power.

Whereas American institutions often appear to be designed to hamper the exercise of power, ours are designed on the whole to facilitate it, though great importance is attached to protecting minorities against its abuse . . . It is in line with the same general attitude to power that, if regulation is required, British opinion tends to be more open-minded than American about the choice between judicial enforcement of rules of law and some form of administrative supervision. . . . In the United States administrative decisions (the "government of men") tend to be unpopular as such, and the search is always for a "government of laws." In Britain the choice is more open; administrative acts, as such, are not so suspect; a government of men subject to law is desired but not a "government of laws" in the American sense.[81]

A similar but more complex historical view of the differences in antitrust attitudes on the European continent is presented by Corwin Edwards:

Whereas American political institutions were formulated after overthrowing colonial status, under the influence of a philosophy that distrusted concentrated governmental power, and in a setting affected by the individualism of the frontier, European political institutions have evolved gradually from origins of monarchy in the state and hierarchy in the church. . . . The European libertarian movements that expressed distrust of state power and sought to curtail state functions found their programs in guarantees of freedom of contract and freedom of association. . . . But as the market economy developed, free association came to mean that businessmen were free to form cartels, and free contract came to include the right to make agreements by which the parties impaired free trade and free competition. Thus the programs that challenged the power of the state tended to strengthen rather than to challenge the power of cartels. It is understandable that as programs to curb cartels developed they tended to accept and rely upon a broad exercise of the regulatory power of the state as a major instrument of control. [These] inherited attitudes . . . have resulted in cartel laws which characteristically grant broad discretion to public officials to amend cartel practices in accord with their own views of the public interest.[82]

The reluctance of the U.S. Congress to discard its cumbersome judicial approach to antitrust is undoubtedly the result of a more fundamental unwillingness to place great discretionary power in the hands of a few officials whose decisions are not controlled by rules of law and judicial review. And because the rule of law is cumbersome, a rule of reason approach to price-fixing cases shows up unfavorably in benefit/cost analyses. The debate between per se rules and the rule of reason turns, therefore, on important questions of political as well as economic philosophy. On such political issues the economist has no special license to prescribe the "correct" public policy.

Oligopoly Pricing and the Conscious Parallelism Doctrine

American law on express agreements to fix prices and restrict output is crystal clear: they are illegal per se. But what if no definite proof of meetings, discussions, and agreements can be established? What if there is in fact no explicit agreement among rivals in the strict sense of the word, but only an implicitly accepted policy of living and letting live to avoid price competition?

Collusion without outright agreement is not likely when market concentration is low; chiseling will sooner or later undermine the effort. But in oligopoly, the situation can be different. With few sellers, each firm recognizes that aggressive actions such as price cutting will induce counteractions from rivals which, in the end, leave all industry members worse off. Although product heterogeneity, financial pressures during a slump, opportunities for secret price cutting, and plain human cantankerousness may prevent oligopolists from maximizing their joint profits with complete success, collusion without explicit meetings and formal agreements is both feasible and attractive in many oligopolistic industries. Its status under the antitrust laws is therefore an important issue.

The relevant principle is the so-called *conscious parallelism* doctrine, whose implications are best discovered by analyzing the key decisions through which it evolved.[83] To keep what is a messy development in perspective, it must be pointed out immediately that the doctrine has at various times been related to two rather different problems: first, with the behavior of oligopolists acting noncompetitively; and second, with the evidentiary burden of proving illegal collusion where only circumstantial evidence, and not direct evidence of meetings and agreements, can be offered.

In the earliest applicable cases, the emphasis was on evidentiary matters. One of the first involved a retail lumber dealers' trade association that published a list of wholesalers who sold at retail (and hence competed with members of the association).[84] Once the list was issued, many retail dealers ceased purchasing from those

81. Neale, *The Antitrust Laws*, supra note 15, pp. 478–479. See also D. P. O'Brien, "Competition Policy in Britain: The Silent Revolution," *Antitrust Bulletin*, vol. 27 (Spring 1982), pp. 217–239, who notes a decline in cases brought before the Restrictive Practices Court and an increase in the amount of administrative discretion exercised by the Office of Fair Trading.

82. Corwin D. Edwards, *Cartelization in Western Europe* (Washington: U.S. Department of State, 1964), pp. 46–47.

83. For analyses of additional cases, see Phillips, *Market Structure*, supra note 5, pp. 47–73; Neale, *The Antitrust Laws*, supra note 15, pp. 71–91; Richard Posner, "Oligopoly and the Antitrust Laws: A Suggested Approach," *Stanford Law Review*, vol. 21 (June 1969), pp. 1562–1606; and Stephen Nye, "Can Conduct-Oriented Enforcement Inhibit Conscious Parallelism?" *Antitrust Law Journal*, vol. 44, no. 2 (1975), pp. 206–230.

84. *Eastern States Retail Lumber Dealers Association* v. *U.S.*, 234 U.S. 600 (1914).

wholesalers. The Justice Department, charging the retailers with an illegal conspiracy, could produce no evidence of an explicit agreement to boycott the blacklisted wholesalers. Nevertheless, the Supreme Court upheld the charge, observing:

[I]t is said that in order to show a combination or conspiracy within the Sherman Act some agreement must be shown under which the concerted action is taken. It is elementary, however, that conspiracies are seldom capable of proof by direct testimony, and may be inferred from the things actually done; and when, in this case, by concerted action the names of wholesalers . . . were periodically reported to the other members of the associations, the conspiracy to accomplish that which was the natural consequence of such action may be readily inferred.[85]

A reiteration and modest extension occurred in another boycott case twenty-five years later.[86] The managers of the Interstate Circuit and another motion picture exhibition chain with a large share of the Texas market wrote identical letters to eight motion picture distributors (for example, Paramount, MGM, and RKO), each letter naming all eight, and each demanding that the distributors not release their first-run films to theaters competitive with Interstate charging less than twenty-five cents admission or using the films in double features. The eight distributors could also benefit by realizing higher exhibition fees as long as all eight adhered to the Interstate proposal. After the letter was sent, independent low-price exhibitors in fact found it impossible to secure first-run films, and many reacted by raising their prices to the twenty-five-cent minimum. When a district court ordered an end to the boycott, the defendants appealed to the Supreme Court, arguing *inter alia* that no evidence showed an agreement or conspiracy among the eight distributors. The Supreme Court rejected their argument, noting the "singular unanimity of action on the part of the distributors" in carrying out the suggested restraint:

It taxes credulity to believe that the several distributors would . . . have accepted and put into operation with substantial unanimity such far-reaching changes in their business methods without some understanding that all were to join, and we reject as beyond the range of probability that it was the result of mere chance.[87]

As proof of illegal conspiracy, the Court said:

It was enough that, knowing that concerted action was contemplated and invited, the distributors gave their adherence to the scheme and participated in it.[88]

Thus, the distributors (along with the two exhibition chains) were found to have violated Sherman Act Section 1 without proof of express agreement, and without even initiating the message that brought about their behavioral change. Yet it is important to see that in both this and the lumber dealers' case, there was an overt act (the publication of a blacklist or receipt of a letter) to which the restraint of trade could be traced.

This requisite seemed to disappear in the 1946 *Tobacco* decision. To recapitulate the facts briefly, the Big Three of the cigarette industry—American Tobacco, Reynolds, and Liggett & Myers—for two decades maintained a pattern of strikingly parallel pricing. Especially noteworthy were the prompt matching of Reynolds' price increase in June 1931, in the depths of the depression, when tobacco leaf prices and labor costs were falling, and the sharp concerted price cuts effected eighteen months later to recapture the market share gained by smaller rivals after the 1931 action permitted "ten-cent" brands to sell at an attractive price differential. In addition, the Big Three brought pressure to bear on retailers to ensure that their products sold at the same price; they declined to participate in leaf tobacco auctions unless buyers from all three were present; they conducted their bidding so that all ended up paying the same price per pound; and each refrained from buying tobacco grades in which the others had a special interest. Although some suspicious incidents came to light,[89] the Justice Department was unable to present any concrete evidence of meetings, messages, or explicit agreements among Big Three members. The evidence was entirely circumstantial, centering on the parallelism in pricing and purchasing behavior. Nevertheless, a jury found the defendants guilty of price fixing and other Sherman Act violations; and in reviewing the case, an appellate court deemed the purely circumstantial evidence sufficient to sustain the criminal charges.[90] On appeal, the Supreme Court declined to review the appellate court's decision on the price-fixing count, thereby approving it implicitly. It also issued a more general pronouncement on the problem of proving guilt in Sherman Act conspiracy cases:

No formal agreement is necessary to constitute an unlawful conspiracy. Often crimes are a matter of inference deduced from the acts of the person accused and done in pursuance of a criminal purpose. . . . The essential combination or conspiracy in violation of the Sherman Act may be found in a course of dealing or other circumstances as well as in an exchange of words. . . . Where the circumstances are such as to warrant a jury in finding that the conspirators had a unity of purpose or a common design and understanding, or a meeting of minds in an unlawful arrangement, the conclusion that a conspiracy is established is justified.[91]

The *Tobacco* decision was viewed by antitrust aficionados as a dramatic new precedent bringing, as William Nicholls speculated, "wholly tacit, nonaggressive oligopoly fully within the reach of the conspiracy provisions of the Sherman Act."[92] From a more distant perspective, it appears that the courts were not going quite as far, but were only extending the possibilities of finding guilt on the basis of circumstantial evidence where there was good reason to believe that outright collusion occurred. It is also likely that the *Tobacco* decision implicitly applied a rule of reason to oligopoly behavior. The firms were found guilty despite weak evidence because their conduct during the 1930s was so flagrantly inconsistent with economic conditions of the time.[93]

---

85. 234 U.S. 600, 612 (1914).

86. *Interstate Circuit, Inc., et al.* v. *U.S.*, 306 U.S. 208 (1939).

87. 306 U.S. 208, 223 (1939).

88. 306 U.S. 208, 226 (1939).

89. On the circumstantial evidence that all three had advance notice of the February 1933 price cut, see note 47, Chapter 7.

90. *American Tobacco Co. et al.* v. *U.S.*, 147 F. 2d 93 (1944).

91. *American Tobacco Co. et al.* v. *U.S.*, 328 U.S. 781, 809–810 (1946).

92. William H. Nicholls, "The Tobacco Case of 1946," *American Economic Review*, vol. 39 (May 1949), p. 285.

93. See *American Tobacco Co. et al.* v. *U.S.*, 147 F. 2d 93, 103 (1944).

Were the law against tacitly collusive oligopoly pricing to follow as strict a line as many persons saw in the *Tobacco* decision, a dilemma would arise. How should oligopolists change their behavior so as to avoid breaking the law? Must they begin ignoring their interdependence in pricing decisions, when to do so would be irrational? As Liggett & Myers attorneys asked rhetorically in their brief before the Court of Appeals, "Is everything the appellants do illegal, or evidence of illegality, if done by more than one of them?" The dilemma is a real one to which we must return in Chapter 12. It suffices here to note that after fines totaling $255,000 were levied upon the tobacco firms and their executives, there was little observable change in their conduct.

Subsequent decisions involving the cement and steel industries carried the conscious parallelism doctrine further, outlawing adherence by mutual tacit consent to a *common system* of pricing — the basing point system, which we shall analyze further in Chapter 13. The problem in both cases was stated succinctly in the Court of Appeals rigid steel conduit decision:

[E]ach conduit seller knows that each of the other sellers is using the basing point formula; each knows that by using it he will be able to quote identical delivered prices and thus present a condition of matched prices under which purchasers are isolated and deprived of choice among sellers so far as price advantage is concerned. . . . Each seller . . . in effect invites the others to share the available business at matched prices in his natural market in return for a reciprocal invitation.[94]

And this, the Court said, was a violation of Federal Trade Commission Act Section 5, which had been stretched in the prior *Cement Institute* decision to cover combinations in restraint of trade as unfair methods of competition.[95] In a subsequent staff memorandum, the Federal Trade Commission pointedly expressed its belief that parallel pricing had become fair game:

[W]hen a number of enterprises follow a parallel course of action in the knowledge and contemplation of the fact that all are acting alike they have, in effect, formed an agreement. . . . The obvious fact [is] that the economic effect of identical prices achieved through conscious parallel action is the same as that of similar prices achieved through overt collusion, and, for this reason, the Commission treated the conscious parallelism of action as a violation of the Federal Trade Commission Act.[96]

As events transpired, 1948 proved to be a high-water mark in the legal construction of conscious parallelism. Erosion took place in still another boycott case. Nine film distributors all refused to grant first-run status to a new theater in a suburban Baltimore shopping center, giving preference instead to established downtown theaters, three of which were owned by distributors. No evidence was adduced to prove express agreement among the distributors. Judgment was rendered for the distributors in a jury trial. In its sustaining decision, the Supreme Court found that the distributors' decisions to deny first-run status could have been taken independently and based upon "individual business judgment motivated by the desire for maximum revenue"[97] — for example, because of the suburban theater's lesser drawing power, the paucity of its newspaper display advertising compared to downtown theaters, and the fact that giving it first-run status would adversely affect rentals to existing customers. The Court went on to administer a rude jolt to those who had construed its *Tobacco* decision broadly:

> The crucial question is whether respondents' conduct toward petitioner stemmed from independent decision or from an agreement, tacit or express. To be sure, business behavior is admissible circumstantial evidence from which the fact finder may infer agreement. . . . But this Court has never held that proof of parallel business behavior conclusively establishes agreement or, phrased differently, that such behavior itself constitutes a Sherman Act offense. Circumstantial evidence of consciously parallel behavior may have made heavy inroads into the traditional judicial attitude toward conspiracy; but "conscious parallelism" has not yet read conspiracy out of the Sherman Act entirely.[98]

A further test came in one of the most closely contested cases in U.S. antitrust history. The facts are complex. Essentially, however, there were two main charges: that the defendant pharmaceutical manufacturers (Pfizer, American Cyanamid, and Bristol-Myers) had during the mid-1950s settled conflicting claims over rights to the tetracycline antibiotic patent by entering a cross-licensing agreement with the explicit or implicit understanding that further entry into the field would be restricted; and that from 1953 to 1961 the three defendants plus two licensees conspired to fix identical and noncompetitive prices. No direct evidence of illegal agreements was produced, and on the witness stand, company executives vehemently denied any wrongdoing. However, contemporary memoranda revealed American Cyanamid's keen awareness and concern that failure to settle their patent dispute might encourage a flood of new competitive entry, with adverse effects on price. The government also showed that prices were stabilized for several years at $30.60 per bottle of 100 capsules to druggists and $19.1884 per bottle to the Veterans Administration, despite unit production costs of only about $3 per bottle. In his instructions to the jury, District Judge Frankel observed that the evidence was entirely circumstantial, and that:

> . . . whether the prosecution has sustained its burden of proving a conspiracy must frequently be judged by what the jury finds the parties actually did rather than from the words they used. The unlawful agreement may be shown if the proof establishes a concert of action, with all the parties working together understandingly with a single design for the accomplishment of a common purpose. . . . It is not sufficient to show that the parties acted uniformly or similarly or in ways that may seem to have been mutually beneficial. If such actions were taken independently as a matter of individual business judgment, without any agreement or arrangement or understanding among the parties, then there would be no conspiracy.[99]

94. *Triangle Conduit and Cable Co. et al.* v. *Federal Trade Commission*, 168 F. 2d 175, 181 (1948). The appellate court's decision was upheld only by a 4-4 tie vote in the Supreme Court. 337 U.S. 956 (1949).

95. *Federal Trade Commission* v. *Cement Institute et al.*, 333 U.S. 683, 712–721 (1948).

96. "Notice to the Staff: In Re: Commission Policy Toward Geographic Pricing Practices," October 1948, cited in U.S. Department of Justice, *Report of the Attorney General's National Committee To Study the Antitrust Laws* (Washington: USGPO, 1955), p. 38.

97. *Theatre Enterprises, Inc.* v. *Paramount Film Distributing Corp. et al.*, 346 U.S. 537, 542 (1954).

98. 346 U.S. 537, 540–541 (1954).

99. *U.S.* v. *Charles Pfizer & Co. et al.*, S.D. New York, from pp. 6200–6201 of the trial record. On an analogous case involving Salk vaccine sales, see *U.S.* v. *Eli Lilly & Co. et al.*, CCH 1959 Trade Cases para. 69,536.

A key point of contention was the large disparity between prices and production costs. Judge Frankel repeatedly cautioned the jury that the reasonableness or unreasonableness of prices charged was irrelevant in a direct sense. But it was relevant indirectly as part of the circumstantial evidence:

I think you will find it helpful to translate the word "unreasonable" to mean "unusual" or "artificial" or "extra-ordinary." By these suggested definitions I am trying to convey the thought that the idea of unreasonableness in the present context is meaningful only if it is understood to refer to kinds of price behavior or price levels which appear to be divorced from variations and differences in available supply or demand or cost or other economic factors that may normally be expected to cause variations or changes in the prices charged in a competitive market. To put the thought in another and slightly shorter way, the charge of unreasonableness in this case is material only insofar as it poses the issue whether the prices involved exhibited qualities or peculiarities of a type that could be deemed evidence that such prices resulted from agreement rather than from competition. . . . Unreasonably or extraordinarily high prices or profits charged uniformly by competing sellers over a substantial period of time may be evidence, taken with all the other circumstances of the case, supporting an inference that the parties had an agreement rather than a competitive situation with respect to prices.[100]

The jury found the defendants guilty on all counts, and maximum fines were imposed.

On appeal, however, the conviction was reversed and a new trial was ordered in a 2-1 split decision of the reviewing judges. The majority stressed the government's claim in its bill of particulars that a conspiracy came into being at certain meetings between Pfizer, American Cyanamid, and Bristol-Myers executives to settle patent rights disputes. Company witnesses denied under oath that they had reached any agreement to limit entry or fix prices at those meetings. Much of the government's evidence was related to pricing, profits, and the disposition of entry-barring patent claims before and after the meetings; and in his charge to the jury, Judge Frankel had dealt at length with that evidence as well as with the testimonial evidence on what happened at the meetings. Noting that its finding might have been different had the government framed its bill of particulars more broadly, the appellate court majority concluded *inter alia* that in devoting substantial attention to such "inflammatory issues" as patents, pricing, and profits, Judge Frankel had failed to focus the jury's attention on the key issue of what happened at the meetings, and he may indeed have diverted it.[101] A 2-1 majority of other second circuit court judges denied a petition for rehearing *en banc*; and on further appeal, the reversal was upheld when the Supreme Court divided 3-3 on the merits.[102] The matter was thereupon returned to the district court for retrial. Nearly six years after the first trial and twelve years after the indictment was filed, Judge Cannella ruled in favor of the companies.[103] In a brief opinion probing beyond what had happened at the meetings, he stated that the Justice Department had not conclusively shown Pfizer's limits on the number of tetracycline patent licensees and the firms' parallel pricing to have resulted from conspiracy, since they might alternatively have stemmed from Pfizer's independent business judgment and a natural tendency toward uniform pricing in the highly concentrated, prescription-oriented market for antibiotics.

In view of the apparent mismatch between the government's bill of particulars and the broader, more interesting conduct patterns at issue, it is difficult to say whether the tetracycline decisions represent an even tighter constriction of the conscious parallelism doctrine. It is clear that more recent decisions have moved far from the mere parallelism of behavior emphasized in cases of the late 1940s. What is not clear is where one draws the line in determining what circumstantial evidence warrants an inference of conspiracy. The accumulated precedents seem to call for "parallelism plus."[104] The key question remains, of what can the "plus" consist?

From the early cases, chain letters and blacklists qualify. A careful reading of the *Tobacco* case facts suggests that when firms have advance knowledge of impending rival actions that could hardly have been gained without covert communications, the necessary "plus" can be inferred.

Another possibility is the adoption by oligopolists of practices facilitating the coordination of pricing behavior. This theory was tested by the Federal Trade Commission in a complaint against the four U.S. producers of tetraethyl lead, an octane-enhancing gasoline additive.[105] Demand for the product was declining during the 1970s as automobiles designed to meet new and more stringent environmental protection rules replaced older models. Excess capacity grew, but prices rose, profit margins remained high, and prices and price changes were highly uniform among the three largest sellers (but not for Nalco, the smallest firm). The Federal Trade Commission found that the tetraethyl lead makers illegally lessened competition by quoting uniform delivered prices, regardless of the shipping distance; by giving customers thirty days' advance notice of price changes and by announcing the warning period in advance, allowing the price leader to back off from a change without loss if others do not follow; and including in sales contracts most-favored-customer clauses ensuring that if the price were cut for any buyer, it would be reduced for all.[106] The two leading sellers, Ethyl and du Pont, were ordered by the FTC to eliminate their most-favored-customer clauses and to offer pickup-at-point-of-origin prices as well as delivered prices. However, the order was overturned on appeal by an appellate court, which stressed evidence showing that all of the "facilitating" practices had been adopted by Ethyl Corporation before it had any competition in the sale of tetraethyl lead and that, beginning with du Pont's entry in 1948, the other companies had "inde-

100. From pp. 6270–6271 and 6275–6276 of the trial record.
101. *Charles Pfizer & Co. et al.* v. *U.S.*, 426 F. 2d 32, 39–43 (1970).
102. 437 F. 2d 957 (1970), 404 U.S. 548 (1972).
103. 367 F. Supp. 91 (1973). Parallel to the criminal proceedings was a Federal Trade Commission action that began in 1958 and ended in 1967 with a finding of illegality on the patent and entry-limiting allegations but not the price fixing allegations. *In the matter of American Cyanamid Co. et al.*, 63 F.T.C. 1747 (1963) and 72 F.T.C. 623 (1967). Reversals were again the order of the day; for

example, the first hearing examiner's dismissal was reversed on all counts by the Commission, whose decision in turn was reversed by an appellate court and remanded for rehearing. 363 F. 2d 757 (1966).
104. *Naumkeag Theatres Co.* v. *New England Theatres, Inc. et al.*, 345 F. 2d 910, 912 (1965).
105. *In the matter of Ethyl Corp. et al.*, 101 F.T.C. 425 (1983).
106. On most-favored-customer clauses as a price-enhancing device, see Chapter 6, pp. 212–213.

pendently adopted its practices for legitimate business reasons."[107] It went on to insist that:

> . . . [P]rice uniformity is normal in a market with few sellers and homogeneous products, such as that in the antiknock compound industry. In view of this . . . the Commission owes a duty to define the conditions under which conduct claimed to facilitate price uniformity would be unfair so that businesses will have an inkling as to what they can lawfully do. . . . The Commission's decision . . . does not provide any guidelines; it would require each producer not only to assess the general conduct of the antiknock business but also that of each of its competitors and the reaction of each to the other, which would be virtually impossible.[108]

This dealt a sharp knock to the FTC's attempt to bring facilitating practices under the conscious parallelism doctrine.

Less settled is whether tacit conspiracy can be found when the conduct and performance of sellers are strikingly different from what one would expect if the firms were independently seeking to maximize their individual profits.[109] An important subissue is how much weight the courts would place on extraordinarily high profits as an indication that sellers' (imperfectly observed) conduct is incompatible with the hypothesis of independent competition. Departing from Judge Frankel's position, both the Second Circuit Court of Appeals and (on retrial) Judge Cannella took a dim view of inferring anything about conduct from the tetracycline profit and price-production cost margin evidence. However, in its *Tobacco* decision, the Supreme Court referred to the Big Three's "tremendous profits" in 1932 as one component of the circumstantial evidence of conspiracy.[110] And in an opinion delivered only a year after the tetracycline reversal, the Ninth Circuit Court of Appeals, in a case involving the pricing of a herbicide used by rice growers, ruled that:

> [I]t may be true that in a two-seller market of fungible products, the products are likely to be priced at the same levels in any given market, and thus no inference of price fixing could be drawn therefrom. . . . However, evidence that pricing schedules were identical for both products warrants a scrutiny of profit margins. Competition could be inferred from a low profit margin in such a market. Similarly, evidence of high profit margins is probative of the existence of a conspiracy.[111]

Yet on retrial the district court found the problems of ascertaining individual product profitability in multiproduct enterprises to be so complex that introducing such evidence, it believed, would do more to confuse than clarify the issues.[112] Thus, a definitive test of how profits enter into the conscious parallelism doctrine must await some future case in which the issues are sharply focused for Supreme Court review.

Price Leadership

One of the most important institutions facilitating tacitly collusive pricing behavior is a well-established system of price leadership. The legality of price leadership was considered by the Supreme Court in cases involving the United States Steel Corp. and the International Harvester Co. The most succinct statement of the Court's viewpoint is found in its *Harvester* decision:

[International Harvester] has not . . . attempted to dominate or in fact controlled or dominated the harvesting machinery industry by the compulsory regulation of prices. The most that can be said as to this, is that many of its competitors have been accustomed, independently and as a matter of business expediency, to follow approximately the prices at which it has sold its harvesting machines; but one of its competitors has habitually sold its machines at somewhat higher prices. . . . [T]he fact that competitors may see proper, in the exercise of their own judgment, to follow the prices of another manufacturer, does not establish any suppression of competition or show any sinister domination.[113]

Under this precedent, which has remained intact, price leadership is not apt to be found contrary to the antitrust laws unless the leader attempts to coerce other producers into following its lead, or unless there is evidence of an agreement among industry members to use the leadership device as the basis of a price-fixing scheme. As long as sellers exercise their own independent judgment in choosing to follow the leader, for example, "because they ma[k]e money by the imitation,"[114] they remain on relatively safe ground.

There is logic in this rule, which avoids making one party's guilt (the price leader's) hang on the autonomous actions of other parties (the followers). Still the rule, along with limits written into the conscious parallelism doctrine since 1950, makes it difficult for the antitrust authorities to deal with the problem of oligopolists quietly but firmly refraining from price competition. We shall return to the question three chapters hence.

Trade Association Price and Cost Reporting Activities

Trade associations have often performed functions that run afoul of the antitrust laws. Their meetings are superb vehicles for getting together and agreeing on prices, outputs, market shares, and the like. This is per se illegal, however difficult it may be to detect, and need not detain us further. But what if the trade association, through its central office staff, merely collects and then distributes to members detailed information on the prices quoted in recent sales transactions, or detailed comparative breakdowns of member production costs?

107. *E.I. du Pont de Nemours Co. et al.* v. *Federal Trade Commission*, 729 F. 2d 128, 140 (1984).

108. 729 F. 2d 128, 139 (1984).

109. This seems to have been a critical consideration in the finding by the Court of Justice of the European Communities that ten aniline dye manufacturers had engaged in illegal "concerted pricing practices," even though there was no direct proof of agreements. See the text of the opinion, *Imperial Chemical Industries, Ltd.* v. *Commission of the European Communities*, in the *Antitrust Bulletin*, vol. 18 (Spring 1973), pp. 117–138.

Amendments to the German antitrust law in 1973 to include "concerted actions" as a violation were stimulated by a court decision overturning a similar national action against the dye producers' parallel pricing. See Kurt Markert, "The New German Antitrust Reform Law," *Antitrust Bulletin*, vol. 19 (Spring 1974), p. 147.

On the (absence of a) British policy, see the Monopolies Commission report, *Parallel Pricing* (London: HMSO, July 1973). On the Canadian policy, which has reach and ambiguities similar to that of the United States, see Dunlop et al., *Canadian Competition Policy*, supra note 66, pp. 131–139.

110. *American Tobacco Co. et al.* v. *U.S.*, 328 U.S. 781 at 805–806 (1946).

111. *Estate of LeBaron et al.* v. *Rohm and Haas Co. et al.*, 441 F. 2d 575, 578 (1971).

112. 506 F. 2d 1261 (1974).

113. *U.S.* v. *International Harvester Co.*, 274 U.S. 693, 708–709 (1927).

114. *U.S.* v. *United States Steel Corp. et al.*, 251 U.S. 417, 447 (1920).

It might seem paradoxical that there could be anything wrong with information dissemination activities, which at first glance appear only to perfect the market. However, perfect information is unambiguously beneficial only in the context of purely competitive markets. When a market is oligopolistic, it may impair rather than invigorate rivalry. As we learned in Chapter 8, secret price shading is the nemesis of effective collusion. When many sellers attempt to capture orders through sub-rosa price cuts, monopolistic price structures tend to collapse. If, on the other hand, every transaction is publicized immediately, all members of the industry will know when one has made a price cut, and each can retaliate on the next transaction. Knowledge that retaliation will be swift serves as a powerful deterrent to price cutting and therefore facilitates the maintenance of tacitly collusive prices.

One of the first persons to recognize this and do something about it was Arthur Jerome Eddy. His solution to the secret price-shading problem was the formation of "open price associations" that would rapidly supply complete information on all sales transactions to all industry members. A few quotations from his 1912 book, *The New Competition*, convey the flavor of his approach. On the book's frontispiece is the theme, "Competition Is War, and War Is Hell." The analysis runs along the following lines:

Of all the rivalries in which man engages, brute competition in the production and distribution of wealth is the most contemptible, since it is the most sordid, a mere money-making proposition, unrelieved by a single higher consideration. . . . Cooperation, whether voluntary or involuntary, . . . is the only regulator of prices. Competition, free and unfettered, is absolutely destructive to all stability of prices.[115]

And now the essence of his message:

The theoretical proposition at the basis of the open price policy is that, Knowledge regarding bids and prices actually made is all that is necessary to keep prices at reasonably stable and normal levels.[116]

Eddy preached his "open price" gospel widely and persuasively, and soon open price associations became a prominent feature of the American industrial landscape. In 1921, there were at least 150 open price associations and possibly as many as 450.[117] After a sharp decline during the late 1920s, the movement thrived again under federal government auspices between 1933 and 1935, when 422 fair competition codes including open price reporting provisions were approved by the National Recovery Administration.

Eddy was an able corporation lawyer. He designed his open price system to stay within the bounds of antitrust law, as he perceived them at the time. On this he was at least partly successful. The law on trade association price and cost reporting activities is one of the most subtle (and some would add the most confused) branches of antitrust. The courts have adopted a rule of reason approach, examining each set of industry practices on its merits.[118] Typically the cases cover such a complex mixture of activities that case-by-case comparison breaks down, and on specific practices some of the judicial pronouncements are downright contradictory.

The first test case to reach the Supreme Court was a defeat for advocates of "the new competition." The American Hardwood Manufacturers' Association, whose members marketed roughly a third of the nation's hardwood lumber, instituted an open price scheme that required each member firm to submit to a central office price lists, a detailed daily report on all sales and shipments (with copies of each invoice), monthly production and stock reports, and various other documents. The central office in turn forwarded to members weekly reports listing each transaction, the price at which it was made, the buyer, the seller, and so on. Special attention was drawn to list price departures. In addition, meetings were held frequently to discuss market conditions, and at both the meetings and in newsletters the association's Manager of Statistics exhorted members to restrict their output and maintain prices. The Supreme Court, finding the system an illegal conspiracy in restraint of trade, observed in its opinion that:

> [G]enuine competitors do not make daily, weekly, and monthly reports of the minutest details of their business to their rivals, as the defendants did; they do not contract . . . to submit their books to the discretionary audit . . . of their rivals for the purpose of successfully competing with them; and they do not submit the details of their business to the analysis of an expert, jointly employed, and obtain from him a "harmonized" estimate of the market as it is and as, in his specially and confidently informed judgment, it promises to be. This is not the conduct of competitors, but is so clearly that of men united in an agreement, express or implied, to act together and pursue a common purpose under a common guide.[119]

Nevertheless, the seeds of subsequent dilution were sown in dissenting opinions by three members of the Court, including Justice Brandeis's suggestion that the Sherman Act did not require business rivals to compete blindly and without the aid of relevant trade information.

Following a second decision striking down an open price plan in the linseed oil industry,[120] the Supreme Court seemingly reversed its field in a case involving the Maple Flooring Manufacturers' Association. The outcome may have been affected by the Justice Department's inadequate preparation, but the facts were also distinguishable from those of previous cases. In particular, evidence of relatively low and nonuniform prices was presented; the members supposedly ceased discussing prices in their association meetings after the Supreme Court found the hardwood lumber and linseed oil operations illegal; the association's weekly report to members stopped linking transactions with specific sellers after the government filed a complaint; and in general, the association made an obvious effort to stay within the letter, if not the spirit, of the antitrust laws. Given these apparent differences, the Supreme Court countermanded a district court decision, showing its willingness to permit trade association activities that went little farther than the dissemination of detailed information:

> We decide only that trade associations . . . which openly and fairly gather and disseminate information as to the cost of their product, the volume of production,

115. A. J. Eddy, *The New Competition* (4th edition; Chicago: McClury, 1917), pp. 18, 29.

116. Ibid., p. 126.

117. See L. S. Lyon and Victor Abramson, *The Economics of Open Price Associations* (Washington: Brookings, 1936), pp. 15–23, for a historical analysis.

118. For a more thorough review of the leading cases, see George W. Stocking, "The Rule of Reason, Workable Competition, and the Legality of Trade Association Activities," *University of Chicago Law Review*, vol. 21 (Summer 1954), pp. 527–619.

119. *American Column and Lumber Co. et al.* v. *U.S.*, 257 U.S. 377, 410 (1921). See also the discussion in Phillips, *Market Structure*, supra note 5, pp. 138–160.

120. *U.S.* v. *American Linseed Oil Co. et al.*, 262 U.S. 371 (1923).

the actual price which the product has brought in past transactions, stocks of merchandise on hand, approximate cost of transportation from the principal point of shipment to the points of consumption, as did these defendants, and who, as they did, meet and discuss such information and statistics without however reaching or attempting to reach any agreement or any concerted action with respect to prices or production or restraining competition, do not thereby engage in unlawful restraint of commerce.[121]

In another decision announced the same day, the Court lent its seal of approval to price-reporting activities of a cement industry trade association, despite its recognition that they tended to bring about uniformity of prices.[122]

The next major case involving open price policies was a victory for the antitrust enforcers, but only because the defendants—fifteen sugar refining companies—had entered into an explicit agreement to adhere to the prices they quoted until they publicly announced changes. While condemning this agreement, the Supreme Court went on to observe that:

. . . [C]ompetition does not become less free merely because of the distribution of knowledge of the essential factors entering into commercial transactions. The natural effect of the acquisition of the wider and more scientific knowledge of business conditions on the minds of those engaged in commerce, and the consequent stabilizing of production and price, cannot be said to be an unreasonable restraint or in any respect unlawful.[123]

During the late 1930s and 1940s, the Federal Trade Commission launched a series of attacks against open price associations that had continued reporting programs initiated under the auspices of the National Industrial Recovery Act (declared unconstitutional in 1935). All but one led to cease-and-desist orders. However, in most of the cases, the trade associations had gone farther than merely disseminating price information—for example, by hiring a consultant who contacted individual firms and lectured them on the irrationality of price cutting,[124] or by encouraging and facilitating rigid adherence to basing point pricing formulas.[125] The sole defeat came in a case against the Tag Manufacturers Institute.[126] The thirty-one companies who formed the institute accounted for 95 percent of the output of price tags, pin tickets, and similar devices used to mark consumer goods. Member firms agreed to file their price lists with the institute, to submit duplicate copies of every shipment invoice, and to report within twenty-four hours any sales that deviated from the list price. Financial penalties were assessed against members who failed to submit the agreed-upon information on time. The institute in turn circulated to all members copies of each member's price lists, periodic summaries of the invoice data (which did not identify specific sellers), and daily reports listing each off-list transaction, the name of the seller, the state in which the buyer operated, the seller's list price, and the price actually quoted. There was no express agreement among institute members to adhere to list prices, and the institute's director scrupulously avoided encouraging members to respect their list prices. Emphasizing the absence of such agreements or encouragement, and noting that 25 percent of the tag manufacturers' sales were made at off-list prices, an appellate court reversed the FTC's decision and found that the tag makers had not acted illegally. The decision was not appealed to the Supreme Court, apparently because of the tag industry's diminutive size.

In 1969 the Supreme Court returned to the open price battlefield, reversing a district court decision that had absolved the price reporting activities of eighteen companies supplying 90 percent of the cardboard cartons used in southeastern United States.[127] No systematic centralized price reporting organization had been formed. Instead, the producers supplied to one another upon request (as often as a dozen times per month, for one firm that kept records) information on prices currently or last quoted to particular customers. Once a company received this information from a rival, it usually quoted the same price to that customer; and it was common for buyers to divide orders among producers offering identical quotations. Sometimes, however, lower prices were quoted, and there was evidence of considerable shifting by purchasers from one supplier to others. Although entry into carton production was easy, the market structure was oligopolistic, with six producers contributing 60 percent of relevant sales. The industry showed signs of excess capacity despite rapidly growing demand. Prices were said to be trending downward between 1955 and 1963, but only gradually and within a narrow band of fluctuation. Speaking for a majority of the Supreme Court, Justice Douglas observed that the facts fit none of the earlier precedents readily. In a brief opinion addressed only to the immediate circumstances, he concluded that the defendants' information exchange practices had tended to stabilize prices, and that this was an anticompetitive effect illegal under Sherman Act Section 1. Three members of the Court dissented, arguing that the government had not presented sufficient evidence of intent to restrain competition or actual anticompetitive effect to support the majority's conclusion.

The majority position in the 1967 cardboard carton case appears to take a somewhat tougher line than earlier decisions, but it was too narrowly drawn to offer clear guidelines for future cases. More generally, it is possible to extract from the leading decisions only a statement of probabilities concerning the boundaries distinguishing legal from illegal price reporting practices. Few certainties exist, except where express agreements to adhere to reported prices have been made. With caution and a bit of luck, producers may be able to stay within the law in maintaining a reporting system sufficiently elaborate to reduce, if not to eliminate altogether, the temptation toward price shading in an oligopolistic market. However, an open price arrangement is less likely to pass legal muster if it provides that extra margin of active encouragement needed to sustain well-disciplined pricing when the industry structure is only loosely oligopolistic or the product is not homogeneous. The chances of withstanding antitrust attack are also impaired when price reporting is carried to extremes of detail.

---

121. *Maple Flooring Manufacturers' Association* v. *U.S.*, 268 U.S. 563, 586 (1925).

122. *Cement Manufacturers' Protective Association* v. *U.S.*, 268 U.S. 588 (1925).

123. *Sugar Institute* v. *U.S.*, 297 U.S. 553, 598 (1936).

124. *Salt Producers' Association* v. *Federal Trade Commission*, 34 F.T.C. 38 (1941), 134 F. 2d 354 (1943); and *United States Maltsters' Association* v. *Federal Trade Commission*, 35 F.T.C. 797 (1942), 152 F. 2d 161 (1945).

125. *Federal Trade Commission* v. *Cement Institute et al.*, 333 U.S. 683 (1948).

126. *Tag Manufacturers' Institute et al.* v. *Federal Trade Commission*, 43 F.T.C. 499 (1947), 174 F. 2d 452 (1949).

127. *U.S.* v. *Container Corporation of America et al.*, 273 F. Supp. 18 (1967), 393 U.S. 333 (1969). During the mid-1970s, the carton makers were found guilty of an explicit nationwide price-fixing conspiracy. See note 36 supra.

The law on trade association reporting activities might be tilted toward encouraging more competition if, in addition to prohibitions applied in the past, the courts were to take a uniformly dim view of price reporting schemes that identify the buyers and/or sellers in individual transactions, have elaborate auditing provisions,[128] or impose penalties for failure to report transactions. It might also be desirable to limit the frequency with which detailed market condition reports are issued, but here delicate judgment is needed. Weekly reports are probably harmless when transactions are small and occur with great frequency, but they may strengthen collusion in industries with large, infrequent transactions.

Price reporting schemes are by no means a uniquely American phenomenon. When the British Restrictive Practices Court handed down its first decisions prohibiting overt price-fixing arrangements, there was a rush to adopt open price agreements, which did not have to be registered under the 1956 Restrictive Practices Act. According to one observer, more than 150 such agreements had already been put into effect by 1960.[129] In 1968 the act was amended to close the loophole, making information agreements subject to registration and challenge. The number of agreements registered was modest, however, which may mean that firms preferred the modest risks of failing to register over the risks of having still another institution facilitating oligopolistic coordination subjected to administrative and judicial scrutiny.

Conclusion

Most industrialized nations have laws discouraging collusive activity among competitors. The United States has gone farther than most in this respect, making all but legislatively exempted price-fixing and market-dividing agreements per se illegal without regard to their reasonableness. The U.S. law is more permissive with respect to subtler forms of conduct that could have the same effect as explicit agreements. Oligopolists who refrain from price competition merely because they recognize the likelihood of rival retaliation do not violate the law as long as their decisions are taken independently. And by avoiding any suggestion of joint decision-making, they may facilitate uniform and nonaggressive pricing through such devices as price leadership, advance notification of price changes, most-favored-buyer clauses, and open price reporting systems. Within these broadly defined bounds, opportunities for significant departures from competitive pricing remain.

128. Following their 1960 conviction on price-fixing charges, electrical turbogenerator makers General Electric and Westinghouse supported most-favored-customer clauses by letting *buyers* audit their records to ensure that no secret price concessions had been granted. A government complaint against the practice was settled by consent decree in October 1962. See also pp. 212 and 258–259 supra.
129. J. B. Heath, "Some Economic Consequences," *Economic Journal*, vol. 70 (September 1960), pp. 74–84. For a broader European survey, see the OECD report, "Report by the Committee of Experts on Restrictive Business Practices on Information Agreements," excerpted in the *Antitrust Bulletin*, vol. 13 (Spring 1968), pp. 225–260. The European Communities Commission has also acted against a variety of information agreements. See the EC's *Seventh Report on Competition Policy* (Brussels: 1978), pp. 18–21 and 90–91; and *Tenth Report on Competition Policy* (Brussels: 1981), pp. 75–76.

The Dynamics of Monopoly and Oligopoly Pricing

To the extent that the profit motive directs business behavior, it is almost surely long-run rather than short-run profits that firms normally seek to maximize. This fact has important performance implications. They are explored in this chapter.

Before we begin, one hazard must be anticipated. Long-run profit maximization requires that the consequences of today's pricing decisions be weighed far into an uncertain future. Entrepreneurs making such decisions may reach divergent conclusions concerning probabilities and contingencies under identical objective conditions. To avoid framing hypotheses that explain everything but predict nothing, we shall for the most part in this chapter emphasize performance variations linked in a systematic and compelling way to observable structural variables.

Substitution and Long-Run Demand Functions

One hypothesis with significant performance implications holds that demand for the products of a firm or interacting group of firms possessing monopoly power is much more price elastic over the long run than in the short run. This was first argued persuasively by J. M. Clark, who suggested that long-run demand schedules might "in numerous cases approach the horizontal so closely that the slope would not be a matter of material moment in the light of all the uncertainties involved."[1]

There are two main reasons for the higher elasticity of long-run demand schedules. First, competition among substitute products is more effective over the long run than during any short period; a given percentage change in price will induce greater shifts in purchases between substitutes over the long pull than in the short. Second, efforts by a particular firm or group of firms to hold its price persistently above cost may attract new entry, which in the long run makes heavy inroads into sales volume. In this section we focus on long-run competition among substitutes. The entry problem will be studied from several angles in later sections.

Competition among substitutes is one of the most universal economic phenomena. Steel, aluminum, magnesium, copper, titanium, high-density polyethylene, fiberglass, western pine, bamboo, and dozens of other raw materials are potential substitutes for one another in thousands of fabricated product applications. Which one wins out in any particular application depends *inter alia* upon relative prices. To be sure, some materials have unique advantages, so the choice is multidimensional, but there is nearly always some combination of price and other features at which custom will shift away from one possibility and toward another. The same is true with respect to virtually every good and service; it is only through failure of imagination that we sometimes consider certain lines to have no substitutes.

Competition among substitutes generally is more effective in the long run than in the short for several reasons, all related to adjustment lags on both the demand and supply sides of the market.

Consumers, for one thing, are creatures of habit. A sharp rise in butter prices will induce only a moderate shift to margarine in the short run, but as homemakers reconsider their budgets and by experimentation find acceptable new uses

1. J. M. Clark, "Toward a Concept of Workable Competition," *American Economic Review*, vol. 30 (June 1940), p. 248. See also Richard B. Heflebower, "Toward a Theory of Industrial Markets and Prices," *American Economic Review*, vol. 44 (May 1954), p. 126; and P. W. S. Andrews, *On Competition in Economic Theory* (London: Macmillan, 1964), pp. 73–85.

for the substitute, the shift will increase in magnitude. Introductory sales are one way through which producers attempt to break the habit barrier. By inducing consumers to try a substitute product at unusually attractive prices, they build up preferences that make it possible to sell more of their product at any given price in the future. Thus, the difference between long- and short-run price elasticities will be especially great for a newly introduced product.[2]

Durable goods in mature markets may offer an exception that reverses this effect. If current purchases reduce the attractiveness of future purchases (How many refrigerators does one family need?), the price elasticity of industry demand will be greater in the short run than in the long run. This effect undoubtedly contributed to the willingness of automobile manufacturers to respond to unexpectedly low demand by cutting prices through rebates. The long-run price elasticity of demand for new automobiles has been estimated at half the short-run level.[3]

Not all consumer lags stem from subjective inertia, however. Some shifts in consumption can occur only after modifications in complementary durable good stocks are accomplished. When, for example, fuel oil and natural gas prices rose rapidly during the 1970s and early 1980s, the most consumers could do in the short run was turn down the thermostat — for example, substituting sweaters for fuel. But as the higher prices persisted, additional home insulation was installed and research on such substitutes as solar energy was precipitated. And over the very long run, one might expect even more drastic substitution effects, such as a shift away from single-family homes and the construction of coal-fired central heating plants that provide steam to a multiplicity of residences. Similarly, the initial impact of rapidly rising gasoline prices was slight, but over the longer run there was a movement toward smaller and more energy-efficient autos both in the United States (where extensive government intervention complicated the analysis of market responses) and in Europe (where price changes had a more pointed effect). The long-run price elasticity of demand for gasoline has been estimated at several times the short-run elasticity.[4]

In an analogous manner, uncertainty creates a switching cost that slows substitution in consumption. When the superiority of a product can be evaluated only after consuming or "experiencing" the good, substitution will depend upon the rate at which consumers sample new products. Trial carries the risk of disappointment. Thus, experience goods will penetrate a market more slowly than goods that can be evaluated by inspection. Particularly where the quality of service is important, buyers accumulate information about the seller (which translates into the asset "goodwill"), and sellers accumulate idiosyncratic information about the buyer. Thus, responsive landlords have less tenant turnover, ceteris paribus, and patients hesitate before leaving the doctor who has seen them through past ills.[5]

Comparable rigidities constrain industrial purchasers. Products must often be redesigned and production processes retooled to substitute one material input for another. Consequently, once production is geared to use a particular input, the demand for that input is relatively inelastic in the short run. But given time and the appropriate incentives, redesign and retooling will take place. For example, in 1966 the American automobile industry began seeking ways to reduce its consumption of copper after sharp price increases added more than $30 million to annual materials costs.[6] The immediate impact was negligible, but the development of new production processes made it possible to displace copper even from such traditional uses as in radiators.

High prices also induce efforts to invent and develop substitute products which, after sometimes substantial lags, provide a powerful new competitive challenge. For instance, during the 1920s natural rubber prices rose as a result of cartel agreements. This triggered intensified research and experimentation on synthetic rubber, which ultimately displaced natural rubber in many applications.[7] Likewise, when the Chilean nitrate cartel drove fertilizer nitrogen prices up during the first two decades of the twentieth century, a search for synthetic sources began, and from 1913 to 1918 the share of the world's fixed nitrogen output supplied by synthetic producers soared from 8 to 23 percent.[8] During the 1950s the aluminum and container industries developed aluminum cans that ended the sovereignty of costly tin-plated steel in the tin can market. The steel industry fought back with research and development on a steel container stock coated with aluminum (at twenty-five cents per pound at the time) in place of tin (at $1.90 per pound).[9] And when sugar prices rose rapidly during the 1970s, vegetable packers and soft drink bottlers found ways of using corn syrup instead. By 1985, sweeteners made from corn had virtually displaced sugar in soft drinks and were used for more than half of all U.S. caloric sweetener applications, measured by weight.[10] More generally, in a comparative analysis of input-output tables for 1947 and 1958, Anne Carter found that rapid developments in technology rendered materials increasingly interchangeable, with steel giving way to aluminum and cement, copper to aluminum, natural fibers to synthetics, wood to paper, and paper to plastics.[11]

The net effect of these influences for most products is to make demand more sensitive to price in the long run than in the short run and, because of this, to constrain the prices firms or oligopolistic groups can charge without inviting sales losses through substitution. If then producers strive to maximize long-run profits, price may depart less from cost than one might expect merely from considering the short-run monopoly power held. The current prices of monopolized products will be kept lower, the more rapidly substitution is expected to occur owing to high prices and the less heavily firms with monopoly power discount future earnings.

2. On this last point, see Frank Bass, "The Relationship between Diffusion Rates, Experience Curves, and Demand Elasticities for Consumer Durable Technological Innovations," *Journal of Business*, vol. 53 (July 1980), pp. S51–S67.

3. Moshe Justman, "Intertemporal Dependence of Demand in an Imperfectly Competitive Market," *International Journal of Industrial Organization*, vol. 4 (September 1986), pp. 271–286.

4. Robert S. Pindyck, *The Structure of World Energy Demand* (Cambridge: MIT Press, 1979), pp. 232–233. Justman cites studies indicating that demand for electricity is six times more price elastic in the long run than in the short run. "Intertemporal Dependence," pp. 271–286.

5. For a discussion of the implications of switching costs related to information, see C. Christian von Weizsäcker, "The Costs of Substitution," *Econometrica*, vol. 52 (September 1984), pp. 1085–1116.

6. See Thomas O'Hanlon, "The Perilous Prosperity of Anaconda," *Fortune*, May 1966, pp. 118–119. On subsequent reactions when aluminum prices rose rapidly, see "Aluminum Gambles on a Higher Price," *Business Week*, August 23, 1976, p. 25.

7. George W. Stocking and Myron W. Watkins, *Cartels in Action* (New York: Twentieth Century Fund, 1964), p. 73.

8. Stocking and Watkins, *Cartels in Action*, p. 127.

9. See "How Steel May Save an Old Market," *Business Week*, December 5, 1964, p. 33.

10. "Sugar's Anguished Plea for More Federal Aid," *Business Week*, August 8, 1977, p. 60; and U.S. Department of Agriculture, Economic Research Service, Situation and Outlook Report, *Sugar and Sweeteners* (Washington: March 1988), Table 16.

11. Anne P. Carter, "The Economics of Technological Change," *Scientific American*, April 1966, pp. 25–31.

There is evidence that many monopolistic and oligopolistic enterprises do exercise pricing restraint to ward off substitution. In late 1919 and early 1920, gasoline marketers on the West Coast resisted price increases, turning instead to rationing to deal with rapid increases in demand. Part of this restraint reflected the fear that high gasoline prices would impede the economic development of the region and hence reduce demand when new supplies became available.[12] During the mid-1960s, the domestic copper oligopoly held its prices in the neighborhood of forty cents per pound, ostensibly to prevent further inroads by aluminum, while prices of secondary (reprocessed scrap) copper and London Metal Exchange quotations reached eighty cents per pound.[13] M. J. Peck found that aluminum producers refrained from raising prices to short-run profit-maximizing levels in order to enhance long-term growth. He concluded that the existence of close substitutes made high long-run price elasticity a permanent feature of the aluminum market.[14] Nevertheless, the aluminum firms' exercise of pricing restraint was clearest where the threat of short-run substitution was most acute — notably, in container stock. Burdened by rapidly rising input costs, they raised aluminum ingot prices by 95 percent between 1974 and 1976 while holding aluminum can stock prices constant. Steel makers at the same time reduced substitute tin plate prices by 2 percent while the average price of all steel products rose 56 percent.[15] In the rayon industry, according to Jesse Markham, strong competition from other fibers limited the leading producers' control over their prices.[16] On the other hand, the absence of close substitutes for bauxite in aluminum production permitted cartel prices well above the competitive level in the 1970s.[17]

It is apparent, however, that fear of long-run substitution has not deterred some firms from setting high prices, paving the way to competitive inroads by alternative products. Steel is the most prominent example. American producers implemented a series of sharp price increases during the 1950s that led to increasing infringement upon traditional steel markets by substitute metals and plastics. This and pricing policies in other industries that encourage substitution could have resulted from upward cost pressures on prices, shortsightedness, conscious decisions to sacrifice long-term market position for higher immediate profits or, most probably, a combination of all three.

The steel experience demonstrates that fear of long-run substitution is no surefire guarantee against excessive prices. But even when producers fail to show restraint, the possibility of turning to substitutes at least gives consumers an escape from severe and extended monopolistic exploitation. And as science makes it possible to create substitutes for more and more products, the combination of these two protection mechanisms — the threat of substitution and its actual occurrence — provides an important check on the social losses attributable to monopoly power.

Limiting Small-Scale Entry

The second major check on industrial pricing power is the threat of entry by new competitors and expansion by smaller existing rivals. We take up the analysis in stages, starting with the small-scale entry faced by a dominant firm. In Chapter 6 (pp. 224–226), we described the short-run equilibrium for an industry in which a dominant firm faces the actual or potential competition of fringe rivals, each too small to exert an appreciable influence on price through its individual output decisions. This structure greatly simplifies the analysis, because fringe behavior can be fully captured by simple decision rules: in the short run, fringe firms expand output until marginal cost equals price. If price exceeds unit costs (including normal profits) at this level of production, fringe firms expand capacity, fringe supply shifts out, the dominant firm's residual demand function shifts to the left, and, if it continues to set its price to maximize short-run profits, the dominant firm's market share and profits will decline. The dominant firm in effect encourages and makes room for an expanded competitive fringe. Its high prices and profits today set in motion a chain of repercussions that reduce the firm's profits in subsequent years.

A Simple Limit Pricing Strategy

In many instances there is only one way for the dominant firm to avert this Greek tragedy: it must abandon its attempt to maximize short-run profits and instead reduce its price to a level at which new entry and the expansion of fringe rivals are discouraged.[18] An overly simple but useful first approximation is to view the dominant firm's decision problem as dichotomous: either it maximizes short-run profits and accepts an eventual market share and profit decline, or it sets prices to deter all entry and expansion by fringe competitors.

Figure 10.1 provides a framework for analyzing the latter strategy. DD' is the dominant firm's initial demand function. (If there is a competitive fringe, its output is assumed to have been subtracted out; if on the other hand the dominant firm is a pure monopolist, DD' is the market demand function. In either case, overall market demand is assumed provisionally to be stable over time.) Now suppose

12. Alan L. Olmstead and Paul Rhode, "Rationing without Government: The West Coast Gas Famine of 1920," *American Economic Review*, vol. 15 (December 1985), pp. 1044–1055. Fear of hostile reactions by the general public and a sense of social responsibility appear to have been motivating factors in a market where the leading firm, Standard Oil of California, controlled 55 percent of gasoline sales and the top four firms 90 percent.

13. Compare J. L. McCarthy, "The American Copper Industry," *Yale Economic Essays*, vol. 4 (Spring 1964), pp. 77–80; and (for a view somewhat more skeptical of the substitution hypothesis) David L. McNicol, "The Two Price Systems in the Copper Industry," *Bell Journal of Economics*, vol. 6 (Spring 1975), especially pp. 59–73.

14. M. J. Peck, *Competition in the Aluminum Industry* (Cambridge: Harvard University Press, 1961), pp. 52–62 and 206–207. For other partly conflicting estimates of short-run and long-run aluminum price elasticities, see the Council on Wage and Price Stability staff report, *Aluminum Prices: 1974–75* (Washington: USGPO, September 1976), pp. 7–8 and 115.

15. "New Threats to the $6 Billion Can Industry," *Business Week* November 22, 1976, p. 78. The battle continued into 1988, with both steel and aluminum producers pricing can stock lower than similar products. See "Prices To Rise on Steel Cans; Beverage Industry Exempt," *New York Times*, August 25, 1988, p. D7.

16. Jesse W. Markham, *Competition in the Rayon Industry* (Cambridge: Harvard University Press, 1952), p. 208.

17. See Robert S. Pindyck, "Cartel Pricing and the Structure of the World Bauxite Market," *Bell Journal of Economics*, vol. 8 (Autumn 1977), pp. 343–360.

18. Seminal works on this problem of "limit pricing" include Nicholas Kaldor, "Market Imperfections and Excess Capacity," *Economica*, vol. 2 (February 1935), pp. 33–50; Clark, "Toward a Concept of Workable Competition," supra note 1, pp. 247–248; Joe S. Bain, "A Note on Pricing in Monopoly and Oligopoly," *American Economic Review*, vol. 39 (March 1949), pp. 448–464; P. W. S. Andrews, *Manufacturing Business* (London: Macmillan, 1949); George J. Stigler, *The Theory of Price*, rev. ed. (New York: Macmillan, 1952), pp. 231–234; R. F. Harrod, *Economic Essays* (London: Macmillan, 1952) especially pp. 139–174; H. R. Edwards, "Price Formation in Manufacturing Industry and Excess Capacity," *Oxford Economic Papers*, vol. 7 n.s. (February 1955), pp. 194–218; Joe S. Bain, *Barriers to New Competition* (Cambridge: Harvard University Press, 1956); Paolo Sylos-Labini, *Oligopoly and Technical Progress*, trans. Elizabeth Henderson (Cambridge: Harvard University Press, 1962); and Franco Modigliani, "New Developments on the Oligopoly Front," *Journal of Political Economy*, vol. 66 (June 1958), pp. 215–232.

Figure 10.1
Pricing to Deter
Small-Scale Entry

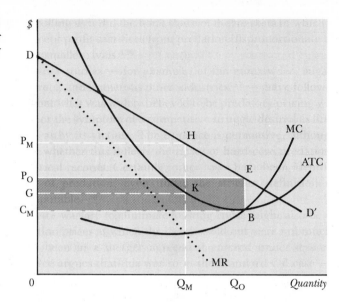

that fringe rivals, actual and potential, are small relative to the total market volume, so they view the dominant firm's price as a parameter essentially unaffected by their output decisions. Suppose too that at their scale of operation, the lowest unit cost (including normal profits attainable by fringe firms) is OP_0. The dominant firm's long-run demand function cannot therefore be DD'. It does include segment ED'. But when the price is held above OP_0, the quantity demanded from the dominant firm falls off more and more as time passes. If the price were held long enough above OP_0, the amount of output demanded from the dominant firm (that is, not supplied by fringe members) will eventually approach zero. P_0E therefore approximates the remaining segment of the dominant firm's long-run demand curve, the whole of which is given by P_0ED'. At the price level above which new entry flows in, the dominant firm's long-run demand function tends to become perfectly elastic. It is this entry phenomenon, more than long-run substitution between different products, that prompted J. M. Clark, Roy Harrod, P. W. S. Andrews, and others to insist that the long-run demand curves confronting monopolists and oligopolistic groups tend to be highly elastic, approaching the horizontal.[19]

To keep the existing competitive fringe in check and deter new entry, the dominant firm must set and maintain a price slightly below OP_0. This price, which we for simplicity represent by OP_0, is called the *limit price* — that is, the price that limits to zero the entry and expansion of fringe rivals. The dominant firm must also ensure that the market demand of OQ_0 at that price is fully satisfied. It must therefore supply output OQ_0 and maintain capacity suited to supplying that output. Figure 10.1 assumes that the dominant firm has chosen a plant capable of supplying OQ_0 at minimum unit cost. The profitability of an entry deterrence strategy depends upon the dominant firm's unit cost at output OQ_0. Figure 10.1 assumes that it is lower than OP_0, and hence lower than actual or potential fringe firms' costs—for example, because the dominant firm can realize scale economies that small fringe members cannot.[20] If this is the case, the dominant firm can set the limit price OP_0, hold fringe rivals in check, and continue year after year to rake in profits given by the shaded rectangle P_0EBC_M.

Is this the most profitable strategy for the dominant firm? In moving toward an answer, let us consider the alternative short-run profit-maximizing strategy. Given the cost functions in Figure 10.1, the short-run profit-maximizing price is OP_M, and the associated output is OQ_M, with profits equal to the rectangular area P_MHKG. These are necessarily higher than the profits under a limit-pricing strategy. But they are also shorter lived. As entry occurs, the profits realized under short-run profit maximization will decline, as shown in the upper panel of Figure 10.2. Under limit pricing, as illustrated in the lower panel, they will be smaller initially but larger eventually. Which time pattern is preferable? The answer turns upon the discount rate applied to future earnings,[21] the rate at which entry occurs and profits decline under short-run profit maximization, and the extent to which the dominant firm is able persistently to maintain a price exceeding unit cost without encouraging fringe expansion. The latter in turn depends (under the assumptions accepted thus far) upon the dominant firm's unit cost advantage over fringe rivals.

If dominant firms discount the future heavily, they may place little weight on the future profits forgone owing to new entry and strive for maximum profits in the short run. According to standard managerial economics texts, high discount rates are especially appropriate when the future is uncertain, as it surely is in planning long-range pricing policy.[22] However, uncertainty might work in the opposite direction. As Harrod observes,

All entrepreneurs . . . have in mind the vast uncertainties of a relatively distant future. The best method of insuring against them is to attach to oneself by ties of goodwill as large a market as possible as quickly as possible. If one can get a substantially larger market by earning no more than a normal profit than one could get by earning a surplus profit . . . one may well choose to do the former, as an insurance against future uncertainties.[23]

It is well known that some decision makers are more shortsighted, or discount the future more heavily, than others. Fog found such differences to be the most important single source of internal conflict and disagreement in Danish price-fixing cartels.[24] Partly because they tap larger pools of savings but also because of cultural

19. See note 1 supra and Harrod, *Economic Essays*, supra note 18, pp. 162–163.

20. If it were contemplating a higher price, lower output policy, the dominant firm would probably invest in less capacity than Figure 10.1 assumes. With lower unit costs at output OQ_M, its profits would be somewhat higher than those shown. Note that ATC is a short-run average cost function, that is, one of many on the long-run envelope curve. The assumption that OP_0 is the lowest unit cost attainable by entrants can be taken to mean that at the largest output an entrant can achieve, OP_0 is the corresponding long-run cost function ordinate.

21. See Chapter 6, note 37.

22. See Lawrence D. Schall and Charles W. Haley, *Introduction to Financial Management*, 2nd ed. (New York: McGraw-Hill, 1980), pp. 269–282.

23. Harrod, *Economic Essays*, supra note 18, pp. 147 and 174.

24. Bjarke Fog, "How Are Cartel Prices Determined?" *Journal of Industrial Economics*, vol. 5 (November 1956), pp. 16–23. Fog observes that larger firms typically placed more weight on long-run considerations — an emphasis possibly related more to objective capital market access differences than entrepreneurial psychology.

Figure 10.2
Comparison of Profit
Streams over Time

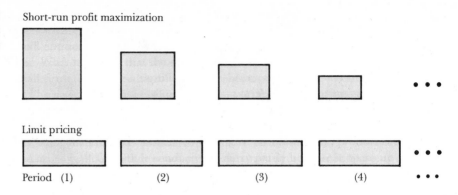

Short-run profit maximization

Limit pricing

Period (1)   (2)   (3)   (4)

and organizational differences, Japanese corporations appear to discount the future less heavily than U.S. firms.[25] The psychology of the decision makers involved may therefore be a relevant variable affecting the pricing strategy choice.

Objective variables also are important, however, and prove more amenable to systematic analysis. Consider, contrary to our assumptions thus far, a situation in which the dominant firm enjoys no unit cost advantage relative to fringe rivals, actual or potential. To deter their entry or expansion, it must maintain a limit price at which it realizes no supra-normal profits. The limit-pricing rectangles in Figure 10.2 will therefore have zero height. Then short-run profit maximization is unambiguously more profitable over the long run too, and unless (Harrod's suggestion to the contrary notwithstanding) its desire for a secure future is extraordinary, the dominant firm will almost surely prefer to set prices at an entry-attracting level.

A crucial role therefore emerges for *barriers to entry* or to the expansion of fringe firms. These can take several forms.[26] For one, the dominant firm (or firms) may enjoy absolute cost advantages over fringe rivals as a consequence of superior patented production methods, the entrepreneurial talent of its managers, or having acquired on favorable terms other superior nonreproducible production inputs (such as ore deposits or hydroelectric power generating rights).[27] Second, as suggested already, the dominant firm's unit costs may be lower because of scale economies in production, physical distribution, purchasing, capital raising,[28] or sales promotion not attainable by smaller fringe rivals. On this we shall have a good deal more to say later. Third, the dominant firm's output may enjoy product differentiation advantages—that is, a brand "image" or accumulation of goodwill that makes buyers willing to pay a higher price than they would for the otherwise comparable products of new entrants or fringe firms. Image advantages are analogous to unit cost advantages in their operation as entry barriers—both act as a wedge between the limit price and the dominant firm's own unit costs. As Chapter 4 brought out, the inability of fringe firms to emulate a dominant firm's image advantages may in turn be related to scale economies in sales promotion efforts.[29] Fourth, capital raising, product differentiation, and information access handicaps might *slow down* the entry and expansion of fringe rivals, altering the time pattern of the dominant firm's profit returns, rather than permitting the dominant firm persistently to enjoy supra-normal profits. Finally, through its conduct the dominant firm may be able to engender expectations in the minds of rivals that discourage entry and fringe expansion. On this too, more must be said later.

Work by William Baumol, Elizabeth Bailey, John Panzar, Robert Willig, and others[30] has extended the analysis of limit pricing by a dominant firm to the multiproduct case. In addition to the product-specific economies realized when turning out more of a particular product reduces unit costs, the ability to deter entry is affected by *economies of scope*, realized when costs are reduced by producing two or more products jointly, rather than in specialized firms. The combination of these two properties determines in a complex way whether the cost function is *subadditive*, that is, whether a single firm can supply a bundle of outputs demanded by the market at lower total cost than some combination of two or more single-product and/or low-volume producers. If subadditivity holds, the dominant firm may (but in special cases cannot) devise a set of prices that is *sustainable*, permitting the incumbent at least to cover its costs while entrants can find no overlapping output bundle at which their costs are covered.[31] Thus, a set of sustainable prices includes limit prices for each product. As in the single product case, sustainable prices yield supra-normal profits only when there are entry barriers. To our list of entry barriers, we therefore add economies of scope and multiproduct cost subadditivity.

A Dynamic Model of Dominant Firm Pricing

We have in hand now most of the analytic pieces one needs to study the dominant firm's long-run pricing strategy choices. But they are not yet put together properly. One problem is that the simple limit-pricing model permits only crude behavioral predictions. Second, it is questionable whether dominant firms face only a dichotomous choice between deterring all fringe entry or raising prices to the short-run profit-maximizing level. Intermediate strategies might be even more

25. See p. 49 supra.

26. Cf. Bain, *Barriers to New Competition*, supra note 18, pp. 1–19; *idem*, *Industrial Organization*, 2nd ed. (New York: Wiley, 1968), pp. 204–205 and 255; and C. Christian von Weizsäcker, *Barriers to Entry: A Theoretical Treatment* (Berlin: Springer-Verlag, 1980).

27. Strictly speaking, supranormal profits gained through such possession are rents imputable to the patent's or input's superiority. What one calls them is less important than what implications they have for structure and performance. Here our concern is with the ability of the incumbent to raise price above cost without attracting entry. Some barriers — such as those that reward innovation — may be socially desirable. We return to this theme later. Seminal contributions to the debate over what constitutes a harmful barrier to entry include George J. Stigler, *The Organization of Industry* (Homewood: R. D. Irwin, 1968), Chapter 6; von Weizsäcker, *Barriers to Entry*; Michael Waterson, "On the Definition and Meaning of Barriers to Entry," *Antitrust Bulletin,* vol. 26 (Fall 1981), pp. 521–539; and Harold Demsetz, "Barriers to Entry," *American Economic Review*, vol. 72 (March 1982), pp. 47–57.

28. Capital market imperfections may also act as a barrier to

entry if they deny potential entrants access to sufficient funds to finance the construction of efficient-size plants — a case not relevant to the small scale entry envisioned here.

29. Cf. pp. 132–134 supra.

30. William J. Baumol, Elizabeth E. Bailey, and Robert D. Willig, "Weak Invisible Hand Theorems on the Sustainability of Multiproduct Natural Monopoly," *American Economic Review*, vol. 67 (June 1977), pp. 350–365; Baumol, John C. Panzar, and Willig, *Contestable Markets and the Theory of Industry Structure* (New York: Harcourt Brace Jovanovich, 1982); and Baumol, "Quasi-Permanence of Price Reductions: A Policy for Prevention of Predatory Pricing," *Yale Law Journal*, vol. 89 (November 1979), pp. 1–26. Critical evaluations include Michael Spence, "*Contestable Markets and the Theory of Industry Structure*: A Review Article," *Journal of Economic Literature*, vol. 21 (September 1983), pp. 981–990; and William A. Brock, "Contestable Markets and the Theory of Industry Structure: A Review Article," *Journal of Political Economy*, vol. 91 (December 1983), pp. 1055–1066.

31. Under this definition of sustainability, the entrant's bundle could be a single product, the same product line as the incumbent's, or a product mix that overlaps the incumbent's.

profitable. A fully dynamic model of dominant firm pricing originating with Gaskins goes far toward eliminating these two problems.[32]

Gaskins argued that a dominant firm facing the prospect of entry or expansion by a competitive fringe will maximize its long-run profits by balancing current profits against the impact of that entry and the resulting reduced market share on future profits. His critical assumption is that the rate at which fringe entry and expansion occurs is neither exogenous nor dichotomous, but varies continuously with the price set by the dominant firm.[33] The higher prices are, the more rapidly potential entrants will perceive the attractiveness of entry. And if, as is common, fringe firms finance plant capacity expansions with retained earnings, fringe expansion will be more rapid, the higher the profit umbrella erected by the dominant firm.[34] Where external finance is available, higher anticipated profit returns make it more likely that interested investors will choose to commit their funds.

If then P_0 is the minimum unit cost at which potential entrants or fringe firms can operate, $P(t)$ is the price set by the dominant firm at time t, and $q(t)$ is the amount of output supplied by the fringe firms at time t, the dynamics of entry are characterized by the simple differential equation:

$$(10.1) \qquad dq/dt = k(t)[P(t) - P_0],$$

where dq/dt is the rate of fringe expansion (or, for negative values of $[p(t) - p_0]$, contraction) per time period and coefficient $k(t)$ reflects the speed at which fringe firms respond to a given profit stimulus.[35] Equation (10.1) is incorporated into the dominant firm's long-run profit-maximization problem, and, using the mathematical techniques of optimal control theory, that problem can be solved to find the time path of prices yielding the highest discounted present value of profits.[36] In this instance, $P(t)$ is known as a control variable — that is, a behavioral variable manipulated over time by the dominant firm to maximize its profit performance functional. The so-called state variable ($q(t)$ in the present case) reflects the structure of the market as it is shaped by the dominant firm's pricing policy. It is worth pointing out that while the value of $q(t)$ influences the dominant firm's pricing policy at any moment in time — that is, structure affects conduct — the choice of a pricing policy in turn affects dq/dt and hence has important feedback effects on market structure.[37]

From an analysis of the basic Gaskins model (as well as more complex variants), a number of strong and plausible conclusions emerge. For one, unless the fringe's unit costs are so high that they exceed the price a monopolist would set to maximize short-run profits — a case Bain called *blockaded entry*[38] — the monopolist *always* finds its long-run profits enhanced by exercising restraint and holding its price below the short-run profit-maximizing level. Thus, when the rate of new entry varies with the dominant firm's price choice, pricing to exclude *some* entry becomes an interesting option alongside pricing to deter *all* entry. The strategy problem is no longer merely a dichotomous choice between blocking all entry or maximizing short-run profits.

What price path over time the dominant firm chooses depends *inter alia*, as one might expect, upon its cost advantage relative to fringe firms, the entry response coefficient $k(t)$, and the discount rate. For dominant firms not subjected to a "sudden death" threat—for example, because a key patent is about to expire—and hence with a reasonably long time horizon, three main cases emerge.

Case I: The Declining Dominant Firm   When the dominant firm has no cost or image advantage over actual and potential fringe rivals, and *a fortiori* when it operates at a cost or image disadvantage, it will maximize long-run profits by setting its price above the limit price P_0 (but below the short-run profit-maximizing price), earning (somewhat constrained) monopoly profits while it can, and letting its market share steadily decline. Its optimal price will gradually converge toward the limit price and eventually equal it as the dominant firm's market share dwindles either to zero or (more plausibly) to a level at which the firm no longer has power over price.[39] A similar strategy is likely to be adopted by dominant firms with only a small unit cost or image advantage. This is more probable as the dominant firm's time discount rate rises. The larger the rival response coefficient $k(t)$ is—that is, the faster entry occurs in response to an above-cost price—the more restraint the

32. Darius W. Gaskins, Jr., "Dynamic Limit Pricing: Optimal Pricing Under Threat of Entry," *Journal of Economic Theory*, vol. 3 (September 1971), pp. 306–322. A fuller exposition covering a broader array of cases is found in his Ph.D. dissertation, "Optimal Pricing by Dominant Firms" (University of Michigan, 1970). For virtually simultaneous contributions with somewhat different assumptions see note 92 *infra*. Useful extensions include N. J. Ireland, "Concentration and the Growth of Market Demand," *Journal of Economic Theory*, vol. 5 (October 1972), pp. 303–305; David Encaoua and Alexis P. Jacquemin, "Degree of Monopoly, Indices of Concentration and Threat of Entry," *International Economic Review*, vol. 21 (February 1980), pp. 87–105; Kenneth L. Judd and Bruce C. Petersen, "Dynamic Limit Pricing: A Reformulation," *Review of Industrial Organization*, vol. 2 (1985), pp. 160–177; and *idem*, "Dynamic Limit Pricing and Internal Finance," *Journal of Economic Theory*, vol. 39 (August 1986), pp. 368–399.

33. For early statistical support, see Edwin Mansfield, "Entry, Gibrat's Law, Innovation, and the Growth of Firms," *American Economic Review*, vol. 52 (December 1962), pp. 1023–1030.

34. Judd and Petersen, "Dynamic Limit Pricing and Internal Finance," supra note 32.

35. It could incorporate the impact of secular growth or decline in the market or a constraint limiting investment in new capacity to some fraction of retained earnings.

36. Assuming that the quantity demanded from all sellers, dominant and fringe, is $Q[P(t)]$, the quantity sold by the dominant firm is obviously $Q[P(t)] - q(t)$. Assuming furthermore that the dominant firm produces at constant unit cost c, the dominant firm's profits in period t are

$$[P(t) - c] \{Q[P(t)] - q(t)\}.$$

If r is the dominant firm's time discount rate, the firm's decision problem is to maximize the functional

$$[P(t) - c] \{Q[P(t)] - q(t)\}e^{-rt}dt,$$

subject to the fringe behavioral condition

$$dq/dt = k(t)[P(t) - P_0],$$

and subject also to various initial and boundary conditions. For a derivation of the solution conditions, which are rather complex, the reader is referred to Gaskins, "Dynamic Limit Pricing," and Judd and Petersen, "Dynamic Limit Pricing and Internal Finance," supra note 32.

37. Cf. Alexis P. Jacquemin and Jacques Thisse, "Strategy of the Firm and Market Structure: An Application of Optimal Control Theory," in Keith Cowling, ed., *Market Structure and Corporate Behaviour* (London: Gray-Mills, 1972), pp. 63–75. For other examples of the bidirectional relationship between variables proxying conduct and structure in dynamic models, see Morton Kamien and Nancy Schwartz, *Dynamic Optimization: The Calculus of Variations and Optimal Control in Economics and Management* (New York: North Holland, 1981).

38. Bain, *Barriers to New Competition*, supra note 18, pp. 21–22. Short-run profit maximization may also occur if the dominant firm's discount rate is infinite, or at the moment the dominant firm's life ends — for example, because its charter expires — or, somewhat more plausibly, because of the expiration of a key patent.

39. In his original work, Gaskins proved this result only for a nongrowing market. For conditions yielding the result in a growing market, see Ireland, "Concentration and the Growth of Market Demand," supra note 32, pp. 303–305; and Judd and Petersen, "Dynamic Limit Pricing," supra note 32, pp. 160–177.

dominant firm will exercise in elevating its price and encouraging fringe expansion.[40]

Case II: Exclusionary Pricing   When there is a competitive fringe of appreciable size and when the dominant firm has a significant unit cost or image advantage over fringe members, the dominant firm's long-run profit-maximizing strategy will often be to set its price initially below the level of fringe firms' unit cost and drive the rivals out. This is more likely, the larger the dominant firm's price-cost advantage is, the lower its time discount rate is, and the more rapidly fringe firms exit in response to prices below their unit cost [that is, the larger $k(t)$ is]. In many instances, given its cost advantage, the dominant firm will continue to earn positive profits as it squeezes rivals out. However, with sufficiently large initial fringe output and values of $k(t)$, the dominant firm may rationally cut the price temporarily below its own unit cost in order to hasten rivals' exit and enhance its market share.[41] In either event, as the fringe dwindles, the dominant firm gradually raises its price, realizing rising profit margins, while the exit of remaining rivals decelerates. It can be shown[42] that there exists an asymptotically optimal market share toward which the dominant firm aspires. That market share is larger, the greater the dominant firm's cost advantage, the lower its discount rate, and the higher the fringe response coefficient $k(t)$. As the dominant firm's actual market share approaches its asymptotic optimum, the firm raises its price toward the limit price and relaxes its efforts to squeeze out additional competition.

Case III: Asymptotic Limit Pricing   Given enough time, the market share of a dominant firm with an appreciable cost advantage over rivals will approach the value at which further market share gains cost more in terms of current profit sacrifices than they add through the generation of profits on a larger future sales volume. From then on, the dominant firm will pursue a classic limit pricing policy, keeping its price $P(t)$ equal to the fringe firms' unit cost P_0. If its cost advantage is slowly eroding over time — for example, because patents are expiring one by one — it may alternatively begin by driving out rivals but later charge a price above the limit price and attract entry. However, Gaskins demonstrates for a range of plausible cases that when this "low-price followed by high-price" strategy maximizes long-run profits, a second-best strategy of maintaining the price consistently at or near the limit price P_0 typically entails only modest profit sacrifices compared to the first-best rule.[43] Because of its simplicity and perhaps also because pricing to drive out rivals could invite antitrust sanctions, the constant limit price strategy may well be favored by dominant firms. As we shall see in Chapter 12, the risk of an antitrust complaint might also increase as the dominant firm's market share exceeds some threshold value — for example, on the order of 65 percent. And in any event, it cannot exceed 100 percent. Gaskins demonstrates that when a dominant firm is charging less than the limit price to drive out fringe competitors and when its market share rises to some such boundary value, its optimal policy shifts abruptly to one of maintaining prices persistently at the limit-price level.[44]

Further Implications   Several additional implications of the basic limit pricing analysis merit attention before we turn to how the model performs in practice. For one, it is entirely possible that equilibrium will occur at a point where industry demand is price inelastic. This is plainly true in Figure 10.1, if we assume the absence of a competitive fringe. At the entry-deterring output OQ_0, dominant firm (and hence industry) short-run marginal revenue is negative. Nearly all *A* students of economic theory (and a few *B* students) have at one time or another written into examination booklets that profit-maximizing monopolists never operate in an inelastic segment of the industry demand function. Yet because after entry their private residual demand function would diverge from the industry demand function, this is not necessarily true.[45] Recent empirical work finds evidence of inelastic industry demand for a range of oligopolistically organized industries.[46]

Second, the threat of fringe entry greatly complicates the coordination problem when an industry is dominated by a group of oligopolists. If the group elects to practice limit pricing, marginalist output determination rules are no longer appropriate. Finding the total amount of output to be produced by the group is a simple task if the group chooses to exclude all new entry — it is the quantity OQ_0 in Figure 10.1. It can also be determined uniquely, following more laborious mathematical derivation, under a Gaskins-type analysis balancing the benefits of a higher current price against eventual erosion of the group's collective market share. However, there is no compelling calculus telling individual group members how much to produce. If each member sets output at the level where its marginal cost equals marginal revenue (derived under the price-matching, constant-shares assumption), too little will be produced. If each equates marginal cost with the price, too much will usually be produced. Ideally, each firm might produce a predetermined share of the total quantity demanded when the price is set at the optimal entry-limiting level. But this requires explicit agreements on market shares, and even that is insufficient in a world of change and uncertainty. When the industry demand function shifts erratically over time (as most demand functions do), member firms could find themselves in the awkward position of planning to produce a known share of an unknown total quantity demanded. As a result, there is no way of ensuring that the quantities member firms plan to supply, either independently or collusively, will add up to a total that just clears the market at the strategically determined price. That price can be sustained only if production

40. For some qualifications to this last point, see Raymond de Bondt, "On the Effects of Retarded Entry," *European Economic Review*, vol. 8 (August 1977), pp. 361–371.

41. This is much less likely when the rate of entry for values of $P(t)$ exceeding P_0 is greater than the rate of exit for equivalent $P(t)$ values below P_0 — for example, when the analogue of Equation (10.1) is a quadratic equation of the form $dq/dt = k_1[P(t) - P_0] + k_2[P(t) - P_0]^2$, with $[P(t) - P_0] \geq -k_1/2k_2$. See Gaskins, "Optimal Pricing," supra note 32, pp. 26–40.

42. Gaskins, "Dynamic Limit Pricing," supra note 32, pp. 311–312.

43. Gaskins, "Optimal Pricing," pp. 22–24. The profit sacrifice is particularly small when the dominant firm enjoys only a moderate cost advantage.

44. Gaskins, "Optimal Pricing," pp. 91–104.

45. For example, Daniel Sullivan concludes that the U.S. cigarette industry's pricing was inconsistent with cartel behavior.

"Testing Hypotheses about Firm Behavior in the Cigarette Industry," *Journal of Political Economy*, vol. 93 (June 1985), pp. 586–598. However, his analysis starts with the assumption that a perfectly coordinated cartel must be pricing in the elastic range of industry demand. If existing firms price to limit expansion by fringe brands, then Sullivan's results may be more a rejection of his assumption than of cartel-like behavior by the industry.

46. See A. Koutsoyiannis, "Goals of Oligopolistic Firms: An Empirical Test of Competing Hypotheses," *Southern Economic Journal*, vol. 51 (October 1984), pp. 540–567, and the subsequent discussion in *Southern Economic Journal*, vol. 52 (April 1986), pp. 1151–1161; and Emilio Pagoulatos and Robert Sorenson, "What Determines the Elasticity of Industry Demand?" *International Journal of Industrial Organization*, vol. 4 (September 1986), pp. 237–250. Pagoulatos and Sorenson find that demand becomes less inelastic as industry concentration rises.

planning errors are absorbed through fluctuations in finished goods inventories and order backlogs. Changes in orders, backlogs, and inventory levels also provide signals to guide member firm production decisions when collusive output determination institutions are lacking. This feedback system, rather than marginalist rules, must be the main basis of output decisions in tacitly collusive oligopolies practicing limit pricing.[47]

In recognizing these problems, we must also be aware that even when oligopolists mutually prefer to adopt an entry-limiting price policy, the desired price may not be attained or maintained. Through miscalculation, the price may be set too high. But more importantly, if the group's discipline is weak, the actual price may fall persistently below the limit price. In this case entry will be deterred, but member firms will realize lower profits than they would under an effectively coordinated deterrence policy.[48]

Once the limit price (or limit-pricing trajectory) has been found, full-cost pricing rules can be effective in facilitating coordinated behavior, and hence maximizing long-run joint profits.[49] When prices of labor and raw materials change, they often do so more or less uniformly for all industry members, actual or potential. The limit price must therefore change correspondingly, and adjustments based upon a full-cost rule will keep actual prices in fairly close step with the altered conditions of entry deterrence. The "conventional profit margin" applied to accounting cost need not be invariant across industry lines; it may be adjusted (as case studies have documented) to reflect the cost or image advantage that established companies have over potential entrants. Thus, when the most profitable long-run strategy for existing producers is to deter new entry, intelligent application of full-cost pricing rules is apt to bring firms as close to the goal of maximum profits as they can hope to come in a world of change and uncertainty.[50]

Some Illustrations

The view of pricing strategy presented thus far is compelling not only because it yields rich predictions but also because those predictions appear to be consistent with a good deal of what we know about U.S. industrial history. Steel provides an especially well-documented illustration.[51] When the United States Steel Corporation was formed by merger in 1901, it accounted for approximately 65 percent of U.S. steel ingot production. No rival was large enough to be seen as anything other than part of a competitive fringe. For example, in 1908 Jones and Laughlin, the second largest producer, controlled only 4.2 percent of ingot capacity. There is reason to believe that U.S. Steel's plants had no operating cost advantage over those of efficient rivals, and in subsequent decades it had clearly higher costs than several rivals. The theory of optimal dynamic pricing predicts that under these circumstances it should set prices inducing entry and a decline in its market share. This it clearly did. Despite acquiring a sizable competitor in 1907 and opening in 1911 the world's largest steel works at Gary, Indiana, U.S. Steel's share of domestic steel ingot production fell to 51 percent in 1915, 42 percent in 1925, and 24 percent in 1967. By that time its behavior had changed sufficiently as to raise doubts about whether the dominant firm analysis continued to be applicable.[52] For the period 1907–1930, the explanatory power of the dynamic limit-pricing model is shown by Hideki Yamawaki's regression analysis. Yamawaki found that prices fell as the fringe market share rose, that higher prices stimulated fringe capacity investment while depressing investment by U.S. Steel, and that higher prices encouraged growth in the fringe's share of production.[53] The U.S. Steel merger led to a highly profitable industry, with steel rail markups on the order of 30 percent.[54] George Stigler shows that, at least in the early years, the high-price, declining market share strategy continued to be quite profitable.[55] In iron ore, on the other hand, U.S. Steel controlled at the time of its creation a considerable share of the nation's richest deposits; and in the subsequent decade, it bought up most of the remaining high-grade reserves, so that only low-quality ore remained for nonintegrated rivals (to whom it sold ore) and fringe entrants. With this cost advantage, U.S. Steel evidently pursued an ore pricing policy under which its share of domestic iron ore production remained fairly constant in the 40 to 45 percent range throughout the first three decades of its existence and probably even longer.[56]

There are many other cases of declining dominant firm market shares over time, in at least some of which corroborating evidence of little or no cost advantage exists. One of the more spectacular involved the Reynolds International Pen Corporation, which sold its pioneering ball-point pens (costing eighty cents to produce) at retail prices of twelve to twenty dollars in late 1945 and precipitated the entry of some one hundred competitors. By 1948 its market share had fallen to zero.[57] In 1919, the American Viscose Company controlled 100 percent of the domestic rayon market. Once key patents expired, new entry and the expansion of entrants caused its share to fall to 42 percent in 1930, after which, according to Markham, it no longer conformed to the dominant firm pricing model.[58] However, it continued to bear the brunt of industry output restriction efforts, and by 1949 its share had fallen further to 26 percent. American Can Company controlled 90 percent of all "tin" can output at the time of its organization in 1901. Its high-price policy encouraged new entry, and its market share fell to 63 percent in 1913 and to roughly 40 percent by 1960.[59] Similar histories are observed in corn

47. See pp. 268–270 supra.

48. In *The Economics of Sellers' Competition* (Baltimore: Johns Hopkins University Press, 1952), p. 537, Fritz Machlup suggested that poorly coordinated oligopolists trying to practice limit pricing are caught on the horns of a dilemma. Lower prices may induce actual competitors to compete belligerently, while high prices will induce new entry.

49. Contrast this observation with the debate (pp. 263–264 supra) over whether the use of full-cost pricing rules, which appear devoid of any attempt to equate marginal revenue with marginal cost, is consistent with profit maximization.

50. For an early reconciliation of full-cost pricing with the equalization of long-run marginal revenue and marginal cost, see Harrod, *Economic Essays*, supra note 18, pp. 161–163.

51. See especially Eliot Jones, *The Trust Problem in the United States* (New York: Macmillan, 1921), Chapter 9, and in particular, on comparative costs, pp. 218–219; George J. Stigler, "Monopoly and Oligopoly by Merger," *American Economic Review*, vol. 40 (May 1950), pp. 23–34; and Donald O. Parsons and Edward J. Ray, "The United States Steel Consolidation: The Creation of Market Control," *Journal of Law & Economics*, vol. 18 (April 1975), pp. 181–220.

52. Cf. pp. 252–254 supra.

53. Hideki Yamawaki, "Dominant Firm Pricing and Fringe Expansion: The Case of the U.S. Iron and Steel Industry, 1907–1930," *Review of Economics and Statistics*, vol. 67 (August 1985), pp. 429–437.

54. Robert C. Allen, "Accounting for Price Changes: American Steel Rails, 1879–1910," *Journal of Political Economy*, vol. 89 (June 1981), pp. 512–528.

55. See George J. Stigler, "The Dominant Firm and the Inverted Umbrella," *Journal of Law & Economics*, vol. 8 (October 1965), pp. 167–173.

56. See Parsons and Ray, "The United States Steel Consolidation," supra note 51, pp. 201–202.

57. Thomas Whiteside, "Where Are They Now?," *New Yorker*, February 17, 1951, pp. 39–58.

58. Markham, *Competition in the Rayon Industry*, supra note 16, pp. 14–20, 46–47, and 103–104.

59. C. H. Hession, "The Metal Container Industry," in Walter Adams, ed., *The Structure of American Industry*, 3rd ed. (New York: Macmillan, 1961), pp. 432–434; and James W. McKie, *Tin Cans and Tin Plate* (Cambridge: Harvard University Press, 1959), pp. 46 and 89.

products refining,[60] farm implements,[61] synthetic fibers,[62] aluminum extrusions,[63] instant mashed potatoes,[64] frozen orange juice,[65] and when dominance in regional markets is taken into account, the gasoline industry.[66]

A particularly sophisticated entry control strategy was pursued by the Xerox Corporation in leasing its copying machines.[67] When the Xerox 914 copier was introduced in 1959, sales efforts were initially directed toward penetrating the low- and medium-volume market segments — that is, serving customers making fewer than 5,000 copies per machine per month. In the low-volume segment, where Xerox had no inherent long-run cost advantage over alternative copying processes, prices were set very close to the short-run profit-maximizing level. According to Xerox executives, this decision was made partly because the company was desperately in need of cash, and therefore discounted the future at a high rate, and partly because they realized that Xerox would eventually have to surrender the market to substitute copiers — notably, to those using the Electrofax process, which is simpler but uses expensive coated paper. Actually, twenty-nine firms entered the low-volume market with Electrofax machines between 1961 and 1967. In the medium- and high-volume ranges, xerography had a modest to substantial cost advantage. Xerox prices were set below the short-run profit-maximizing level, but above the entry-deterring level, in the expectation that a share of the market would gradually be handed over to Electrofax producers. The entry rate was in fact much less than in the low-volume market. In 1967, there were ten firms offering Electrofax machines designed for medium-volume applications and only four firms in the high-volume range. Finally, in the very high volume field (above 100,000 copies per month), Xerox's comparative cost position left entry essentially blockaded until its basic patents expired or would-be rivals succeeded in the formidable task of inventing around its patent portfolio. As it moved into this market with new high-speed machines during the 1960s, it was able for nearly a decade to charge prices exceeding cost by a substantial margin without experiencing appreciable entry.

More generally, in a regression analysis of forty-two once-dominant U.S. manufacturing firms, Richard Caves et al. found that conduct and performance over the period 1905-1929 were substantively consistent with the predictions of dynamic limit-pricing theory.[68] The erosion of dominant market shares was slowest when the dominant firm started with a high market share in an industry where economies of scale were important and where the minimum efficient scale was a large fraction of industry demand. Economies of scale were also important in achieving higher profits over the entire period — more important than capital cost and product differentiation entry barriers.

Cases in which dominant firms retained their dominant positions over an extended period are rarer, perhaps because it is exceptional for a single company to enjoy a persistent and substantial cost or image advantage.[69] One important exception is IBM's control of the general-purpose mainframe computer industry. Estimating the Gaskins optimal dynamic pricing model econometrically, Gerald Brock found that IBM could charge prices roughly 10 to 15 percent higher than its costs without sacrificing market share.[70] The dominant firm dynamic pricing model tracks IBM's pricing trajectory well, but fails to cope with details of the strategies IBM adopted in introducing new computer models and peripheral equipment. We shall have more to say about those strategies, including some evidently aimed at driving rivals from the market, in Chapters 12 and 13.

With control of superior domestic bauxite reserves and low-cost hydroelectric power rights, the Aluminum Company of America (Alcoa) maintained a 100 percent share of U.S. primary aluminum production from 1893 to 1940. There is reason to believe that Alcoa followed a conscious policy of charging less than the market would bear at any moment in time in order to maintain its long-run market position.[71] The International Nickel Company controlled 75 to 90 percent of the Western world's nickel supply through the first half of the twentieth century. Its dominance was based upon the ownership of uniquely rich sulphide ore deposits in the Sudbury, Ontario, area, which afforded it a cost advantage great enough to make a limit pricing strategy highly profitable.[72] However, as Inco's best ore reserves approached exhaustion, it raised nickel prices to a level permitting the profitable mining of inferior but abundant laterite ores, and this encouraged new entry and expansion by existing rivals. As a result, its noncommunist

60. Simon N. Whitney, *Antitrust Policies*, vol. II (New York: Twentieth Century Fund, 1958), pp. 258–260.

61. A. D. H. Kaplan, Joel B. Dirlam, and R. F. Lanzillotti, *Pricing in Big Business* (Washington: Brookings Institution, 1958), p. 69.

62. See R. W. Shaw and S. A. Shaw, "Patent Expiry and Competition in Polyester Fibers," *Scottish Journal of Political Economy*, vol. 24 (June 1977), pp. 117–132; and "Sagging du Pont Casts Shadow over the Dow," *Business Week*, April 8, 1967, p. 120.

63. Peck, *Competition in the Aluminum Industry*, supra note 14, p. 70.

64. Lester C. Telser, *Competition, Collusion, and Game Theory* (Chicago: Aldine-Atherton, 1972), pp. 299–304.

65. Telser, *Competition, Collusion, and Game Theory*, pp. 304–305.

66. Kaplan et al., *Pricing in Big Business*, supra note 61, pp. 86 and 157; Edmund P. Learned and Catherine C. Ellsworth, *Gasoline Pricing in Ohio* (Boston: Harvard Business School Division of Research, 1959), pp. 23–24 and 161; and (on the entry-inducing strategy of British petroleum refiners) R. W. Shaw, "Price Leadership and the Effect of New Entry on the U.K. Retail Petrol Supply Market," *Journal of Industrial Economics*, vol. 23 (September 1974), pp. 65–79. For subsequent developments in the U.K., see R. M. Grant, "Pricing Behaviour in the UK Wholesale Market for Petrol, 1970–80: A 'Structure-Conduct' Analysis," *Journal of Industrial Economics*, vol. 30 (March 1982), pp. 271–292.

67. Erwin A. Blackstone, "Limit Pricing and Entry in the Copying Machine Industry," *Quarterly Review of Economics and Business*, vol. 1 (Winter 1972), pp. 57–65.

68. Richard E. Caves, Michael Fortunato, and Pankaj Ghemawat, "The Decline of Dominant Firms, 1905–1929," *Quarterly Journal of Economics*, vol. 99 (August 1984), pp. 525–546. Their analysis provides more support for limit pricing models that assume lumpy entry (to be described below) than for the continuous entry flow assumed by Gaskins.

69. For a dissenting view, see Paul A. Geroski and Alexis Jacquemin, "Dominant Firms and Their Alleged Decline," *International Journal of Industrial Organization*, vol. 2 (March 1984), pp.

1–27; and Donald Hay and John Vickers, eds., *The Economics of Market Dominance* (Oxford: Basil Blackwell, 1987).

70. Gerald W. Brock, *The U.S. Computer Industry* (Cambridge: Ballinger, 1975), pp. 71–87. Brock underestimates the tendency for IBM's market share to erode (from 75 percent in 1956 to 68 percent in 1967). However, estimates based on a discrete-time version of Gaskins' limit pricing model and more detailed data for 1962 through 1969 largely eliminate this bias. Jati K. Sengupta, John E. Leonard, and James P. Vanyo, "A Limit Pricing Model for the US Computer Industry: An Application," *Applied Economics*, vol. 15 (June 1983), pp. 297–308.

71. See Leonard W. Weiss, *Economics and American Industry* (New York: Wiley, 1963), pp. 189–204.

72. See O. W. Main, *The Canadian Nickel Industry* (Toronto: University of Toronto Press, 1955); "The Beguiling New Economics of Nickel," *Fortune*, March 1970, pp. 100–104; "With Its Long Sway in Nickel Fading, Inco Gears Up To Fight," *Wall Street Journal*, April 20, 1978, p. 1; and "INCO: Guarding its Edge in Nickel," *Business Week*, June 9, 1980. For an attempt to estimate the socially optimal pricing trajectory for nickel, see Robert D. Cairns, "An Application of Depletion Theory to a Base Metal: Canadian Nickel," *Canadian Journal of Economics*, vol. 14 (November 1981), pp. 635–648.

Francois Melese extends the dominant firm dynamic limit pricing model to the general problem of a depletable resource. "Deregulation, Endogenous Expectations, and the Evolution of Industry Structure," *Southern Economic Journal*, vol. 51 (January 1985), pp. 793–803. Similar results are obtained when von Stackelberg leader-follower rivalry is played out for the extraction of a depletable resource. Richard J. Gilbert, "Dominant Firm Pricing Policy in a Market for an Exhaustible Resource," *Bell Journal of Economics*, vol. 9 (Autumn 1978), pp. 385–395. For analyses of the pricing strategies of depletable resource cartels in crude oil, bauxite, and copper, see Robert S. Pindyck, "Gains to Producers from the Cartelization of Exhaustible Resources," *Review of Economics and Statistics*, vol. 60 (May 1978), pp. 238–251.

world market share fell to approximately 50 percent in the late 1960s and continued to fall to 30 percent by 1977. By the early 1980s, Inco had shed the trappings of industry leadership.

From the end of World War II to the early 1980s, General Motors managed to maintain its share of U.S. domestic auto production in the 45 to 60 percent range and its share of U.S. market sales above 40 percent. Both its dominance and decline can be explained by changes in its image and cost advantages over smaller manufacturers. During most of this period, GM earned very high profit returns while Ford's profits exceeded the average for all U.S. manufacturers by only a slight margin and firms smaller than Chrysler teetered on the brink of failure.[73] When the first wave of automobile imports arrived in the late 1950s, GM (and the other domestic producers) were able to stem the tide primarily by introducing and promoting autos in the small car niche.[74] At first, GM held a delivered cost advantage over foreign producers and could afford to blockade substantial entry. By the 1970s, however, Japanese small car producers had reversed GM's cost advantage. Since then, consistent with dynamic limit pricing theory, GM accommodated entry by small car importers and raised small car prices whenever favorable changes in the exchange rate and barriers to imports permitted.[75] Initially, GM was better able than its domestic rivals to absorb the impact of imports. GM's 1980 market share was virtually unchanged from its 1974 level, while Ford's fell 8 percentage points and Chrysler's was cut in half. However, with downsizing and vertical disintegration in the early 1980s, Ford largely eliminated GM's domestic cost advantage, and GM lost ground relative to its rivals.

Except for the added complication of intragroup coordination, the pricing problem faced by a cartel or a group of oligopolists acting jointly is analogous to that of a single dominant firm. Fritz Voigt found that most of the thousands of German cartels formed between 1873 and 1933 collapsed quickly, often after only a few months of operation. The reason was that "if they succeeded in raising prices, new firms entered the industry, operating as outsiders, which led to a decline in sales by the cartel members; the cartel collapsed and a price war set in. . . ." Only the cartels with strong patent protection or other effective entry barriers were able to hold prices up while retaining their market shares, but they were the exceptions.[76] As Machlup put it, cartel members often "find themselves 'holding the umbrella' over outsiders and getting increasingly wet feet."[77]

The pricing behavior of the U.S. steel industry during the 1960s and 1970s is better described as that of a well-disciplined oligopolistic group than by the dominant firm model. As Japanese and West European steel producers rebuilt and expanded their industries with modern equipment following World War II, and with the dollar significantly overvalued during the 1960s, U.S. steel makers found themselves at a cost disadvantage relative to importers. Their most profitable strategy was to set U.S. prices above the entry-excluding level. Imports rose from 1.5 percent of U.S. demand in 1957 to nearly 17 percent in 1967, after which government-supported import quotas stemmed the tide. Devaluation of the dollar reversed a renewed trend toward rising imports in 1971. After that, the picture has been sufficiently blurred by price controls, worldwide escalation of energy costs, rapid U.S. price increases following the end of controls, and the reimposition of import restraints when imports soared anew that it is difficult to discern a clear long-run pricing strategy. The evidence is not inconsistent with the declining dominant group model's predictions.

The U.S. brewing industry illustrates the opposite case of a leading group pricing to drive out existing rivals. The principal nationally advertised brewers enjoyed an image advantage over local and regional beers and, after building large new decentralized breweries during the 1960s, they also gained an appreciable unit cost advantage.[78] Their strategy, with Anheuser-Busch playing an increasingly dominant role, was to squeeze the price differential between premium and popular beers. As a result of these developments, the number of companies brewing beer in the United States fell from 404 in 1947 to 108 in 1972 and sixty-seven in 1982, and the combined national market share of the four leading brewers rose from 21 percent in 1947 to 85 percent in 1987.

The dynamic limit pricing model also helps explain the impact of exchange rate fluctuations on highly concentrated domestic markets. From the perspective of the dominant domestic producers, imports, when not highly differentiated, supplement domestic fringe production. A rise in the real domestic exchange rate or a reduction in tariffs or other trade barriers will exert downward pressure on the domestic prices of tradable goods. If the domestic industry is purely competitive, the price adjustment will be immediate and complete. However, dominant domestic producers will maximize profits by setting prices that encourage gradually rising import penetration. Robert Feinberg found that the level of exchange rate pass-through was less in concentrated than in unconcentrated German industries for the years 1977–1983.[79] More generally, the level of import penetration and its rate of growth will constrain the ability of dominant firms to elevate prices above cost. A standard finding of industry cross-section statistical studies is that measures of profitability are negatively associated with the level of import penetration, and that this negative effect is stronger in more concentrated markets.[80]

Other Dynamic Influences on Dominant Firm Behavior	The basic Gaskins model yields a rich set of predictions about how the pricing behavior and profits of firms with monopoly power will vary both statically and dynamically with cost conditions, factors affecting the speed of entry, and market shares. This analytic power is achieved by accepting some important simplifications of reality — notably, the assumption of a deterministic entry function such as

73. Cf. Lawrence J. White, *The Automobile Industry Since 1945* (Cambridge: Harvard University Press, 1971), especially Chapters 4, 8, and 15.

74. U.S. manufacturers resisted introducing small cars because of the lower profit margins on such vehicles.

75. John E. Kwoka, Jr., "Market Power and Market Change in the U.S. Automobile Industry," *Journal of Industrial Economics*, vol. 32 (June 1984), pp. 509–522. See also pp. 255–256 supra.

76. Fritz Voigt, "German Experience with Cartels and Their Control during Pre-War and Post-War Periods," in John Perry Miller, ed., *Competition, Cartels and Their Regulation* (Amsterdam: North-Holland, 1962), pp. 171–72, 181, and 184.

77. Machlup, *The Economics of Sellers' Competition*, supra note 48, pp. 527–529.

78. See p. 134 supra.

79. Robert Feinberg, "The Interaction of Foreign Exchange and Market Power Effects on German Domestic Prices," *Journal of Industrial Economics*, vol. 35 (September 1986), pp. 61–69.

80. Among the first careful attempts to assess the impact of imports was Louis Esposito and Frances F. Esposito, "Foreign Competition and Domestic Industry Profitability," *Review of Economics and Statistics*, vol. 53 (November 1971), pp. 343–353. See also Thomas A. Pugel, "Foreign Trade and US Market Performance," *Journal of Industrial Economics*, vol. 29 (December 1980), pp. 119–129; and companion articles in Richard E. Caves, ed., "Symposium on International Trade and Industrial Organization," *Journal of Industrial Economics*, vol. 29 (December 1980).

Equation (10.1), the assumption that entry and exit occur in small (that is, infinitesimal) quantities rather than large lumps, and the closely related assumption that fringe firms and potential entrants are price takers, ignoring the effect of their own actions on the behavior of the dominant firm. Much of our remaining agenda in this chapter involves relaxing these assumptions.

However, before we do, we note that fringe entry is only one of several factors affecting long-run profits (hence eliciting a strategic response by dominant firms), and that price is not the only strategic variable at the firm's disposal. Thus, the intensity of future competition, and therefore the level of future profits, depends also upon investments in advertising, research and development, and the like. These are more conveniently taken up in later chapters.

A particularly important class of long-run strategy problems arises when there are product-specific economies associated with "learning by doing."[81] The essence of the matter is that one learns how to reduce production costs through actual production experience.[82] The more a firm has produced, the lower its unit costs tend to be, all else equal. To the extent that such experience is not readily transferable to other enterprises, this means that the first company to enter some new product line begins with a natural cost advantage over subsequent rivals, for by the time the latter enter or consider entering, the pioneer has already progressed some distance down its learning curve. More important for our present concerns, the pioneer's pricing policy also affects the magnitude of its advantage.[83] By keeping its price low initially, the pioneer can stimulate rapid expansion of demand for its product and therefore progress farther down its learning curve before others begin competing. Thus, a limit-pricing dominant firm enjoying learning-by-doing economies tends to see its cost advantage growing, reinforcing its exclusionary pricing incentive.[84]

It is conceivable that when learning economies are important, the capturing of an initial advantage by some company could set in motion a dynamic process that ends with the relevant product more or less permanently monopolized. However, several circumstances may mitigate such a tendency. For one, the rate of unit cost reduction with repeated doublings and redoublings of cumulative output does appear to taper off eventually.[85] As the leading firm approaches the bottom of its learning curve, its incentive to constrain price in the hope of gaining future cost advantages weakens, and it will be tempted to price less aggressively and reap the profit fruits of its prior pricing restraint. Second, some of the cost reduction benefits associated with cumulative experience are likely to spill over to other firms as skilled employees are hired away, patents expire, and production techniques become public knowledge.[86] Although rivals with a lower cumulative volume may not catch up completely, their eventual cost disadvantage may be much less than the assumption of strictly firm-specific learning implies. Third, some of the product lines in which learning by doing is most important (such as semiconductors, aircraft, and computers) are also characterized by rapid technological obsolescence of product designs. The development of a completely new design often permits an initially handicapped producer to jump to a new learning curve in a position of equality or even superiority. And finally, antitrust fears or the desire of industry buyers to ensure that multiple, competing sources of supply survive may lead firms with a cumulative learning advantage to stop short of a pricing strategy yielding an exclusive monopoly position.[87] Nevertheless, when learning-by-doing economies are substantial, it seems clear that there will be a heightened tendency toward high concentration in narrowly defined product lines. For example, Richard and Susan Shaw found that most of the firms which had established leading market shares in the European synthetic fibers industry were able to maintain that leadership over the next twenty years.[88]

That such interactions between experience-related cost advantages and pricing policies exist is supported by considerable evidence.[89] Pricing to enhance one's market position and hence gain learning curve advantages has been especially prevalent in the semiconductor and related electronics industries, including

81. In addition to the references in Chapter 4, note 1, see William Fellner, "Specific Interpretations of Learning by Doing," *Journal of Economic Theory*, vol. 1 (August 1969), pp. 119–140; and L. E. Yelle, "The Learning Curve: Historical Review and Comprehensive Survey," *Decision Sciences*, vol. 10 (1979), pp. 302–328.

82. A similar case occurs with a newly introduced experience good when the rate of sales grows exponentially with the number of customer trials. See Frank M. Bass, "A New Product Growth Model for Consumer Durables," *Management Science*, vol. 15 (January 1969), pp. 215–227; Bruce Robinson and Chet Lakhani, "Dynamic Price Models for New Product Planning," *Management Science*, vol. 21 (June 1975), pp. 1113–1122; Robert J. Dolan and Abel P. Jeuland, "Experience Curves and Dynamic Demand Models," *Journal of Marketing*, vol. 45 (Winter 1981), pp. 52–62; and Frank H. Clarke et al., "Optimal Pricing Policy in the Presence of Experience Effects," *Journal of Business*, vol. 55 (October 1982), pp. 517–530.

83. The monopoly (or dominant firm) problem has been solved by I. Steedman, " 'Learning by Doing' and the Theory of the Firm," *Journal of Economic Studies*, vol. 4 (1969), pp. 47–59; Sherwin Rosen, "Learning by Experience as Joint Production," *Quarterly Journal of Economics*, vol. 86 (August 1972), pp. 366–382; R. W. Latham and D. A. Peel, "Profit Maximizing Firms and Inelastic Demands," *Applied Economics*, vol. 7 (Spring 1975), pp. 161–165; Wayne Y. Lee, "Oligopoly and Entry," *Journal of Economic Theory*, vol. 11 (August 1975), pp. 35–54; A. Michael Spence, "The Learning Curve and Competition," *Bell Journal of Economics*, vol. 12 (Spring 1981), pp. 49–70; Drew Fudenberg and Jean Tirole, "Learning-by-Doing and Market Performance," *Bell Journal of Economics*, vol. 14 (Autumn 1983), pp. 522–530; Chaim Fershtman and Uriel Spiegel, "Monopoly Versus Competition: The Learning by Doing Case," *European Economic Review*, vol. 23 (November 1983), pp. 217–222; and Ronald S. Saunders, "Learning by Doing and Dominant Firm Pricing Strategy," *Review of Industrial Organization*, vol. 2 (1985), pp. 32–39.

84. Small scale entry is particularly handicapped when learning economies exist, since small firms have relatively little cumulative production and hence are slow to progress down learning curves in the absence of substantial spillovers.

85. Harold Asher, *Cost-Quantity Relationships in the Airframe Industry* (Santa Monica: Rand Corporation, 1956), p. 129; Nicholas

Baloff, "The Learning Curve — Some Controversial Issues," *Journal of Industrial Economics*, vol. 14 (July 1966), pp. 275–282; Paul A. David, "Learning by Doing and Tariff Protection: A Reconsideration of the Case of the Ante-Bellum United States Cotton Textile Industry," *Journal of Economic History*, vol. 30 (September 1970), pp. 521–601; G. R. Knecht, "Costing, Technological Growth and Generalized Learning Curves," *Operational Research Quarterly*, vol. 25 (September 1974), pp. 487–491; and R. B. Zevin, "The Use of a 'Long Run' Learning Function: With Application to a Massachusetts Cotton Textile Firm, 1823–1860," in R. B. Zevin, ed., *The Growth of Manufacturing in Early Nineteenth Century New England* (New York: Arno Press, 1975), pp. 1–21.

86. Pankaj Ghemawat and A. Michael Spence, "Learning Curve Spillovers and Market Performance," *Quarterly Journal of Economics*, vol. 100 (Supplement 1985), pp. 839–852; and David R. Ross, "Learning To Dominate," *Journal of Industrial Economics*, vol. 34 (June 1986), pp. 337–353.

87. On the desire for multiple sources of supply even when higher costs were the consequence, see F. M. Scherer, Alan Beckenstein, Erich Kaufer, and R. D. Murphy, *The Economics of Multi-Plant Operation: An International Comparisons Study* (Cambridge: Harvard University Press, 1975), pp.134–135; and John Newhouse, *The Sporty Game* (New York: Knopf, 1982). There is reason to believe that competition in the production of particular World War II aircraft types accelerated the rate of learning. See F. M. Scherer, *The Weapons Acquisition Process: Economic Incentives* (Boston: Harvard Business School Division of Research, 1964), pp. 119–126.

88. Richard W. Shaw and Susan A. Shaw, "Late Entry, Market Shares, and Competitive Survival: The Case of Synthetic Fibers," *Managerial and Decision Economics*, vol. 5 (June 1984), pp. 72–79.

89. Indeed, a consulting firm thrived on advising industrial enterprises how to take advantage of learning-by-doing effects in their pricing decisions. See "Selling Business a Theory of Economics," *Business Week*, September 8, 1973, pp. 85–90; Boston Consulting Group, Inc., *Perspectives on Experience* (Boston: January 1972); and idem, *The Cross Sectional Experience Curve* (Boston: 1978). For cautionary notes, see William J. Abernathy and K. Wayne, "Limits to the Learning Curve," *Harvard Business Review*, vol. 52 (September 1974), pp. 109–120.

personal computers, hand-held electronic calculators, and video cassette recorders.[90] Consumers benefited during the early years of those product life cycles from relatively low prices charged by producers vigorously striving for a market share advantage. Although concentration in specific product lines tended to be high, sometimes after an intense competitive shakeout, rapid technological progress kept downward pressure on prices even when some firms did achieve a significant advantage in a narrow line. This is consistent with formal models predicting that economic performance will be better (with lower prices and more rapid cost reductions) for an industry dominated by a large long-run profit-maximizing firm than it would be in a more atomistically structured industry during periods when significant learning economies are present.[91] Longer-term economic performance depends upon the market structure that evolves at the foot of the learning curve and the rate at which technological innovations yield new product introductions.

Deterring Large-Scale Entry

Thus far we have assumed that new entrants or existing fringe firms add output on such a small scale relative to total market volumes that the effect on price of any single firm's entry decision is negligible. When impressive economies can be realized by entering or expanding on a large scale, however, this assumption is likely to be violated. Lumpy entry exposes incumbents to sudden price cuts and/or the need to absorb large production decreases. Morton Kamien and Nancy Schwartz developed independently of Gaskins a dominant firm entry deterrence model that makes uncertainty and lumpiness a central analytic feature.[92] They assume that if entry takes place, it occurs in a sizable lump, and that the probability of its occurrence in any given time period increases, the higher the price charged by the dominant firm. Like Gaskins, they find that the dominant firm reduces price more to retard entry, the lower its time discount rate is and the more probable entry is in response to a given price (which embodies both the cost advantage and entry speed features of the Gaskins model).

However, unless a potential entrant lacks information about demand and cost conditions (more on this below), it is hard to rationalize why the entrant should be influenced by the prevailing market price. It is the *postentry* price and the entrant's market share that determine the attractiveness of entry. The problem, in essence, is that a firm contemplating entry on a large scale has reason to fear that its incremental output contribution will be absorbed by the market only if the price is reduced. As a result, even though the entrant's costs may be just as low as those of enterprises already in the industry, and even though the preentry price exceeds the entrant's full expected unit cost, the price after entry may fall below that cost, and entry will prove to be unprofitable. If this is anticipated, entry will be deterred.

Contestability Theory   William Baumol et al. have proposed an analytic structure in which, contrary to this caveat, it *is* appropriate to relate the large-scale entry decision to the prevailing preentry price.[93] They postulate a form of hit-and-run entry entailing several key assumptions. Suppose a potential entrant can identify a group of potential customers who would buy the relevant product from the entrant at a price less than or equal to the prevailing market price. Suppose further that the entrant is able to sell to these customers before incumbents have an opportunity to change their price. Finally, suppose that at the price quoted, the entrant earns enough revenue to cover all variable and fixed costs of production, including all truly sunk costs. Sunk costs are fixed costs resulting from irreversible investments. For example, laying railroad track imposes a sunk cost, since the investment cannot be transferred economically to some other use, while investing in railroad rolling stock imposes little or no sunk cost, since the engines and cars can be transferred to a different railroad line at modest cost. When investments are reversible, an entering firm need not worry about how long it will be in business, since it can sell its capital assets for the purchase price less wear-and-tear depreciation. However, when an investment is irreversible, how long the asset will be used becomes crucial. If the asset can be used solely in the current period, then the total value of the sunk and irreversible investment constitutes a current fixed cost. If, before incumbents can react, the entrant can sell enough output at a price high enough to cover variable, reversible fixed, and irreversible sunk costs, then the firm will find "hit-and-run" entry to be profitable, and it will occur. Recovering all sunk costs in the first period is important because *after* that period, Baumol et al. assume that the incumbent firms can react strategically (for example, reducing their prices enough to win back their lost sales) to make the entrant's *continuing* operation unprofitable. But if entry for one period only is profitable, the entrant can "hit," take its profits, and then "run" when the incumbents react.

When potential entrants have access to the same technology as incumbents, when there are no sunk costs, and when a firm can enter and exit the market before incumbents can respond, the market is said by Baumol et al. to be *perfectly*

90. See "The Complexities of Electronics Pricing," *Business Week*, April 6, 1974, pp. 44–45; "New Leaders in Semiconductors," *Business Week*, March 1, 1976, pp. 43–44; Ernest Braun and Stuart MacDonald, *Revolution in Miniature*, 2nd ed. (New York: Cambridge University Press, 1982); and Richard C. Levin, "Innovation and Public Policy in the Semiconductor Industry," in Richard R. Nelson, ed., *Government and Technical Progress: A Cross-Industry Analysis* (New York: Pergamon Press, 1982). Significant learning curves have been found in many other industries. See R. W. Conway and A. Schultz, Jr., "The Manufacturing Progress Function," *Journal of Industrial Engineering*, vol. 10 (1959), pp. 131–150; Yelle, "The Learning Curve," supra note 81, pp. 302–328; and Marvin B. Lieberman, "The Learning Curve and Pricing in the Chemical Processing Industries," *Rand Journal of Economics*, vol. 15 (Summer 1984), pp. 213–228.

91. See note 83 supra and Robert H. Smiley and S. A. Ravid, "The Importance of Being First," *Quarterly Journal of Economics*, vol. 98 (May 1983), pp. 353–362.

92. Morton I. Kamien and Nancy L. Schwartz, "Limit Pricing and Uncertain Entry," *Econometrica*, vol. 39 (May 1971), pp. 441–454. Extensions include Kamien and Schwartz, "Uncertain Entry and Excess Capacity," *American Economic Review*, vol. 62 (December 1972), pp. 918–927; Kamien and Schwartz, "Cournot Oligopoly with Uncertain Entry," *Review of Economic Studies*, vol. 42 (January 1975), pp. 125–131; David P. Baron, "Limit

Pricing, Potential Entry, and Barriers to Entry," *American Economic Review*, vol. 63 (September 1973), pp. 666–674; and Raymond R. de Bondt, "Limit Pricing, Uncertain Entry, and the Entry Lag," *Econometrica*, vol. 44 (September 1976), pp. 939–946.

93. Baumol et al., *Contestable Markets*, supra note 30; Baumol, "Contestable Markets: An Uprising in the Theory of Industry Structure," *American Economic Review*, vol. 72 (March 1982), pp. 1–15; Baumol and Robert D. Willig, "Contestability: Developments Since the Book," *Oxford Economic Papers*, vol. 38 supplement (November 1986), pp. 9–36; Martin L. Weitzman, "Contestable Markets: An Uprising in the Theory of Industry Structure: Comment," *American Economic Review*, vol. 73 (June 1983), pp. 486–487; W. G. Shepherd, " 'Contestability' vs. Competition," *American Economic Review*, vol. 74 (September 1984), pp. 572–587; Elie Appelbaum and Chin Lim, "Contestable Markets Under Uncertainty," *Rand Journal of Economics*, vol. 16 (Spring 1985), pp. 28–40; Marius Schwartz, "The Nature and Scope of Contestability Theory," *Oxford Economic Papers*, vol. 38 Supplement (November 1986), pp. 37–57; and R. D. Cairns and D. Mahabir, "Contestability: A Revisionist View," *Economica*, vol. 55 (May 1988), pp. 269–276.

An early statement of the theory's logic was Richard E. Caves, *Air Transport and its Regulators* (Cambridge: Harvard University Press, 1962), pp. 79–80, 343, and 428–433.

contestable. The only sustainable price[94] available to incumbents under these conditions is one that just covers average cost.[95] This result holds regardless of the industry's structure. In a perfectly contestable market, economies of scale and scope may limit the number of firms operating to some small cost-minimizing group, but they will not allow incumbents to elevate prices above average cost. Thus, where perfect contestability holds, even a natural monopoly[96] will set prices so as to realize only competitive returns on investment.

Experiments designed to replicate the conditions of perfect contestability have tended to confirm this logic.[97] A repeated game structure was simulated in which potential contestants for the same natural monopoly market offered price-quantity pairs in the face of uncertain demand. If the quantity offered by the low-price firm was less than the quantity demanded, buyers turned to the next lowest-price seller for their requirements (unless that firm's price exceeded the buyers' reservation price). Through repetition, the firms acquired information about demand and other firms' strategies. With blockaded entry (that is, with one firm designated the monopoly seller, confident that no entry would occur), incumbents succeeded in coming very close to the theoretical profit-maximizing monopoly price. Under perfectly contestable conditions, early stages of the game were characterized by market sharing (often with losses for all sellers) and cycling (with contestants taking turns supplying the entire market). In a few games, contestants managed through signaling behavior to achieve and maintain positive-profit outcomes.[98] However, the prevailing tendency was for prices to approach average cost.

The key question concerning contestability theory is not whether the internal logic holds, but whether the conditions required are likely to be found in practice.[99] At first glance, it is easy to identify cases where sunk costs seem to be low or nonexistent. In transportation industries such as airlines, ocean shipping, and trucking, flying, sailing, or driving one's capital from one market to another as conditions change seems plausible. However, sunk costs have a way of popping up in the form of effort incurred to negotiate airport landing rights and gate fees, advertising needed to gain initial sales, and the sustained performance that underlies a reputation for reliability. It has been even harder to document significant cases in which strategic response lags are long enough to permit true hit-and-run entry. Baumol et al. cite the example of charter airlines, which often sold tickets conditional on filling the plane, allowing the entrant to obtain business before committing significant resources.[100] However, for commercial air service in general, incumbent firms have been quick to react to new pricing initiatives from either entrants or other incumbents.[101] Statistical analyses of the U.S. domestic airline industry since deregulation in the late 1970s have found that prices and profits were much more sensitive to existing market structure and actual entry than to the presence of potential entrants—a result incompatible with the predictions of contestability theory.[102]

Of course, markets may be imperfectly contestable in the sense that limited opportunities for hit-and-run entry prompt incumbents to set prices below the level they would choose if entry were blockaded, but above the level that would prevail following large-scale entry. However, it has proved impossible thus far to distinguish such behavior from other strategies for deterring large-scale entry,[103] which we now investigate. Perhaps the most valuable insight of contestability theory will be the distinction between fixed and sunk costs. While economies of scale and scope limit the number of firms that can be supported by market demand at minimum cost, unless most fixed costs are sunk, pricing by seemingly monopolistic incumbents may be significantly restrained by fear of less than permanent new entry.

Classic Limit Pricing   Absent conditions conducive to perfect contestability, incumbents and potential entrants alike will expect prices to fall following entry. The amount by which the price falls depends *inter alia* upon the surplus of postentry over preentry output. This in turn depends not only upon the entrant's output but also upon any output changes effected by the original industry members. Here we run squarely into the problem of oligopolistic interdependence. How will the established sellers react? Conceivably, they could reduce their own outputs to make room for the newcomer. If so, the price might not decline at all. At the other extreme, they could hold their production constant or even increase it to make life as difficult as possible for the interloper. Some assumption has to be made by a potential entrant calculating the profitability of entry. The economist too must build a theory upon assumptions conforming, one hopes as closely as possible, to the thought processes of real-world entrepreneurs. Although there is a slightly different British tradition

94. See page 361 supra.

95. Since an entrant can by assumption replicate what the incumbent was doing, the entrant can sell the output the incumbent intended to sell in any period at a price between average cost and the incumbent's preentry price.

96. See pp. 30–31 supra.

97. See Don Coursey, R. Mark Isaac, and Vernon L. Smith, "Natural Monopoly and Contested Markets: Some Experimental Results," *Journal of Law & Economics*, vol. 27 (April 1984), pp. 91–114; Coursey, Isaac, Margaret Luke, and Smith, "Market Contestability in the Presence of Sunk (Entry) Costs," *Rand Journal of Economics*, vol. 15 (Spring 1984), pp. 69–84; and Glenn W. Harrison and Michael McKee, "Monopoly Behavior, Decentralized Regulation, and Contestable Markets: An Experimental Evaluation," *Rand Journal of Economics*, vol. 16 (Spring 1985), pp. 51–69.

98. Participants were far less successful at achieving cooperative solutions in the natural monopoly environment than in similar games that assumed constant or increasing unit costs. Harrison and McKee, "Monopoly Behavior," p. 64. The ability to reach cooperative solutions fell as the number of potential entrants rose.

99. Spence, "Contestable Markets," supra note 30; Brock, "Contestable Markets," supra note 30; Shepherd, " 'Contestability' vs. Competition," supra note 93; and Schwartz, "The Nature and Scope," supra note 93.

100. William J. Baumol, John Panzar, and Robert Willig, "Contestable Markets: An Uprising in the Theory of Industry Structure: Reply," *American Economic Review*, vol. 73 (June 1983), p. 493.

101. For example, in 1984 Delta Airlines assigned a number of staff members to monitor rival prices. Once Delta learned of a price change, it could adjust prices in its computer reservation system within two hours. "In Airline's Rate War, Small Daily Skirmishes Often Decide Winners," *Wall Street Journal*, August 24, 1984.

102. David R. Graham, Daniel P. Kaplan, and David S. Sibley, "Efficiency and Competition in the Airline Industry," *Bell Journal of Economics*, vol. 14 (Spring 1983), pp. 118–138; Gregory D. Call and Theodore E. Keeler, "Airline Deregulation, Fares and Market Behavior: Some Empirical Evidence," in Andrew Daughety, ed., *Analytical Studies in Transport Economics* (New York: Cambridge University Press, 1985), pp. 221–247; Steven A. Morrison and Clifford Winston, "Empirical Implications and Tests of the Contestability Hypothesis," *Journal of Law & Economics*, vol. 30 (April 1987), pp. 55–66; and Samuel H. Baker and James B. Pratt, "Experience as a Barrier to Contestability in Airline Markets," *Review of Economics and Statistics*, vol. 71 (May 1989), pp. 352–356. An earlier study, which reported evidence that performance in some airline markets was not influenced by existing market structure, may have been biased by the fact that it occurred in the early stage of the transition to a deregulated industry. Elizabeth E. Bailey and John C. Panzar, "The Contestability of Airline Markets During the Transition to Deregulation," *Law and Contemporary Problems*, vol. 44 (Winter 1981), pp. 125–145.

103. See the discussion in Schwartz, "The Nature and Scope," supra note 93, pp. 47–50.

following the work of P. W. S. Andrews,[104] we emphasize here the approach pioneered by Joe S. Bain and Paolo Sylos-Labini and extended by Franco Modigliani.[105]

Both Bain and Sylos-Labini emphasize maintenance of output by established firms as the most likely reaction to new entry. Bain's principal defense of output maintenance is that it is a relatively pessimistic assumption from the standpoint of the new entrant.[106] And, of course, a certain amount of pessimism is in order when one is contemplating entering a new industry on a large scale. According to Sylos-Labini, existing firms maintain their output partly in an effort to discourage entry and partly because assumed cost structure rigidities encourage full utilization of capacity.[107] If we provisionally accept the output maintenance assumption, we can derive from it several testable generalizations. For simplicity we assume in all cases that new entrants can, by building a plant of minimum efficient scale, produce at unit costs just as low as those of existing firms. We also ignore price premiums associated with brand image differences, in effect assuming the absence of appreciable product differentiation. The problem is, how much can existing firms elevate prices above their own (minimum) unit costs without attracting new entry?

Suppose initially that the new entrant chooses to enter at minimum efficient scale (MES), that is, to produce an output volume just sufficient to realize all economies of scale. Then the larger the MES is relative to the overall size of the market, the more the price will be depressed by a new entrant, other things (such as the elasticity of demand) being equal. Assume, for example, that demand has unit elasticity in the relevant neighborhood. If entry at MES requires the entrant to produce (and hence dispose of) 10 percent of the total quantity demanded at the postentry price, price will be depressed by 10 percent owing to entry.[108] So unless the preentry price exceeds the potential entrant's expected unit costs by more than 11 percent,[109] entry will be unprofitable. A preentry price exceeding minimum unit cost by about 11 percent will be just sufficient to deter entry. If, alternatively, entry at MES requires the entrant to produce only 5 percent of the total quantity demanded at the postentry price, price will fall by only 5 percent upon entry; and existing firms can hold their price no higher than 5.25 percent above minimum unit cost without encouraging entry. Generalizing, the smaller the MES is relative to the output volume demanded at a price equal to minimum unit cost (that is, at the competitive price), the less price can be held persistently above the competitive level without attracting new entry, ceteris paribus.

Suppose now that the scale of entry continues to be 10 percent of total market volume at the competitive price. If the elasticity of demand is 2 instead of 1, the price will fall by only about 5 percent instead of 10 percent upon entry. If the elasticity is 5, the price will fall by only about 2 percent, and a preentry price exceeding minimum unit cost by more than 2 percent will attract entry. Thus, the more elastic market demand is — that is, the more readily the market will absorb an increment of supply without a large fall in price — the less price can be held persistently above the competitive level without attracting new entry, ceteris paribus.

Finally, we relax the assumption that the new entrant must enter at the least-cost scale. By entering at a size smaller than MES, a newcomer incurs the disadvantage of higher unit costs but gains the advantage of adding a smaller output increment and thus precipitates a milder price decline. Recognizing this possibility, output-maintaining incumbent sellers must set their output and price at levels such that the market demand curve segment not satisfied by their supply — that is, the segment to the right of their output on a conventional industry demand diagram — lies at no point above the potential entrant's cost curve, whose zero-output point is set to coincide with the existing firms' total output point. To comprehend this notion and its implications, consider Figure 10.3. Panel (a) displays two alternate long-run cost functions b and c.[110] Both exhibit economies of scale over their full illustrated range; both reach the minimum efficient scale at the same output OM and unit cost OY; and both have the same vertical intercept OZ. The only difference between them is that curve c has unit costs declining at first more rapidly with scale increases than curve b. Now let us in effect slide the cost curves horizontally to the right — curve b until it just touches the market demand function

a. The Cost Curves

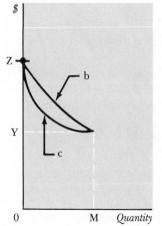

b. Deterrence with Cost Curve b

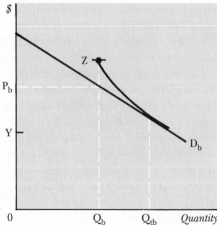

c. Deterrence with Cost Curve c

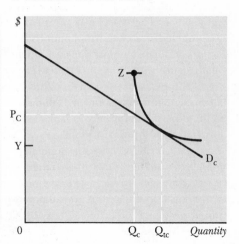

Figure 10.3
Deterring Large-Scale Entry
with Cost Functions
of Various Curvature

104. See especially Andrews, *Manufacturing Business,* supra note 18; and Jagdish N. Bhagwati, "Oligopoly Theory, Entry-Prevention, and Growth," *Oxford Economic Papers*, vol. 22 n.s. (November 1970), pp. 297–310.

105. Supra note 18.

106. Bain, *Barriers to New Competition,* supra note 18, p. 105. Bain did explore alternative output behavior assumptions in the course of his analysis.

107. Sylos-Labini, *Oligopoly and Technical Progress,* supra note 18, p. 43.

108. If the price elasticity of demand is 1 over the relevant range, then total sales revenue must be the same for all price-output levels in this range, that is, $P_0Q_0 = P_1Q_1$, where Q is the quan-

tity demanded in the market and the 0 and 1 subscripts indicate pre- and post-entry periods. If entry accounts for 10 percent of post-entry industry production and incumbent output remains fixed, then $Q_0 = .9Q_1$. This implies that $P_0(.9Q_1) = P_1Q_1$, hence $P_1 = .9P_0$. The change in price as a fraction of the pre-entry price $(P_1 - P_0)/P_0 = -.1$.

109. If the entrant's expected unit costs equal the post-entry price, then $(P_1 - C_1)/C_1 = -.1$. Hence, $(P_1 - C_1) = -.1C_1$, and $P_1 = .9C_1$. Substitution yields the result: $(P_1 - C_1)/P_1 = -.1/.9 \cong -.11$.

110. This method of presentation is adapted from Modigliani, "New Developments," supra note 18.

D_b in panel (b), and curve c until it is similarly tangent to market demand curve D_c. Tangency in both cases implies that if the output of established firms ends where the output of the entrant begins [that is, at Q_b in panel (b) and Q_c in panel (c)] and if the entrant makes the only output choice at which the market price is not below its unit costs—that is, the output associated with its demand curve tangency position Q_{tb} or Q_{tc}—the entrant will just cover its costs (including the opportunity cost of capital). Entry will therefore be barely attractive. In view of this, the incumbents must commit themselves to maintaining output at slightly more than OQ_b or OQ_c and charge (in the absence of entry) a corresponding price just below OP_b or OP_c to leave no room in the market for profitable suboptimal scale entry. Note that this entry-deterring price is higher in case (b), with more slowly falling unit costs, than it is in case (c), where the entrant can realize most of the economies of scale at an output smaller in relation to the MES. Quite generally, the less disadvantaged by above-minimum unit costs an entrant is when operating at some suboptimal fraction of the minimum efficient scale, the less insiders can hold the price persistently above the competitive level without attracting new entry, ceteris paribus.

To sum up, when potential entrants expect existing firms to maintain their output in the face of sizable new entry, prices can be held persistently above the competitive level by a greater percentage margin without attracting entry: (1) the less elastic demand is, (2) the higher the proportion of total industry output a firm of minimum efficient scale must produce, and (3) the more a firm operating at less than MES is disadvantaged by high unit costs. We see then that even when new entrants are physically able to operate just as efficiently as existing firms, the interaction between the necessity of large-scale entry and price effects can be a significant deterrent to new entry. Because of this deterrent effect, existing firms may command supra-normal profits more or less permanently.[111]

This conclusion depends upon the assumption that existing sellers maintain their output in the face of new entry. Will they in fact do so? If, despite pricing at a level calculated to deter new entry under the output maintenance assumption, new entry does take place, maintaining output normally will *not* be the most profitable strategy for the original firms. Indeed, if entry occurs at the least-cost scale and established firms maintain their output, the price will fall to the competitive level and the original firms' supra-normal profits will be wiped out altogether. To enforce this outcome—or the only marginally more profitable outcome following sub-MES entry—when higher profits could be earned by reducing output would be like cutting off one's nose to spite the face. Sooner or later, it can be argued, the original firms will react to entry by backing off and allowing the price to rise.[112] If a potential large-scale entrant recognizes that the existing firms have no economic incentive to adopt and maintain an uncooperative price-output policy following its entry, it will not be deterred by the belief that its addition to industry output will depress the price severely. Established firms use the limit price as a threat—to signal their intention to inflict losses on the entrant. But threats that are not credible do not deter.

Rational Entry
Deterrence

To make their threat credible, incumbents can turn the threat into a commitment. The distinguishing characteristic of a commitment to deter entry is that, if entry actually occurs, it is in the incumbent's self-interest to choose a price-output policy that prevents the entrant from achieving at least zero economic profits.[113] We now consider investment strategies available to the incumbent that can create such a commitment, that is, that can credibly deter entry. The essence of these strategies is "some voluntary but irreversible sacrifice of freedom of choice. They rest on the paradox that the power to constrain an adversary may depend on the power to bind oneself. . . ."[114] By investing to alter the environment in which rivalry occurs following entry, the incumbent binds itself to behavior that eliminates the profitability of entry.

To create a commitment to deter: (1) an incumbent's investment must be durable, that is, it must be in place long enough to constrain the entrant; (2) it must be irreversible — otherwise the potential entrant could reasonably expect the incumbent to discard its aggressive posture post-entry; and (3) its implications must be clear to the entrant, that is, the entrant must be able to observe the investment and recognize that entry following the investment is unlikely to be profitable. Expansion of plant capacity to reduce the marginal cost of post-entry production by the incumbent has received the most attention from theorists. However, many other investments have been suggested as vehicles by which an incumbent can commit itself to deter entry.[115] We will return to some of them later.

111. For variations on this theme, see Donald Dewey, "Industrial Concentration and the Rate of Profit: Some Neglected Theory," *Journal of Law & Economics*, vol. 19 (April 1976), pp. 67–78.

112. If the entrant's market share is small, the original firms may choose to set either the short-run profit-maximizing price or the limit price (modified, perhaps, to reflect their prior unsuccessful experience). If the entrant seems likely to become a major rival, its interests will need to be accommodated as the industry solves its revised pricing problem, with all the complications discussed in Chapters 6 through 8.

113. The strategic distinction between threat and commitment was emphasized by Thomas C. Schelling, *The Strategy of Conflict* (Cambridge: Harvard University Press, 1960), Chapter 5.

114. Schelling, *The Strategy of Conflict*, p. 22.

115. In addition to variables analyzed elsewhere in this chapter, these include:

Finished goods inventories: Lanny Arvan, "Some Examples of Dynamic Cournot Duopoly with Inventory," *Rand Journal of Economics*, vol. 16 (Winter 1985), pp. 569–578; and Garth Saloner, "The Role of Obsolescence and Inventory Costs in Providing Commitment," *International Journal of Industrial Organization*, vol. 4 (September 1986), pp. 333–345.

Financial structure: James A. Brander and Tracy R. Lewis, "Oligopoly and Financial Structure: The Limited Liability Effect," *American Economic Review*, vol. 76 (December 1986), pp. 956–970.

Customer service staff, trading stamps, frequent flyer discounts and other investments designed to cement customer loyalty: Richard Schmalensee, "Advertising and Entry Deterrence," *Journal of Political Economy*, vol. 91 (August 1983), pp. 636–653; Paul Klemperer, "Collusion via Switching Costs: How 'Frequent Flyer' Programs, Trading Stamps, and Technology Choices Aid Collusion," Stanford University Graduate School of Business Research Paper No. 786 (1984); and *idem*, "The Welfare Effects of Entry

into Markets with Consumer Switching Costs," Oxford University, St. Catherine's College, mimeo.

Cost-reducing research and development: James A. Brander and Barbara Spencer, "Strategic Commitment with R&D: The Symmetric Case," *Bell Journal of Economics*, vol. 14 (Spring 1983), pp. 225–235; and A. Michael Spence, "Cost Reduction, Competition, and Industry Performance," *Econometrica*, vol. 52 (January 1984), pp. 101–121.

Labor and management compensation contracts: Chaim Fershtman and Kenneth Judd, "Equilibrium Incentives in Oligopoly," Northwestern University Center for Mathematical Studies in Economics and Management Science, Discussion Paper No. 642, December 1984; and S. Sklivas, "The Strategic Choice of Managerial Incentives," University of Pennsylvania Center for the Study of Organizational Innovation, Discussion Paper No. 184, May 1985.

Raising rivals' costs through the manipulation of regulatory agencies or control of key inputs: Stephen C. Salop, "Raising Rivals' Costs," *American Economic Review*, vol. 73 (May 1983), pp. 267–271; and Thomas G. Krattenmaker and Salop, "Anticompetitive Exclusion: Raising Rivals' Costs to Achieve Power Over Price," *Yale Law Journal*, vol. 96 (December 1986), pp. 209–293. Compare Timothy J. Brennan, "Understanding 'Raising Rivals' Costs,'" U.S. Department of Justice Economic Analysis Group, Discussion Paper No. 86-14, September 1986.

Influencing domestic trade policies (tariffs, quotas, and export subsidies) to affect market conditions: Avinash Dixit, "International Trade Policy for Oligopolistic Industries," *Economic Journal*, vol. 94 (Supplement 1984), pp. 1–16; Paul Krugman, "Import Protection as Export Promotion: International Competition in the Presence of Oligopoly and Economies of Scale," in Henryk Kierzkowski, ed., *Monopolistic Competition and International Trade* (Oxford: Clarendon Press, 1984), pp. 180–194.

We use investment in plant capacity to introduce a stylized two-stage game-theoretic model that captures the strategic essence of the incumbent's commitment problem and that can be extended to describe a wide range of strategic cases.[116] In the first stage Firm 1, the incumbent, chooses the level of plant capacity K_1 it will carry. In the second stage, Firm 2 observes K_1 and chooses whether to enter the industry, producing a product identical to that sold by Firm 1. If entry occurs, each firm chooses its output, q_1 and q_2, respectively,[117] to maximize its profit, given its conjecture about how the other will respond. This returns us to the complexities of oligopolistic interdependence, the subject of Chapters 6 through 8. Since our focus here is the impact of the incumbent's investment, we assume a rudimentary model of post-entry rivalry — the quantity-Cournot model.[118] (Later we will relax the assumption that incumbent and entrant can project the post-entry rivalry's outcome with certainty.) The incumbent's capacity choice affects the post-entry equilibrium by altering the incumbent's marginal cost. Let $q_1(K_1)$ and $q_2(K_1)$ be the post-entry equilibrium outputs, given alternative capacity levels chosen by Firm 1 in the first stage. By lowering the incumbent's marginal cost, an increase in K_1 raises Firm 1's equilibrium output, which in turn reduces Firm 2's output.[119] If no entry occurs, Firm 1 produces the short-run profit-maximizing output $q_1^M(K_1)$ consistent with its chosen level of capacity.

Panel (a) of Figure 10.4 depicts Firm 1's profit as a function of K_1 both in the absence of entry (π_1^M) and with entry (π_1^E). Panel (b) depicts Firm 2's post-entry profit, also as a function of K_1. In post-entry rivalry, the strategic impact of lower marginal cost is to encourage Firm 1 to expand production for any given value of q_2, driving the price down and hence reducing Firm 2's output and profit. At low capacities, Firm 1's profit is depressed by its high marginal cost of production, while investment in very high capacity is not justified by the incremental operating profit it would yield — hence the $\cap$-shape of Firm 1's profit functions. Firm 2, of course, would prefer to have Firm 1 exit the industry entirely ($K_1 = 0$). Capacity K_1^M, hence output $q_1(K_1^M)$, would maximize Firm 1's profits (at level OA in Figure 10.4) before entry occurs. However, if Firm 1 had invested in that level of capacity, Firm 2 would earn profits of OE in the post-entry quantity-Cournot rivalry. Since Firm 1 cannot credibly deter entry by choosing capacity K_1^M, profit level OA cannot be sustained in the long run.

Is there a value of K_1 that will deter entry? By expanding capacity, Firm 1 reduces its marginal cost. By raising its capacity to K_1^D, Firm 1 drives Firm 2's post-entry profit value to an intersection with the zero ordinate, assuring that Firm 2 will do no better than break even should it enter.[120] Hence, for capacity greater than or equal to K_1^D, entry is deterred. Of course, Firm 1 has no incentive to expand capacity beyond K_1^D, where it earns OB dollars of profit pre-entry and OD dollars if its deterrence effort fails.

Does it always pay to deter entry? We have assumed that if Firm 2 could do no better than break even, it would choose not to enter. If Firm 2 did enter when Firm 1 chose capacity K_1^D, Firm 1's profit would be reduced to OD. If it knew that entry was going to occur in any event, the incumbent could accommodate the entry in advance by restricting its pre-entry capacity to K_1^A, raising its post-entry profits to OC dollars. Whether it is in Firm 1's interest to deter entry depends on whether the maximum profit it could earn successfully deterring entry [OB in Figure

10.4(a)] is greater than the maximum profit OC it could expect to earn after the entry it has accommodated occurs. In the example illustrated by Figure 10.4, entry deterrence is in fact the more profitable strategy. However, examples in which accommodation is preferred are easily constructed.[121]

Even when it is not in the incumbent's interest to deter entry completely, it may be worth while investing to alter the post-entry environment to its advantage, for instance, inducing Firm 2 to enter with a relatively small plant in the expectation that any larger output would, with Firm 1's low-cost capacity, depress the price unduly. Similarly, the pioneering firm in an industry characterized by substantial learning-by-doing economies is assured higher profit per unit than its rivals through its lead down the learning curve. However, by pursuing an aggressive low-price policy that higher-cost rivals have difficulty emulating, the pioneer will almost surely maintain a dominant market share, and with a larger market share, it will enjoy more of the learning-by-doing economies, reinforcing its dominant position into the period when learning-by-doing cost savings are exhausted.[122]

Whether the incumbent's profit-maximizing investment strategy is to deter or accommodate entry, once its investment is in place, the incumbent is assumed to

116. The analysis here follows A. Michael Spence, "Entry, Capacity, Investment, and Oligopolistic Pricing," *Bell Journal of Economics*, vol. 8 (Autumn 1977), pp. 534–544; idem, "Investment Strategy and Growth in a New Market," *Bell Journal of Economics*, vol. 10 (Spring 1979), pp. 1–19; Avinash Dixit, "A Model of Duopoly Suggesting a Theory of Entry Barriers," *Bell Journal of Economics*, vol. 10 (Spring 1979), pp. 20–32; and *idem*, "The Role of Investment in Entry-Deterrence," *Economic Journal*, vol. 90 (March 1980), pp. 95–106. See also John T. Wenders, "Excess Capacity as a Barrier to Entry," *Journal of Industrial Economics*, vol. 20 (November 1971), pp. 14–19; idem, "Collusion and Entry," *Journal of Political Economy*, vol. 79 (November/December 1971), pp. 1258–1277; B. Curtis Eaton and Richard G. Lipsey, "Exit Barriers are Entry Barriers: The Durability of Capital as a Barrier to Entry," *Bell Journal of Economics*, vol. 10 (Autumn 1980), pp. 721–729; Eaton and Lipsey, "Capital, Commitment, and Entry Equilibrium," *Bell Journal of Economics*, vol. 12 (Autumn 1981), pp. 593–604; James W. Friedman, "Limit Pricing and Entry," *Journal of Economic Dynamics and Control*, vol. 3 (August 1981), pp. 319–323; Drew Fudenberg and Jean Tirole, "Capital as Commitment: Strategic Investment to Deter Mobility," *Journal of Economic Theory*, vol. 31 (December 1983), pp. 227–250; Stylianos Perrakis and George Warskett, "Capacity and Entry under Demand Uncertainty," *Review of Economic Studies*, vol. 50 (July 1983), pp. 495–511; Jeremy Bulow, John Geanakoplos, and Paul Klemperer, "Holding Idle Capacity to Deter Entry," *Economic Journal*, vol. 95 (March 1985), pp. 178–182; and Stanley S. Reynolds, "Capacity Investment, Preemption, and Commitment in an Infinite Horizon Model," *International Economic Review*, vol. 28 (February 1987), pp. 69–88.

117. Firm 2 must also choose its scale of entry K_2; however, unlike Firm 1, Firm 2 gets no strategic advantage from this choice. It will choose K_2 to minimize the cost of producing the level of q_2 that maximizes its profits, given q_1. Hence, in the structure of the model, Firm 2's capacity cost is subsumed within its profit function.

118. Each firm chooses production on the assumption that changes in its own production will induce no response from the other. See pp. 200–204 supra. For a discussion of how changes in second-stage behavior affect the incumbent's investment decision, see Eaton and Lipsey, "Capital, Commitment, and Entry Equilibrium," supra note 116; Daniel F. Spulber, "Capacity, Output, and Sequential Entry," *American Economic Review*, vol. 71 (June 1981), pp. 503–514; and Stanley S. Reynolds, "Strategic Capital Investment in the American Aluminum Industry," *Journal of Industrial Economics*, vol. 34 (March 1986), pp. 225–245.

119. See equations (6A.5) and (6A.6) on p. 228 supra.

120. Whether investment in capacity K_1^D is in Firm 1's interest *ex post* plays no role here. As long as the investment is irreversible, Firm 1 cannot back off from the commitment it made in the first stage of the game.

121. See Drew Fudenberg and Jean Tirole, "The Fat Cat Effect, the Puppy Dog Ploy and the Lean and Hungry Look," *American Economic Review*, vol. 74 (May 1984), pp. 361–368, who distinguish conditions leading to "tough" entry-precluding investment and "soft" entry-accommodating behavior. See also Jean Tirole, *The Theory of Industrial Organization* (Cambridge: MIT Press, 1988), pp. 314–337; and Jeremy Bulow, John Geanakoplos and Paul Klemperer, "Multimarket Oligopoly: Strategic Substitutes and Complements," *Journal of Political Economy*, vol. 93 (June 1985), pp. 488–511.

122. See Ross, "Learning to Dominate," *supra* note 86. For a discussion of the impact of other investment strategies open to market pioneers, see Marvin B. Lieberman, "First-Mover Advantages," *Strategic Management Journal*, vol. 9 (1988), pp. 41–58.

Figure 10.4
Choosing Plant Capacity
to Deter Entry

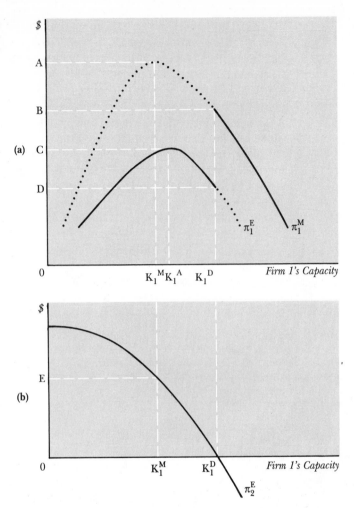

set its price at the short-run profit-maximizing level. To be sure, with more capacity, the incumbent's pre-entry profit-maximizing price will be lower than it would have been if capacity had not been expanded to confront would-be entrants with a credible deterrent. However, there is no intrinsic reason for setting the pre-entry price below the profit-maximizing level, *given* the level of capacity chosen. In other words, the incentive for limit pricing below the short-run profit-maximizing level seems to vanish. What happens then to limit-pricing logic when dominant firms invest to create *post-entry* conditions that credibly deter entry?

Imperfect Information,
Signaling, and
Irrationality

There are at least three possible answers, none of which has clear pride of place. First, one may conclude that limit pricing is an ineffective means of deterring large-scale entry and is therefore unlikely to be observed. Second, setting pre-entry prices below the profit-maximizing level might be seen as a means of signaling the likelihood of rational post-entry responses unprofitable to the would-be entrant. Or third, limit pricing could be a way of warning rivals that the dominant firm's turf will be defended, rationally or not.

The objective of game theory is to devise behavioral models that are consistently rational, implying *inter alia* that if firms make a threat, they are better off carrying it out than backing off if the target of the threat chooses to undertake the action (for example, entry) against which the threat is directed. If deterrence threats are not credible in this sense, would-be entrants will see through them and enter despite them. But in fact, the information available to would-be entrants is imperfect. Game theorists have therefore constructed models in which entrants are uncertain as to whether the incumbent has sufficiently low costs rationally to drive the post-entry price down to levels that wipe out an entrant's profits.[123] If the would-be entrant makes inferences from the incumbent's pre-entry behavior about probable post-entry conditions, setting a pre-entry price below the short-run profit-maximizing level might signal that the incumbent's costs are sufficiently low to render the post-entry environment unprofitable for the interloper. Under appropriate assumptions, this limit pricing strategy can succeed in either of two quite different cases: by discouraging would-be entrants from making a mistake, entering a market in which the incumbent has a rational incentive to obliterate the entrant's profits; and by discouraging entrants when a high-cost incumbent only mimics a low-cost posture, but lacks a rational incentive to render the entrant unprofitable if the bluff is called. The difficulty with such models is that there may be much less costly and risky ways by which entrants can distinguish between rational entry deterrents and bluffs. In particular, by observing the movement of trucks and workers into an incumbent's plants, obtaining from capital goods suppliers information on the incumbent's capacity, hiring away a key employee from the incumbent, or other tactics of business espionage, a would-be entrant can find out how great the incumbent's capacity is and how low its marginal costs are without placing on the betting table the large investment stake associated with actual full-scale entry.

A more plausible role exists for using pre-entry prices to signal not the incumbent's capacity and costs, but the behavior likely to follow a large-scale entry. The example surrounding Figure 10.4 *assumed* Cournot-type pricing behavior in the post-entry environment. But the actual environment could be more or less hospitable to entry — more hospitable if the incumbent reduced its output to accommodate output increases by the entrant, less if the incumbent reacts with von Stackelberg leadership or chooses, perhaps irrationally, to "punish" the interloper. By setting a low pre-entry price, the incumbent signals its deep interest in maintaining the status quo and warns the would-be entrant of serious risks if it enters.

That the possibility of an irrational response can deter has been a central tenet of superpower relations since World War II. For decades, the United States' strategy for defending Western Europe against feared Soviet aggression has called for

123. See Paul Milgrom and John Roberts, "Limit Pricing and Entry under Incomplete Information: An Equilibrium Analysis," *Econometrica*, vol. 50 (March 1982), pp. 443–459; Steven Matthews and Leonard Mirman, "Equilibrium Limit Pricing: The Effects of Private Information and Stochastic Demand," *Econometrica*, vol. 51 (July 1983), pp. 981–996; and I. K. Cho, "Equilibrium Analysis of Entry Deterrence: A Reexamination," mimeo, 1986.

the possible use of nuclear weapons if conventional forces were overwhelmed. But would it be rational for the United States to retaliate against Eastern Europe and the Soviet Union with nuclear weapons, knowing that the situation could escalate, leading the Soviets to respond in kind against the American homeland? Sober analysis suggests that it would not. If this were believed by the Soviets, they would not be deterred, if indeed they sought to bring additional unruly satellites under their wing. If, however, U.S. leaders have committed their reputations to a nuclear response, or decentralized decision-making so that field commanders would initiate the response under the pressures of combat, or if emotional behavior for any other reason could displace "rational" thinking, escalation might plausibly progress to the large-scale use of nuclear weapons. With the cost of a miscalculation about the U.S. response so high, fear by the Soviets of such an irrational response contributes to deterrence. Furthermore, the United States has something to gain by cultivating the impression that it will act irrationally, or that events will get out of control, if aggression occurs, for this too contributes to deterrence. By making irrational actions seem more likely in a contingency one seeks to avert, one may move nearer the rational goal of averting the contingency. This is the so-called *rationality of irrationality*.[124]

So also with deterring market entry. There is always a chance that industry discipline will break down when new entry occurs. Even if they hope to avoid irrational pricing, established firms can enhance their deterrent by concealing that hope and communicating that they will fight to maintain market share if challenged. One way of signaling that intention is to exhibit irrationality pre-entry by holding prices below the short-run profit-maximizing level. This seems a frail reed for explaining limit pricing behavior, however, since there may be other ways to exhibit one's willingness to fight without incurring potentially large ongoing profit sacrifices. Before reaching a final verdict on the question, we explore some of those possibilities.

Deterrence Through Predation An answer comes in part from recognizing that the struggle for strategic position is seldom a two-party, two-stage game, as assumed in the analysis of Figure 10.4. Rather, it is played out repeatedly over time as diverse newcomers try their hand at entering some market, and it may also be repeated over space if a dominant incumbent firm serves numerous distinguishable geographic markets or product segments. Then a response that is "predatory" at some time in a particular market may signal to would-be entrants the likelihood of equally rapacious responses in other markets at later dates.[125]

The logic and ambiguities of the problem are best illuminated by describing and expanding upon what is called "the chain store paradox."[126] Suppose a food retailing chain is the dominant supplier in 1, . . . , N local markets. Each of the markets might be entered by an outsider, but entry must take place in a well-ordered sequence, for example, first in market 1 and last (if at all) in market N. We assume that before entry occurs, short-run profit maximization yields an annual profit of 100 in each market. If entry is attempted, the incumbent can fight, incurring losses (a payoff of -10) and causing the entrant to lose money too, or give way, in which case (assuming some loss of scale economies) each participant makes profits of $+35$ per year. The payoff matrix for a single play of the game, with incumbent profits listed first and entrant profits second, is:

		ENTRANT	
		Stay Out	**Enter**
INCUMBENT	Business as usual	+100, 0	n.a., n.a.
	Give way	n.a., n.a.	+35, +35
	Fight	n.a., n.a.	−10, −10

The entrant perceives that if it fails to venture, it gains nothing. If it enters, the incumbent will retain some profits by giving way but suffer losses if it fights. If the game is viewed as a one-shot isolated case, it is rational for the incumbent to give way, and the entrant, seeing this, enters.

We know instinctively that the difficulty here is treating the entry as an isolated case and ignoring the precedential effect of early moves. Taking the next logical step, Reinhard Selten formulated the problem as a sequence of ordered entry and response decisions from market 1 to market N. Applying the standard technique for solving repeated games of this kind,[127] Selten asked what behavior would be rational in the *last*, that is, the Nth, stage. Clearly, since there would be no more entries, what happens at stage N can have no precedential effect, and so the only rational behavior at that stage would be for the entrant to enter and the incumbent to give way. If so, then at the N-1th stage, what is done cannot influence behavior at stage N, so the participants would choose the rational strategies for that stage only — entering and giving way. The same reasoning is iterated at stages N-2, N-3, and so on back to stage 1. Thus emerges the paradox: if the participants foresee rationally what will ensue at each stage all the way to the end of the game, not fighting is a Nash equilibrium solution. The incumbent lacks incentive to discourage subsequent entry, and, as a result, it ends up sharing its profits with entrants in every market.

The paradox is easily escaped if the sequence of entries is neither clearly bounded in number nor ordered in time, or, more importantly, if the incumbent's response to early entries alters would-be entrants' assessment of the profitability of entry. If potential entrants estimate the probability that an incumbent will fight additional entry, rationally or irrationally, on the basis of the behavior they observe in connection with early entry attempts, then it may pay the incumbent to react to early entries by fighting, despite the loss of profits in the markets entered. The more often the incumbent responds by fighting, the higher is the updated probability of fighting, as perceived by uncertain would-be entrants. Kreps and Wilson show that a relatively small probability that the incumbent will fight at the

124. See Schelling, *The Strategy of Conflict*, supra note 113, Chapter 8; and Herman Kahn, *On Thermonuclear War* (Princeton: Princeton University Press, 1960), pp. 291–295. Compare Henry A. Kissinger, *Nuclear Weapons and Foreign Policy* (New York: Harper, 1957), Chapters 5 and 6, who advocates building conventional forces — the (costly) analogue of investing in capacity with low production costs — to repel an invasion without resort to nuclear weapons.

125. We enclose "predatory" in quotes because there has been vigorous debate about the term's definition in the context of antitrust cases. See Chapter 12 infra.

126. The phrase and the original formulation are from Reinhard Selten, "The Chain-Store Paradox," *Theory and Decision*, vol. 9 (1978), pp. 127–159.

127. Cf. pp. 214–215 supra.

first stage is sufficient, if there are numerous stages, to make fighting rational for the incumbent.[128] In effect, the incumbent fights to engender a reputation for toughness that deters additional entrants. If the game has a finite number of well-ordered stages, the incumbent's incentive to react by fighting diminishes as the set of unchallenged markets declines, and eventually, the incumbent will give way to some entrant, after which deterrence will fail repeatedly. But if each market is subject to a continuing stream of entry threats, the desire to maintain a reputation for toughness may rationally induce the incumbent to fight any entry, which in turn makes each entry prospect unattractive.

This view of the payoffs from rapacious responses to entry is consistent with events in the U.S. coffee industry during the 1970s. Through its Maxwell House and related brands, General Foods controlled approximately 45 percent of regular coffee sales in the Eastern United States. Folger's (owned by Procter and Gamble), the leading brand in Chicago and points west but little known in the East, began a campaign to expand eastward. Maxwell House countered the invasion with sharp (possibly below-cost) price reductions and increased promotional spending in selected key cities, evidently with the intent of persuading Folger's that its inroads would be vigorously resisted. The counterattack was initially successful, for although Folger's remained in the cities it entered and continued expanding into the Southeast, it drew back for several years from its original plan to move aggressively into New York City and other densely populated Northeast seaboard markets. However, in the 1980s, Folger's advance resumed. One interpretation of the 1980's sequel is that antitrust actions restrained the aggressiveness of General Foods' response.[129] Nevertheless, early rapaciousness followed by accommodation once few additional markets remain to be occupied is precisely what the theory of multimarket deterrence through reputation-building predicts.

Predation Against Already Established Firms

This line of analysis raises the question of how effective sharp below-cost pricing and related strategies are against firms that are already well established in a market.[130] We have seen earlier that when such firms are price takers, a dominant firm may price to squeeze them out if it has a strong cost advantage and exit is reasonably rapid. But are there further strategic ramifications?

The most famous case of allegedly predatory pricing is that of the old Standard Oil Company. Under the leadership of John D. Rockefeller, the Standard Oil trust between 1870 and 1899 attained and maintained a 90 percent share of the U.S. petroleum refining industry through a vigorous program of mergers, combined with various sharp practices that supposedly increased the willingness of independent refiners to sell out. These included securing discriminatory rail freight rates and rebates, foreclosing supplies of crude oil through the control of pipelines, business espionage, price warfare waged both overtly and secretly through bogus independent distributors, and (although never proved) astute placement of an occasional stick of dynamite. Regarding predatory price warfare, the conventional wisdom, handed down from generation to generation of economists, tells us that Standard cut prices sharply in specific local markets where there was competition while holding prices at much higher levels in markets lacking competition. Thereby it presumably softened up its rivals until they were receptive to merger offers. In a precedent-setting opinion, Supreme Court Justice Edward White enumerated the predatory practices of which Standard was accused and cited approvingly the prosecution's contention that "the pathway of the combination . . . is strewn with the wrecks resulting from crushing out, without regard to law, the individual rights of others."[131]

This interpretation stood virtually unchallenged until 1958, when it was attacked by John McGee on two main grounds: (1) that there was little evidence to support the contention that Standard achieved its monopoly position through predatory price cutting, and (2) that such a strategy by Standard would have been irrational because it demanded an excessive sacrifice of profits.[132]

McGee's criticism of the supporting evidence was based solely upon an analysis of the voluminous Standard Oil antitrust case record. It is not convincing, since antitrust investigations labor under such severe evidentiary difficulties that they frequently fail to elicit proof of the main points at issue. Had McGee cast his net further into historical works drawing upon the Rockefeller papers, he would have found that Standard tried in some instances to drive out its rivals through price cutting. As Rockefeller wrote to an associate in 1891:

We want to watch, and when our volume of business is to be cut down by the increase of competition to fifty percent, or less, it may be a very serious question whether we had not better make an important reduction, with a view of taking substantially all the business there is.[133]

McGee's second point is better taken, for independent evidence suggests that Rockefeller apparently recognized the futility of trying to drive rivals out of business through predatory pricing in all but exceptional cases.[134] Absent substantial barriers to entry, there was nothing to stop old and new competitors from starting up operations once Standard returned prices to profitable levels;[135] and Standard,

128. David Kreps and Robert Wilson, "Reputation and Imperfect Information," *Journal of Economic Theory*, vol. 27 (August 1982), pp. 253–279. See also the simultaneous contribution of Paul Milgrom and John Roberts, "Predation, Reputation, and Entry Deterrence," *Journal of Economic Theory*, vol. 27 (August 1982), pp. 280–312; and Milgrom and Roberts, "Limit Pricing and Entry under Incomplete Information," supra note 123. Variations and extensions include David Easley, Robert T. Masson, and Robert J. Reynolds, "Preying for Time," *Journal of Industrial Economics*, vol. 33 (June 1985), pp. 445–460; and Drew Fudenberg and David M. Kreps, "Reputation in the Simultaneous Play of Multiple Opponents," *Review of Economic Studies*, vol. 54 (October 1987), pp. 541–568. As is common with games of imperfect information (see pp. 219–220 supra), the equilibria emerging in these models are sensitive to the assumptions made.

129. *In the matter of General Foods Corporation*, 103 F.T.C. 204 (filed 1976, decided 1984); and *Indian Coffee Corp. et al.* v. *Procter & Gamble et al.* (W.D. Pennsylvania, October 1976).

130. The distinction here is the same as that made by Thomas C. Schelling between "deterrence" ("If you cross the line we shoot . . ." and "compellence" ("We move, and you get out of the way . . ."). *Arms and Influence* (New Haven: Yale University Press, 1966), pp. 69–78.

131. *Standard Oil Company of New Jersey* v. *U.S.*, 221 U.S. 1, 47, 76 (1911).

132. John S. McGee, "Predatory Price Cutting: The Standard Oil (N.J.) Case," *Journal of Law & Economics*, vol. 1 (October 1958), pp. 137–169. See also Lester G. Telser, "Cutthroat Competition and the Long Purse," *Journal of Law & Economics*, vol. 9 (October 1966), pp. 259–277; and McGee, "Predatory Pricing Revisited," *Journal of Law & Economics*, vol. 23 (October 1980), pp. 289–330.

133. Letter to H. A. Hutchins, quoted in Allan Nevins, *Study in Power: John D. Rockefeller*, vol. II (New York: Scribner's, 1953), p. 65.

134. See the second edition of *Industrial Market Structure and Economic Performance*, pp. 336–337, for a discussion of this point.

135. See Wayne A. Leeman, "The Limitations of Local Price-Cutting as a Barrier to Entry," *Journal of Political Economy*, vol. 64 (August 1956), pp. 329–332. For evidence of similar reentries into the sugar refining industry, see Richard Zerbe, "The American Sugar Refinery Company, 1887–1914: The Story of a Monopoly," *Journal of Law & Economics*, vol. 12 (October 1969), pp. 355–356.

controlling as it did the lion's share of the markets in which it sold, inevitably had to accept profit sacrifices from predation disproportionate to the harm it inflicted upon smaller rivals.[136]

Other studies — for example, of the gunpowder, sugar refining, ready-mix concrete, and numerous other industries[137] — have followed McGee in concluding that what was widely believed to be predatory pricing was in fact rare, ineffective, or the symptom of a competitive struggle desired as little by the alleged predators as by its victims. The evidence is persuasive, although it is not completely clear whether this reflects the rarity of hard-core predation or the barrenness of historical records. Certainly, other cases have been identified in which an inference of predation, even under the strictest definition of the term, appears indisputable.[138]

Price warfare to eliminate existing rivals might also be unprofitable if the liquidation prices at which the victims sold out were not much less than they would have been in a merger agreement entered under less coercive conditions.[139] McGee argues that this was so in the Standard Oil case — that Standard could have acquired rival facilities in any event by paying only a modest premium over their competitive value. But this is doubtful. A successful price war could spell the difference between paying the nuisance value of a firm, which most entrepreneurs opposing Standard believed to be high, and the distress price, which for narrowly based specialists suffering a liquidity crisis in imperfect capital markets would be appreciably lower. In the most careful analysis of this point, Malcolm Burns offers persuasive evidence that the American Tobacco Company successfully used predatory pricing to reduce the cost of acquiring rivals between 1891 and 1906.[140]

A related argument known as the "deep pocket" hypothesis holds that financially powerful conglomerate corporations may use predatory pricing to drive out or discipline smaller but efficient rivals, cross subsidizing their predatory operations with profits from other lines of business.[141] Although clear-cut examples are hard to find, the argument could be valid to the extent that conglomerates can obtain capital at lower costs, or in larger quantities, than small specialist firms. Much less plausible is the further contention that when losses are incurred in some lines for predatory reasons, prices in other lines are elevated to generate the needed subsidies. Normally, one would expect the conglomerate to set prices at profit-maximizing levels in high-profit lines, whether or not there are low-profit lines to be subsidized. To do otherwise would be to accept needless profit sacrifices. However, cross subsidization of losing operations *can* lead to price increases in other lines if a multimarket company is subject to an overall profitability constraint because it is a regulated public utility,[142] because of governmental price controls (like those enforced during the early 1970s) targeted on consolidated corporate profitability,[143] or because it fears a public outcry if its aggregate profits exceed some "reasonable" level. Then incremental losses in one line will be offset through price increases on other products whose prices had not previously been raised to the profit-maximizing level.

Recapitulation   Let us bring together the strands of our analysis. The surest way for dominant incumbent firms to erect a credible deterrent against large-scale entry is to commit themselves through irreversible investments to a posture that makes a rapacious response to entry rational. Undertaking such investments in advance of actual entry is costly and may not be profitable. If so, dominant firms may instead react to actual entry attempts by cutting prices well below the level that is rational in the sense of maximizing post-entry profits, thereby seeking to create a reputation for toughness that frightens off future would-be entrants. Holding prices persistently below profit-maximizing levels *before* entry is attempted — that is, limit pricing — does not play an essential role in either of these strategies. Low pre-entry prices may in some instances signal the incumbent's seriousness about defending its market and hence communicate that a rapacious response may occur with ominous probability. However, the theoretical rationale for limit pricing on such signaling grounds is less than clear-cut. Recognizing this brings us full circle to our original approach to limit pricing. The synthesis that emerges is a two-pronged strategy of deterrence. Incumbent sellers have an incentive to restrain prices sufficiently to deter inefficiently small price-taking firms and fringe rival expansion, or to optimize the rate of entry by such firms. The more important economies of scale and absolute cost advantages possessed by the leading incumbents are, the higher is the margin by which prices can exceed the insiders' unit costs without encouraging fringe competition. On the other hand, implicit or explicit threats of price warfare that may or may not be embodied in low pre-entry prices are brandished to deter entry at large, relatively efficient scales.

Modes of Entry and Deterrence

This conclusion is consistent with the systematic evidence available on actual patterns of entry into concentrated industries. Measured by the sheer number of entities making the decision to enter, most new entry involves relatively small firms — too small, as a rule, to achieve all conventional economies of scale.[144] Entry at or

136. In the words of one Rockefeller associate, Standard "gained or lost on a titan's scale while its opponents did so on a pygmy's." Nevins, *Study in Power*, supra note 133, p. 66.

137. See Kenneth G. Elzinga, "Predatory Pricing: The Case of the Gunpowder Trust," *Journal of Law & Economics*, vol. 13 (April 1970), pp. 223–240; Zerbe, "The American Sugar Refinery Company," supra note 135, pp. 351–375; and David R. Kamerschen, "Predatory Pricing, Vertical Integration and Market Foreclosure: The Case of Ready Mix Cement in Memphis," *Industrial Organization Review*, vol. 2, no. 3 (1974), pp. 143–168. See also Roland H. Koller II, *Predatory Pricing in a Market Economy* (New York: Arno Press, 1978), who studied the materials from 123 antitrust case records and found that examples of clear, hard-core price predation were rare.

138. For example, on the China steamship trade in the 1880s, see Basil S. Yamey, "Predatory Price Cutting: Notes and Comments," *Journal of Law & Economics*, vol. 15 (April 1972), pp. 129–142.

139. See Telser, "Cutthroat Competition," supra note 132, pp. 259–277.

140. Malcolm R. Burns, "Predatory Pricing and the Acquisition Costs of Competitors," *Journal of Political Economy*, vol. 94 (April 1986), pp. 266–296. See also Garth Saloner, "Predation, Mergers and Incomplete Information," *Rand Journal of Economics*, vol. 18 (Summer 1987), pp. 165–186.

141. See Corwin D. Edwards, "Conglomerate Bigness as a Source of Power," in the National Bureau of Economic Research conference report, *Business Concentration and Price Policy* (Princeton: Princeton University Press, 1955), pp. 334–335.

142. See Harvey Averch and Leland L. Johnson, "Behavior of the Firm under Regulatory Constraint," *American Economic Review*, vol. 52 (December 1962), pp. 1058–1059. Alleged cross-subsidization was an issue in the AT&T antitrust case, discussed in Chapter 12.

143. For an alleged episode of predatory pricing influenced by the overall profit ceiling imposed under government renegotiation of defense contractor profits, see *Pacific Engineering & Production Co.* v. *Kerr-McGee Corp. et al.*, 551 F. 2d 790 (1977), cert. den. 434 U.S. 879 (1977). The role of profit renegotiation is brought out in Pacific Engineering's petition for a writ of certiorari, 1977, p. 8.

144. See Robert McGuckin, "Entry, Concentration Change, and Stability of Market Shares," *Southern Economic Journal*, vol. 38 (January 1972), p. 369; Scherer et al., *Multi-Plant Operation*, supra note 87, pp. 147–54; and George S. Yip, *Barriers to Entry: A Corporate-Strategy Perspective*, (Lexington: D.C. Heath and Co., 1982). Small-scale entry may of course be undertaken by a division of a much larger corporation.

near the minimum efficient scale into significant oligopolistic markets is a rarer phenomenon. Whether the aggregate volume of output contributed by many small entrants equals the contribution of occasional but large entrants is uncertain. What is clear is that the sum of many small entries, or expansions by many small firms, can have a significant concentration-reducing effect.[145]

The systematic statistical evidence on variables influencing rates of entry remains somewhat contradictory. The weight of the evidence suggests that the rate of entry is higher when pre-entry profits are ample, when demand is growing rapidly, and when barriers associated with scale economies and product differentiation are low.[146] Growth is conducive to entry partly because it opens up sales opportunities not exploited rapidly enough by established enterprises and partly because capacity constraints, and satisfaction with the business already in hand, may prevent industry leaders from carrying a retaliatory price war very far.[147] Where scale and differentiation barriers are high, outsiders are more likely to enter by acquiring a fringe producer, which in the first instance adds nothing to industry supply and hence is not entry in the strict sense of the word.[148]

It is much more difficult to observe systematically the actions taken by incumbents to deter entry. Important insights into the incidence of entry-deterring behavior are provided by Robert Smiley's survey of 293 product managers and similarly placed executives in manufacturing and service industry firms.[149] The respondents were asked to comment on the prevalence of nine possible strategies for deterring entry:

1. Set prices and market products to exploit learning and scale economy effects aggressively;
2. Expand capacity;
3. Advertise to cement customer loyalty;
4. Seek patents on likely substitute products and technologies;
5. Talk tough about responding to entry;
6. Set limit prices to block entry;
7. Set limit prices to slow the rate of entry;
8. Introduce new product varieties to fill all product niches; or
9. Avoid disclosing profit data on individual product lines.

Fifty-eight percent of the respondents reported that one or more of these strategies were used frequently in their industry to defend existing products, while 98 percent reported at least occasional use. Although only 9 percent indicated that entry was an extremely important concern in their decision making, 52 percent rated entry as at least equal in importance compared to other concerns. Of the companies that did not pursue any entry-deterring strategies, the majority (62 percent) viewed entry as inevitable or too costly to deter. Another 33 percent viewed existing oligopolistic rivalry as so intense as to dissuade entry, while only 5 percent considered entry to be blockaded.

Perhaps the most striking result of the Smiley survey is that only 9 percent of the respondents reported frequent use of limit-pricing strategy (6) or (7) to protect existing products, and only 4 percent perceived frequent use to protect new products. Instead, advertising and patent protection (32 and 31 percent of respondents

for new products) and disguising profitability (31 percent of respondents on existing products) were the most commonly used strategies. Expanding the question to
include at least occasional use, Smiley found that advertising, masking profitability, and filling available product niches were the most commonly cited strategies, while limit pricing and maintaining excess capacity ended up at the bottom
of the list.[150] Thus, strategies that raise barriers to entry or keep outsiders unin-
formed about market conditions are preferred over efforts to signal aggressive
entry-impeding responses.

When entry does occur at a substantial scale, the reactions to it by leading established firms appear to vary widely in ways predictable only if one has rich information on demand and cost conditions, industry traditions, and perhaps even per-
sonalities, if indeed confident predictions are possible at all. The choice facing
incumbents was succinctly put by one brand manager, "Should we bomb them
back to the stone ages or just hope they'll go away?"[151] William Robinson's survey
evidence suggests that at least half the time, they choose the latter option.[152]

145. See McGuckin, "Entry," pp. 363–370; and Roger Sherman, "Entry Barriers and the Growth of Firms," *Southern Economic Journal*, vol. 38 (April 1971), pp. 238–247. Compare Daniel Shapiro and R. S. Khemani, "The Determinants of Entry and Exit Reconsidered," *International Journal of Industrial Organization*, vol. 5 (March 1987), pp. 15–26, who found that overall entry rates are among the most important determinants of rates of exit.

146. The determinants of entry have been estimated for industry cross-sections and specific industry groups in numerous countries, including the United States, Canada, Germany, Sweden, and the United Kingdom. See Paul K. Gorecki, "The Determinants of Entry by New and Diversifying Enterprises in the UK Manufacturing Sector, 1958–1963," *Applied Economics*, vol. 7 (June 1975), pp. 139–147; Maury N. Harris, "Entry and Long-Term Trends in Industry Performance," *Antitrust Bulletin*, vol. 21 (Summer 1976), pp. 295–312; Larry L. Duetsch, "Entry and the Extent of Multiplant Operations," *Journal of Industrial Economics*, vol. 32 (June 1984), pp. 477–488; John C. Hause and Gunnar Du Rietz, "Entry, Industry Growth, and the Microdynamics of Industry Supply," *Journal of Political Economy*, vol. 92 (August 1984), pp. 733–757; Richard Highfield and Robert Smiley, "New Business Starts and Economic Activity: An Empirical Investigation," *International Journal of Industrial Organization*, vol. 5 (March 1987), pp. 51–66; Robert T. Masson and Joseph Shaanan, "Stochastic-Dynamic Limiting Pricing: An Empirical Test," *Review of Economics and Statistics*, vol. 64 (August 1982), pp. 413–422; Masson and Shaanan, "Optimal Oligopoly Pricing and the Threat of Entry," *International Journal of Industrial Organization*, vol. 5 (September 1987), pp. 323–339; Joachim Schwalbach, "Entry by Diversified Firms into German Industries," *International Journal of Industrial Organization*, vol. 5 (March 1987), pp. 43–50; and additional references cited in Paul Geroski and Robert T. Masson, "Dynamic Market Models in Industrial Organization," *International Journal of Industrial Organization*, vol. 5 (March 1987), pp. 11–13.

147. Cf. Sylos-Labini, *Oligopoly and Technical Progress*, supra note 18, pp. 61–62. Three-fourths of the entrants surveyed in one study entered during the start-up or high growth phases of product life cycles, when annual sales growth averaged 35 percent. William T. Robinson, "Marketing Mix Reactions to Entry," *Marketing Science*, vol. 7 (Fall 1988), pp. 368–385.

148. Mergers or expansion by existing firms accounted for just over half of the "entrants'" sales observed in Canada by John R. Baldwin and Paul K. Gorecki, "Plant Creation Versus Plant Acquisition," *International Journal of Industrial Organization*, vol. 5 (March 1987), pp. 27–41. "Entrants" here include firms that entered by acquiring existing market participants.

149. Robert Smiley, "Empirical Evidence on Strategic Entry Deterrence," *International Journal of Industrial Organization*, vol. 6 (June 1988), pp. 167–180.

150. Two econometric studies support Smiley's finding that few firms choose excess capacity to deter entry: Marvin Lieberman, "Excess Capacity as a Barrier to Entry: An Empirical Appraisal," *Journal of Industrial Economics*, vol. 35 (June 1987), pp. 607–627; and Robert T. Masson and Joseph Shaanan, "Excess Capacity and Limit Pricing: An Empirical Test," *Economica*, vol. 53 (August 1986), pp. 365–378. Lieberman finds that excess capacity in chemical processing industries can be explained largely by demand volatility, and that incumbents and entrants fill capacity niches in growing markets at virtually identical rates. Both studies do suggest that excess capacity slows entry. Masson and Shaanan find support for the hypothesis that the presence of excess capacity raises the price at which entry would be forestalled.

151. Quoted in John Hauser, "Theory and Application of Defensive Strategy," in L. G. Thomas, ed., *Economics of Strategic Behavior* (Lexington: Heath-Lexington, 1986), p. 113.

152. William Robinson reports that 57 percent of entrants encountered no significant response from incumbents two years after their entry. "Marketing Mix Reactions," supra note 147. See also E. R. Biggadike, *Corporate Diversification: Entry, Strategy, and Performance* (Cambridge: Harvard University Press, 1979), p. 179; and Yip, *Barriers to Entry*, supra note 144.

Incumbents appear least likely to respond to small-scale and very large scale entry, while intermediate-scale entry attracts retaliation. Incumbents are most likely to respond to entry in fast-growing markets, or where the entrant threatens to transform the nature of the market through product innovation or effective advertising.

An example of the last case is provided by the entry of Datril into the analgesic drug market.[153] By the early 1970s, Johnson & Johnson's Tylenol acetaminophen pain reliever had achieved a reasonable share of the market, largely through physicians' recommendations. In 1975 Bristol-Myers introduced acetaminophen-based Datril, advertising it nationally and pricing it below Tylenol. Johnson & Johnson responded by matching Datril's price, escalating its national advertising, expanding its sales force, introducing related Tylenol brands, and charging Bristol-Myers with false advertising. It succeeded not only in limiting Datril's penetration but in expanding acetaminophen's segment of the analgesic drug market at the expense of aspirin and other drugs.

One of the most extreme examples of a passive response to entry was the behavior of the Canadian Cement Company, which in 1946 controlled an 80 percent share of the cement trade in Canada.[154] It pursued a consistent price maintenance, give-way policy in the face of repeated entry, on occasion choosing to operate at only 40 to 55 percent of capacity rather than fighting. As a consequence, its national market share fell to 34 percent by 1970. Similar propensities to avoid price warfare following large-scale new entry were evident in the nickel industry and the once-monopolized British tin can industry,[155] among others. Near the other extreme were IBM's response to inroads by such computer peripheral equipment manufacturers as Telex,[156] the price wars following the start-up of large polyethylene and anhydrous ammonia plants,[157] and the localized price war in 1967 and general shift to discount pricing in 1970 that accompanied entry by new grocery chains into the concentrated Washington, D.C., retail food market.[158] The most that can be said with confidence from this and other qualitative evidence is that sizable new entrants can by no means be certain that existing firms will give ground.

Potential entrants are well aware of this, and when they consider entering a market, they devote a good deal of thought to finding an entry strategy that strikes the best compromise between securing scale economies and minimizing the risk of price warfare.[159] One common strategy is to enter at a small scale with a plant that can be expanded gradually when and if demand growth permits. This is done more readily in industries with flexible, divisible production processes (such as in textile manufacturing and most retail trades) than in continuous process industries like petroleum refining and cement, where major equipment items may come only in large chunks. When indivisibilities compel large-scale entry, other devices to soften the output expansion blow may be sought. For example, when the Dundee Cement Company opened an unprecedentedly large new plant near St. Louis in 1968, it tried to minimize the price repercussions by barging its cement as far south as Mobile, Alabama, so that no single local market had to absorb more than a 5 percent supply increment.[160] Its luck was bad, however, because a general cement demand slump aggravated the absorption problem, and as a result widespread price cutting followed. A frequent concomitant of both large- and small-scale entry is seeking out some qualitative or geographic niche in the market where one will have an advantage over existing suppliers. On this we shall have more to say shortly.

How effective entry deterrence is depends also upon the characteristics of the entrant. The threat of price warfare is not apt to be credible against companies entering through upstream vertical integration. Major food packers and beverage producers, for example, have repeatedly entered or threatened to enter the "tin" can and glass bottle industries. Even if such entry touched off a price war, the integrated entrant would not be adversely affected, since it enjoys a captive market influenced only indirectly by outside price levels.[161] Because of this credible entry threat, the prices of food and beverage containers have undoubtedly been held much lower than one might have anticipated merely from observing the high levels of seller concentration in regional container markets.

Over a broad range of sizes, foreign firms entering a market through importation are appropriately analyzed as fringe producers. Like small local entrants, importers may be able to sell in sufficiently small quantities, or reduce their supply with sufficient ease in the event of adverse price reactions, that it is reasonable for them to view the import market price as a parameter. Consequently, it is difficult to deter import entry or expansion unless the domestic price is held below importers' home market costs (or under GATT antidumping rules, prices) plus freight and duties. For importers, unlike local entrants, the realization of production scale economies does not normally hinge upon selling a large quantity of output in any single target market. This observation applies with equal force to firms interpenetrating regional and local markets separated within national boundaries by moderate to high transportation costs. If anhydrous ammonia producers in Iowa set their prices above the level of production costs plus transportation from Louisiana, they risk "import entry" from Gulf Coast firms already taking more or less full advantage of scale economy opportunities and who, under more restrained pricing, would not have been viewed as obvious competitors of the Iowa firms.

Just as entrants seek strategies minimizing the price repercussions of sizable entry, they commonly attempt to exploit any advantages they might already possess to offset or minimize their absolute cost, scale economies, or product differentiation handicaps vis-à-vis already established sellers. This often means that the

153. See "A Painful Headache for Bristol-Myers?" *Business Week*, October 6, 1975, pp. 78–80; and Hauser, "Theory and Application," supra note 151, pp. 119–122.

154. Scherer et al., *Multi-Plant Operation*, supra note 87, pp. 151–152.

155. "A U.S. Canmaker Breaks a Stranglehold," *Business Week*, February 3, 1973, p. 37.

156. See Brock, *The U.S. Computer Industry*, supra note 70, pp. 114–134; and Chapters 12 and 13 infra.

157. See "Polyethylene Is Up Off the Floor," *Business Week*, November 8, 1969, p. 76; and George C. Sweeny, Jr., "The U.S. Nitrogen Industry," *Agricultural Chemicals*, February 1970.

158. Russell C. Parker, *Discount Food Pricing in Washington, D.C.*, Federal Trade Commission staff report (Washington: USGPO, March 1971).

159. Scherer et al., *Multi-Plant Operation*, supra note 87, p. 153. Foreign producers may elect to enter a market by gradually increasing the level of their exports until the market share achieved justifies the construction of a minimum efficient scale plant. This is the pattern followed by a number of Japanese firms in the United States. For a discussion of exporting companies' incentives, see Hideki Yamawaki, "Exports, Foreign Market Structure, and Profitability in Japanese and U.S. Manufacturing," *Review of Economics and Statistics*, vol. 68 (November 1986), pp. 618–627.

160. Scherer et al., *Multi-Plant Operation*, supra note 87, p. 150.

161. If outside suppliers' prices fall after upstream integration, one might say that an opportunity cost has been incurred by not taking advantage of the new, lower price. But the opportunity might not have materialized had the packer not integrated vertically.

most plausible new entrants into some market are companies already well established in another more or less closely related field.[162] Thus, when full-scale entry demands a large investment, corporations with an ample cash flow and/or good links to capital markets are more likely entrants than some totally new enterprise. The organization whose salespeople visit supermarkets weekly is more apt to enter a food product line in which it was previously inactive than is a ball bearing or shoe manufacturer. The firm with a plant that die-casts and machines refrigerator compressors is a more likely entrant into small gasoline engine production than is a computer assembler. And, more generally, a substantial proportion of the new large-scale entry into the markets of many nations since World War II has been by companies well established in the design, production, and marketing of similar products abroad — first, with U.S. corporations serving as a leading source of entrants overseas, but more recently, with European and Japanese enterprises interpenetrating the U.S. and each others' national markets as well.[163]

All this means, as Professor Bain recognized in his seminal work,[164] that there may in effect be an upward-sloping supply schedule for new entrants, with some potential entrants being deterred only if established firms set prices yielding themselves no more than the opportunity cost of their capital, while other would-be entrants face substantial entry barriers. This complicates the strategy problem of established sellers, but does not change it fundamentally.[165] To oversimplify, if there is an abundant supply of potential entrants at prices approximating existing sellers' costs and if the scale of individual entry is likely to be small, there is not much the existing industry leaders can do but take their profits and watch their market shares decline. If only one or a small number of potential entrants are as well situated as the leading incumbents, the latter may choose to let them enter the club while pursuing a strategy that deters all others. If every potential entrant faces significant barriers owing to cost or image disadvantages or credible adverse price reactions, deterrence of all entry may be attempted. Thus both the height of entry barriers generally and how they vary with respect to different potential entrants are critical.

Entry Deterrence Through Plant Location Strategy

Up to this point we have focused almost exclusively on how established sellers can deter competitive entry by charging low prices and offering correspondingly increased outputs, either before entry or after it occurs. However, as the empirical studies discussed in the preceding section reveal, price is not the only strategic variable manipulatable to impede entry and restrain rivals. We consider now some of these other possibilities, beginning with the location of plants in geographic space.

As noted earlier, new entrants often try to circumvent entry barriers by seeking market niches where they have an advantage over established producers. Geography generates one set of possible niches. When transportation costs are a significant component of total product costs, either because the goods are of low value in relation to their shipping weight or because consumers must make a special trip to receive the goods or services at their supply origin, markets tend to be localized or regionalized. Potential entrants may then seek out some local market, or set of markets, inadequately served by existing firms and locate there, deriving an advantage over incumbents by their proximity to customers. Recognizing this threat, established producers anxious to maintain their dominance must decide how to cope with it. Preempting the niches by locating plants or other outlets in them may be the answer.

To explore the theory of such preemption, let us consider an extended example kept as simple as possible without sacrificing essential features.[166] Suppose that the commodity with which we are concerned is ready-mix concrete. We assume for mathematical convenience that the market lies along a continuous straight line — for example, a road in otherwise uninhabited space — of unspecified but considerable length, and that population and hence demand is of uniform density along the road. A fixed price is quoted at each plant and buyers pay the delivery charges, amounting to twenty-five cents for each ton-mile of transportation from the plant to the demand locus.[167] Buyers' demand varies inversely and linearly with the sum of the ex-plant price plus transport charges. We assume that if this sum is zero, the total quantity demanded per month over a unit in geographic space (that is, over one linear mile) is 500 tons. If the sum rises to $40 per ton, the quantity demanded drops to zero. These assumptions permit us to determine the total demand for any monopolist plant's output.[168] Economies of scale will play an

162. In Robert Smiley's survey, 71 percent of the respondents named existing rivals in a subset of respondent product markets as the most likely potential entrants in the remaining markets. "Empirical Evidence," supra note 149, p. 177. Producers of similar products in other nations were the next most frequently cited potential entrants (13 percent). See also Howard H. Hines, "Effectiveness of 'Entry' by Already Established Firms," *Quarterly Journal of Economics*, vol. 71 (February 1957), pp. 132–150; and Richard E. Caves and Michael E. Porter, "From Entry Barriers to Mobility Barriers," *Quarterly Journal of Economics*, vol. 91 (May 1977), pp. 241–261.

163. For a diversity of views, see John H. Dunning, ed., *Economic Analysis and the Multinational Enterprise* (New York: Praeger, 1974), especially Chapters 1 through 6. See also Richard E. Caves, "Causes of Direct Investment: Foreign Firms' Shares in Canadian and United Kingdom Manufacturing Industries," *Review of Economics and Statistics*, vol. 56 (August 1974), pp. 279–293; and Paul K. Gorecki, "The Determinants of Entry," supra note 146, pp. 485–488.

164. Bain, *Barriers to New Competition*, supra note 18, pp. 8–10.

165. Compare Roger Sherman and Thomas D. Willett, "Potential Entrants Discourage Entry," *Journal of Political Economy*, vol. 75 (August 1967), pp. 400–403; Victor Goldberg and Sharon Moirao, "Limit Pricing and Potential Competition," *Journal of Political Economy*, vol. 81 (November/December 1973), pp. 1460–1466; Lionel Kalish, Jerry Hartzog, and Henry Cassidy, "The Threat of Entry with Mutually Aware Potential Entrants: Comment," *Journal of Political Economy*, vol. 86 (February 1978), pp. 147–150; Kalish et al., "Potential Competition: The Probability of Entry with Mutually Aware Potential Entrants," *Southern Economic Journal*, vol. 44 (January 1978), pp. 542–555; and Timothy H. Hannan, "Mutual Awareness Among Potential Entrants: An

Empirical Examination," *Southern Economic Journal*, vol. 47 (January 1981), pp. 805–808.

166. The analysis here closely follows Donald A. Hay, "Sequential Entry and Entry-Deterring Strategies in Spatial Competition," *Oxford Economic Papers*, vol. 28 n.s. (July 1976), pp. 240–257. Such models have a tradition dating back to Harold Hotelling, "Stability in Competition," *Economic Journal*, vol. 39 (March 1929), pp. 41–57. Newer extensions dealing with important dynamic questions include Edward C. Prescott and Michael Visscher, "Sequential Location among Firms with Foresight," *Bell Journal of Economics*, vol. 8 (Autumn 1977), pp. 378–393; Dennis R. Capozza and Robert Van Order, "A Generalized Model of Spatial Competition," *American Economic Review*, vol. 68 (December 1978), pp. 896–908; B. Curtis Eaton and Richard G. Lipsey, "The Theory of Market Pre-emption: The Persistence of Excess Capacity and Monopoly in Growing Spatial Markets," *Economica*, vol. 46 (May 1979), pp. 149–158; Ram C. Rao and David P. Rutenberg, "Preempting an Alert Rival: Strategic Timing of the First Plant by Analysis of Sophisticated Rivalry," *Bell Journal of Economics*, vol. 10 (Autumn 1979), pp. 412–428; and Damien J. Neven, "Endogenous Sequential Entry in a Spatial Model," *International Journal of Industrial Organization*, vol. 5 (December 1987), pp. 419–434.

167. This is known as ex-works or F.O.B. pricing, which will be analyzed further from a different perspective in Chapter 13.

168. The price m miles from the plant is the ex-works price P plus 0.25 m. The quantity demanded over a mile's span m miles from the plant is $q_m = 500 - 12.5P - 3.125m$. The total quantity demanded Q on both sides of the plant out to Z miles is

$$\int_0^z q_m dm = 1{,}000Z - 25ZP - 3.125Z^2.$$

important role in the analysis, so we assume a simple long-run cost function with unit costs falling continuously as output is increased. Specifically, establishing a plant is assumed to entail fixed investment outlays whose unavoidable monthly carrying cost is $60,000. The marginal cost of output is assumed constant at $10 per ton.[169]

Now suppose Firm A seeks to dominate the ready-mix business along our hypothetical linear market or road. Suppose it sets out to do so by building plants at evenly spaced intervals along the road — for example, every eighty miles, as illustrated by plant locations A_1, A_2, and A_3 in Figure 10.5, with distance calibrated from the location of plant A_2.[170] With this spacing, the monopoly profit-maximizing price at each (identical) plant is $22.50 per ton.[171] As a consumer's distance from the nearest plant increases, the total paid per ton — that is, the ex-works price plus delivery charges — rises linearly until, at the boundary between plants, it is $32.50. The quantity demanded falls accordingly with greater distance and hence a higher effective price. The total quantity demanded from any plant selling out to forty miles in both directions is 12,500 tons per month, and the total profit per plant (after the deduction of fixed costs) is $96,250 per month.

The realization that Firm A is making profits amounting to more than a third of its sales is likely to attract the interest of potential entrants. Also, and more important, by locating at the boundary between two of Firm A's plants, an entrant Firm B can take advantage of the high effective prices consumers in that vicinity pay. Suppose entry does occur at locations B_{12}, B_{23}, and similar points not shown. Suppose too that each such entrant quotes the same ex-works price as Firm A — that is, $22.50 per ton. The consumers nearer a Firm B plant than a Firm A plant will patronize Firm B, and demand will be divided equally between the A and B plants, with the boundary lying twenty miles from each plant. There will also be an overall increase in demand, since the effective price paid by customers near Firm B plants has been reduced because their concrete is now shipped a shorter distance. A typical entrant plant (for example, at B_{23}) will experience demand of 7,500 tons per month.[172] With an assumed cost function identical to Firm A's, and hence with a gross margin of $12.50 per ton and fixed costs of $60,000, the entrant plant will realize profits of $33,750. Clearly, if matters work out in this way, entry will have proved to be highly profitable, and if they can anticipate such profits, competitors will indeed enter.

Figure 10.5
Plant Locations in
Geographic Space

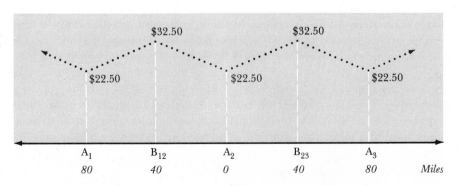

This entry is not, of course, advantageous from the original dominant Firm A's perspective. Each of its plants impacted by entry will be restricted to a selling radius of twenty miles, and like an entrant's plant, each will have profits of $33,750 instead of the $96,250 experienced before entry. Firm A might react to entry by cutting its price and trying to maintain a disproportionate territorial share, but this is costly when entrant Firm B has a delivery cost advantage on its own side of the twenty-mile boundary. Also, Firm B might respond with a matching price cut that restores an equal territorial division. Recognizing the futility of such price warfare, Firm A is likely to refrain from initiating it, and if potential entrant Firm B realizes this, the threat of price warfare will not be credible as an entry deterrent. Indeed, if Firm A accepts entry at B_{12}, B_{23}, . . . as a fait accompli, it will raise its price to $23.75, which maximizes joint profits (at $34,531 per plant) with the smaller twenty-mile plant shipping radius. In the spirit of collective profit maximization, Firm B plants will presumably follow the price lead.

To avert the loss of profit and market share resulting from competitive entry, Firm A will surely consider preempting the entrants by establishing its own plants at B_{12}, B_{23}, and similar locations. Its profits will be less (by some $27,188 per eighty miles of market supplied) than they would be if a single plant shipped forty miles in each direction, but they will be twice the $34,531 realized per eighty-mile segment if competitive entry occurred at each node. Preemption will indeed be an attractive option.

The question then arises, Will this new 40-mile plant spacing be sufficient to deter entry, or will entry now occur at the boundaries of the more closely spaced Firm A plants — for example, 20 miles from each? Figure 10.6 reassesses the situation from Firm A's revised perspective. It has plants 40 miles apart at A_2, A_{23}, A_3, and analogous locations along the market road. Its short-run profit-maximizing price at each is $23.75, and the effective price including delivery charges rises to $28.75 at the plants' shipping boundaries. Given the possibility of winning away customers served at relatively high delivered prices by locating at such boundary points as B_{223} and B_{233}, will potential entrant Firm B in fact enter? Let us assume that if it does, Firm A will not try to wage a price war, but will instead raise its price to $24.375, consistent with short-run joint profit maximization when the markets are divided equally and its plants deliver to customers no

---

169. Thus, total cost TC = 60,000 + 10Q. More complex cost functions — for example, with a U-shape — complicate the mathematics formidably.

170. In "Sequential Entry and Entry-Deterring Strategies," supra note 166, pp. 244–245 and 254, Hay implies that profits are maximized by building plants at a spacing that leaves zero demand at the boundary between plants when the profit-maximizing price is set. In the present example, this would entail a distance of 160 miles between plants, which does not in fact maximize Firm A's profits. That is, profits are $280,000 for 320 miles of market covered with 160-mile spacing and $385,000 for the same coverage with eighty-mile spacing. Hay's conclusion appears to stem from a misinterpretation of second-order conditions. Spacing of eighty miles comes within a mile of maximizing profits per mile served, assuming no threat of entry.

171. Profits per plant are (price minus marginal cost) times quantity less fixed costs. Thus, $\pi = (P - 10)(1{,}000Z - 25ZP - 3.125Z^2) - 60{,}000$. For a maximum, $d\pi/dP = 1{,}250Z - 50\,ZP - 3.125Z^2 = 0$. Solving for the profit-maximizing price P^*, we obtain $P^* = 25 - .0625Z$. With $Z = 40$ (that is, the distance to the plant boundaries), $P^* = \$22.50$. From the expression in note 168, it can be ascertained that $Q^* = 12{,}500$ tons. $\pi = (22.50 - 10)(12{,}500) - 60{,}000 = \$96{,}250$.

For a more general analysis of cases in which entry leads to price increases, see Capozza and Van Order, "A Generalized Model," supra note 166, pp. 896–908.

172. From note 168, $Q = 1{,}000 \times 20 - 25 \times 20 \times 22.50 - 3.125 \times 20^2 = 7{,}500$ tons.

Figure 10.6
Closer Plant Spacing
to Deter Entry

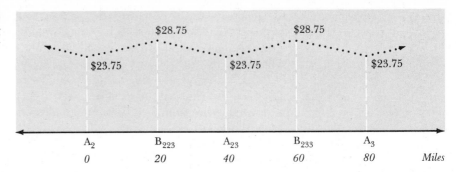

more distant than ten miles. The typical entrant plant follows suit. It too will have a shipping radius of ten miles, and output per plant will be 3,594 tons per month. The entrant plant's profit will be ($24.375 − 10.000)(3,594) − $60,000 = −$8,336. Entry will not be profitable, even though each plant of Firm A is realizing pre-entry profits of $34,531 (that is, 21 percent of sales) at forty-mile spacing.[173] Supra-normal profits persist, and yet entry is deterred.[174]

This happens for reasons analogous to those underlying the more traditional large-scale entry deterrence analysis of Figure 10.3. Economies of scale resulting from irreversible investments in plant capacity are the key. If a market niche could be entered on a very small scale at no significant unit cost disadvantage, no deterrence strategy by established sellers would be effective.[175] Economies of scale create a lumpiness problem — the entrant must either add to the market a large, low-cost lump of output for which insufficient absorption capacity exists, or it must enter on such a small scale that its unit costs are elevated above any feasible price it can charge. In other words, given Firm A's strategy of packing geographic space with plants, whatever demand curve might be left over for an entrant to capture lies at all points below the entrant's (lumpy) long-run cost curve. There is, however, an important difference between the spatial entry case and the Bain-Sylos-Modigliani case described by Figure 10.3. The latter assumed one common homogeneous product market, so the entrant added its output to the output of all existing sellers' plants and hence interacted competitively with all those plants. Under such circumstances, it is not unusual for a minimum efficient scale capacity lump to be small relative to the total output volume of established sellers. Therefore, the percentage by which output can be held below the competitive level without leaving room for a new entrant may be similarly small, all else equal. But in one-dimensional geographic space with substantial transportation costs, entrants impinge upon the markets of only two plants — one on each side of the entering plant's chosen location. An entering plant's output contribution is almost certain to be large in relation to the market served by those two plants; consequently, the difference in the revenue-cost balance before versus after an entry lump will also be considerable. Or in the more realistic case of entry into two-dimensional geographic space, the company filling the niche will impinge upon the demand of only a half dozen or so nearby established plants. Its lump will again be sizable in relation to the volume of established sellers, and so the latter may be able persistently to restrict output and hold prices above costs by an appreciable margin without leaving sufficient room for the entrant's output to be absorbed profitably.[176]

Would it be possible for established firms to accomplish the same entry deterrence result by other means — notably, by reducing price and expanding output at more widely scattered plants? To do so successfully, they must convince the potential entrant that the demand curve it will secure following entry lies at all points below its cost curve or, in the borderline case, that its demand and cost functions will be tangent. Much depends in this instance upon the assumptions made about the postentry reactions of established sellers. As we saw in the preceding section and in Chapters 6 through 8, there are many possibilities.[177] Given the delivery cost advantage a niche-filling entrant enjoys and the corresponding advantage of established sellers near their own plants, the Bain output maintenance assumption seems excessively pessimistic. A more plausible but still conservative assumption is that the established sellers will maintain their (already restrained) price in the face of new entry and that the new entrant, occupying a relatively small niche and recognizing the self-defeating nature of a price war, will charge the higher price that maximizes its profits. Then Firm A, while maintaining eighty-mile plant spacing (as in Figure 10.5) can keep potential entrant Firm B at the zero-profit level, with its postentry demand function tangent to its cost curve, by charging an ex-works price of $20.1625. The best response open to the entrant is to charge a price of $24.2625 and sell no farther than 11.8 miles from its plant.[178]

If no entry occurs as a consequence of this limit-pricing strategy, Firm A's profit per plant with plants eighty miles apart is $90,786. This is considerably more than the total of $69,062 earned from two plants spaced forty miles apart under the geographic space-packing deterrence strategy analyzed previously. However, it is arguable whether the $20.1625 limit pricing strategy is as credible as the plant proliferation strategy. Should entry occur despite the $20.1625 price, Firm A's profits will fall to $56,870 — less than under the forty-mile space-packing strategy. They will be even lower if Firm B can expand its selling radius beyond 11.8 miles — for example, by threatening a price war if Firm A matches its price

173. Note that if Firm B did enter, Firm A's plants would experience similar losses owing to the decrease in sales volume.

174. The entrant might alternatively try to enter with an ex-works price higher than the existing firm's, letting Firm A maintain its preentry price and retain more than an equal share of the market between two plants. Although such a strategy might work when demand is relatively price inelastic and shipping costs are very high, it does not make sense at this stage in the present example. Thus, if the entrant charges a price of $26 per ton while Firm A charges $24.375, the entrant's shipping radius is cut to 6.75 miles, output falls to 2,220 tons, and the monthly loss increases to $24,478.

Another possibility is for the entrant to enter immediately adjacent to a Firm A plant — for example, at location A_{23} — and attempt to share the market from there. But at best this gives the entrant no larger sales volume than with B_{223} or B_{233} entry, and indeed, sales must be smaller because less will be demanded by customers in the B_{223} or B_{233} vicinity owing to higher delivery charges. Therefore, profits are lower with side-by-side entry.

175. Deterrence also depends upon the degree to which plant investments constitute sunk costs. If it were feasible for incumbents to shut down plants, the presence of those plants cannot be a barrier to entry. Kenneth L. Judd, "Credible Spatial Preemption," *Rand Journal of Economics*, vol. 16 (Summer 1985), pp. 153–166.

176. See B. Curtis Eaton and Richard G. Lipsey, "The Non-Uniqueness of Equilibrium in the Löschian Location Model," *American Economic Review*, vol. 66 (March 1976), pp. 71–93.

177. For a discussion of the special difficulties associated with attempting to characterize the nature of price rivalry where transportation costs are important, see M. L. Greenhut and H. Ohta, "Spatial Configurations and Competitive Equilibrium," *Weltwirtschaftliches Archiv*, vol. 109 (March 1973), pp. 87–104; C. d'Aspremont, J. Jaskold-Gabszewicz, and J. F. Thisse, "On Hotelling's 'Stability in Competition,' " *Econometrica*, vol. 47 (September 1979), pp. 1145–1150; and Simon Anderson, "Spatial Competition and Price Leadership," *International Journal of Industrial Organization*, vol. 5 (December 1987), pp. 369–398.

178. This result is obtained by solving simultaneously the entrant's normal price equation $P^* = 25 - .0625 Z$ and the entrant's profit function set equal to zero. The solution involves a third-degree polynomial.

reductions. Given Firm B's unsought but now unavoidable competition on its flanks, it would be both easy and tempting for Firm A to raise its price and accept a more equal division of the market with Firm B. If Firm B recognizes this, its entry will not be deterred by Firm A's low $20.1625 price. In contrast, once Firm A has packed the market with plants at forty-mile spacing, withdrawing — that is, shutting down the plants — is likely to be quite costly and hence improbable. Because plants have a permanence that prices cannot match, the strategy of entry deterrence by packing geographic space with plants is more credible than a strategy of quoting a low price and offering a correspondingly expanded supply. Even though the latter strategy is more profitable as long as the bluff is not called, the plant proliferation strategy may well be adopted for its superior credibility.

Limit pricing combined with wider spacing of plants is not unambiguously more profitable than entry deterrence through close spacing with prices set at short-run profit-maximizing levels. The forty-mile spacing of Figure 10.6 perpetrates some overkill, imposing upon in-between entrants $8,336 losses rather than the infinitesimal losses assumed sufficient for deterrence under limit pricing with eighty-mile spacing. If we change our assumptions to let fixed costs be only $52,000 instead of $60,000, the entrant between plants spaced forty miles apart loses $340. Two Firm A plants spaced forty miles apart and deterring entry under this lower fixed-cost variant realize combined profits of $85,063. A single eighty-mile plant practicing optimal limit pricing earns $94,675 covering the same market segment. Thus, even without overkill, limit pricing is somewhat more profitable — if it succeeds. However, analysis of additional entry deterrence scenarios with different parameters revealed that plant proliferation could, under some conditions, be more profitable than limit pricing. This was more likely, the higher transport costs were in relation to other costs and to the ex-works price.

The relative importance of plant proliferation versus limit pricing strategies is illuminated by a sprinkling of case study research. An interview study of plant size and location decisions in twelve industries across six nations revealed by far the strongest emphasis on geographic space packing as an entry-deterring strategy in the cement industry.[179] Transport costs for cement in 1963 averaged forty-five cents per dollar of ex-works product value on a representative 350-mile haul.[180] However, a statistical study of U.S. cement markets found no evidence of successful preemption in plant locations, above-normal economic profits, or dissipation of profits through excessive investment in plant capacity.[181] On the other hand, Douglas West detected evidence of locational clustering consistent with preemption (and beyond the level explicable by economizing on distribution costs) among Vancouver's retail food supermarket stores.[182]

The question remains, How does entry deterrence through geographic niche filling affect overall economic performance? And, in particular, Is it more or less desirable than a limit pricing approach? Not surprisingly, the answer depends upon the level of pricing that accompanies the space packing strategy.[183] Where the cost penalty for producing below minimum efficient scale is particularly great, encouraging entry to the point where no firm makes positive profits yields lower combined consumers' plus producers' surplus than the case where incumbents combine Cournot pricing with entry-deterring space packing.[184] Would less intensive space packing, combined with a limit pricing approach, be more desirable? Several considerations are relevant. The proliferation of smaller plants associated with a pure space-packing strategy is likely to entail significant scale economy sacrifices and hence higher production costs, but transportation costs are reduced. In our original (that is, $60,000 fixed cost) example, combined average production plus delivery costs (the latter borne by customers) are $21.20 per ton with the forty-mile spacing deterrence strategy, compared to $18.60 with eighty-mile spacing and a limit price of $20.1625.[185] Second, with the limit pricing strategy, consumers near Firm A's more widely spaced plants benefit from lower delivered prices; and although the most distant customers pay more than they would if entry were deterred by geographic space packing, they cannot be really badly treated under limit pricing or deterrence will fail. In fact, total consumers' surplus is clearly higher under the eighty-mile spacing limit pricing strategy, given the assumptions of our example.[186] Third, to the extent that the limit pricing strategy is less credible as a deterrent, fresh competition is more apt to develop, bringing

179. Scherer et al., *Multi-Plant Operation*, supra note 87, pp. 152–153. Second but far behind in its emphasis on space packing was the glass bottle industry, with transport costs averaging ten cents per dollar of product value on a 350-mile haul. In none of the other ten industries, all with lower transport cost indices, was plant proliferation by itself viewed as an effective deterrent strategy.

180. Scherer et al., *Multi-Plant Operation*, p. 90.

181. Ronald N. Johnson and Allen Parkman, "Spatial Monopoly, Non-Zero Profits and Entry Deterrence: The Case of Cement," *Review of Economics and Statistics*, vol. 65 (August 1983), pp. 431–439.

182. Douglas S. West, "Testing for Market Preemption Using Sequential Location Data," *Bell Journal of Economics*, vol. 12 (Spring 1981), pp. 129–143; and *idem*, "Tests of Two Locational Implications of a Theory of Market Pre-Emption," *Canadian Journal of Economics*, vol. 14 (May 1981), pp. 313–326.

183. Dennis R. Capozza and Robert Van Order, "Unique Equilibria, Pure Profits, and Efficiency in Location Models," *American Economic Review*, vol. 70 (December 1980), pp. 1046–1053; and Klaus Schöler, "The Welfare Effects of Spatial Competition under Sequential Market Entry," *Southern Economic Journal*, vol. 52 (July 1985), pp. 265–273.

184. Capozza and Van Order, "Unique Equilibria," pp. 1051–1052.

185. With more modest scale economies than assumed here, the comparison is apt to be closer. There is reason to believe that combined unit production plus transportation cost curves tend to be rather flat over a broad range. See Figure 4.4, p. 108 supra; and Scherer et al., *Multi-Plant Operation*, supra note 87, pp. 368–381.

In a simulation analysis that ignores production costs, J. M. A. Gee found that sequential entry into imperfectly competitive spatial markets leads to transportation costs substantially above those associated with pure (but unrealizable) competition. "A Model of Location and Industry Efficiency with Free Entry," *Quarterly Journal of Economics*, vol. 90 (November 1976), pp. 557–574. On the generality of Gee's findings, see the discussion in the *Quarterly Journal of Economics*, vol. 93 (August 1979), pp. 447–454.

186. At any given delivery distance m, consumers' surplus with linear demand is one-half the difference between the demand function's delivered price intercept less the sum of F.O.B. price plus delivery cost times the quantity demanded. Thus, let:

(1) $$q_m = a - b(P + tm),$$

where in our example, $a = 500$, $b = 12.5$, and $t = 0.25$. Consumers' surplus at m is:

(2) $$CS_m = 1/2 q_m[a/b - (P + tm)].$$

Substituting (1) into (2), we obtain:

(3) $$CS_m = 1/2(bt^2m^2 + bP^2 + 2tbPm - 2aP - 2atm + a^2/b).$$

This is the consumers' surplus at a point in space m. Consumers' surplus for a plant selling Z miles in each direction is $2\int_0^Z CS_m dm$. Integrating by parts, we obtain:

(4) $$CS_{2z} = \frac{bt^2 Z^2}{3} + bP^2Z + tbPZ^2 - 2aPZ - atZ^2 + (a^2/b)Z,$$

which has been known to make stoics weep! However, substituting in $a = 500$, $b = 12.5$, and $t = 0.25$, we have:

(5) $$CS_{2z} = 0.2604\, Z^3 + 12.5\, P^2Z + 3.125\, PZ^2 - 10,000\, PZ - 125\, Z^2 + 20,000.$$

This is readily solved for the appropriate values of Z and P. Under limit pricing, $Z = 40$ and $P = 20.1625. Total consumers' surplus in serving a space eighty miles wide is $114,240. With entry deterrence through geographic space packing, $Z = 20$ and $P = 23.75. Recalling that it takes two plants to cover an eighty-mile space, we find consumers' surplus to be $95,570.

It is uncertain how general this result is. Even though there is a simple linear relationship between P and Z in the short-run profit-maximizing (that is, non-limit pricing) case, the mathematics of consumers' surplus comparisons appear intractable, especially when a comparison is to be made with the limit pricing conditions, introducing an additional third-degree polynomial. The most that can be said is that an attempt was made to select parameters representative of situations with fairly high transportation costs. Extensive computer simulation would undoubtedly yield interesting insights.

with it the possibility (although, in view of the oligopolistic interdependence among adjacent sellers, not a certainty) of invigorated price competition. Thus, it is doubtful whether an entry deterrence strategy emphasizing geographic space packing is as beneficial to society as strategies that involve keeping prices low and outputs high.

Entry Deterrence Through Product Differentiation

In addition to seeking unfilled niches in geographic space, would-be entrants often look for unfilled product design or brand image niches to facilitate their entry. Consumers' desire for products of diverse characteristics is in this respect analogous to their desire to buy from geographically proximate suppliers.[187] The buyer of wine, for instance, may be interested in dryness, tartness, fruitiness, alcohol content, prestige, and diverse other attributes as well as price. Each of these can be mapped as a dimension in N-dimensional product characteristics space, just as the set of possible plant locations is mapped in two-dimensional geographic space. A product with specific characteristics is in effect located at a point in that N-space. Products with similar characteristics are located near one another, while products with quite different characteristics are located far apart, appealing to different consumers or different facets of a given consumer's tastes. The loss of utility consumers experience from having to consume products located some distance from their ideal bundle of desired characteristics is analogous to the delivery costs consumers must pay when buying from geographically distant plants. A firm attempting to gain a product differentiation advantage to facilitate its entry will seek some unfilled or poorly filled locus in product characteristics space, just as companies in industries with high transport costs gravitate toward locations with no nearby competing plant. To deter entrants pursuing this product niche-filling strategy, established sellers may seek to pack product characteristics space with a sufficient diversity of product variants so that no room for profitable new entry remains. The analogy to geographic space packing is quite close, and so the formal logic developed in the previous section can be applied with little modification to analyze what appears to be an important aspect of real-world firms' entry deterrence strategy.

Although economists were slow to recognize this point, entrepreneurs were not. A key 1921 strategy decision of the reorganized General Motors Corporation was to establish a complete spectrum of automobile offerings. As its chairman at the time, Alfred Sloan, later described the move:

It seemed to me that the intelligent approach would be to have a car at every price position, just the same as a general conducting a campaign wants to have an army at every point he is likely to be attacked. We had too many cars in some places and no cars in other places. One of the first things we did was to develop a line of products that met competition in the various positions in which competition was offered.[188]

An unusually clear illustration of the product space-packing strategy is found in the history of the government-owned Swedish Tobacco Company.[189] Until 1961, the company had a legal monopoly over cigarette production and distribution in Sweden. Then its control over distribution was terminated, and non-Swedish firms began to capture a rapidly growing market share with cigarettes imported duty-free from other European Free Trade Association nations. An important component of Swedish Tobacco's effort to contain this entry threat was to identify through marketing research and then fill in every significant point in the cigarette taste and image spectrum. Between 1961 and 1969 it moved from having twelve brands to twenty-five, redesigned its packages, and increased its advertising roughly twelvefold. The strategy was apparently successful, for Swedish Tobacco managed to maintain a market share on the order of 80 percent.

As in the case of geographic space packing, the lumpiness associated with irreversible investments in plant capacity and (in this case) new product varieties and the resulting economies of scale are what makes product variety proliferation a profitable entry deterrence strategy. Developing a new product variety costs a more or less fixed sum, and there may also be product-specific economies of scale in production. Perhaps even more important, threshold effects in advertising and other sales promotional methods mean that a sizable lump must be invested in launching a new product into a branded consumer goods market.[190] If a new entrant comes in with too small a launching campaign, the effort may be ineffective, or the sales gained insufficient to cover high unit development and production costs. If, on the other hand, established sellers can "crowd" product characteristics space densely enough, the amount of demand left over for any differentiated new brand will be too small to permit entrants to cover the costs of a full-scale launching campaign. As in geographic space, the number of existing product varieties or brands upon which a new entrant impinges may be small, and so the size of the entry lump is large in relation to the volume of demand with which it interacts competitively. Because of this lumpiness, established products may be able to command continuing supra-normal profits while expected profits for an additional new product remain negative.[191]

Assuming a market in which differentiation is sufficiently strong that new products impinge only upon the sales of immediately adjacent brands and assuming also price-matching behavior on the part of entrants, Richard Schmalensee

187. The pioneer in utilizing the analogy between geographic and product characteristics space was Hotelling, "Stability in Competition," supra note 166. The notion of characteristics space was significantly extended by Kelvin Lancaster in "A New Approach to Consumer Theory," *Journal of Political Economy*, vol. 74 (April 1966), pp. 132–157, and in numerous subsequent works by him. For an admirable survey plus extensions of direct relevance to the analysis here, see Richard Schmalensee, "Entry Deterrence in the Ready-to-Eat Breakfast Cereal Industry," *Bell Journal of Economics*, vol. 9 (Autumn 1978), pp. 305–327. More recent variations on this approach include Steven C. Salop, "Monopolistic Competition with Outside Goods," *Bell Journal of Economics*, vol. 10 (Spring 1979), pp. 141–156; W. J. Lane, "Product Differentiation in a Market with Endogenous Sequential Entry," *Bell Journal of Economics*, vol. 11 (Spring 1980), pp. 237–260; Takasi Omori and George Yarrow, "Product Diversification, Entry Prevention and Limit Pricing," *Bell Journal of Economics*, vol. 13 (Spring 1982), pp. 242–248; Kenneth L. Judd, "Credible Spatial Preemption," supra note 175, pp. 153–166; and Neven, "Endogenous

Sequential Entry," supra note 166, pp. 419–434.

188. Quoted in Alfred D. Chandler, Jr., *Strategy and Structure: Chapters in the History of the American Industrial Enterprise* (Cambridge: MIT Press, 1962), p. 143.

189. Cf. Scherer et al., *Multi-Plant Operation*, supra note 87, p. 157.

190. The size of the lump can to some extent be influenced by the conduct of established sellers. By advertising more heavily, they increase "media clutter," above which entrants can be heard only by advertising at a similarly intensified level. See John C. Hilke and Philip B. Nelson, "Noisy Advertising and the Predation Rule in Antitrust Analysis," *American Economic Review*, vol. 74 (May 1984), pp. 367–371; and Charles F. Mason, "Predation by Noisy Advertising," *Review of Industrial Organization*, vol. 3 (1987), pp. 78–92.

191. See Schmalensee, "Entry Deterrence," supra note 187, who develops the product space-packing and lumpiness logic to explain the high sustained profitability of ready-to-eat cereal brands.

has shown that limit pricing is less profitable than brand proliferation as a deterrence strategy.[192] He observes too that moving products in characteristics space, like moving plants in geographic space, is costly; and with "backing off" relatively unlikely,[193] the space-packing strategy deters sizable entry more credibly than limit pricing. Thus, the use of a brand proliferation strategy appears plausible, especially in consumer goods lines amenable to strong product differentiation.

Whether society is well served when entry is deterred in this way is arguable. To the extent that tastes are highly varied, the proliferation of product varieties adds to consumers' utility. But if there are persistent product-specific scale economies in production, it also increases production costs. And perhaps more important in consumer goods fields, advertising and other marketing costs are likely to escalate. How these benefits and costs balance out is a difficult question we must defer for more systematic analysis in Chapter 16. To anticipate a part of our conclusions, when most or all sellers forgo price competition and emphasize the proliferation of high-priced product variants, more product variety is apt to materialize than the amount that maximizes social welfare.

Other product differentiation barriers to entry of a less complex nature might also permit established firms to hold prices above their own costs without attracting new entrants or fringe rival expansion. It is sometimes argued that through heavy advertising, established firms can build up consumer loyalty to their products, and that the loyalty created in this way makes entry difficult for newcomers.[194] Deferring to Chapter 16 the question of whether advertising actually does on balance cement loyalties, this view is too simple unless it is accompanied by an explanation of why new entrants cannot play the loyalty-winning game on equal terms. As we have seen in Chapter 4 and reiterated here, it may be necessary to achieve a certain minimum threshold level of advertising or other promotional activity to have much effect on consumer behavior. The firm with a large market share can spread the cost of reaching that threshold over a larger sales volume than a small (possibly new) rival. The smaller enterprise might aspire to reach a size at which it suffers no such unit promotional cost disadvantage. However, the effort may take a long time, or it may not be feasible at all if high unit advertising costs, the failure to realize production scale economies, and capital market access difficulties interact with the pursuit of a limit pricing strategy or space-packing strategy by established firms to retard the entrant's attainable growth.[195]

Paradoxically, the threat of entry may lead incumbents to underinvest in advertising relative to the joint profit-maximizing level. To the extent that heavy advertising cements customer loyalties, it reduces the willingness of incumbents to allow prices to fall following entry. Lower advertising outlays might alternatively raise the credibility of aggressive price cutting following entry.[196] On the other hand, heavy advertising may alter the distribution of customers in characteristics space, inclining consumers toward existing brands and narrowing the remaining niches available to potential entrants. This can occur if incumbents have an advantage in changing consumers' perceptions of how products meet their tastes, and hence the location of consumers in product characteristics space.

A final reason why new entrants may be disadvantaged is the tendency for history to endow companies with different promotional cost-sales response functions. Pioneering brands often possess significant advantages over subsequent entries.[197] There may be no practical promotional strategy by which a latecomer can acquire a product image equivalent to the image of the firm that pioneered the field, or that had the good luck to capture consumers' imagination with a unique advertising campaign. With an inferior image, new entrants and fringe firms may be condemned more or less permanently to receiving prices lower than those of well-established firms and/or spending more on promotion per dollar of sales to cultivate and maintain whatever brand loyalty they enjoy. In a statistical study of 103 large company operating units, Robert Buzzell and Paul Ferris found that having been the pioneer in a consumer goods market permitted average advertising and sales promotion cost savings amounting to 1.45 percent of sales relative to early nonpioneer suppliers, all else being equal.[198] Late entrants, on the other hand, had to spend 2.12 cents per sales dollar *more* on promotion than early, but not first, suppliers. With promotional cost and price advantages, well-established sellers may indeed find it profitable to set their prices at levels that impede the entry and growth of fringe rivals.

Other Dynamic Influences Affecting Price

A few further dynamic considerations affecting pricing decisions must be mentioned to round out the picture. One is the whole set of influences associated with public opinion and the threat of government intervention. Clear and blatant exploitation of monopoly power leads to a bad press, which most business managers prefer to avoid. The executive concerned about a place in the history books can scarcely ignore the fact that William H. Vanderbilt is remembered more for his "the public be damned" outburst (in 1883) than for his substantial entrepreneurial and philanthropic accomplishments. Persistently high prices and profits may also provoke direct government intervention in the form of price controls or antitrust proceedings. Robert Feinberg reports that most of the effect of antitrust actions in reducing prices occurred soon after the onset of an investigation, rather than at the

192. Schmalensee, "Entry Deterrence," pp. 311–313 and 323–324. Whether profit-maximizing incumbents will combine limit pricing with brand proliferation depends upon the extent of scale economies. See Omori and Yarrow, "Product Diversification," supra note 187.

193. On this point, see Judd, "Credible Spatial Preemption," supra note 175, pp. 153–168.

194. For an early conceptualization of this view, see Oliver E. Williamson, "Selling Expense as a Barrier to Entry," *Quarterly Journal of Economics*, vol. 77 (February 1963), pp. 112–128. The most comprehensive treatment is by William S. Comanor and Thomas A. Wilson, *Advertising and Market Power* (Cambridge: Harvard University Press, 1974).

195. See A. Michael Spence, "Notes on Advertising, Economies of Scale, and Entry Barriers," *Quarterly Journal of Economics*, vol. 95 (November 1980), pp. 493–507.

196. See Richard Schmalensee, "Advertising and Entry Deterrence: An Exploratory Model," *Journal of Political Economy*, vol. 91 (August 1983), pp. 636–653. For an alternative model in which lower advertising expenditures are associated with higher entry barriers, see John Cubbin, "Advertising and the Theory of Entry Barriers," *Economica*, vol. 48 (August 1981), pp. 289–298.

197. Richard Schmalensee, "Product Differentiation Advantages of Pioneering Brands," *American Economic Review*, vol. 72 (June 1982), pp. 349–365; and Cecilia A. Conrad, "The Advantage of Being First and Competition Between Firms," *International Journal of Industrial Organization*, vol. 1 (December 1983), pp. 353–364. See also Chapter 16 *infra*.

198. Robert D. Buzzell and Paul W. Farris, "Marketing Costs in Consumer Goods Industries," in Hans B. Thorelli, ed., *Strategy + Structure = Performance* (Bloomington: Indiana University Press, 1977), pp. 128–129.

time an indictment was brought or the case tried.[199] A study of the bread industry found that the negative effect of antitrust prosecutions on prices extended beyond the geographic markets in which cases were brought.[200] The desire to maintain a favorable public image and fear of government intervention undoubtedly induce some companies to avoid squeezing all they can out of a monopolistic market position.

Concern about legal action or other government intervention may sometimes work in the opposite direction, dissuading firms from cutting prices. Rivals injured when a more efficient firm prices below their costs may charge the firm with predatory behavior. Although recent developments in antitrust law (considered further in Chapter 12) make it hard for aggrieved rivals to win such cases — at least, as long as the predator is pricing above its own marginal cost — a firm seeking the quiet life will avoid price cuts that squeeze rivals too tightly. Similarly, importing firms may hesitate to take full advantage of favorable exchange rate swings out of concern that rapid market share growth at the expense of domestic firms may lead to the imposition of tariffs or quotas.

Uncertainty also affects pricing in a variety of ways. Output may be expanded beyond the level at which short-run profits are maximized in order to cement customer relations and ensure room for maneuvering, should some adverse contingency materialize in the future. On such aspects of dynamic strategy economic theory has little to contribute; its significance is an empirical question. However, theoretical analysis provides some interesting insights into the links among demand uncertainty, inventory policy, and pricing behavior.

A firm in a purely competitive market can by definition sell as much output as it wishes at the ruling market price. Uncertainty pertains only to the price that will prevail. This is not so for the firm possessing monopoly power. At any given quoted price, the monopolistic firm will be able to sell more if demand turns out to be strong than if it is weak. Unless production to order is practical, the firm must decide how much to produce before it knows how strong demand will be. If it produces too much, it will be left holding a large inventory, incurring higher storage, capital, and possibly obsolescence costs, or else it will have to dispose of its surplus at distress prices. If it produces too little, it will lose sales and perhaps drive disappointed customers permanently into the arms of rival sellers. It must decide then upon an optimal price, production, and inventory policy to make the best of demand uncertainties.

Do price and output decisions differ under these conditions from what they would be in a world of certainty? Pioneering mathematical analyses by Mills, Karlin and Carr suggest that they do, although numerical simulation studies by Nevins show that under plausible assumptions the deviations are not very large.[201]

Unfortunately, few sweeping generalizations are possible. The output of an enterprise with a downward-sloping demand function may be either greater or less under uncertainty than under certainty; it depends upon the amount and character of the uncertainties faced, the shapes of cost and demand functions, the costs and risks of maintaining an inventory position, the costs of adjusting production, and whether the firm is risk neutral or risk averse. One fairly general result relates inventory policy to market structure. When errors in predicting demand are symmetrically distributed about their mean, the monopolistic firm will tend to produce and hold more output for inventory (reducing the probability of shortages and dissatisfied customers), the higher is the ratio of price to marginal cost.[202] This is so because the more price exceeds marginal cost, the more profitable it is to satisfy an extra unit of demand from inventory in times of peak demand, amply repaying inventory holding costs. This is one sense in which monopoly power confers some compensating benefits. To keep the phenomenon in perspective, it should be noted that monopolistic firms will never find it optimal to produce an output that makes marginal cost exceed price — for example, more than the competitive output — merely to hedge against demand uncertainties.[203]

The dependence of price upon inventory behavior is even more complex. As we have seen in Chapter 7, the main function of inventory policy in oligopoly may be to support the price at a value chosen for strategic reasons, and not to maximize profits in any narrower sense. But if we limit our attention to profit maximization efforts that ignore oligopolistic interdependence, mathematical studies of optimal inventory policy become relevant. Mills, Karlin, and Carr demonstrated that when demand is uncertain, only by coincidence will firms with monopoly power set their price at the same value as that which maximizes profit under uncertainty. Nevins clarified this conclusion by showing that the certainty and uncertainty pricing strategies will be identical, ceteris paribus, in the unlikely event of zero time discount rates and inventory carrying costs. Excluding this case, producers must make a complicated tradeoff decision balancing the effects of price changes on expected demand against the effects of price and inventory variations on the probability of costly shortages or surplus production. The price resulting from this tradeoff may be above or below the price that would be set by a monopolist under certainty; it depends mainly upon the shape of the marginal cost function and the character of the demand uncertainties, for example, whether the error distribution is additive or multiplicative relative to mean expected demand.[204] In the case of rising short-run marginal costs, which is most typical of real-world conditions when production is not greatly below capacity, the optimal price under uncertainty

199. Robert M. Feinberg, "The Timing of Antitrust Effects on Pricing," *Applied Economics*, vol. 16 (June 1984), pp. 397–409.
200. Michael K. Block, F. C. Nold, and J. G. Sidak, "The Deterrent Effect of Antitrust Enforcement," *Journal of Political Economy*, vol. 89 (June 1981), pp. 429–445. See also Robert M. Feinberg, "Antitrust Enforcement and Subsequent Price Behavior," *Review of Economics and Statistics*, vol. 62 (November 1980), pp. 609–612.
201. Edwin S. Mills, "Uncertainty and Price Theory," *Quarterly Journal of Economics*, vol. 59 (February 1959), pp. 116–130; idem, *Price, Output and Inventory Policy* (New York: Wiley, 1962), Chapters 5 through 7; Samuel Karlin and Charles Carr, "Prices and Optimal Inventory Policy," in Kenneth Arrow et al., eds., *Studies in Applied Probability and Management Science* (Stanford: Stanford University Press, 1962), pp. 159–172; and Arthur J. Nevins, "Some Effects of Uncertainty: Simulation of a Model of Price,"

Quarterly Journal of Economics, vol. 80 (February 1966), pp. 73–87. For extensions raising doubts about the generality of certain earlier results, see Edward Zabel, "Monopoly and Uncertainty," *Review of Economic Studies*, vol. 37 (April 1970), pp. 205–219; and Robert S. Pindyck, "Adjustment Costs, Uncertainty, and the Behavior of the Firm," *American Economic Review*, vol. 72 (June 1982), pp. 415–427.
202. Mills, "Uncertainty and Price Theory," pp. 121–122.
203. Mills, *Price, Output, and Inventory Policy*, supra note 201, p. 90.
204. When inventory carry-overs are infeasible, another critical variable is whether the firm must determine its price, its output, or both before actual demand is known. See Hayne E. Leland, "Theory of the Firm Facing Unknown Demand," *American Economic Review*, vol. 62 (June 1972), p. 289.

tends to be less than the certainty price. At the same time, however, production is likely to be restricted so that out-of-stock situations occur more frequently than surpluses.

Much more research on the implications of demand uncertainty for business pricing behavior remains to be done. The theory can be extended, and perhaps more important, empirical studies of actual inventory and price policies and their effects are needed. Among other things, difficult welfare problems arise when demand is inadequately satisfied, not because of high monopoly prices, but because production and inventory levels are inadequate to meet peak demands at the (possibly restrained) prices set.[205] Much depends then upon the nonprice rationing system adopted — that is, to what extent supplies go to high, as compared to low, reservation price consumers. The more the latter are favored over the former, the larger the resource misallocation losses will be. On what actually happens when rationing of this sort occurs, we know all too little.

Conclusion

We concluded from our discussion of oligopoly pricing in Chapters 6 through 8 that when sellers are few in number, there are incentives for them to recognize their interdependence and to cooperate in policies that lead toward maximum group profits. Institutions such as outright collusion, price leadership, pricing by rules of thumb, and focal point pricing facilitate the maintenance of prices above the competitive level. However, we observed also that there are important limits on the ability of monopolists and oligopolists to hold prices at highly profitable levels. Oligopolistic coordination may break down owing to conflicts over the most suitable price, heterogeneity of products, the pressure of under-absorbed fixed costs, secret price cutting, or simple cussedness on the part of some maverick producer. To this list we now add long-run substitution and the threat or actuality of entry by new competitors. Both place a ceiling — sometimes a low one — on producers' pricing discretion.

The performance implications of this complicated picture are themselves complex. It is clear that under conditions favorable to the exercise of monopoly power, prices may be held substantially above competitive levels for extended periods of time. Still this result does not follow automatically from the mere existence of a concentrated market structure. Prices often hover closer to cost than one would predict from an analysis that takes into account only the fewness of sellers, ignoring coordination obstacles and long-run constraints. These more subtle structural and behavioral variables help explain why pricing performance in modern industrial markets has on the whole been fairly satisfactory despite significant departures from the structural ideal of pure economic theory.

205. Cf. Dennis W. Carlton, "Uncertainty, Production Lags, and Pricing," *American Economic Review*, vol. 67 (February 1977), pp. 246–247.

Market Structure and Performance: Empirical Appraisal

Recent years have seen a dramatic expansion in the range and intensity of empirical industrial organization research. The primary focus has remained the same: evaluating the impact of market structure on the pricing behavior of firms.[1] Improvements in the quality of data and statistical techniques have significantly altered our appraisal of the relevant theory. In this chapter, we survey the premises, methodology, results, and unresolved puzzles of economists' attempts to confront theory with the statistical evidence on industrial performance.

As we observed in Chapter 1, the paradigm traditionally employed by industrial organization economists holds that structure affects conduct, which in turn determines ultimate economic performance. Within this paradigm, the classic testable hypothesis has been that, given the pricing behavior expected under monopoly or tight oligopoly, the average profit return realized by firms in highly concentrated industries will tend to be significantly higher than that of firms in less concentrated oligopolies or atomistically structured industries. The pioneering test of this hypothesis came in two studies by Joe Bain.[2] In the first, he found that in manufacturing industries with eight-firm concentration ratios of 70 or higher, the average profit rate (12.1 percent of the largest firms' stockholders' equity) was significantly greater than the 6.9 percent rate for industries with seller concentration ratios below 70 percent. In the second, he found more generally that industry profitability is significantly correlated with the concentration ratio and a subjectively estimated categorization of the height of barriers to new entry. Since then, several hundred studies (varying widely in statistical sophistication) in this Bainian tradition have been carried out. Most found that industry profits, variously measured, rise with industry concentration, variously measured. The strength of this finding contributed in part to a reduction of interest in empirical industrial organization research. Why bother, when the main question has been answered?

However, recent work has demonstrated that most, if not all, of the correlation between profitability and concentration found by Bain and his descendants (at least for the United States) was almost surely spurious—the result of aggregating a positive relationship between sellers' market shares and profitability to the industry level. This finding complicates the evaluation of the structure-conduct-performance paradigm, because, as we will see below, it is consistent with several alternative explanations of firm behavior and industrial performance.

The importance of market share was confirmed with the availability of data at the line of business level, that is, data segmenting company operations by industry. These and other new data sets, the development of new game-theoretic models of oligopoly behavior (and hence, the appearance of new testable hypotheses), and the availability of improved statistical techniques (and computer programs for implementing them) have prompted renewed interest in empirical

---

1. Of course, industrial performance has many dimensions, including allocative efficiency, technical efficiency of resource use, equity of the income distribution, speed of technological innovation, and a broad range of social and political concerns. In this chapter we focus primarily on the first two: on the degree to which market structure, by influencing pricing behavior, leads to allocative and resource use inefficiency. We discuss the interaction of market structure and technological innovation in Chapter

17 and review studies of the impact of market structure on income distribution and the remaining dimensions of performance in Chapter 18.

2. Joe S. Bain, "Relation of Profit Rate to Industry Concentration: American Manufacturing, 1936–1940," *Quarterly Journal of Economics*, vol. 65 (August 1951), pp. 293–324; and *Barriers to New Competition* (Cambridge: Harvard University Press, 1956).

industrial organization research. We cannot possibly do justice to all the studies here, and such an attempt would be redundant, since several convenient surveys exist.[3] What we shall do instead is focus on the main substantive and methodological issues and attempt to convey what is known and still unknown as a result of the accumulated research.

Basic Paradigm

Let us begin with first principles. It is hypothesized that certain market structures are conducive to monopolistic conduct — that is, the raising of price above costs. Without detailed observations over time, this conduct in itself may be difficult to analyze quantitatively, but its consequences are believed to be observable in profit and price data. We saw in Chapter 6 that the ability of Firm i to elevate price above marginal cost, captured by the Lerner index,[4] depends upon the industry price elasticity of demand (e), the firm's market share (s_i), and the firm's conjectural variation (dQ_i/dq_i) — its assumption about how rivals will respond to changes in its production level:[5]

$$(11.1) \qquad \frac{(P - MC_i)}{P} = \frac{s_i}{e}(1 + dQ_i/dq_i).$$

Depending upon conduct[6] — that is, depending upon the value of the conjectural variation — price can range anywhere between the level that would prevail under conditions of pure competition $(P = MC_i)$[7] and the level that would be chosen by a profit-maximizing monopolist: $(P - MC_i)/P = 1/e$. The conjectural variation acts as an index of the extent of coordination among industry members: the more positive the firms' conjectural variations, the more closely the industry will approximate a joint profit-maximizing cartel. The resulting divergence between price and marginal cost, we learned in Chapter 2, underlies the tendency for resources to be misallocated when some prices are set monopolistically. Theoretical analysis suggests that the most important structural variables that could influence conduct are seller concentration and barriers to entry for the industry (j) in which Firm i operates. Thus,

$$(11.2) \qquad dQ_i/dq_i = f_1(C_j, B_j, X_{ij}),$$

where C_j measures seller concentration in industry j, B_j denotes a set of entry barrier measures, and X_{ij} represents other industry or firm characteristics affecting Firm i's conjectural variation. Theory offers little insight into the precise functional form of f_1. Even if it did, we are rarely able to observe the Lerner index, elasticity of demand, and the component measures of f_1 with great precision.

In practice, researchers estimate a statistical model of the following form:

$$(11.3) \qquad \pi_i = f_2(s_i, C_j, B_j, X_{ij}, OS_{ij}, D_j, \epsilon_i),$$

where π_i is a measure of profitability correlated with Firm i's unobserved Lerner Index, OS_{ij} denotes other structural characteristics that explain the discrepancy between π_i and the Lerner index, D_j is a set of measures characterizing the state of demand, and ϵ_i is an error term reflecting a host of unmeasured factors and the discrepancy between f_2 and the true (but unknown) function relating π_i to the other variables. In many studies, the data were aggregated to the industry level, so the statistical model becomes

$$(11.4) \qquad \pi_j = f_3(C_j, B_j, X_j, OS_j, D_j, \nu_j).$$

The most common statistical approach to estimating Equations (11.3), (11.4), and related models is to use multiple regression analysis,[8] which seeks to evaluate the degree to which deviations of a *dependent variable*, π_i in Equation (11.3), from its mean are "explained by" or associated with variations in each of a set of *independent* or *explanatory variables*, for example, the arguments of f_2. The nature of this association is captured by *regression coefficients* or *parameters* relating π_i to each independent variable, allowing us to determine the effect, for example, of a 10 percent increase in seller concentration on Firm i's profit, holding all other explanatory variables constant. Where the error term ϵ_i is a random variable satisfying diverse statistical conditions, it is possible to test whether the size and sign of estimated regression coefficients are statistically significant at some arbitrarily chosen level of confidence.

Many potential problems can interfere with the reliable estimation of regression models, leading to incorrect inferences about the statistical significance and economic importance[9] of explanatory variables. Suppose, for example, that our profitability measure is positively associated with the firm's capital/sales ratio, because with a larger capital stock the firm must earn more to compensate owners for

3. See Leonard W. Weiss, "Quantitative Studies of Industrial Organization," in Michael D. Intriligator, ed., *Frontiers of Quantitative Economics* (Amsterdam: North-Holland, 1971), pp. 362–411; Weiss, "The Concentration-Profits Relationship and Antitrust," in Harvey J. Goldschmid et al., eds., *Industrial Concentration: The New Learning* (Boston: Little, Brown, 1974), pp. 201–220; R. Alton Gilbert, "Bank Market Structure and Competition: A Survey," *Journal of Money, Credit and Banking*, vol. 16 (November 1984), pp. 617–644; Richard E. Caves, "International Trade and Industrial Organization: Problems, Solved and Unsolved," *European Economic Review*, vol. 28 (August 1985), pp. 377–395; Paul A. Geroski, "In Pursuit of Monopoly Power: Recent Quantitative Work in Industrial Economics," *Journal of Applied Econometrics*, vol. 3 (April 1988), pp. 107–123; John Cubbin, "Industry Structure and Performance: the Empirical Work," London Business School mimeo, 1988; and Richard Schmalensee, "Inter-Industry Studies of Structure and Performance," in Schmalensee and Robert D. Willig, eds., *Handbook of Industrial Organization* (Amsterdam: North-Holland, 1989).

4. The ratio of price minus marginal cost to price. See pp. 70 and 206 supra.

5. Equation (11.1) reproduces Equation (6.4) supra. We can expand our interpretation of dQ_i to represent the response of Firm i's rivals, including potential entrants.

6. The conjectural variation is a relatively narrow indicator of firm conduct, covering only the firm's evaluation of the output (or price) response of rivals and entrants to its current price-output choice. As we saw in Chapter 10, the firm has a wide range of strategic variables at its disposal, including investments in cost-reducing plant capacity, learning-by-doing economies, and research and development; investments in product differentiation through brand proliferation, advertising, and enhanced customer services; and efforts to induce favorable government regulations. It is common in statistical studies to treat such strategies as affecting performance by altering market structure and limit the focus on the conduct-performance linkage to price-output strategies.

7. As discussed in Chapter 2, there are conditions under which the elevation of price above marginal cost may not signal unduly poor economic performance. In a monopolistically competitive industry, price will remain elevated above marginal cost at the point where free entry drives profit to zero. The resulting allocative inefficiency may be offset by the greater choice of products facing consumers. When economies of scale are pervasive, the best that can be expected from free entry or, more plausibly, government regulation, is a price approximating average cost, but above marginal cost.

8. An elementary introduction to regression analysis appears as the appendix to Chapter 3 of the second edition of *Industrial Market Structure and Economic Performance*. For a textbook treatment assuming no formal background in statistics, see Thad W. Mirer, *Economic Statistics and Econometrics*, 2nd ed. (New York: Macmillan, 1988). More advanced coverage is provided by a number of texts, including George G. Judge et al., *The Theory and Practice of Econometrics*, 2nd ed. (New York: John Wiley & Sons, 1985); and Jan Kmenta, *Elements of Econometrics*, 2nd ed. (New York: Macmillan, 1986).

9. Even if a regression coefficient is significantly different from zero, it may be so small that the impact on the dependent variable of reasonable variations in the associated explanatory variable will be slight.

their investment. Suppose further that high capital/sales ratios for industry members signal the presence of substantial scale economies, limiting the number of firms that can profitably enter those industries. Hence, capital/sales ratios will tend to be positively correlated with industry seller concentration. If the capital/sales ratio were excluded from the equation being estimated, a significant positive association between π_i and C_j would be reported, even if none existed independent of the capital stock influence. Thus, it is important to capture within the analysis all variables that might reasonably be expected to be causally related to dependent and independent variables alike.

A second problem arises if the statistical function f_2 is a poor approximation to the function relating π_i to its explanatory variables. For example, suppose that the only significant variable affecting profitability were market share and that it did so quadratically, as shown in the scatter plot of data depicted by Figure 11.1. That is, increases in market share initially raise profitability through scale economies, but eventually inefficiencies cause profits to fall:

(11.5) $$\pi_i = a - bs_i + cs_i^2 + \epsilon_i.$$

Researchers estimating a model that assumes a linear relationship between profit and market share will find no apparent relationship. The estimated coefficient on market share ($\hat{b}$) will be insignificantly different from zero.

While this is an extreme example, the general problem is of concern, since Equation (11.1) suggests that the correct functional form is likely to be highly nonlinear in the explanatory variables. Most researchers estimate linear (or log-linear) versions of Equation (11.3) and related models, in part because such models are easier to interpret, and because they serve as good approximations to the true model for observations near the means of the dependent and explanatory variables.[10] It is important to test the robustness of model estimates for extreme value effects and for the inclusion of various quadratic and interactive terms.[11]

Figure 11.1
Mismeasurement of a
Nonlinear Relationship

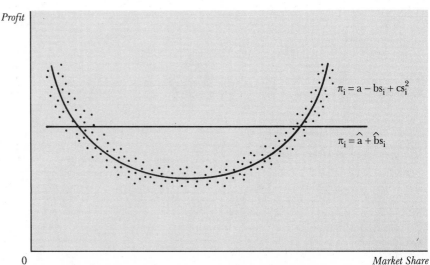

Profit

$\pi_i = a - bs_i + cs_i^2$

$\pi_i = \hat{a} + \hat{b}s_i$

0

Market Share

A third problem with estimating Equations (11.3) or (11.4) arises from the fact that many determinants of profitability may not be truly independent variables. Our analysis of limit pricing models in Chapter 10 suggests that market structure, as characterized by the concentration ratio C_j, may itself be influenced by the pricing policies sellers choose, taking into account entry barriers, for example, as prices are either set high with the expectation of inducing substantial new entry or held low to retard entry. Industry members' prices and profits will influence the rate of change in concentration over time:

$$(11.6) \qquad dC_j/dt = g(\pi_1, \pi_2, \ldots, \pi_i, \ldots, B_j, \zeta_{jt}),$$

with barriers to entry and other unmeasured or random influences also playing a role. Particularly where the π_i variable is defined, as it was in Bain's original study, over a time interval long enough for appreciable structural change to occur, concentration and profitability will be simultaneously determined. Unless Equations (11.3) and (11.6) are estimated as part of a system of equations, it is not clear whether the estimated relationship between profitability and concentration will be positive [because of the coordination-enhancing effect hypothesized in Equation (11.1)], negative [through the entry-inducing effect captured in Equation (11.6)], or insignificantly different from zero (because the two effects cancel each other out).

These three problems illustrate the complications met when one seeks a statistical method compatible with a rich theoretical conception of industrial reality. We leave a discussion of additional points until later, turning now to the more mundane problem of finding appropriate measures for performance, structure, and other relevant variables.

Measurement Problems

Because monopoly power presumably permits sellers to hold prices above the levels that would prevail under competition, one might wish to focus one's statistical analysis directly upon prices. But this is seldom possible. A single firm may set dozens or even thousands of prices on different product variants and to different customers. And even if this were not a problem, it is difficult to directly compare the prices of aluminum, turbogenerators, and ice cream cones. Some common denominator is needed. We shall see that under ideal conditions prices of identical products *can* be compared across different market structures, but such cases are exceptional.

Profitability   The usual common denominator for evaluating prices is costs — ideally, in a short-run analysis, marginal cost. Unfortunately, it is difficult to obtain systematic data on business firms' marginal costs, or to estimate Lerner indices. As a surrogate, researchers have chosen diverse profitability measures that can be used, with

---

10. For the data in Figure 11.1, the slope of the estimated regression line ($\hat{b} = 0$) approximates the slope of the true curve near $(\bar{\pi}, \bar{s})$.

11. On the importance of sensitivity tests, see Edward Leamer, "Let's Take the Con out of Econometrics," *American Economic Re-*view, vol. 73 (March 1983), pp. 31–43; and James L. Bothwell, Thomas F. Cooley, and Thomas E. Hall, "A New View of the Market Structure — Performance Debate," *Journal of Industrial Economics*, vol. 32 (June 1984), pp. 397–417.

varying degrees of reliability, as proxies for the elevation of price above marginal cost.

Economic profit is the surplus of revenue over cost, including the cost of attracting capital from alternative uses. A purely competitive or monopolistically competitive industry can realize positive economic profits under short-run disequilibrium (for example, boom) conditions. However, in the long run, competitive entry should erode such supra-normal profits, leaving nothing more than a normal return on invested capital. A monopoly does not necessarily secure economic profits,[12] but one ordinarily expects the two to coincide, and if there are appreciable barriers to entry, monopoly profits may persist for a long time or even indefinitely. On the average, and especially outside business boom periods, producers are expected to utilize their capacity optimally in a range of constant returns to scale. Under these conditions, a good long-run approximation to the Lerner index would be the ratio of supra-normal profit to normal cost. This is approximated by the ratio:

$$\pi_S = \frac{\text{Supra-normal profit}}{\text{Sales revenue}},$$

where supra-normal profit = sales revenue − noncapital costs − depreciation − (total capital × competitive cost per unit of capital). Because the cost of capital under competition is not recorded in firms' accounting statements and can only be imputed with difficulty, few researchers have developed accounting-based estimates of π_s.[13] Economists seeking to avoid that difficulty have usually opted for second-best surrogates falling into three categories.

One is the accounting rate of return on stockholders' equity:[14]

$$\pi_E = \frac{\text{Accounting profit attributable to stockholders}}{\text{Book value of stockholders' equity}},$$

or on capital:

$$\pi_C = \frac{\text{Accounting profits + interest payments}}{\text{Total assets}}.$$

The stockholders' equity measure, although loosely related to what the firm's owners seek to maximize, is sensitive *inter alia* to debt/equity ratio variations (since stockholders must be paid higher average returns to compensate for the increased risk associated with higher debt). Accounting rates of return also vary in their handling of taxes and depreciation. However, correlations among alternative rate of return measures are generally quite high.[15]

A second measure, Tobin's q ratio, captures the deviation between the market value of a firm and the replacement value of its assets:

$$q = \frac{M_C + M_P + M_D}{A_R},$$

where the numerator is the sum of the market value of a firm's common and preferred stock $M_C + M_P$ plus the total value of outstanding debt M_D, and the denominator is the cost of replacing total assets.[16] In an industry that meets all the conditions of pure competition, the q ratio should be 1, i.e., the market value of the firm would just equal the value of the capital resources owned by the firm. The q ratio will exceed 1 in the long run if the firm is able to earn supra-normal profits by elevating prices above cost.[17] Calculating replacement cost is difficult, and stock value data, available only for publicly traded firms, are subject to substantial market valuation errors.[18] Nevertheless, the q ratio tends to be highly correlated with accounting rates of return. Simulation analysis suggests that neither measure is innately superior to the other in detecting supra-competitive profits.[19]

Before describing the third alternative measure of profitability, we note a significant drawback of both the q ratio and most rate of return measures: they usually reflect the operations of whole companies. Company-specific profit data must somehow be meshed with *industry*-specific structural variables. Several approaches exist.

In early studies, the so-called primary industry method was the most widely used. A given firm's primary industry — that is, the industry in which the largest single share of its sales occurs — is identified, and accounting values for the whole firm are assigned entirely to that industry. When economists do the assignment using published company data, their sample is limited to the relatively few corporations whose securities are traded on public exchanges. To the extent that smaller nonpublic companies differ, biases can intrude.[20]

12. Cf. p. 22 supra.

13. See P. David Qualls, "Concentration, Barriers to Entry, and Long Run Economic Profit Margins," *Journal of Industrial Economics*, vol. 20 (April 1972), pp. 146–158.

14. Stockholders' equity is the residual accounting value obtained when one subtracts from total assets all short-term liabilities, long-term debt, and other nonowner claims. It usually consists of the original or par value of outstanding common and preferred stock plus the value of retained earnings.

15. Before-tax measures are undistorted by the peculiarities of tax systems, which can affect reported rates of depreciation. However, it is after-tax rates of return that should be equalized across industries by free entry. See S. J. Liebowitz, "What Do Census Price-Cost Margins Measure?" *Journal of Law & Economics*, vol. 25 (October 1982), pp. 231–246; Richard Schmalensee, "Intra-Industry Profitability Differences in US Manufacturing," *Journal of Industrial Economics*, vol. 37 (June 1989), pp. 337–357; and the references in Schmalensee, "Inter-Industry Studies," supra note 3, his note 10.

16. The measure was suggested and applied by James Tobin in a series of macroeconomic studies. See Tobin, "A General Equilibrium Approach to Monetary Theory," *Journal of Money, Credit and Banking*, vol. 1 (February 1969), pp. 15–29; and Tobin and William Brainard, "Pitfalls in Financial Model Building," *American Economic Review*, vol. 58 (May 1968), pp. 99–122. Applications in industrial organization started with the path-breaking article, "Tobin's q Ratio and Industrial Organization," *Journal of Business*, vol. 54 (January 1981), pp. 1–32, by Eric B. Lindenberg and Stephen A. Ross. See also Michael Smirlock, Thomas Gilligan, and William Marshall, "Tobin's q and the Structure-

Performance Relationship," *American Economic Review*, vol. 74 (December 1984), pp. 1051–1060; and Steven Lustgarten and Stavros Thomadakis, "Mobility Barriers and Tobin's q," *Journal of Business*, vol. 60 (October 1987), pp. 519–537.

17. Tobin's q could fall below 1 in the short-run if the firm is "dying," for example, because of a permanent decline in demand, or because a technological innovation has made its capital stock obsolete. In a new, fast-growing industry, bottlenecks in the supply of capital goods could cause a firm's market value to exceed replacement cost even under atomistic conditions.

18. See Fischer Black, "Noise," *Journal of Finance*, vol. 41 (July 1986), p. 533, who suggests that efficient capital markets value company stocks within half to twice their true but unknown level 90 percent of the time.

19. See Henry McFarland, "Evaluating *q* as an Alternative to the Rate of Return in Measuring Profitability," *Review of Economics and Statistics*, vol. 70 (November 1988), pp. 614–622. McFarland finds the q ratio to have an edge, ignoring the substantial market valuation errors described in the previous note. Compare William G. Shepherd, "Tobin's q and the Structure-Performance Relationship: Comment," *American Economic Review*, vol. 76 (December 1986), pp. 1205–1210.

20. However, some large companies are also private — for example Deering-Milliken, one of the largest U.S. textile makers; Mars Inc., the largest U.S. candy producer; Hoffmann-LaRoche, a leading pharmaceutical manufacturer; and Cargill, the largest U.S. grain elevator operator. The growing incidence of leveraged buy-outs has increased the number of large corporations for which data are not publicly available.

The sample coverage limitation prompted many analysts to use industry data aggregations compiled by government statistical agencies — for the United States, the Internal Revenue Service's annual *Statistics of Income: Corporation Income Tax Returns* series and the Census Bureau's *Census of Manufactures* and *Annual Survey of Manufactures*. These, however, do not avoid significant problems.

With minor exceptions,[21] the Internal Revenue Service (IRS) employs the primary industry method. Large industrial corporations, we have seen, tend to be diversified into many lines of business.[22] This means that vast amounts of irrelevant or "contaminating" activity are loaded into the primary industry totals along with correctly classified primary industry profits, sales, and assets. Thus, General Motors' data are classified to the automobile industry, mixing with activities more or less closely related to GM's primary line more than $12 billion of 1988 guided missile, radar, satellite, computer service, locomotive, and other sales. This contamination problem became increasingly severe as the diversification wave of the 1960s gathered momentum.[23] It is hardly an exaggeration to say that any study using data for the years since the early 1960s classified by the primary industry method, without elaborate quality controls, is virtually worthless.[24]

The U.S. Census Bureau reduces the contamination problem by collecting manufacturing activity statistics at the level of individual plants. Each plant is assigned to its primary industry, but since plants are on average much more specialized than companies, the problem of contamination is greatly reduced. The Census Bureau also publishes coverage and specialization ratios that allow one to assess the degree to which industry data include the activities of nonprimary industries. From the aggregated census statistics it is possible to compute an average *price-cost margin*

$$PCM = \frac{TS - CM - PR}{TS},$$

where TS is total plant sales, CM is material costs, and PR is in-plant payroll costs. The index is a poor measure of net profitability because census data do not capture with any precision such out-of-plant outlays as advertising, central office costs, sales force expenditures, separate research and development expenditures, and the cost of capital. By including industry aggregates for these measures as controls[25] in statistical studies, PCM can be made to serve as a crude proxy for the Lerner index, signaling the ability of firms in the industry to elevate price above average cost, if not marginal cost.[26] The correlation between PCM and the other measures of profitability discussed above tends to be far weaker than correlations among the other measures. This suggests important differences across industries in the magnitude of non-plant-specific costs and in the treatment of the cost of capital.[27] A principal attraction of the price-cost margin is its ready availability at a level of aggregation that exactly matches the level at which industry concentration indices are published.

Ideally one would like to obtain data on PCM and other profit measures segregated for each industry in which the companies operate. Several steps have been made in this direction. For the years 1974–1977, the U.S. Federal Trade Commission's Line of Business Program obtained data on sales, costs, profits, and assets from the 471 largest U.S. manufacturing enterprises broken down into 261 standardized manufacturing industry categories. Nearly 4,000 individual company/industry segments reported per year. These line of business data have proved to be a rich basis for new studies during the 1980s. There was bitter industry opposition to the program as it was getting under way,[28] and the Reagan administration halted data collection for the years after 1977.

Outside this 1974–1977 period, the most richly subdivided data available are the so-called PIMS (Profit Impact of Market Strategy) data set.[29] Beginning with 1970, a group of typically large corporations began supplying to a private organization elaborately detailed performance and structure data on certain of their individual "businesses," defined as company units selling a distinct set of products or services in competition with a well-defined set of competitors. The PIMS data set has grown to cover 2,900 such businesses (for varying time periods) operated by more than 450 corporations. Its principal limitations are twofold. First, there is an element of self-selection for both the cooperating companies and the businesses on which they choose to report, and in some quantifiable respects the sample is clearly not representative.[30] Second, the data are subjected to stringent confidentiality restrictions so that an analyst cannot ascertain what companies and industries are being studied or what the absolute size of any given business is. Despite these limitations, very important research has been done using the PIMS data.

The analyst who has obtained appropriately adjusted industry or line of business data must still be concerned about biases that might intrude as a result of the diverse accounting conventions companies adopt.

---

21. For example, when multi-unit corporations file unconsolidated tax returns.

22. See pp. 90–94 supra.

23. Beginning in 1977, U.S. corporations were required by the Financial Accounting Standards Board (FASB) to report profits, sales, and assets broken down by "industry segments" that accounted for 10 percent *or more* of total company sales or profits. See FASB, Statement of Financial Accounting Standards No. 14, *Financial Reporting for Segments of a Business Enterprise* (Stamford, 1978). A significant limitation of the FASB approach is that companies have broad discretion to define their segments as they please, and so large diversified corporations like General Electric report their profits for such meaninglessly broad segments as "consumer products," "industrial products," "materials," "technical products and services," and "aerospace," along with a few narrower breakdowns such as "aircraft engines" and "major appliances." This means *inter alia* that the industry segments are not comparable from firm to firm.

24. See Liebowitz, "Census Price-Cost Margins," supra note 15, pp. 238–239, for a discussion of efforts to circumvent the diversification problem with IRS data. IRS data also suffer from the duplication of returns and time mismatches when amended returns are filed.

25. To control for the cost of capital, the standard approach is to include the capital/sales ratio as an explanatory variable. This approach is not entirely satisfactory, since it amounts to assuming that the competitive cost of capital (including depreciation), as well as any entry-barrier or coordination-impairing effects associated with increments to the capital/sales ratio, are the same for all industries in the sample.

26. The use of census PCMs in structure-performance studies was pioneered by Norman Collins and Lee E. Preston, "Price-Cost Margins and Industry Structure," *Review of Economics and Statistics*, vol. 51 (August 1969), pp. 271–286; and *Concentration and Price-Cost Margins in Manufacturing Industries* (Berkeley: University of California Press, 1968). For a precursor that found a similar positive price-cost margin-concentration relationship for the years 1931 and 1933, see Alfred C. Neal, *Industrial Concentration and Price Inflexibility* (Washington: American Council on Public Affairs, 1942), pp. 130–134.

27. For criticisms of the PCM as an indicator of profitability, see S. J. Liebowitz, "Census Price-Cost Margins," supra note 15; and Stanley I. Ornstein, "Empirical Uses of the Price-Cost Margin," *Journal of Industrial Economics*, vol. 24 (December 1975), pp. 105–117.

28. For a debate on the substantive issues, see F. M. Scherer, "Segment Financial Reporting: Needs and Trade-offs," and George J. Benston, "The Segment Reporting Debate," in Harvey J. Goldschmid, ed., *Business Disclosure: Government's Need to Know* (New York: McGraw-Hill, 1979), pp. 3–118.

29. Robert D. Buzzell and Bradley T. Gale, *The PIMS Principles: Linking Strategy to Performance* (New York: Free Press, 1987); and Cheri T. Marshall, "PIMS and the FTC Line-of-Business Data: A Comparison," DBA dissertation, Harvard University, 1986.

30. For example, in 57 percent of the sample businesses, the reporting company claimed to be one of the pioneers in its market.

How companies value their assets—the denominator in many rate of return measures and a key element in the imputed capital cost component of π_S—poses several potential problems. Whatever it is that gives the sellers in an industry monopoly power is in a sense an asset that might be sold and purchased. If a company holding or sharing in monopoly power is acquired, or if its acquisition by another enterprise will enhance the power to maintain elevated prices, the acquiring firm is apt to pay a higher price for the acquisition than if no such monopoly potential were present. After the merger, the value of assets may be written up so much that profit returns appear to be only normal. This is more likely if the acquiring firm uses purchase accounting methods, bringing the acquired firm's assets onto its books at market value, than if it uses pooling of interest accounting, incorporating the acquired assets at their book value.[31] The more extensive merger activity has been in an industry, the more likely it is that monopoly profit expectations will have been capitalized, so that accounting figures provide a downward-biased picture of monopoly power. Inflation also complicates matters. If the rate of inflation exceeds the rate at which technological advances raise the productivity of assets, older assets will tend to be undervalued relative to newly acquired assets. This can among other things cause the profitability of more slowly growing firms or industries to be overstated relative to that of entities with a comparatively young asset portfolio.

Varying or inappropriate depreciation policies also engender difficulties. Most companies keep at least two sets of books—one for the tax collector and another for financial reporting purposes. Profit returns reported in the Internal Revenue Service's *Statistics of Income* series are much more apt to be reduced by accelerated depreciation than those appearing in company annual reports. Studies of the public accounting methods firms employ suggest that, at least for the United States, large firms are more likely than small ones to adopt financial accounting practices such as accelerated depreciation that depress current profits.[32] It is not clear what implication this has for efforts to measure the association between intra-industry profitability and market share, since an industry's market leader could be a small specialist firm, while low market shares might be held by divisions of large conglomerate firms.[33] In any event, there is no evidence of a correlation between accounting method choices and industry concentration.[34]

Also contributing to biased accounting rates of return is the convention that treats outlays for advertising, research and development, and oil and mineral exploration as current costs. Such outlays might actually be more in the nature of an investment yielding benefits over an extended time frame. To the extent that this is true, economic reality would be portrayed better by capitalizing the outlays and then depreciating them at an appropriate rate. Current costing tends to understate assets and, with the rate of economic profit consistently exceeding the growth rate of the relevant outlays, economic profit is overstated.[35]

Owner-managed corporations pose additional problems. Owner-managers may pay themselves unrealistically high salaries in order to avoid double taxation (of corporate earnings and then dividends), although they might underpay themselves when corporate profits can be shielded by accelerated depreciation and capital gains are taxed at preferential rates. A smaller proportion of concentrated industries' sales and profits tend to be contributed by owner-managed small firms.

Thus, systematic biases correlated with market structure may intrude unless appropriate exclusions and adjustments are effected.[36]

Finally, when the profits of a corporation are broken out by line of business, as for the PIMS data and FTC Line of Business reporting program, a certain amount of arbitrariness in allocating common costs—for example, the cost of maintaining central offices, joint sales forces, and broad ranging basic research—is inescapable. Distortions may also arise through the setting of arbitrary transfer prices.[37]

There are various possible reactions to this formidable array of accounting problems. One is to hope that the errors introduced by varying or inappropriate accounting conventions are not systematically correlated with the industry structure characteristics under investigation, so that estimated structure-performance relationships are only attenuated by statistical noise but not biased in one direction or another. In certain cases, however, such optimism is clearly unwarranted. Thus, capitalization of monopoly returns through merger leads to a systematic underestimation of profit-concentration relationships, while any tendency for excessive owner-manager salaries to be paid on a more widespread scale in unconcentrated industries imparts the opposite bias. Another response is to throw up one's hands and despair of doing any meaningful research using accounting data.[38] A more constructive course is to devise methods of detecting and, if possible, adjusting for systematic biases. For example, the effects of inflation can be

31. See David J. Ravenscraft and F. M. Scherer, *Mergers, Sell-Offs, and Economic Efficiency* (Washington: Brookings Institution, 1987), pp. 12–14, 78–80, and 229–238. Pooling of interest accounting was used extensively for mergers consummated during the 1960s, but less frequently thereafter.

32. See Robert L. Hagerman and Mark E. Zmijewski, "An Income Strategy Approach to the Positive Theory of Accounting Standard Setting/Choice," *Journal of Accounting and Economics*, vol. 3 (August 1981), pp. 129–149; and Robert Holthausen and Richard Leftwich, "The Economic Consequences of Accounting Choice: Implications of Costly Contracting and Monitoring," *Journal of Accounting and Economics*, vol. 5 (August 1983) pp. 77–117.

33. But see Gerald L. Salamon, "Accounting Rates of Return," *American Economic Review*, vol. 75 (June 1985), pp. 495–504.

34. Holthausen and Leftwich, "Economic Consequences," supra note 32, pp. 77–117.

35. See Franklin M. Fisher and John J. McGowan, "On the Misuse of Accounting Rates of Return to Infer Monopoly Profits," *American Economic Review*, vol. 73 (March 1983), pp. 82–97; Schmalensee, "Inter-Industry Studies," supra note 4; and Thomas R. Stauffer, "The Measurement of Corporate Rates of Return: A Generalized Formulation," *Bell Journal of Economics and Management Science*, vol. 2 (Autumn 1971), pp. 434–469.

36. For example, see Robert W. Kilpatrick, "Stigler on the Relationship between Industry Profit Rate and Market Concentration," *Journal of Political Economy*, vol. 76 (May–June 1968), pp. 479–487.

37. For evidence on the sensitivity of statistical structure-performance estimates to alternative allocation and transfer pricing strategies in the FTC line of business data, see William F. Long, "Impact of Alternative Allocation Procedures on Econometric Studies of Structure and Performance," mimeo, September 1981; David J. Ravenscraft, "Transfer Pricing and Profitability," mimeo, December 1981; and Ravenscraft and Scherer, *Mergers*, supra note 31, pp. 103–106.

38. For arguments along this line, see Fisher and McGowan, "On the Misuse of Accounting Rates of Return," supra note 35, pp. 82–97; Franklin M. Fisher, "The Misuse of Accounting Rates of Return: Reply," *American Economic Review*, vol. 74 (June 1984), pp. 509–517; and George J. Benston, "The Validity of Profits-Structure Studies with Particular Reference to the FTC's Line of Business Data," *American Economic Review*, vol. 75 (March 1985), pp. 37–67.

For more sanguine views of the utility of accounting data, see William F. Long and David J. Ravenscraft, "The Misuse of Accounting Rates of Return: Comment," *American Economic Review*, vol. 74 (June 1984), pp. 494–500; Stephen Martin, "The Misuse of Accounting Rates of Return: Comment," *American Economic Review*, vol. 74 (June 1984), pp. 501–506; J. A. Kay and C. P. Mayer, "On the Application of Accounting Rates of Return," *Economic Journal*, vol. 96 (March 1986), pp. 199–207; and F. M. Scherer et al., "The Validity of Studies with Line of Business Data: Comment," *American Economic Review*, vol. 77 (March 1987), pp. 205–217.

compensated by including in one's analysis capital stock vintage and growth variables.[39] Mergers pose more difficult problems, but a crude adjustment is possible by introducing variables measuring their extent and currency, or by estimating the values that would prevail if assets were entered into the books at preacquisition figures. Adjustments can be made for owner-manager salary biases, or the effect of excluding very small companies from one's analysis can be tested and reported. Sophisticated techniques have been developed to capitalize advertising and research and development outlays improperly charged off as current costs. When profit data for multiple segments of companies are analyzed, the sensitivity of one's conclusions to alternative common cost allocation formulas can be tested. Vertically related segments with substantial transfers can be reintegrated for similar sensitivity tests, or separate variables measuring the relative volume of intersegment sales and purchases can be introduced to detect systematic transfer biases. In short, much can be done if sufficient care and imagination are exercised. At the very least, the person analyzing structure-performance relationships statistically must be sensitive to the possible intrusion of biases so that their direction and probable magnitude can be acknowledged.

Concentration   Careful attention must also be devoted to measuring the explanatory variables. We begin with measures of market share and concentration. As we have seen in Chapter 3, the two most widely used measures of concentration are the leading firm concentration ratio (for example, CR4 for the U.S., CR5 for the U.K., CR3 for West Germany) and the Herfindahl-Hirschman index (H). The former was used almost exclusively in early studies, primarily because of its availability, and it remains the most widely used measure.[40] Ideally, the appropriate measure would be suggested by oligopoly theory. But existing theories provide ambiguous guidance. We saw in Chapter 6 that by restricting the interaction of firm conjectural variations, one can write average industry profitability as a linear function of H.[41] Thomas Saving shows that if an industry consists of a dominant group containing n firms and a competitive fringe, industry and dominant firm profits will rise with CR*n*,[42] the share of industry sales produced by the group. However, empirical reality may not follow specific assumed mathematical models, so too strong a restriction *ex ante* may impose a high misspecification price. Alternative concentration measures are highly correlated with one another, and efforts to assess the sensitivity of statistical results to the concentration measure choice present a mixed picture.[43] Until theory offers better guidance, a certain amount of pragmatic empiricism, guarded against spurious inference by retesting across diverse samples using alternative specifications, seems warranted.

Nothing in oligopoly theory suggests that the concentration-performance link must be continuous. Rather, the hypothesis is that coordination of industry pricing is more likely to occur where seller concentration is high — perhaps discontinuously above some threshold.[44] Thus, in his 1951 study, Bain focused on whether firms operating in industries with CR8 greater than 70 (corresponding approximately to CR4 above 50 for U.S. data) were more profitable than firms operating in lower-concentration industries. Subsequent studies of U.S. data also have found such a "critical level" of concentration for CR4 between 45 and 60; that is, there is little evidence that increases in seller concentration to CR4 levels below 50 have any effect on profitability.[45] Bradburd and Over found that the critical level depends upon concentration trends. Where concentration had previously been low, CR4 must exceed 68 before there is a discernible increase in profitability; where concentration had been high, estimated profits do not fall until CR4 falls below 46.[46] However, most studies continue to estimate models in which profitability depends linearly upon concentration.

Much more important than the choice of concentration index is ensuring that the index reflects economically meaningful market definitions. As we saw in Chapter 3, the industry definitions embodied in government statistical classifications often fall short of satisfying this criterion. More often than not, four-digit Standard Industrial Classification industries are too broadly defined, and therefore, their concentration ratios understate the true level of structural monopoly or oligopoly. Failure to control for this bias leads to inflated measurement errors and

39. See George J. Stigler, *Capital and Rates of Return in Manufacturing Industries* (Princeton: Princeton University Press, 1963), pp. 59–61 and 125–127. Few subsequent studies have followed Stigler's example.

40. The U.S. Census Bureau began publishing H indices with data for 1982. For earlier years, see Chapter 3, note 43. It is possible to estimate H by combining concentration ratios for different leading firm groups. See Richard Schmalensee, "Using the H-Index of Concentration with Published Data," *Review of Economics and Statistics*, vol. 59 (May 1977), pp. 186–193; and Claudio Michelini and Michael Pickford, "Estimating the Herfindahl Index from Concentration Ratio Data," *Journal of the American Statistical Association*, vol. 80 (June 1985), pp. 301–305.

41. See Chapter 3, note 48.

42. Thomas R. Saving, "Concentration Ratios and the Degree of Monopoly," *International Economic Review*, vol. 11 (February 1970), pp. 139–146.

43. See John E. Kwoka, Jr., "Does the Choice of Concentration Measure Really Matter?" *Journal of Industrial Economics*, vol. 29 (June 1981), pp. 445–453; and Leo Sleuwaegen and Wim Dehandschutter, "The Critical Choice Between the Concentration Ratio and the H-Index in Assessing Industry Performance," *Journal of Industrial Economics*, vol. 35 (December 1986), pp. 193–208.

44. On the difficulty of inferring the ease of pricing coordination from seller concentration indices, see Almarin Phillips, "A Critique of Empirical Studies of Relations Between Market Structure and Profitability," *Journal of Industrial Economics*, vol. 24 (June 1976), pp. 241–249.

45. See Collins and Preston, *Concentration and Price-Cost Margins*, supra note 26; James A. Dalton and David W. Penn, "The Concentration-Profitability Relationship: Is There a Critical Concentration Ratio?" *Journal of Industrial Economics*, vol. 25 (December 1976), pp. 133–142; Frederick E. Geithman, Howard P. Marvel, and Leonard W. Weiss, "Concentration, Price, and Critical Concentration Ratios," *Review of Economics and Statistics*, vol. 63 (August 1981), pp. 346–353; John E. Kwoka, Jr., "The Effect

of Market Share Distribution on Industry Performance," *Review of Economics and Statistics*, vol. 61 (February 1979), pp. 101–109; James W. Meehan, Jr., and Thomas D. Duchesneau, "The Critical Level of Concentration: An Empirical Analysis," *Journal of Industrial Economics*, vol. 22 (September 1973), pp. 21–30; Stephen A. Rhoades and Joe M. Cleaver, "The Nature of the Concentration-Price Cost Margin Relationship for 352 Manufacturing Industries: 1967," *Southern Economic Journal*, vol. 40 (July 1973), pp. 90–102; and Lawrence J. White, "Searching for the Critical Industrial Concentration Ratio: An Application of the 'Switching of Regimes' Technique," in Stephen Goldfeld and Richard E. Quandt, eds., *Studies in NonLinear Estimation* (Cambridge: Ballinger, 1976), pp. 61–75. Compare Paul A. Geroski, "Specification and Testing the Profits-Concentration Relationship: Some Experiments for the U.K.," *Economica*, vol. 48 (August 1981), pp. 279–288; and Sleuwaegen and Dehandschutter, "Critical Choice," supra note 43. The general approach of these studies is to find the critical concentration level that maximizes the regression equation's goodness of fit. As a rule, estimates within a 10 to 20 percentage point range are indistinguishable in explanatory power from the "best" estimate, and the particular estimate that emerges is sensitive to the choice of other explanatory variables and the way those variables enter the regression.

Additional support for the critical concentration hypothesis is provided by Weiss, who concludes that variations in CR4 below 50 appear to have little effect on observed *pricing* differences among geographically separated markets for identical commodities. *Concentration and Price* (Cambridge: MIT Press, 1989), p. 277.

46. Ralph M. Bradburd and A. Mead Over, Jr., "Organizational Costs, 'Sticky' Equilibria and Critical Levels of Concentration," *Review of Economics and Statistics*, vol. 64 (February 1982), pp. 50–58. They argue following Bain that cooperative pricing behavior will emerge only in highly concentrated industries, but that, once established, a major loss in the dominant group's share of industry sales will be required before cooperation begins to disintegrate.

a concomitant tendency not to detect systematic relationships that might, if correctly measured, be statistically significant.[47]

Poorly defined industries must be excluded, or adjustments made, if sensible analysis is to be done. Theory suggests that the relevant market should contain the smallest group of firms that could, by joining together in a joint profit-maximizing cartel, raise prices substantially above costs.[48] However, applying this reasoning to adjust concentration indices to reflect perceived market realities can lead to spurious correlations. Ideally, adjustments should be based upon objective information independent of the performance indicators.[49]

Regional and local markets for manufactured products can be identified by a low sales value per unit of weight, a high ratio of transportation cost per dollar of sales over a standardized distance, or a short average shipment radius. Researchers have dealt with this problem either by adjusting the concentration index[50] or by including transportation cost and geographic dispersion measures as explanatory variables.[51]

It is common practice to account for the influence of imports by including the ratio of imports to domestic production or consumption as an additional explanatory variable.[52] The theoretical justification for doing so has never been clear, although the coefficient on the ratio is typically negative and statistically significant. Where import penetration is constrained by high transport costs, tariffs or quotas, (1 − the import ratio) should interact multiplicatively with the concentration ratio.[53] Where trade barriers are low, Leitzinger and Tamor argue for using a world concentration index rather than the domestic measure.[54]

Other Explanatory Variables

Theory states that entry barriers also should be important in explaining profitability differences. Concentration may be conducive to high prices and high profits, but unless there are appreciable barriers to entry, the profits will attract new entrants, and sooner or later pricing coordination will be undermined. Monopoly returns may be realized despite low concentration if entry has been restricted and individual sellers' output cannot readily be expanded. Medical practice is the classic example.

There are two main approaches to measuring entry barriers. One entails a more or less careful study of an industry's technology, raw material availability, spatial configuration, consumer buying practices, and legal environment followed by subjective judgments as to whether entry barriers are, say, *very high, substantial,* or *moderate to low*.[55] As with the adjustment of concentration ratios, there is a danger that these judgments will be colored by awareness of industries' profit records, leading to spurious correlations.

The other approach seeks objectively measurable indices consonant with the theory of entry deterrence. For example, scale economies limit the number of firms that can operate in an industry at minimum average cost. The Bain-Sylos-Modigliani theory suggests that prices can be held persistently above costs by a greater margin, the larger a minimum efficient scale firm is relative to the size of the market, the steeper the cost curves are at less than minimum efficient scale, and the less elastic demand is.[56] Minimum efficient *plant* scales have been estimated by engineering methods for at least thirty-three industries, and statistical studies reveal that these estimates are significantly correlated with more readily accessible indices, such as the ratio of sales of plants at the midpoint of industry plant size distributions to total industry sales.[57] Caves, Khalilzadeh-Shirazi, and Porter argue that even large minimum efficient scales are unlikely to deter entry unless unit cost curves impose a significant penalty for sub-MES entry. They formulate a *cost disadvantage ratio* that can be interacted with the MES ratio to identify

47. Coefficient estimates are biased toward zero in a regression analysis when an independent variable is subject to random errors of measurement. See Peter Kennedy, *A Guide to Econometrics*, 2nd ed. (Cambridge: MIT Press, 1985), pp. 113–123. Usually, however, the errors measuring concentration are not random. There is a bias toward underestimation, and "true" concentration values that are large probably tend to be understated by a larger absolute amount than small values. When this occurs, regression coefficient estimates may be inflated relative to their true values, but standard errors will be inflated even more, biasing the test toward a finding of statistical insignificance.

It is not excessively cynical to observe that economists who believe market structure does not influence prices and profitability—a group that might be loosely identified as the University of Chicago school—tend to spend little time or effort worrying about faulty market definitions. As a result, their research frequently conforms all too closely to the "garbage in, garbage out" principle.

48. See pp. 73–76 and 178–184 supra.

49. See David R. Ross and Ralph M. Bradburd, "The Effect of Industry Heterogeneity in Structure-Performance Studies," Williams College Department of Economics Research Paper, RP–111, December 1987.

50. For example, see David Schwartzman and Joan Bodoff, "Concentration in Regional and Local Industries," *Southern Economic Journal*, vol. 37 (January 1971), pp. 343–348; and Leonard W. Weiss and George A. Pascoe, Jr., "Adjusted Concentration Ratios in Manufacturing, 1972 and 1977," (Washington: Federal Trade Commission, 1986).

51. See F. M. Scherer, Alan Beckenstein, Erich Kaufer, and R. D. Murphy, *The Economics of Multi-Plant Operation: An International Comparisons Study* (Cambridge: Harvard University Press, 1975), pp. 183–187, 201, 408–413, and 429–439; Leonard W. Weiss, "The Geographic Size of Markets in Manufacturing," *Review of Economics and Statistics*, vol. 54 (August 1972), pp. 245–257; and the discussion on pp. 78–79 supra. When the data needed to compute regional market concentration ratios are unavailable, Weiss's market count indices or the Scherer-Murphy transportation cost indices can be used as shift variables interacting multiplicatively with the uncorrected concentration ratios. A commonly used alternative with much less theoretical justification is an index reflecting the degree to which employment or sales in an industry's plants is dispersed geographically in proportion to population. To the extent that it has any logical validity, the dispersion index should interact multiplicatively with the unadjusted concentration ratios. This point is uniformly overlooked.

52. For example, see Louis and Frances Esposito, "Foreign Competition and Domestic Industry Profitability," *Review of Economics and Statistics*, vol. 53 (November 1971), pp. 343–353; Stephen Martin, "Advertising, Concentration and Profitability: The Simultaneity Problem," *Bell Journal of Economics*, vol. 10 (Autumn 1979), pp. 639–647; Jaime de Melo and Shujiro Urata, "The Influence of Increased Foreign Competition on Industrial Concentration and Profitability," *International Journal of Industrial Organization*, vol. 4 (September 1986), pp. 287–304, for Chile; Paul A. Geroski, "Simultaneous Equations Models of the Structure-Performance Paradigm," *European Economic Review*, vol. 19 (September 1982), pp. 145–158, for the U.K.; and Manfred Neumann, Ingo Böbel, and Alfred Haid, "Domestic Concentration, Foreign Trade, and Economic Performance," *International Journal of Industrial Organization*, vol. 3 (March 1985), pp. 1–19, for West Germany.

53. Several studies *have* found that the negative impact of imports on domestic profitability is stronger when domestic concentration is high. See, for example, Thomas A. Pugel, "Foreign Trade and US Market Performance," *Journal of Industrial Economics*, vol. 29 (December 1980), pp. 119–129; and the references in Richard Schmalensee, "Inter-Industry Studies," supra note 3, his note 23.

54. Jeffrey J. Leitzinger and Kenneth L. Tamor, "Foreign Competition in Antitrust Law," *Journal of Law & Economics*, vol. 26 (April 1983), pp. 87–102.

55. See Bain, *Barriers to New Competition*, supra note 2, pp. 170–171.

56. See pp. 378–379 supra.

57. See p. 115 supra; Scherer, et al., *Economics of Multi-Plant Operation*, supra note 51, pp. 182–183; Stanley I. Ornstein, et al., "Determinants of Market Structure," *Southern Economic Journal*, vol. 39 (April 1973), pp. 612–625; and Leonard W. Weiss, "Optimal Plant Scale and the Extent of Suboptimal Capacity," in Robert T. Masson and P. D. Qualls, eds., *Essays on Industrial Organization in Honor of Joe S. Bain* (Cambridge: Ballinger, 1976), pp. 126–134. See also Peter F. Cory, "A Technique for Obtaining Improved Proxy Estimates of Minimum Optimal Scale," *Review of Economics and Statistics*, vol. 63 (February 1981), pp. 96–106.

For an attempt to measure minimum efficient *firm* scale, see Neuman, Böbel, and Haid, "Domestic Concentration," supra note 52, pp. 1–19.

industries where scale-related entry barriers are high.[58] Since it may be harder to enter an industry requiring a massive capital investment,[59] the capital/sales ratio multiplied by the sales volume associated with MES production has been used as a proxy for what Bain called absolute capital requirement barriers to entry. The height of product differentiation barriers to entry has been proxied by the ratio of advertising expenditures to sales—a variable that will compel more careful scrutiny in the next section.[60]

Other independent variables with a claim to inclusion in multiple regression equations "explaining" profitability must be mentioned more briefly. Equation (11.1) predicts that firms with monopoly power will be able to gain larger supra-normal returns when demand is relatively inelastic, all else being equal. However, obtaining demand elasticity estimates for a sizable sample of industries is extremely difficult, and only one study has made a serious effort to do so.[61] For intermediate goods industries, whose output is an input to some other industry, the degree of *buyer* concentration may influence profitability.[62] Since even atomistically competitive industries can realize supra-normal profits under disequilibrium conditions, the structural relationships from boom years should be estimated separately from those for normal or recession periods. Disequilibrium may also be specific to a particular industry. Therefore, a variable that measures industry growth over the past several years is often included in the expectation that profits will be abnormally high in fast-growth industries because investment in additional capacity has not caught up with demand.[63] In periods of rapid inflation, on the other hand, this relationship may be offset by a tendency for rapidly growing industries to have a younger, higher-cost plant and equipment mix than slowly growing industries. One might also expect profits to be higher in industries characterized by particularly high risks. Many studies have therefore attempted to include a measure of risk more or less solidly rooted in the theory of corporate finance.[64] We saw in Chapter 8 that the temptation to chisel on price agreements may be especially strong during business slumps for firms bearing a heavy burden of fixed costs. Thus high values of an industry's capital/sales ratio may signal a tendency for pricing below the level that would otherwise be expected. However, we have already seen that the capital/sales ratio is also interpreted as capturing the cost of capital included in PCM measures and signaling the size of absolute capital requirements for entry. Thus, as with a number of other variables suggested for inclusion in profit-structure statistical models, it is not clear what sign one would expect the coefficient on this variable to have.

Cross-Section Studies

Bain's initial claims of a statistically significant profit-concentration relation, found for small samples of large firms,[65] became accepted wisdom when they were replicated by studies using virtually exhaustive U.S. manufacturing industry samples[66] and data drawn from several different nations.[67] Typical of the studies for the United States, and still among the most comprehensive, is one by Weiss.[68] Analyzing 1963 data on 399 census industries, and correcting for poorly defined markets only through the inclusion of a geographic dispersion index, he estimated *inter alia* the following regression equation, with the price-cost margins and other ratios expressed in percentage terms:

$$(11.7) \quad \text{PCM} = 16.3 + \underset{(2.08)}{.050} \text{ CR4} - \underset{(2.00)}{.029} \text{ DISP} + \underset{(7.44)}{.119} \text{ CAP/S}$$

$$+ \underset{(7.2)}{1.30} \text{ A/S} - \underset{(.42)}{1.9} \text{ CAO} + \underset{(.169)}{.023} \text{ INV/S}$$

$$+ \underset{(2.9)}{.26} \text{ GROW} + \underset{(2.7)}{.00083} \text{ CONS} \times \text{CR4}$$

$$+ \underset{(.38)}{.095} \text{ MID} - \underset{(1.65)}{.033} \text{ PLANTCAP};$$

$$N = 399, \quad R^2 = .427.$$

58. Richard E. Caves, J. Khalilzadeh-Shirazi, and M. E. Porter, "Scale Economies in Statistical Analyses of Market Power," *Review of Economics and Statistics*, vol. 57 (May 1975), pp. 133–140. Their cost disadvantage ratio, the ratio of census value added (sales − payroll and materials costs) per worker in sub-MES plants to value added per worker in large plants, overstates the disadvantage of small plants to the extent that the ratio of capital (the implicit cost of which is included in value added) to labor rises with scale. See Richard E. Caves and Thomas A. Pugel, *Intraindustry Differences in Conduct and Performance: Viable Strategies in U.S Manufacturing Industries* (New York: Salomon Brothers Center, New York University, 1980).

59. Capital market imperfections arguably raise the cost of capital to new entrants, and absolute capital requirements may arguably signal the size of sunk costs, which limits the willingness of firms to risk entry. On the last point, see the discussion on pp. 374–376 supra and Ioannis N. Kessides, "Advertising, Sunk Costs, and Barriers to Entry," *Review of Economics and Statistics*, vol. 67 (February 1986), pp. 84–95.

60. See William S. Comanor and Thomas A. Wilson, *Advertising and Market Power* (Cambridge: Harvard University Press, 1974).

61. Comanor and Wilson, *Advertising and Market Power*, pp. 82–92 and 123–127. For an attempt to use intra-industry profit-market share relations to derive a proxy for elasticity differences across industries, see William F. Long and David J. Ravenscraft, "The Impact of Concentration and Elasticity on Line of Business Profitability," *Economic Letters*, vol. 16 (1984), pp. 345–350.

62. Large buyers may be able to destabilize collusive behavior or bid down industry prices. On the other hand, if the downstream industry itself engages in cartel pricing, its input demand may become less elastic, allowing prices to rise. See Chapter 14 *infra*.

63. See Bothwell, Cooley, and Hall, "A New View," supra note 11, pp. 397–417; Ralph M. Bradburd and Richard E. Caves, "A Closer Look at the Effect of Market Growth on Industries'

Profits," *Review of Economics and Statistics*, vol. 64 (November 1982), pp. 635–645; and S. J. Liebowitz, "Measuring Industrial Disequilibria," *Southern Economic Journal*, vol. 49 (July 1982), pp. 119–136. We will return later to the question of cyclical influences on the profit-structure relationship.

64. See, for example, Frederick H. deB. Harris, "Market Structure and Price-Cost Performance under Exogenous Profit Risk," *Journal of Industrial Economics*, vol. 35 (September 1986), pp. 35–59; and the second edition of *Industrial Market Structure and Economic Performance*, pp. 292–293.

65. Bain, "Relation of Profit Rate"; and *Barriers to New Competition*, supra note 2.

66. See the references in Weiss, "Quantitative Studies of Industrial Organization," supra note 3, pp. 362–411.

67. For examples of studies that found a positive profit-concentration relation, see, for Canada, J. C. H. Jones, Leonard Laudadio, and M. Percy, "Market Structure and Profitability in Canadian Manufacturing Industry: Some Cross-Section Results," *Canadian Journal of Economics*, vol. 6 (August 1973), pp. 356–368; for France, Frederic Jenny and A. P. Weber, "Profit Rates and Structural Variables in French Manufacturing Industries," *European Economic Review*, vol. 7 (February 1976), pp. 187–206; for Japan, Richard E. Caves and Masu Uekusa, *Industrial Organization in Japan* (Washington: Brookings Institution, 1976), pp. 72–82 and 92–96; for Pakistan, Lawrence J. White, *Industrial Concentration and Economic Power in Pakistan* (Princeton: Princeton University Press, 1974), pp. 138–146; and for West Germany, Manfred Neumann, Ingo Böbel, and Alfred Haid, "Profitability, Risk and Market Structure in West German Industries," *Journal of Industrial Economics*, vol. 27 (March 1979), pp. 227–242; and the second edition of *Industrial Market Structure and Economic Performance*, p. 294.

68. "The Concentration-Profits Relationship," supra note 3, p. 229. Revised coefficient values were kindly provided by Professor Weiss.

(T-ratios for the regression coefficients are given in parentheses.) Price-cost margins were positively and significantly associated with seller concentration CR4, the ratio of capital to sales CAP/S, the ratio of advertising expenditures to sales A/S, past output growth GROW, and the multiplicative interaction of seller concentration with the percentage of industry sales going to consumer goods markets CONSxCR4. Margins were significantly lower, the less dispersed production was geographically, as indicated by high values of DISP. Coefficients for variables estimating the ratio of central office employment to total employment CAO and the ratio of inventories to sales INV/S were insignificantly different from zero. So also were the coefficients associated with the variables included to account for entry barriers: the ratio of midpoint plant sales to total industry sales MID and the estimated amount of capital PLANTCAP required by a midpoint plant.

One could quibble at length about the results of these and many other studies attempting to explain variations in profitability indices using measures of concentration, entry barriers, and other available variables. No simple statistical summary can do justice to the diversity of methods, subsamples, and results, but Equation (11.7) is broadly consistent with the weight of evidence from statistical studies of the determinants of profitability at the industry level. We note only two exceptions. First, numerous studies have found that import/consumption ratios are negatively associated with profitability. However, failure to include an import variable does not appear to bias the coefficients on the other explanatory variables. Second, concentration indices and scale-related barriers to entry, such as MID and PLANTCAP, are often highly correlated with one another. It is therefore difficult to isolate the effect of each measure on profitability independent of the other. The effect of this "multicollinearity" among explanatory variables is to raise the standard errors on the regression coefficients associated with the correlated variables and to heighten the sensitivity of coefficient estimates to the inclusion of a few deviant observations. Thus, whether the coefficients on CR4, on individual scale and capital-related entry barrier variables, or on all of these variables are significant depends largely upon the degree to which those variables are intercorrelated.

The CR4 coefficient in Equation (11.7) implies that, holding all else fixed, an increase in four-seller concentration from 20 to 70 percent of industry sales would have raised an industry's weighted average price-cost margin by about 2.5 percentage points in 1963.[69] Whether this is considered a large magnitude relative to a sample average PCM value of around 25 percent requires subjective value judgment. We have seen that census price-cost margins fail to net out such costs as central office expenses, the cost of capital, and expenditures on advertising, research and development, and sales and customer service. The coefficient of determination R^2 indicates that some 57 percent of the variation of PCM from its sample mean remains unexplained after controlling for variations in all of the independent variables. And with the exception of the CONS $\times$ CR4 term, Equation (11.7) is at best a linear approximation to the unknown model of Equation (11.4). In light of these factors, it may be considered remarkable that any significant relation between profitability and concentration was detected at all.

Until the early 1980s, most scholars accepted the positive associations found between concentration and profitability as evidence supporting the conduct hypothesis embedded in Equation (11.3): higher concentration facilitates the ability of firms to coordinate their behavior and to hold prices above marginal cost. Critics,[70] however, observed that Equation (11.3) implied a second channel for market structure to influence profitability — through an association between profits and *market share*. Suppose that pricing conduct is unaffected by concentration, but that individual firm profits are positively associated with market share, as implied by Equation (11.1). Concentrated industries by definition contain high market share firms. The *average* level of profits will be higher in highly concentrated industries than in low-concentration industries: (1) because large firms in high-concentration industries have high profits as a result of their large market shares, and (2) because large-firm profits are accorded more weight in calculating industry profitability. Therefore, a positive profit-market share relation at the firm level will imply a positive profit-industry concentration relation, even if higher concentration has no effect on conduct. This argument was viewed skeptically by most industrial organization economists[71] until statistical studies using line of business (LB) data confirmed that the effect of own-market share on LB profitability dominates industry concentration effects.

Definitive evidence was supplied by Ravenscraft's estimate of Equation (11.3) for 3,186 lines of business in 258 FTC industry categories for 1975:[72]

$$(11.8) \qquad PCM = -22.3 + \underset{(4.95)}{.183\ S} - \underset{(1.38)}{.022\ CR4}$$

$$+ (21\ \text{other industry and LB variables});$$

$$N = 3186, R^2 = .208.$$

Price-cost margins were positively associated with lines' market shares S, but if anything, *negatively* associated with seller concentration CR4. Although Ravenscraft included twenty-one additional explanatory variables to control for other industry, LB, and company characteristics, nearly 80 percent of the variation in profitability remained unexplained. This, combined with uncertainty over the

69. Strictly speaking, this estimate applies only to an industry having no sales to consumer goods markets, and hence underestimates the profit-concentration relation for a typical industry. To the extent that an industry sells in consumer goods markets, we would need to add the effect of the interactive term CONS × CR4.

70. See, in particular, Yale Brozen, "Concentration and Structural and Market Disequilibria," *Antitrust Bulletin*, vol. 16 (Summer 1971), pp. 244–248; Harold Demsetz, "Industry Structure, Market Rivalry, and Public Policy," *Journal of Law & Economics*, vol. 16 (April 1973), pp. 1–9; Demsetz, "Two Systems of Belief About Monopoly," in Goldschmid, ed., *Industrial Concentration*, supra note 3, pp. 175–181; and Richard B. Mancke, "Causes of Interfirm Profitability Differences: A New Interpretation of the Evidence," *Quarterly Journal of Economics*, vol. 88 (May 1974), pp. 181–193.

71. The positive association between profitability and industry concentration was cited in support of policies calling for public

intervention to nullify the price-raising effects of monopoly and tight oligopoly. That the association was driven by a profit-market share association was one of a number of arguments raised by economists opposed to public intervention.

72. David J. Ravenscraft, "Structure-Profit Relationships at the Line of Business and Industry Level," *Review of Economics and Statistics*, vol. 65 (February 1983), pp. 22–31. The PIMS data yield similar findings. See Bradley T. Gale and Ben S. Branch, "Concentration versus Market Share: Which Determines Performance and Why Does it Matter?" *Antitrust Bulletin*, vol. 27 (Spring 1982), pp. 83–105. Earlier studies using firm-level data had suggested that both market share and industry concentration were important explanatory variables. Bradley Gale, "Market Share and Rate of Return," *Review of Economics and Statistics*, vol. 54 (November 1972), pp. 412–423; and William G. Shepherd, "The Elements of Market Structure," *Review of Economics and Statistics*, vol. 54 (February 1972), pp. 25–37.

correct functional form, raises questions about the reliability of the estimated coefficients.[73] However, when similar models were estimated using different disaggregated samples with different profitability measures and different combinations of explanatory variables, there were robust findings that (1) LB profitability was positively associated with market share, and (2) neither the four-seller concentration ratio nor the Hirschman-Herfindahl index was positively associated with LB profitability when market share was included as an explanatory variable.[74] Hence, the positive association found in most studies between industry profitability and seller concentration, at least for the United States, appears to have been spurious, a construct of aggregating from the line of business to the industry level.[75]

The Causal Nexus: Pricing Power or Efficiency?

The dominance of the estimated relationship between market share and profitability poses a theoretical challenge, since it is consistent with diverse alternative hypotheses concerning the profitability of individual firms. To explore the matter, we consider alternative characterizations of an industry consisting of five firms, whose market shares range from 4 to 40 percent of total industry sales. Figure 11.2 depicts four possible relationships between prices and unit costs, with the position of each firm shown by the numbered circles. In panels (a) through (c), we assume that the firms produce a homogeneous product; whereas panel (d) illustrates a case where Firms 1 and 2 can differentiate their products.

In panel (a), economies of scale are exhausted quickly, after which production occurs at constant long-run cost of $2 per unit. Only Firm 5 operates at any cost penalty. Through high barriers to entry and explicit or implicit collusion, the price is elevated to $3.50. Each firm earns substantial and more or less uniform supranormal profits.

In panel 11.2(b), economies of scale persist out to market shares of roughly 40 percent. At the assumed uniform price of $3.50, the largest seller, Firm 1, has the highest profit rate, and small firms realize no supra-normal profits (for example, Firm 4) or even negative returns (like Firm 5). Within industries described well by panel (b), we observe a positive association between market share and profitability. This association should be magnified when data on many diverse industries are analyzed in *industry* cross sections. With such compelling scale economies, one would expect industries like that in panel (b) to be, or become, tightly oligopolistic. The pull toward concentration is much weaker in panel (a) (although mergers, the operation of Gibrat's law, and other influences could lead to concentration levels higher than those needed for minimum-cost operation). If panel (a) firms fail to become much larger than Firms 4 or 5, concentration will be modest, and it will be difficult to sustain price levels much above the minimum cost of $2.00. Panel (b) type industries will thus gravitate toward concentrated structures and high profit margins, while panel (a) type industries are more apt to have atomistic structures and low profit margins.

Why don't the smaller firms in panel (b) expand to attain equally low unit costs, in the process driving prices down to competitive levels? One answer is that they may in fact be doing so, and that panel (b) represents a snapshot of an industry moving toward a long-run equilibrium in which supra-normal profits are competed away by the expansion of fringe firms. If true, then the observed profit-market share correlation is a disequilibrium phenomenon: In the short-run, high

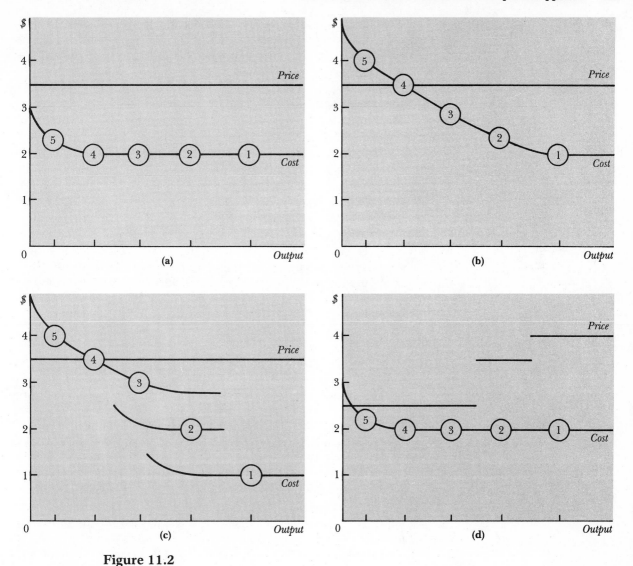

Figure 11.2
Price-Cost Relationships

73. Equation (11.8) implies that the shift from being a follower firm, with market share of 5 percent, to a leading firm, with a market share of 45, would raise PCM by 7.3 percentage points. Ravenscraft adjusted his price-cost margin measure to net out advertising, other selling expenses, depreciation, and allocated research and development and administrative expenses. Thus, except for the inclusion of capital costs, it approximates the ratio of price minus average cost to price. The simple average value of PCM in the sample was 6.5 percent—a result influenced by the large number of unprofitable tiny LBs in the sample. Weighting the average by sales, but not subtracting out allocated administrative expenses, raises the average to 21.9 percent.

74. See Scherer et al., "The Validity of Studies," supra note 38, p. 208.

75. It is, of course, possible that the 1970s, with a particularly steep recession in 1975, are atypical—that both market share *and* concentration would have been found to be positively associated with profitability were line of business data available for the 1950s and 1960s. Time series evidence, described later in this chapter, suggests that concentration effects on industry profitability were weaker, and size effects on firm profitability were stronger, in the 1970s than in earlier periods.

prices resulting from cooperation among the small number of firms that produce at minimum efficient scale attract entry at sub-MES levels by firms that slowly expand (or induce expansion by incumbent firms), driving price down toward cost. An alternative explanation for firm size differences in industries with substantial scale economies is that there may be some barrier to fringe firm expansion or the entry of new low-cost firms. If so, why don't large Firms 1 and 2 expand their own output further, again driving down price? The most reasonable response to this question is another question: why should they? In a panel (b) environment, leading firms must recognize the monopoly power conferred upon them by whatever influences condemn Firms 4 and 5 to sub-MES operations. They will maximize profits by setting relatively high prices after taking into account the residual supply of fringe firms. Indeed, to do so is the essence of exploiting monopoly power.

Either explanation for the positive association between line of business profitability and market share rests in part upon the premise that industries sufficiently oligopolistic to sustain high leading firm profit margins have cost structures more like those of panel (b) than panel (a). Doubts on this point are raised by the evidence reviewed in Chapter 4 that minimum efficient plant scales and even minimum efficient multiplant firm scales are characteristically small in relation to the size of U.S. markets, and that leading firms tend to be much larger than they need to be to realize all or most of the advantages of size.[76] Harold Demsetz has urged in response that the greater profitability of leading firms may have little or nothing to do with scale economies in the conventional sense and, indeed, that the scale economies hypothesis may assume the wrong chain of causation.[77] He argues that, for reasons possibly unrelated to its initial size, a firm may come up with methods of reducing cost significantly, or with superior new products that permit it to enjoy unusually high profits. Given this element of superiority, which for some reason may be difficult to imitate, the firm grows rapidly to a position of industry leadership. Examining the situation after this process has been in effect for a while, the statistical analyst sees a correlation between size and profitability. The scale economies hypothesis implies that size has conferred an advantage, but in fact, superior innovativeness or managerial skill has led to size *and* supranormal profits.

Examples appear in panels (c) and (d) of Figure 11.2. In panel (c), Firms 3, 4, and 5 operate on the same long-run unit cost curve as depicted in panel (b), while Firms 1 and 2 have managed to reach lower long-run cost curves. The firms in panel (d) have costs identical to those in panel (a). However, consumers view their products differently. In equilibrium, Firms 3, 4, and 5 are able to charge no more than $2.50; Firm 2 can charge $3.50; while Firm 1 maximizes its profits by charging just over $4.00.

Richard Mancke recast this argument in the spirit of the Gibrat-type processes we considered in Chapter 4.[78] He postulated that all firms start from identical positions and periodically reinvest their profits in lumpy, uncertain business opportunities. Each faces the same probability distribution of investment payoffs. Those that are particularly lucky—realizing cost-saving innovations or popular new products—will grow more rapidly. After some time, the largest firms will be the luckiest ones who will also have been reporting relatively high profit returns.

Again, the patterns in panels (c) and (d) will emerge, implying a positive correlation between market share and profitability. Its basis is neither economies of scale nor superiority in any conventional sense, but plain luck.

In an ingenious use of PIMS data, Richard Caves and associates tested the Mancke hypothesis.[79] They reasoned that if above-average size and profitability were the consequences of past chance events, one would expect the positive association between market share and profitability to be stronger, the more uncertain or turbulent is the environment within which firms operate. Distinguishing between high- and low-turbulence situations on the basis of seven qualitative characteristics as well as the observed instability of leading-firm market shares, they found support for the random effect hypothesis only in businesses whose products underwent regular model changes. For other characteristics such as newness of the business, the importance of technological change, and being in the early stages of the product life cycle, the evidence was either inconsistent with the Mancke hypothesis or, paradoxically, consistent with it only for industries of low market share instability.

Thus, appreciable market share and concentration increases are not merely the result of Gibrat-like processes. The firms experiencing rapid market share gains are frequently found to have been doing something different with their products, services, promotional or distribution methods, price strategies, production processes, or the like. It is not a difficult leap to infer that if they were successful, they must have been exhibiting superiority of some sort. With the proper amount of faith and another leap, one reaches the further conclusion that if their success was achieved in a marketplace where buyers and sellers could choose freely, any correlation between profitability and market share that emerges from the ensuing dynamics must reflect superiority and hence, in a broader sense, economic efficiency. One need not question why other firms failed to enter and compete away supra-normal profits, whether the industry's structure might have been so transformed that wholly different pricing behavior patterns resulted, or whether the structural transformations that followed were indispensable expectationally in triggering the initial innovation. To quote John McGee's extreme view, in freely functioning markets:

> such economies as there are will assert themselves, and no one need be concerned with how large or small they are. . . . [A]part from those industries dominated by State controls, there is the strongest presumption that the existing structure is the efficient structure.[80]

Although there are also factual and interpretational quarrels, whether or not one accepts this view — that is, that whatever happens in the marketplace must be for the best — is the most fundamental point of disagreement separating the diverse

76. See pp. 138–141 supra.

77. Demsetz, "Industry Structure," supra note 70, pp. 1–5. For antecedents, see Brozen, "Concentration and Structural Market Disequilibria," supra note 70, pp. 244–248; and especially John S. McGee, *In Defense of Industrial Concentration* (New York: Praeger, 1971).

78. Mancke, "Causes of Interfirm Profitability Differences," su-

pra note 70, pp. 181–193. Cf. pp. 141–146 supra.

79. Richard E. Caves, Bradley T. Gale, and Michael E. Porter, "Interfirm Profitability Differences: Comment," with a reply by Mancke, *Quarterly Journal of Economics*, vol. 91 (November 1977), pp. 667–680.

80. From his commentary in Goldschmid, ed., *Industrial Concentration*, supra note 3, p. 104.

schools of economists debating the meaning of structure-performance relationships. It is doubtful that the disagreements would vanish even if statistics on performance and structure were available in unlimited quantity and impeccable quality. We shall nonetheless have a good deal more to say about the issues when product differentiation and technological innovation are subjected to detailed study in Chapters 16 and 17.

A somewhat different view of the world emerges from the theoretical analysis developed in Chapter 10. It says that market structure and the pricing behavior flowing from it do not occur only through chance or simple acts — for example, of innovation. Rather, they are consciously shaped as firms with a sufficiently dominant position in some market choose business policies that maximize long-run profits. When a dominant seller (or group of sellers acting in concert) obtains for one reason or another a significant cost or price advantage over rivals, it can raise prices to maximize short-run profits and see its market share decline; set prices high enough to realize unit profits commensurate with its advantage while maintaining its market share; or it can temporarily reduce prices and profit margins to enhance its share and ability to earn even higher profits later. This view suggests that, when intra-industry profitability differences are observed, as in panels (b) through (d) of Figure 11.2, they reflect *inter alia* strategic behavioral choices by leading firms calculated to maximize the payoffs from whatever advantages the sellers have succeeded in achieving.

Thus, the positive profit-market share relationships observed in line of business studies represents a still-unknown mixture of temporary efficiency differences and more or less durable monopoly power. Disentangling the relative importance of the two effects and identifying the relative incidence of alternative intra-industry price-cost relationships, such as those illustrated in Figure 11.2, is the great challenge facing empirical industrial organization researchers. A complete, unbiased statistical analysis of the dynamic interdependence among profitability, concentration, market share, and product differentiation can only be carried out in a dynamic framework. We turn to work along these lines later. First, however, we must examine some additional insights into the nature of the performance-structure relations emerging from cross-sectional line of business research.

For one, complex and perhaps unsystematic inter-industry differences have much to do with profitability differences among sellers' lines of business. This is shown by regression analyses that added zero-one industry and firm intercept dummy variables to LB-specific variables in "explaining" profitability.[81] Replacing the zero-one variables distinguishing each industry from all others with continuously scaled measures of industry concentration, barriers to entry, growth, and other characteristics reduces the explanatory power of the analyses by about one-half (from $R^2 \simeq .40$ to $R^2 \simeq .20$). In contrast, market share differences alone account for a very small share of the variation in LB profitability explained by regression models.

Second, the strong positive effect of market share on profitability is related at least as much to product differentiation advantages as to economies of scale. One expects key aspects of product differentiation to be stronger for consumer goods than for goods sold to well-informed industrial buyers, while there is no particular reason to believe that scale economies should be greater in either industry category. Dividing Ravenscraft's line of business sample into producer and consumer goods categories, Ross found a significant positive profit – market share relation for consumer goods industries, but *no* association between LB profitability and market share for producer goods industries.[82] This is consistent with the finding in inter-industry cross sections that the profit-concentration relation is stronger for consumer goods industries than for producer goods, for example, in Equation (11.7) above. It suggests that the case in panel (d) of Figure 11.2 may occur often in the industrial world.

Third, several important insights about the nature of intra-industry rivalry emerge from a study by Kwoka and Ravenscraft.[83] Profitability differences among *leading* firms are uncorrelated with differences in their market shares; that is, leading firm profitability depends more upon industry characteristics than upon the leader's share of industry sales. However, having a relatively large number two firm in the industry tends to intensify rivalry, squeezing the leading firm's profits. An increase in the leading firm's market share tends to *depress* follower firm profits in industries with sizable minimum efficient scales, but not in small-plant industries. This almost surely reflects some form of price leadership in which the leader enjoys greater discretion in high-MES industries.[84] However, the profit disadvantages of followers is lessened, even in industries with sizable minimum efficient scale requirements, when smaller rivals are able to establish differentiated product niches.[85]

These results from line of business research do not imply the absence of monopoly power. Monopoly power is the power to choose the price that is most profitable. What the new evidence suggests is that such power is exercised not collectively by some large group, but primarily by leading firms, especially when these firms have a cost or price advantage over rivals. In such market structures, a social tradeoff may be implied. An alternative structure with lower leading firm market shares may mean high unit costs (although when the leading firm's advantage comes from product differentiation, as illustrated in panel (d) of Figure 11.2, this is not necessary). Whether a more fragmented market structure yields lower prices depends upon the extent to which the leading firm's power (and desire) is

81. See Richard Schmalensee, "Do Markets Differ Much?" *American Economic Review*, vol. 75 (June 1985), pp. 341–351; John T. Scott and George Pascoe, "Beyond Firm and Industry Effects on Profitability in Imperfect Markets," *Review of Economics and Statistics*, vol. 68 (May 1986), pp. 284–292; Ioannis Kessides, "Do Firms Differ Much? Some Additional Evidence," University of Maryland, mimeo, June 1987; and David R. Ross, "Do Firms Differ Much? Markets Differ by Stage of Processing," Williams College, mimeo, November 1986. Scott and Pascoe and Kessides also report significant firm-specific effects. Similar conclusions emerge from a study of pooled industry cross sections by David T. Levy, "Variation in the Concentration-Profit Relationship Across Industries," *Southern Economic Journal*, vol. 51 (July 1984), pp. 267–273.

82. Ross, "Do Markets Differ Much?" See also Gale and

Branch, "Concentration versus Market Share," supra note 72.

83. See John E. Kwoka, Jr., and David J. Ravenscraft, "Cooperation vs. Rivalry: Price-Cost Margins by Line of Business," *Economica*, vol. 53 (August 1986), pp. 351–363.

84. See p. 239 supra.

85. Ralph M. Bradburd and David R. Ross, "Can Small Firms Find and Defend Strategic Niches? A Test of the Porter Hypothesis," *Review of Economics and Statistics*, vol. 71 (May 1989), pp. 258–262. See also Howard H. Newman, "Strategic Groups and the Structure-Performance Relationship," *Review of Economics and Statistics*, vol. 60 (August 1978), pp. 417–427; Michael E. Porter, "The Structure Within Industries and Companies' Performance," *Review of Economics and Statistics*, vol. 61 (May 1979), pp. 214–227; and Caves and Pugel, *Intraindustry Differences,* supra note 58.

constrained versus the degree to which unit costs are elevated with smaller-scale operation.

Advertising and Product Differentiation

We have seen that the market share-profit relationship depends upon the degree of product differentiation in at least some markets. A standard approach to capturing the role of product differentiation is to include the ratio of advertising expenditures to total sales as an explanatory variable in line of business or industry profitability regressions. Comanor and Wilson did the pioneering research.[86] They hypothesized that in industries with substantial advertising expenditures, product differentiation barriers to entry would be relatively high for several reasons: (1) newcomers would have to incur disproportionately high advertising outlays per dollar of sales to win patronage away from established sellers enjoying significant brand preferences, (2) economies of scale in advertising favored firms with sizable market positions, and (3) the absolute amount of capital needed for successful entry was higher when an entrant had to advertise intensively along with setting up production operations. Interpreting the coefficient on the industry advertising/sales variable A/S requires care when profitability is measured by census price-cost margins from which advertising outlays have not been deducted. If the Comanor-Wilson hypothesis holds, the coefficient on A/S should be significantly greater than unity. Thus, we interpret the coefficient on A/S in Equation (11.7) as indicating that a 10 percentage point increase in A/S would increase PCM by 10 percentage points to cover the cost increase and by another 3 percentage points as supra-normal returns.[87]

The Comanor-Wilson hypothesis has been tested many times using diverse profitability measures for widely varying firm and industry samples. The results have proved to be quite robust, at least for manufacturing industries.[88] Profitability indices appear consistently to be positively correlated with industry advertising/sales ratios. Nevertheless, these results could conceivably be affected by subtle biases. Three possibilities deserve attention.

First, as we have observed before, advertising spending might properly be viewed as a capital outlay with potentially long-lasting effects. Treating it as a current expense, as is standard accounting practice, can lead to upward-biased profitability values when profit rates exceed the growth rate of advertising outlays.[89] This in turn implies upward-biased estimates of the effect advertising has on profitability. Thus, the positive profitability-advertising association could be an accounting artifact. Some attempts to correct for this problem by capitalizing and then depreciating advertising outlays show that the findings remain essentially unaltered.[90] However, the positive correlation between the advertising/sales ratio and profitability fades to insignificance when the effects of advertising are assumed to be very long lived, that is, when the applicable depreciation rate is quite low.[91] The crucial question is whether the effects of advertising depreciate fairly rapidly, for example, at a rate of 33 to 90 percent per year, or slowly, for example, at the 5 percent rate favored by Bloch. The higher range of depreciation rates appears more plausible, but the issue is still disputed.[92]

Second, there is a problem in ascertaining the direction of causation.[93] As the margin between price and unit production cost rises, sellers have a heightened incentive to compete for additional business on nonprice bases, for example, by increasing their advertising outlays.[94] Ample gross profit margins induce high advertising — the reverse of the hypothesis that high advertising reflects barriers to entry, which in turn implies high profits. To disentangle these differing chains of causation, one needs a properly specified simultaneous equations model, preferably using data for narrowly defined lines of business spanning a considerable period of time. Tests falling appreciably short of this data quality ideal provide consistent but generally weak support for the hypothesis that higher firm and industry profits do *flow from* relatively high advertising/sales ratios.[95]

Third, the positive association between advertising and profitability does not hold up consistently when samples are subdivided into smaller subsets.[96]

86. William S. Comanor and Thomas A. Wilson, "Advertising, Market Structure, and Performance," *Review of Economics and Statistics*, vol. 49 (November 1967), pp. 423–440; and *Advertising and Market Power*, supra note 60.

87. A similar problem of interpretation arises when the ratio of operating income to sales or assets is used as the profitability measure.

88. For a comprehensive critical survey of profitability-advertising studies up to 1974, see James M. Ferguson, *Advertising and Competition: Theory, Measurement, Fact* (Cambridge: Ballinger, 1974), especially Chapters 6 and 7. See also the references in Schmalensee, "Inter-Industry Studies," supra note 3. Among the most recent replications of the Comanor-Wilson finding are, for the United States, Bothwell, Cooley, and Hall, "A New View," supra note 11, pp. 397–417; for Australia, David K. Round, "Intertemporal Profit Margin Variability and Market Structure in Australian Manufacturing," *International Journal of Industrial Organization*, vol. 1 (June 1983), pp. 189–209; for Japan, Caves and Uekusa, *Industrial Organization in Japan*, supra note 67, pp. 72–82 and 92–96; and for the U.K., Paul A. Geroski, "Simultaneous Equations Models," supra note 52, pp. 145–158.

In producer goods industries, advertising intensity has been found to be *negatively* associated with profitability. Bradburd and Caves, "A Closer Look," supra note 63, pp. 635–645; and Ian Domowitz, R. Glenn Hubbard, and Bruce C. Petersen, "Business Cycles and the Relationship between Concentration and Price-Cost Margins," *Rand Journal of Economics*, vol. 17 (Spring 1986), pp. 1–17. This presumably reflects measurement error, since advertising is rarely the dominant component of selling expenses in such industries. See Leonard W. Weiss, George A. Pascoe, and Stephen Martin, "The Size of Selling Costs," *Review of Economics and Statistics*, vol. 65 (November 1983), pp. 668–672.

Evidence for nonmanufacturing industries presents a mixed picture. See Kenneth D. Boyer, "Information and Goodwill Advertising," *Review of Economics and Statistics*, vol. 56 (November 1974), pp. 541–548; and Michael E. Porter, "Interbrand Choice, Media Mix and Market Performance," *American Economic Review*, vol. 66 (May 1976), pp. 398–406.

89. See p. 420 supra.

90. See the extension of work by Comanor and Wilson in *Advertising and Market Power*, supra note 60, Chapter 8; Allyn D. Strickland and Leonard W. Weiss, "Advertising, Concentration, and

Price-Cost Margins," *Journal of Political Economy*, vol. 84 (October 1976), pp. 1109–1121; and Henry G. Grabowski, "Industrial Research and Development, Intangible Capital Stocks, and Firm Profit Rates," *Bell Journal of Economics*, vol. 9 (Autumn 1978), pp. 328–343.

91. See Harry Bloch, "Advertising and Profitability: A Reappraisal," *Journal of Political Economy*, vol. 82 (March/April, 1974), pp. 267–286.

92. For a literature survey suggesting that the weight of evidence favors relatively high depreciation rates, see G. Assmus, J. U. Farley, and D. R. Lehmann, "How Advertising Affects Sales: A Meta-Analysis of Econometric Results," *Journal of Marketing Research*, vol. 21 (1984), pp. 65–74.

93. See Richard Schmalensee, "Advertising and Profitability: Further Implications of the Null Hypothesis," *Journal of Industrial Economics*, vol. 25 (September 1976), pp. 45–54. If there are diminishing returns in the ability of advertising to increase sales — that is, if $dS/dA > 0$ and $d^2A/dA^2 < 0$ — then the more price exceeds marginal cost, the more profitable an additional sale is, and hence the higher is the profit-maximizing advertising/sales ratio. See also Chapter 16 *infra*, note 65.

94. See Chapter 16 *infra*.

95. See Comanor and Wilson, *Advertising and Market Power*, supra note 60, pp. 153–163; Strickland and Weiss, "Advertising, Concentration, and Price-Cost Margins," supra note 90, pp. 1109–1121; Stephen Martin, "Advertising, Concentration and Profitability: The Simultaneity Problem," *Bell Journal of Economics*, vol. 10 (Autumn 1979), pp. 639–647; and Ian Domowitz, R. Glenn Hubbard, and Bruce C. Petersen, "The Intertemporal Stability of the Concentration-Margins Relationship," *Journal of Industrial Economics*, vol. 35 (September 1986), pp. 13–33.

96. For example, Michael Porter found a positive advertising-profitability relation for convenience goods, but not for nonconvenience goods (on which retailers' salespersons provide substantial in-store assistance to consumers, thereby influencing product choices); for network television, but not for other media; and for leading firms but not for follower firms. "Consumer Behavior, Retailer Power and Market Performance in Consumer Goods Industries," *Review of Economics and Statistics*, vol. 56 (November 1974), pp. 419–436; "Interbrand Choice," supra note 88; and "The Structure Within Industries," supra note 85.

However, splitting industry samples too finely risks losing sight of important theoretical considerations, since if heavy advertising reflects product differentiation barriers to entry, it is the differences *among* industries that primarily matter. The closer one comes to analyzing purely intra-industry differences, the more any positive inter-industry effects will be attenuated. Indeed, if there are economies of scale in advertising, as seems plausible, and if firms within an industry have similar markups of price over production cost, one would expect to find a *negative* correlation between profit rates and advertising/sales ratios at the intra-industry level of analysis. In profit regressions using firm and line of business data that include industry and firm or LB advertising/sales ratios, the coefficients on the industry ratio are significantly positive, while those on the own line of business ratio are negative but insignificantly different from zero.[97]

In sum, there is reason to believe that, for at least an important group of industries, intense advertising is associated with relatively high profits. This relationship presumably reflects the ability of sellers to hold the prices of strongly differentiated products above costs. We shall return for a fuller exploration of the phenomenon in Chapter 16.

Monopoly Power and Costs

Usually, statistical studies seeking to isolate the impact of market share and seller concentration on monopoly power and hence prices assume costs to be unaltered. However, if the conditions that strengthen monopoly power lead also to the inflation of costs, then the relationship between concentration and monopoly power may be understated.

One possibility is that high prices in concentrated industries could attract inefficiently small producers, so that average industry profit margins understate the ability of firms to elevate price above minimum unit cost. For example, in panel (b) of Figure 11.2, Firms 4 and 5 are operating where unit costs are well above minimum levels (approximated by Firm 1's unit cost of $2.00). The lower profits of these inefficient firms depress the industry average. Several studies have found that the fraction of industry output produced by such firms, that is, in plants operating below minimum efficient scale, is *negatively* related to concentration. This suggests that the downward bias in industry price-cost margins is *less* for concentrated industries.[98] However, other studies have found that this result is reversed for industries with substantial tariff barriers to imports.[99]

The absence of competition may also permit slack and inefficiencies that raise costs.[100] Efforts to quantify the extent of such "X-inefficiency" systematically have proved difficult.[101] The weight of the evidence, to be examined further in Chapter 18, leans in favor of a conclusion that operations are tighter under more intense competitive pressure.

Finally, profits in concentrated industries could be captured by input suppliers — notably, by workers. Evidence of wage reductions when the airline and trucking industries were deregulated and exposed to new competition provides anecdotal support.[102] Inter-industry studies also support the "monopoly rent capture" hypothesis, but there is wide disagreement about the fraction of what would otherwise be monopoly profits gained by workers.[103] Two statistical difficulties complicate sorting out the issues. First, the determinants of unionization and seller concentration tend to be highly correlated, at least for the United

States.[104] Second, where monopoly profits are partially captured by workers, the determinants of both must be estimated simultaneously: profits are negatively correlated with "excess" wages, and wages are positively correlated with monopoly profits. Pugel estimated that workers capture between 7 and 14 percent of excess profits, while Karier calculated the figure at about 60 percent.[105] Although some studies report no bias in estimated profit-concentration relationships resulting from labor's capture of excess profits, Michael Salinger suggests that complete unionization could eliminate any observed profit-concentration relationship.[106]

We conclude that some of the monopoly power derived from large market shares or high seller concentration probably leads to higher costs, reducing observed profit differences. Pinpointing the magnitude of the resulting bias awaits more detailed data and improved statistical techniques.

Cross-Sectional Evidence on Price-Structure Relationships

Even if one could correct for this bias, it may be difficult through the statistical analysis of profit data to distinguish monopolistic price-raising effects from the cost-depressing effects of scale economies and other efficiencies realized by firms with relatively large market shares. An alternative approach is to analyze price-structure relationships directly, ruling out the impact of efficiency-related cost variations. High prices might still indicate superiority of product or service quality. But this can be mitigated by focusing on industries where product differentiation opportunities are relatively limited, for example, by studying cement rather

97. John M. Vernon and R. E. M. Nourse, "Profit Rates and Market Structure of Advertising Intensive Firms," *Journal of Industrial Economics*, vol. 22 (September 1973), pp. 1–20; and Ravenscraft, "Structure-Profit Relationships," supra note 72, p. 26.

98. See Leonard W. Weiss, "Optimal Plant Size and the Extent of Suboptimal Capacity," in Robert T. Masson and P. David Qualls, eds., *Essays in Honor of Joe S. Bain* (Cambridge: Ballinger, 1976), pp. 123–142; F. M. Scherer, et al., *The Economics of Multi-Plant Operation*, supra note 51, Chapter 3; and John R. Baldwin and Paul K. Goreki, "The Determinants of Small Plant Market Share in Canadian Manufacturing Industries in the 1970s," *Review of Economics and Statistics*, vol. 67 (February 1985), pp. 156–161.

99. Harry Bloch, "Prices, Costs and Profits in Canadian Manufacturing: The Influence of Tariffs and Concentration," *Canadian Journal of Economics*, vol. 7 (November 1974), pp. 594–610; and Baldwin and Gorecki, "Determinants of Small Plant Market Share."

100. See Harvey Leibenstein, "Allocative Efficiency vs. X-Efficiency," *American Economic Review*, vol. 56 (June 1966), pp. 392–415; and *Beyond Economic Man: A New Foundation for Microeconomics* (Cambridge: Harvard University Press, 1976). See also Chapter 18 *infra*.

101. For examples, see Walter J. Primeaux, Jr., "An Assessment of X-efficiency Gained Through Competition," *Review of Economics and Statistics*, vol. 59 (February 1977), pp. 105–108; and John J. Siegfried and Edwin H. Wheeler, "Cost Efficiency and Monopoly Power: A Survey," *Quarterly Review of Economics and Business*, vol. 21 (Spring 1981), pp. 25–46.

102. See, for example, Nancy L. Rose, "Labor Rent-Sharing

and Regulation: Evidence from the Trucking Industry," *Journal of Political Economy*, vol. 95 (December 1987), pp. 1146–1178. The evidence is less clear in the airline industry: Wallace Hendricks, Peter Feuille, and Carol Szerszen, "Regulation, Deregulation, and Collective Bargaining in Airlines," *Industrial and Labor Relations Review*, vol. 34 (October 1980), pp. 67–81; and David Card, "The Impact of Deregulation on the Employment and Wages of Airline Mechanics," *Industrial and Labor Relations Review*, vol. 39 (July 1986), pp. 527–538.

103. For surveys of the literature, see W. T. Dickens and L. F. Katz, "Interindustry Wage Differences and Industry Characteristics," in Kevin Lang and J. Leonard, eds., *Unemployment and the Structure of Labor Markets* (New York: Basil Blackwell, 1987), pp. 48–89; Schmalensee, "Inter-Industry Studies," supra note 3; and Geroski, "In Pursuit of Monopoly Power," supra note 3, pp. 110–111.

104. See Dickens and Katz, "Interindustry Wage Differences and Industry Characteristics," pp. 62–63.

105. Thomas A. Pugel, "Profitability, Concentration and the Interindustry Variation in Wages," *Review of Economics and Statistics*, vol. 62 (May 1980), pp. 248–253; and Thomas Karier, "Unions and Monopoly Profits," *Review of Economics and Statistics*, vol. 67 (February 1985), pp. 34–42.

106. See Kim B. Clark, "Unionization and Firm Performance: The Impact on Profits, Growth, and Productivity," *American Economic Review*, vol. 74 (December 1984), pp. 893–919; Domowitz, Hubbard, and Petersen, "Intertemporal Stability," supra note 95; and Michael A. Salinger, "Tobin's q, Unionization and the Concentration-Profits Relationship," *Rand Journal of Economics*, vol. 15 (Summer 1984), pp. 159–170.

than wine or computers. It is seldom possible to analyze structure-price relationships cross-sectionally because of an apples and oranges problem in comparing the prices of diverse industries' products.[107] However, when the same commodity is sold in numerous well-defined regional or local markets, meaningful comparisons can be made.

Money is an unusually homogeneous product and, at least for consumer-type loans, the relevant markets are local. There have been numerous studies of the relationship between local market structure and the prices consumers pay for money (that is, the interest rate on loans), as well as the prices consumers receive for money (that is, the interest on saving and checking accounts), taking into account also diverse bank operating cost-influencing variables.[108] They reveal quite uniformly that loan interest rates and service charges tend to be higher, and deposit interest rates tend to be lower, the more concentrated local banking markets are.[109]

Similar studies have been conducted for a number of other industries.[110] The findings are generally consistent with those of industry-level profit-concentration studies. An increase in four-seller concentration from 20 to 70 percent would raise prices by about 5 percent on average.[111] The resulting impact on *profits* will be less to the extent that firms in more concentrated markets allow costs to rise, and greater to the extent that high concentration permits firms to exploit scale economies and other size-related efficiencies.

One can, as always, quarrel with the samples, controls, and methods employed in these studies. Perhaps the most difficult challenge is controlling for differences in product mix and input costs among regional markets that might bias the estimated price-concentration relationship. Nevertheless, industry-specific studies offer important complementary observations to the evidence generated by inter-industry studies.

Time Series Studies

Until the 1980s, nearly all statistical studies of structure-performance relationships used cross sections of industries, firms, or business units. The presumption was that inter-industry variations in profitability or prices associated with variations in the independent variables reflect long-run systematic differences. At any particular time, many industries are in disequilibrium, with firms entering, growing, and dying. But these deviations from long-run equilibrium positions were assumed to enter the residual error term of the regression equations without substantially biasing the estimated relationships between dependent and independent variables.[112]

What happens, however, if this assumption is violated? Suppose, to take an extreme example, that all firms produce at minimum efficient scale, except for a transition period of several years during which a typical firm slowly expands its production to MES. Suppose further that the ability of industries to coordinate pricing decisions is unrelated to the number of firms in the industry, so that there is no equilibrium relationship between firm profitability and market shares or industry concentration. In any particular cross section, some firms would be found moving down their long-run cost curves, earning lower profits than their larger rivals. If there are a sufficient number of industries in which small firms find themselves in transition, then a statistically significant positive relationship between market share and profitability will be found.

Only time series studies can control for disequilibrium effects. Further, only through such studies can changes in structure-performance relationships be detected. However, a number of special problems attend the construction of a time series panel.[113] Old firms may drastically alter their product mix, declare bankruptcy, or merge with other related or unrelated firms.[114] New enterprises may not have enough of a history to be useful. Working with census data is complicated by the fact that industry definitions change over time, and certain data (such as concentration indices) appear only at five-year intervals.

Researchers are beginning to overcome these problems, creating the prospect of promising new avenues for analysis in the years ahead. Three strands of research utilizing time series merit discussion.

Cyclical Effects and Trends

In a 1974 survey, Leonard Weiss observed that the strength of the profit-concentration relationship observed in earlier industry cross sections seemed to vary systematically over time.[115] Because the industry samples also varied over time, Weiss had no way of confirming his hunch. Domowitz, Hubbard, and Petersen were able to do so, using a panel of 284 census industries for the years 1958–1981.[116] They found that over this period, the observed relation between industry average price-cost margins and seller concentration weakened dramatically. In addition, the profit-concentration relation appeared to be procyclical, reflecting greater variation of price-cost margins in highly concentrated industries

107. For an exception involving 135 census industries, see Christina M. L. Kelton, and Leonard W. Weiss, "Change in Concentration, Change in Cost, Change in Demand, and Change in Price," in Weiss, ed., *Concentration and Price,* supra note 45, Chapter 3. Controlling for differences in costs, they find a positive association between price and seller concentration.

108. For surveys, see Gilbert, "Bank Market Structure and Competition," supra note 3; and Leonard W. Weiss, "Concentration and Price in Banking," in Weiss, ed., *Concentration and Price,* Chapter 12.

109. Exceptions to the significant association finding arise when interest rate movements were limited by state usury laws and federal regulations. It should be noted also that few banking studies are able to control adequately for portfolio differences among banks, that is, the relative mix of long-term and short-term consumer loans, and the mix of checking, saving, and saving certificate of deposit accounts.

110. In *Concentration and Price,* supra note 45, Weiss presents or summarizes studies for airline fares between city pairs, beef slaughter houses, cement, gasoline, retail food stores, and railroad freight.

111. Weiss, *Concentration and Price,* Chapter 13.

112. Succinct statements of the long-run equilibrium hypothesis underlying cross-sectional studies appear in Caves and Pugel, *Intraindustry Differences,* supra note 58, pp. 9–11; and Schmalensee, "Inter-Industry Studies," supra note 3.

113. At present, researchers who wish to work with line of business panels are stymied. The FTC Line of Business Program contains complete data only for 1974–1977. Confidentiality restrictions and a tendency for business units to remain in the panel only for short periods limit one's ability to trace the impact of changes in market structure over time in the PIMS data.

114. In *Profits in the Long Run* (Cambridge: Cambridge University Press, 1986), p. 5, Dennis Mueller found that of the 1,000 largest U.S. manufacturing companies in 1950, 384 were acquired, nineteen were liquidated, and no information could be found on fourteen others as of 1972.

115. Weiss, "The Concentration-Profits Relationship," supra note 3.

116. Ian Domowitz, R. Glenn Hubbard, and Bruce C. Petersen, "Business Cycles and the Relationship Between Concentration and Price-Cost Margins," *Rand Journal of Economics,* vol. 17 (Spring 1986), pp. 1–17; "The Intertemporal Stability," supra note 95, pp. 13–34; and "Market Structure and Cyclical Fluctuations in U.S. Manufacturing," *Review of Economics and Statistics,* vol. 70 (February 1988), pp. 55–66. Generally consistent results using much more aggregated data are reported by Robert E. Hall, "The Relation Between Price and Marginal Cost in U.S. Industry," *Journal of Political Economy,* vol. 96 (October 1988), pp. 921–947.

than in industries with average or low concentration. This suggests that cross-sectional studies done for relatively prosperous years (such as 1963) will observe a stronger link between concentration and profitability than will cross-sectional studies of samples drawn from recession years (such as the mid-1970s). Alternatively, one can view the Domowitz et al. findings as driven by the possibly unique stagflation of the 1970s, when weak demand combined with rising costs (magnified by union contracts indexed for inflation) to squeeze concentrated industry profit margins.

Domowitz et al. also identify important differences in industry subsamples. The procyclical pattern is much more pronounced in producer goods industries than in consumer goods industries.[117] In fact, no significant relation between industry profitability and seller concentration was observed for producer goods industries over the period 1974–1981. Another categorization of the data found that the procyclical pattern is strongest for concentrated nondurable goods industries. Price-cost margins in concentrated durable goods industries showed little cyclical sensitivity.

These findings raise as many questions as they answer. The census data do not permit Domowitz et al. to distinguish between the effects of market share and concentration. Some suggestive evidence is provided by Schmalensee's study of Internal Revenue Service *Statistics of Income* data for 1953–1983.[118] He observed differences in twelve alternative profitability measures among firms classified into asset size categories over the thirty-one-year period. Even though the twelve measures were not on average highly correlated with one another, all were significantly positively associated with asset size categories, that is, larger firms were more profitable, and variations in this association over the sample period *were* highly correlated for all twelve measures. Consistent with the Domowitz et al. results, the profit-size relationship weakened with the passage of time. However, profit differences between large and small asset categories moved *counter-cyclically* over the sample period, that is, the profit advantage of large firms was greater in recessions than in boom periods.[119] This seems inconsistent with arguments that large firms are likely to be more heavily burdened by fixed costs in recessions.[120] However, it is consistent with evidence that large firms lose fewer sales in recessions and expand output less in booms than smaller rivals.[121]

Persistence of Profitability

The great promise of time series data lies in permitting analyses of dynamic structure-performance relationships. For example, in his criticism of early concentration-profitability cross-sectional studies, Brozen showed *inter alia* that there was a tendency for the profits of firms located in high-concentration, high-profit industries to decline in subsequent time periods.[122] He argues that the samples caught concentrated industry leaders during a period of disequilibrium — for example, before smaller rivals had been able to expand to take advantage of scale economies, as in panel (b) of Figure 11.2, and thereby erode supra-normal returns. There are alternative explanations for his findings, such as the tendency for returns to converge toward the all-manufacturing average as particularly profitable companies diversify into less profitable lines. Nevertheless, a properly formulated dynamic theory indicates that one should indeed expect to see especially profitable firms' returns decline *unless* entry barriers are sufficiently high to warrant an entry-deterring or exclusionary-pricing strategy. The bulk of the carefully derived evidence on this point suggests that, contrary to the Brozen hypothesis, profitability differences among firms tend to persist over long periods for the United States and a number of other countries.[123] However, important international differences appear. For example, rates of convergence are faster in Japan than in the United States and faster in France and Germany than in the United Kingdom.

To understand the linkages that allow profitability differences to persist for long periods, one must capture the dynamic interdependence among profitability, concentration, market share, and barriers to entry—each of which is simultaneously determined. If definitive results are to be obtained, they will have to come from joining solid realistic theory, sophisticated econometric technique, and broadly representative, intertemporally comparable performance and structure data covering individual lines of business. This objective remains out of reach.[124] Perhaps it will always be so, but optimism is a pardonable folly, even for economists.

Preliminary attempts have generated sufficiently provocative results to whet one's appetite for more. The first known effort to estimate a three-equation system with industry profitability (from census price-cost margin data), concentration, and advertising/sales ratios as the endogenous variables had difficulty, like many less ambitious studies, disentangling the profitability effects of concentration and scale- and capital-related entry barrier measures.[125] The most ambitious effort estimated a nonlinear system of five equations using data on 184 census industries for 1963 and 1967, adding the long-run equilibrium level of seller concentration and the speed of adjustment to that level as endogenous (that is, internally

117. The classification is based on input-output table estimates of the uses of industry shipments. An industry is classified as a producer goods industry if more than 50 percent of the industry's output was classified as materials input or investment by some other industry. If 50 percent or more of output was classified as being used for consumption, the industry was classified as a consumer goods industry.

118. Richard Schmalensee, "Intra-Industry Profitability Differences in U.S. Manufacturing," supra note 15, pp. 337–357. However, note that firm size and market share generally are weakly correlated at best.

119. Cf. Chapter 4, Table 4.1.

120. Large corporations have higher capital/sales ratios than smaller rivals. Caves and Pugel, *Intraindustry Differences,* supra note 58. If this signals a higher ratio of fixed to variable costs, one would expect large firms' profits to fall more than the profits of small firms in recessions. See the analysis on p. 288 supra.

121. David E. Mills and Laurence Schumann, "Industry Structure with Fluctuating Demand," *American Economic Review,* vol. 75 (September 1985), pp. 758–767.

122. "The Antitrust Task Force Deconcentration Recommendations," *Journal of Law & Economics,* vol. 13 (October 1970), pp. 279–292; and "Concentration and Structural and Market Disequilibria," supra note 70, pp. 241–248. See also the exchange among Brozen, John T. Wenders, Paul W. MacAvoy, James McKie, and Lee E. Preston in the *Journal of Law & Economics,* vol. 14 (October 1971), pp. 485–512.

123. For the United States, David Qualls, "Stability and Persistence of Economic Profit Margins in Highly Concentrated Industries," *Southern Economic Journal,* vol. 40 (April 1974), pp. 604–612; Dennis C. Mueller, "The Persistence of Profits Above the Norm," *Economica,* vol. 44 (November 1977), pp. 369–380; Robert A. Connolly and Steven Schwartz, "The Intertemporal Behavior of Economic Profits," *International Journal of Industrial Organization,* vol. 4 (December 1985), pp. 379–400; and Mueller, *Profits in the Long Run,* supra note 114. For Japan and the United States, see Hiroyaki Odagiri and Hideki Yamawaki, "A Study of Company Profit-Rate Time Series: Japan and the United States," *International Journal of Industrial Organization,* vol. 4 (March 1986), pp. 1–23. For France, West Germany, and the U.K., see Paul A. Geroski and Alexis Jacquemin, "The Persistence of Profits: A European Comparison," *Economic Journal,* vol. 98 (June 1988), pp. 375–389. Also for the U.K., see John Cubbin and Paul Geroski, "The Convergence of Profits in the Long Run: Inter-Firm and Inter-Industry Comparisons," *Journal of Industrial Economics,* vol. 35 (June 1987), pp. 427–442.

124. In addition to the low probability of locating usable line of business data, it is difficult to find enough truly exogenous variables—variables whose values are not influenced by other variables in the analysis—to identify the system of simultaneous equations required to estimate any fully realized dynamic structure-performance model. See Schmalensee, "Inter-Industry Studies," supra note 3.

125. Strickland and Weiss, "Advertising, Concentration, and Price-Cost Margins," supra note 90.

determined) variables.[126] Controlling for disequilibrium conditions, the study found that most of the interactions reported in cross-sectional regressions continue to hold. However, few industries operate in long-run equilibrium (where no incumbent firm has an incentive to alter its market share and no outsider has an incentive to enter) in any single period. The estimated equations suggest a tendency for seller concentration to rise toward levels well above the average actually observed. Although the estimated speed of adjustment to this level varied greatly across industries, for most industries it was quite slow. The study predicted that over a five-year period, seller concentration would move on average 12.3 percent of the distance between the initial level and the estimated long-run level.[127] What one should conclude from these efforts is uncertain. They are certainly a step in the right direction. Much more work needs to be done to test the sensitivity of these results to alternative model specifications and data samples.

Industry-Specific Studies

We have already seen that studies of individual industries can provide an important check on the conclusions of inter-industry studies. However, the cross-sectional studies discussed above were limited to industries selling comparable products in geographically isolated markets. Time series data allow one to analyze industries that sell in national markets, or whose products differ greatly across regions. Some researchers see an additional opportunity in time series data, arguing that by focusing on single-industry firms' responses to changing conditions, one can characterize conduct directly by estimating the firms' conjectural variations.[128]

The relevant theory starts with the profit-maximizing condition embodied in Equation (11.1), which we can rewrite to obtain price at time t as a function of Firm i's marginal cost MC_{it}, the slope of the industry demand curve dP_t/dQ_t, an index of firm production q_{it}, and the firm's conjectural variation dQ_{it}/dq_{it}:[129]

$$(11.9) \qquad P_t = MC_{it} - (dP_t/dQ_t)q_{it}(1 + dQ_{it}/dq_{it}).$$

Since, by assumption, price and production data are available, the principal impediment to calculating conjectural variations is our inability to observe marginal cost and the slope of the industry demand curve. Each of these, however, can in principle be derived from estimates of the determinants of industry demand and firm costs emerging from the following statistical model:

$$(11.10) \qquad P_t = f_4(Q_t, D_t, \epsilon_{Dt}); \text{ and}$$

$$(11.11) \qquad C_{it} = f_5(q_{it}, W_t, \epsilon_{Cit}).$$

Equation (11.10) estimates industry demand, relating the market price to total industry output Q_t, a vector of variables shifting the demand curve D_t, and a random error term. Equation (11.11), estimated for each firm, defines total cost to depend upon the firm's output q_{it}, input prices W_t, and a random error term. If the unobservable demand and cost functions can be closely approximated by f_4 and f_5, then the conjectural variation of Firm i will emerge as a regression coefficient from estimating Equations (11.9) through (11.11) as a nonlinear simultaneous system.[130]

There are a daunting list of complications that make this approach difficult to implement in practice. As in industry price-concentration cross sections, the range of brands, sizes, and other features of a firm's product mix complicates the definition of price and output. The usual approach is to ignore the heterogeneity problem and calculate a single "price" by averaging revenue over a measure of units sold, adjusted for any product size differences.[131] Similar problems occur in obtaining data on the costs of inputs, which typically are grouped into a few large categories such as materials, fuel, production workers, and central office staff. Although theory provides more of the characteristics of the demand and cost functions than it does for the profit-structure models (11.3) and (11.4), many alternative representations of Equations (11.10) and (11.11) are possible.

Nevertheless, a number of studies have attempted to estimate simplified versions of the model.[132] Virtually all have focused on industries where the researcher

126. Paul A. Geroski, Robert T. Masson, and Joseph Shaanan, "The Dynamics of Market Structure," *International Journal of Industrial Organization*, vol. 5 (March 1987), pp. 93–100. This study extended work of Stephen Martin, "Advertising, Concentration and Profitability," supra note 95.

127. For a survey of other studies estimating dynamic models of the structure-performance relationship, see Paul A. Geroski and Robert T. Masson, "Dynamic Models in Industrial Organization," *International Journal of Industrial Organization*, vol. 5 (March 1987), pp. 1–13.

128. This research grows out of Leonard Weiss's observation, following an early survey of interindustry cross sections, that "perhaps the right next step is back to the industry study, but this time with regression in hand." "Quantitative Studies of Industrial Organization," supra note 3, p. 398. An introduction to, and survey of, research in this area appears in Timothy J. Bresnahan, "Empirical Studies of Industries with Market Power," in Richard Schmalensee and Robert Willig, eds., *Handbook of Industrial Organization*, supra note 3.

129. We multiply through by P_t and decompose the elasticity and market share terms:

$$P_t \frac{s_{it}}{e} = P_t \frac{q_{it}}{Q_t} \frac{dP_t}{dQ_t} \frac{Q_t}{P_t} = (dP_t/dQ_t)q_{it}.$$

130. If there are N firms in the industry, Equations (11.9) through (11.11) form a system of $2N + 1$ separate equations (industry demand, each firm's cost function, and each firm's profit-maximization condition) estimated over T periods. Unless some restrictions are imposed on the possible values of dQ_{it}/dq_{it}, the conjectural variations cannot be estimated econometrically. Typically, researchers assume that a firm's conjectural variation is constant over time or shifts between two values, for example, representing cooperative behavior and price wars.

131. For an effort to allow for quality differences within the range of products offered by a firm, see Timothy F. Bresnahan, "Departures from Marginal-Cost Pricing in the American Automobile Industry: Estimates for 1977–1978," *Journal of Econometrics*, vol. 17 (November 1981), pp. 201–227.

132. Aluminum: Valerie Suslow, "Estimating Monopoly Behavior with Competitive Recycling: An Application to Alcoa," *Rand Journal of Economics*, vol. 17 (Autumn 1986), pp. 389–403. Automobiles: Timothy F. Bresnahan, "Departures from Marginal-Cost Pricing," supra note 131; "Competition and Collusion in the American Automobile Industry: The 1955 Price War," *Journal of Industrial Economics*, vol. 35 (June 1987), pp. 457–482; and John Cubbin, "Quality Change and Pricing Behaviour in the United Kingdom Car Industry," *Economica*, vol. 42 (February 1975), pp. 45–58. Banking: Pablo Spiller and Edgardo Favaro, "The Effects of Entry Regulation on Oligopolistic Interaction: The Uruguayan Banking Sector," *Rand Journal of Economics*, vol. 15 (Summer 1984), pp. 244–254. Beer: Jonathan B. Baker and Timothy F. Bresnahan, "The Gains from Merger or Collusion in Product-Differentiated Industries," *Journal of Industrial Economics*, vol. 33 (June 1985), pp. 427–444; and "Estimating the Residual Demand Curve Facing a Single Firm," *International Journal of Industrial Organization*, vol. 6 (September 1988), pp. 283–300. Cigarettes: Daniel Sullivan, "Testing Hypotheses About Firm Behavior in the Cigarette Industry," *Journal of Political Economy*, vol. 93 (June 1985), pp. 586–598; Orley Ashenfelter and Daniel Sullivan, "Nonparametric Tests of Market Structure: An Application to the Cigarette Industry," *Journal of Industrial Economics*, vol. 35 (June 1987), pp. 483–498; and Elie Appelbaum, "The Estimation of the Degree of Oligopoly Power," *Journal of Econometrics*, vol. 19 (August 1982), pp. 283–294. (Appelbaum also estimates models for the rubber, textile, and electrical machinery "industries.") Coffee: Paul Geroski, "The Empirical Analysis of Conjectural Variations in Oligopoly," Université Catholique de Louvain, mimeo, 1982; Frank Gollop and Mark Roberts, "Firm Interdependence in Oligopolistic Markets," *Journal of Econometrics*, vol. 10 (August 1979), pp. 313–331; and Mark Roberts, "Testing Oligopolistic Behavior: An Application of the Variable Profit Function," *International Journal of Industrial Organization*, vol. 2 (December 1984), pp. 267–383. Food Processing: R. E. Lopez, "Measuring Oligopoly Power and Production Responses of the Canadian Food Processing Industry," *Journal of Agricultural Economics*, vol. 35 (1984), pp. 219–230. Gasoline: Margaret Slade, "Conjectures, Firm Characteristics and Market Structure: An Empirical Assessment," *International Journal of Industrial Organization*, vol. 4 (December 1986), pp. 347–370. Flat glass: Gyoichi Iwata, "Measurement of Conjectural Variations in Oligopoly," *Econometrica*, vol. 42 (September 1974), pp. 947–966. Petroleum products: Elie Appelbaum, "Testing Price Taking Behavior," *Journal of Econometrics*, vol. 9 (February 1979), pp. 283–294. Railroads: Robert H. Porter, "A Study of Cartel Stability: The Joint Executive Committee, 1880–1886," *Bell Journal of Economics*, vol. 14 (Autumn 1983), pp. 301–314.

expected to find evidence of monopoly power—for instance, where there were known or suspected cartels, where case study research suggested anticompetitive conduct, or simply where seller concentration was high. Not surprisingly then, many have found evidence of price elevated substantially above marginal cost and conjectural variations significantly above the level associated with competitive behavior. Such findings alone are not particularly informative, except perhaps as a validation of the statistical model. One expects to observe price above long-run marginal cost in industries where a substantial share of production occurs in plants operating below minimum efficient scale. Conjectural variations will be above the competitive level in these and in monopolistically competitive industries. More indicative of the potential value of industry-specific time series data are studies that have detected occasional shifts in conjectural variations from a "normal" cooperative level to conditions approximating pure competition—suggesting the outbreak of price wars.[133]

An important next step requires linking these and other changes in the measured conjectural variations to market structural characteristics.[134] And much more needs to be done to perfect statistical techniques and locate usable data. Until then, industry-specific statistical studies can do little more than confirm the lessons of careful descriptive case studies.

Conclusion

Statistical studies reveal that substantial differences in the profitability of firms exist both within and between industries. These differences tend to persist for long periods of time, particularly where barriers to entry are high. Profitability is positively associated with a seller's own market share, but there is little evidence, at least in recent richly disaggregated data, of a positive association between profitability and indices of seller concentration independent of the profit – market share correlation. Evidence of the exercise of monopoly power—the power to raise price above marginal costs—arises in concentrated industries. That power appears to be wielded not collectively but rather by the leading seller, especially when that firm has a cost or price advantage over its rivals. This raises a possible tradeoff for policy makers. Whether lower prices would result from policies designed to reduce seller concentration depends upon the degree to which the resulting reduction in monopoly power is offset by elevated unit costs.

These conclusions must be leavened with appropriate caveats, for the results are not uniform, the data have many shortcomings, the statistical estimates leave much more variation in profitability unexplained than they explain, and we are still some distance away from disentangling fully the relative importance of price-raising and cost-reducing linkages. One cannot help recalling the Princeton physics professor who concluded a research report by noting, "The experiments indicate that the negative mesons are absorbed only one billionth as rapidly as calculated by the theoretical physicists. This would be a major error even for an economist."[135] Against that modest standard, at least, industrial organization theory has done well.

A certain amount of art is unavoidable in statistical studies of structure-performance relationships—for example, in choosing meaningful indices of market concentration and entry barriers, in devising a proper econometric structure, and even in interpreting what has been observed. This poses risks of conscious or inadvertent bias, or, as Harold Demsetz has warned, that "believing is seeing."[136] Still it seems clear that statistical studies of structure and performance reveal the existence of important relationships whose presence stands out more sharply, the better is the quality of the data analyzed. A future research agenda must stress obtaining data of high quality and assaulting them imaginatively with high-powered econometric tools to discriminate among the still-contending behavioral hypotheses.

133. For example, see Bresnahan, "Competition and Collusion"; and Porter, "A Study of Cartel Stability." Gollop and Roberts, "Firm Interdependence in Oligopolistic Markets," found evidence of conduct approaching competitive pricing in the highly concentrated coffee industry during the period in which General Foods was cutting price in an attempt to slow market penetration by Procter and Gamble's Folgers brand. See the discussion on p. 388 supra.

134. For an important step in this direction, although outside the estimation framework described in the text, see Ralph G. M. Sultan, *Pricing in the Electrical Oligopoly*, vol. 2 (Boston: Harvard Business School Division of Research, 1975), especially Chapter 14.
135. Quoted from Jacob Viner, "The Economist in History," *American Economic Review*, vol. 53 (May 1963), p. 16.
136. Demsetz, "Two Systems of Belief About Monopoly," supra note 70, p. 164.

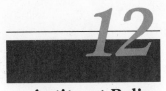

12

Antitrust Policy Toward Monopoly Market Structures

Sooner or later, monopoly power atrophies. Unless there are substantial barriers to new entry, it is eroded relatively quickly if dominant firms or tightly knit oligopolistic groups attempt to maximize short-run monopoly profits. Through the use of limit pricing or other entry-deterring strategies, the emergence of competitive market structures can be delayed, sometimes for decades. Through strategies more aggressive than limit pricing, a dominant position can be attained or strengthened, although this is more difficult when government policies discourage concentration-increasing mergers.

Our question in this chapter is, how does antitrust policy deal with dominant market positions and the behavior through which they are achieved and defended or surrendered? In the United States, the principal policy instrument (other than the merger laws, discussed in Chapter 5) is Section 2 of the Sherman Act.

Monopoly and Monopolization

Sherman Act Section 2 proclaims in part:

Every person who shall monopolize, or attempt to monopolize, or combine or conspire with any other person or persons, to monopolize any part of the trade or commerce among the several states, or with foreign nations, shall be deemed guilty of a felony . . .

The language suggests concern primarily with structural conditions rather than conduct. But why did Congress choose the word *monopolize* to describe what it condemned, and not some more conventional phrase such as "obtain or possess monopoly power"? When does a firm or group of firms monopolize? How large a share of the market must it control? Is it illegal to dominate an industry merely because one is so much more efficient than rivals that they all disappear in the face of one's competitive efforts? These are questions that cannot be answered merely by reading the statute. It is necessary to analyze the intent of Congress and interpretations rendered by the courts.

Unfortunately, the historical record affords only limited insight into what Congress had in mind in enacting Section 2.[1] The original bill proposed by Senator Sherman was debated briskly on the Senate floor, but it was altered in major respects by the Judiciary Committee, and passage of the amended bill was preceded by only a cursory debate. It appears probable, however, that the choice of the unorthodox word *monopolize* reflected the mixed emotions of legislators at the time toward big business.[2] They were acutely aware of abuses by the "trusts." But they also believed that many combinations brought economies of large-scale operation, benefiting the consumer. As a way out of a perceived dilemma, the Sherman Act drafters wrote into the law a prohibition only of monopolizing, which they apparently intended to mean an active process of securing to oneself a monopoly, going

1. For various views, see Hans B. Thorelli, *The Federal Antitrust Policy* (Stockholm: Stockholms Högskola, 1954), pp. 166–210; William Letwin, *Law and Economic Policy in America* (New York: Random House, 1965), pp. 88–89; Harlan M. Blake and William K. Jones, "Toward a Three-Dimensional Antitrust Policy," *Columbia Law Review*, vol. 65 (March 1965), pp. 423–425; and

Robert H. Bork, "Legislative Intent and the Policy of the Sherman Act," *Journal of Law & Economics*, vol. 9 (October 1966), pp. 7–48.

2. See the characterization of President Roosevelt's views on p. 12 supra.

beyond the mere possession of monopoly power as a consequence of superior efficiency.

The Emergence of a Rule of Reason

Efforts to apply the new law and probe its boundaries were halfhearted under Presidents Harrison, Cleveland, and McKinley. An early action against the Whiskey Trust was dismissed at the district court level, first because of a procedural error and then on various substantive grounds.[3] A case involving the sugar refining trust was carried all the way to the Supreme Court, only to be thrown out on the technical question of what constituted interstate commerce.[4] An indictment against the notorious cash register trust was sustained by a district court on four out of eighteen counts, but then the case was dropped by the government.[5] The first real government victory over a close-knit combination, spearheaded by Theodore Roosevelt's accession to the presidency, came when a merger consolidating control over the Northern Pacific and Great Northern railroads was declared illegal.[6]

A more important step followed in 1911, when the Supreme Court held that the Standard Oil Company of New Jersey had illegally monopolized the petroleum refining industry.[7] "The Standard" had been organized as an Ohio corporation in 1870 by the Rockefeller brothers. It pioneered the trust form of consolidation during the 1880s and then, after a skirmish with the Ohio antitrust laws, was incorporated as a New Jersey holding company in 1889. From its inception, it seemed determined to dominate the refining and sale of petroleum products—notably, in that prehorseless carriage era, kerosene and lubricating oil. It managed to maintain a 90 percent share of those markets throughout most of the 1880s and 1890s. This it accomplished by acquiring more than 120 former rival companies, securing discriminatory rail freight rates and rebates, foreclosing crude oil supplies to competitors by buying up pipelines, conducing business espionage, and allegedly waging predatory price warfare to drive rivals out of business or soften them up for takeover. Whether Standard actually cut prices deeply to destroy or discipline rivals on any widespread scale has been disputed.[8] Careful analysis suggests that more frequently it pursued a sophisticated region-by-region limit-pricing strategy. This subtlety, however, eluded contemporary jurists and economists.

Sustaining a district court's finding of guilt, the Supreme Court stated that the crime of monopolization involves two elements: the acquisition of a monopoly position, and the intent to acquire that position and exclude rivals from the market. The Court went on to articulate a rule of reason for ascertaining whether or not actions by accused firms exhibited the essential element of intent: if the acts unduly restrained competition, going beyond normal business practice, intent could be inferred. Finding "the pathway of the combination . . . strewn with the wrecks resulting from crushing out . . . the individual rights of others," the Court ruled that Standard's

> . . . intent and purpose to exclude others . . . was frequently manifested by acts and dealings wholly inconsistent with the theory that they were made with the single conception of advancing the development of business power by usual methods, but which on the contrary necessarily involved the intent to drive others from the field and to exclude them from their right to trade and thus accomplish the mastery which was the end in view.[9]

To remedy matters, the courts ordered that the Standard Oil holding company be dissolved, its controlling shares in thirty-three geographically dispersed operating subsidiaries to be distributed on a pro rata basis to Standard Oil of New Jersey stockholders. At first this led to no appreciable increase in competition, for the spun-off units operated for the most part in nonoverlapping geographic markets, and a controlling interest in the fragments remained in the hands of John D. Rockefeller and associates who had managed the original Standard Oil trust.[10] But as the dominant stockholders distributed their shares among numerous heirs and gave substantial blocks to nonvoting philanthropic institutions, as expansion to meet rapidly growing gasoline demands necessitated issuing new stock to a broader base of investors, and as some of the fragments merged with Standard competitors, competition among the surviving entities gradually developed, and each interpenetrated markets that were dominated by its former affiliates.[11]

Two weeks after the Supreme Court handed down its *Standard Oil* decision, it reinforced the rule of reason doctrine in a decision against the American Tobacco Company, also called the Tobacco Trust.[12] American was found guilty of monopolizing the cigarette and related tobacco products trades through such unreasonable business practices as excluding rivals from access to wholesalers, engrossing supplies of leaf tobacco, buying out some 250 former rivals, and predatory pricing. In the cold light of hindsight, its pricing behavior appears more swashbuckling than Standard Oil's.[13] It frequently established "fighting brands" that were sold in rivals' local markets at less than cost, and on at least one occasion at an effective after-tax price of zero, forcing the hapless competitors to sell out. The Supreme Court found these practices to be clear evidence of illegal monopolistic intent. A district court subsequently ordered that the Tobacco Trust be split into sixteen pieces, including a successor American Tobacco Company (now American Brands), Liggett & Myers, P. Lorillard, Reynolds (now RJR Nabisco, which

3. *U.S.* v. *Greenhut et al.*, 50 Fed. 469 (1892); 51 Fed. 205 (1892); and *In re Greene*, 52 Fed. 104 (1892). See also Letwin, *Law and Economic Policy*, pp. 111–113 and 145–149.

4. *U.S.* v. *E.C. Knight Co. et al.*, 60 Fed. 306 (1894), 60 Fed. 934 (1894); 156 U.S. 1 (1895).

5. *U.S.* v. *Patterson et al.*, 55 Fed. 605 (1893). On its links to the formation of IBM, see Richard T. DeLamarter, *Big Blue: IBM's Use and Abuse of Power* (New York: Dodd Mead, 1986), pp. 5–10.

6. *U.S.* v. *Northern Securities Co. et al.*, 193 U.S. 197 (1904). See p. 174 supra.

7. *U.S.* v. *Standard Oil Co. of New Jersey et al.*, 173 Fed. 177 (1909), 221 U.S. 1 (1911).

8. Compare Allan Nevins, *Study in Power: John D. Rockefeller*, vol. II (New York: Scribner's, 1953), pp. 54–67; John S. McGee, "Predatory Price Cutting: The Standard Oil (N.J.) Case," *Journal of Law & Economics*, vol. 1 (October 1958), pp. 137–169; Wayne A. Leeman, "The Limitations of Local Price-Cutting as a Barrier to Entry," *Journal of Political Economy*, vol. 64 (August 1956), pp. 329–332; and Randall Mariger, "Predatory Price Cutting: The Standard Oil of New Jersey Case Revisited," *Explorations in Economic History*, vol. 15 (October 1978), pp. 341–367.

9. *U.S.* v. *Standard Oil Co. of New Jersey et al.* 221 U.S. 1, 47, 76

(1911). For a fuller discussion of earlier state actions, the Federal suit, and its aftermath, see Bruce Bringhurst, *Antitrust and the Oil Monopoly: The Standard Oil Cases, 1890–1911* (Westport: Greenwood, 1979); and Joseph A. Pratt, "The Petroleum Industry in Transition: Antitrust and the Decline of Monopoly Control in Oil," *Journal of Economic History*, vol. 40 (December 1980), pp. 815–837.

10. On the benign stock market reaction to Standard's dissolution, see Malcolm R. Burns, "The Competitive Effects of Trust-Busting," *Journal of Political Economy*, vol. 85 (August 1977), pp. 717–739.

11. In 1987, the largest 15 U.S. industrial corporations by asset value included five Standard fragments: Exxon (Standard Oil of New Jersey), Mobil (Standard Oil of New York), Chevron (Standard Oil of California), Amoco (Standard Oil of Indiana), and BP America (acquirer of Standard Oil of Ohio).

12. *U.S.* v. *American Tobacco Co.*, 221 U.S. 106 (1911).

13. See Malcolm R. Burns, "Outside Intervention in Monopolistic Price Warfare," *Business History Review*, vol. 56 (Spring 1982), pp. 33–53; "Predatory Pricing and the Acquisition Cost of Competitors," *Journal of Political Economy*, vol. 94 (April 1986), pp. 266–296; and "New Evidence on Predatory Price Cutting," *Managerial and Decision Economics*, vol. 10 (1989).

at the time had no cigarette brand), and the American Snuff Company (which even today dominates its declining field under a new name, the Conwood Corporation).[14]

During the next few years, the government scored further but less spectacular victories against the Powder Trust,[15] the glucose and cornstarch trust,[16] Eastman Kodak Company,[17] the thread trust,[18] and a group of railroads dominating the anthracite coal industry.[19] The next important step by way of precedent occurred, however, when the government was defeated in its suit against the United States Steel Corporation.[20]

U.S. Steel was formed through a billion-dollar merger in 1901, consolidating control over 65 percent of domestic steel ingot output. It added to its holdings in 1907 by acquiring, with the permission of President Roosevelt, the Tennessee Coal and Iron Corporation. In that same recession-impacted year Judge E. H. Gary, its chairman, initiated a four-year series of dinners with rival company leaders, persuading them that sharp price competition could be avoided if they followed U.S. Steel's leadership, which they in fact chose to do. Unlike Standard Oil and American Tobacco, U.S. Steel was not accused of trying to drive rivals from the industry through cutthroat pricing and other predatory practices. Instead, it set prices sufficiently high to encourage the gradual entry and growth of other steel makers. Partly because of this, its share of the market had fallen to 52 percent in 1915, despite the sizable Tennessee Coal and Iron merger, and was continuing to fall in 1920.

After winning the *Standard Oil* case, the government brought suit in 1911 to break up U.S. Steel. A district court, applying the *Standard Oil* rule of reason, found in favor of the steel company in 1915. The Justice Department appealed to higher authority. With two justices abstaining because they had criticized or prosecuted U.S. Steel in the past, a four-member majority of the Supreme Court ruled for the corporation. They argued that since Judge Gary felt compelled to meet with competitors in order to fix and control steel prices (a practice discontinued before the suit was initiated), U.S. Steel had not attained monopoly power. They noted further that a multitude of witnesses representing competitors, dealers, and customers had paraded before the district court, and none had anything but good to say about U.S. Steel's conduct.[21] Competitors in particular testified that they were in no way restrained by the corporation's pricing. From this evidence, the majority concluded that U.S. Steel had not monopolized in the Sherman Act sense, and that even if the corporation did possess monopoly power, it had certainly not exercised that power. There followed the famous *obiter dictum* that:

. . . the law does not make mere size an offense or the existence of unexerted power an offense. It . . . requires overt acts. . . . It does not compel competition nor require all that is possible.[22]

Thus, despite the vigorous dissent of a three-justice minority, the greatest consolidation in contemporary U.S. industrial history escaped antitrust censure. Moreover, it became settled that dominant firms would subject themselves to monopolization convictions only if they behaved in a predatory or aggressive manner toward rivals, and not if they merely held a price umbrella over them. And the first seeds were sown for a cynical view that Sherman Act Section 2 protects competitors, not competition.

The *Steel* precedent was solidified in three parallel cases. Two years earlier, the Supreme Court held in a similar 4-3 decision that the United Shoe Machinery Corporation was innocent of monopolization.[23] It found *inter alia* that the five-company merger underlying United's formation in 1899 involved producers of complementary and hence noncompeting machines, that fifty-nine subsequent acquisitions were "justified by exigencies or conveniences of the situation," and that United's 80 to 95 percent share of the relevant markets had been maintained largely through superior efficiency and the legitimate exploitation of patent rights. The government also suffered a 1916 defeat at the district court level in its suit against the American Can Company. The facts were strikingly similar to those of the *Steel* case. American Can had been formed through a 1901 merger of some 120 independent entities. Competitors thrived under the umbrella of its high prices, eroding its market share from 90 percent in 1901 to roughly 50 percent in 1913. The district court observed that American "had done nothing of which any competitor or any consumer of cans complains, or anything which strikes a disinterested outsider as unfair or unethical," adding that it was "frankly reluctant to destroy so finely adjusted an industrial machine."[24] After the Supreme Court rendered its *Steel* decision, the Justice Department dropped its appeal of the *American Can* judgment along with a number of other pending and planned monopolization suits. It persevered in prosecuting only one other major monopolization case, seeking to extend the modest divestiture ordered in an earlier court judgment against the International Harvester Company.[25] Here again it was rebuked by the Supreme Court, which reiterated its *U.S. Steel* rule that mere size unaccompanied by unlawful conduct was not illegal.[26] Discouraged by these defeats, the Justice Department for more than a decade gave up trying to attack consolidations of monopoly power under Sherman Act Section 2.

The Alcoa Case and Its Aftermath

Two developments altered the course of structural antitrust during the 1930s. For one, disillusioned with the results of his cartel-friendly policy under the National Recovery Act, President Franklin D. Roosevelt appointed a vigorous trustbuster, Thurman Arnold, to head a revitalized Antitrust Division of the Department of

14. On the stock market's reaction, see M. R. Burns, "An Empirical Analysis of Stockholder Injury under Sec. 2 of the Sherman Act," *Journal of Industrial Economics*, vol. 31 (June 1983), pp. 333–362.

15. *U.S.* v. *E. I. du Pont de Nemours & Co.*, 188 Fed. 127 (1911).

16. *U.S.* v. *Corn Products Refining Co. et al.*, 234 Fed. 964 (1916).

17. *U.S.* v. *Eastman Kodak Co. et al.*, 226 Fed. 62 (1915).

18. *U.S.* v. *American Thread Co.*, settled by consent decree in 1913.

19. *U.S.* v. *Reading Co. et al.*, 253 U.S. 26 (1920); and *U.S.* v. *Lehigh Valley Railroad Co. et al.*, 254 U.S. 255 (1920).

20. *U.S.* v. *United States Steel Corporation et al.*, 223 Fed. 55 (1915), 251 U.S. 417 (1920).

21. See, for example, Naomi R. Lamoreaux, *The Great Merger Movement in American Business, 1895–1904* (Cambridge: Cambridge University Press, 1985), pp. 176–177.

22. 251 U.S. 417, 451 (1920).

23. *U.S.* v. *United Shoe Machinery Co. of New Jersey et al.*, 247 U.S. 32 (1918). An earlier criminal case against United's officers was also unsuccessful. *U.S.* v. *Winslow et al.*, 195 Fed 578 (1912), 227 U.S. 202 (1913).

24. *U.S.* v. *American Can Company et al.*, 230 Fed. 859, 861, 903 (1916).

25. *U.S.* v. *International Harvester Co. et al.*, 214 Fed. 987 (1914), with settlement effected in a 1918 consent decree.

26. *U.S.* v. *International Harvester Co.*, 10 F. 2d 827 (1925), 274 U.S. 693 (1927). It is remarkable how well the fragments of early divestiture actions survived through the 1980s, whereas the winners of early Sherman Act suits atrophied and by 1988 had shed all or most of their original businesses.

Justice.[27] Arnold initiated a flurry of suits in important industries. Also, Roosevelt's control over judicial nominations gradually "packed" the courts with jurists more inclined to support interventions aimed at correcting perceived business shortcomings. These changes culminated in the *Alcoa* case, resolved twenty-five years after the *Steel* decision.

The Aluminum Company of America, or Alcoa, was formed in 1888 to exploit the Hall electrolytic reduction patents. It bought out the competing Bradley patents in 1903. There were several attempts to enter the industry after the basic patents expired in 1909, but none was successful until 1940. Reasons for the dearth of new entry included the difficulty of obtaining conveniently located high-grade bauxite ore reserves, most of which Alcoa controlled; plain bad luck by two would-be entrants; and the general unattractiveness of entering at a cost disadvantage while Alcoa practiced moderation in pricing.

Over the years Alcoa had been in and out of the courts frequently in patent disputes and on antitrust charges concerning mergers, international cartel agreements, and price discrimination, but it was never seriously discommoded. However, in 1937 (before Thurman Arnold took office) the Justice Department charged the company with monopolization. Culminating a district court trial lasting 358 hearing days, Alcoa was absolved on all counts, with the *U.S. Steel* and *International Harvester* cases stressed as precedents. The government appealed, but because four Supreme Court justices had been associated with the earlier litigation, a quorum could not be obtained. Consequently, the appeal was heard by a three-member panel of circuit court judges as court of last resort. Its decision in 1945 reversed the lower court and found Alcoa guilty of monopolization. The opinion focused on two central issues: whether Alcoa possessed a monopoly, and whether it had exhibited the intent essential to find monopolization.

The first question turned on how the market was defined. As we have seen in Chapter 5, it is not always easy to identify meaningful market boundaries. In the *Alcoa* case, unlike most of its Section 2 predecessors, this proved to be so. There was no problem of local versus national market definitions, for aluminum was sold nationally on a uniform delivered price basis. The key issue was, What substitutes on the demand side should be included?

Because of aluminum's unique properties, other metals such as steel, copper, and magnesium were summarily excluded, despite the fact that aluminum and other metals are viewed by users as feasible substitutes in many applications.[28] The appellate court limited its analysis to the following three alternative definitions of Alcoa's aluminum ingot market share, where the numerator denotes the output credited to Alcoa and the denominator the output attributed to all sources of supply within the relevant market:

$$S_1 = \frac{\text{Alcoa's output of primary ingots less the primary metal Alcoa used internally to fabricate end products}}{\text{All primary ingot production plus all secondary ingot production plus aluminum ingot imports}}$$

$$S_2 = \frac{\text{Alcoa's output of primary ingots}}{\text{All primary ingot production plus all secondary ingot production plus aluminum ingot imports}}$$

$$S_3 = \frac{\text{Alcoa's output of primary ingots}}{\text{All primary ingot production plus aluminum ingot imports}}$$

Under the first definition, which was accepted as correct by the district court, Alcoa was found to have possessed only a 33 percent share of the market during the 1930s; under the second, its share was calculated at 64 percent; and under the third, 90 percent. The appellate panel rejected the first definition, which deducts from the ingot production of Alcoa the metal used internally by Alcoa to fabricate aluminum sheets, panels, pots, pans, and the like because "all intermediate, or end, products which 'Alcoa' fabricates and sells, *pro tanto* reduce the demand for ingot itself."[29] This makes sense, although one might have nagging doubts, given evidence that Alcoa found it desirable to stimulate aluminum demand by pioneering many new fabricated product applications. The only difference between definitions S_2 and S_3 is the inclusion of secondary (that is, reprocessed scrap) metal, accounting for roughly 40 percent of all domestic aluminum supplies, in the denominator of S_2 but not S_3. Judge Learned Hand, one of the most respected U.S. jurists and opinion writer for the appellate panel, favored the third definition, arguing that since Alcoa had produced the metal reappearing as reprocessed scrap, it would have taken into account in its output decisions the effect of scrap reclamation on future prices. Hence, it exerted effective monopolistic control over the supply of secondary metal. Here again, economic analysis supports the court's choice, especially when one recognizes that a considerable fraction of the secondary metal, as defined by the court, came from "factory scrap" melted down only a short time after it left Alcoa's primary reduction works.[30]

How the court decided these market definition issues had a crucial bearing on the case's outcome, for Judge Hand went on to observe that 90 percent "is enough to constitute a monopoly; it is doubtful whether sixty or sixty-four percent would be enough; and certainly thirty-three percent is not."[31]

Concluding that Alcoa did possess a monopoly of the aluminum market, the court had to determine whether it had exhibited the intent to achieve its position that proof of monopolization under Section 2 demands. In his opinion, Judge Hand acknowledged that Alcoa's profits had not been extortionate, but added that whether or not profits were "fair" was irrelevant to proving monopolization. He admitted also that Alcoa would be within the bounds of legality if its monopoly position had merely been "thrust upon" it by the failure of rivals to enter the market, or because it had outlasted its rivals owing to superior skill, foresight, and

27. See Ellis W. Hawley, *The New Deal and the Problem of Monopoly* (Princeton: Princeton University Press, 1966), Chapters 22–23.

28. In a later study, aluminum's cross elasticity of demand with respect to steel was estimated to be roughly 2.0. See M. J. Peck, *Competition in the Aluminum Industry* (Cambridge: Harvard University Press, 1961), pp. 31–34.

29. *U.S.* v. *Aluminum Co. of America et al.*, 148 F. 2d 416, 424 (1945).

30. See Darius W. Gaskins, "Alcoa Revisited: The Welfare Implications of a Secondhand Market," *Journal of Economic Theory*, vol. 7 (March 1974), pp. 254–271; Franklin M. Fisher, "Alcoa

Revisited: Comment," *Journal of Economic Theory*, vol. 9 (November 1974), pp. 357–359; Peter L. Swan, "Alcoa: The Influence of Recycling on Monopoly Power," *Journal of Political Economy*, vol. 88 (February 1980), pp. 76–99; Robert E. Martin, "Monopoly Power and the Recycling of Raw Materials," *Journal of Industrial Economics*, vol. 30 (June 1982), pp. 405–419; and Valerie Y. Suslow, "Estimating Monopoly Behavior with Competitive Recycling," *Rand Journal of Economics*, vol. 17 (Autumn 1986), pp. 389–403.

31. *U.S.* v. *Aluminum Co. of America et al.*, 148 F. 2d 416, 424 (1945).

industry. "The successful competitor," he warned, "having been urged to compete, must not be turned upon when he wins."[32] But he found that Alcoa had gone farther. He pointed to Alcoa's building up of ore reserves and electric power contracts and production capacity in advance of demand:

It was not inevitable that it should always anticipate increases in the demand for ingot and be prepared to supply them. Nothing compelled it to keep doubling and redoubling its capacity before others entered the field. It insists that it never excluded competitors, but we can think of no more effective exclusion than progressively to embrace each new opportunity as it opened and to face every newcomer with new capacity already geared into a great organization, having the advantage of experience, trade connections and the elite of personnel.[33]

And this, said the court, was sufficient to show intent to maintain a monopoly position:

"Alcoa" meant to keep, and did keep, that complete and exclusive hold upon the ingot market with which it started. That was to "monopolize" that market, however innocently it otherwise proceeded.[34]

This decision, broadly endorsed by the Supreme Court a year later in the latter-day *American Tobacco* case,[35] in effect overthrew the *Standard Oil* and *U.S. Steel* precedents, making it possible to infer illegal monopolization without evidence of unreasonable practices driving competitors from the market. It did not exactly make the possession of monopoly power by means other than the receipt of invention patents *per se* illegal, but it came close. And it is possible to read into the decision, with its references to "fair" profits and expanding capacity to meet demand, a condemnation of dominant market positions maintained merely through limit pricing.

Remedial action was deferred until the disposition of war plants built with government funds and operated by Alcoa could be settled. Alcoa was barred from bidding to buy the plants, and as a result the primary ingot supply industry was transformed from a monopoly into a triopoly through the acquisition of integrated facilities by Reynolds Metals and Kaiser Aluminum. This, a district court concluded later, was almost sufficient, so Alcoa was not fragmented.[36] The principal additional remedy ordered was the divestiture of joint stockholdings in Alcoa and Aluminium, Ltd., of Canada by the Davis, Hunt, and Mellon families, removing the possibility that these across-the-border competitors would be jointly controlled.

A series of cases following on the heels of the *Alcoa* decision contributed to the strengthening of Section 2. Two deserve special mention.

Shortly after bringing suit against Alcoa, the Justice Department also moved against several motion picture exhibition chains, charging them with monopolizing first-run film exhibition. Some were said to have threatened not to exhibit certain producers' films in towns where they operated the only theaters unless the producers gave them first-run preference in cities where they faced competition. In every such instance the Supreme Court ruled that illegal monopolization existed.[37] This was no large step beyond *Standard Oil* of 1911. However, speaking for a 6-1 majority upholding the government's case against a chain absolved of making such threats, Justice Douglas stated that specific intent to achieve monopoly need not be proved if monopoly has in fact resulted from the defendant's conduct, and that "monopoly power, whether lawfully or unlawfully acquired, may itself constitute an evil and stand condemned under Section 2 even though it remains unexercised."[38] That the old *U.S. Steel* doctrine had been overturned could scarcely have been reaffirmed more pointedly.

A decision paralleling *Alcoa* came in a renewed attack against the United Shoe Machinery Corporation. This time United was found guilty of monopolization because certain of its business policies, although not objectionable per se, tended to prevent new entry and to perpetuate United's dominance.[39] These included the refusal to sell machines, which were instead only leased for long (for example, ten-year) terms; a price structure that accepted lower profit margins on machines exposed to competition than on those shielded by United's extensive patent portfolio; and pricing, service, and machine replacement provisions that made it advantageous for shoe manufacturers to employ the full line of United machines. This array of practices appears to stray farther from orthodox business conduct than Alcoa's "embracing each new opportunity," and so the *United Shoe Machinery* decision cannot be considered as daring a departure from earlier precedents.

The *Alcoa* and motion picture exhibition chain decisions of the late 1940s appear to have been a high-water mark in judicial willingness to infer monopolization without proof of oppressive business practices, just as the conscious parallelism doctrine under Sherman Act Section 1 reached its zenith in nearly contemporaneous decisions. Any illusion that the courts had shifted to a uniformly tough line against dominant firms was shattered in 1956, when the Supreme Court found du Pont innocent of monopolizing cellophane production. Again, the crucial issue was definition of the relevant market. Emphasizing cellophane's unique properties, the substantial price differences between cellophane and other packaging materials, and the unusually high profits du Pont sustained, the Justice Department argued for a narrow definition embracing only cellophane sales. These du Pont clearly dominated by virtue of patents it acquired from a French company, patents it secured on its own improvement inventions, and licensing arrangements it worked out with an American company that challenged its patent

---

32. 148 F. 2d 416, 430 (1945).

33. 148 F. 2d 416, 431 (1945). The court's conclusion on this crucial issue may have been wrong factually. In his study of the aluminum industry, Donald H. Wallace found that Alcoa's capacity had *lagged behind demand* on numerous occasions. *Market Control in the Aluminum Industry* (Cambridge: Harvard University Press, 1937), pp. 252, 259–260, 291–292, 307–308, and 331.

34. 148 F. 2d 416, 432 (1945).

35. *American Tobacco Co. et al.* v. *U.S.*, 328 U.S. 781, 813–814 (1946).

36. *U.S.* v. *Aluminum Company of America et al.*, 91 F. Supp. 333 (1950).

37. *U.S.* v. *Crescent Amusement Co.*, 323 U.S. 173 (1944); and *Schine Chain Theatres* v. *U.S.*, 334 U.S. 110 (1948).

38. *U.S.* v. *Griffith Amusement Co.*, 334 U.S. 100, 105, 107 (1948).

39. *U.S.* v. *United Shoe Machinery Corporation*, 110 F. Supp. 295 (1953), affirmed in 347 U.S. 521 (1954). Later the case was reopened when the Justice Department insisted that the remedies ordered in 1954 — compulsory licensing of patents and divestiture of minor subsidiary operations — had been insufficient to restore competition. A divestiture program to reduce USM's market share to 33 percent was agreed upon in a consent decree. See 391 U.S. 244 (1968) and CCH 1969 Trade Cases Para. 72,688. On the aftermath, see "USM's Hard Life as an Ex-Monopoly," *Fortune*, October 1972, pp. 124–130. In 1975, USM was acquired in a hostile takeover by Emhart. After a continuation of its declining fortunes, USM's shoe machinery operations were sold off in May 1987 to managers of its British subsidiary, and USM's ancient plant in Beverly, Massachusetts, was closed.

claims.[40] Attorneys for du Pont argued that there was a high cross elasticity of demand between cellophane and other flexible packaging materials, and therefore that cellophane ought to be considered only a part of that broader market, in which its share was roughly 18 percent. The issues were analogous to those analyzed in connection with the *Owens-Illinois* glass bottle merger case in Chapter 5, except that technological changes at the time were causing cellophane to gain ground on other packaging materials, not lose it.[41] A Wilmington, Delaware, district court accepted the broader market definition, acquitting du Pont. In a 4-3 split decision, the Supreme Court affirmed the lower court's decision, concluding that:

> While the application of the [market definition] test remains uncertain, it seems to us that du Pont should not be found to monopolize cellophane when that product has the competition and interchangeability with other wrappings that this record shows.[42]

During the late 1950s and through the 1960s, there was little judicial action on the Section 2 front involving charges of market domination untainted by other prohibited practices.[43] Several important actions were initiated by the Department of Justice, but these were settled not with a bang but a whimper through *consent decrees* — remedial agreements negotiated out of court by the adversaries in a case. A consent decree leaves unresolved the question of guilt versus innocence, but it is binding upon the parties once the decree has been approved by a federal court. A suit alleging monopolization of color film processing by Eastman Kodak, for example, was settled with an agreement that Eastman would unbundle processing services from the price of film, and that it would reduce its share of the processing market to below 50 percent within seven years, helping new firms enter by licensing its patents and conveying its know-how to them.[44] A consent decree with similar provisions affecting tabulating card production ended a suit against IBM charging monopolization of the keypunch and related mechanical (but not electronic) data processing equipment industry.[45] The Radio Corporation of America emerged from a suit challenging its domination of television technology by agreeing to license large numbers of patents on a royalty-free basis.[46] Western Electric, the manufacturing arm of AT&T, consented to a program of patent licensing and the divestiture of minor subsidiary operations, escaping the three-way structural breakup originally sought by the government.[47] In 1958 the United Fruit Corporation agreed to relinquish a part of its banana barony by establishing and spinning off a new firm capable of handling 35 percent of all U.S. banana imports.[48] And in an action attacking General Motors' 85 percent share of the domestic intercity bus manufacturing industry, the consent settlement specified several actions by GM to enhance the viability of existing competitors, plus the possibility of future divestiture if any existing rival failed or if GM retained its dominant share despite market growth.[49]

Renaissance and Decline

Structural antitrust runs in cycles. In the 1970s, there was an upsurge in monopolization cases — this time marked by contending party decisions to fight their battles out to the bitter end in court. One reason for the renaissance of "big cases" was what appeared briefly to be an emerging consensus that high concentration led on average to abnormally high profitability, which in turn implied the attenuation of vigorous price competition.[50] We learned in Chapter 11 that this consensus soon broke down, but its ascendance lent impetus to the invigoration of structural antitrust. Also, the Federal Trade Commission was severely criticized for wasting its resources on unimportant cases.[51] New members appointed by President Nixon sought to do better, and in particular, to initiate imaginative cases against perceived concentrations of monopoly power. Meanwhile, the Department of Justice began in 1965 to strengthen its economics staff, one result of which was a series of industry studies that led eventually to major monopolization complaints.

The IBM Case

The salvo that signaled a new era was a Justice Department complaint challenging IBM's dominance of the computer industry, filed on the last day of the Johnson administration in 1969. Then, in 1974, the department alleged monopolization of

---

40. Also at issue was the question of whether the patent practices through which du Pont maintained its dominance justified an inference of intent to monopolize. The district court thought not, but the Supreme Court, concluding that du Pont had no monopoly, did not consider the question.

For fascinating new insights based upon company documents, see David A. Hounshell and John K. Smith, Jr., *Science and Corporate Strategy: DuPont R&D, 1902–1980* (Cambridge: Cambridge University Press, 1988), pp. 170–180.

41. See pp. 180–184 supra. After the period covered by the antitrust case, cellophane lost ground to newer materials such as vinyl, polyethylene, and the like. In 1954, cellophane sales exceeded those of all other plastic films. By 1967, other plastic films had sales 9.2 times those of cellophane.

42. *U.S.* v. *E. I. du Pont de Nemours and Co.*, 351 U.S. 377, 404 (1956). See also the critical analysis by G. W. Stocking and W. F. Mueller, "The Cellophane Case and the New Competition," *American Economic Review*, vol. 45 (March 1955), pp. 29–63.

43. The principal litigated government victories were *U.S.* v. *International Boxing Club of New York*, 358 U.S. 242 (1959), 171 F. Supp. 841 (1959); and *U.S.* v. *Grinnell Corporation et al.*, 236 F. Supp. 244 (1964), 384 U.S. 563 (1966). The *Grinnell* case is noteworthy both for its strained definition of a national market for fire and burglar alarm services monitored by local central stations, and for a restatement of what is required to constitute monopolization under Section 2, viz:

. . . the possession of monopoly power in the relevant market and . . . the willful acquisition or maintenance of that power as distinguished from growth or development as a consequence of a superior product, business acumen, or historic accident.

384 U.S. 563, 570–571 (1966).

Significant defeats included *U.S.* v. *National Malleable & Steel Castings Co. et al.*, CCH 1957 Trade Cases, Para 68,890; and *U.S.* v. *General Motors Corporation* (the diesel locomotive case), dropped by the Justice Department in 1967 owing to insufficient evidence. On the latter, see Thomas G. Marx, "Economic Theory and Judicial Process: A Case Study," *Antitrust Bulletin*, vol. 20 (Winter 1975), pp. 775–802.

44. *U.S.* v. *Eastman Kodak Co.*, CCH 1954 Trade Cases, Para. 67,920; CCH 1961 Trade Cases, Para. 70,100. Although the *Kodak* case was a probable exception, compulsory patent licensing decrees appear for the most part to have had little discernible impact on market structure. See F. M. Scherer, *The Economic Effects of Compulsory Patent Licensing* (New York: New York University Graduate School of Business Administration Monograph Series in Finance and Economics, 1977), pp. 75–78.

45. *U.S.* v. *International Business Machines Corp.*, CCH 1956 Trade Cases, Para. 68,245; CCH 1963 Trade Cases, Para. 70,628.

46. *U.S.* v. *Radio Corporation of America*, CCH 1958 Trade Cases, Para. 69,164.

47. *U.S.* v. *Western Electric, Inc., et al.*, CCH 1956 Trade Cases, Para. 68,246. Included among the licensed patents were those covering the basic principles of semiconductors. On the tactics by which AT&T played off the Department of Defense against the Justice Department to secure the settlement, see the House Committee on the Judiciary, Antitrust Subcommittee, report, *Consent Decree Program of the Department of Justice* (Washington: USGPO, 1959), pp. 29–120.

48. *U.S.* v. *United Fruit Corporation*, CCH 1958 Trade Cases, Para. 68,941.

49. *U.S.* v. *General Motors Corporation*, CCH 1958 Trade Cases, Para. 71,624. In 1987 GM, still one of the two industry leaders, sold its bus making operations to Greyhound Corp.

50. See, for example, *Report of the White House Task Force on Antitrust Policy* (the Neal Report), July 1968, reproduced in *Journal of Reprints for Antitrust Law and Economics*, vol. 1 (Winter 1969), pp. 663–668.

51. *Report of the ABA Commission To Study the Federal Trade Commission*, September 1969, reprinted in *Journal of Reprints for Antitrust Law and Economics*, vol. 1 (Winter 1969), pp. 885–1009; and Mark J. Green et al., *The Closed Enterprise System* (Ralph Nader's Study Group Report on Antitrust Enforcement) (New York: Grossman, 1972), pp. 321–437.

telecommunications services and equipment markets by AT&T and its subsidiary, Western Electric. On January 9, 1982, an end was announced to both suits. The case against IBM was abandoned unilaterally as "without merit" by the Reagan Administration's antitrust chief. In the AT&T case, a mutually negotiated settlement called for massive reorganization, with twenty-two Bell "local operating companies" to be divested (ultimately into seven groups) from parent AT&T, which was to retain long-distance communications services and Western Electric's manufacturing functions.[52] How these two "great cases"[53] came to such disparate conclusions tells much about both the substance and process of antitrust.

Whether IBM monopolized an economically meaningful market, and whether its position was willfully acquired and maintained, were both contested tenaciously.[54]

The government emphasized a market defined as "general purpose electronic digital computer systems," in which IBM's share ranged from 82 percent in 1962 to 72 percent in 1972. IBM argued in reply for a broad computer industry definition, including along with "mainframes" special-purpose process control, message switching, and military computers; programmable hand-held calculators, and computer leasing and service activities. In this broader market, its 1972 share was 32 percent—too small to imply monopolization.

On the conduct side, it seems clear that IBM vaulted to a dominant position in the infant computer industry during the 1950s by recognizing the potentialities of electronic business data processing, promoting them aggressively, providing superior applications engineering to tap the potential, and offering machines that, although no more advanced technically than those of rivals, performed well. Also, the first computer maker to win an organization's data processing business—in more cases than not, IBM—had an advantage in placing its next generation of machines because of the close working relationships established and "software lock-in," that is, the difficulty of rewriting programs to run on other manufacturers' operating systems.

The crucial question was whether IBM's continued dominance, if indeed it existed, merely reflected these advantages plus sustained good performance, or whether IBM went out of its way to erect obstacles to the entry and growth of rivals. The government saw unnecessary barriers to entry in IBM's policy of selling computer hardware, applications programming, and maintenance at a single package price, requiring independent service and programming firms to compete against an effective price of zero. IBM, unlike United Shoe Machinery Corp., offered both to lease or sell its computers, but it manipulated the relative prices to its own advantage. At first, leasing was strongly encouraged, and this, the government argued, increased the amount of capital rivals needed to compete with IBM. With the introduction of IBM's System 360 in 1965, the terms were shifted to favor purchase, but when this stimulated the rapid growth of computer leasing companies who attached non-IBM peripheral equipment to the IBM mainframes, lease prices were reduced and sale prices increased, undermining the leasing companies' profitability. Also, alarmed at the rapid ascendance of Control Data Corporation into top-of-the-line scientific computers, IBM conducted a crash program to develop the System 360/90 model, which, internal studies showed, was expected to incur substantial out-of-pocket losses.[55] Like United Shoe Machinery

Corp., IBM maintained a discriminatory pricing structure. Customers were hooked on bottom-of-the-line machines priced at thin profit margins, but as they later recognized the need for more core memory, disk storage, and the like, the upgrades carried high margins. This strategy attracted competitive entry from "plug-compatible" add-on memory, disk, and tape drive manufacturers (PCMs). But when the PCMs began to make significant inroads, IBM commissioned detailed studies of their financial vulnerability and effected sharp and often discriminatory price reductions to contain them. Or when price reductions were insufficient to stem the tide, IBM changed peripheral equipment interface designs to make interconnection difficult.

Broadly characterized, IBM's pricing policies were more complex and more sophisticated than those encountered in earlier monopolization cases. Unlike Alcoa, IBM did not restrain its prices continuously to deter entry. Rather, like Standard Oil and United Shoe Machinery, it sought high prices and profits whenever it could achieve them, but when competition threatened, it reacted with carefully calculated strategic adjustments. Unlike Standard Oil and United Shoe Machinery, it did not achieve its dominant position by merger, nor did it acquire rivals wounded by its strategic reactions. And because the computer technology was evolving so rapidly, its aggressive policies did not stem the flow of entry; as one threat was contained, others appeared in new and sometimes unexpected quadrants. As a result, by any definition, its market share declined over time. Another distinction is perhaps equally important. IBM had throughout its history been in and out of the antitrust courts with some frequency, and the rules of the game had become reasonably well known. In antitrust wars, paper is a key weapon. The *IBM* case record reveals that strategic decisions were carefully reviewed by internal attorneys—arguably, to ensure that the law was respected, but in some instances, quite clearly to see that the paperwork would not be embarrassing in an anticipated antitrust challenge.[56] Thus, it was peculiarly difficult to determine after the fact where the truth lay.

The *IBM* case had another crucial distinguishing characteristic. IBM fought the government's charges with unsurpassed ferocity. The court trial began in 1975 and was continuing when the government withdrew in 1982. One government economist testified for 78 days. The slow pace of adjudication was aggravated by inept government team management and failure of the presiding judge to focus the issues. Meanwhile, the technology advanced relentlessly. The mainframe computers of 1982 were vastly more powerful than their System 360 precursors,

52. See the multipage analysis in the *New York Times*, January 9, 1982. It is undoubtedly coincidental that the previous major antitrust cases against AT&T and IBM were concluded only a day apart in January 1956.

53. The allusion is to the famous dissent of Justice Oliver Wendell Holmes, "Great cases like hard cases make bad law." *U.S. v. Northern Securities Co. et al.*, 193 U.S. 197, 400 (1904).

54. Books published by members of the contending parties' economics teams provide the equivalent of analytic briefs: for the government, DeLamarter, *Big Blue*, supra note 5; for IBM, Franklin M. Fisher, John McGowan, and Joen Greenwood,

Folded, Spindled, and Mutilated: Economic Analysis and U.S. v. IBM (Cambridge: MIT Press, 1983). Co-author Scherer was a witness for the government.

55. See Russell W. Pittman, "Predatory Investment: U.S. v. IBM," *International Journal of Industrial Organization*, vol. 2 (December 1984), pp. 341–366.

56. See Pittman, "Predatory Investment," pp. 348 and 356; DeLamarter, pp. 122, 177–182, 185–186, 203, 216, and 367–368; and Gerald W. Brock, *The U.S. Computer Industry* (Cambridge: Ballinger, 1975), pp. 128–134.

on which the case initially focused. Minicomputers (pioneered by firms other than IBM) had made substantial inroads, and the microcomputer revolution (led by Apple) was under way. Whatever the market was, it was vastly different from what existed when the *IBM* case was filed, and IBM was beset by competition more pervasive and subtle than in 1969. The case had become a historical relic, and the government had good reasons for withdrawing. Yet by so doing, it set a bad precedent: it rewarded antitrust targets who, by fighting a war of attrition, delayed the administration of justice until the issues were overtaken by events.

The AT&T Case

Although similar to *IBM* in some respects, *AT&T* was radically different on one point: the technological and institutional changes that precipitated the case were moving along trajectories that made the key issues more, not less, important in the future.[57] Advances in microwave radio and satellite technology encouraged newcomers to offer services that bypassed and competed with Bell's traditional near-monopoly in intercity communications. Advances in other areas of electronics brought forth a stream of newcomers offering wireless telephones, answering machines, automatic dialers, and switchboards for connection by customers into the Bell network or for purchase by the local Bell operating companies. The case turned on how AT&T reacted to these challenges.

In long-distance services, Bell sought to retard competitive entry by urging the Federal Communications Commission (FCC) to forbid it, on one occasion (involving a proposed digital business data transmission network) arguing that the service was technically and financially infeasible when its internal studies showed the opposite. When such tactics failed, Bell refused to interconnect the interlopers' lines with its local distribution facilities, or offered interconnection only on unfavorable and discriminatory terms. It also made radical changes in its price structure to discriminate in favor of the high-volume customers who might otherwise defect to new competitive microwave communication systems. In this it faced a dilemma stemming from a major regulatory failure. The technological changes following World War II reduced costs much more on long-distance transmission than on intracity switching and final distribution. The FCC encouraged AT&T to use part of the intercity cost savings to keep basic local service charges low. It also encouraged uniformity of intercity rates across heavily and sparsely populated areas. But the new technologies yielded substantial scale economies, so uniform rates meant that profit margins would be much larger on dense-traffic routes than on the links between smaller cities. This encouraged competitors to "cream skim," entering the high-volume but not the low-volume routes. Given the threat of entry, if AT&T failed to cut prices, it lost profitable business with which it had cross subsidized low-volume and local service; if it cut prices, it also sacrificed revenues used previously for cross subsidies, but if its costs were lower than those of the would-be entrants, it could retain more subsidy funds than if it failed to stem the entry challenge. The characteristically adversary relationship between AT&T and its regulators permitted no rational cooperative solution to this pricing problem.

On so-called foreign attachments, AT&T was obstinate. With a protected monopoly position, it was slow to introduce new equipment desired by customers. When competitors came forward to fill the gap, AT&T asked the FCC to prohibit the use of their products, arguing that they would flood the telephone network with harmful signals. When the FCC refused, AT&T attempted to force customers to connect "foreign" devices through a protective connecting arrangement that was poorly designed and priced to make the competitors' attachments prohibitively costly. When the FCC eventually ordered that foreign devices be certified for their compatibility with the telephone network before connection, AT&T delayed implementing the program until it could offer its own competitive alternatives.

Parent AT&T owned and controlled its intercity Long Lines operating division, its local operating companies, and Western Electric, which manufactured equipment for both. This arrangement created severe conflicts of interest, for when other manufacturers sought to sell their equipment to the operating units, Western Electric could write specifications that favored its own apparatus or delay approval until its offerings were redesigned or repriced to retain an advantage.

AT&T responded to these charges with four main counter arguments: (1) that they were untrue (on which it was at best only partly successful); (2) that its conduct was necessary to preserve the integrity of the U.S. telephone system, which was both technically delicate and a natural monopoly; (3) that its conduct was approved by the Federal Communications Commission, or when typically long delays occurred before FCC decisions emerged, a legitimate exercise of its rights as a regulated firm; and (4) that the end result was good, that is, that the United States had the best telephone system in the world.

After the government's case was completed, AT&T moved for dismissal. Rejecting the motion in September 1981, district judge Harold Greene concluded that the evidence demonstrated "that the Bell System has violated the antitrust laws in a number of ways over a lengthy period of time."[58] He left for AT&T the burden of refuting those findings and showing that its refusals to interconnect and pricing choices were reasonable in view of broader regulatory policy. He rejected the government's contention that AT&T had abused the regulatory process in its efforts to impede competitive entry.

Nevertheless, the regulatory abuse theory probably had much to do with the Justice Department's determination to litigate the AT&T case "to the eyeballs."[59] Prominent in the dogma of Reagan Administration appointees was a belief that government regulation was the source of much, if not most, monopoly power and that "Predation by abuse of governmental procedures . . . presents an increasingly dangerous threat to competition . . . [with] almost limitless possibilities."[60] And to repeat, the AT&T case in many respects was the consequence of regulatory failure. Judge Greene pointed to testimony that the Federal Communications Commission "may realistically be incapable of efficiently regulating a company of

57. For diverse book-length analyses of the case, its precursors, and its consequences, see David S. Evans, ed., *Breaking Up Bell* (Amsterdam: North-Holland, 1983); Harry M. Shooshan, ed., *Disconnecting Bell: The Impact of the AT&T Divestiture* (New York: Pergamon, 1984); Peter Temin, *The Fall of the Bell System: A Study in Prices and Politics* (Cambridge: Cambridge University Press, 1987); and Gerald R. Faulhaber, *Telecommunications in Turmoil: Technology and Public Policy* (Cambridge: Ballinger, 1987).

58. *U.S.* v. *American Telephone and Telegraph Co. et al.*, 524 F. Supp. 1336, 1381 (1981).

59. See "Government Watchdog," *New York Times*, January 9, 1982, p. 24.

60. See Robert H. Bork, *The Antitrust Paradox* (New York: Basic Books, 1978), p. 347; quoted by Judge Greene in 524 F. Supp. 1336, 1362 (1981).

AT&T's size, complexity, and power."[61] By severing the local Bell operating companies from their parent, the Justice Department hoped that the invisible hand of competition could replace regulation in significant ways. Whether its hopes will be realized remains to be seen. The early postdivestiture experience suggests that new, equally complex, regulatory institutions were substituted for the old.[62]

Had AT&T fought as vigorously as IBM, it could have delayed its breakup for many years. The question remains why it did not. There were several probable reasons. Judge Greene's preliminary decision implied a reasonably high probability that it would eventually lose, and if it did, a formal conviction could pave the way for later treble damages suits. Also, there is reason to believe that the settlement was not unattractive to AT&T's top management.[63] Contrary to the government's original petition, AT&T was allowed to retain Western Electric and its research and development powerhouse, Bell Telephone Laboratories. The negotiated settlement ended a previous order prohibiting Western Electric from selling nontelephone equipment in commercial markets. AT&T's management apparently believed (in hindsight — wrongly) that this new freedom would permit it to become an important and profitable challenger to IBM in computer markets. Also, because of regulatory lag, state and local regulatory bodies allowed Bell operating companies to secure rates of return on their invested capital far below the extraordinarily high interest rates prevailing at the time in the United States. As a result, new investment in the operating companies was unprofitable, and the stock market reacted unfavorably to such investment, despite its necessity.[64] By divesting the local operating companies, AT&T made itself more attractive to the market. Here too, however, it probably erred, for when interest rates fell sharply over the next five years, the operating companies moved from "dog" to "star" status in stock market investors' eyes.

The Breakfast Cereal Case

While the Department of Justice struggled with IBM and AT&T, the Federal Trade Commission pursued its own antitrust initiatives. The most ambitious effort sought to fragment the three leading ready-to-eat (RTE) cereal manufacturers into eight more evenly matched firms and to require compulsory licensing of significant cereal formulas and trademarks.[65] The proposed trademark licensing remedy was unorthodox, as were several other facets of the case. Most importantly, the charge of monopolization was levied not against a single dominant firm, but against four (later three) companies who together controlled 90 (later 81) percent of RTE cereal sales.[66]

Charges of collective monopolization were not entirely new to antitrust. They were an important component of the tetracycline and the 1946 *American Tobacco* cases, analyzed in Chapter 9. But in only one prior case, involving the five leading motion picture producers, had multifirm structural reorganization been ordered. The five controlled 70 percent of the first-run theaters in cities with population exceeding 100,000, and they were required to sever their vertical ownership ties for 1,197 theaters.[67] With its cereal case, the FTC sought for the first time horizontal fragmentation of collectively monopolizing sellers. In this it was attempting to advance antitrust law beyond the awkward state in which it was left following the *American Tobacco* decision. That is, if oligopolists behave noncompetitively because of the very market structure in which they operate, punishing them without altering the underlying structural conditions may do little to improve economic performance.[68]

The situation in cereals was similar to that of *Tobacco*. Prices were maintained at persistently high levels — twice manufacturing costs, and high enough to let the cereal makers spend sixteen cents per sales dollar on advertising and still realize an after-tax return on assets between 1958 and 1970 roughly twice the average for all manufacturing corporations. Kellogg normally exercised price leadership, and although price matching was less close than in cigarettes owing to greater product differentiation, discipline was strong, list price reductions were rare, and sub-rosa price cutting was unknown.[69] The closest thing to aggressive pricing during this period was an isolated price cut to contain (but not eliminate) private-label corn flake competition. As a matter of policy, Kellogg and General Mills refused to engage in private-label production, which was seen as a threat to branded product price levels. Post (General Foods) acquired one of the leading private-label producers in 1943 and let its operations atrophy, choosing during the 1960s not to compete actively for additional business, even though it had substantial excess capacity and internal analyses showed sizable private-label accounts to be quite profitable. There was circumstantial evidence that the Big Three reached an agreement in 1957 to limit stringently the use of in-pack premiums, which they considered a potent but mutually cancelling marketing tool. At the same time, but for unexplained reasons, the granting of trade deal cash discounts to retailers — one of the most common forms of price competition among other food processors — declined sharply and indeed vanished except with respect to new products. During the late 1960s the Big Three mutually shunned the extension of vitamin fortification to most of their standard products. When criticized before a congressional committee for the low nutritional content of their offerings, they discussed concerted action at a Cereal Institute meeting, reportedly without reaching a conclusion. Yet afterward all implemented nearly simultaneous fortification programs.

Despite high prices and profits, the cereal makers' collective market share did not decline. To the contrary, it rose slightly between 1950 and 1970. The explanation of how new entry and the expansion of fringe firms were restrained without the kinds of exclusionary practices condemned in earlier monopolization cases was another unorthodox facet of the case. Economies of scale were no answer, for the minimum efficient scale appeared to entail a market share of only 4 to 6 percent.

61. 524 F. Supp. 1336, 1359 (1981).

62. For an optimistic view, see Roger G. Noll, "The Twisted Pair: Regulation and Competition in Telecommunications," *Regulation*, vol. 11 (1987, no. 3/4), pp. 15–22; for a pessimistic view, Paul W. MacAvoy and Kenneth Robinson, "Winning by Losing: The AT&T Settlement and Its Impact on Telecommunications," *Yale Journal on Regulation*, vol. 1 (1983, no. 1), pp. 1–42.

63. See Alvin Toffler, *The Adaptive Corporation* (New York: McGraw-Hill, 1984), pp. 25–29 and 129–138.

64. See p. 10 supra and (on the mathematics) the first (1970) edition of this volume, pp. 524–527.

65. Co-author Scherer was a witness for the Federal Trade Commission.

66. Quaker was dropped after the FTC completed its case in 1978, leaving respondents Kellogg, with 45 percent of 1970 sales, General Mills, with 21 percent, and General Foods, with 15 percent.

67. *U.S.* v. *Paramount Pictures, Inc., et al.*, 334 U.S. 131, 167–175 (1948), 85 F. Supp. 881 (1949). In the 1980s there was a new flurry of integration by producers into distribution. See "Studios' Bid To Own Theaters Raises Old Antitrust Concerns," *Philadelphia Inquirer*, April 17, 1988, p. 2–C.

68. Cf. pp. 339–346 supra.

69. See pp. 256–258 supra.

The FTC staff contended that opportunities for profitable new entry had been preempted by proliferation of product varieties—a theory explored more fully in Chapter 10. The number of brands distributed nationally by the six leading firms rose from twenty-seven in 1950 to seventy-four in 1971. There was almost no evidence that the cereal makers channeled their rivalry into product proliferation with the explicit intent of precluding new entry, but the entry-deterring effects of brand proliferation were well known to marketing managers during the 1960s, if not earlier. The cereal companies argued that in their brand proliferation, as in other facets of their conduct, they were merely competing vigorously and responding to the demand of consumers for variegated breakfast fare.[70]

In addition to denying virtually all the FTC's allegations, the cereal companies took their battle outside the courtroom.[71] Using a consultant's study alleging that union workers would lose their jobs if the government prevailed, support from the AFL-CIO was won. Company lobbyists then invaded Capitol Hill, securing bills (eventually dropped) that would have halted the case or removed the FTC's power to impose a divestiture remedy. During the week before he was elected President of the United States, Ronald Reagan released a letter to the president of Kellogg, observing, "It is clear to me that the [cereal] case under consideration has very little basis in fact and that a favorable ruling on behalf of the FTC would have a chilling effect on American industry.[72] A similar statement was made by then-President Carter while he was campaigning in Michigan.

As the trial neared completion, the administrative law judge who had presided over it for four years was disqualified on procedural grounds. A replacement judge heard the final defense witnesses, drew the threads, and ordered that the case be dismissed.[73] Except for rejecting the cereal makers' "all breakfast foods" proposal and accepting RTE cereals as a relevant market, which he found to be highly concentrated, he resolved virtually every contested issue of fact or theory in favor of the companies.[74] What followed was even more unprecedented. As is common in important FTC proceedings, the losing side (that is, the FTC enforcement staff) sought to appeal to the commission as a whole. But their superiors, chosen by Reagan administration appointees, refused to transmit the appeal. The staff then bypassed their bureau directors and appealed directly to the commission. Under a cloud of continuing congressional criticism concerning both the case's substance and the administrative law judge replacement, the commission elected to receive the appeal but dismiss it without addressing its factual merits. Speaking for a divided majority, Commissioner Patricia Bailey cited "congressional stormwaters of imposing magnitude" and concluded:

The paradox we are left with is that while there may be a legitimate concern with the anticompetitive effects of the exercise of oligopoly power, it is rarely true that these concerns will mandate an administrative agency to restructure an industry, short of a legislative warrant to that effect. Therefore, I will vote that this appeal be terminated, not for the reasons relied upon by the Administrative Law Judge, but because the promulgation of relief by this agency will not, in any eventuality, conceivably lead to a restructuring of the cereal firms.[75]

Other FTC Cases Other Federal Trade Commission cases reached more clear-cut conclusions concerning the permissible bounds of dominant firm conduct. Particularly important in this respect was a complaint concerning du Pont's strategy in pricing titanium dioxide (TiO_2), widely used as a whitening pigment in paints, plastics, paper, and other materials.

During the early 1970s, du Pont found itself with a unit cost advantage of 20 to 40 percent over its principal rivals. Two decades earlier it had developed a new ilemite chloride process for producing TiO_2 from abundantly available domestic ore. Recent events drove up the costs of the two previously competitive processes — ilemite sulphate, whose vast quantities of waste had become costly to dispose, as required under newly passed environmental protection laws, and rutile chloride, which was dependent upon increasingly scarce and high-priced Australian ore. Du Pont refused to license rivals to use its ilemite chloride technology, much of which was embodied in secret know-how accumulated over the years through learning by doing. Beginning in 1971, du Pont task forces recommended, and management approved, a strategy under which TiO_2 prices would be set at levels profitable for du Pont, but too low to yield profits to rivals, whose replacement of obsolete ilemite sulphate and rutile chloride plants would therefore be strongly discouraged. Meanwhile, du Pont would expand its ilemite chloride capacity aggressively, raising its market share from 30 percent in 1970 to 52 percent in 1977 and 65 percent in 1988. Because of price controls, import threats, and unexpectedly slow demand growth, implementation of the plan did not go smoothly, but du Pont did resist price increase attempts by rivals, and by 1977, its market share had risen to 42 percent, with a continuing upward trend in sight. At this point the Federal Trade Commission charged du Pont with unfair and monopolistic practices, asking for the divestiture of two du Pont plants and royalty-free licensing of du Pont's technology.

Du Pont's conduct was similar to Alcoa's, but more aggressive. Both practiced a form of limit pricing and "embrace[d] each new opportunity," but Alcoa's strategy merely kept outsiders from entering, whereas du Pont's squeezed insiders out. Considering the case on appeal, the Federal Trade Commission approved an administrative law judge's order to dismiss, stating *inter alia* that:

[T]he essence of the competitive process is to induce firms to become more efficient and to pass the benefits of the efficiency along to consumers. That process would be ill-served by using antitrust to block hard aggressive competition that is solidly based on efficiencies and growth opportunities, even if monopoly is a possible result.[76]

70. Compare Richard Schmalensee, "Entry Deterrence in the Ready-To-Eat Breakfast Cereals Industry," *Bell Journal of Economics*, vol. 9 (Autumn 1978), pp. 305–327; F. M. Scherer, "The Welfare Economics of Product Variety: An Application to the Ready-To-Eat Cereals Industry," *Journal of Industrial Economics*, vol. 28 (December 1979), pp. 113–124; and Brian F. Harris, *Shared Monopoly and the Cereal Industry* (East Lansing: Michigan State University Graduate School of Business Administration, 1979); and Lacy Glenn Thomas, "Asymmetries in Entry Competence: A Revisionist Analysis of the RTE Cereals Industry," Columbia University Graduate School of Business working paper FB-89-14 (March 1989).

71. This paragraph and the next are condensed from F. M. Scherer, "The Breakfast Cereal Industry," in Walter Adams, ed.,

The Structure of American Industry (7th edition; New York: Macmillan, 1986), pp. 195–197.

72. See "Candidates Hit FTC Cereal Action," *Washington Post*, November 4, 1980, p. D7.

73. *In the matter of Kellogg et al.*, initial decision dated September 1, 1981, reprinted in 99 F.T.C. 8,16 (1982).

74. Compare p. 337 supra.

75. Dismissal order dated January 15, 1982, 99 F.T.C. 8, 289 (1982).

76. *In the matter of E. I. du Pont de Nemours & Company*, 96 F.T.C. 653 (1980). See also William G. Shepherd, "Anatomy of A Monopoly," *Antitrust Law and Economics Review*, vol. 11 (December 1979), pp. 93–104, vol. 12 (March 1980), pp. 76–93, and (June 1980), pp. 93–106.

Clearly, this was an important step back from *Alcoa*. Yet had the FTC ruled against du Pont, it would have conveyed a signal that firms with sizable market shares and significant cost advantages should hold a price umbrella over less efficient rivals. This would have conformed more closely to the 1920 *U.S. Steel* doctrine, which hardly merited such reinforcement.

Other efforts by the FTC to pursue important structural cases must be considered more briefly. In a 1975 consent decree, the Xerox Corporation's extensive portfolio of copying machine patents was made available for licensing at a royalty rate not exceeding 1.5 percent of using firm copier sales.[77] A collective monopolization suit against the eight leading U.S. petroleum companies, launched in the heat of passion following gasoline shortages attributable to clumsy government price controls, was abandoned in 1981.[78] The Borden Company was found to have monopolized the processed lemon juice market (excluding fresh lemons) by selling its ReaLemon® juice at sharply reduced and discriminatory prices in metropolitan areas where its principal rival, Golden Crown, was gaining market share. After finding Borden culpable, an administrative law judge ordered compulsory licensing of the ReaLemon® trademark to rivals—an unprecedented remedy adopted because the trademark was seen as the heart of Borden's monopoly power.[79] On appeal, the Commission validated the monopolization finding, but eliminated the controversial trademark licensing remedy. Borden was ordered not to sell ReaLemon® juice below cost or at "unreasonably low" prices and to refrain from granting price concessions that discriminated among retail food store customers serving the same geographic area.[80] While Borden was unsuccessfully appealing to a higher court, Reagan administration appointees gained a majority in the FTC and secured the Supreme Court's permission to substitute a weaker order negotiated with Borden attorneys.[81] Under it, Borden was barred for seven years from selling ReaLemon® in any sales district below its average variable cost, including the cost of spot television advertisements in the district. Two additional cases alleging predatory pricing by leading sellers came to the FTC on appeal after Reagan members held the majority. One complaint, involving General Foods Corporation's pricing of Maxwell House coffee in response to the eastward expansion of Procter & Gamble's Folger's coffee, had been dismissed by an administrative law judge. The dismissal was upheld.[82] The second, concerned with the pricing of Wonder Bread and private-label substitutes by the Continental Baking Company, had been upheld by the administrative law judge, but was reversed and dismissed by the commission.[83]

The Predatory Pricing Problem

In many of the monopolization cases pursued by the Justice Department and Federal Trade Commission during the 1970s, predatory pricing allegations occupied a prominent role. The FTC's dismissal of the Maxwell House and Wonder Bread complaints reflected a new skepticism about the likelihood that allegedly predatory pricing harmed competition, whatever its impact on individual competitors might be. ReaLemon® was an exception, probably because its substance was decided before skeptics gained the majority.

Predatory pricing and analogous practices were even more intensely scrutinized in private treble damages suits, usually brought by one or more firms who perceived themselves to be the victims. Such actions typically emphasize attempted monopolization as the claimed Sherman Act Section 2 violation. To prove attempted monopolization, the plaintiff must show that there was exclusionary or anticompetitive conduct, that the firm(s) engaging in the conduct had a specific intent to monopolize the market in question, and that there was a dangerous probability it (or they) would succeed.[84] Among the many suits of this sort litigated during the 1970s and 1980s, only one was reviewed substantively by the Supreme Court. There too, a skeptical stance was adopted.[85]

During the 1950s, with the encouragement of Japan's Ministry of International Trade and Industry (MITI), numerous Japanese consumer electronic goods makers formed an export cartel. The principal product affected was television sets, on which we focus. The aim of the cartel was allegedly to set prices high in Japan and low in the United States. At MITI's insistence, the cartel arrangement included provisions to prevent producers from competing too vigorously for U.S. wholesale distributor access or driving prices below certain "check points," presumably to reduce the likelihood of dumping charges. The television manufacturers offered rebates that undercut the check point prices and attempted to keep them secret, presumably from U.S. customs authorities and perhaps also from MITI and each other. The consequence of all this was that prices in the U.S. market were kept at low levels, the Japanese gained substantial market shares, and many U.S. producers exited after sustaining substantial losses. This pattern of behavior continued at least until 1974, when aggrieved U.S. companies sued under the antitrust laws to recover damages (and also induced the Treasury Department to bring antidumping charges).

77. *In the matter of Xerox Corporation*, decision and order, 86 F.T.C. 364 (1975). On the effects, see Timothy F. Bresnahan, "Post-Entry Competition in the Plain Paper Copier Market," *American Economic Review*, vol. 75 (May 1985), pp. 15–19.

78. *In the matter of Exxon Corporation et al.*, complaint filed January 24, 1972, dismissal order filed September 16, 1981, 98 F.T.C. 453 (1981). It is interesting that the remedy sought by the FTC — separation of crude oil operations from refining and marketing — was viewed by stock market investors as a desirable form of petroleum industry restructuring in the 1980s. See, for example, "Sun Co. Applauded for Moves," *Philadelphia Inquirer*, July 10, 1988, p. 1-E.

79. *In the matter of Borden, Inc.*, 92 F.T.C. 669 (1978). For various views, see Richard Schmalensee, "On the Use of Economic Models in Antitrust: The ReaLemon Case," *University of Pennsylvania Law Review*, vol. 127 (April 1979), pp. 994–1050; J. T. McCarthy, "Trademarks, Antitrust and the Federal Trade Commission," *John Marshall Journal of Practice and Procedure*, vol. 13 (Fall 1979), pp. 151–162; Clement G. Krouse, "Brand Name as a Barrier to Entry: The ReaLemon Case," *Southern Economic Journal*, vol. 51 (October 1984), pp. 495–502; and David I. Rosenbaum, "Predatory Pricing and the Reconstituted Lemon Juice Industry," *Journal of Economic Issues*, vol. 21 (March 1987), pp. 237–256.

80. *In the matter of Borden, Inc.*, 92 F.T.C. 669 (1978), affirmed in 674 F. 2d 498 (1982).

81. *In the matter of Borden, Inc.*, 102 F.T.C. 1147 (1983), revised order issued on remand from 461 U.S. 940 (1983). Complying with the Supreme Court's mandate to issue a new order, Commissioner and former FTC Chairman Michael Pertschuk stated that "[T]his modified order represents for all practical purposes an abandonment of the Commission's role in policing predatory pricing by a monopolist. . . . The provisions are so lenient that it is highly unlikely we could ever establish a violation no matter what Borden did." 102 F.T.C. 1147, 1150. On the background, see "FTC To Relax Pricing Order Against Borden," *Wall Street Journal*, March 2, 1983, p. 54.

82. *In the matter of General Foods Corp.*, 103 F.T.C. 204 (1984). See also p. 388 supra.

83. *In the matter of International Telephone & Telegraph Corp. et al.*, 104 F.T.C. 280 (1984).

84. See Phillip Areeda and Donald F. Turner, *Antitrust Law* (Boston: Little, Brown, 1978), vol. III, pp. 312–355.

85. *Matsushita Electric Industrial Co. Ltd. et al.* v. *Zenith Radio Corp. et al.*, 475 U.S. 574 (1986).

A five-member majority of the Supreme Court rejected the claim that U.S. producers had been injured in the sense required under monopolization law. To be rational (that is, profit-maximizing), the majority said, a predatory price-cutting campaign must have the prospect of a payoff when, after the targets have exited, sufficient monopoly power exists to elevate prices. But at the time the record was closed, the Japanese cartel had not achieved a monopoly position, nor was there evidence of price elevation. "Two decades after their conspiracy is alleged to have commenced," the majority continued, "[the Japanese firms] appear to be far from achieving this goal: the two largest shares of the retail market in television sets are held by RCA and respondent Zenith."[86] Citing a collection of scholarly articles lopsidedly biased on the skeptical side, the majority said "there is a consensus among commentators that predatory pricing schemes are rarely tried, and even more rarely successful."[87] Since the goal of predation had not been reached and seemed out of reach, the majority concluded, they had to infer, unless contradictory evidence were brought forward, that the Japanese producers "underpriced . . . to compete for business rather than to implement an economically senseless conspiracy."[88]

Four Supreme Court justices dissented, arguing that the majority had ignored an alternative theory of the Japanese producers' behavior: price discrimination in the form of export market dumping. The majority accepted as facts that the Japanese firms had capacity beyond domestic market needs, that they had higher fixed but lower variable costs than their American counterparts, and that their home market was both cartelized and protected from import competition. Under these circumstances, it was profitable and hence rational to dump at low prices abroad.[89] Home market cartelization was directly relevant, a consultant's report correctly observed, because "If the Japanese manufacturers had competed in both domestic and export markets, they would have sold more in the domestic market and less in the United States. . . . [This] would have resulted in reducing exports to the United States and United States prices would have risen."[90] If television set production were subject to pervasive scale economies (which is unlikely) or if there were enduring economies associated with learning by doing (which seems likely), a high-domestic-price, low-export-price strategy would have been profitable even when continued for more than a decade as capacity was expanded. It would not have been necessary for the Japanese producers eventually to raise U.S. prices to realize the pot of gold at the end of the predatory pricing rainbow. Japanese government support for such a scheme, which at first glance seems so unfair to Japanese consumers and so altruistic toward U.S consumers, could be gained with three further assumptions: (1) that home demand for television sets was relatively price-inelastic, implying low dead-weight welfare losses; (2) that the adverse income distribution consequences from high domestic prices were mitigated by extensive worker sharing in the profits from price discrimination; and (3) that strong manufacturing export performance was valued for its own sake by raw materials-poor Japan. At least two of the three are highly plausible,[91] and indeed, this alternative story of what happened and why seems to provide the needed explanation so patently lacking in the majority's opinion.

The question remains, was the Japanese producers' conduct predatory or in some analogous manner inconsistent with the monopolization laws? The answer hinges on how one defines *predation,* and providing such definitions is the essential business of lawmakers. The Supreme Court chose a narrow definition: conduct is not predatory unless prices are cut sharply with the expectation of being elevated later. By this standard, consumers benefit in the short run but lose in the long run, whereas in *Matsushita,* U.S. consumers appeared to benefit over the long run too. Different definitions are possible, however. U.S. producers were injured by the Japanese cartel's conduct. The Supreme Court majority was reluctant to make predation depend only upon such injury, recognizing that injury to competitors is not necessarily injury to the vigor of competition, which is presumably what the antitrust laws seek to protect.[92] But the *Matsushita* case, and many other alleged predatory pricing cases, contained more: systematic price discrimination as a proximate cause of the injury. Price discrimination requires, as we shall see in the next chapter, monopoly power; and systematic discrimination precipitating the exit of otherwise viable competitors might legitimately be defined as predatory on either efficiency or fairness grounds (or both). Or it could be declared illegal with some other descriptive adjective attached, for example, under the antitrust laws governing price discrimination. But here we encounter a Catch 22, for as we shall learn in Chapter 13, the tests of actionable price discrimination have gravitated toward requiring consequences similar to those essential for proving attempted monopolization. Since the issue should not be escaped through semantic shell games, we pursue it here.

The common element unifying the diverse arguments encountered here is that prices differ significantly from one regime in time or space to another. What the Supreme Court majority looked for in *Matsushita,* but did not find, is low prices in one time interval followed by high prices in another. What existed in *Matsushita* and many other alleged predatory pricing cases was low prices in a relatively competitive geographic market and high prices in a less competitive one. Or in cases like *United Shoe Machinery* and *IBM,* there were high prices on parts of the product line insulated from competition and low prices on other parts exposed to competition. The question is, what is a low price? How far can one go in driving prices to low levels before one is found to predate? And upon what does the threshold depend?

In *Matsushita,* there were allegations that Japanese television set prices in the U.S. market were below cost. The record is unclear, but the implication seems to be that prices were below average total cost. It is perfectly rational (that is, profit-maximizing) for a discriminating monopoly (or cartel) to charge prices below

86. 475 U.S. 574, 591 (1986).

87. 475 U.S. 574, 589 (1986).

88. 475 U.S. 574, 597–598 (1986).

89. See, for example, Jacob Viner, *Dumping: A Problem in International Trade* (Chicago: University of Chicago Press, 1923) pp. 23–30. Viner observes (p. 28) that dumping to "obtain the economies of operation at full capacity without surrendering the profits to be derived from the sale of part of . . . output in the domestic market" is probably "the most prevalent type of dumping."

90. From a report by economic consultant Horace DePodwin, cited in minority opinion footnote 2, 475 U.S. 574, 602 (1986).

91. See, for example, Clyde V. Prestowitz, *Trading Places: How We Allowed Japan To Take the Lead* (New York: Basic Books, 1988), pp. 199–206.

92. The *Matsushita* case was special in the sense that the injured parties were U.S. firms and the injurers foreign firms. One might argue that the injured firms should turn to international trade law for relief. But at the time, the relevant U.S. law was weak, and the U.S. television makers were unable to recover damages under it — hence the resort to antitrust.

average total cost in some markets. If, however, prices in any market were below the *marginal cost* of providing the good or service, an unnecessary profit sacrifice is being accepted. Beginning from this correct premise, Professors Areeda and Turner argued in an influential article that predation exists only when prices are held below marginal cost.[93] But recognizing that it is difficult in practice for a court to measure marginal cost, they urged that predation be inferred only when prices are set below more readily ascertained average variable cost.

The Areeda-Turner contribution precipitated a storm of critical analyses seeking the proper test of predation.[94] The most fundamental problem is that the rationale for setting price equal to marginal cost presupposes myopic short-run welfare maximization criteria, but pricing that alters the structure of an industry is a long-run phenomenon. It is easily demonstrated that if pricing at marginal cost but below average total cost (for example, when there is excess capacity) drives out (or keeps out) competitors, so that prices are raised above marginal costs in some other market, or over some later period in time, overall long-run welfare (that is, the discounted sum of producers' plus consumers' surpluses) can be reduced.[95] Moreover, the rules specified for distinguishing predatory from legal behavior affect the decisions taken by powerful firms with respect to capacity and other strategic variables. Setting the wrong rule could elicit strategic reactions that make matters worse, not better.

To see this, let us compare the consequences of three proposed rules: the Areeda-Turner rule, holding that price may not be held below marginal cost; an analogous rule substituting average total cost for marginal cost; and the *Quantity rule* (or Q rule) advocated by Oliver Williamson, stating that an incumbent monopolist confronted with new entry may not produce a quantity greater than what it was supplying prior to entry.[96] Several simplifying assumptions are adopted. Contrary to the *Matsushita* facts, we focus on an incumbent monopolist with short-run cost functions ATC and MC in Figure 12.1(*a*) optimally adapted to supplying the profit-maximizing quantity of 100 output units, with a resulting price of \$30 per unit.[97] The initial question is, how effectively can the incumbent deter entry under each of the three rules?

It is answered by finding the would-be entrant's residual demand curve, that is, the demand curve left over for the entrant, assuming that the incumbent takes full advantage of, but does not overstep, whatever rule binds its behavior.[98] The analysis is simplest for Williamson's Q rule, so we begin there. The rule says, the incumbent may not increase its output if entry occurs. Thus, the incumbent's quantity is fixed at the preentry profit-maximizing level of 100 units. This means that all of the demand curve for quantities in excess of 100 units, that is, the segment BEHMLYD, is ceded to the entrant. What will happen to price upon entry now depends entirely upon the entrant, since the incumbent's output is fixed. If the entrant adds 50 units, point H will be reached on the Figure 12.1(*a*) market demand curve and the price will fall to \$25. If the entrant adds 100 units, point Y will be reached, and price will fall to \$20. These price-quantity reactions map the entrant's residual demand curve BEHMLYD, which we lift up and transport to panel 12.1(*b*), labelling it R_Q (for residual demand curve, quantity rule). Panel (*b*) has a somewhat larger scale than panel (*a*).

Deriving the entrant's residual demand under the cost rules is more subtle. Suppose the incumbent must adhere to the MC rule. If the entrant places 100 units of output on the market (white-line segment ZY), price will be driven into equality with the incumbent's marginal cost if and only if the incumbent produces 100 units too, so point Z is the incumbent's marginal cost rule point at a price of $20 per unit and ZY = 100 is the entrant's residual demand quantity. Suppose the entrant offers a smaller quantity — enough to bring the price to $22.50, assuming an incumbent pushing the MC rule to its limit. In this case, the firms' combined supply will equal the quantity demanded when the entrant offers quantity KL (approximately 65 units) while the incumbent *expands* its output to point K, that is, by JK (approximately 10 units). At point K, the incumbent has marginal cost of $22.50, and with price at the same level, it is on the razor's edge of the rule. By similar reasoning, at a postentry price of $25, assuming the incumbent to be on the MC rule's razor's edge, the incumbent will produce at G (approximately 119 units) and the market will clear, with supply equal to demand, only when the entrant offers GH (approximately 31 units). If the price were to be at the $27.22 level of point E, the incumbent could abide by the rule with a still larger output of 128 units, and there will be *zero* demand left over for the entrant. Point E therefore defines the *choke price* or zero-quantity ordinate of the entrant's residual demand curve, while the segments GH, KL, and ZY define the quantities left for the entrant at progressively lower prices. We transport these (and intermediate) values to panel (b), obtaining the marginal cost rule demand curve R_{MC} for the entrant.[99]

93. Phillip Areeda and Donald F. Turner, "Predatory Pricing and Related Practices under Section 2 of the Sherman Act," *Harvard Law Review*, vol. 88 (February 1975), pp. 697–733.

94. See, for example, Oliver E. Williamson, "Predatory Pricing: A Strategic and Welfare Analysis," *Yale Law Journal*, vol. 87 (December 1977), pp. 284–340; William J. Baumol, "Quasi-Permanence of Price Reductions: A Policy for Preventing Predatory Pricing," *Yale Law Journal*, vol. 89 (November 1979), pp. 1–26; Paul L. Joskow and Alvin K. Klevorick, "A Framework for Analyzing Predatory Pricing Policy," *Yale Law Journal*, vol. 89 (December 1979), pp. 213–270; J. Timothy Lefever, "Predatory Pricing Rules: A Comment on Williamson's Output Restriction Rule," *Yale Law Journal*, vol. 90 (June 1981), pp. 1639–1645; Frank H. Easterbrook, "Predatory Strategies and Counterstrategies," *University of Chicago Law Review*, vol. 48 (Spring 1981), pp. 263–337; Joel B. Dirlam, "Marginal Cost Pricing Tests for Predation: Naive Welfare Economics and Public Policy," *Antitrust Bulletin*, vol. 26 (Winter 1981), pp. 769–814; James D. Hurwitz and William E. Kovacic, "Judicial Analysis of Predation: The Emerging Trends," *Vanderbilt Law Review*, vol. 35 (January 1982), pp. 63–157; and Charles W. McCall, "Rule of Reason versus Mechanical Tests in the Adjudication of Price Predation," *Review of Industrial Organization*, vol. 3 (Spring 1988), pp. 15–44.

95. See F. M. Scherer, "Predatory Pricing and the Sherman Act: A Comment," *Harvard Law Review*, vol. 89 (March 1976), pp. 883–888.

96. See Williamson, "Predatory Pricing," supra note 94. Williamson's "Q rule" requires that an incumbent dominant firm conform to the output-maintaining assumption central to the limit pricing theories of Bain and Sylos-Labini. See pp. 378–380 supra.

97. To get the curves right and illuminate the analyses, specific mathematical forms are assumed. The total cost function in Figure 12.1(*a*) is:

$$TC = 800 + 7.5\,Q + 0.01\,Q^2 + 0.00035\,Q^3,$$

where Q is the quantity of output. Note that at Q = 100, the fixed costs of 800 are 40 percent of total cost. The demand function is:

$$P = 40 - 0.1\,Q.$$

98. This analysis follows Phillip Areeda and Donald F. Turner, "Scherer on Predatory Pricing: A Reply," *Harvard Law Review*, vol. 89 (March 1976), pp. 897–900, who in turn acknowledge the assistance of Michael Spence and Richard Caves. Note that the residual demand curve here is different from the one derived in Figure 6.4, which was residual for the *incumbent*, not for the *entrant*.

99. The curve should be convex downward, but the curvature is so mild that we ignore it and approximate R_{MC} (and later R_{ATC}) as a more easily constructed straight line.

Figure 12.1(a)
Derivation of the Entrant's
Residual Demand from the
Monopolist's Cost Conditions

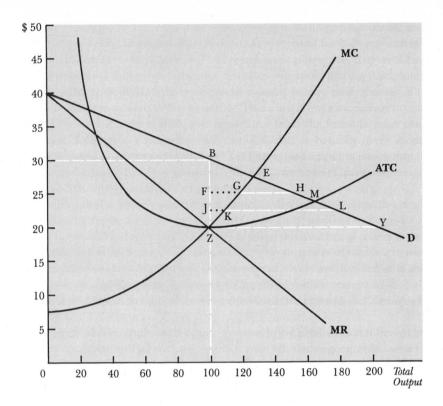

By analogous reasoning, we derive the ATC rule demand curve. Note that at a price of about $23.50, the incumbent is allowed under the ATC rule to expand all the way out to point M (roughly 165 units), leaving zero residual demand for the entrant. This large output expansion is possible under the rule because average costs rise more slowly than marginal costs with increased output, so the incumbent is held back less from an aggressive output-expanding response by the pressure of falling price on rising unit cost. Point M is the zero-output ordinate of the entrant's R_{ATC} demand curve in panel (*b*). Should the entrant supply ZY = 100 units, the incumbent would be forced by the P = ATC rule to back off to 100 units of its own output. Thus, when entrant behavior forces the price down to $20, the incumbent exactly satisfies the Q, MC, and ATC rules at identical outputs of 100 units, leaving 100 units for the entrant. This is why the three residual demand curves cross at an entrant's output of 100.

Now let us superimpose on the entrant's residual demand panel 12.1(*b*) the entrant's *long-run* unit cost function $LRATC_E$ (dotted curve). (The long-run function is applicable because, before entering, the entrant has an open choice of plant capacities.) We have drawn it to imply a minimum efficient scale, that is, a bottoming out, at 100 units of output. We also show the entrant to operate at a slight disadvantage relative to the incumbent; at a plant capacity of 100, the entrant's minimum unit cost is $20.50, or 2.5 percent more than the incumbent's minimum unit cost. The question is, is it profitable for the entrant to enter, given an incum-

Figure 12.1(b)
Residual Demand Curves
under the Q, MC,
and ATC Rules

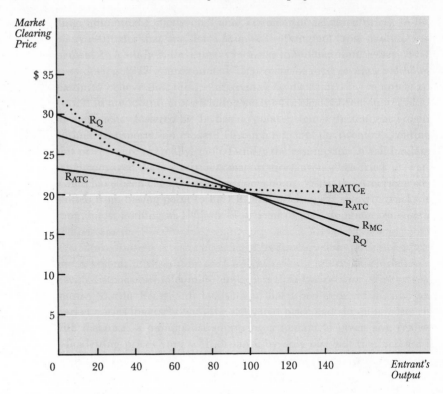

bent who lives by the rule? If either the Q rule or MC rule applies, profitable entry *is* possible, since the entrant's demand functions R_Q and R_{MC} lie above the cost function, revealing the possibility of an output choice with price above average cost. But entry is not profitable if the incumbent conforms to the ATC rule, since $LRATC_E$ lies above R_{ATC} (though only a hair's breadth above at their nearest conjunction). Quite generally, the ATC rule leaves the least strong residual demand for the entrant, and therefore allows the strongest deterrence. The Q rule leaves the most lucrative demand for the entrant and is therefore the *weakest* deterrent. This is so because the Q rule does not allow the incumbent to expand at all in response to entry, whereas the ATC rule permits the most expansion, squeezing the entrant's opportunity set. The MC rule occupies an intermediate position.

But this is not the end of the story. Suppose the incumbent is forced to conform to the weakly deterring Q rule, but wants very much to protect its highly profitable position. Can it deter? Yes, but only by investing in additional capacity. This is shown in Figure 12.2(a), which replicates the cost curves of Figure 12.1(a), but adds new cost functions ATC_{127} and MC_{127} (dotted lines) for a larger incumbent plant network designed to produce 127 units of output at minimum cost. If the incumbent installs this larger capacity and in fact operates before entry at 127 units, the would-be entrant has its Q rule residual demand curve's zero-output ordinate shifted from point B to point T. This means that in Figure 12.2(b), the

Figure 12.2(a)
Strategic Propositioning to
Deter Entry under the Q Rule

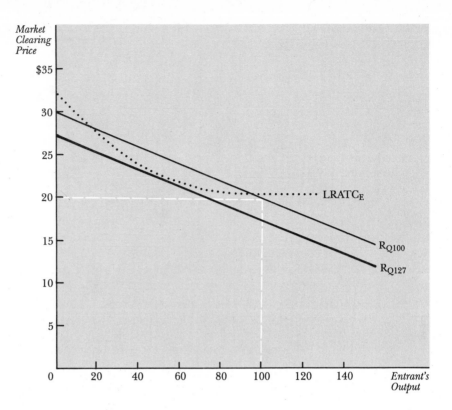

entrant's residual demand curve R_{Q127} with incumbent output of 127 is shifted down and to the left relative to the curve R_{Q100} carried over without change from Figure 12.1(*b*). R_{Q127} lies at all points below the would-be entrant's long-run cost curve, taken without change from Figure 12.1(*b*). By investing in and utilizing a higher level of capacity, the incumbent can deter entry even when forced to abide by the relatively weak Q rule. Indeed, even if the would-be entrant could in principle produce at unit costs just as low as those of the incumbent, contrary to our initial assumption with Figure 12.1(*b*), the incumbent could, by expanding its capacity enough (that is, beyond 127 units) deter entry.

By making deterrence relatively more difficult for the incumbent, the weak Q rule makes life better for consumers. More preentry output is required to deter under the Q rule than under the MC or ATC rules; thus, preentry prices are lower and dead-weight welfare losses (with constant long-run costs beyond 100 units of output, triangle BYZ in Figure 12.1[*a*]) are smaller. There are also more subtle differences. Suppose, contrary to the assumptions embodied in Figure 12.1(*b*), the incumbent could also not deter entry under the marginal cost rule if its capacity were optimized to produce 100 units. As in the Q rule case, it could achieve a deterrent posture by increasing capacity, shifting R_{MC} down and to the left. Although less capacity expansion would be required than under the Q rule, suppose, to avoid proliferating diagrams, the ultimate MC rule deterrent capacity were consistent with the dotted cost curves of Figure 12.2(*a*). Before entry, the MC rule

Figure 12.2(b)
Q Rule Deterrence

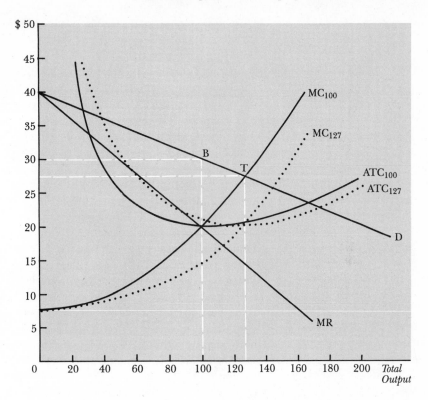

adherent would not maximize profits by operating at full minimum-unit-cost capacity output 127. Rather, since its preentry output does not bind its postentry
output, it would reduce output until MC_{127} equals marginal revenue, that is, at an
output of roughly 113 units, with a correspondingly higher price of $28.70. Only
after entry occurred would the MC rule incumbent expand its output aggressively
beyond 127 units. Thus, compared to the Q rule, the incumbent's preentry deterrent posture under the MC rule entails less capacity, less full utilization of that
capacity, higher prices, and higher average costs. Preentry, the MC rule advocated by Areeda and Turner is unambiguously inferior to the Q rule.

Deterrence is not always successful, and so we must consider what would happen if the incumbent tried to deter, adhering to the appropriate rule, but failed.
Postentry, the dominant firm's costs will be closer to their minimum possible
value, and its output is likely (but not certain) to be greater, under the quantity
rule than under the MC (or ATC) rule. In this respect, the quantity rule has superior welfare properties postentry as well as preentry. However, for the defiant entrant, a different story unfolds. From Figure 12.2(*b*), we observe that R_Q has
steeper slope than R_{MC}, whose slope in turn is greater than R_{ATC}. This means
that if entry does occur, the entrant's profits will be maximized by entering at a
larger scale under the MC rule than under the Q rule and at the largest scale of all
under the ATC rule. With larger-scale entry, the entrant's costs will be lower and
its contribution to industry output will be larger, exerting more of a depressing

effect on the postentry price. Thus, in its influence on the entrant's behavior, the MC rule has properties superior to those of the Q rule, while the ATC rule is still better. For plausible cost and demand curve assumptions, Timothy Lefever has shown that the MC rule's relatively favorable postentry welfare effects on the entrant's side tend to outweigh the Q rule's superior effects on the incumbent's side.[100] Thus, of the two, the Q rule is superior preentry but the MC rule is superior postentry. And of the three, the ATC rule tends to be worst preentry but best postentry. One must therefore weight their relative pre- and postentry dead-weight losses by the probabilities that entry will not, or will, occur, choosing the rule with the smallest probability-weighted dead-weight loss.

It is not clear in general which rule dominates in this respect. What *is* clear is that what started as a quite simple analysis by Areeda and Turner can become extremely complicated — too complicated to be handled competently by the antitrust courts. Legal scholars and economists have therefore sought rules that would be simple enough to enforce, but with a better claim to economic rationality. The rule adopted most often by U.S. courts has been the Areeda-Turner marginal cost rule or its average variable cost surrogate.[101] This choice cannot be attributed to demonstrably superior welfare effects. More likely explanations are the prestige of the authors or the fact that they, unlike many subsequent contributors to the debate, argued their point in plain English rather than plane geometry. A somewhat more complicated but less mechanistic approach has been proposed by Joskow and Klevorick.[102] They would analyze predatory pricing claims in two stages. In the first stage, market structure, entry barriers, and the dynamics of industry technology would be examined to determine whether sufficient monopoly power existed, or might be gained, to make predatory pricing a plausible and socially harmful strategy. In markets where "there is no significant evidence of a monopoly problem . . . [firms] can do anything they please with price."[103] But if conditions conducive to predatory pricing were found, the second-stage analysis would proceed. Predation would be inferred if:

a. Prices were cut below average variable cost; or
b. Prices were set below average total cost but above average variable cost, to be rebutted if the dominant firm showed that its pricing maximized short-run profits (for example, because substantial excess capacity existed); or
c. Prices were cut, but not below average total cost, and then were raised significantly within two years without a corresponding increase in production costs or market demand.

Scenario (c) corresponds to a proposal made by William J. Baumol aimed at encouraging dominant firm limit pricing policies that may exclude entry, but are justified by cost advantages and hence can be sustained more or less permanently.[104] Like Areeda and Turner, Joskow, Klevorick, and Baumol would bar consideration of intent evidence, such as documents evaluating the vulnerability of rivals to particular strategies, or sales managers' declarations that they are out to crush the competition, even though such evidence could help an appropriately skeptical court determine the expected consequences of conduct under scrutiny.

These are reasonable solutions to an extremely difficult antitrust adjudication problem. The Joskow-Klevorick and Baumol proposals would not be easy to enforce, and as the proponents concede, errors would be made. They would not catch all behavior that might under some criteria be deemed undesirable. Thus, it is likely that the Japanese television set producers would have found in the logic of price discrimination a profit-maximizing rationalization for setting U.S. prices persistently below average total cost. Rules of thumb are helpful and perhaps even essential to the resolution of complex competition policy questions. Yet there is something to be said for tossing the rulebook aside and undertaking a less-constrained rule of reason analysis for conduct that has potentially serious adverse consequences but conforms poorly to the standard models.

Price cutting is by no means the only strategic weapon dominant incumbents can deploy to repel or deter competitive entry challenges. As we have seen in Chapter 10, the threat of price cutting may be less credible than nonprice actions that leave insufficient room in the market for profitable new entry. Entry deterrence through product proliferation was scrutinized and found unobjectionable in the breakfast cereal case,[105] but procedural infirmities make the case an unreliable precedent. On such questions, much remains to be learned. Attempting to develop a generalized approach to exclusionary behavior using variables other than price, Steven Salop and colleagues have proposed that attempted monopolization be inferred when firms gain profit or injure competitors by pursuing strategies aimed at "raising rivals' costs."[106] Although specific applications can be gleaned from past antitrust cases, the broad concept has not been tested or accepted by the U.S. courts.

Proposals to Reform Sherman Act Section 2

With the exception of the *AT&T* case, the wave of monopolization suits brought by government antitrust agencies during the late 1960s and 1970s came to little. Some were lost, others were abandoned, and except in *AT&T*, intended restructuring remedies were not implemented even when the government achieved a nominal victory. The Reagan administration was inclined to believe that few significant private sector monopoly problems exist, and no new monopolization suits seeking restructuring were filed. Thus, as before, the wave came to an end. Whether the cycle will turn again remains to be seen.

It is difficult to tell how much impact existing monopolization doctrines have had on American industry. It seems reasonable to suppose that they discourage particularly rapacious conduct by enterprises with substantial market positions, but the large number of predation suits brought during the 1970s impels skepticism. Fear of Sherman Act Section 2 and related treble damages suits may also have induced some leading sellers to restrain their competitive efforts so as not to exceed that magic 60 to 64 percent market share identified by Judge Hand as the

---

100. See Lefever, "Predatory Pricing Rules," supra note 94.

101. See Dirlam, "Marginal Cost Pricing Tests," supra note 94, pp. 777–779.

102. Joskow and Klevorick, "A Framework," supra note 94.

103. Ibid., p. 245.

104. Baumol, "Quasi-Permanence," supra note 94.

105. *In the matter of Kellogg et al.*, supra note 73.

106. See Steven C. Salop and David T. Scheffman, "Raising Ri-

vals' Costs," *American Economic Review*, vol. 73 (May 1983), pp. 267–271; and Thomas G. Krattenmaker and Steven C. Salop, "Anticompetitive Exclusion: Raising Rivals' Costs To Achieve Power over Price," *Yale Law Journal*, vol. 96 (December 1986), pp. 209–293. For a critical view, see Timothy J. Brennan, "Understanding 'Raising Rivals' Costs,'" Discussion Paper EAG 86–16, Economic Analysis Group, U.S. Department of Justice (September 1986).

threshold of actionable monopoly. That General Motors was once so inhibited in selling its automobiles has been claimed, but denied by the company's management.[107] Similar claims have been made concerning the impact of pending antitrust suits on IBM's aggressiveness, but there is also contradictory evidence.[108] Kaplan and associates heard officials of several large corporations report in interviews that they prefer to concentrate their energy on invading new markets rather than building legally vulnerable positions in traditional markets.[109] To the extent that such statements are true, they lend support to the adage, "The ghost of Senator Sherman sits at the board table of every large corporation."

Apart from indirect behavioral effects, the *direct* impact of Sherman Act Section 2 in lessening market concentration has been modest. Since 1890, the courts have ordered structural reorganization in only thirty-three Section 2 cases — all but eight of them before 1950.[110] A few of the orders were drastic, such as the separation of Bell local operating companies from AT&T, the division of New Jersey Standard Oil into thirty-three pieces, and the splitting of du Pont into three separate powder manufacturing enterprises. But most have been mild, such as the order requiring Alcoa shareholders to shed their stock interest in Aluminium Ltd. of Canada or the dissolution of A&P's food brokerage subsidiary. One reason for the relative paucity of major reorganizations is a natural reticence by the federal courts to impose what were considered harsh remedial measures without compelling cause. As Judge Wyzanski cautioned in his first *United Shoe Machinery* decision:

In the antitrust field the courts have been accorded . . . an authority they have in no other branch of enacted law. . . . They would not have been given, or allowed to keep, such authority in the antitrust field, and they would not so freely have altered from time to time the interpretation of its substantive provisions, if courts were in the habit of proceeding with the surgical ruthlessness that might commend itself to those seeking absolute assurances that there will be workable competition.[111]

Although corporate surgery continues to be strong medicine, it has become a less radical course of action than it was when Judge Wyzanski wrote. During the 1970s and 1980s, *voluntary* restructuring was an everyday occurrence in U.S. industry. On average, 1,138 corporate divestitures (defined as the sale of product lines, subsidiaries, or divisions) were reported annually between 1970 and 1987.[112] If objections remain, they must turn on principle or on the belief that government is a much clumsier surgeon than corporate leaders.

Clumsy or not, government-induced surgery is costly. Restructuring actions have also been held back by the prodigious complexity and cost of major monopolization suits. Legal and related costs in *U.S.* v. *IBM* are said to have exceeded $200 million. Responsibility for such enormous costs is multisided. Attorneys, including government lawyers, are risk averters. When they represent plaintiffs, they strive to support every conceivable allegation in the hope that some will be decided in their favor. With large stakes in the balance, defense attorneys do everything in their power to block or delay the discovery and introduction of prejudicial documents, to pick apart or obscure the testimony of opposing witnesses through protracted cross-examination, and to present a thoroughly hedged rebuttal case. Judges often contribute by failing to force attorneys to focus on the central issues. And at bottom, the system is at fault for procedural rules that do more to advance the income of antitrust practitioners than the quest for truth.

Widespread dissatisfaction with the status quo has inspired numerous proposals for reform. There have, of course, been suggestions that Sherman Act Section 2 be scrapped without replacement.[113] On the other side, a task force established by President Johnson recommended in 1968 a "Concentrated Industries Act" under which the leading sellers in "oligopoly industries" exhibiting certain structural characteristics would be subjected to reorganization proceedings before a specially constituted court.[114] The case for reorganization could be rebutted by proving that substantial scale economies would be forfeited. Bills implementing such restructuring through an Industrial Reorganization Commission were introduced by Senator Philip Hart in 1972 and 1973.[115] The commission would also have been charged with investigating the appropriateness of structural reorganization in the chemical, drug, electrical equipment, energy, steel, motor vehicle, and nonferrous metals industries. In 1976 Senator Hart proposed an alternative "no-fault" monopolization bill under which Sherman Act Section 2 proceedings would be simplified by eliminating the government's need to prove intent to monopolize.[116] Companies shown to possess monopoly power could escape fragmentation only by demonstrating that their power came solely from valid patents or that divestiture would cause a loss of substantial scale economies. None of these or similar proposals gained sufficient support in Congress to be voted out of committee.

The Johnson task force and Hart proposals came at a time when statistical studies were showing that high seller concentration led systematically to elevated profits, implying the exercise of shared oligopoly power. Similar proposals now would sail on more troubled intellectual waters. As we learned in Chapter 11, new research tapping more finely disaggregated data has changed our view of the relationships. What was once seen as a fairly simple relationship between industry concentration and profitability is now recognized to follow mostly from the tendency for individual firms, or lines of business within firms, with relatively high market shares to be more profitable. The superior profitability of lines with high market shares could reflect the price leader's power to choose a pricing policy, product differentiation advantages that permit their holders to enjoy both higher

107. See, for example, Simon Whitney, *Antitrust Policies*, vol. 1 (New York: Twentieth Century Fund, 1958), pp. 482–483; Martin Shubik, *Strategy and Market Structure* (New York: Wiley, 1959), pp. 304–307; and "G.M. Reported To Centralize To Avert Antitrust Moves," *New York Times*, September 22, 1971, p. 65.

108. Compare David Levy and Steve Welzer, "System Error: How the IBM Antitrust Suit Raised Computer Prices," *Regulation*, September/October 1985, pp. 27–30; with the letter to the editor from Ross Petty, *Regulation*, September/October 1986, p. 4.

109. A. D. H. Kaplan, Joel B. Dirlam, and R. F. Lanzillotti, *Pricing in Big Business* (Washington: Brookings, 1958), p. 268.

110. See Richard A. Posner, "A Statistical Study of Antitrust Enforcement," *Journal of Law & Economics*, vol. 13 (October 1970), p. 406; and U.S. Department of Justice, *Report of the Attorney General's Committee To Study the Antitrust Laws* (Washington: USGPO, 1955), p. 354n.

111. *U.S.* v. *United Shoe Machinery Corporation*, 110 F. Supp. 295,

348 (1953). See also *Timken Roller Bearing Co.* v. *U.S.*, 341 U.S. 593, 603 (1951).

112. See W. T. Grimm & Co., *Mergerstat Review: 1987* (Chicago: 1988), p. 63.

113. See, for example, Richard A. Posner, *Antitrust Law: An Economic Perspective* (Chicago: University of Chicago Press, 1976), Chapters 1, 5, and 8; Bork, *The Antitrust Paradox*, supra note 60, Chapters 7 and 8; and Dominick T. Armentano, *Antitrust and Monopoly: Anatomy of a Policy Failure* (New York: Wiley, 1982), Chapters 3, 4, and 9.

114. *Report of the White House Task Force*, supra note 50, Section II and Appendix A.

115. For the text, see Appendix B of Harvey J. Goldschmid et al., eds., *Industrial Concentration: The New Learning* (Boston: Little, Brown, 1974), pp. 444–448. A debate on the issues among distinguished economists, legislators, and attorneys occurs on pp. 340–426.

116. S. 3429, 94th Cong., 2nd sess., introduced May 13, 1976.

prices and higher market shares, greater operating efficiency, or (most likely) some complex combination of these and other phenomena. Even though the leading sellers in most American manufacturing industries owe their size to the operation of multiple plants, and although there is reason to believe that the efficiencies flowing from multiplant operation tend to be small,[117] the new statistical results advise caution in plant divestiture actions lest subtle product-specific or other economies of scale be sacrificed. Reorganization measures that failed to cope with entrenched product differentiation advantages might leave the sources of monopoly power undisturbed, create nonviable firms (that is, those deprived of access to well-accepted brand names), or both.

Caution is also advised by the lessons of recent history. Many of the industries singled out for investigation in Senator Hart's industrial reorganization bill have since then experienced massive restructuring, primarily in response to import competition and other market forces. The automobile industry has been revolutionized as Japanese producers gained significant market shares, first by importing and then by establishing plants in the United States. Steel has been restructured through import competition, plant closings, and the rise of low-cost, independently owned mini-mills. The expropriation of multinational oil companies' overseas reserves and the emergence of a world crude oil market, however effectively cartelized by OPEC, has undermined much of the rationale for the major refiners' vertical integration from wellhead to gasoline pump. The computer industry has been changed radically by the ascendance of the microchip and the microcomputer. Time and market forces are powerful restructurers—more powerful than U.S. antitrust has ever been. Yet these lessons cut in two directions. On one hand, they counsel against hasty restructuring actions to achieve what competition would do anyway. On the other hand, some changes wrought by market forces in the 1970s and 1980s were a reaction to structural imperfections of long standing. Had the United States Steel Corporation been broken up in 1920, it is at least arguable that the industry would not have performed so sluggishly in the 1950s and 1960s, falling behind technologically and setting the stage for rapidly increasing imports. Had U.S. automobile production not been concentrated in the hands of four companies, all with headquarters in Detroit, it seems likely that high-quality compact cars would have been available from domestic sources sooner, reducing the need for Japanese competition as a corrective force. The problems in these and other industries were long evident. Timely competition-enhancing structural measures might have yielded benefits sooner, with less subsequent hardship for workers and stockholders when the forces of import competition finally did their job.

Whether industrial efficiency would be enhanced, degraded, or little changed by antitrust-based restructuring actions must be evaluated carefully in deciding whether to strengthen the law on monopolization. In addition, noneconomic considerations are relevant. The dispersion of power as an end in itself has from the beginning been an objective of antitrust, as it was in the drafting of the U.S. Constitution. As Senator Sherman said in his principal speech supporting his 1890 bill:

If the concentrated powers of [a trust] are intrusted to a single man, it is a kingly prerogative, inconsistent with our form of government, and should be subject to the strong resistance of the State and national authorities. If anything is wrong this is wrong. If we will not endure a king as a political power we should not endure a king over the production, transportation, and sale of any of the necessaries of life.[118]

Whether this is what U.S. citizens continue to want, and if so, how vigorously they wish to see the dispersion of economic power pursued, has become increasingly unclear as the size and complexity of the economy have grown and the accumulation of power, private and governmental, has been taken for granted. If monopolization law is to be reformed, it will have to be accompanied by a fundamental reexamination of values.

Even without a broad social consensus, procedural reform is clearly needed. Litigation costs like those borne in *U.S.* v. *IBM*, *Kellogg*, *AT&T*, and less dramatic monopolization suits are an intolerable waste. The waste is compounded by delay. Valid competitive problems might have been alleviated through timely action in cases like *IBM*, but when a decision is delayed for thirteen years or more,[119] changes in industry structure and technology often create such a gap between the conditions originally challenged and current realities that no constructive alternatives remain. A revised approach might work as follows. Following a limited period of evidence discovery, the contending parties would submit polished briefs documenting their views on both the mandate for structural reorganization and the probable consequences. The presiding judge, assisted by a panel of impartial economic experts subject to questioning by the contending parties,[120] would then narrow the issues and allow testimony covering only those relevant disputed issues on which further useful illumination is deemed probable. Counseled in open court by a panel of experts, the judge would then hear final arguments and render a decision. In addition to moving more swiftly and costing less, such a procedure would almost surely lead to decisions that better satisfy the important goals of truth and equity.

Policy toward Monopoly Positions Abroad

To put American policy toward monopolistic positions in perspective, it is useful to compare it with analogous policies in other industrialized nations.

For quite some time, structural antitrust was one of the United States' less successful postwar exports. At the end of World War II, the U.S. occupation forces imposed upon defeated Germany and Japan stringent antitrust laws, including deconcentration measures directed toward breaking up such consolidations as the Krupp and I.G. Farben empires and the Japanese Zaibatsu. The deconcentration program had two purported objectives: to punish the leading industrial groups for their complicity in the war, and to weaken the industrial bases of Germany and Japan so they would be less able to pursue militaristic adventures again.[121] The

---

117. See pp. 138–141 supra.

118. *Congressional Record*, vol. 21 (1890), p. 2457. See also pp. 18–19 supra.

119. Over the Sherman Act's history, the average length of monopolization proceedings averaged seven years. See Posner, "A Statistical Study," supra note 110, pp. 404–406.

120. An economist was used as "clerk" in *U.S.* v. *United Shoe Ma-*

chinery, supra note 39, and also in an action determining the size of treble damages awards following proven price fixing in the folding carton industry.

121. The German ordinance stated that its objective was in part "to destroy Germany's economic potential to wage war." Gesetz Nr. 56, "Verbot der übermässigen Konzentration deutscher Wirtschaftskraft," February 1947.

second objective, although not universally accepted as logically valid, implied a curious contradiction of the conventional American wisdom. If one breaks up monopolistic concentrations to weaken industrial might, what should be done to strengthen it? Contributing to the paradox was the fact that when the United States reversed its field and resolved to build up West German and Japanese industry as bulwarks against communism, one of the first occupation policies to be relaxed was the deconcentration program. These developments did not escape the attention of business leaders eager to effect monopolistic restrictions, who drew support for their views from the U.S. policies. More generally, the postwar antitrust serum inoculations engendered a reaction of hostility to such measures after the occupation measures were relaxed. And as we have seen in Chapter 5, the belief, particularly in relatively small nations, that domestic enterprises had to achieve greater scale to compete effectively in world markets led to policies favoring mergers and at odds with vigorous structural antitrust.

Gradually, however, attitudes changed, and confidence in giant market-dominating enterprises as sources of international competitive advantage ebbed. Competition policy laws were passed and extended to include features paralleling the merger and monopolization provisions of U.S. law. Although a few national laws now have provisions that in principle permit structural reorganizations like those that occurred in the U.S. *Standard Oil* (1911) and *AT&T* (1982) cases, no such divestiture other than those undoing prohibited mergers has been recorded. The emphasis abroad is instead on preventing *abusive* conduct by firms or groups of firms possessing monopoly power.

The difference between nations is illustrated by considering how the U.K. Monopolies Commission approached a problem that also commanded the attention of U.S. antitrust authorities. In the United States, we saw earlier, the Federal Trade Commission tried (unsuccessfully) to attack the bases of the three leading ready-to-eat cereal makers' monopoly power through the divestiture of plants and the compulsory licensing of formulas and trademarks. In the United Kingdom, the Monopolies Commission found in 1972 that an evident reluctance to compete on the basis of price, along with 1967–1971 profit returns on the Kellogg Company's capital ranging between 37 and 58 percent before taxes, were "largely attributable to the [highly concentrated] structure of the industry."[122] Concluding that structural change was infeasible, at least in part because industry leader Kellogg operated only one factory, but overlooking the possibility of trademark licensing, the commission recommended, and the Ministry of Trade ordered, that Kellogg be required to seek government approval before effecting any further breakfast cereal price increases.[123] Continuing governmental surveillance of Kellogg prices, costs, and profit rates followed.

Similarly, the commission recommended a 20 percent reduction in the prices of household detergents sold by Procter & Gamble and Unilever, but the government settled after negotiations for a remedy under which the two companies introduced new unadvertised detergents priced 20 percent lower than existing products.[124] Finding prices and profits of the tranquilizers Valium and Librium excessive, the commission recommended 75 and 60 percent price reductions.[125] Price cuts averaging 40 percent were urged following a Monopolies Commission investigation of the condom industry.[126]

West German law was first amended to deal with abuses of monopoly power in 1973, with extensions added in 1980.[127] The Federal Cartel Office soon commenced a program of interventions to force price reductions or rollbacks by market dominating enterprises. According to the statute, market domination exists when a single firm controls a third or more of some relevant market, or for oligopolies, when three or fewer enterprises have a combined market share of 50 percent or more, or when five or fewer firms have a combined share of two-thirds or more. Early targets of the Cartel Office's effort included Merck, the leading producer of vitamin B-12; Hoffmann-LaRoche of Valium fame; the leading West German petroleum refiners; and the automobile industry.[128] Many of the firms against whom actions were initiated complied voluntarily, for example, when the automobile companies rolled back contemplated, but not yet announced, price increases in 1977.[129] However, Hoffmann-LaRoche fought the Valium case to the German Supreme Court, eventually winning dismissal of the charges against it by showing that the Dutch generic company price "yardstick" with which its prices were compared was not representative.[130] Similarly, in its action against petroleum companies following the 1973–1974 OPEC shock, the Cartel Office was unable to penetrate the companies' internal transfer pricing mysteries and thereby obtain a clear picture of how profitable their operations were in Germany. As a result, the suit was dismissed by the Berlin Court of Appeals. There is reason to believe that following these and other setbacks, the Cartel Office reoriented its enforcement policy, devoting more attention to restraining mergers and other structural changes that could confer monopoly power and saving direct attacks on abusive pricing "for exceptional cases."[131]

The British and West German experiences reveal two difficulties in the abuse-oriented approach to monopoly power. For one, determining whether or not prices are excessive and what price level is reasonable calls for judgments in which the antitrust enforcers invariably operate at an information disadvantage vis-à-vis those whose prices they seek to control. It is hard to avoid arbitrary judgments, as

122. Monopolies Commission, *Report on the Supply of Ready Cooked Breakfast Cereal Foods* (London: HMSO, 1973), p. 25. Since 1965 the Monopolies Commission has had the power to recommend structural reorganization.

In 1989 the Monopolies and Mergers Commission recommended extensive divestiture of the "tied house" pubs from their brewing company owners. See "The Last Days of the Beerage," *The Economist,* May 20, 1989, pp. 69–70. But compare "British Pubs Get New Rules," *New York Times,* July 11, 1989, p. D5, concerning the weaker remedy actually imposed.

123. Ibid., p. 30. See also "Britain: A Chill on Kellogg's Pricing Policies," *Business Week,* March 3, 1973, p. 35.

124. See Alister Sutherland, *The Monopolies Commission in Action* (Cambridge: Cambridge University Press, 1969), pp. 48–49. Few consumers bought the new unadvertised products.

125. Monopolies Commission, *Chlordiazepoxide and Diazepam* (London: HMSO, 1973), p. 70.

126. See "A Classic in the History of Monopoly," *London Financial Times,* February 7, 1975. The reductions ultimately negotiated by the Office of Fair Trading were in the range of 2 to 11 percent.

127. See Ingo Schmidt, "Different Approaches and Problems in Dealing with Control of Market Power: A Comparison of German, European, and U.S. Policy Towards Market-Dominating Enterprises," *Antitrust Bulletin,* vol. 28 (Summer 1983), pp. 417–460.

128. See the OECD *Annual Reports on Competition Policy in OECD Member Countries, 1977,* No. 2 (Paris: 1977), pp. 30–31.

129. See "Preemptive Jawboning Astonishes Business," *Business Week,* March 28, 1977, p. 36.

130. See Schmidt, "Different Approaches," supra note 127, pp. 426–429; and Erich Kaufer, "The Control of the Abuse of Market Power by Market-Dominant Firms under the German Law Against Restraints of Competition," *Zeitschrift für die gesamte Staatswissenschaft,* vol. 136 (September 1980), pp. 510–532.

131. See OECD, *Competition Policy in OECD Countries, 1984–1985* (Paris: 1987), p. 108.

the round percentage reductions recommended by the U.K. Monopolies Commission suggest. Second, and perhaps more important, as the U.S. Supreme Court recognized long ago, today's reasonable price may through economic changes become the unreasonable price of tomorrow.[132] Therefore, an abuse-oriented approach requires, if it is to be anything more than an occasional lightning bolt, continuous monitoring of dominant firms' behavior. Intervention of this sort is inconsistent with the principles (although not always with the practice) of U.S. antitrust. It is better, runs the logic of Sherman Act Section 2, to take once and (one hopes) for all whatever structural actions are needed to restore effective competition and then stand back and let market processes do their job. Although there has been gradual convergence of the U.S. and European approaches, it remains true that Europeans are more willing to involve government authorities in a more or less permanent price controller's role.

Article 86 of the European Economic Communities Treaty, adopted in 1957, prohibits "any improper exploiting . . . of a dominant position" affecting Common Market trade. The approach is clearly abuse-oriented. In an important precedent, the European Commission fined the United Brands Company $1.2 million in 1975 and ordered it to reduce banana prices in Germany, Denmark, and the Benelux Countries by 15 percent.[133] The fine (penalizing several other abusive practices as well) was upheld by the European Court of Justice. However, the price reduction order was nullified because the Irish prices to which comparisons had been made were considered unrepresentative, and because an alternative means of judging abuse, an analysis of United Brands' profitability, had not been pursued. Despite this setback, the commission continued to pursue pricing abuse cases, and in 1988, the European Court of Justice ruled that a group of French funeral directors could be found to violate Article 86 by using their exclusive burial rights in 2,800 cemeteries to overcharge customers.[134]

Several other practices have been found by the European Common Market authorities to be abuses of dominant positions under Article 86.

Price discrimination between different groups of banana distributors was found by the Court of Justice to be one basis for levying a fine on United Brands. In another case, AKZO, a Dutch chemical maker, was fined heavily in 1985 when, in response to entry by a smaller firm into a West German product market AKZO dominated, AKZO's subsidiary cut prices sharply and discriminatorily, but not below average variable cost, in a British market where the smaller firm was relatively strong.[135] This precedent appears to adopt a tougher line toward alleged predatory pricing than concurrent court decisions in the United States. And in 1988, the commission fined British Sugar, Ltd., for attempting to squeeze a small company out of the U.K. retail sugar market. The size of the fine was mitigated when British Sugar agreed to fire managers involved in the exclusionary action.[136]

Refusals by firms with dominant positions to sell to, or deal with, certain other firms have been found in several cases to violate Article 86. A key precedent was set in a 1974 Court of Justice opinion sustaining the commission's judgment against the Italian subsidiary of the Commercial Solvents Corporation.[137] CSC was the sole commercial-scale supplier in the Common Market of a raw material used both in paint and as a necessary intermediate for producing a drug effective against tuberculosis. When CSC's Italian subsidiary began producing the profitable drug, it ceased supplying the raw material to other Common Market firms. This was ruled an abuse of CSC's dominant position, and in addition to paying a $215,000 fine, CSC was ordered to resume supplying independent would-be buyers. Using the antitrust laws to attack such refusals to deal has for the most part been avoided by U.S. courts, although there have been exceptions requiring access to bottleneck facilities such as railroad terminals and electric power transmission lines that are both essential to outsiders and not easily duplicated.[138] A difficulty with such actions is that a monopolist who chooses not to sell can do so either by proclaiming its refusal to deal or by setting its announced price so high that no one will buy. To police such abuses effectively, the antitrust agencies may again have to play a continuing role as price controllers.

Finally, a negotiated remedy settled charges that IBM abused its dominant position in European markets by bundling computer hardware with software and taking unfair advantage of its role as interface standards-setter for products that plugged into the IBM System 370. IBM agreed to sell main memory units separately from System 370 central processor units and to make available upon request interface specifications within four months of the first announcement of a new mainframe design.[139] Although limited in scope, the settlement at least accomplished more than the massive *U.S* v. *IBM* litigation.

As a last stop on this Cook's tour, we turn to Canada, which in 1986 amended its laws to permit injunctive actions against anticompetitive acts by business entities that "substantially or completely control . . . a species of business" in all or part of Canada.[140] Along with prohibitions against undesirable conduct, the newly created Competition Tribunal is authorized to seek divestiture as a remedy.[141] The new law is unusual in providing a fairly detailed list of abuses against

132. *U.S.* v. *Trenton Potteries Co. et al.*, 272 U.S. 392, 397 (1927).

133. See Schmidt, "Different Approaches," supra note 127, pp. 429–432; and Eleanor M. Fox, "Monopolization and Dominance in the United States and the European Community: Efficiency, Opportunity, and Fairness," *Notre Dame Law Review*, vol. 61, no. 5 (1986), pp. 981–1020.

134. "May in the EEC," *The Economist*, May 28, 1988, p. 52.

135. See Fox, "Monopolization," p. 1012, note 114; and OECD, *Competition Policy in OECD Countries, 1985–86* (Paris: 1987), p. 261. In 1989, the case was on appeal before the European Court of Justice.

136. "Careful, Careful," *The Economist*, July 23, 1988, p. 53.

137. The European Court's opinion is excerpted in "Refusal by a Dominant Firm To Sell Raw Materials," *Antitrust Bulletin*, vol. 19 (Fall 1974), pp. 605–618. For an analysis of this and other refusals to deal cases, see Fox, "Monopolization," pp. 994–1004.

138. *U.S.* v. *Terminal Railroad Association*, 224 U.S. 383 (1912); and *Ottertail Power Co.* v. *U.S.*, 410 U.S. 366 (1973). For a critical view, see David Reiffen and Andrew Kleit, *"Terminal Railroad Revisited: Foreclosure of an Essential Facility or Simple Horizontal Monopoly?"* Federal Trade Commission Bureau of Economics working paper no. 172 (April 1989). A new and more anomalous

case is *Aspen Skiing Co.* v. *Aspen Highlands Skiing Corp.*, 105 S. Ct. 2847 (1985), in which the owner of skiing facilities on three Aspen, Colorado, mountains was required to cooperate with the owner of facilities on a fourth mountain in offering joint multi-mountain lift tickets.

139. "IBM Settles Antitrust Suit With Common Market; Rivals Welcome Concessions, But Hoped for More," *Wall Street Journal*, August 3, 1984, p. 2.

140. See Bruce Dunlop, David McQueen, and Michael Trebilcock, *Canadian Competition Policy: A Legal and Economic Analysis* (Toronto: Canada Law Book Inc., 1987), pp. 188–190 and 198–204; and Bruce C. McDonald, "Abuse of Dominant Position: A New Monopoly Law for Canada," *Antitrust Bulletin*, vol. 32 (Fall 1987), pp. 795–827.

141. In an action against the leading Canadian petroleum companies, the Director of Combines Investigation and Research recommended restructuring legislation, but the Restrictive Practices Commission found the recommendation unwarranted. See *The State of Competition in the Canadian Petroleum Industry* (Hull: Canadian Government Publishing Centre, 1981), vol. I, pp. 9–12; and Restrictive Practices Commission, *Report on Competition in the Canadian Petroleum Industry* (June 1986).

which action might proceed, including the use of fighting brands and below-cost selling to discipline or eliminate competitors, price squeezes by vertically integrated firms against nonintegrated competitors, the preemption of scarce resources or facilities to keep them out of competitors' hands, inducing suppliers not to sell to one's competitors, and adopting product specifications that prevent the entry of competing firms. The Canadian law takes an approach generally similar to that of U.S. monopolization precedents, and on its face, it suggests a somewhat tougher line than U.S. courts have adopted during the 1980s. Its reach will become clear only as experience in case-by-case adjudication accumulates.

Price
Discrimination

Most of the analysis up to this point has assumed that sellers quote a uniform price to all buyers during any short period of time. This is a tolerable first approximation for retail product pricing in the United States and Europe (but not in the Middle East) and for much wholesale and intermediate goods pricing. Yet many exceptions are encountered. When a seller charges diverse prices to different buyers of products that are essentially identical (in terms of subsidiary services such as packaging and delivery, as well as physically), the seller is engaging in price discrimination.

No simple, all-inclusive definition of price discrimination is possible. Succinctly, price discrimination is the sale (or purchase) of different units of a good or service at price differentials not directly corresponding to differences in supply cost. Note that this definition includes not only the sale of identical product units to different persons at varying prices, but also the sale of identical units to the same buyer at differing prices (for example, when electric utilities charge less for additional kilowatt-hour blocks), and asking the same price on transactions entailing different costs (for example, when universities extract the same tuition from honors seminar participants and students taught only through large lectures).

For a seller to practice price discrimination profitably, three conditions must be satisfied. First, the seller must have some control over price—some monopoly power. A purely competitive firm cannot discriminate profitably. It can of course sell some units at less than the prevailing market price (for example, for altruistic reasons), but it need not do so to sell as much as it wants, and it sacrifices profit in doing so. Second, the would-be discriminator must be able to segregate its customers into groups with different price elasticities of demand, or into discrete classes with varying reservation prices (the highest prices buyers will pay for any specific unit of output). Third, opportunities for *arbitrage*—resale by low-price customers to high-price customers—must be constrained. Reselling personal services such as medical care and education to make an arbitrage profit is virtually impossible, and so the service industries lend themselves particularly well to price discrimination. Because most *goods*, on the other hand, can be stored, transported, and resold, arbitrage is more easily practiced. Thus, the possibilities for price discrimination are more limited, although by no means negligible.[1]

Standard Theoretical Cases

It is customary, following the lead of A. C. Pigou, to speak of three main price discrimination cases: first degree, second degree, and third degree.[2] With first-degree, or perfect, discrimination, each unit is sold at its reservation price, so that

---

1. In a classic case, duopolists du Pont and Rohm & Haas charged 85 cents per pound to general industrial users of the plastic molding powder methyl methacrylate, while special mixtures of the same compound were offered for use in denture manufacture at $22 per pound. The opportunity for making an arbitrage profit attracted firms who bought at the industrial price, incurred moderate conversion costs, and undercut the duopolists' denture price. To thwart the arbitragers, Rohm & Haas considered mixing some arsenic into the industrial powder so it would be unsuit-

able for oral use. It ultimately rejected the idea, but did plant rumors that the industrial powder had been adulterated. G. W. Stocking and M. W. Watkins, *Cartels in Action* (New York: Twentieth Century Fund, 1946), pp. 402–404.

2. A. C. Pigou, *The Economics of Welfare* (London: Macmillan, 1920), pp. 240–256. For a comprehensive modern treatment of the economic theory of price discrimination, see Louis Phlips, *The Economics of Price Discrimination* (Cambridge: Cambridge University Press, 1983).

every customer is milked of the largest outlay he or she would be willing to commit for the good in question and still consider its purchase worthwhile. In other words, the perfect discriminator leaves no consumers' surplus, but appropriates it all as producer's surplus. Second-degree discrimination is similar, only cruder. It is illustrated in Figure 13.1. The standard demand curve is given by DD', the marginal revenue curve by D MR, and the marginal cost curve by MC. A simple monopolist would equate marginal cost with marginal revenue, setting the uniform price OP_M for all buyers and selling OX_M units. A discriminating monopolist, however, is able to partition demand into ten blocks in order of descending reservation prices. There are consumers willing to buy P_1K units at the highest discernible reservation price OP_1; an additional EF units will be taken at the lower price OP_2, and so on. The seller, charging each block its approximate reservation price, finds it worthwhile to expand output until there are no remaining blocks whose reservation price exceeds marginal cost. Thus, OX_D units will be sold at a total of seven different prices. Total profit is the sum of the declining margins of price over average unit cost OC_D for all units sold. It is shown by the shaded area. This discriminatory profit is considerably larger than the profit realized under simple nondiscriminatory monopoly (shown by the area of the rectangle with height CMP_M and width OX_M).

Third-degree discrimination is quite different. It is assumed that the seller can divide customers into two or more independent groups, each of which has its own continuous demand function reflecting quantities sold to that group at alternative prices.[3] If these demand functions have different elasticities at common prices, it will pay to discriminate. To see this, suppose the firm charges the uniform price P* to each of two groups, at which price the demand elasticity for Group A is 2.0 and for Group B 4.0. This strategy does not maximize profits. We recall from Chapter 2 that marginal revenue is related to price by the formula $MR = P(1 - 1/e)$, where e is the elasticity of demand.[4] Thus, marginal revenue is one-half of price P* in selling to Group A and three-fourths of P* in selling to Group B. It

Figure 13.1
Second-Degree Price
Discrimination

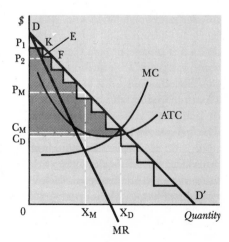

must then pay to reallocate some output away from Group A and toward Group B, for the marginal revenue from selling an extra unit to Group B customers exceeds the marginal revenue lost from selling one unit less to Group A customers. This reallocation can continue profitably until prices in the two markets have changed by a sufficient amount to equalize marginal revenue. Generalizing, a third-degree discriminator maximizes profits by charging the highest price in the market whose demand elasticity at the simple monopoly price is lowest and the lowest price in the market with the highest elasticity at the simple monopoly price.

Figure 13.2 presents the conventional geometric analysis of third-degree discriminating monopoly for two markets A and B, whose demand and marginal revenue curves are given in panels (*a*) and (*b*). The problem is to ensure that the last unit sold in Market A adds the same amount to revenue as the last unit sold in Market B, that is, to equalize the marginal revenues. To accomplish this, the marginal revenue curves of the two markets are summed horizontally, yielding the combined marginal revenue function CMR in panel (*c*). CMR is equated to marginal cost MC, indicating the profit-maximizing combined output OX_c. To equalize marginal revenue in the separate markets at the profit-maximizing value, we construct a horizontal line from the point where MC = CMR. The output in each market is found where this horizontal line intersects a market's MR function, and the prices are found (as usual) by reading off the relevant demand functions the prices at which the profit-maximizing quantities are demanded. Thus, the higher price OP_A is charged in the less elastic market A and the lower price OP_B in the more elastic market B.

Types of Discrimination Found in Practice

Although the soporific effect of exhaustive categorization normally outweighs any educational value, a systematic list of ideal types provides useful insight into the tremendous variety of real-world price discrimination practices. We can do no better than follow, with some modifications, the classification scheme articulated by Fritz Machlup.[5] Three main classes are identified: personal discrimination, based upon differences ascertained among individual customers; group discrimination, in which intergroup differences are exploited; and product discrimination, under which different products are priced discriminatorily. For each broad class we list the principal types with a brief explanation and example.

Personal Discrimination   *Haggle-every-time.*   Each transaction is a separately negotiated bargain. Examples include the typical pricing practice in Middle Eastern bazaars and the sale at retail of most new and used cars.

3. On violations of the independence assumption, see Stephen Enke, "Some Notes on Price Discrimination," *Canadian Journal of Economics and Political Science*, vol. 30 (February 1964), pp. 104–109; and C. A. Lovell and Kenneth L. Wertz, "Price Discrimination in Related Markets," *Economic Inquiry*, vol. 19 (July 1981), pp. 488–494.

4. See note 36, p. 35 supra.

5. Fritz Machlup, "Characteristics and Types of Price Discrimination," in the National Bureau of Economic Research conference report, *Business Concentration and Price Policy* (Princeton: Princeton University Press, 1955), pp. 400–423. Machlup in turn borrowed some of his categories from Ralph Cassady, Jr., "Techniques and Purposes of Price Discrimination," *Journal of Marketing* (October 1946), pp. 135–150.

Figure 13.2
Third-Degree Price
Discrimination

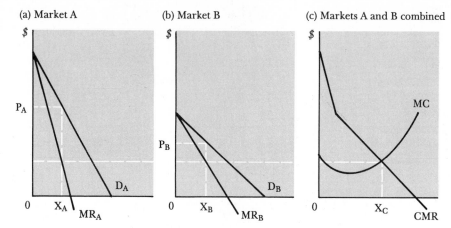

(a) Market A   (b) Market B   (c) Markets A and B combined

Give-in-if-you-must. Secret departures are made from list prices when buyers play one seller off against the others. Examples were given in Chapter 8, and more will be added in the next chapter.

Size-up-their-income. Wealthier customers with inelastic demand are charged more than the less affluent, who at high prices would restrict consumption disproportionately. Standard examples are the pricing of legal and medical services.

Measure-the-use. Customers who use a good or service more intensively are charged more, even though differences in cost may be negligible. For instance, Xerox machine rental charges are based upon the number of copies made, and the volume-related charge more than compensates incremental maintenance costs.

Group Discrimination

Absorb-the-freight. Delivery costs are absorbed or overcharged to customers located at varying distances from one's production or warehousing site. Since such discrimination will be analyzed more fully later, we defer examples.

Kill-the-rival. Prices are systematically reduced, perhaps below cost, only in the geographic market served by a rival the discriminator is trying to drive out of business. During the 1900s, the American Tobacco Company sold fighting brands of plug and smoking tobacco at prices below its production costs with the acknowledged intent to render rivals unprofitable.[6]

Dump-the-surplus. Goods in excess supply are offered at reduced prices overseas so as not to depress domestic monopoly prices. Although nations adhering to GATT (the General Agreement on Tariffs and Trade) are bound by anti-dumping rules, allegations of dumping continue, for example, as in the *Zenith* v. *Matsushita et al.* case examined in the previous chapter.

Get-the-most-from-each-region. Prices are persistently held higher in regions where competition is weak than where it is strong. Wide differences in the prices of bananas across member nations of the European Common Market were the subject of an important EC competition policy action during the 1970s.[7]

Promote-new-customers. New customers are offered prices lower than those paid by established customers in the hope of developing permanent brand loyalty.

Newspapers and magazines are avid practitioners of this art, for example, in the discounts offered new college student subscribers.

Keep-them-loyal. Special discounts or prizes are offered to customers who concentrate a large cumulative amount of business with one seller. The U.S. airlines' "frequent flyer" programs during the 1980s are illustrative.[8]

Sort-them-by-time-value. Coupons are distributed that offer a discount when presented in buying a product at the supermarket, or rebate coupons are attached to products, to be redeemed by mail. Since time is required to clip or send in the coupons, these offers favor customers who have a low opportunity cost of time, which is correlated with low reservation prices.[9]

Divide-them-by-elasticity. Group discrimination may also be practiced whenever groups readily classifiable by age, sex, occupation, and so on have different reservation prices or demand elasticities. U.S. airlines' requirement that trips span Saturday night to qualify for bargain fares, for instance, is an attempt to separate business travelers from vacationers and persons on family business, many of whom would not travel if they had to pay full fares. Similarly, lower prices are charged for children's haircuts (despite the higher labor input to shear a wiggling object) because of stronger do-it-yourself competition.

Product Discrimination

Appeal-to-the-classes. Differences in price more than proportional to differences in cost are associated with premium quality. For example, much higher margins between price and incremental production cost are realized on clothbound as compared to paperbound books. Cadillacs command higher price markups than Oldsmobiles and Chevrolets of comparable size and mechanical equipment.

Make-them-pay-for-the-label. Manufacturers distribute a physically homogeneous product under various brands, charging more for the better-known brands. Examples abound on the shelves of any supermarket.[10]

Clear-the-stock. Price concessions are granted at special times of the year, or continuously in special sections of a retail store, in order to reduce inventories or increase sales to customers with weak budgets and strong elbows. Filene's Basement in Boston remains a breathtaking example.[11]

Switch-them-to-off-peak-times. Lower prices are charged for services identical except with respect to time of consumption in order to encourage fuller and

6. See Malcolm R. Burns, "New Evidence on Predatory Price Cutting," *Managerial and Decision Economics*, vol. 10 (1989).

7. See Chapter 12, p. 486 supra.

8. See Abhijit Banerjee and Lawrence H. Summers, "On Frequent Flyer Programs and Other Loyalty-Inducing Economic Arrangements," working paper, Harvard University, August 1987.

9. See J. William Levedahl, "Marketing, Price Discrimination, and Welfare: Comment," *Southern Economic Journal*, vol. 50 (January 1984), pp. 886–891; idem, "Profit Maximizing Pricing of Cents Off Coupons," *Quarterly Journal of Business Economics*, vol. 25 (Autumn 1986), pp. 56–70; Douglas A. Houston and John S. Howe, "An Economic Rationale for Couponing," *Quarterly Journal of Business Economics*, vol. 24 (Spring 1985), pp. 37–50; Raymond Chiang and Chester S. Spatt, "Imperfect Price Discrimination

and Welfare," *Review of Economic Studies*, vol. 49 (April 1982), pp. 155–181; and "Rebates: The Attraction Quickly Fades," *New York Times*, April 9, 1988, p. 56.

10. See Asher Wolinsky, "Brand Names and Price Discrimination," *Journal of Industrial Economics*, vol. 35 (March 1987), pp. 255–268.

11. See Hal R. Varian, "A Model of Sales," *American Economic Review*, vol. 70 (September 1980), pp. 651–659; Abel P. Jeuland and Chakravarthi Narasimhan, "Dealing — Temporary Price Cuts — by Seller as a Buyer Discrimination Mechanism," *Journal of Business*, vol. 58 (July 1985), pp. 295–308; and Edward P. Lazear, "Retail Pricing and Clearance Sales," *American Economic Review*, vol. 76 (March 1986), pp. 14–32.

more balanced utilization of capacity. Resort prices varying with the season and the late night/weekend discounts on long-distance telephone rates are examples.[12]

Bundle-the-outputs.   Diverse goods and services are sold together at a single package price, even though many customers do not consume all components of the bundle. Thus, in classical music concert series, the best seats are offered to season subscribers, and performances featuring "stars" are mixed with less attractive offerings to ensure that the whole package will be purchased.

Get-the-most-from-each-group.   In this final catch-all category we include such practices as charging higher railroad freight rates on more valuable commodities; offering additional blocks of electricity at lower rates to encourage home owners to install electric water and space heaters; and the realization by multiproduct firms of higher price-cost margins on items for which demand is relatively inelastic and/or less competitive.[13] Also noteworthy is *skimming*—introducing a new and superior product at a high price designed to extract the highest possible revenue from eager buyers with high reservation prices, and then gradually reducing the price to penetrate a broader market.[14]

The Implications of Discrimination for Economic Welfare

With such a diversity of types, it is impossible to reach any simple blanket judgment about the social desirability of price discrimination. We can, however, formulate some guidelines for assessing specific types in terms of three criteria: income distribution, efficiency effects, and impact on market structure and the intensity of competition.

Income Distribution Effects   Price discrimination causes a redistribution of income toward the discriminator and away from its customers. In the absence of legal quirks, no firm with monopoly power *has* to discriminate. It will do so only if a system of discriminatory prices yields higher expected profits than uniform pricing, ceteris paribus.[15]

Whether this is a bad thing or not hinges on value judgments over which reasonable (as well as self-interested) persons may disagree. Many people believe that social welfare would be enhanced if monopoly profits gained through price discrimination were redirected into the hands of the consuming public and away from corporate stockholders, the majority of whom (by dollar holdings) are already well off. But this is a subjective judgment, and there is no iron-clad way to demonstrate its correctness. Furthermore, the practitioners of price discrimination are not always the great corporations. Physicians are the most highly paid professional class in the United States, with mean earnings for full-time male practitioners of $60,247 in 1979, compared to $41,362 for lawyers, $25,986 for electrical and electronic engineers, $23,865 for accountants and auditors, $19,499 for athletes, and $17,662 for secondary school teachers.[16] The relative affluence of the medical profession (and also attorneys) can be attributed in part to their discrimination in fees charged to patients of widely varying ability to pay.[17] It is debatable whether such differentials are equitable, although we must return to the question in a different context shortly.

Efficiency Effects   Price discrimination is sometimes condemned because it is symptomatic of monopoly, and the exploitation of monopoly power implies a misallocation of resources. This is an inappropriate criticism if monopoly power would be present whether or not discrimination were practiced. The correct question is, are resources allocated more or less efficiently under discriminating monopoly than under simple (uniform price) monopoly? The answer depends in part upon the type of discrimination exercised.

First- or second-degree discrimination usually leads to larger outputs than under simple monopoly, and from there to lower dead-weight losses and improved allocative efficiency. To see this, consider Figure 13.1 again. The simple monopolist, recognizing that any price reduction made to customers on the margin between buying and not buying must also be offered to customers who would buy even if the price were not reduced, maximizes profits by equating marginal cost with marginal revenue, producing output OX_M. Needing to offer a price reduction only to marginal buyers, the second-degree discriminating monopolist finds it profitable to expand output all the way to OX_D. Indeed, in the special case portrayed by Figure 13.1, the discriminator's output is the same as that of a competitive industry with a short-run supply curve identical to the monopolist's marginal cost function. There is no dead-weight loss in this instance, even though there is a massive redistribution of wealth in favor of the discriminator. First- and second-degree discriminators supply more than the simple monopoly output unless adverse income effects associated with their pricing policies are extraordinarily large[18] or their ability to segregate marginal customers by reservation prices is quite imperfect.[19] Thus, the output restriction inefficiencies for which simple monopoly is criticized tend to be reduced, perhaps greatly.[20]

Third-degree discrimination is probably the most widely used of the three main theoretical types. Its efficiency implications are also the most difficult to evaluate. The clearest case occurs when all demand functions are straight lines, as in Figure 13.2. Then if all relevant markets are served under both simple monopoly pricing

12. Price differentials just sufficient to repay the cost of building facilities capable of satisfying peak demands are not strictly discriminatory in a long-run sense. See Peter O. Steiner, "Peak Loads and Efficient Pricing," *Quarterly Journal of Economics*, vol. 71 (November 1957), pp. 585–610. Indeed, failure to charge peak-load demanders for the cost of maintaining peaking capacity would be discrimination in favor of such users.

13. See, for example, Eli W. Clemens, "Price Discrimination and the Multiple-Product Firm," *Review of Economic Studies*, vol. 19, no. 1 (1951), pp. 1–11; Bruce Yandle, "Monopoly-Induced Third-Degree Price Discrimination," *Quarterly Review of Economics and Business*, vol. 11 (Spring 1971), pp. 71–75 (on retailing); and W. Duncan Reekie, "Price and Quality Competition in the United States Drug Industry," *Journal of Industrial Economics*, vol. 26 (March 1978), pp. 223–237.

14. See, for example, Darral G. Clarke and Robert J. Dolan, "A Simulation Analysis of Alternative Pricing Strategies for Dynamic Environments," *Journal of Business*, vol. 57 (January 1984), pp. S179–198; and Nancy L. Stokey, "Intertemporal Price Discrimination," *Quarterly Journal of Economics*, vol. 93 (August 1979), pp. 355–371.

15. An exception may occur when secret discriminatory price cuts by oligopolists made with the intention of raising individual profits induce spreading retaliation that reduces *group* profits.

16. U.S. Bureau of the Census, *1980 Census of Population*, "Earn-

ings by Occupation and Education," PC80–2–8B (Washington: USGPO, May 1984), Table 1.

17. See Reuben A. Kessel, "Price Discrimination in Medicine," *Journal of Law & Economics*, vol. 1 (October 1958), pp. 20–59; and Elton Rayack, *Professional Power and American Medicine* (Cleveland: World, 1967), especially Chapters 3, 4, and 5.

18. For all but inferior goods, the income redistribution associated with discrimination shifts demand curves to the left, usually only slightly except when the good or service represents a large fraction of consumers' budgets.

19. Segregating customers into reservation price classes may entail costs that could conceivably outweigh the dead-weight losses from output restriction under single-price monopoly.

20. Similar but more attenuated conclusions hold for commodity bundling and for "two-part tariffs" — a form of second-degree discrimination under which consumers are charged a flat entry fee plus a fixed price per unit bought. See W. J. Adams and Janet L. Yellen, "Commodity Bundling and the Burden of Monopoly," *Quarterly Journal of Economics*, vol. 90 (August 1976), pp. 475–498; Walter Y. Oi, "A Disneyland Dilemma: Two-Part Tariffs for a Mickey Mouse Monopoly," *Quarterly Journal of Economics*, vol. 85 (February 1971), pp. 77–96; H. E. Leland and R. A. Meyer, "Monopoly Pricing Structures with Imperfect Discrimination," *Bell Journal of Economics*, vol. 7 (Autumn 1976), pp. 449–462; and the references in Chapter 14, note 84 infra.

and discrimination, output remains the same, with or without discrimination. But since discrimination drives a profit-enhancing wedge among the prices paid by marginal consumers in the segregated markets, dead-weight losses are increased relative to the simple monopoly case, and so economic welfare is unambiguously worse.[21] When one or more of the demand functions is nonlinear, output under discrimination may either rise or fall relative to the simple monopoly pricing case. If output contracts, the welfare consequences are even worse than with straight-line demand functions. If output rises, on the other hand, consumers' and/or producer's surpluses are increased, and unless the output change is small, the output-linked gain in surplus is likely to (but does not necessarily) exceed the deadweight loss stemming from nonequalization of prices to marginal consumers, and so overall welfare is increased. In the two-market case, an output increase can occur when the more elastic (that is, low-price) market's demand curve is convex downward while the less elastic demand function is linear or concave downward, or when the demand curve in the more elastic market is less convex than the curve in the less elastic market.[22] How often these output-increasing conditions coincide is difficult to determine. Finally, third-degree discrimination often permits (price-elastic) markets to be served that would not be served under single-price monopoly, especially when the discriminator segments its markets richly. In this case too, output and net consumers' plus producer's surplus increases are likely to follow from discrimination.

Any type of discrimination may have desirable allocative consequences in special situations where demand is too weak to permit profitable operation of a service under simple monopoly pricing. It is possible, for instance, that no physician would be attracted to a small town if he or she were required to charge the same fee to rich patients as to poor. The added revenue gained through price discrimination may be sufficient to make the difference in whether or not a service is supplied.[23] In the same vein, it is probable that railroad service would not have been provided to remote areas of the American frontier during the nineteenth century had rate discrimination between high-value and low-value commodities been impossible.

Price Discrimination and Natural Monopoly

Price discrimination can also provide ways out of an efficiency dilemma encountered in regulated natural monopoly industries. The problem is illustrated in Figure 13.3. Under natural monopoly, the long-run average total cost curve LRATC is continuously falling, so the long-run marginal cost curve LRMC lies below it. Efficient resource allocation requires that if a uniform price is charged, it must be set at the marginal cost level OP_M in Figure 13.3, with output OX_M being supplied. But then average cost $X_M C = OB$ exceeds the price, and the enterprise incurs a deficit equal to the rectangular area $P_M ECB$. To induce capital investment in the industry under these circumstances, public subsidies might be provided. But the taxes out of which subsidies come cause new and more subtle allocative distortions, and the political barriers to such subsidization may also be potent.

One solution is to permit second-degree price discrimination, as shown in Figure 13.4. One block of output OX_1 is sold to consumers with high reservation

Figure 13.3
Marginal Cost Pricing with
Falling Long-Run Costs

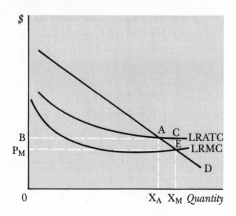

Figure 13.4
Discriminatory Marginal
Cost Pricing with Falling
Long-Run Costs

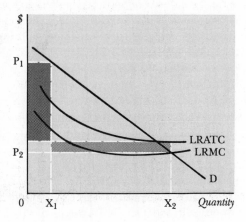

21. See Stephen Layson, "Third-Degree Price Discrimination, Welfare, and Profits: A Geometrical Analysis," *American Economic Review*, vol. 78 (December 1988), pp. 1131–1132; and Richard Schmalensee, "Output and Welfare Implications of Monopolistic Third-Degree Price Discrimination," *American Economic Review*, vol. 71 (March 1981), pp. 242–247.

22. See W. James Smith and John P. Formby, "Output Changes under Third Degree Price Discrimination: A Reexamination," *Southern Economic Journal*, vol. 48 (July 1981), pp. 164–171; Songken Hsu, "Monopoly Output and Economic Welfare under Third-Degree Price Discrimination," *Southern Economic Journal*, vol. 50 (July 1983), pp. 234–239; and Jun-ji Shih, Chao-cheng Mai, and Jung-chao Liu, "A General Analysis of the Output Effect under Third-Degree Price Discrimination," *Economic Journal*, vol. 98 (March 1988), pp. 149–158. Contrary to the usage found in some of the price discrimination literature, downward convexity here refers to a demand curve whose slope on conventional coordinates becomes less steep with higher output.

23. For a geometric treatment of this problem, see Pigou, *Economics of Welfare*, supra note 2, pp. 950–951. To be sure, if price discrimination were not practiced in larger cities, the potential small town physician's opportunity cost would be lower, and he or she might settle in the small town with a lower income expectation.

prices at the price OP_1, while a second block X_1X_2 moves at the marginal cost price OP_2. On the second block, accounting losses shown by the lightly shaded rectangle occur, but these are offset by the profits sustained from the first block (darker rectangle). The result is the simultaneous attainment of allocatively efficient output levels and financial self-sufficiency.

An alternative approach called *Ramsey pricing* invokes the logic of third-degree price discrimination. The agency regulating the natural monopoly could seek to enforce prices such that in any given market segment i:[24]

$$(13.1) \qquad \frac{P_i - MC_i}{P_i} = R \left(\frac{1}{e_i}\right)$$

where R is a *Ramsey number* with values in the interval from 0 to 1 and e_i is the price elasticity of demand in the ith market segment. When $R = 1$, the outcome in any given market segment is identical to the solution that would be chosen voluntarily by price-discriminating monopolists.[25] When $R = 0$, the numerator of the price-cost margin must be zero, which means that price equals marginal cost — the competitive equilibrium. Ramsey numbers intermediate between 0 and 1 would be applied when some degree of monopoly pricing is necessary for a natural monopoly to cover its costs, but in which going all the way to the unconstrained monopoly solution would provide more revenue than is necessary. Thus, the Ramsey solution approximates what a profit-maximizing monopolist would do naturally, but constrains the monopolist in the amount of revenue it can extract.[26]

The efficiency rationale of Ramsey pricing is illustrated by Figure 13.5.[27] Suppose, to keep matters as simple as possible, two market segments 1 and 2 are served at the same constant marginal cost level $MC_{1,2}$ and are of the same "size," that is, with identical quantities demanded when price equals marginal cost. Thus, their demand curves intersect at point J, associated with output OX_C. But as the divergent demand curve slopes at J reveal, the elasticities of demand differ between segments, with segment 2 having the less price-elastic demand D_2. Now suppose some elevation of price above marginal cost is necessary to cover the natural monopolist supplier's costs. If the elevation is the same in each segment, for example, to price OP_A, dead-weight loss triangle KJL will result in market segment 2 while the dead-weight loss in segment 1 will be MJN. Because of the much larger quantity response to the price distortion in segment 1, with its more elastic demand, the dead-weight loss there is much larger than the loss in segment 2. This means that a different set of elevated prices could yield the same surplus of revenue above marginal costs but with smaller dead-weight losses. From starting price OP_A, the price must be reduced in elastic-demand segment 1 to OP_1, causing the dead-weight loss triangle to shrink to area YJT. In segment 2, the price is raised to OP_2, causing a modest expansion of the dead-weight loss triangle ZJS. The general moral is that if price distortions must be accepted, it is better to load them more heavily into the market segments with less elastic demand, leading to relatively modest output contractions and hence relatively small dead-weight loss triangles, all else equal. Third-degree price discrimination points firms' price adjustments naturally in the correct directions, while the Ramsey number constraint ensures that the resulting second-best solution adds no more to total revenues than is necessary to cover costs.

Figure 13.5
The Rationale
of Ramsey Pricing

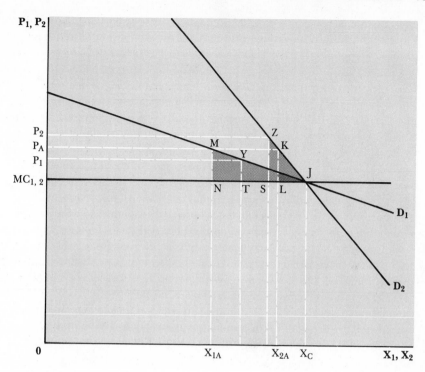

The Effects
of Discrimination
on Competition

Price discrimination is a two-edged sword. It can improve the performance of industries that are unavoidably monopolistic, but it can also alter the extent of monopoly power wielded by sellers. In addition to minimizing the allocative distortions associated with natural monopolies, discrimination can enhance

24. For a derivation of the proof, see William J. Baumol and David Bradford, "Optimal Departures from Marginal Cost Pricing," *American Economic Review*, vol. 60 (June 1970), pp. 265–283. The long-ignored originator was Frank J. Ramsey, "A Contribution to the Theory of Taxation," *Economic Journal*, vol. 37 (March 1927), pp. 47–61.

Creating price differentials enhances welfare with Ramsey pricing but reduces it in the unregulated linear demand case because in the latter, additional profits are extracted from consumers' surplus, whereas with Ramsey pricing, the regulated firm is held at some constant level or rate of profits. Layson, "Third Degree Price Discrimination," supra note 21, shows that in the linear demand case, the greater the increase in profits, the larger is the welfare loss from discrimination.

The relationships in equation (13.1) hold only for goods or services that are not substitutes. When there is substitution, the appropriate Ramsey formula is:

$$\frac{P_i - MC_i}{P_i} = \frac{R}{e_i - \left[\dfrac{P_i}{Q_i} \sum_{j \neq i} \dfrac{\partial Q_j}{\partial P_i}\right]},$$

where the term in brackets corresponds to the inverse of the cross elasticity of demand between market segment i and other segments $j \neq i$. In a two-segment case, the solution reduces to:

$$\frac{P_1 - MC_1}{P_1} = \frac{R}{e_1 - e_{21}}$$

where e_{21} is the cross elasticity of demand for market segment 2's product with respect to product 1's price.

25. Recall from equation (2.2) in Chapter 2 that in any given market, a profit-maximizing monopolist sets its price-marginal cost margin equal to $1/e$.

26. For a remarkably prescient rail freight pricing analysis that captures the essence of the Ramsey pricing approach, see Arthur Hadley, *Railroad Transportation* (New York: Putnam's, 1886), pp. 76–77, 111–124, and 261–265.

27. The figure is adapted from Baumol and Bradford, "Optimal Departures," supra note 24, p. 272.

competition by facilitating experimentation in pricing. The best way to determine whether the demand for one's products is price elastic is to try out selected price changes. Sellers may be reluctant to engage in such experimentation if the changes must be implemented across the board—for example, in every geographic market. They will be more willing if changes can be tried in restricted test markets, so that the consequences of an adverse rival or consumer reaction are less serious.

Another important procompetitive effect is the tendency of unsystematic price discrimination to undermine oligopoly discipline. The dynamics of this process have already been sketched in Chapter 8. In order to utilize capacity more fully, producers grant secret, discriminatory price concessions to a few aggressive buyers. Sooner or later the word leaks out, often through the efforts of buyers to extract similar concessions from additional suppliers, and others match or undercut the cuts. As the price concessions spread, list prices become increasingly unrealistic, and eventually they are reduced formally, benefiting all buyers and not just the favored few. When secret price shading of this sort occurs frequently, sellers may lose all confidence in their rivals' willingness to cooperate toward a common price policy, and the resulting loss of discipline makes joint oligopoly profit maximization impossible.[28]

For price discrimination to stimulate competition in this way, it is vital that the discriminatory concessions be *unsystematic*. Systematic price discrimination can have the opposite effect of weakening competition. There are several possible linkages.

For one, it may entrench firms in their positions of power by creating strong buyer-seller ties and raising barriers to the entry of new competitors. The tin can industry illustrates this point.[29] American Can's dominant position was bolstered both by the discriminatory price concessions it received from suppliers of tin-plated steel and the discriminatory price reductions it granted to large canners. As a buyer, American received discounts on the order of 7.5 percent from tin plate manufacturers until the practice became illegal in 1936. Smaller tin can makers, who were denied these discounts on an input accounting for roughly 70 percent of their costs, were at an obvious disadvantage. Other things being equal, American could set prices yielding excess profits approximating 5 percent of costs before smaller companies could enter and earn a normal return. As a seller, American granted discounts as high as 14 percent to large customers. These were usually tied in with long-term contracts covering a larger annual volume of cans than smaller can makers could supply. By making it difficult for small producers to secure can orders from large packers, this combination of discriminatory discounts with long-term, high-volume requirements contracts turned "what would have been a fairly innocuous practice into a rather formidable obstacle to open competition."[30]

A different sort of systematic discriminatory pricing was practiced in the U.S. shoe machinery industry. For decades United Shoe Machinery Corporation successfully defended its 85 percent market share in part by accepting much lower rates of return on machines that faced competition than on those it supplied exclusively.[31] In this way it could take full advantage of its monopoly power in lines it dominated, while the low prices in lines with competition made it difficult for rivals to maintain a foothold. By discouraging the entry and expansion of rivals,

USM in turn was able to remain the only shoe machinery manufacturer offering a full line — an advantage that strengthened its position with customers.

Accepting lower rates of return on product lines facing competition shades into more predatory kill-the-rival types of price discrimination. In actual cases the line between meeting competition and destroying it is seldom sharp, and unsuccessful kill-the-rival discrimination may cause nothing more than an interlude of intensified competition.

A spectrum of cases, some tending clearly toward the kill-the-rival type, came to light through antitrust actions waged against IBM during the 1970s. (Most ended in IBM's acquittal.) Unlike United Shoe Machinery, IBM faced *some* competition on each of its mainframe computer lines. But like USM, IBM accepted slimmer profit margins or even losses on computers facing particularly strong competition — for example, on its 360/90 superpower machine (with Control Data Corporation as the prime competitor) and the 360/67 time-sharing machine (aimed especially at General Electric).[32] Even more pointed were its reactions to competitive threats from certain plug-compatible peripheral equipment manufacturers (PCMs). Thus, when the Telex and Memorex Corporations began capturing appreciable shares of IBM's disk drive business in 1970, IBM repackaged an existing disk drive and offered it at a 26 percent discount to price-conscious customers. A half year later IBM announced a revised pricing policy for peripheral devices, offering 16 percent discounts to customers accepting two-year term leases instead of the traditional leases cancellable on a month's notice. Since competing peripheral device manufacturers could not achieve technical compatibility with new IBM computer mainframes until after the mainframes had been delivered, this in effect locked computer users into IBM peripheral leases for the first two years of a new computer model's life. And since technological change in computer designs and their related peripheral devices was rapid, the two-year lock-out left too short a remaining peripheral device life span for competing PCMs to recoup their investment. The result of the two-year lease discount strategy, in the words of an IBM staff analysis, was therefore expected to be "PCM corporate revenues lower — no funds for [manufacturing, engineering] — dying company!"[33]

28. Conversely, MacAvoy concluded that the prohibitions against price discrimination contained in the Interstate Commerce Act of 1887 provided the foundations for successful collusive pricing among U.S. railroads. Paul W. MacAvoy, *The Economic Effects of Regulation: The Trunkline Railroad Cartels and the ICC Before 1900* (Cambridge: MIT Press, 1965), p. 204.

29. James W. McKie, *Tin Cans and Tin Plate* (Cambridge: Harvard University Press, 1959), pp. 58–64 and 160–182.

30. McKie, *Tin Cans*, p. 175. For similar examples from ocean shipping and the West German electric light bulb industry, see the United Nations Conference on Trade and Development interim report, *Restrictive Business Practices* (New York: United Nations, 1971), pp. 11–13.

31. Carl Kaysen, *United States* v. *United Shoe Machinery Corporation* (Cambridge: Harvard University Press, 1956), especially pp. 126–134. USM's pricing strategy closely resembled that of a mul-

tiproduct natural monopoly setting Ramsey prices at levels low enough on average to deter entry undermining its monopoly position. On the relevant theory, see William J. Baumol, Elizabeth E. Bailey, and Robert D. Willig, "Weak Invisible Hand Theorems on the Sustainability of Multiproduct Natural Monopoly," *American Economic Review*, vol. 67 (June 1977), pp. 350–365.

32. Compare Gerald W. Brock, *The U.S. Computer Industry* (Cambridge: Ballinger, 1975), pp. 114–124; Franklin M. Fisher, John J. McGowan, and Joen E. Greenwood, *Folded, Spindled, and Mutilated: Economic Analysis and U.S.* v. *IBM* (Cambridge: MIT Press, 1983), pp. 277–288; Richard T. DeLamarter, *Big Blue: IBM's Use and Abuse of Power* (New York: Dodd Mead, 1986), pp. 86–96, 128–131, and 161–198; and Russell W. Pittman, "Predatory Investment: U.S.* v. *IBM*," *International Journal of Industrial Organization*, vol. 2 (December 1984), pp. 341–365.

33. Brock, *The U.S. Computer Industry*, p. 121.

In sum, systematic price discrimination can preserve and strengthen monopoly positions by permitting large firms to buy inputs at lower prices than their smaller rivals, by tying buyers together with sellers giving discounts for concentrated purchases, and by making entry into narrow segments of a market more difficult. On the other hand, systematic discrimination can improve the efficiency of pricing in situations where monopoly is inevitable, while unsystematic discrimination can invigorate competition by undermining oligopolistic pricing discipline.

The Special Problems of Geographic Price Discrimination

To a consumer in Indianapolis, a ton of hot-rolled steel from Pittsburgh is not the same as a ton of the same steel in South Chicago. When producers are located at different points on the map, their products are said to be *spatially differentiated*. When in addition transport costs are significant in relation to total product value, as in steel, cement, petroleum, and many other commodities, pricing practices often entail significant elements of discrimination.[34]

There are several broad approaches to freight pricing. One is the so-called postage stamp system, under which a uniform delivered price is charged to every buyer, regardless of distance from the production source. Or in a variant, buyers in a particular zone — for example, west of the Mississippi — all pay the same delivered price. The producer may then absorb higher freight costs on shipments to distant customers, in whose favor discrimination occurs. Postage stamp pricing is used most frequently with commodities whose value is high relative to transportation costs.

An approach better suited to bulky, low-value commodities is uniform F.O.B. mill pricing.[35] With it, producers announce a mill price at which customers may buy, paying their own freight bills or, if delivery by the producer is preferred, having actual delivery charges added to the mill price. This is the only system that entails no geographic price discrimination. The seller receives a *uniform mill net price* after outbound freight expenses are covered.

Some important properties of uniform F.O.B. mill pricing can be illustrated with a simple diagram. In Figure 13.6, the horizontal axis represents geographic distance between points. One mill is assumed to be located at point C (for example, Chicago), selling at the announced F.O.B. mill price CA. As it sells to customers located to the east, the delivered price rises (somewhat exaggeratedly) along the trajectory AR, reflecting increasing freight costs for shipment over greater distances. Another mill is located at point P (Pittsburgh), selling at the F.O.B. mill price PB, with delivered prices rising along the line BT. Given these assumptions, customers from Dayton westward enjoy lower delivered prices buying from the Chicago mill, and so (if the product is otherwise homogeneous) they will give all their orders to Chicago. The spatial market segment CX is Chicago's *freight advantage territory*, while in the corresponding segment XP Pittsburgh enjoys a delivered price advantage. If each mill adheres strictly to its F.O.B. mill pricing policy, neither can sell in the other's territory.

This seems a curious kind of competition, in which the two mills quote matching mill prices and vie directly for orders only in Xenia, Ohio (point X) (1987 population 23,800). How can the Chicago mill increase its sales, say, by capturing some orders in Columbus?

Figure 13.6
F.O.B. Mill Pricing

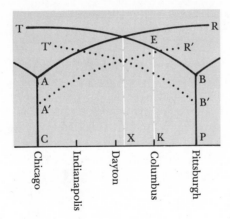

If a uniform F.O.B. mill system is retained, there is only one way—cutting the mill price, for example, to CA'. Then the delivered price locus shifts downward to A'R', the Chicago mill's freight advantage territory is expanded through Columbus, and the Pittsburgh mill's territory contracts accordingly. But this approach has two obvious disadvantages. First, the Chicago mill is not apt to be very enthusiastic about cutting price to all the customers between Chicago and Xenia, to whom it can otherwise sell at mill net price CA, merely to expand sales between Xenia and Columbus. Second, the Pittsburgh mill will be even less enthusiastic about losing its customers between Columbus and Xenia. If Chicago reduces its mill price to CA', Pittsburgh will probably respond with a matching cut in its own price to PB'. With the new F.O.B. Pittsburgh delivered price function B'T', the market division point is once again Xenia. Each seller finds itself serving the same market territory as before the round of price cuts, but at a lower mill net price. And each will soon recognize that they will not endow many libraries through such uncooperative tactics.

One way around the problem is to shift to a system of F.O.B. mill pricing coupled with unsystematic discrimination through freight absorption. Each mill then quotes its F.O.B. mill price: CA for Chicago and PB for Pittsburgh. Normally each delivers output at this mill price plus freight, but if an especially attractive sales opportunity arises in Columbus, Chicago may choose to absorb freight discriminatorily and meet or even undercut the Pittsburgh delivered price KE. Such freight absorption will be attractive to Chicago if marginal production costs are less than or equal to CA'. Of course, two or more can play at this game, and so Pittsburgh is likely to meet or undercut Chicago's prices by absorbing freight in Indianapolis and Dayton. If the discrimination is unsystematic, both mills will be

---

34. For excellent analyses of spatial differentiation and the pricing practices to which it gives rise, see Martin Beckmann, *Location Theory* (New York: Random House, 1968), especially Chapter 3; and Melvin L. Greenhut, George Norman, and Chao-shun Hung, *The Economics of Imperfect Competition: A Spatial Approach* (Cambridge: Cambridge University Press, 1987).

35. F.O.B. means free on board; that is, the price quoted to load a product on board the transporting vehicle, after which the buyer becomes responsible for freight costs.

uncertain how low a price they must quote to win an order in their home territories. This uncertainty can precipitate a breakdown in oligopoly discipline, culminating in a general erosion of the price structure.

Again, this is not the way to endow libraries and symphony halls. To minimize the temptation toward independent pricing initiatives, the firms may adopt some sort of *basing point system*, as the U.S. steel, cement, lead, corn oil, plywood, wood pulp, automobile, sugar, and many other industries have at one time or another.[36] The most striking variety is the *single basing point system*—for example, the Pittsburgh-plus system used in the American steel industry until 1924, when it was abandoned following an antitrust order, and the Portland-plus system used for plywood and other lumber into the 1970s. One production point is accepted by common consent as the basing point, and *all* prices are quoted as the announced mill price at that point plus freight (traditionally, rail freight) to destination.

Although the geometry is similar, a new diagram (Figure 13.7) will illustrate the system. Pittsburgh is the basing point, at which the announced mill price is PB. Delivered prices are quoted according to the Pittsburgh-plus-freight line BT not only by Pittsburgh mills, but also by Chicago (as well as Birmingham, Los Angeles, and all other) mills. Thus, the Chicago mill will quote the price CG to its local customers, IL to Indianapolis customers, and KE to Columbus customers— a clearly discriminatory pattern. On nearby shipments, Chicago charges customers the high freight from Pittsburgh, whereas its actual freight costs (rising along the path AR) are modest. The surplus of billed over actual freight under basing point pricing is called *phantom freight*. At Indianapolis, buyers pay phantom freight of DL if they buy from a Chicago mill (although there is no phantom freight if they buy from Pittsburgh).[37] Only when it sells in the territory east of Xenia does Chicago receive no phantom freight. Then its actual freight costs exceed billed freight charges, so that in selling to Columbus customers it absorbs freight equal to NE dollars per unit. It will be willing to do this if its marginal cost of producing the units for Columbus is less than CA minus NE. With sufficiently low marginal costs, Chicago might find it worthwhile to absorb freight and penetrate all the way to Pittsburgh or even farther east. Pittsburgh at the same time receives full compensation for its freight when selling at the Pittsburgh-plus price in Chicago and farther west. Obtaining the same mill net price on such sales as those at home, it has every incentive to seek a share of the Chicago business. Each mill may therefore ship products into the other's home territory, incurring freight charges higher than those required if the order were filled locally. This practice is known as *cross-hauling*.

The incidence of phantom freight is reduced, perhaps greatly, under a *multiple basing point system*. Here more than one producing mill is designated as a basing point, and the delivered price quoted to any given customer reflects the lowest applicable basing point price plus freight from that point. In the steel industry after 1924, there were several basing points (typically including Pittsburgh, Chicago, and Birmingham) for most products. The U.S. cement industry had 79 basing point mills and 86 nonbasing point mills during 1937.[38] To illustrate the system's operation, suppose in Figure 13.7 that both Chicago and Pittsburgh are basing points, with CA the Chicago base price and PB the Pittsburgh base price. Then the delivered price ID will be quoted on *all* sales to Indianapolis customers,

Figure 13.7
Basing Point Pricing

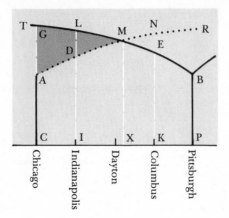

whether made by Pittsburgh or Chicago mills, and KE will be quoted to all Columbus buyers. When Chicago sells to Indianapolis it receives no phantom freight if it is its own basing point, and when it sells to Columbus it must absorb freight equal to EN dollars per unit. Phantom freight is gained only by nonbase mills—for example, by a mill located at Dayton and selling in its home territory at the delivered price quoted from Pittsburgh or Chicago.

Basing Point Pricing and Competition

Superficially, the multiple basing point system is similar to F.O.B. mill pricing with discriminatory freight absorption, and it is often difficult to place actual borderline cases in one category or the other. There are some important differences in principle, however. For one, buyers under any form of F.O.B. pricing have the option of paying only the mill price, taking delivery at the producing mill, and providing their own transportation. This is seldom advantageous under strict basing point systems, since all prices are quoted as *delivered* prices. Also, freight absorption may be unsystematic under discriminatory F.O.B. mill pricing. Producers do not necessarily match the rival mill's delivered price to the penny when they seek orders in the rival's home territory; they may match it, undercut it, or try to gain an order at their full list F.O.B. mill price plus freight. But under basing point pricing, producers *systematically* adhere to pricing rules that enable each to quote identical delivered prices at every destination. By following the basing point

36. For a more extensive list of industries, see Fritz Machlup, *The Basing Point System* (Philadelphia: Blakiston, 1949), p. 17. Other early classics on basic point pricing include Carl Kaysen, "Basing Point Pricing and Public Policy," *Quarterly Journal of Economics*, vol. 63 (August 1949), pp. 289–314; George J. Stigler, "A Theory of Delivered Price Systems," *American Economic Review*, vol. 39 (December 1949), pp. 1143–1159; Arthur Smithies, "Aspects of the Basing Point System," *American Economic Review*, vol. 32 (December 1942), pp. 705–726; and J. M. Clark, "Basing Point Methods of Price Quoting," *Canadian Journal of Economics and Political Science*, vol. 4 (November 1938), pp. 477–489. Newer contributions include David D. Haddock, "Basing-Point Pricing: Competitive vs. Collusive Theories," *American Economic Review*,

vol. 72 (June 1982), pp. 289–306; Dennis W. Carlton, "A Reexamination of Delivered Pricing Systems," *Journal of Law & Economics*, vol. 26 (April 1983), pp. 51–70; and Jacques-Francois Thisse and Xavier Vives, "On the Strategic Choice of Spatial Price Policy," *American Economic Review*, vol. 78 (March 1988), pp. 122–137.

37. There is a certain amount of ambiguity in defining the amount of phantom freight, since the Chicago mill has no announced mill price. We assume here an implicit Chicago base price equal to the Pittsburgh base price PB. Other writers (for example, Smithies) have defined CA as the marginal cost in Chicago.

38. Machlup, *The Basing Point System*, supra note 36, p. 80.

rules, for example, eleven manufacturers were all able to submit quotations of $3.286854 per barrel in response to a government request for bids on cement delivered to Tucumcari, New Mexico.[39] Through such adherence, they avoid independent initiatives that might otherwise threaten oligopoly pricing discipline.

To be sure, collusion might be ineffective under basing point pricing if producers chose not to adhere to the formulas. There are always incentives to chisel, especially when business is slack and departures from the formula price can be kept secret. Examples of nonadherence can be found in virtually every industry that has adopted a basing point system.[40] Yet basing point pricing has clearly contributed to oligopoly discipline in such U.S. industries as steel, primary lead, and cement and in European steel and cement markets.

Assuming that a more competitive method is desired, how attractive are the alternatives to the basing point approach? It is doubtful whether uniform F.O.B. mill pricing would induce more competition when the number of sellers is small, since producers at each shipping point are the sole suppliers of customers within their freight advantage territories. Unless several rivals are located at a single shipping point, there is little interfirm competitive contact except in the zones where mill prices plus freight charges are equalized (for example, at Xenia in Figure 13.6).

Both single and multiple basing point systems bring producers at different locations into rivalrous contact with one another over a broader geographic area than under uniform F.O.B. mill pricing. However, the rules of the game discourage using price as a competitive weapon, and so the greater interfirm contact leads mainly to more intense nonprice rivalry — at best, diligence in providing good service; at worst, inflated customer entertainment outlays.

F.O.B. mill pricing with unsystematic discriminatory freight absorption appears to be the best compromise between the available extremes when market structures are oligopolistic. Unlike uniform F.O.B. mill pricing, it permits sellers to shade mill net prices and invade each others' territories in search of additional business. And unlike multiple basing point pricing, this market interpenetration is achieved through explicit price rivalry, not passive acceptance of prices ordained by the system.

Spatial Pricing and Efficiency
The diverse spatial pricing methods also have significant efficiency consequences. One problem is excessive transportation expense. In principle, single basing point systems should be the worst offenders, since mills located at the basing point incur no mill net price disadvantage even when they serve customers located next door to a distant rival's plant. Also, nonbase mills can be expected to focus their sales efforts on customers located to the far side of the basing point, for example, west of Chicago in Figure 13.7, rather than toward it, where increasing freight absorption is necessary. Such a nonoptimal delivery pattern was observed in the U.S. plywood industry.[41] Some cross-hauling is also expected under multiple basing point and discriminatory F.O.B. mill pricing. Only a uniform F.O.B. mill approach has negligible cross-hauling.

Evidence on the magnitude of cross-hauling costs under basing point systems is sparse. One study of the U.S. steel industry estimated that in February 1939 freight absorption, which in a multiple basing point system is a rough indicator of cross-hauling, amounted to between 3 and 5 percent of delivered prices.[42] Two later company estimates that may have been self-serving put cross-hauling costs nearer 1 percent.[43] A study of the cement industry found that unnecessary cross-hauling costs during 1927 approximated 15 percent of total revenue, although there is reason to believe that this estimate may be overstated by as much as a factor of two.[44] In any event, cross-hauling costs have clearly been appreciable.

Another inefficiency fostered by the basing point system is the tendency to employ nonoptimal transportation media. Through much of the twentieth century, basing point prices were normally quoted under the assumption of rail haulage. This in fact encouraged the use of rail transportation, even when truck or water routings would have been cheaper or more convenient. When the American steel industry shifted from basing point to F.O.B. mill pricing, the share of trucks increased from almost nothing in 1953 to 44 percent of total shipment tonnage in 1963 and 63 percent in 1977.[45]

Excessive transportation is also encouraged by postage stamp delivered price systems and a system of discriminatory freight pricing under which delivered prices rise with distance from the mill, but by less than the amount of increase in shipping costs. Martin Beckmann has shown that when demand in any geographic market varies inversely with the delivered price and shipping costs rise linearly with distance, a monopolist supplying a market of given size realizes higher profits letting prices vary with distance by only one-half the increase in shipping cost than with either straight F.O.B. mill pricing or postage stamp pricing.[46] Such a scheme is the spatial analogue of profit-maximizing third-degree price discrimination with richly segregatable markets. Nevertheless, transportation costs are lower with F.O.B. mill pricing, and the sum of consumers' plus producer's surplus is higher, making the F.O.B. mill approach superior in terms of economic efficiency, given Beckmann's assumptions. When markets of variable rather than fixed size are assumed, however, and when firms crowd competitively into the markets until supra-normal profits are eliminated, freight-absorbing discriminatory pricing may, by increasing the output delivered to relatively distant

39. Machlup, *The Basing Point System*, p. 2.
40. On the U.S. maple flooring industry, see Almarin Phillips, *Market Structure, Organization and Performance* (Cambridge: Harvard University Press, 1962), pp. 153–160. On plywood, see the initial findings of a Federal Trade Commission administrative law judge, *In the matter of Boise Cascade Corp. et al.*, 91 F.T.C. 1, 34–49, and 63–67 (1978). On the western European steel industry, see Klaus Stegemann, "The Functions of Basing Point Pricing and Article 60 of the E.C.S.C. Treaty," *Antitrust Bulletin*, vol. 13 (Summer 1968), pp. 411–421.
41. *In the matter of Boise Cascade*, 91 F.T.C. 1, 49 (1978).
42. Cited in Kaysen, "Basing Point Pricing," supra note 36, p. 299. See also McKie, *Tin Cans*, supra note 29, p. 71; and Machlup, *The Basing Point System*, supra note 36, pp. 56–57, 72, and 82–83.
43. United States Steel and Jones & Laughlin estimates cited in Simon N. Whitney, *Antitrust Policies*, vol. I (New York: Twentieth Century Fund, 1958), p. 283.

44. Compare Samuel M. Loescher, *Imperfect Collusion in the Cement Industry* (Cambridge: Harvard University Press, 1959), pp. 208–213; and Clark, "Basing Point Methods," supra note 36, p. 482. To keep cross-hauling costs from rising further, cement firms sometimes swapped orders. For example, a central Ohio producer would have a Cleveland mill fill its orders in northern Ohio and vice versa. In this way both increased their mill nets. See Loescher, pp. 139–141.
45. See Louis Marengo, "The Basing Point Decisions and the Steel Industry," *American Economic Review*, vol. 45 (May 1955), p. 521; U.S. Bureau of the Census, *Census of Transportation: 1963*, vol. III, Part 2 (Washington: USGPO, 1966), p. 301; and *Census of Transportation: 1977*, "Commodity Transportation Survey: Summary," TC77–CS (Washington: USGPO, 1981), p. 206.
46. Martin J. Beckmann, "Spatial Price Policies Revisited," *Bell Journal of Economics*, vol. 7 (Autumn 1976), pp. 619–629.

customers, lead to superior welfare results.[47] The conditions under which discrimination is more efficient in this sense are quite complex, rendering conclusions as to the best system hazardous.

Under basing point pricing another kind of resource misallocation — the distortion of industrial location decisions — can also occur. A seller planning to build new capacity in an industry operating under the basing point system must weigh the advantages of building at a basing point against those of a nonbase location. Favoring the basing point location is the possibility of serving more customers without having to absorb freight. Nonbase mills benefit from their ability to realize phantom freight on sales near home, but they suffer an increasing freight absorption burden as they try to expand and serve more distant customers. How this tradeoff is resolved depends upon specific industry and firm conditions, although the consensus appears to place the advantage more commonly with concentrating production at basing points. In the U.S. steel industry, there was a distinct acceleration in the rate of capacity growth at Chicago, Birmingham, and California as the industry moved away from Pittsburgh-plus pricing and established new basing points in those areas.[48] Basing point pricing could also distort customer locational choices. It is said, for example, that the Pittsburgh-plus system retarded the development of steel fabricating operations in the American South and West, although it is difficult to isolate the effects of the geographic price structure from a host of other elements affecting industrial location decisions.[49]

Conclusion   There are so many kinds of price discrimination, with such diverse consequences, that simple generalizations about their economic effects are apt to be misleading. Some forms of discrimination increase the efficiency of resource allocation compared to simple monopoly pricing, others are essentially neutral, while still other types such as single basing point systems lead to possibly serious inefficiencies. Unsystematic discrimination can increase the vigor of competition, while systematic discrimination may bolster the monopoly power of already powerful firms and facilitate adherence to collusive price structures. Discrimination always causes a redistribution of income whose merits cannot be assessed without invoking strong value judgments. In view of these complexities, it is necessary to judge specific cases of discrimination on their individual merits.

Antitrust Policies Toward Price Discrimination

With such a complex array of consequences, laws regulating the use of price discrimination must be sophisticated and discerning to encourage desirable practices and discourage undesirable ones. The actual enforcement of U.S. antitrust law has fallen visibly short of this ideal.

Legislative History   The first statutory pronouncement on price discrimination for U.S. industries other than railroading was Section 2 of the 1914 Clayton Act.[50] It outlawed price discrimination between different purchasers where the effect "may be to substantially lessen competition or tend to create a monopoly." However, discrimination on account of differences in the grade, quality, or quantity of the commodity sold was exempted, as was discrimination that merely made due allowance for differences in cost, or that was carried out in good faith to meet competitive pressures. The quantity loophole proved to be a gaping one. Because of it and other exclusions, enforcement of the law was not particularly active. Between 1914 and 1936 the Federal Trade Commission, with primary enforcement responsibility, initiated forty-three discrimination complaints. Only eight led ultimately to cease-and-desist orders not overturned on appeal to the courts.[51]

Recognition of these limitations played some role in stimulating the enactment of a tougher law. However, other considerations had a more direct and potent influence. During the 1920s and 1930s, chain stores like A&P began to rise to the forefront of retail distribution, displacing small independent retailers. A 1934 Federal Trade Commission report on the chain store movement stated that one reason for the decline of the independents was the ability of chains to wrest discriminatory price concessions from their suppliers. These savings were passed along to consumers, and because of the chains' low prices, sales were drawn away from the smaller retailers.[52] Under heavy pressure from food wholesaler, independent grocer, and drug store lobbies, Congress passed the Robinson-Patman Act, substantially amending Clayton Act Section 2, in 1936. There is virtual unanimity among students of the act that, in sharp contrast to the other antitrust laws, its motivation was mainly a desire to limit competition, not to enhance it. In this respect the Robinson-Patman Act was not inconsistent with the spirit of the times, for in 1936, with recovery from the Great Depression not yet in sight, there were serious doubts afoot concerning the efficacy of unfettered competitive market processes.

The Robinson-Patman Act was enforced much more aggressively and with greater prosecutorial success than the original Section 2. Between 1936 and 1957, the Federal Trade Commission concluded 429 cases under the new law. In 311 of these cases, or 72 percent, cease-and-desist orders were issued.[53] Only four of the

47. Compare Melvin L. Greenhut and Hiroshi Ohta, "Output Effects of Spatial Price Discrimination under Conditions of Monopoly and Competition," *Southern Economic Journal*, vol. 46 (July 1979), pp. 71–84; Greenhut et al., *Imperfect Competition*, supra note 34, pp. 115–130; Phlips, *Price Discrimination*, supra note 2, pp. 51–61; and Benjamin F. Hobbs, "Mill Pricing versus Spatial Price Discrimination under Bertrand and Cournot Spatial Competition," *Journal of Industrial Economics*, vol. 35 (December 1986), pp. 173–191.

48. Compare A. R. Burns, *The Decline of Competition* (New York: McGraw-Hill, 1936), pp. 340–345; Leonard W. Weiss, *Economics and American Industry* (New York: Wiley, 1961), pp. 302–303; and "Billions Build Chicago into a Steel Titan," *Business Week*, November 19, 1966, p. 68; with the more skeptical view of Walter Isard and William M. Capron, "The Future Locational Pattern of Iron and Steel Production in the United States," *Journal of Political Economy*, vol. 57 (April 1949), pp. 131–133.

49. See Weiss, *Economics and American Industry*, pp. 300–303; Machlup, *The Basing Point System*, supra note 36, pp. 237–247; Kaysen, "Basing Point Pricing," supra note 36, pp. 304–305; and

John S. Hekman, "An Analysis of the Changing Location of Iron and Steel Production in the Twentieth Century," *American Economic Review*, vol. 68 (March 1978), pp. 123–133.

50. The Interstate Commerce Act of 1887 prohibited "undue" discrimination in railroad rates, with special bars against personal discrimination and rates that were lower on the same line for longer than shorter hauls "under substantially similar circumstances and conditions."

51. See Corwin D. Edwards, *The Price Discrimination Law* (Washington: Brookings, 1959), p. 6. For further background see Frederick M. Rowe, *Price Discrimination under the Robinson-Patman Act* (Boston: Little, Brown, 1962).

52. U.S. Federal Trade Commission, *Final Report on the Chain Store Investigation* (Washington: USGPO, 1934), p. 55. The investigation also revealed that the pecuniary gains from induced price discrimination accounted for only about 15 percent of the chains' selling price advantage over independents; the rest could be traced to operating cost efficiencies.

53. Edwards, *The Price Discrimination Law*, pp. 66–91.

twenty-three commission decisions appealed to higher courts during this twenty-one-year period were reversed. Between 1960 and 1972, 758 cease-and-desist orders followed.[54]

The Robinson-Patman Act's Substance

The core of the Robinson-Patman Act is embodied in Sections 2(a) and 2(b). They prohibit charging different prices to different purchasers of "goods of like grade and quality" where the effect "may be substantially to lessen competition or tend to create a monopoly in any line of commerce, or to injure, destroy, or prevent competition with any person who either grants or knowingly receives the benefit of such discrimination, or with customers of either of them." Three potential escape routes are then specified. Discrimination may be justified through proof (1) that it was carried out to dispose of perishable or obsolescent goods, or under a closeout or bankruptcy sale; (2) that it merely made due allowance for differences in "the cost of manufacture, sale, or delivery resulting from the differing methods or quantities" in which the commodity was sold or delivered; or (3) that it was effected "in good faith to meet an equally low price of a competitor."

The act also reached out to deal with several practices ignored in the original Section 2. Robinson-Patman Section 2(c) flatly prohibits the receipt (or payment) of brokerage commissions or any allowance or discount in lieu thereof except by (or to) middlemen actually performing services as independent brokers. No defenses—for example, on the basis of cost differences or meeting competition—are permitted. In this respect the law appears to enforce price discrimination *against* direct buyers, who might have to pay for services not rendered, even when they incur internal costs carrying out tasks otherwise performed by middlemen.[55] To enforce the section it is necessary to make distinctions between brokerage commissions, which are illegal if received by a company buying for its own needs, and wholesalers' functional discounts, which can under certain conditions be justified under Robinson-Patman Act Sections 2(a) and 2(b).[56] In the 1930s, the distinction was often obvious from industry traditions. But as marketing institutions changed, it became increasingly vague, particularly for firms serving as agents for buyers as well as for sellers, and for enterprises simultaneously purchasing goods to be distributed through their own retail outlets and performing middleman services for other retailers. Large companies have managed to escape Section 2(c) by purchasing their suppliers' entire output, or by purchasing only from suppliers who employ no brokers.

Section 2(d) prevents sellers from making payments (such as advertising allowances) to buyers for promotional and other services rendered by the buyer, unless the payment is available to all buyers "on proportionally equal terms." Section 2(e) prohibits sellers from providing services (such as the use of special display racks, or the supply of inventories on a consignment basis) unless the service is made available to all customers on proportionally equal terms. These rules were intended to prevent discrimination on nonprice as well as price dimensions. In enforcing them it has not been easy to determine when buyers of widely varying characteristics were in fact accorded "proportionally equal" treatment.[57]

Section 2(f) makes it illegal for a buyer "knowingly to induce or receive a discrimination in price" prohibited by other parts of the law. It reflects the belief of

Congress that powerful buyers were mainly to blame for the discriminatory practices inspiring the Robinson-Patman Act's passage. Its enforcement has not mirrored this apportioning of responsibility. Out of the more than 1,100 Robinson-Patman cease-and-desist orders issued by the Federal Trade Commission between 1936 and 1966, only thirty were brought under Section 2(f). One reason was the stringent standard of proof demanded by the Supreme Court in a key case. The phrase "knowingly to induce" requires, said the Court, proof not only that the buyer received illegal price concessions, but that it had good reason to believe the concessions were illegal.[58]

Whether such knowledge was present was one of the many questions addressed in a case that nearly ensnared the A&P Company, whose purchasing practices had been a prime target of the Robinson-Patman Act's passage forty years earlier. Bargaining hard over the procurement of private-label milk for its Chicago area stores, A&P told its supplier, Borden, that a price offer from rival dairy Bowman was sufficiently attractive that "You [Borden] people . . . are not even in the ball park." Needing the A&P business to keep its new plant operating at satisfactory levels, Borden thereupon submitted a new offer that increased A&P's annual milk discount savings from $410,000 to $820,000, or roughly 15 percent of the total value of A&P's Chicago area purchases from Borden. Borden informed A&P that it was offering the large discount solely to meet the competitive bid described in vague terms by A&P, implying that the discount was discriminatory and could not be cost-justified. Emphasizing A&P's knowledge of Borden's probable discrimination and its knowledge (which Borden lacked) that Borden's bid not only met, but undercut, Bowman's quotation, the Federal Trade Commission found that A&P had illegally induced discrimination.[59] However, A&P was exonerated when the Supreme Court ruled that seller Borden had a valid defense to charges of price discrimination because of the imprecise competitive threat with which it was confronted. The Court concluded further that buyers (that is, A&P) could not be held liable for violating Section 2(f) unless their suppliers' discriminatory prices were illegal, having no valid defense under other sections of the Robinson-Patman Act.[60]

54. U.S. House of Representatives, Committee on Small Business, Ad Hoc Subcommittee on Antitrust, the Robinson-Patman Act, and Related Matters, hearings, *Recent Efforts To Amend or Repeal the Robinson-Patman Act,* Part 2 (Washington: USGPO, 1976), pp. 186–191.

55. See, for example, Morris A. Adelman, *A&P: A Study in Price-Cost Behavior and Public Policy* (Cambridge: Harvard University Press, 1959), pp. 160–161.

56. The key precedent on the latter is *Federal Trade Commission* v. *Standard Oil Co. of Indiana et al.,* 355 U.S. 396 (1958).

57. See, for example, *Fred Meyer, Inc.* v. *Federal Trade Commission,* 390 U.S. 341 (1968); *In re Marpos Network, Inc.,* advisory opinion 88, September 3, 1971; withdrawn June 29, 1972; reinstatement refused, February 6, 1976; and *In re Dan Odessky, Inc.,* advisory opinion dated February 6, 1976, revoked February 1, 1979; and

"F.T.C. Plans Rule Change on Co-op Ads," *New York Times,* Feb. 21, 1989, p. D13.

58. *Automatic Canteen Co.* v. *Federal Trade Commission,* 346 U.S. 61 (1953).

59. *In the matter of the Great Atlantic & Pacific Tea Co. et al.,* 87 F.T.C. 962 (1976). An irony of the case was that the net price at which A&P ultimately bought its milk from Borden was apparently not appreciably lower than the unit cost at which Jewel, the leading food retailer in the Chicago area, obtained milk from its own vertically integrated dairy. At the time, A&P had only the fifth largest Chicago area market share.

60. *Great Atlantic & Pacific Tea Co., Inc.* v. *Federal Trade Commission,* 440 U.S. 69 (1979).

Some Interpretations of Section 2(a)

We return now to Section 2(a), under which many of the most important Robinson-Patman Act cases have been brought. The basic prohibition covers charging diverse prices to different customers on goods of "like grade and quality." An important point of contention concerns price differences between products unlike only in terms of brand name or some other aspect of image differentiation. The issue came to a head in 1966, when the Supreme Court ruled that the Borden Company had engaged in price discrimination by selling physically homogeneous canned evaporated milk at two prices, one for cans sold under the Borden label and a lower price for milk to which retailers affixed their own brand labels.[61] This opinion evoked a cry of protest from those who feared that the competitive challenge of low-priced, high-quality unbranded consumer products might be blunted. However, the case was shorn of its potentially revolutionary impact when an appellate court ruled on remand that no injury to competition resulted if "a price differential between a premium and nonpremium brand reflects no more than a consumer preference for the premium brand," since it merely represents "a rough equivalent of the benefit by way of the seller's national advertising and promotion which the purchaser of the more expensive branded product enjoys."[62]

One of the most complex and controversial features of the Robinson-Patman Act is the Section 2(a) requirement that price discrimination, to be found illegal, must injure competition in some manner. Injury can be shown at any of three levels: the primary line, the secondary line, and the tertiary line. A primary line injury involves competition among firms that are direct rivals to the seller practicing discrimination. A secondary line injury involves firms competing with buyers to whom a discriminatory price has been granted. A tertiary line injury involves firms competing with customers of the buyer in whose favor discrimination occurred. Different standards have evolved for handling primary as opposed to secondary and tertiary line injuries.

The central issue in all cases is whether the injury essential for a violation is injury to the *vigor of competition* or to particular *competitors*. These are usually not synonymous, although they might be, for example, when individual competitors have been injured so lethally that they withdraw from the market, leaving fewer firms competing more cautiously.

In secondary and tertiary line cases, the emphasis has been much more on injury to competitors than to the vigor of competition. The Supreme Court's decision in the *Morton Salt* case set the standard. Morton systematically sold its table salt at $1.60 per case in less-than-carload lots, at $1.50 per case for carload purchases, and at still lower prices when larger quantities were purchased over the span of a year. Observing that the discounts permitted large buyers to set retail salt prices below those of smaller rivals, the Court found an illegal injury to competition. It went on to note that "Congress was especially concerned with protecting small businesses which were unable to buy in [large] quantities . . . whether the particular goods constituted a major or minor portion of [their] stock."[63] This statement was amplified in subsequent secondary line cases to indicate that actionable injury would not be inferred when the price differentials were too small to have any significant effect on sales and market shares, or when they existed for too short a period to affect industry member positions. Returning to the question in 1983, the Supreme Court found that when a brewer sold beer at consistently lower prices to a Kentucky wholesaler than to a nearby Indiana wholesaler, when the lower Kentucky wholesale prices led to lower retail prices, and when there was evidence that Indiana consumers crossed the border into Kentucky to take advantage of the lower-priced beer, the competitive injury required for a *prima facie* case under Section 2(a) was "more than established."[64]

In primary line cases alleging that one or more firms were injured by their competitor's discrimination, a significantly higher threshold of injury has been set.

In one key decision, an appellate court observed that the Robinson-Patman Act was "not concerned with mere shifts of business between competitors." It concluded that Anheuser-Busch, having sold beer at discriminatorily low prices in the St. Louis area for fifteen months, "used restraint in its competitive efforts" and refrained from "the predatory misconduct" condemned in other primary line cases, and therefore had not violated the law.[65]

Where the magic line was overstepped seemed to be clarified in another case. In late 1957 the Utah Pie Company, a tiny family-owned and operated firm, began producing and marketing frozen dessert pies in the Salt Lake City area. Its principal rivals were three nationwide concerns—Continental Baking, Pet Milk, and the Carnation Company. All had entered the frozen pie business before Utah, shipping their products into Salt Lake City from California plants. Utah enjoyed a significant transportation cost advantage over the three, and through aggressive price competition it was able to build its Salt Lake City area market share to 67 percent in 1958. Each of the three cut prices sharply in response to Utah's gains, selling pies in Salt Lake City at prices below average total cost (including overhead allowances) and (at least occasionally) below the levels quoted in markets nearer their production sources. Utah's share of the market thereupon fell to 34 percent in 1959, rising to 45 percent again in 1961. Its absolute volume of frozen pie sales expanded steadily in the rapidly growing market, and it operated profitably throughout the period. Utah sued its three rivals for damages resulting from their alleged price discrimination. The Supreme Court found on appeal that the jury could rationally have inferred the requisite injury to competition. It stressed the sales of the three rivals below cost, the fact that Pet Milk management had identified Utah Pie as an "unfavorable factor" that "dug holes in our operation," and the fact that Pet had sent a spy into Utah's plant to seek evidence of quality deficiencies. Recognizing in a footnote the possible claim that Pet, Continental, and Carnation were only displaying "fierce competitive instincts," the Court nevertheless pointed to the evidence of predatory intent and argued that:

[A]ctual intent to injure another competitor does not . . . fall into that category, and neither . . . do persistent sales below cost and radical price cuts

61. *Federal Trade Commission* v. *Borden Co.*, 383 U.S. 637 (1966).

62. *Borden Co.* v. *Federal Trade Commission*, 381 F. 2d 175, 181 (1967). The appellate court also noted approvingly that Borden offered all buyers the opportunity to buy unlabeled milk at the lower price.

63. *Federal Trade Commission* v. *Morton Salt Co.*, 334 U.S. 37, 47, 49 (1948).

64. *Falls City Industries, Inc.* v. *Vanco Beverage, Inc.*, 460 U.S. 428, 437–438 (1983).

65. *Federal Trade Commission* v. *Anheuser-Busch, Inc.*, 289 F. 2d 835 (1961).

themselves discriminatory. . . . We believe that the Act reaches price discrimination that erodes competition as much as it does price discrimination that is intended to have immediate destructive impact.[66]

The *Utah Pie* decision was criticized by scholars for reading too much into evidence of intent and for excessively protecting a seller whose cost advantage made it quite able to fend for itself.[67] Perhaps because of that criticism, but more probably because the Court's membership became increasingly conservative, the primary line injury standards have subsequently coalesced with those set for judging Sherman Act predatory pricing cases. As we have seen in Chapter 12, the burden of proof imposed upon plaintiffs claiming predation has become increasingly heavy, so *Utah Pie* appears to have set a high-water mark in the willingness of the courts to find injury to competition from primary line discrimination.

The Discriminator's Defenses

Affirmation that competition has been injured through price discrimination does not complete a Robinson-Patman Act Section 2(a) proceeding. The burden of proving that its prices were legally justifiable then shifts to the discriminator. This is normally attempted under either the cost justification or "good faith meeting of competition" defenses.

Price differentials that merely reflect differences in the costs of serving particular customers are clearly unobjectionable, and to forbid them would be to encourage reverse discrimination. However, companies attempting to sustain a Robinson-Patman Act cost justification defense have seldom been successful because of stringent standards set by the Federal Trade Commission, that is, requiring detailed documentation of full (not marginal) costs and causing the defense to fail if less than 100 percent of the price differential is shown to result from cost differences.[68]

Section 2(b) of the Robinson-Patman Act permits a seller to rebut the *prima facie* presumption of illegality by showing that its discriminatory price was quoted "in good faith to meet an equally low price of a competitor." Interpretation of this "good faith meeting" defense has presented a tangle of legal and economic problems.

A few of the early contested decisions involved the use of basing point pricing systems. In the leading case, A. E. Staley Co., a central Illinois producer of glucose and corn syrup, systematically matched the delivered prices set from a Chicago basing point by its principal rival. For sales in the Chicago area Staley therefore quoted lower delivered prices than in downstate Illinois, even though its shipping costs were higher on Chicago orders. Staley argued that its discrimination was justifiable, since it merely met in good faith the prices of its Chicago rival. Sustaining an FTC cease-and-desist order, the Supreme Court ruled that the good faith meeting of competition defense could not apply when the prices met were themselves illegal, stemming from an illegal discriminatory system.[69]

In another case appealed twice to the Supreme Court, the FTC argued that the Standard Oil Company of Indiana could not plead good faith meeting of competition when it granted 1.5 cents per gallon functional discounts to four Detroit gasoline jobbers who took delivery in rail carload lots (instead of the much smaller truckload lots accepted by retailers) and then sold the gasoline in their own retail outlets as well as to independent retail gas stations. Stressing the *Staley* precedent, the Commission insisted that Standard's functional discounts were made pursuant to a discriminatory pricing system, and therefore did not qualify as good faith meeting of "individual competitive situations." The Supreme Court rejected this view, noting that Standard had lost three of its jobbers by not meeting competitors' discounts during a price war and that it granted the jobber's discount to one distributor only after prolonged haggling. It found that "Standard's use of . . . two prices, the lower of which could be obtained under the spur of threats to switch to pirating competitors, is a competitive deterrent far short of the discriminatory pricing of Staley," and thus the good faith meeting defense was sustained.[70]

Equally baffling questions have arisen in determining what it means to meet a competitor's price. A literal reading of the statutory language, endorsed explicitly by the Supreme Court in 1983, indicates that firms practicing discrimination may match rival prices exactly but not undercut or "beat" them.[71] Widespread seller adherence to such a rule could smother the forces that undermine oligopoly price structures. In the same case, the Supreme Court rejected an interpretation that prices had to be *reduced* to meet those of competitors; good faith meeting might also occur when prices were raised less in one location than in another.[72]

Finally, the Federal Trade Commission urged in some early cases that sellers could escape under the good faith meeting clause only when they discriminated in self defense to retain existing customers, but not to attract new ones. This view was rejected in 1983 by the Supreme Court, which stated flatly that "Section 2(b) . . . does not distinguish between one who meets a competitor's lower price to retain an old customer and one who meets a competitor's lower price in an attempt to gain new customers."[73]

Evaluation   The Robinson-Patman Act is a complex and imperfect instrument. If it has not reduced the vigor of competition in American industry,[74] credit must go more to the resilience of the forces of competition than to the act itself or its enforcement.

There is an irony in the record of the Federal Trade Commission, which is the government's primary enforcer. As we have seen, the act was passed to help small

66. *Utah Pie Co.* v. *Continental Baking Co. et al.*, 386 U.S. 685, 702–703 (1967).

67. See, for example, Ward S. Bowman, "Restraint of Trade by the Supreme Court: The *Utah Pie* Case," *Yale Law Journal*, vol. 77 (November 1967), pp. 70–85; *Report of the White House Task Force on Antitrust Policy*, July 1968, Appendix C, reprinted in the *Journal of Reprints for Antitrust Law and Economics*, vol. 1 (Winter 1969), pp. 753–765; Phillip Areeda and Donald F. Turner, "Predatory Pricing and Related Practices under Section 2 of the Sherman Act," *Harvard Law Review*, vol. 88 (February 1975), pp. 736–737; and Robert H. Bork, *The Antitrust Paradox* (New York: Basic Books, 1978), pp. 386–387.

68. See Edwards, *The Price Discrimination Law*, supra note 51, pp. 587–591; R. A. Lynn, "Is the Cost Defense Workable?" *Journal of Marketing*, vol. 29 (January 1965), pp. 37–42; and U.S. Department of Justice, *Report of the Attorney General's National Committee To Study the Antitrust Laws* (Washington: USGPO, 1955), p. 171.

69. *Federal Trade Commission* v. *A.E. Staley Mfg. Co. et al.*, 324 U.S. 746 (1945). See also *Corn Products Refining Co.* v. *Federal Trade Commission*, 324 U.S. 726 (1945); *Federal Trade Commission* v. *Cement Institute et al.*, 333 U.S. 683 (1948); and *In the matter of Boise Cascade Corp. et al.*, 91 F.T.C. 1 (1978). See also Chapter 9, notes 94–96.

70. *Federal Trade Commission* v. *Standard Oil Co.*, 355 U.S. 396, 404 (1958).

71. *Falls City Industries* v. *Vanco Beverage*, 460 U.S. 428, 446 (1983).

72. 460 U.S. 428, 444–445 (1983).

73. 460 U.S. 428, 446 (1983).

74. That it had not done so was the conclusion of the only empirical study of actual case outcomes. Robert C. Brooks, Jr., "Report of Pilot Field Survey on Market Effects of Robinson-Patman Orders," in *Recent Efforts To Amend*, supra note 54, Part 1, pp. 276–282.

businesses. However, of the 564 companies named in FTC Robinson-Patman complaints between 1961 and 1974, only thirty-six, or 6.4 percent, had annual sales of $100 million or more at the time of complaint.[75] More than 60 percent had sales below $5 million. Thus, the brunt of the Commission's effort fell upon the small businesses Congress sought to protect. Moreover, when large companies *were* caught in the net, their greater incentive and financial resources allowed them to resist the Commission's efforts more strenuously and with greater success. Consent settlements were accepted without any litigation by between 84 and 95 percent of the respondents with sales of less than $10 million, but by only 37 percent of the $100 million-plus companies. And 23 percent of the corporations with sales exceeding $100 million ultimately succeeded in having the complaints against themselves dismissed, whereas none of the companies with sales of less than $10 million did.

FTC commissioners were of divided mind about the efficacy of their enforcement efforts. Following a change in membership, the Commission reduced the number of companies charged in Robinson-Patman Act complaints from an average of seventy-four per year in 1960-1965 to 5.6 in 1966–1970.[76] A further drop ensued in the 1970s as attempts were made to reform the Commission's case selection procedures and screen out specious or downright anticompetitive actions. Between 1975 and 1982, only six formal complaints were issued, and from 1983 to 1986, only one additional complaint emerged.[77]

Thus, Robinson-Patman Act enforcement has become an activity pursued mainly by private treble damages litigants. A sample survey estimated that 18.1 percent of all private federal antitrust suits initiated between 1973 and 1983 included Robinson-Patman Act claims (often accompanied by allegations that other antitrust laws were also violated).[78] Inflating the sample figures to estimated population levels implies that 233 private actions alleging Robinson-Patman Act violations were filed in the average year. Judgments favoring the plaintiffs—in 35 percent of the cases by a broad definition and 11 percent by a narrow definition— did not occur significantly more frequently in price discrimination cases than in others.[79] How much effect this amount of litigation and the threat it carries have on business firms' pricing practices remains uncertain. What is certain is that, despite efforts by the federal courts to make sense of the Robinson-Patman Act's complexities, legislative reform merits support.

75. See the testimony of F. M. Scherer in *Recent Efforts To Amend*, supra note 54, Part 2, pp. 145–148, and Part 3, pp. 19–22. Section 2(c) complaints were excluded from the count.

76. *Recent Efforts To Amend*, Part 2, p. 147. Section 2(c) brokerage commission cases, whose incidence also declined sharply, are excluded because comparable statistics were unavailable.

77. Richard A. Whiting, "R-P: May It Rest in Peace," *Antitrust Bulletin*, vol. 31 (Fall 1986), p. 711. Several other papers commemorating the Robinson-Patman Act's fiftieth anniversary and interpreting new developments are found in that issue. On an important new complaint concerning book publishers' discounts issued in 1988, see "Industry Partners Disagree on Favoring of Chain Stores," *New York Times*, January 9, 1989, p. D6.

78. Steven C. Salop and Lawrence J. White, "Private Antitrust Litigation: An Introduction and Framework," in Lawrence J. White, ed., *Private Antitrust Litigation* (Cambridge: MIT Press, 1988), p. 6.

79. Ibid., p. 42.

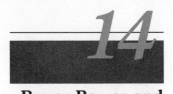

14

Buyer Power and Vertical Pricing Relationships

We turn now from concern with the pricing power of sellers to the buyers' side of the power ledger. In this chapter we consider four main topics—the extent of buyer concentration, how monopsony (that is, buyer) power affects pricing, the links between vertical integration and pricing behavior, and the hypothesis that countervailing power by strong buyers mitigates the pricing distortions otherwise associated with monopoly.

The Extent of Buyer Concentration

A quantitative picture of how much buyer concentration exists is difficult to secure, for there are no statistical series analogous to the abundant data on seller concentration. An impressionistic view suggests that concentration on the buyers' side is generally more modest than concentration on the sellers' side, although appreciable pockets of monopsony or oligopsony power (the power associated with fewness of buyers) can be found.

Roughly two-thirds of the gross national product flows ultimately to consumers for personal consumption. Buyer concentration in this vast consumer goods market is clearly low. Yet most goods pass through numerous intermediate transactions before reaching the consumers' hands. Consumers buy from retailers, who sometimes obtain their supplies from wholesalers, who buy from consumer goods manufacturers, who obtain raw materials, equipment, and parts from other manufacturing and mining enterprises, who in turn purchase from still other companies, and so on. Within manufacturing industry alone, each dollar of final product sales at wholesale generates on average more than a dollar's worth of additional manufacturers' sales for parts, materials, and the like. At any point in this chain of transactions monopsony power might intrude.

Although local market definitions are appropriate in measuring retail sellers' concentration, retailers as buyers normally purchase all but perishables and bulky, low-value commodities in something approximating a national (or even world) market. The largest U.S. retailing firm in 1986 was Sears, Roebuck, with domestic merchandise sales of $22 billion. Total U.S. retail sales in the fields most closely related to Sears' merchandising interests—auto and home supplies, hardware, furniture and appliances, apparel, and general merchandise—amounted in that year to $352 billion.[1] If Sears' share of sales in each product line were the same as its overall share, it would account for approximately 6.3 percent of wholesale purchases in each line. But since it is stronger in some fields than others, its share of purchases no doubt ranges from as little as 1 percent in certain clothing lines to as much as 20 percent on such items as washing machines and auto accessories.

The U.S. sales of Safeway, the largest food chain, were $16.2 billion in 1986, or 5.5 percent of total food store sales. Taking into account restaurant and institutional demands, its share of most food product purchases must have been somewhat less than 4 percent. The four largest food chains together made 15.4 percent

1. U.S. Bureau of the Census, *Statistical Abstract of the United States: 1988* (Washington: USGPO, 1988), p. 737.

of all food store sales in 1982 and hence some 9 to 11 percent of food product purchases.[2]

Buyer concentration in other lines of retailing appears to be even lower. The four largest retail shoe chains made 27 percent of such outlets' sales in 1982, but they competed in procuring their stock with the shoe departments of many general-line retailers, including Sears. Walgreen, the largest drug chain, made 7.4 percent of all drug store sales in 1986; the four largest drug store chains together accounted for 19.2 percent of their trade's 1982 sales. However, hospitals and government agencies are also important wholesale buyers of drug products. The 36 percent of Walgreen's sales comprising prescription and proprietary drug products amounted to 3.8 percent of the U.S. drug industry's total 1986 output.[3] On most of the other products it retailed, Walgreen's competed at wholesale for supplies with food chains, restaurants, and diverse other soft goods and appliance retailers, so its purchasing share must have been even lower. Similar overlaps lead to low buyer concentration in most other major retailing fields.

The degree of buyer concentration among manufacturers purchasing from other manufacturers is harder to assess quantitatively. If each supplying industry specialized in providing inputs to a single buying industry, the concentration of buying power could be estimated directly from seller concentration ratios in the buying industries. This is seldom the case, however. Three complications arise.

First, inspection of input-output tables for the American economy shows that most raw materials and intermediate goods manufacturing industries sell their products to many other using industries and are dependent upon any single class of industrial buyers for only a small fraction of their sales. The steel industry's best customer is typically the automotive (that is, automobile, truck, and bus) industry, which absorbed 15 percent of domestic steel output in 1987, a year of relatively strong auto demand.[4] This fact in isolation suggests that because manufacturers' interindustry sales are spread over so many fields, buyer concentration is much lower on average than end product seller concentration. Such spreading is less extensive at the raw materials stage, where outputs are often specialized to a single using industry. Thus, virtually all domestic iron ore supplies are used by steel makers, and most of the roughly half of U.S.-grown leaf tobacco not exported is purchased by a very few domestic cigarette manufacturers.

A minor qualification to this first point stems from the diversification of many industrial corporations. Since General Motors accounted for nearly half of domestic auto and truck output, we might expect its share of all steel purchases directly or indirectly (that is, through parts suppliers) to have been about 7 percent. However, GM bought steel not only for automotive products, but also for locomotives, construction equipment, and military vehicles. Its total share of steel purchases must have been somewhat higher than the figure for automotive products alone.

The third complication is more compelling. The industry definitions in available input-output tables are often too broad to reflect the true amount of seller dependence. The glass industry (excluding containers) sold 18.5 percent of its output to motor vehicle producers in 1977.[5] Yet a handful of auto and truck makers purchase most of the output of plants specializing in laminated and tempered glass. Similarly, a few refrigerator and air conditioner producers are the main outlets for small compressors; and IBM, Apple, and Compaq in 1987 together bought nearly three-fourths of all miniaturized disk drives for microcomputers. When plants and equipment are specialized to meet the needs of a single concentrated buying industry, the buying firms may possess considerable monopsony power. But such narrow specialization in serving a single buying industry appears to be more the exception than the rule among producers' good and intermediate material manufacturers. Thus, average concentration on the buyers' side in manufacturing is undoubtedly lower than seller concentration.

The Exercise of Buyer Power: Theory

The economist with a Teutonic obsession for classifying things into neat categories can identify at least six main market structure types involving power on the buyer's side, including a single buyer facing a single seller (bilateral monopoly), a single buyer facing many purely competitive sellers (pure monopsony), a few buyers facing a few sellers (bilateral oligopoly), a few buyers facing many sellers (oligopsony), and so on. Only for the first two cases, which are seldom encountered in a pure form in the real world, do we possess much in the way of compelling economic theory.

Bilateral Monopoly   The theory of bilateral monopoly is indeterminate with a vengeance. It carries all the problems we met in our study of oligopoly theory in Chapter 6: for example, do the parties attempt to maximize their individual profits, ignoring their interdependence, or do they cooperate to maximize joint profits? And unlike oligopoly, even if buyer and seller do collaborate to establish a joint profit-maximizing output, the price is indeterminate over a potentially wide range.

Figure 14.1 presents the standard diagrammatic analysis.[6] The curve marked MC, S_C represents either the marginal cost function of a monopolistic supplier or the supply function of a competitively producing industry. Since end consumers seldom have significant monopsony power, the demand side of the picture must for realism reflect a derived demand, or the average net value of the product (AVP, D_C) produced by the *buying* firm using the input X, whose quantity is measured on the horizontal axis of Figure 14.1. If both supply and demand were competitive, input purchases would be expanded until supply equals demand at OX_C, with a resulting price of OP_C. However, if the buyer is a monopsonist and if it faces *either* competitive sellers or a monopolistic supplier accepting the buyer's quoted price as a parameter and making the best of it, the buyer must recognize that the more of X it seeks to buy, the higher its purchase price will be. It therefore reckons the marginal cost of its purchases in terms of the curve MMC marginal to

2. U.S. Bureau of the Census, *1982 Census of Retail Trade*, summary volume, "Establishment and Firm Size," RC82-I-1 (Washington: February 1985), Table 6.

3. Estimated from company annual reports and U.S. Bureau of the Census, *1986 Annual Survey of Manufactures*, "Statistics for Industry Groups and Industries," M86(AS)–1 (Washington: May 1988).

4. American Iron and Steel Institute, *Annual Statistical Report: 1987* (Washington: 1988), p. 31.

5. U.S. Department of Commerce, Bureau of Economic Analysis, *The Detailed Input-Output Structure of the U.S. Economy, 1977* (Washington: USGPO, 1984), pp. 166 and 226.

6. The original standard exposition is A. L. Bowley, "Bilateral Monopoly," *Economic Journal*, vol. 38 (December 1928), pp. 651–659. The most thorough analysis of complications is James N. Morgan, "Bilateral Monopoly and the Competitive Output," *Quarterly Journal of Economics*, vol. 63 (August 1949), pp. 371–391.

Figure 14.1
Bilateral Monopoly

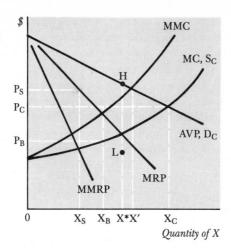

the supply function MC,S_C. Let us provisionally assume that the monopsonist also has monopoly power in its output market, so it perceives that the more of input X it buys and hence the more output it puts on the market, the lower its output's price must be and hence the lower will be the average value derived from the inputs it purchases. It therefore sees the benefits from purchasing more input in terms of the curve marginal to AVP,D_C — that is, the marginal revenue product curve MRP. To maximize profits, it equates MMC with MRP, buying OX_B units and offering the price OP_B sufficient to call forth the desired supply.

If, on the other hand, the *seller* is a monopolist and sets a price to which the buyer responds, the seller will recognize that the buyer maximizes profit by purchasing until its marginal revenue product has fallen into equality with the quoted price. Therefore, MRP is the derived demand function confronting the monopolist seller to the monopsonist-monopolist buyer. The seller's relevant marginal revenue function is the curve marginal to MRP, or MMRP, and it will maximize its own profits by equating its marginal cost with MMRP at output OX_S, quoting the price OP_S that induces the buyer to purchase that quantity.

We see then that what happens under bilateral monopoly depends in part upon whether the buyer or the seller exercises price leadership. Neither of these leadership solutions, however, is consistent with joint profit maximization. If maximum profit is to be extracted from a bilateral monopoly situation, the quantity of input supplied and used must be set at the level OX^*, where marginal cost equals marginal revenue product. A full mathematical proof is provided in Part 1 of the appendix to this chapter. One way to achieve the joint profit maximizing result is for the parties to agree through bargaining that OX^* will be transferred. They must then agree on a price. There is no compelling calculus indicating what that price should be. It could conceivably be so high that the buyer derives no profit from the transaction — that is, when the price equals the buyer's average value product at point H in Figure 14.1. Alternatively, it could be so low that it equals the seller's average cost of production — for example, at point L in Figure 14.1. Within this range, the price is theoretically indeterminate, depending upon the relative bargaining power and skill of the protagonists, which in turn may hinge upon diverse institutional variables, some of which will be considered later. The joint profit-maximizing quantity might also be achieved if one party can successfully pursue a take-it-or-leave-it strategy, for instance, with the buyer saying in effect, "I will buy OX* units from you at a price 5 percent above X*L, and if you won't go along, I just won't bargain any more and we can both shut down and lose money." Again, if output OX* can be set through such tactics, combined profits will be higher than they would be if one party quoted a price and the other adjusted its output to make the best of it. Moreover, unlike the case of collusion in duopoly, consumers benefit along with producers from such cooperative behavior. The amount of the relevant input transferred is necessarily higher with joint profit maximization than it would be with either buyer or seller price leadership, leading to outputs OX_B and OX_S respectively in Figure 14.1. And barring extreme production or cost function assumptions, if the amount of input is greater, the amount of end product will also be greater, which necessarily means lower prices to consumers.

Vertical Integration and Efficiency

Clearly, cooperative behavior can benefit all parties concerned when a monopolist deals with a monopsonist-monopolist. Nevertheless, reaching a cooperative solution may not be easy, especially when the parties find themselves engaging in the brinkmanship of take-it-or-leave-it threats. Bargaining stalemates can arise, leading to a cessation of trade injurious to both parties' interests (as well as to consumers). Recognizing this, parties to a bilateral monopoly frequently seek to create a more stable relationship through the vertical integration of successive production stages.[7]

When monopsony and monopoly stages are integrated vertically, decisions regarding how much of an input to use can be guided by the actual marginal cost of the input, rather than by bargaining stratagems or by the monopsonist's concern for restraining the volume of its purchases to avoid driving up the supply price. Consequently, vertical integration facilitates arriving at the input choice that extracts maximum profits from whatever monopoly power exists at either stage — that is, the choice consistent with joint profit maximization under unintegrated bilateral monopoly. A mathematical proof is provided in Part 2 of the appendix to this chapter. For the ultimate consumer, vertically integrated monopoly is less satisfactory than competitive behavior at *all* stages. But as we have seen, it is an improvement over the even greater output restrictions and end product price elevations that can occur under imperfect bargaining or a price leadership solution to the bilateral monopoly problem. If then bargaining difficulties preclude joint profit maximization under bilateral monopoly, vertical integration can make everyone — producers *and* consumers — better off. Economic efficiency is unambiguously improved.

This point has implications transcending the bilateral monopoly case. Indeed, in the prior case where a monopolistic input supplier quoted a price to which the buyer reacts, monopsony power on the buyer's side was irrelevant, for in accepting the seller's price lead, the buyer essentially waived the use of its monopsony

---

7. See also Chapter 4, pp. 109–111 supra.

power. What induced an excessive restriction of output in that case was not monopsony, but the vertical pyramiding of two *sellers' monopolies*—one at the input stage and one at the output stage. Each monopolist's decision was guided by the marginal revenue derived from the demand curve it directly faced, and through cumulated myopic marginalization, a greater restriction of output resulted than that which maximizes the joint profits of all firms in the vertical chain.[8] By exercising monopsony power, the buyer might break the monopolistic supplier's price leadership and move toward higher output and joint profits. But success is uncertain, and because vertical integration of pyramided sellers' monopolies also helps avoid the pyramided restrictions from repeated marginalization, it has been singled out as a compelling welfare-enhancing solution to the vertical chain monopoly problem.

Recapitulating, three arguments have been advanced thus far: (1) that vertical integration can break bilateral monopoly stalemates and increase output; (2) that piling one monopoly on top of another in a vertical chain can lead to *lower*, not higher, profits; and (3) that integrating such monopolies vertically can enhance both profits and economic efficiency. Although originally proved by a Duke University economist,[9] propositions (2) and (3) have come to be known as the "Chicago" propositions on vertical integration because they were invoked in a vigorous criticism of U.S. legal precedents that inhibited mergers between firms with strong positions in vertically related markets.[10] To them, a fourth proposition was added: (4) that if a firm has a monopoly over the supply of some indispensable input (that is, one without substitutes) at any stage in a vertical chain of markets, the firm's monopoly power cannot be enhanced by vertical integration into other *competitive* stages. For wherever it is in the chain, the monopoly can take full advantage of all output-restricting, profit-enhancing opportunities by correctly deriving its own monopoly demand function from the demand functions and costs of competitive stages nearer the consumer, that is, downstream. See the proof in Part 3 of the appendix to this chapter. If downstream vertical integration by a monopolist into competitive industries cannot enhance monopoly power (proposition [4]) but if it can improve efficiency when the downstream industry is monopolistic (proposition [3]), how can the antitrust laws find fault with vertical integration mergers?

Vertical Integration as a Monopoly Power Source

One answer is that the world is a good deal more complex than assumed in the models generating the Chicago propositions. In particular, those models ignore the possibility of substitution between monopolized and competitive upstream inputs, consider only the polar extremes of pure monopoly and pure competition, and abstract from market dynamics. Relaxation of the simplifying assumptions shows that monopoly power *may be* (but is not necessarily) enhanced through vertical combinations.

Figure 14.2 introduces one aspect of the input substitution question.[11] It depicts the choice possibilities for an unintegrated downstream firm able to substitute along isoquant Q_D between competitively supplied input Y and monopolized input X in producing a given quantity of output. Because X is monopolized, its price will be high in relation to its marginal cost, and the isocost line C_M confronting the buying firm will be relatively steep, leading to the input mix choice M. If, however, the input monopolist integrates vertically downstream, then as a user of

Figure 14.2
Choice of Monopolized
and Competitive Inputs

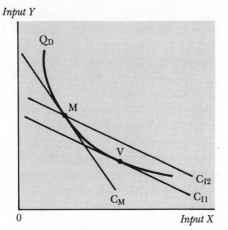

X it perceives the cost of X not as its monopoly price, but as the lower true marginal cost of X. Its isocost line will have a less steep slope, as in C_{I1}, leading to the more X-intensive input combination choice V. Since the unintegrated input choice bundle M lies on a higher parallel isocost line C_{I2}, assuming (contrary to the facts of the arms-length monopoly case) X to be priced at marginal cost, it follows that elimination of input choice distortions through integration yields real cost savings proportional to the distance between C_{I2} and C_{I1}. With more efficient input choices and lower costs, the vertically integrated firm might be able to reduce prices relative to those prevailing before integration occurred. This is a further plus for vertical integration.

However, there is also a minus that works contrary to the Chicago propositions. By extending its monopoly to downstream operations, the integrated firm gains control over the downstream industry's use of *all* inputs, and not merely the use of input X. In addition to controlling the proportions in which X and Y are used, the integrated monopolist can determine the *amount* of previously competitive input Y used and hence increases its control over the amount of downstream output.[12] The result may be a restriction of output relative to the preintegration case, and thus an increase in the downstream product's price. The mathematical

8. This follows directly from equations (2), (9), and (10) in the mathematical appendix to this chapter.

9. Joseph J. Spengler, "Vertical Integration and Antitrust Policy," *Journal of Political Economy*, vol. 58 (August 1950), pp. 347–352.

10. See, for example, Richard A. Posner, *Antitrust Law: An Economic Perspective* (Chicago: University of Chicago Press, 1976), pp. 196–201; and Robert H. Bork, *The Antitrust Paradox* (New York: Basic Books, 1978), Chapter 11. Important precedents were *U.S. v. Columbia Steel Co. et al.*, 334 U.S. 495 (1948), and *Brown Shoe Co.* v. *U.S.*, 370 U.S. 294 (1962).

11. It is drawn with minor modifications from John M. Vernon and Daniel A. Graham, "Profitability of Monopolization by Vertical Integration," *Journal of Political Economy*, vol. 79 (July/August 1971), pp. 924–925.

12. In "Vertical Integration Revisited," *Journal of Law & Economics*, vol. 19 (April 1976), p. 28, John S. McGee and Lowell R. Bassett observe correctly that the monopolist could achieve similar control by extending its upstream monopoly position to cover all substitute inputs instead of integrating downstream.

conditions underlying this result are complex, with formidable nonlinearities.[13] What happens following integration depends upon at least four variables: the elasticity of substitution between monopolized input X and other inputs (for example, Y);[14] the extent to which X is important as an input into the downstream production process; the elasticity of demand for the downstream product; and the structure of the downstream market before integration.

When the elasticity of substitution has a value of unity or above, and/or when the elasticity of substitution exceeds the downstream product's price elasticity of demand in absolute value, price increases are almost certain to occur when an upstream input monopoly is extended downstream. Price increases are somewhat more likely, the *less* important the monopolized input is relative to other inputs, shown, for example, when it receives only a relatively modest share of total input payments at competitive price levels. The seeming paradox in this result is easily resolved when one recalls that integration downstream by an upstream monopolist extends the monopolist's usage control to other inputs, and the less important the originally monopolized input was, the more significant is the extension of control to other inputs.

When downstream integration occurs into a monopolized industry with substitutable inputs, there are two output-increasing effects, the elimination of double marginalization and the increased efficiency of input choices, and one output-reducing effect, the increased control over the use of competitive inputs. If the downstream industry was competitive before vertical integration, one of the two output-increasing effects (avoiding double marginalization) is absent. It follows that the more competitive the downstream industry was before integration, the more likely it is that price increases will occur after integration. Using numerical simulation methods to evaluate a model in which the downstream firms are Cournot output-setters, Michael Waterson has shown that with elasticities of substitution in the low range of 0.2 to 0.3, postintegration price increases are likely *only* if the preintegration structure and pricing approach purely competitive norms.[15] With elasticities of substitution near unity, postintegration price increases are likely for nearly all preintegration market structures, monopolistic and competitive.

Substitution elasticities of unity and less normally imply that inputs are indispensable, that is, that no output can be produced until at least some use is made of each relevant input. When the monopolist of an input indispensable in this sense integrates downstream, it can make life difficult for remaining downstream competitors. It can refuse to sell the input to them, driving them out of business.[16] Or it can sell to them at monopoly prices, meanwhile transferring input at marginal cost to its affiliated downstream units, which, with their lower costs, can set end product prices at levels sufficiently low to squeeze the rivals out of the market.[17] On the other hand, an elasticity of substitution exceeding unity often implies that production can occur without the monopolized input. In this case, a limit price exists which, if exceeded, induces downstream rivals to do without the monopolized input. The integrated monopolist then has a two-stage limit pricing problem: it must decide whether, given its cost advantage in using the monopolized input, it should set end product prices that drive nonintegrated rivals from the market or allow them to survive, and if the latter, it must set its input price below the price at which the downstream rivals defect totally to substitute inputs. If the substitution elasticity's value is well above 1.0, other inputs will displace the monopolized input when its price is elevated only modestly above competitive levels, so the monopolist's cost advantage will be small. If in addition the exit of nonintegrated rivals in response to a price squeeze is slow, dynamic considerations like those analyzed in Chapter 10 most likely favor a policy of leaving end product prices at preintegration levels, so that rivals neither expand nor leave the market.

Our analysis reveals that under plausible circumstances, vertical integration downstream by an input monopolist *can* lead to enhanced monopoly power and price increases. The implications for economic efficiency are even more complex. Integration improves the efficiency of downstream input choices. On the other hand, if downstream product prices are raised owing to integration, output is restricted and classic dead-weight monopoly misallocation losses occur. Which set of effects dominates depends upon the parameter values determining the extent of postintegration price increase. When the elasticity of substitution is zero, economic efficiency is either improved (if double marginalization is eliminated[18]) or

13. The relevant theory has evolved in a sequence of increasingly generalized contributions. See Frederick R. Warren Boulton, "Vertical Control with Variable Proportions," *Journal of Political Economy*, vol. 82 (July/August 1974), pp. 783–802; Richard Schmalensee, "A Note on the Theory of Vertical Integration," *Journal of Political Economy*, vol. 81 (March/April 1973), pp. 442–449; Parthsaradhi Mallela and Babu Nahata, "Theory of Vertical Control with Variable Proportions," *Journal of Political Economy*, vol. 88 (October 1980), pp. 1009–1025; Kwang S. Chung, "Forward Integration by a Monopolist: Some Extensions," *Southern Economic Journal*, vol. 50 (January 1984), pp. 690–710; Seung Hoon Lee, "The Price of Final Product after Vertical Integration," *American Economic Review*, vol. 77 (December 1987), pp. 1013–1016; Michael A. Salinger, "Vertical Mergers and Market Foreclosure," *Quarterly Journal of Economics*, vol. 103 (May 1988), pp. 345–356; and (for an extension to the case of multiple downstream firms offering differentiated products), Martin K. Perry and Robert H. Groff, "Resale Price Maintenance and Forward Integration into a Monopolistically Competitive Industry," *Quarterly Journal of Economics*, vol. 100 (November 1985), pp. 1293–1311.

14. The elasticity of substitution measures the percentage change in the ratio of the quantity of one input used to that of another, in response to a given percentage change in the ratio of the inputs' prices. For inputs X and Y in Figure 14.2, it is $[\,\partial\,(Y/X)\,/\,\partial\,(P_X/P_Y)]\,\times\,[(P_X/P_Y)\,/\,(Y/X)]$. It in effect describes the curvature of the isoquant Q_D, which in Figure 14.2 is drawn with an elasticity of substitution slightly below unity. A zero elasticity of substitution is associated with L-shaped isoquants; an infinite elasticity with \ -shaped isoquants. Time may be an important influence in this respect. In the short run, substitution elasticities are often low, but as time passes and technical changes are induced, elasticities on the order of 1.0 appear to be common. See Hans P. Binswanger and Vernon W. Ruttan, *Induced Innovation: Technology, Institutions, and Development* (Baltimore: Johns Hopkins University Press, 1978), Chapters 2, 3, 5, and 8.

15. Michael Waterson, "Vertical Integration, Variable Proportions and Oligopoly," *Economic Journal*, vol. 92 (March 1982), pp. 129–144.

16. European law has been tougher on such refusals to deal than U.S. antitrust law. See p. 487 supra.

17. On the dynamics of price movements while the squeeze is under way, see Herman C. Quirmbach, "The Path of Price Changes in Vertical Integration," *Journal of Political Economy*, vol. 94 (October 1986), pp. 1110–1119. Quirmbach ignores the total substitution limit-pricing constraint.

When a monopolized input is used in two or more different end product markets, price discrimination may be required to extract maximum profit from each use. If arbitrage prevents discrimination, vertical integration can help attain a similar result.See J. R. Gould, "Price Discrimination and Vertical Control: A Note," *Journal of Political Economy*, vol. 85 (October 1977), pp. 1063–1071; Martin K. Perry, "Price Discrimination and Forward Integration," *Bell Journal of Economics*, vol. 9 (Spring 1978), pp. 209–217; Perry, "Forward Integration by Alcoa, 1888–1930," *Journal of Industrial Economics*, vol. 29 (September 1980), pp. 37–53; David L. McNicol, "The Two Price System in the Copper Industry," *Bell Journal of Economics*, vol. 6 (Spring 1975), pp. 64–72; Richard E. Romano, "A Note on Vertical Integration," *Economica,* vol. 55 (May 1988), pp. 261–268; and "Prices To Rise on Steel Cans; Beverage Industry Exempt," *New York Times*, August 25, 1988, p. D1. On other ways of achieving results like those under vertical integration, see Roger D. Blair and David L. Kaserman, "Vertical Control with Variable Proportions: Ownership Integration and Contractual Equivalents," *Southern Economic Journal*, vol. 46 (April 1980), pp. 1118–1128. See also more generally Blair and Kaserman, *Law and Economics of Vertical Integration and Control* (New York: Harcourt Brace Jovanovich, 1983).

18. This case is stressed by M. L. Greenhut and H. Ohta in "Vertical Integration of Successive Oligopolists," *American Economic Review*, vol. 69 (March 1979), pp. 137–141.

(if not) remains unchanged. When substitution is possible, the efficiency gain from improved input proportion choices at least partly offsets the efficiency loss from elevated end product prices, and so the set of cases in which overall efficiency is reduced by the extension of monopoly downstream is smaller than the set of cases in which downstream price increases occur. Waterson has shown through numerical simulations that net efficiency losses can nevertheless occur under plausible conditions, especially when the downstream market is competitively structured before integration, when substitution elasticities are 0.8 or higher, and the monopolized input is relatively unimportant.[19]

The standard analyses of vertical integration's effects assume almost uniformly that the upstream stage is a pure monopoly. To the extent that upstream structure and pricing are more (even if not purely) competitive, double marginalization and input choice distortion problems are likely to be less severe, leaving a weaker rationale for integration as an efficiency-enhancing instrument. If, on the other hand, vertical integration led to *increased* upstream monopoly power, those problems, as well as the possibility of higher end product prices, could be aggravated. This could happen if, for example, the conduct of vertically integrated firms increased risks for nonintegrated firms by exposing downstream specialists to regular or occasional price squeezes or made it difficult for upstream specialists to find markets for their output in times of depressed demand. To avoid these hazards, firms entering either of the markets in question might feel compelled to enter both, increasing the amount of capital investment required for entry. If, in addition, unit capital costs were higher with larger-scale entry attempts or if there were absolute barriers to raising the amount of capital needed for integrated entry, a chain of causation would run from vertical integration to increased risk of nonintegrated operation to the need for large-scale entry to capital cost barriers to entry. The elevated entry barriers could in turn lead to higher product prices and corresponding allocative inefficiency. How often this chain of consequences coalesces is an empirical question. To the extent that entry is mainly by well-established corporations diversifying into new fields, rather than by newcomers, capital cost barriers to integrated entry are not likely to be very significant. On the other hand, emphasizing entry by newcomers, W. S. Comanor has argued that integrated incumbents might view harassment of nonintegrated competitors as a profitable "investment in entry barriers."[20] Whatever their likelihood, cases in which the resulting vertical integration significantly raises entry barriers by necessitating multistage entry have been singled out by the U.S. Department of Justice as a basis for opposing vertical integration mergers.[21]

It is also possible that business firms undertake vertical integration mergers not to enhance the level of monopoly power at some stage, but to redistribute it. Oligopolies often settle down into behavioral patterns in which price competition atrophies, even though some or all sellers suffer from excess capacity. Nonprice rivalry then becomes crucial to the distribution of sales. One form of nonprice competition is the acquisition of downstream enterprises which, all else (such as prices) being equal, will purchase from their upstream affiliates. If acquisitions of this sort deflect significant amounts of sales, disadvantaged rivals are apt to acquire other potential customers in self-defense, and reciprocal fear of foreclosure precipitates a bandwagon effect in which the remaining independent downstream enterprises are feverishly sought. This seems to be what happened in the late 1950s and early 1960s when U.S. cement manufacturers acquired numerous ready-mix concrete companies, despite an evident dearth of efficiency-increasing or monopoly-enhancing possibilities and the stated unhappiness of cement makers over the course they found themselves pursuing.[22]

Such explanations of the motives for vertical integration, some implying the aggrandizement of monopoly power and some not, are less elegant theoretically and messier empirically than the original Chicago propositions. Emphasizing oligopoly rather than pure monopoly and dynamics rather than statics, they are less easily hammered into a mathematically tractable mold. Because both benign and rapacious motives can seldom be ruled out conclusively and because the outcomes of strategic moves in oligopoly often diverge from what was originally intended, a good deal of skepticism is warranted in evaluating claims that monopoly power is being enhanced through vertical integration. Yet dogmatic insistence that it cannot happen is equally unwarranted.

Countervailing Power and Consumer Prices

We advance now to a rather different perspective on the exercise of monopsony power. In a popular 1952 book, J. K. Galbraith argued *inter alia* that in modern oligopolistically structured industries, the *main* force compelling sellers to conform to consumer wants and hold prices near cost is not sellers' competition, but countervailing power exercised by strong buyers.[23] As examples, Galbraith cited A&P's use of power to extract price concessions from grocery manufacturers; the discounts won from oligopolistic tire makers by Sears, Roebuck; the auto industry's reputed success in curbing the pricing power of steel mills; and (on the other side of the market) the ability of strong unions to win large wage and fringe benefit concessions from powerful employer groups.

The Pure Theory   In the analysis of bilateral monopoly accompanying Figure 14.1, we found that although joint profit maximization by a strong buyer facing a monopolistic seller led to higher output and lower prices than alternative price leadership strategies, output was nonetheless substantially restricted compared to the competitive equilibrium level. Under what circumstances might countervailing power lead to still better results for the consumer? The answer must involve an asymmetry on the buyer's side: The buyer must be powerful enough to constrain the monopolistic seller's prices, but lack the power as a reseller to charge monopoly prices. If in the terms of Figure 14.1 the buyer lacks monopoly power, it will expand its purchases

19. "Vertical Integration," supra note 15, p. 136.

20. William S. Comanor, "Vertical Mergers, Market Power and the Antitrust Laws," *American Economic Review*, vol. 57 (May 1967), pp. 259–262.

21. U.S. Department of Justice, *Merger Guidelines* (Washington: June 14, 1984), pp. 26–28.

22. Compare Bruce T. Allen, "Vertical Integration and Market Foreclosure: The Case of Cement and Concrete," *Journal of Law & Economics*, vol. 14 (April 1971), pp. 251–274; the comment by James W. Meehan and reply by Allen in the *Journal of Law & Economics*, vol. 15 (October 1972), pp. 461–471; Mark E. McBride, "Spatial Competition and Vertical Integration: Cement and Concrete Revisited," *American Economic Review*, vol. 73 (December 1983), pp. 1011–1022; and the comment by Ronald N. Johnson and Allen M. Parkman and reply by McBride, *American Economic Review*, vol. 77 (September 1987), pp. 750–756.

23. John Kenneth Galbraith, *American Capitalism: The Concept of Countervailing Power* (Boston: Houghton Mifflin, 1952). For a critical view, see George J. Stigler, "The Economist Plays with Blocs," *American Economic Review*, vol. 44 (May 1954), pp. 7–14.

until the perceived marginal cost of input X rises into equality with the average value AVP (not the marginal value MRP, as with downstream monopoly). Thus, it will buy OX′ units of X — more, as Figure 14.1 is constructed, than the joint profit-maximizing bilateral monopoly quantity OX*.[24] With more input purchased, more output will presumably be produced, and consumers will benefit from lower prices. Should the supply of X be perfectly elastic (that is, with curve MC,S_C horizontal) because the monopolist producer of X operates at constant unit costs, a buying firm with monopsony power but no monopoly power would expand its purchases all the way out to the level associated with pure competition at both the input and end product producing stages. We see then that countervailing power is most likely to benefit consumers when three conditions hold simultaneously: when upstream supply functions are highly elastic, when buyers can bring substantial power to bear on the pricing of monopolistic suppliers, and when those same buyers face substantial price competition in their end product markets.

Bilateral Oligopoly

The simultaneous attainment of all three conditions is unlikely under pure bilateral monopoly, which in any event is rare in the real world. However, bilateral oligopoly — with a few powerful buyers facing oligopolistic sellers — is more promising. It is entirely conceivable that a few end product sellers could have sufficient power as buyers to hold the price of intermediate products supplied by upstream oligopolists at or near competitive levels. At the same time, for any of the reasons analyzed in Chapters 8 through 10, they might find themselves unable to depart appreciably from competitive pricing in their end product markets.

Strong buyers restrain the pricing power of oligopolistic sellers in several ways. One was identified in Chapter 8, where we saw that oligopolists are prone to cut prices in order to land an unusually large order, especially when they have excess capacity. Large buyers can exploit this weakness by concentrating their orders into big lumps, dangling the temptation before each seller, and encouraging a break from the established price structure. It is perhaps surprising that the U.S. automobile manufacturers grasped this point and began concentrating their steel orders only in the 1980s, when they came under heavy price and cost pressure from Japanese imports.[25] It is not always necessary to be one of the largest buyers to play the countervailing power game, and mere size is insufficient if wielded ineffectively. In the U.S. cement industry, for example, the largest buyers were often state governments procuring supplies for their highway construction programs. But during the depressed 1930s, even when all requirements of a state were lumped together into a single giant purchase, cement makers refused to undercut each other because, when the state purchasing agency made public an aggressive winning bid, as required by law, rival cement makers instituted retaliatory cuts against the price chiseler on nongovernmental business. Large construction contractors, who normally purchased less cement than the state governments, were more successful in breaking the producers' pricing discipline because they shopped around and bargained for *secret* concessions before placing their sizable, irregularly occurring orders. Recognizing this, many states ceased buying cement directly, decentralizing the procurement function to highway contractors.[26]

Large buyers also play one seller off against the others to elicit price concessions. For instance, each of the major U.S. automobile manufacturers has traditionally had a principal tire supplier, but each also spreads its business around to other tire makers so that it can threaten to shift, or actually shift, its distribution of orders in favor of the supplier who offers more attractive terms. A similar stance was taken by truck makers toward the suppliers of heavy-duty transmissions. But product-specific scale economies are undoubtedly more significant in transmission manufacturing than in tire production, and in 1985, Ford and General Motors announced new policies under which a single low bidder would be awarded a long-term contract for the entire supply of a given truck line's transmission requirements. Learning-by-doing economies are important in the production of guided missiles and submarines, but the U.S. Department of Defense consciously accepted scale economy sacrifices to maintain parallel competitive production sources for its Sidewinder, Maverick, and Sparrow missiles and for Los Angeles class attack and Trident missile-firing submarines. As each new contract's award date approached, the competing firms submitted price bids, and the percentage division of quantity orders was adjusted to favor the lower bidder.[27]

A ploy complementary to the playing-off game is considered unethical if not illegal in business circles, but it occurs with some frequency.[28] When sellers lack confidence in each other's determination to maintain pricing discipline, they are easy prey to the purchasing agent who fabricates convincing but fictitious claims of concessions offered by unnamed rivals. Once a single supplier is taken in, the actual quotation (and the favorable shift in patronage with which it was rewarded) provides a lever to extract lower prices from additional sellers.

These tactics are pursued most successfully when demand is slack, so that producers have excess capacity that can be utilized profitably if an increased share of some major buyer's business can be captured through price cuts, or when the loss of business to a price-cutting rival would leave previously favored sellers with a substantial burden of underabsorbed overhead costs. The balance of power is clearly in the hands of the buyer, and especially the large buyer, during a downturn. One might expect a bargaining power reversal during booms, when demand is outracing capacity. On this symmetry conjecture we have meager and conflicting evidence. Morris Adelman's rough estimates show that A&P won proportionately larger special price concessions from its suppliers during the depressed early 1930s than in prosperous 1929, and there were faint indications of a decline in concessions as the onset of World War II revived demand.[29] James McKie, on the other hand, found no evidence that tin-plated steel manufacturers were able to play one large tin can maker off against the others to escalate prices when steel was

24. This result depends upon the moderately high supply elasticity assumed. With less elastic supply and hence a sharper monopsony restriction, the amount of X purchased could be less than OX*.

25. "Now Steel's Customers Are Taking Their Turns at Jolting the Industry," *Wall Street Journal*, May 21, 1982, p. 1; and "G.M. To Pay More for Its Steel," *New York Times*, September 8, 1988, p. D1.

26. Samuel M. Loescher, *Imperfect Collusion in the Cement Industry* (Cambridge: Harvard University Press, 1959), pp. 54–55, 112–113, and 130–134.

27. See Donald L. Pilling, *Competition in Defense Procurement* (Washington: Brookings, 1989).

28. On the legal difficulties resulting from A&P's use of the tactic, see *Great Atlantic & Pacific Tea Co.* v. *Federal Trade Commission*, 440 U.S. 69 (1979).

29. Morris A. Adelman, *A&P: A Study in Price-Cost Behavior and Public Policy* (Cambridge: Harvard University Press, 1959), pp. 237 and 242.

in short supply following the war. His explanation was that "sellers hesitate to give buyers their own medicine at such times, fearing the imminent return of a buyer's market. Thus, there tends to be an asymmetry of bargaining power in bilateral oligopoly, other things being equal."[30]

Large buyers can also issue credible threats to integrate vertically upstream, producing their own requirements of an input unless prices are held close to cost. Unlike potential outside entrants, they have an assured market, and therefore have no reason to fear strategic pricing reactions from established producers. When the buyer's demand is large enough to permit realization of all scale economies in producing for its own use and when (contrary to experience in several U.S. industries during the early 1980s) the buyer and outside vendors pay similar wages, the buyer can scarcely lose: Either sellers restrain their prices in response to its threat, or, if the threat fails, the buyer displaces them and consumes its own low-cost production. Numerous examples of this dual strategy are recorded in industry studies. Although some scale economies are apparently unattainable to firms integrating vertically, tin-plated steel prices were restrained before aluminum became an important substitute by the ability of can manufacturers to begin plating flat-rolled steel purchased outside. Tin can prices were in turn held in check by the threat (and in some cases the actuality) of upstream integration by large food canners and beer brewers.[31] The U.S. auto manufacturers have kept downward pressure on prices for transmissions, windows, electrical components, fabricated parts, and even cold-rolled sheet steel by their demonstrated willingness to produce for their own use whenever the prospect of cost savings becomes attractive.[32] General Motors and Ford have been especially likely to integrate components with unique designs requiring special engineering, since on such components, suppliers might otherwise have strong bargaining power because of the investments that gave them a sole-source position.[33]

Surprisingly, Adelman found only one clear instance of a successful vertical integration threat by A&P to win price concessions, despite the once-leading food retailer's extensive entry into food manufacturing operations.[34] Whether this reflects inadequacies in the available evidence or A&P's belief that threats of potential competition would have little effect on food suppliers already under heavy pressure from their many existing competitors is not certain. The A&P history does demonstrate, however, that the desire to countervail oligopoly pricing power is not the only motive for vertical integration into suppliers' fields. Integration can also confer real economies in transferring goods from one stage to another—for example, minimization of sales representation and contracting functions, better coordination of production with requirements, streamlining of distribution channels, lower spoilage, and the like.[35]

A further approach to upstream integration merits more extended comment. Some firms, including aircraft and automobile manufacturers in the United States and a broad array of large Japanese companies, engage in what is called *tapered integration*.[36] That is, they produce a portion of their materials and parts requirements and farm out the remainder to independent specialists. This strategy gives the buyer a powerful bargaining position relative to suppliers, for the buyer can threaten credibly to increase internal production at their expense unless prices are held in check. Internal production also gives the buyer a good feel for costs, which is most useful in bargaining. In addition, the buyer can transfer the risk of demand fluctuations to suppliers. In both good times and bad, internal production lines are kept operating as near capacity as possible. Peak requirements are met by loading outside suppliers with orders, while in a slump outside orders are cut back sharply. As a result, the outsiders bear nearly all the brunt of output swings, and the percentage variation in their employment over the business cycle is much greater than it would be if they produced the buyer's full requirements. Needless to say, overflow suppliers will be reluctant to accept this precarious existence without being compensated for their risks, and one might expect them to hold out for high prices in periods of peak demand. The available evidence fails to support this hypothesis, apparently because the suppliers recognize that when the boom ebbs, their ability to keep going at all depends upon the good will of their customer. The main connection between risk and profits in such cases works through the mechanism of entry. New firms will not enter unless buyers are paying prices sufficiently high over the cycle to compensate the risks. If buyers desire to maintain a flow of new outside investment to satisfy their needs, they must refrain from frightening would-be entrants by taking full advantage of their bargaining power over companies whose investments are already committed. Large Japanese companies appear to be particularly proficient in sustaining viable long-term relationships with their overflow suppliers, in part by taking minority equity positions in the suppliers but also by recognizing the importance of a far-sighted strategy.[37] When, on the other hand, firms pursuing a tapered integration policy believe there is too much investment in supplier capacity — for example, because demand is secularly declining, as it was in the military manned aircraft field since the 1960s and in guided missiles and spacecraft during the early 1970s — they can extract unusually favorable bargains from overflow suppliers, whose lot is not a happy one.

30. James W. McKie, *Tin Cans and Tin Plate* (Cambridge: Harvard University Press, 1959), pp. 24–25 and 63.

31. McKie, *Tin Cans and Tin Plate*, pp. 50–54, 110–114, and 291–292.

32. See Simon N. Whitney, *Antitrust Policies*, vol. I (New York: Twentieth Century Fund, 1958), pp. 496–500; A. D. H. Kaplan, Joel B. Dirlam, and R. F. Lanzillotti, *Pricing Practices in Big Business* (Washington: Brookings, 1958), p. 172; and (for an instance in which countervailing power failed) "Move To Sidetrack Steel's Price Rise Dropped by G.M.," *New York Times*, August 6, 1969, p. 47.

33. Kirk Monteverde and David J. Teece, "Supplier Switching Costs and Vertical Integration in the Automobile Industry," *Bell Journal of Economics*, vol. 13 (Spring 1982), pp. 206–213. On other countervailing power-enhancing methods adopted by the auto makers, see Monteverde and Teece, "Appropriable Rents and Quasi-Vertical Integration," *Journal of Law & Economics*, vol. 25 (October 1982), pp. 321–328.

34. *A&P*, supra note 29, pp. 269–271 and Chapter 12 generally.

35. Adelman, *A&P*, pp. 253–258. For a more skeptical view of

the opportunities for economies through integration of manufacturing and retailing stages, see F. M. Scherer, Alan Beckenstein, Erich Kaufer, and R. D. Murphy, *The Economics of Multi-Plant Operation: An International Comparisons Study* (Cambridge: Harvard University Press, 1975), pp. 269–271 and 319–320.

36. On the U.S. aircraft industry, see M. J. Peck and F. M. Scherer, *The Weapons Acquisition Process: An Economic Analysis* (Boston: Harvard Business School Division of Research, 1962), pp. 386–404; and Jacques S. Gansler, *The Defense Industry* (Cambridge: MIT Press, 1980), pp. 128–148. On the U.S. auto industry, see Whitney, *Antitrust Policies*, supra note 32, pp. 496–498; and "UAW Mounts Campaign Against 'Monopsony,'" *Business Week*, July 24, 1965, pp. 43–44. On the use of tapered integration in Japan as a means of increasing flexibility when large-company workers have lifetime employment tenure, see Richard E. Caves and Masu Uekusa, *Industrial Organization in Japan* (Washington: Brookings, 1976), pp. 112–115.

37. That U.S. firms emulate Japanese practice in this domain is urged in the National Research Council panel report, *Toward a New Era in U.S. Manufacturing: The Need for a National Vision* (Washington, DC: National Academy Press, 1986), pp. 50–52.

Pass-on Dynamics   It seems clear that countervailing power can and does lead to lower prices, at least in that middle ground of oligopolistic market structure where sellers are few enough to recognize their interdependence, but too weak to maintain a disciplined front against the whipsaw tactics of a strong, shrewd buyer. The question remains — Who benefits, the strong buyer, or the consuming public? Are prices to consumers reduced because retailers and consumer goods manufacturers have struck unusually favorable bargains on the procurement side of their operations?

The answer depends in part upon whether price reductions gained by one large buyer or by a very few spread more widely through the buying industry. Three main cases can be distinguished. First, if the concessions reflect real production and distribution economies associated with large-scale ordering and production, there is no reason to believe that smaller buyers will receive the same opportunities as their more sizable counterparts. Second, if the concessions are exacted not because of cost differences, but because the large buyer has bargaining leverage smaller buyers lack, the large buyer may again retain a persistent advantage over its less powerful rivals (absent such compulsion as that intended, but seldom achieved, through the Robinson-Patman price discrimination law[38]). A striking example was the Champion Company's sale of identical spark plugs to Ford Motor Company at six cents per unit for original equipment installation and twenty-two cents for replacement part use, while independent wholesalers paid 26.1 cents per unit.[39] But third, when several aggressive buyers purchase substantial quantities of an intermediate product, a concession unrelated to cost offered by an oligopolistic supplier to one buyer will sooner or later be found out by other buyers and sellers and, unless discipline in the oligopoly is strong, the concession stands a high probability of spreading. Here what begins as isolated price discrimination touches off a chain reaction that ultimately affects the whole structure of prices.

It is in this last case that countervailing power is most apt to have favorable effects for consumers. As McKie observes from his study of vertical price relationships in the tin can industry:

When there is moderate or low concentration among sellers — a "loosely" oligopolistic structure — and there are some large buyers, the result is likely to be a pattern of behavior more effectively competitive than if there were atomistic competition on the buying side.[40]

Similarly, Adelman concluded that:

A limited degree of monopoly ("substantial bargaining power"), on one side of the market, can be of great service in maintaining competition on the other. A strong, alert buyer, large enough so that the loss of his patronage is not a matter of indifference, constantly on the watch for a break which he can exploit by rolling up the whole price front, able to force concessions first from one and then from all, and followed by other buyers, can collapse a structure of control or keep it from ever coming into existence.[41]

Whether *all* the benefits of countervailing power are passed on to consumers, or whether some gains are trapped within the vertical price structure, depends upon the absence or presence of power on the selling side of the market. The essential combination of power on the buying side with lack of it on the resale side appears especially compatible with conditions in the retail trades, suggesting that Galbraith's emphasis on retailing to illustrate workable countervailing power was not misguided.[42] As buyers, the large food and drug chains, discount outlets, and mail order houses can engage in all the bargaining tactics discussed earlier. These do not always work — for example, against pharmaceutical manufacturers with strong patent protection or cereal and detergent companies offering heavily advertised, trademarked brands. But under favorable conditions they can succeed, and the result is a reduction in wholesale prices. The chains in turn are under competitive pressure to pass along their gains. Entry into retailing is not particularly difficult, in part because stores traditionally operating in one field (such as groceries or clothing) can with a minimum of bother add a whole new line (for example, appliances or drugs) if the prospects are attractive. Incentives for independent pricing behavior are also strong in retailing, since it is difficult, with thousands of different products, to play the price-matching game characteristic of oligopolists selling a few homogeneous items.[43] Given these conditions, there is a good chance that gains made through the exercise of buying power will sooner or later be squeezed out and passed along to the consumer.

Still the competitive steamroller does not operate flawlessly even in retailing. Pockets of monopsony profit may persist for extended periods of time. A&P did not, for example, pass along to customers all the gains derived from its superior purchasing power and efficiency during the late 1920s and early 1930s. Because of organizational inertia and internal pricing policy disputes, its prices were adjusted downward more slowly than the fall in costs, and profits climbed to new peaks. But A&P's very success created incentives for others to imitate its methods and introduce their own innovations (such as the modern supermarket). As they did, A&P's volume declined, dragging profits along. By "pursuing a policy of making too much money," A&P "was slowly drowning in its own good fortune."[44] This slow-acting dynamic competition forced A&P to reassess its business policies, and one result was a concerted effort to reduce retail price-cost margins and prices. Ultimately then, even if not immediately, consumers were the beneficiaries.

Statistical Evidence   Supplementing the qualitative evidence on countervailing power and its effects is a smattering of statistical analyses. As is often the case, doubts have arisen about what originally appeared to be clear-cut results, and our insights have not yet been sharpened by a clarification of the remaining ambiguities.

A key problem in such analyses is devising an appropriate index of buyer power. The approach used most frequently is to compute from input-output tables

38. See Chapter 13 supra.

39. See H. L. Hansen and M. N. Smith, "The Champion Case: What Is Competition?" *Harvard Business Review*, vol. 29 (May 1951), pp. 89–103. On the rationale of this practice, which continued at least into the 1970s, see Allan Zelenitz, "Below-Cost Original Equipment Sales as a Promotional Means," *Review of Economics and Statistics*, vol. 59 (November 1977), pp. 438–446.

40. *Tin Cans and Tin Plate*, supra note 30, pp. 20–21.

41. M. A. Adelman, "Effective Competition and the Antitrust Laws," *Harvard Law Review*, vol. 61 (September 1948), p. 1300.

42. See also Michael E. Porter, *Interbrand Choice, Strategy, and Bi-*

lateral Market Power (Cambridge: Harvard University Press, 1976), pp. 11–13, 28–30, and 49–53.

43. For evidence on the independent pricing of advertised items by Philadelphia retail food chains, see William J. Baumol, Richard E. Quandt, and Harold T. Shapiro, "Oligopoly Theory and Retail Food Pricing," *Journal of Business*, vol. 38 (October 1965), pp. 346–362.

44. Adelman, *A&P*, supra note 29, pp. 36 and 45. The first quotation is from A&P president John Hartford; the second is Adelman's interpretation, shown by later history to be correct.

for any given selling industry a weighted average buyer concentration ratio, that is, the average concentration ratio of the industries to which it sells, weighted by the fraction each buying industry's purchases are to the selling industry's total sales. However, unless the selling industry serves only a single buying industry, this index is biased upward, the more so, the more the selling industry's output is dispersed across numerous buying industries. It is important therefore to take into account not only the average concentration of buying industries, but also the number or dispersion of buying industries.

Steven Lustgarten was the first to test the structural influence of buyer power on selling industries' profitability using both of these measures.[45] His measure of profitability, drawn from U.S. Census data, was the price-cost margin (PCM), estimated for 327 manufacturing industries in 1963. As in similar studies reviewed in Chapter 11, he found PCMs to be higher, the higher *seller* concentration in an industry was and the more capital-intensive its operations were. But in addition, industry profitability was significantly *lower*, the more concentrated, and the fewer (or less dispersed) were the industries to which it sold. Thus, the countervailing power hypothesis was supported. A reworking of Lustgarten's data by LaFrance revealed that the negative impact of buyer concentration on price-cost margins was greater in industries with high seller concentration, where there was arguably more oligopoly power to countervail, than in atomistically structured industries.[46] Stephen Martin's analysis of 1972 PCM data using a more complex array of buyer concentration variables and a more elaborate econometric structure yielded results similar to those of Lustgarten and LaFrance[47]. Thus, strong buyers do appear to restrain sellers' price-cost margins.

Much weaker or even contradictory results have been obtained when measures of net profit (obtainable only from company accounts), rather than the gross margins derived from census reports, were taken as the performance index. Analyzing data on 3,186 disaggregated lines of business, David Ravenscraft found that after controlling for buyer dispersion and twenty-one other structural influences, the ratio of operating income to sales *increased* with higher weighted average buying industry concentration — the opposite of what the countervailing power hypothesis predicts.[48] The sample year was 1975, a period of sharp recession, when we should expect the hypothesis to have held particularly strongly. When gross margin ratios were substituted for operating income as the performance index, the positive relationship faded to insignificance. This suggests a possible reconciliation of the conflicting results. With few buyers, sellers can economize on advertising and field selling costs. Gross margins (or PCMs) can therefore be smaller without adversely affecting *net* profitability. Independent support for this conjecture comes from Cowley, who analyzed 828 disaggregated lines of business in the PIMS data base.[49] Consistent with earlier studies using census price-cost margins, he found that gross margins increased with the number of buyers directly served, holding other structural variables equal. However, the ratio of marketing, research and development, and corporate overhead costs to sales increased almost commensurately with the number of buyers. His analysis does not state directly whether any residual correlation remains between net profitability and the buyer count. An earlier but less well-controlled analysis of PIMS data showed that the ratio of net operating income (after deduction of selling, R&D, and overhead costs) to assets was systematically higher for business units with fragmented customer bases.[50] This supports the countervailing power hypothesis, leaving us perplexed about the conclusion to be drawn from such widely divergent results.

More consistent support exists for another hypothesis in the countervailing power spirit: that a seller is better off being unimportant to its buyers, in the sense that the inputs it supplies make up only a small fraction of its buyers' total purchases, and hence do not receive priority in buyers' efforts to exert pressure on input prices. That census price-cost margins were lower in producer goods industries whose supplies were relatively "important" to their customers was first shown by Ralph Bradburd.[51] The relationship has been confirmed in two studies using more finely disaggregated and more precisely measured PIMS data.[52]

The ability of retailers to exert pressure on consumer goods suppliers under certain conditions has been investigated statistically by Michael Porter.[53] Porter argues that retailers have more power to extract price concessions for products such as shoes and appliances, on which the retail salesperson's expertise often influences choices, than for so-called convenience goods (for example, food products and books) "pulled" through into the consumer's hands by advertising and past consumption experience without the intervention of sales clerks. He found that seller profitability was more strongly correlated with seller concentration ratios and advertising expenditure intensity in convenience goods industries than in industries whose consumer products were sold with appreciable point-of-sale input by retailer employees.

Conclusion

Our evidence on the links from buyer concentration and the vertical organization of markets to performance is less richly developed than the evidence concerning market structure on the sellers' side. It seems clear, however, that vertical structure

45. Steven H. Lustgarten, "The Impact of Buyer Concentration in Manufacturing Industries," *Review of Economics and Statistics,* vol. 57 (May 1975), pp. 125–132.

46. Vincent A. LaFrance, "The Impact of Buyer Concentration — An Extension," *Review of Economics and Statistics,* vol. 61 (August 1979), pp. 475–476.

47. Stephen Martin, "Vertical Relationships and Industrial Performance," *Quarterly Review of Economics and Business,* vol. 23 (Spring 1983), pp. 6–18. For an argument that Martin's and earlier studies confounded buyer power with low-margin intra-firm transfer pricing, see Craig M. Newmark, "Administrative Control, Buyer Concentration, and Price-Cost Margins," *Review of Economics and Statistics,* vol. 71 (February 1989), pp. 74–78.

48. David J. Ravenscraft, "Structure-Profit Relationships at the Line of Business and Industry Level," *Review of Economics and Statistics,* vol. 65 (February 1983), pp. 22–31. For similar but weaker results investigating returns on stockholders' equity measured at the industry aggregate level, see H. Landis Gabel, "The Role of Buyer Power in Oligopoly Models: An Empirical Study," *Journal of Economics and Business,* vol. 35, part 1 (1983), pp. 95–108. Consistent with the countervailing power hypothesis, both Ravenscraft and Gabel found profitability to be lower, the less dispersed buyers were.

49. Peter R. Cowley, "Business Margins and Buyer/Seller Power," *Review of Economics and Statistics,* vol. 68 (May 1986), pp. 333–337.

50. Robert D. Buzzell, Bradley T. Gale, and Ralph G. M. Sultan, "Market Share — A Key to Profitability," *Harvard Business Review,* vol. 53 (January-February 1975), p. 103.

51. Ralph M. Bradburd, "Price-Cost Margins in Producer Goods Industries and 'The Importance of Being Unimportant,' " *Review of Economics and Statistics,* vol. 64 (August 1982), pp. 405–412.

52. Cowley, "Business Margins," p. 336; and Robert D. Buzzell and Bradley T. Gale, *The PIMS Principles: Linking Strategy to Performance* (New York: Free Press, 1987), pp. 47, 62–65, and 274.

53. Michael E. Porter, "Consumer Behavior, Retailer Power and Market Performance in Consumer Goods Industries," *Review of Economics and Statistics,* vol. 56 (November 1974), pp. 419–436.

matters. By bringing their bargaining power to bear, strong buyers are in at least some cases able to restrain the price-raising proclivities of oligopolistic sellers. If the buyers in turn face significant competition as resellers, consumers benefit. Vertical integration can also alleviate the distortions caused by bilateral monopoly bargaining stalemates and pyramided chains of monopoly power. Under other circumstances, however, especially when competitively priced inputs are moderately good substitutes for monopolized inputs, vertical integration into downstream input-buying industries can bolster monopoly power rather than taming it. We have made some progress toward isolating the structural conditions under which one or another of these diverse forces predominates.

1. Profitability of Alternate Vertical Pricing Structures

We wish to show that both output and profitability are greater under joint profit maximization by vertically linked firms than under either buyer or seller price leadership. For simplicity, we assume that the supplying firm has a linear marginal cost function $MC_S = a + 2bX_S$, so that the total cost function is $TC_S = k + aX_S + bX_S{}^2$. Let one unit of the input X be transformed by the buying firm into one unit of output Q after a processing cost of c per unit is incurred. The inverse demand function for the buying firm's output Q is assumed to be $P(Q) = d - fQ$, where $d > (a + c)$. The buying firm's profits as a supplier of output is written:

$$(14A.1) \qquad \pi_B = Q(d - fQ) - cQ - P_x Q,$$

where P_x is the price charged by the supplier for a unit of X. Maximum profits for the buying firm occur where:

$$(14A.2) \qquad \frac{\partial \pi_B}{\partial Q} = d - c - P_x - 2fQ = 0.$$

Given that $Q = X$, this can be solved for the derived demand curve MRP confronting a price-announcing supplier, that is, $P_x = d - c - 2fX$. Henceforth we shall use the 1 to 1 assumed relationship between Q and X to write all functions in terms of input quantities X rather than end product output Q.

Joint profits π_j are the sum of the buying firm's profits $\pi_B = X(d - fX) - cX - P_xX$, plus the supplier's profits $\pi_S = P_x - k - aX - bX^2$. Thus,

$$(14A.3) \quad \pi_j = dX - fX^2 - cX - P_xX + P_xX - k - aX - bX^2.$$

Setting the derivative of this function equal to zero and solving for the joint profit-maximizing value of X^*, we have:

$$(14A.4) \qquad X^* = \frac{d - c - a}{2(f + b)}.$$

Let $M = d - c - a$ and $N = f + b$. Then total profits:

$$(14A.5) \quad \pi^*_j = d\left(\frac{M}{2N}\right) - f\left(\frac{M}{2N}\right)^2 - c\left(\frac{M}{2N}\right) - k - a\left(\frac{M}{2N}\right) - b\left(\frac{M}{2N}\right)^2$$

$$= (d - c - a)\left(\frac{M}{2N}\right) - (f + b)\left(\frac{M}{2N}\right)^2 - k$$

$$= M\left(\frac{M}{2N}\right) - N\left(\frac{M}{2N}\right)^2 - k$$

$$= \frac{M^2}{4N} - k .$$

Assume now that the buyer is price leader, proposing a price P_x to which the supplier reacts by equating its marginal cost with P_x. Its supply function is therefore $P_x = a + 2bX$, which becomes the *average* input cost function for the buyer.

The buyer now chooses a level of input purchase (and a value of P_x consistent with the input supply function) so as to maximize its profits:

(14A.6) $$\pi_B = X(d - fX) - cX - X(a + 2bX).$$

Differentiating, setting the derivative equal to zero, and solving, we obtain:

(14A.7) $$X_B = \frac{d - c - a}{2(f + 2b)}.$$

Comparing this quantity with the joint profit-maximizing X^* in equation (4), note that $(f + 2b) > (f + b)$, so the amount of X used under buyer price leadership is less than under joint profit maximization. To determine total profits, let M $= d - c - a$ as before and let $ZN = f + 2b$, with $Z > 1$. Thus,

(14A.8) $$\pi_B = M\left(\frac{M}{2ZN}\right) - N\left(\frac{M}{2ZN}\right)^2 - k$$

$$= \left(\frac{2ZM^2}{4Z^2N}\right) - \left(\frac{M^2}{4Z^2N}\right) - k$$

$$= \left(\frac{2Z - 1}{Z^2}\right)\left(\frac{M^2}{4N}\right) - k.$$

Since $(2Z - 1)/Z^2 < 1$ for $Z > 1$, profits with buyer price leadership (equation [8]) must be less than profits with joint profit maximization (equation [5]).

Alternately, let the monopolist supplier confront the buyer with a price P_x, leading the buyer to maximize its profits according to equation (2). The supplier's perceived demand function is $P_x = d - c - 2X$. The supplier's profit function is:

(14A.9) $$\pi_S = X(d - c - 2fX) - k - aX - bX^2.$$

Setting the derivative equal to zero and solving for X, we obtain:

(14A.10) $$X_S = \frac{d - c - a}{2(2f + b)}.$$

Again, this is less than the joint profit-maximizing X^* in equation (4). And by a proof analogous to equation (8), it is readily shown that joint profits are also lower under seller price leadership.

2. Profitability under Vertical Integration

Extending the analysis above, an integrated monopolist views its total revenue as $X(d - fX)$ and its total costs as $cX + k + aX + bX^2$. Its profit function is therefore $\pi_{VI} = dX - fX^2 - cX - k - aX - bX^2$. Since this is identical to equation (3) above, maximizing π_{VI} is the same as maximizing π_j.

3. Profitability of an Upstream Monopolist with Competitive Buyers

To show that an upstream monopolist can extract all the profits available in a vertically linked chain of markets, we assume now, in contrast to the previous analysis, that the input supplier is a pure monopolist but that the end product market is competitive, with demand function $P(Q) = d - fQ$. No changes are made in cost assumptions. The competitive industry will expand until its end product price $P(Q)$ equals its unit processing cost c plus the input price P_x. Thus, in equilibrium $P(Q) = d - fQ = c + P_x$. Recalling that $Q = X$, it follows that $P_x = d - c - fX$. This is the demand for the monopolist supplier's output. Its profits are:

(14A.11) $$\pi_S = X(d - c - fX) - k - aX - bX^2.$$

Setting the derivative equal to zero and solving for X, we obtain:

(14A.12) $$X_S = \frac{d - c - a}{2(f + b)},$$

which is identical to the joint profit-maximizing output X^* in equation (4) above. With identical output and costs, total profits must be the same as under joint profit maximization, that is, those given in equation (5) above. And since the competitive stage earns zero profits, the monopolist input supplier realizes all of those maximum profits.

Vertical Restraints: Law and Economics

Vertical restraints are restrictions a firm at one stage in a chain of transactions (usually the seller) imposes upon the conduct of firms at another stage (usually the seller's customers). They include prescribing the prices at which the customer may resell a purchased product (resale price maintenance, or RPM), limiting the geographic territory in which the buyer may resell what it has purchased (territorial restrictions), inducing the buyer to deal only in the seller's products (exclusive dealing), and making the availability of one product contingent upon the purchase of other goods or services (tying or bundling). United States law on the permissibility of vertical restraints has had an unusually tumultuous history, marked by abrupt changes in legislated policy and judicial interpretations. Paralleling these changes, and sometimes influencing them, have been sharply conflicting interpretations of the economic motivations for, and consequences of, vertical restraints. Since the 1960s, few questions in the field of industrial organization economics have been debated more heatedly. Happily, the heat has generated a considerable amount of light, which we attempt to bring into focus here.

As on several other fronts, the debate over vertical restraints can be characterized with only mild imprecision as a contest between the University of Chicago, with its extensive farm club network, and the rest of the world. And as in other areas, the "Chicago school" has through superior organization, fervor,[1] and timing, if not superior access to revealed truth, sent the rest of the world reeling. But as competition in the marketplace of ideas continued, serious weaknesses in the Chicago position materialized.

The Theoretical Paradox and Its Resolution

In Chapter 14 we learned that when a monopolistic supplier sells to a monopolistic buyer, serious output restrictions and allocative distortions can result from the repeated marginalization of revenue functions. Greater profit can be gained by an upstream monopolist if it sells to a competitive downstream sector or, failing that, integrates vertically to bring the downstream sector under its internal control. Vertical restraints represent a diametrically opposite thrust. Instead of seeking *more* competitive behavior downstream, the upstream firm attempts to make the downstream sector *less* competitive by creating pockets of monopoly power, or by widening the wedge between upstream prices and the prices at which products are resold. That Chicagoans stress the benefits of avoiding vertically pyramided monopoly power and at the same time argue for letting upstream sellers impose restraints that enhance downstream monopoly power seems paradoxical, unless the common thread is a belief that *whatever* upstream firms do in their efforts to maximize profits must be efficient, and hence not to be discouraged. *Laissez faire, laissez passer.*

There are several avenues of escape from the paradox. Vertical integration, we have seen, can avoid the repeated marginalization problem, although not always without harming consumers. In principle, vertical integration might also let upstream producers achieve whatever downstream behavioral changes they seek in

---

1. *Fervor* may be the key. It is easy to be fervent in advancing simplistic theories of economic behavior. It is much more difficult to work up passion over the view, held by the authors of this work, that the industrial world is quite diverse and complex, requiring complex theories if it is to be understood.

implementing such vertical restraints as resale price maintenance or exclusive dealing. However, most of the vertical restraints we will analyze in this chapter are clustered at the retail distribution stage, into which vertical integration by upstream producers is often impractical. Retailers commonly secure economies of scope by offering the consumer under one roof dozens or even thousands of products, often gathered together from a diversity of manufacturers. It would be prohibitively costly for the manufacturer of paper towels, crescent wrenches, or antibiotics to establish its own retail distribution facilities in order to control the conditions under which its product is resold to consumers. And even when there is a reasonably close fit between manufacturer product lines and retail outlets' scope, as in automobiles, major appliances, or photo supplies, the two stages require quite different skills, attitudes, and spans of managerial focus, and the advantages of specialization typically require that retailers be kept separate organizationally from their primary suppliers. Thus, the leading auto manufacturers operate only a handful of company stores, relying mainly on independently owned dealers for their retail distribution. General Electric once maintained a network of company-owned appliance outlets, but found it advantageous to withdraw in favor of independent broad-line retailers. The petroleum refiners' appreciable, but far from complete, integration into gasoline retailing remains an exception to the general rule.

An alternative escape is to assume away any complications that interfere with the point one wishes to make; for example, to assume that retailing is always competitive and hence not subject to double marginalization, when analyzing vertical restraints, but to ignore the rationale for vertical restraints when evaluating the motives for vertical mergers. This is useful and sometimes even necessary for clarity of exposition, but one must recognize that balance and realism may suffer.

A third possibility is to admit that manufacturers often face complex and conflicting problems getting their products into consumer hands. On one hand, too much monopoly power at the retailing stage can raise prices and restrict demand so much that the manufacturer's profits suffer. On the other hand, if retailing is highly competitive, retailers' margins may be squeezed so much that inventories are too low, product promotion too lethargic, and/or direct customer service too meager to maximize the upstream firm's profits. One type of manufacturer intervention, for example, the setting of *maximum* resale prices, may advance the producer's interests best under one constellation of retailing conditions and a quite different one, for example, the setting of *minimum* resale prices, under another. To deal with this diversity of conditions, a rich analytic model is required.[2]

Let us nevertheless begin our analysis by focusing on the simplified pure case in which retailing is so competitive that, from the manufacturer's point of view, too few services are provided. Figure 15.1 introduces the problem. The consumer demand for a manufacturer's product is given by D_1. With manufacturing costs (assumed for simplicity to be constant per unit) of MC_M, the manufacturer enjoys advantages over its competitors sufficient to sustain a wholesale price to retailers of OP_o. The retailers in turn have selling costs of P_1P_o per unit sold, and since the retailing industry is competitive, their equilibrium price settles at OP_1, yielding them zero economic profit. Now suppose that the manufacturer is dissatisfied with the level of service provided, and hence implicitly with the level of selling cost incurred, by its retailers. To remedy matters, it imposes upon them resale price maintenance, insisting that they not sell the product in question for less than OP_2 per unit.

Figure 15.1
Welfare-Neutral Resale
Price Maintenance

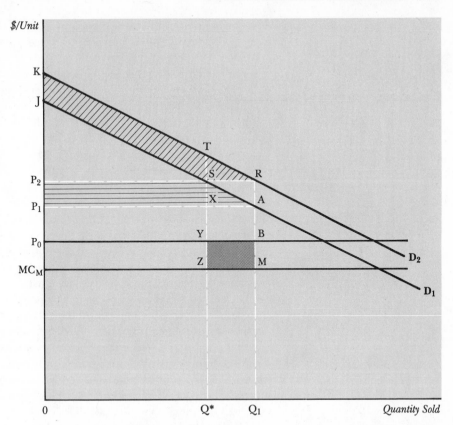

Now the increase P_2P_1 in the retailing margin will, if the manufacturer's instincts are correct, lead to more spending on services by the retailers. How much more depends upon diverse circumstances. The simplest view, more consistent with a long-run than short-run analysis, recognizes that under purely competitive conditions, the retailing industry can sustain no supra-normal profits.[3] Therefore,

2. Contributions in this vein that lead to complex prescriptions, depending upon parameter values, include G. F. Mathewson and R. A. Winter, "An Economic Theory of Vertical Restraints," *Rand Journal of Economics*, vol. 15 (Spring 1984), pp. 27–38; idem, "The Economics of Vertical Restraints in Distribution," in Joseph E. Stiglitz and G. Frank Mathewson, eds., *New Developments in the Analysis of Market Structure* (Cambridge: MIT Press, 1986), pp. 211–236; and Martin K. Perry and Robert H. Porter, "Resale Price Maintenance in the Presence of Retail Service Externalities," working paper, March 1987.

3. An alternative approach is to invoke the Dorfman-Steiner theorem, from Robert Dorfman and Peter O. Steiner, "Optimal Advertising and Optimal Quality," *American Economic Review*, vol. 44 (December 1954), pp. 826–836. Then the profit-maximizing ratio of service expenditure to sales $(A/S)^*$ will be:

$$\left(\frac{A}{S}\right)^* = E_A\left(\frac{P - MC}{P}\right)$$

where $(P - MC)/P$ is the margin between price and nonservice marginal costs and E_A is the elasticity of the quantity of output sold with respect to changes in the amount of service expenditure. Thus, the more price exceeds nonservice marginal costs, the larger the ratio of service outlays to sales will be. $(P - MC)$ is manipulated (in this case, raised) through resale price maintenance. Also, E_A implies that the more responsive quantities sold are to service outlays, the more the retailer will increase its service outlays. Diminishing marginal returns in the sales-service relationship imply that supra-normal profits will follow an increase in price-cost margins unless additional retailers are induced to enter, squeezing each retailing firm to a zero-profit Chamberlinian equilibrium. See note 65, Chapter 16.

the *entire* amount of the increased retail margin will be spent on additional services.[4] With the price to consumers at OP_2, output will as a first approximation be OQ^*, the area P_1XYP_0 will be costs incurred by retailers for the kinds of services they provided without resale price maintenance, and the area P_2SXP_1 will be costs incurred for services induced by the wider retail margins mandated under RPM.

This is an incomplete picture, however, because there is no gain to the manufacturer from its price-raising action. Indeed, if output fell from OQ_1 to OQ^*, the manufacturer's profit would be reduced by rectangular area YBMZ, so the manufacturer would choose not to impose RPM. But with increased retailer service effort, demand does not remain fixed at D_1. Instead, it shifts to the right. Figure 15.1 is rigged to show a borderline case in which there is a parallel demand curve shift, to D_2, just sufficient to maintain output constant at OQ_1. With no change in output or the wholesale price OP_o, there is no change in the manufacturer's profits. Thus, the manufacturer is indifferent between RPM and no RPM.

What about consumers? The price is now higher, which is unfavorable from consumers' perspective. But consumers get more service from their retailers. To determine the value of those services, we must think deeply about the information demand curves contain. Any point on a demand curve, we recall from Chapter 2, tells the maximum amount a consumer would be willing to pay for not forgoing that specific unit of consumption.[5] It therefore measures the value of that extra unit to the consumer. When the provision of additional retailer services shifts demand curves outward and, more importantly for present purposes, upward, as in Figure 15.1, the products sold *with* services have become more valuable to consumers. The increase in consumers' surplus from the enhanced service, given retail price OP_2 and output quantity OQ_2, is shown by the diagonally cross-hatched trapezoidal area KRSJ in Figure 15.1. Consumers continue to realize consumers' surplus triangle JSP_2, which they were enjoying before RPM was imposed. However, there is an incremental loss to consumers of horizontally cross-hatched trapezoid P_2SAP_1, which was consumers' surplus before prices were raised. In the first instance, P_2SAP_1 is a pure transfer from consumers to retailers. But then, after that wash-out, it is offset by the added costs retailers incur providing the services that shifted demand upward and outward. Thus, P_2SAP_1 is a net cost to society, while KRSJ is a net gain in the form of consumers' surplus.[6] To determine whether consumers are better off, we must compare gain area KRSJ against loss area P_2SAP_1. As Figure 15.1 is constructed, the consumer gain trapezoid KRSJ has exactly the same area as the consumer loss trapezoid P_2SAP_1.[7] We have therefore identified the borderline case: neither consumers nor manufacturers have gained or lost surplus as a result of RPM. And since by assumption the revenue gains to retailers are fully offset by additional service costs, RPM under the conditions assumed in Figure 15.1 is welfare-neutral.

Consider now Figure 15.2, in which an RPM-backed price increase from OP_1 to OP_2 (by construction, equal in magnitude to that of Figure 15.1) induces a larger parallel demand shift to D_2, so that output OQ_2 after the imposition of RPM is higher than it was before. Now, because of the output increase, manufacturers' profits are increased by the cross-hatched area BLNM. Thus, resale price maintenance (or some analogous vertical restraint) is attractive to the manufacturer because the elevated retail price induces retailers to provide more services,

Figure 15.2
Welfare-Increasing RPM

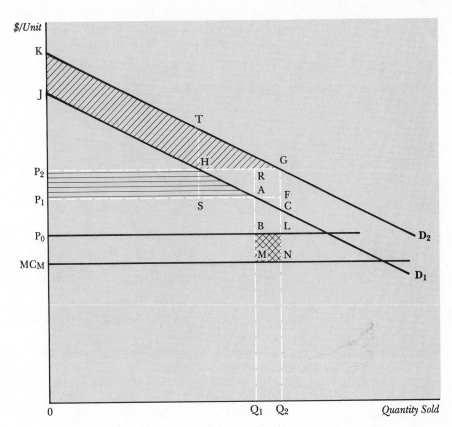

which stimulates (shifts) consumer demand, leading to higher total quantities sold and increased manufacturer profits.

Again we must ask, how does the consumer fare? Thanks to the valuable services provided by retailers, the shift in demand adds diagonally cross-hatched trapezoid KGHJ to consumers' surplus. However, the increase in price causes consumers to lose horizontally cross-hatched surplus trapezoid P_2HAP_1, which is transformed into increased selling costs. Comparing the two, it is plain that the

---

4. This equilibrium can also be described as an example of the economics of rent-seeking. That is, when monopoly margins are created, firms will compete for the opportunity to earn them, in the present case, by spending additional amounts on services, until the rents are transformed into costs. See Gordon Tullock, "The Welfare Costs of Tariffs, Monopolies and Theft," *Western Economic Journal*, vol. 5 (June 1967), pp. 224–232; and Anne O. Krueger, "The Political Economy of the Rent-Seeking Society," *American Economic Review*, vol. 64 (June 1974), pp. 291–303.

5. See pp. 23–24 supra.

6. Triangle SRA is a pure washout, representing newly created surplus that is exactly offset by increased retailer costs. P_2SAP_1 is

different because it is not newly created; old surplus is merely redistributed and then offset by retailer costs.

7. Proof: Let segment TSX divide the trapezoids into a parallelogram and a triangle. The area of a parallelogram is equal to base times height. Because the demand lines are parallel and the price lines parallel, RA = TS = SX. The bases of the parallelograms (turned on their sides) are therefore equal. The heights are also equal (at P_2S), so area KTSJ = area P_2SXP_1. Because TS = SX and the parallel demand curves cut off equal angles, triangle TRS is congruent to triangle SAX. Thus, the two trapezoidal surplus areas are equal.

gain KGHJ exceeds the loss P_2HAP_1, so there is a net consumers' surplus gain.[8] In addition, we saw earlier, there is a manufacturer's surplus gain of doubly cross-hatched rectangle BLMN. Since consumers' surplus is larger, the manufacturer's surplus is larger, and (by assumption) retailers have costs equal to revenues; total consumer plus producer surplus is greater under resale price maintenance than without it. Output-increasing RPM is therefore not only profit-enhancing, but welfare- (or synonymously, efficiency-) enhancing.

In a seminal article, Robert Bork argued, as we have shown geometrically, that manufacturers will not adopt vertical restraints unless they increase output and hence profit.[9] He went on to insist that:

No manufacturer will desire r.p.m. for the mere purpose of giving his resellers a greater-than-competitive return. The extra return would be money out of his pocket and we may safely assume that manufacturers are rarely moved to engage in that variety of philanthropy. The manufacturer who imposes r.p.m., therefore, must be attempting to purchase something for it. What he gets is usually increased activity by the reseller in providing information, promotional services, and the like. These are means of increasing distributive efficiency and should be permitted on grounds of efficient resource allocation.[10]

Bork's conclusion that "since vertical restraints are not means of creating restriction of output, we must assume that they are means of creating efficiencies" became the foundation for the Chicago school view favoring such restraints.[11] The inference is consistent with the geometric analysis presented thus far. However, it is not generally true.

Figure 15.3 provides a counterexample.[12] The introduction of RPM, increasing retail prices by the same amount P_2P_1 and output by the same amount Q_1Q_2 as in Figure 15.2, leads to increased service and a shift in demand from D_1 to D_2. However, the demand shift is not parallel, but "isoelastic."[13] Now the gain to consumers is the diagonally cross-hatched triangle KGH and the loss the horizontally cross-hatched trapezoid P_2HAP_1. The loss is visibly larger than the gain — about half again as large, if one measures carefully. Even after adding to KGH the manufacturer's profit gain BLNM, the sum of gains is less than the losses, so we must conclude that total social welfare has been *reduced* in this case. Although the balance of gains and losses does not always turn out unfavorably, there is a wide array of cases in which it does. This unfavorable tendency is stronger, the larger is the price increase attributable to resale price maintenance. For a given amount of price elevation, the welfare outcome is less likely to be unfavorable, the more demand shifts rightward.

With one seemingly innocent choice of demand curve shift patterns, resale price maintenance turns out to be welfare-increasing, while with another, it is welfare-reducing. Clearly, the nature of the shift is important. What do differences in the two alternatives (Figures 15.2 and 15.3) mean?

Geometrically, the demand curve shifts upward by smaller absolute amounts at relatively high consumer reservation prices in Figure 15.3 than in Figure 15.2. For Figure 15.2, the economic intuition is that consumers willing to pay a high price to obtain the product even without service have the intensity of their demand augmented as much by the additional service as consumers at, say, point A, just on the margin between purchasing a unit and not purchasing at pre-RPM price

Figure 15.3
Welfare-Reducing RPM

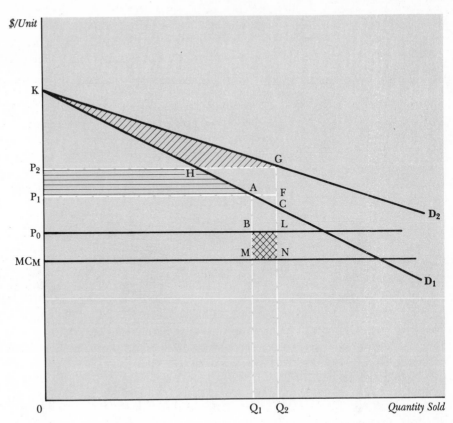

OP$_1$. In Figure 15.3, the intensity of demand is augmented more by extra service to those with low reservation prices than to those who would buy the product even at much higher prices. If the service is information, there is an even more pointed meaning. Consumers with high pre-RPM reservation prices presumably know

8. Proof: Comparing parallelograms KTHJ and P$_2$HSP$_1$ (turned on their sides), the heights are equal, but the base of KTHJ is greater because TH = GC, HS = GF, and GC>GF. Lost surplus triangle HAS equals triangle HRA, which in both base and height is smaller than triangle TGH.

9. Robert H. Bork, "The Rule of Reason and the Per Se Concept: Price Fixing and Market Division," *Yale Law Journal*, vol. 75 (January 1966), pp. 402–403 and 424.

10. "A Reply to Professors Gould and Yamey," *Yale Law Journal*, vol. 76 (March 1967), p. 731. See also his "Resale Price Maintenance and Consumer Welfare," *Yale Law Journal*, vol. 77 (April 1968), pp. 950–960.

11. Bork, *The Antitrust Paradox* (New York: Basic Books, 1978), p. 290. See also Richard A. Posner, "The Rule of Reason and the Economic Approach: Reflections on the *Sylvania* Decision," *University of Chicago Law Review*, vol. 45 (Fall 1977), p. 18; and How-

ard P. Marvel and Stephen McCafferty, "The Welfare Effects of Resale Price Maintenance," *Journal of Law & Economics*, vol. 28 (May 1985), pp. 370–371. Marvel and McCafferty attempt to rescue the Chicago view's generality by showing that resale price maintenance does not raise prices, but they commit a logical error. See the comment on their paper by Keith Leffler in the same volume at p. 383.

12. It is drawn from F. M. Scherer, "The Economics of Vertical Restraints," *Antitrust Law Journal*, vol. 52, no. 3 (1983), p. 700; and William S. Comanor, "Vertical Price Fixing and Market Restrictions and the New Antitrust Policy," *Harvard Law Review*, vol. 98 (March 1985), pp. 990–998. Comanor's version achieves even larger and less ambiguous net welfare losses.

13. Isoelastic because at any given price, the price elasticity of demand is the same on the two curves.

enough about the product that they are eager to purchase it even without information provided by the dealer. If so, we should expect additional information services to enhance their willingness to pay by less than it does for consumers on the margin between buying and not buying at price OP_1. The extra information is of greater value to marginal consumers than to the more confirmed inframarginal buyers. In effect, the uniform elevation of prices under RPM makes inframarginal consumers pay a premium for something of little value to them. Alternatively, if the service is retailers' willingness to carry abundant inventories, one might expect consumers with high reservation prices, absent RPM, to trade off some of their consumers' surplus by incurring the cost of back-order delay, and/or additional shop visits, if the product they want is temporarily out of stock. For consumers with low reservation prices, this tendency will be weaker, and the likelihood of no purchase at all will be greater. In both the information provision and inventory stocking cases, Figure 15.3 seems to describe the demand-shifting effects of resale price maintenance more realistically.

In sum, we have examined in broad terms the motivation for, and consequences of, vertical restraints, discovering that even in the purest cases, those restraints can be either welfare-enhancing or welfare-reducing, depending upon the circumstances. Under plausible conditions, a tendency toward welfare reductions seems more likely than the opposite. The Chicago dogma that *all* profitable vertical restraints are welfare-increasing is false. With this background firmly in mind, we can advance to examine more complex and realistic cases and see how public policy has dealt with them.

Resale Price Maintenance in Theory and Practice

Resale price maintenance has had a checkered legal history in the United States. In the early days of American antitrust, vertical price-fixing agreements were condemned as Sherman Act Section 1 violations.[14] In response, retailer and some manufacturers' groups banded together for a lobbying campaign they euphemistically called the "Fair Trade Movement." They received intellectual support from such eminent figures as Supreme Court Justice Louis Brandeis, an archenemy of big business but friend of the small merchant.[15] Bills were introduced in every session of Congress from 1914 to 1936, but none was enacted. The movement experienced its first legislative success in 1931, when the State of California passed a statute authorizing fair trade. By 1935 nine other states had enacted resale price maintenance laws; and within five years after a 1936 U.S. Supreme Court decision upholding the California and Illinois statutes, every state but Texas, Missouri, and Vermont had climbed aboard the fair trade bandwagon.

The state laws, however, were effective only with respect to goods sold in intrastate commerce. The retail merchants' lobby, led by the druggists, continued to exert pressure; and in 1937 Congress passed the Miller-Tydings Resale Price Maintenance Act, appending it as a rider to the District of Columbia appropriations bill to avert a presidential veto. It amended Section 1 of the Sherman Act, exempting from antitrust prohibition contracts prescribing minimum prices for the resale of trademarked or branded commodities "in free and open competition with commodities of the same general class produced or distributed by others" where such contracts were authorized under state laws.

Given this permissive mandate, vertical price fixing thrived in the consumer goods industries. Nevertheless, there was a loophole in the Miller-Tydings law. Not all retailers were interested in adhering to the manufacturer's specified prices. The fraction of U.S. retail sales covered by RPM in its heyday has been variously estimated at from 4 to 10 percent.[16] Retailers who preferred to seek high sales volume through low markup policies refused to sign RPM contracts with their suppliers. To bring these intransigents into line, most states added *nonsigner clauses* to their fair trade statutes, making adherence to a manufacturer's price floors binding upon *all* retailers in the state if any *single* retailer signed an RPM contract with the manufacturer. However, the Supreme Court ruled in 1951 that the Miller-Tydings Act exempted only express contracts to maintain minimum prices, and that the exemption did not cover nonsigning retailers.[17] The retail lobby again went to work; and in the following year Congress passed by overwhelming majorities the McGuire Act. It reiterated the Miller-Tydings policy and extended it to permit the enforcement of resale price maintenance upon nonsigning sellers where state laws permit. A challenge to the law's constitutionality was rejected by two of the three judges on an appellate panel, and the Supreme Court, reluctant to interfere when Congress had expressed its intent so forcefully, chose not to review the decision.[18] As a result, resale price maintenance enforced unilaterally by manufacturers on both willing and nonsigning retailers was immune from federal antitrust attack in states with nonsigner clauses. On the other hand, any attempt by retailers collectively to enforce price maintenance among themselves continued to be strictly illegal, like all other horizontal price-fixing conspiracies.

Eventually, we shall see later, major changes came, but for a considerable period, the U.S. policy toward resale price maintenance was more permissive than that of other leading industrialized nations whose antitrust laws were in other respects much weaker.[19] Canada passed an unconditional ban on RPM in 1951, although it was amended in 1960 to allow exceptions when loss leader pricing or other abuses could be proved. France has had a law against RPM since 1953, but there is some question as to how vigorously it has been enforced. In 1964 the British, after extended debate, passed a Resale Prices Act. It adopted a *prima facie* presumption that vertical price fixing is illegal, to be relaxed only if the producer can bear the burden of proving before the Restrictive Practices Court that the

14. A key decision was *Dr. Miles Medical Co.* v. *John D. Park and Sons Co.*, 220 U.S. 373 (1911). For an excellent historical and legal survey, see Thomas R. Overstreet, *Resale Price Maintenance: Economic Theories and Empirical Evidence* (Washington: Federal Trade Commission Bureau of Economics staff report, November 1983).

15. See his article (written before he ascended the bench), "Cut-Throat Prices: The Competition That Kills," *Harper's Weekly*, November 15, 1913.

16. Overstreet, *Resale Price Maintenance*, pp. 6–7.

17. *Schwegemann Bros. et al.* v. *Calvert Distillers Corp.*, 341 U.S. 384 (1951).

18. *Schwegemann Bros. Giant Super Markets et al.* v. *Eli Lilly & Co.*, 205 F. 2d 788 (1953), cert. den. 346 U.S. 856 (1953). See also *Hudson Distributors, Inc.* v. *Eli Lilly & Co.*, 377 U.S. 386 (1964), in which the Supreme Court did explicitly review the legality of non-signer clauses and bowed to the will of Congress.

19. For surveys, see Basil S. Yamey, ed., *Resale Price Maintenance* (Chicago: Aldine, 1966), and Overstreet, *Resale Price Maintenance*, supra note 14, pp. 148–157.

benefits of resale price maintenance outweigh the detriments. The Court's decisions took a generally tough line, with only proprietary drugs and books receiving exemptions.[20] In 1973 West Germany joined the ranks of nations with strong prohibitions, although nonbinding "recommended prices" (*Empfehlungspreise*) continue to be legal and widely used. At the time the German law was strengthened, 810 companies had resale price maintenance stipulations covering 174,000 branded articles registered with the Federal Cartel Office.[21] In Japan, RPM agreements are inconsistent with several provisions of the 1947 and 1953 antitrust laws, but antitrust enforcers have the power to exempt certain commodities, and they have done so on a blanket basis for cosmetics, drugs, toothpaste, soaps, and synthetic detergents.[22]

The Economic Arguments

From our brief history of U.S. experience, several points stand out: (1) that retailers have been in the vanguard of the effort to legalize fair trade; (2) that, given the apparent necessity of nonsigner clauses, not all retailers of fair-traded products favored RPM; and (3) that even under favorable legal conditions, RPM was far from ubiquitous.

There are several theories of why RPM is adopted. One is the so-called retailer collusion theory. Retailers are said to cajole or coerce supplying manufacturers into writing and enforcing RPM contracts. They do this to prevent the margin between retail and wholesale prices from being eroded by competition, whether that competition comes from conventional retailers unable to restrain their cutthroat pricing proclivities, or new types (such as discount stores) with cost structures that threaten traditional outlets' very existence. Clearly, retailers have been active politically in support of RPM, and equally clearly, they cannot be unsympathetic to the suppression of margin-eroding competition. However, it is questionable whether RPM benefits small retailers as much as one might suppose. Entry into the retailing of specific fair-traded goods is typically easy. If retailers are earning supra-normal profits because of RPM, additional sellers will in the long run enter and/or stock the fair-traded items, squeezing the sales volume of the original outlets until unit merchandising costs have risen to wipe out the surplus. The representative retailer ends up operating at smaller than optimal scale, but earning no more than a normal profit return. Whether for this reason or others, studies of numerous RPM cases suggest that only a minority, and perhaps a small minority, of the adoptions for particular products came as a primary consequence of organized dealer pressures.[23]

This leads us to ask why manufacturers initiate fair trade contracts with their retailers. Here too there is a collusion hypothesis. Vertical price fixing, if adopted sufficiently widely to cover most of an industry's products, removes some of the incentive for price chiseling at the manufacturers' level, since with retail prices fixed, secret wholesale price reductions have only an attenuated effect in expanding the chiseler's sales. Thus, the pricing discipline of oligopolistic producers may be strengthened. Although the logic is persuasive, there are few documented cases of the use of RPM to strengthen manufacturer cartels.[24] Also, a quantitative analysis of the U.S. manufacturing industries in which RPM was actively employed suggests that in most, concentration ratios were too low to believe that price-fixing conspiracies were likely to thrive.[25]

The other main explanation is that manufacturers see RPM as an effective marketing instrument. The basic logic has been laid out already: an increase in retailer margins induces greater retailer outlays on service, more investment in inventories, and other retailer actions that shift product demand curves. Or alternatively, the wider margins may be a kind of bribe offered to induce retailers to stock the product of a fair-trading manufacturer rather than lower-margin substitutes. Setting this alternative possibility aside for the moment, the service-inducing explanation nevertheless leaves important questions unanswered. In particular, why must the manufacturer take the initiative in raising retail prices and hence margins? If superior service sells more goods, why don't retailers choose a high-margin, high-service policy on their own initiative? And why are high prices forced upon *all* retailers, including those who prefer different policies, through the enforcement of nonsigner clauses?

An answer was advanced in an influential 1960 article by Lester Telser.[26] Telser argued that the incentive of retailers to provide desirable presale services might be undermined as a result of "free-riding" by retailers who provided no comparable service but lured customers into their shops with lower prices made possible by the avoidance of heavy service costs. Thus, a personal computer retailer (to advance Telser's story into the 1990s) might spend an hour demonstrating the merits of various machines to a would-be customer who, after saying "I'll think it over," drives down the street to a discount house and buys the now-preferred computer at a cut-rate price. If this experience occurs repeatedly, high-service retailers will tire of seeing their clerks' time wasted, cease providing full demonstrations, and the market will implode into one in which low service prevails even though the sale of computers would be enhanced if full demonstrations were available.

It is necessary to recognize the limitations of Telser's scenario. First, only presale service (including advertising, on-site demonstration, and generous inventory stocking) qualifies. On postsale services, the free rider problem is less likely to arise. If, for example, nonwarranty repairs are needed after the sale is made, the high-service outlet can charge for them without fearing the competition of low-service rivals. Or if the customer discovers *after* the purchase that she needs tutoring in the use of a complex software package, the high-service retailer can say, "We'll be delighted to help—for $30 per hour."[27] Second, most of the presale

20. See J. F. Pickering, "The Abolition of Resale Price Maintenance in Britain," *Oxford Economic Papers*, vol. 26 (March 1974), pp. 120–146. In 1989, the book exemption came under attack. See "British Book Industry Debates Elimination of Ban on Discounts," *New York Times*, March 13, 1989, p. D1.

21. "Vor dem endgültigen 'Aus' für die Preisbindung," Berlin *Tagesspiegel*, June 13, 1973.

22. In 1984 the Fair Trade Commission's guidelines were clarified and probably made more stringent. See Organisation for Economic Co-Operation and Development, *Competition Policy in OECD Countries, 1984–1985* (Paris: 1987), pp. 134–135.

23. See Overstreet, *Resale Price Maintenance*, supra note 14, pp. 13–19, 80, 140–144, and 161–163; and Stanley I. Ornstein, "Resale Price Maintenance and Cartels," *Antitrust Bulletin*, vol. 30 (Summer 1985), pp. 401–432.

24. A prominent probable exception was the U.S. electric lamp

manufacturers' cartel. See Lester G. Telser, "Why Should Manufacturers Want Fair Trade?" *Journal of Law & Economics*, vol. 3 (October 1960), p. 86. Compare Ward S. Bowman, "Resale Price Maintenance — A Monopoly Problem," *Journal of Business*, vol. 25 (July 1952), pp. 152–155.

25. Overstreet, *Resale Price Maintenance*, pp. 71–82.

26. "Why Should Manufacturers Want Fair Trade?" supra note 24.

27. More realistically, most consumers recognize that some postsale service is provided without charge, and that there is a correlation between the quality of "free" pre- and postsale service. The individual who knows nothing about computers and is intimidated by users' manuals written in pidgin Japanese, or worse, in Hacker-speak 4.2, is well advised to avoid discount houses and purchase from a full-service outlet.

service implied in Telser's argument is unnecessary when the customer already knows what she wants and why, for example, because past experience consuming the product or advertising by the manufacturer has already informed the choice, or because the product's attributes are sufficiently transparent that the normally experienced consumer can evaluate them without help from sales personnel. Thus, most of the goods sold in supermarkets, clothing stores, furniture outlets, and much else are ruled out. Third, the free-riding argument applies mainly for purchases of reasonably high value. The consumer who secures from her friendly local hardware store a ten-minute demonstration of a $1.79 potato peeler's merits and then makes a special trip to the discount house to buy one is a candidate for something other than center stage in the economic theory of shopping behavior.

Recognizing that relatively few products qualify under this strict construction of Telser's free-rider theory, Marvel and McCafferty advanced the argument to a new and more plausible sphere.[28] They propose that certain retailers perform a valuable service by identifying "good" products and certifying to consumers, through the fact that they stock the products, that they are indeed a good purchase. Such certification activities are costly, Marvel and McCafferty continue; they entail at least the careful evaluation of alternative products, and they may also require that a relatively high level of in-store amenities be maintained (as in Neiman-Marcus or Bonwit Teller) so that the consumer places high credence in the store's stocking judgments. In addition to expanding greatly the universe of products to which the Telser argument might apply, the Marvel-McCafferty apologetic is consistent with a product life cycle interpretation of how innovative products gain wide consumer acceptance.[29] And although the fit is imperfect, it helps integrate a justification for RPM that was advanced long before Telser focused the debate on free riders: the argument that when some retailers sell a product at bargain prices as *loss leaders,* they injure the manufacturer by impairing its reputation for quality (since consumers allegedly judge quality from price) and limiting its access to the market (since high-amenity retailers will be reluctant to stock items sold at much lower prices by others).

The certification free-rider argument has several limitations. For one, how do low-amenity stores actually free ride on the stocking decisions of a Neiman-Marcus? If low-price outlets advertise, "This product is sold at Neiman-Marcus, but you can get it here cheaper," Neiman-Marcus could sue. If, on the other hand, retailer reputation and amenities are the key, an enterprise like Neiman-Marcus must have a consumer draw that has value in itself, and for which a price premium can be charged. How often do consumers actually visit a high-status store, observe that a product is stocked there, and then prance off to buy the product at a discount house? In all but extreme cases, the leakage is typically small. Most discussions of free riding severely underestimate the ability of high-service, high-cost outlets to coexist with discount houses, each catering to its specialized clientele.

A dynamic model is needed to avoid these difficulties.[30] Quite plausibly, innovative but not easily evaluated products are stocked first by high-quality, high-margin outlets. Avant-garde consumers buy them, are satisfied with them, and gradually the product's reputation becomes sufficiently well-established, among other things through word-of-mouth, that there is enough informed demand to support stocking by low-price chains. But if this is true, a problem analogous to the central question of invention patent protection, to be examined in Chapter 17, is posed. Do the high-quality stores need the special protection of resale price maintenance to warrant their stocking of innovative products? Clearly, their head start and the advantage they have in serving pioneering but wary consumers provide a period during which they can charge premium prices before discount store competition takes hold. Are those advantages, plus the reputation advantage they enjoy in serving their normal well-heeled clientele, sufficient to cover the costs of certification, or must the head start be extended by forcing outlets with fewer amenities to charge equally high prices? If extension is necessary, for how long? Indefinite protection through permanent RPM could be both unnecessary and, by slowing products' movement into the mature, price-competitive stages of their life cycles, cost consumers much while providing few incremental benefits.

Robert Steiner embroiders this important set of issues further.[31] If resale price maintenance becomes widespread, discount merchandisers will have difficulty obtaining high-quality products. Their inability to offer well-accepted brands will prevent them from surmounting threshold barriers to rapid growth, which in turn means that consumers may be deprived of retailing innovations which, under more favorable circumstances, would prove highly beneficial. There is a fair amount of evidence that in Europe, where resale price maintenance was once employed much more widely than in the United States, the appearance of supermarkets was significantly retarded until laws discouraging resale price maintenance were passed.[32] Also, manufacturers for whom RPM is sales-increasing in the early stages of their products' lives may find it difficult to kick the habit, delaying the transition to retail competition beyond the time when it would have been beneficial to both themselves and consumers. There are two reasons.

For one, if most of their manufacturing rivals pursue similar policies, each producer may find itself caught in a prisoners' dilemma situation. If any single firm abandons RPM, but its rivals do not, serious volume losses may be experienced as high-margin dealers abandon its products and favor nondeviators. Even though all might benefit by securing wider distribution in low-margin outlets, RPM persists beyond its joint profit-maximizing time until some firm (usually one with particularly strong brand acceptance) takes the first dangerous step. When most of the firms selling a mature product retain RPM, it should be emphasized, the sales increase advantages each seeks by enforcing high dealer margins and high expenditure on service tend to be cancelled out by the matching outlays on rival products, and until the prisoner's dilemma is broken, a high-service, high-cost equilibrium holds *without* appreciable collective output increases. This, our previous theoretical analysis teaches, is almost surely inefficient.

The abandonment of RPM may also be postponed past the time when it becomes unprofitable because of manufacturers' inertia or erroneous evaluation of

28. Howard P. Marvel and Stephen McCafferty, "Resale Price Maintenance and Quality Certification," *Rand Journal of Economics*, vol. 15 (Autumn 1984), pp. 346–359.

29. See Robert L. Steiner, "The Nature of Vertical Restraints," *Antitrust Bulletin*, vol. 30 (Spring 1985), pp. 143–197.

30. See Steiner, "The Nature of Vertical Restraints," who, as a

former consumer goods marketing executive, has unusually perceptive insights.

31. Ibid., pp. 171–187.

32. See, for example, Overstreet, *Resale Price Maintenance*, supra note 14, pp. 151–157.

the uncertain alternatives. The experience of Levi, Strauss is a likely illustration.[33] The company had long fair-traded the prices of its blue jeans, and it was actively policing retailer deviations from its policy when a Federal Trade Commission suit persuaded it in 1977 to cease its enforcement efforts. Price cutting soon proliferated, led by such jeans specialty chains as County Seat, who were major outlets for Levi's jeans. The result was a sharp increase in jeans sales in general and especially for Levi's, whose earnings and stock price soared. However, the story has a less happy sequel from which conflicting interpretations might be drawn. During the early 1980s, the boom faded and the profits of Levi, Strauss (and of other jeans makers) fell. Whether this had anything to do with the abandonment of resale price maintenance is unclear. In 1979, when retail price competition on Levi's had become widespread, a new type of jeans—designer jeans—made their appearance.[34] It is arguable whether this would have happened under any circumstances, or whether it was induced by the loss of prestige as Levi's moved to popular price levels, leaving an up-market gap to be filled by such makes as Gloria Vanderbilt, Jordache, and Calvin Klein. The newcomers clearly captured market share from Levi, Strauss. However, the company's problem was also attributable to a general slump in jeans demand, from 30.8 million dozen in 1977 to 29.8 million dozen in 1982, due to demographic changes.[35] Whether the combination of new product competition and a fading of the boom will have a permanently depressing effect on the fortunes of Levi, Strauss is difficult to ascertain, since in September 1985 the company went private, ceasing publication of relevant financial reports.[36]

The Levi's story suggests another perplexity in the Marvel-McCafferty certification theory. Especially for fashion goods, an important benefit that certification by a high-price retail outlet conveys is imparting to the manufacturer's product a high-status image. Levi's may have had that image tarnished by the abandonment of RPM; Izod's alligator sport shirt image also faded as the product became more and more widely available.[37] But what is the wider economic significance of a high-status image that comes from the high prices at which a product is sold, and not from the product's intrinsic superiority? If an individual consumer derives utility from exclusiveness, and if the utility declines when a product enters mass distribution, there must be external diseconomies in consumption, violating one of the fundamental assumptions on the basis of which the efficiency of market processes is judged.[38] The argument that product quality certification through resale price maintenance is efficiency-enhancing becomes even more dubious.

To sum up, the free-rider justification of resale price maintenance has severe limitations. Its plausibility is palpably low in many product areas where RPM is used. Even when RPM helps new products become established in the market, its use can be carried too far in time and space, giving rise to prisoners' dilemma equilibria in which high-cost distribution strategies neutralize each other and to the delayed emergence of desirable retailing innovations.

Moreover, manufacturers' marketing objectives can often be reached through means less clumsy than RPM and less likely to yield high-cost equilibria when other manufacturers respond in kind. Manufacturer payments to the retailer specifically linked to the performance of desired advertising or demonstration tasks are believed to induce more retailer effort per dollar of cost than across-the-board retail price raising, although they may also be more vulnerable to abuse through exaggerated reporting by retailers.[39] If free riding is common, but when presale services add significantly to consumers' utility and demand, retailers can find ways of charging for them. For example, automobile dealers, audio equipment retailers, and a New York bicycle shop in 1983 charged consultation fees for providing varying amounts of expert advice to shoppers.[40] In many cases, the fees were refundable against the purchase price for those who chose to buy. Some computer retailers deflect free riding by selling lessons in the elements of computer operation to would-be buyers. The need for presale consultation in the retailer's shop can also be circumvented by the manufacturer's informative advertising, and the retailer's role in image certification can be bypassed through image-oriented advertising. Steiner argues that deviations from high-RPM industry equilibria are usually led by manufacturers who have built strong consumer loyalty through direct advertising.[41] Once such leaders defect to a strategy that fully exploits the potentialities of low-price mass merchandisers, other industry members have been forced to follow.

Further Policy Gyrations

Few propositions about resale price maintenance are uncontroversial. Even on the question of whether RPM raises retail prices, there is dispute.[42] The weight of the evidence, however, supports a conclusion that prices are on average elevated, perhaps appreciably. Comparisons of the retail prices of fair-traded product market baskets in diverse U.S. cities, some bound by strong RPM laws and some not,

---

33. See Steiner, "The Nature of Vertical Restraints," pp. 178–183; Overstreet, *Resale Price Maintenance*, pp. 120–122; and Sharon Oster, "Levi Strauss," in R. N. Lafferty, R. H. Lande, and John B. Kirkwood, eds., *Impact Evaluations of Federal Trade Commission Vertical Restraints Cases* (Washington: Federal Trade Commission, August 1984), pp. 47–90. The Lafferty et al. volume also contains informative case studies on RPM's application to Florsheim shoes, audio components, and hearing aids.

34. See "Designer-Brand Jeans Aren't Likely To Unseat Makers of Basic Denim Wear, Analysts Believe," *Wall Street Journal*, December 31, 1979, p. 19.

35. Shipments of women's and misses' jeans, most affected by the designer jeans phenomenon, rose from 5.83 to 7.26 million dozen. Shipments of men's and boys' jeans fell from 24.99 to 22.56 million dozen. The average wholesale price per unit for women's jeans rose by 79 percent while the price for men's jeans rose by 45 percent. *1982 Census of Manufactures*, Industry Reports, "Men's and Boys' Apparel" and "Women's and Misses' Outerwear," MC82-I-23A and B (Washington: March 1985).

Demographic changes and fading of the designer jeans boom underlay declining jeans sales during the mid-1980s. See "Faded Youth," *The Economist*, November 19, 1988, p. 80.

36. That its sales and profits subsequently revived is suggested in "Levi Strauss and UPS Name New Chiefs," *Business Week,* March 20, 1989, p. 46; and "Jeans Fade but Levi Strauss Glows," *New York Times,* June 26, 1989, p. D1.

37. See "Has Izod's Alligator Peaked?" *New York Times*, September 8, 1983, p. D1.

38. See pp. 29–30 supra.

39. See Robert L. Steiner, "Vertical Restraints and Economic Efficiency," Federal Trade Commission Bureau of Economics working paper no. 66 (June 1982), p. 6.

40. "Consumer Saturday: Stores Charge for Advice," *New York Times*, October 1, 1983, p. 52.

41. "Vertical Restraints," supra note 39, p. 11.

42. Thus, with a model in which wholesale prices are determined residually after manufacturers choose profit-maximizing retail prices, assuming retailers' service costs to be fixed and hence not marginal, Marvel and McCafferty argue that RPM affects only the differential between prices in RPM and non-RPM territories, and not the average price level. "The Welfare Effects of Resale Price Maintenance," supra note 11; and "The Political Economy of Resale Price Maintenance," *Journal of Political Economy*, vol. 94 (October 1986), pp. 1074–1095. However, the crucial fixed cost assumption is almost surely wrong. Compare the comment by Leffler, supra note 11, p. 383; and Bork, "A Reply to Professors Gould and Yamey," supra note 10, pp. 732–733.

The higher costs of service under RPM might be offset by lower manufacturing costs owing to the realization of scale economies. However, if most manufacturers employ RPM, the expanded service efforts may be mutually cancelling, yielding only meager sales and hence scale gains.

suggest average price differentials of 10 to 23 percent.[43] A particularly well-controlled study of liquor prices found that the 1978 income redistribution specifically attributable to RPM was $227 million, or 4.5 percent of retail liquor sales in the affected states.[44]

Price differentials such as these were influential in undermining the legal foundations of RPM. The U.S. federal fair trade law was born during the Great Depression of the 1930s. It died in the recession of 1975. With unusually severe price inflation persisting despite rapidly rising unemployment, the balance of power between consumer and retail business interests shifted, and in December 1975, a bill repealing the Miller-Tydings and McGuire acts was signed. After the new law took effect, manufacturers risked violating Sherman Act Section 1 if they attempted to enforce resale price maintenance on goods moving in interstate commerce.

Although death came swiftly and unexpectedly, it was preceded by a long illness. Two forces—legal setbacks at the state level and the pressures of competition—had been slowly sapping RPM's vitality.

RPM laws were never passed in Texas, Missouri, Vermont, and the strategically located District of Columbia. In several other jurisdictions, state courts ruled the applicable fair trade statutes inconsistent with state constitutions and/or legally unenforceable. In more than a dozen additional venues, the nonsigner provisions of state laws were declared unconstitutional, typically on the ground that they deprived nonsigners of property without due process of law. These developments created a number of islands where it was possible to ignore manufacturers' prescribed minimum prices. Entrepreneurs took advantage by locating mail-order houses in non-RPM areas, building a lively business in shipping branded merchandise at reduced prices to customers in fair trade states. This practice was encouraged by federal court decisions in 1957 holding that such shipments could not be enjoined in the receiving states.[45] And even where retailers were clearly bound by state laws, some of the more aggressive outlets chose to ignore them. Faced with this challenge, manufacturers often decided not to initiate the legal proceedings available for enforcing compliance, partly because the burden of proving actionable departures was difficult and costly, and partly because they were reluctant to alienate important high-volume retailers.

When a significant fraction of the transactions in some product line began taking place at prices undercutting the fair trade minimum, the whole RPM system in that line tended to crumble. Manufacturers who did enforce their minimums found themselves losing sales to those who did not or who refused altogether to play the fair trade game. Some abandoned RPM completely. Others like the Sunbeam Corporation brought out new product lines to be sold at uncontrolled retail prices alongside their fair-traded items. With enforcement weak and retailers stocking products of comparable quality, some fair-traded and some not, one of the most serious objections to resale price maintenance was defused. Consumers were no longer deprived of the opportunity to choose what mix of price and product differentiation attributes they preferred.

By 1975, the processes of erosion had advanced farther. Only thirteen states had valid nonsigner laws still in effect. And although twenty-three others retained fair trade laws without nonsigner provisions, competition had undermined manu-facturers' enforcement incentives, and the volume of retail sales covered by RPM had fallen sharply. Strong RPM programs persisted in only a few lines such as high-fidelity equipment, cosmetics, liquor, televisions, glassware, and prescrip-tion drugs. Thus, for the most part, the effects of the federal law's abolition were imperceptible because the forces of competition had already repealed the law in their own quiet way.

Still the controversy did not cease. Although attempts to specify price mini-mums below which retailers could not sell had become illegal per se, manufac-turers could still suggest retail prices. They could also choose the retailers to whom they would sell and, if they wanted to achieve the substance of resale price main-tenance, deny supplies to retailers known to be price cutters. The termination of supply arrangements with price-cutting retailers became a subject of manufacturer-dealer litigation, with allegations by the excluded retailers that it constituted de facto resale price fixing. In a key case, two issues, one broad and one narrow, came before the Supreme Court: (1) whether resale price mainte-nance should be judged on the basis of a rule of reason rather than being held illegal per se when proved; and (2) whether the existence of de facto RPM could be inferred when a dealership was terminated after the manufacturer received from other (nonterminated) dealers complaints that the terminated dealer had been cut-ting prices. Choosing to ignore the broader issue, the Supreme Court ruled that illegal RPM could not be inferred merely from evidence of complaints and dealer terminations; there had to be proof of an actual agreement on resale prices be-tween the manufacturer and nonterminated dealers.[46] In 1988, the Court took a further step, concluding that an agreement between a manufacturer and a com-plaining dealer to terminate another dealer who undercut the complaining dealer's prices was not per se illegal, absent proof that the complaining dealer's prices had been set in collusion with the manufacturer. Rather, the matter (which had origi-nated fifteen years earlier!) had to be judged on rule of reason grounds.[47] Influen-tial members of Congress reacted to these developments by proposing the Retail Competition Enforcement Act of 1987 (S. 430), which would ease the burden of proving illegal price maintenance for dealers terminated as a result of complaints about their price cutting from other dealers. Following threats of a filibuster that would disrupt an already crowded Senate agenda, the bill failed to emerge for floor debate.

Whether resale price maintenance agreements quite generally should be evalu-ated under a rule of reason, rather than under the per se rules embedded in the

---

43. For a survey, see Overstreet, *Resale Price Maintenance*, supra note 14, pp. 106–112.

44. Stanley I. Ornstein and Dominique M. Hanssens, "Resale Price Maintenance: Output Increasing or Restricting?" *Journal of Industrial Economics*, vol. 36 (September 1987), pp. 1–18.

45. *Bissell Carpet Sweeper Co.* v. *Masters Mail Order Co. of Washing-ton*, 240 F. 2d 684 (1957); and *General Electric Co.* v. *Masters Mail Order Co. of Washington*, 244 F. 2d 681 (1957), cert. den. 355 U.S. 824 (1957).

46. *Monsanto Corporation* v. *Spray-Rite Service Corp.*, 465 U.S. 752 (1984). The Department of Justice had filed an *amicus curiae* brief asking the Court to rule that all resale price maintenance agree-ments should be treated under a rule of reason.

47. *Business Electronics Corp.* v. *Sharp Electronics Corp.*, 99 S. Ct. 808 (1988).

main U.S. legal precedents, recalls many of the difficult issues addressed for horizontal price fixing in Chapter 9. On one hand, some resale price maintenance arrangements facilitate new entry or the provision of desirable services, and except when RPM spreads to cover the bulk of an industry's output, depriving consumers of a meaningful choice between high-service and low-price outlets, most are probably innocuous. On the other hand, Chicagoans' claims that strictly vertical RPM cannot impair economic efficiency are plainly wrong, and their estimates of the benefits from RPM are correspondingly exaggerated. The overall balance between benefits and costs is probably close. The remaining question is whether the courts are able to sort out desirable from harmful conduct under a rule of reason approach without excessive litigation cost and error rates. If one is pessimistic on that point, the main alternatives are to make RPM per se legal, as some Chicago school adherents have proposed, or to leave the existing presumption of per se illegality intact.

On another facet of the question, there is much more agreement among scholars. The per se prohibition of resale price maintenance under U.S. law covers agreements to fix *maximum* prices as well as minimum prices.[48] The most plausible reason why a manufacturer would wish to prescribe price ceilings binding its resellers is to avoid repeated marginalization by vertically pyramided monopolists — a problem analyzed fully in Chapter 14. Unless the ceilings are used as focal points to discourage undercutting, and hence to support price-*raising* collusion, it is hard to see how such behavior could harm competition or consumers. Quite clearly, it should not be illegal per se.

Exclusive Franchising

A practice with many similarities to resale price maintenance is the granting by manufacturers of exclusive franchises to their dealers. These generally place some limit on the amount of competition the dealer will have to face from other outlets distributing the manufacturer's line — for example, by restricting the number of dealers operating in a particular area, or by confining dealers to specific territories or customer classes. For the dealer, exclusivity is attractive because, by lessening competition, it permits wider price-wholesale cost margins than could be sustained under an unrestricted access policy. From the manufacturer's perspective, the wider margin encourages dealers to carry larger inventories and spend more money on advertising and other promotional activities. The dealer with a profitable franchise may be better able, and more willing, to provide high-quality maintenance and repair services. Offering the prospect of supra-normal returns may also permit manufacturers to attract dealers of superior ability. And once an entrepreneur has taken on a profitable franchise, he or she will be reluctant to lose it and will therefore be responsive when the manufacturer suggests changes in operating methods.

Exclusive franchising is often coupled with another quite different restriction, an exclusive dealing arrangement. Under it, the retailer or wholesaler agrees to devote its efforts exclusively to handling the product line of a particular manufacturer. Exclusive dealing often appeals to manufacturers because it ensures that their products will be merchandised with maximum focus and enthusiasm.[49] It may also help avoid free riding on advertising or informational services provided by the manufacturer,[50] allow strong manufacturers to preempt the most able distributors and hence make entry or survival more difficult for less-advantaged firms,[51] and sustain systematic price discrimination that might otherwise be undermined through arbitrage by dealers.[52] Distributors may also find it advantageous to deal exclusively in the products of a single producer, although the benefit from contract provisions compelling them to specialize is dubious, as numerous suits by dealers seeking to break free from such restrictions testify.

For consumers, the benefits and costs of exclusive franchising and dealing are qualitatively similar to those that must be evaluated in judging resale price maintenance. The central question is, under which of the alternatives is the net balance more favorable?

Exclusive franchising has the advantage in principle of greater flexibility to deal with variations in local conditions. If demand is thin, dealers can be assigned large territories and broad product spans to ensure that they realize maximum feasible economies of scale and scope; in large metropolitan areas, smaller territories can be designated and, if interdealer competition yields advantages, territories or customer assignments can be designed to overlap. No such fine-tuning is possible with resale price maintenance, and if margins are set too high, entry can squeeze individual dealers to inefficiently small scales. Dynamically, however, it is less clear that exclusive franchising can cope flexibly with major shifts in demand and technology. Once territorial assignments are made, the dealers often consider their exclusive domain to be a valuable property right, and changes are vigorously opposed. The U.S. soft drink industry offers a prime example.[53] In the early decades of the twentieth century, Coca-Cola, Pepsi-Cola, and other syrup makers assigned their bottlers exclusive territories on the basis of demand and cost conditions prevailing at the time. But with the shifting emphasis from bottles to cans, general advances in bottling technology, and the gradual fall in transportation costs as interstate highway networks were improved, the minimum efficient scale of a soft drink bottling plant rose sharply, and as a result, the old territorial allocations became wildly uneconomic. Also, the rise of supermarket chains offered potential economies through shipping soft drinks from the bottling plant to supermarket warehouses for final distribution. But the chains' warehouse delivery

48. See, for example, *Albrecht* v. *Herald Co.*, 390 U.S. 145 (1968).

49. Distribution through exclusive dealers is attractive only for specialty and shopping goods. For convenience goods, the manufacturer's best strategy is to get its product into as many retail outlets as it can, even though competing brands are also carried. See Chapter 1, footnote 6, for definitions.

50. See Howard P. Marvel, "Exclusive Dealing," *Journal of Law & Economics*, vol. 25 (April 1982), pp. 1–25; and Marvel's case study of hearing aid distribution practices in Lafferty et al., eds., *Impact Evaluations*, supra note 33, pp. 271–377.

51. Compare William S. Comanor and H. E. Frech, "The Competitive Effects of Vertical Agreements," *American Economic Review*, vol. 75 (June 1985), pp. 539–546; the comments by G. Frank Mathewson, Ralph Winter, and Marius Schwartz and reply by Comanor and Frech in *American Economic Review*, vol. 77 (December 1987), pp. 1057–1072; and Thomas G. Krattenmaker and

Steven C. Salop, "Anticompetitive Exclusion: Raising Rivals' Costs To Achieve Power over Price," *Yale Law Journal*, vol. 96 (December 1986), pp. 231–238 and 259–260.

52. See the case study of compressed industrial gas distribution by Gerald Brock in Lafferty et al., eds., *Impact Evaluations*, supra note 33, pp. 386–422.

53. For various views, see Robert Larner, "The Economics of Territorial Restrictions in the Soft Drink Industry," *Antitrust Bulletin*, vol. 22 (Spring 1977), pp. 145–155; Barbara G. Katz, "Territorial Exclusivity in the Soft Drink Industry," *Journal of Industrial Economics*, vol. 27 (September 1978), pp. 85–96; Louis W. Stern, E. F. Zelek, and T. W. Dunfee, "A Rule of Reason Analysis of Territorial Restrictions in the Soft Drink Industry," *Antitrust Bulletin*, vol. 27 (Summer 1982), pp. 481–515; and Posner, "The Rule of Reason," supra note 11, p. 6.

territories did not coincide with bottling company territorial assignments, and rigidities in the soft drink makers' franchise contracts made it difficult to rectify the imbalances, so more costly bottler-to-store delivery continued. The syrup makers might have been rescued from this obsolete equilibrium when the Federal Trade Commission declared their exclusive franchise arrangements illegal in 1978.[54] However, the bottlers — in part because of their geographic dispersion, a powerful political force — secured from Congress in 1980 special legislation invalidating the FTC's decision. The national syrup makers were forced to attack their problem in a different way, buying out franchised bottling companies or having their largest franchisees buy them out and then, after the mergers were consummated, closing down obsolete plants and reallocating territories.[55]

Robert Steiner argues that the exclusive franchise approach is also less flexible than RPM dynamically because industrywide RPM usage tends to break down completely when a few key manufacturers decide to make their products available to mass merchandisers without price floors.[56] Also, he notes, when exclusive franchises are parceled out selectively, the consumer visiting any given retail outlet is confronted with a severely limited array of products, making side-by-side price and quality comparison difficult. Resale price maintenance without franchise limitations permits more comparison shopping at a given shoe leather cost. William Comanor adds that when the retailers of a given brand are prevented from competing with one another through territorial assignments, there is less pressure for them to use their widened margins to support service efforts.[57] Thus, unless the manufacturer stimulates its franchisees in other ways, a given elevation of consumer prices is likely to induce more spending on services under competitive RPM than under noncompetitive franchising. In sum, despite the fine-tuning advantages exclusive franchising offers in principle, it can engender inefficiencies at least as serious as those imposed upon the consumer by resale price maintenance.

Franchise arrangements that restrict competition among a manufacturer's outlets can be challenged as illegal contracts in restraint of trade under Sherman Act Section 1. Under prevailing interpretations, a manufacturer is fully within the law in limiting the number and location of outlets to which franchises are granted. But when exclusive territorial and/or customer assignments are made, a danger line is approached. There are two main subcases, depending upon whether the restrictions are imposed horizontally or vertically.

When the dealers agree *among themselves* not to interpenetrate each others' markets, or when they collectively induce the manufacturer to impose upon them such restrictions, the law is clearly violated. Thus, a joint effort by Los Angeles Chevrolet dealers and General Motors officials to prevent some dealers from bootlegging cars to unfranchised automobile supermarkets was called "a classic conspiracy" in restraint of trade by the Supreme Court.[58]

More complex issues were faced in a series of cases concerning Sealy mattress distribution.[59] Under the Sealy system, Sealy, Inc., granted exclusive territorial licenses to some twenty-nine geographically dispersed manufacturers of mattresses carrying the Sealy brand and meeting Sealy design specifications. Sealy, Inc., was in turn owned by eight of the licensees, so decisions to maintain territorial exclusivity (and also to set resale prices) were taken by agents of franchisees whose competition among themselves was restricted by the decisions. Viewing the arrangement as "an aggregation of trade restraints," including unlawful price fixing and policing, the Supreme Court pronounced it per se illegal.[60] Applying Chicago vertical restraints dogma without much appreciation of the underlying facts, Professor (and later Supreme Court nominee) Robert Bork wrote that the Court's decision illustrated "the needless destruction of an efficiency-creating system of ancillary restraints."[61] He was wrong on at least two counts. First, Sealy, Inc., chose not to have its system destroyed. It adopted a new and more complex set of licensing practices, including payments by licensees who shipped out of their home territories to the licensees whose territories they invaded, that preserved the spirit of the old exclusive territory system. But second and more important, a few aggressive Sealy licensees saw the territorial limitations as an impediment to their efficiency and growth. They sought to break out by shipping into others' territories, opening bulk warehouses where production facilities were prohibited by the franchise restraints, and merging, contrary to the wishes of Sealy, Inc., with other franchise holders. More litigation ensued, leading ultimately to rulings that the new system also violated the Sherman Act.[62] Contrary to claims that the Sealy system was output-enhancing and hence efficiency-increasing, the trial record revealed that prices were lower, and Sealy's share of the relevant markets was higher, in cities where competitive interterritorial penetration was most extensive.[63] Thus, consumers apparently benefited from the erosion of exclusivity.

Purely vertical restrictions—those imposed unilaterally by the manufacturer upon independent dealers—have experienced a more turbulent history, but are now viewed more sympathetically than horizontal restrictions. In 1963, a 5-3 majority of the Supreme Court refused to condemn out of hand the territorial and customer restrictions placed in dealer franchise contracts by the White Motor Company, a truck manufacturer with sales exceeding half a billion dollars at the time. The Court acknowledged that it did not "know enough of the economic and business stuff out of which these arrangements emerge" to be certain whether they merely stifle competition, or whether they may be "the only practicable means a small company has for breaking into or staying in business."[64] It therefore remanded the action to the district court for a thorough exploration of the facts, that is, for the application of a rule of reason. The case was settled through a negotiated

54. *In the matter of Coca Cola Co. et al.*, 91 F.T.C. 517 (1978); *In the matter of Pepsico, Inc.*, 91 F.T.C. 680 (1978). Appeals were taken but voided when Congress intervened.

55. See "Coke's Big Marketing Blitz," *Business Week*, May 30, 1983, pp. 59–64; and "Coke Bottling Unit Sets Richest Stock Offering," *New York Times*, October 15, 1986, p. D1.

56. "The Nature of Vertical Restraints," supra note 29, pp. 190–192.

57. William S. Comanor, "Vertical Arrangements and Antitrust Analysis," *New York University Law Review*, vol. 62 (November 1987), p. 1160.

58. *U.S.* v. *General Motors Corp. et al.*, 384 U.S. 127 (1966).

59. This account draws heavily upon Willard F. Mueller, "The Sealy Restraints: Restrictions on Free Riding or Output?" *Wisconsin Law Review*, vol. 1989, No. 5 (1989).

60. *U.S.* v. *Sealy, Inc.*, 388 U.S. 350, 356–358 (1967). See also *U.S.* v. *Topco Associates, Inc.*, 405 U.S. 596 (1976), which involved analogous exclusive territorial assignments by a cooperatively owned grocery wholesaling organization. Despite modest post-judgment changes in its franchising practices, Topco continued to thrive. See Mueller, "The Sealy Restraints."

61. *The Antitrust Paradox*, supra note 11, p. 270.

62. The most recent of several reported decisions was *Ohio-Sealy Mattress Mfg. Co.* v. *Kaplan et al.*, 745 F. 2d 441 (1984), cert. den. 471 U.S. 1125 (1985).

63. Mueller, "The Sealy Restraints." See also "Behind High Price for Ohio Mattress," *New York Times*, March 7, 1989, p. D17.

64. *White Motor Co.* v. *U.S.*, 372 U.S. 253, 263 (1963); CCH 1964 Trade Cases Para. 71,195.

consent decree in which White agreed to terminate certain restrictive provisions in its dealer franchises.

In 1967 the Court tightened the screws, ruling, with no coherent attempt to rationalize its change, that manufacturers selling their products subject to territorial and other restrictions upon resale committed per se violations of the Sherman Act.[65] Withering criticism by legal scholars, economists, and even lower courts followed.

A decade later, the Court returned to the problem and admitted error. At issue were certain actions following from franchise contracts limiting selected retailers of Sylvania television sets to store locations specified by the manufacturer. Sylvania had initiated the program of winnowing out weak retailers and concentrating its distribution efforts on a limited number of aggressive franchised outlets after a decline in its national market share into the 1 to 2 percent range. The Supreme Court articulated its newly acquired belief that vertical restrictions can promote interbrand competition by allowing the manufacturer to achieve distribution efficiencies.[66] It observed further that there had been no showing, either generally or in the specific case of Sylvania, that vertical restrictions have or are likely to have "a pernicious effect on competition" or that they lack "any redeeming value."[67] It therefore concluded that although particular vertical restrictions might well be anticompetitive, vertical restrictions (other than resale price maintenance) should be judged under a rule of reason.

Assuming that the courts can cope with the substantive complexities, this is a reasonable solution. Yet if nonprice vertical restraints are treated on a rule of reason basis, one might ask, shouldn't purely vertical resale price maintenance arrangements be handled symmetrically? As we have seen, the Supreme Court inched in that direction during the 1980s, precipitating a sharp Congressional counter reaction. Debate on the issue is likely to continue.

In the European Economic Community, what is best described as a rule of reason approach to exclusive franchising has evolved. The Community's original objective was to develop free trade among member nations, and in a key early decision, the EC Commission struck down an arrangement under which a tape recorder maker's exclusive distributors were precluded from exporting or reexporting to other distributors' national territories.[68] Evidence had been presented that the practice had led to large sustained price differentials on Grundig products between France and Germany. On the other hand, a block exemption was granted in 1983 to strictly vertical exclusive territorial and/or product arrangements that permit distributors to sell, even if not actively to solicit orders, in other distributors' territories.

Exclusive Dealing, Requirements Contracts, and Tying

Section 3 of the U.S. Clayton Act prohibits contracts for the sale or lease of commodities imposing a condition that the purchaser or lessee "shall not use or deal in the goods, . . . supplies, or other commodities of a competitor . . . of the lessor or seller" where the effect "may be to substantially lessen competition or tend to create a monopoly." It applies to three main types of practices: exclusive dealerships, requirements contracts, and tying arrangements.

Exclusive Dealing As we have seen earlier, exclusive dealing is often employed in conjunction with exclusive franchising. It has a variety of possible rationales, some efficiency-oriented and some not. The limits to which sellers may legally go have been progressively narrowed through a series of U.S. antitrust decisions. In a 1922 opinion, the Supreme Court found an exclusive dealership to be illegal under Clayton Act Section 3 when it encompassed 40 percent of all dress pattern outlets in the United States.[69] Subsequent pronouncements in analogous requirements contract cases (to be considered in a moment) shifted the allowable affected market share thresholds to a much lower level. However, manufacturers with modest market shares are not likely to run afoul of the law when they urge exclusive dealing without actually coercing their dealers to eschew competitive products. For instance, the J. I. Case Company, selling roughly 7 percent of all U.S. farm machinery in 1948, avoided censure when a district court found that it had not made exclusive dealing an inviolable condition of its franchises, that 2,600 of its 3,738 dealers handled at least some competitive products, and that other farm machinery manufacturers experienced no difficulty obtaining outlets for their products.[70]

In the automobile industry, dealerships have often been exclusive in fact if not by contractual compulsion, although the number of multimanufacturer dealers increased sharply in the United States during the 1970s and 1980s. Efficiencies can be attained when dealers focus on a single car line for which sufficient demand exists, but overhead-spreading argues for multimake dealing when demand is weak, and exclusivity almost surely operated to raise auto manufacturing entry barriers during the 1950s and 1960s.[71] In a case testing the extent to which exclusivity could be carried, an appellate court found that the Hudson Motor Company was within its rights in refusing to renew a dealer's contract because the dealer diffused its efforts over too many competing makes.[72] It is unlikely that the Big Three would have emerged as favorably from such a test. Although no systematic analysis of the question is known, it seems reasonable to suppose that U.S. manufacturers' fear of overstepping the allowable exclusivity bounds facilitated the

65. *U.S.* v. *Arnold, Schwinn & Co. et al.*, 388 U.S. 365 (1967). Following the decision, Schwinn terminated the contracts with its twenty-two independent wholesale distributors and established a vertically integrated wholesaling subsidiary.

66. *Continental T.V., Inc., et al.* v. *GTE Sylvania, Inc.*, 433 U.S. 36, 54 (1977).

67. 433 U.S. 36, 58 (1977).

68. *Grundig Consten* case, discussed in the European Communities Commission's *First Report on Competition Policy* (Brussels: April 1972), pp. 55–56. For compact surveys of further interpretations, see Alexis P. Jacquemin and Henry W. de Jong, *European Industrial Organisation* (London: Macmillan, 1977), pp. 211–214; and John Agnew, *Competition Law* (London: Allen & Unwin, 1985), pp. 155–160.

69. *Standard Fashion Co.* v. *Magrane-Houston Co.*, 258 U.S. 346 (1922).

70. *U.S.* v. *J.I. Case Co.*, 101 F. Supp. 856 (1951). Compare *Federal Trade Commission* v. *Brown Shoe Co.*, 384 U.S. 316 (1966), in which less than completely exclusive dealing arrangements of

seemingly innocuous scope were condemned. See also John L. Peterman, "The Federal Trade Commission v. Brown Shoe Company," *Journal of Law & Economics*, vol. 18 (October 1975), pp. 361–419.

71. See pp. 135–136 supra. On the vertically stacked monopoly problems arising when powerful manufacturers sell to dealers with appreciable power, see B. P. Pashigian, *The Distribution of Automobiles: An Economic Analysis of the Franchise System* (Englewood Cliffs: Prentice-Hall, 1961); and Richard L. Smith, "Franchise Regulation: An Economic Analysis of State Restrictions on Automobile Distribution," *Journal of Law & Economics*, vol. 25 (April 1982), pp. 125–157.

72. *Hudson Sales Corporation* v. *Waldrip*, 211 F. 2d 268 (1954). On the special regulations adopted by the European Communities for exclusive arrangements in automobile retailing, see Organisation for Economic Co-Operation and Development, *Competition Policy in OECD Countries, 1984–1985* (Paris: 1987), pp. 243–244.

entry of Japanese auto makers into the U.S. market. By 1984, one-fourth of all U.S. auto dealers handled both domestic and foreign cars.[73]

Requirements Contracts

Under a requirements contract, the buyer agrees to purchase all its requirements for some product or group of products from a particular seller. Such arrangements have the possibly undesirable effect of foreclosing a distribution channel to competing sellers during the life of the contract. They also offer a number of potential advantages, however, as the Supreme Court acknowledged in its 1949 *Standard Stations* opinion:

> In the case of the buyer, they may assure supply, afford protection against rises in price, enable long-term planning on the basis of known costs, and obviate the expense and risk of storage in the quantity necessary for a commodity having a fluctuating demand. From the seller's point of view, requirements contracts may make possible the substantial reduction of selling expenses, give protection against price fluctuations, and—of particular advantage to a newcomer to the field to whom it is important to know what capital expenditures are justified—offer the possibility of a predictable market. . . . They may be useful, moreover, to a seller trying to establish a foothold against the counterattacks of entrenched competitors.[74]

The Court went on to observe that jurists are seldom in a good position to weigh the anticompetitive effects of specific requirements contracts against their economic advantages. It therefore ruled that contested contracts should be judged primarily in terms of their structural impact, and that a violation of Clayton Act Section 3 could be found when there is proof "that competition has been foreclosed in a substantial share of the line of commerce affected."[75] In the case at issue, Standard Oil of California had entered into requirements contracts with 5,937 independent franchised Standard gasoline retailers, comprising 16 percent by number of all gas stations in a seven-state western U.S. area and making 6.7 percent of 1946 gasoline sales in that area. Some contracts required the stations to purchase only their gasoline supplies exclusively from Standard; others covered tires, batteries, and similar products in addition to gasoline. Emphasizing the 6.7 percent market share and the $58 million volume of annual gasoline sales, the Supreme Court held that a substantial share of commerce had in fact been foreclosed and that the contracts were therefore illegal.[76] This decision served not only to constrain the use of requirements contracts in many fields, but also established the structural criteria upon which subsequent merger decisions were based.

The manufacturers of automobiles and other complex equipment have often insisted that their dealers refrain from selling or installing repair parts produced by competing firms, which in effect means that they must purchase their full requirements from the original equipment maker. Such vertical restrictions tread close to the uncertain limits of the law. In a 1936 opinion, the Supreme Court affirmed a lower court decision approving General Motors' requirement that GM dealers install only GM replacement parts. It accepted the argument that installation of inappropriate or defective parts could impair an automobile's functioning and thereby damage the manufacturer's reputation.[77] Five years later the Federal Trade Commission ordered General Motors to cease insisting that dealers stock and sell only GM supplies and accessories. However, an exception was permitted for "parts necessary to the mechanical operation of an automobile, and which are not available, in like quality and design, from other sources of supply."[78] Following the tightening of Clayton Act Section 3 criteria in the *Standard Stations* decision, the early General Motors parts decisions were criticized by some courts.[79] And in 1959, an appellate court ruled that attempts by Ford Motor Company to force its dealers to sell or install only Ford-made or approved parts might be found illegal if they substantially lessened competition.[80]

Tying and Bundling

Under a tying arrangement, the purchaser of some article—for example, a machine—agrees as a condition of purchase (or lease) to buy from the seller supplies of some other commodity, such as raw materials processed by the machine. The agreement in effect forecloses competing materials suppliers from selling the *tied* commodity to that purchaser. Conceptually related are *bundling* practices, under which the seller insists that the buyer take a package of products, bundled together and offered at a single price per bundle.

There are some good reasons why business firms may tie or bundle their products. For example, the producer of a technically complex machine may tie to control the quality of raw materials used with its machine, so that its reputation is not sullied by breakdowns caused through the use of faulty supplies. Cost savings may also be realized by producing or distributing the tied and tying goods together. Supplies of special copying machine toner or paper might be delivered by maintenance personnel in the course of routine service visits, saving separate delivery visits. In practice, however, it is doubtful that the savings realized in this way could be very significant.

Tying is also used to increase the profits derived from monopoly power.[81] In what is probably the most important and common case, tying permits a firm with monopoly power to discriminate in price according to the intensity of demand. Suppose, for instance, that one copying machine user makes 3,000 copies per month while another makes 20,000 copies per month. It would be difficult for a company selling only copying machines to price its machines in such a way as to

73. U.S. Bureau of the Census, *Statistical Abstract of the United States: 1986* (Washington: USGPO, 1987), p. 783.
74. *Standard Oil Co. of California et al.* v. *U.S..*, 337 U.S. 293, 306–307 (1949). Note that the last two advantages would be described in modern parlance as making markets more contestable.
75. 377 U.S. 293, 314 (1949).
76. But see Richard A. Miller, "Exclusive Dealing in the Petroleum Industry: The Refiner-Lessee Dealer Relationship," *Yale Economic Essays*, vol. 3 (Spring 1963), pp. 223–247, who argues that petroleum refiners had alternative ways to achieve the objectives of prohibited requirements contracts.
In 1984, thirteen leading petroleum refining companies settled a private Clayton Act Section 3 case by agreeing to let some 50,000 of their franchised dealers sell gasoline from other refiners. Appropriate labeling was required to distinguish the substitute from a station's advertised brand. See "13 Refiners Agree Stations May Sell Any Brand of Gas," *New York Times*, September 25, 1984, p. 1.

77. *Pick Manufacturing Co.* v. *General Motors Corp. et al.*, 80 F. 2d 641 (1935), affirmed *per curiam*, 299 U.S. 3 (1936).
78. *In re General Motors Corp. and General Motors Sales Corp.*, 34 F.T.C. 58, 86 (1941).
79. *Dictograph Products, Inc.* v. *Federal Trade Commission*, 217 F. 2d 821, 828 (1954).
80. *Englander Motors, Inc.* v. *Ford Motor Co.*, 267 F. 2d 11 (1959). The case was apparently settled out of court before the district court determined whether competition had in fact been lessened. See also *Alles Corp.* v. *Senco Products, Inc.*, 329 F. 2d 567 (1964).
81. For diverse views, see Ward S. Bowman, Jr., "Tying Arrangements and the Leverage Problem," *Yale Law Journal*, vol. 67 (November 1957), pp. 19–36; M. L. Burstein, "A Theory of Full-Line Forcing," *Northwestern University Law Review*, vol. 55 (March–April 1960), pp. 62–95; and Martin J. Bailey, "Price and Output Determination by a Firm Selling Related Products," *American Economic Review*, vol. 44 (March 1954), pp. 82–93.

extract more revenue from the more intensive user. But if the machine maker can tie the purchase of special ink (toner) to the purchase of its machine, and if it can price the supplies so as to realize a supra-normal profit margin on them, it will be able to extract additional profits from the higher-volume user. This sort of tying is called *metering* because the sale of supplies serves as a substitute for placing a meter on the machine itself and billing the customer (who leases the machine rather than buying it) on the basis of metered usage. It can be highly profitable; thus, copying machine makers often refer to their toner as "black gold."

If the tied good is used in fixed proportions with the tying good — that is, when exactly one sheet of paper and 0.1 gram of toner are used to make a normal copy — tying is unlikely to cause allocative inefficiency. In the first instance, it merely transfers surplus from consumers to producers. Moreover, by securing a result that approximates first-degree price discrimination, it can actually increase output and total (consumers' plus producer's) surplus relative to the case in which the machine is priced sufficiently high to extract a simple monopoly profit. If able to tie, the machine monopolist reduces the price of its machine to a level near marginal cost, thereby encouraging more machine purchases than would occur if the machines were priced as simple monopoly products. It then more than makes up for the sacrifice of machine profits through the intensity-of-use-linked profits on the tied good.

When inputs are substitutable, matters become more complex in ways directly analogous to those examined in Chapter 14, where the focus was downstream vertical integration by the monopolist of an input against which other inputs were substitutable.[82] Suppose a firm has a monopoly on input X_1. If substitute input X_2 is supplied competitively, users will substitute away from high-priced X_1 and toward X_2, minimizing their exploitation by the monopolist but using the inputs (one priced monopolistically, the other competitively) in less than the most efficient proportions. When the monopolist successfully ties the sale of X_2 to the purchase of X_1, there are two main effects: prices are readjusted so that X_1 and X_2 are used in more efficient proportions, thus encouraging the sale of X_1; and the monopolist's control is extended to the usage of X_2, so that more profits can be extracted from the inputs' *combined* sale. Whether the amount of end product obtained using X_1 and X_2 (or, in the case of consumption goods, consumers' utility) increases or decreases following such tying depends, following logic similar to that developed in Chapter 14, upon the elasticities of substitution, end product price elasticity, and the relative importance of the tying and tied goods. Under a plausible array of conditions, consumers are worse off when X_2 is tied than when X_1 alone is sold monopolistically.[83] At the same time, the firms that would have supplied X_2 but for the tie are excluded from the marketplace; although when X_1 is not indispensable, the X_1 monopolist must take care not to exceed the limit price at which buyers choose to meet their needs using only X_2, competitively supplied, without any X_1.

When, instead of having systematically varying intensities of demand for one monopolized good, buyers have differing and imperfectly correlated reservation prices for two or more goods, bundling the goods and selling them at a package price often permits a multiproduct monopolist to extract greater profits than it would if each product were priced separately. The welfare implications of bundling are complex. Sellers clearly gain at the expense of buyers, but the sum of producer's plus consumers' surplus may either rise or fall, depending upon the particular facts of the case.[84]

Finally, tying contracts may be employed to evade governmental price controls—for example, when a firm supplying some commodity such as natural gas or telephone service whose price is regulated requires customers to buy from it fixtures and attachments whose prices are not effectively controlled. Then the firm will set the fixture prices above competitive levels, capturing profits that regulation prevented it from retaining in its core monopolized business.

Under early U.S. legal precedents, companies requiring purchasers of their patented machines to purchase unpatented supplies were allowed to enforce their tying contracts and secure injunctions against the use of competing supplies.[85] However, the situation changed after the Clayton Act was passed. From then on, tying arrangements have been dealt with severely not only in Clayton Act Section 3 cases, but also in Sherman Act Section 1 and patent infringement actions.[86] In a decision setting forth general guidelines for the interpretation of Clayton Act Section 3, the Supreme Court observed that "[t]ying agreements serve hardly any purpose beyond the suppression of competition."[87] In a nearly contemporaneous case tried under both Clayton and Sherman Act charges, the Court ruled that it is "unreasonable, *per se*, to foreclose competitors from any substantial market" by means of tying contracts.[88]

These statements have the ring of a per se prohibition, but the presumption against tying is not quite as strong as the per se rule against price-fixing conspiracies. After moving toward a more lenient position in a series of somewhat confused decisions, the Supreme Court in 1984 articulated three criteria, all of which had to be met to infer per se illegality: (1) the tying and tied products had to be distinct; (2) the firm tying the products had to have sufficient power in the tying good market to force the purchase of the tied good; and (3) the tying agreement

82. See Roger D. Blair and David Kaserman, "Vertical Integration, Tying, and Antitrust Policy," *American Economic Review*, vol. 68 (June 1978), pp. 397–402; and (for a particularly clear and comprehensive analysis limited to numerically computable cases) John S. McGee, "Compound Pricing," *Economic Inquiry*, vol. 25 (April 1987), pp. 315–339.

83. Significant inefficiencies persist when the purchase of input X_2 is tied to the sale of monopolized input X_1, but when additional substitutes (for example, X_3 and X_4) remain competitively available. See McGee, "Compound Pricing," p. 333. Assuming plausible substitution relationships of this sort, McGee shows that the sum of consumers' plus producers' surplus is greatest under competitive pricing of all inputs, second-greatest when the monopolist of X_1 enforces an all-or-nothing scheme that is tantamount to first-degree price discrimination; third-greatest under simple monopoly pricing of X_1; worse yet under monopoly tying of X_2 to X_1; and worst when the X_1 monopolist secures a contract precluding its customers from using any X_2 from any source.

84. See William J. Adams and Janet L. Yellen, "Commodity Bundling and the Burden of Monopoly," *Quarterly Journal of Economics*, vol. 90 (August 1976), pp. 475–498; Richard Schmalensee, "Gaussian Demand and Commodity Bundling," *Journal of Business*, vol. 57 (January 1984, Part 2), pp. S211–230; Robert E. Dansby and Cecelia Conrad, "Commodity Bundling," *American Economic Review*, vol. 74 (May 1984), pp. 377–381; Roy W. Kenney and Benjamin Klein, "The Economics of Block Booking," *Journal of Law & Economics*, vol. 26 (October 1983), pp. 497–540; and R.P. McAfee, John McMillan, and Michael D. Whinston, "Multiproduct Monopoly, Commodity Bundling, and Correlation of Values," *Quarterly Journal of Economics*, vol. 104 (May 1989), pp. 371–382.

85. *Heaton Peninsular Button-Fastener Co.* v. *Eureka Specialty Co.*, 77 F. 288 (1896); and *Henry* v. *A.B. Dick Co.*, 224 U.S. 1 (1912).

86. The turning point was *Motion Picture Patents Co.* v. *Universal Film Manufacturing Co.*, 243 U.S. 502 (1917).

87. *Standard Oil Co. of California et al.* v. *U.S.*, 337 U.S. 293, 305–306 (1949).

88. *International Salt Co.* v. *U.S.*, 322 U.S. 392, 396 (1947).

must foreclose a substantial volume of trade, or have the potential to do so.[89] When the tying firm's position in the relevant market is insufficiently strong to warrant an inference that it could force its buyers into accepting tied purchases, the severity of the restraint is to be judged under a rule of reason. For sellers with relatively small market shares, especially when the tying product is unpatented, the per se criteria are not likely to be satisfied. Small companies attempting to break into a new market under the protection of tying contracts may also escape censure. And the courts have been willing to consider extenuating circumstances such as the need to exercise control over complementary goods or services to ensure satisfactory operation of the tying product.

Quality control was a central issue in a case involving IBM's requirement that its unpatented tabulating cards be used exclusively in the keypunch, card-sorting, and other mechanical data processing equipment it leased before electronic computers were available. IBM argued that the use of faulty cards could cause machine jams and processing errors, damaging its reputation. The Supreme Court rejected this contention. It found that other suppliers were capable of manufacturing cards conforming to IBM's specifications and that IBM was not prevented under the law from "proclaiming the virtues of its own cards" or even from making its leases conditional upon the use of cards meeting the necessary quality standards.[90] What it could not do was make its machine lease contracts conditional upon the use of IBM cards. In a later case, a more tolerant judgment was rendered. The Jerrold Electronics Corporation, a pioneer in the development and installation of cable television systems, required purchasers of its system to also accept five-year maintenance contracts. This was supposedly done to avoid breakdowns that could result if the complex, delicate equipment were serviced by inadequately trained personnel. In a decision broadly endorsed by the Supreme Court, a district court ruled that the service tying arrangement was not unreasonable at the time of its inception, but that it came to violate Sherman Act Section 1 as the industry "took root and grew."[91]

The effects of legal bans against tying contracts vary among industries, depending upon the degree to which producers can sustain informal ties by "proclaiming the virtues" of complementary goods and services. On one hand, the 1936 decree requiring IBM to end its tying contracts had little effect, for twenty years later, IBM still accounted for 90 percent of greatly expanded tabulating card production.[92] On the other hand, an attack on tying practices appears to have had a major impact in the metal container industry. Prior to 1950, the American Can Company tied the sale of tin cans to the lease of its patented can-closing machines by arranging to have the expiration dates of machine leases and long-term can requirements contracts coincide, and by refusing to conclude new machine lease contracts unless the canner also accepted a can requirements contract. After the courts found this subterfuge illegal, American was required to offer its machines for sale at attractive prices and to limit the life of its can supply contracts to one year.[93] Similar injunctions bound Continental Can, American Can's leading rival. Within four years, customers responsible for 75 percent of the two firms' machine leases had taken advantage of the opportunity to own their own can-closing machines. Price competition in the can-making trade intensified, and the market share of can sellers other than the Big Four increased from 20 percent in 1954 to 34 percent in 1972 and 50 percent in 1982.

Conclusion

The restraints sellers attempt to impose on their customers and on those customers' conduct toward buyers even farther downstream are extremely complex, with equally complex economic consequences. Economic efficiency may be increased, reduced, or left essentially unchanged by such vertical restraints, depending upon the facts. Economic theory has had a difficult time keeping up with real-world practice, but during the 1970s and 1980s, the relevant body of theory advanced more rapidly than in most other areas of industrial organization analysis. Legal doctrine has lagged even more seriously behind. In its 1977 *Sylvania* decision, the Supreme Court took a major step toward endorsing a University of Chicago world view just as new work was beginning to illuminate its limitations. In 1985 the Justice Department's Antitrust Division, having been captured by Chicago school attorneys, published "Vertical Restraints Guidelines" adopting a more permissive posture toward vertical restraints than was embodied in the standing judicial precedents.[94] The attorneys general of the various states responded by issuing tougher guidelines for their own growing intervention into antitrust matters.[95] Vigorous confrontation in the marketplace of ideas must occur before the diverse parties converge upon a new consensus policy. Such a policy must integrate the insights offered by theory on a problem whose real-world complexities make it difficult for fallible courts to sort out desirable from undesirable conduct.

89. *Jefferson Parish Hospital District No. 2 et al.* v. *Hyde*, 466 U.S. 2, 15–18 (1984).

90. *International Business Machines Corp.* v. *U.S.*, 298 U.S. 131, 139–140 (1936).

91. *U.S.* v. *Jerrold Electronics Corp.*, 187 F. Supp. 545, 557 (1960), affirmed *per curiam* at 363 U.S. 567 (1961).

92. *U.S.* v. *International Business Machines Corp.*, CCH 1956 Trade Cases, Para. 68,245. On subsequent developments in *IBM* and similar cases, see William L. Baldwin, "The Feedback Effect of Business Conduct on Industry Structure," *Journal of Law & Economics*, vol. 12 (April 1969), pp. 123–153.

93. *U.S.* v. *American Can Co. et al.*, 87 F. Supp. 18 (1949). See also James W. McKie, "The Decline of Monopoly in the Metal Container Industry," *American Economic Review*, vol. 45 (May 1955), pp. 499–508; and Charles H. Hession, "The Metal Container Industry," in Walter Adams, ed., *The Structure of American Industry*, 3rd ed. (New York: Macmillan, 1961), pp. 430–467.

94. U.S. Department of Justice, *Vertical Restraints Guidelines* (Washington: January 1985).

95. National Association of Attorneys General, *Vertical Restraints Guidelines* (Washington: December 1985).

16

Product Differentiation, Market Structure, and Competition

We advance now to firms' product policies—that is, to the important strategic choices they make in differentiating their goods and services from rival offerings. Four main product differentiation modes can be identified.[1] First, sellers may select plant or store locations more convenient (in terms of travel time and/or transportation costs) than rival locations. The locational advantages of the corner drugstore and the local gravel quarry are illustrations. Second, there are physical differences in product attributes. A suit may incorporate the most finely woven wool worsted or a coarser substitute; the design of an appliance may be mundane or reflect the genius of a Henry Dreyfuss; beer may be hops-laden or bland; a computer may be addressed through complex logical codes or simple pictograms; and so forth. Third, firms may offer exceptionally good (or bad) service. As the previous chapter's discussion of the links between manufacturers and their distributors revealed, some retailers maintain large and well-trained staffs to provide prompt, intelligent, and courteous service; others are better known for long checkout lines and grumbling cashiers, mollifying the effect with rock-bottom prices. Some microcomputer software writers maintain hot lines to advise users how to overcome problems in using their products; others are unreachable. Finally, products are differentiated in terms of the subjective image they impress on the consumer's mind. Sellers attempt to enhance the image of their products through brand labeling, advertising, the design of attractive packages, and by distributing only through prestigious retail outlets.

Most of the product differentiation effort observed in a modern private-enterprise economy is a natural and healthy response to consumer demands. Peoples' wants are diverse. It is a rare consumer who doesn't value convenience in the location of suppliers, and many will pay a price premium for a certain amount of locational convenience. Nearly every consumer prefers good service over poor, although the prices individuals are willing to pay for extra service vary widely. The diversity of preferences with respect to physical design and performance attributes is especially great. Some men prefer cotton shirts, some silk shirts, some hair shirts, and some no shirt at all. Some want to fly supersonically; others would just as soon walk in the woods. Likewise, different consumers assign varying weight to the subjective image that accompanies the products they buy.

This rationale for product differentiation is generally accepted by consumers and scholars. To the extent that debate persists, it focuses on *how much* differentiation there should be and whether certain market conditions might lead to excessive (or inadequate) differentiation. Most controversial and important in this respect is image differentiation, especially the image differentiation created or reinforced through advertising.[2] In this chapter we direct our inquiry mainly to various facets of the image differentiation question, probing the bounds to which economic analysis can carry our insights and identifying the value judgments that

1. Compare Richard E. Caves and Peter J. Williamson, "What Is Product Differentiation, *Really?*" *Journal of Industrial Economics*, vol. 34 (December 1985), pp. 113–132, who use factor analysis to identify five dimensions.

2. For systematic expositions of economists' strongly differing views on the effects of advertising, see the papers by Yale Brozen and H. Michael Mann in Harvey J. Goldschmid et al., eds., *In-*

dustrial Concentration: The New Learning (Boston: Little, Brown, 1974), pp. 115–156; William S. Comanor and Thomas A. Wilson, "The Effect of Advertising on Competition: A Survey," *Journal of Economic Literature*, vol. 17 (June 1979), pp. 453–476; Jules Backman, *Advertising and Competition* (New York: New York University Press, 1967); and Robert E. McAuliffe, *Advertising, Competition, and Public Policy* (Lexington: Lexington Books, 1987).

underlie contending viewpoints. We then examine more briefly how market structure affects firms' product variety and durability choices.

Advertising, Information, and Persuasion

In 1986, it is estimated, $102 billion were spent on advertising in the United States. How those expenditures were distributed across the various advertising media is shown in Table 16.1. In 1977—the last year for which detailed industry breakdowns are available—the median manufacturing industry (among 225 candidates) devoted 0.66 percent of its sales revenue to advertising.[3] However, a few industries are much more advertising-intensive. Table 16.2 lists the ten leading industries, ranked in the order of their media advertising/sales ratios for 1977. Prominent among the leaders are industries supplying repetitively purchased consumers goods advertised heavily on television, including (in tenth place) the industry from which the term *soap opera* comes.

Advertising can perfect competition by helping consumers make better-informed choices, or it can make competition less perfect by persuading consumers to favor a particular brand over alternatives. Drawing a line between these modes is often difficult, since information and persuasion are combined in widely varying proportions. Newspaper advertising, accounting for a fourth of U.S. outlays in 1986, is preponderantly informative, although some insertions mislead more than they inform,[4] and as any erstwhile home seller knows, even classified ads are written in persuasive fashion. Television advertising in the United States probably occupies the opposite extreme. A 1976 study examined 378 television commercials to determine whether they contained information on fourteen points such as price, quality, product performance, taste, nutrition, new ideas, warranties, etc.[5] Only 49 percent of the insertions were found to be informative in the sense of satisfying at least one of the fourteen information content criteria. The

Table 16.1   Estimated U.S. Advertising Expenditures by Media in 1986

Medium	Billions of Dollars
Newspapers	26.99
Television	22.59
Radio	6.95
Magazines	5.32
Direct mail	17.15
Business papers	2.38
Farm publications	.19
Outdoor	.99
Miscellaneous	19.60
Total	102.14

Source: U.S. Bureau of the Census, *Statistical Abstract of the United States: 1988* (Washington: USGPO, 1988), p. 530, drawing upon McCann-Erickson compilations. The miscellaneous category includes the estimated cost of corporate advertising departments, art work, subsidized signs and advertising novelties, and such true miscellanea as the Goodyear Blimp.

Table 16.2 The Ten Leading Manufacturing Industries in Terms of
Media Advertising/Sales Ratios, 1977

Industry	Industry Advertising as a Percent of Sales
Over-the-counter drugs	20.2
Perfumes, cosmetics, and other toilet preparations	14.6
Soft drink syrups and other flavorings	13.8
Cutlery (including razor blades)	12.9
Cereal breakfast foods	11.4
Dog, cat, and other pet foods	11.0
Distilled liquors	11.0
Magazines and similar periodicals	10.3
Cigarettes	8.8
Soap and other cleaning preparations	8.0

Source: Federal Trade Commission, *Statistical Report: Annual Line of Business Report, 1977* (Washington: 1985), p. 17.

highest rate of informative advertising (60 percent) occurred during the evening; the lowest rate (33 percent) during weekday afternoons.

Search, Advertising, and Price Dispersion

If consumers lack information on the prices charged by alternative sources of a desired product or service, the vendors' ability to charge higher prices is enhanced. This imperfection can be lessened when consumers search, by foot or telephone, for the lowest price. In a seminal article, George Stigler showed that more search was warranted, and hence competition was more apt to drive prices toward equality, the larger the amount of the consumer's intended expenditure.[6] When vendors advertise their prices, Stigler continued, "Search now becomes extremely

3. Federal Trade Commission, *Statistical Report: Annual Line of Business Report, 1977* (Washington: April 1985), pp. 26–41. Total selling expenses, including the cost of sales representatives, point of sale displays, coupons, samples, advertising allowances to retailers, and trade allowances as well as media advertising expenses, tend to be much larger, with a median value of 7.75 percent of manufacturers' sales in 1977. On reasons for the differing emphasis across industries on media advertising versus other selling expenses, see Leonard W. Weiss, George Pascoe, and Stephen Martin, "The Size of Selling Costs," *Review of Economics and Statistics*, vol. 65 (November 1983), pp. 668–672; and Richard E. Caves, "Information Structures of Product Markets," *Economic Inquiry*, vol. 24 (April 1986), pp. 195–212.

4. See, for example, "New York and Other States Cracking Down on Auto Ads," *New York Times*, November 19, 1988, p. 52, which observed that advertisements for new and used automobiles had become "so deceptive that dealers themselves can't live with them anymore."

5. Alan Resnik and Bruce L. Stern, "An Analysis of the Infor-

mation Content in Television Advertising," *Journal of Marketing*, vol. 41 (January 1977), pp. 50–53.

In a 1976 Harris poll, 46 percent of the 1,510 respondents believed that all or most television advertisements were seriously misleading. "Business, Public Out of Sync," *Advertising Age*, May 23, 1977, p. 102.

Explaining the content of television advertisements for automobiles, General Motors advertising executive Sean Fitzpatrick observed that "Image is not one way to differentiate yourself . . . It's the only way." The Chevrolet "Heartbeat of America" advertisements aired in 1988, he continued, "may look unorganized . . . but every detail is cold-heartedly calculated. People see the scenes they want to identify with; there's a Chevy for everyone. It's not verbal. It's not rational. It's emotional, just the way people buy cars." "On the Road Again, With a Passion," *New York Times*, October 10, 1988, p. A-10.

6. George J. Stigler, "The Economics of Information," *Journal of Political Economy*, vol. 69 (June 1961), pp. 213–225.

economical," and the tendency for price dispersion to vanish is limited only by the fact that not all consumers read the relevant advertisements.[7] However, despite the considerable amount of price advertising in local newspapers and the opportunities for search, substantial price differences persist in consumer goods markets. Pratt, Wise, and Zeckhauser obtained price quotations on thirty-nine standardized consumer goods and services from an average of twelve suppliers each in the Boston metropolitan area during 1978. They found that on average, the standard deviation of quoted prices averaged 21.6 percent of average price quotations.[8] Maximum quoted prices exceeded minimum quotations by an average of 120 percent. Our own regression analysis of their data reveals that the standard deviation of prices as a percentage of average prices was smaller for nationally known brands than for other items.[9] Consistent with Stigler's search hypothesis, prices deviated less from their average, the larger the average transaction was. Contrary to the expectation that quality might vary more widely for services, the deviation was lower for services than for goods. However, the search and quality relationships were not statistically significant.

Advertising, Price Levels, and Quality

Despite the persistence of substantial price dispersion, there is reason to believe that advertising, and especially price advertising, can lead to lower service prices in local markets. The richest evidence on this point exists for the fitting of eyeglasses, since optometrists' and opticians' professional codes of ethics vary widely from state to state in the extent to which advertising is permitted. Analyzing the results of an unusually well-controlled Federal Trade Commission experiment, John Kwoka found that the examination prices of optometrists advertising in media other than the Yellow Pages were roughly 45 percent lower than comparable prices in cities where advertising was prohibited.[10] In the cities permitting advertising, even the prices of nonadvertisers were lower, although only slightly so, than the averages for cities with no advertising. Nonadvertisers in cities permitting advertising provided examinations of somewhat higher quality than those of their peers in no-advertising cities, while the active advertisers conducted significantly less thorough examinations. Thus, consumers in cities with advertising had a choice between less thorough but much less expensive service and more thorough, higher-priced service. However, holding quality constant, consumers in the cities with advertising were served at prices that were lower on average.

Local consumer-oriented advertising could lead to lower prices by intensifying price competition among contending suppliers, or by permitting suppliers to attract more business than would otherwise be possible, thereby facilitating the realization of scale economies and hence cost savings.[11] Large chain optometrists in the Federal Trade Commission experiment had slightly lower prices than small-firm advertisers, suggesting that both effects may have been at work. Whether this result generalizes to other trades and to national as well as local markets is unknown, compelling us to reiterate Neil Borden's conclusion from an early comprehensive survey of the evidence that "it is impossible from cost data to trace a clear causal relationship between decreased production costs and advertising."[12]

A line of analysis articulated most fully by Robert L. Steiner suggests that even when it assiduously avoids mentioning prices, *national* advertising significantly affects consumer goods prices by altering the power relationships between manufacturers and their retailers.[13] When a product appeals directly and successfully to consumers through advertising, the relevant retailers are virtually forced to stock it or suffer a loss of customers to competitors who do carry the best-known brands. Facing relatively high elasticity of demand for such products because of the inter-retailer competition, monopolistically competitive retailers maximize their profits by accepting relatively slender price-cost margins.[14] This proclivity is reinforced by two other phenomena: the belief by retailers that stocking well-known brands draws customers who, once attracted, will also buy higher-margin items; and the demonstrated tendency, at least with food store products, for nationally advertised brands to have higher shelf turnover, and hence to yield more profit per unit

7. Ibid., p. 223.

8. John W. Pratt, David A. Wise, and Richard Zeckhauser, "Price Differences in Almost Competitive Markets," *Quarterly Journal of Economics*, vol. 93 (May 1979), pp. 206–207.

9. The estimated regression equation was:

$$\text{SIGMA/MEAN} = \underset{(3.73)}{56.3} - \underset{(0.60)}{.021} \quad \text{VALUE}$$

$$- \underset{(0.68)}{3.78} \quad \text{SERVICE} - \underset{(1.92)}{11.97} \text{ NATBRD}$$

$$- \underset{(2.05)}{8.36} \text{ SQRTNR}, \quad R^2 = .224, \quad N = 39;$$

where SIGMA/MEAN is the ratio of the standard deviation of prices to mean reported prices (in percent), VALUE is the average value of the quoted transaction, SERVICE is a dummy variable for service (as contrasted to goods) quotations, NATBRD is a dummy variable with value of unity when nationally known branded items were requested, and SQRTNR is the square root of the number of price quotations sought. The values in parentheses are t-ratios. The SQRTNR variable is included because the number of quotations appears the denominator of the calculated standard deviations.

10. John E. Kwoka, Jr., "Advertising and the Price and Quality of Optometric Services," *American Economic Review*, vol. 74 (March 1984), pp. 211–216, extending an analysis by Ronald Bond et al., *Effects of Restrictions on Advertising and Commercial Practice in the Professions: The Case of Optometry*, Federal Trade Commission staff report (Washington: USGPO, 1980). An earlier study with similar findings for the dispensing of eyeglasses was Lee Benham, "The Effect of Advertising on the Price of Eyeglasses," *Journal of Law & Economics*, vol. 15 (October 1972), pp. 337–352. Similar results were obtained with less satisfactory controls for the type and magnitude of advertising by attorneys in John R. Schroeter, Scott L. Smith, and Steven R. Cox, "Advertising and Competition in Routine Legal Services Markets," *Journal of Industrial Economics*, vol. 36 (September 1987), pp. 49–60.

In "Advertising, Information, and Prices—A Case Study," *Economic Inquiry*, vol. 19 (October 1981), pp. 661–671, Amihai Glazer reports that supermarket food prices in Queens, New York, rose relative to those on Long Island when a 1978 strike caused the three leading New York City newspapers to suspend publication while *Newsday* of Long Island continued to publish.

11. There is an extensive but ultimately inconclusive theoretical literature on Edward H. Chamberlin's contention that product

differentiation, supported in part by advertising, leads firms into equilibrium on the falling segment of their long-run average total cost function, thereby sacrificing some scale economies. *The Theory of Monopolistic Competition* (Cambridge: Harvard University Press, 1933), Chapter 7. Significant contributions include Nicholas Kaldor, "The Economic Aspects of Advertising," *Review of Economic Studies*, vol. 18 (1950), pp. 1–27; Harold Demsetz, "The Nature of Equilibrium in Monopolistic Competition," *Journal of Political Economy*, vol. 67 (February 1959), pp. 21–30; Richard Schmalensee, "A Note on Monopolistic Competition and Excess Capacity," with a reply by Demsetz, *Journal of Political Economy*, vol. 80 (May/June 1972), pp. 586–597; Arthur S. De Vany and Thomas R. Saving, "The Economics of Quality," *Journal of Political Economy*, vol. 91 (December 1983), pp. 979–1000; and Melvin L. Greenhut, George Norman, and Chao-shun Hung, *The Economics of Imperfect Competition: A Spatial Approach* (Cambridge: Cambridge University Press, 1987), especially Chapters 18–20.

12. Neil H. Borden, *The Economic Effects of Advertising* (Chicago: Irwin, 1942), pp. 121–123.

13. Robert L. Steiner, "Does Advertising Lower Consumer Prices?" *Journal of Marketing*, vol. 37 (October 1973), pp. 19–26; and "Basic Relationships in Consumer Goods Industries," *Research in Marketing*, vol. 7 (1984), pp. 165–208. For a mathematical treatment, see Michael Lynch, "The 'Steiner Effect': A Prediction from a Monopolistically Competitive Model Inconsistent with any Combination of Pure Monopoly or Competition," Federal Trade Commission Bureau of Economics working paper no. 141 (August 1986).

That *price* advertising in national magazines is infrequent is shown through a survey by Alfred Arterburn and John Woodbury, "Advertising, Price Competition and Market Structure," *Southern Economic Journal*, vol. 47 (January 1981), pp. 763–775. The fraction of insertions mentioning price averaged 29 percent, with a range of from 0 percent in several food categories to 100 percent for games and toys (the original locus of Steiner's manufacturer-retailer power observations). Price advertising was more common in less concentrated industries. It fell with the intensity of advertising in convenience goods industries (those in which small purchases are made repetitively) but rose in nonconvenience goods industries.

14. See the profit-maximizing price-cost margin formula derived in Chapter 2, note 36, and p. 229 supra.

of shelf space with a given price-cost markup.[15] Whether the lower retail margins on advertised items translate into lower prices for consumers is less clear. Products with strong consumer franchises can command relatively high wholesale prices, all else (including manufacturing and distribution scale economies) held equal, and the sum of the high wholesale price plus a thin retailing margin may be a high retail price. However, the outcome can reverse if a product line has entered a relatively mature life cycle phase in which highly advertised brands face strong price competition from other advertised brands or unadvertised (for example, private-label) brands recognized by consumers to be of comparable quality. Then the combination of strong competition among retailers to stock well-known brands plus strong competition among manufacturers for consumers' patronage may mean that consumer prices will be lower than they would be in the absence of national advertising.[16] We shall have more to say about these tendencies in a later section.

A quite different explanation of the informational role advertising plays was advanced initially by Phillip Nelson.[17] He argued that no matter how little solid information advertisements contain, they at least signal to would-be consumers that a product exists and that the originator is sufficiently confident of the product's merits to spend money advertising it. For experience goods, that is, products whose quality can only be ascertained through actual consumption experience rather than prepurchase inspection, the advertisements say in effect, "Try me, you'll like me." If trial is induced and the consumer finds the product satisfactory, repeat purchases ensue. The greater a product's superiority, the higher will be the probability of repeat purchases, and hence the larger is the stream of continuing profits anticipated by a firm using advertising to induce trial, and thus the more it pays to advertise. From this, Nelson concludes that the most highly advertised products are in fact the best buys.

The Nelson theory has been subjected to rich elaboration, revealing that its implications are sensitive to variations in the assumptions. When consumers have difficulty assessing quality even after trial, or when prices rise less rapidly than production costs with increasing product quality, paradoxes may arise, for example, poor-quality brands may advertise as heavily as the best brands.[18] If some consumers choose products on the basis of advertising while others search for the best buys, advertising may signal goods to be of more uniform quality, but not of the best quality.[19] And consumers may be guided by high prices as well as, or instead of, high advertising as signals of high quality.[20]

Tests of these "signaling" theories of advertising and price have yielded equivocal results. One problem is that quality is often multidimensional, and a product superior on one attribute is commonly inferior on another, so no unambiguous correlation with unidimensional signals such as advertising outlays or price may exist. Investigating 10,162 brands in 685 product categories, Peter Reisz found only a weak average correlation of 0.26 between prices and the quality ratings assigned through Consumers Union tests.[21] In a more narrowly focused study, Archibald and colleagues found that prices and advertising levels for 187 individual runners' shoe designs were only weakly correlated with quality ratings by the magazine *Runner's World* before those ratings were published, but *after* the ratings were published, the advertising correlation jumped to $+0.61$.[22] The price correlations, on the other hand, changed only slightly. The implication appears to be that the availability of an authoritative, "advertisable" mark of superior quality stimulated advertising by the high-quality producers. However, this finding may not generalize to other products, at least in the United States, since the leading source of objective quality evaluations, *Consumer Reports*, unlike *Runner's World*, does not allow advertisers to quote its ratings.

Other Reputation Effects   Whether or not it is related in any close way to advertising levels, the information created through image differentiation can help consumers select products of high quality and reliability and motivate producers to maintain adequate quality standards. If there were no brand names and trademarks, the consumer might never be sure who made a product, and she would have difficulty rewarding through repeat purchases manufacturers who achieve high quality, or cater to her special tastes. This is a lesson that dawned late but forcefully upon Soviet Union economic planners, who found that requiring consumer goods manufacturers to imprint their individual "production marks" on products helped guard against

15. For new survey evidence that retail margins are lower on nationally advertised food items, see Mark S. Albion, *Advertising's Hidden Effects: Manufacturers' Advertising and Retail Pricing* (Boston: Auburn House, 1983). For statistical evidence that the relationship may not carry over to products sold in other specialized retail outlets, see Weiss et al., "The Size of Selling Costs," supra note 3, p. 670.

16. In a survey of 2,700 *Harvard Business Review* subscribers, 82 percent of them business managers, 49 percent believed that on balance advertising led to higher prices, while 35 percent believed it led to lower prices. Stephen A. Greyser and Bonnie B. Reece, "Businessmen Look Hard at Advertising," *Harvard Business Review*, vol. 49 (May-June 1971), p. 26.

17. Phillip Nelson, "Advertising as Information," *Journal of Political Economy*, vol. 82 (July/August 1974), pp. 729–754.

18. See Richard Schmalensee, "A Model of Advertising and Product Quality," *Journal of Political Economy*, vol. 86 (June 1978), pp. 485–503; Yehuda Kotowitz and Frank Mathewson, "Advertising, Consumer Information, and Product Quality," *Bell Journal of Economics*, vol. 10 (Autumn 1979), pp. 566–588; Carl Shapiro, "Consumer Information, Product Quality, and Seller Reputation," *Bell Journal of Economics*, vol. 13 (Spring 1982), pp. 20–35; and Richard E. Kihlstrom and Michael Riordan, "Advertising As a Signal," *Journal of Political Economy*, vol. 92 (June 1984), pp. 427–450.

The paradoxes that arise here are a variant of the "lemons" problem formalized by George Akerlof in "The Market for 'Lemons': Quality Uncertainty and the Market Mechanism," *Quarterly Journal of Economics*, vol. 84 (August 1970), pp. 488–500. See also Hayne E. Leland, "Quacks, Lemons, and Licensing: A Theory of Minimum Quality Standards," *Journal of Political Economy*, vol. 87 (December 1979), pp. 1328–1346. Tests of the lemons hypothesis for used truck and car markets have been equivocal. See Eric W. Bond, "A Direct Test of the 'Lemons' Model: The Market for Used Pickup Trucks," *American Economic Review*, vol. 72 (September 1982), pp. 836–840, with comment by Michael D. Pratt and George Hoffer and reply by Bond, *American Economic Review*, vol. 74 (September 1984), pp. 798–804; and James M. Lacko, *Product Quality and Information in the Used Car Market*, Federal Trade Commission Bureau of Economics staff report (Washington: April 1986).

19. Steven N. Wiggins and W. J. Lane, "Quality Uncertainty, Search, and Advertising," *American Economic Review*, vol. 73 (December 1983), pp. 881–894.

20. Paul Milgrom and John Roberts, "Price and Advertising Signals of Product Quality," *Journal of Political Economy*, vol. 94 (August 1986), pp. 796–821; Benjamin Klein and Keith B. Leffler, "The Role of Market Forces in Assuring Contractual Performance," *Journal of Political Economy*, vol. 89 (August 1981), pp. 615–641; Asher Wolinsky, "Prices as Signals of Product Quality," *Review of Economic Studies*, vol. 50 (October 1983), pp. 647–658; and Alan Schwartz and Louis Wilde, "Product Quality and Imperfect Information," *Review of Economic Studies*, vol. 52 (April 1985), pp. 251–262.

21. Peter C. Riesz, "Price versus Quality in the Marketplace, 1961–1975," *Journal of Retailing*, vol. 54 (Winter 1978), pp. 15–28. See also Christian Hjorth-Anderson, "Price and Quality of Industrial Products: Some Results of an Empirical Investigation," *Scandinavian Journal of Economics*, vol. 83, no. 3 (1981), pp. 372–389, who obtained similar results in a study of 87 Danish products. Thomas Russell and Richard Thaler, "The Relevance of Quasi Rationality in Competitive Markets," *American Economic Review*, vol. 75 (December 1985), pp. 1078–1080, summarize two studies showing that the highest-priced air conditioners had the best energy efficiencies and the highest-priced dishwashing liquids the greatest washing power per ounce and penny. The implication drawn by Russell and Thaler is that consumers often focus on product dimensions (e.g., bulk or price per se) that are imperfect indicators of value.

22. Robert B. Archibald, C. A. Haulman, and C. E. Moody, "Quality, Price, Advertising, and Published Quality Ratings," *Journal of Consumer Research*, vol. 9 (March 1983), pp. 347–353.

deteriorating quality standards.[23] And although there may be incentives to cash in on a good reputation by letting the quality of infrequently purchased durable goods deteriorate,[24] the costs of quality failures serious enough to attract public attention are plainly significant. When pharmaceuticals and automobiles were recalled or taken off the market because of late-emerging product hazards, company stock prices declined much more than the cost of remedying the problems, suggesting that the companies also suffered reputation effects impairing the sale of other, possibly unrelated products.[25] A market survey revealed that 90 percent of the buyers experiencing costly problems with purchased durable goods did not make additional purchases from the offending manufacturer if nothing was done to correct the problem, but that 54 percent remained loyal when complaints were satisfactorily handled.[26]

For an auto manufacturer, the discounted present value of sales gained by keeping buyers satisfied over their lifetimes was estimated at $142,000; for a supermarket, $22,000 over a five-year period.[27] The research that yielded these estimates was motivated in part by recognition that in the past, manufacturers did not take sufficient precautions to control quality at levels maintaining their reputations. Whether image-preserving performance will improve in the future remains to be seen.

Trademarking and brand labeling also contribute in subtle ways to distributional efficiency.[28] Without them, the conscientious shopper would have to make repeated inquiries about experience goods susceptible to quality or taste variations, asking whether a particular product was good, what its distinguishing characteristics were, and perhaps (as in the almost bygone days of the pickle barrel) whether he might try a sample. This takes a great deal of time for both merchants and shoppers, increasing transaction costs—the more so, the more prosperous consumers are, and hence the greater is the opportunity cost of their time. The information conveyed by brand names on goods whose characteristics vary little from week to week makes it possible to have convenient self-service shopping and hence to realize the efficiencies of supermarkets. Whether mere trademarking is sufficient to achieve this desirable end, or whether brand images must be reinforced by advertising of greater or lesser intensity, remains uncertain.

Advertising and Product Innovation

Whether or not information on price and other objective attributes is provided, advertising also communicates the availability of new products, accelerating first trial and helping innovators tap larger markets more rapidly. This in turn enhances the profits from innovation and strengthens incentives for timely investment in product R&D.[29] How intense advertising must be to achieve this function is debatable. As a glance at Table 16.2 reveals, the fields in which advertising outlays are highest in relation to sales are not exactly those in which human welfare has taken giant strides through technological change. Statistical investigations suggest that R&D/sales ratios are higher in industries with relatively intense advertising. However, the estimated relationship is weakest, falling short of statistical significance, in the study using the highest-quality data and the most extensive controls for other R&D-influencing variables.[30] Thus, although advertising almost surely facilitates the introduction of technologically new products, the effect probably operates within modest thresholds, subject to attenuation at high advertising intensities.

More Global Effects

Advertising also has several broader effects on the provision of information and the quality of life. For one, it is an important source of revenue to the mass communications media, upon which citizens depend for information on many things other than the products they consume. During the late 1970s, the sale of advertising space or time provided roughly 71 percent of American newspapers' gross revenues, half of general periodicals' revenues, and (excluding educational stations) virtually all the revenue of radio and television broadcasters.[31] For the typical newspaper, the marginal cost of printing an extra copy is less than the revenue received from readers, but newsstand and subscription revenue is profitably supplemented by the higher advertising charges that can be levied with additional readership. Such contributions are a mixed blessing. They may undermine what might otherwise be an important external benefit of the mass media — the cultivation of a sensitive, informed public. Consumer goods advertisers tend to favor media that will transmit their message to the largest relevant audience, and when radio frequency band restrictions or economies of scale severely limit the number of television stations or newspapers, the media attempt to maximize audience size by appealing to the lowest common denominator. The result is the scandal sheet and television's "vast wasteland," to quote the words of Federal Communications Commission chairman Newton Minow, as true now as when they were uttered in 1961. Indeed, many TV programs are of such low intellectual caliber that the commercials stand out as a refreshingly sophisticated interlude.

On a quite different plane, there has been a lively but thus far inconclusive debate over whether advertising, and especially the persuasive advertising that alters consumers' preferences, adds more to economic welfare than its costs.[32]

23. See Marshall Goldman, "Product Differentiation and Advertising: Some Lessons from Soviet Experience," *Journal of Political Economy*, vol. 68 (August 1960), pp. 346–357. For a more skeptical view, see Philip Hanson, *The Consumer in the Soviet Economy* (London: Macmillan, 1969), pp. 204–206.

24. See, for example, Kotowitz and Mathewson, "Advertising," and Shapiro, "Consumer Information," supra note 18. Compare C. C. von Weizsäcker, *Barriers to Entry* (Berlin: Springer, 1980), Chapters 5 and 6.

25. Gregg Jarrell and Sam Peltzman, "The Impact of Product Recalls on the Wealth of Sellers," *Journal of Political Economy*, vol. 93 (June 1985), pp. 512–536.

26. See "Making Service a Potent Marketing Tool, *Business Week*, June 11, 1984, p. 165; and "Complaints? I Love 'em," *The Economist*, November 5, 1988, p. 78.

27. "Making Service," p. 167. See also Borden, *The Economic Effects*, supra note 12, pp. 631–632 and 866.

28. See, for example, William M. Landes and Richard A. Posner, "Trademark Law: An Economic Perspective," *Journal of Law & Economics*, vol. 30 (October 1987), pp. 265–309.

29. See F. M. Scherer, "Research and Development Resource Allocation under Rivalry," *Quarterly Journal of Economics*, vol. 81 (August 1967), pp. 368 and 388; and Yehuda Kotowitz and Frank Mathewson, "Informative Advertising and Welfare," *American Economic Review*, vol. 69 (June 1979), pp. 284–294.

30. John Lunn and Stephen Martin, "Market Structure, Firm Structure, and Research and Development," *Quarterly Review of Economics and Business*, vol. 26 (Spring 1986), pp. 31–44. See also Stephen Farber, "Buyer Market Structure and R&D Effort: A Simultaneous Equations Model," *Review of Economics and Statistics*, vol. 63 (August 1981), pp. 336–345; David G. Hula, "Advertising, New Product Profit Expectations, and the Firm's R&D Investment Decisions," *Applied Economics*, vol. 20 (January 1988), pp. 125–142; and (on pharmaceuticals only) Keith B. Leffler, "Persuasion or Information? The Economics of Prescription Drug Advertising," *Journal of Law & Economics*, vol. 24 (April 1981), pp. 45–74.

31. U.S. Bureau of the Census, *Statistical Abstract of the United States: 1979* (Washington: USGPO, 1979), p. 591. Later editions lack comparable data.

32. See Avinash K. Dixit and Victor D. Norman, "Advertising and Welfare," *Bell Journal of Economics*, vol. 9 (Spring 1978), with comments by Franklin Fisher, John McGowan, and Carl Shapiro and replies by Dixit and Norman, *Bell Journal of Economics*, vol. 10 (Autumn 1979), pp. 726–729 and vol. 11 (Autumn 1980), pp. 749–754. The debate encroaches on, but in the end misses the point of, the analysis in Chapter 15, pp. 542–548 supra.

For analyses of advertising's effects from more qualitative perspectives, see Jules Henry, *Culture Against Man* (New York: Random House, 1963), Chapters 2 and 3; Walter Taplin, *Advertising: A New Approach* (Boston: Little, Brown, 1963); and Michael Schudson, *Advertising, the Uneasy Persuasion* (New York: Basic Books, 1984).

Often overlooked in such debates is the fact that advertising can destroy utility along with creating it. Much advertising leads consumers to make introspective comparisons between their own well-being and that of people they admire or would like to emulate. Translated into economic jargon, advertising seeks to make the utility of individual consumers depend not only upon the goods and services they themselves consume, but also upon the consumption decisions of their peers. It renders utility functions interdependent, generating external diseconomies in consumption. To be sure, by purchasing an advertised product in response to the message that they are not consuming what the "right" people consume, individuals may feel they are gaining something worthwhile. But it is not clear they have done any more than return to the satisfaction level they would have maintained without the persuasive assault on their preference structures.

Finally, it is sometimes urged that advertising has macroeconomic effects, for example, through the direct contribution advertising activity makes to aggregate demand and the indirect impact of persuasive advertising in altering marginal propensities to consume. On the first point, the evidence is clear. Advertising expenditures are mildly destabilizing to the macroeconomy, rising in booms and falling during recessions.[33] On the second point, a mixed and more uncertain verdict must be rendered. Analyses of the time-series relationship between aggregate advertising outlays and changes in national consumption or saving have yielded conflicting results, with negative findings emerging *inter alia* from the most recent studies using relatively new Granger-Sims techniques for ascertaining causal priority.[34] It is questionable, however, whether there is enough year-to-year variation in national aggregates for even the most powerful time-series methods to extract conclusive results. A more promising but largely neglected approach might be the analysis of differences in advertising and savings rates across nations. Advertising expenditures as a percent of gross national product, averaged over the years 1977 to 1980, varied widely among relatively industrialized nations, for example, 0.33 percent for Italy, 0.45 percent for Sweden, 0.84 percent for West Germany, 0.93 percent for Japan, 1.28 percent for the United Kingdom, and 1.59 percent for the United States.[35] For fifteen such nations, the simple correlation between 1977-1980 advertising/GNP ratios and the ratio of 1978–1981 personal saving to disposable household income was -0.35. The more intense national advertising was, the lower the savings rate. However, advertising intensities were positively correlated with gross national product per capita, which in turn was negatively correlated with savings rates ($r = -0.50$). When both advertising intensities and GNP per capita were included as independent variables in a regression seeking to explain international savings rate differences, both had negative coefficients, but neither was statistically significant.[36] Further work with richer data and a more fully specified econometric model is needed to determine whether advertising in fact tends to raise consumption propensities.[37]

Advertising, Image, and Monopoly Power

Some advertising, by increasing consumers' objective knowledge about product alternatives and prices, helps perfect competition. Other advertising, by creating or reinforcing consumer preferences for particular brands and making the demand for those differentiated brands less elastic, can increase monopoly power. How these effects balance out is vigorously disputed. Here we begin our analysis of the monopoly nexus.

That prices are affected when a product has a superior image linked (in ways yet to be pinpointed) with advertising is readily apparent from a trip through any supermarket. One of the clearest cases is old-fashioned liquid laundry bleach, which is offered as a rigidly standardized 5.25 percent sodium hypochlorite solution. Visits to five retail food stores in the western Philadelphia suburbs during October 1988 revealed prices for two-quart containers of nationally advertised Clorox of $.99 (twice), $1.09, and (in a Seven-Eleven convenience outlet) $1.15. Local and private-label brands were available in the three larger stores, in each instance in an adjacent shelf position, at prices 14 to 40 percent lower than that of Clorox. An older example particularly well documented because of an (ultimately unsuccessful) antitrust suit concerns reconstituted bottled lemon juice. The product is easy to make, and (with minor exceptions) the diverse producers' offerings were physically identical. The leading seller's 1971 marketing plan stated as its objective:

> Although reconstituted lemon juice is virtually indistinguishable one brand from another, heavy emphasis on the ReaLemon® brand through its media effort should create such memorability for the brand, that an almost imaginary

33. See Borden, *The Economic Effects*, supra note 12, pp. 735–736 and 865–866; Julian Simon, *Issues in the Economics of Advertising* (Urbana: University of Illinois Press, 1970), pp. 67–74; Richard Schmalensee, *The Economics of Advertising* (Amsterdam: North-Holland, 1972), pp. 58–75; and Ingo Böbel, "Advertising and Economic Development: The West German Experience During the 1970s," *Journal of Advertising*, vol. 1 (July-September 1982), pp. 237–252.

34. Advertising was found to have a positive influence on aggregate consumption in Lester D. Taylor and Daniel Weiserbs, "Advertising and the Aggregate Consumption Function," *American Economic Review*, vol. 62 (September 1972), pp. 642–655; William S. Comanor and Thomas A. Wilson, *Advertising and Market Power* (Cambridge: Harvard University Press, 1974), Chapter 5; and (for Australia) M. M. Metwally and H. U. Tamaschke, "Advertising and the Propensity To Consume," *Oxford Bulletin of Economics and Statistics*, vol. 43 (August 1981), pp. 273–284. Negative inferences were drawn by Richard Schmalensee, *The Economics of Advertising*, supra note 33, pp. 48–86; Simon, *Issues*, supra note 33, pp. 193–206; R. Ashley, C. W. J. Granger, and R. Schmalensee, "Advertising and Aggregate Consumption: An Analysis of Causality," *Econometrica*, vol. 48 (July 1980), pp. 1149–1167; and Brian T. Sturgess and Nicholas Wilson, "Advertising Expenditure and Aggregate Consumption in Britain and West Germany: An Analysis of Causality," *Managerial and Decision Economics*, vol. 5 (December 1984), pp. 219–227.

35. "Trends in Total Advertising Expenditures in 29 Countries, 1970-1980," *Journal of Advertising*, vol. 1 (January-March 1982), pp. 57–88. Only the data for OECD member nations (that is, the more industrialized nations) are analyzed here. Personal saving data were obtained from Organization for Economic Cooperation and Development, *Historical Statistics: 1960–82* (Paris: 1984), Table 6–18; and GNP per capita data from U.S. Bureau of the Census, *Statistical Abstract of the United States: 1980* (Washington: USGPO, 1980), p. 910.

36. The regression was:

$$\text{SAVING} = \underset{(5.15)}{22.6} - \underset{(0.93)}{3.03} \text{ ADVERT}$$
$$- \underset{(1.73)}{0.77} \text{ GNP/CAP}, \quad R^2 = .303$$

where SAVING is 1978–1981 personal saving as a percent of personal disposable income, ADVERT is 1977–1980 advertising as a percent of gross national product, and GNP/CAP is 1978 gross national product in thousands of dollars per capita. T-ratios are in parentheses. Despite one chance in three that the true effect is zero, the ADVERT effect is not trivial; a two standard deviation increase in advertising implies a 2.4 percentage point reduction in the savings rate.

37. For a much more richly specified model explaining advertising/GNP ratios for 1968–1979 samples covering forty-three nations, see Seymour Banks, "Cross-National Analysis of Advertising Expenditures: 1968–1979," *Journal of Advertising Research*, vol. 26 (April/May 1986), pp. 11–16. Banks finds a cluster of variables closely associated with the level of economic development (for example, GNP per capita) to be the strongest positive predictor of advertising intensities.

superiority would exist in the mind of the consumer, a justification for paying the higher price we are asking.[38]

Recognizing their name as "one of the greatest brand names in the history of the supermarket," ReaLemon's producers were able in 1973 to command a sixty-two-cent price for their product and capture 80 percent of all reconstituted lemon juice sales while the price of the principal competitive brand, Golden Crown, was forty-six to forty-eight cents.[39]

These cases are apparently not exceptional. Double-blind experiments have repeatedly demonstrated that consumers cannot consistently distinguish premium from popular-priced beer brands, but exhibit definite preferences for the premium brands when labels are affixed—correctly or not.[40] More generally, the staff of the National Commission on Food Marketing found through a sample survey of ten canned and bottled food products that the price of the most popular nationally advertised brand sold in chain stores was 21.5 percent higher on average than the prices for private-label items of comparable quality.[41] A survey of from forty-six to fifty-seven products sold by three food chains in 1974 revealed that private-label product prices averaged 8 to 13 percent less than national brand prices.[42]

Price differentials between nationally branded and less well-known items appear to be especially large for medicinal products. A 1989 shopping trip in the Western Philadelphia suburbs revealed 100-tablet bottles of Bayer aspirin to be priced between $4.39 and $4.59 in three drug stores and at $7.11 in an outlet serving the captive Swarthmore College student market. Generic aspirin could be obtained at prices between $1.19 and $2.19 per 100 tablets, the highest price again prevailing in the store adjoining Swarthmore College's campus. In a similar experiment eleven years earlier, the cheapest brand was purchased and found to have a binder inferior to Bayer's; its dissolving time on the tongue was roughly thirty-five seconds, compared to twenty-two seconds for Bayer. That the level of prices depends upon the strength of one's trademark position is suggested through an international comparison. In West Germany, the Bayer Company (which held the original patent) has exclusive rights to the name "Aspirin" as well as "Bayer;" others must use different brand designations or the generic name acetylsalicylic acid (equally jaw-breaking in German). A survey of three West German pharmacies in 1989 revealed the prices of Bayer "Aspirin" clustered tightly about an average value of $6.03 for 100 tablets.[43]

How Premium Brand Images Arise

How does a firm obtain a superior brand image, permitting the maintenance of price differentials relative to less well-known brands? And what role does advertising play in image creation?

That advertising matters is shown by the history of the U.S. beer industry. The industry is unique in the sense that more than 700 participants came off the starting blocks virtually simultaneously in 1933, when the thirteen-year constitutional ban on the production and sale of alcoholic beverages was repealed. Unlike the vast majority of brewers, who viewed their markets as essentially local, a few Midwestern brewers—notably, Anheuser-Busch (Budweiser), Schlitz, Pabst, and Miller—chose at that time to market their products nationally. Since transportation costs from the Midwest to the east and west coasts added 25 to 30 percent to costs, higher prices had to be charged, and to justify the higher prices absent recognizable taste or quality differences, the national sellers advertised their brands as "premium," justifying a price differential over "popular" local brands. At first this strategy allowed the premium brands to capture only a few percent of the national market, but as increasingly prosperous consumers sought to trade up to higher quality during the 1950s and 1960s, the national brewers gained market share rapidly, reinforcing their growth with heavy advertising. The retention of a premium image was not, however, automatic. After encountering marketing setbacks during the 1960s, Pabst experimented with systematic reductions in its price to "popular" levels. At first this paid off in significant volume gains, but as the price reductions were extended, Pabst found that its premium image had been eroded, and in most states it was unable to return to premium-price levels. The image of Schlitz, once the nation's leading seller, was tarnished during the 1970s through a product reformulation that failed to capture consumers' approval.[44] The field was left to Budweiser and Miller, joined by Coors, which had pursued a later move to national premium status.

Equally informative is the story of the U.S. industry's most significant post-Prohibition innovation, "light" beer. When it was acquired by Miller in 1972, Meister Brau, Inc. had been selling small quantities of a light beer, one of several on the market, targeted toward diet-conscious women. Reconsidering the acquired brand's potential, Miller discovered through in-depth marketing research that an important market segment was badly served: its members wanted to guzzle numerous beers in a sitting, but were concerned about the weight gain consequences. Miller therefore retargeted its acquired "Lite" brand toward heavy drinkers, supporting it with a massive television advertising campaign featuring charismatic sports heroes proclaiming that with Miller Lite, they could drink as much as they wanted without feeling filled up. Its success was spectacular. By

38. Quoted in the initial decision of the administrative law judge *In the Matter of Borden, Inc.*, 92 F.T.C. 669 (1978), para. 83. For a dissenting view, suggesting that lower-priced brands may on occasion have experienced random or deliberate quality variations, see Clement G. Krouse, "Brand Name as a Barrier to Entry: The ReaLemon Case," *Southern Economic Journal*, vol. 51 (October 1984), pp. 498–492.

39. *In re Borden*, para. 75, 81, and 82.

40. Douglas F. Greer, *Industrial Organization and Public Policy* (New York: Macmillan, 1980), pp. 87–90.

41. U.S. National Commission on Food Marketing, *Special Studies in Food Marketing*, Technical Study No. 10 (Washington: USGPO, June 1966), p. 65.

42. Willard F. Mueller et al., *The Profit and Price Performance of Leading Food Chains, 1970–74*, report issued by U.S. Congress, Joint Economic Committee (Washington: USGPO, April 1977), p. 67.

43. The German tablets were in a 500-mg. dosage size while the standard American tablets contained only 324 mg. A price adjustment was made to compare identical dosage sizes. The prevailing exchange rate of $1 = DM 1.88 was used. If the U.S. market basket purchasing power parity rate of approximately DM 2.30 is used, the Bayer price average for Germany was $4.93. Non-Bayer branded acetylsalicylic acid tablets were available at an average price of $2.59 at prevailing exchange rates or $2.11 at purchasing power parity.

For a fascinating history of the discovery and marketing of aspirin and its newer substitutes and an analysis of the continuously misleading advertising used to differentiate brands, see Charles C. Mann and Mark L. Plummer, "The Big Headache," *The Atlantic Monthly*, October 1986, pp. 39–57.

44. Carling's, once the leading beer brand in Canada, lost its position when an additive used in Quebec proved to be lethal to a few consumers who drank prodigious quantities daily.

In automobiles, inept styling and inattention to other aspects of quality caused Cadillac to lose its image as the premier U.S. luxury car to Mercedes and BMW. See "Europe's Luxury Models Defy the Sales Slump," *Business Week*, August 9, 1982, p. 25; "Cadillac Seeks Sales To Match Its Image," *Advertising Age*, September 9, 1985, p. 10; and "Cadillac's Allante Struggles," *New York Times*, November 16, 1987, p. D–1.

1986, every major brewer had its own imitation, and the light beer market had expanded to 37 million barrels, or 19 percent of all beer sold nationally. Yet Miller's "Lite," costing less to produce than premium beer but selling at premium prices, retained 54 percent of the product segment it had pioneered.

In beer, premium images rested upon what (in hindsight) proved to be astute product positioning reinforced by appropriate advertising. New technology played no significant role. For a different perspective, we draw upon a Federal Trade Commission study of pharmaceuticals that yielded results radically different from the hypotheses with which it began.[45] Believing that technological advance and patent protection were crucial variables in establishing leading pharmaceutical market positions, the FTC staff selected for detailed research two quite different product groups, one with significant technological breakthroughs and heavy patenting and one without.

In the oral diuretic (that is, body fluid- and hence hypertension-reducing) drug field, Merck made a key technical advance leading to the introduction in 1958 of the product Diuril (chlorothiazide). Inventing around Merck's patent proved to be easy, and within two years ten other firms were offering therapeutically equivalent substitutes. Yet thirteen years later, after further entry had occurred and improved products had been fielded by several competitors, Merck retained a 33 percent share of the oral diuretic market, despite the fact that it spent only three-eighths as much per sales dollar as its rivals on sales promotion and charged a price four times as high as Abbott Laboratories' chemically equivalent brand of hydro-chlorothiazide. Among Merck's competitors, those who captured the largest market shares were for the most part those whose products first offered important therapeutic advantages over the pioneering diuretics.

The experience of Warner-Lambert with its pioneering drug Peritrate (that is, pentaerythritol tetranitrate — PETN) for angina pectoris therapy was surprisingly similar. Warner-Lambert introduced Peritrate in 1952, attracted nearly one hundred competitors, charged prices averaging five to six times higher than chemically identical substitutes, and spent less on promotion per sales dollar than rivals; and yet two decades later, it retained a 30 percent share of the antianginal drug market. Compared to the oral diuretic case, there were only two noteworthy differences. First, Warner-Lambert was neither the technological inventor nor the first to use PETN in treating angina pectoris. Rather, its contribution was to take that already known and unpatented entity, give it a brand name, and promote it vigorously to physicians for anginal therapy, in which nitroglycerin and various nitrites had previously been the drugs of choice. Second, the promotion of Peritrate and similar nitrates emphasized their use in long-term prophylactic therapy, but objective studies cast doubt over whether the early versions were in fact more effective than older entities or even a placebo.[46] Thus, in the case of Peritrate, as in beer, it was marketing innovation, not technological innovation, that gave Warner-Lambert a highly profitable image advantage.

Innovation is the key word emerging from these and other studies of leading brands' image advantages. It is questionable whether a superior image can be created simply by advertising vigorously. Rather, something more is needed. That "something more" is usually an innovative act of some sort. The innovation may be technological, as in the case of Diuril, or it may be rooted in advertising, but add new insights into the uses of a product, as with Peritrate and Lite beer. Whatever its source, the image advantage that comes from consumer recognition as the first mover in some product category may permit its possessor to hold prices above costs for significant periods of time while retaining a large share of the relevant market.

The links between image advantages, market share, and a history of having been a first mover have received impressive statistical confirmation. The PIMS (Profit Impact of Market Strategies) data base is unique in providing quantitative information on all three variables (plus many others) for numerous narrowly defined business units. Participating units were asked *inter alia* whether, at the time they first entered the relevant market, they were "one of the pioneers in first developing such products or services," "an early follower," or a later entrant. They also estimated the percentage of their sales volume comprising products *perceived by consumers* to be superior in quality to those of their three leading competitors.[47] The "relative quality" variable is avowedly subjective, emphasizing consumers' perception rather than imposing an objective standard, and hence corresponds closely to the notion of product image. For a sample of consumer goods industries, Robinson and Fornell found that having been a pioneer added 21 percentage points to a business unit's relative product quality index (whose overall sample mean was 24).[48] The pioneer's image impact was only half as great, however, for mature products — that is, those in which the pioneering occurred twenty or more years earlier. In a separate analysis, Robinson found that perceived relative quality rose by only 7.6 percentage points on average in pioneering businesses selling *industrial* products, whose customers are more apt to judge sellers on the basis of careful objective analysis than from subjective reputation.[49] In both consumer goods and industrial product businesses, pioneers also had significantly broader product lines than their followers. Higher perceived quality led in turn to prices higher than those of competitors and (in conjunction with product line breadth) to substantially greater market shares. With all influences combined, pioneers had market shares 23.6 percentage points higher than those of late entrants in consumer goods lines and 17.2 points higher in industrial goods lines, although the advantages declined to 12.8 and 13.0 percentage points respectively in lines where the pioneering had occurred twenty or more years earlier. The pioneers' market share gains were greatest in consumer product lines with low purchase prices and low

45. Ronald S. Bond and David F. Lean, *Sales, Promotion, and Product Differentiation in Two Prescription Drug Markets*, Federal Trade Commission staff report (Washington: USGPO, February 1977); and idem, "Consumer Preference, Advertising, and Sales: On the Advantage from Early Entry," Federal Trade Commission Bureau of Economics working paper no. 14 (October 1979).

46. See Bond and Lean, *Two Prescription Drug Markets*, pp. 47–49; and (on more recent developments) Peter O. Oberender, "Cost-Benefit Analysis of Angina Prophylaxis in the Federal Republic of Germany," in W. van Eimeren and B. Horisberger, eds., *Socioeconomic Evaluation of Drug Therapy* (Berlin: Springer, 1988), pp. 132–140.

47. Strategic Planning Institute, *PIMS Data Manual* (Cambridge: February 1978), p. 3–50.

48. William T. Robinson and Claes Fornell, "Sources of Market Pioneer Advantages in Consumer Goods Industries," *Journal of Marketing Research*, vol. 22 (August 1985), pp. 305–317. An earlier but more limited analysis in the same spirit was Robert D. Buzzell and Paul Ferris, "Marketing Costs in Consumer Goods Industries," in Hans Thorelli, ed., *Strategy + Structure = Performance* (Bloomington: Indiana University Press, 1977), pp. 122–145. They found that consumer goods pioneers spent 1.45 cents per sales dollar less on advertising and promotion than early followers, who in turn had a 2.1 cent advantage over late entrants, all else equal.

49. William T. Robinson, "Sources of Market Pioneer Advantages: The Case of Industrial Goods Industries," *Journal of Marketing Research*, vol. 25 (February 1988), pp. 87–94.

purchase frequencies — that is, those for which search may be more trouble than it is worth and learning by trial and error relatively slow. They were lower in consumer product lines with annual or periodic design changes and even more so in lines with seasonal product changes — those in which reputation or image might be considered a less reliable basis for judging new offerings.

The Pricing Implications of Image Advantages

A clear recognition of the links between being a first mover in some product line and monopoly power — that is, the ability to hold prices above costs while defending a sizable market share — emerged from several empirical studies during the 1970s. The next task was to shape a theory that fit the facts. There have been several contributions. Here we characterize the work of the first mover, Richard Schmalensee.[50]

Schmalensee's analysis focuses on experience goods, whose properties can be ascertained by trial. The first key question is, when will a consumer try some product? Trial will occur, Schmalensee argues, when the discounted present value of consumer's surplus expected through trial exceeds the similarly discounted consumer's surplus expected from continuing to use the product already accepted. The surplus anticipated from trial is the probability-weighted sum of the benefits from a successful trial, followed by switching to the new brand, plus the disbenefits of an unsuccessful trial (including the money wasted buying the tried product and the money value of any unpleasantness, pain, and/or embarrassment incurred) followed by a return to the old brand. These considerations are compressed into a single variable τ, which we shall call the *risk-cost factor*. τ is greater, the larger the probability, and the higher the cost to the consumer, of a bad consumption experience and the less frequently repeat purchases occur. Trial will occur then when:

$$(16.1) \qquad P < V(1 - \tau) - S$$

where P is the price at which the challenging product is offered, V is the value of the new product to the consumer if it turns out to be satisfactory, and S is the consumer's surplus realized on the product currently used, if any, in the relevant category. (For the first entrant into a new category, S = 0.) If there were no risk-cost factor τ, trial would occur whenever consumer's surplus on the new product (that is, the difference between V and P) exceeded the consumer's surplus on the old product.

However, the risk-cost factor drives a wedge between consumers' valuations of the challenging product, given pretrial uncertainty about its true merits, and their valuations assuming full posttrial information about its quality. The relevant valuations in these two cases are nothing more or less than consumers' reservation prices for the product in the pre- and posttrial states. As we learned in Chapter 2, a demand curve arrays all products consumed in descending order of consumers' reservation prices. Thus, the would-be seller of a product faces two quite different demand curves, as Figure 16.1 shows: the upper function V(Q), assuming that consumers are fully informed through trial of the well-functioning product's quality, and the lower curve $V(1 - \tau)$, assuming that consumers lack trial information and believe there is a finite probability of a bad consumption experience.

Consider now the behavior of Firm 1, the first to offer a product satisfying the demands of the consumers with tastes described by demand functions V(Q) and

Figure 16.1
Pre- and Post-trial Demand
Functions Faced by Pioneer
and Late Mover

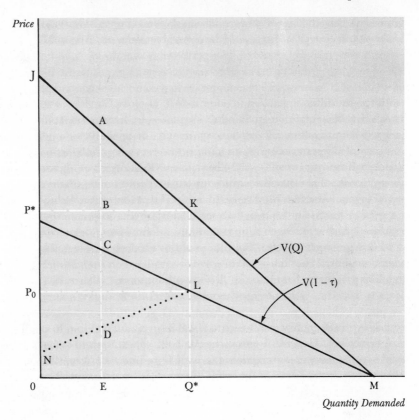

V$(1 - \tau)$. Before trial has occurred, its demand curve is V$(1 - \tau)$. Suppose the firm makes an introductory trial offer at price OP$_o$. Consumers over the output range OQ* will find their reservation prices (read along V$(1 - \tau)$ to exceed the introductory price and will try the product. Once they do, they will jump to full-information demand curve V(Q) segment JK—knowing that the product is good, they are willing to pay more for it. After the introductory period is over, first moving Firm 1 will take advantage of this demand change, raising its price to OP* and retaining the consumers it has hooked through its trial offer.

Suppose Firm 2 later markets a product of equal quality whose merits, however, can only be ascertained through trial. It faces two classes of potential customers: those who were not hooked by the first mover (arrayed over output space Q*M) and those who tried Firm 1's product and liked it (output range OQ*). Note that Firm 1's introductory offer captured all the consumers with high full-information reservation prices, leaving only less eager would-be consumers unhooked. The only unhooked consumers ceded to Firm 2 have risk-impacted reservation prices arrayed along segment LM of V$(1 - \tau)$. To win *any* of them, Firm 2

50. Richard Schmalensee, "Product Differentiation Advantages of Pioneering Brands," *American Economic Review*, vol. 72 (June 1982), pp. 349–365. See also Carl Shapiro, "Optimal Pricing of Experience Goods," *Bell Journal of Economics*, vol. 14 (Autumn 1983), pp. 497–507; Cecelia A. Conrad, "The Advantage of Being First and Competition Between Firms," *International Journal of Industrial Organization*, vol. 1 (December 1983), pp. 353–364; and Paul Klemperer, "Entry Deterrence in Markets with Consumer Switching Costs," *Economic Journal*, vol. 97 supplement (1987), pp. 99–117.

must offer an introductory price below the price OP* charged by the first mover, and to win many of them, the price will have to be much lower. This is one sense in which the second mover operates at a disadvantage. But more importantly, suppose Firm 2 targets its introductory offers at the consumers Firm 1 has already hooked. Before they were hooked, they had no alternatives in the relevant product category, so they were willing to try Firm 1's product as long as the trial price was less than their pretrial reservation prices (read off $V(1 - \tau)$). But after they are hooked, equation (16.1) (and common sense) tells us, they will try another product only if the trial price is less than their pretrial reservation price *less* the consumer's surplus they would forgo by not consuming Firm 1's tried-and-true product. To illustrate, consider a consumer whose full-information reservation price is located at point A in Figure 16.1. With pretrial reservation price EC, it was easily hooked by Firm 1 at introductory price OP_o. But despite Firm 1's posttrial price increase, it is enjoying consumer's surplus AB on Firm 1's product, and it will try Firm 2's product only if the price offered by Firm 2 is less than its pretrial reservation price EC *less* surplus AB; that is, at a price of ED or less (where by construction CD = AB). Thus, Firm 2 can win away Firm 1's customers only by offering introductory prices lower than those at which Firm 1 won them. This informational asymmetry gives the first mover an advantage over latecomers at the introductory marketing stage. Furthermore, unless Firm 2 offers very low introductory prices (approaching ON),[51] it will not be successful in unhooking the customers of Firm 1 who have the highest reservation prices. Thus, even after Firm 2 has made some market inroads, the customers it has captured will tend to be those with less willingness to pay than those patronizing first mover Firm 1, permitting Firm 1 to choose pricing strategies that extract more from consumers than the strategies open to latecomer Firm 2.

An Example: Pharmaceuticals

Schmalensee's model of first-mover pricing advantages and its offspring are starkly simplified, assuming a high degree of consumer rationality, the ability to ascertain quality differences through trial, no risk aversion or habit formation, a limited or unclear role for status considerations, and (among other things) the implicit belief that trying new goods is burdensome, not a pleasurable challenge.[52] Our insight into the roots and strength of first-mover advantages can be honed by returning to the case of pharmaceuticals, on which particularly rich evidence exists.

Pharmaceuticals approach an extreme in the extent to which first-mover advantages confer pricing power, at least in part for reasons captured by the Schmalensee model. For one, the cost of a bad consumption experience can be particularly high—for the patient, prolonged illness or adverse side effects, and for the prescribing physician, a malpractice suit. Second, absent information sources to be discussed in a moment, there is considerable ex ante uncertainty as to whether a second-mover (for example, generic) product has the same quality as the extensively tested pioneer drug. But third, pharmaceuticals differ from Schmalensee's experience goods in the extent to which quality can be ascertained through trial. The prescription drug taker commonly lacks the knowledge to evaluate therapeutic efficacy, and placebo effects cloud self-evaluations of both efficacy and contraindications. Prescribing physicians rarely take the time to monitor observable effects, and in many instances, there are no inexpensive means for determining whether one drug is more effective or safer than another, even when the observer is highly trained. Finally, as a key decision maker in the choice process, the prescription-writing physician bears no financial cost from selecting higher-priced brand names, and the patient with generous health insurance coverage may also be indifferent to the price implications.

For a sample of thirty-seven drugs available from two or more sources, Masson and Steiner found that U.S. retailers' invoice costs for leading branded drugs exceeded the costs of generic substitutes by 83 percent on average.[53] For a sample of twenty-nine drugs that had been patented before becoming multisource, Hurwitz and Caves found the average manufacturer's price to be 127 percent higher for branded leaders than for their late-arriving substitutes.[54] Despite these price differentials, the average leader held a market share of 63 percent in the Hurwitz-Caves sample. Regression analyses indicated that an extra year of head start added on average 1.6 percentage points to the first mover's market share. First movers' market shares were sensitive to the size of their price premium over generic substitutes, but not much — a 10 percent increase in the price premium reduced the leader's market share by less than a half percentage point. Hurwitz and Caves found that leaders' market shares rose with their spending on sales promotion (including detailing and advertising). The promotional effect was greater for drugs prescribed only sporadically than for those used to treat chronic conditions, presumably because patients who must refill a prescription regularly become more price-sensitive and less loyal to the best-known product.[55] Thus, promotional effort helps preserve first-mover advantages, but with effectiveness varying for economically plausible reasons.

During the 1970s, most states of the United States and all of the Canadian provinces enacted laws permitting the substitution of generic drugs when the physician prescribed a higher-priced branded product. The degree of permissiveness varied widely from state to state and province to province. In Canada, when a branded drug was prescribed, substitution by pharmacists was impermissible only when the physician took the trouble to write, "no substitution" on the prescription form.[56] In the United States the physician's action required to bar substitution varied from state to state, but characteristically entailed less effort than in Canada. In the United States during 1980, approximately 80 percent of the prescriptions for drugs with multiple sources were written for a particular brand.[57] "No substitution" injunction rates varied widely from state to state, but averaged approximately 10 percent. In Canada, 79 percent of prescriptions were for specific brand names, but only about 1 percent of the prescribers barred substitution.[58] One

51. By construction, segment LN subtracts consumers' surplus from $V(1 - \tau)$ for any given unit of consumption.

52. Compare Tibor Scitovsky, *The Joyless Economy* (New York: Oxford University Press, 1976), pp. 212–215 and 232–276.

53. Alison Masson and Robert L. Steiner, *Generic Substitution and Prescription Drug Prices*, Federal Trade Commission staff report (Washington: October 1985), p. 36. Because surveyed retailers took larger absolute markups on generic than on branded drugs, the retail prices of the leading brands averaged 32 percent more than generic prices.

54. Mark A. Hurwitz and Richard E. Caves, "Persuasion or Information? Promotion and the Shares of Brand Name and Generic Pharmaceuticals," *Journal of Law & Economics*, vol. 31 (October 1988), pp. 299–320.

55. Compare Leffler, "Persuasion or Information," supra note 30, pp. 60–66.

56. Paul K. Gorecki, *Regulating the Price of Prescription Drugs in Canada*, Technical Report no. 8 of the Economic Council of Canada (Ottawa: May 1981), pp. 15–16.

57. Masson and Steiner, *Generic Substitution*, supra note 53, pp. 24–26.

58. Paul K. Gorecki, "The Importance of Being First: The Case of Prescription Drugs in Canada," *International Journal of Industrial Organization*, vol. 4 (December 1986), p. 377, note 19.

might interpret "no substitution" orders as evidence that the prescribing physician had reason to believe the branded product might be superior to generic alternatives. But in the United States, "no substitution" was mandated about as often for drugs that had no substitutes and on prescriptions written in a generic name (for which barring substitution had no effect) as for prescriptions written with a brand name when generic substitutes did exist.[59] Thus, a more plausible explanation is that physicians prescribe the brand name mainly because it is easier to remember and write—that is, by force of habit or to save a few seconds of valuable time.

Canada provides a natural experiment for testing other determinants of generic substitution because the legal mandates varied unusually widely among provinces and because, between 1969 and 1987, a compulsory licensing law made drugs available for low-price generic sale long before their patents had expired.[60] The provincial regulations varied in at least three important ways. All provinces permitted substitution, but in Quebec, only with the patient's explicit consent. If substitution occurred, some provinces gave the pharmacist considerable discretion in making the choice, whereas Ontario and New Brunswick *required* that the lowest-cost substitute be dispensed. Second, most provinces published *formularies* listing branded and generic drugs certified by an expert panel as being biologically equivalent. But British Columbia had none as of 1986; others began publishing them only during the early 1980s, and the inclusiveness of the formularies varied widely. In most provinces with a formulary, physicians prescribing and pharmacists dispensing generic drugs were exempted from malpractice liability when they chose listed products, but in Quebec, they continued to bear responsibility for any adverse consequences from substitution. Third, under Canada's national health insurance system, provincial governments pay pharmacies directly for the drugs dispensed under many conditions. The rules governing the amount of such payment ranged from full reimbursement of the pharmacist's procurement cost to covering only the cost of the lowest-priced substitute (in all cases, plus a fixed dispensing fee). In minimum-price provinces, the pharmacist who dispensed a high-priced drug when substitution was permitted could expect to be reimbursed less than his or her wholesale cost, and thus had strong incentives to substitute.

McRae and Tapon focused their analysis on three provinces, Saskatchewan, with the strongest regulatory inducements for substitution, Ontario, following close behind, and Quebec, with by far the weakest provisions. For twenty-one important drugs with multiple sources, the simple average reimbursed prescription market shares captured by firms *other than* the branded first mover in the three provinces in 1980 were as follows:

Saskatchewan	61.6 percent
Ontario	82.5 percent
Quebec	23.5 percent

In Quebec, which reimbursed the full cost of even high-priced branded drugs and provided no legal protection for substituters, first movers were by far quite successful in defending their positions. Although Saskatchewan was predicted to have higher generic inroads than Ontario, the positions were reversed, apparently because "no substitution" prescribing was unusually commonplace in Saskatchewan.[61]

When Quebec shifted from full cost reimbursement for pharmacists to a fixed (median) price rule in 1982, the average market share of late entrants in seven important drug categories jumped in a year's time from 18.7 to 54.7 percent.[62] Thus, when a profit-conscious entity has to absorb the cost of high-priced brand choices, behavior changes radically. Paul Gorecki reveals the informational and liability-limiting effect of formulary listing through a further analysis.[63] Newfoundland and Saskatchewan both had product choice and cost reimbursement rules strongly favoring substitution in 1983. But of seven multisource drugs with generic products listed as interchangeable in Saskatchewan's formulary, three of the generics were not included as authorized substitutes on Newfoundland's list. The reimbursed prescription market shares of the late entrants were as follows for the two provinces:

	Newfoundland	Saskatchewan
Three drugs not listed as interchangeable in Newfoundland but listed in Saskatchewan	9.7%	59.2%
Four drugs listed in both provinces	76.0%	57.2%

Listing made a thumping difference in Newfoundland, but in Saskatchewan, where all seven drugs were listed, the market share differences were trivial. Gorecki repeated the same analysis for New Brunswick and Nova Scotia, where pharmacists are not required to substitute the lowest-priced brand and the costs of high-priced brands were reimbursed. In four product categories, generic substitutes were not included in the New Brunswick formulary, but were included (along with the generics of three other groups) in the Nova Scotia formulary. The late entrants' market shares were:

	New Brunswick	Nova Scotia
Four drugs not listed as interchangeable in New Brunswick but listed in Nova Scotia	3.2%	13.9%
Three drugs listed in both provinces	5.1%	5.8%

Here the most striking statistic is the low share of all generics — the result of weak substitution mandates. Failure to make it into the formulary affects generic sales in the expected direction, but the effect is necessarily small. Thus, legal mandates

---

59. Masson and Steiner, *Generic Substitution*, p. 25.

60. This analysis is drawn from Gorecki, *Regulating the Price* and "The Importance of Being First;" and James J. McRae and Francis Tapon, "Some Empirical Evidence on Post-Patent Barriers to Entry in the Canadian Pharmaceutical Industry," *Journal of Health Economics*, vol. 4 (March 1985), pp. 43–61.

61. For an explanation, see Gorecki, "The Importance of Being First," pp. 389 and 393.

62. Ibid., pp. 390–391.

63. Ibid., pp. 380–382.

and having to pay for high-priced choices seem to be the most important determinants of generic market shares, but given encouragement for substitution, the information provided by a formulary assumes a crucial role.

The moral to be drawn is that under conditions like those found in pharmaceuticals, first movers have natural product differentiation advantages that permit them to charge high prices and retain substantial market shares—the essence of monopoly power. That power appears to rest as much upon force of habit as upon fears that serious adverse consequences will follow an inappropriate choice. It can be reinforced by advertising. But the power is not impregnable. It can be eroded and perhaps even undermined when two conditions coexist: when consumers have substantial financial incentives to make cost-saving choices, for example, on "big ticket" transactions and purchases repeated sufficiently often that sizable cumulative outlays result; and when objective information about the competing products' quality is available.

The Role of Market Structure

Establishing a strong brand image creates monopoly power. Advertising expenditures contribute to image formation. Market structure may also affect the level of advertising and other promotional outlays, or it may be affected by them. We proceed to explore the links.

Market Structure and Advertising Outlays

Insight into the profit-maximizing level of advertising (or other product differentiation) outlays is provided by the Dorfman-Steiner theorem and extensions.[64] Consider a firm that, as a first approximation, monopolizes its market. The quantity of output demanded from it depends functionally upon both price and the dollar volume of advertising A it undertakes:

(16.2) $$Q = q(P,A)$$

The conditions for profit maximization on the price dimension are conventional, as derived in earlier chapters. However, there is in addition a first-order condition indicating the profit-maximizing amount of advertising A^*. Letting $R = PQ$ be the firm's sales revenue, the Dorfman-Steiner result is commonly written as:[65]

(16.3) $$A^* / R = e_a / e_p,$$

where e_p is the well-known elasticity of demand with respect to price while e_a is the elasticity of quantity demanded with respect to advertising outlays. Intuition is sharpened by recalling from Chapter 2 that the profit-maximizing price-cost margin $(P - MC)/P$ under monopoly (unconstrained *inter alia* by limit-pricing considerations) is equal to the inverse of the price elasticity of demand, that is, $1/e_p$.[66] Substituting the inverse price-cost margin for e_p in (16.3), we obtain:

(16.4) $$\frac{A^*}{R} = e_a \left(\frac{P - MC}{P} \right).$$

Thus, the profit-maximizing ratio of advertising to sales revenue is greater, the wider is the equilibrium gap between price and marginal cost relative to price, and the more responsive the quantity sold is to an increase in advertising outlays.

Advertising in this formulation, and surely also in the real world, acts as a shifter of demand curves. As with other inputs, the purchase of advertising will normally continue into the stage of diminishing marginal returns. For a given e_a and hence a given shift in the quantity demanded from spending a certain amount on advertising, it pays to carry the advertising farther into the diminishing returns stage when the additional sales are highly profitable, that is, with high price-cost margins, than when the marginal sales add only meager contributions to profit.

At the limit, in the purely competitive case, marginal cost is equal to price, so $(P - MC) / P = 0$. From (16.4), the profit-maximizing A^*/R is zero. It does not pay to advertise for a pure competitor because, by definition, the competitor can sell as much or as little as it wants at the market-determined price without advertising. The more conditions depart from pure competition, that is, the larger the equilibrium price-cost ratio, the more intensely firms will advertise.

There is another reason why advertising is inhibited under atomistic competition. If individual sellers' products are essentially undifferentiated, as in the case of Florida oranges, national advertising by any single firm tends to expand the demand for all oranges, and even if the resulting increase in equilibrium prices and quantities is appreciable, the individual advertiser will realize only a tiny fraction of the benefits. The remaining benefits redound as an externality to other growers. To overcome this potential incentive failure, firms join together in trade

64. Robert Dorfman and Peter O. Steiner, "Optimal Advertising and Optimal Quality," *American Economic Review*, vol. 44 (December 1954), pp. 826–836. A dynamic variant focusing on stocks rather than flows is Marc Nerlove and Kenneth J. Arrow, "Optimal Advertising Policy under Dynamic Conditions," *Economica*, vol. 29 (May 1962), pp. 129–142.

65. Proof: The firm's objective is to maximize profits, defined as:

$$(1) \qquad \pi = P \, Q(P) - C(Q) - A,$$

where P is price, Q is quantity sold, C(Q) is total cost except for advertising, and A is advertising expenditure. The first-order condition with respect to price is:

$$(2) \qquad \frac{\partial \pi}{\partial P} = P \left(\frac{\partial Q}{\partial P}\right) + Q - \frac{\partial C}{\partial Q} \frac{\partial Q}{\partial P} = 0.$$

The differentiation is with respect to price rather than the more customary quantity variable, hence the unfamiliar form.
The first-order condition with respect to advertising is:

$$(3) \qquad \frac{\partial \pi}{\partial A} = P \left(\frac{\partial Q}{\partial A}\right) - \frac{\partial C}{\partial Q} \frac{\partial Q}{\partial A} - 1 = 0.$$

Factoring out the $\partial Q/\partial A$ terms and multiplying both sides by A, we obtain:

$$(3a) \qquad A \left[\frac{\partial Q}{\partial A}\right] \left[P - \frac{\partial C}{\partial Q}\right] = A.$$

Multiplying the terms in brackets by Q/Q (= 1), we obtain:

$$(3b) \qquad \left[\frac{\partial Q}{\partial A} \frac{A}{Q}\right] \left[PQ - \left(\frac{\partial C}{\partial Q}\right)Q\right] = A.$$

Note that the first bracketed term is the elasticity of demand with respect to advertising.
We similarly rewrite pricing condition (2) to the form:

$$(4) \qquad \frac{\partial Q}{\partial P} \left[P - \frac{\partial C}{\partial Q}\right] = - Q.$$

Multiplying both sides by P and the bracketed terms (as before) by Q/Q, we obtain:

$$(4a) \qquad \left[\frac{\partial Q}{\partial P} \frac{P}{Q}\right] \left[PQ - \left(\frac{\partial C}{\partial Q}\right)Q\right] = -PQ,$$

noting that the first bracketed term is the *price* elasticity of demand and the second bracketed term is identical to the second bracketed term of (3b). Dividing (3b) by (4a), we obtain as the profit-maximizing condition for the advertising/sales ratio:

$$(5) \qquad \frac{A^*}{-PQ} = \frac{\left(\frac{\partial Q}{\partial A} \frac{A}{Q}\right)}{\left(\frac{\partial Q}{\partial P} \frac{P}{Q}\right)} \left[1\right] = \frac{e_a}{e_p}.$$

The minus sign on the left-hand side is transferred to the right-hand side, letting the price elasticity of demand (normally with a negative sign) have a positive value.

66. See p. 35 supra.

associations such as the Florida Citrus Commission and the Sunkist Growers, which undertake collective advertising programs aimed at shifting industrywide demand. The situation is different when roadside stands advertise the availability and price of their oranges in local newspapers, since then the firms are of appreciable size in relation to their natural markets. The stands' offerings are differentiated *inter alia* in terms of locational convenience, so even when there are many vendors, monopolistic competition, not pure competition, prevails. It is also different when, even though there are many firms selling nationally, each firm's products are differentiable in design or image from those of others, as in fashion garment manufacturing. Again, competition is monopolistic, not pure, and if the price-cost margin is not zero, advertising may occur.

Advertising Under Oligopoly

These special cases shade into the general problem of advertising under oligopoly. To investigate incentives for advertising under oligopoly, we must redefine some of the notation in equations (16.2–4) above. Specifically, the output of the ith firm is now q_i, Firm i's advertising is A_i, its share of total market output $Q = \Sigma q_i$ (and, assuming symmetry, advertising) is $m_i = (q_i / Q)$, and its demand elasticity with respect to its own advertising becomes e_{ai}. Then the advertising elasticity e_a in equation (16.4) must be replaced by e_{ia}. If sellers conform to Cournot-Nash assumptions, expecting rivals' advertising outlays to be unchanged in response to their own outlays, e_{ia} can be decomposed into two terms:

$$(16.5) \qquad e_{ai} = \left(\frac{A_i}{Q}\frac{\partial Q}{\partial A_i}\right) + \left(\frac{A_i}{m_i}\frac{\partial m_i}{\partial A_i}\right),$$

where the first term gives the elasticity of Firm i's output with respect to the industry output-expanding impact of Firm i's advertising, while the second term is the elasticity of changes in Firm i's market share to changes in its advertising.[67] The first term can be called the industry expansion effect, the second term the rivalrous capture effect. Especially when pricing is cooperative, so that price-cost margins remain high, oligopolists have strong dual incentives to advertise. With sizable market shares, they appropriate a substantial fraction of the industrywide benefits from their own advertising, while at the same time, if rivals are not expected to respond effectively to their campaigns, they take away market share from their rivals. As George Washington Hill, swashbuckling president of the American Tobacco Company from 1925 to 1946, explained regarding his company's advertising in the highly concentrated cigarette industry, "Of course, you benefit yourself more than the other fellow . . . but you help the whole industry if you do a good job."[68]

If, contrary to the assumptions thus far, rivals *are* expected to retaliate in kind to increases in advertising, equation (16.5) remains incomplete, requiring a third (negative) term embodying the elasticity of Firm i's output with respect to the changes in rival advertising induced by changes in Firm i's advertising. The more one firm's advertising initiatives are expected to be countered by aggressive responses, the weaker oligopolists' incentives to advertise heavily will be, all else equal. When rival reactions are taken into account fully, the second (rivalrous capture) term in equation (16.5) may be completely offset by the rival retaliation term, and as a result, oligopolists' advertising may be held cooperatively at or near joint profit-maximizing levels.[69]

In Chapters 6 through 8, we saw that Cournot-Nash pricing behavior, that is, ignoring plausible rival countermoves, is fairly unlikely. Rival retaliation to aggressive price cutting is apt to come quickly, and recognizing this, firms in tightly knit oligopolies are often drawn toward policies that are either explicitly cooperative or that emulate the joint profit-maximizing cooperative result. But advertising appears to be different in important respects.[70] First, price cuts can be matched almost instantaneously as soon as secrecy breaks down, whereas it takes weeks or even months to set a retaliatory nationwide advertising campaign in motion. During the interim, the initiator may enjoy market share and profit gains at the laggard's expense. Second, success in advertising depends at least as much upon the way the appeal is presented as on the amount of money spent. Any fool can match a price cut, but counteracting a clever advertising gambit is far from easy. In this unpredictable clash of creative power, sellers often overestimate their own ability to make market share gains and underestimate their rivals' ability to retaliate successfully, exhibiting little concern for mutual interdependence. Third, since price competition is unappealing in oligopoly, business managers may seek an outlet for their aggressive instincts on nonprice dimensions such as advertising, where the threat to collective profits is less certain. And if prices are held comfortably above marginal production and distribution cost, equation (16.4) amended by (16.5) informs us, the quest for additional orders through nonprice rivalry is stimulated.

There is considerable evidence that oligopolists often carry their advertising expenditures beyond the levels at which joint profits would be maximized.[71] In cigarettes, advertising outlays rose from \$4.3 million in 1910 to \$13.8 million in 1913 after the American Tobacco Company, with 90 percent of the U.S. market,

67. Alternatively, the first term in parentheses can be written

$$\left(\frac{\Sigma A}{\Sigma q_i} \frac{\partial \Sigma}{\partial \Sigma A q_i} \right) \frac{A_i}{\Sigma A},$$

where the Σs indicate industry sums, so that the first term (in parentheses) is the elasticity of industry output with respect to total industry advertising, and the second term is firm i's share of industry advertising (or output). Here we follow Michael Waterson, *Economic Theory of the Industry* (Cambridge: Cambridge University Press, 1984), p. 132.

68. Quoted in William H. Nicholls, *Price Policies in the Cigarette Industry* (Nashville: Vanderbilt University Press, 1951), p. 60.

69. We ignore the scale economy and diversity effects from dividing up advertising efforts among several oligopolists rather than having a single entity do the entire job. If scale economies are sacrificed, joint profit-maximizing outlays may be excessive; if a greater diversity of approaches under oligopoly stimulates industrywide demand more effectively than a monolithic campaign, joint profits may be higher under oligopoly than monopoly.

70. For diverse views, see William Fellner, *Competition Among the Few* (New York: Knopf, 1949), pp. 183–191; Nicholls, *Price Policies*, supra note 68, pp. 187–203; Alexander Henderson, "The Theory of Duopoly," *Quarterly Journal of Economics*, vol. 69 (November 1954), pp. 580–581; James M. Ferguson, *Advertising and Competition: Theory, Measurement, Fact* (Cambridge: Ballinger, 1974), pp. 21–27; Simon, *Issues*, supra note 33, pp. 93–103; Dixit and Norman, "Advertising and Welfare," supra note 32, pp. 2–6; and James W. Friedman, "Advertising and Oligopolistic Equilibrium," *Bell Journal of Economics*, vol. 14 (Autumn 1983), pp. 464–473.

71. Sales promotion by retailers through the use of trading stamps, premiums, and sweepstakes tickets may be subject to similar dynamics. See, for example, the Federal Trade Commission staff report, *On the Use and Economic Significance of Trading Stamps* (Washington: USGPO, 1966); B. M. LaLonde and J. Herniter, "The Effect of Trading Stamp Discontinuance on Supermarket Performance," *Journal of Marketing Research*, vol. 7 (May 1970), pp. 205–209; and E. M. Tauber, "The Oligopolistic 'Lock-In,' " *Applied Economics*, vol. 2, no. 3 (1977), pp. 225–229.

was broken into several pieces under an antitrust judgment.[72] Further escalation followed during the 1920s as American attempted to regain industry leadership through an all-out promotional assault. Advertising spending settled down during the 1930s and 1940s, only to rise sharply in the 1950s as new filter tip and king-size brands were introduced, upsetting the prior market share equilibrium.[73] After a new plateau was attained, Congress banned cigarette advertising on television (until then, the most heavily used medium) and radio beginning in January 1971. Total outlays dropped from $315 million in 1970 to $252 million in 1971 while profits rose commensurately.[74] For three years expenditures hovered near that lower figure, but then there was another escalation, accompanied by unusually costly free sample distribution. That repeated rivalrous escalations of cigarette advertising have carried outlays far beyond the short-run joint profit-maximizing point seems indisputable. It is less certain whether long-run profits have been sacrificed or whether, by stimulating consumption, higher advertising outlays have more than paid their way. The weight of evidence indicates that the long-run growth attributable to advertising has been modest, and thus that much of the industry's advertising is self-cancelling and unprofitable even in the long run.[75]

In the soap industry, the principal savings anticipated by Lord Leverhulme from his 1906 proposal to create a soap monopoly in Great Britain were to be realized by eliminating "the frenzied competitive advertising" undertaken by competing producers.[76] A study of several U.S. small-town motion picture markets found that total display ad lineage fell significantly when the number of theaters was reduced from two to only one.[77] Another U.S. study found that the ratio of advertising and other promotional expenses to sales was higher in markets with two private electric utilities than in markets with a municipally owned monopoly.[78] And although U.S. cement manufacturers successfully enforced agreements to avoid price and quality competition, they found themselves "helpless in combatting excessive selling costs" during the 1930s, with outlays covering salesmen's compensation, entertainment, gifts for cement buyers, and other nonfreight distribution costs mounting to 16 percent of net sales in 1939.[79]

More generally, from an ambitious econometric analysis of advertising behavior in sixteen consumer goods product lines across diverse European national markets, Lambin found that in many cases observed levels of advertising might be consistent with profit maximization, short-run or long-run. But for others, and particularly for gasoline, coffee, yogurt, insecticides, deodorants, detergents, and (less clearly) soft drinks, he concluded:

The limited capacity of advertising to increase primary demand, the reciprocal cancellation of brand advertising effects combined with the interdependence of advertising policies leading to an escalation in advertising expenditures constitute a built-in mechanism of advertising competition which has undesirable effects from the consumer point of view. . . . [T]his [advertising] duplication does not benefit the consumer in the long run, as does a price war or technological race.[80]

Nevertheless, exceptions can be found to the tendency for advertising rivalry to be noncooperative. During the 1960s, the U.S. cigarette manufacturers, following prodding by the Federal Trade Commission, collectively adhered to an advertising code discouraging claims with respect to product tar and nicotine content.

However, in 1966 the Commission reversed its stance, and immediately thereafter, with the sales of its Kent cigarettes falling, P. Lorillard Co. withdrew from the code despite industry opposition. Others soon followed suit.[81] In 1957, the U.S. auto producers agreed to deemphasize horsepower in their advertisements and to refrain from direct participation in auto racing, ostensibly as a public service gesture but no doubt also to slow the growth of advertising outlays. The agreement was subsequently honored more in the breach than the keeping. They experienced somewhat greater success in avoiding competitive advertising of safety features.[82] Whether this reflects a spirit of oligopolistic forbearance, or merely the belief (based upon Ford's experience during the 1950s) that advertising safety features didn't pay, is unclear.[83] Still these cases appear to be exceptional. As Fellner suggests, nonrivalrous handling of advertising expenditures is most apt to be seen in relatively rare mature oligopolies, where the strategy options of member firms have been reduced to a matter of routine and demand is fairly stable.[84]

72. See Borden, *The Economic Effects*, supra note 12, pp. 212–216. Likewise, the entry of a second firm into the Australian cigarette industry in 1956 led to a trebling of advertising outlays in the first year of entry and 22 to 48 percent increases in each of the next four years. M. A. Alemson, "Advertising and the Nature of Competition in Oligopoly over Time," *Economic Journal*, vol. 80 (June 1970), p. 293.

73. See Lester G. Telser, "Advertising and Cigarettes," *Journal of Political Economy*, vol. 70 (October 1962), pp. 494–498; and Henry G. Grabowski and Dennis C. Mueller, "Imitative Advertising in the Cigarette Industry," *Antitrust Bulletin*, vol. 16 (Summer 1971), pp. 257–292.

74. Federal Trade Commission, *Report to Congress pursuant to Public Health Cigarette Smoking Act* (Washington: USGPO, December 31, 1974), Statistical supplement Table 7.

The ban on such advertising, which had been accompanied by counter advertising emphasizing health hazards (some of which helped "switch" consumers to low-tar brands), is believed to have slowed the movement away from smoking. See, for example, James L. Hamilton, "The Demand for Cigarettes, Advertising, the Health Scare, and the Cigarette Advertising Ban," *Review of Economics and Statistics*, vol. 54 (November 1972), pp. 401–411; Eugene M. Lewit, Douglas Coate, and Michael Grossman, "The Effects of Government Regulation on Teenage Smoking," and Lynne Schneider, Benjamin Klein, and Kevin Murphy, "Governmental Regulation of Cigarette Health Information," both in *Journal of Law & Economics*, vol. 24 (December 1981), pp. 545–612; and John E. Calfee, "Cigarette Advertising, Health Information and Regulation before 1970," Federal Trade Commission Bureau of Economics working paper no. 134 (December 1985). The Calfee paper contains a particularly thorough bibliography of the extensive literature.

75. Compare Simon, *Issues*, supra note 33, pp. 104–105; Schmalensee, *The Economics of Advertising*, supra note 33, pp. 187–215; Telser, "Advertising and Cigarettes," pp. 498–499; Schneider et al., "Governmental Regulation," p. 594; M. M.

Metwally, "Advertising and Competitive Behavior of Selected Australian Firms," *Review of Economics and Statistics*, vol. 57 (November 1975), pp. 417–427; and "Ad Ban Might Help Cigarette Makers," *New York Times*, January 2, 1989, p. 33.

76. P. Lesley Cook, *Effects of Mergers* (London: George Allen & Unwin, 1958), p. 233.

77. Simon, *Issues*, supra note 33, pp. 108–109.

78. Walter J. Primeaux, "An Assessment of the Effect of Competition on Advertising Intensity," *Economic Inquiry*, vol. 19 (October 1981), pp. 613–625.

79. Samuel M. Loescher, *Imperfect Collusion in the Cement Industry* (Cambridge: Harvard University Press, 1959), pp. 135–136 and 213–216. In 1977, by which time the cartel agreements were ancient history, the cement industry's total selling expenses were 2.9 percent of sales. Federal Trade Commission, *Statistical Report*, supra note 3, p. 33.

80. Jean Jacques Lambin, *Advertising, Competition and Market Conduct in Oligopoly over Time* (Amsterdam: North-Holland, 1976), p. 167. See also pp. 107–113 and 141–147. For similar U.S. results see Jeffry M. Netter, "Excessive Advertising: An Empirical Analysis," *Journal of Industrial Economics*, vol. 30 (June 1982), pp. 361–373.

81. Calfee, "Cigarette Advertising," supra note 74, pp. 41–57.

82. "The Race for Safety Is On," *Business Week*, June 11, 1966, pp. 186–190. Asked by a reporter whether Ford would capitalize in its advertising on safety features its rivals lacked, president Arjay Miller replied, "Probably not. It wouldn't be fair because the others are not antisafety. They'll move as fast as they can. But we plan to compete like hell on the safety features themselves."

83. As industry wags put it at the time, "McNamara (at the time, head of Ford's U.S. auto operations and later U.S. Secretary of Defense) is selling safety, but Chevy is selling cars." See Dan Cordtz, "The Face in the Mirror at General Motors," *Fortune*, August 1966, p. 208.

84. *Competition Among the Few*, supra note 70, pp. 188–189.

Advertising and Seller Concentration

The simple monopoly version of equation (16.4) implies that advertising/sales ratios should be larger, all else equal, as market structures move from competition (with low price-cost margins) to monopoly (with high margins). When the possibility that oligopolists can capture market share from their rivals through advertising is recognized, one might anticipate a nonlinear, inverted U-shaped relationship between advertising/sales ratios and concentration, with peak advertising intensities occurring under more or less tight oligopoly rather than monopoly.[85]

There have been numerous statistical tests of this hypothesis. Virtually all such studies using data of reasonable quality have discovered advertising/sales ratios and seller concentration ratios to be positively correlated, at least in consumer goods industries.[86] The relationship also appears to hold for selling expenditures other than advertising.[87] Those who have tested for a nonlinear ∩-shaped relationship have found it, with peak advertising-sales ratios occurring at four-seller concentration ratios in the range of 46 to 53 (for the United States) and 64 percent (for the United Kingdom).[88]

Other analyses have shown that consumer goods market shares and industry concentration ratios tend to be more variable over time in advertising-intensive lines.[89] This relationship has been interpreted by some scholars as evidence of weak or non-existent monopoly power in high-advertising industries. However, the conclusion does not follow. As we have seen, any fool can match a price cut, whereas a successful advertising campaign may be difficult to duplicate, leading to rapid market share gains whose beneficiary enjoys appreciable pricing discretion, at least until the equilibrium is disrupted by another innovation.

Intensive advertising can also have feedback effects on market structure. Accelerated market share turnover could, under most variants of Gibrat's law, lead to increasing concentration over time.[90] Economies of scale in advertising could have the same effect. On the other hand, if advertising facilitates entry by helping newcomers make their products known quickly, the concentration-increasing effect of turnover could be dissipated or even reversed.[91] The U.S. evidence reviewed in Chapter 4 suggests that the balance lies on the side of rising concentration over time with more intense advertising, especially for industries relying heavily upon television advertising.[92]

Advertising, Monopoly Power, and Profitability

One of the more durable empirical relationships uncovered in statistical investigations of firm and industry profitability, we discovered in Chapter 11, is the tendency for profitability to be relatively high in high-advertising consumer goods industries. We reconsider those results now in the light of what we have learned here.

Image advantages associated more or less closely with being a first mover almost surely underlie much of what has been observed. An image advantage is an asymmetry that presents a barrier to the entry of new firms and a barrier to the upward mobility of less-favored existing firms. It allows its possessor to charge prices higher than those of rivals without ceding market share. Image advantages can also raise the productivity of their possessor's advertising or, by enlarging market shares, permit the realization of advertising scale economies, in both instances letting sellers maintain their market positions at lower advertising/sales ratios than those of less-favored firms.[93] Both the price-raising and cost-saving implications are consistent with evidence that industry advertising/sales ratios are correlated with profitability mainly for leading firms, and not for followers.[94]

Exactly what role advertising per se plays in this chain of causation remains imprecisely illuminated. The qualitative evidence reviewed earlier suggests that intensive advertising contributed to the achievement of first-mover images in at least some important cases. Once a superior image is attained, prices can be held above costs, and under the Dorfman-Steiner theorem, more intensive advertising is encouraged. Such advertising in turn reinforces and prolongs the image advantage. Thus, high advertising is related to superior profitability both as cause and effect.

Two caveats to this general line of reasoning remain to be evaluated. First, whether one concludes that profitability is correlated with advertising intensity depends in part upon the depreciation rates applied to good will stocks built up through advertising.[95] It might be urged that the high profit returns found in advertising-prone industries occur because the seminal advertising took place in earlier, nonobserved periods, and if that early advertising had been capitalized and then depreciated in the periods under observation, supra-normal profit returns would fall or even vanish. This argument is implausible when applied to specific cases. It seems undeniable that success in achieving a strongly differentiated product image can yield properly discounted returns on investment far above competitive norms. A more telling criticism is raised by Glazer, who argues that correlations of profitability with first-mover assessments impose a selection bias,

85. See, for example, John Cable, "Market Structure, Advertising and Intermarket Differences in Advertising Intensity," in Keith Cowling, ed., *Market Structure and Corporate Behaviour* (London: Gray-Mills, 1972), pp. 111–124.

86. See John R. Meisel, "Demand and Supply Determinants of Advertising Intensity Among Convenience Goods," *Southern Economic Journal*, vol. 46 (July 1979), pp. 233–243; and Ralph M. Bradburd, "Advertising and Market Concentration: A Reexamination of Ornstein's Spurious Correlation Hypothesis," *Southern Economic Journal*, vol. 47 (October 1980), pp. 531–539.

87. Weiss et al., "The Size of Selling Costs," supra note 3, p. 671.

88. Stephen Martin, "Advertising, Concentration, and Profitability: The Simultaneity Problem," *Bell Journal of Economics*, vol. 10 (Autumn 1979), pp. 639–647; A. J. Buxton, S. W. Davies, and B. R. Lyons, "Concentration and Advertising in Consumer and Producer Markets," *Journal of Industrial Economics*, vol. 32 (June 1984), pp. 451–464; and Noel D. Uri, "A Re-Examination of the Advertising and Industry Concentration Relationship," *Applied Economics*, vol. 19 (April 1987), pp. 427–435.

89. See Lester G. Telser, "Advertising and Competition," *Journal of Political Economy*, vol. 72 (December 1964), pp. 547–551; Richard E. Caves and Michael E. Porter, "Market Structure, Oligopoly, and Stability of Market Shares," *Journal of Industrial Economics*, vol. 26 (June 1978), p. 308; and E. Woodrow Eckard, "Advertis-

ing, Competition, and Market Share Stability," *Journal of Business*, vol. 60 (October 1984), pp. 539–552.

90. See pp. 143–146 supra.

91. For evidence that conflicts, but favoring a conclusion that entry rates are lower in high-advertising industries, see Daniel Shapiro and R. S. Khemani, "The Determinants of Entry and Exit Reconsidered;" Joachim Schwalbach, "Entry by Diversified Firms into German Industries;" and Richard Highfield and Robert Smiley, "New Business Starts and Economic Activity," all in the *International Journal of Industrial Organization*, vol. 5 (March 1987); Ionnis N. Kessides, "Advertising, Sunk Costs, and Barriers to Entry," *Review of Economics and Statistics*, vol. 68 (February 1986), pp. 84–95; and Zoltan Acs and David Audretsch, "Small-Firm Entry into U.S. Manufacturing," *Economica* (forthcoming in 1989).

92. See pp. 137–138 supra.

93. See pp. 131–134 supra; and note 48 supra in this chapter.

94. See John E. Kwoka and David J. Ravenscraft, "Cooperation vs. Rivalry: Price-Cost Margins by Line of Business," *Economica*, vol. 53 (August 1986), pp. 359–360; and Lawrence J. Gromes, "The Competitive and Anticompetitive Theories of Advertising: An Empirical Analysis," *Applied Economics*, vol. 18 (June 1986), pp. 599–613.

95. See pp. 420–436 supra.

counting only the firms that succeeded in building premium images and overlooking the many firms that tried to do so, invested money in the process, but failed.[96] It is questionable whether in any single product category, the losses of those who failed offset with any precision the supra-normal profits of those who succeeded, since an early (perhaps lucky) success may create such strategic asymmetries that latecomers are discouraged from spending heavily on their own innovations and then, by failing, dissipating the winners' gains. However, it is conceivable that, averaging across all industries, the losses from product differentiation failures do roughly offset the gains of those who succeed. J. A. Schumpeter may have captured the essence of dynamic capitalism in observing that:

Spectacular prizes much greater than would have been necessary to call forth the particular effort are thrown to a small minority of winners, thus propelling much more efficaciously than a more equal and more "just" distribution would, the activity of that large majority of businessmen who receive in return very modest compensation or nothing or less than nothing, and yet do their utmost because they have the big prizes before their eyes and overrate their chances of doing equally well.[97]

How the profits of the winners and losers in this broader sense balance out, we simply do not know.

It has also been argued that advertising leads to supra-normal profitability by building brand loyalty. The semantic distinction between an image advantage and brand loyalty is far from clear. Presumably, the latter is more ephemeral and based less on having been a pioneer. If advertising is an effective instrument for creating profitable brand loyalty, one must ask why *all* sellers do not advertise to establish their own specialized monopoly franchises, through their actions fragmenting markets and driving costs up until a profitless Chamberlinian equilibrium emerges. Something more—that is, something like first-mover advantages—is needed to explain the persistence of supra-normal profits where advertising is high. Also, there is reason to question whether high advertising/ sales ratios are associated in any simple way with strong brand loyalty. In his econometric study of sixteen European consumer product lines, Lambin found *negative* but weak correlations between a measure of consumers' loyalty to particular brands and three different indices of advertising intensity.[98]

Advertising could lead to elevated profitability because it generates barriers to entry other than those embodied in the asymmetry of first-mover images and other brand loyalties. If advertising helps entrants become recognized, intensive counter advertising by incumbents has been known to drown out entrants' messages, lessening the volume of sales they can capture.[99] By raising required entry costs or leaving smaller niches for outsiders to fill, advertising can make markets too crowded to sustain profitable entry.[100] And as we have seen in Chapter 4, there may be economies of scale that give leading advertisers a cost and hence profit advantage over smaller firms. Still these hypotheses almost surely have less power in explaining the observed advertising-profitability associations than image advantages linked to some kind of innovative behavior.

Market Structure and Product Variety

We advance now to the important question of whether other dimensions of product differentiation—for example, in physical product features, convenience, and service — are systematically linked to differences in market structure. As E. H. Chamberlin emphasized long ago, consumers have varied tastes, and to satisfy those tastes necessitates variety in the menu of goods and services offered.[101] But variety imposes costs of two main kinds. Product differentiation gives sellers some control over price, and hence leads to monopolistic resource misallocation. Perhaps more significant, carrying the quest for variety very far conflicts with the realization of scale economies in production and marketing. Were it not for scale economies, every street corner would have its own conveniently located grocery, pharmacy, and lumber yard, and every household would brew its own beer to taste and weave its own blue denim in the precisely desired texture and weight. Within certain bounds, then, a tradeoff must be struck among variety, cost, and price. The question we explore here is, How do diverse market structures affect the outcome of that tradeoff?

One facet that imparts complexity to the problem is the diversity of structural and behavioral assumptions one might make. Plausible candidates for investigation include monopoly with blockaded entry; monopolists deterring entry through either pricing or investment policy (for example, on the latter, as they choose how many product variants to offer and how densely to pack geographic space with plants); unfettered oligopolistic nonprice rivalry with cooperation in pricing; rivalry among firms ignoring their interdependence on both price and quality dimensions, that is, classic Chamberlinian monopolistic competition; and various "ideal" cases in which monopolists or monopolistic competitors are induced by diverse government interventions (such as subsidies or controls) to behave optimally in both price and quality decisions. Not all of these cases and their manifold variants have been explored theoretically. Nevertheless, a good deal can be said about some of the most interesting cases.

Some Examples One of the surest ways to call forth the wrong amount of variety is to set, either through governmental regulation or a rigid cartel mechanism, a uniformly high monopoly price and then let individual producers compete for business on non-price bases. Two kinds of distortions result, both of which are illustrated by U.S. airline regulation during the 1960s and early 1970s.[102] First, the offering of

96. Amihai Glazer, "The Advantages of Being First," *American Economic Review*, vol. 75 (June 1985), pp. 473–480.

97. Joseph A. Schumpeter, *Capitalism, Socialism, and Democracy*, 3rd ed. (New York: Harper, 1950), pp. 73–74.

98. *Advertising*, supra note 80, pp. 115–118.

99. See John C. Hilke and Philip B. Nelson, "Noisy Advertising and the Predation Rule in Antitrust Analysis," *American Economic Review*, vol. 74 (May 1984), pp. 367–371; and Charles F. Mason, "Predation by Noisy Advertising," *Review of Industrial Organization*, vol. 3, no. 1 (1986), pp. 78–88. For an application to political campaigns, see Jeffry M. Netter, "Political Competition and Advertising as a Barrier to Entry," *Southern Economic Journal*, vol. 50 (October 1983), pp. 510–520.

100. See John Cubbin, "Advertising and the Theory of Entry Barriers," *Economica*, vol. 48 (August 1981), who argues that there is no reason for such entry-deterring tendencies to be correlated with advertising intensity.

101. *The Theory of Monopolistic Competition*, supra note 11. See also pp. 32–33 supra.

102. On the experience before deregulation, see George W. Douglas and James C. Miller, III, *Economic Regulation of Domestic Air Transport* (Washington: Brookings, 1974), Chapters 4–6; and Lawrence J. White, "Quality, Competition, and Regulation: Evidence from the Airline Industry," in Richard E. Caves and Marc Roberts, eds., *Regulating the Product: Quality and Variety* (Cambridge: Harvard University Press, 1975), pp. 17–35. On the experience after deregulation, see D. R. Graham, D. P. Kaplan, and D. S. Sibley, "Efficiency and Competition in the Airline Industry," *Bell Journal of Economics*, vol. 14 (Spring 1983), pp. 118–138; and Steven Morrison and Clifford Winston, *The Economic Effects of Airline Deregulation* (Washington: Brookings, 1986).

no-frills flights with high seating density was discouraged, and so consumers who preferred to sacrifice convenience or luxury to save money were badly served. Second, even for the average consumer, the level of quality was often not optimal. Under the prevailing regulated, cartelized rate structure, price-cost margins tended to rise with distance. This encouraged airlines to offer too many flights over long hauls and too few on short hauls relative to the flight frequency — fare preferences of the average air traveler. After the Airline Deregulation Act of 1978 was implemented, both problems were largely solved, and although other new problems emerged, the consensus is that consumers were for the most part substantially better served under deregulated rate-setting and flight scheduling.

More generally, society is usually better off when consumers enjoy a wide range of choices between high-quality, high-priced and low-quality, low-priced opportunities than when they face a severely restricted choice set. Something approximating the desired level of variety in this sense is likely to emerge whenever entry is relatively easy, as it is, for example, in most of the retail trades. Thus, if the typical consumer can choose among several well-stocked, price-competitive supermarkets within ten minutes' driving distance from home and friendly but high-priced "Mom and Pop" grocery and drug stores within a few blocks' walking distance; or between a low-priced, minimum-service gasoline station and a high-priced station offering advertised brands, accepting credit cards, and checking tire air pressure, the state of welfare can hardly be seriously amiss.

The Theory of Optimal Product Variety

A more general perspective on the links between market structure and product variety can be gained by extending the analogy introduced in Chapter 10 between product characteristics space and geographic space.[103] Most products and services have multidimensional characteristics, but the essence of the matter can be grasped by considering a situation in which there is only one more or less continuously variable characteristic—for example, the maneuverability of a car, or the color of a garment (varying over a spectrum), or the speed of a restaurant's service. Figure 16.2 provides the initial framework. The horizontal axis represents a one-dimensional space over which real or perceived product characteristics can vary. Consumers' preferences are mapped by their location in product characteristics space. If, for example, the relevant dimension is the bitterness of a beer, derived from the amount and type of hops used, consumers whose most favored beers are relatively bitter (for example, Pilseners) would have their preferences located farther to the right on the diagram, while those preferring blander beers would be located more to the left. We assume without serious loss of generality a uniform distribution and intensity of preferences over the relevant portion of product characteristics space.

Figure 16.2 looks somewhat like the geographic pricing diagrams presented in Chapters 10 and 13, but its vertical dimension is quite different conceptually. It measures not prices, but consumers' and producers' surpluses. Concretely, the upper (solid) tent-shaped line shows at any abscissa point the total surplus, consumers' plus producers', realized from sales to consumers with preferences located at the corresponding point in horizontal characteristics space.[104] The lower (dotted) line shows the producers' surplus, and so the vertical distance between the upper and lower functions reveals the total consumers' surplus derived by consumers at any given point in product characteristics space.

Figure 16.2
The Surplus Implications of
Product Location in
Characteristics Space

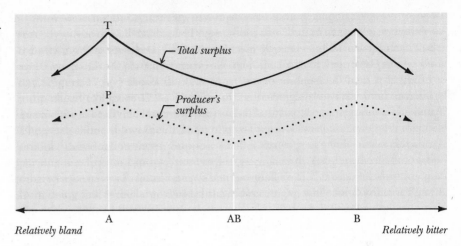

In Figure 16.2, the supply of only two product variants, **A** and **B**, is assumed. These products have characteristics exactly matching the preferences of consumers located at points A and B in characteristics space. By assumption, however, consumer preferences are distributed uniformly over space. Those whose preferences are imperfectly satisfied by **A** or **B** must either buy **A** or **B** or spend more of their income on unrepresented (perhaps quite different) products—for example, wine, or orange juice, or sleeping pills. The loss of utility experienced by consumers at, say, boundary point AB from having to make do with imperfect substitutes **A** or **B** leads to a lower quantity demanded. Demand is choked off

103. This analysis is drawn with only minor modifications from F. M. Scherer, "The Welfare Economics of Product Variety: An Application to the Ready-To-Eat Cereals Industry," *Journal of Industrial Economics*, vol. 28 (December 1979), pp. 113–134.
104. Concretely, let D_A below be the conventional demand function for consumers whose preferences are located *exactly* at point A in Figure 16.2. Then the *length* of the line AT is equal to the total surplus *area* MKJLM in the demand diagram below, where OP is the price charged, OM is marginal cost, and quantity OX is supplied. The line segment TP in Figure 16.2 corresponds to con-

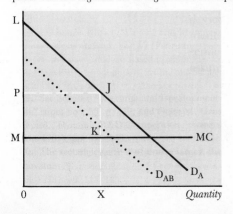

sumers' surplus area LJP and the line segment PA in Figure 16.2 to producer's surplus area PJKM. For a different consumer located at point AB in Figure 16.2, the corresponding demand curve below would be D_{AB}, with appropriately reduced surpluses (assuming the same price OP to be paid). The *areas* under the curves in Figures 16.2 and 16.3 sum (integrate) the surplus areas under all such demand curves for consumers located at all points in characteristics space.

For the mathematics of mapping from individual demand curves to surplus curves like those in Figures 16.2 and 16.3, see Steven S. Wildman, "A Note on Measuring Surplus Attributable to Differentiated Products," *Journal of Industrial Economics*, vol. 33 (September 1984), pp. 123–132. See also Alan Randall and John R. Stoll, "Consumer's Surplus in Commodity Space," *American Economic Review*, vol. 70 (June 1980), pp. 449–455.

more, the farther the consumer's preferences lie from the characteristics of available products. This, combined with the assumption of a uniform distribution of preferences over characteristics space, gives rise to the tent shape of the surplus functions, whose maximums are the points in space where product characteristics exactly match some consumers' preferences.

Let us consider now the introduction of a third product, **C**, at the point in characteristics space intermediate between **A** and **B**, as in Figure 16.3. This means that consumers in the neighborhood of C will be satisfied better, leading to an increase in consumption by those consumers, and hence to increases in consumers' and producers' surplus represented by the new tent-shaped functions with maximums above point C. If the prices of the various products are equal, consumers whose tastes lie within the range AC to CB will buy product **C**, those whose tastes lie to the left of CB will buy **B**, and those who prefer a beer blander than AC will buy **A**.

Whether or not product **C** will be offered depends critically upon the fixed costs of supplying it — that is, the required investment in research, development, plant and equipment, and introductory marketing — and upon market structure. Market structure matters in the following way. If the market is at least locally monopolized and entry by outsiders at C is blockaded, the relevant gross payoff to the producer of **A** and **B** contemplating the introduction of **C** is the diamond-shaped area consisting of triangles T_A and T_B.[105] Assuming the variable unit production and distribution costs of **C** to be the same as for **A** and **B**, T_A and T_B represent increased contributions to profits from the producer's perspective, although as Figure 16.3 is drawn, they are actually redistributions from what would be consumers' surplus in the absence of **C** to producers' surplus. If the sum of T_A plus T_B exceeds the fixed cost of supplying **C**, our monopolist will offer **C**; if fixed costs exceed $T_A + T_B$, **C** will not be offered, at least under the monopoly conditions postulated.

Let us however relax the assumption that entry is blockaded. A monopolistic competitor considering offering **C** in competition with other sellers' products **A**

Figure 16.3
Consequences of Introducing
an Additional Product
Variant **C**

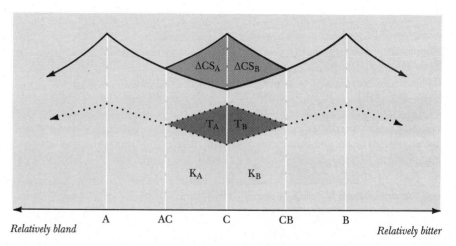

and **B** and assuming, Bertrand-like, that **C** is priced at the same level as the unchanged prices of **A** and **B**,[106] perceives itself as gaining the diamond-shaped surplus $T_A + T_B$ *plus* the surpluses K_A and K_B, which are transfers of producers' surplus from the maker(s) of **A** and **B** to the producer of **C**. Such transfers are sometimes referred to as *cannibalization*. The monopolistic competitor unconcerned about whence K_A and K_B come views itself as gaining a larger surplus through product introduction than does the monopolist of **A** and **B**. It is entirely possible that fixed costs exceed $T_A + T_B$, in which case the monopolist enjoying blockaded entry will not launch product **C**, while they are less than $T_A + T_B + K_A + K_B$, in which case a monopolistic competitor *will* offer **C**. Such reasoning lies at the heart of economists' conclusion that a greater variety of substitute products is likely to appear under monopolistic competition, with entry open, than under monopoly with closed entry.[107]

If there is monopoly but entry into space C is open, the monopolist may choose also to offer **C** and preempt entry that would otherwise cause it to lose surpluses K_A and K_B. If so, as much product variety may arise under such entry-deterring monopoly (or oligopoly) as under monopolistic competition, other things (such as pre- and postentry prices) being equal.

This seeming virtue of monopolistic competition and entry-deterring monopoly can be carried so far that it becomes a vice. From the standpoint of society as a whole, assuming that a dollar's worth of costs, consumers' surplus, or producers' surplus are equally valued, a new product *should* be introduced if its net addition to surplus—that is, $CS_A + CS_B$ in Figure 16.3—exceeds the fixed cost of introduction. (T_A, T_B, K_A, and K_B are irrelevant to the calculation of social benefit because, as transfers, they cancel out.) The diamond-shaped consumers' surplus addition may be either larger or smaller than the wall tent-shaped surplus guiding the decisions of monopolistic competitors or entry-deterring monopolists. As Figure 16.3 is drawn, $CS_A + CS_B$ is considerably smaller than $T_A + T_B + K_A + K_B$, and so if fixed costs are substantial (that is, greater than $CS_A + CS_B$), but less than the T, K sum, monopolistic competition is likely to lead to *too much* product variety relative to the social welfare-maximizing level.

How can one tell whether the optimal amount of product variety will be overshot in this way? Two sets of considerations provide guidance.

First, the relative flatness or steepness of the surplus functions matters. With relatively flat surplus functions, the net social gain $CS_A + CS_B$ is likely to be small

105. To be more precise, the producer will view as its gross benefit from introducing **C** the discounted present value of the surpluses T_A and T_B over all years in which product **C** is expected to be sold.

106. On alternative pricing assumptions, see Steven C. Salop, "Monopolistic Competition with Outside Goods," *Bell Journal of Economics*, vol. 10 (Spring 1979), pp. 141–156; and Motoshige Itoh, "Monopoly, Production Differentiation, and Economic Welfare," *Journal of Economic Theory*, vol. 31 (October 1983), pp. 88–104.

107. See Kelvin Lancaster, "Socially Optimal Product Differentiation," *American Economic Review*, vol. 65 (September 1975), pp.

580–585; Michael Spence, "Product Selection, Fixed Costs, and Monopolistic Competition," *Review of Economic Studies*, vol. 43 (June 1976), pp. 217–235; Michael C. Lovell, "Product Differentiation and Market Structure," *Western Economic Journal*, vol. 8 (June 1970), pp. 137–139; J. E. Meade, "The Optimal Balance Between Economies of Scale and Variety of Products," *Economica*, vol. 41 (November 1974), pp. 359–367; Roger W. Koenker and Martin K. Perry, "Product Differentiation, Monopolistic Competition, and Public Policy," *Bell Journal of Economics*, vol. 12 (Spring 1981), pp. 217–231; and Norman J. Ireland, "Product Diversity and Monopolistic Competition under Uncertainty," *Journal of Industrial Economics*, vol. 33 (June 1985), pp. 501–513.

relative to the amount of cannibalization $K_A + K_B$, and so excessive product proliferation is apt to be encouraged. The surplus function slopes cannot be measured directly, but they have observable correlates. A steep surplus function slope means that people shun products located some distance from their most preferred characteristics; a flat slope means that consumers readily substitute a product of less than ideal characteristics if they cannot get exactly what they want. Strong qualitative preferences imply steep slopes and sizable consumers' surplus gains; fickleness among consumers toward substitutes implies small gains. Also, with steep surplus function slopes, the net noncannibalized sales (or more precisely, gross margin) increase $T_A + T_B$ that results from introducing a new product is likely to be relatively large.

Second, cannibalization will be greater, all else held equal, the higher the elevation of the producers' surplus functions (dotted lines) is in relation to the total surplus functions (solid lines), or more simply, the greater is the ratio of producers' surplus to consumers' surplus. This in turn depends upon two factors. If producers maximize profit in the short-run sense, setting marginal cost equal to marginal revenue, the ratio of producers' surplus to consumers' surplus will be higher when the demand function for an individual product is concave downward (that is, with a relatively flat top) than when it is convex downward.[108] With concave-downward demand functions, it should be noted, the quantity of a product demanded falls off sharply as the product's price is increased, holding the prices of substitute products constant, which means that the products are relatively close substitutes, and hence that one product is likely to cannibalize considerable surplus from the other. Producer's surplus is also apt to be relatively high when the oligopolistic sellers of substitute products respect their mutual interdependence in pricing, cooperating in a joint profit-maximizing policy, as compared to behaving in the Cournot-like manner of monopolistic competitors.

In sum, excessive product variety is most likely to be forthcoming when there is open entry or the threat of entry that insiders choose to preempt; high substitutability among product variants; relatively high gross profit margins (that is, before the deduction of fixed costs); modest sales growth as a consequence of adding an additional product to the existing set; and fixed product introduction costs that are substantial but less than the amount of potential producers' surplus cannibalization. There is little systematic evidence on how frequently this constellation of conditions occurs. It is certainly possible to find cases in which product proliferation appears to have been carried beyond the point at which marginal social benefits equaled social costs. The U.S. ready-to-eat cereal industry during the 1960s, with close respect for mutual interdependence in pricing, price-manufacturing cost margins in excess of 50 percent, fickle consumers, and modest real (noncannibalized) growth despite intensive launching of new products, is a probable example.[109] So is the U.S. soft drink industry during the 1980s, in which numerous new low-calorie and decaffeinated products cannibalized each others' surpluses extensively.[110] Exploring a wide range of parameters with a simple partial equilibrium simulation model, Michael Spence found a tendency for the number of product variants under monopolistic competition to exceed the social optimum in all cases except those with both high fixed product launching costs and low cross elasticities of demand (that is, poor substitutability).[111] How general his results are is unclear. On this important question, more theoretical and (especially) empirical research is needed.[112]

Product Standardization

Variety is not always a good thing. Wholly apart from the cost savings attainable through longer production runs, there are cases in which standardization serves consumers better than diversity. The adoption of common technical standards for records and compact discs, so that any product can be played on any manufacturer's audio equipment, is one example. Similarly, typewriter keyboards are standardized on the QWERTY system so that users can move easily from one machine to another, even though appropriately trained persons could type much faster on alternative keyboard layouts.[113] The use of computers would be facilitated in numerous applications if compatible data coding conventions and programming languages were adopted, although in 1989, the computer world remained a Tower of Babel despite occasional standardization attempts.[114]

Convergence upon a common industry standard can be difficult when early adopters incur costs, or lose sales to rivals, as a result of pioneering the way.[115] Once they are established, standards may persist beyond their useful lives because the first firms to change encounter resistance from already committed users and are unable to capture the benefits accruing to the customers of rivals who might follow suit. Recognizing the difficulties of standard changing, industry members often form cooperative standards committees to coordinate product specifications and interfaces. These can have negative as well as positive effects; for example, they may serve as a forum for collusion, or insiders may influence the standards adopted so as to make entry more difficult for outsiders.[116] Even without such formal coordination, entrenched incumbents may, by preempting the announcement of new standards or taking predatory actions inhibiting the growth of smaller

108. See Spence, "Product Selection," pp. 224–225.

109. See Scherer, "The Welfare Economics," supra note 103; and Richard Schmalensee, "Entry Deterrence in the Ready-To-Eat Breakfast Cereal Industry," *Bell Journal of Economics*, vol. 9 (Autumn 1978), pp. 305–327. For an industry analysis that draws no welfare conclusions, see R. W. Shaw, "Product Proliferation in Characteristics Space: The UK Fertiliser Industry," *Journal of Industrial Economics*, vol. 31 (September/December 1982), pp. 69–91.

110. See "Coke's Big Marketing Blitz," *Business Week*, May 30, 1983, p. 61, in which 30 to 35 percent of the sales of Diet Coke were found to have come from Coca-Cola's own previous brand, Tab, in addition to cannibalizing Diet Pepsi sales. See also "It's Coke vs. Pepsi—Again," *Business Week*, August 2, 1982, p. 65, in which it was predicted that one-fourth of Diet Coke's sales would come by cannibalizing Coca-Cola products and three-fourths "from somebody else's."

111. Michael Spence, "Product Differentiation and Welfare," *American Economic Review*, vol. 66 (May 1976), pp. 407–414.

112. Marketing researchers have begun to analyze the sales of specific new products in the framework of characteristics space

models. See John Hauser, "Theory and Application of Defensive Strategy," in L. G. Thomas, ed., *The Economics of Strategic Planning* (Lexington: Heath-Lexington, 1986), pp. 113–139.

113. See Paul David, "Clio and the Economics of QWERTY," *American Economic Review*, vol. 75 (May 1985), pp. 332–337.

114. See "Computer 'Gangs' Stake Out Turf; Each Hopes To Set Industry Standards," *New York Times*, December 13, 1988, p. D1.

115. See Joseph Farrell and Garth Saloner, "Standardization, Compatibility, and Innovation," *Rand Journal of Economics*, vol. 16 (Spring 1985), pp. 70–83; and idem, "Installed Base and Compatibility: Innovation, Product Preannouncements, and Predation," *American Economic Review*, vol. 76 (December 1986), pp. 940–955.

116. A standards committee's exclusion of newcomers with an allegedly superior solid-state circuitry approach to fluorescent lamp ballasts was a central issue in an antitrust case, *L.M.P. Corp. et al.* v. *Universal Manufacturing Corp. et al.*, Superior Court of the State of California, Alameda County, no. 590001-7, filed in 1987. See also Federal Trade Commission Bureau of Consumer Protection, final staff report, *Standards and Certification* (Washington: April 1983).

rivals, prevent the emergence of standards that would prove to be superior if they could gain a sufficient foothold. Little is known about the distribution of benefits and costs from such standard-setting activities under diverse market structural conditions.

Market Structure and Product Durability

In addition to determining how many product variants to offer, sellers must decide how much quality to build into a given product. Among other things, this entails a choice as to how durable the product will be. As a rule, it costs more to produce a more durable product, but the product then yields its services to buyers over a longer period of time, which means that the seller must wait longer for replacement sales. Does market structure affect the tradeoff sellers make on this point?

Perhaps the most interesting point of departure is the work of Peter Swan, who, after correcting important omissions in earlier analyses, concluded that with perfect foresight, perfect capital markets, and the absence of either economies or diseconomies of scale in production, monopolists and competitors would choose identical product durability.[117] The essence of his argument is best captured by considering separately the cases in which durable goods are leased or rented out by the producer, as compared to selling them outright.

In the leasing case, how often the good wears out and has to be replaced is mainly a concern of the lessor. Ignoring possible disruption costs while the good is replaced, durability should be a matter of indifference to the lessee. A monopolistic lessor will of course restrict the supply of its durable good's services more than a set of competitive lessors would, but that classic monopoly restriction is effected by setting the rental rate higher than the competitive rate. Given the choice of price and service levels over time, both the competitor and the monopolist maximize their profits by choosing the degree of durability that minimizes the discounted cost of providing the chosen stream of durable good services. And with no economies or diseconomies of scale, that cost-minimizing durability level will be the same under either market structure.

Results for the sales case follow from the leasing logic. With perfect capital markets and foresight, the profit-maximizing sales price for a durable good will equal the discounted present value of the benefits to marginal users under an optimally priced leasing policy.[118] Ignoring complications to be introduced in a moment, the producer under either monopoly or competition should therefore be indifferent between selling and leasing, and the optimal level of durability is therefore the same when the product is sold as when it is leased. And that choice, to repeat, is the same with either market structure.

These conclusions do not survive the modification of important assumptions, especially when there are reasons why durable goods producers must sell their products rather than leasing them. For one, when capital markets are imperfect and durable good buyers have a higher discount (that is, interest) rate than producers, durability will be lower under monopoly than under competition.[119] This is so because future replacement outlays are discounted more heavily by buyers than by sellers, and a monopolist will take advantage of this asymmetry by reducing durability to stimulate replacement sales. Second, if buyers *fear* that the durable good seller will reduce the value of their purchases by flooding the market, they will restrict their purchases, and the durable goods seller reacts by slanting its production decisions toward lower durability than it would choose as a lessor.[120] Third, the Swan analysis ignores the possibility that buyers incur maintenance costs to prolong the life of their equipment. If the cost of maintenance is beyond the durable good supplier's control, the ratio of the cost of an hour's maintenance effort to the cost of the good will be lower under monopoly (with elevated goods sale prices) than under competition. Thus, relatively more maintenance will be done under monopoly and the good's life will be extended, ceteris paribus. Taking this into account, the monopolist is likely to adjust its choices in the directin of reduced durability (and lower prices).[121] Finally, it is common for the costs of using a durable good to rise over time as the good gradually deteriorates. The more frequently the durable good is replaced, the lower average operating costs will be, but the higher capital (that is, replacement purchase) costs will be. Under a high-price monopoly, this tradeoff will be biased more toward later replacement than under competitive pricing.[122] Recognizing this, the monopolist seller will adjust its durability choice, although the direction of the change cannot be predicted unambiguously without additional information on the pattern of operating costs.

Because the pure monopolies assumed in these models are rare in the real world, it is difficult to find evidence permitting a clear-cut test of the theory. One illustration is AT&T's shift, forced by the Federal Communications Commission in 1981, from leasing to selling its telephone handsets. Durability clearly fell, although it is unclear how much of the change was attributable to the move from leasing to selling and how much to the concomitant transition from monopoly to competition.[123] Robert Avinger reports four cases—electric lamps, phonograph styli, stainless steel razor blades, and electronic vacuum tubes—consistent with the hypothesis that monopoly considerations inhibited the introduction of more durable product variants.[124] However, product durability limitations were arguably attributable at least as much to the complexities of coordination in cartelized

117. Peter L. Swan, "Durability of Consumption Goods," *American Economic Review*, vol. 60 (December 1970), pp. 884–894; and E. Sieper and Peter L. Swan, "Monopoly and Competition in the Market for Durable Goods," *Review of Economic Studies*, vol. 40 (July 1973), pp. 333–351.

118. Among other things, arbitrage by firms buying durable goods and then leasing them competitively will help ensure this result. For instance, when IBM reduced the sales prices of its System 360 computers by 6 percent relative to lease prices in 1966, it induced the rapid expansion of computer leasing companies who ultimately brought competitive pressure to bear on IBM's lease rates.

119. See, for example, Robert J. Barro, "Monopoly and Contrived Depreciation," *Journal of Political Economy*, vol. 80 (May/June 1972), pp. 598–602.

120. See Jeremy I. Bulow, "Durable-Goods Monopolists," *Journal of Political Economy*, vol. 90 (April 1982), pp. 314–332.

121. See Richard Schmalensee, "Market Structure, Durability, and Maintenance Effort," *Review of Economic Studies*, vol. 41 (April 1974), pp. 277–286. See also S. J. Liebowitz, "Durability, Mar-

ket Structure, and New-Used Goods Models," *American Economic Review*, vol. 72 (September 1982), pp. 816–824; and John Rust, "When Is It Optimal To Kill Off the Market for Used Durable Goods?" *Econometrica*, vol. 54 (January 1986), pp. 65–86.

In this and the next case, the monopolist would prefer to lease, all else equal, which would permit undistorted durability choices. The problems here are analogous to those under which vertical integration by a monopolist whose product has imperfect downstream substitutes improves the efficiency of downstream production. See Chapter 14 supra.

122. Teddy T. Su, "Durability of Consumption Goods Reconsidered," *American Economic Review*, vol. 65 (March 1975), pp. 148–157.

123. In an unpublished speech, an AT&T official observed that one of the most difficult lessons the company had to learn following various deregulation measures was how to make a telephone that lasted only three years.

124. Robert L. Avinger, "Product Durability and Market Structure: Some Evidence," *Journal of Industrial Economics*, vol. 29 (June 1981), pp. 357–374.

oligopoly structures as to the kinds of reasoning assumed in the pure monopoly vs. competition theories. On this question, as on how market structure affects the provision of product variety, much remains to be learned.

Conclusion

Product differentiation is both desirable and inescapable. Yet advertising and product proliferation can be overdone, and that is cause for concern. Advertising campaigns can be carried far beyond the point where they are informative or add spice to consumption, serving merely to barrage the consumer with mutually conflicting or even misleading claims. Image differentiation reinforced through intensive advertising can be an important barrier to entry, permitting the sustained realization of monopoly profits. Product varieties can be proliferated until launching costs outweigh the gains from the more complete satisfaction of diverse consumer demands. Thus, high prices, waste, resource misallocation, and income redistribution are the consequences of excessive product differentiation.

The market system has no fully satisfactory built-in mechanism for curbing advertising abuses and the provision of defective goods and services. At the local community level, agencies such as Better Business Bureaus attempt to mediate complaints on a voluntary basis. In the mid-1970s, the Better Business Bureau of New Haven, Connecticut, received approximately one complaint per year for each 500 resident citizens. The highest complaint frequencies were recorded in home furnishings, automobile sales and service, floor coverings, and roofing. Eighty percent of the complaints were reported to have been settled.[125] At the national level in the United States, claims that advertising is deceptive can be referred either to a voluntary business group, the National Advertising Division of the Council of Better Business Bureaus, which investigates 100 to 150 cases per year,[126] or to the government's Federal Trade Commission. The FTC can enjoin misleading practices, compel corrective advertising, and in extreme cases, seek fines against repeat violators. There is evidence that formal FTC legal actions have sharp "teeth," reducing complained-of companies' stock market values and (less consistently) market shares appreciably.[127] The Commission's task is not an easy one, for the line between misleading and merely persuading is fuzzy, and too heavy a hand at the controls could suppress desirable initiative and creativity.

In cases where advertising is patently excessive, the government might intervene to induce a reduction. The 1971 ban on television and radio advertising of cigarettes is an example, but not a successful one. A considerable volume of expenditures was deflected into other media, and an important source of health hazard warnings was eliminated. There is little reason to believe that cigarette consumption fell as intended. Another example was set in 1966 when the British Monopolies Commission recommended a 40 percent cut in advertising by Unilever and Procter & Gamble accompanied by a 20 percent reduction in household detergent prices.[128] However, the government settled for a milder compromise under which the two companies agreed to introduce new, less heavily promoted products priced 20 percent lower than existing brands. The effort is said to have accomplished little, largely because the companies refused to admit that the unadvertised products' quality was equivalent to that of their main brands. As a result, consumers showed little interest in purchasing the new products. Other expenditure-discouraging policy alternatives include imposing a progressive excise tax on advertising, requiring advertisers to capitalize and then depreciate their advertising outlays in computing income taxes rather than writing them off in the year they are incurred,[129] or attacking under the price discrimination laws the quantity discounts received by large advertisers. All such policies run the risk of evasion and evoking undesirable side effects. It is difficult to be sanguine about the ability of government staff charged with policy enforcement to outwit their business counterparts and ensure that after companies have taken adaptive steps, the situation is significantly improved.[130]

The adverse effects of advertising can be mitigated by making available to consumers objective information on the relative qualities of competing products. Much is already done along these lines; part of the problem is simply to do it better. The government might subsidize the activities of such organizations as the Consumers Union, permitting them to conduct more frequent and extensive product tests and to disseminate reports to a broader audience.[131] The wider implementation of uniform quality grading systems, enforced through inspection and supplemented by programs to inform the consumer, might be encouraged. Reports of quality and suitability tests conducted on thousands of consumer items by federal procurement agencies could be published and distributed on a massive scale. And finally, appropriate government agencies might take the more radical step of subpoenaing the extensive consumer panel test information in company files and making it available to the press and public in comprehensible form.

Whether problems of excessive product proliferation or insufficient product durability can be corrected through governmental action is debatable. As we have seen, product durability can be optimal or downward-biased under monopoly, and market processes can lead to too much, too little, or the right amount of product variety. The key question is, Can government agencies or courts outperform the market in determining how much variety or durability is correct? Considerable skepticism seems warranted. Intervention is best saved for the most severe market failures—for example, as in the U.S. government's actions during the early 1970s to require automobile bumper designs sufficiently durable to withstand specified crash impacts, or the Air Force's insistence in 1987 that all computers purchased under its $4.2 billion modernization program use the Unix operating system.

125. Sharon Oster, "The Determinants of Consumer Complaints," *Review of Economics and Statistics*, vol. 62 (November 1980), pp. 603–609.

126. "In Advertising, It's No More Mr. Nice Guy," *Philadelphia Inquirer*, Sept. 21, 1986, p. 9-D. For comparisons to other nations, see J.J. Boddewyn, *Advertising Self-Regulation and Outside Participation: A Multinational Comparison* (New York: Quorum, 1988).

127. Sam Peltzman, "The Effects of FTC Advertising Regulation," *Journal of Law & Economics*, vol. 24 (December 1981), pp. 403–448. That issue of the *Journal* is devoted entirely to consumer protection regulatory questions. See also Pauline Ippolito and David Scheffman, eds., *Consumer Protection Economics*, Federal Trade Commission conference report (Washington: 1986).

128. Monopolies Commission report, *Household Detergents* (London: HMSO, 1966). See also "Britain and 2 Soap Makers End Price Battle with Compromise," *New York Times*, April 2, 1967, p. 65.

129. See "Curb on Ad Write-Offs Is Opposed," *New York Times*, March 8, 1986, p. 35.

130. For a case study in chronic failure, see Mann and Plummer, "The Big Headache," supra note 43.

131. During the mid-1980s, *Consumer Reports* had nearly three million subscribers.

Market Structure, Patents, and Technological Innovation

Making the best use of resources at any moment in time is important. But in the long run, it is dynamic performance that counts. As we observed in Chapter 2, an output handicap amounting to 10 percent of gross national product owing to static inefficiency is surmounted in twenty years if the output growth rate can be raised through more rapid technological progress from 3.0 to 3.5 percent. Or if the growth rate can be increased to 4.0 percent, the initial disadvantage is overcome in 10.6 years.

To Adam Smith, the pin factory was the epitome of static efficiency.[1] Through mechanization and the division of labor, an average output per worker of 4,800 pins per day could be achieved in the 1770s. Two centuries later, thanks to countless technological changes, output per worker had risen to 800,000 pins per day.[2] The increase seems astounding at first glance, but it implies an average annual work-day productivity growth rate of only 2.56 percent per year — a rate matched by many industries over substantial periods of time.

From the time of Smith's successor David Ricardo, and especially after the Neoclassical breakthrough of the 1870s, until well into the twentieth century, the mainstream of (non-Marxian) economic theory exhibited remarkably little sensitivity to the importance of compound productivity growth through technological innovation. Emphasis was on the result of combining labor and capital with production functions of an essentially static character. Not until the 1950s did technological change become more than a side-show attraction. For the shot that signaled a revolution in economic thought, Robert Solow received the Nobel Prize.[3] He set out to measure the extent to which increases in the amount of capital employed were responsible for the rise of U.S. nonfarm output per labor hour between 1909 and 1949. To the surprise of economists mired in the static tradition, he found that increased capital intensity accounted for only 12.5 percent (later corrected to 19 percent) of the measured growth in output per work hour. The rest of the observed 1.79 percent average annual productivity gain was evidently attributable to improvements in production practices and equipment (technological change in the strictest sense) and to the increased ability of the labor force. In a subsequent extension, Edward Denison estimated that 13 percent of the gain in output per worker between 1929 and 1982 could be credited to increased capital intensity, 34 percent to improved work force education, 22 percent to the greater realization of scale economies, and 68 percent to advances in scientific and technological knowledge, broadly construed.[4] Although one can quibble with the detailed estimates, it is hard to dispute the main thrust of Solow's and Denison's conclusion: that the growth of output per worker in the United States (and also in other industrialized lands[5]) has come predominantly from the

1. Adam Smith, *An Inquiry into the Nature and Causes of the Wealth of Nations* (1776), Book I, Chapter I.

2. Clifford F. Pratten, "The Manufacture of Pins," *Journal of Economic Literature*, vol. 18 (March 1980), pp. 93–96.

3. Robert M. Solow, "Technical Change and the Aggregate Production Function," *Review of Economics and Statistics*, vol. 39 (August 1957), pp. 312–320.

4. Edward F. Denison, *Trends in American Economic Growth,*

1929–1982 (Washington: Brookings, 1985) p. 30. The percentages add to more than 100 because there are also negative factors, for example, a decrease in hours worked by the average employee (−25 percent) and the effects of government regulation (−4 percent).

5. See, for example, Edward F. Denison, *Why Growth Rates Differ* (Washington: Brookings, 1967).

application of new, superior production techniques by an increasingly skilled work force. It seems clear too that imperfectly understood declines in the pace of technological innovation were responsible in part for a fall in the growth of U.S. business-sector productivity from 2.92 percent per year over 1947–1973 to 1.01 percent per year over 1973–1987.[6]

The introduction of better production methods is one main arm of technological advance. The other is the creation of new and superior consumer goods. Because of measurement difficulties, it is doubtful whether the full effect of consumer product innovations is captured by available productivity growth statistics. Consequently, the impact of technological change on consumer well-being is probably understated by those statistics.

Several further effects of technological change can be identified. For one, advanced industrialized nations like the United States, Japan, and Sweden derive much of their comparative advantage in international trade not from the land, labor, and capital endowments stressed in neoclassical economic theory, but from superiority in developing and producing technologically advanced products such as aircraft, machine tools, electronic appliances, pharmaceuticals, and computers.[7] Second, international differences in the ability to develop and apply modern technology have a crucial impact on the balance of military power. Third, process innovation alters the structure of labor demands, most likely strengthening the demand for skilled workers and weakening demand for the unskilled, with troubling implications for income distribution. Finally, technological change affects market structure, for major innovations often bring new firms to the fore and displace laggards, defining the structural conditions within which price and other more static forms of rivalry are conducted for decades to come.

Here we are concerned largely with a possible causal flow in the opposite direction: from market structure to innovation. Is progress faster or slower under monopolistic conditions, or does it make no difference? A leader in stressing the important role technological change plays in capitalistic economies was Joseph A. Schumpeter. In a widely read and controversial book, he argued that market structure does make a difference. Despite their restrictive pricing behavior, he asserted, large monopolistic firms are ideally suited for introducing the technological innovations that benefit society:

What we have got to accept is that [the large-scale establishment or unit of control] has come to be the most powerful engine of [economic] progress. . . . In this respect, perfect competition is not only impossible but inferior, and has no title to being set up as a model of ideal efficiency.[8]

Whether or not this "Schumpeterian" view is correct is the question we tackle in this chapter. More precisely, we explore several narrower issues: the incentive role of patents, the links between market structure and innovation, and the climate for innovation in large, diversified firms.

Industrial Innovation

Before addressing these questions, we must pause and examine more carefully what the process of technological change is all about.

Organized Industrial R&D

Technical innovations do not fall like manna from heaven. They require effort — the creative labor of invention, development, testing, and introduction into the stream of economic life. To some extent innovative effort is a haphazard thing, conducted by individuals and firms as a digression from routine workaday activities. But to an increasing degree, the task of creating and developing new products and processes has been institutionalized through the establishment of formal research and development (R&D) laboratories. This phenomenon evolved gradually. In the 1770s and 1780s, the firm of Boulton & Watt had the equivalent of an R&D laboratory for work on steam engines.[9] The genesis of the modern R&D laboratory in America is commonly traced to 1876, when Thomas Edison opened his famed laboratory in Menlo Park and Alexander Graham Bell established a similar facility in Boston. Wherever the starting point is placed, the idea spread rapidly until research and development came to be big business. In 1987, U.S. companies expended some $91 billion on research and development activities — 2.4 percent of business-sector gross national product.[10] Real (that is, inflation-adjusted) total industrial R&D spending rose at an average rate of 6.6 percent per year between 1953 and 1970 and at the slower 3.4 percent rate from 1970 to 1987. Thirty-six percent of 1987 industrial R&D outlays were financed under government contracts, mostly covering military and space systems development, while for the balance, company funds were directly at risk. Our emphasis here is on the company-financed component.[11]

The intensity with which companies pursue privately financed research and development varies widely from industry to industry. The manufacturing sector conducts 97 percent of all industrial R&D and hence is the prime mover in generating technological progress. Among 238 U.S. manufacturing industries in 1977, the median industry devoted 0.8 percent of sales to company-financed R&D. The eight R&D/sales leaders were:[12]

Ethical drugs	10.2%
Electronic computing equipment	8.9

6. See Martin Baily, "What Has Happened to Productivity Growth?" *Science*, October 24, 1986, pp. 443–451; and F. M. Scherer, "The World Productivity Growth Slump," in Rolf Wolff, ed., *Organizing Industrial Development* (Berlin: de Gruyter, 1986), pp. 15–27. The data here are from the *Economic Report of the President* (Washington: USGPO, 1988), p. 300.

7. See Edward M. Graham, "Technological Innovation and the Dynamics of the U.S. Comparative Advantage in International Trade," in Christopher T. Hill and James M. Utterback, *Technological Innovation for a Dynamic Economy* (New York: Pergamon, 1979), pp. 118–160; Leo Sveikauskas, "Science and Technology in United States Foreign Trade," *Economic Journal*, vol. 93 (September 1983), pp. 542–554; Kirsty S. Hughes, "Exports and Innovation," *European Economic Review*, vol. 30 (April 1986), pp. 383–399; David B. Audretsch and Hideki Yamawaki, "R&D Rivalry, Industrial Policy, and U.S.-Japanese Trade," *Review of Economics and Statistics*, vol. 70 (August 1988), pp. 438–447;

and U.S. National Science Board, *Science & Engineering Indicators: 1987* (Washington: USGPO, 1988), pp. 15, 124–136, and 313–326.

8. Joseph A. Schumpeter, *Capitalism, Socialism, and Democracy* (New York: Harper, 1942), p. 106.

9. See F. M. Scherer, *Innovation and Growth: Schumpeterian Perspectives* (Cambridge: MIT Press, 1984), Chapter 2.

10. *Science & Engineering Indicators*, supra note 7, p. 294.

11. On structure-performance links in federally supported programs, see William Burnett and F. M. Scherer, "The Weapons Industry," in Walter Adams, ed., *The Structure of American Industry* (8th ed.; New York: Macmillan, 1989).

12. Federal Trade Commission, *Statistical Report: Annual Line of Business Report, 1977* (Washington: April 1985), p. 21. The FTC Line of Business reports for 1974 through 1977 are the only reliable source of R&D spending data disaggregated to the four-digit level of detail.

Aircraft engines and parts	8.4
Calculating and accounting machines	7.3
Photographic equipment and supplies	6.3
Semiconductors	6.1
Photocopying equipment	5.7
Optical instruments and lenses	5.5%

What R&D Laboratories Do

Approximately 3 percent of U.S. industry's R&D effort goes into basic research, defined by the National Science Foundation as "original investigation for the advancement of scientific knowledge, without specific commercial objectives." Most basic research by this definition is done not in industry, but by academic and non-profit institutions (56 percent of the total in 1985) and government laboratories (24 percent). Industry's forte is applied research and the development of new or improved products and processes. From a count of the patents resulting from the 1974 R&D efforts of 443 large U.S. corporations, the distribution of industrial inventions by intended user orientation was as follows:[13]

Production processes for internal company use	26.2%
Capital goods for use by other industries	44.8
Same, with consumer usage too	7.8%
Materials for use by other industries	21.6
Same, with consumer usage too	8.7%
Consumer goods only	7.4%

What is particularly striking is the revealed emphasis on inventions by one industry that flow to other industries to improve the recipients' products and production processes.[14] Thus, a new fiber from du Pont improves the fabrics sold by textile weavers to garment makers, which only then enter the consumer's wardrobe; or a new aircraft engine from General Electric is sold to the airlines to let their planes operate more reliably, quietly, and economically. A surprisingly small fraction of industrial R&D is oriented toward improving products that will serve solely as consumer goods.

Another useful way of viewing what goes on in industrial R&D laboratories is to extend a trichotomy originally proposed by Schumpeter into a five-function schema: invention, entrepreneurship, investment, development, and diffusion.[15] Invention is the act of insight by which a new and promising technical possibility is worked out (at least mentally, and usually also physically) in its essential, most rudimentary form. Development is the lengthy sequence of detail-oriented technical activities, including trial-and-error testing, through which the original concept is modified and perfected until it is ready for commercial introduction. The entrepreneurial function involves deciding to go forward with the effort, organizing it, obtaining financial support, and cultivating the market. Investment is the act of risking funds for the venture. These creative functions need not be performed by the same person or even by the same organization. Indeed, they are often organizationally separate. Finally, diffusion (or imitation) is the process by which an innovation comes into widespread use as one producer after another follows the pioneering firm's lead.

Two Illustrations   To illustrate the first four functions, it is helpful to consider two brief examples. No case is completely typical. The histories presented here were chosen because they reflect unusually important and ambitious technical changes and because the stages and functions stand out with particular clarity. One, the Watt-Boulton steam engine venture of the 1770s, is ancient; the other, xerography, relatively new.

It is generally accepted that James Watt "invented" his improved steam engine in 1765, when he repaired a Newcomen steam engine model owned by Glasgow University and perceived that its efficiency could be greatly enhanced by condensing the steam outside the operating cylinder. He wrote later that "In three days, I had a model at work nearly as perfect . . . as any which have been made since that time."[16] But much remained to be done before he could supply a machine useful in industrial practice. Full-scale models had to be built, condenser concepts had to be devised and tested, valves designed, methods of machining and sealing the operating cylinder perfected, and so forth. All this required time and money, and for want of both financial support and entrepreneurial initiative, Watt twice abandoned the venture to work as a salaried engineer. Not until Matthew Boulton came forward to provide these missing ingredients was a full-scale model completed, and the first commercially useful Watt-Boulton steam engine was installed only in 1776, eleven years after the original invention. Expenditures preparing the way for operating the first commercial engine amounted to the equivalent of at least 60 person-years of skilled labor.

While working as a patent attorney, Chester Carlson was impressed by the difficulty of copying documents efficiently.[17] For several years he spent much of his spare time after work mulling over the problem and browsing in potentially relevant technical literature, eventually (in 1938) conceiving the basic idea of xerography. With the assistance of an unemployed physicist, he successfully tested his concept through an extremely crude model. After numerous fruitless attempts to interest industrial firms in helping him develop a commercially practical copying system, he enlisted in 1944 the cooperation of the Battelle Development Company, a subsidiary of the nonprofit Battelle Institute. From two years' labor by a Battelle research physicist and his aides came two key inventions building upon Carlson's original principle: the use of a selenium-coated plate to store the electrostatic image, and the corona discharge method for sensitizing the plate and applying

---

13. Scherer, *Innovation and Growth*, supra note 9, p. 36.

14. Strictly defined, R&D aimed at improving one's own productivity is *process* R&D. When a new machine is developed for sale to enhance another industry's productivity, the work is *product* R&D for its performer.

15. See Joseph A. Schumpeter, *The Theory of Economic Development*, trans. by Redvers Opie (Cambridge: Harvard University Press, 1934), Chapter 2; and Scherer, *Innovation and Growth*, supra note 9, Chapters 1 and 2.

16. Quoted in Scherer, *Innovation and Growth*, p. 10.

17. This example is drawn from John Jewkes, David Sawers, and Richard Stillerman, *The Sources of Invention*, 2nd ed. (New York: Norton, 1969), pp. 321–323; and Erwin Blackstone, "The Economics of the Copying Machine Industry" (Ph.D. diss., University of Michigan, 1968).

ink to the copying paper. With these inventions, xerography began to show distinct signs of commercial promise.

At this point the Haloid Corporation (later renamed the Xerox Corporation) took over developmental responsibility. By 1950 its engineers had completed a prototype system useful primarily for making offset lithography masters. This was a cumbersome, three-machine contraption, however, with limited market potential. The company then devoted its resources to developing a single-unit console copier—a task that required surmounting a difficult lens design problem and numerous lesser engineering challenges. The result was the 914 copier, which took the world by storm after its introduction in 1959. By that time, Xerox had accumulated a portfolio of nearly 300 issued and pending patents on its copying machine inventions.

During the more than two decades preceding the 914 copier's debut, formulation of the basic xerographic copying concept consumed the inventor's energies part-time for a very few years. The selenium plate and corona discharge inventions came from an only slightly greater increment of effort. After Haloid entered the picture, it expended roughly $4 million on research and development up to 1953, when it redirected attention to devising a console model. To attain that goal, further R&D outlays estimated at $16 million, severely straining the company's financial resources, were committed.

Several generalizations can be extracted from these and other innovation case studies. First, the initial invention that precipitates a major innovative effort is typically inexpensive, both relatively and absolutely. Its money cost is often so modest that almost any well-prepared imaginative individual thrown into contact with the problem might achieve the essential insight. The inventive challenge may be recognized as a result of formal work assignments, as a by-product of work or leisure pursuits, or from any of the 101 experiences a person has each day. If industrial R&D laboratories enjoy comparative advantage in generating inventions, it is because they are more likely to put together the critical combination of a fertile mind, a challenging problem, and the will to solve it.

Second, there is a substantial random component in fundamental invention. Thousands of persons may recognize an unsolved problem or unmet need, but only a fraction will be sufficiently intrigued to devote serious thought to it, and an even smaller fraction will have the ingenuity and good luck to gain a correct insight by viewing the problem in exactly the right way—that is, in the proper gestalt.[18] After the insight is achieved, the solution may seem obvious, but before the fact invention is largely unpredictable. If this were not so, every problem, once recognized, would be solved quickly.

Third, supporting inventions of greater or lesser creative magnitude may be required before the innovation begins to look technically and economically viable. Once the original insight is attained, however, it forms a gestalt within which such supporting inventions will tend inevitably to emerge if good minds are focused on the problem.

Fourth, when the necessary conceptual advances have occurred and when their essential correctness has been demonstrated, typically through crude model tests requiring only a modest resource investment, the uncertainties associated with innovation are transformed qualitatively and quantitatively. The question, "Is there something interesting and technically feasible here?" is no longer a serious issue. Uncertainty centers on such questions as: What will the detailed configuration be? How well can it be made to work? How much will perfecting it cost? How long will it take? At what price can it be sold? What will be the market demand at that price? These are not negligible uncertainties, but usually they are not overwhelming or outside the bounds of entrepreneurial experience. The vast majority of all industrial R&D projects, it should be noted, begin at this stage, since they embody no fundamental new concepts, or build upon insights achieved elsewhere.

Finally, once the sequence has progressed this far, outlays much greater than those incurred during the early conceptual stages are necessary before an innovation is brought to the point of commercial utility. The investment decision at this juncture entails committing possibly substantial resources in the face of moderate technological uncertainties. It is quite different from the earlier stage, where the amounts of money at risk are small, but the technical uncertainties are great. If inexpensive conceptual work has not reduced the degree of technical uncertainty to tolerable levels, a decision to move into full-scale development will be taken only under the most unusual pressures (as in the atomic and hydrogen bomb programs[19]). Normally, conceptual work will be continued at a low spending level until the main technical uncertainties have been resolved.

The Costs and Risks of R&D	The costs of individual industrial R&D projects vary widely. Most projects entail fairly modest outlays. Since 1963 the magazine *Research & Development* (earlier, *Industrial Research*) has conducted an annual competition to name the one hundred most significant technical advances of the year. On average, the winners in the years 1984 to 1986 had an average R&D cost of $2.47 million, with a range from $1,000 to $110 million.[20] However, the survey excludes some of the most complex and costly innovations. The original version of the F-18 fighter aircraft cost roughly $1 billion to develop during the late 1970s, and the B-2 Stealth bomber, first flown in 1989, absorbed $22 billion of R&D funds. Such military projects are so expensive and risky that they almost always go forward only with more or less full financing under government contracts. The most expensive projects undertaken under private initiative have been commercial airliners. In the late 1980s, developing a completely new long-range subsonic airliner was estimated to cost nearly $3 billion.

It is useful to think about R&D project costs in terms of a frequency distribution. A census would undoubtedly reveal the distribution to be highly skewed. The spectacularly costly projects that receive the most press attention are few in number, forming the distribution's long thin tail.[21] Smaller projects are much more numerous, giving rise to a peak or mode in a spending range near $1 million

18. This interpretation of the inventive act is based upon Abbott P. Usher, *A History of Mechanical Inventions*, rev. ed. (Cambridge: Harvard University Press, 1954), Chapter 4; N. R. Hanson, *Patterns of Discovery* (Cambridge: Cambridge University Press, 1958); and Thomas S. Kuhn, *The Structure of Scientific Revolutions* (Chicago: University of Chicago Press, 1962).

19. See Richard Rhodes, *The Making of the Atomic Bomb* (New York: Simon & Schuster, 1986).

20. "Developers of 100 Significant Products Feted," *Research & Development*, October 1986, p. 55. For earlier cost data, see F. M.

Scherer, *The Economic Effects of Compulsory Patent Licensing* (Monograph 1977–2, New York University Graduate School of Business Administration, 1977), p. 15, pulling together the results of several surveys by Edwin Mansfield and associates.

21. The distribution's extreme skewness is indicated by the wide range of values reported for the most costly of the 100 annual *Research & Development* citation winners: $40 million in 1981, $8 million in 1982, $960 million in 1983, $30 million in 1984, $50 million in 1985, and $110 million in 1986.

at 1987 price levels. The parameters of this distribution have been shifting over time; that is, the modal R&D project today is more expensive in constant-dollar terms than its counterpart thirty years ago.

However, the sizes of business enterprises have also been rising. In 1987, the two hundred fiftieth firm on *Fortune*'s list of the 500 largest industrials had sales of $1.39 billion. The average manufacturing corporation spent roughly 2.3 percent of its sales on R&D in that year. These two statistics imply an annual R&D budget of $40 million. Assuming an average R&D project to entail total expenditures of $2.5 million spread over three years,[22] our two hundred fiftieth industrial company could maintain a portfolio of roughly forty-eight projects. Thus, unless it inhabits an industry in which "big ticket" developments are the norm, the typical medium-sized corporation could hedge its risks with a fairly sizable and well-diversified R&D project portfolio.

The riskiness of individual corporate R&D projects has been illuminated in a series of studies by Edwin Mansfield and colleagues. In one such survey, they discovered that among projects carried out during 1963 to 1965, the average fraction fulfilling their technical objectives was 70 percent in seven chemical laboratories, 32 percent in five drug companies, 73 percent in three electronics organizations, and 50 percent in the laboratories of four petroleum companies.[23] The reason for the characteristically high rate of technical success has been brought out already: firms do not as a rule begin new product or process development until the principal technical uncertainties have been whittled down through inexpensive research, conducted either by their own personnel or by outsiders. Still the possibility of technical failure is not the only risk borne in industrial R&D. Consumer reactions and/or the size of the cost reductions achieved with new production processes may also be misjudged. Analyzing the fate of projects undertaken in the laboratories of sixteen chemical, pharmaceutical, electronics, and petroleum companies, Mansfield and associates identified three different success probabilities: (1) the probability that technical goals would be achieved; (2) the probability that, conditional upon technical success, the resulting product or process would be commercialized; and (3) given commercialization, the probability that the project yielded a return on investment at least as high as the opportunity cost of the firm's capital.[24] For all sixteen firms combined, the average conditional probabilities were:

Technical success	0.57
Commercialization, given technical success	0.65
Financial success, given commercialization	0.74

The firms' overall track record is assessed by multiplying the three conditional probabilities. Thus, on average, 27 percent of the projects initiated ultimately achieved financial success. For the prototypical *Fortune* 250 firm whose portfolio was characterized above, this means that its R&D laboratories would deliver four financial successes in a typical year. To be sure, the averages derived by Mansfield et al. were attended by considerable variation, so some of the firms studied did even better than average while others reaped barren harvests.

The Logic of Patent Protection

To reward those who invest their time and money in technological invention and innovation, and thus to encourage such investment, has been the classic function of invention patents since the first patents were granted in fifteenth-century Italy.[25] Modern patents, awarded to the first inventor of some new and useful product or process, give their holder the right to exclusive use of the invention for a specified period of time. This right includes the right to enjoin others from using the invention, or to license as few or as many other users as the patent holder chooses.

Most nations conferring patent rights accept broad guidelines stemming, with subsequent amendments, from the Paris Convention of 1883. In 1987, the Paris Convention had been adopted by ninety-seven member states, including thirty industrialized western nations, twelve eastern (that is, communist) nations, and fifty-five less-developed nations. Under the prevailing law of most western European nations, which was harmonized by the European Patent Convention in 1977, patents are issued to the first person to file an application validly claiming to have made an invention. The exclusive right they confer lasts for twenty years from the day of application. Under U.S. law, the normal life is seventeen years following the date a patent is issued. Priority under the U.S. system (emulated only by Canada and the Philippines) goes to the "first to invent," whose determination in contested cases entails a complex admixture of three criteria — who was first to conceive the idea, who was first to reduce it to practice, and whether the party exercised reasonable diligence in reducing the invention to practice. Between the application and issue dates is an examination period averaging roughly two years, but sometimes lasting as long as fifteen years, during which the Patent Office decides whether the claimed invention is indeed new, inventive, and useful, and, in cases of dispute, who the true inventor is.

Between 1980 and 1986, the U.S. Patent Office issued an average of 64,580 patents per year.[26] From the late 1960s until 1986, there was a declining trend in the total number of patents issued. There has also been a drop in the fraction of U.S. patents gained by domestic inventors. During the 1950s, foreign inventors received only 7 percent of U.S. patents. By 1980–1986, their share had increased to 42.6 percent, with Japanese inventors alone achieving a 15 percent share. A trend that predated the increasing internationalization of U.S. patenting was the shift from individual to corporate invention. When an employee makes an invention in the course of normal duties, the inventor typically "assigns" his or her rights

22. The mean outlay assumed here exceeds the mode because of the disproportionate influence of the largest projects.

23. Edwin Mansfield et al., *Research and Innovation in the Modern Corporation* (New York: Norton, 1971), pp. 34–35. See also Mansfield, *Industrial Research and Technological Innovation* (New York: Norton, 1968), pp. 56–61.

24. Edwin Mansfield, Samuel Wagner, et al., *The Production and Application of New Industrial Technology* (New York: Norton, 1977), pp. 22–32.

25. For new insights into the early history of patent grants and a thorough exploration of the underlying economic logic, see

Erich Kaufer, *The Economics of the Patent System* (Chur: Harwood, 1988). An earlier classic is Fritz Machlup, *An Economic Review of the Patent System*, Study No. 15 of the Senate Committee on the Judiciary, Subcommittee on Patents, Trademarks, and Copyrights (Washington: USGPO, 1958).

26. Recent data are summarized in *Science & Engineering Indicators*, supra note 7, pp. 302–303. Longer time series on a slightly different classification basis are found in the annual *Statistical Abstract of the United States*. The most comprehensive source on other nations' patent grants is the annual statistical report in the World Intellectual Property Organization's journal, *Industrial Property*.

to the employing corporation, in whose name the patent is then issued. Thus, a distinction is made between corporate and "individual" patent grants. The share of all U.S. patents issued to individual inventors was 91 percent in 1901, 72 percent in 1921, 42 percent in 1940, 25 percent during the 1960s, and 18.5 percent during the early 1980s.

The Basic Logic The funds supporting invention and the commercial development of inventions are front-end "sunk" investments; once they have been spent, they are an irretrievable bygone. To warrant making such investments, an individual inventor or corporation must expect that once commercialization occurs, product prices can be held above postinvention production and marketing costs long enough so that the discounted present value of the profits (or more accurately, quasi rents) will exceed the value of the front-end investment. In other words, the investor must expect some degree of protection from competition, or some monopoly power. The patent holder's right to exclude imitating users is intended to create or strengthen that expectation. Patents also confer a property right which the original patent holder can sell, recouping its original investment and letting another entity exclusively commercialize the patented subject matter. Partial "sale" is also possible, for example, when the patent holder licenses others to exploit the invention and charges a royalty for the right.[27]

The simplest case of a product innovation covered by patent protection is shown in Figure 17.1(a). If the product is really new and useful, it creates a wholly new demand curve D_1 — one that did not exist previously. With an exclusive right to make and sell its product, the patent holder is a monopolist. It derives its marginal revenue MR_1, equates marginal revenue with marginal production and distribution cost MC, and sets price OP_1, realizing "monopoly" profits in the amount of rectangular area P_1AXM. These are not pure profits, however, because the innovator's sunk R&D costs must be taken into account. To make that one-time lump sum consistent with Figure 17.1(a), which is expressed in annual "flow" terms, let us assume that the innovator finances its R&D investment by taking out a seventeen-year mortgage whose annual payment obligation is given by the area of the inset rectangle IJKL.[28] If the patent monopoly lasts for seventeen years, the annual "profit" P_1AXM will more than cover the annual R&D debt service cost, and the innovator will be well compensated for its efforts. It is not true, however, that the monopoly innovator is the only one to gain. The ordinates of demand curve D_1 array the values diverse consumers place upon having the new product to consume. The product's availability on monopolized terms generates not only producer's surplus P_1AXM, but also consumers' surplus BAP_1. With linear demand and constant marginal production and distribution costs, as shown in Figure 17.1(a), the monopolist is said to "appropriate" to itself only two-thirds of the total surplus its product creates.[29] The remaining third goes to consumers.

Suppose, however, that there were no patent protection and no other barriers to the imitation of the innovator's invention. Then a scenario like the one shown in panel (b) of Figure 17.1 might unfold. Soon after the new product appears, competing firms will introduce their imitating products, squeezing the demand schedule left for the original innovator to D_2. With less residual demand, the innovator must derive a new marginal revenue function MR_2 and set a new, lower price

(a) with Patent Protection

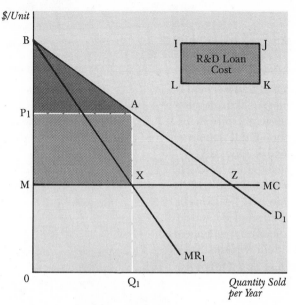

(b) without Patent Protection

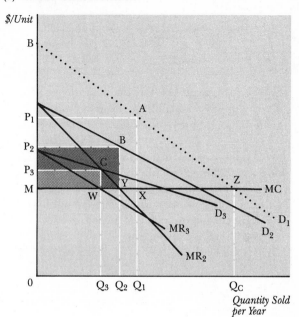

Figure 17.1
New Product Pricing With and
Without Patent Protection

OP_2, which yields profit rectangle P_2BYM barely covering the innovator's R&D debt service cost. However, the imitator firms may have had to incur little or no R&D cost on their own, "free riding" on the innovator's R&D, and thus, with unit costs of only OM, they will realize supra-normal profits at price OP_2. More competitors will be drawn in by this price and profit lure, squeezing the innovator's residual demand curve further to D_3. The innovator must reoptimize again, setting profit-maximizing price OP_3 and capturing "profit" rectangle P_3CWM, which is now smaller than the continuing R&D debt service obligations. If this

27. On the economics of licensing, see John S. McGee, "Patent Exploitation: Some Economic and Legal Problems," *Journal of Law & Economics*, vol. 9 (October 1966), pp. 135–162; Richard E. Caves, Harold Crookell, and J. Peter Killing, "The Imperfect Market for Technology Licenses," *Oxford Bulletin of Economics and Statistics*, vol. 45 (August 1983), pp. 249–267; and Morton I. Kamien, Y. Tauman, and I. Zang, "Optimal License Fees for a New Product," *Mathematical Social Sciences,* vol. 16 (August 1988), pp. 77–106.

28. Where RD is the original R&D investment, the yearly mortgage payment will be given by:

$$M(t) = \frac{RD}{\frac{1 - (1 + i)^{-17}}{i}}$$

with i the annual rate of interest and 17 the number of years over which the mortgage is paid down. If the R&D investment is $1 million and the interest rate i is 10 percent, the annual debt service will be $124,664.

29. Proof: From footnote 13, Chapter 2, MR falls by twice as much as D_1 over output range OQ_1. Thus, BM = 2 BP_1 and BP_1 = P_1M. With height and base equal to those of rectangle P_1AXM, triangle BAP_1 has half the rectangle's area.

diffusion process were to unfold rapidly and if the innovator correctly foresaw its course, the innovator would perceive that its R&D costs will not be recouped and would therefore choose not to invest in the R&D. Consumers will be deprived of a valuable new product — one that, even under pure monopoly conditions, could yield them a sizable consumers' surplus.

Pursuing the analysis a step further, we see a kind of dilemma. *If* the R&D investment were incurred and the innovation made, imitative entry might, absent patent protection, continue until the price is driven all the way down to the competitive level, ignoring the innovator's front-end costs — that is, to OM. If this happens, surplus P_1AXM, originally captured by the innovator, will be transformed into consumers' surplus. In addition, the competitive expansion of output to OQ_C leads to the emergence of still more consumers' surplus, measured by triangle AZX. In this limiting case, the innovator appropriates none of the (now larger) surplus its invention has created — consumers get it all. If the innovator is allowed to monopolize the new product's sale, its profit-maximizing output restriction means that total surplus will be less than it might ideally be by dead-weight loss triangle AZX. In this sense, granting patent monopolies imposes a cost upon society. Seeing this, consumers might urge that the government renege on its patent monopoly grant so they can have the best of all worlds — the new product, competitive pricing, and maximum surplus. But if this occurs with any frequency, would-be innovators will expect rapid imitation to erode their surpluses, causing them to lose money on their R&D investments, so they will not invest in additional new products. The technological well will run dry. The patent system makes a deliberate tradeoff, accepting during the patent grant's life dead-weight surplus losses in order to ensure that new products and processes, along with the surpluses they create, will not be discouraged by fear of rapid imitation. Only after the patent expires, when competitive imitation can run its full course, are consumers able to have their new product along with the extra surplus competitive pricing brings.[30]

Complications

Although devised to solve an important incentive problem, the patent system is a crude and imperfect instrument. Because of diverse real-world complications, the patent protection given an innovator may be too little, too much, or of the wrong kind.

The protection provided is often weak because there can be many viable solutions to a technical problem, so other firms can "invent around" a given patented solution. Individual patents that solidly protect a whole field of product or process technology are rare, and when such cases occur, the credit is frequently due as much to the skill of the patent attorney as to the breadth of the inventor's vision. To be sure, companies often seek to fence in their technological domain by patenting every conceivable variation on a product or process.[31] Yet fences are also permeable. Du Pont, for example, took out hundreds of patents on variants of its nylon synthetic fiber technology. But even in the directly applicable polyamide molecule family it left a gap into which Germany's I.G. Farben moved with Perlon L, and other companies invented competitive fibers using polyester and polyolefin molecules.

Further complications emerge because the growth of technology is cumulative and richly interactive. Company B may patent an improvement on Company A's invention, or Companies C and D may each hold patents on diverse features, all of which a state-of-the-art product should ideally incorporate. Each might if it wishes block the other from using desired complementary technology. Under Chinese patent law and Japanese practice, firms holding improvement patents on others' inventions can demand a license to the original patent by reciprocally offering to license their improvement. This logjam-breaking provision, absent from U.S. and European law, engendered considerable conflict between U.S. and Japanese industry leaders during the 1980s.[32] In the United States and Europe, the holders of complementary patents often agree voluntarily to cross license each other.[33] This enables all to achieve state-of-the-art technology but lessens the exclusionary power of patents. However, such cross licensing agreements have sometimes been used as a fulcrum for industrywide price-fixing and entry-excluding cartels that suppress competition more than would have been possible if each firm independently exploited its own patented technology. In the United States, cartelization through reciprocal licensing of patents has for the most part been dealt with harshly under the antitrust laws.[34]

For smaller and especially less-developed countries (LDCs), patent holders' power to block use of their inventions by others poses a special problem. Multinational corporations commonly patent their most important inventions in dozens of national jurisdictions. The quest for scale economies leads them to produce in one

30. Extending this logic, William D. Nordhaus developed a pioneering model to determine the optimal patent life tradeoff— that is, one that maximizes the discounted present value of consumers' plus producers' surpluses. See his *Invention, Growth, and Welfare: A Theoretical Treatment of Technological Change* (Cambridge: MIT Press, 1969), Chapter 5. He shows that the optimal patent life is longer: (1) the less price-elastic demand is (and hence the smaller the dead-weight loss AYX incurred until the patent expires); (2) the smaller the overall benefit from invention is in relation to the chosen R&D outlay; and (3) the more responsive the amount of invention is to an increase in R&D expenditures. In extensions, it has been shown that the optimal patent life is longer than Nordhaus' computations when patents provide imperfect protection against imitation or when there is compulsory licensing at controlled (that is, low) royalty rates. It is shorter when preinnovation competition raises R&D costs and reduces the net profitability of innovation. See, for example, Scherer, *Innovation and Growth*, Chapter 7; Pankaj Tandon, "Optimal Patents with Compulsory Licensing," *Journal of Political Economy*, vol. 90 (June 1982), pp. 470–486; D. G. McFetridge and M. Rafiquzzaman, "The Scope and Duration of the Patent Right and the Nature of Research Rivalry," with a comment by Roger Beck, in *Research in Law and Economics*, vol. 8 (Greenwich, CT; JAI Press, 1986), pp. 91–129; and Brian D. Wright, "The Economics of Invention Incentives," *American Economic Review*, vol. 73 (September 1983), pp. 691–707.

31. Under U.S. antitrust precedents, this is not in itself illegal. See *Automatic Radio Mfg. Co.* v. *Hazeltine Research, Inc..*, 339 U.S. 827, 834 (1950). However, when collusive or abusive practices were used in conjunction with the accumulation of patents, or

when the accumulation was achieved through merger rather than one's own R&D, licensing of the accumulated patents has been required. See, for example, U.S. Senate, Committee on the Judiciary, Subcommittee on Patents, Trademarks, and Copyrights, staff report, *Compulsory Patent Licensing under Antitrust Judgments* (Washington: USGPO, 1960); and F. M. Scherer, *The Economic Effects of Compulsory Patent Licensing*, supra note 20, pp. 59–78.

32. See "An American Views Japan's Copycat Culture," *Wall Street Journal*, July 12, 1988, p. 33.

33. In "The Learning Curve, Technology Barriers to Entry, and Competitive Survival in the Chemical Processing Industries," *Strategic Management Journal* (1989), Marvin B. Lieberman reports that the licensing of technology to new entrants was more common in unconcentrated than in concentrated industries. On the licensing practices of West German firms, see Klaus Grefermann and K. C. Roethlingshöfer, *Patentwesen und technischer Fortschritt*, Teil II, "Patent- und Lizenzpolitik der Unternehmen" (Göttingen: Schwartz, 1974).

34. See U.S. Senate, *Compulsory Patent Licensing*, supra note 31; Floyd L. Vaughan, *The United States Patent System* (Norman: University of Oklahoma Press, 1956); and Louis Kaplow, "The Patent-Antitrust Intersection," *Harvard Law Review,* vol. 97 (June 1984), pp. 1813–1892. During the 1980s some backpedaling occurred, following arguments first emphasized by Ward S. Bowman, *Patent and Antitrust Law: A Legal and Economic Appraisal* (Chicago: University of Chicago Press, 1973), especially Chapter 10. See also Roger B. Andewelt, "Analysis of Patent Pools under the Antitrust Laws," *Antitrust Law Journal,* vol. 53, no. 3 (1985), pp. 611–638.

or a few preferred locations, exporting elsewhere and preventing the local exploitation of their technology in export markets by asserting their patent rights. For an LDC, this typically means that high prices will be paid for imported patented products, while opportunities to build a home industry using first-line technology are restricted. Many LDCs and some more industrialized nations have therefore included in their patent laws provisions requiring that the technology on which they issue patents be "worked" domestically within a few years or be subjected to compulsory licensing. Such provisions have been a focus of conflict between multinational corporations, stressing the rationale of patent incentives and efficiently centralized production, and LDCs, emphasizing their need to escape from backwardness by building dynamic modern industries.[35]

Alternative Protection from Imitation

The patent grant is a tradeoff, but if an invention would be made and commercialized without patent protection, the terms are altered. The power to impose monopolistic restrictions remains, but what consumers get in the bargain would have been available on less restrictive terms. There are several reasons why competitive imitation might be impeded even without patents, leaving sufficient incentive for investments in research and development.

For one, to imitate one must know about the innovation and its advantages, and knowledge is almost always imperfect. Firms often protect their technological advances by keeping them secret for as long as they can.[36] Even when patent protection is sought, there is a lag from the time of invention to the time the patent (or under European and Japanese procedures, its application) is published. And once a new technology is made public, it takes time for potential imitators to learn about it and decide whether it is worth copying. Some are quicker than others in this respect. Studies of the diffusion process reveal that adoption spreads, first slowly and then more rapidly, in a pattern characterized well by an ogive curve such as the cumulative logistic.[37] For a sample of twelve significant innovations, lags ranging from one to twenty years and averaging ten years occurred before 60 percent of all relevant producers adopted the new technology.[38] Edwin Mansfield found the speed of imitation to be positively correlated with the profitability of adopting the new technology. For product innovations in particular, this means that the pace of imitation is a variable under the innovator's control. Companies pricing their new products to make a quick killing will encourage rapid imitation, while those pursuing dynamic limit-pricing strategies like those analyzed in Chapter 10 may be able to retain sizable market positions for a considerable period.

Second, free riding on an innovator's technical contribution is often far from free. An appreciable but varying fraction of the original R&D may have to be replicated. At one extreme in this respect are airliners. One can inspect a rival's design, but to build a similar aircraft, one must generate detailed engineering drawings for each part, program machine tools to produce the parts, build prototypes, and subject them to static and dynamic testing to ensure that unnoticed design flaws do not lead to catastrophe. Only the innovator's most basic conceptual work and wind tunnel testing can be circumvented. At the other extreme are new prescription drugs. To introduce a new drug to the U.S. market during the late 1980s entailed research, development, and testing costs of $50 to $100 million. Most of these costs were incurred discovering molecules with desirable therapeutic effects in humans and proving through extensive clinical testing that the substances were effective and safe. Once these formidable information-generating hurdles are surmounted, it typically costs only a few hundred thousand dollars for an able biochemist to develop production methods. Thus, if there is no patent (or regulatory) barrier,[39] imitators can free ride on most of the innovator's investment.

Through a broad-ranging survey of company research and development decision makers, Richard Levin and colleagues learned that the R&D costs of duplicating a major *unpatented* new product exceeded 50 percent of the original innovator's R&D costs in 86 percent of the 127 covered industries.[40] Duplication costs exceeded 75 percent of the original costs in 40 percent of the industries. Patenting does, however, affect the cost of duplication. Levin et al. estimated that patent protection increased imitation costs by 40 percentage points in pharmaceuticals (relative to a scale on which equally costly imitation is 100), by 25 points for typical chemical products; by 7 to 15 points for semiconductor, communications equipment, and computer products; and by an average of 17 percentage points for machine tools, pumps, and compressors.[41] Timely duplication of a major patented new product was reported to be impossible in only twelve of the 127 surveyed industries.[42]

Third, as we have seen in Chapter 16, being the first to bring a new product onto the market, with or without patent protection, often confers a substantial reputational advantage over imitators, permitting the innovator to maintain elevated prices while defending a sizable market share. Also, as Chapter 10 revealed, the first mover has a head start in the race down learning curves, gaining cost advantages which, if exploited sufficiently aggressively, can be used to deter entry and enjoy supra-normal profits until the relevant technology matures.

35. For various views, see Edith T. Penrose, "International Patenting and the Less Developed Countries," *Economic Journal,* vol. 83 (September 1973), pp. 768–786; the articles by S. J. Patel, Pedro Roffe, and Peter O'Brien in *World Development*, vol. 2 (September 1974), pp. 2–36; Michael Berkowitz and Y. Kotowitz, "Patent Policy in an Open Economy," *Canadian Journal of Economics*, vol. 15 (February 1982), pp. 1–17; and Helena Stalson, *Intellectual Property Rights and U.S. Competitiveness in Trade* (Washington: National Planning Association, 1987).

36. The number of patents obtained per million dollars of R&D varies widely from industry to industry, in part because of differing emphases on secrecy. See F. M. Scherer, "The Propensity to Patent," *International Journal of Industrial Organization*, vol. 1 (March 1983), pp. 107–128. In an analysis of the data underlying that paper, Swarthmore College student Laurie Laird found that the propensity to patent declined significantly with the importance surveyed corporate R&D officials attached to keeping their inventions secret. On the survey, see note 40 infra.

37. See William L. Baldwin and John T. Scott, *Market Structure and Technological Change* (Chur: Harwood, 1987), pp. 128–144; and Colin Thirtle and Vernon W. Ruttan, *The Role of Demand and Supply in the Generation and Diffusion of Technical Change* (Chur: Harwood, 1987), pp. 77–124. Recognition appears to occur much more rapidly than implementation. See Edwin Mansfield, "How Rapidly Does New Technology Leak Out?" *Journal of Industrial Economics,* vol. 34 (December 1985), pp. 217–223. Empirical

studies reveal fairly consistently that large firms tend to imitate new technologies more rapidly than small firms, all else equal. Baldwin and Scott conclude (p. 143) that diffusion is likely to proceed more rapidly in industries of relatively low seller concentration, but find (p. 132) that the relationship is "blurred."

38. Estimated (with assistance from the author) from Edwin Mansfield, *Industrial Research and Technological Innovation* (New York: Norton, 1968), pp. 134–135.

39. On regulatory barriers, see Edmund W. Kitch, "The Patent System and the New Drug Application," in Richard L. Landau, ed., *Regulating New Drugs* (Chicago: University of Chicago Center for Policy Study, 1973), pp. 81–109.

40. Richard C. Levin, Alvin Klevorick, Richard R. Nelson, and Sidney G. Winter, "Appropriating the Returns from Industrial Research and Development," *Brookings Papers on Economic Activity* (1987, no. 3), p. 809. Altogether, the survey encompassed 650 executives.

41. Ibid., p. 811. The mechanical product average is derived by us from the Levin et al. raw data. Their results are similar to those obtained from a study of forty-eight specific new products by Edwin Mansfield, Mark Schwartz, and Samuel Wagner, "Imitation Costs and Patents: An Empirical Study," *Economic Journal*, vol. 91 (December 1981), pp. 907–918.

42. See also Mansfield et al., "Imitation Costs," p. 913, who found that 60 percent of the successful patented inventions in their sample were imitated within four years.

Finally, imitation may be held back by the very structure of the market. For all but innovations that define a completely new field,[43] the most likely early imitators are companies already operating in the industry to which the innovation pertains. Lack of production facilities, managerial experience, and channels of distribution impedes the entry of outsiders. If in addition the market is moderately or tightly concentrated, postimitation pricing discipline may remain firm for a considerable period. The innovator can then expect to retain at least its historical share of the industry's enhanced profits, and if innovation confers first-mover advantages, an already sizable share may be augmented.

In sum, competitive elimination of innovators' profits is often delayed because of natural secrecy and recognition lags, imitators' need to duplicate some or all of the innovator's R&D effort, first-mover advantages accruing to the innovator, and the protection an oligopolistic market structure affords. As a result, the profit expectations associated with a prospective innovation may be sufficient to warrant going ahead even when no patent protection is anticipated.

This conclusion is supported by the findings from several surveys of R&D executives, revealing quite uniformly that in most industries, patents are not very important compared to other incentives for innovation. In the most recent and comprehensive effort, Levin et al. asked 650 U.S. R&D executives to evaluate on a scale of from 1 ("not at all effective") to 7 ("very effective") the effectiveness of alternative means of protecting the competitive advantages from new and improved products and processes.[44] Averaging across 130 industries, the scores on six questionnaire items were as follows:

Method of Appropriating the Benefits from Innovation	New and Improved Product Average	New and Improved Process Average
Patents to prevent duplication	4.33	3.52
Patents to secure royalty income	3.75	3.31
Secrecy	3.57	4.31
Being first with an innovation	5.41	5.11
Moving quickly down the learning curve	5.09	5.02
Superior sales or service efforts	5.59	4.55

For both products and processes, the nonpatent strategic advantages from being an innovator were found to be substantially more important than patent protection.[45] In only twenty-five of the 130 industries did the average score for product patents as a means of preventing duplication exceed 5 on a 7 point scale (that is, between "moderately effective" and "very effective"). R&D executives placed greatest stress on product patent protection in the pharmaceuticals industry, agricultural chemicals (for example, pesticides and herbicides, subject to analogous federal testing regulations), and industrial organic chemicals.

Pursuing a different survey thrust, Edwin Mansfield asked the chief R&D executives of one hundred U.S. firms what proportion of the inventions they developed during 1981 through 1983 would not have been developed had they been unable to obtain patent protection. The results for eight surveyed industry groupings were as follows:[46]

Pharmaceuticals	60%
Other chemicals	38
Petroleum	25
Machinery	17
Fabricated metal products	12
Electrical equipment	11
Primary metals	1
Instruments	1

In four other groups, office equipment, motor vehicles, rubber products, and textiles, the average score was 0 percent. Weighting the responses according to 1982 company-financed R&D expenditures in the reporting groups, the aggregate loss of inventions without patent protection would have been roughly 14 percent of those actually made.[47]

Thus, a world without patents quite clearly would not be a world without innovation. Other incentives for innovation would fill most gaps. Some inventions would be lost, especially when the output of R&D is mostly information on whether the product works, upon which free riding is easy, and not on the details of product design and manufacturing. Patent protection appears also to be relatively important where the coverage is an all-or-nothing affair, for example, on particular chemical molecules or the features of a unique mechanism. The absence of patents might have particularly serious negative effects for independent inventors and small fledgling firms, who were not included in the surveys reported here. On this the evidence is more sparse, but offsetting tendencies can be identified. Small firms are at a severe disadvantage trying to claim patent rights, or enforce them against large rivals better able to sustain the multimillion-dollar costs of a protracted patent litigation.[48] Thus, even though they need patent

43. For field-creating innovations, new outside entry is more likely, but only after a period of slow entry averaging fourteen years in an analysis of forty-six new product histories by Michael Gort and Steven Klepper. "Time Paths in the Diffusion of Product Innovations," *Economic Journal*, vol. 92 (September 1982), pp. 640–642. The slow-entry stage was found to have declined over time to five years on average for products introduced after 1940.

44. "Appropriating the Returns," supra note 40, pp. 794–796. Similar earlier studies include F. M. Scherer, S. E. Herzstein, Alex Dreyfoos, et al., *Patents and the Corporation* (rev. ed.; Boston: privately published, 1959); and C. T. Taylor and Z. A. Silberston, *The Economic Impact of the Patent System* (Cambridge: Cambridge University Press, 1973).

45. Among eight reasons why the effectiveness of patents in protecting new technology was limited, the ability of competitors legally to "invent around" patented inventions was accorded by far the greatest weight. Levin et al., "Appropriating the Returns," supra note 40, p. 803.

46. Edwin Mansfield, "Patents and Innovation: An Empirical Study," *Management Science*, vol. 32 (February 1986), p. 175. Earlier surveys yielding similar results include, for the United Kingdom, Taylor and Silberston, *The Economic Impact*, supra note 44, pp. 195–199; for Germany, Klaus Grefermann, K. H. Oppenländer, et al., *Patentwesen und technischer Fortschritt*, Teil I, "Die Wirkung des Patentwesens im Innovationsprozess" (Göttingen: Schwartz, 1974), pp. 47–52 and Appendix Tables 75–78; and Mansfield et al., "Imitation Costs," supra note 41, pp. 915–916.

47. The weights are from U.S. National Science Foundation, *National Patterns of Science and Technology Resources: 1984* (Washington: USGPO, 1984), p. 52.

48. In a rarer "David slays Goliath" case, a former graduate student inventor, supported by a venture capital firm, won basic laser patent rights after an eighteen-year legal struggle against Bell Telephone Laboratories. See "Now the Father of the Laser Can Get Back To Inventing," *Business Week*, February 17, 1986, p. 98; "Patlex Wins Suit on Laser Patent," *New York Times*, November 6, 1987, p. D4; and "Ex-Astronaut To Lead Small Laser Company," *New York Times*, June 16, 1988, p. D4.

protection more than well-established companies, the protection they actually receive is more fragile. Wherever the balance lies for both small and large corporations, it is clear that we must seek deeper insight into the stimuli for innovation in a world where patents provide at best partial protection against rapid imitation, and where other barriers to imitation are at least as important as patents. To that task we proceed.

The Links Between Market Structure and Innovation

Under the logic of the patent grant, the expectation that successful innovation will lead to a monopoly position induces firms to invest in R&D. Now we turn the tables to examine a series of hypotheses inspired by Joseph A. Schumpeter.[49] They suggest that the *possession* of monopoly power is conducive to innovation in the kind of turbulent environment associated with, and often caused by, technological change. The chain of causation is said to run from existing market structure to the pace of innovation, though it must be recognized at once that there are feedback effects from innovation to market structure.

One hypothesis is that profits accumulated through the exercise of monopoly power are a key source of funds to support costly and risky innovation. The predictions of economic theory on this point are ambiguous,[50] so the matter can only be resolved empirically. Carrying out clear-cut statistical tests is difficult because, while profits may lead to innovation, innovation also leads to profits, and it is crucial to get both the timing and the shapes of the lags right.[51] Also, increases in demand are believed to "pull" increased inventive effort,[52] and since outward demand shifts normally increase short-run profits, one must disentangle demand-pull from financing influences. There is considerable evidence that augmented R&D activity follows increases in profitability with typically short lags,[53] but in view of the conceptual problems, it is hard to be sure that the cause was enhanced financing ability. Especially in the United States, the growth of a thriving venture capital industry channeling investment into new high-technology firms shows that past monopoly profits are no *sine qua non* for supporting innovation.[54]

Monopoly and Oligopolistic Rivalry

Economic theory has yielded numerous insights on firms' incentives to innovate under market structures ranging from pure monopoly with blockaded entry to pure competition, with diverse empirically important oligopoly variants in between. We focus here on incentives for *product* innovation, on which in the United States roughly three dollars are spent for each dollar of internal *process* R&D.[55]

Introducing a product innovation is usefully viewed as tapping into a market with some potential for earning profits, which means that there must be a surplus of sales over production and distribution costs so that front-end R&D costs can be recouped. Precision of terminology is important here, so despite the awkwardness, let us call that transitory surplus by its correct name, a *quasi rent*. The quasi-rent potential has a significant time dimension. It is approximated by the line b(t) in Figure 17.2 as being constant over time, for example, $800,000 per year, year after year. If demand-pull influences were at work, the quasi-rent potential b(t) would instead be rising steadily over time or jumping discontinuously at certain moments in time (for example, when an energy shock occurs). How innovators and their rivals tap into the stream's potential is crucial to the analysis of incentives.[56] Absent government or similar subsidies, no gains can be realized until research and development are completed and the product is commercially introduced. This introduction date is shown as T* in Figure 17.2. Usually it takes time to build up to the new product's full quasi-rent potential, so the innovator's annual gain *if it subsequently monopolizes the new product market* is shown by the rising line v_M. However, as we have seen, neither patents nor being first with a new product are normally sufficient to exclude competitive imitation. Suppose another firm imitates at time T_{ii}. Then the rival begins chewing away some of the quasi rents the innovator would otherwise capture. The effect on the innovator's quasi-rent realizations is shown by the dotted line v_{ii}. The distance between v_M and v_{ii} is the quasi rent realized by the imitator, assuming that the total profit pool is not shrunk by price competition; so the distance under v_{ii} is what remains for the innovator. Suppose alternatively that the imitator delays its product introduction even more to time T_{iii}. This will presumably strengthen the innovator's first-mover advantage. If so, the imitator will not only tap the market later, but will capture a

49. *Capitalism, Socialism, and Democracy*, supra note 8, especially Chapter VIII.

50. See Morton I. Kamien and Nancy L. Schwartz, "Self-Financing of an R&D Project," *American Economic Review*, vol. 68 (June 1978), pp. 252–261.

51. See David J. Ravenscraft and F. M. Scherer, "The Lag Structure of Returns to Research and Development," *Applied Economics*, vol. 14 (December 1982), pp. 603–620.

52. See Jacob Schmookler, *Invention and Economic Growth* (Cambridge: Harvard University Press, 1966); and for a survey of subsequent studies, many critical, see Thirtle and Ruttan, *The Role of Demand*, supra note 37, especially pp. 6–11.

53. The most careful attempts to estimate both forward and backward lag structures are Ben S. Branch, "Research and Development Activity and Profitability," *Journal of Political Economy*, vol. 82 (September/October 1974), pp. 999–1011; and Ariel Pakes, "On Patents, R&D, and the Stock Market Rate of Return," *Journal of Political Economy*, vol. 93 (April 1985), pp. 390–409. See also Dennis C. Mueller, "The Firm Decision Process: An Econometric Investigation," *Quarterly Journal of Economics,* vol. 81 (February 1967), pp. 71–73; Albert N. Link, "An Analysis of the Composition of R&D Spending," *Southern Economic Journal*, vol. 49 (October 1982), pp. 343–349 (suggesting that basic and applied research are more responsive to prior profitability than development); and Lorne Switzer, "The Determinants of Industrial R&D," *Review of Economics and Statistics*, vol. 66 (February 1984), pp. 163–168.

54. For data on the growth of technology-oriented venture capital activity, see U.S. National Science Board, *Science Indicators: The 1985 Report* (Washington: USGPO, 1985), pp. 260–261. Updated expenditures data and other current reports appear in a periodical, the *Venture Economics Journal*. For an international view, see OECD, *Venture Capital: Context, Development and Policies* (Paris: 1986).

55. In addition to the approach taken here, there are two main alternative lines of theorizing. One, focusing on outlays that shift

the firm's cost curve (that is, process invention), began with Kenneth J. Arrow, "Economic Welfare and the Allocation of Resources for Invention," in the National Bureau of Economic Research conference volume, *The Rate and Direction of Inventive Activity* (Princeton: Princeton University Press, 1962), pp. 609–625. A recent extension with comprehensive references to earlier Arrow progeny is Thomas F. Cosimano, "The Incentive To Adopt Cost Reducing Innovation in the Presence of a Non-Linear Demand Curve," *Southern Economic Journal*, vol. 48 (July 1981), pp. 97–104. Another line invokes the Dorfman-Steiner theorem (see Chapter 15, note 3; and Chapter 16, notes 64 and 65) to determine an overall R&D budget (undifferentiated by project types) that maximizes profits. See Douglas Needham, "Market Structure and Firms' R&D Behavior," *Journal of Industrial Economics*, vol. 23 (June 1975), pp. 241–255; and Takeo Nakao, "Product Quality and Market Structure," *Bell Journal of Economics*, vol. 13 (Spring 1982), pp. 133–142.

56. The analysis here follows F. M. Scherer, "Research and Development Resource Allocation under Rivalry," *Quarterly Journal of Economics*, vol. 81 (August 1967), pp. 359–394, and two related articles reproduced in Scherer, *Innovation and Growth*, supra note 9, Chapters 4 and 6. Rich variations and extensions are presented in Morton I. Kamien and Nancy L. Schwartz, "On the Degree of Rivalry for Maximum Innovative Activity," *Quarterly Journal of Economics*, vol. 90 (May 1976), pp. 245–260; Kamien and Schwartz, "Potential Rivalry, Monopoly Profits and the Pace of Inventive Activity," *Review of Economic Studies*, vol. 45 (October 1978), pp. 547–557; Jennifer Reinganum, "A Dynamic Game of R&D: Patent Protection and Competitive Behavior," *Econometrica*, vol. 50 (May 1982), pp. 671–688; Marion B. Stewart, "Noncooperative Oligopoly and Preemptive Innovation without Winner-Take-All," *Quarterly Journal of Economics*, vol. 98 (November 1983), pp. 681–694; and Michael L. Katz and Carl Shapiro, "R&D Rivalry with Licensing or Imitation," *American Economic Review*, vol. 77 (June 1987), pp. 402–420.

Figure 17.2
Innovator's Quasi-rents
Without and With Imitation

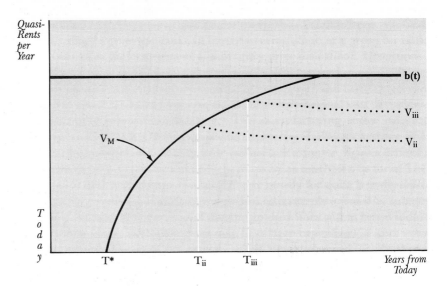

smaller share of the total quasi-rent potential, leaving the innovator with a gain function like v_{iii} in Figure 17.2.

The question remains, How rapidly should a firm that believes it will (or in a more uncertain world, might) be the innovator conduct its R&D project? In other words, what determines the position of T* in Figure 17.2?

To find out, we must first introduce the cost side of the picture. This is done through the *time-cost tradeoff function* C(T) in Figure 17.3. It shows the cost of conducting the R&D effort over a continuous array of alternative time schedules, assuming that the effort begins at time 0 (that is, today). Accelerating the pace of R&D, that is, achieving lower values of T, increases the cost of R&D for three reasons: because one may have to pursue parallel experimental approaches to find a good solution quickly under uncertainty, because moving on to design and production tooling steps before early experiments have yielded their information saves time but increases the number of false starts, and because of conventional diminishing marginal returns in allocating talent to a given technical assignment.[57] The more uncertain the technological environment is, the more curvature the time-cost tradeoff function is likely to have.[58]

The line V_M in Figure 17.3 integrates (literally) the data in Figure 17.2 to show the discounted present value of the *total* quasi rents expected over time by an innovating firm on the assumption that it will be a monopolist, experiencing no competition from imitators. It is downward sloping because the longer the firm takes to carry out its development, the longer it will have to wait to tap the stream of potential quasi rents, and the more heavily discounted the benefits it anticipates will be. To maximize profits, the firm must find a development schedule that leaves the maximum vertical distance between quasi-rent function V_M and R&D cost function C(T). This is achieved where the slopes of the two functions are equal, that is, with a planned project time of five years, leaving a surplus AB of quasi rents over R&D costs.

Figure 17.3
Profit-maximizing R&D
Schedule Choices

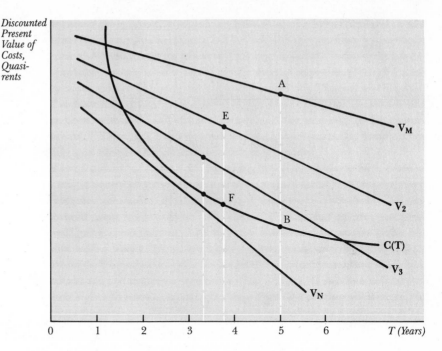

Let us now relax our assumption that the innovator monopolizes its product's sales after innovating. Moving step by step, we consider first the case in which innovative rivalry is duopolistic. If one firm is an imitator, reaching the market with its new product later than the innovator, an uneven division of quasi rents like those shown by curves v_{ii} or v_{iii} in Figure 17.2 will occur. But if the firms start from symmetric structural positions, there is no reason to believe that one rival will consciously choose to accept second place. Instead, each may struggle to be the first mover. We saw in Chapter 6 that Cournot-Nash rivalry in price-setting duopolies is implausible; at best, the parties may jump without intervening moves to an equilibrium position. But each new product rivalry is *sui generis,* not a repeated game, and there are lags between observation, reaction, and further reaction. It is much more realistic, therefore, to assume that something like Cournot reactions will ensue.

Figure 17.4(*a*) shows the R&D schedule reaction pattern in a completely symmetric duopolistic new product rivalry. The horizontal axis measures Firm 1's R&D time, the vertical axis Firm 2's time. Quasi-rent functions like those shown in Figure 17.2 and cost functions like C(T) in Figure 17.3 give rise to reaction functions like R_1 (for Firm 1) and R_2 in Figure 17.4(*a*). Suppose Firm 1 starts the new product development at the leisurely pace implied by point A. Seeing its rival

57. For statistical estimates, see Edwin Mansfield et al., *Research and Innovation*, supra note 23, Chapters 6 and 7; and *Technology Transfer, Productivity, and Economic Policy* (New York: Norton, 1982), pp. 87–96.

58. Scherer, *Innovation and Growth*, supra note 9, Chapter 4.

(a) Fully Symmetric
    Duopoly

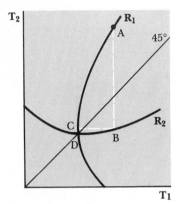

(b) Asymmetric Starting Dates,
    Symmetric Structure

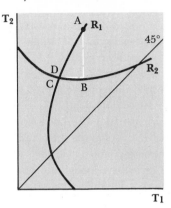

(c) Symmetric Starting Dates,
    Asymmetric Strategic Position

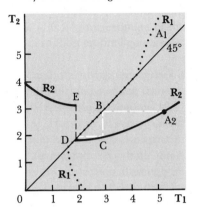

Figure 17.4
R&D Rivalry Reaction
Functions

ahead (that is, on the northwest side of the 45° equal-times line), Firm 2 gets going and moves to point B on its reaction function. Seeing Firm 2 pull ahead, Firm 1 accelerates to point C. Firm 2 reacts to Cournot equilibrium point D, where both firms are symmetrically pursuing much faster R&D schedules than they would have chosen in the absence of rivalry. Except to the extent that chance factors intervene, they will enter the market with their new products in a dead heat.

The effects of two-firm rivalry can be shown more summarily for a representative firm through the discounted total quasi-rent line V_2 in Figure 17.3. It slopes downward more steeply than monopoly function V_M because of the stimulus rivalry provides. With steeper slope, the maximum distance between V_2 and $C(T)$ occurs at a more compressed R&D schedule—for example, in Figure 17.3, 3.75 years, with total quasi rents exceeding R&D costs by the distance EF. V_2 is nearer the origin than V_M because the gains from innovation are shared by two firms, each of which appropriates less than a single monopolist would for any given market introduction date.

Symmetry in Figure 17.4(a) implies two tacit assumptions: equal natural strengths in the market, reflected for instance in equal market shares for the most closely related existing products, and equal (or insignificantly different) R&D project starting times. Panel (b) of Figure 17.4 relaxes the second but not the first assumption. Now Firm 1 gets a jump on its rival, scheduling its project at A. When Firm 2 wakes up, it moves to B on its own reaction function. But with its head start, Firm 1 can accelerate to C, putting Firm 2 at a hopeless disadvantage. Laggards like Firm 2 under these conditions commonly turn *submissive*, slowing down to point D on their reaction function to reduce their otherwise high R&D costs and giving up a bit more market share in compensation.[59]

Now we relax the symmetry assumption in a more important way. Suppose that, by virtue of well-established reputation, distribution channels, and other attributes in related markets, Firm 1 would win 80 percent of the new product's sales and Firm 2 only 20 percent if each rolled out the fruits of their R&D on the same day. Figure 17.4(c) shows the reactions, but to understand them it is useful to jump ahead to Figure 17.5. The size of the rectangle shows the total amount of quasi rents to be divided between the rivals if both had the same innovation date.[60] The vertical line shows the division of quasi rents between the two with identical product introduction dates. Suppose further that a year's first-mover advantage permits one firm to capture more or less permanently one-fourth of what would otherwise be its rival's quasi rents. Then for small Firm 2, the cannibalization gain from being first is the large darkest shaded rectangle, while for dominant Firm 1, the gain is the much smaller shaded rectangle. The small firm has more to gain from being first than the large firm. Turning back to Figure 17.4(c), this shows up in different reaction function positions on that side of the 45° equal-times diagonal where a firm leads its rival. If Firm 1 saw no competition on the horizon, it would choose a point like A_1 on its reaction function (marked by large dots), corresponding to a 4.75 year R&D schedule. With more to gain by being first, smaller Firm 1 will choose A_2, implying a 2.8 year schedule. If both firms choose strategies at the same time, Firm 2 will set the pace. But now Firm 1 realizes that it has much to lose — the darkest shaded rectangle in Figure 17.5 — if it lags significantly behind Firm 2. It does not want to force the pace, but if forced, it reacts along the 45° line to point B. Firm 2, perceiving that hope is not yet lost, accelerates to C. But Firm 1 responds in kind by accelerating to D, in effect preempting its challenger. It is possible, depending upon the circumstances, that Firm 2, seeing it cannot be first, then reacts submissively to a point like E.

This asymmetric model provides insight into the frequently observed tendency for market-dominating firms to be slow in developing important new products, but to roar back like tigers when smaller rivals — often new entrants with no historical market share at all — challenge their dominance. Examples include Gillette's lag behind Wilkinson on stainless steel razor blades in 1962–1963; IBM's slow start and (sometimes) fast finish in developing its first digital computers and their transistorized, super-, mini-, and microcomputer descendants;[61] AT&T's record in developing microwave radio relay systems and communications satellites; the reactions of Kellogg and General Mills to small firms' success in selling granola-type cereals; NCR's shift from mechanical cash registers to electronic point-of-sale devices; Boeing's reaction to European "Airbus" competition; and Texas Instruments' response to the pace-forcing efforts of Japanese dynamic random-access semiconductor memory makers, among others.[62] However, variations in the assumptions can change the outcome in important ways. In particular, we have

59. See Scherer, "Research and Development Resource Allocation," supra note 56, p. 379; and Gene M. Grossman and Carl Shapiro, "Dynamic R&D Competition," *Economic Journal*, vol. 97 (June 1987), pp. 376–379.

60. The rectangle's size is of course larger, the earlier both innovate.

61. For a similar but more richly structured model explaining IBM's leased computer development incentives, see Gerald W. Brock, *The U.S. Computer Industry* (Cambridge: Ballinger, 1975), pp. 211–215.

62. For references on some of these illustrations, see the second edition of this work, pp. 433–435.

Figure 17.5
Division of Quasi-Rents with
Equal R&D Times and Shifts
when One Firm Gains a
First-Mover Advantage

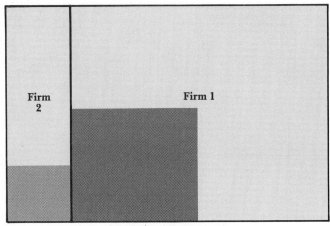

Total Quasi-Rents (Area)

assumed thus far that both rivals must operate on identical time-cost tradeoff functions. But if a laggard can shift its time-cost tradeoff function inward by hesitating, observing, and avoiding the first movers' false technical starts, and if small interlopers initially penetrate the market only slowly, dominant firms may find it more profitable to pursue a "fast second" strategy—not so fast that they must blaze the trail, but sufficiently fast that smaller pioneers achieve only modest inroads into their dominant positions before their aggressive response occurs.[63]

The asymmetric market positions logic helps us understand what happens when we relax the assumption that only two rivals compete with new products. For small Firm 2 in Figure 17.5, the gains it can capture *if* it can reach the market first do not really depend upon whether the (large) rest of the market is held by a single dominant firm or by several firms—for example, four others, each with 20 percent related market shares like its own. If being first mover confers lasting market share gains, the larger the share of the market *all* other firms would command if they exactly matched Firm 2's new product introduction date, the more Firm 2 has to gain by being first and capturing some of what otherwise would be rivals' quasi rents. Or to accentuate the negative, the smaller a company's share will be if it only ties others to the market, the more it has to gain by leading. If firms' preinnovation market positions are symmetric, the more rivals there are, the smaller will be a representative firm's simultaneous-innovation market share, and so the larger will be the gains from being first mover for any given head start over the others. Returning to Figure 17.3, this means that the more symmetric firms there are, the steeper a representative firm's discounted quasi-rent function V will be.[64] Thus, V_3 (for three symmetric rivals) has a steeper slope than V_2, whose slope is steeper than with the blockaded monopolist V_M. The steeper the slope, the quicker is the profit-maximizing R&D schedule. An increase in the number of symmetric rivals accelerates product research and development!

As Figure 17.3 reveals, there is a hitch. As the number of would-be innovators increases to some critical value N, the representative firm's discounted quasi-rents function is not only steeper, but lies at all points below the time-cost tradeoff function. If R&D is to be undertaken at all, it will be done quickly. But it is not profitable, and so if firms correctly see what is happening, there will be a market failure. Each firm will refrain from investing in R&D in the expectation that if all invest, the market will be divided up into so many pieces that each firm's discounted quasi rents are too small to cover R&D costs.

This problem is reinforced by another that we have kept in abeyance. As the market structure moves from monopoly to duopoly to looser oligopoly, the ability of firms to hold prices at monopoly levels will break down. When that happens, the quasi rents per firm will be too small to cover R&D costs not only because the new product market is divided into so many slices, but also because price competition has eroded the market's profitability.

We find therefore a clash of structural propensities, giving rise to a dualism in the links between market structure and incentives for innovation. Up to a point, increased fragmentation stimulates more rapid and intense support of R&D. This influence is called the *stimulus factor*. But when the number of firms becomes so large that no individual firm can appropriate quasi rents sufficient to cover its R&D costs, innovation can be slowed or even brought to a halt. This influence can be called the *market room* factor.

Dynamics and Welfare Implications

To carry the analysis further, we need a broader dynamic conception of the process of technological advance. The profitability of innovation depends most fundamentally upon demand and supply conditions. On the demand side, as population grows, per capita incomes rise, and (less certainly) input cost ratios change, the quasi-rent potential b(t) in Figure 17.2 increases over time, leading in Figure 17.3 to upward shifts in discounted total quasi-rent functions V for any given number of firms. On the supply side, as scientific and technological knowledge advances, what may be impossible today will be feasible but costly next year and easy several years hence. This means that time-cost tradeoff functions, recalibrated periodically in current time, shift toward the origin of Figure 17.3 (that is, in a southwesterly direction) as knowledge accumulates. An innovation becomes profitable when, as a result of changes in knowledge and/or demand, the discounted total quasi-rent function comes to lie at least partially above the time-cost tradeoff function. Innovations induced mainly by advances in knowledge are called *technology-push innovations*. Those rendered attractive by rising demand are called *demand-pull inventions*.

63. See William L. Baldwin and G. L. Childs, "The Fast Second and Rivalry in Research and Development," *Southern Economic Journal*, vol. 36 (July 1969), pp. 18–24. Later contributions show that the dominant firm will be more inclined to preempt than lag, the more perfect patent protection is, the more the innovation threatens its rents in existing markets, the less uncertain R&D completion time is, the less likely licensing of the challenger's technology is, and the less likely multiple challenges are. See Richard J. Gilbert and David Newberry, "Preemptive Patenting and the Persistence of Monopoly," *American Economic Review*, vol. 72 (June 1982), pp. 514–526; Jennifer Reinganum, "Uncertain Innovation and the Persistence of Monopoly," *American Economic*

Review, vol. 73 (September 1983), pp. 741–748; Jonathan Cave, "A Further Comment on Preemptive Patenting and the Persistence of Monopoly," *American Economic Review*, vol. 75 (March 1985); Christopher Harris and John Vickers, "Patent Races and the Persistence of Monopoly," *Journal of Industrial Economics*, vol. 33 (June 1985), pp. 461–481; and Partha Dasgupta, "The Theory of Technological Competition," in Joseph Stiglitz and G. Frank Mathewson, eds., *New Developments in the Analysis of Market Structure* (London: Macmillan, 1986), pp. 519–547.

64. A formal proof is found in Scherer, "Research and Development," supra note 56, pp. 389–390.

Suppose now that the advance of knowledge and increases in demand occur smoothly and continuously. At some moment in time, an innovation that was not profitable before will suddenly become profitable for a pure monopolist as the shifting V_M quasi-rent and C(T) cost functions fleetingly become tangent to one another. At this same moment, the development would not yet be profitable if the market were divided among oligopolists, each of whom (assuming imperfect patent protection) anticipates having to share the new product's sales with rivals. If innovation is to occur as rapidly as is practically feasible under the conditions postulated, monopoly is essential!

The story is different when the functions shift discontinuously by large amounts, as when a scientific breakthrough (for example, the discovery of the transistor effect, or low-temperature superconductivity, or gene splicing) occurs, *or* when there are significant lags in the recognition of profitable innovation opportunities. Then the quasi-rent functions may lie above the time-cost tradeoff function even for firms in relatively atomistic industries. If so, firms' behavior is dominated by the stimulus factor, and the pace of innovation will almost surely be faster when there is rivalry than under a securely monopolized market structure.

Although a monopolist *could* go faster when demand and knowledge advance continuously, it remains to be seen whether its incentives lead it actually to do so. Also, we have tacitly assumed that faster is better, but that assumption must be probed. Both of these questions are illuminated by the pioneering contribution of Yoram Barzel.[65]

Barzel's innovators inhabit a world similar to the one we postulated in our initial exploration of the patent grant's logic. Once a patent is gained, it is assumed to provide its owner perfect protection. Among other things, inventing around the patent is assumed impossible. But before invention occurs, a wide array of market structures, ranging from monopoly with blockaded entry to a form of all-out competition, can exist. Dynamics are introduced by assuming (in our adaptation) that the cost of developing a new product or process falls steadily over time. If the development were carried out today, it would cost $10 million. The advance of science reduces that cost at a rate of 5 percent per year. Thus, the cost of development follows the time trajectory $C_o(T) = \$10^7 \times e^{-.05T}$. We ignore demand-pull influences, assuming that the stream of tappable quasi rents has a constant depth of $800,000 per year. The question is, how long should firms wait before innovating? And how does market structure matter?

The problem can be characterized in simple graphic form with a further assumption: that when the development is carried out, it is financed by taking out a loan at an interest rate *r* of 10 percent per year. To keep the geometry and algebra simple, we assume further that both the resulting patent and the loan have perpetual life.[66] Then the yearly cost of carrying the development loan beginning at time T and continuing in perpetuity will be $0.1 \times C_o(T)$. This annual cost declines exponentially over time as R&D is postponed, as shown by the declining solid curve in Figure 17.6. If the development were undertaken today (at year 0), loan carrying costs would exceed annual quasi rents b(T), so any profit-maximizing firm would wait. After 4.5 years, $C_o(T)$ has declined sufficiently with the advance of knowledge that break-even is achieved; loan carrying costs equal annual quasi rents. But a profit-maximizing monopolist would not innovate at this time if it anticipates a further fall in development costs, because if it waits, it can make a

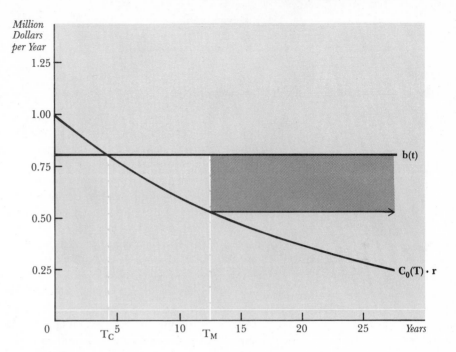

Figure 17.6
Innovation Date Choices and
Profits Under Competition
and Monopoly

profit. Even though the profit *margin* rises continuously over time with waiting, the monopolist will not wait forever because early profits are preferred to later profits. The discounted present value of its profits under the assumptions of Figure 17.6 is maximized when it innovates at year $T_M = 12.5$.[67] Then its annual quasi rents will start and continue at $800,000 per year. Incurring a one-time R&D cost reduced to $5.35 million, its annual financing costs will be $535,000 per year, and it will realize the darker-shaded profit rectangle in perpetuity.

This is the solution for the extreme case of a monopolist so secure in its position that it can wait until the profit-maximizing moment to innovate. How does the opposite extreme—pure competition—compare? Barzel invokes here the classic equilibrium definition: competition is characterized by such free entry that expected profits (after covering fixed R&D costs) are zero. This can only occur at the

---

65. "Optimal Timing of Innovations," *Review of Economics and Statistics*, vol. 50 (August 1968), pp. 348–355.

66. This is unrealistic, but its impact on the results is transparent. The shorter the patent life, the longer firms will delay innovating.

67. Generalization: Let b be the annual quasi rent realized after innovation occurs, r the rate of interest, C_o the one-time cost of development at time $t = 0$, and p the rate at which development costs fall over time. Then the cost of development at time T is $C_o e^{-pT}$. The monopolist maximizes the discounted present value of quasi rents less costs:

$$(1) \qquad \pi = \int_T^\infty b\, e^{-rt}\, dt - C_o\, e^{-(p+r)T};$$

$$(2) \qquad \pi = \frac{b\, e^{-rT}}{r} - C_o\, e^{-(p+r)T}.$$

Differentiating with respect to T, the first-order condition for a maximum is:

$$(3) \qquad b\, e^{-rT} = (p+r)\, C_o\, e^{-(p+r)T}.$$

break-even point T_C = 4.5 years.[68] Just how the competitive process evolves to achieve this zero-profit equilibrium need not concern us in detail yet. It cannot be through postinnovation price competition, for a perfect patent permits monopoly pricing then. So the competition is at the preinnovation stage, for example, in Barzel's original schema, as a single firm preempts its less bold rivals with an R&D project conducted so early that its costs equal discounted quasi rents.

Thus, pure competitors in the Barzel sense innovate sooner than secure monopolists. The question remains, what is best for society? A natural criterion for evaluating society's interest is that the sum of all surpluses, consumers' plus producers', should exceed development (and other fixed) costs by as much as possible. Normally, we saw in our discussion of Figure 17.1,[69] innovations generate both consumers' and producers' surplus. Let us define a coefficient of appropriation k, measuring the ratio of the total surplus from innovation, producer's plus consumers', to the producer's surplus alone.[70] Under the assumptions of Figure 17.1, consumers' surplus was half as great as the monopolist producer's surplus, so k would have a value of 1.5. If instead k = 1, the monopolist's gains coincide with society's gains, and so the monopolist's timing choice is socially optimal. In the more realistic case where k > 1, the monopolist proceeds too slowly, the more so, the larger k is.[71]

How well do competitive innovators perform in comparison? A useful way of proceeding is to ask, Under what conditions does break-even competition in the Barzel sense innovate at exactly the social welfare-maximizing date? It is not difficult to show that given the assumptions accepted here, the competitive and social welfare-maximizing choices coincide when k equals the sum of the rate at which development costs fall (which we call p) plus the interest rate r, divided by r.[72] Figure 17.7 relates the values of k consistent with social optimality to the range of

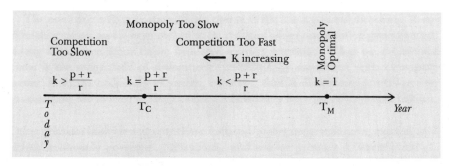

Figure 17.7
How the Optimality
of R&D Plans Varies
with Appropriability
Coefficient k under
Competition and Monopoly

possible monopoly and competitive innovation date choices. When $k = (p+r)/r$, the competitive break-even date T_C is optimal.[73] Leisurely innovation dates between T_M and T_C are socially optimal for $1 < k < (p+r)/r$; that is, when the innovator appropriates a large fraction of the total surplus. Dates faster than the pace set by competition are optimal when k is large, that is, when there are large external benefits not captured by the innovator. In this case, competitive innovators' inability to appropriate a sufficient share of the benefits from their R&D causes a market failure delaying the introduction of the new technology. When the degree of appropriability is low (k is large), the competitive break-even solution tends to be optimal when the rate of advance in knowledge is fast, that is, p is relatively high. For high appropriability, competition tends to be optimal when knowledge advances slowly.

Needless to say, k will exactly equal $(p+r)/r$, and break-even competition will be socially optimal, only by happenstance. There is no invisible hand assuring that competition will set the right pace for innovation. This result parallels our finding in Chapter 16 that monopolistic competition with free entry might lead to either too much or too little product variety.[74] Still pure monopoly with blockaded entry has no better claim; indeed, it is always too slow when appropriability is

---

68. From equation (2) of note 67 above, break-even occurs where:

$$(1) \qquad \frac{b\,e^{-rT}}{r} = C_o\,e^{-(p+r)T} .$$

Multiplying both sides by r, we obtain a condition analogous to profit maximization condition (3) of note 67:

$$(2) \qquad b\,e^{-rT} = r\,C_o\,e^{-(p+r)T},$$

except that the premultiplier on the right-hand side is r rather than $(p+r)$. To satisfy equation (2) here, T must be lower than it needs to be to satisfy equation (3) in note 67. Thus, the break-even competitive T_C is shorter than the monopoly T_M.

69. And also in our discussion of optimal product variety in Chapter 16, whose parallels with the present analysis should become evident.

70. Some important problems must be dodged here. In principle, k should depend on both market structure and pricing conduct. Under monopoly pricing (absent first-degree price discrimination), total surplus is less than it would be under competitive pricing. If k is approximated as a parameter, should the total surplus measured for the numerator of k be the total actually realized, or the total possible under competitive pricing? Since without postinnovation monopoly pricing there could be no innovation, the solution must be second best, and so the proper measure of total surplus is the surplus actually realized.

71. Proof: A social planner would maximize the difference between discounted total surplus and R&D costs. By definition, total surplus is k times the innovator's surplus (from equation [2] of note 67, be^{-rT}). Assuming that the discount rate is the same for innovators and society at large, we wish to maximize:

$$(1) \qquad k\,(be^{-rT})\,/\,r - C_o\,e^{-(p+r)T}$$

with respect to T. The first-order condition is:

$$(2) \qquad k\,(be^{-rT}) = (p+r)\,C_o\,e^{-(p+r)T},$$

which differs from profit-maximizing condition (3) in footnote 67 only by the k premultiplier. If $k = 1$, the two solutions are identical. The more k exceeds unity, the more T must be reduced relative to the monopolist's profit-maximizing T_M to satisfy the equality.

72. T must satisfy equation (3) of note 67 and equation (2) of note 71 simultaneously. Let $Z = C_o\,e^{-(p+r)T}$ and $X = b\,e^{-rt}$. Then we must simultaneously have:

$$(1) \qquad X = rZ,\ so\ Z = X/r,\ and$$

$$(2) \qquad kX = (p+r)\,Z.$$

Substituting (1) for Z in (2), we obtain:

$$(3) \qquad kX = (p+r)\,X/r;$$

$$(4) \qquad k = (p+r)\,/\,r.$$

73. In a study of seventeen innovations, Edwin Mansfield and associates found the median social/private surplus ratio to be on the order of 2.25. "Social and Private Rates of Return from Industrial Innovations," *Quarterly Journal of Economics*, vol. 91 (May 1977), pp. 221–240.

74. The parallelism holds even more strongly. The high surplus appropriation associated with cartelized pricing tips the balance toward excessive product variety, just as preinnovation "competitors" are likely to innovate excessively quickly when a high fraction of the postinnovation benefits will be appropriated.

incomplete, as it must be if consumers are to enjoy the fruits of technological progress. Barzel's model is silent on the intermediate oligopoly case. From our previous analysis, oligopolists (or monopolists reacting to preempt smaller firms' R&D challenge) are likely to innovate more quickly than Barzel's secure monopolist unless the number of rivals is so large that profit expectations turn negative. Profitable oligopoly is most apt to sustain an innovation pace preferable to that of monopoly and competition in the range of Figure 17.7 appropriability values where competition is too fast.

Further Theoretical Insights

Economists have extended the above theoretical skeleton with a rich profusion of variants—perhaps too rich to satisfy the criteria for optimal model variety. Through an astute choice of assumptions, virtually any market structure can be shown to have superior innovative qualities. This may only mirror the complexity of the real world. Yet some strong generalizations persist across a wide range of assumptions.

Thus far, we have assumed innovations to be one-time events. However, most industries experience a continuing stream of innovations over time, and in many cases, each completed new product or process sets an agenda focusing improvement work for the next technological generation. This has two consequences.[75] Since the next generation often makes previous innovations obsolete, the degree to which any innovation can expect to appropriate the future surpluses it generates is lessened, that is, k rises. This weakens incentives to innovate and extends the range of outcomes (in Figure 17.7) over which even competitive markets proceed too slowly. Second, to the extent that subsequent R&D is focused and informed, becoming more productive than it otherwise would have been, an innovation at time T confers benefits upon innovators at stages $T+1$, $T+2$, etc., in the chain. Except in the most extraordinarily tightly monopolized industries, it is unlikely that the firms generating such benefits will capture them exclusively in their own future R&D, and so the benefits spill over as positive externalities to other firms. This too extends the range of outcomes over which competitive markets innovate too slowly or in excessively modest qualitative steps, although, since Barzel competition may proceed too rapidly for other reasons, it yields no precise guidance as to the optimal market structure.

Barzel's competitive case was offered in the spirit of an extreme among alternatives; and his explanation of how zero profits emerged, through a particularly aggressive firm's preemption of potential rivals before they started their own R&D efforts, ignored alternative but plausible possibilities. These lacunae stimulated several further contributions.[76]

A common thread is the assertion that the zero-profit outcome is not simply an extreme case, but the natural state toward which research and development rivalry gravitates in the absence of artificial entry barriers. Thus, the market structure *affecting* R&D decisions is not a given, but is endogenously determined by technology and competition. If the cost per firm of conducting R&D is small relative to the size of appropriable quasi rents, many firms will join in, and an atomistic zero-profit equilibrium will emerge. If project costs are large relative to quasi rents, there will be few participants, but the number will be large enough again to drive profits to zero. This view is plausible as a gross approximation. Within a year of the first announcement of high-temperature superconductivity, hundreds of firms had commenced R&D projects to explore its perceived high potential—far more than the number of firms working to devise a more easily opened sardine can. Yet the approximation is indeed rough. Firms are limited by managerial know-how, channels of distribution, production capabilities, and patiently accumulated R&D staff skills in the innovation challenges to which they can respond. In a dynamic world, these change, and can be changed, much more slowly than the rate at which the technological knowledge base and demand conditions shift. Especially when the quasi-rent potential of an innovation could support far more firms than the number possessing the capabilities needed to exploit it, convergence to a zero-profit R&D equilibrium seems highly implausible. A zero-profit result is more readily imagined when there are more firms with relevant capabilities than the quasi-rent potential can accommodate. But even then, history teaches, some firms recognize an opportunity more quickly than others, and the first movers characteristically gain advantages that prevent imitators from driving the industry to a symmetric zero-profit equilibrium.[77]

A more significant contribution of the "endogenous market structure" analyses is their extension of the Barzel schema to alternative quasi-rent eroding scenarios. In particular, when the success of a given R&D project is highly uncertain,[78] but the payoffs are large relative to the cost of a single project, something resembling a lottery may occur. Multiple firms will undertake one or more projects, and in the limiting case, the number of projects will be such that the expected value of the winning ticket(s) equals the sum of all firms' project costs. If the first or most successful participants acquire patents, and if the patents provide strong protection, there may be many losers and only one winner, or a very few winners. That in itself is uninteresting, unless firms are risk-averse. But in addition, under some conditions, the lessened probability of being a winner as the number of rivals rises may cause individual firms to reduce the intensity of their R&D efforts.[79] This does not mean that the rate of innovation is retarded by competition, since the increase in the number of rivals normally raises the joint probability of an early success, more than offsetting the reduced probability that any single firm will be successful.

75. See especially C. C. von Weizsäcker, *Barriers to Entry* (Berlin: Springer, 1980), Chapters 8 and 9; and Jennifer F. Reinganum, "Innovation and Industry Evolution," *Quarterly Journal of Economics*, vol. 100 (February 1985), pp. 81–99.

76. See Glenn C. Loury, "Market Structure and Innovation," *Quarterly Journal of Economics*, vol. 93 (August 1979), pp. 395–410; Tom Lee and Louis Wilde, "Market Structure and Innovation: A Reformulation," *Quarterly Journal of Economics*, vol. 94 (March 1980), pp. 429–436; Partha Dasgupta and Joseph Stiglitz, "Uncertainty, Industrial Structure, and the Speed of R&D," *Bell Journal of Economics*, vol. 11 (Spring 1980), pp. 1–28; Dasgupta and Stiglitz, "Industrial Structure and the Nature of Innovative Activity," *Economic Journal*, vol. 90 (June 1980), pp. 266–293; Pankaj Tandon, "Rivalry and the Excessive Allocation of Resources to Research," *Bell Journal of Economics*, vol. 14 (Spring 1983), pp.

152–165; and Tandon, "Innovation, Market Structure, and Welfare," *American Economic Review*, vol. 74 (June 1984), pp. 394–403.

77. Simulation results showing how R&D affects market structure in the long run, assuming varying degrees of appropriability and rates of exogenous (or cumulative) knowledge growth, are presented in Richard R. Nelson and Sidney G. Winter, *An Evolutionary Theory of Economic Change* (Cambridge: Harvard University Press, 1982), Chapters 13 and 14. See also Carl A. Futia, "Schumpeterian Competition," *Quarterly Journal of Economics*, vol. 94 (June 1980), pp. 675–695.

78. This is more the exception than the rule, Mansfield's research shows. See note 23 supra.

79. Compare Loury, "Market Structure," with Lee and Wilde, "A Reformulation," supra note 76.

Even more importantly, if the prospect of large gains to a successful innovator induces many firms to undertake R&D, there may be extensive duplication of R&D approaches. This is not per se wasteful. When the success of any single project is uncertain, running duplicated projects hastens success unless the rivals conduct exactly identical experiments, which is unlikely. The greater the social gains from a successful innovation, the larger is the optimal number of parallel but uncertain approaches.[80] But if firms independently proliferate R&D approaches until profits are driven to zero, individual projects may be reduced to inefficiently small scales, and total costs may rise to inefficient levels. A coordinated (more monopolistic) approach might use the R&D resources more efficiently.[81]

From this it does not necessarily follow that competition proceeds too rapidly, for as we have seen, the economic welfare analysis yields no simple generalizations except that secure monopoly proceeds too slowly. Favoring competitive duplication are two further considerations not yet incorporated into the formal analyses of R&D rivalry. First, any single firm (that is, monopolist) coordinating parallel but uncertain R&D approaches is likely to have perceptual blind spots, overlooking some promising avenues and putting too much stress on a committee's favorites. By propagating a greater diversity of approaches, competition often evokes winning solutions at lower cost despite seemingly inefficient duplication.[82] Second, the multiple solutions emerging from duplicated R&D are usually not identical, and among other things, they may add desirable product variety. Product variety, like speed in reaching the market, can of course be carried too far. No simple generalizations are possible, but these considerations strengthen the case for at least some degree of rivalry in research and development.

The Evidence

The theory of how market structure affects the vigor of technological innovation provides a rich array of predictions, some conflicting. To sort out the most likely tendencies, qualitative and especially quantitative evidence must be marshaled. Considerable progress has been made toward this objective. In reviewing the evidence, we consider first relationships at the industry level and then investigate how firm size, both within an industry and spanning multiple industries, matters.

Several general problems must be conquered to study market structure-innovation links statistically. For one, ways must be found to measure the vigor or success of innovative activity. Early investigations focused, for want of better data, on *inputs* into the innovative process—for example, in the first studies, counts of scientists and engineers employed by companies or industries, and later, on expenditures devoted to research and development. Other work, usually possible only after new data development efforts had been completed, analyzed such measures of innovative *output* as the number of invention patents received, tallies of new products and processes introduced by industry members, and the growth of productivity. Here we emphasize the results of the typically more recent studies taking advantage of superior data sources.[83]

Second, to avoid biased inferences, it is necessary to take into account variables other than market structure that affect the pace of innovation. Particularly important in this respect is some measure of what has come to be called *technological opportunity* — that is, the rate at which more or less exogenous and cumulative advances in science and technology generate profitable new innovative possibilities.

As always, one must get the direction of causation right. Our theories reveal that market structure can affect the pace of innovation, but innovation in turn can shape market structure. The structure-to-innovation linkage probably operates over a much shorter time span than the innovation-to-structure linkage, but especially in industries blessed with rich technological opportunities, powerful links of the second type also exist, and so, as we shall see, controlling for opportunity takes on added importance.

The Role of Market Concentration

In the long run, improved standards of living track productivity growth, that is, the growth of real output per hour of work. At first glance, it might seem surprising to postulate a link between market structure and productivity growth. In a modern economy, there are rich interrelationships among industries. Some industries specialize in producing technologically advanced machines, components, and materials which, when purchased by other industries, enhance the buying industry's productivity.[84] Concentrated or atomistic, for an industry not to take advantage of such externally supplied advances would be like refusing a free lunch. However, closer scrutiny reveals that while *non*manufacturing industries do rely almost exclusively upon manufacturers for their capital goods, a majority of the *special-purpose* production equipment used by U.S. manufacturers is internally developed.[85] Thus, the stronger the incentives for internal development are, the more rapid manufacturers' productivity growth should be.

A positive and statistically significant correlation between productivity growth and seller concentration ratios has been found for U.S. manufacturing industries over time periods ranging from 1919 through 1978.[86] However, when industry expenditures on product and process research and development per dollar of sales were included as additional explanatory variables, the R&D variables took away the concentration indices' explanatory power, reducing them to statistical insignificance. Thus, the chain of causation appears to run from higher R&D spending, which is correlated with seller concentration, to higher productivity growth. The question remains, what is the nature of the R&D-concentration relationship?

80. See Scherer, *Innovation and Growth*, supra note 9, Chapter 4.

81. An alternative to monopoly could be a research and development joint venture. See, for example, Barry Bozeman, Albert Link, and Asghar Zardkoohi, "An Economic Analysis of R&D Joint Ventures," *Managerial and Decision Economics*, vol. 7 (December 1986), pp. 263–266; John T. Scott, "Diversification versus Co-operation in R&D Investment," *Managerial and Decision Economics*, vol. 9 (June 1988), pp. 173–186; Alexis Jacquemin, "Cooperative Agreements in R&D and European Antitrust Policy," *European Economic Review*, vol. 32 (March 1988), pp. 551–560; and Thomas M. Jorde and David J. Teece, "Innovation, Cooperation, and Antitrust," paper presented at a University of California, Berkeley, conference on Antitrust, Innovation, and Competitiveness, October 1988.

82. This is the pervasive message of Burton Klein, *Dynamic Economics* (Cambridge: Harvard University Press, 1977).

83. For more thorough surveys of earlier empirical research, see the first and second editions of this text, Chapter 15, and Baldwin and Scott, *Market Structure*, supra note 37, pp. 64–113.

84. See p. 614 supra; Scherer, *Innovation and Growth*, supra note 9, Chapters 3 and 15; and Albert Link, "Alternative Sources of Technology: An Analysis of Induced Innovations," *Managerial and Decision Economics*, vol. 4 (March 1983), pp. 40–43.

85. Scherer, *Innovation and Growth*, p. 250.

86. See *Innovation and Growth*, pp. 250–252; Douglas F. Greer and Stephen A. Rhoades, "Concentration and Productivity Changes in the Long and Short Run," *Southern Economic Journal*, vol. 43 (October 1976), pp. 1031–1044; and Louis Amato and J. Michael Ryan, "Market Structure and Dynamic Performance in U.S. Manufacturing," *Southern Economic Journal*, vol. 47 (April 1981), pp. 1105–1110.

Our earlier theoretical analysis predicts that more rivalry, approximated by lower concentration indices, invigorates R&D spending up to a point, but that too atomistic a market structure discourages R&D by causing would-be innovators to appropriate an insufficiently large share of the ensuing benefits to expect positive profits from their innovations. Multiseller rivalry is more apt to stimulate R&D spending when advances in the underlying science and technology base occur quickly and unexpectedly, generating large quasi-rent opportunities for the tapping, than when the pace of advance is slow and continuous. Both predictions have received statistical support.

Most studies for the United States and other leading nations reveal a positive correlation between concentration and industry R&D/sales ratios, or cruder proxies for that ratio.[87] A test for nonlinearities using 1960 U.S. employment data showed an "inverted-U" relationship, with peak R&D/sales ratios occurring at average four-digit industry, four-seller concentration indices of 50 to 55.[88] Industries with four-firm shares below 15 percent appeared to have fatally defective incentives for supporting R&D.

Since then, the inverted-U hypothesis has been tested repeatedly as richer data have become available, especially from the Federal Trade Commission's Line of Business statistical surveys covering the years 1974 to 1977. Working with FTC data aggregated to the industry level, Richard Levin and associates found strong initial support for the inverted U, with the maximum R&D/sales ratio occurring at a four-firm concentration ratio of 52.[89] From their survey of research and development executives, Levin et al. had parallel, subjectively measured, indices of the rate at which new products and processes had been introduced into 130 manufacturing industries during the 1970s. Concentration was found to influence those measures in ways nearly identical to those for the R&D/sales ratios. Disaggregating FTC R&D/sales data to the level of 3,388 individual lines of business, John Scott also observed an inverted U in two-variable regressions, with the maximum intensity of R&D at (adjusted) four-firm concentration ratios of 64.[90]

However, the inverted U hypothesis fares less well when additional variables are introduced to account for technological opportunity and other innovation-affecting influences. Using simple dummy variables at the two-digit industry level to control for interindustry differences, Levin et al. found their results virtually unchanged; the inverted U persisted. They then introduced a battery of survey-derived indices assessing the relevance of diverse scientific fields to the industries' R&D efforts, the extent to which outside R&D performers contributed to industry technological progress, and the strength of various innovative reward appropriation mechanisms (such as patents, secrecy, and lead time). With these variables added, the concentration coefficients fell to insignificant values, and the existence of an inverted U could no longer be inferred. Similarly, the "U" disappeared when Scott added to his 3,388-line analysis twenty two-digit industry dummy variables and 437 dummy variables permitting each sample company to have its own best-fitting R&D/sales relationship.[91] Evidently, the U-shaped concentration influence captured by relatively simple statistical analyses is correlated with a set of more complex industry and firm effects. Whether those effects influence concentration causally, are affected by it, or are spuriously correlated with it, is unclear, so one cannot be certain whether the inverted U is a phenomenon important in its own right or an accident of the data. That the underlying theory points to its existence suggests that the phenomenon should not be dismissed too quickly.

Interindustry differences in the richness of technological opportunities might affect concentration-R&D relationships in another way. Inability to appropriate a sufficient share of an innovation's quasi rents because of excessive rivalry is more likely when the relevant science base is advancing slowly and predictably than when it moves forward rapidly and discontinuously, that is, in break-throughs. Therefore, we expect R&D/sales ratios to be more strongly correlated with seller concentration indices, the less rich an industry's technological opportunities are. Typically, the role of technological opportunity is investigated by classifying industries either dichotomously or into more elaborate subdivisions reflecting the principal technologies exploited. Most U.S. and European studies that have attempted such a test support the differential correlation hypothesis.[92] A particularly rich categorization was possible using data on 1974 company-financed R&D/sales ratios from the FTC's Line of Business survey. The industry technology groupings, the number of industries in each, and the simple correlation

87. See again Baldwin and Scott, *Market Structure*, supra note 37. Examining the composition of 108 relatively large U.S. companies' R&D portfolios, Edwin Mansfield found the percentage of company expenditures devoted to basic research, long-term projects, and entirely new products and processes to be inversely correlated with seller concentration in industries occupied by the firms. "Composition of R and D Expenditures: Relationship to Size of Firm, Concentration, and Innovative Output," *Review of Economics and Statistics*, vol. 63 (November 1981), pp. 610–613. For similar results, see Albert N. Link, "An Analysis of the Composition of R&D Spending," supra note 53.

88. Scherer, *Innovation and Growth*, supra note 9, p. 246. See also Thomas M. Kelly, "The Influences of Size and Market Structure on the Research Efforts of Large Multiple-Product Firms," Ph.D. diss., University of Oklahoma, 1969, pp. 85–86; and (on the food processing industries) John D. Culbertson, "Should Antitrust Use the Schumpeterian Model?" in Robert L. Wills et al., ed., *Issues After a Century of Federal Competition Policy* (Lexington: Heath, Lexington, 1987), pp. 106–107.

89. Richard C. Levin, Wesley M. Cohen, and David C. Mowery, "R&D, Appropriability, and Market Structure: New Evidence on Some Schumpeterian Hypotheses," *American Economic Review*, vol. 75 (May 1985), pp. 20–24.

90. John T. Scott, "Firm versus Industry Variability in R&D Intensity," in Zvi Griliches, ed., *R&D, Patents, and Productivity* (Chicago: University of Chicago Press, 1984), pp. 233–240. See also Reinhard Angelmar, "Market Structure and Research Intensity in High-Technological-Opportunity Industries," *Journal of Industrial Economics*, vol. 34 (September 1985), pp. 69–79, who analyzed disaggregated PIMS data on 160 relatively high-

technology business units and found an inverted U, with maximum R&D/sales ratios at four-digit four-firm concentration ratios of 44. For evidence of a logistic relationship for Finland peaking at a three-firm concentration ratio of roughly 80, see B. Wahlroos and M. Backström, "R&D Intensity with Endogenous Concentration," *Empirical Economics*, vol. 7 (1982, no. 1/2), pp. 13–22.

91. Because company diversification occurs largely through merger and high-R&D companies tend to acquire companies with similarly high R&D/sales ratios, such company dummy variables are undoubtedly mirroring complex industry effects. See David J. Ravenscraft and F. M. Scherer, *Mergers, Sell-offs, and Economic Efficiency* (Washington: Brookings, 1987), p. 51.

92. Supporting studies include Scherer, *Innovation and Growth*, supra note 9, pp. 241–246; William S. Comanor, "Market Structure, Product Differentiation, and Industrial Research," *Quarterly Journal of Economics*, vol. 85 (November 1967), pp. 524–531; Ronald Shrieves, "Market Structure and Innovation: A New Perspective," *Journal of Industrial Economics*, vol. 26 (June 1978), pp. 329–347; John Lunn, "An Empirical Analysis of Process and Product Patenting: A Simultaneous Equation Framework," *Journal of Industrial Economics*, vol. 34 (March 1986), pp. 319–328; John Lunn and Stephen Martin, "Market Structure, Firm Structure, and Research and Development," *Quarterly Review of Economics and Business*, vol. 26 (Spring 1986), pp. 31–44; and (for the Netherlands) Alfred Kleinknecht and Bart Verspagen, "R&D and Market Structure: The Impact of Measurement and Aggregation Problems," *Small Business Economics*, vol. 1 (December 1989). For supporting Canadian and French studies and a contrary Belgian analysis, see the second edition of this text, p. 437, note 112.

coefficients between industry R&D/sales ratios and 1972 four-firm concentration indices were as follows:

Technology Grouping	Number of Industries	Correlation Coefficient
All industries	236	0.347*
Traditional technologies	78	0.305*
General and mechanical	106	0.404*
Organic chemicals	6	0.210
Other chemicals	12	0.101
Metallurgical	12	0.165
Electronics	9	0.362
Electrical	13	−0.158

Positive and statistically significant correlations (denoted by asterisks) are found for all industries together, the least progressive "traditional" technologies (for example, dairies and brick making), and the general and mechanical technologies. For industries rooted more firmly in fast-moving chemical and electrical technologies, the correlations are small and in one case negative. Only the electronics industry stands out as a contradiction to the hypothesis, with the second-highest correlation. However, that correlation is strongly influenced by a single concentrated industry's values (for computers), and with only nine industries in the subsample, the correlation falls far short of being statistically significant. Thus, there appears to be a rough tendency for concentration to be more conducive to technological vigor in relatively slow-moving fields. In no case, it must be recognized, are the concentration-R&D correlations strong. A conclusion that emerges from every such study is that interindustry differences in technological opportunity, however measured, have much greater power in explaining varying R&D or innovation intensities than differences in such market structure indices as concentration.

A more novel approach to the problem of relating market structure and technological opportunity has been taken by Paul Geroski.[93] He used extraordinarily rich data tallying 1,203 product and process innovations emerging from seventy-three British manufacturing industries (defined at the three-digit level) over the period 1970 to 1979. Splitting the sample into two time segments, he used the level of innovative activity in an industry during one time period as a predictor of innovation in the other period. When this approach to controlling for technological opportunity was adopted, he found higher seller concentration (and increases in other monopoly-related variables) to have a significant *negative* impact on the emergence of innovations. When no such controls were included, the impact of concentration was positive but statistically insignificant. However, in addition to the negative direct influence of concentration with opportunity controls, Geroski discovered that greater monopoly power led to larger time-lagged profit margins, and the expectation of those higher margins had a *positive* influence on innovation.

In this indirect way, monopoly favored innovation. But when the direct and indirect influences were combined, the negative direct effect substantially outweighed the positive indirect influence (operating through expected profitability). Thus, on balance, Geroski's results indicate that high market concentration was more likely to retard innovation than to stimulate it.

It would be premature to conclude that this new U.K. evidence overturns the weight of prior evidence suggesting a modest positive influence for concentration, especially in low-opportunity industries. Much remains to be learned.

A particularly important loose end is the chain of causation leading from innovation to market structure. If vigorous innovation induces appreciable market structure changes, and if the need for concentration to appropriate quasi rents depends upon technological opportunity, opportunity and structural feedback effects might be confounded. Figure 17.8 lays out the connections in simplified form. In Figure 17.8(*a*), two technological opportunity regimes are postulated. Seller concentration (measured on the horizontal axis) is assumed to have no causal influence on the intensity of innovation (vertical axis), so the "true" relationships between concentration and innovation are given by the upper line H_1 (for high-opportunity industries) and L_1 (for low-opportunity industries). Random deviations about the true tendency lines are shown by the scatter of dots, one per industry. However, if vigorous innovation leads to increasing concentration, the industry observations in high-opportunity fields will be shifted over time in a rightward direction, as shown by the arrows. As the center of gravity for the high-opportunity industry observations shifts to the right, a regression line fitted to the shifted data without controls for opportunity will approximate dotted line F_1, showing a weak but spurious positive concentration-innovation association. Figure 17.8(*b*) illustrates a case more consistent with theory: concentration has no effect on innovation in high-opportunity fields, but a positive effect when opportunities are weak. If (reversing our previous assumption) rapid innovation leads to *lower* concentration, a regression analysis that fails to control for opportunity will show a weak but spurious *negative* concentration-innovation association: the opposite of reality in low-opportunity industries.[94]

To avoid biases under these circumstances, a well-specified simultaneous equation system is needed. If differences in technological opportunity are not controlled properly, if concentration is favorable to innovation, and if rapid innovation raises concentration levels over time, a "virtuous circle" dynamics will ensue, and cross-sectional regression analyses will underestimate concentration's beneficial long-run effects. Or, alternatively, if innovation thrives in relatively atomistic markets and rapid innovation *reduces* concentration, the virtuous circle dynamics will again be underestimated even when there are perfect controls for opportunity.

93. P. A. Geroski, "Innovation, Technological Opportunity, and Market Structure," *Oxford Economic Papers*, forthcoming in 1989.

94. Other biases can result if opportunity is improperly inferred from high innovation intensity. For example, point Z in Figure 17.8(*b*) is in the low-opportunity set, but has relatively high innovation because of favorable market structure. If Z is put in a medium-opportunity class because of its observed performance, the effect of concentration will be underestimated. This bias could occur with Geroski's control technique.

Figure 17.8
Biases Resulting from
Innovation-Induced
Concentration Changes

a. Growing concentration, no true market
   structure effect

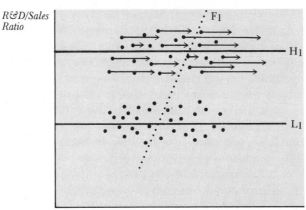

Seller Concentration

b. Declining concentration, positive
   concentration effect in low-opportunity
   industries

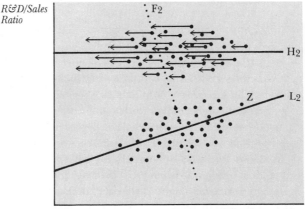

Seller Concentration

Innovation could be concentration-increasing if successful innovators rise to market dominance and can defend themselves successfully from imitators,[95] or if vigorous innovation increases the variance of firms' growth rates under many versions of Gibrat's Law.[96] However, the standard Gibrat formulations assume no entry. If innovation stimulates the entry of new competitors, concentration could tend to fall in high-opportunity industries.

Historical studies reveal that high concentration in such American and European industries as synthetic fibers, synthetic rubber, synthetic dyestuffs and derivative organic chemicals, electric lamps, telephone equipment, aircraft engines, and photographic supplies was caused in part by vigorous innovation combined with patent and/or know-how barriers to imitation. However, it is less clear that these tendencies have survived into more recent times. Using the British innovation count data described earlier, Geroski found a strong tendency for concentration to fall during the 1970s with more vigorous innovative activity.[97] A U.S. study using less satisfactory data also found a tendency toward falling concentration in high-opportunity industries.[98] John Lunn discovered that U.S. market concentration tended to rise with innovation when innovative activity emphasized internal production process changes, but to fall when new product work predominated.[99] In the United States, it will be recalled, roughly three-fourths of industrial R&D is oriented toward products and one-fourth toward processes. Lunn's findings are reinforced by those of Gort and Konakayama, who found that new entry rates were much higher than exit rates in the early life cycle stages of major product innovations.[100] Although much remains to be learned on this important question, the weight of existing evidence favors a conclusion that innovation under late twentieth-century conditions has tended to be more concentration-reducing than the opposite. This in turn implies possible underestimation of concentration's R&D-supporting role if the statistical controls for technological opportunity are inadequate.

The Advantages of Large and Small Firms

We move now from the industry to the firm level. Within a given industry, are relatively large or relatively small firms the more potent innovators? And do diversified companies — those that span multiple industries — pursue research and development more aggressively than those that specialize in a single line of business?

Theory offers ambiguous predictions on one aspect of the firm size question. As we have seen, firms with relatively small or (for new entrants) zero market shares have incentives to force the innovative pace when they can anticipate gaining first-mover advantages and capturing substantial chunks of market share. However, dominant firms subjected to such threats are motivated to respond aggressively, minimizing the fringe firms' lead or even preempting them. Which pattern is more common can only be ascertained empirically.

95. This is the scenario emphasized by Nelson and Winter in *An Evolutionary Theory*, supra note 77, Chapters 13 and 14.

96. See pp. 141–146 supra.

97. "Innovation," supra note 93, footnote 11; and P. A. Geroski and R. Pomroy, "Innovation and the Evolution of Market Structure," London Business School Centre for Business Strategy, working paper no. 36 (November 1987).

98. Arun Mukhopadhyay, "Technological Progress and Change in Market Concentration in the U.S., 1963–77," *Southern Economic Journal*, vol. 52 (July 1985), pp. 141–149. See also Micha Gisser, "Price Leadership and Dynamic Aspects of Oligopoly in U.S. Manufacturing," *Journal of Political Economy*, vol. 92 (December 1984), pp. 1035–1048, who found rising productivity to be accompanied by Galtonian tendencies toward rising concentration in low-concentration industries and falling concentration in high-concentration industries.

99. "An Empirical Analysis," supra note 92, pp. 324–328. In an elaborately structured model, Richard C. Levin and Peter C. Reiss found greater R&D efforts to induce *higher* concentration. See "Cost-Reducing and Demand-Creating R&D with Spillovers," National Bureau of Economic Research working paper no. 2876 (March 1989), and for similar results with more aggregated data, "Tests of a Schumpeterian Model of R&D and Market Structure," in Griliches, ed., *R&D, Patents and Productivity*, supra note 90, pp. 175–202.

100. Michael Gort and Akira Konakayama, "A Model of Diffusion in the Production of an Innovation," *American Economic Review*, vol. 72 (December 1982), pp. 1111–1119. Compare note 43 supra.

Large companies have noteworthy advantages in supporting research and innovation. Their size permits them to maintain a diversified portfolio of R&D projects, hedging the risks that any given project will fail. The ability to exploit scale economies is another potential advantage. A large laboratory can justify purchasing highly specialized equipment such as wind tunnels, supercomputers, differential scanning calorimeters, and much else. It can employ specialists in many disciplines to cross-fertilize one another and lend temporary assistance when a team working on some project bogs down on a technical problem outside its normal sphere of competence.[101] Scale economies may also accrue in other parts of the large firm's operations. As we have seen in Chapter 4, large corporations can attract capital at lower cost than their smaller cousins and may therefore be better able to finance ambitious R&D undertakings. This has probably become less important over time, at least in the United States, with the growth of venture capital firms seeking to invest in small high-technology enterprises. Large corporations usually have well-established marketing channels and may realize scale economies in advertising and other promotional activities (such as the "detailing" of new drugs by field salespersons). Such promotional advantages permit them to penetrate markets more rapidly with new products, enhancing the products' expected profitability. And finally, large producers have stronger incentives to develop internal process improvements. A new process that reduces costs by a given percentage margin yields larger total savings, the larger the developing firm's affected output is.[102]

Against this impressive array of actual and conjectured advantages, the disadvantages of corporate size must be weighed. For one, research in large laboratories can become overorganized. If too many people are involved in a project, they spend a disproportionate amount of their time writing memoranda to each other at the expense of more creative endeavor. Also, the quickest path to higher status and pay in a large firm's R&D establishment often entails giving up work at the bench and becoming a member of the management team. Although some companies have tried to combat this tendency by creating well-paid positions for senior research fellows, it is still commonplace to find the most able people in a laboratory devoting nearly all their time to supervising others. This is not the way truly creative work gets done.

Even more important, small firms may be more adept at risk taking. Their decisions to go ahead with an ambitious project typically are made by a handful of people who know one another well. In a large corporation, on the other hand, the decision must filter through an elaborate chain of command—the person with the idea, his or her section chief, the laboratory manager, the vice president for research, and if substantial financial commitments are required, several members of top management. Under these circumstances there is a distressingly high probability that some member of the chain will be what C. Northcote Parkinson has called "an abominable no-man," objecting decisively to ideas that are untried or that stray too far from accepted ways of doing business.

One consequence of this syndrome, which has been noted time and again in case histories and treatises on research management, is a bias against really imaginative innovations in the laboratories of large firms. Inability to get ideas approved by higher management drives creative individuals out of large corporate

R&D organizations to go it alone with their own ventures. Thousands of research-based new enterprises have been founded by frustrated expatriates from the laboratories of such U.S. giants as IBM, Sperry-Rand (now Unisys), Western Electric, Hughes Aircraft, and Texas Instruments.[103]

Jewkes, Sawers, and Stillerman compiled case histories of seventy important twentieth-century "inventions" and learned that only twenty-four had their origin in industrial research laboratories.[104] More than half were pioneered by individuals working either completely independent of any formal research organization or in an academic environment. However, one must be wary of carrying this insight too far. Further analysis by Jewkes et al. revealed that sizable corporations often shouldered the burden of *developing* independent inventors' ideas for commercial utilization. And for complex innovations like high-performance aircraft, high-definition television equipment, and nuclear reactor systems requiring R&D expenditures of tens or even hundreds of millions of dollars before commercialization can commence, only very large firms can undertake the tasks of technical development with something approaching equanimity.[105]

It is nevertheless well-established that new entrants without a commitment to accepted technologies have been responsible for a substantial share of the really revolutionary new industrial products and processes. The illustrations are legion: arc lighting (Brush), the incandescent lamp (Edison), radio telegraphy (Marconi), radio telephony (Fessenden and de Forest), FM radio (Armstrong), the photoflash lamp (Wabash), the dial telephone (Automatic Electric), the turbojet engine (Whittle in England, Heinkel and Junkers in Germany), sound motion pictures (Western Electric and Warner Brothers), catalytic cracking of petroleum (Houdry), the electric typewriter (IBM), the ball-point pen (Reynolds), self-developing photography (Polaroid), electrostatic copying (Haloid), supine dentistry (Den-Tal-Ez), the microwave oven (Raytheon), the microprocessor chip (Intel),[106] the microcomputer (Altair and Apple), polytetrafluoroethylene arterial grafts (IMPRA), and (unsuccessfully) laser-actuated hydrogen fusion (KMS Industries), to name only a few. In several of these cases, well-established firms flatly rejected invitations to collaborate with the inventor of a concept that later revolutionized

101. This large firm advantage is minimized when small firms have ready access to outside specialists such as university science and engineering faculty. It is not clear, however, whether outside expertise is tapped as willingly as internal expertise.

102. See Albert N. Link, "Firm Size and Efficient Entrepreneurial Activity: A Reformulation of the Schumpeter Hypothesis," *Journal of Political Economy*, vol. 88 (August 1980), pp. 771–782, who found that productivity growth returns to R&D expenditures rose with company size within the broadly defined chemicals industry.

103. For an early study of the phenomenon, see Edward B. Roberts, "Entrepreneurship and Technology," *Research Management*, vol. 11 (July 1968), pp. 249–266. On the efforts of large corporations to stem the tide, see Gifford Pinchot III, *Intrapreneuring: Why You Don't Have To Leave the Corporation To Become an Entrepreneur* (New York: Harper and Row, 1986).

104. *The Sources of Invention*, supra note 17, pp. 65–78. See also

Dan Hamberg, "Invention in the Industrial Research Laboratory," *Journal of Political Economy*, vol. 71 (April 1963), pp. 95–115; and Willard F. Mueller, "The Origins of the Basic Inventions Underlying du Pont's Major Product and Process Innovations, 1920 to 1950," in the National Bureau of Economic Research conference report, *The Rate and Direction of Inventive Activity* (Princeton: Princeton University Press, 1962), pp. 323–346.

105. Surprisingly, the fraction of business lines' patent portfolios devoted to (relatively complex) systems and subsystems inventions was observed to increase only weakly with unit size, for example, from 51.0 percent with sales of $100 million to 53.8 percent with sales of $1 billion. Scherer, "The Propensity To Patent," supra note 36, pp. 124–125.

106. For a detailed analysis of the innovative role of small new firms in computers and semiconductors, see Nancy Dorfman, *Innovation and Market Structure* (Cambridge: Ballinger, 1987).

their industry. Many other cases can be found in which the threat of entry through innovation by a newcomer stimulated existing members to pursue well-known technical possibilities more aggressively. Examples include General Electric's handling of the fluorescent lamp; AT&T's development of microwave radio relay systems, cordless telephones, and electronic office switchboards; IBM's response to the electronic computer innovations of Sperry Rand, Control Data, Digital Equipment, and Compaq; and the sudden awakening of old-line aircraft makers' interest in basic research and systems engineering when the U.S. Air Force chose the infant Ramo-Wooldridge Corporation to oversee its Atlas ICBM development program.

The qualitative evidence supports a preliminary conclusion that no single firm size is uniquely conducive to technological progress. There is a place for firms of all sizes. Technical progress thrives best in an environment that nurtures a diversity of sizes and, perhaps especially, that keeps barriers to entry by technologically innovative newcomers low.

A Quantitative Perspective

With this qualitative generalization in mind, we move to the evidence on such quantitative indicators of innovative performance as research and development expenditures, patenting, and the origination of significant product and process innovations.

In 1982, there were approximately 294,000 manufacturing enterprises in the United States. National Science Foundation surveys reveal that only about 12,000 had expenditures on formally organized research and development programs. The fraction of companies conducting formal R&D rises with firm size. Thus, R&D programs were sustained in 1982 by 293 of the 300 manufacturing companies with 10,000 or more employees, by 184 of the 223 companies with from 5,000 to 9,999 employees, and by 693 of the 1,352 firms with 1,000 to 4,999 employees.[107] Enterprises with 10,000 or more employees performed 81.3 percent of all company-financed R&D in that year while employing 45 percent of the persons engaged in manufacturing. Companies with fewer than 1,000 employees had an employment share of 35 percent and a company-financed R&D share of 5 percent. Thus, formally organized R&D is much more the forte of relatively large than small firms. As a qualification to this conclusion, it must be recognized that inventive and innovative activities are also pursued outside the context of formal R&D programs, particularly in smaller corporations.[108]

Among the manufacturing corporations that conduct sufficient amounts of company-financed R&D to report the sums spent to their stockholders, there is no tendency for the very largest firms to contribute disproportionately. *Business Week's* tabulation of R&D expenditure disclosures for 1987 included 915 corporations.[109] When the companies were ranked on the basis of 1987 sales, the cumulative fractions of sales and R&D outlays for various size cohorts were as follows:

Number of Firms, Ranked by Sales	Percentage of All 915 Firms'	
	Sales	R&D Outlays
Top 10	32.5	32.3
Top 25	47.1	44.4

Top 50	60.9	59.7
Top 100	76.2	74.4
Top 200	89.1	86.7
All 915	100.0	100.0

There is a hint that the ten largest corporations had an R&D share closer to their sales share than companies of less gigantic size, but the differences are sufficiently small throughout the size distribution that we cannot confidently reject an inference that R&D outlays were proportional to sales.

This rough proportionality seems to be a phenomenon of long standing. David Mowery traced the spread of industrial R&D activity in the United States from 1921, when only 35 percent of the 200 largest manufacturers reported formal programs, to 1946, when 84 percent of the top 200 had programs.[110] Except in the chemicals industry, R&D employment increased less than proportionately with company size (measured by asset values). For chemical manufacturers, R&D employment rose more than proportionately with size in 1921 and 1933 but roughly proportionately in 1946.

R&D spending is a measure of inputs into the process of advancing industrial technology. At least as vital to assessing the role firm size plays is how effectively those inputs are transformed into outputs.[111] Patent counts are the most comprehensive quantitative indicator of industrial technology outputs. The Federal Trade Commission's Line of Business survey for 1974 included the 250 largest U.S. manufacturing corporations in that year, ranked by domestic sales, plus 193 additional (uniformly sizable) producers. The 443 surveyed corporations obtained 61 percent of the invention patents issued to U.S. industrial corporations in

107. U.S. National Science Foundation, *Research and Development in Industry, 1982*, NSF 84–325 (Washington: microfiche, 1984), pp. 14 and 19; and U.S. Bureau of the Census, *1982 Enterprise Statistics*, vol. 1, "General Report on Industrial Organization (Washington: USGPO, October 1986), Table 3.

108. See, for example, Jacob Schmookler, "Bigness, Fewness, and Research," *Journal of Political Economy*, vol. 67 (December 1959), p. 630, who found that for every eight inventions stemming from full-time R&D employees, companies obtained five inventions from employees engaged only part-time in inventive activity. On the undercounting of R&D in the Netherlands, see Alfred Kleinknecht, "Measuring R&D in Small Firms: How Much Are We Missing?" *Journal of Industrial Economics*, vol. 36 (December 1987), pp. 253–256. For a case study, see Samuel Hollander, *The Sources of Increased Efficiency* (Cambridge: MIT Press, 1965), Chapters 7 and 8.

109. "A Perilous Cutback in Research Spending," *Business Week*, June 20, 1988, pp. 139–160. Companies classified to the service and financial industries are excluded. The *Business Week* listing is confined to companies with sales of $35 million or more and R&D expenses of at least $1 million or 1 percent of sales. This selection criterion (and the corporate reporting practices that underlie it) biases the list in favor of relatively research-oriented

companies, excluding many others, small and large. Among the excluded large corporations were Philip Morris, Shell Oil, RJR Nabisco, Tenneco, and BP America — all on *Fortune*'s list of the 25 largest U.S. industrial corporations in 1987. For a similar analysis of 1975 data, see the second edition of this text, p. 420.

110. David C. Mowery, "Industrial Research and Firm Size, Survival, and Growth in American Manufacturing, 1921–1946," *Journal of Economic History*, vol. 43 (December 1983), pp. 953–979.

111. On the importance of having output data and the theory underlying the interpretation of input–output relationships, see Franklin M. Fisher and Peter Temin, "Returns to Scale in Research and Development: What Does the Schumpeterian Hypothesis Imply?" *Journal of Political Economy*, vol. 81 (January-February 1973), pp. 56–70; Meir Kohn and John T. Scott, "Scale Economies in Research and Development: The Schumpeterian Hypothesis," *Journal of Industrial Economics*, vol. 30 (March 1982), pp. 239–249; and John Lunn, "Research and Development and the Schumpeterian Hypothesis: Alternate Approach," *Southern Economic Journal*, vol. 49 (July 1982), pp. 209–217. On Australian input-output relationships, see Ian W. McLean and David K. Round, "Research and Product Innovation in Australian Manufacturing Industries," *Journal of Industrial Economics*, vol. 27 (September 1978), pp. 1–12.

the lagged time period when patents from 1974 R&D were granted.[112] They accounted for 73 percent of company-financed research and development expenditures, 68 percent of the value of plant and equipment in manufacturing, and 52.4 percent of U.S. manufacturers' sales in 1974. Thus, the largest firms received patents more than proportionate to their sales, but less than proportionate to their capitalization and R&D outlays.[113] The same 443 FTC sample members won 55 percent of the "most significant technical advance of the year" citations bestowed upon U.S. corporations by the magazine *Research & Development* for the years 1976 through 1980.[114] Evidently, the largest manufacturers derived fewer patents and significant technical advances from their R&D money than smaller firms.

Another view of large versus small firm innovative output propensities emerges from a survey that sought to compile a comprehensive list of technical innovations introduced by U.S. manufacturing firms in 1982. Of the 4,531 innovations so identified, 42 percent came from small firms, defined as those with fewer than 500 employees. Those small firms averaged 322 innovations per million employees, while companies with 500 or more employees averaged 225 innovations per million employees.[115] Again, the implication is that relatively small enterprises make a disproportionate contribution to innovative output, especially in view of their modest formal R&D expenditures share.

The superior innovative performance of smaller firms does not persist across all industries. In some fields, firms with fewer than 500 employees contributed a share of innovations lower than their employment share; in others, as the overall averages require, they surpassed their employment share. Analyzing the relative innovative performance of large as compared to small companies, Acs and Audretsch discovered that small firms had higher innovation-per-employee ratios than their larger counterparts in four-digit industries with high innovation rates, an employment mix rich in professional workers, and modest small-firm employment shares.[116] The first two variables reinforce the prediction from theory that firms with small market shares do well when technical progress is rapid. Companies with 500 or more employees "out-innovated" their smaller compatriots in industries where consumer goods advertising was important, production processes were capital intensive, and (for the most innovative industries only) four-firm concentration ratios were relatively high.

Evidence from an international survey of major innovations introduced between 1953 and 1973 suggests that the superior innovative record of small enterprises in the United States is not always mirrored elsewhere. From that survey, the percentages of innovations credited to companies with sales at the time of less than $50 million for various nations were as follows:[117]

United States	50%
France	57
West Germany	37
United Kingdom	33
Japan	20

The low fraction for Japan is consistent with well-known facts about that nation's culture: the most able technical graduates favor lifetime jobs in large companies, venture capital sources are meager, and those who leave a large corporation to start their own high-technology ventures suffer ostracism from former colleagues.[118] The United Kingdom's experience is particularly interesting. For it, a comprehensive tally of more than 4,000 significant industrial innovations commercialized between 1945 and 1983 exists. Between 1956 and 1970, companies with fewer than 500 employees contributed a lower share of innovations than their share of industrial employment. But since then, firms in the 100 to 499 employment range have innovated more than proportionately to their employment shares, and indeed, by growing margins.[119] How much this change owes to the emergence of a high-technology venture capital market in the UK is unknown.[120] In contrast to patterns observed for the United States, British companies with 25,000 or more employees have consistently originated a much larger share of innovations than their employment share, while companies in the 2,000 to 9,999 employee range are notable technological laggards. Evidently, the relative roles of small and large businesses depend more upon variations in business culture and the supply of entrepreneurial talent than upon hard-and-fast technological imperatives.

R&D Activity within Large, Established Firms

A more detailed picture of R&D performance within large, well-established companies can be gleaned by tapping once again the data assembled under the Federal Trade Commission's Line of Business surveys. In those surveys, to reiterate, U.S. manufacturing companies disaggregated information on their operations to individual *lines of business,* defined homogeneously at the three- or four-digit Standard Industrial Classification industry level. For each of the 196 industries in which there were five or more reporting units with nonzero company-financed R&D expenditures in 1974, nonlinear regression equations were computed with the form:

$$(17.1) \qquad R_i = a + b_1 S_i + b_2 S_i^2 + e_i,$$

where R_i is the level of R&D expenditures for the ith company's line, S_i is that line's sales, and e_i is an error term.[121] Interpretation of the squared sales variable's coefficient (and in a few cases, the value of the *a* term) permitted the industries to be

112. F. M. Scherer, "Technological Change and the Modern Corporation," in Betty Bock et al., ed., *The Impact of the Modern Corporation* (New York: Columbia University Press, 1984), pp. 284–284; and Federal Trade Commission, *Statistical Report: Annual Line of Business Report, 1974* (Washington: 1981), p. 47.

113. Within the FTC sample, patenting tended to rise most frequently in rough proportion to line of business R&D outlays, but in the nonconforming cases, patenting rose less than proportionately with R&D more often than disproportionately. See Scherer, "The Propensity To Patent," supra note 36, p. 115.

114. Scherer, "Technological Change," pp. 282–283. At the time, the journal was called *Industrial Research & Development.*

115. See Zoltan J. Acs and David B. Audretsch, "Innovation, Market Structure, and Firm Size," *Review of Economics and Statistics,* vol. 69 (November 1987), p. 568.

116. "Innovation," pp. 571–573.

117. Stephen Feinman and William Fuentevilla, *Indicators of International Trends in Technological Innovation,* Final Report to the National Science Foundation, NTIS document PB-263-738

(Jenkintown, PA: Gelman Research Associates, April 1976). The sample sizes for some nations were quite small.

118. See also Edwin Mansfield, "Industrial R&D in Japan and the United States," *American Economic Review,* vol. 78 (May 1988), p. 227, who observed that R&D expenditures on entirely new products and processes increased more than proportionately with firm size in Japan, whereas the opposite was true in the United States.

119. Keith Pavitt, Michael Robson, and Joe Townsend, "The Size Distribution of Innovating Firms in the UK: 1945–1983," *Journal of Industrial Economics,* vol. 35 (March 1987), pp. 302–304. The innovation tallies are the same as those used in Geroski's analyses, supra notes 93 and 97.

120. See "Venture Adventures," *The Economist,* December 19, 1987, p. 67. The U.K. venture capital market is sufficiently new that one might appropriately view it more as a response than an inducement to the change.

121. Lines of business with no R&D were retained in the analysis if the five non-zero line criterion was satisfied.

classified into one of three categories, as illustrated in Figure 17.9. When b_2 and a were insignificantly different from zero, R&D performance increased proportionately with line of business sales, so the situation described in Figure 17.9(a) as *constant returns* prevailed. When $b_2 > 0$, one has the increasing returns case of Figure 17.9(b); that is, R&D performance increases more than proportionately with size. With $b_2 < 0$, the Figure 17.9(c) diminishing returns case holds.[122]

The results of this curve fitting for 196 industries yielded the following breakdown of cases:

	Number of Industries
No significant departure from constant returns	140
Increasing returns	40
Diminishing returns	16

The constant returns case was predominant, indicating that firms with relatively small market shares invested as intensively relative to their size as market leaders. Deviations from the constant returns pattern were biased on the side of increasing returns, implying that leading firms were more aggressive R&D supporters than counterparts with lower market shares.[123]

A similar analysis was carried out for 124 industries in which five or more firms had nonzero patenting. The distribution of cases was as follows:

	Number of Industries
No significant departure from constant returns	91
Increasing returns	14
Diminishing returns	19

a. Constant Returns

b. Increasing Returns

c. Diminishing Returns

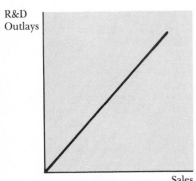
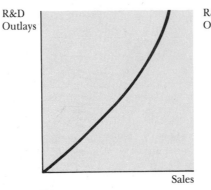
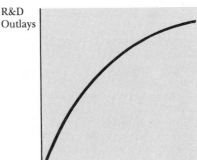

Figure 17.9
Three Firm Size–Innovative
Activity Cases

Here the story is somewhat different. The tendency toward constant returns was slightly stronger — 73 percent of the cases, as contrasted to 71 percent for R&D expenditures. And for the cases that departed from constant returns, the bias was on the side of diminishing rather than increasing returns. To the extent that patent counts are better measures of innovative output than R&D input data, the indicated conclusion is that leading firms were not on average more vigorous innovators. But again, the overriding implication from both the R&D and patent analyses is that large and small units contributed roughly proportionately to the advance of technology.[124]

These results are for activity within lines of business, which for diversified corporations were often much smaller than the corporate whole. The question remains, Does size beyond the line of business level, that is, diversified size, affect the vigor with which innovative activity is pursued? Diversification might contribute affirmatively if firms with many lines were better able to exploit unexpected results emerging from their research laboratories, achieve richer cross-fertilization among specialized technical talent, secure lower-cost R&D financing, and/or utilize common channels of distribution to market new products. On the other hand, it could hold back progress if it meant greater bureaucratization of decision-making processes.

The most powerful tests of the diversification hypothesis have been conducted using FTC Line of Business data. In one such analysis, a Herfindahl numbers-equivalent index of diversification[125] was added to the analysis of 1974 R&D-sales and patent-sales regression equations described above. The diversification index was found to have minute and statistically insignificant effects on the intensity of R&D and patenting.[126] Cohen et al. focused on R&D/sales ratios by line of business averaged over the years 1975 to 1977.[127] Their diversification measure was the amount of companywide domestic sales *not* originating from the line of business being observed. They found diversification to have a slight but statistically

122. For a more complete discussion of the classifications when a ≠ 0, see Scherer, "Technological Change," supra note 112, pp. 287–289, from which the results here are drawn.

123. For similar results from analyses of R&D/sales ratios as a function of line of business, see Wesley M. Cohen, Richard C. Levin, and David C. Mowery, "Firm Size and R&D Intensity: A Re-Examination," *Journal of Industrial Economics*, vol. 35 (June 1987), pp. 543–565; and Ravenscraft and Scherer, *Mergers*, supra note 91, pp. 120–121. In all these analyses, inter-industry differences are found to have a much more powerful effect on R&D expenditures than intra-industry size differences.

124. These results, it must be reemphasized, relate innovative activity to size at the line of business level, not the whole-company level. But they are generally similar to the results of earlier, less well-controlled studies using observations measured at the whole-company level. See, for example, Scherer, *Innovation and Growth*, supra note 9, Chapter 9 and pp. 213–215; Albert N. Link, Terry G. Seaks, and Sabrina R. Woodbery, "Firm Size and R&D Spending: Testing for Functional Form," *Southern Economic Journal*, vol. 54 (April 1988), pp. 1027–1038; J. D. Howe and D. G. McFetridge, "The Determinants of R&D Expenditures," *Canadian Journal of Economics*, vol. 9 (February 1976), pp. 57–71; W. J. Adams, "Firm Size and Research Activity: France and the

United States," *Quarterly Journal of Economics*, vol. 84 (August 1970), pp. 386–409; Jörg Tabbert, *Unternehmensgrösse, Marktstruktur und technischer Fortschritt* (Göttingen: Vandenhoeck & Ruprecht, 1975), pp. 56–108; Louis Phlips, *Effects of Industrial Concentration: A Cross-Section Analysis for the Common Market* (Amsterdam: North-Holland, 1971), pp. 121–132; D. J. Smyth, J. M. Samuels, and J. Tzoanos, "Patents, Profitability, Liquidity and Firm Size," *Applied Economics*, vol. 4 (June 1972), pp. 77–86; Bengt Johanisson and Christian Lindström, "Firm Size and Inventive Activity," *Swedish Journal of Economics*, vol. 73 (December 1971), pp. 427–442; Noriyuki Doi, "Diversification and R&D Activity in Japanese Manufacturing Firms," *Managerial and Decision Economics*, vol. 6 (September 1985), pp. 147–152; and K. Gannicott, "The Determinants of Industrial R&D in Australia," *Economic Record*, vol. 60 (September 1984), pp. 231–235.

125. See p. 92 supra.

126. Scherer, "Technological Change," supra note 112, pp. 292–293. But see Scott, "Diversification versus Cooperation," supra note 81, who found that R&D spending increased with *purposive* diversification, identified as diversification across apparently complementary fields.

127. "Firm Size and R&D Intensity," supra note 123.

significant positive effect on R&D intensity in one version of their regression model, but it faded to insignificance when seven extreme-valued observations (out of 1,797) were removed or when variables controlling for technological opportunity and appropriability were included. These ambiguities led them to conclude that no significant relationship existed between company size and R&D intensity. In still another study using Line of Business data for 1977, Ravenscraft and Scherer found that R&D/sales ratios were slightly lower in lines with a history of diversification mergers, although the result fell short of statistical significance by conventional standards.[128]

It seems clear that firm size increases associated with greater diversification do not in general have a favorable effect on the vigor of research and development efforts. To this finding, one noteworthy qualification must be added. There is statistical evidence that the fraction of total industrial R&D outlays devoted to basic research rises with overall corporate size and greater diversification.[129] Vigorous support of basic research in turn appears to be positively correlated with higher innovative output across individual firms and higher productivity growth across broadly defined industry sectors, although the underlying chain of causation remains poorly understood.[130]

Conclusion

Viewed in their entirety, the theory and evidence suggest a threshold concept of the most favorable climate for rapid technological change. A bit of monopoly power in the form of structural concentration is conducive to innovation, particularly when advances in the relevant knowledge base occur slowly. But very high concentration has a positive effect only in rare cases, and more often it is apt to retard progress by restricting the number of independent sources of initiative and by dampening firms' incentive to gain market position through accelerated R&D. Likewise, given the important role that technically audacious newcomers play in making radical innovations, it seems important that barriers to new entry be kept at modest levels. Schumpeter was right in asserting that perfect competition has no title to being established as the model of dynamic efficiency. But his less cautious followers were wrong when they implied that powerful monopolies and tightly knit cartels had any stronger claim to that title. What is needed for rapid technical progress is a subtle blend of competition and monopoly, with more emphasis in general on the former than the latter, and with the role of monopolistic elements diminishing when rich technological opportunities exist.

128. *Mergers*, supra note 91, pp. 120–121.

129. See Albert N. Link and James E. Long, "The Simple Economics of Basic Scientific Research: A Test of Nelson's Diversification Hypothesis," *Journal of Industrial Economics*, vol. 30 (September 1981), pp. 105–109; Link, "The Changing Composition of R&D," *Managerial and Decision Economics*, vol. 6 (June 1985), pp. 125–128; Mansfield, "Composition of R&D Expenditures," supra note 87, pp. 612–613; and Richard R. Nelson, "The Simple Economics of Basic Scientific Research," *Journal of Political Economy*, vol. 67 (June 1959), pp. 297–306.

130. Edwin Mansfield, "Basic Research and Productivity Increase in Manufacturing," *American Economic Review*, vol. 70 (December 1980), pp. 863–873; and Zvi Griliches, "Productivity, R&D, and Basic Research at the Firm Level in the 1970s," *American Economic Review*, vol. 76 (March 1986), pp. 141–154.

Market Structure and Performance: Overall Appraisal

It is time now to stand back and assess what we have learned about the dependence of industrial performance on market structure and conduct. This is best accomplished by addressing the question introduced at the end of Chapter 2: Is competition workable? Or, alternatively, how serious are the performance deficiencies resulting from monopolistic structure and conduct?

No profound analytic vision is needed to discern that industrial performance in the U.S. economy, which has been our principal focus, is not at all bad. Even though the economy is shot through with monopolistic and oligopolistic elements that might lead one to predict dire consequences, performance has in fact been rather good.

This exhausts our complacency quota. Although performance has been good, it is far from perfect. Nor need we embrace what Professor Demsetz has called the "nirvana approach" to perceive that performance could be better,[1] even though the policy measures one might select in attempting to improve matters are themselves quite imperfect. How large are the social losses associated with monopolistic structure and conduct? What keeps performance from departing farther from the norm of workability? These are the questions to which we devote the balance of our attention. We must consider several dimensions of performance in our appraisal: allocative efficiency, efficiency of resource use, equity of income distribution, progressiveness, and diverse broader social concerns.

The Welfare Losses Attributable to Resource Misallocation

One adverse consequence of monopoly, the theory of welfare economics instructs, is the misallocation of resources. By raising price above marginal cost, monopolists restrict output, divert resources to less valued demands, and reduce consumer welfare.

By making a number of simplifying assumptions, economists have obtained a foothold for estimating the social losses associated with resource misallocation owing to elevated monopoly prices. Figure 18.1 provides a frame of reference. Suppose that in the neighborhood of output levels attainable by sellers of appropriate size, neither economies of scale remain unexploited, nor have diseconomies of scale set in. Suppose also, as is common in manufacturing, inputs are supplied at more or less constant prices, so that the long-run marginal (and average) cost function for an industry is the horizontal line LRC. The equilibrium price under pure competition would be OP_C, the output OX_C, and the total realized consumers' surplus the triangular area FEP_C. If the industry were monopolized but without blockaded entry, the price would be raised, say, to OP_M and output would be restricted to OX_M. (We assume that entry threats or imperfections in the collusion among oligopolists preclude the elevation of prices all the way to the short-run monopoly profit-maximizing level.) Consumers' surplus is reduced to the triangular area FBP_M, and what was consumers' surplus given by the rectangular area P_MBAP_C is transformed into monopoly profit or producers' surplus.

1. Harold Demsetz, "Information and Efficiency: Another Viewpoint," *Journal of Law & Economics*, vol. 12 (April 1969), p. 1.

Figure 18.1

The Welfare Loss Attributable
to Monopolistic Resource
Misallocation

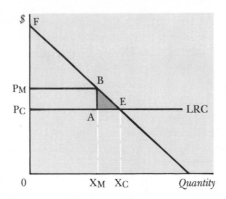

If the marginal utility of income to consumers and the industry's stockholders is identical, or if one has no basis for determining which group has higher marginal utility, the redistribution $P_M BAP_C$ can be regarded as a washout without significance for allocative efficiency. There remains, however, the triangle BEA, whose area was consumers' surplus under competition, but which is lost to consumers under monopoly pricing and not captured by (nondiscriminating) monopolists. In effect, it vanishes into thin air and therefore represents the *dead-weight welfare loss* attributable to the misallocation of resources under monopolistic output restriction.

A bit of algebra will help put these geometric results into more useful form. Let ΔP denote the dollar amount by which the monopoly price deviates from the competitive price P_c and ΔQ the amount (in units of output) by which the monopoly output differs from the competitive output. Since the area of a triangle equals one-half its base times its height, we measure the dead-weight welfare loss W by:

$$(18.1) \qquad\qquad W = 1/2 \; \Delta P \; \Delta Q.$$

The *relative price distortion* under monopoly, the ratio by which the monopoly price deviates from the competitive price, is defined as $d = \Delta P/P_c$. Ignoring signs and assuming ΔP and ΔQ to be small, we define the elasticity of demand to be approximately:

$$(18.2) \qquad\qquad e = \frac{\Delta Q/Q}{\Delta P/P} = \frac{\Delta Q/Q}{d} \; ,$$

which can be rearranged to:

$$(18.3) \qquad\qquad \Delta Q = e \, d \, Q_c.$$

Substituting $P_c d = \Delta P$ and Equation (18.3) into Equation (18.1), we obtain:

$$(18.4) \qquad\qquad W = (1/2) \, P_c \, Q_c \, e \, d^2.$$

Thus, the dead-weight welfare loss from monopoly rises as a quadratic function of the relative price distortion d and as a linear function of the demand elasticity e.

All of the variables in Equation (18.4) are potentially measurable. The first to seize upon the measurement possibilities was Arnold Harberger.[2] His wedge into the problem was a study of profit returns on capital in seventy-three manufacturing industries, originating 45 percent of all manufacturing output, for the more or less normal years 1924 through 1928. Assuming that equating price with long-run unit cost implied earning a profit return neither greater nor less than the full sample's average return, he took individual industry deviations from the sample profit mean as an estimate of the relative monopoly price distortion d. Using available industry sales (PQ) data, and accepting the further assumption that demand was of unit elasticity in every industry, he had all the variables required by Equation (18.4), plugging them in to arrive at an estimated dead-weight welfare loss of $26.5 million for the industries sampled. Expanding this estimate to cover the whole of manufacturing industry raised the estimated welfare loss to $59 million — about 0.06 percent of gross national product at the time. Further adjustments to compensate for inadequacies in his data led to a final judgment that eliminating monopolistic resource misallocation in manufacturing during the 1924–1928 period would have increased social welfare by slightly less than 0.1 percent of GNP. At 1988 levels of output, this implies a dead-weight loss of about $4.8 billion, or roughly $20 per capita — enough to treat everyone in the land to a prime steak dinner at a good (monopolistically competitive) restaurant.

Not surprisingly, Harberger's article, with its implication that economists were wasting their time (and that of students) studying quantitatively insignificant phenomena, stimulated a considerable flurry of methodological criticism[3] and attempts to reassess the dead-weight loss using different data sets and conceptual assumptions. Several empirical studies yielded figures in the same general range as Harberger's.[4] Others, however, came up with much larger estimates — in the range of 4 to 7 percent of U.S. GNP.[5] It repays some effort to explore the principal grounds for disagreement.

Harberger's study was limited to the manufacturing sector. This introduces two biases. For one, the average return on capital tends to be lower in agriculture

2. Arnold C. Harberger, "Monopoly and Resource Allocation," *American Economic Review*, vol. 44 (May 1954), pp. 77–87.

3. See for example George J. Stigler, "The Statistics of Monopoly and Merger," *Journal of Political Economy*, vol. 64 (February 1956), pp. 33–35; Dean A. Worcester, Jr., *Monopoly, Big Business, and Welfare in the Postwar United States* (Seattle: University of Washington Press, 1967), pp. 210–227; Charles K. Rowley, *Antitrust and Economic Efficiency* (London: Macmillan, 1973); Abram Bergson, "On Monopoly Welfare Losses," *American Economic Review*, vol. 63 (December 1973), pp. 853–870; the exchange among R. Carson, Worcester, and Bergson in the *American Economic Review*, vol. 65 (December 1975), pp. 1008–1031; John A. Kay, "A General Equilibrium Approach to the Measurement of Monopoly Welfare Loss," *International Journal of Industrial Organization*, vol. 1 (December 1983), pp. 317–331; Björn Wahlroos, "Monopoly Welfare Losses under Uncertainty," *Southern Economic Journal*, vol. 51 (October 1984), pp. 429–442; and G. K. Yarrow, "Welfare Losses in Oligopoly and Monopolistic Competition," *Journal of Industrial Economics*, vol. 33 (June 1985), pp. 515–529.

4. See David Schwartzman, "The Burden of Monopoly," *Journal of Political Economy*, vol. 58 (December 1960), pp. 627–630; Dean A. Worcester, Jr., "New Estimates of the Welfare Loss to Monopoly," *Southern Economic Journal*, vol. 40 (October 1973), pp. 234–245; John J. Siegfried and Thomas K. Tiemann, "The Welfare Cost of Monopoly: An Inter-Industry Analysis," *Economic Inquiry*, vol. 12 (June 1974), pp. 190–202; and Wahlroos, "Monopoly Welfare Losses under Uncertainty."

5. David R. Kamerschen, "An Estimation of the Welfare Losses from Monopoly in the American Economy," *Western Economic Journal*, vol. 4 (Summer 1966), pp. 221–236; and Keith Cowling and Dennis C. Mueller, "The Social Costs of Monopoly Power," *Economic Journal*, vol. 88 (December 1978), pp. 724–748, with comment by S. C. Littlechild, *Economic Journal*, vol. 91 (June 1981), pp. 348–363, and reply by Cowling and Mueller, *Economic Journal*, vol. 91 (September 1981), pp. 721–725. See also Dennis O. Olson and Donald L. Bumpass, "An Intertemporal Analysis of the Welfare Costs of Monopoly Power," *Review of Industrial Organization*, vol. 1 (Winter 1984), pp. 308–323; and Frederic Jenny and Andre-Paul Weber, "Aggregate Welfare Loss Due to Monopoly Power in the French Economy," *Journal of Industrial Economics*, vol. 32 (December 1983), pp. 113–130. The percentages in the text are confined to the dead-weight loss triangle only and not other possible loss components included in the Cowling-Mueller and Jenny-Weber analyses.

and many divisions of the retail and service trades than in manufacturing. Consequently, using the average return in manufacturing alone as a proxy for normal profits leads to an understatement of monopoly price distortions. Distortions attributable to monopoly also exist in sectors other than manufacturing, although they are more difficult to isolate because data are scarcer and because profit figures do not necessary reflect the magnitude of price/marginal cost deviations in monopolistically competitive markets.[6] The manufacturing sector originated about one-fourth of U.S. GNP in the period studied by Harberger and one-fifth in the 1980s. To arrive at an economy-wide welfare loss estimate, figures derived for manufacturing alone must be inflated—perhaps by as much as a factor of 3 or 4.

The profit data available to Harberger were mostly for quite broadly defined industries. Aggregation biases dead-weight loss estimates downward by submerging the high monopoly distortions of narrow product lines within broad industry averages. Also, some monopoly gains may have been capitalized in asset values, reducing indicated returns on capital, when assets changed hands through merger. Nevertheless, not all the profit deviations observed in the Harberger study (or others) were necessarily the result of monopoly. Many may have reflected transient influences, special risks, or superiority rents. Harberger made crude adjustments in his estimates to compensate for these problems, but it is hard to know whether the biases were netted out. Using a methodology generally similar to Harberger's, Cowling and Mueller found that aggregating up from the individual firm to the three-digit industry level led to a 47 percent reduction in the computed welfare loss.[7] Wahlroos, on the other hand, concluded that failure to eliminate systematic risk premiums from U.S. industry profit data caused welfare loss estimates to be overstated by 24 to 36 percent.[8]

A key assumption—differences in which account for much of the variation in diverse scholars' welfare loss estimates—is the value given the demand elasticity coefficient *e*. Harberger rather arbitrarily assumed a ubiquitous unit elasticity. At the other extreme, Kamerschen and Cowling and Mueller attempted to estimate elasticities for individual industries or firms by invoking a formula which, as we have seen in Chapters 2, 6, and 7, emerges from the conventional calculus of monopoly profit maximization:

$$(18.5) \qquad e = P / (P - MC).$$

When, for example, price is 10 percent higher than unit cost, the implied value of *e* for a profit-maximizing monopolist is $1.1/(1.1 - 1) = 11$. The smaller the observed deviation is between price and cost, the larger the imputed demand elasticity must be. Since the data used in monopoly misallocation studies rarely show price-cost deviations in excess of 15 to 20 percent, this method gives rise to much larger elasticities and hence, following Equation (18.4), much larger welfare estimates than the Harberger method. Indeed, the imputed elasticities appear inconsistent with reality in at least two significant ways. First, respect for mutual interdependence in oligopoly is often imperfect, leading to prices below the joint monopoly profit-maximizing level. The less successful oligopolists are at achieving joint profit maximization, the more they will fall short of satisfying Equation (18.5), and yet the larger will be the imputed elasticity (and welfare loss estimate) derived by the unwarranted application of Equation (18.5). Second, even when coordination among oligopolistic insiders is perfect, limit pricing leads to a price below the level satisfying Equation (18.5) except when entry is blockaded. Firms seeking to maximize their long-run profits may even set prices in the range of *inelastic* industry demand — a result completely inconsistent with the application of Equation (18.5).[9] Examining thirty-seven relatively highly concentrated industries, Masson and Shaanan found that welfare losses at actually observed prices were only one-fourth of what would have been estimated had joint profit maximization occurred in the absence of entry threats.[10] Thus, the 4 to 7 percent welfare loss estimates by Kamerschen and Cowling and Mueller are almost certainly exaggerated.

A point emphasized by Abram Bergson suggests that relatively high demand elasticities might nonetheless be relevant in at least some cases.[11] When the products of an industry are moderately differentiated, each product's individual ceteris paribus demand curve is likely to be quite elastic. Pricing that distorts consumer choices could, as a consequence, lead to large intraindustry output shifts and hence sizable welfare losses. There are, however, important limiting factors. Confronted with high demand elasticities, monopolistic competitors selling close substitute products are apt to pursue similar pricing policies. If no close substitute's price is much higher in relation to marginal cost than that of other substitutes, the misallocation of resources *within* the industry will be modest. In a collusive differentiated product oligopoly protected by appreciable entry barriers, this state of affairs could conceivably coexist with relatively high (but uniform) price-marginal cost disparities for the whole range of the industry's products, while *inter*industry misallocation losses are held down by low *industry* (as distinguished from individual product) demand elasticities. These relationships are quite complex, and little is known about their real-world significance. The most one can say with confidence is that Harberger-type welfare loss estimates that assume unit demand elasticities are biased downward more, the more important the misallocation among relatively close substitute products is.

An equally complicated problem overlooked by most authors concerns the transmission of monopoly distortions through successive vertical stages.[12] To illustrate, suppose there are two industries, A and B, each with sales of $1 billion per year and constant long-run marginal costs (including a normal return on capital) of $900 million. With $d = 100/900 = 0.11$ in each, and assuming unit demand elasticity, we obtain by applying Equation (18.4) a combined welfare loss

6. For a multimarket equilibrium estimate of allocative efficiency losses (mostly attributable to price regulation) in the U.S. railroad and truck transportation sectors, see Ronald R. Braeutigam and Roger G. Noll, "The Regulation of Surface Freight Transportation: The Welfare Effects Revisited," *Review of Economics and Statistics*, vol. 66 (February 1984), pp. 80–87. Estimates following deregulation of the late 1970s and early 1980s would undoubtedly be much lower.

7. "The Social Costs of Monopoly Power," Table 3.

8. Wahlroos, "Monopoly Welfare Losses under Uncertainty," supra note 3, p. 439.

9. See p. 365 supra.

10. Robert T. Masson and Joseph Shaanan, "Social Costs of Oligopoly and the Value of Competition," *Economic Journal*, vol. 94

(September 1984), pp. 528–530. Similar limits on welfare losses are obtained in an analysis by Micha Gisser, who assumes that the pricing of a dominant group is constrained by fringe supply and that collusion within the dominant group may be imperfect. "Price Leadership and Welfare Losses in U.S. Manufacturing," *American Economic Review*, vol. 76 (September 1986), pp. 756–767.

11. "On Monopoly Welfare Losses," supra note 3, p. 860, and his reply in the *American Economic Review*, vol. 65 (December 1975), pp. 1024–1031.

12. See pp. 36 and 521–526 supra. See also V. A. Dickson, "Deadweight Loss and Stage of Production Influences," *Atlantic Economic Journal*, vol. 10 (December 1982), p. 104.

estimate of $12 million. However, suppose Industry A supplies some of its output as raw material to Industry B — for example, that half of Industry B's $900 million costs are for purchases from A. Then the long-run marginal social cost of B's output is not $900 million, but $450 million + 0.9 × $450 million = $855 million. With B's relative price distortion raised to 145/855 = 0.17, our estimate of the total dead-weight loss increases to $17.9 million ($3.4 million on final goods sales by A plus $14.5 million on sales by B).

Since every dollar's worth of final output sales by manufacturing enterprises is supported on average by an additional dollar or more of intermediate transactions, one might suppose that welfare loss estimates derived using Equation (18.4) should at least be doubled to take this bias into account. However, this is probably not a correct approximation. Michael Klass has estimated the direct impact of vertical pricing distortions by computing price distortion ratios for both intermediate and final goods industries and then flowing the distortions through an input-output matrix of the U.S. economy for 1958.[13] It turns out that industries with exceptionally low and perhaps even subnormal returns, such as coal mining, transmitted a disproportionate share of their output ultimately to finished goods industries like automobile manufacturing with unusually high returns, mitigating to some extent the misallocations at the later stages. When price distortion estimation techniques similar to Harberger's were employed, taking vertical distortion effects into account actually *reduced* Klass's final estimate of the total welfare losses attributable to monopoly, given the U.S. economy's 1958 structure. When an alternative distortion measurement technique that smoothed unsystematic interindustry pricing behavior was used, taking vertical distortions into account *raised* welfare loss estimates by roughly 40 percent compared to the figure obtained with a model assuming that all outputs satisfied final consumer demands.

Labor is also an intermediate input. Its pricing poses analogous and other difficulties. At least for the United States, there is evidence that as much as two-thirds of the gains from monopoly power are realized in the form of higher wages to the monopolistic firms' workers rather than, or in addition to, higher profits for capitalists.[14] At minimum, this means that studies evaluating only observable supranormal profitability miss an important part of the monopoly-based distortions, and hence underestimate welfare losses. Also, to the extent that the higher wages paid to such workers are passed on to the purchasers of intermediate products in the form of prices higher than they would be if profits alone were elevated, there can be pyramided vertical distortions of the type identified in the preceding two paragraphs. This compels an additional upward adjustment, but the size of the effect is too conjectural to permit any informed guess on how large the adjustment should be.

One more complication lurks in the shadows. Any attempt to measure the dead-weight loss attributable to monopolistic resource misallocation rests ultimately upon an assumption that resources are worth no more (and no less) in alternative uses than their marginal cost in the specific industry exercising monopoly power. This implies a partial equilibrium context in which, among other things, second-best considerations are irrelevant.[15] But in a world of oligopolies and monopolistic competition, second-best effects *should* ideally be taken into account, even though the necessary data are virtually unattainable. Thus, in the strictest sense, we operate with a measuring rod (or triangle) of distressingly elastic rubber. In principle we cannot even tell the direction of the measurement error imparted by neglecting second-best and other general equilibrium repercussions, but it seems more likely to be on the side of exaggerating monopoly welfare losses.[16]

Faced with this reality, we have two options. We can give up trying to measure the allocative burden of monopoly, or we can cross our fingers and hope the errors from proceeding in a partial equilibrium framework are not too serious. Leaning toward the second alternative more on faith than with strong logical support, we conclude that Harberger's estimate was biased downward. Applying the multiplicative correction factors suggested in our critique of Harberger's results, it appears that the dead-weight welfare loss attributable to monopolistic resource misallocation in the United States lies somewhere between 0.5 and 2 percent of gross national product.[17]

Other Inefficiencies

Thus far we may have glimpsed only the tip of the iceberg. It is hard to think of realistic circumstances under which the dead-weight loss triangle BEA would be very large, for it involves the square of the relative price distortion ratio d, whose average value was only 0.036 in the Harberger sample and 0.084 in seven industries with high barriers to entry analyzed by David Qualls.[18] More serious consequences follow if monopoly affects costs as well as prices. Then the welfare loss has as its major dimension the whole output of the monopolized industry, not just the *change* in output associated with an elevated price. Inefficiencies might proliferate to fill or perhaps even overflow the trapezoidal area $P_M BEP_C$ in Figure 18.1 instead of its triangular right-hand extremity.

There are two broad sets of reasons why costs under monopoly might be excessive. First, absent competitive pressure on profit margins, cost controls may become lax. Adam Smith recognized this danger two centuries ago: "Monopoly . . . is a great enemy to good management."[19] The refrain has been taken up and refined by Harvey Leibenstein, who argues that when competitive pressure is

13. Michael W. Klass, "Inter-Industry Relations and the Impact of Monopoly" (Ph.D. diss., University of Wisconsin, Madison, 1970).

14. See Thomas Karier, "Unions and Monopoly Profits," *Review of Economics and Statistics*, vol. 67 (February 1985), pp. 34–42, and, for an earlier analysis based upon cruder data, Frederick W. Bell, "The Effect of Monopoly Profits and Wages on Prices and Consumers' Surplus in U.S. Manufacturing," *Western Economic Journal*, vol. 6 (June 1968), pp. 233–241.

15. Compare pp. 25–27 and 33–35 supra.

16. For a simulation exercise suggesting that partial equilibrium analyses significantly overestimate the welfare losses caused by monopoly, see Thomas S. Friedland, "The Estimation of Welfare Gains from Demonopolization," *Southern Economic Journal*, vol. 45 (July 1978), pp. 116–123.

17. A best-guess partial equilibrium estimate is derived as follows. Raise Harberger's estimate of 0.06 percent to 0.12 to take into account excessive aggregation and the use of too high a normal profit return. Inflate this by a multiplier of 2 for monopoly gains captured by labor, by a multiplier of 3 to cover the entire economy, by a multiplier of 1.5 to reflect more plausible demand elasticities, and by a multiplier of 1.2 to take into account vertical distortions. The resulting estimate is 1.3 percent of GNP.

18. P. David Qualls, "Stability and Persistence of Economic Profit Margins in Highly Concentrated Industries," *Southern Economic Journal*, vol. 40 (April 1974), p. 608.

19. Adam Smith, *The Wealth of Nations* (New York: Modern Library edition, 1937), p. 147.

weak, business organizations may tolerate and maintain what he named "X-inefficiency."[20] Second, the lure of monopoly profits can induce "rent seeking" — that is, incurring substantial and possibly wasteful expenditures to obtain, strengthen, and defend monopoly positions.[21] Included here are certain outlays on product differentiation, the maintenance of excess capacity, and political lobbying and litigation, among others.

X-Inefficiencies Whether business enterprises actually indulge in so-called X-inefficiency has been debated on various theoretical and semantic grounds, but those who oppose the concept in general terms have by far the poorer case.[22] Anyone with experience in real-world organizations must recognize that something resembling X-inefficiency exists. The important questions for our purposes are, to what extent is there a systematic relationship between monopoly power and X-inefficiency, and of what general magnitude is the monopoly-correlated component?

Great Britain in the 1950s and 1960s provided a unique laboratory for observing the effects of a transition from monopoly to competition. Before 1956, there were no effective legal barriers to price-fixing arrangements, and cartelization was widespread. But by 1960, strong judicial decisions interpreting a new antitrust law undercut the bases of most cartels. Many cartels found other ways to maintain pricing discipline.[23] But some did not, and significant price competition broke out. It in turn triggered a search for ways to reduce costs. The glass bottle industry illustrates the latter reaction.[24] After price competition wiped out previously comfortable profit margins, a cost-cutting drive was implemented by the leading producers, outmoded plants were closed, and modern bottle-making equipment (long available on the market) was introduced, making it possible to produce with 750 to 900 employees the same output that had previously occupied 1,400 workers. Similar reactions were observed in the transformer, automobile battery, galvanized tank, surgical dressings, and sanitary ware industries, among others.[25] Likewise, Britain's Imperial Chemical Industries Ltd. reacted to new domestic and import competition with a strenuous effort to reduce its patently excessive costs. As its chairman explained the situation in 1966:

We had been in existence thirty-four years and had been having a comfortable time. We were doing well without too much exertion and had been favored by a good deal of scientific discovery. Then we ran into competition and had to learn to deal with it.[26]

Further evidence on cartelization's effects exists for a handful of industries in other nations. Bruce Erickson studied illegal price-fixing conspiracies in three U.S. industries and found signs of deficient cost controls in all three. When, for instance, the gymnasium bleacher price-fixing agreement broke down in 1959, newly initiated cost reduction efforts led to a decline of approximately 23 percent in manufacturing costs.[27] The U.S. steel industry stands out for its chronic avoidance of price competition and for the sluggishness of its leading firm. Thus, the report of a management consulting firm hired during the 1930s to study the United States Steel Corporation's operations has been summarized as follows:

[T]he report of the industrial engineers . . . pictured the Steel Corporation as a big sprawling inert giant whose production operations were improperly coordinated; suffering from a lack of a long-run planning agency; relying on an antiquated system of cost accounting; with inadequate knowledge of the costs or of the relative profitability of the many thousands of items it sold; with production and cost standards generally below those considered everyday practice in other industries; with inadequate knowledge of its domestic market and no clear appreciation of its opportunities in foreign markets; with less efficient production facilities than its rivals had; slow in introducing new processes and new products.[28]

It is significant that United States Steel began visibly to improve its operations during the late 1960s, after it was exposed to severe import competition and it relaxed its efforts to maintain industry price leadership. Similarly strenuous cost-cutting reactions were evident in the U.S. automobile industry and other previously sheltered oligopolistic industries when they experienced a sharp increase in import competition during the early 1980s. And in Sweden, significant behavioral changes followed 1961 legislation ending the Swedish Tobacco Company's exclusive control over wholesale distribution of imported cigarettes. One manifestation was the closure of small, obsolete plants and the construction of a modern plant. The explicit goal was to minimize Swedish Tobacco's cost disadvantage relative to newly emerging competitors from other European Free Trade Association nations.[29] An interview revealed company managers' belief that they could no longer sustain the quiet life that characterized their earlier legal monopoly era.

20. Harvey Leibenstein, "Allocative Efficiency vs. 'X-Efficiency,' " *American Economic Review*, vol. 56 (June 1966), pp. 392–415; and *Beyond Economic Man: A New Foundation for Microeconomics* (Cambridge: Harvard University Press, 1976).

21. The phrase was apparently coined by Anne O. Krueger in "The Political Economy of the Rent-Seeking Society," *American Economic Review*, vol. 64 (June 1974), pp. 291–303. For applications related more directly to monopoly questions, see Gordon Tullock, "The Welfare Costs of Tariffs, Monopolies, and Theft," *Western Economic Journal*, vol. 5 (June 1967), pp. 224–232; Richard A. Posner, "The Social Costs of Monopoly and Regulation," *Journal of Political Economy*, vol. 83 (August 1975), pp. 807–827; Robert E. McCormick, William F. Shugart, and Robert D. Tollison, "The Disinterest in Regulation," *American Economic Review*, vol. 74 (December 1984), pp. 1075–1079; Franklin M. Fisher, "The Social Costs of Monopoly and Regulation: Posner Reconsidered," *Journal of Political Economy*, vol. 93 (April 1985), pp. 410–416; and John T. Wenders, "On Perfect Rent Dissipation," *American Economic Review*, vol. 77 (June 1987), pp. 456–459.

22. See, for example, Ross M. Parish and Y. K. Ng, "Monopoly, X-Efficiency, and the Measurement of Welfare Loss," *Economica*, vol. 39 (August 1972), pp. 301–308; George J. Stigler, "The Xistence of X-Efficiency," *American Economic Review*, vol. 66 (March 1976), pp. 213–216; Leibenstein's reply, "X-Inefficiency Xists — Reply to an Xorcist," *American Economic Review*, vol. 68 (March 1978), pp. 203–211; and Louis De Alessi, "Property Rights, Transaction Costs, and X-Efficiency," *American Economic Review*, vol. 73 (March 1983), pp. 64–81. For a survey of the debate tapping a vast array of empirical studies, see Roger S. Frantz, *X-Efficiency: Theory, Evidence and Applications* (Dordrecht:

Kluwer, 1988). See also John J. Siegfried and Edwin H. Wheeler, "Cost Efficiency and Monopoly Power: A Survey," *Quarterly Review of Economics and Business*, vol. 21 (Spring 1981), pp. 25–46.

23. See Dennis Swann et al., *Competition in British Industry* (London: George Allen & Unwin, 1974), Chapter 4.

24. This discussion is based upon Swann et al., *Competition*, pp. 167 and 185–186, supplemented by F. M. Scherer's interviews with British glass bottle company executives.

25. On the more general statistical association between apparent inefficiency and restrictive agreements in the U.K., see Jack Downie, *The Competitive Process* (London: Duckworth, 1958), Chapters 13 and 14; and the interpretation by Richard E. Caves in *Britain's Economic Prospects* (Washington: Brookings, 1968), pp. 287–293.

26. "The British Company That Found a Way Out," *Fortune*, August 1966, pp. 104–105. See also "Reshaping a Chemical Giant for Common Market Competition," *Business Week*, December 2, 1972, pp. 55–60.

27. W. Bruce Erickson, "Price-Fixing Conspiracies: Their Long-Term Impact," *Journal of Industrial Economics*, vol. 24 (March 1976), pp. 189–202.

28. Statement of George Stocking in U.S. House of Representatives, Committee on the Judiciary, hearings, *Study of Monopoly Power* (Washington: USGPO, 1950), pp. 966–967.

29. Based upon an interview reported in F. M. Scherer et al., *The Economics of Multi-Plant Operation: An International Comparisons Study* (Cambridge: Harvard University Press, 1975), especially p. 157.

Attempts to explore the X-inefficiency hypothesis beyond the bounds of anecdotal evidence have commonly used some variant of a *frontier production function* approach. Figure 18.2 illustrates the basic methodology. The two axes measure labor per unit of output (on the horizontal) and capital per unit of output (on the vertical).[30] For the set of plants observed within an industry (or the set of similarly defined industries across a sample of nations), there is a scatter of points reflecting actual input usage to obtain a unit of output. Using appropriate statistical techniques, the *frontier unit isoquant* Q_oQ_o* is fitted through the observations for plants using the least inputs at varying capital/labor ratios. Points located to the northeast of the frontier isoquant represent plants producing inefficiently, the more so the farther they are from the frontier. Industries whose input use observations cluster tightly near the frontier isoquant are characterized as achieving a higher average level of efficiency than those, as in Figure 18.2, with many observations a considerable distance from the (best practice) frontier isoquant. The length of the segment AZ relative to segment OA measures the extent to which actual practice departs from best practice and hence provides a crude index of X-inefficiency.

Cross-country comparisons for a given industry show large departures from the frontier isoquant, especially for nations characterized as less developed. Investigating 1965 input-output relationships in agriculture, for example, Binswanger and Ruttan found Australia, Canada, the United States, New Zealand, West Germany, Denmark, Belgium, the Netherlands, Japan, and Taiwan to be on or near the frontier.[31] Less-developed nations such as Venezuela, South Africa, Mexico, Syria, and Colombia used roughly ten times as much input as the frontier nations to produce equivalent units of output. Their inefficient use of inputs cannot be attributed in any important degree to the subject of our inquiry — monopoly power — since most nations' agricultural sectors, though protected from import competition, are organized more or less competitively internally. Rather, the profligate use of resources stems mainly from the classic correlates of underdevelopment — failure to implement modern production methods, which comes in turn from deficient entrepreneurship, inadequate accumulation of human capital, and various more subtle cultural and governmental institutions impeding enterprise.

These handicaps are largely absent when one examines differences in X-efficiency within the industries of highly developed nations. In a pioneering investigation of competition's role, Bo Carlsson found that the plants within twenty-six Swedish industries departed *less* on average from the production frontier, implying less X-inefficiency, the *higher* seller concentration was.[32] This result, contrary to the hypothesis that competition stimulates X-efficiency, could have a trivial statistical explanation. The more concentrated an industry is, the fewer plants it tends to contain; and the smaller the number of plants, the less likely it is statistically that sizable deviations from the frontier will occur. However, Carlsson discovered further that the higher the tariffs or other barriers to import competition were, the greater the amount of measured X-inefficiency was.[33] From the observed relationships, he concluded that as long as import competition was vigorous, high seller concentration did not impede the attainment of X-efficiency and may in fact have facilitated it by permitting scale economies to be realized despite

Figure 18.2
Illustration of Frontier
Production Function Method
for Measuring X-Inefficiency

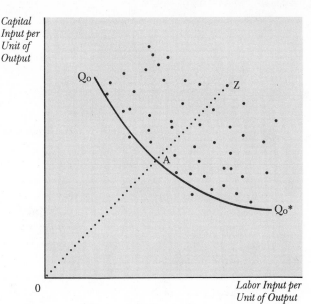

*Capital
Input per
Unit of
Output*

Q_0

Z

A

$Q_0{}^*$

0

*Labor Input per
Unit of Output*

the small size of the Swedish market.[34] But blunted import competition permitted X-inefficiency to rise.

Richer insights emerge from a study by Caves and Barton of U.S. Census data for 1977 on some 285 four-digit manufacturing industries.[35] For each industry, frontier production functions were estimated using individual plant data, and X-inefficiency indexes measuring average and maximum deviations of sample plant observations from the frontier were computed. As anticipated, the amount of measured X-inefficiency increased with the number of plants within an industry, which in turn was inversely correlated with seller concentration, making it difficult to isolate concentration-efficiency links. Controlling for the number of plants, concentration appeared to have a significant nonlinear impact, with X-inefficiency being minimized in industries with four-firm concentration ratios of

30. In statistical analyses, other inputs can also be taken into account.

31. Hans P. Binswanger and Vernon W. Ruttan, *Induced Innovation: Technology, Institutions and Development* (Baltimore: Johns Hopkins University Press, 1978), p. 28. The nations are listed here in descending land/labor ratio order. See also T. Y. Shen, "The Estimation of X-Inefficiency in Eighteen Countries," *Review of Economics and Statistics*, vol. 66 (February 1984), pp. 98–104.

32. Bo Carlsson, "The Measurement of Efficiency in Production: An Application to Swedish Manufacturing Industries, 1968," *Swedish Journal of Economics*, vol. 74 (December 1972), pp. 468–485.

33. For similar results using different methodologies, see Ronald Saunders, "The Determinants of Productivity in Canadian Manufacturing Industries," *Journal of Industrial Economics*, vol. 29 (December 1980), pp. 167–184; and M. Pickford, "A New Test for Manufacturing Industry Efficiency: An Analysis of the Results of Import Licence Tendering in New Zealand," *International Journal of Industrial Organization*, vol. 3 (June 1985), pp. 153–177.

34. See also p. 117 supra.

35. Richard E. Caves and David R. Barton, *Technical Efficiency in U.S. Manufacturing Industries* (Cambridge: MIT Press, forthcoming in 1990).

approximately 40 and rising as market structures became more tightly oligopolistic.[36] Increased import penetration tended weakly to constrain the amount of X-inefficiency. A further analysis revealed that the constraining influence of imports was strongest in industries that were more concentrated than they needed to be to achieve scale economies at the single-plant level—that is, in industries where monopoly power might have afforded producers discretion to run a loose ship, absent an import threat. This result for 1977 seems to have foreshadowed the intensified efforts of concentrated industries to improve their efficiency when import competition escalated unexpectedly during the 1980s. A variable measuring the number of Sherman Act price-fixing violations found in the industry between 1958 and 1977 was only erratically correlated with X-inefficiency. A persistently strong finding was that industries whose plants were owned by highly diversified parent companies tended to experience more X-inefficiency than industries populated by specialist producers. This is consistent with the evidence in Chapter 5 that the conglomerate merger wave of the 1960s and early 1970s was a failure, atrophying acquired units' ability to manage emerging challenges within their home industries and leading eventually to widespread divestiture of previously acquired entities.

Other evidence that competition matters comes from a study of electric power costs in forty-nine U.S. cities where there were two competing companies. Walter Primeaux found significantly lower unit costs—by about 11 percent on average—in municipally owned firms facing such competition than in an otherwise matched sample of monopoly municipal electrical utilities.[37] Rodney Stevenson discovered that U.S. electric power utilities also operating local gas distribution companies had electricity-generating costs 6 to 8 percent higher than companies that had no such control over natural gas competition.[38] In a statistical study covering thirty-four U.S. metropolitan areas, Franklin Edwards observed that banks maintained larger staffs and incurred higher labor expenses when they operated in highly concentrated markets, taking into account also a variety of urban size, bank demand, and bank branching characteristics.[39] This "expense preference" behavior, he surmised, explained a tendency for banks' prices (that is, interest rates on loans) but not their net profits to be positively correlated with concentration.

The evidence is fragmentary, but it points in the same general direction. X-inefficiency exists, and it is more apt to be reduced when competitive pressures are strong than when firms enjoy insulated market positions. What we do not yet know is the magnitude of differences systematically correlated with monopoly power. It seems eminently plausible, however, that X-inefficiencies attributable to monopoly are at least as large as the welfare losses from resource misallocation.

Monopoly-Induced Waste

Other relevant inefficiencies are those induced by the attempt to gain, extend, and defend monopoly positions. Advertising and similar product differentiation efforts provide an important example, although here we must tread warily for reasons articulated in Chapter 16. Some advertising is informative or otherwise beneficial, some is conducted in the hope of enhancing product differentiation and securing monopoly profits, and some results from producers' attempts to increase sales through nonprice rivalry when the suppression of price competition has left price-cost margins at temptingly high levels.

An illustration of the inverse link between price and nonprice competition comes from the experience of the Kellogg Company.[40] During much of the 1960s there was little price competition among American breakfast cereal manufacturers, and the margin between price and unit production costs averaged roughly 50 percent. This stimulated intensive spending on advertising. Kellogg's Corn Flakes was no exception; advertising outlays ranged from 16 to 22 percent of sales between 1965 and 1967. But then growing private-label corn flake sales began bringing competitive pressure to bear on prices, at first squeezing margins and then provoking Kellogg in 1971 to announce a sizable list price reduction. As its margins were reduced, Kellogg lowered its corn flakes advertising to 11 percent of relevant sales in 1968 and then, after the list price reduction, to 6 percent in 1972. Similar advertising cuts were effected by rival General Foods on its Post Toasties corn flakes.

Considering the mutually canceling nature of much advertising by oligopolists, the inducement provided by high price-cost margins, and the fact that producers in highly developed nations such as West Germany, Japan, and Sweden manage to sell their wares despite per capita advertising outlays roughly one-half those of their U.S. counterparts,[41] it does not seem too extreme to propose that one-fourth of the $102 billion spent on advertising in the United States during 1986, or 0.6 percent of GNP, represented a waste more or less directly attributable to monopoly.[42] To this estimate must be added the amounts spent on dysfunctionally elaborate packaging,[43] personal sales calls unsolicited and unwanted by buyers,[44] administering premium giveaway programs and sweepstakes, and accelerated styling changes that do nothing more than render last year's model obsolete. The sum of these items is unknown and, because tastes differ, unknowable. In the authors' opinion, the total annual expenditures on wasteful sales promotion could not be less than 1 percent of gross national product.

It is natural to proceed another step and ask whether product differentiation efforts might lead to an excessive proliferation of product variants. "Excessive"

36. Also included in this and other Caves-Barton regression equations were variables measuring the intraindustry variance in capital/labor ratios, the size of an industry's median plant in relation to total industry output, the percentage of employees working only part-time, and the ratio of company-financed research and development outlays to industry sales.

37. Walter J. Primeaux, "An Assessment of X-Efficiency Gained through Competition," *Review of Economics and Statistics*, vol. 59 (February 1977), pp. 105–108.

38. Rodney E. Stevenson, "X-Efficiency and Interfirm Rivalry: Evidence from the Electric Utility Industry," *Land Economics*, vol. 58 (February 1982), pp. 52–66.

39. Franklin R. Edwards, "Managerial Objectives in Regulated Industries: Expense-Preference Behavior in Banking," *Journal of Political Economy*, vol. 85 (February 1977), pp. 147–162.

40. Drawn from F. M. Scherer's testimony *in re Kellogg Company et al.*, Federal Trade Commission docket no. 8,883, December 1977, pp. 28,013–28,018.

41. See p. 580 supra.

42. Nonprice competition among television stations for viewers (success at which permits the stations, limited in number by regulation, to charge higher advertising rates) also appears to induce rent-seeking outlays on programming. See Gary M. Fournier, "Nonprice Competition and the Dissipation of Rents from Television Regulation," *Southern Economic Journal*, vol. 51 (January 1985), pp. 754–765.

43. See the package-opening scene in the German film, *Männer* (winner of the 1986 Palme d'Or at Cannes).

44. In "The Welfare Loss of Excess Nonprice Competition: The Case of Property-Liability Insurance Regulation," *Journal of Law & Economics*, vol. 23 (October 1980), pp. 429–440, H. E. Frech and Joseph Samprone found that service-intensive insurance sales methods were used more extensively in states with insurance rates held at high levels owing to regulation. Netting out the value of the extra service to consumers, they estimate that welfare losses amounting to 11 percent of mean competitive demand per capita were stimulated by the high-price regime.

here means that the costs of development and product launching and the sacrifice of product-specific economies owing to small-lot production outweigh the surplus that consumers derive from variegated product offerings catering to special tastes.[45] Judging whether the right balance has been struck is extremely difficult. Social losses from excessive product variety are most likely when a cartel or tight-knit oligopoly maintains uniformly high price-cost margins, thereby stimulating efforts to capture additional business through nonprice rivalry, and when it refrains from offering low-price options of lower real quality, or with less prestigious images. A further symptom of wasteful product proliferation is the absence of strong consumer preferences for one product variant over others, manifested *inter alia* in frequent brand switching or high price elasticities of demand, holding the prices of close substitutes constant.[46] It is certainly possible to find industries exemplifying these conditions.[47] It is unclear, however, how widespread they are, and since a certain amount of monopoly power (under monopolistic competition) is necessary to call forth sufficient product variety, no general conclusions seem possible.

Price-fixing agreements, tacit oligopolistic collusion, and monopoly pricing can also stimulate the wasteful accumulation of excess capacity. There are four main mechanisms.

First, offering ample reserve capacity provides another kind of nonprice rivalry advantage—for example, as travelers patronize airlines with the most flights and seats available at the last moment, or as industrial buyers favor suppliers who were able to meet their demands in unusually tight gray markets. Second, when cartel sales quotas are allocated in proportion to capacity, as they were under the U.S. crude oil prorationing system until the early 1970s, investment in excess capacity to get a higher quota is encouraged. Third, excess capacity may be carried to strengthen the credibility of a monopolistic group's entry deterrent. And fourth, monopolistic pricing cushions the survival of capacity in secularly declining industries.

There is reason to believe that the relationship between monopoly power and certain of these propensities is nonlinear. Thus, ocean shipping cartels that perfected their monopoly through controls over entry, investment, and scheduling were less prone toward costly excess capacity or "overtonnaging" than the looser "open" cartels serving U.S. routes. Two studies revealed unit-cost elevations on the order of 38 percent as a result of excess capacity on U.S. routes.[48] Similarly, cement producers using the basing point system as a collusive device were apparently unable to control the tendency toward excess investment stimulated by their high prices. Between 1909 and 1946, the fraction of practical production capacity utilized by the U.S. industry averaged 68 percent, and in only three years out of thirty-eight did the level of capacity utilization climb above 90 percent.[49] In a statistical analysis of 273 U.S. manufacturing industries, Frances and Louis Esposito found excess capacity levels in periods of peak demand to be 2.8 percentage points higher on average in middling oligopolies than in either atomistically structured or tightly oligopolistic industries, taking into account also demand variability, demand growth, capital intensity, and plant durability.[50] Caves et al. confirmed this result for a smaller sample and discovered that concentrated industries also tended to hold larger inventories, other relevant variables being held equal.[51] In addition, they found excess capacity to be greater in industries engaging in intense advertising. Some excess capacity, it must be recognized, serves a useful purpose by enhancing producers' ability to meet peak demands.[52] But most of the studies cited here attempted to control for peak demand levels and variability, identifying nevertheless a tendency toward overshooting and hence high costs, especially in loose oligopolies and weak cartels.

Excessive costs can also be induced by government regulation of industries in which, for good reasons or bad, lawmakers have concluded that market forces cannot be counted upon to operate unfettered. Three rather different sources of waste must be distinguished. For one, classic public utility industries such as electric power generation and distribution, telecommunications, and (less clearly) some branches of transportation gravitate toward natural monopoly, causing market failures that motivate the imposition of various governmental controls. There is reason to believe that the price and profit regulations distort producers' incentives, leading to deficient cost control and excessive investment.[53] Second, companies spend substantial sums attempting to use political and regulatory processes to erect artificial entry barriers, impose other limitations on competition, and defend themselves when their monopolistic conduct or structure runs afoul of antitrust or similar laws.[54] Third, even when markets would function well if left alone, business enterprises often succeed in securing protective and/or regulatory laws that simultaneously restrict competition and distort incentives in wasteful directions. Not all the costs associated with these phenomena can be attributed directly to monopoly power. Indeed, distortions of the third type stem more from a failure of government than from market failure. It is widely believed that the

45. See pp. 604–606 supra.

46. Note the link to our earlier discussion of allocative efficiency and demand elasticities. When intraindustry demand elasticities are high, interindustry elasticities are low, and producers pursue uniformly high markup policies, the welfare losses associated with conventional allocative inefficiency may, as we have seen, be small. But these conditions are precisely the ones under which product proliferation is most likely to be socially wasteful.

47. See F. M. Scherer, "The Welfare Economics of Product Variety: An Application to the Ready-to-Eat Cereals Industry," *Journal of Industrial Economics*, vol. 28 (December 1979), pp. 113–134.

48. J. W. Devanney, V. M. Livanos, and R. J. Stewart, "Conference Ratemaking and the West Coast of South America," *Journal of Transportation Economics and Policy*, vol. 9 (May 1975), pp. 154–177; and University of Wales, Institute of Science and Technology, *Liner Shipping in the U.S. Trades* (April 1978), pp. 46–50 and 251.

49. Samuel M. Loescher, *Imperfect Collusion in the Cement Industry* (Cambridge: Harvard University Press, 1959), pp. 168–169. Loescher's analysis is contested by Gerald Aranoff, "John M. Clark's Concept of Too Strong Competition and a Possible Case: The U.S. Cement Industry," manuscript, Lehman College of the City University of New York, December 1988. After the basing point system was abandoned, periods of high capacity utilization became more common.

50. Frances F. Esposito and Louis Esposito, "Excess Capacity

and Market Structure in U.S. Manufacturing: New Evidence," *Quarterly Journal of Business and Economics*, vol. 25 (Summer 1986), pp. 3–14. On an earlier study with similar results, see their "Excess Capacity and Market Structure," *Review of Economics and Statistics*, vol. 56 (May 1974), pp. 188–194, with a critical comment by H. Michael Mann et al. and reply by the Espositos, *Review of Economics and Statistics*, vol. 61 (February 1979), pp. 156–160. On pricing reactions to excess capacity in Norway, see Sigbjørn Atle Berg, "Excess Capacity and the Degree of Collusion," *International Journal of Industrial Organization*, vol. 4 (March 1986), pp. 99–108.

51. Richard E. Caves, J. Peter Jarrett, and Michael K. Loucks, "Competitive Conditions and the Firm's Buffer Stocks: An Exploratory Analysis," *Review of Economics and Statistics*, vol. 61 (November 1979), pp. 485–496.

52. See Arthur De Vany and N. G. Frey, "Stochastic Equilibrium and Capacity Utilization," *American Economic Review*, vol. 71 (May 1981), pp. 53–57.

53. See note 17, p. 11 supra.

54. See, for example, W. Mark Crain and Asghar Zardkoohi, "X-Inefficiency and Nonpecuniary Rewards in a Rent-Seeking Society," *American Economic Review*, vol. 70 (September 1980), pp. 784–792, who found that private water supply companies persuaded their regulators to award higher rate-of-return increases in states where the utilities were allowed to incur political expenditures in the rate-setting process.

total social costs imposed by all such forms of governmental regulation are very large — perhaps even greater than the costs traceable to monopolistic market failures unprovoked by government intervention.[55] Even if the tally is confined, as it should be in the context of this chapter, to inefficiencies stemming directly from natural monopoly regulation and attempts to secure legal monopolies, significant costs must be recognized. An extremely rough estimate would place them between 0.5 and 2.0 percent of GNP, with a best guess of 1.0 percent.

Finally, it must be recognized that monopolistic market structure can reduce costs as well as impose them — notably, when high concentration is conducive or necessary to the full realization of scale economies. Several complex considerations must again be integrated. Consumers' desire for variety makes it inevitable that some plants will be smaller than what appears from a technological standpoint to be the minimum efficient scale (MES) of production. Small geographic markets will be served at lowest total cost by small plants when transportation costs are high, and specialized products and services can often be supplied at lower cost by firms below the MES of general-line producers. No social cost can properly be counted for such cases of sub-MES operation. Second, when prices are elevated well above minimum unit costs through monopoly, cartels, or tacit oligopolistic collusion, an umbrella is held up to attract and sustain small, high-cost fringe producers.[56] Similar phenomena were evident in abundance in such trades as retail pharmacies, liquor stores, and gasoline retailing when prices were sustained at generous levels through the imposition of resale price maintenance, especially before its exemption from U.S. antitrust law ended in 1975. But third, holding technology, product mix, and geographic variables constant, sellers with large market shares appear better able to capture sufficient demand to justify building large-scale least-cost plants.[57]

How these conflicting influences balance out is an empirical question. We have systematic evidence only for U.S. manufacturing industry. It appears to be clearly established that average plant sizes tend to be larger, and the incidence of suboptimal scale operations lower, when seller concentration is high than when it is low.[58] In this regard, concentration is cost saving. A crude estimate of the potential magnitudes involved can be derived from research by Weiss and Scherer. On average in U.S. manufacturing during the 1960s, between 48 and 58 percent of all capacity was smaller than the general-line plant minimum efficient scale. For the median of twelve industries on which consistent estimates were available, plants one-third the MES incurred a 5 to 6 percent unit-cost penalty. A percentage point increase in the average industry's four-firm concentration ratio appears to have been accompanied by a decrease of 0.56 to 0.95 points in the percentage of sub-MES capacity. In estimating the consequences of higher concentration, one must recognize that cost functions are nonlinear, that some sub-MES plants would surely survive in small spatial and specialized product niches and under monopolists' price umbrellas, that plant size distributions tend to be approximately log normal in shape, and that many of the shifts would involve plants already close to the minimum efficient scale. Given such assumptions, we estimate that a doubling of average four-firm concentration ratios for four-digit manufacturing industries — that is, from 40 to 80 — would, over the long run, cause a bit less than one-third of total capacity to move from the sub-MES into the MES range, with an average unit-cost reduction of 1.5 to 2.5 percent for the shifted plants. The average cost reduction relative to total manufacturing sector costs would be on the order of 0.50 to 0.85 percent.[59] In addition, we recall from Chapter 4 that firms in concentrated industries had lower general and administrative (for example, central office) costs.[60] Raising average four-firm concentration ratios from 40 to 80 was found to reduce G&A costs as a percentage of sales by 0.90 percentage point, other variables being held equal. Such a doubling of concentration levels is about as extreme a structural change as can reasonably be imagined. Whether unit-cost reductions of equal magnitude would result from comparable structural changes in nonmanufacturing industries is doubtful. Since economies of scale are probably less compelling outside manufacturing, the economy-wide unit-cost reduction would most likely be somewhat smaller than the 1.40 to 1.75 point combined range found for manufacturing.

Considerations similar in principle apply to the relationship between concentration and the realization of product-specific scale economies. On one hand, cartelization and rigid oligopolistic pricing undermine firms' incentives to specialize and achieve long production runs. Respect for mutual interdependence inhibits price cutting to win a large share of a product variant's demand, and buyers confronted with uniform oligopoly prices have a natural tendency to split their orders rather than concentrate them with a single low-cost supplier.[61] On the other hand, it is conceivable that sellers with large market shares in concentrated industries would manage to aggregate orders in such a way as to realize larger lot sizes and longer production runs than they would if concentration were lower, all else being

55. For various views, see Posner, "The Social Costs," supra note 21, pp. 818–821; Almarin Phillips, ed., *Promoting Competition in Regulated Markets* (Washington: Brookings, 1975), especially Chapters 2, 3, 8, and 9; Murray Weidenbaum and Robert De Fina, *The Cost of Federal Regulation of Economic Activity* (Washington: American Enterprise Institute for Public Policy Research, 1978); F. M. Scherer, "Regulatory Dynamics and Economic Growth," in Michael Wachter and Susan Wachter, eds., *Toward A New U.S. Industrial Policy?* (Philadelphia: University of Pennsylvania Press, 1981), pp. 289–320; and B. Peter Pashigian, "The Number and Earnings of Lawyers: Some Recent Evidence," *American Bar Foundation Research Journal* (Winter 1978), pp. 77–81.

56. For additional theoretical perspectives, see Martin K. Perry, "Scale Economies, Imperfect Competition and Public Policy," *Journal of Industrial Economics*, vol. 32 (March 1984), pp. 313–334; and James A. Brander and Barbara A. Spencer, "Tacit Collusion, Free Entry and Welfare," *Journal of Industrial Economics*, vol. 33 (March 1985), pp. 277–294.

57. See p. 124 supra.

58. For the United States, see Scherer et al., *Multi-Plant Operation*, supra note 29, Chapter 3; and Leonard W. Weiss, "Optimal Plant Size and the Extent of Suboptimal Capacity," in Robert T. Masson and P. D. Qualls, eds., *Essays on Industrial Organization in Honor of Joe S. Bain* (Cambridge: Ballinger, 1976), pp. 123–141. On Canada, see Vinod K. Gupta, "Suboptimal Capacity and Its Determinants in Canadian Manufacturing Industries," *Review of Economics and Statistics*, vol. 61 (November 1979), pp. 506–512; V.

A. Dickson, "Sub-optimal Capacity and Market Structure in Canadian Industry," *Southern Economic Journal*, vol. 46 (July 1979), pp. 206–217; and John R. Baldwin and Paul K. Gorecki, "The Determinants of Small Plant Market Share in Canadian Manufacturing Industries in the 1970s," *Review of Economics and Statistics*, vol. 67 (February 1985), pp. 156–161. On the U.K., see D. K. Round, "Monopoly Power and Inefficiency in United Kingdom Manufacturing Industries," *Bulletin of Economic Research*, vol. 26 (November 1974), pp. 130–132.

59. A much larger estimate in the 2.6 to 4.1 percent range for eliminating *all* sub-MES capacity is presented by Kaye D. Evans, John J. Siegfried, and George H. Sweeney, "The Economic Cost of Suboptimal Manufacturing Capacity," *Journal of Business*, vol. 56 (September 1983), pp. 55–76. Their estimate is higher because they eliminate more sub-MES capacity, including very small fringe plants, and because they assume somewhat steeper long-run cost curves. On the upward bias in some of the scale economies data included in their sample, see Aubrey Silberston, "Economies of Scale in Theory and Practice," *Economic Journal*, vol. 82 (March 1972), Supplement, p. 379.

60. See pp. 122–123 supra.

61. See Scherer et al., *Multi-Plant Operation*, supra note 29, pp. 311–316; Martin Howe, "Competition and the Multiplication of Products," *Yorkshire Bulletin of Economic and Social Research*, vol. 12 (November 1960), pp. 57–72; and Howe, "A Study of Trade Association Price Fixing," *Journal of Industrial Economics*, vol. 21 (July 1973), p. 250.

equal.[62] There is very little evidence on this point, and as a result it is impossible to tell whether on balance monopolistic market structures worsen or improve the attainment of product-specific economies.

Economies of scale in advertising and sales promotion pose equally difficult problems. They surely exist, and, for a given pattern of conduct, increasing concentration undoubtedly brings savings. The trouble is, conduct does not remain constant, and if price-cost margins rise, expenditures on advertising and other forms of nonprice competition will also tend to escalate, perhaps overwhelming the savings attributable to larger scale. Again, our knowledge is too meager to estimate a net cost effect.

Overall Assessment

In the first edition of this work, estimates of the diverse social costs attributable to domestic monopoly were brought together into a single composite total. The combined estimate was roughly 6 percent of U.S. gross national product, with a range of uncertainty running from 3 to 12 percent of GNP. No attempt is made here to present a similar revised estimate. There are two main reasons. The composite estimate in the first edition was surrounded by appropriate caveats, yet these were assiduously ignored by journalists and politicians seeking to enliven an article or speech with a seemingly precise magic number. Truth was not well served. Also, no cost reductions stemming from higher concentration were netted out, largely because the negative associations with the incidence of suboptimal scale plant capacity and G&A cost levels had not yet been discovered. It seems certain now that partly offsetting benefits do exist. The authors' best estimate is that they are a good deal smaller than the burdens imposed by monopolistic conduct, but there is considerable uncertainty on this point, and truth is better served by shunning a spuriously precise net social cost figure.

The most that can be said with reasonable confidence is that the social costs directly ascribable to monopoly power are modest. It is appropriate to inquire why this is so. From our analysis in foregoing chapters, several explanations emerge. They are listed in descending order of importance. First, a large fraction of the American economy—perhaps as much as half—consists of industries whose structures, although seldom atomistically competitive, include enough sellers to sustain a vigorous, workable species of competition as long as outright collusion is neither tolerated nor encouraged by the government. Second, many of the industries with oligopolistic structures possess little or no collective power to hold prices substantially above costs for extended periods because barriers to new entry, fringe firm expansion, and the incursion of imports are modest. Obversely, pricing performance is *least* satisfactory in concentrated industries sealed off by very high scale economy, product differentiation, resource control, import restraint, and/or patent barriers to entry. Third, high long-run price elasticities of demand reflecting the threat of product substitution frequently discourage maximum exploitation of short-run monopoly power, even when new entry with a perfect substitute is blockaded. This constraint has become increasingly important with industrial firms' growing sophistication in harnessing science to create new and superior synthetic materials. Fourth, the exercise of power by large buyers may countervail the pricing power of sellers, preventing the pyramiding of price distortions through a chain of vertical transactions and often (but not always) transmitting the savings to consumers. Finally, public policy has played a role. Except in some special case industries, the United States has since the late 1930s maintained a fairly vigorous antitrust program, striking down restrictive agreements, preventing the consolidation of power through mergers and predation, and raising legal and financial obstacles in the path of countless monopolistic arrangements.

Other Effects of Monopoly Power

To round out our assessment, we must consider the impact of monopoly power on other dimensions of performance.

Monopoly Profits   One is income distribution. Monopoly profits represent a redistribution of income from the consuming public to the owners—as a first approximation, the stockholders—of monopolistic enterprises.[63] The impact of monopoly profits on various strata in the income distribution depends upon both consumption and profit claim patterns. In the most thorough study, Irene Powell found that middle-income American consumers spent a slightly larger fraction of their incomes on goods from high-concentration manufacturing industries than either the poorest or most affluent consumers.[64] Not surprisingly, the highest-income stratum of her sample claimed the lion's share of profits attributed to high seller concentration. Powell's analysis indicates that if four-firm concentration ratios in high-concentration manufacturing industries were reduced uniformly to 40 percent, the resulting decline in profits (predicted statistically on the basis of 1963 price-cost margin relationships) would mean a 1.8 percent fall in average income for the wealthiest of six income distribution strata. Reducing concentration to atomistic levels, with four-firm ratios at (impossibly low) zero values, would imply a 7.6 percent loss of income for the wealthiest stratum. Netting out the gains to consumers if manufacturing concentration ratios were reduced to 40 percent against the losses to monopoly rent recipients, Powell estimated that the wealthiest of the six income distribution strata would suffer a net income loss of 1.45 percent. The five less affluent groups would gain on average by from 0.3 to 0.7 percent of their pre-deconcentration income.

To obtain a more complete picture of monopoly power's distributional consequences, several further ramifications must be taken into account. First, if we examine only the extremes of the income distribution, we find that some, but by no means all or even a majority of, great wealth positions were derived from industries in which the exploitation of monopoly power was prominent. Thus, among the twenty-five wealthiest American families listed in *Forbes* magazine's 1988 tally

---

62. See pp. 123–125 supra.

63. For a survey of the literature, see Robert Smiley, "Firm Size, Market Power, and the Distribution of Income and Wealth," in the Federal Trade Commission conference volume, *The Economics of Firm Size, Market Structure, and Social Performance* (Washington: July 1980), pp. 90–103.

64. Irene Powell, "The Effect of Reductions in Concentration on Income Distribution," *Review of Economics and Statistics*, vol. 69 (February 1987), pp. 75–82. See also Katherine McElroy, John J. Siegfried, and George H. Sweeney, "The Incidence of Price

Changes in the U.S. Economy," *Review of Economics and Statistics*, vol. 64 (May 1982), pp. 191–203; Ralph Lankford and John F. Stewart, "The Distributive Implications of Monopoly Power: A General Equilibrium Analysis," *Southern Economic Journal*, vol. 46 (January 1980), pp. 918–924; and (for a simulation analysis) Lankford and Stewart, "A General Equilibrium Analysis of Monopoly Power and the Distribution of Income," in Federal Trade Commission, *The Economics of Firm Size*, supra note 63, pp. 113–128.

of the 400 richest families,[65] only six owed their fortunes primarily to industries in which profitability depended crucially upon monopoly positions—notably in newspapers (often local monopolies) and broadcasting (whose oligopolistic structures were the result of restricted franchise grants by the government). Six others (Sam Walton of Wal-Mart Stores, Ross Perot of Electronic Data Systems, David Packard of Hewlett-Packard, Ted Arison of Carnival Cruise Lines, the Mars family of candy makers, and Charles Feeney of Duty Free Shoppers) became rich by building great enterprises in industries characterized for the most part by vigorous competition, although successful product differentiation also had a role. Most of the others achieved their fortunes playing the great American speculation game— buying assets (such as oil extraction rights or real estate) cheap and selling dear, more often than not in industries that, even though turbulent and strongly affected by government intervention, were more competitive than monopolistic in structure.[66]

Second, many of the great fortunes of the 1980s can be traced to inheritance. In a regression analysis of the *Forbes* 400 list for 1982, Canterbery and Nosari discovered that persons with a substantial inheritance were on average $100 million wealthier than those who made the top 400 list but had no inheritance.[67] Many of the inherited fortunes were attributable in turn to monopolistic consolidations that took place around the turn of the century, before antitrust constraints became effective, and to later enterprises built upon strong patent protection or other first-mover advantages. Typically, families that gained fortunes linked at least in part to monopoly power have long since diversified their portfolios and no longer dominate the corporations from which they profited.

That the reinvestment of monopoly profits made long ago can have an important and indeed increasing impact on the distribution of wealth is shown by Comanor and Smiley.[68] Over most of the twentieth century, average rates of return on corporate common stock have been considerably higher than the rate of growth of personal income per capita. If wealthy corporate stockholders invested their income in an average portfolio of corporate stocks and avoided excessive dissipation of their gains through consumption, inheritance taxes, and the proliferation of heirs,[69] they could command a growing share of the total wealth distribution. Making what appear to be plausible assumptions about savings and dissipation rates, Comanor and Smiley found that in the absence of monopoly profits amounting to 3 percent of GNP between 1890 and 1962, the share of total personal wealth controlled by the wealthiest 2.4 percent of all U.S. families in 1962 would have been reduced from 41 percent to somewhere between 17 and 27 percent. Or if the eliminated monopoly profits amounted to only 2 percent of GNP, the same families' share of personal wealth would have been reduced to between 31 and 34 percent.

One might suppose that the growing participation of ordinary workers in stock ownership through pension fund entitlements mitigates the tendency for monopoly profits to increase the inequality of wealth distribution. In 1985, 51 percent of the common stock shares of the leading one hundred U.S. corporations, ranked by the market value of shares outstanding, and 44 percent of the shares of the one thousand most valuable corporations were held by financial intermediary institutions.[70] A large but not precisely known share of those institutional holdings was for pension and life insurance funds, whose ultimate beneficiaries were a fairly representative cross section of the income-earning population (although low-income wage earners participated less than proportionately). To the extent that such pension recipients share in monopoly gains, the redistribution of income is likely to be more equitable than it would be if the profits flowed only to direct individual stockholders. The 2 percent of individual stockholders with the highest incomes in 1983 owned 50 percent of all personally held corporate stocks.[71] However, pension funds are compelled by "prudent investor" rules to emphasize the shares of seasoned, well-known corporations in their portfolios. As such, they invest only small amounts in enterprises passing through their early formative phases, when monopoly power is being built. If the monopoly potential of a relatively new enterprise is recognized by the stock market when the original investors begin diversifying their own holdings and selling new shares, new secondary investors (such as pension funds) will pay high prices for the capitalized value of the anticipated monopoly profits, realizing only normal returns on their investments. It is the early birds who capture the principal capital gains from monopoly. Pension fund beneficiaries do profit when seasoned enterprises add new lines with monopoly power through internal development (as contrasted to acquisition, when a high capitalized value will again be paid). Although very little is known about the quantitative distribution of cases, it seems likely that pension fund beneficiaries capture only a modest fraction of the capital gains that are attributable to monopoly.

Wages and Salaries

Monopoly also affects the distribution of wage and salary income in three identifiable ways.

For one, we have seen in Chapter 2 that managerial salaries are correlated at least weakly with profitability, holding company size constant,[72] and from Chapter 11, we know that profitability rises with market share, which in turn reflects some complex blend of monopoly power and efficiency advantages. It should not be surprising that salaries are correlated with concentration.[73] The salaries plus short-term bonuses of chief executive officers for one thousand U.S. corporations surveyed by *Business Week* in 1988 averaged $685,000 — more than forty times the average 1987 earnings of nonsupervisory workers.[74] To the extent that top

65. "The Forbes Four Hundred," *Forbes*, October 24, 1988, pp. 149–164.

66. That the industries in which great fortunes were gained recently were more competitive than monopolistic is implied in John Siegfried, "Could a Score of Industrial Organization Economists Agree on Competition?" *Review of Industrial Organization*, vol. 3 (Fall 1988), pp. 139–148.

67. E. Ray Canterbery and E. Joe Nosari, "The Forbes Four Hundred: The Determinants of Super-Wealth," *Southern Economic Journal*, vol. 51 (April 1985), pp. 1073–1083.

68. William S. Comanor and Robert H. Smiley, "Monopoly and the Distribution of Wealth," *Quarterly Journal of Economics*, vol. 89 (May 1975), pp. 177–194.

69. On the crucial role of dissipation in limiting tendencies toward rising concentration of wealth, see Stanley Lebergott, "Are the Rich Getting Richer? Trends in U.S. Wealth Concentration," *Journal of Economic History*, vol. 36 (March 1976), pp. 147–162.

70. See F. M. Scherer, "Corporate Ownership and Control," in John R. Meyer and James M. Gustafson, eds., *The U.S. Business Corporation: An Institution in Transition* (Cambridge: Ballinger, 1988), pp. 44–46.

71. Robert B. Avery et al., "Survey of Consumer Finances, 1983," *Federal Reserve Bulletin*, September 1984, p. 689.

72. See pp. 49–50 supra.

73. For the only known confirmation, see Oliver E. Williamson, "Managerial Discretion and Business Behavior," *American Economic Review*, vol. 53 (December 1963), pp. 147–162.

74. "A Portrait of the Boss," *Business Week*, October 21, 1988, p. 28; and *Economic Report of the President* (Washington: USGPO, January 1989), p. 359.

managers' salaries are enhanced as a consequence of monopoly power, inequality of income distribution is clearly increased.

Second, there is evidence that the wages of rank-and-file employees tend to be higher in concentrated industries, other variables being held equal. For nonunion workers, increased wages appear to flow causally from higher concentration; for unionized workers, high seller concentration is conducive to a stronger union presence, which in turn leads to higher wages.[75] Since unionization tends also to increase the equality of wage payments among workers *within* a firm or industry, the full distributional implications of these relationships remain unclear.

Third, one way business firms might indulge the discretion they enjoy when competitive pressures are weak is by practicing racial or religious discrimination in hiring—for instance, by not hiring or promoting up to the profit-maximizing point blacks or other minorities against whom prejudice exists. Statistical tests of this hypothesis reveal no clear discriminatory wage pattern among manufacturing industries of varying structure. However, there is evidence, mostly from the period before federal government efforts to enforce equal employment opportunity gained momentum, of somewhat more favorable wage levels for blacks in government and nonprofit organizations than in profit-oriented enterprises.[76] Other studies disclose that for given worker characteristics and wage levels, more highly concentrated and/or profitable industries tended to hire a disproportionately small number of black workers, especially for administrative and other white-collar jobs.[77]

Technological Progress

In the long run, we have urged repeatedly, good economic performance depends much more critically upon sustaining a vigorous pace of technological progress than upon plausible variations in allocative efficiency or income distribution. However, a considerable volume of research suggests that the links between market structure and innovation are weak, surrounded by much "noise" associated with other measured and unmeasured influences. Beyond this, four summary observations are warranted. First, some of the most strikingly profitable monopoly positions were the result, not the cause, of successful innovation attended by strong patent protection. The rewards realized in these instances serve an indirect incentive function. However, much corporate inventive and innovative effort does not require a patent stimulus, and abuses and extensions over time of patent positions appear more often than not to be dysfunctional. Second, in some atomistic industries, concentration is too low and representative firm sizes are too small for ambitious research and innovation efforts to thrive. Whether the technological needs of these industries are adequately served by materials and equipment suppliers operating under more conducive structural conditions is not certain. Third, in other industries, especially those marked by rich technological opportunity, concentration is higher, and leading firm sizes are larger, than they need to be to support the most vigorous pace of invention and innovation. But fourth, our knowledge remains too limited to predict confidently whether the rate of technical progress could be accelerated significantly by structural reforms—for example, by forcing the deconcentration of highly concentrated industries and permitting joint ventures or concentration of atomistic industries. The authors' best reading of the evidence is that such measures, taking the current structure of American industry as a point of departure, would make very little difference.

Other Effects Finally, there are implications of concentration and monopoly to which we have devoted little or no attention in previous chapters, partly because the evidence on them is so fragmentary and partly because they lie outside the conventional domain of economics.

For one, there is inconclusive evidence that large plants and large firms propagate working conditions that instill a greater sense of alienation among workers.[78] However, wages also rise with plant and firm size, and the wage premiums must at least compensate, and may even overcompensate, workers for the loss of job satisfaction associated with a large-scale organization. Whether this compensation eliminates any basis for complaint, or whether one might wish to place more weight on avoiding alienation than the market itself chooses to apply, is debatable.

Market structure could also affect firms' efforts to avoid polluting the environment. On a priori grounds, the effects could run in either of two directions: concentration could help firms coordinate their efforts to avoid the imposition of stringent standards by regulatory authorities, but, since each significant firm in a concentrated industry is a relatively large and hence promising enforcement target, it could facilitate more potent government enforcement efforts. The only available evidence on these conflicting hypotheses shows that 1977 air and water pollution abatement outlays were significantly higher in more highly concentrated industries.[79]

Quantitative analyses of U.S. income tax data reveal that corporate contributions to philanthropic causes rise with profitability, although probably less than proportionately and by only six to nine dollars for each $1,000 of additional profits.[80] Given the links between monopoly and profitability, this means that positive but small fringe benefits flow from enhanced power.[81] There is also evidence that large corporations allocate a disproportionate share of their contributions to

75. Recent contributions on this nexus include Karier, "Unions and Monopoly Profits," supra note 14; John S. Heywood, "Labor Quality and the Concentration-Earnings Hypothesis," *Review of Economics and Statistics*, vol. 68 (May 1986), pp. 342–346; Dale Belman, "Concentration, Unionism, and Labor Earnings: A Sample Selection Approach," *Review of Economics and Statistics*, vol. 70 (August 1988), pp. 391–397; and Richard B. Freeman and James L. Medoff, *What Do Unions Do?* (New York: Basic Books, 1984), especially Chapters 3–5.

76. See William R. Johnson, "Racial Wage Discrimination and Industrial Structure," *Bell Journal of Economics*, vol. 9 (Spring 1978), pp. 70–81; and Edwin T. Fujii and John M. Trapani, "On Estimating the Relationship between Discrimination and Market Structure," *Southern Economic Journal*, vol. 26 (January 1978), pp. 556–567.

77. See William G. Shepherd and Sharon G. Levin, "Managerial Discrimination in Large Firms," *Review of Economics and Statistics*, vol. 55 (November 1973), pp. 412–422; William S. Comanor, "Racial Discrimination in American Industry," *Economica*, vol. 40 (November 1973), pp. 363–378; Walter Haessel and John Palmer, "Market Power and Employment Discrimination," *Journal of Human Resources*, vol. 13 (Fall 1978), pp. 545–560; and Marshall

H. Medoff, "On the Relationship Between Discrimination and Market Structure: Comment," *Southern Economic Journal*, vol. 46 (April 1980), pp. 1227–1234.

78. See the papers by Frank P. Stafford, Lucia F. Dunn, John E. Kwoka, Orley Ashenfelter, and Daniel S. Hamermesh in the Federal Trade Commission conference volume, *The Economics of Firm Size*, supra note 63, pp. 325–388; the papers by Lucia F. Dunn, Jon M. Shepard, and James G. Hougland in Betty Bock et al., eds., *The Impact of the Modern Corporation* (New York: Columbia University Press, 1984), pp. 5–78; and Lucia F. Dunn, "Work Disutility and Compensating Differentials," *Review of Economics and Statistics*, vol. 68 (February 1986), pp. 67–73.

79. S. C. Farber and R. E. Martin, "Market Structure and Pollution Control under Imperfect Surveillance," *Journal of Industrial Economics*, vol. 35 (December 1986), pp. 147–160.

80. See Katherine M. McElroy and John J. Siegfried, "The Effect of Firm Size and Mergers on Corporate Philanthropy," in Bock et al., eds., *The Impact of the Modern Corporation*, pp. 99–138.

81. In "The Effect of Economic Structure on Corporate Philanthropy," *The Economics of Firm Size*, supra note 63, p. 220, Maddox and Siegfried show that corporate contributions rise with seller concentration, holding firm size and profitability constant.

beneficiaries in the cities where their central offices are located.[82] Although the evidence is not completely clear, this may mean that when mergers concentrate the control of industry in a relatively few large cities, charitable causes may suffer reduced support in smaller cities that otherwise would have been headquarters locations.

Along similar lines, there is reason to believe that positive business participation in community affairs is less vigorous when plants and other establishments are owned by firms headquartered elsewhere.[83] Here too, concentrated control, especially when accompanied by high levels of multiplant operation, may have adverse repercussions for the quality of civic life.

On the other hand, in political forums that they find important, large firms in concentrated industries may marshal their resources with unique effectiveness to secure favorable legislation and regulatory actions. The higher seller concentration is, the more attenuated will be the discouraging effect of noncontributing firms free riding on the political efforts of active participants. Empirical tests of this hypothesis for the United States have shown that large corporations were more successful in obtaining tax breaks;[84] that larger, more profitable firms with sizable market shares spent more heavily on lobbying in California;[85] that large companies in more concentrated industries contributed greater amounts to federal election campaign funds;[86] and that firms in more highly concentrated industries enjoyed greater success in securing federal legislation they favored and blocking legislation they opposed.[87] In this respect, high concentration aggravates the "mischiefs of faction" about which the drafters of the United States Constitution worried.[88]

Finally, the sensitivity of oligopolists to the adverse price effects of output expansion in their home markets may drive them to search not only for domestic diversification opportunities but also for investment outlets abroad. However beneficial this modern brand of imperialism may be on grounds of technology transfer and the efficiency of resource allocation, it is a source of concern in target nations—especially when it is coupled with political subversion or the exercise of overt military power.[89]

Conclusion

Industrial market structure does matter in a host of ways. Our efforts to map the links between structure and performance have made considerable progress, although much remains to be learned. On the relationships to which we have devoted the most attention, we find that the small amounts of full-fledged monopoly and generous quantities of oligopoly evident in the U.S. economy have for the most part had only modest performance-impairing effects. Performance outcomes have been relatively favorable because structural and behavioral constraints that would operate under any circumstances limit the adverse consequences of monopoly power, and because public policy has often, but not consistently, been exercised in such a way as to impose further limits. Yet more can be done, both to understand how structure, conduct, and performance are affected by public policy and to improve the policy instruments at hand.

82. See Maddox and Siegfried, "The Effect of Firm Size," in *The Impact of the Modern Corporation*, pp. 124–129; and (in the same volume) Ivar Berg and Janice Shack-Marquez, "Corporations, Human Resources, and the Grass Roots: Community Profiles," pp. 248–250.

83. Compare Robert N. Stern and Howard Aldrich, "The Effect of Absentee Firm Control on Local Community Welfare," in the FTC conference volume, *The Economics of Firm Size*, pp. 162–181; and Jon M. Shepard and James G. Hougland, "Organization Size, Managerial Mobility, and Corporate Policy: A Study of the Community Participation of Managers," in Bock et al., eds., *The Impact of the Modern Corporation*, pp. 163–190.

84. Lester M. Salamon and John J. Siegfried, "Economic Power and Political Influence: The Impact of Industry Structure on Public Policy," *American Political Science Review*, vol. 71 (September 1977), pp. 1026–1043.

85. H. Michael Mann and Karen McCormick, "Firm Attributes and the Propensity To Influence the Political System," in FTC conference proceedings, *The Economics of Firm Size*, pp. 300–313.

86. See Russell W. Pitman, "The Effects of Industry Concentration and Regulation on Contributions in Three 1972 U.S. Senate Campaigns," *Public Choice*, vol. 27 (Fall 1976), pp. 71–80; and Pitman, "Market Structure and Campaign Contributions: Does Concentration Matter?" U.S. Department of Justice Economic Policy Office discussion paper 85–11 (September 1985).

87. Daniel C. Esty and Richard E. Caves, "Market Structure and Political Influence," *Economic Inquiry*, vol. 21 (January 1983), pp. 24–38.

88. Federalist Paper No. 10 (by James Madison), in *The Federalist Papers* (New York: Mentor Books, 1961), p. 81.

89. For various views, see K. W. Rothschild, "Price Theory and Oligopoly," *Economic Journal*, vol. 57 (September 1947), pp. 318–319; Paul A. Baran and Paul M. Sweezy, *Monopoly Capital* (New York: Monthly Review Press, 1966), pp. 178–217; Stephen Hymer and Robert Rowthorn, "Multinational Corporations and International Oligopoly: The Non-American Challenge," in Charles P. Kindleberger, ed., *The International Corporation* (Cambridge: MIT Press, 1970), pp. 57–91; United Nations Department of Economic and Social Affairs, *Multinational Corporations in World Development* (New York: United Nations, 1973), especially Chapter 3; Bertrand Russell Peace Foundation, *Subversion in Chile: A Case Study in U.S. Corporate Intrigue in the Third World* (Nottingham: Spokesman Press, 1972); and U.S. Senate, Committee on Foreign Relations, Subcommittee on Multinational Corporations, Report, *Multinational Oil Corporations and American Foreign Policy* (Washington: USGPO, 1975), especially pp. 58–74.

Author Index

Subject Index